D0722830

THE LINGUISTIC ATLAS OF SCOTLAND

THE LINGUISTIC ATLAS of SCOTLAND

SCOTS SECTION VOLUME 1

Edited with an introduction by J.Y. MATHER and H.H. SPEITEL
Cartography by G.W. LESLIE
Editorial Assistant I.E. MATHER

ARCHON BOOKS, HAMDEN, CONNECTICUT

Published in the United States of America as an Archon Book, an imprint of The Shoe String Press, Inc., Hamden, Connecticut 06514

Library of Congress Cataloging in Publication Data
Mather, J.Y.
The linguistic atlas of Scotland.
Based on the archives of the Scots section of the Linguistic Survey of Scotland.
1. English language—Dialects—Scotland.
I. Speitel, H.H., joint author. II. Leslie, George W., joint author. III Linguistic Survey of Scotland.
IV. Title.
PE2102. M3 427'.9'41 74-22345

ISBN 0-208-01475-6

Printed in Great Britain by Redwood Burn Limited,
Trowbridge & Esher

memoriae sacrum
Iohannis Orr
talium antistitis studiorum
huius operis
hortatoris fautorisque

CONTENTS

FOREWORD

Just twenty years ago I was setting down in a small book — *An Introduction to a Survey of Scottish Dialects* — a plan of campaign for a somewhat challenging and hazardous enterprise. This had to take into account, so far as was in my power, both what was theoretically desirable and what in practice it was reasonable to hope to achieve. I attempted on this basis to lay down general lines of approach without unduly cramping the activities of anyone subsequently engaged on the project. It is with some satisfaction, two decades later, that I pen a foreword to this first volume of the Scots Section of *The Linguistic Atlas of Scotland.*

The Linguistic Atlas of Scotland will cover both Gaelic and Scots but I am concerned here only with the Scots side. The first two volumes will be devoted to word-geographical material, and the introduction which comes after this foreword is an introduction to both these volumes, besides providing a sketch of the intellectual background to dialectological study as a whole in this country. The publication of the word-geographical material will be followed by that of the mainly phonological findings gradually assembled and ordered over a period of more than twenty years; these will probably appear in a single large third volume. In it, whatever additional analysis and comment there may be, the presentation of the data will once more be cartographic; no other method can make the same powerful and effective impact, not least because a map is itself a piece of analysis of a kind which the dialectologist responsible is himself most competent to carry out. In this way the reader is relieved from subsequent recourse to the makeshift and time-consuming construction of basic maps of his own.

When the publication of the bulk of the material relating to the whole Scots-speaking area of the country is completed, it is hoped to publish some of the main findings in a more popular form; indeed a valuable handbook on the word-geography of Scotland might well follow the second main volume. Before long it may be that historians, demographers and others will have drawn on the main work for studies which go far beyond dialectology in the narrow sense.

The introduction to this (and the next) volume sets forth what I believe to be compelling arguments in favour of dialectological studies being non-terminating in character; one does not just 'do' the dialectology of Scotland. Much for example remains to be done on the study of urban dialect-complexes from a sociological point of view on the continuing impact of 'standard' forms of pronunciation on regional ones, on dialect problems relating to particular types of community, e.g. the fishing villages. There are also very good reasons for making a thorough dialectal investigation of Scots in its earlier stages, on the lines of work at present being done on Middle English. *The Linguistic Atlas of Scotland* (including the Gaelic material) will provide part of the essential broad framework for such further studies. One may rejoice that other parts of the framework will include an actively progressing full-scale Gaelic dictionary, the *Scottish National Dictionary,* the *Dictionary of the Older Scottish Tongue,* a large and continuing archive of Scottish place-names and a massive and still growing collection of information about material culture and folk traditions. The picture was very different in 1951.

An attempt has been made below to acknowledge our debt to those who have made it possible to assemble and co-ordinate so much information about Scots dialects. For my part I would wish to pay tribute to the authors of the present volume and to their predecessors on the survey itself. But above all I would like to express appreciation to the many hundreds of people all over Scotland and Northern Ireland and in Northumberland, Cumberland and the Isle of Man who have given of their unique knowledge not only freely, but with a wonderful sensitivity and interest: in a very real sense what we are publishing is *theirs.* Finally I do not forget our debt to my friend and mentor John Orr, without the force of whose immense authority and commanding personality the undertaking of dialect and related studies in this country on an adequate scale might never have come about.

ANGUS McINTOSH

INTRODUCTION

THE CONCEPT OF LINGUISTIC GEOGRAPHY IN SCOTLAND

In publishing the first lexical part of the Linguistic Survey of Scotland's material (Scots Section) the editors have, in this Introduction, set themselves the additional task (i) of considering the historical development of such a survey in Scotland, (ii) of setting out the main theoretical concepts upon which its present activities depend, and (iii) of providing an apparatus for guidance and interpretation in the use of the material.

The Linguistic Survey of Scotland is a department in the Faculty of Arts in the University of Edinburgh, and this of itself might be sufficient to emphasise that its general concern is to uphold and develop a continuing and coherent academic discipline in linguistic geography as much as to systematise and publish the results of its lexical or phonological researches which is its immediate but not, in our opinion, its final and sufficient task. Moreover, the study of linguistic geography in the University of Edinburgh is both helped by, and gives help to, a far-reaching ramification of other linguistic disciplines, now generally gathered together in the Department of Linguistics and the Department of English Language; and in the same way it also sustains a particular and mutual relationship with the Dictionary of the Older Scottish Tongue, the Scottish National Dictionary, and the School of Scottish Studies, all of which are located within the University.

It will be convenient to stress at this point that researches in vocabulary and phonology have been approached by the Survey as two separate tasks. That is to say, the gathering of material, the editing, and finally the publication of the lexical material which now appears have been kept apart, editorially, from the phonological material which has been gathered on other occasions, with a different questionnaire, and by a different technique. There is, furthermore, a very considerable *potential* programme in such studies as intonation, grammar, 'standard' Scots, and so on, which must be regarded as future, and separate, tasks. In this division of labour, and of techniques, as well as in some other material points,[1] the LSS differs from linguistic surveys in some other parts of the English-speaking world — in those of England or America, for instance — where both tasks have been combined in one concentrated effort of field-work and by the use of some form of combined lexical and phonological questionnaire.

Nevertheless, the material on which a linguistic survey works, as well as the manner of its collection, are matters of more importance than simple internal working arrangement. Nor is it sufficient merely to presume that in Scotland there is a rich and almost inexhaustible mine of unworked material for dialectology which it is only necessary to exploit in some not very clearly defined direction. There is a very fundamental sense in which the data can only be defined by the intention in gathering the data, and such commonplaces of modern descriptive linguistics as 'there is no such thing as "pure" description', or 'there are no brute facts', are obviously relevant here. For what is being asserted is that the order of activity is not, first, collection of data, *and then* their interpretation, from some 'pure' or detached viewpoint, any more than that this is the necessary order of activity in the study of history. Dialectologists, at least, have been reminded by Ernst Pulgram that they cannot expect to attain to new knowledge from linguistic material other than that which must come from a new *ordering* of their material, and the new insight which follows. Hence, 'what the linguist has to do is to state his purpose, to explain why he expects benefits from pursuing it, and what these benefits will be, and then select and delimit his material accordingly.'[2] Similarly, W.S. Allen has said that the linguist's work is a *creative*, rather than an observational activity. He must deny himself 'the satisfaction of presuming to deal in realities.'[3] And thus for the linguistic geographer, whose business is commonly held to be collection of material (and sometimes little else) it is necessary to assert that he will not first collect and then interpret. He will approach his problem with a declared intention and as a single creative act.

The approach will be true in another direction. For a linguistic geographer engaged in a project like the LSS it will be true not only for his work as an academic codification and systematisation of 'raw' linguistic material but also as one possible complement to a general, and often very vague, reflection on Scots by Scotsmen. It is clear that this reflection can take (and has taken) almost any form from the nostalgic and sentimental to the scientific or pseudo-scientific. It is equally clear that much is to be gained by trying to understand the nature of this reflection in this or that historical situation. Over a hundred years ago A.J. Ellis noted that 'collecting country words is looked upon as an amusement, not as laying a brick in the temple of science',[4] but it is our experience, in Scotland at least, that there has been a certain seriousness of purpose among informants, together with (and perhaps more important) what Franz Boas in his investigation into American Indian culture called 'secondary reasoning and reinterpretation'.[5] Boas considered that in the culture which he studied, specifically *linguistic* phenomena did not rise into consciousness, although other ethnological phenomena (having 'the same unconscious origin') very often did, and were followed by 'secondary reasoning' etc. In Scotland it is clear that linguistic phenomena have certainly, although possibly gradually, risen into consciousness. Historically, it seems to be true that the onset of conscious reinterpretation of the English language in Scotland was preceded by a long period of unanalytical acceptance of 'Inglis' as the language of Lowland Scotland; and the subsequent use of the term 'Scottis' is clearly the product of a reasoned, if also impassioned, reinterpretation. The first native writer to use the term has generally been given as Gavin Douglas (for example, by Sir James Murray).[6] What seems to be of considerable importance in assessing the significance of the term is an observation by Marjorie Bald: 'Just before the Scots dialect entered on its period of decline', she wrote, 'the term "Scottis" was applied.'[7] In fact, in a series of articles Miss Bald analysed the later (sixteenth-century) anglicising influences at work on 'Inglis' in Scotland, especially in the *written* form of the language, and for our purpose here in tracing the history of linguistic activity in Scotland since that period, this will be the first of two categories (the other will be the *spoken* form) about which some account must be given.

From its own type of linguistic codification and systematisation the benefit which the Linguistic Survey of Scotland reasonably expects from its lexical research, and the expectancy which has guided the form of its questionnaires is a cartographical display of word distributions. This is what is now presented. It is, of course, at least conceivable that the contemporary historical situation will set a term to the usefulness of the investigation of distributions. Obviously, much of the value of continuing studies in a lexical linguistic survey must lie in the demonstration of whatever distributional changes take place; and as traditional activities like farming or fishing, for instance, which have always been considered to be high in distributional yield, adopt new techniques or find new rewards in new enterprises, actual *uniformity* of usage may prove to be significant and chiefly worthy of study.

A further point must be made here: it is that a linguistic survey, by definition, can only work out a certain theoretical approach by active and practical investigation. This takes time. It is true that the most penetrating questionnaire can be devised only *après l'enquête,* but even so there is a point where some sort of halt has to be called in the working-out of theoretical advance in the interests of practical achievement in work already undertaken. This, we believe, is the justification for the notion of a linguistic survey as a continuing academic discipline within a university. Its published results will be given greater definition by being set within this continuing framework, and will properly be compared, eventually, with new work on new theoretical bases. Nothing, therefore, can be defined as final except in the special sense that a specific piece of work, like Jakob Jakobsen's in Shetland,[8] for example, has been accomplished in a specific and dissolving situation.

THE HISTORICAL DEVELOPMENT OF LINGUISTIC REFLECTION IN SCOTLAND

All situations are, of course, dissolving, and it is obvious that reflection (formal or informal) by Scotsmen on their language must necessarily be interpreted as it exists within a given historical situation. Even so, it is perfectly possible to represent some sort of continuity between one defined situation and another in Scotland, where reflection on language can be seen to have been transmitted, perhaps adapted or re-stated in some way, and finally re-applied. In looking for such continuity in their studies in Scotland, most dialectologists would put Sir James Murray's *Dialect of the Southern Counties of Scotland* (1873) in a place of central importance. We would maintain here that this can be justified because from this particular vantage point it is possible to look both before and after and with considerable penetration. It is clear, first of all, that the work developed under the widely held and contemporary academic discipline of comparative historical linguistics. So too did Murray's thinking in lexicography. Following the lines both of lexicography and dialectology, therefore, it is not difficult to discern Murray's influence on subsequent formal and scientific linguistic studies in Scotland. But there is also an antecedent native tradition in which the *Dialect of the Southern Counties of Scotland* itself clearly stands. This is not the powerful antiquarian tradition of John Jamieson's *Dictionary* (1808), but a scientific and linguistic tradition which reaches back to the early seventeenth century to Alexander Hume's *Of the Orthographie and Congruitie of the Britan Tongue.*[9]

The written tradition

The link between the seventeenth century and the nineteenth century is to be found in Murray's declared determination to represent systematically what he has to say about Scottish dialects. He stands, therefore, in that tradition in Scotland which has attended specifically to the *written* language as a means of rational linguistic analysis. His intention, he tells us, is defined by three main principles:[10]

> First, to make the spelling systematic; without indeed representing each sound by one invariable symbol in all positions, to provide that the same letter, or combination of letters, should always have the same sound. Secondly, to represent to the eye the differences patent to the ear between the Dialect and the Standard English; to spell words in such a way as at least to suggest that they are not identical in sound with their English representatives. And, thirdly, as far as consistent with the other two principles, to use forms for which a precedent already exists in Scotch usage.

Finally, and in the further interest of exact representation of sounds, Murray gives A.M. Bell's universal table of sounds from his 'Visible Speech' (which also stands in the native Scottish tradition) together with Ellis's 'Palaeotype'.

Alexander Hume was not concerned with Scottish dialects but with the problem of what he called 'uncertentie in our men's wryting'. This was the central linguistic problem of his time, and it was twofold: first, a practical phonemic problem for writers and printers, and, second, a taxonomic problem for philosophers.[11] Both problems were presented by the demands of a particular historical situation – the first by the political and diplomatic revolution of a recently united kingdom, the second by the problem of classification in an increasingly complicated body of knowledge of the physical world. Hume was therefore concerned with 'king's language' as a *written* language, that is, as a powerful, unifying political instrument. 'Thus I have brieflie handled the letteres and their soundes', he wrote, 'quilk . . . I wald wish the printeres in their a, b, c to expresse thus'.[12]

The taxonomic problem was also linguistic. It was, furthermore, a problem for the *written* language inasmuch as contemporary thought was concerned with devising a 'real character' whereby similar phenomena might be represented by similar symbols. An early and somewhat eccentric exponent of the idea, the Scotsman Sir Thomas Urquhart of Cromarty[13] (who is chiefly known as a translator of Rabelais) theorised on a 'world of words [which] hath but two hundred and fifty prime radices upon which all the rest are branched'. So that in considering one of the words a person might 'after a most exact prying into all its letters . . . punctually hit upon the very proper thing it represents in its most special signification.'

Contemporary thought was also much concerned with a *language* (which might even be spoken) as well as with a 'character'. In the mind of another Scotsman, George Dalgarno, less exuberant in temperament than Urquhart, his 'chaine of thought,' as he tells us, connected both character and speech. He began by reflecting that 'the Hebrew does often contract a whole sentence into one word'. And then, 'this compendium did first exite me to do something for improving the art of shorthand; that drove me before I was aware upon a Real character; that again . . . resolved itself into an effable language.'[14]

Dalgarno's intention is 'to frame a language by art from the principles of nature.' Thus, in the construction of this philosophical, and effable, language he proposes to do the best he can with what is left in these latter days, 'of that primitive and Divine or purely rational Sematology, taught by almight God or invented by Adam before the Fall.'[15] The pristine word pattern was an invariable C+V+C+V . . ., but now in the 'defaced reliques' of this first language there are such features as consonant clusters and diphthongs which are the result of the working of art on primitive nature. This is Dalgarno's rationalisation of a usage in word structure which he finds necessary in his philosophical language and, accordingly, he proceeds (in his 'Ars Signorum') to an elaborate phonetic analysis.[16]

The spoken tradition

Dalgarno's introspection into the development of his own thought epitomises a whole sequence of development in linguistic reflection after his own time. As we have seen, certain linguistic problems were implicit in the historical circumstances of a united kingdom. But, for our present purpose of tracing the influence of seventeenth-century linguistic thought on Scotland, by far the greatest impact was made considerably later — in the early nineteenth century — by a revival of the very name of George Dalgarno.

He died in 1687 at Oxford after having spent thirty years teaching in England.[17] In Scotland, his name and reputation seem also to have died, for in 1815 Dugald Stewart declared that he felt 'called on to lay hold of the . . . opportunity . . . of rescuing from oblivion the name of George Dalgarno.'[18] The rescue was timely and appropriate, for by Stewart's time a new concentration of attention, amounting to something like an obsession, had appeared in Scotland, and especially in Edinburgh, on Dalgarno's end point of an 'effable language'. The occasion of this concentration of attention was not the construction of an 'effable philosophical language'.[19] It took the form, rather, of a more ordinary and more manageable and apparently more teachable doctrine of *correctness* in the pronunciation of English in eighteenth-century Scotland. The efforts of Edinburgh's *intelligenzia* in this direction, from Principal Robertson downwards, are well known.[20] But underneath these often ludicrous surface phenomena was something more serious — more serious even than the most dignified essays in correctness. The Scots, observed an Englishman (the Reverend Thomas Morer) in 1715, 'are great critics in Pronunciation and often upbraid us for not giving evry word its due sound.' And he went on to note how they complained when a word like *enough* was pronounced 'neglecting the *gh* as if not written.'[21]

It seems, therefore, that serious 'secondary reasoning and reinterpretation' was concerned with the *due sound* and its manifestation both in speech and writing; and that this was the link between the particular linguistic activities of the seventeenth and eighteenth centuries. There was also an important ancillary activity, namely, remedial speech and the training of the deaf and dumb. In fact, the revival by Dugald Stewart of Dalgarno's name and significance appeared in his paper, given before the Royal Society of Edinburgh, on the celebrated case of the boy James Mitchell, the son of a Morayshire clergyman, and born (1795) blind and deaf.[22] This was, obviously, a clear instance of Dalgarno's postulated case of 'The soul . . . deprived of her principal Secretaries the Eye and the Ear . . . [who] must be contented with the service of her lackeys and scullions, the other senses; which are no less true . . . but not so quick for dispatch',[23] and therefore an important occasion for the study of the *media* of communication.

THE NEW APPROACH IN SCOTTISH PHONETICS AND DIALECTOLOGY

After Dugald Stewart, and continuing in the tradition of this study in Scotland, although not now as a philosopher but as a practical phonetician, stands the commanding figure of Alexander Melville Bell. Already, at the London Alphabetic Congress of 1854, he had rejected the use of the roman alphabet as a universal 'graphic exponent'. Ten years later he wrote: 'My daily professional work in correcting faults of articulation has accustomed me to a very minute discrimination of sounds independently of letters . . . I constructed from the mouth itself a new set of representative letters . . . displaying to the eye the exact position of each sound in the physiological circuit.'[24]

It is important to notice that it was the *generality* of this 'new set of representative letters' which commended itself to a critic like A.J. Ellis,[25] who had himself made one or two essays in the consideration of the linguistic sign. Furthermore, Dugald Stewart's reflections in the case of the boy Mitchell turned on the rejection of a *particular* sign (namely, the articulatory sign) so that the best intention came to be ' . . . not to astonish the vulgar by the sudden conversion of a dumb child into a speaking *automaton;* but by affording scope to those means which Nature herself has provided for the gradual evolution of our intellectual powers to convert [the] pupil into a rational and moral being.'[26]

Out of this new-found generality, particularly in linguistic symbolism, came a concept of *relationship* which was of profound importance for dialectological studies in Scotland. It is this which is new and arresting in Sir James Murray's *Dialect of the Southern Counties of Scotland.* Bell had already argued for his 'Visible Speech' that 'shades of diversity in vowel sound — such as *wheep* for "whip", *doag* for "dog", varieties of *win, wan, won,* for "one" and all minor differences among the elements will ultimately correct each other by the VISIBLE RELATIONS of the alphabetic characters.'[27] Murray reproduced in his work Bell's 'Visible Speech Alphabet' (together with Ellis's 'Palaeotype') in order, he said, 'to show the exact value of the sounds used in the Scottish dialect of the Southern Counties and their relation to the English sounds.'[28] He spoke, expressly, of 'the vowel system of the dialect' which 'is not the English vowel system',[29] and he proceeded to give a minute analysis and comparison in these chosen fields of reference, and, eventually, to an actual grouping of dialects (into North East, Central, and Southern) which he also displayed on a simple map together with 'The present limits of the Gaelic Tongue'.

Linguistic geography in Europe

The 'exact value of the sounds' which Bell and Murray claimed, was not universally conceded even as a new and more precise tool in linguistic geography. There was, it is true, a considerable demand for some sort of phonetic precision in contemporary dialectological work. In Europe, for example, there was Tourtoulon and Bringier's *Étude sur la limite geographique de la langue d'oc et de la langue d'oïl* an investigation on a phonological basis and, in the same year (1876), Winteler's *Die Kerenzer Mundart des Kantons Glarus* which Henry Sweet described as 'an exact analogue of Dr. J.A.H. Murray's "Dialect of the Southern Counties of Scotland", . . . an English and a German philologist arriving independently at precisely the same method of dealing with a living dialect.'[30] Nevertheless, claims to phonetic exactness through physiological analysis were severely criticised by Moritz Trautmann of Bonn[31] who attacked both Bell and Sievers. Bell's system, was 'ein ausgetifteltes system'; whereas, his own, based on a combined physiological/harmonic analysis of vowels 'ruht auf den grundlagen eines naturgesetzes'. These views, expressed in 1881, were no doubt some sort of rejoinder to Sweet's 'Preface' in his *Handbook of Phonetics*[32] which charged German phonetic scholarship with being particularly defective in its treatment of vowels — a charge probably all the more pointed because both Bell and Murray had given these especial attention and had used the image of a 'skeleton' with which to treat quickly of the relatively minor function of consonants.

The Scottish Dialect Committee

Nevertheless, and in spite of controversies such as these, it is possible to judge (of course after the event, but from the point of view of a modern linguistic survey) that problems of *scope* in the extent of a survey and of *display*, analysis, and communication in its results were left relatively untouched by essays in phonetic 'exactness' — or 'hair-splitting' as Henry Sweet was cheerfully prepared to call it.[33] In Scotland, at least, it was as if Murray's *alter idem* — that is to say, the linguistic geographer who existed side by side with the lexicographer — had inexplicably receded, or at least had not advanced, after the publication of *The Dialect of the Southern Counties of Scotland.* Murray proceeded to the editorship of the *New English Dictionary;* and when in 1909 William Grant (eventually to become the first editor of the *Scottish National Dictionary)*[34] published a pamphlet with the title: *What Still Remains to be Done for the Scottish Dialects,*[35] there was no clear theoretical or methodological advance proposed or discussed (either then or later) other than on lexicography or on the recording of pronunciation as part of lexicography. Grant restated the three headings under which the Scottish Dialect Committee was prepared to proceed: '(1) by gathering in words, meanings and usages which have not yet been recorded in any dictionary; (2) by an exact description of the pronunciation of existing Scottish words; (3) by dividing the country into dialect areas corresponding to differences of pronunciation.' Under (1) there was to be a clear advance over Jamieson's *Dictionary* especially in the treatment of etymologies. Under (2) Grant, who was himself a phonetician and lectured on the subject in the Aberdeen Training College, envisaged a type of 'correspondent' in dialect research in Scotland who should have had proper phonetic training; and, in fact, the lecturers in phonetics in the Edinburgh and Dundee Training Colleges joined the Scottish Dialect Committee and engaged to enlist their best students. 'With their help,' Grant went on, 'the Committee hope to dot the country with correspondents who have an expert knowledge of sounds.'

The problem of a dialect atlas

Under heading (3), however, there was no mature thought or discussion on any of the actual *problems* — especially problems in interpretation — involved in 'dividing the country into dialect areas.' This was in very marked contrast with the general climate of dialectological opinion and debate in Europe. The twenty years before Grant's pamphlet had seen (at the very least) Gaston Paris's celebrated paradox: 'Dans une masse linguistique de même origine que la nôtre, il n'y a *reellement pas de dialectes*[36] Hermann Fischer's 'Verkehrsgrenzen'; and Karl Haag's 'Kernlandschaften'.[37] Above all, and preceding all these, the problems of linguistic geography had been given practical consideration in Georg Wenker's *Sprachatlas des Deutschen Reiches.*[38] In discussing these problems a few years later, A.J. Ellis seized on what he believed to be Wenker's most significant contribution, which was to solve the problem of the communication of the results of research in linguistic geography cartographically. Certainly, Ellis argued, in one respect 'his attempt falls short of mine, because I aim at the utmost possible phonetic exactness'. Nevertheless, when he considered Wenker's scope (30,000 localities) and his system of reference which broke down the forty sentences of his questionnaire into 274 linguistic 'facts', Ellis was bound to ask the most important question of all, namely, 'how to make this enormous mass of information available', and was satisfied that Wenker's maps provided an effective answer.[39]

Even so, there were very great problems for the reader in the handling of the large number of maps in the *Sprachatlas* and in the establishment of any sort of relatively quick synoptic view of a particular usage. Yet no such problems of scope or display were mentioned or considered in Scotland even as late as 1908. Grant merely noted it as 'a reproach to our scholarship that Sir James Murray's treatise on Border Scotch is still, after thirty-five years' interval, almost *sui generis.*'[40] It is clear that Grant continued to stand in the tradition of Bell, Murray and Ellis for the 'utmost possible phonetic exactness' and in the tradition of Murray for lexicography 'on historical principles'. In point of fact, Scotland had to wait another thirty years before any sort of basic problem in linguistic geography, especially the supremely important problem of cartographic display in some form of dialect atlas, was actively and adequately discussed. It is true that in 1914 the first of the *Transactions of the Scottish Dialect Committee* proposed in future issues to give an 'Account of the distribution of peculiar pronunciations over different districts with maps to illustrate'. But this did not happen. The financial resources of the Committee were, in fact, consumed in the publication of four numbers of its *Transactions* (1914-21). Yet important theoretical and practical problems in the linguistic geography of Scotland were revived in the 1930s, and from another direction. It is significant that they were reintroduced, and refreshed in some sense from Europe, through the activity and influence of John Orr, Professor of French Language and Romance Linguistics in the University of Edinburgh, and Gilliéron's pupil.

The Orr Memorandum

In 1936 Professor Orr prepared a Memorandum[41] on the idea of a comprehensive Linguistic Survey of Scotland for the guidance of the Language Survey Committee (of which he was chairman) of the Scottish Archive for Ethnological, Folkloristic and Linguistic Studies — a co-ordinating archive for various established societies in Scotland with these general aims. A sub-committee had already discussed the project earlier in the year. Earlier still, in 1935, a possible 'Survey of the dialects of the British Isles' had received some attention from a committee under the chairmanship of Professor Wilhelm Horn at the Second International Phonetic Congress in London.[42] Orr's Memorandum took as a model what was described as 'the best existing Atlas', namely Jaberg and Jud's *Sprach- und Sachatlas Italiens und der Südschweiz* (1928-40) and set out some of the problems involved in any full-scale essay in linguistic geography: (i) it was probable that a full and definitive questionnaire could only be used after some considerable initial investigation because, in order to concentrate field-work to the best advantage, it was necessary to determine as far as possible in advance of the final and formal investigation 'where regional differences in speech are marked and numerous, and . . . where speech is less diversified'; (ii) it was necessary always to register the 'immediate response' of an informant (this was, and is, 'controversial and was not adopted by the LSS); (iii) the questionnaire should be comprehensive (1,500 words) and should cover both Scots and Gaelic areas in the proportion of one hundred Scots to fifty Gaelic points (a pilot survey using a short questionnaire of fifty-six words was actually distributed; see p. 10 below; (iv) it was essential to map the information obtained so that a complete map for any item 'would consist of an outline map of Scotland with 150 forms of [the] word or its local equivalent, each inscribed close to the number standing on the map for the locality where the form is current. The complete Atlas would therefore contain as many maps as there are words in the questionnaire' (see our map type (1), p. 20).

The Memorandum did not explicitly require quite separate investigations in Scots and Gaelic, nor did it envisage a division of activity into separate lexical and phonological concentrations which eventually came to be one of the defining characteristics of the Scots section of the LSS. There were, however, to be phoneticians as 'observers' and it was also foreseen that 'for any detailed investigation of the speech of a given locality in all its aspects of pronunciation, rhythm, intonation, syntax, etc., the information supplied by the Atlas would of course be inadequate and would need to be supplemented and checked by prolonged study in the locality'. In the event, and as we have already tried to make clear, problems like these involving particular and local study have been met, at least for the phonological side of our research, by work done in the field by a member of the LSS staff.

The Linguistic Survey of Scotland

The possibility of a linguistic survey for the British Isles was diminished by the outbreak of war in 1939, but not wholly obliterated. After the war, in 1946, the project was taken up within the Philological Society and Professor Dieth of Zürich and Professor Orton of Leeds contributed a paper: 'A new survey of English dialects' which was not published in the Society's *Transactions,* although an essay with the same title appeared in 1947 under the auspices of the English Association and under Dieth's name. There, he insisted on the need for a survey which would ultimately cover the whole of Britain — 'her great Linguistic Domesday Book', as he called it — and he continued to point out, as a European critic, the poverty of dialect studies in Britain. The culmination, for England at least, of this stimulation was the active collaboration of Dieth and Orton, at the University of Leeds, on a linguistic atlas of England and, as a first step, the publication in 1952 of their joint work, *A Questionnaire for a Linguistic Atlas of England.* Scotland, which had already engaged Dieth's attention in Volume I of his *Grammar of the Buchan Dialect* (1932), continued to attract his pupils — Zai published a study of a dialect in Roxburghshire and Wettstein of Berwickshire. Twenty years later, and independently of the LSS which was by then actively working, the German Wolfgang Wölck (a pupil of Herbert Pilch) also worked in Dieth's own area of Buchan. So, indeed, had another German, Mutschmann, as early as 1909.[43]

There were, nevertheless, other influences on Scotland from Europe, broader than dialectology but with ultimate reference to dialectological procedures and techniques. These were the influences of Trubetzkoy, de Saussure and Hjelmslev which were mediated and assayed in Edinburgh in the early 1950s through a broadening of linguistic disciplines in the University, and thus through scholars established either in an existing department extended in scope, as with the appointment in 1948 of Angus McIntosh as the first Professor of English Language and General Linguistics, or in the formation of a new department, as with the appointment of David Abercrombie (now Professor) as head of the Department of Phonetics. Professor McIntosh and Professor Abercrombie, together with Professor Kenneth H. Jackson, Professor of Celtic since 1949, have in committee administered the LSS.

Two important influences from within Britain itself also added their own particular character to the general linguistic climate in the University. These were the influences of the thought of J.R. Firth who, in the University of London, occupied the first chair of General Linguistics in Britain, and of the development and realignment (in the direction, for example, of the significance of the phonematic unit) of the native phonetic tradition. This was the living and direct phonetic tradition of Bell, Ellis, Sweet, Daniel Jones and David Abercrombie. For linguistic geography this development also meant a rediscovery and reassessment of certain latent features, like synchronicity of approach for instance, in the work of Sir James Murray; and the rediscovery was all the more cogent when, as an outcome both of the constant effort of Professor John Orr and of the widening linguistic activity in the University, the LSS was finally instituted in 1949. It began by being administered by the University Court through an executive committee, and then in 1965 it became a department within the Faculty of Arts, with its executive committee continuing.

We have already urged once or twice in this introduction our own particular opinion that the LSS should be seen to be an academic basis for a continuing discipline in linguistic geography. We would observe now that the linguistic climate of opinion in Edinburgh which has surrounded it since its inception fully justifies this. And it would seem clear that current attitudes in linguistics and related fields support the concept of something more than a survey disposed only to accomplish a defined task in a given time like (to use the example we have already given) Jakob Jakobsen's in Shetland. The characteristic *ramification* of contemporary linguistic studies (indeed of all modern scientific studies) was already becoming clear in a series of formative linguistics seminars held within the University in the early 1950s; and the synchronic and systemic approach of the Scots survey in the LSS was thus worked out within a wider atmosphere of linguistic thought. It is also worth noticing in this connection that in a directly related way synchronic techniques have been developed and applied in a *historical* situation by

Professor Angus McIntosh and Professor Michael Samuels in their studies in Middle English dialectology.[44] Members of the LSS staff have usually had extensive, ramified, linguistic interests. The first appointment, that of H.J. Uldall (Hjelmslev's collaborator) in 1950, was not made directly to the LSS but to the Department of English Language and General Linguistics. Uldall gave up his lectureship in the following year to work in Copenhagen, and succeeding appointments have been made directly to the LSS. At present (1974) the academic staff (for the Scots section) comprises J.Y. Mather and H.H. Speitel. Former members (Scots section) have been J.S. Woolley, J.C. Catford and Trevor Hill. Contributions to the theory of linguistic geography have therefore been made from within a much wider linguistic discipline. At the same time the Survey has been fortunate that theory has at no point been dissociated from practical field-work.[45]

THE THEORETICAL APPROACH OF THE LSS

In its theoretical background the LSS is a product of the second half of the 1940s. There has been some advantage in this late start in Scottish dialectological studies in that these have benefited from certain theoretical developments, especially in phonological work. In the last twenty years most of the theoretical concepts underlying the Scottish Survey e.g., synchronicity and systemicity, have been widely accepted and developed but the emphasis of linguistic analysis has now shifted to the syntactical level. As has been pointed out above, it is an inherent feature of linguistic investigations to be 'out of step' when their projects are carried to an end[46] and to this the LSS is no exception. This makes it all the more important to state explicitly their presuppositions.

We should accordingly consider the lexical investigations of the LSS within the framework of general dialectology. Many of the ideas were, of course, not formulated in their present form at the beginning of the research. We believe that in many ways we are perhaps much more aware of the limitations of the methodology of postal enquiry, which will be discussed later. But we are firmly convinced that, in spite of necessary qualifications, we have been able to establish valid and important results within the scope of our enquiry.

Dialectology

Dialectology is not a well-defined and clearly delimited discipline within linguistics. Even the term 'dialect' is itself not very precise. There is also a good deal of confusion between the terms 'dialectology' and 'dialect geography'; this is understandable, because in the past the aim of dialect studies has often been simply to publish dialect maps and atlases. It is therefore necessary to define these terms.

It might be useful to start with a rather wide definition of dialectology which can be narrowed down to suit particular circumstances:[47]

Dialectology is the study of permanent linguistic varieties within a language community

Three terms need clarification and expansion: (1) language community, (2) permanent linguistic varieties, and (3) study.

(1) By a *language community* we mean a group of people who can be shown to share the same language. Language, in this sense would be the total[48] of permanent (and, of course, transient) speech varieties (cf. next paragraph) for which there exist linguistically relevant reasons for grouping them together.[49]

(2) We have accepted J.C. Catford's classification of *speech varieties* into *permanent* and *transient.* A language variety is defined by Catford as 'a subset of formal and/or substantial features which correlates with a particular type of socio-situational feature'.[50]

In a speaker's idiolect there will be features which can be affiliated to his regional or social provenance (permanent characteristics), and others which will depend on the immediate situation in which the speech act occurs (transient characteristics). Dialectology has been mainly interested in permanent regional features. Permanent *social* characteristics have been rather neglected and have only recently received more attention.[51]

This division is purely heuristic. In fact, most present-day speakers may be said to have more than one permanent variety at their disposal (e.g. 'dialect' and 'standard', see p. 8) and their choice of one rather than the other (or, in the case of a mixing of varieties, the predominance of features of one rather than the other) will depend largely on the situation in which the speaker produces his utterance. A speaker or a group of speakers has what can be called a *potential to perform* in one, two, or more varieties and the linguist can test the competence in any of them and try to assign it to a geographical area and/ or social group (by whichever criteria the latter might be established).

So far we have stated the case for the spoken medium, but the classification is also meant to be applicable to the written medium. In a written text a person may reveal permanent regional and social features as well as transient features.[52] To attribute them to one or the other will depend on what we can gather from similar texts and, where possible, from inferences from the spoken medium.

At this point the dimension of time must be introduced. The linguist will either look at varieties over a period of time in which they have undergone changes (diachronic method) or he will look at them at any point of time and describe them as more or less static phenomena in terms of the internal interdependence of their linguistic elements (synchronic method).

Diachronically, speech varieties are said to belong to the same language if a great number of their present-day linguistic characteristics can be traced back to a common ancestor. In this case they are said to be genetically related. The emphasis is, from this point of view, on changes from the 'base'[53] (i.e., the earliest available or postulated variety) over periods of time, which account (partially) for the present linguistic speech varieties. Stages in this development are called *temporal* dialects (e.g., Old English, Middle English, Early Modern English etc.) and the thread which holds them together is their gradual change. There must, therefore, have been *continuity* in time. This is the method of historical dialectology.[54]

Synchronically, the most commonly used criterion for proving affiliation to a common language is *mutual intelligibility* between linguistic varieties in space and society, either directly, or along a chain of other linguistic varieties.[55] It might be better to speak about a *linguistic continuity* in space and society which is actually *established* by a linguist. The concept of mutual intelligibility, which is often difficult to apply, would then be one reflex of this. This also leaves open

the possibility of non-contiguity of speech varieties.
Difficulties may arise in the exact definition of one *language* from another genetically related one,[56] but this is not a complicating issue in our case. The synchronic viewpoint has been adopted in the present work.

It must be remembered that the two ways of looking at language are a construct by the linguist, and are in fact interdependent: continuity in space and in society is only possible, if there is a sufficiently large body of common core[57] linguistic features at all linguistic levels[58] of analysis between the language varieties under consideration. This common core owes its origin to a large extent to the common history of these varieties.

(3) In the *study* of varieties we can perhaps distinguish between three processes: (i) the establishment of varieties, (ii) the comparison and classification of these, and (iii) the interpretation. These can take place at any of the linguistic levels at which these varieties are studied: phonetic/phonological, lexical, grammatical.[59] For the first two processes the main tool is the *questionnaire* which makes it possible to achieve *comparability* of material, a necessity for all branches of dialectology.

Linguistic Geography

Within the discipline of dialectology this is only one particular, if very interesting, subdivision. It is concerned with the study of elements of language varieties in their relative geographical positions and tries to establish linguistic distribution areas, which can be shown on maps,[60] by a comparison of linguistic data. This is the approach chosen by the LSS for the present project.

In achieving this aim extensive use is made of the concept of the *isogloss* which is defined as a line that surrounds an area in which a particular linguistically defined phenomenon (or set of phenomena) is found.

Outside the isogloss the particular phenomenon is (a) absent or (b) does not form a coherent linguistic area i.e., it is not sufficiently concentrated. The absence can be due to various factors: (i) Another linguistic area abuts (or overlaps). (ii) There are no returns from informants in that area and the isogloss is then drawn on the basis of an *argumentum ex silentio* and therefore difficult to interpret. (Where informants do not respond, there has either been some misunderstanding of the question or the question itself makes no sense in that area, e.g. the 'thing' asked for may not be known). (iii) The area outside the isogloss is uninhabited. We believe that it is important to take physical geographical features which often condition (iii) into consideration, so that our isoglosses often follow geographical contours.[61]

To attempt to establish the causes which shape linguistic areas is one of the goals of linguistic geography. (See p. 16 study (iii) interpretation). Nevertheless, we have intentionally not dealt with this because our knowledge is still so limited. To try to do this even cursorily would take us beyond linguistics into fields where fundamental work has still to be done in Scotland in other branches of scholarship. Many of the long accepted hypotheses put forward by linguistic geographers during the last century have been severely (perhaps too severely) criticised,[62] and they will require further thought.

Terms for speech varieties of English

It is now possible to sketch the particular linguistic situation in the United Kingdom and especially in Scotland against the foregoing general remarks. To do this we shall employ a number of terms which are in general use, but will be defined here more precisely in a technical sense.[63] Although our proposed classification of varieties is, of course, a fairly rough and simplified construct which is at the moment being considerably refined by the application of some of the recent developments in sociology, it has nevertheless proved useful in our investigations.

To the English language community in our area the following general terms are relevant: 'Standard English', 'accents', 'dialects'.

Standard English: the variety found all over the area, considered to be the 'same' at the grammatical and lexical levels [SE].

Accents: varieties of pronunciation of Standard English (i.e. differing from each other phonetically and/or phonologically).

Dialects: varieties differing from Standard English at all levels and usually deviating from SE accents much more radically than these accents amongst each other.

These terms are rather flexible in that they do not specify what degree of similarity is required to attribute a variety to one or the other category. This explains why there is often some confusion[64] when the criteria are not set out. Thus there are clearly differences in vocabulary and usage between the Standard English in Scotland and that in Southern England or in the Midlands and within these wide geographical regions one could establish further regional subclasses in which each class comprises varieties which are more similar to each other than the varieties in another class (which covers a different area). Linguists speak about Scottish, Southern English, Midland etc., *dialects* in this sense, but we should prefer to restrict the use of dialect to varieties as defined above and we will neglect certain minor regional differences in the Standard English of our area.

Varieties in the atlas area. Our investigation covered the whole of Scotland, the two northern counties of England bordering on Scotland (Cumberland and Northumberland), the six counties of Northern Ireland, and some neighbouring parts of Eire.

Apart from immigrant minorities there are two distinct languages which the LSS has set out to investigate, *English* and *Gaelic.*[65] There are no difficulties in keeping the two separate historically as well as synchronically (they are, for example, mutually unintelligible). Map A shows from which localities the first postal questionnaire was returned by Gaelic speakers. These do not concern us further as the Scots Section of the LSS is only dealing with varieties of the English language. Standard English is found all over the atlas area and there are now only few mono-lingual Gaelic speakers left. An investigation of the accents i.e., phonetic/phonological differences of the SE in the area is still outstanding, but there is one important subvariety of accent in Scotland which is SE on a Gaelic substratum (both in the formerly Gaelic speaking areas and also, where the language is still spoken). This is usually called *Highland English.* The term 'Highland' refers to the present geographical area in which this accent is found and also to the historic (but, of course, shifting) border between Gaelic and English and their dialects, the Highland Line. Map A shows some attempts which have been made to define the line linguistically. This includes our own interpretation, which is based on the phonological sections of PQ1 and indicates the maximal extension of certain phonological features of Scots dialects. It may suffice to say here that north, east, and south of the line we find the speech varieties which we call *Scots dialect(s)* proper. Even a quick glance at the bulk of our maps in this volume will show that dialect vocabulary is found far beyond this phonological line in the (formerly) Gaelic area. This illustrates one of the commonplaces of dialectology: that words travel more easily than sounds: that is that words are more easily borrowed from one language (or language variety) into another than, say, sound systems. Thus we find, in many cases, Scots dialect words or expressions in Highland areas and, on the other hand, especially in Inverness-shire and further north, Gaelic words persisting in English speech varieties. As the first two volumes of this atlas are concerned with linguistic phenomena at the lexical level, dialect is here mainly defined as deviation from SE vocabulary. Synchronically it does not matter whether a dialect item is of Germanic or Celtic or other origin. We have therefore included dialect vocabulary from areas which are inside the Highland area, if the informants were speakers of English.

Similar problems of division exist in Northern Ireland, but they have not yet been fully explored and even the terminology used by research workers is rather varied. We have tried on Map A to adapt the researches of R.J. Gregg and G.B. Adams.[66] It is possible to distinguish between Ulster dialects of Scots provenance and those of English provenance. Gregg has investigated the areal extension of certain Scots features and established a linguistic dividing line. Detailed work on the Ulster dialects of English provenance has not yet appeared.[67] We prefer to call the SE spoken in Ulster *Ulster English,* although there are possible groupings into geographically distributed accents. The Gaelic area in the west of Ulster is based on the 1951 census.[68]

Lastly, we must mention Orkney and Shetland which are separated, like Ireland and some islands on the west coast of Scotland, from the Scottish mainland, but belong to the same (English) language community in spite of strong Norse linguistic influence.

Bilingualism For the understanding of our methodology some discussion of the term is essential. It is usually applied to speakers of two or more distinct languages, say, Norwegian and English or Gaelic and English. For our purpose we propose to extend the term to cover speakers with more than one permanent language variety at their disposal. It must be assumed that the majority of our informants (i.e., those who completed the lexical questionnaire themselves) were bilingual in the sense that they had (1) knowledge of SE and one of its accents, since at least they had to be able to read and understand the questions, and (2) that they spoke the local dialect i.e., if we leave non-lexical questions aside, that they used vocabulary which differed from SE completely (different consonontal skeleton, see p. 16 below, Interpretation of the Informants' Spelling) or differed from the locally acceptable pronunciation of the item as given in the SE question (ibid).

We will discuss the details of this in the sections on the questionnaire and on spelling, but we think it is important to stress a point we have made in general terms above: bilingualism in our extended sense usually leads to the mixing of features, at all linguistic levels, of the two (or more) permanent language varieties involved; it is very seldom the case that a speaker keeps these varieties rigorously apart. Field-work experience has taught us that it is very difficult to find informants who speak 'pure' dialect in the sense of using consistently in all situations and contexts all the maximally deviant features from SE which have been observed over a period of time. It might be more realistic to consider the 'pure' dialect in our area as a *potential* which the linguist has to investigate as best he can. This requires considerable skill at the phonetic/phonological level, but is perhaps most readily understood by informants and collaborators with regard to vocabulary, although at least in Scotland we have found a great deal of sophistication at the phonological level too. What is presented in the first two volumes, therefore, is regional difference from SE at the lexical level. It is necessary to remember that we do not attempt to say how many or which people in a certain locality know or would use the word which actually appears in our list or how often and in which situation a given informant would actually produce this word himself. There are often one or more alternative expressions available to him for a SE item. Which they are is largely determined by his regional provenance. Our material will give, we believe, ample exemplification of this.

Map A.

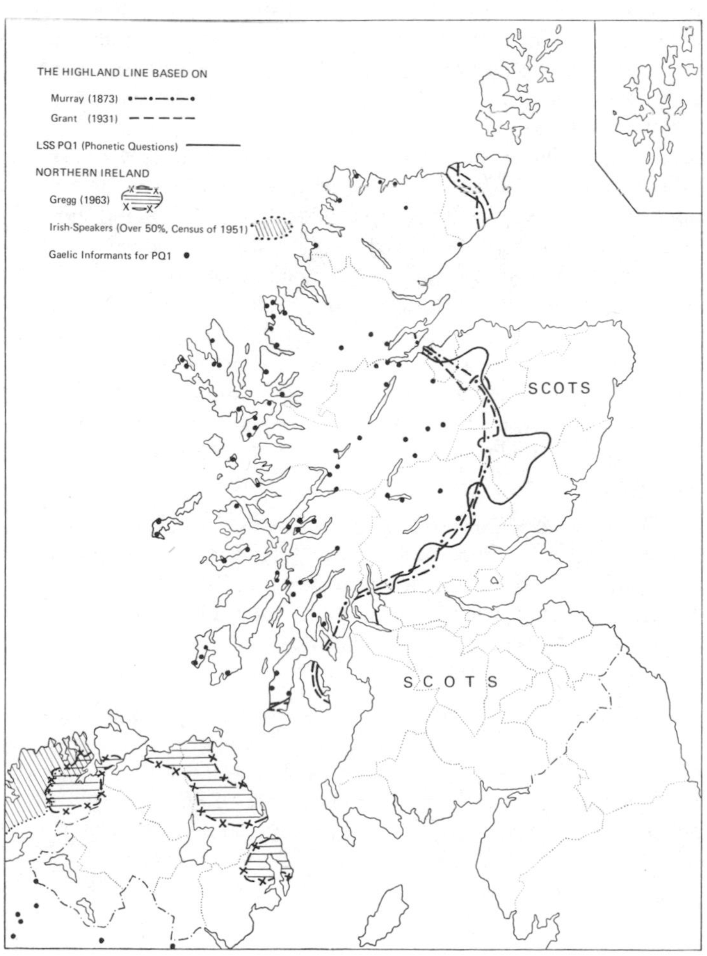

The place of the questionnaire in dialectology

The questionnaire is of great importance as a tool in dialectology (cf. p. 8). Its set of questions must be appropriate to the purpose of the enquiry, and the success or failure of the investigation depend largely upon it. It reflects a certain state of knowledge before the beginning of the enquiry together with the presuppositions of its author. Gilliéron seems to have realised this fully, when he said, *'le questionnaire . . . pour être sensiblement meilleur, aurait dû être fait après l'enquête.*[69] The progressive elimination of error must be the aim in dialectology as in other sciences: each enquiry fails partially, but carries at the same time the seeds for further investigation and the extension of knowledge. Accordingly, our questionnaire and atlas can best be considered as a tentative step towards the acquisition of knowledge.[70]

The postal questionnaire method

The distinguishing factor of the postal questionnaire method (also called 'indirect' method) is that there is *no direct contact* between the investigator and the informant and that literate, but (predominantly) linguistically untrained *intermediaries* have to be involved who are responsible for the selection of informants and, in many cases, the written form of the answers. The method has a long tradition which has been traced back to the sixteenth century.[71] It was first employed for the purpose of linguistic geography on a national scale by Georg Wenker for the German *Sprachatlas* in its various stages from the 1870s onwards. Wenker used the national primary school teachers as intermediaries or informants. As it was aimed at eliciting material for which the 'indirect method' is least suitable, namely for phonetic transcriptions of common core vocabulary,[72] it incurred a great deal of criticism and subsequent linguistic surveys, especially the Romance *enquêtes,* preferred personal interview by trained field-workers ('direct' method). This method subsequently became part of a school of dialectology where the field-work method and the way of questioning (see below) were of the first importance, sometimes, in our opinion, to the neglect of the selection and organisation of the actual questionnaire material. One of the major projects using the postal method in this century was W. Mitzka's *Deutscher Wortatlas* (material collected in 1939-40) which concentrates, as the name suggests, on lexical problems.[73] It was also employed in regional investigations in Germany. In the United States[74] it mainly supplemented field-work findings.

There are obvious advantages in the direct method, since an investigator can then attend directly to the selection of informants, the accuracy of the phonetic details of the collected material, the evaluation of answers, the possibility of sorting out difficulties on the spot, of investigating additional problems not sufficiently provided for in the questionnaire, etc.[75]

The postal questionnaire, on the other hand, can reach a far greater number of places and informants more quickly[76] and at less expense and can provide useful information in certain linguistic fields.[77] It seems especially suitable in the collection of lexical data[78] and is cheaper than using field-workers who might in any case then devote themselves to more intricate investigations.[79] If it could in future benefit from the rather sophisticated questionnaires developed more recently in other fields of human enquiry (e.g. sociology, market research) the results might more favourably compare with those obtained by direct contact with the informants.[80]

The LSS postal questionnaire

We turn now to a discussion of the LSS postal questionnaire I [PQ1]. General points regarding the indirect approach will be made at the appropriate stage.

Sources. It has already been made clear that each survey has to draw actively at its beginnings on particular previous knowledge. It cannot be constructed on generalised lines, but only with reference to the cultural and linguistic background of the region and people. For this reason the two LSS postal questionnaires benefited largely from lexicographical knowledge available in Scotland and explored and developed possibilities which were known to exist (see pp 3-4 above). In the first place, therefore, assistance was obtained from the editors of the *Scottish National Dictionary*[81] (D. D. Murison) and the *Dictionary of the Older Scottish Tongue* (A. J. Aitken) who provided word lists of potentially useful questionnaire items.

There exists in the LSS files a lexical questionnaire, which was distributed some time after 1936 by the Scottish Archive for Ethnological, Folkloristic, and Linguistic Studies, Language Survey Committee of which the chairman was John Orr.[82] It consisted of five pages and was divided into various topics. There were altogether fifty-six questions, many of which appear also in PQ1.[83]

Another short lexical questionnaire was constructed by John Orr and used in the first LSS pilot field-work project by his former pupil J. C. Catford in 1950. As it is of some historical interest, it is reproduced here:

1. A CROWD/ 2. of CHILDREN/ 3. followed the PEDLAR.
4. They were playing TRUANT.
5. One of the BOYS/ 6. STUMBLED and fell
7. into the OPEN DRAIN/ 8. near the PIGSTY
9. and SPRAINED/ 10. his ANKLE.
11. Under the HENCOOP/ 12. we saw a GREAT LOT
13. of SPIDERS/ 14. and EARWIGS.
15. One of the GIRLS/ 16. fell into the MUD
17. and SPOILED/ 18. her CLEAN APRON.
19. There were enough CRUMBS/ 20. to make a POULTICE
21. for a SPLINTER.

Further pilot schemes were tested by Angus McIntosh in his English language classes and some short trial questionnaires were sent out by post. Assistance was also obtained from those working on the *Atlas of the United States of America,* especially with regard to lexical postal questionnaire techniques as developed by A. L. Davis and Fred G. Cassidy.[84]

Contents of PQ1. In Appendix E we give a condensed list of the complete number of items in PQ1 (numbered consecutively). Questions included in Orr's two preliminary questionnaires are maked + ((+) where the identification is doubtful or difficult).

Arrangement and selection of items. It will be seen that the questionnaire items are mainly chosen from the vocabulary of the parts of the human body and its ailments, names for people of various age groups, everyday life and activities (especially of farming communities), children's games, insects, birds, etc. Related questions are kept together (topical arrangement), some forming semantic fields. These topics were chosen because the LSS was here interested by definition in areal distributions and therefore tried not only to cover as many localities and groups of people as possible but also to select such groups for their known variation in lexical usage. By these criteria agriculture seems to offer the most suitable field for investigation. Mining and fishing communities also use a great variety of terms, but are restricted to certain parts of the country. Likewise, urban communities are restricted to certain areas and tend, moreover, not to show such a great variety of terms eligible for an overall lexical questionnaire. This is not, of course, to say that these sections of society should or could be neglected by dialectology; in fact, the LSS has been carrying out some research in these fields[85] and will eventually produce specialised questionnaires for detailed investigation of smaller areas.

The layout of the questionnaire book. The questionnaire was produced in book form (11 in. x 8 in.) with a stiff cardboard cover bearing on its front an embossed University of Edinburgh crest and the words *Linguistic Survey of Scotland, University of Edinburgh.* This formal and official exterior was chosen to impress on collaborators and informants the fact that they were being involved in a serious and important enquiry.[86]

The book contained forty-four leaves of thick stiff paper (in view of their frequent eventual use as slips). Pages 1-2 (our pagination) were taken up by the General Information, pages 3-5 (our pagination) by the Detailed Instructions. Except for the last five leaves (general questions, Gaelic questions; see item 211, App. E) each leaf was subdivided into six 2in x 3in. rectangles, thus yielding six slips of equal size, when the questionnaire was cut up with a printer's guillotine.[87] Each of the slips bore one question (the back was reserved for comments which could not be accommodated on the front).

001662

NAME
(Mr, Mrs, Miss)

ADDRESS

How long have you lived in the above place ?

Born : Place Year

Father's Birthplace

Mother's Birthplace

001662

GRID
(nothing to be written here)

NAME

ADDRESS

COUNTY

001662

1. CHILD Line 1

USUAL LOCAL WORD(S) Line 2

LESS COMMON LOCAL WORD(S) Line 3

BY WHOM USED Line 4

COMMENTS Line 5

001662

2. BOY (aged about 12)

USUAL LOCAL WORD(S)

LESS COMMON LOCAL WORD(S)

BY WHOM USED

COMMENTS (Have you different words for a boy according to his age ?)

001662

3. GIRL (aged about 12)

USUAL LOCAL WORD(S)

LESS COMMON LOCAL WORD(S)

BY WHOM USED

COMMENTS (Have you different words for a girl according to her age ?)

001662

4. YOUNG MAN (around 20)

USUAL LOCAL WORD(S)

LESS COMMON LOCAL WORD(S)

BY WHOM USED

COMMENTS

We reproduce as a sample of the first page of the questionnaire (Fig. 1). Every book has a number which appears in the top right-hand corner of each slip and facilitates its identification. The first two slips on the left-hand side, the 'name-slip' and the 'grid-slip' respectively, contain the *personalia* of the informant and overlap partially, but are essential for cross-indexing. The national grid (see p. 15) was entered on both these slips on the return of the books to the Survey.

The 'Detailed Instructions' and the question slips. The construction of the rest of the slips which are numbered consecutively from 1-207 and contain the actual linguistic questions is best examined in connection with the Detailed Instructions [DI] (pp. 3-5 of the questionnaire according to our pagination).[88]

DETAILED INSTRUCTIONS.

In the top left-hand corner of most of the six rectangles numbered 1 to 184 in the booklet is a word or phrase, e.g. HARE or PANE (of glass), and underneath you are asked to give the word or words commonly used for this in your own locality. The following points should be noted, BUT IF THEY SEEM TOO COMPLICATED, REMEMBER THAT ONLY 1 and 2 ARE VITALLY IMPORTANT :—

1. The word or words used in your district should be spelt as far as possible in such a way as to indicate your local pronunciation of them. Please write all such words in BLOCK CAPITALS. Comments, etc., can be written in ordinary writing. Always use INK if possible.
2. In the part of the booklet where the pages are divided into rectangles, only words and phrases used in YOUR OWN district should be entered (except under COMMENTS, where you are free to give other information). By thus drawing on your intimate knowledge of ONE dialect, we shall get a clear and detailed picture of where certain words are used and where they are not.
3. Do not worry if you cannot supply an answer to some of the questions; just leave these blank. But in cases where you definitely use the same word as that given at the top of a rectangle, put it down, using a spelling which will indicate how it is pronounced.
4. The words in brackets which are sometimes to be found before or after the "main" word, e.g. SOAKED (with rain), are just put there to make the meaning of the main word as clear as possible; they need not be "translated."
5. If two or more words are in common use in your district, you should list them. This applies to very similar words like *quean* and *quine* or *webster* and *wabster*, as well as to quite distinct words like *bairn*, *wean*, and *chiel* or *doit* and *gomeril*. If the words you list are not equally common, you are asked to put the less usual one(s) on the line below, and on the line below this (opposite BY WHOM USED) to say whether these are used, say, only by old people, or by children, or by incomers, or by people of some particular occupation. A typical reply would then look like this :

   8. CROWD

   USUAL LOCAL WORD(s) *Crood*

   LESS COMMON LOCAL WORD(s) *bourach*

   BY WHOM USED *Mostly by old people only*

   COMMENTS *My mother often used the word "mardle" but it is never heard here now.*

6. In some cases you may happen to know that a word you have given is used with a different meaning in some other place. If so, you should give this information under COMMENTS. E.g. :

   176. EARWIG (the fork-tailed insect with six legs)

   USUAL LOCAL WORD(s) *Cloaker, scodgible*

   LESS COMMON LOCAL WORD(s) *forkietail*

   BY WHOM USED *Younger people mostly*

   COMMENTS *In Bo'ness, West Lothian, "cloaker" means "beetle," not "earwig."*

7. If you list more than one word as being in local use, you may find that, though they all more or less correspond to the English word, they differ slightly in meaning from one another. If so, you are asked to try to indicate how they differ (under COMMENTS).
8. It may also happen that you give only one word and that this does not *exactly* correspond in meaning to the English word; if this is so, you might try to show how they differ in meaning. In this case and in 7 you may sometimes find it easiest to do this by giving an example of how the word is used in a phrase or a sentence.
9. If necessary, your various comments may be continued within the same rectangle on the back of the page.
10. Towards the end of the booklet there is space for further cases you may happen to know of where the form or the meaning of a word in some other place differs from your own. There is also space for noting down any rare words you may know. However, the most important thing is the information about your own speech, *i.e.*, what is asked for in rectangles 1-207.
11. Some questions, especially those after No. 184, are a little different from those so far discussed, but there are no special difficulties connected with them.
12. Most of the questions are intended both for speakers of Scots and speakers of Gaelic, but a few have no application to Gaelic and are marked as such. Those who fill in the booklet with information about their own dialect of Gaelic should not attempt in the same booklet to give any information about Scots, and *vice versa*. On the other hand, those who either speak Gaelic themselves or are in contact with Gaelic speakers are asked to answer the questions listed under No. 211.

We have asked you to fill in your name and address twice because they have to be filed twice, in different places : alphabetically under your name, and also according to the geographical grid-reference of the place you come from.

UNIVERSITY OF EDINBURGH
1951

ANGUS McINTOSH
H. J. ULDALL
Department of English Language and General Linguistics
KENNETH JACKSON
Department of Celtic

We can now look at slip PQ1, 1 CHILD* in Fig. 1. The informant is asked to 'give the word or words commonly used for this in [his] own locality'. Here use is made of the bilingualism of most of the informants. He is requested to 'translate' (DI 4) the Standard English word 'child' (line 1), henceforward to be called the *source item*[89] (in our terminology), into his own dialect i.e., he is to supply, where possible, a different word or words, the *target item(s)*, known to and used by him and other members of the speech community. This is to be entered in line 2 USUAL LOCAL WORD(S). Lines 3-4 LESS COMMON LOCAL WORD(S) and BY WHOM USED belong together and are referred to in DI 6-9.

The Informant and the Detailed Instructions. Although the phrasing of DI and the layout of the slips had been a matter of careful concern for the editors of the questionnaire some problems nevertheless arose for a number of informants. The editors themselves, realising that this section might be confusing for some people, pointed out that only points 1 and 2 were 'vitally important'. On looking back, we could have wished that points 3 and 5 had also been emphasised and elaborated.

DI 3. In a great number of cases informants left a slip blank. This might have been because: (1) the informant did not know a dialect word for the source item or could not think of it at the time; (2) he used the Standard English form (e.g., spider) or a dialect pronunciation of it (e.g., speeder) and did not trouble to repeat the source item. Some informants gave the answer 'same'. In this case the source item has been entered in the list; (3) the source item was not known or was badly phrased.

In the text of the atlas all blanks are listed under *Nil.* If appropriate boxes for these three possibilities had been provided on the slips which the informant could have ticked, a great deal of additional and valuable information might have been collected.

DI 5. The informants were perhaps overtaxed by being asked to distinguish between *usual* and *less common.* As field experience has shown such classifications are usually highly impressionistic and often quite wrong. But the success of this instruction was further impaired by the layout of the slip in PQ1 (see Fig. 1). Many informants, who had probably only read DI 1 and 2, took line 4, BY WHOM USED, to refer to both USUAL LOCAL WORD(S) and LESS COMMON LOCAL WORD(S) instead of just to the latter. Thus we sometimes find the entry 'by all', 'everybody' etc., in line 4 for a usual local word. This was amended in PQ2 where the third and fourth lines of Fig. 1 appear as one: LESS COMMON LOCAL WORD(S) AND BY WHOM USED.

The distinction was, moreover, understood by some people in such a way as to repeat the Standard English form under USUAL WORD(S) and the dialect form under LESS COMMON LOCAL WORD(S).[90] As all these factors have made the distinction between 'usual' and 'less common' rather unproductive, it was decided to disregard it and to treat, in general, all forms entered under these categories as being of equal status.

The space for COMMENTS (line 5) was used rather sparingly by informants except where a specific additional question was asked as e.g., PQ1, 112 'hay rack' (Are there different words according to the animal it is for? Is there a different word if it is in the fields?)'. In such cases the information has been incorporated in the text of the atlas, wherever it seemed appropriate and helpful (see e.g. items 52-53 (PQ1, 112-13)). Again, if the importance of context which the informant might have been able to supply had been stressed more urgently, a great number of apparent synonyms on a slip could have been differentiated (see DI 7). This is a close parallel to the deficiencies of answers due to insufficient contextualisation of a source item (see below).

Question types and some problems of translation. It is of particular linguistic interest that most questions concern 'picturable', 'concrete' *nouns.* The emphasis on this particular word-class is shared by most existing lexical surveys. It seems that abstract nouns, verbs, adjectives etc., are less suitable for this kind of investigation in dialectology.[91]

Most items selected for the atlas are of the same question *type* as PQ1, 'child'. As with most types of translation, in this case from one speech variety (SE) into another (dialect), certain familiar difficulties arise: often, for example, the translation is complicated in that in either SE or dialect there is no one word to describe the 'thing meant', the referent. Thus we have SE definitions in 17 (PQ1, 67) 'two pailfuls carried together' or 31 (PQ1, 89) 'broken pieces of china (used as playthings)', on the other hand many dialects have no single word for 36 (PQ1, 95) 'leap frog' and use phrases like 'cuddie loup the dyke' etc. Frequently an explanation was added to narrow down the context in which it might occur as in 3 (PQ1, 19) 'blister (on skin)', 91 (PQ1, 27) 'to sprain (a muscle, the ankle etc.)'. Where the context was not made sufficiently clear the answers have been rather confused as for example in PQ1, 7 'foolish person', PQ1, 47 'to intend' etc. and are therefore not suitable for inclusion in the atlas. *Pictures* were not used in PQ1 or PQ2 to elicit data. This could have been a help in some cases as e.g., 13 (PQ1, 60) 'three legged stool', PQ1, 61 'four legged stool', 52 (PQ1, 112) 'hay rack', 53 (PQ1, 113) 'hay stack', because more informants might have been stimulated to comment. On the other hand, however, informants might have rejected items because an idealised picture might not have fitted their own experience of the 'thing'.

There were other types of question in the questionnaire. Although none of these have been included in the present volume, some must be briefly mentioned. Four questionnaire items were translations in the reverse direction, from Scots into Standard English, PQ1, 9 'bourach', PQ1, 23 'branks' PQ1, 26 'stob', and PQ1, 82 'stoor'. These words are known widely within the atlas area and occur more or less in the same phonetic shapes, but refer to different things in different areas. They were all listed with a SE source item in the same word-field, namely, PQ1, 8 'crowd', PQ1, 22 'mumps', PQ1, 25 'splinter', and PQ1, 81 'dust' respectively. It is evident that, for example, in English counties where *bourach* is not known i.e., the source is not understood, no 'translation' or target item can be supplied.

Then there were a number of supplementary, often less specific, items like PQ1, 151 'Any other calls to animals' or PQ1, 158 'Any other words telling a horse what to do', PQ1, 135 'Any other words which are traditionally avoided for some superstitious reason, and say by whom' etc.

* We prefix items referred to by this questionnaire with PQ1 followed by a comma and the number.

Questions 185-96 concerned problems of idiomatic use and grammar, 197-207 were phonetic items.[92] The latter have yielded some very valuable and reliable data when compared with the Survey's formal phonological field-work and have also been used in the establishment of the Highland Line (see Map A).

Finally, items 208-10 were meant to elicit certain specialised types of lexical information and 211 A-J enquired into the status of Gaelic in the community.

Some other types of questionnaires and question procedures. Other types of question procedure have been developed which it is only possible to sketch here in a short *excursus.*

Basically our method confronts the informant, in most cases, with a one word stimulus to which he is expected to give a *one word response.* The same procedure is used by the LSS in its field-work. Thus the informant is put in a rather artificial situation. There is a school of thought in dialectology, mainly in Romance linguistics, but also in England and Switzerland, which seeks to collect all information by direct investigation and to avoid using the source items in questions by employing a variety of 'question types', like defining, pointing, completing etc.[93] This is done, it is argued, to eliminate the possibility of influencing the informant by the standard form. There remains, however, the question frame which is expressed in the standard speech form and which will still contribute to the artificiality of the interview situation. Our view is that the linguistic problem facing a survey, especially at the interview stage, is too great to be eliminated by a uniform mode of questioning.[94]

Other surveys, like G. Wenker's *Sprachatlas* or A. J. Ellis's *On Early English Pronunciation,* vol. V, construct coherent sentences from their source items and ask for translation. Both these texts, however, sound extremely stilted and artificial.[95] J. Orr's short questionnaire (see p. 10) is another more reasonable, example of this kind.

Ellis's questionnaire is also noteworthy in that it was used largely for postal enquiry. It was, however, accompanied by a special phonetic dialect alphabet which the intermediary was expected to learn and use. Experiments in this direction have not been altogether successful.

Questionnaires also differ in the order in which they ask their questions. Most current field-work books attempt to cover as many aspects of linguistics as possible at once. Phonetics/phonology, morphology, grammar are, for example, closely interwoven in the topically ordered Survey of English Dialects questionnaire. The LSS has taken a different point of view in this respect by investigating mainly one linguistic aspect in one particular type of questionnaire and by letting the linguistic requirements determine the order in which items appear.[96]

Distribution of PQ1. Selection of informants. Like the questionnaires of Wenker and Mitzka, PQ1 was mainly distributed through the headmasters of primary schools (except in Northern Ireland)[97] with the approval and support of the respective educational authorities, which also published articles in their journals on the intention and progress of the undertaking. A letter drafted by the LSS and signed by the secretaries of the institutions accompanied each book. It drew attention to the *General Information*[98] section in the questionnaire, which explains the idea of a linguistic survey and some of its tasks, and continued with advice on the selection of informants:

> It is not the intention of those responsible for the Linguistic Survey to burden you personally with the task of filling this in, though, of course, if you have an urge to undertake it, *and are a native of the district,* they will be very happy if you do. In every part of the country, it is felt, teachers are almost sure to know of some local person who is willing and competent to undertake this work. All that is asked is that you will be good enough to put the questionnaire into the hands of such a person without much delay and then make sure, after a few weeks, that it has been sent back to Edinburgh. The person chosen should if possible be middle aged or older and a lifelong inhabitant of your district. In most cases some such person should be available who will be able to write the whole thing himself or herself, but — especially where Gaelic is involved — it may be necessary in certain cases for you or someone else to assist with the actual writing down of the answers.

It was assumed — and our atlas will show how far this assumption was correct — that dialect was generally understood in the sense we have defined it (see p. 8) which is based on popular usage, and that informants were selected and instructed accordingly. Without this general concept of a deviant speech variety our work would have been impossible.

The other qualifications of an informant (middle aged or older, lifelong inhabitant of the district, literate) were meant as a rough guide and proved quite successful although from the viewpoint of present socio-linguistic methods they are rather crude. Nowadays problems such as *availability* v. *representativeness* are more usually discussed.[99]

We should like to stress again (cf. above, bilingualism) that dialect in Scotland today is often no more than a potential speech variety (beside some variety of SE). It is used or actualised mainly in intimate family situations or amongst friends and workmates. In our investigations we make use of most Scots' linguistic sophistication[100] and awareness of their bilingualism. Our experience is that dialect is more readily accessible to investigators through older people (see the list of informants) and often through children. The age group between fifteen and fifty-five is usually less available for consultation and often less communicative about linguistic matters.

From this it follows that our enquiry is directed to a numerical minority of speakers of a socially restricted speech variety in Scotland; our atlas reflects a potential of dialect available in the early 1950s but it does not tell the reader how many people in a locality would use it and in which specific situations. Our questionnaire techniques were not powerful enough to deal with these important questions.[101] It remains to be seen, whether a postal questionnaire could be developed which might handle problems of this kind.

Returns and coverage. The great majority (two-thirds) of the nearly 3000 copies of PQ1 distributed in 1952 were returned in a prepaid envelope (enclosed in each book) within the next two years. They were examined by the Survey staff on their arrival and checked for inclusion in the archive. The 1774 informants (this means about 59 per cent of the books distributed or about 88 per cent of all books returned) listed in Appendix C as having provided the data for this atlas are those left after a necessary process of elimination. Reasons for exclusion ranged from the lack of information on the name-slip (which meant that the provenance of the book could not be established) to insufficient or unsatisfactory information (many books were sent back blank) and general misunderstanding of the purpose of the enquiry or wrong selection of informant (e.g., if all target items were SE for a locality known to have dialect-speakers). For Scotland the final coverage is one book for about every 3800 inhabitants, or, if the four big cities are excluded, one book for about 2400 inhabitants.[102]

The filing of the slips. After cutting up the books all slips with the same source item were sorted into one file. They were ordered by counties as these appear in the text of the atlas. The key map (App. C) shows that the order of the localities within each county was obtained roughly by scanning the map from top left along successively descending parallels to bottom right.[104] Informants' localities were then given numbers from 1 onwards. Where several informants fell under the same grid reference i.e., lived at the same place, they were distinguished by adding small letters (a, b, c etc.) after the number.

> Thus all informants Fife 44abcdef live at Kirkcaldy, which has the grid reference 36/2791.

Another convention had to be adopted for Northern Ireland, where additional questionnaires were distributed by a LSS field-worker in 1966 to fill in some important gaps. These slips had to be added to a previously established numerical order, and this we have indicated by putting capital letters (A, B, C etc.) after numbers.

> County Donegal 1A refers to the locality Carrickart, grid reference C 1236, which would, according to our method of numeration, have been given the locality number 2, if it had been available earlier. Carrickart had now to be fitted in between the previously established locality numbers 1 and 2 and this is indicated by 1A.

The information from the slips thus classified was transferred on to work sheets from which the lists of the atlas were prepared.

The questionnaire in Gaelic areas. In parts of Scotland where Gaelic was still spoken in 1951 two copies of PQ1 were distributed with the instruction that one should be completed in Scots (if spoken) and the other in Gaelic. The questionnaire made provision for this and indicated that certain questions (e.g., the phonetic section 197-209 should not be answered, others (e.g., 211) should only be answered by native Gaelic speakers. However, the questionnaire is designed essentially for the investigation of 'English' dialects.

Those books marked 'Gaelic' have not been included in this atlas, which is only concerned with dialectal varieties of English.

THE LISTS

The bulk of the material presented in the atlas consists of lists and their interpretation on maps (items 1-90). The lists present the data as returned by the informants in PQ1 in an editorially condensed form.

Editorial conventions

It has been our policy to keep our conventions, which are set out below, as flexible as possible so as to give the fullest information within the limits imposed on us by space and without burdening the work with elaborate rules or symbols.

The introductory notes. These appear at the beginning of lists and are used (i) to supplement the map(s) (for instance by naming an item which appears uniformly nearly everywhere), (ii) to point out variants of items which have been subsumed (see Subsumptions, p. 16 below), (iii) to refer to other questionnaire items which have yielded similar or identical areas of target items and are therefore not included in the atlas (e.g., 'four legged stool'),[105] or (iv) to give cross-references to atlas (source) items whose maps show some similar or identical target items,[106] and (v) to describe any major deviations from the editorial conventions.

The arrangement of the material. Each list is broken up into *counties* which appear in the same order as in the lists, App. C. The *target items* within each county are arranged alphabetically and *Nil* entries appear at the end.

The *figures* refer to the localities from which the entry has been reported, or, in the case of Nil, localities from which no target item has been returned. The code is explained in Appendix C.

Figures in italics and the round brackets. The round brackets allow a number of space-saving conflations of items especially where these consist of two elements. Thus *(pig)sty, (muck) hoe, palin(g) (posts),* stand for *sty* and *pigsty, hoe* and *muck hoe, palin(g)* and *palin(g) posts.* Sparing use has been made of this convention. In general only words which are also SE source items, or elements of SE source items and sometimes other SE target items, have been bracketed, but where the list required further abbreviation, we have in some cases gone beyond this rule.

Although the original plan was to let these bracketed forms stand without comment, we have since then adopted the convention of *italicising* those figures or letters in the locality code, for which the full (unbracketed) form of an item is attested (although a very few places of these may also have given the shorter forms).

> *(Muck)hoe 1* 2 *3-9* 10-12 15a*c*d *21bd*
>
> e.g., implies that the fully expanded form *muck hoe* occurs in the following localities: 1, 3-9, 12, 15c, 21bd. All localities between two italicised figures linked by a hyphen, e.g. *3 - 9* have the unbracketed form and figures have been italicised if all succeeding letters im-

plied the full form, e.g. *21bd* (as compared with 15a*c*d, where only *c* shows the full form).
Where an italicised figure is linked by a hyphen with a non-italicised one, only the former has the fully expanded form. None of the intermediate figures have it.

Where only one letter is bracketed as in pig('s) or in the suffix -in(g), we have not indicated fully expanded forms. In examples like *(pig('s)) riv* or *palin(g) (posts)* the full forms may be *pig riv, pig's riv* or *palin posts, paling posts.*

Obliques (/). *Replacements of elements.* Oblique lines have not been used frequently. Their purpose is the same as in the case of brackets, namely conflation:

(Big/black) beetle

The element of an item immediately following the oblique *(black)* can replace the element immediately preceding it *(big).* 'Element' is here defined as an orthographical unit delimited by a space or, as in this example, a bracket. The notation *(Big/black) beetle* implies therefore the following possibilities: *beetle, big beetle,* and *black beetle.*

Note also the following example:

Jennie with/and the/a hundred legs

is to be interpreted as

Jennie with the hundred legs, Jennie and the hundred legs, Jennie with a hundred legs, Jennie and a hundred legs.

Where more than one element replaces a single element *or* is inserted.

(Big *or* big black) beetle

is to be interpreted as

beetle, big beetle, big black beetle.

(Large/black *or* big black) beetle

is to be interpreted as

beetle, large beetle, black beetle, big black beetle.

Orthographic word boundaries. For compound items (consisting of more than one free morpheme) informants varied considerably in their indication of orthographic boundaries. Where they used the SE source item, they often followed the convention of the questionnaire: *pigsty, mouldboard, meal bin.* In other cases the choice seems to have been completely random: *pick*maw, *pick*-maw, *pick* maw (see 74 'seagull'). As in the case of orthographic subsumptions (see below) we have in general followed the majority decision of informants within each county, but hyphens have been replaced by spaces and items have been separated or reduced to one orthographic entry where it was editorially convenient.

Indications of informants' comments. As we have indicated elsewhere (p. 13) informants comments have in general been disregarded, but there are instances to the contrary where further information was specifically requested in the COMMENTS and the results are classifiable and helpful. This is the case for example in 16 ' "pail" (Be sure to specify names for different types, according to shape, material and purpose)'. Where we decided to include comments these have been grouped by the use of a code which is explained at the beginning of the particular item and takes the form of small *raised* letters or symbols *after* the locality to which it refers. If more than one response was given, letters are separated by commas.

E.g., 16 'pail'

flag(g)on 9^{s,i}, 12a^{i}

Informant 9 had the comments 'small, for milk';

Informant 12a said that *flag(g)on* was used as a container for milk.

Some other problems of the list. Some other changes had to be made in the lexical entries as returned in the questionnaire. Where the source item had been explained or contextualised and the informant translated or repeated these expansions in his answer these do not in general appear in the lists. Thus, *gizzard of a fowl* appears as *gizzard* because the source item is 67 'gizzard (of fowl)'.

On the other hand we have changed certain entries e.g., *flake of snow* (for 69 'snowflake') to *snowflake* because most people give the latter form. Similarly, a few forms of *mouth of the drain* (for 48 'the drain opening itself') are changed to *drain mouth* as this was the usual answer supplied.

In general no attempt was made to change word-classes which did not agree with the word-class of the source item (but see 33 'shooting a marble').

Varying uses of apostrophes (') have often been conflated under one form; e.g., *sheep's, sheeps', sheeps* (as in 63 'sheep's dung') all appear as *sheep's.*

The Interpretation of the informants' spelling

Because of the postal method of communication used in the lexical work of the LSS, all relevant information has been transmitted by the written word. It is, accordingly, necessary to give some account of the ways in which this has been interpreted.

It is worth noticing, first of all, that the LSS stands here within that tradition of analysis of the written word about which something has already been said in the historical background to linguistic studies in Scotland, and where Sir James Murray's 'three principles' were quoted: 'to make the spelling systematic . . . to represent to the eye the differences patent to the ear . . . to use forms for which a precedent already exists in Scotch usage.' It is also proper to notice in this connection that lexicography, as well as dialectology, in Scotland has continued to give some analytical attention to the written word. *The Scottish National Dictionary,* at least, has from the beginning systematically absensed the value of the graph used in Scottish orthography, in the first article in each of its alphabetical sections.

Subsumption of variants of dialect items. In the material which we present here the spellings given by informants are not in all cases reproduced exactly. We have, that is to say, intervened to the extent of subsuming certain spellings under a normalised type where we judge that little or no ambiguity could follow. When, for instance, the entries *lems, lemms* and *laims* appear in our files in a given area for item 31 'broken pieces of china', the first two are subsumed and the last kept separate. The principle on which this is based will be shown presently. One point however will be made clear at once: it is that, for each county, our method is to choose the *majority* spelling where two graphs refer, in our judgement, to the same sound. To use the simplest possible illustration, drawn from item 6 'left-handed' the forms *car* and *kar* both occur. The majority form in most counties is *car.*

Theoretically, there appear to be two main problems in interpretation: 1. where the informant's spelling suggests distinctions which do not exist in his dialect; 2. where the informant's spelling does not convey phonemic distinctions which do exist in his dialect. In practice, and as we have tried to interpret our material, we have found (chiefly under 2) that the pattern *imposed* by the adoption of a particular spelling convention has conditioned the information. An informant, we may suppose, may *wish* to make certain distinctions but if he is committed, say, to the Standard English orthography he cannot necessarily do this.[107] (In some areas near to the Highland Line — in the middle of the Black Isle, for instance, 'week' is [wik̑] and 'weak' is [wi:k].[108] But, short of stating the convention explicitly, how is this to be shown?) If the informant also uses another orthography — Scots for example — we cannot be sure at what precise point he adopts this, unless it is in one of the conventions which are quite certain, like the adoption of <ö>or <φ>in Shetland, or <eu> in Orkney, for a front rounded vowel. Thus *göd, gφd, geud* for 'good'. In point of fact, it is in vowels rather than in consonants that difficulties in interpretation mainly occur.

These considerations imply that there are some specifically local problems which do not necessarily apply elsewhere. Hence, for their solution, some knowledge of the distinction of phonological systems is presumed; and in this, of course, the LSS is able to draw on its own phonological material. Nevertheless, it is not necessary to set out a minute and systematic scale of correspondences between phonemic and graphemic units in order to demonstrate beyond doubt the value of the lexical material. For it is clear that, considered simply as 'eye language', this material has distinctions large enough and patent enough to show clear distributions. For instance, in item 82 'earwig' the responses *scotchibell, clipshear,* or *hornie gellock* can be displayed without comment; and the bulk of all responses presented in this lexical atlas are differentiated in this obvious way. There is a further point: it is that in a given response, the skeletal framework of written consonants (graphs or digraphs) is of more general utility in the display of lexical distinctions than written vowels. Thus, it is not only clear that for item 13 'three legged stool' the forms *stuil* or *steel* or *still* or *stule* are distinct from forms like *creepie* or *cracket* or *coppie,* but also that the first four forms have a regular st+V+l framework into which certain vowel graphs have been inserted.

Consonants. This is not to say that the consonant framework is always unambiguous. Even if, in the construction of this framework a Scottish informant usually employs, and at random, both the orthographical conventions which he has at his disposal, namely, the convention of modern English and the convention of Scots dialect literature — which also uses some of the historical conventions of literary Middle Scots — difficulties occur at limited and well-known points in the framework and are often common to both conventions.

It seems a little surprising that in our material popular phonetic terms like 'hard g' or 'soft g' have been used by our informants hardly at all. In Caithness, popular dialect literature has neutralised the ambiguity which exists between [g] and [dʒ] as represented by<g>by writing <ch>for [dʒ] (corresponding to the local dialect pronunciation, which is [tʃ] at least in certain clearly defined phonetic contexts). Caithness informants have not followed this convention in their spelling. The form *jeck* for item 73 'jackdaw' occurs which is presumably to be interpreted by the Caithness [tʃ] corresponding to the more usual [dʒ]. On the whole there has been very little uncertainty throughout the material in interpreting <g>. Through analogy, and through some of the lexical by-products which the personal method of the phonological work has necessarily thrown up, it has been possible to build up a consonantal framework of near certainty. Thus the response to item 98 'the call used when calling pigs' was very often given as *geese* by informants, and this has been accepted as [gis] at least partly on the analogy of the word 'geese'. Similarly, a form like *gellock* (item 82 'earwig') has been accepted as [ˈgɛlək] through a general acquaintance with the word, both in the field and in general lexicographical studies.

The interpretation of <ch> in certain contexts — the common representation in the Scots convention of the voiceless velar fricative — is perhaps a little more difficult. There is, first of all, the obvious difficulty that <gh> may also be used, and the confusion with what it now represents in ordinary English orthography is apparent. Both <ch> and <gh> occur in the common response *sheuch* or *sheugh* for item 46 'a gutter', and especially in Renfrewshire, Lanarkshire, Perthshire, Stirlingshire, West Lothian and Midlothian. We do not consider it to be possible that <gh> should, in this final position in a word and with this geographical distribution, represent anything other than [x].

The form <gh> can also represent [f] and in our material the forms *draught, draft,* and *dracht,* for instance, appear in item 15 'down draught'. Here, our opinion is that *dracht* is the [x] form and the other two [f] forms. It may not, of course, be so. It may be that *draught* is a 'logographic' shortcut (so to speak) for the more specific *dracht* in the representation of [x], and that therefore, *draft* is the only indubitable [f] form. And, admittedly, the same sort of argument may also apply to *sheugh.*

In the matter of <ch> and <gh>, therefore, the only certainty in interpretation which can be offered is the sort of statistical certainty which the Linguistic Survey of Scotland claims for the density of its coverage. The map of the graphs used in item 93 (PQ1, 33) 'sudden fright', in the general form *fri+C+t,* shows that <ch> forms are concentrated everywhere except in Inverness-shire, Sutherland and Orkney which have <gh> forms and which are certainly to be explained on historical grounds as representing the adoption of English as a relatively new language. Shetland, incidentally, has been omitted from the above exceptions because the actual lexical item with the general form *fri+C+t* was only given twice (in Fair Isle and Dunrossness) and in both cases with <ch>. It is to be emphasised, in trying to interpret the word *fri+C+t* in our material, that it is a secondary (although still very frequent) choice. (The first word given by informants was usually some form of 'fleg', 'gliff' etc.) We propose, therefore, to interpret *fri+C+t* not as a Scots 'dialect' word, but as a 'standard English word with a dialect pronunciation'. We treat it, that is to say, as a 'common core' item

In the representation of the consonantal framework

there are additional complexities for informants from areas with a Gaelic or Norse language substratum. Some responses from formerly Gaelic-speaking areas were given with spellings which we have interpreted as the attempt of a Scots informant to direct attention to a particular, and probably non-Scots, quality in the *consonant.* Thus, *gullyack, gull-yuchan, goilleach, golyachan* are forms which appear for item 82 'earwig' for Ross and Cromarty and Inverness, and they seem to be the informants' attempts to represent a palatal 'l'.

There is a further and somewhat more ambiguous example in the consonant framework in this area which concerns the labial, alveolar and velar plosives. In Gaelic these can be voiceless and aspirated (or pre-aspirated) or voiceless and unaspirated. Very commonly, in the representation of Highland English in Scots dialect literature, it is voicelessness which is specially featured (as opposed to the voicing in the English or Scots counterpart) – hence *coot* for 'good' etc. It happens that in Scots the voiceless plosives are unaspirated (but there are, of course, also voiced plosives). When, therefore, in our material a Gaelic loan-word like 'bodach-rocais' (item 57 'scarecrow') is variously rendered (as a Scots response) as *bodach* or *botach* or *bottach* in Ross and Cromarty and Inverness, there can be no real certainty about the precise significance of the <t> or <d>, since we do not know to which particular feature the informant is trying to direct attention – whether to voicelessness, or to aspiration, or to non-aspiration.

In an area of Norse substratum – like Shetland, for example – there is occasional, but quite clear, evidence of representation in the informants' spelling of the (in certain circumstances) characteristic palatalisation of [d] [l] and [n]. Thus, in item 50 'gutter (the kind running through a byre)' there occurred several instances of forms like *oiler* or *oilick* which can only be interpreted as ['ɔiljər] and ['ɔiljık]. The absurdity of interpreting phonetically such words on the basis of strictly *English* conventions will be apparent.

Stressed vowels. The vowel core which the informant uses to fill in the consonant framework is also based on the two conventions of English and Scots orthography which he normally employs. Thus, all informants were obviously intuitively aware of such basic principles of English orthography as the use of final <e> to modify an antecedent vowel, on the general principle of -V:Ce *versus* -VC, in, for instance, *mat* versus *mate*, or *sit* versus *site*. Similarly, informants generally accepted and used the spelling convention of the doubled, or double, consonant as *matting* versus *mating,* and *sitting* versus *siting.* There are, of course, certain ambiguities in this as in *pasty* which represents either ['pastı] or ['pestı] – and *fasten* and *hasten, castle* and *bastle.* Our informants, in fact, sometimes spell with a doubled consonant in an obvious attempt to avoid ambiguity. Thus, in item 16 'pail', in all counties from Ross and Cromarty to Angus, there are entries both of *flagon* and *flaggon.* In interpreting these it is clear that we cannot know if the *flagon* entry is meant to represent the Standard English pronunciation, or to be a deliberate attempt to represent an [e] type vowel which stands in opposition to the vowel represented by *flaggon.*

There are, however, more serious ambiguities. As we have suggested, the most obvious and practical difficulties arise in the first of the two main problems in interpretation, namely, where the spelling of an entry suggests distinctions which do not exist in the informant's dialect. In the north-east, for instance (Aberdeenshire) in item 76 'ant' spellings like *emert* and *emmert, emerteen* and *emmerteen, emertine* and *emmertine* occur. A strict application of the general English spelling convention would, of course, give an ['imərt] ['ɛmərt] dichotomy. There are, however, no spellings of *eemert,* which might have corroborated the first of these possibilities and we might therefore assume that both spellings represent ['ɛmərt]. or ['emərt]. We cannot, however, rule out completely yet another possibility suggested by two cases of *aimerteen.* Since in the north-east the vowels in words like *met* and *mate* often fall together in [met], both *emerteen* and *emmerteen* might stand for ['emərtin]. For all these considerations taken together, we have not subsumed *emert* and *emmert* under a general type which would signify a single phoneme. There is, nevertheless, an entry – item 31 'broken pieces of china' – where for Aberdeenshire and Kincardineshire the response is *lems, lemms,* and *laims.* Here we have subsumed the first two under what we consider to be an unambiguous front vowel, opener than, and in opposition to, the third item.

In Aberdeenshire, the case for our not subsuming *emert,* and *emmert* as representing a single phoneme rested partly on the lack of corroborative evidence from an *eemert* spelling which would have enabled us to assign the *emert* spelling to the /i/ phoneme. We have to admit that Aberdeenshire may be a special case: first, there are in fact *eemert* spellings from Banff, Nairn and Moray (the comment from one Aberdeenshire informant was that the form 'is *eemert* in Moray'); second, in item 11 'undervest (man's)' similar problems occur for Aberdeenshire e.g., *semit, semmit,* but now we also have a fairly large number of *seemit* forms. This means, we believe, that we can equate the *semit* and *seemit* forms as representing an /i/ and interpret the *semmit* form as an opposed, and lower, front vowel.

There are further instances of spelling distinctions which appear to demonstrate phonemic distinctions but which must be considered to be doubtful. In item 38 'swing', the spellings *shog* and *shoag* appear from informants in the counties of Moray, Banff, Kincardine, Angus, and Perth. The phonemic reality, however, seems to be that only one phoneme occurs i.e., [ɔ], thus [ʃɔg]. This we know from our phonological research.[109]

Another complication which is also exemplified by this item occurs in Aberdeenshire where forms like *shoud* and *showd* are given. On the basis of an English orthography the graph <ow> may represent either [o] or [ʌu]. In Scots orthography both <ou> and <ow> also represent [u] as in *down/doun* [dun]. In either case there will be ambiguities and uncertainties, even if in general our informants throughout Scotland seem to have preferred the graph <oo> for [u]. Nevertheless, in instances like *shoud/showd* we have not ventured to subsume and have retained both forms.

For item 83 'maggot' there is a very widespread use of spellings which appear to suggest phonemic oppositions. The most general is *mauk/mawk* as against *mack*. It is sometimes varied to *mauch/mawch* and *mach* especially in the east, and the form *maak* or *maach* also occurs. The <au / aw> forms predominate overall to the extent of probably 70 per cent of occurrences. A first, and minor, point is that we have subsumed the <au> and <aw> forms. We have not, however, subsumed the forms *mauk/mawk* and *mack*. There is a problem here which ought to be discussed. Briefly, it concerns the notion of what we called a 'logographic short cut' in the discussion on the use of digraphs like <ch> or <gh> and the reason why one might be preferred. The argument can be expanded and reapplied here, and in the following way: the OSc form for this word was *mauch* or *mauk* and the vowel-element of this is still phonemically represented in some dialects (though not in all) by a long rounded back vowel [ɔ]. Even though, historically, this vowel has always been distinguished from a short and unrounded back vowel [a], the development in the remaining dialects has been to a levelling of both historical vowels. In Berwickshire, for example, this has resulted in [a:] and in Selkirkshire in [ɔ:]. Even so, this difference is not always discernible, and rounding and spreading often tend to be indefinitive. The point we wish to make is that the graphic and historic <au> form has probably been kept as the traditional orthographic representation and has been used here to depict *any* of these developments in any of these dialects, and this rather than a phonemic opposition explains the predominance of the <au/aw> form (as opposed to <a/aa>).

In item 19 'porridge stick', forms like *theevil* and *theivil* regularly appear and these we have subsumed under the majority spelling for each county, on the assumption that both represent ['θivəl]. There are, it is true, forms in English orthography in common English words like *veil* or *reign* which would not corroborate this, but we have preferred to assume (aided by our phonological field research) that Scots orthography is the criterion here, that is, the <ei> digraph (the only one which need be in doubt) is the historic <ei> as in *heid, Reid* etc. One local complication arises out of this however. In Caithness, local dialect literature usually uses <ei> to represent the characteristic diphthongal pronunciation [ei] as in *lead* (noun) [leid]. We have mapped the first element in item 27 'lead pencil' (Appendix A) and our Caithness material shows one instance each of *leid, leyd,* and *lide.* The *lide* form seems to be a clear indication of the diphthongal pronunciation and corroborates the others. We accept, therefore, a specifically local usage here.

There are even clearer instances of the validity of a local form. It will be recalled that when we posed the problem of the precise point at which it might be assumed that an informant began to use a given orthographic device or system, use of <ϕ> or <ö> for Shetland was cited as a definitive example where we are to understand, at least for these localities, a front rounded vowel and nothing else. In item 13 'three-legged stool' wherever the response involved the use of the word stool at all, <ö> (together with <ü> and <üi> and <ϕ> (which we regard as Norse conventions) are given for Shetland together with some instances of <ui> which is the Scots convention for this front rounded vowel. It is necessary to bear in mind at this point that the form *stool* is our SE, not our dialect subsumption and that we use the variant forms here because they can conveniently be consulted on a display map (see map 4, Appendix A).

For dialect items our conventions are different: in the item *c+V+t* or *k+V+t* (for item 17 'ankle'), V appears as a front rounded vowel in Shetland and Orkney. In cases like this the graphs <ϕ>, <ö>, <ü>, <üi> in Shetland have for typographical reasons *always* been given the <ui> graph (which also occurs in Shetland). Thus *küt, kϕt, küit* etc. appear as *kuit.* In Orkney where <eu> (which is the common spelling in local dialect literature) and <ui> appear in otherwise the same item, the majority spelling <ui> has been adopted and the subsumed form is therefore *cuit* in accordance with our general policy.

Our subsumption for item 13 'three legged stool' has been under the form *stool*. The individual forms which we had from our informants are shown in the map in Appendix A. It is necessary to notice, first of all, that the *still* forms represent the unrounded forms of the reflex of OE ō OSc ü, which, in the rounded representation is *stuil* or *stule* (these were varigraphs in OSc). The localisation of the rounded forms in Roxburghshire and Shetland will be noticed, together with the significant instances in the Strath Earn/Strathmore area and in Kirkcudbrightshire, all of which correspond to what is known of these distributions from our phonological field-work. The ambiguity of an <eu> form appears from the map to be possible only in Cumberland where the form *steul* appears. But this must be interpreted as [stjʌl] since the other possible interpretation is localised only in Orkney. (The graph <eu> is of course also found frequently in Scotland in items like *speug* (for 71 'sparrow') where it must be interpreted as [jʌ] which is often confirmed by corresponding spellings such as *spyug*).[110]

There is, finally, the rather special case in Scotland of vowels preceding the graph <r>. Most speech varieties in Scotland (including accents of Standard English) have [r] in syllable-final position. This means that wherever <r> occurs in the spelling it is invariably pronounced. In the accents of the Standard English of England this <r> is not pronounced; what occurs is simply [ɜ] where in Scotland words like *fir, fur, pearl, journey* very often appear as [fɪr], [fʌr], [perl̩], [dʒʌrnɪ]. It is necessary to stress, however, that these vowels are not usually consistently distributed in different speakers, nor is the number of contrasting phenomena stable. For these reasons we have left graphs before <r> as they were presented by the informants: thus, *spirtle, spurtle, spirkle, spurkle* in 19 'porridge stick'.

Unstressed vowels. Variants of unstressed vowels in dialect words are more numerous than those in stressed vowels, and they occur less regularly. They have therefore been treated more cursorily in our lists. Where there are forms like *gellack, gellock, gelluck, gellick* (for item 176 'earwig') in one area we assume that the variants represent one type of unstressed vowel, presumably ['gɛlək]. In such cases we have subsumed the graphs under the majority spelling in each county. There are other examples, however: (i) where the variants are extremely numerous, (ii) where there is no clear majority spelling. Here the variants were conflated under one form (e.g. *gollach* out of forms like *gollach, golluch, gollech*) for the whole area where they occur. This procedure has been stated in the introductory notes (see 82 'earwig'; the A in *gollAch* in the note draws special attention to the subsumption.)

The suffix spelt variously <y>, <ie>, <ey> as in *stoolie, housie* etc. has usually been represented in the lists by <ie> throughout the area except where there was a SE form with <y>, as in *granny*.

Subsumptions of SE spellings. When an informant gives in his response a SE item in *SE orthography*, there is the possibility that he is using it in a 'logographic' form. Thus *spider* may stand for [ˈspaedər] or for [ˈspɛidər] which are acceptable pronunciations in Standard Scottish English. On the other hand, it may represent the dialect pronunciation [ˈspidər] which other informants spell *speeder.* Such logographic forms of common core items are very common in Scottish dialect literature.

At an earlier stage of the editorial work the policy regarding variant spellings of SE items had been to subsume them under their SE orthography in an extension of the 'logographic principle', especially where the SE target item appeared also as a source item (e.g. *spider* in 84 'spider'), part of a source item (e.g., *cow* in 60 'cow dung'), or part of an explanation of a source item (*down* in 51 'PIPE down the side of a house draining water from the roof'). The subsumption also took place where the SE item occurred with a dialect element (e.g. *cow* in the expression *cow sharn* for 60 'cow dung') and in some cases where the SE item was a SE synonym of a SE source item (e.g., *droppings* in 60 'cow dung'). This procedure stressed the emphasis of the atlas on non-SE vocabulary and its variants.

Later it was decided to retrieve variants of SE items wherever a good deal of information, especially about stressed vowels, would otherwise have been lost. This was done:

(1) by including maps of variants in Appendix A and referring to them in the introductory notes.

(2) by pointing out variants in the introductory notes

e.g. 46 'gutter'. Variants of GUTTER have been subsumed (*guitter* Roxburghshire; a few *gitter, gaetter* Fife).

Where a 'logographic' form is used in the introductory notes it appears in capital letters (GUTTER). Variants appear in italics, often followed by a rough indication of the areas where they are concentrated.

(3) in many instances, by putting the variants into the list. This method was often chosen (if the overall length of the list allowed this) when –

(i) the consonantal skeletons showed a significantly different structure from SE: e.g., *pottage* and *poddish* for 'porridge' in 18 'porridge bowl'; w(h)ol(l) for 'hole' in 91 'hole (used in playing marbles)'; *gerse, girs* for 'grass' in 87 'couchgrass'.

(ii) there were other problems of identifying a variant with the SE form.

Cases of lesser subsumptions of SE forms have not been stated explicitly. The same applies to *unstressed* vowels (cf. e.g. 71 'sparrow') and the suffix '-ed' which appears as <-it>, <-ed>, <-et> etc., on the slips (e.g. *legged* in 13 'three legged stool').

[i]	<ee, e-e,[1] ea,[2] ei[3]>
[ɩ]	<i>
[e]	<ai, ay, ae, a-e, ey[4]>
[y, ϕ]	<ui>
	Shetland also <ö, ϕ, ü, üi[5]>
	Orkney also <eu>
[ɛ]	<e>
[a]	<a>
[ä:]	<aa, ah>
[ɔ:]	<au, aw>
[ɔ]	<o>
[o]	<oa, o-e, ow[6]>
[ʌ]	<u>
[u]	<oo; ou, ow[6]>
[ae, ɛɩ]	<i-e, y-e>; in word final position <y, ye, ey[4]>
[oɩ]	<oi, oy>
[ʌu]	<ow, ou[6]>
[ju]	<u-e, eu[7]; ew>
[jʌ]	<eu[7]>

Fig. 2 Table of Common Stressed Vowel Equivalents

Symbols in [ ] suggest a phonetic interpretation for the graphs standing next to it in the same line i.e., graphs which have been treated as equivalent and have therefore often been subsumed under a majority spelling. Special graphs have been discussed in the preceding text.

1. 'e' as indicating the 'long' value of a vowel is shown by <-e>, e.g. <e-e>, <a-e>, etc.
2. <ea> also stands for [e] in Scots dialect literature as in *feat* 'smart' [fet].
3. For <ei> in Caithness see p. 19
4. In word final position this may occasionally stand for [ɛɩ] as in *hey* 'hay'
5. The Shetland graphs are subsumed under <ui> in the lists.
6. For the interpretation of <ou, ow> see p. 18
7. For <eu> in items like *speug, pleuch* see p. 19

THE MAPS

In the selection of items from PQ1 for publication the main criterion, it will be remembered, was their suitability for the display of areal distributions. We propose therefore to discuss briefly the function of maps in linguistic geography.

Maps used in linguistic geography

Different kinds of maps have been developed in linguistic geography to display lexical and phonological distributions. We shall mention only four types here, but it should be kept in mind that there are other possibilities.[111]

(1) The information, in our case the word or phrase, is printed in its entirety on the map for every locality. This solution was used by Gilliéron in his *Atlas linguistique de la France (1902-10)* and has been widely accepted in Romance dialectology. There are serious disadvantages in this kind of map. It

is difficult and expensive to produce and can only be used for surveys with a sparse coverage (see Gilliéron's 639 points for the whole of France) because of the physical space the printed items cover. Otherwise a very large-scale map is required. Moreover, it is rather difficult to read, as coherent areas are difficult to recognise at a glance, especially on phonological maps where one often wants to look at individual segments of variants of a lexical item rather than the whole word or phrase. This kind of map reproduces the collected material; it replaces a list, but in many cases it does not really offer a clearer picture.

(2) The linguistic focus of interest (phrase/word/'sound'/etc.) is represented by symbols in each locality which the survey has covered. In contrast to type (1), this method allows any length of segment of an item to be picked out. The symbols take up less space and facilitate mapping of denser coverage surveys. By using the same shape or colour of symbol for the same linguistic feature, coherent distribution areas can be recognised immediately. On the other hand, it becomes necessary to provide an extensive legend and often supplementary information without which the map is not always intelligible. If the survey coverage is very dense, however, the symbol-maps may become very intricate and rather difficult to read: if ill-chosen, the shape and colour of some symbols tend to dominate the rest. The legends to the maps, too, will tend to get more and more complicated and therefore more exacting for the reader.

(3) Some, for example the editors of the German *Wortatlas* (1951-), have tried to improve (2) by introducing isogloss lines into the symbol-map. This enables the cartographer to omit the symbols which constitute the basis for his isogloss and there is then more room for the display of minor groups of symbols in that area. This method has been successful in a number of cases, but very often it makes great demands on, and even confuses, the reader.

The question is, in fact, whether a map alone can satisfactorily convey all the linguistically relevant information to the reader. In the LSS we have after careful and thorough consideration decided that the uses of maps of types (1)-(3) are, at least for the present volume, limited and that in general separate lists should carry all the available material. We have been guided in this mainly by (a) our initial decision to concentrate in this publication on the linguistic problem of distributional lexical *areas*, (b) the great disadvantages of the big map-format that would have been required and the increased expense of producing such maps, and (c) our belief that the reader might find it easier to consult this work if the information is split up into a map and a text section. Providing *all* the information in a text or list means that the function of the map can be rather more restricted, and that it can then be used to illustrate much more clearly some particular focus of interest. It need not, however, present a full and exhaustive picture for any one item. Scholars interested in smaller areas may want to draw their own micro-maps in any case and have been given the necessary details for doing so.[112]

(4) These considerations have led us to adopt a fourth type of map which is a variation of (3). We only map distribution areas, i.e. we use the isogloss method, but omit minor and scattered groups of symbols.

Producing the LSS lexical maps

The problems inherent in the concept of the isogloss have been mentioned above. Here we wish to describe the various stages in the production of the maps published and to add some cautionary remarks. We arrived at our lexical maps in three stages:

Stage 1: After a preliminary examination of the work-sheets, target items which seemed promising for our purpose were plotted on a map using different colours and, occasionally, different shapes.

Stage 2: Isoglosses were drawn on tracing paper superimposed on the previous map. A certain degree of arbitrariness cannot be avoided in determining their course. Not all linguistic areas on our maps are of the same 'weight', because the density of symbols varies considerably over the geographical region. This is due to (a) extra-linguistic factors (i.e. the fluctuating number of atlas localities in each ten mile square), (b) the number of answers received for a particular source item (see the many 'Nil' returns for some items), and (c) the variation in number of mappable target items in different parts of the country. Furthermore, there was a technical limit to the number of overlapping areas which could be depicted by our means of representation. This is why in certain cases an extensive area has been left off the map and described in general terms in the introductory notes to the lists of the items concerned. It should be remembered that the fact that a map does not show a certain item in some parts of the atlas region does not necessarily mean that it is not known there, but only that its *concentration,* its number of occurrences in the particular area, is not sufficiently high to warrant drawing an isogloss. Our attention is focused on *concentrated* distributional areas of target items. The text should therefore in all instances be consulted.

Stage 3: A reduced map of distribution areas was produced from the isogloss tracing. For the sake of clarity the linguistic areas circumscribed by isoglosses were filled in with Letraset patterns. The isoglosses do not appear as lines on the finished product, but can be inferred from the boundaries of the different patterns. Where overlapping occurs, two or more Letraset shadings will form a new shading when superimposed.

The arrangement of the lexical maps

Maps 1-90 form the essential part of the atlas. The lists belonging to these maps have been separated from them and appear in the second half of the volume. Occasionally the complexity of an item has made it necessary to present its distribution areas on two maps.

Maps 91-100 have been published without lists, because these are excessively long and do not add much to the understanding of the maps, although they do obviously contain a considerable amount of additional (but not mappable) lexical information.

Finally, there is in the appendices A and B a set of maps in which symbolic interpretation (map type (2) above) is used. Most of these are spread over two pages. Appendix A has been introduced to retrieve from the text variant (dialect) pronunciations of SE words (see p. 19) for which the text simply gives the 'logographic' SE orthography. Appendix B presents some items which are of phonetic interest, but of which no list appears in the atlas. Some interesting material which we have not been able to present here still remains in our files.

The base map and specialised map

The ordinary base map used in this atlas is on the scale of approximately 1:2,000,000. Note that because of its extreme position Shetland has had to appear as an inset map in the top right-hand corner. Non-linguistic features mapped have been restricted to a minimum: coastlines, county boundaries, main lochs, the Scottish-English Border, and the border between Northern Ireland and Eire. For further information, reference should be made to the *physical map* of Scotland (App. D) and the *population density map* (App. D). By consulting these together the reader should get a fairly clear picture about the areal coverage of PQ1. He will also find there an explanation for certain areas which recur consistently as blanks east and south of the Highland Line (see map A): the physical feature of an area conditions its settlement and this, in turn, is reflected by the number of atlas localities or their complete absence. The *key maps* (App. C) enable the reader to compile specialised maps from the lists, by using tracing paper and plotting the data locality by locality.

Some advice on how to use the maps

As pointed out above, the maps show distributional areas by means of various Letraset patterns or shadings. Where areas overlap, different types of pattern were superimposed thus forming a distinct composite configuration which the reader can analyse by reference to the legend which gives the non-composite patterns. In the analysis the reader is further helped by clues on the actual map itself as most non-composite shadings occur on their own in the proximity of the regions where they overlap.

The shadings usually appear in the following order in the key:

I Line patterns
(a) vertical lines
(b) horizontal lines
(c) slanted lines

Within (a)-(c) the order is determined by the *distance* between lines: wide comes before narrow, and the *degree of blackness:* thick lines come before thin ones.

(d) broken lines

II Dots
These are ordered by
(a) the distance between dots: a wide pattern comes before a narrow one.
(b) their size: open circles come first, thick (black) dots precede thinner ones.

The map legends

In order to save space abbreviations have been used where dialect terms consist of more than one element and one of these also occurs in the (English) source item.

Thus the legend to map 20 *meal bin* shows entries like *(M) ark, (M) tun, (M) garnel* where *M* stands for *meal.*

Where it was convenient items were conflated beyond the style adopted in the lists but on similar editorial principles as outlined above. To establish the exact forms of a particular item in a given county the reader should refer to the list giving special consideration to merged forms (italicised figures).

NOTES

1. See The theoretical approach.
2. 'Structural comparison, diasystems, and dialectology', *Linguistics,* 4,1964, pp.66-82, p.75.
3. *On the Linguistic Study of Languages: An Inaugural Lecture,* Cambridge, 1957, p.15.
4. *On Early English Pronunciation,* Part IV, London, 1875, p.1087, n.2.
5. *Handbook of American Indian Languages,* Part I, Washington, 1911, p.67.
6. *The Dialect of the Southern Counties of Scotland,* Philological Society, London, 1873, p.46. Douglas's use of the word 'Scottis' is in the well-known passage in the prologue to his verse translation of the *Aenid,* which was first 'imprinted at London' 1553. Although he wrote (111-18), Kepand na sudron bot our awyn langage. nevertheless . . . sum word I pronunce as nyghtbouris doys;

   Lyke as in Latyn beyn Grew termys sum,
   So me behufyt quhilum or than be dum
   Sum bastard Latyn, French or Inglis oyss
   Quhar scant was Scottis — I had nane other choys.

   Mr. A. J. Aitken, in his article 'Scottish language', in *Chambers' Encyclopaedia* (1967) has, however, cited Adam Loutfut, a heraldic scribe, as having used the term in 1494.
7. 'Contemporary references to the Scottish speech of the sixteenth century', *Scottish Historical Review,* 25, 1928, pp.163-79. The other articles in Miss Bald's series are: 'The anglicisation of Scottish printing', ibid., 23, 1926, pp.107-15; 'The pioneers of anglicised speech in Scotland', ibid., 24, 1927, pp.179-93.
8. *An Etymological Dictionary of the Norn Language in Shetland* (Eng. trans.), London and Copenhagen,1928, Introduction, especially ch.II.
9. *Of the Orthographie and Congruitie of the Britan Tongue; A Treates, noe shorter then necessarie for the Schooles* [?1619], H.B. Wheatley (ed.), EETS, London, 1865.
10. op. cit., p.98.
11. On the general linguistic problems of the seventeenth century see: Otto Funke, *Zum Weltsprachenproblem in England im 17. Jahrhundert,* Anglist. Forsch. 69, Heidelberg, 1929; Jonathan Cohen, 'On the project of a universal character', *Mind,* 63, 1954, pp. 49-63; Vivian Salmon, ' Language planning in seventeenth century England; Its context and aims', in *In Memory of J. R. Firth,* C. E. Bazell et al. (eds.), London, 1966, pp.370-97.
12. op. cit., p.16.
13. *The Works of Sir Thomas Urquhart of Cromarty, Knight,* Maitland Club, vol. 30, Edinburgh, 1834. 'The Logopandecteison or introducduction to the universal language' (1653) is given at p.299. The quotations are from para. 73 of the first book, namely *Neandethaumata or Wonders of the New Speech.* See also J. Willock, *Sir Thomas Urquhart of Cromartie, Knight,* Edinburgh and London, 1899; F. C. Roe, *Sir Thomas Urquhart and Rabelais,* Oxford, 1957.
14. George Dalgarno, 'A discourse of the nature and number of double consonants', in *Works,* Maitland Club, vol.29, Edinburgh, 1834, pp.161-79, at p.163. This edition of the *Works of George Dalgarno* was reviewed by Sir William Hamilton in the *Edinburgh Review,* 61, July 1835. For the known facts of Dalgarno's life see Anthony à Wood, *Athenae Oxonienses,* vol. II, London,1691-2, p. 506.
15. 'A discourse of the nature and number of double consonants', in op. cit., p.164. For what Dalgarno has to say on 'Real character', see B. M. MS. Sloan 4377, esp. f. 143, 'News to the whole world of the discovery of an universal character, and a new rational language'; f.148 'A copy of the Dalgarno's letter, written to Mr. Hartlib', Oxford, 20 April 1657; f.149 St. John's Gospel, ch. XVI, vv. 1-13 written in 'Real character'; f.145 and 146 Various tables under two heads: (i) 'Radical character and points of affixes', (ii) 'Their gramatical flexion, circumstantiating particles and rational derivations'.
16. 'Ars Signorum', in op. cit., pp. 1-109. See especially ch.I, 'De Primis Signorum elementis speciatim vero de sonis simplicibus'. (The 'Ars Signorum' was published in London, 1661).
17. Anthony a Wood, *Athenae Oxonionses,* vol. II, p.506.
18. 'Some account of a boy born blind and deaf, collected from authentic sources of information; with a few remarks and comments', *Transactions of the Royal Society of Edinburgh,* 7, 1815, pp.5-78, at p.48.
19. For what Stewart had to say on 'philosophical language' see *Elements of the Philosophy of the Human Mind.* In two Parts, G. N. Wright (ed.), London, 1877, p.108 and note L, p.561. (The first part of the work was published in 1792 and the second in 1814.)
20. In Edinburgh these are almost legendary and, accordingly, not particularly well documented and even less well interpreted. See T. E. Ritchie, *Account of the Life and Writing of David Hume,* London, 1807, p.94 and cf. Horace Walpole, *Letters,* III, p.202 (quoted Henry Gray Graham, *Scottish Men of Letters in the Eighteenth Century,* London, 1901, p.91) and S. A. Leonard, 'The doctrine of correctness in English usage, 1700-1800', *University of Wisconsin Studies in Language and Literature,* no.25, Madison, 1929.
21. Reverend Mr. Thomas Morer, Minister of St. Anne's within Aldersgate . . . when he was chaplain to a Scotch Regiment, *A Short Account of Scotland,* London, 1715, p.13.
22. See n.18.
23. Quoted Dugald Stewart in *Transactions of the Royal Society of Edinburgh,* 7, 1815, p.49. See also Dalgarno's 'Didascalocophus' (esp. chs. I and II), in *Works,* Maitland Club edition, Edinburgh, 1834, p.111. ('Didascalocophus or the deaf and dumb man's tutor' was first 'Printed at the theater, Oxford' in 1680.)
24. Alexander Melville Bell, *Visible Speech: A New Fact Demonstrated,* London and Edinburgh, 1865, p.45. (This was a pamphlet. Bell's *Visible Speech, The Science of Universal Alphabetics* appeared in 1867, inaugural edition, London.)
25. Ellis's views on what he calls Bell's 'general positions' are given in the pamphlet mentioned in n.24 at p.25.
26. In *Transactions of the Royal Society of Edinburgh,* 7, 1815, p.39. Stewart in this passage was noting, with approval, the methods of the Abbé Sicard in the treatment of the deaf and dumb (usually, of course, dumb *because* deaf). In the hypothetical case of *Aveugle-Sourd-Muet,* Sicard advocated the use of as many of the senses as possible, especially of *touch*. Stewart regretted that he did not also include *smell.*
27. Alexander Melville Bell, *English Visible Speech for the Million,* London, 1868, p.3. (This was a short, popular pamphlet which appeared after the inaugural edition of *Visible Speech,* London, 1867.)
28. op. cit., p.98. Murray had studied under Bell in Edinburgh, probably in the early 1860s, and again met him in London in 1864. He seems to have become a close friend of Bell and his family, especially the son Alexander Graham Bell for whom he made his first electric battery and introduced him generally to the study of electricity. Graham Bell eventually called him 'the grandfather of the telephone'. James Clerk Maxwell once referred to Graham Bell as

'not an electrician who has found out how to make a tin plate speak, but a speaker who to gain his private ends has become an electrician.' This seems to be a most interesting link in the chain which connects the study of speech in Edinburgh with much that came after – the Bell Telephone Laboratories, information theory, and its general influence on the study of linguistics.(Harold J. R. Murray, 'Sir James Murray of the Oxford English Dictionary', *Transactions of the Hawick Archaeological Society,* 1934, pp.35-41; J. Clerk Maxwell, *Scientific Papers,* W. D. Niven (ed.), Cambridge, 1890, vol.2, p.742).

29. op. cit., p.94. Murray did not, of course, use 'system' in the modern sense of a structured system. But in his work there are sufficient indications of notions like minimal pairs or synchronicity in method to warrant a more than sentimental look at his use of the term 'vowel system'.
30. *Transactions of the Philological Society.* London, 1877-9, p.9, cf. p.423.
31. *Anglia,* 4, 1881, p.56 (Anzeiger), review by Moritz Trautmann of *Grundzüge der Phonetik* by Eduard Sievers. (Winteler was Sievers's pupil.)
32. *Handbook of Phonetics,* Oxford, 1877, p.vii. Sweet of course, had been Bell's pupil.
33. Loc. cit. under n.30.
34. *The Scottish National Dictionary* began its work in 1931 under Grant's editorship. The present editor (since 1946) is David D. Murison. The dictionary is (sub-title): 'Designed partly on regional lines and partly on historical principles, and containing all the Scottish words known to be in use or to have been in use since c. 1700.' *The Dictionary of the Older Scottish Tongue* ('From the twelfth century to the end of the seventeenth') also began in 1931 under the editorship of W. A. Craigie. The present editor (since 1957) is A. J. Aitken. See also David D. Murison, 'A survey of Scottish language studies', *Forum for Modern Language Studies,* 3, no.3, July 1967. A. J. Aitken, 'Completing the Record of Scots', Scottish Studies, 8, 1964.
35. The English Association, Leaflet no. 11, June 1909.
36. In paper given to the 'Réunion des Sociétés savantes', 26 May, 1888 and published in *Revue des patois gallo-romans,* 2, 1888, pp.161-75; cf. Edwin C. Roedder, 'Linguistic Geography', *Germanic Review,* 1, no.4, October 1926.
37. Hermann Fischer, *Geographie der schwäbischen Mundart,* Tübingen, 1895; Karl Haag, *Die Mundarten des oberen Neckar- und Donaulandes,* Programm Reutlingen, 1898.
38. Wenker began his atlas in 1876. In 1881 the first instalment appeared: *Sprachatlas von Nord- und Mitteldeutschland,* Strassburg. See also Walther Mitzka, *Handbuch zum Deutschen Sprachatlas,* Marburg, 1952, esp. p.9 ff.
39. A. J. Ellis, President of the Philological Society, 'On dialect, language, orthoepy, and Dr. G. Wenker's speech atlas', *Transactions of the Philological Society* (1882-4), pp.20-32, p.28.
40. op. cit., p.3.
41. A copy of the Memorandum is in the files of the LSS in Edinburgh. See also I. Iordan and J. Orr, *An Introduction to Romance Linguistics,* London, 1937 and the revision, together with a supplement, 'Thirty years on' by R. Posner, Oxford, 1970.
42. Wolfgang Viereck, 'Englische Dialektologie', *Germanische Dialektologie: Festschrift für Walther Mitzka zum 80.Geburtstag,* L. E. Schmitt (ed.), II, Wiesbaden, 1968, p.552.
43. For a map showing the areas in Scotland in which various dialectologists have worked, see H. H. Speitel and J. Y. Mather, 'Schottische Dialektologie', in op. cit., p.537, n.42. See R. Zai, *The Phonology of the Morebattle Dialect, East Roxburghshire,* Luzern, 1942; P. Wettstein, *The Phonology of a Berwickshire Dialect,* Bienne, 1942; W. Wölck, *Phonematische Analyse der Sprache von Buchan,* Heidelberg, 1965; H. Mutschmann, *A Phonology of the North-eastern Scotch Dialect,* Bonn, 1909; and O. Ritter's critical review of this, 'Zur Mundart des nordöstlichen Schottland', *Englische Studien,* 46, 1912-13, pp.9-65, at p.9.
44. In his paper 'A new approach to Middle English dialectology', *English Studies,* 44, no.1, 1963, Professor McIntosh specifically mentioned the link between his approach to problems in Middle English dialectology and the problems of the LSS upon which he had already been engaged. See his *Introduction to a Survey of Scottish Dialects,* Edinburgh, 1952. This was the first of a series *University of Edinburgh, Linguistic Survey of Scotland Monographs.* The second was K. H. Jackson, *Contributions to the Study of Manx Phonology,* Edinburgh, 1955. Also of interest for the development of techniques in the LSS are the following: J. S. Woolley, *Bibliography for Scottish Linguistic Studies,* Edinburgh, 1954; David Abercrombie, 'The recording of dialect material', *Orbis,* 3, 1954, pp.231-5, and 'English accents', ch.iv. of *Problems and Principles: Studies in the Teaching of English as a Second Language,* London, 1956; Angus McIntosh, 'The study of Scots dialects in relation to other subjects', *Orbis,* 3, 1954, pp.173-7.
45. J. Y. Mather was appointed to the staff of the LSS in 1956 and H. H. Speitel in 1964. J. S. Woolley was on the staff in 1950-6, J. C. Catford in 1952-7, Trevor Hill in 1954-66. H. J. Uldall died in 1957. See in particular H.J. Uldall, *Outline of Glossematics,* Part I, *General theory,* Copenhagen, *TCLC* X, 1957 (second edition 1967) has an introduction by Eli Fischer-Jørgensen); J. C. Catford, 'Vowel systems of Scots dialects', *Transactions of the Philological Society,* 1957, pp.107-17, and 'The Linguistic Survey of Scotland' *Orbis,* 6, 1957, pp.105-21; Trevor Hill, 'Institutional Linguistics' *Orbis,* 7, 1958, pp.441-55, and 'Phonemic and prosodic analysis in linguistic geography', *Orbis,* 12, 1963, pp.449-55.
46. This does not exclude the possibility that an investigator with a different point of view might not interpret the material in a completely new way. But he would in most cases set up a different set of questions, if he had an opportunity to do so.
47. Within the framework of this short introduction we cannot, of course, treat fully all the aspects of the subject. See n.62.
48. We wish to emphasise here that we would include standard varieties in our definition. T. Hill, 'Institutional linguistics', *Orbis,* 7, 1958, pp.441-55, suggests the term 'dialect continuum' for our language community, but this seems to exclude standard varieties (his 'koines'). By avoiding the word 'continuum' we also do not have to talk about 'divided continuum' (see p.443).
49. It must be pointed out that, in practice, extra-linguistic (e.g. historical, political, ethnic, nationalistic) criteria are often involved in the definition of language.
50. J. C. Catford, *A Linguistic Theory of Translation,* London, 1965, pp.83-92, especially p.84; see also M. Gregory, 'Aspects of varieties differentiation', *Journal of Linguistics,* 3, 1967, pp.177-98.
51. A seminal work in this field is W. Labov, *The Social Stratification of English in New York City,* Washington D.C., 1966. There is now also considerable activity in the investigation of urban speech at the University of Newcastle-upon-Tyne (under B. H. M. Strang) and, also at the postgraduate level, in other places in Britain.
52. Catford accounts for 'medium' only under the transient characteristic 'mode' (op. cit., p.85).
53. This emphasis on the underlying base has often led to the neglect of other aspects of language change like accretion, borrowing, convergence etc., which may change a language much more drastically.
54. There are close resemblances in the methodology of diachronic (genetic) dialectology and comparative philology. The distinction is really only one of degree. See J. Ellis, *Towards a General Comparative Linguistics,* The Hague, 1966, p.17.

55. C. F. Hockett, *A Course in Modern Linguistics,* New York, 1958, p.323 ff.
56. Cf. e.g. Dutch and German.
57. C. F. Hockett, op. cit., p.332 ff.
58. The recognition of levels and their number will, of course, depend on one's linguistic theory.
59. In practice, it is mainly the segmental elements at the phonetic/phonological and the lexical levels that have been studied.
60. This restricts the display of the material to two dimensions and does not give enough scope to indicate, say, social stratifications in localities or systemic relationships of phonological material. It has been seriously questioned whether the map is a suitable means for displaying the complexity of dialectology. As we will discuss further below, we hope to have countered some of the criticism by the introduction of the term 'dialect potential' and our claims for the representativeness of our maps are perhaps less strong than those of some of our predecessors in linguistic geography.
61. See H. H. Speitel, 'A typology of isoglosses. Isoglosses near the Scottish-English border', *Zeitschrift für Dialektologie und Linguistik,* 1969, pp.49-66.
62. Full bibliographies on dialectological studies in nearly all countries of the world are found in S. Pop, *La Dialectologie,* 2 vols., Louvain, 1950 (now supplemented by *Germanische Dialektologie,* Festschrift für Walther Mitzka, L. E. Schmitt (ed.), 2 vols., Wiesbaden, 1968); while the classical German approach is summarised by A. Bach, *Deutsche Mundartforschung,* 2nd ed., Heidelberg, 1950, and criticised and developed by G. H. Hard, 'Zur Mundartgeographie', *Beihefte zur Zeitschrift Wirkendes Wort,* 17, Düsseldorf, 1966, and by J. Goossens, *Strukturelle Sprachgeographie,* Heidelberg, 1969; the influential Romance school of dialectology is described in I. Iordan and J. Orr, op. cit.; for the Netherlands see A. Weijnen, *Nederlandse dialectkunde,* Aasen, 1958 (2nd ed., 1966); for Scotland see A. McIntosh, *Introduction to a Survey of Scots Dialects,* Edinburgh, 1952 (2nd ed., 1961).
64. H. H. Speitel, 'Dialect', *Problems of Language and Learning,* Alan Davies, (ed.), London, 1974, pp.34-60.
'accent', for which they use 'dialect'. What we call 'dialects' they call 'languages'.
65. Research is in general carried out separately.
66. R. J. Gregg, 'The Scotch-Irish dialect boundaries in Ulster', in *Patterns in the Folk Speech of the British Isles,* Martyn F. Wakelin (ed.), London, 1972; G. B. Adams, 'Ulster dialects' in *Ulster Dialects,* Holywood, 1964, pp.1-4.
67. But see P. L. Henry, 'A linguistic survey of Ireland, preliminary report', *Lochlann,* I, *Norsk Tidsskrift for Sprogvidenskap,* suppl. vol. V, 1958, pp.49-208. This is now supplemented by our atlas.
68. As interpreted by G. B. Adams, see n.21.
69. *Etude de géographie linguistique, Pathologie et thérapeutique verbales,* I, Neuveville, 1915, p.45.
70. A full although sometimes indiscriminate treatment of questionnaire-making, methods of enquiry, etc., can be found in Sever Pop's *La Dialectologie* (see n.62) especially vol. II, p.1133 ff.
71. Sever Pop, op. cit., vol. II, pp.1179-82.
72. Common core vocabulary contains lexical items found all over the area of a 'language' as e.g. *take, make, sit* in English. See C. F. Hockett, op. cit., p.332f.
73. On the work of the German survey and the postal method, see Walther Mitzka, *Handbuch zum Deutschen Sprachatlas,* Marburg, 1952.
74. See Raven McDavid, review of PQI, *Journal of English and Germanic Philology,* 52, 1953, pp.568-70.
75. See the discussion of the shortcomings of PQI.
76. The shortness of the time span of the investigation is important for the concept of synchronicity, although this is often undermined (as in our case and most other enquiries) by the greatly varying age-groups of informants, who are, in a sense, representative of different periods of time.
77. The data thus obtained may supplement previous field-work (see n. 6), or, as in the case of the present volume, yield material which can be cartographically interpreted and displayed, but raises new problems for field-work coverage.
78. But cf. J. Goossens, *Strukturelle Sprachgeographie,* Heidelberg, 1969, who makes out a good case for direct and simultaneous investigation of lexical fields and material culture and its function.
79. See n. 6.
80. We are thinking here mainly of evaluation procedures, i.e. specific questions in which the informant is called upon to comment on his linguistic responses.
81. The Scottish National Dictionary sends out check-lists to voluntary helpers (at present *c.* 300) in all counties of Scotland for verification and supplementation of printed material, and these provide a rough and ready guide to the distributions of a particular word.
82. How many of the questionnaires were actually distributed and returned is not known.
83. See Appendix E, list of items in PQ1, where they have been specially marked.
84. See n.5.
85. See J. Y. Mather, 'Aspects of the linguistic geography of Scotland', I, *Scottish Studies*, 9, 1965, pp.129-44; II, ibid., 10, 1966, pp.129-53; III, ibid., 13, 1969, pp.1-16.
86. In some cases this may have saved the book from the fate of many circulars.
87. This technical detail is of great importance for the storage and accessibility of the questionnaire. Many surveys have paid no attention to it and are therefore awkward to consult because each individual questionnaire has to be handled to obtain the relevant information on one item. We must admit, however, that where the emphasis of the survey is on systemic relationships, as in our phonological questionnaire, it may be more appropriate to keep each book together. Although our procedure has been most useful in the preparation of the atlas, it is difficult to judge the material of individual informants. Perhaps some means of duplicating each slip and a double filing system should have been considered.
88. See first paragraph of DI.
89. The 'main word' in DI 4.
90. This probably accurately reflects in many cases, the position of 'dialect' spoken by a minority or restricted to certain situations as against the 'standard' speech variety.
91. Note the exclusion of items of this kind from the atlas (e.g. a number of items between PQ1, 34-44). A number of these might have been more productive for areal distribution, if the context had been more narrowly defined.
92. In these cases the questioning method is self-explanatory.
93. See H. Orton, *Survey of English Dialects (A), Introduction,* Leeds 1962.
94. See dialect v. standard.
95. Wenker is said to have constructed his forty sentences merely for the convenience of the schoolchildren, who had to act as informants if the teacher was not a native of the locality (cf. L.E. Schmitt, *Das Forschungsinstitut für deutsche Sprache . . .* mit wissenschaftlichem Jahresbericht, Marburg, 1964, p.8).
96. It must be admitted, however, that a topically ordered field questionnaire can hold the informants' interest much longer, whereas with the LSS phonological field questionnaire (set out to elicit phonological systems) there is, in the majority of cases, a maximum length of two hours for an interview. Perhaps a combina-

tion of the two possibilities should be tried out using question cards rather than books so that the material could be easily re-ordered.

97. In Northern Ireland the distribution was carried out by the dialect section of the Belfast Naturalists' Field Club.

98. Pp. 1-2 of our pagination. The text reads as follows:

Reference has already been made from time to time in the press to the Linguistic Survey of Scotland which the University has undertaken. Such surveys have already been made or are in process of being made in a number of other countries, and the purpose of the present one may be summarised as follows. We wish to discover as much as possible about the characteristics of each Scottish and Gaelic dialect and also to analyse the various ways in which one dialect differs from another. It is hoped that what we shall learn in this way will enlighten us about many problems connected with Scots and with Gaelic, and that this in turn will help us to know more about the cultural and historical background to the different parts of this country, and the neighbouring areas of Northern England and Northern Ireland.

A study of the characteristics of a dialect and a comparison of these characteristics with those of neighbouring dialects is quite a complicated business, because it involves an examination of a large number of diverse features. Among these we might mention the following:—

1. How words are pronounced, e.g. whether you pronounce the word *two* as *twa* or *twaw* or *tway* or *too.*
2. What form a word has in a particular grammatical function, e.g. whether you say "he's *brocht* it" or whether you use *brung* or *brochten* instead; whether you say *shin* or *shen* or *shoes,* and so forth.
3. Whether one and the same word varies in meaning from place to place, and in what way. E.g. in some parts of Scotland, the words *stirk* and *stot* are used only of the male animal, while in other parts they are used of both sexes; again, in some places the phrase "half three" means "half past two," but in others it means "half past three."
4. How different words are used to refer to one and the same thing, often according to the part of the country you are in. E.G. the word *bourach* "a crowd" is common in many areas north of the Tay but rare anywhere else. Similarly the word *gellick* "a crowbar" is hardly found anywhere except in Kirkcudbrightshire and Dumfriesshire; elsewhere other words are used, of which the commonest is *pinch.*

Some of these questions can best be examined by detailed investigation on the spot; in particular, it is difficult to get down precise information about exactly how words are pronounced except by sending an expert phonetician to look into the matter. But there are many problems which can better be solved on the evidence of material sent in by a large number of local correspondents, and the enclosed booklet contains questions intended to throw light on just over 200 such problems. These are mostly of the kind mentioned in 4 above, but a few are of types 1, 2, and 3. It is not realised by all dialect speakers that certain words are strictly confined to particular areas, or that others, though used almost everywhere, differ quite sharply in meaning from one district to another. This booklet contains only a small selection of words of these kinds, and space is therefore left at the end for you to note down any others that may have struck you, so that use may be made of them in another enquiry similar to the present one at some later date.

We hope that several thousands of these booklets will be returned to us, duly filled in, in the course of the next few weeks. The success of the whole undertaking depends on the co-operation of those people in all parts of the country who have an intimate knowledge of their local variety of Scots or Gaelic. We therefore hope that those who receive this document will help us by giving us as much, and as accurate, information as possible. When it comes back to us, your booklet will be taken apart and each page (except those at the end) will be cut up into six sections. The information we get from all over the country about each basic word will then be filed. The distribution of the various words supplied by your answers to each question will afterwards be plotted in great detail on maps. A full analysis will take a considerable time, but the information we hope to receive in this way will be very vital to the Linguistic Survey as a whole. We realise that the work of filling in the booklet means a good deal of time and trouble, but we hope that those who undertake it will feel recompensed by the knowledge that they are making a direct and important contribution to the better understanding of their own language and the traditions behind it.

99. More recent developments in linguistics with a strong sociological interest would support the argument that it is not sufficient to select one informant in one place picked more or less accidentally, but that a representative sample on non-linguistic criteria of the speech community should be taken (which might not include our kind of informant, as in many localities the dialect in our sense is spoken only by a small minority which might slip through the meshes of the 'sample net'). See also p. 00, n. 51, and D.J. Trudgill, 'The Social Differentiation of English in Norwich', Cambridge 1974.

100. See p. 21.

101. See our comments on the failure of informants to distinguish between usual and less common words

102. These figures are based on the census of 1951 (Scotland 5,096,415 inhabitants). The four cities are Glasgow (1,089,767), Edinburgh (466, 761), Aberdeen (182,729) and Dundee (177,340). 1337 questionnaires were returned from localities in Scotland.

103. Slips returned by Gaelic-speaking informants were filed separately.

104. For this purpose the map was divided into 10 km squares.

105. See item 13 'three legged stool'.

106. These cross-references have been confined to items which are mapped. There are, of course, more examples in the various lists, above all in those of related items as, e.g. birds, insects etc. The full extent of the recurrence of target items under different source items will be revealed by the *Index* which is proposed for inclusion in volume II.

107. For an exhaustive analysis of Standard English orthographic conventions see Axel Wijk, *Regularized English,* Stockholm, 1959.

108. Square brackets, i.e. [ ] show phonetic transcriptions; obliques i.e., / / show phonemic transcriptions; small acute brackets, i.e. <> enclose orthographies where these are graphs or digraphs. Where the orthography of a word is represented, this is in italics. Further below, 'C' stands for any consonant and 'V' for any vowel, 'V:' for a long vowel

109. The same point was made at the end of the eighteenth century by the contributor to the First Statistical Account for the parish of Duffus (Morayshire) in a note (vol. VIII, p.396): 'No Morayshire man of the lower ranks ever pronounces . . . long *o . . .* [He says] *clo͝os* for *clōse, ro͝od* for *rōad* and *rōde'* etc.

110. The matter is further complicated by a not uncommon <eu> usage in dialect literature for [u], [ju] as in *pleuch* = 'plough' etc.

111. See Jan Goossens, *Strukturelle Sprachgeographie,* Heidelberg, 1969.

112. See Appendices C and D.

ACKNOWLEDGEMENTS

The editors wish to acknowledge the work of their predecessors on the staff of the LSS, H.J. Uldall, J.S. Woolley, J.C. Catford and Trevor Hill, in the ordering of the word-geographical material. Before he left in 1966, Trevor Hill was also involved in matters of editorial principle and in the working out of a theoretical background for the interpretation of informants' spelling.

They also wish to thank the numerous succession of clerical workers (mostly post-graduate students), together with the secretarial staff of the LSS, who did much of the early routine work especially in the general processing of complete questionnaires. They would also like to thank the committee of the Scottish National Dictionary for the use of their mailing-list.

Finally, they thank the committee of the LSS, Professor D. Talbot Rice (Convenor), Professor Angus McIntosh, Professor Kenneth H. Jackson and Professor David Albercrombie for their support; and in particular Professor McIntosh who has also read the Introduction to the Atlas in manuscript, and from whose criticism they have greatly benefited.

Corrigenda

p.8 l.h. col., last para., line 2 for 'p.16' *read* 'above'
p.10 r.h. col., last para., line 4 for 'maked' *read* 'marked'
p.16 r.h. col., 7th para., line 12 for 'absensed' *read* 'observed'
p.25 n.64 for '64' *read* '63' and insert after line 2
'64. It must be pointed out particularly that many American linguists and following them European scholars dispense with the term'
p.27, last para., line 3 for 'Albercrombie' *read* Abercrombie'

MAPS AND LISTS

A map should always be examined in conjunction with its list (particularly the introductory note at the beginning of the list).

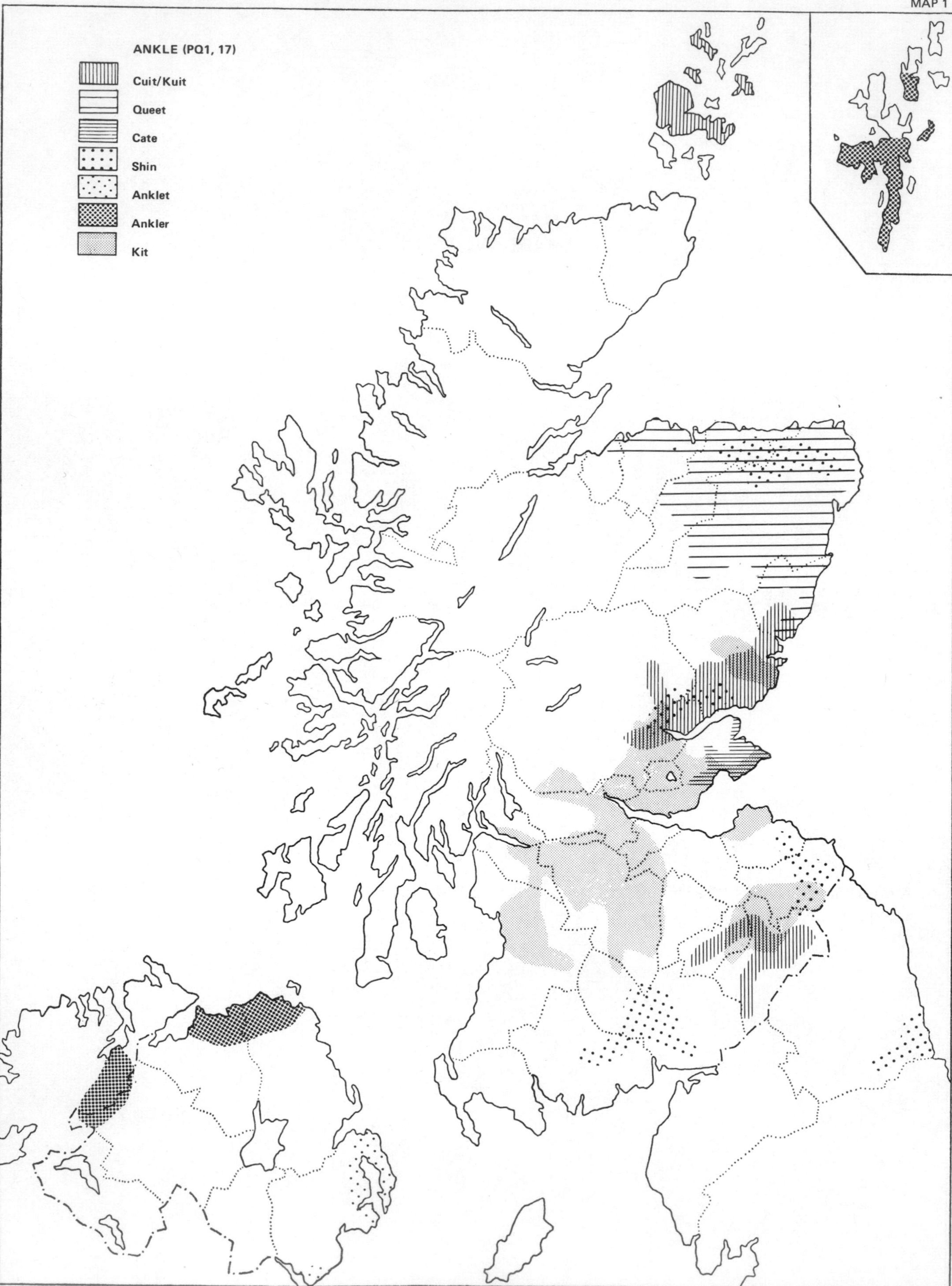
ANKLE (PQ1, 17)
Cuit/Kuit
Queet
Cate
Shin
Anklet
Ankler
Kit

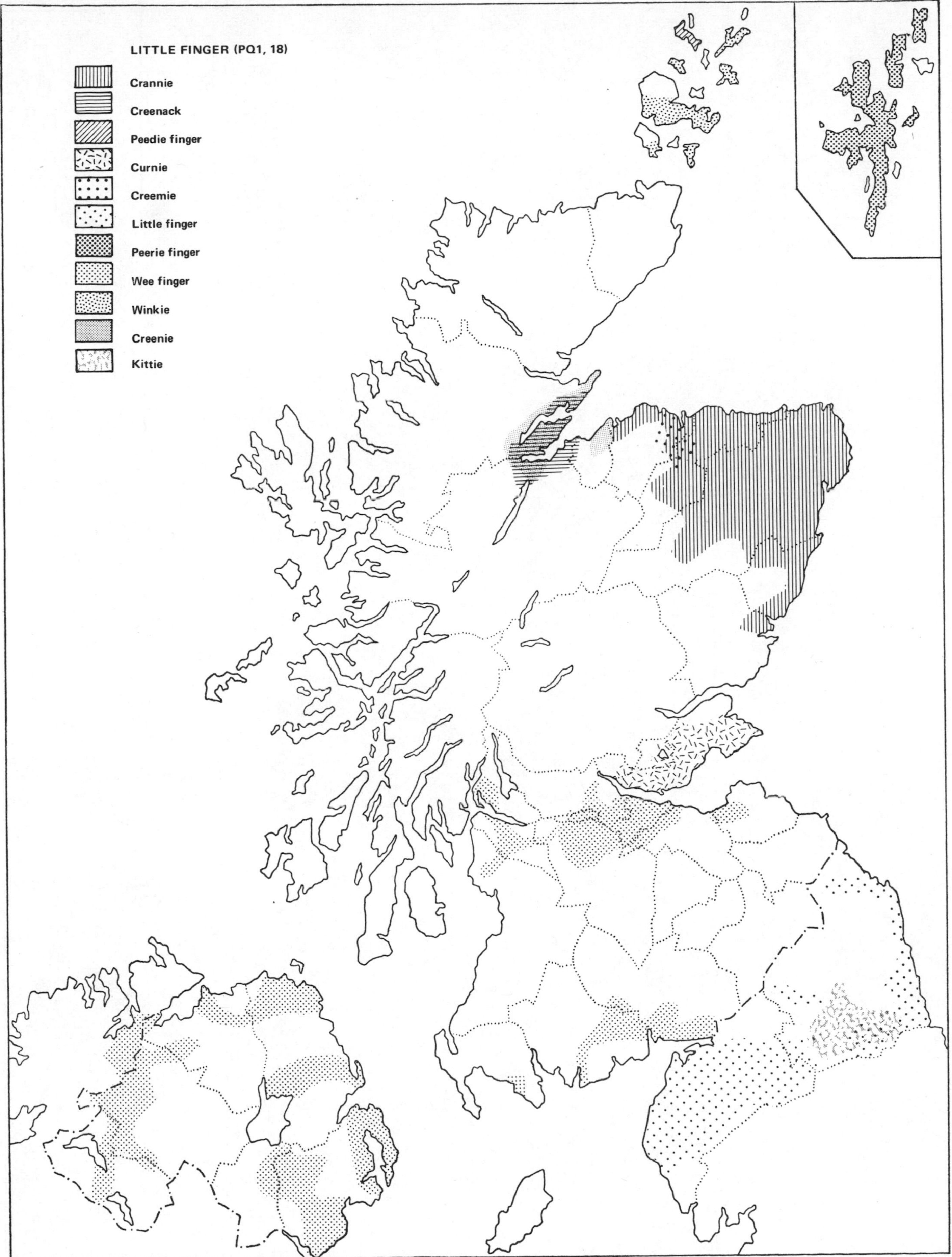
LITTLE FINGER (PQ1, 18)
Crannie
Creenack
Peedie finger
Curnie
Creemie
Little finger
Peerie finger
Wee finger
Winkie
Creenie
Kittie

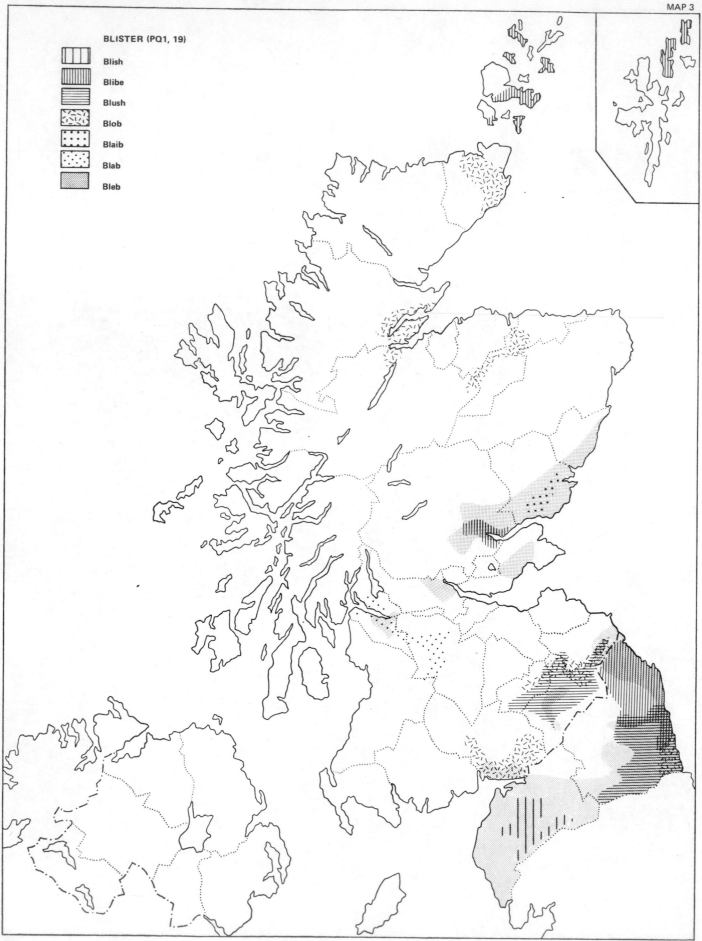

BLISTER (PQ1, 19)

Blish
Blibe
Blush
Blob
Blaib
Blab
Bleb

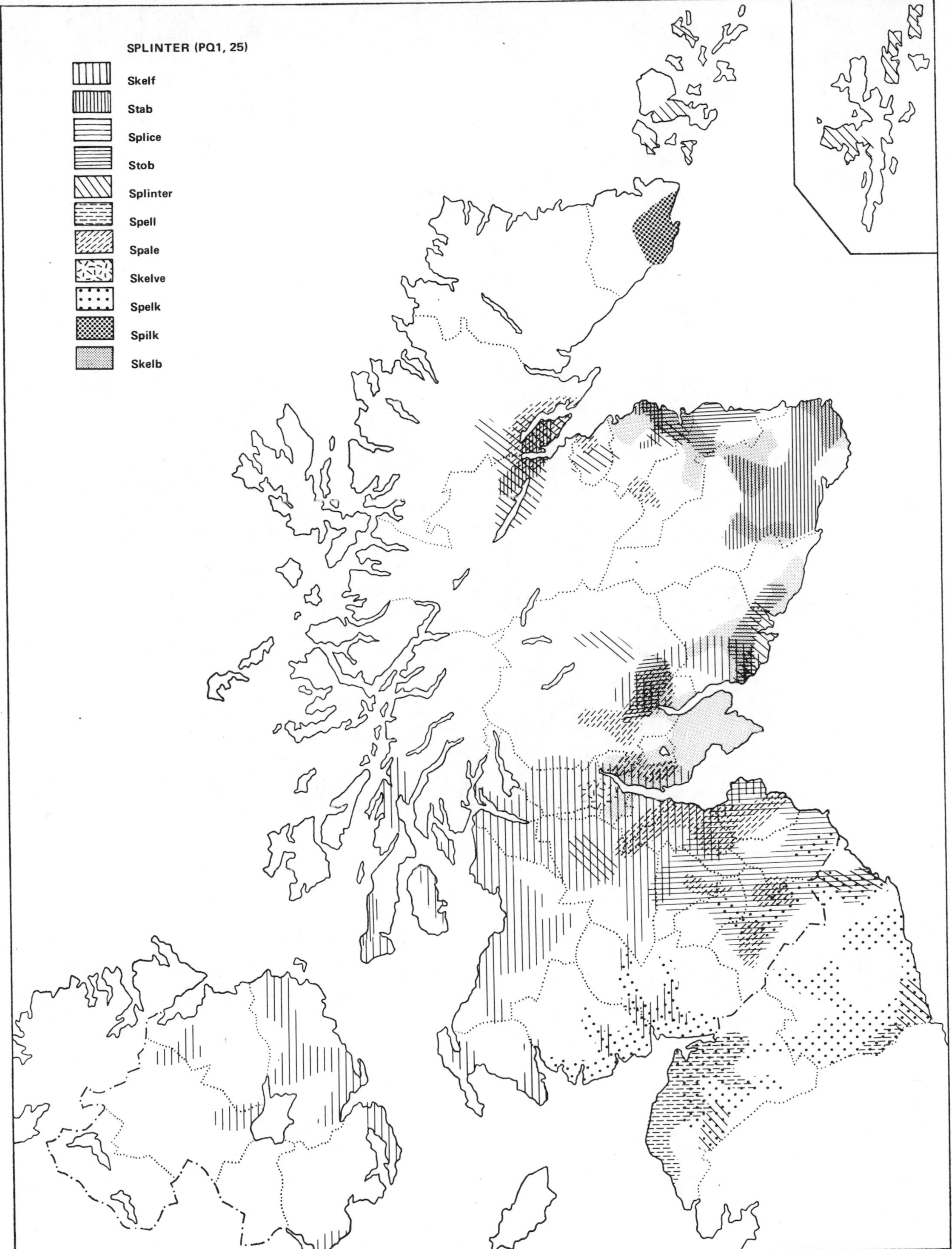
SPLINTER (PQ1, 25)
Skelf
Stab
Splice
Stob
Splinter
Spell
Spale
Skelve
Spelk
Spilk
Skelb

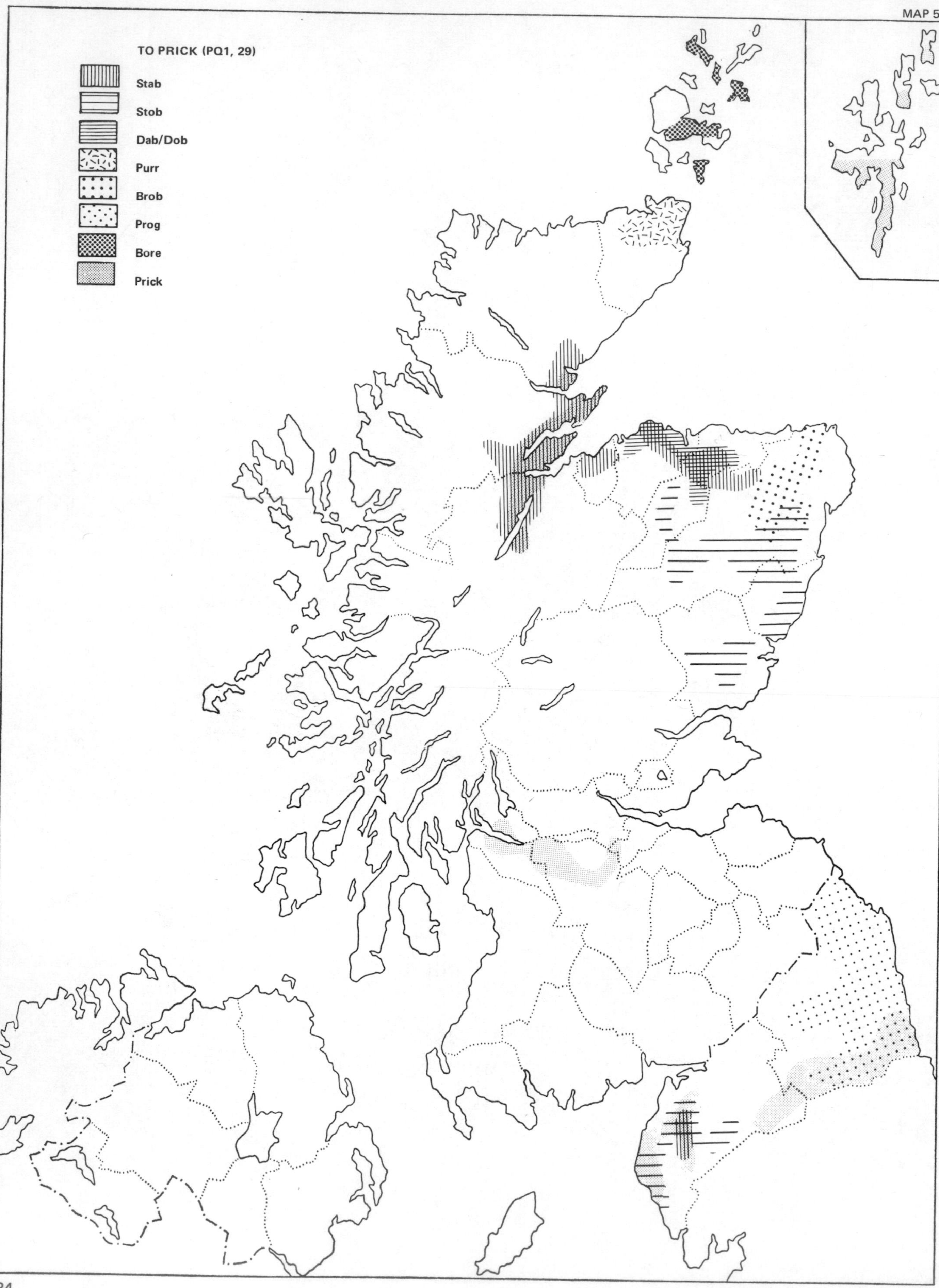

MAP 5
TO PRICK (PQ1, 29)
Stab
Stob
Dab/Dob
Purr
Brob
Prog
Bore
Prick

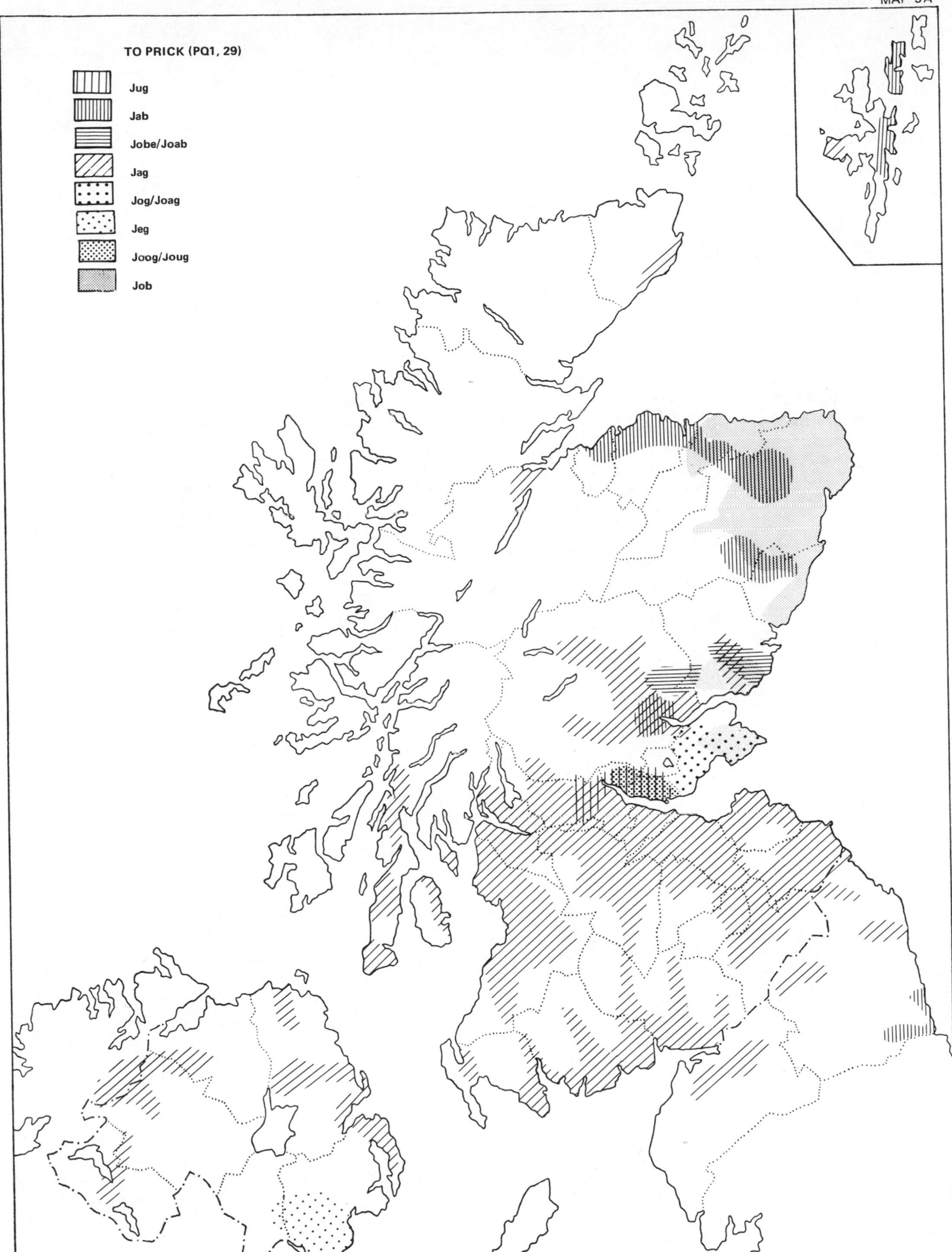
TO PRICK (PQ1, 29)
Jug
Jab
Jobe/Joab
Jag
Jog/Joag
Jeg
Joog/Joug
Job

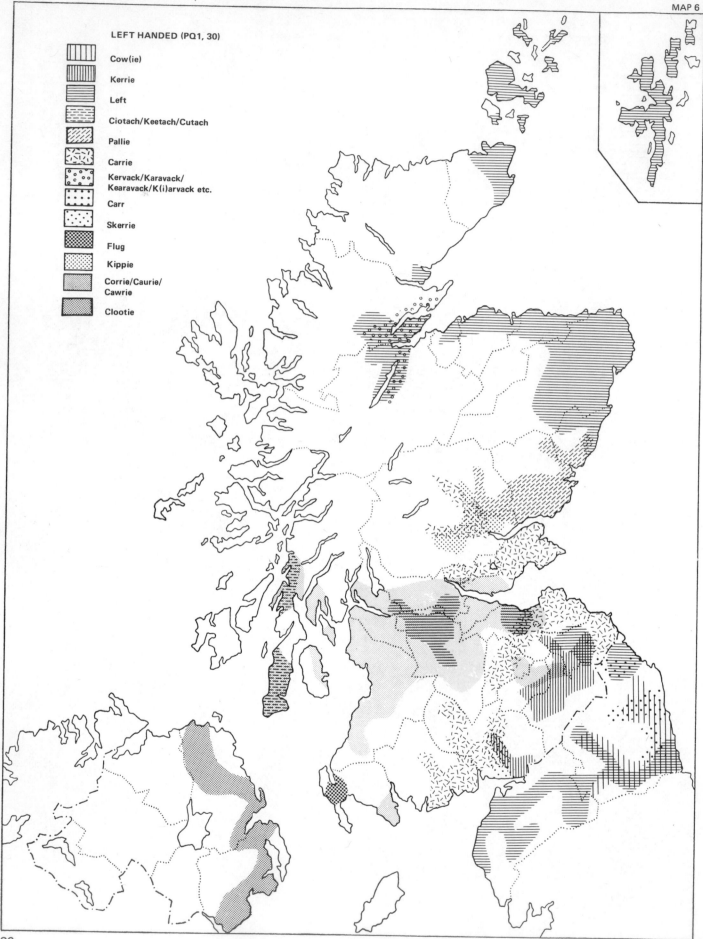

LEFT HANDED (PQ1, 30)

Cow(ie)
Kerrie
Left
Ciotach/Keetach/Cutach
Pallie
Carrie
Kervack/Karavack/
Kearavack/K(i)arvack etc.
Carr
Skerrie
Flug
Kippie
Corrie/Caurie/
Cawrie
Clootie

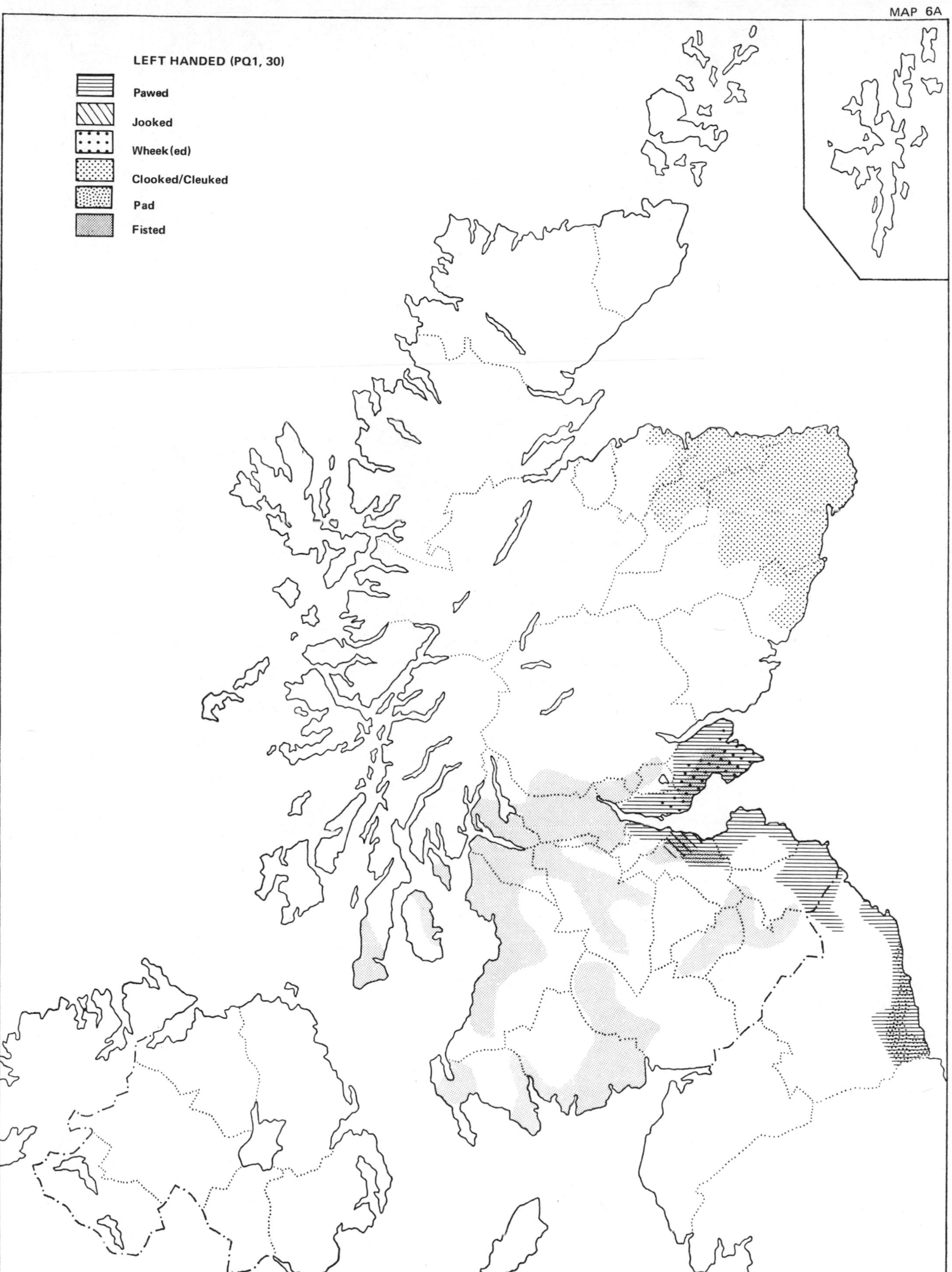
LEFT HANDED (PQ1, 30)
Pawed
Jooked
Wheek(ed)
Clooked/Cleuked
Pad
Fisted

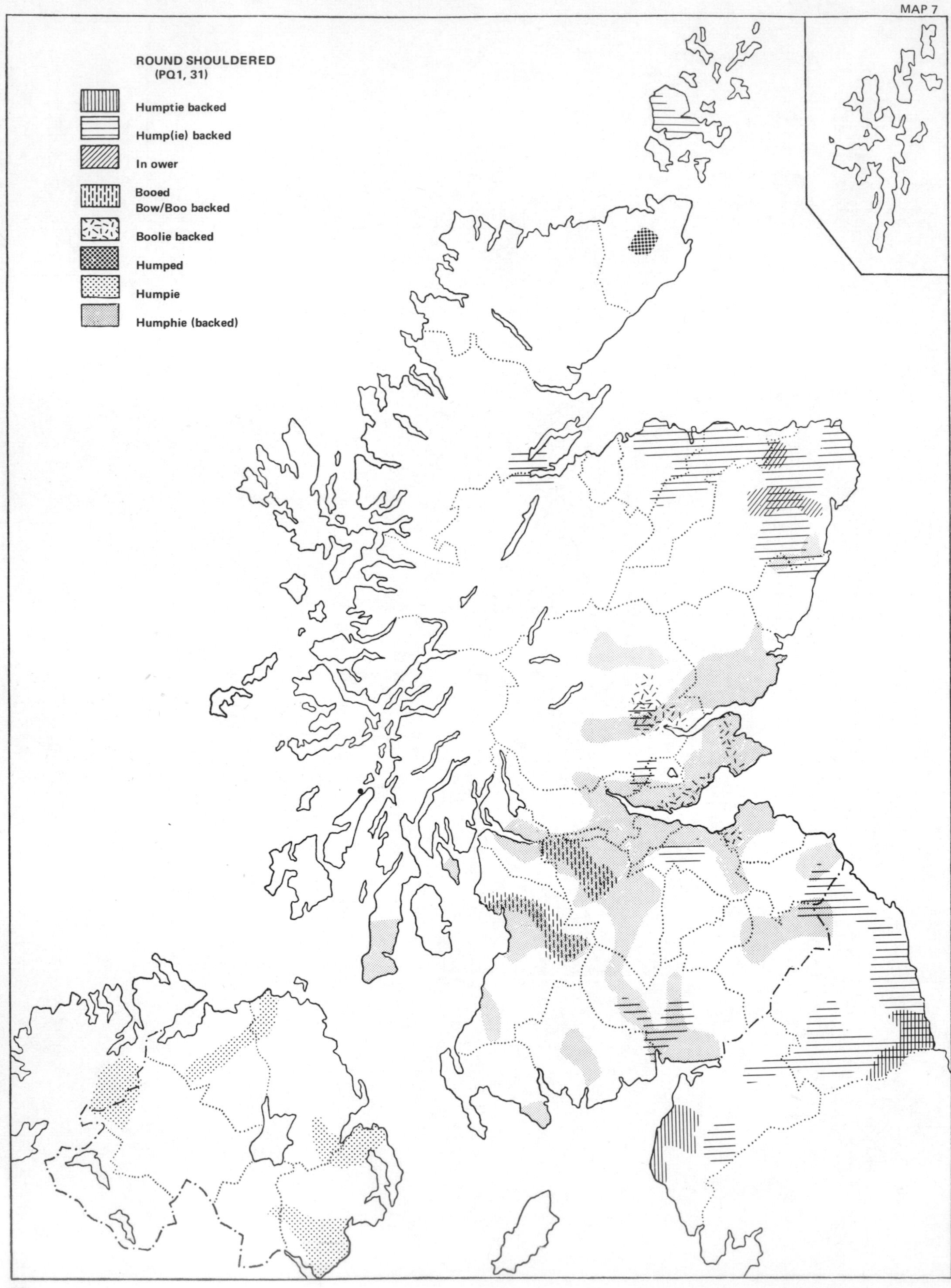
ROUND SHOULDERED
(PQ1, 31)
Humptie backed
Hump(ie) backed
In ower
Booed
Bow/Boo backed
Boolie backed
Humped
Humpie
Humphie (backed)

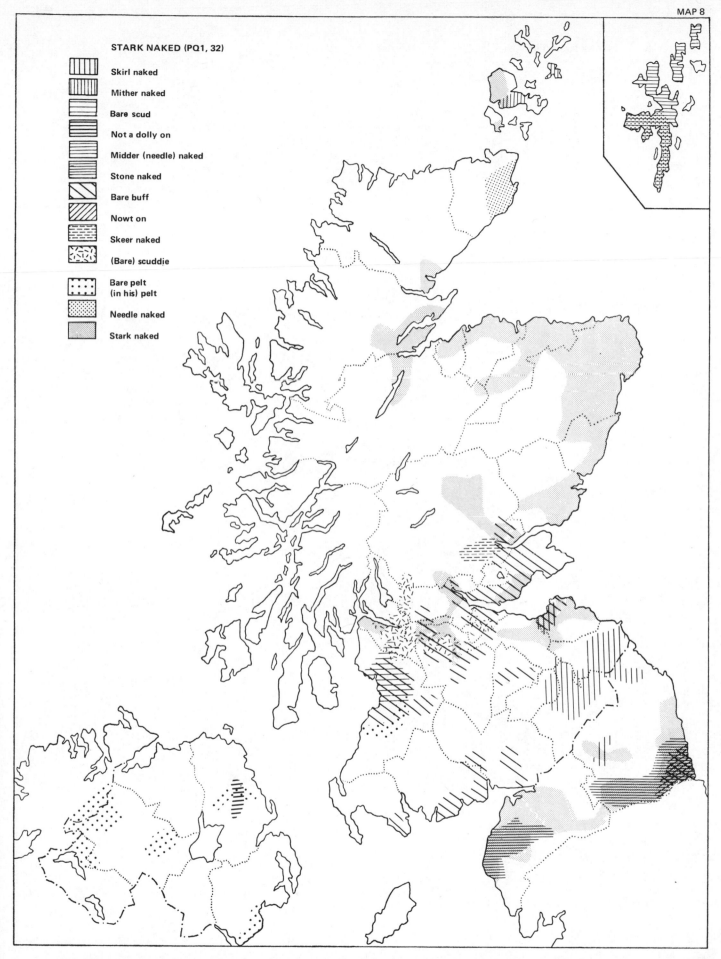

STARK NAKED (PQ1, 32)

Skirl naked

Mither naked

Bare scud

Not a dolly on

Midder (needle) naked

Stone naked

Bare buff

Nowt on

Skeer naked

(Bare) scuddie

Bare pelt
(in his) pelt

Needle naked

Stark naked

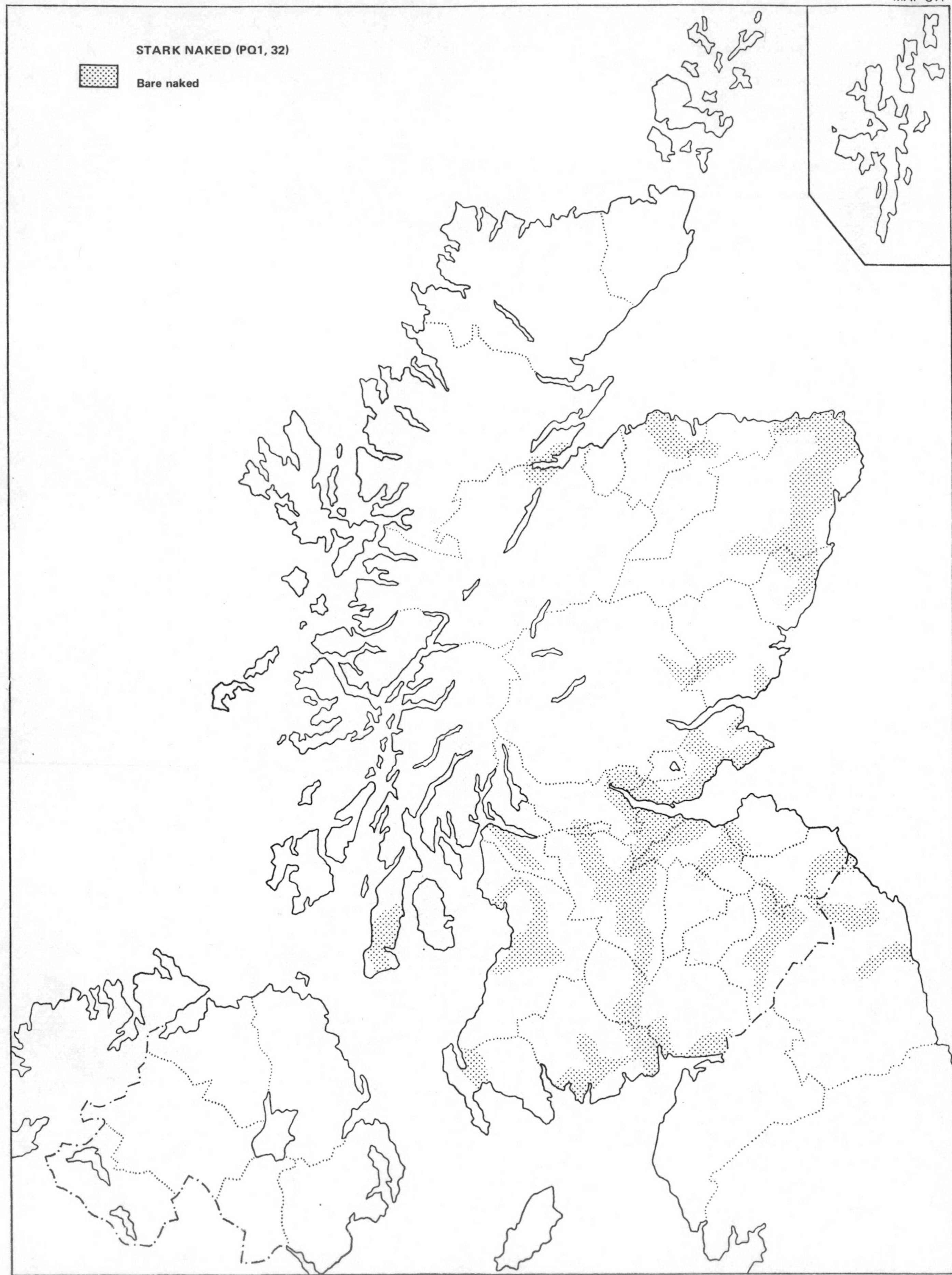
STARK NAKED (PQ1, 32)
Bare naked

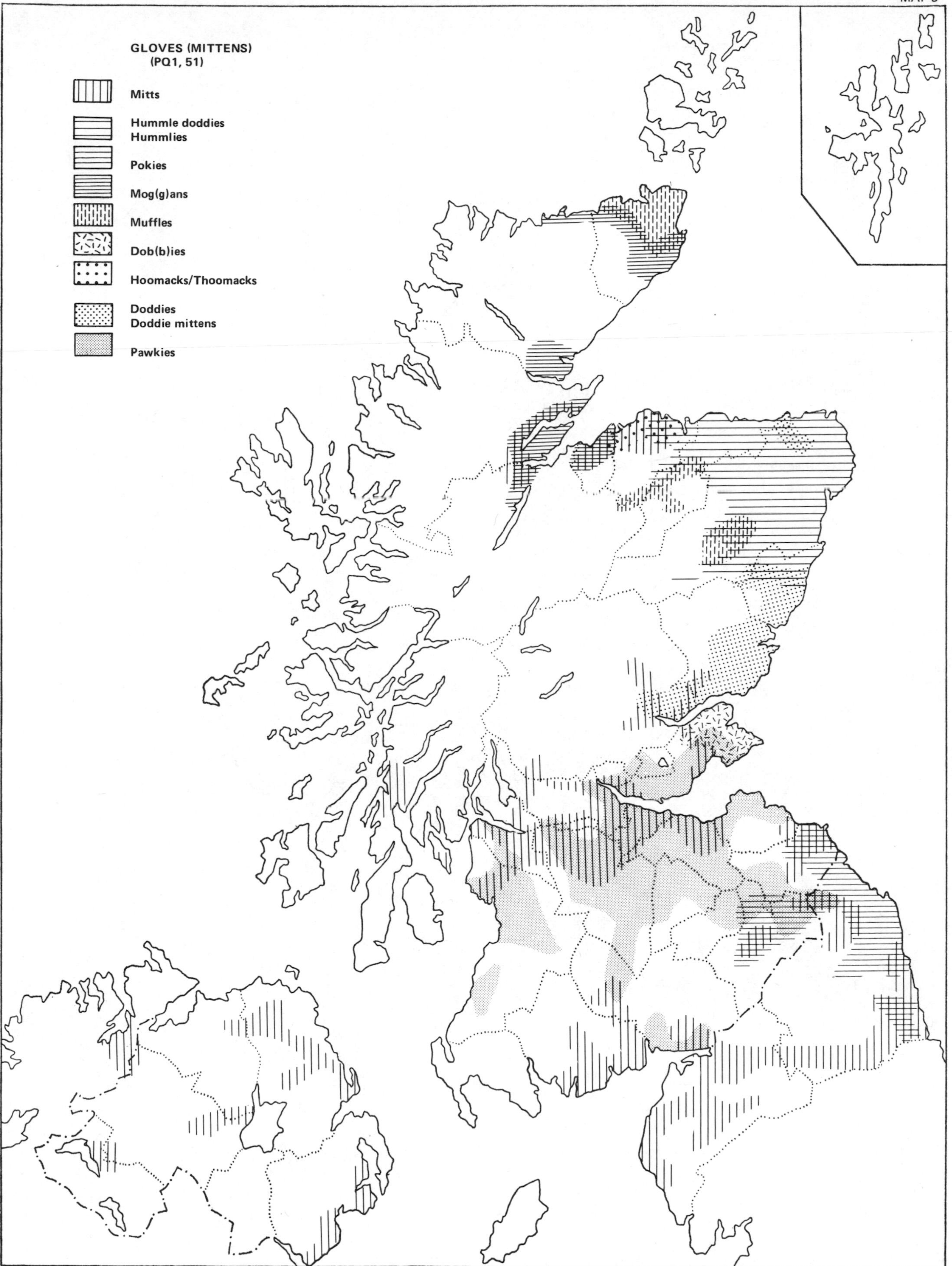
GLOVES (MITTENS)
(PQ1, 51)
Mitts
Hummle doddies
Hummlies
Pokies
Mog(g)ans
Muffles
Dob(b)ies
Hoomacks/Thoomacks
Doddies
Doddie mittens
Pawkies

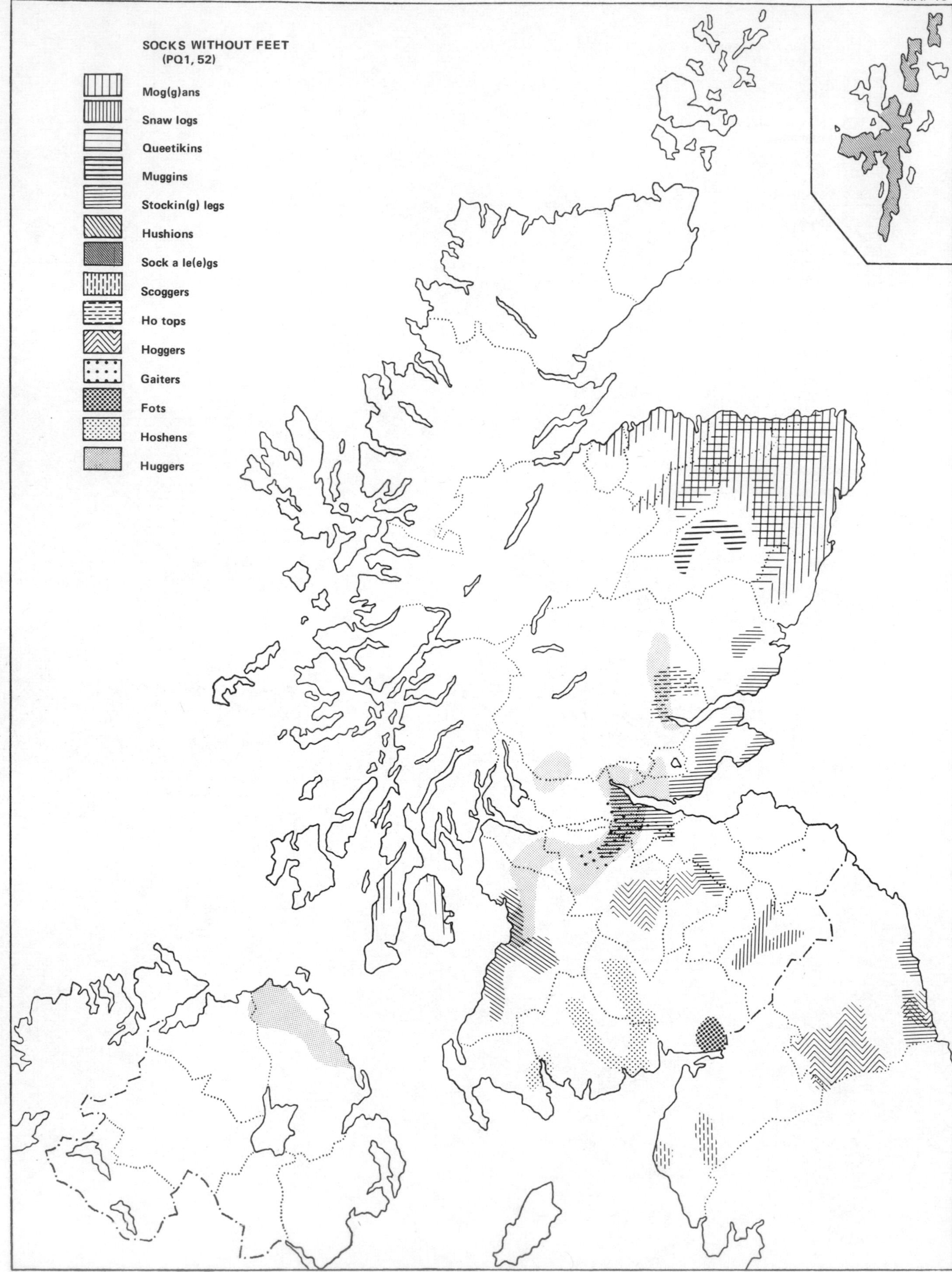
SOCKS WITHOUT FEET
(PQ1, 52)
Mog(g)ans
Snaw logs
Queetikins
Muggins
Stockin(g) legs
Hushions
Sock a le(e)gs
Scoggers
Ho tops
Hoggers
Gaiters
Fots
Hoshens
Huggers

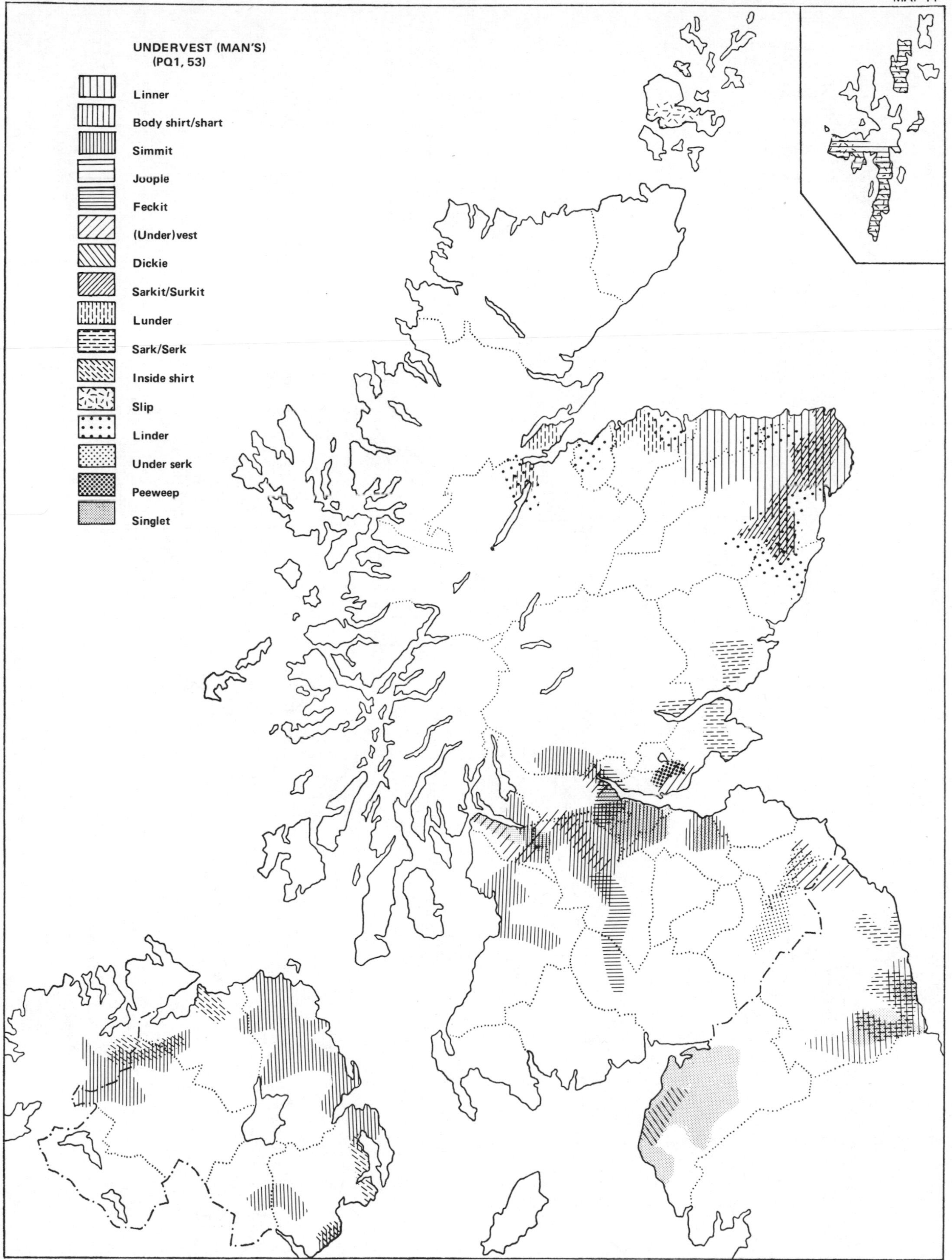
UNDERVEST (MAN'S)
(PQ1, 53)
Linner
Body shirt/shart
Simmit
Joople
Feckit
(Under)vest
Dickie
Sarkit/Surkit
Lunder
Sark/Serk
Inside shirt
Slip
Linder
Under serk
Peeweep
Singlet

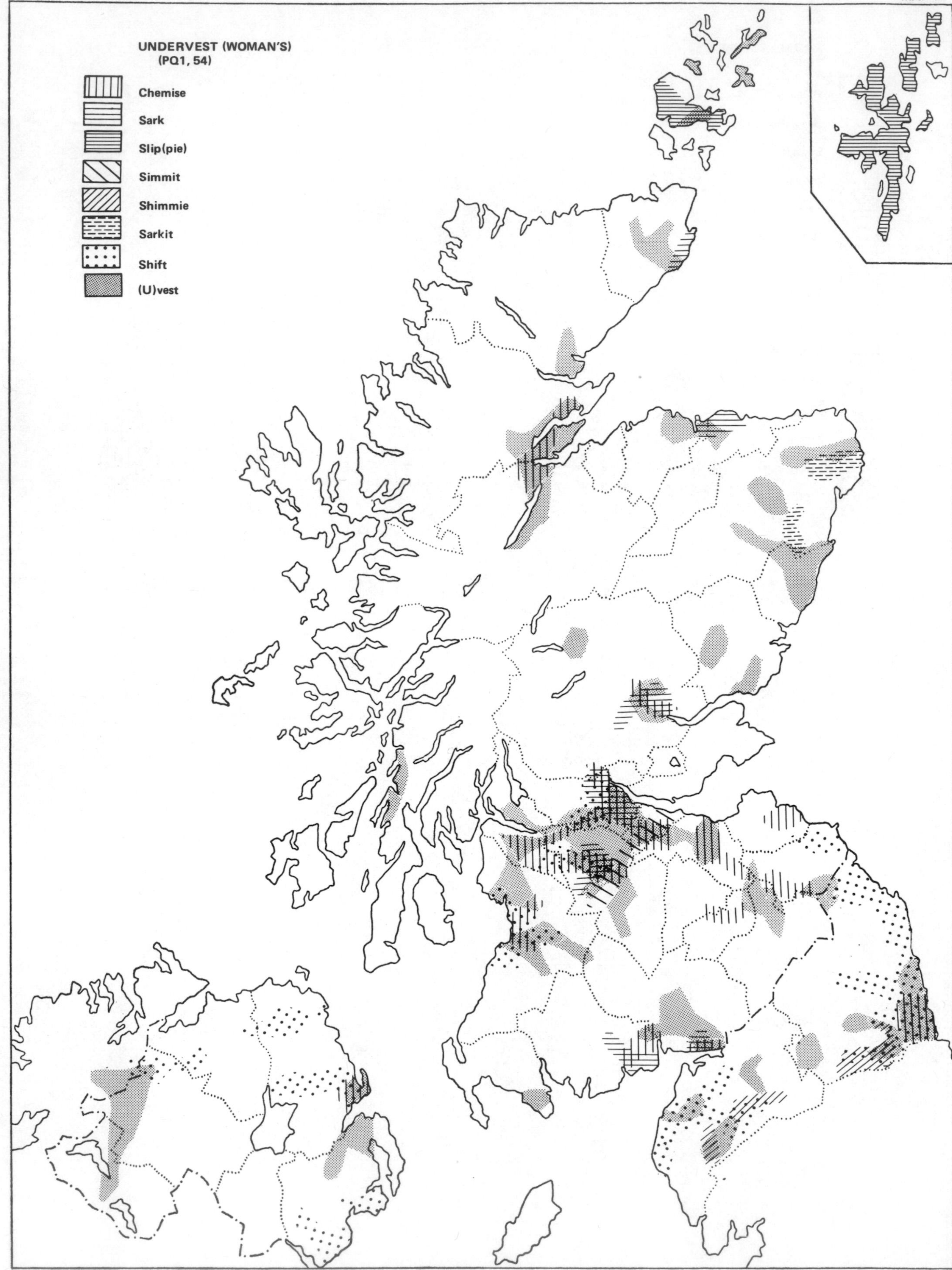
UNDERVEST (WOMAN'S)
(PQ1, 54)
Chemise
Sark
Slip(pie)
Simmit
Shimmie
Sarkit
Shift
(U)vest

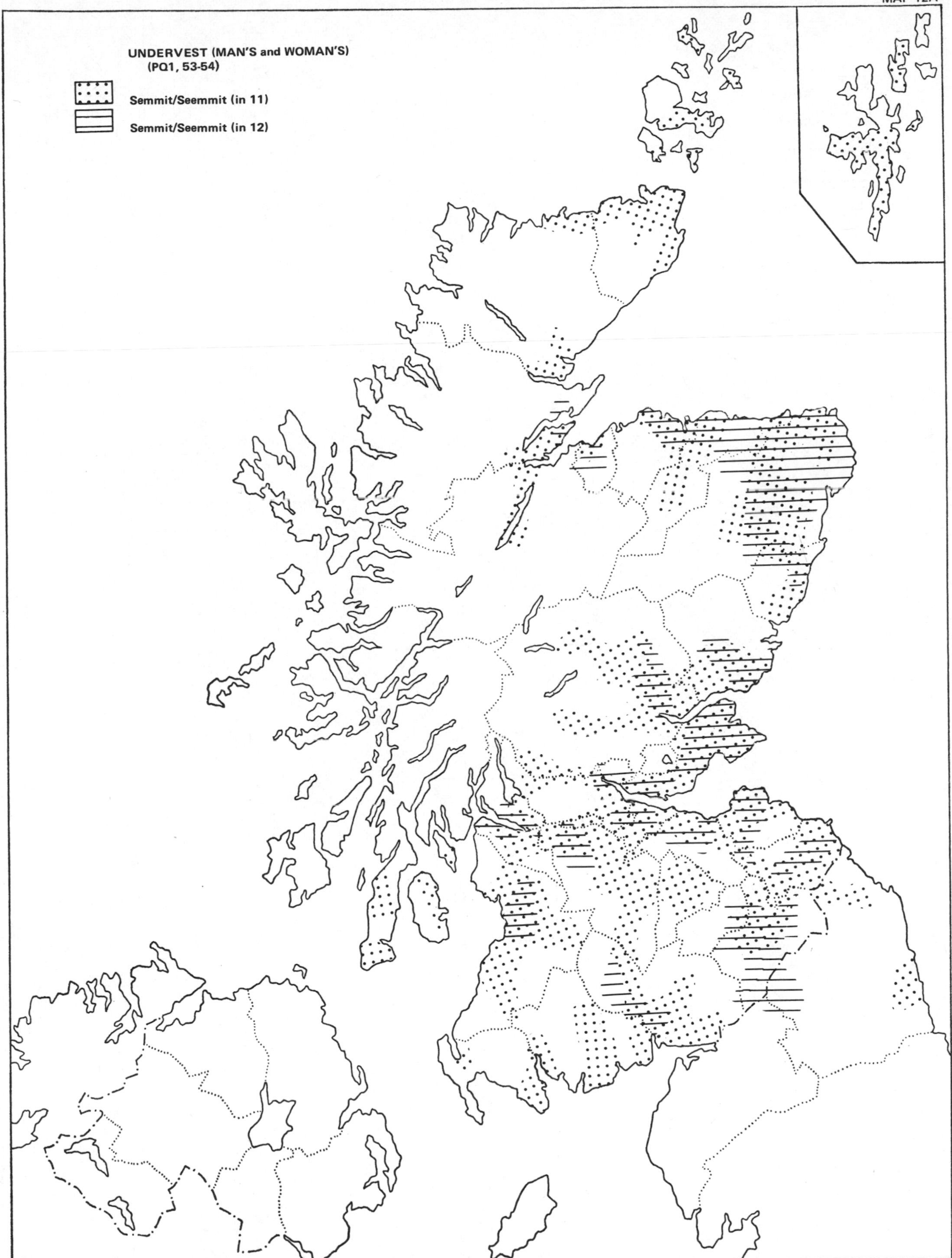
UNDERVEST (MAN'S and WOMAN'S)
(PQ1, 53-54)
Semmit/Seemmit (in 11)
Semmit/Seemmit (in 12)

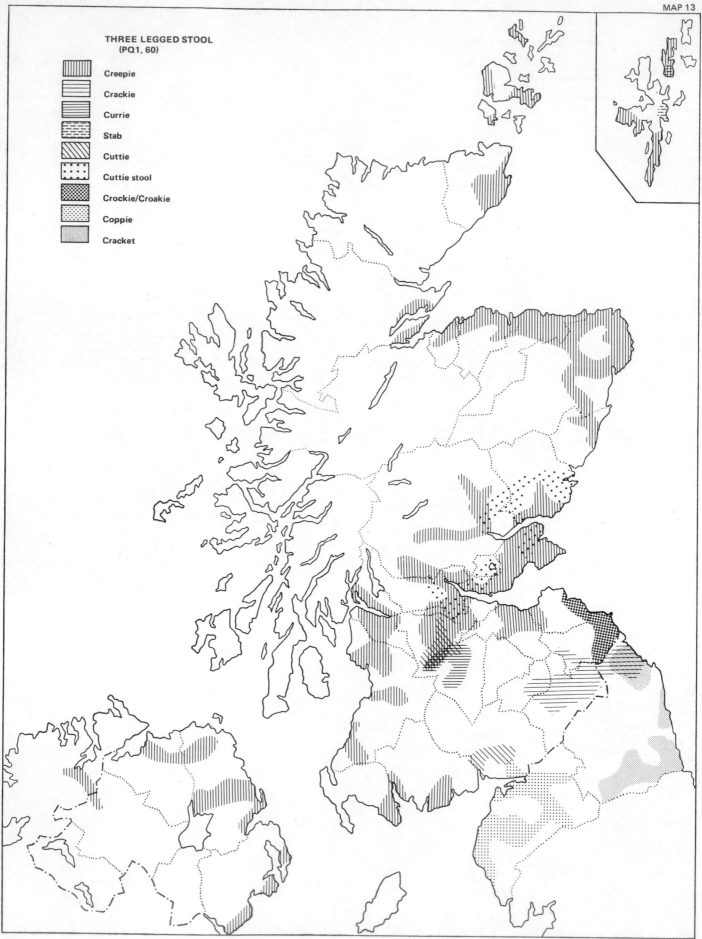

THREE LEGGED STOOL
(PQ1, 60)

Creepie
Crackie
Currie
Stab
Cuttie
Cuttie stool
Crockie/Croakie
Coppie
Cracket

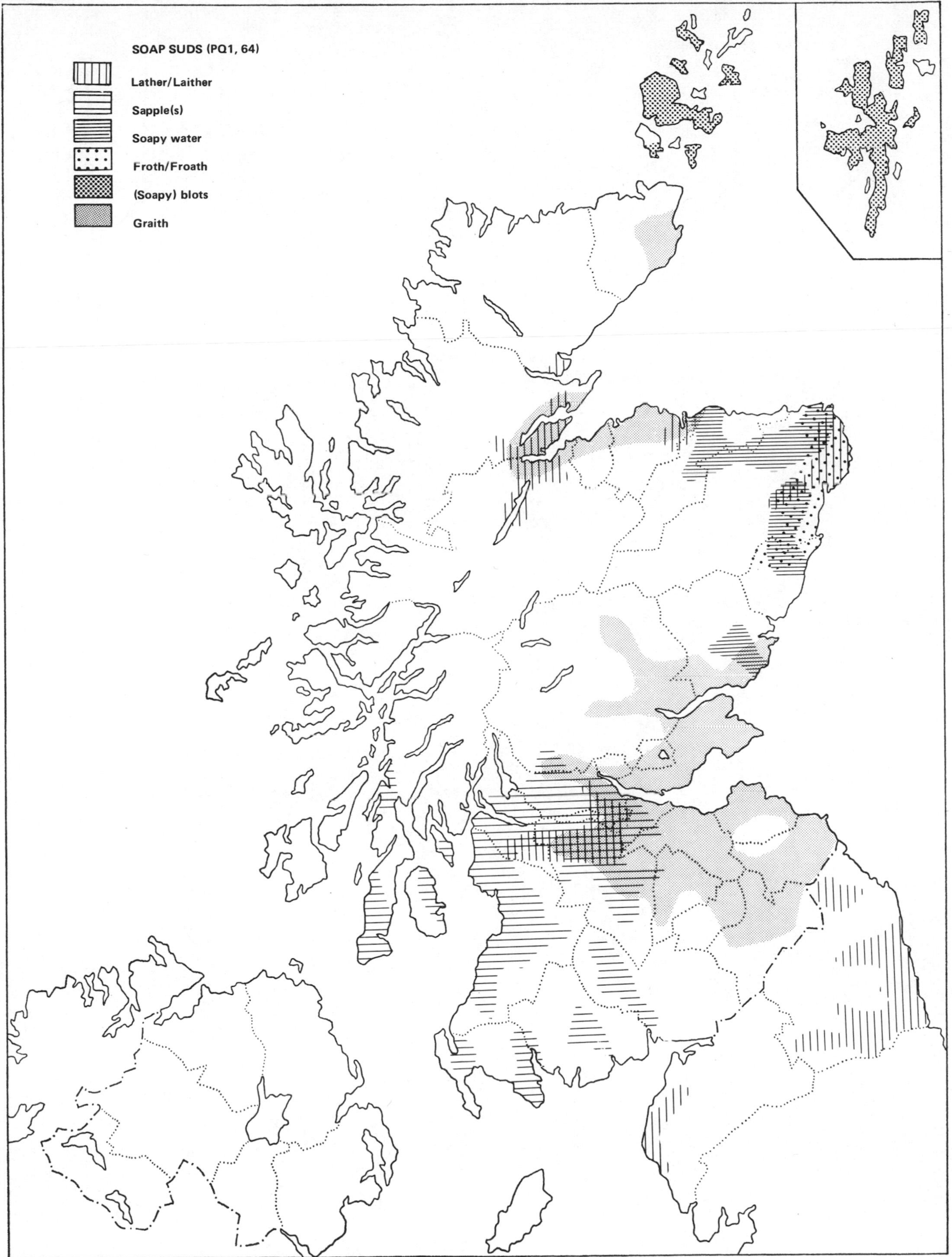
SOAP SUDS (PQ1, 64)
Lather/Laither
Sapple(s)
Soapy water
Froth/Froath
(Soapy) blots
Graith

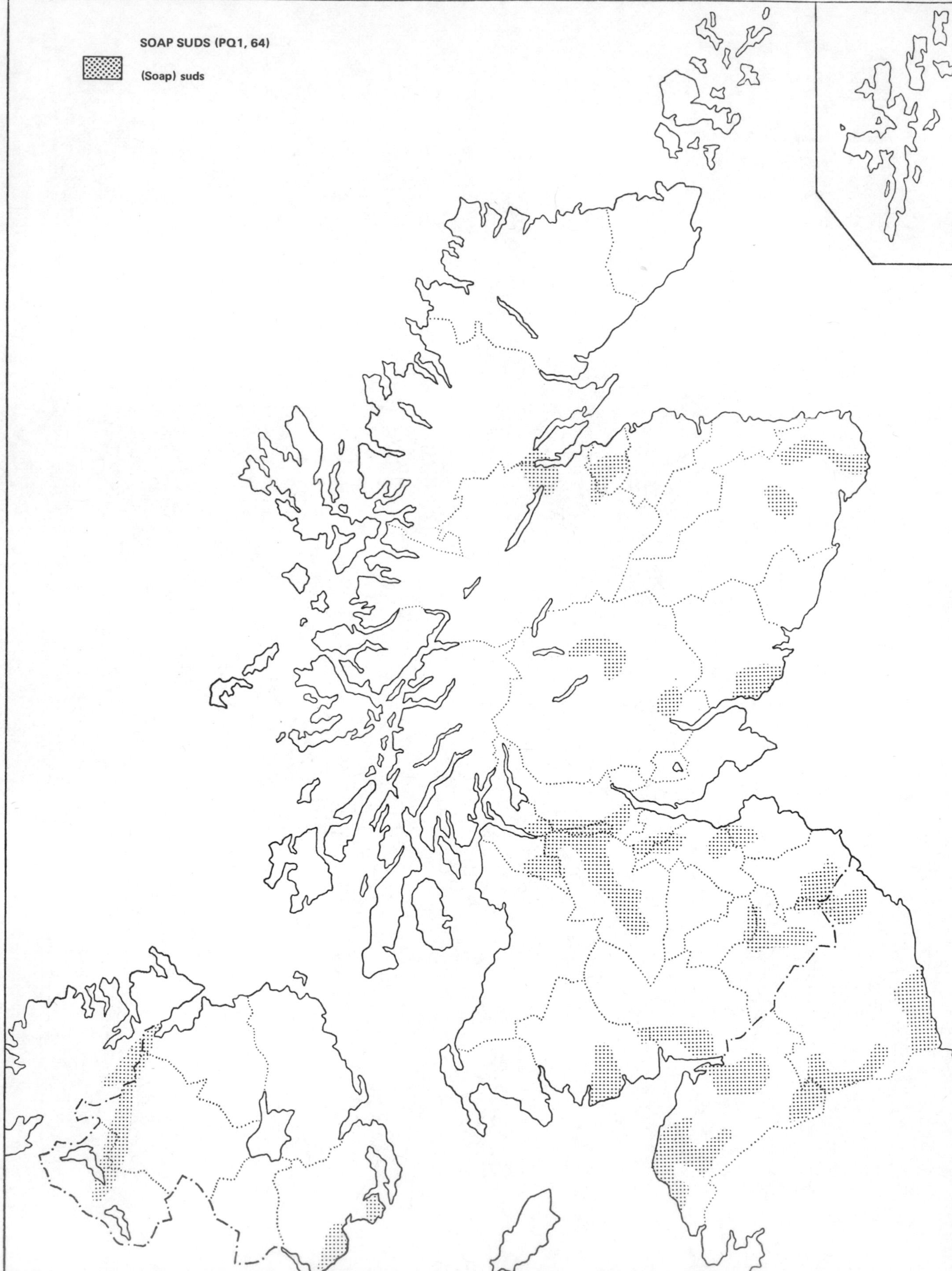

SOAP SUDS (PQ1, 64)
(Soap) suds

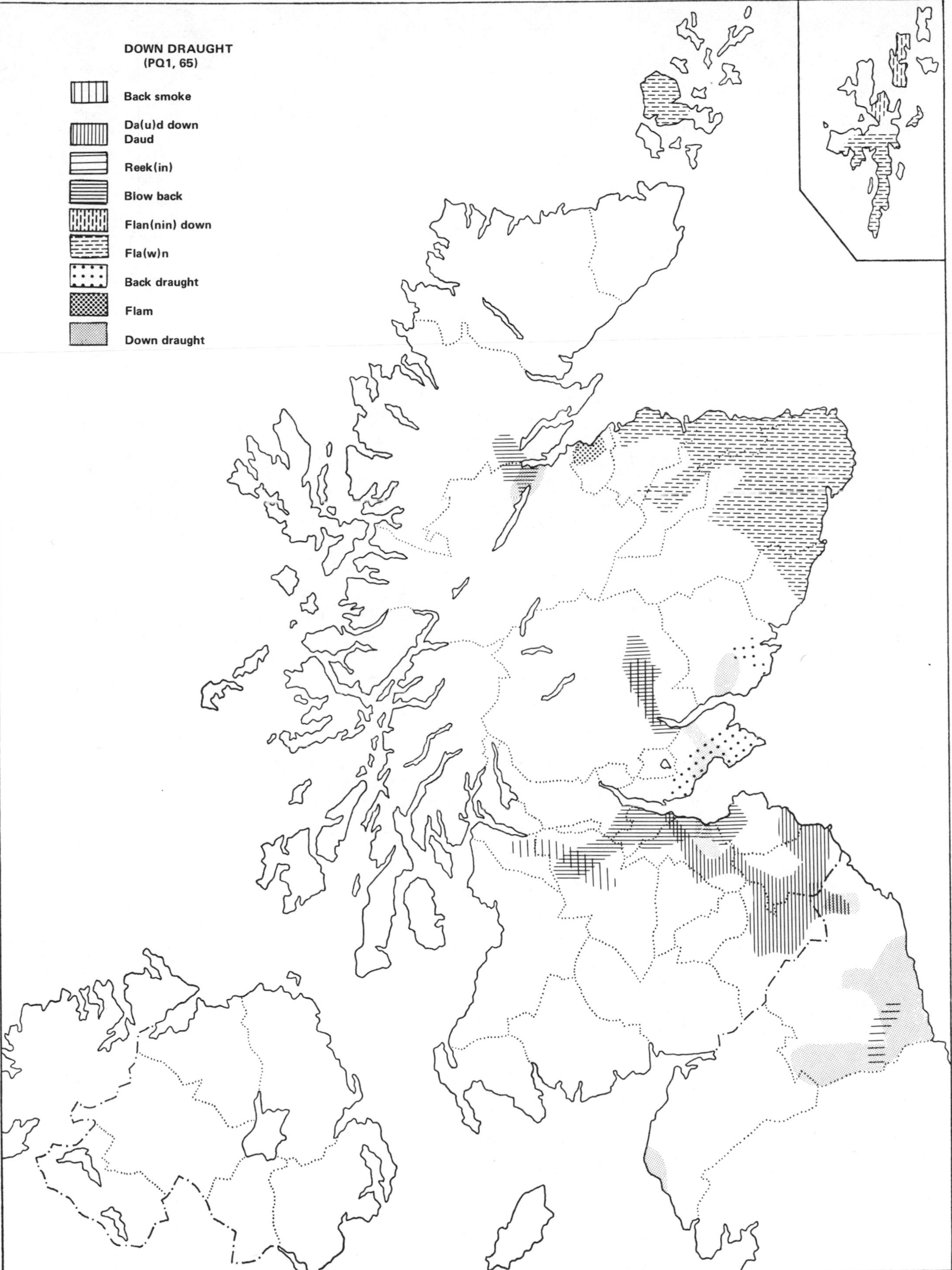
DOWN DRAUGHT
(PQ1, 65)
Back smoke
Da(u)d down
Daud
Reek(in)
Blow back
Flan(nin) down
Fla(w)n
Back draught
Flam
Down draught

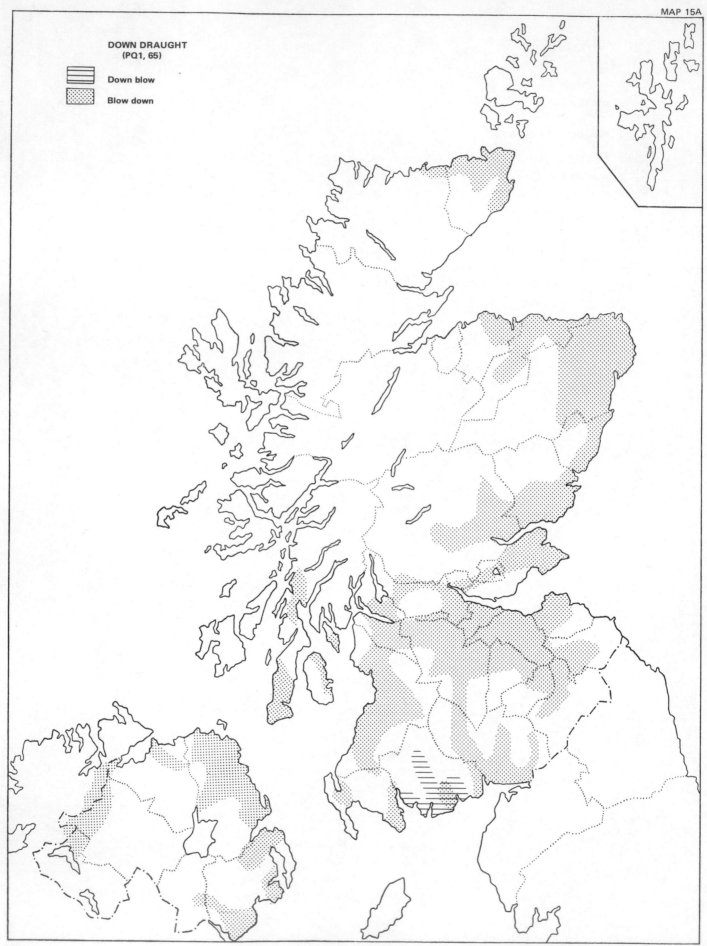

DOWN DRAUGHT
(PQ1, 65)
Down blow
Blow down

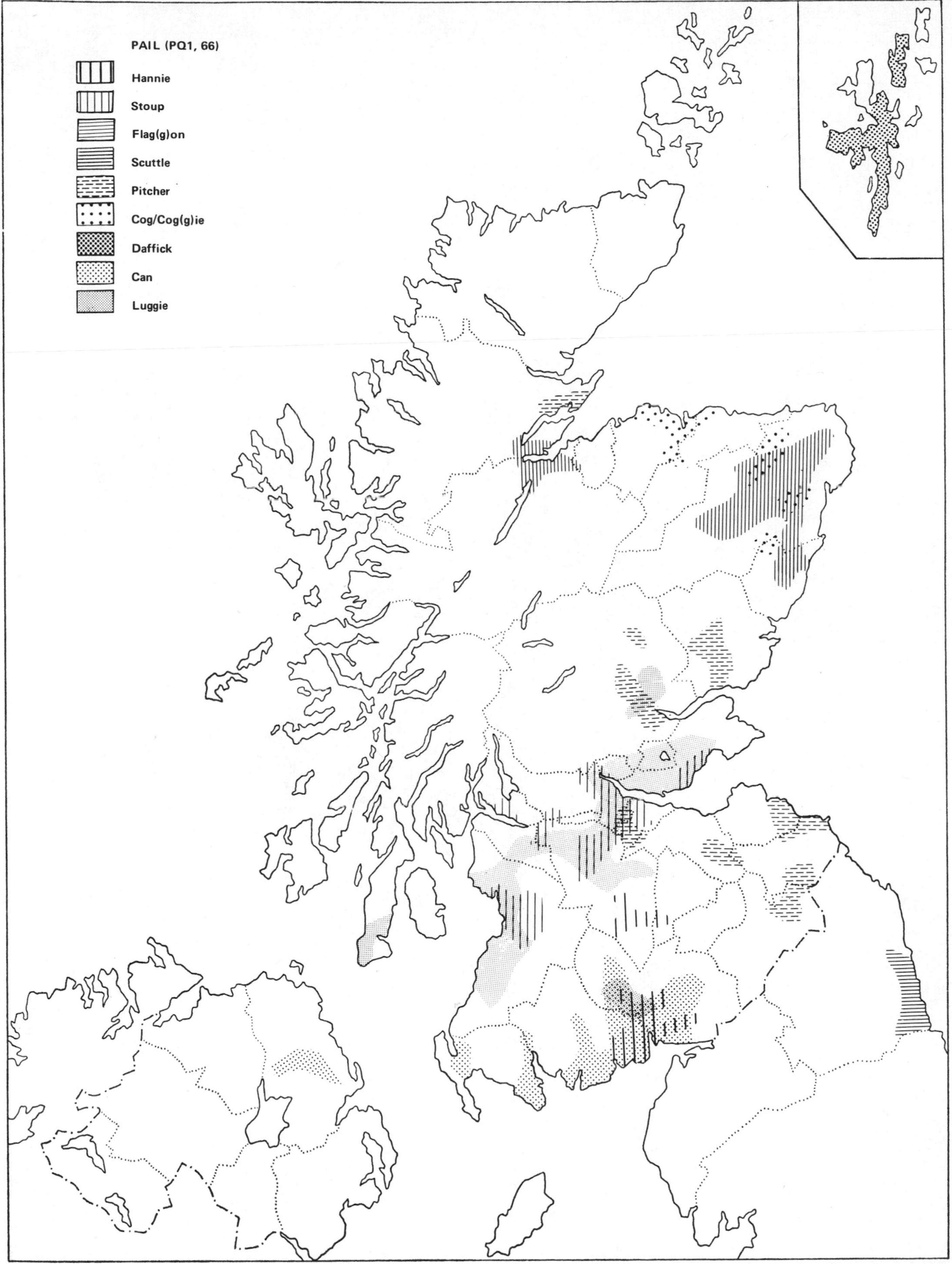
PAIL (PQ1, 66)
Hannie
Stoup
Flag(g)on
Scuttle
Pitcher
Cog/Cog(g)ie
Daffick
Can
Luggie

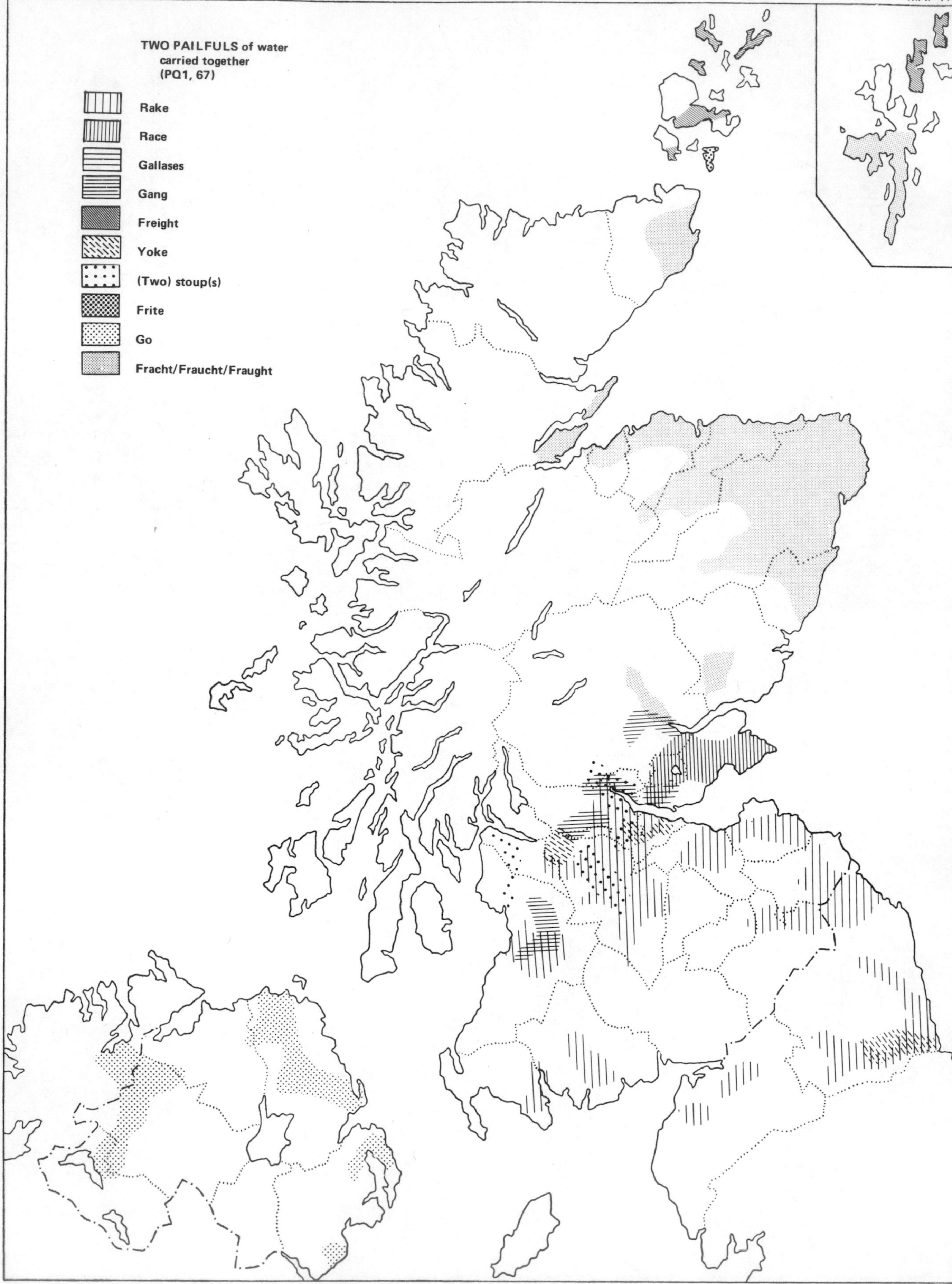
TWO PAILFULS of water
carried together
(PQ1, 67)
Rake
Race
Gallases
Gang
Freight
Yoke
(Two) stoup(s)
Frite
Go
Fracht/Fraucht/Fraught

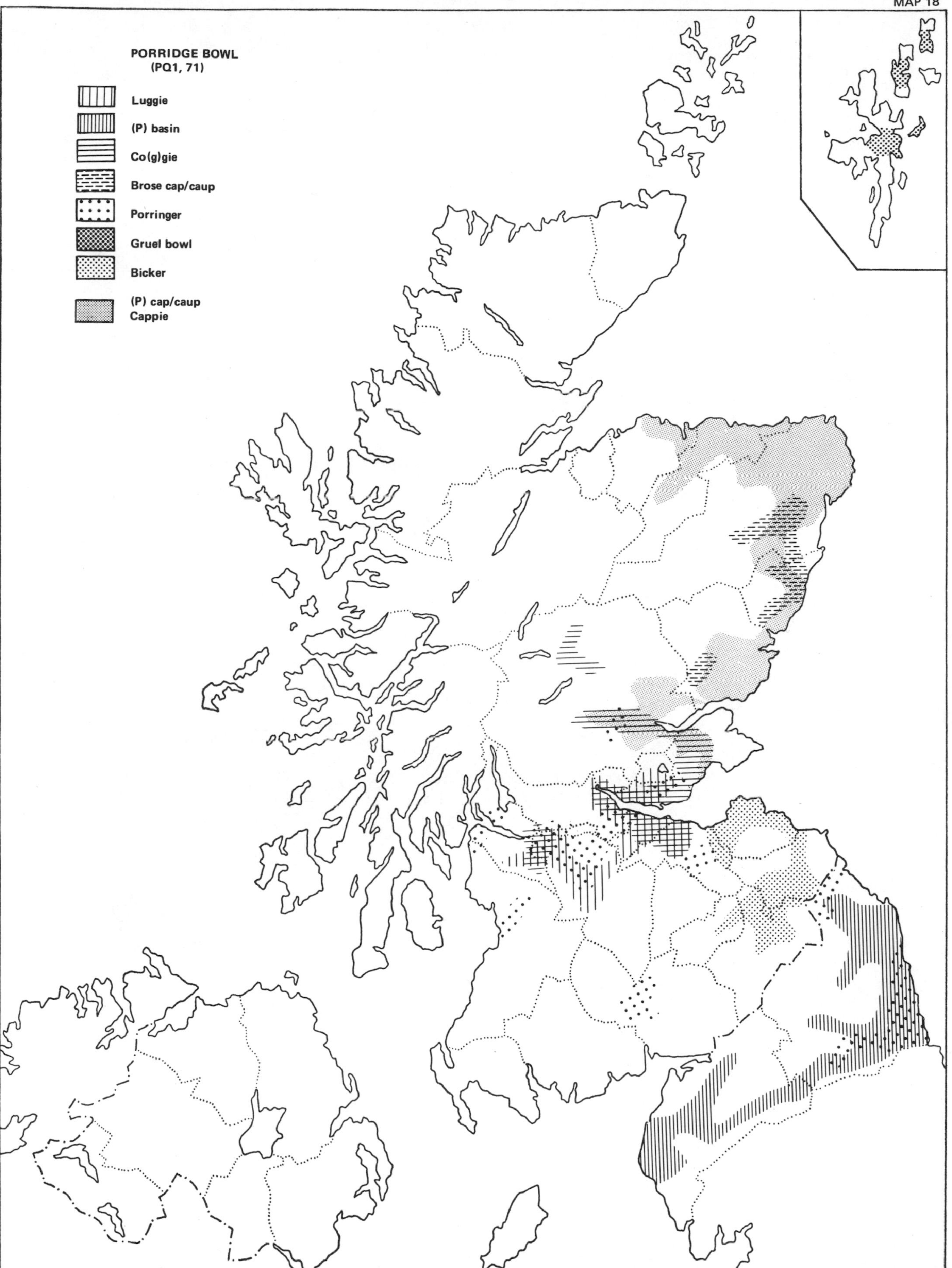
PORRIDGE BOWL
(PQ1, 71)
Luggie
(P) basin
Co(g)gie
Brose cap/caup
Porringer
Gruel bowl
Bicker
(P) cap/caup
Cappie

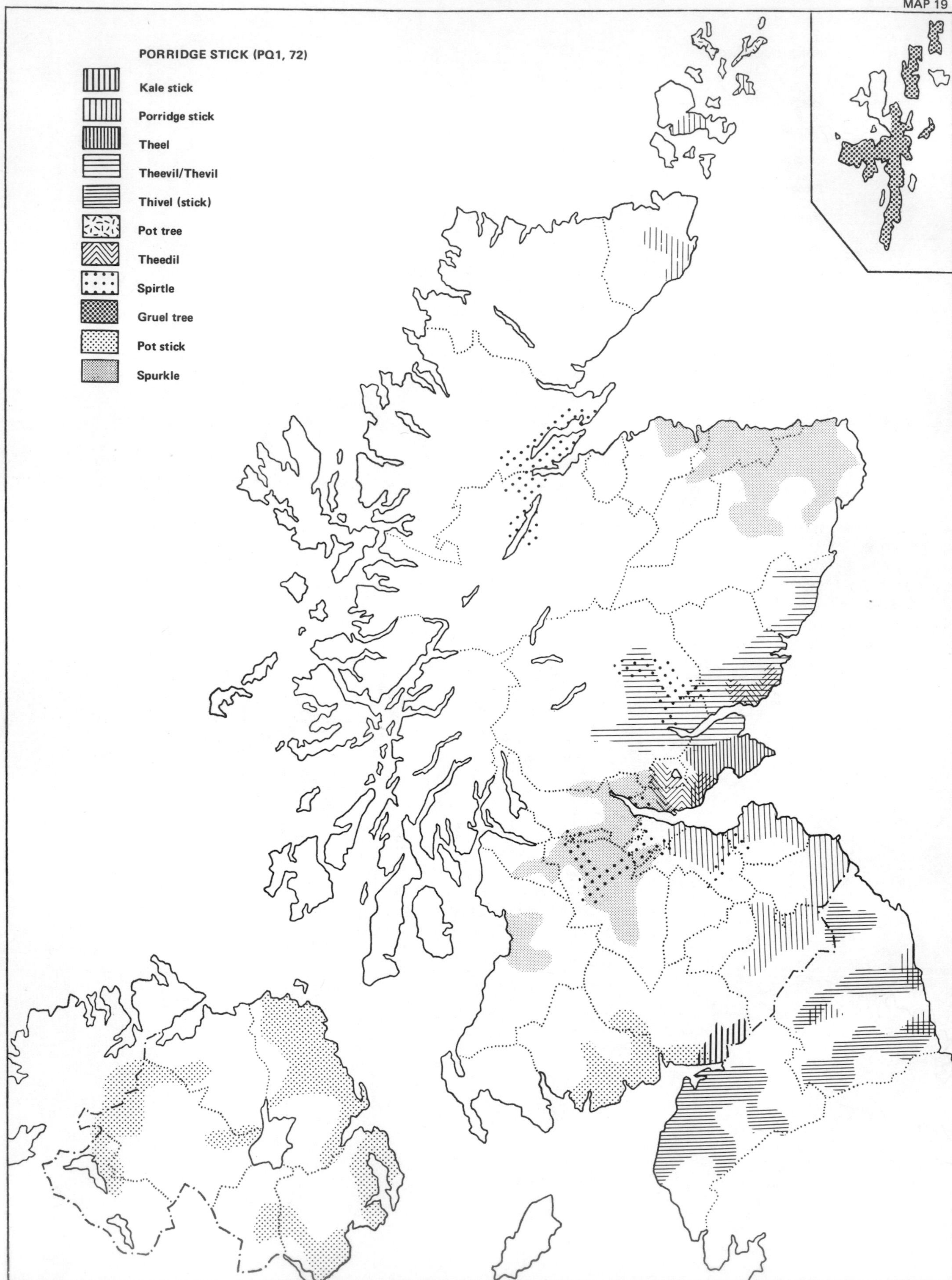
PORRIDGE STICK (PQ1, 72)
Kale stick
Porridge stick
Theel
Theevil/Thevil
Thivel (stick)
Pot tree
Theedil
Spirtle
Gruel tree
Pot stick
Spurkle

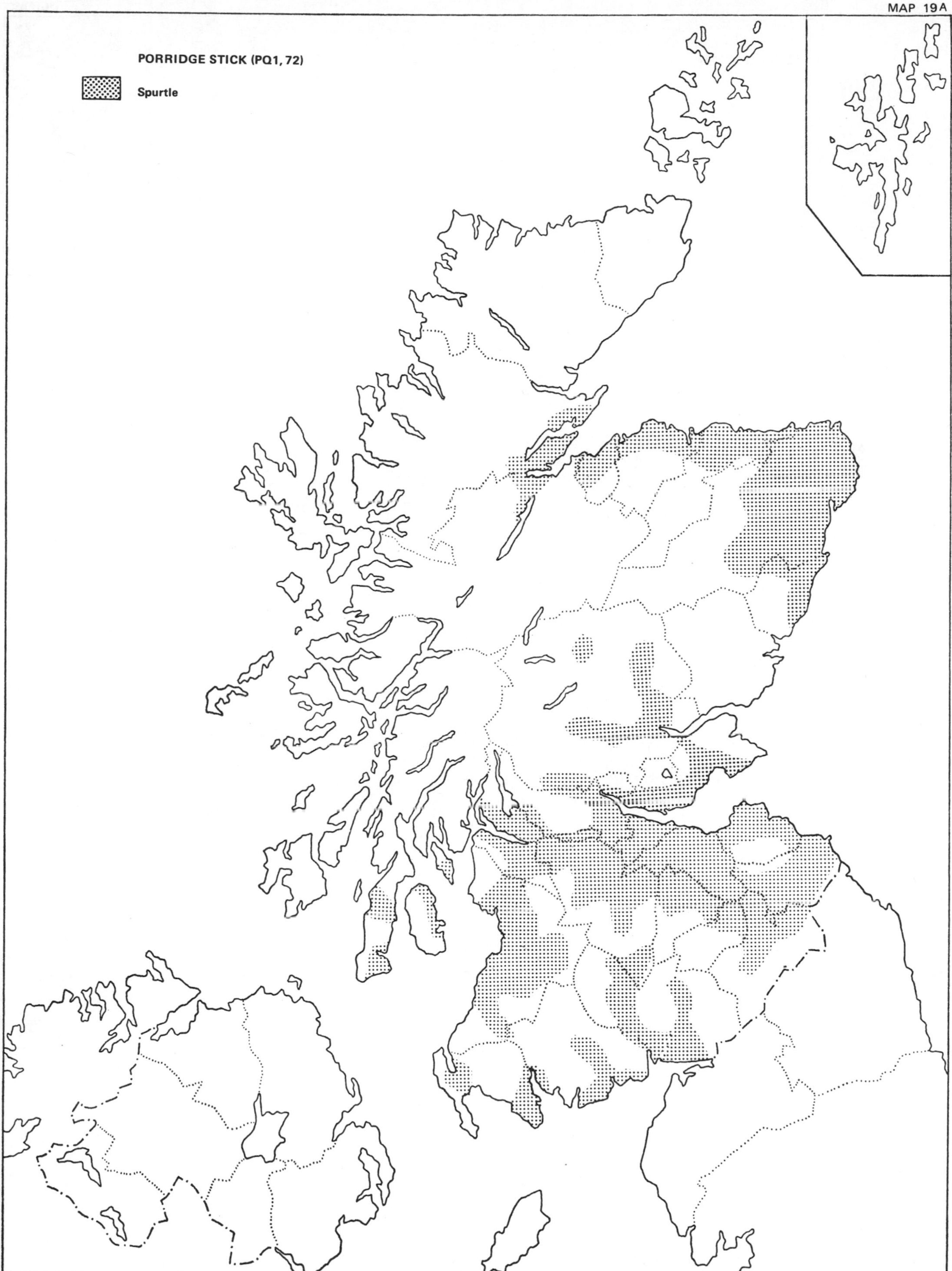
PORRIDGE STICK (PQ1, 72)
Spurtle

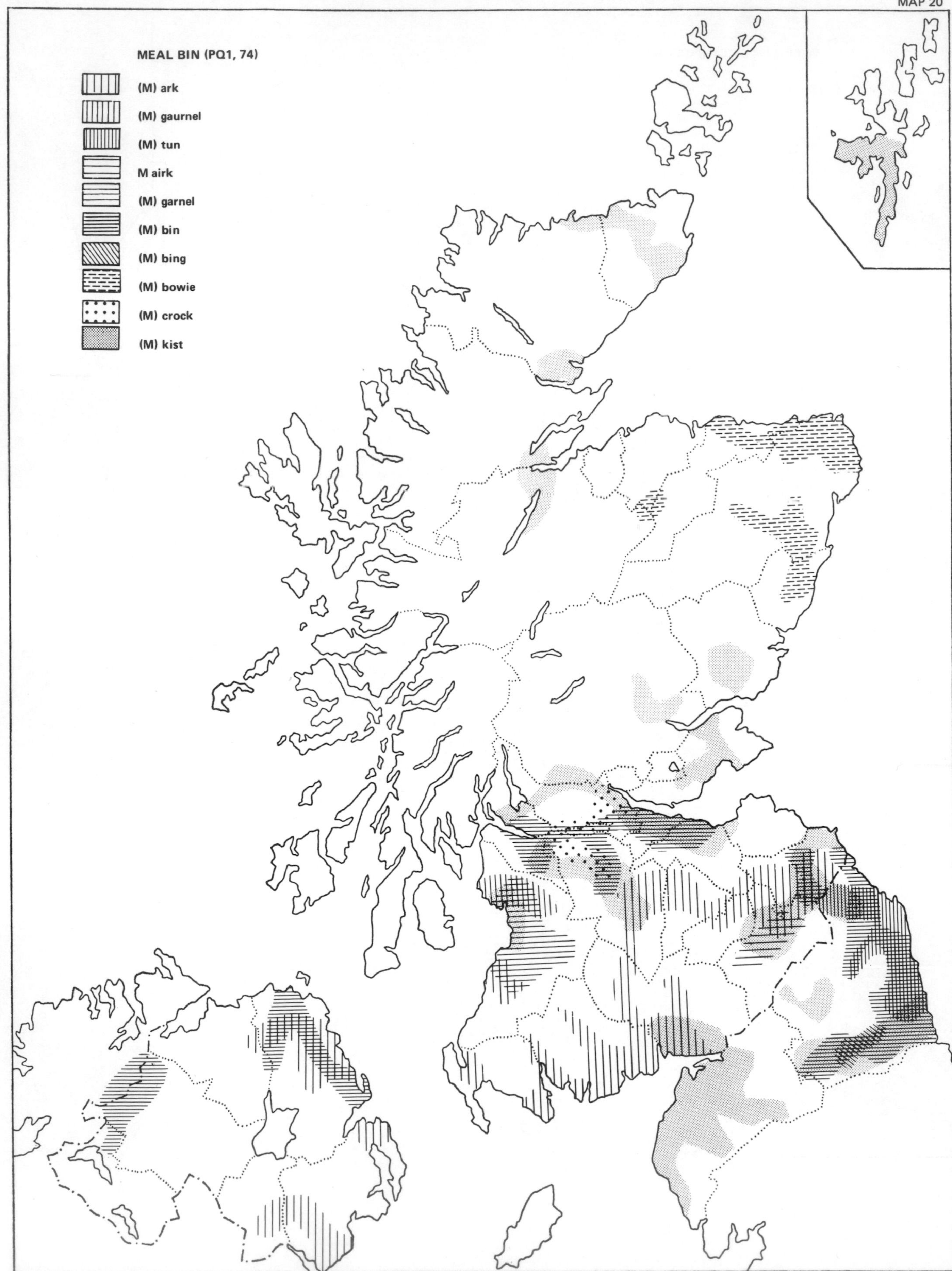
MEAL BIN (PQ1, 74)
(M) ark
(M) gaurnel
(M) tun
M airk
(M) garnel
(M) bin
(M) bing
(M) bowie
(M) crock
(M) kist

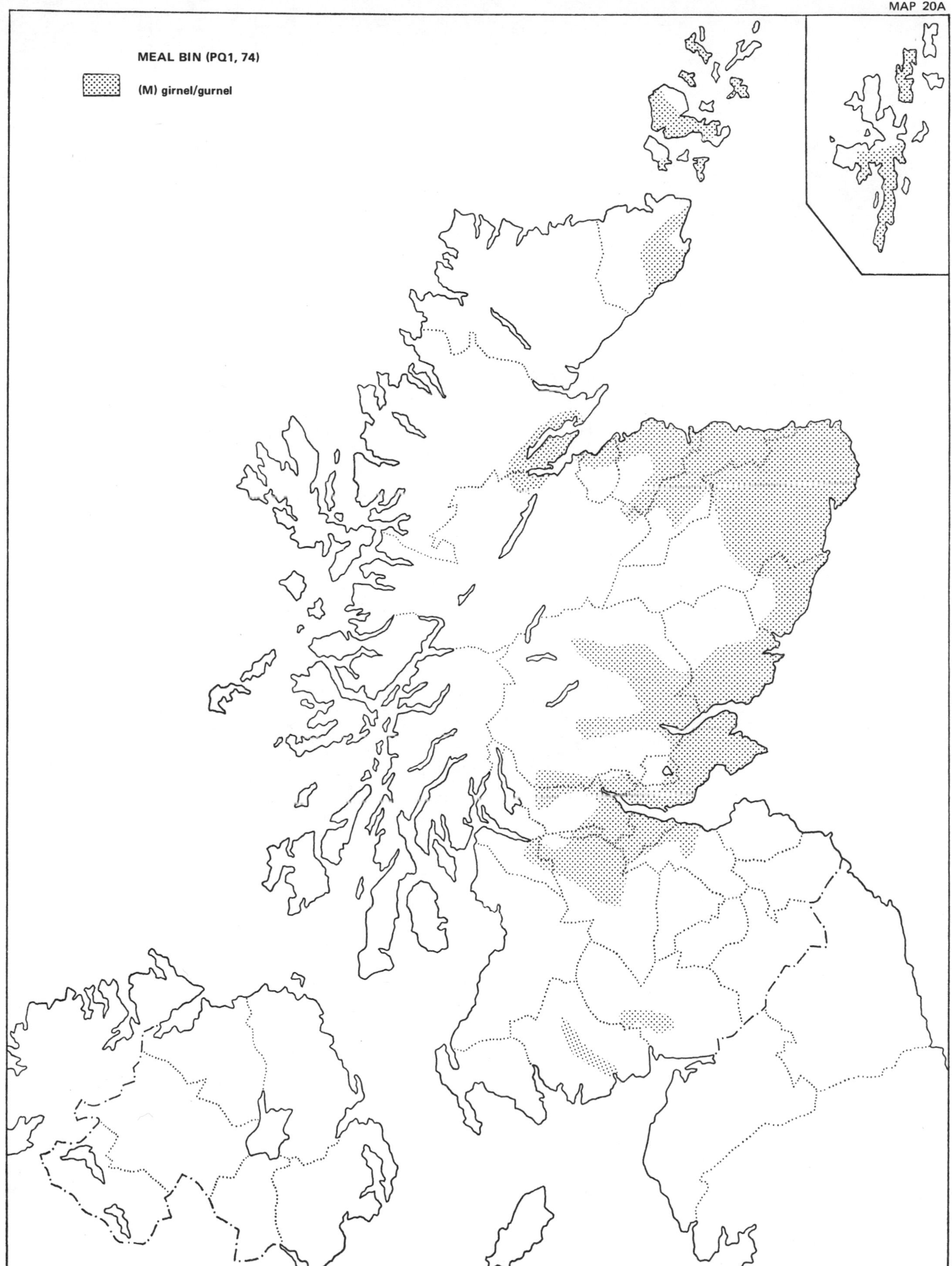
MEAL BIN (PQ1, 74)
(M) girnel/gurnel

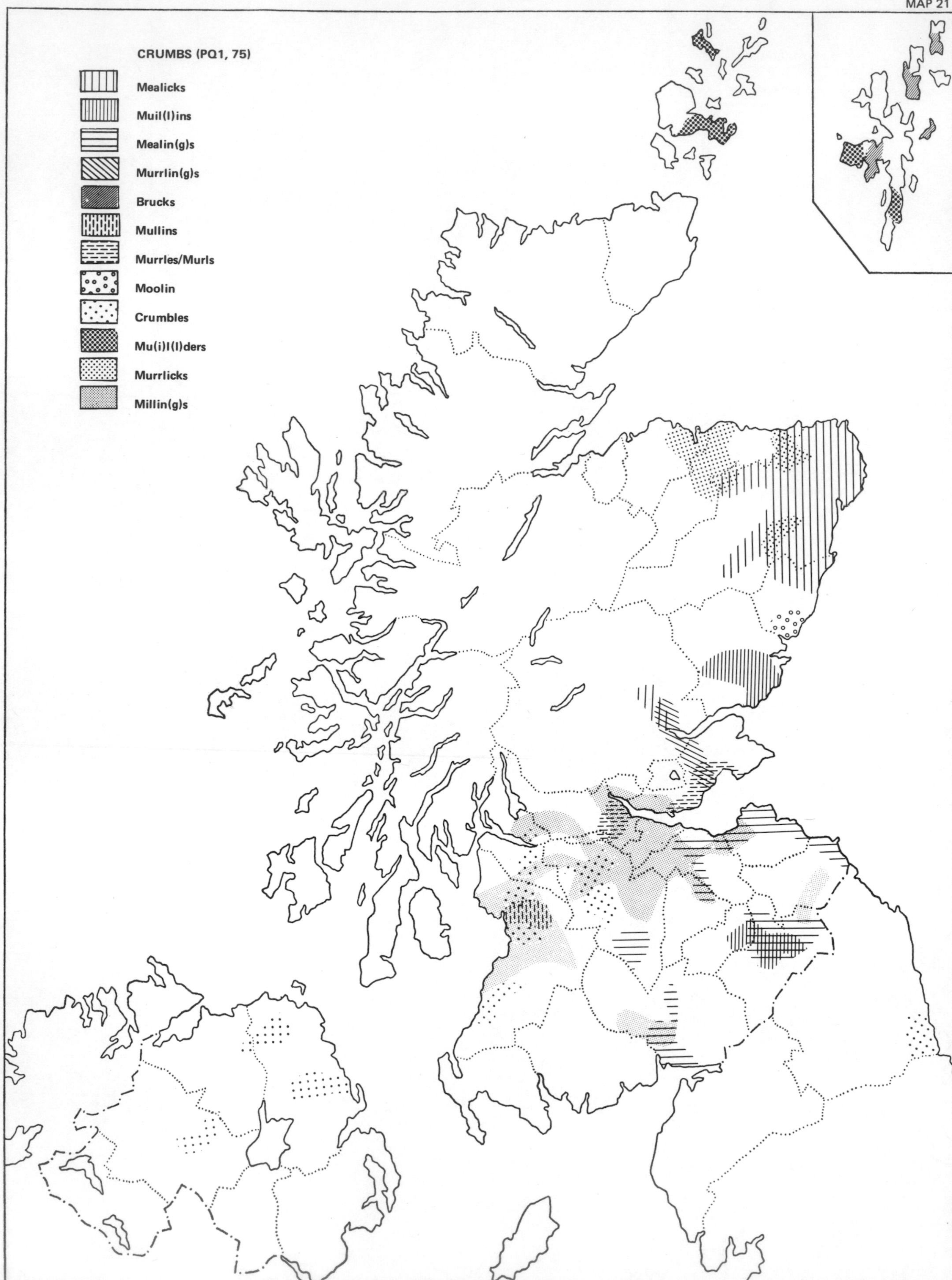
CRUMBS (PQ1, 75)
Mealicks
Muil(l)ins
Mealin(g)s
Murrlin(g)s
Brucks
Mullins
Murrles/Murls
Moolin
Crumbles
Mu(i)l(l)ders
Murrlicks
Millin(g)s

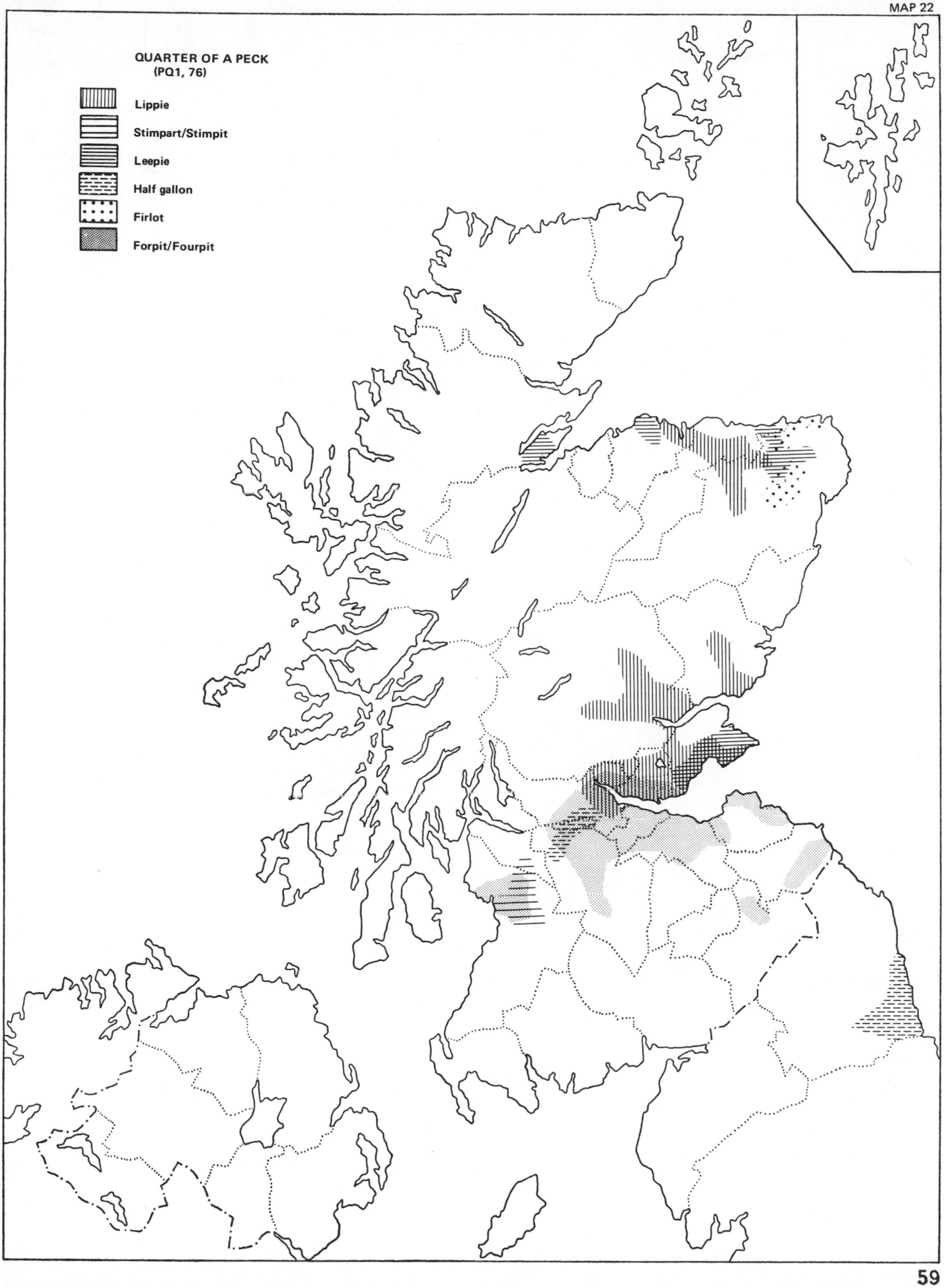

QUARTER OF A PECK
(PQ1, 76)

Lippie

Stimpart/Stimpit

Leepie

Half gallon

Firlot

Forpit/Fourpit

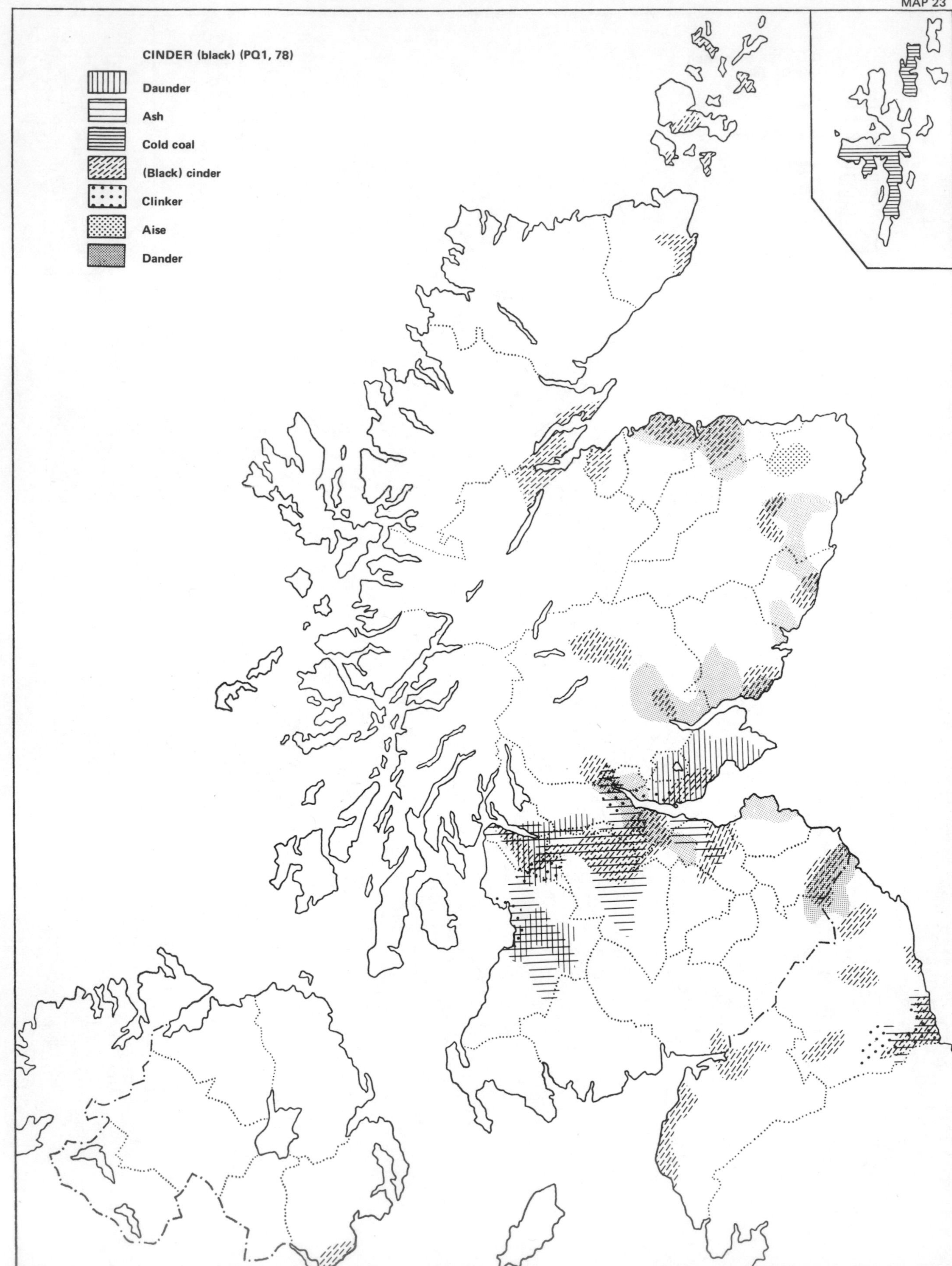
CINDER (black) (PQ1, 78)
Daunder
Ash
Cold coal
(Black) cinder
Clinker
Aise
Dander

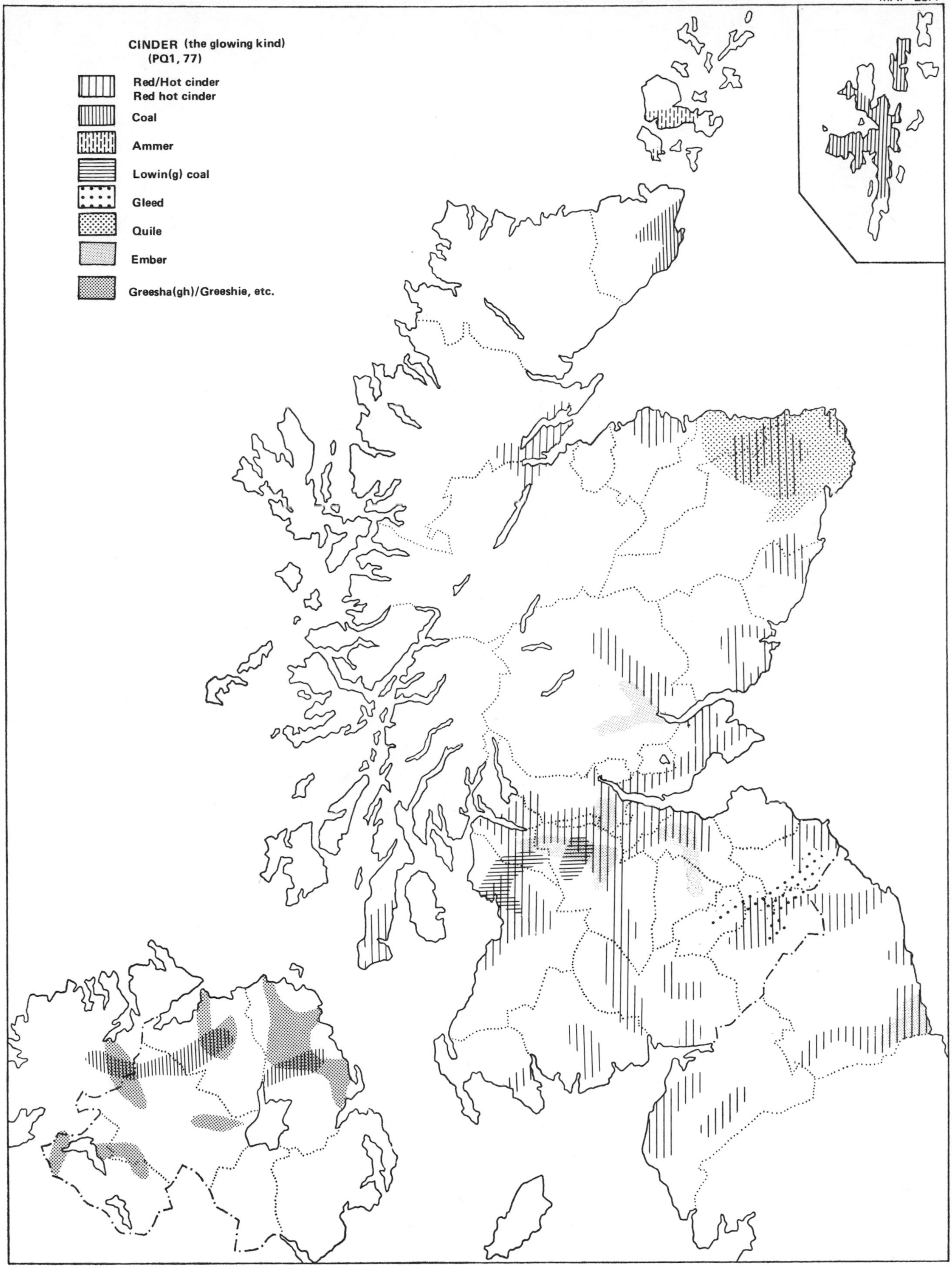

CINDER (the glowing kind)
(PQ1, 77)
Red/Hot cinder
Red hot cinder
Coal
Ammer
Lowin(g) coal
Gleed
Quile
Ember
Greesha(gh)/Greeshie, etc.

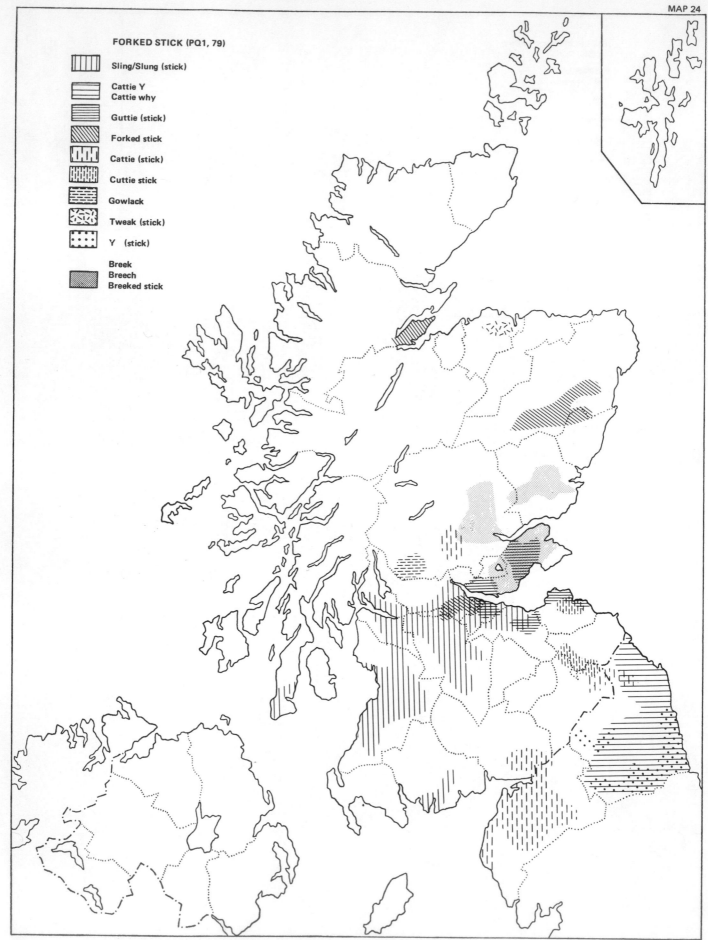

FORKED STICK (PQ1, 79)

Sling/Slung (stick)
Cattie Y
Cattie why
Guttie (stick)
Forked stick
Cattie (stick)
Cuttie stick
Gowlack
Tweak (stick)
Y (stick)
Breek
Breech
Breeked stick

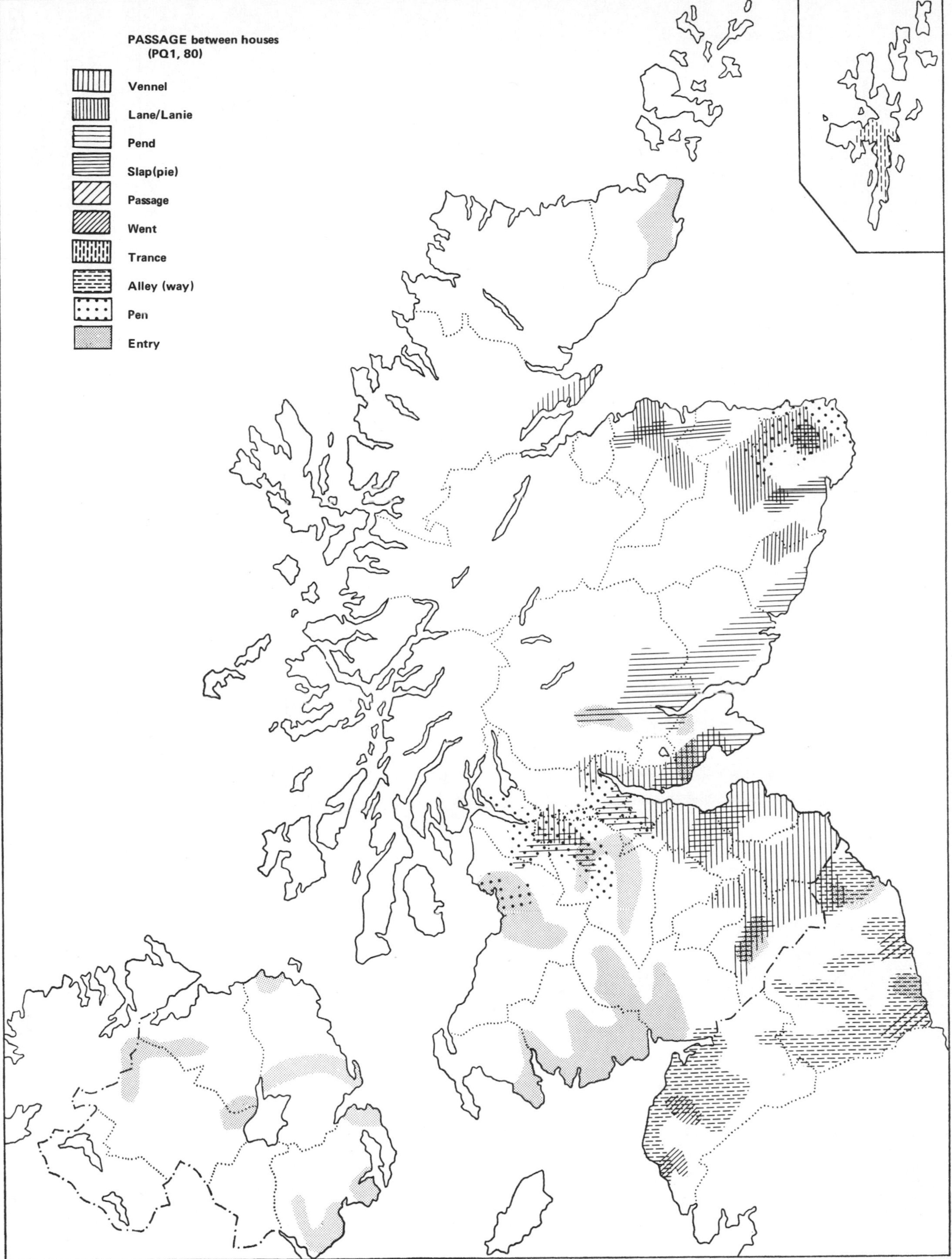
PASSAGE between houses
(PQ1, 80)
Vennel
Lane/Lanie
Pend
Slap(pie)
Passage
Went
Trance
Alley (way)
Pen
Entry

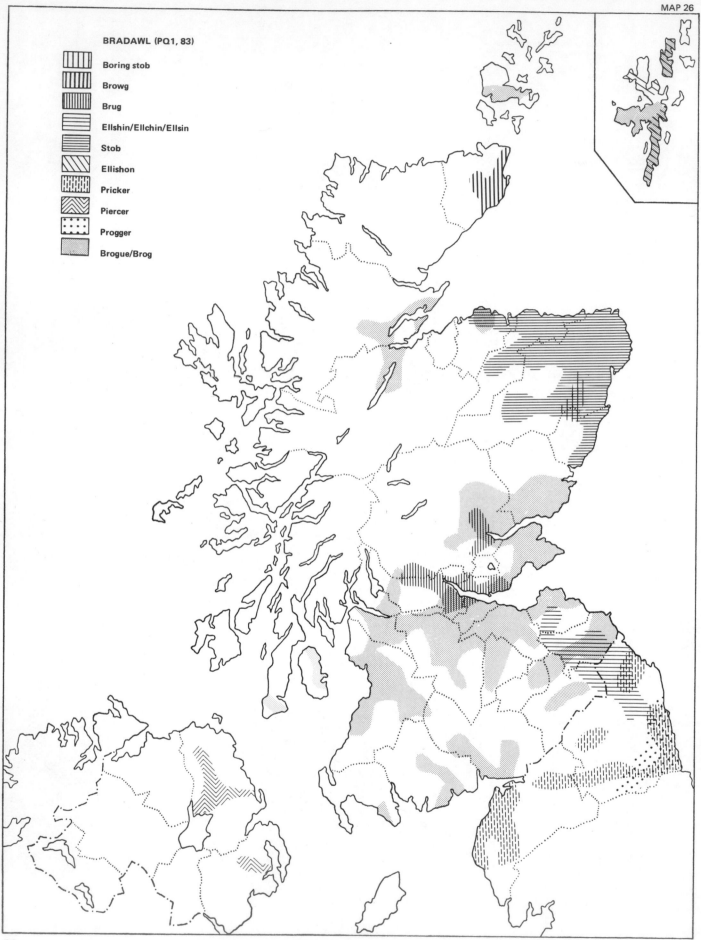

BRADAWL (PQ1, 83)

- Boring stob
- Browg
- Brug
- Ellshin/Ellchin/Ellsin
- Stob
- Ellishon
- Pricker
- Piercer
- Progger
- Brogue/Brog

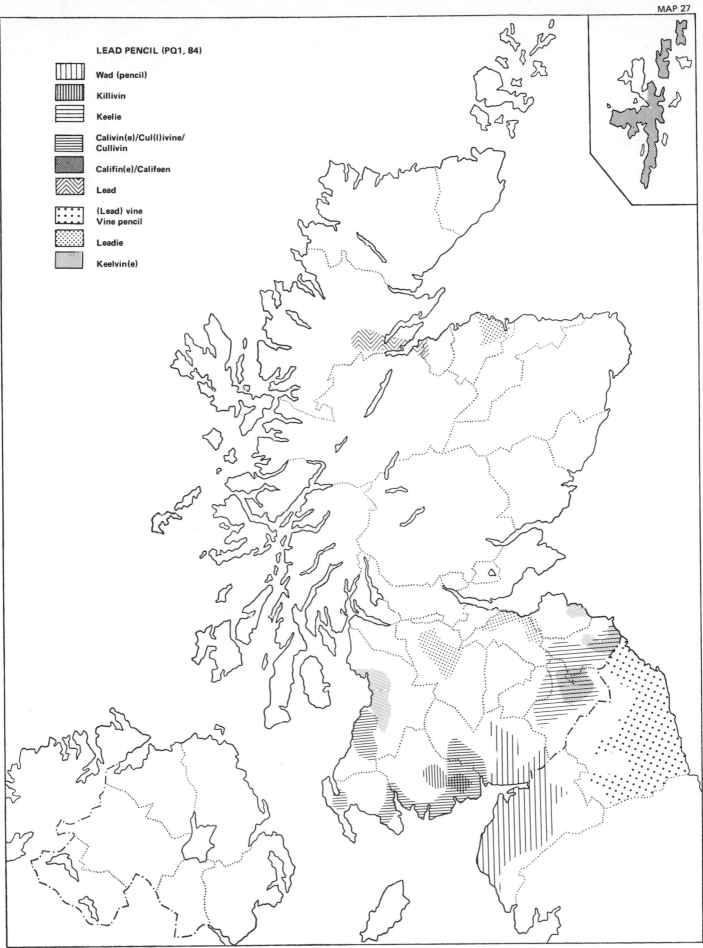

LEAD PENCIL (PQ1, 84)
Wad (pencil)
Killivin
Keelie
Calivin(e)/Cul(l)ivine/
Cullivin
Califin(e)/Califeen
Lead
(Lead) vine
Vine pencil
Leadie
Keelvin(e)

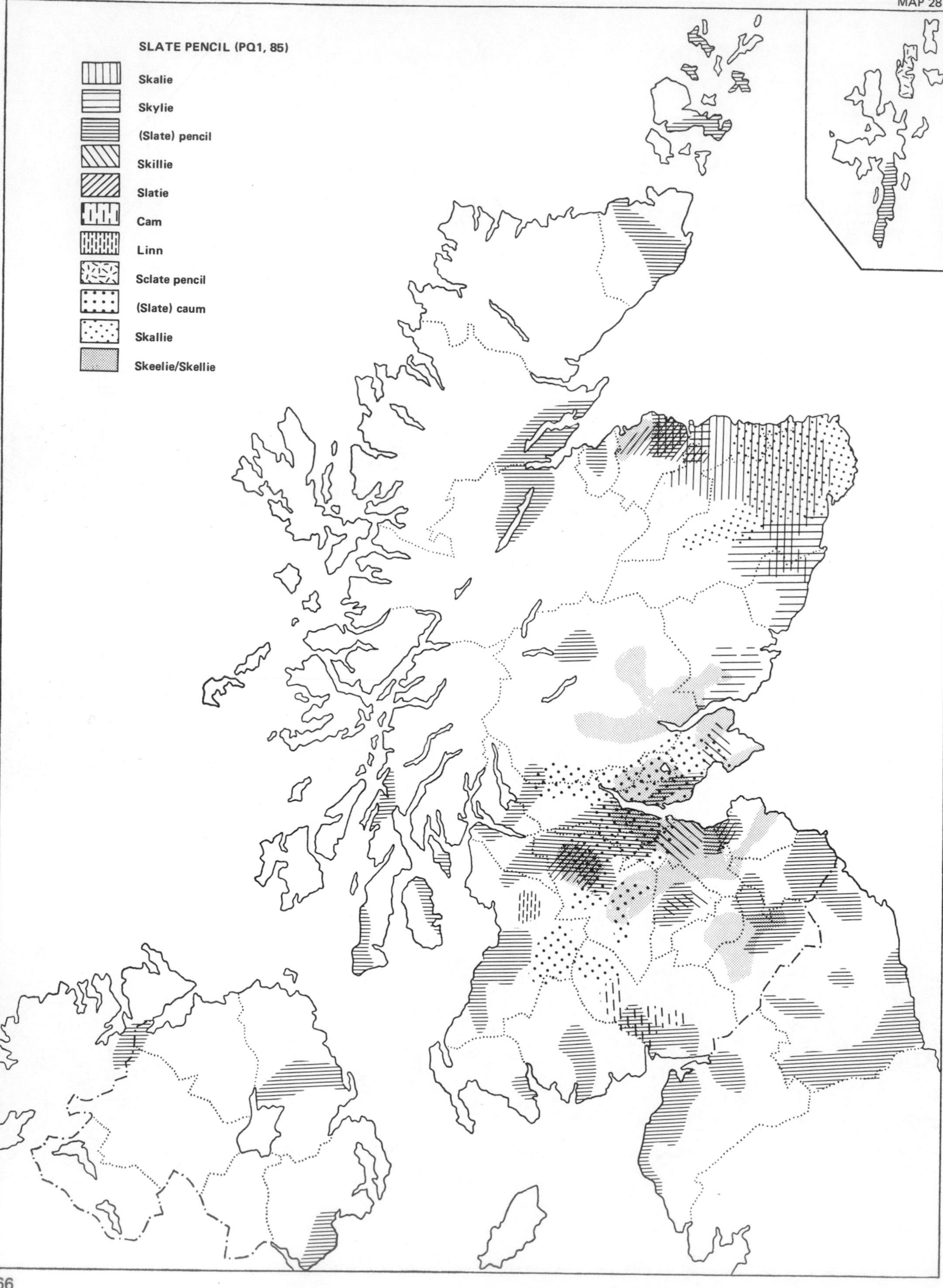
SLATE PENCIL (PQ1, 85)
Skalie
Skylie
(Slate) pencil
Skillie
Slatie
Cam
Linn
Sclate pencil
(Slate) caum
Skallie
Skeelie/Skellie

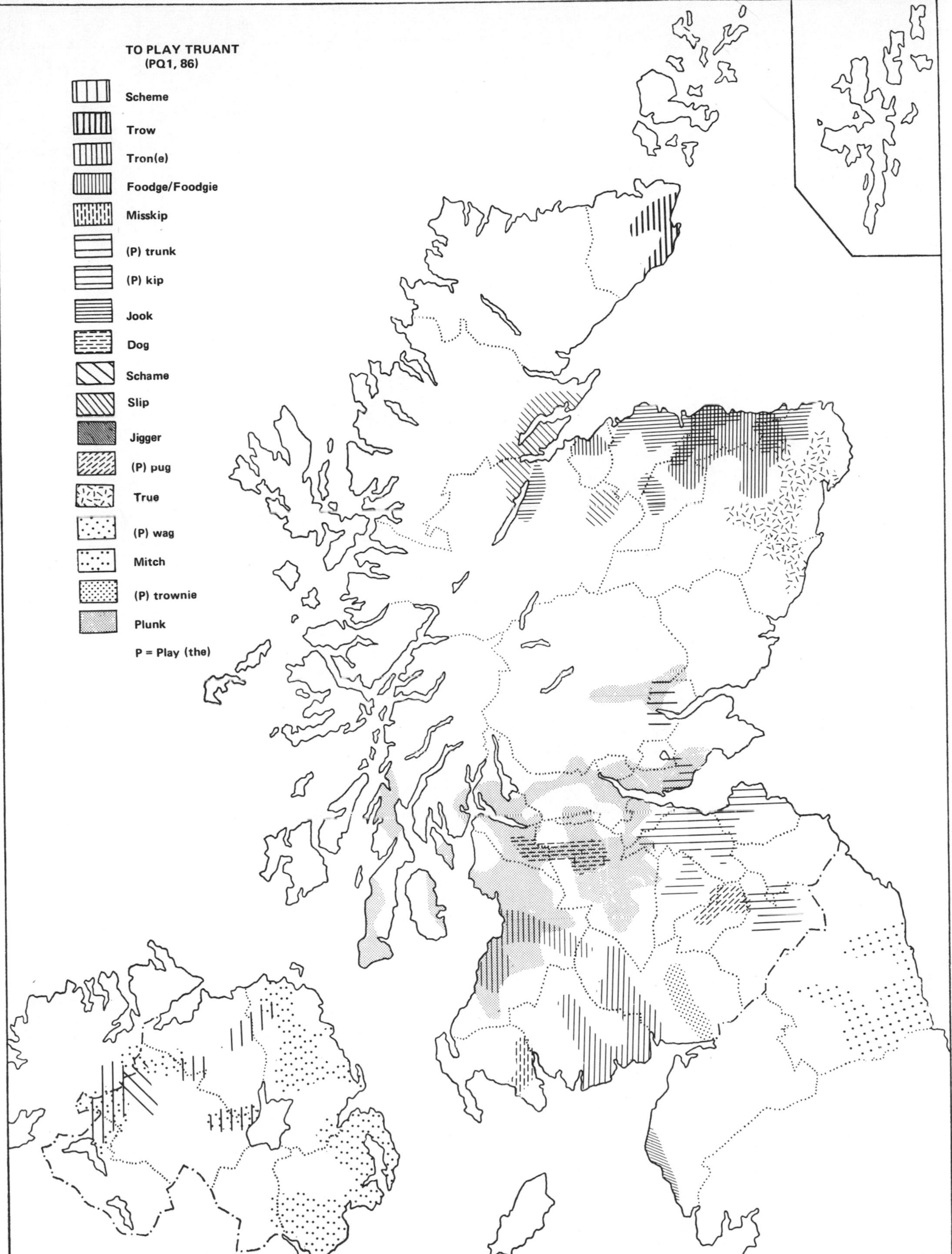
TO PLAY TRUANT
(PQ1, 86)
Scheme
Trow
Tron(e)
Foodge/Foodgie
Misskip
(P) trunk
(P) kip
Jook
Dog
Schame
Slip
Jigger
(P) pug
True
(P) wag
Mitch
(P) trownie
Plunk
P = Play (the)

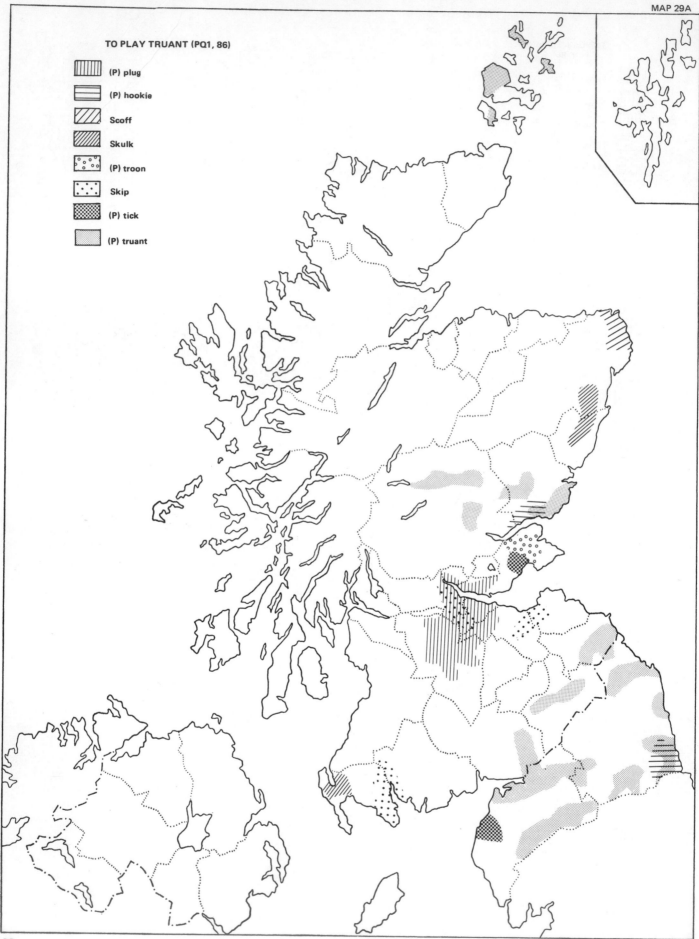

TO PLAY TRUANT (PQ1, 86)

(P) plug
(P) hookie
Scoff
Skulk
(P) troon
Skip
(P) tick
(P) truant

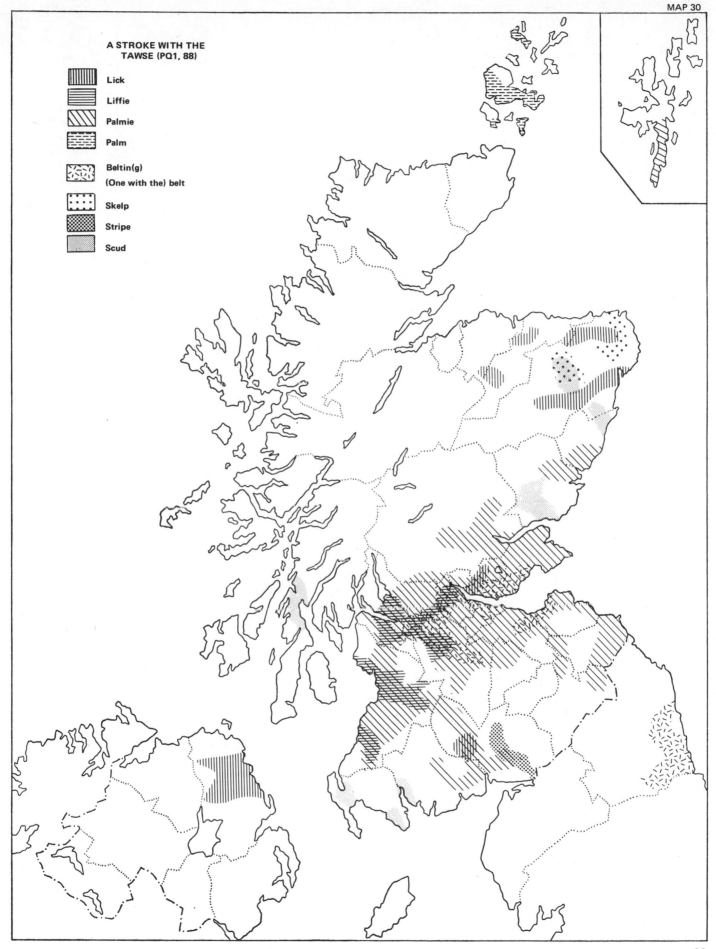

A STROKE WITH THE TAWSE (PQ1, 88)
Lick
Liffie
Palmie
Palm
Beltin(g)
(One with the) belt
Skelp
Stripe
Scud

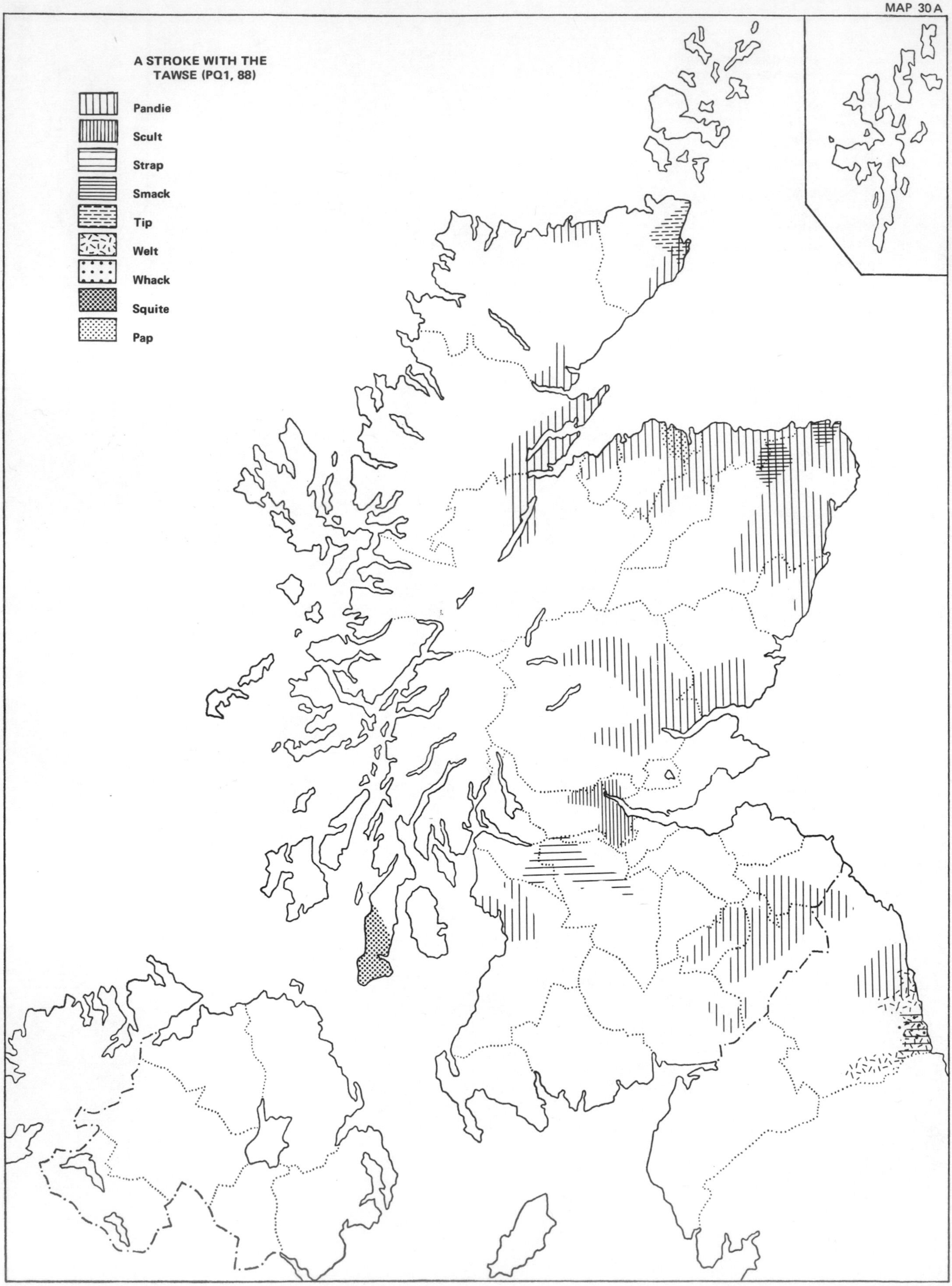

A STROKE WITH THE
TAWSE (PQ1, 88)
Pandie
Scult
Strap
Smack
Tip
Welt
Whack
Squite
Pap

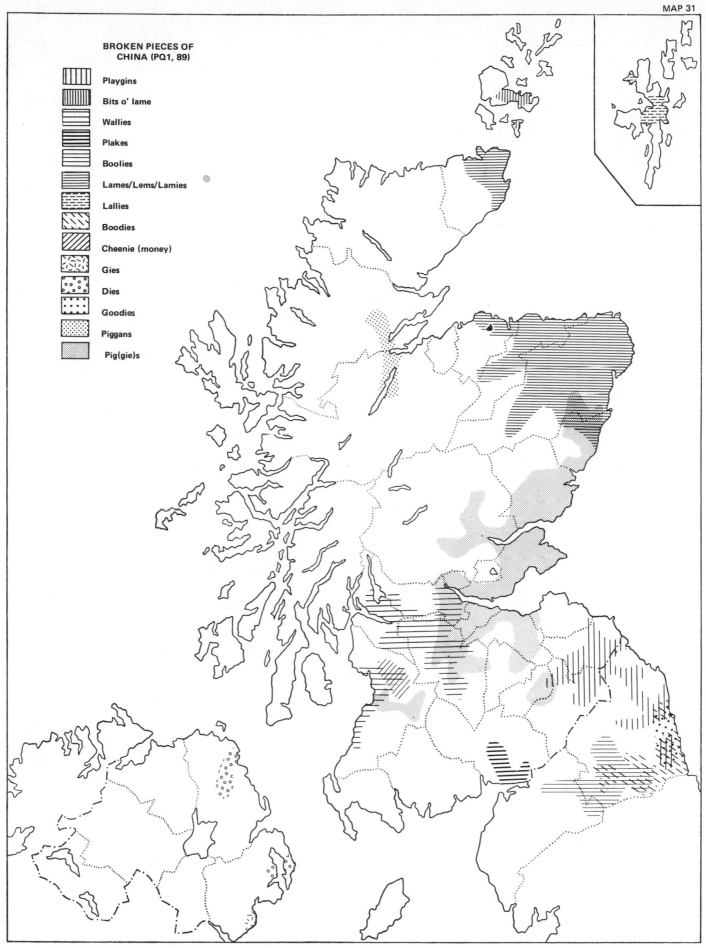

BROKEN PIECES OF CHINA (PQ1, 89)

- Playgins
- Bits o' lame
- Wallies
- Plakes
- Boolies
- Lames/Lems/Lamies
- Lallies
- Boodies
- Cheenie (money)
- Gies
- Dies
- Goodies
- Piggans
- Pig(gie)s

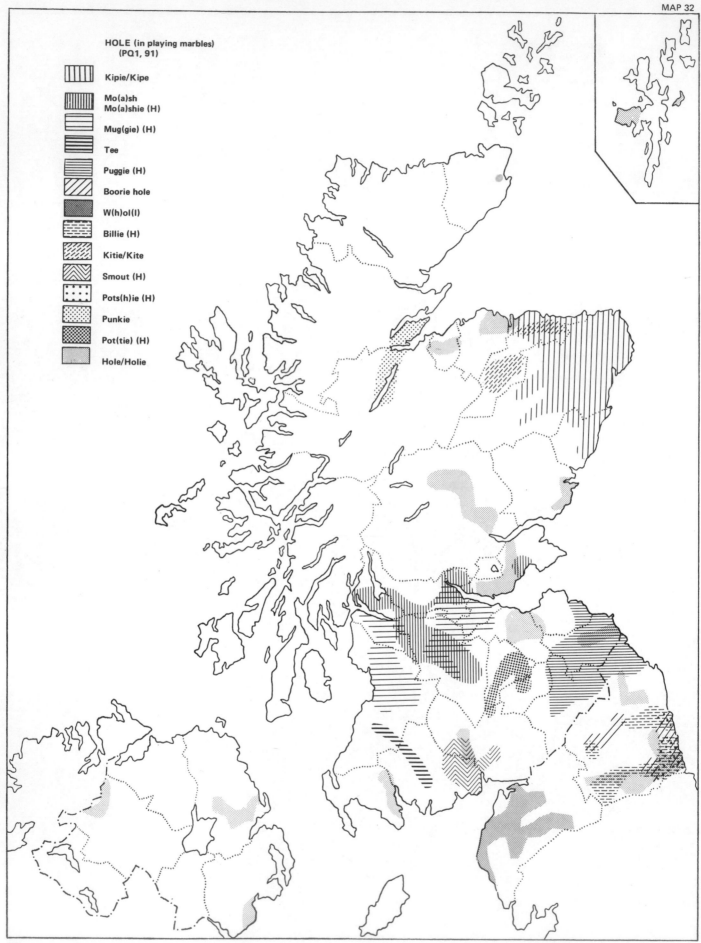

HOLE (in playing marbles)
(PQ1, 91)

Kipie/Kipe
Mo(a)sh
Mo(a)shie (H)
Mug(gie) (H)
Tee
Puggie (H)
Boorie hole
W(h)ol(l)
Billie (H)
Kitie/Kite
Smout (H)
Pots(h)ie (H)
Punkie
Pot(tie) (H)
Hole/Holie

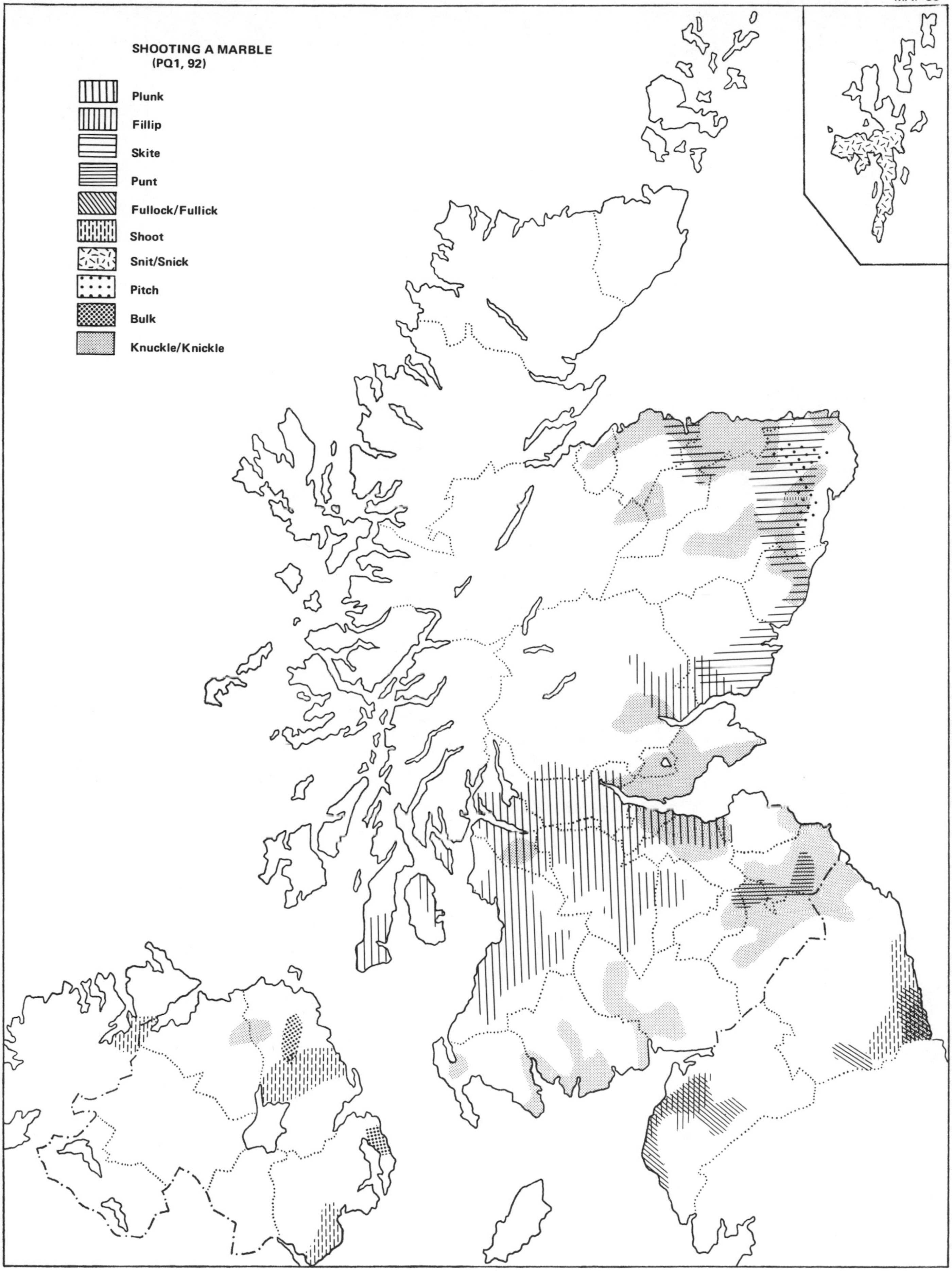

SHOOTING A MARBLE
(PQ1, 92)

- Plunk
- Fillip
- Skite
- Punt
- Fullock/Fullick
- Shoot
- Snit/Snick
- Pitch
- Bulk
- Knuckle/Knickle

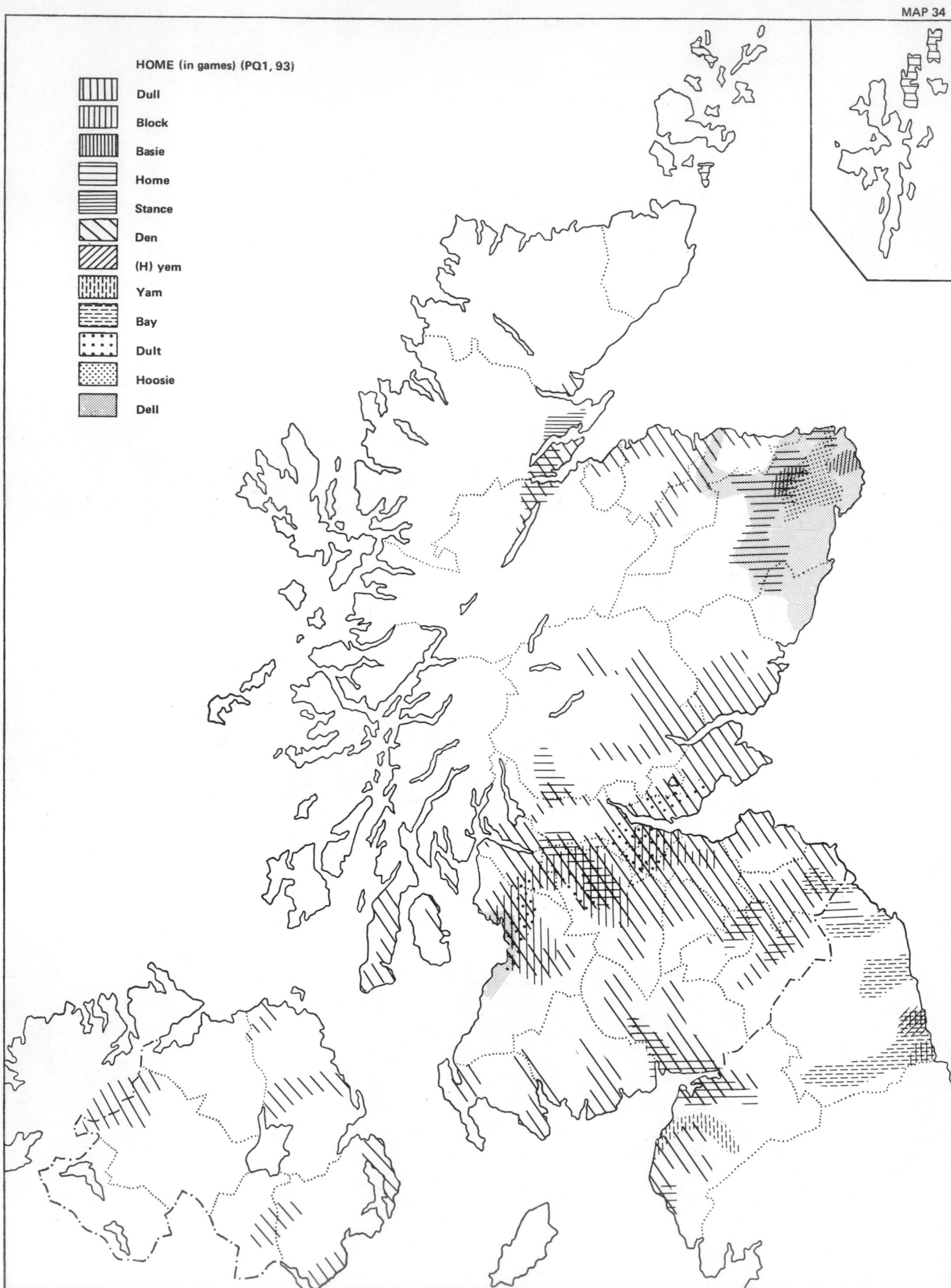
HOME (in games) (PQ1, 93)
Dull
Block
Basie
Home
Stance
Den
(H) yem
Yam
Bay
Dult
Hoosie
Dell

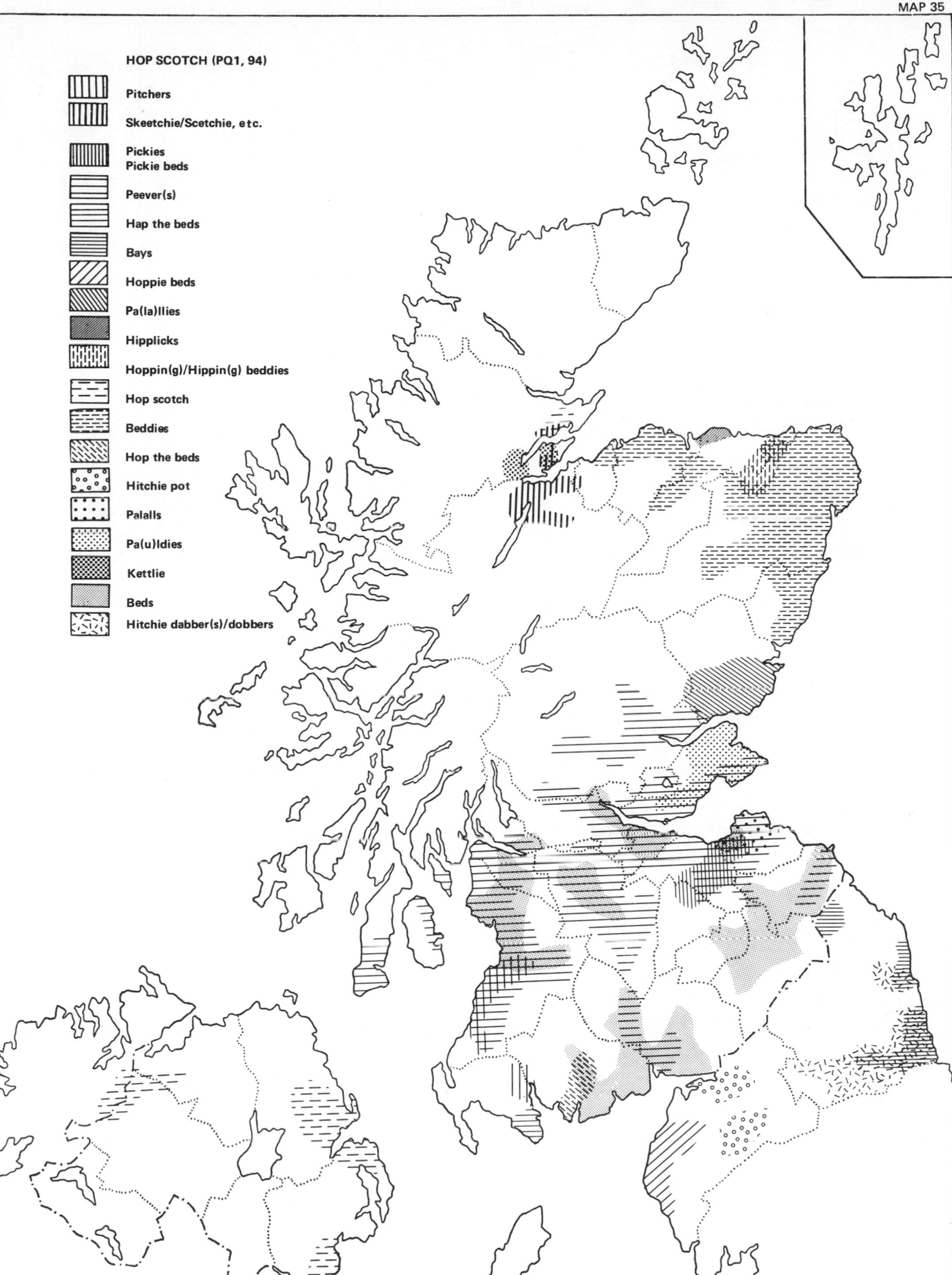
HOP SCOTCH (PQ1, 94)
Pitchers
Skeetchie/Scetchie, etc.
Pickies
Pickie beds
Peever(s)
Hap the beds
Bays
Hoppie beds
Pa(la)llies
Hipplicks
Hoppin(g)/Hippin(g) beddies
Hop scotch
Beddies
Hop the beds
Hitchie pot
Palalls
Pa(u)ldies
Kettlie
Beds
Hitchie dabber(s)/dobbers

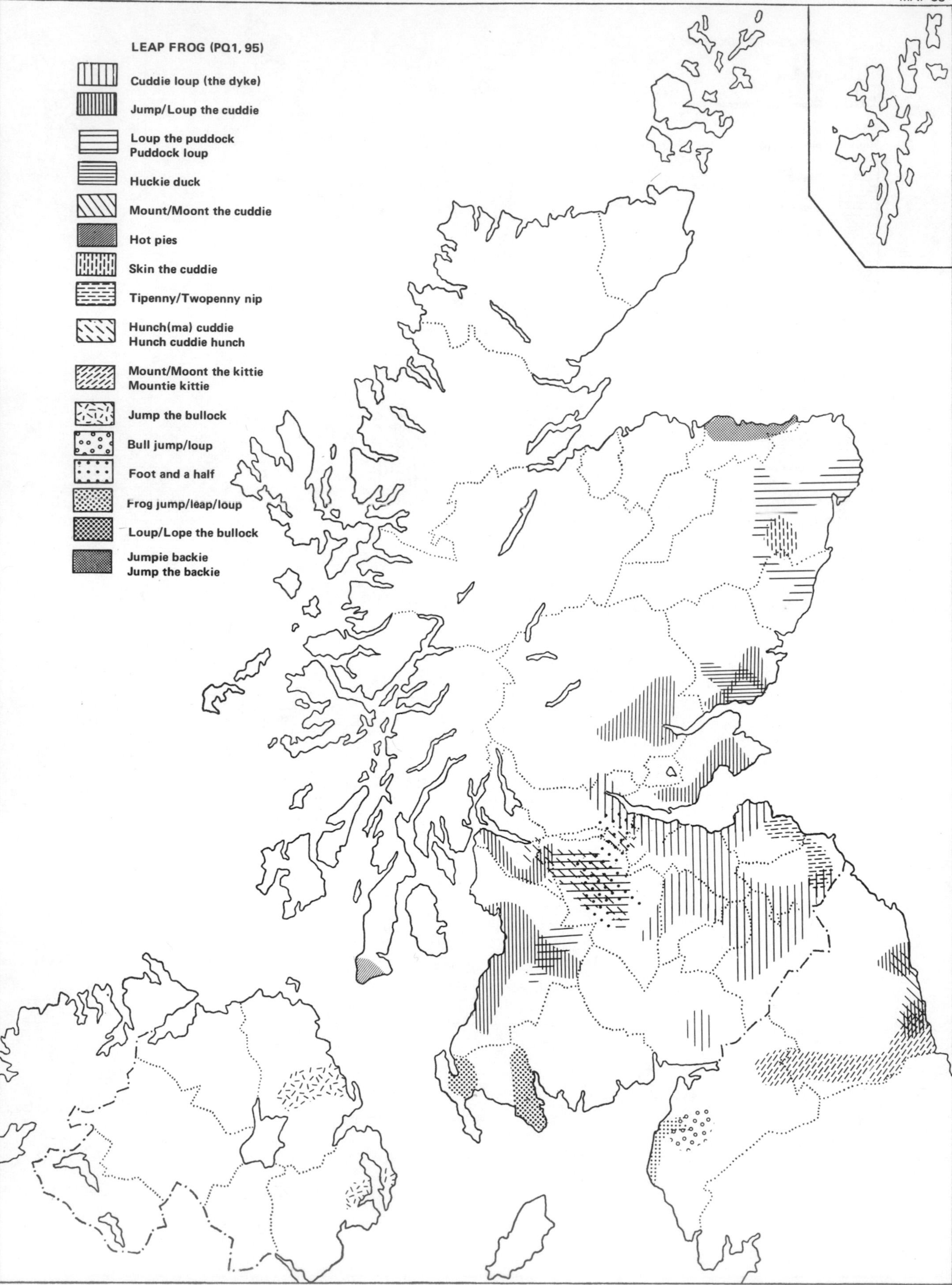
LEAP FROG (PQ1, 95)
Cuddie loup (the dyke)
Jump/Loup the cuddie
Loup the puddock
Puddock loup
Huckie duck
Mount/Moont the cuddie
Hot pies
Skin the cuddie
Tipenny/Twopenny nip
Hunch(ma) cuddie
Hunch cuddie hunch
Mount/Moont the kittie
Mountie kittie
Jump the bullock
Bull jump/loup
Foot and a half
Frog jump/leap/loup
Loup/Lope the bullock
Jumpie backie
Jump the backie

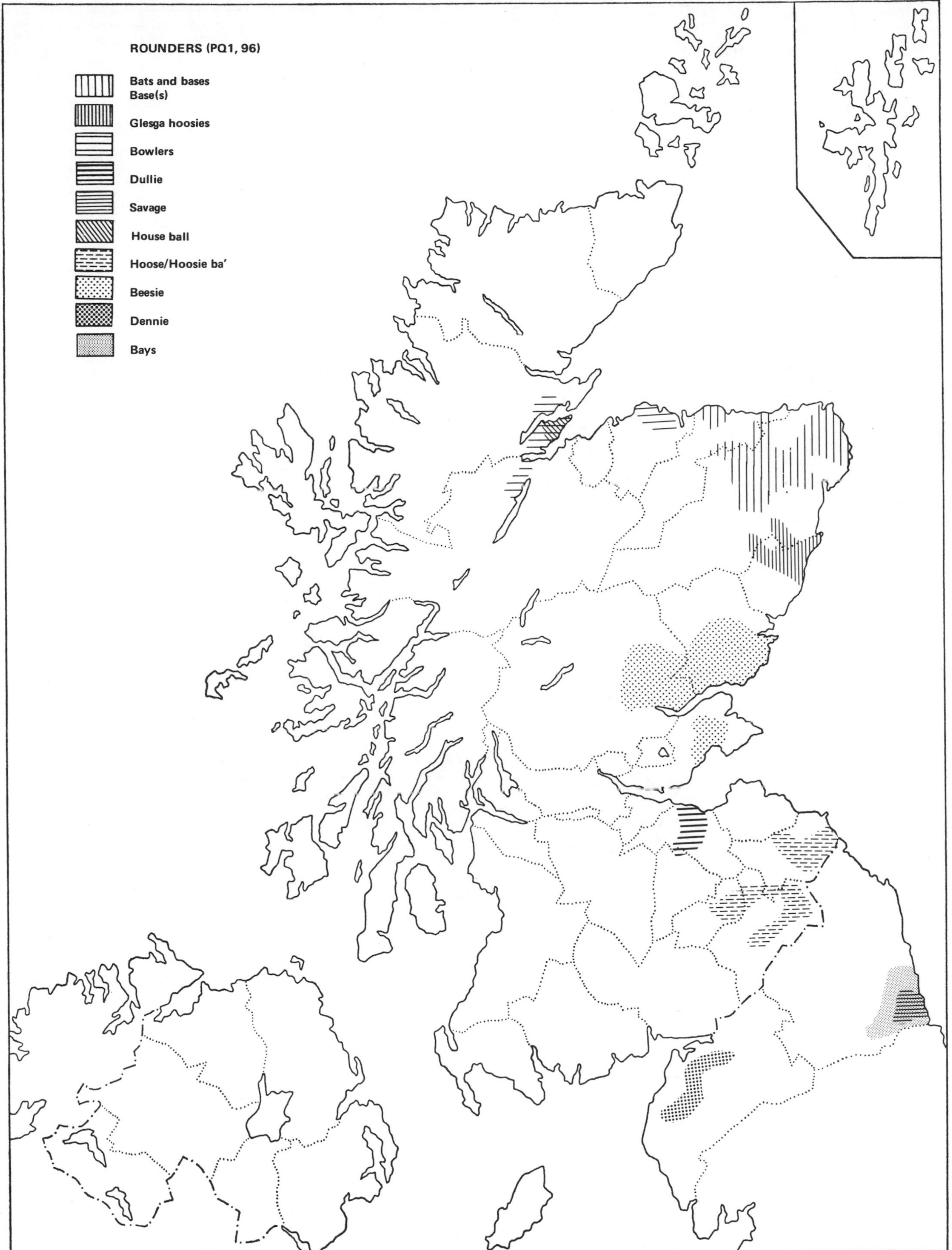
ROUNDERS (PQ1, 96)
Bats and bases
Base(s)
Glesga hoosies
Bowlers
Dullie
Savage
House ball
Hoose/Hoosie ba'
Beesie
Dennie
Bays

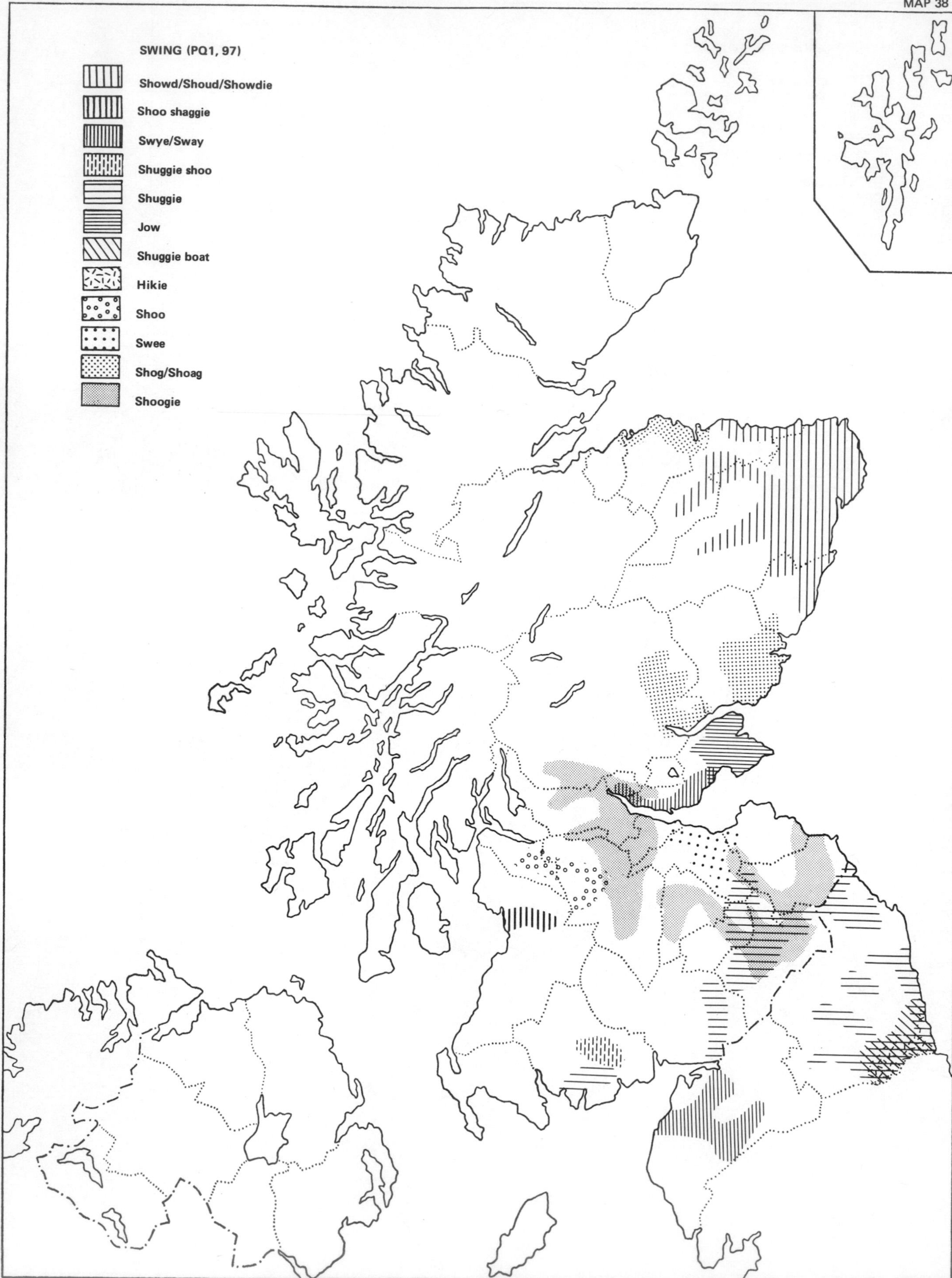

SWING (PQ1, 97)
Showd/Shoud/Showdie
Shoo shaggie
Swye/Sway
Shuggie shoo
Shuggie
Jow
Shuggie boat
Hikie
Shoo
Swee
Shog/Shoag
Shoogie

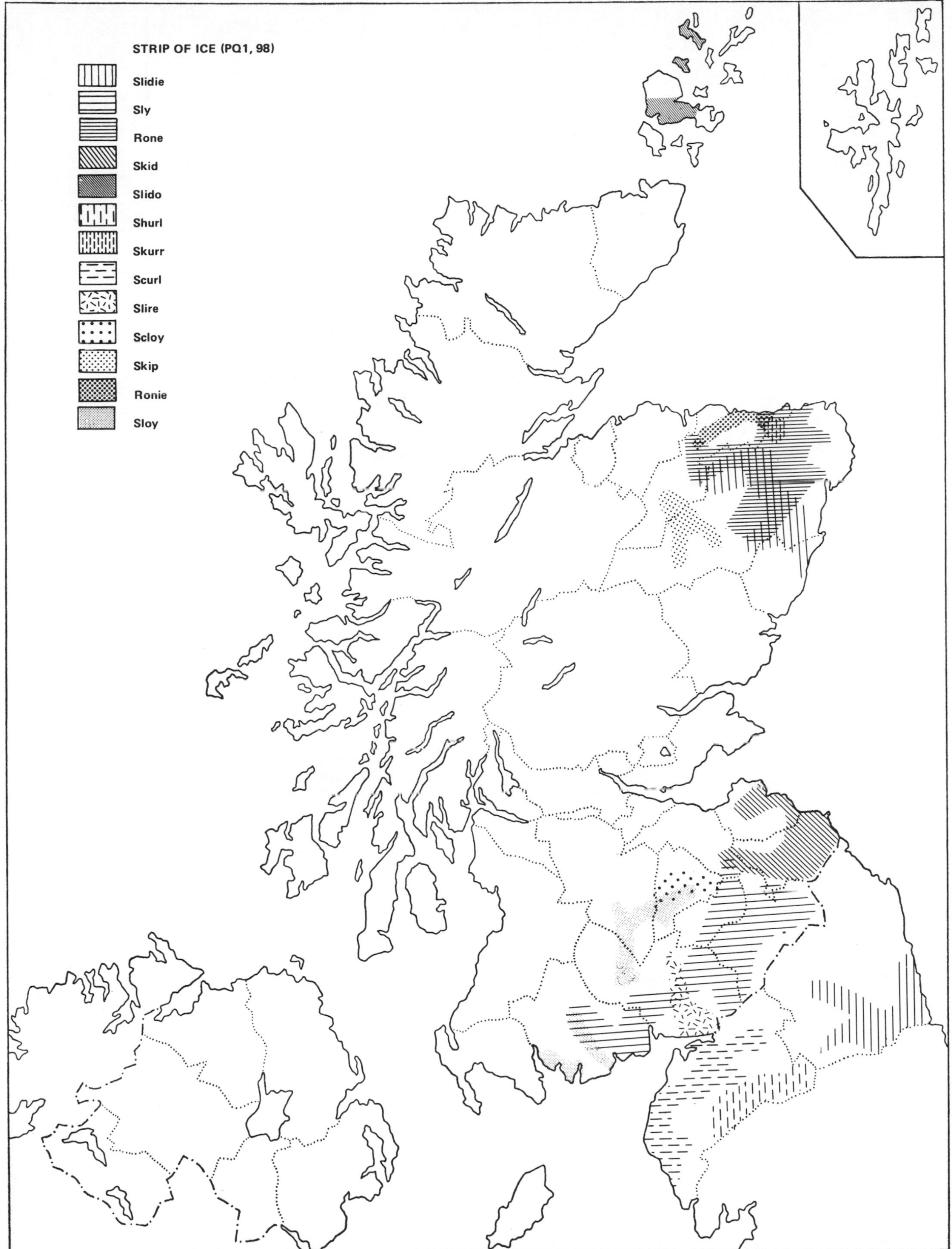
STRIP OF ICE (PQ1, 98)
Slidie
Sly
Rone
Skid
Slido
Shurl
Skurr
Scurl
Slire
Scloy
Skip
Ronie
Sloy

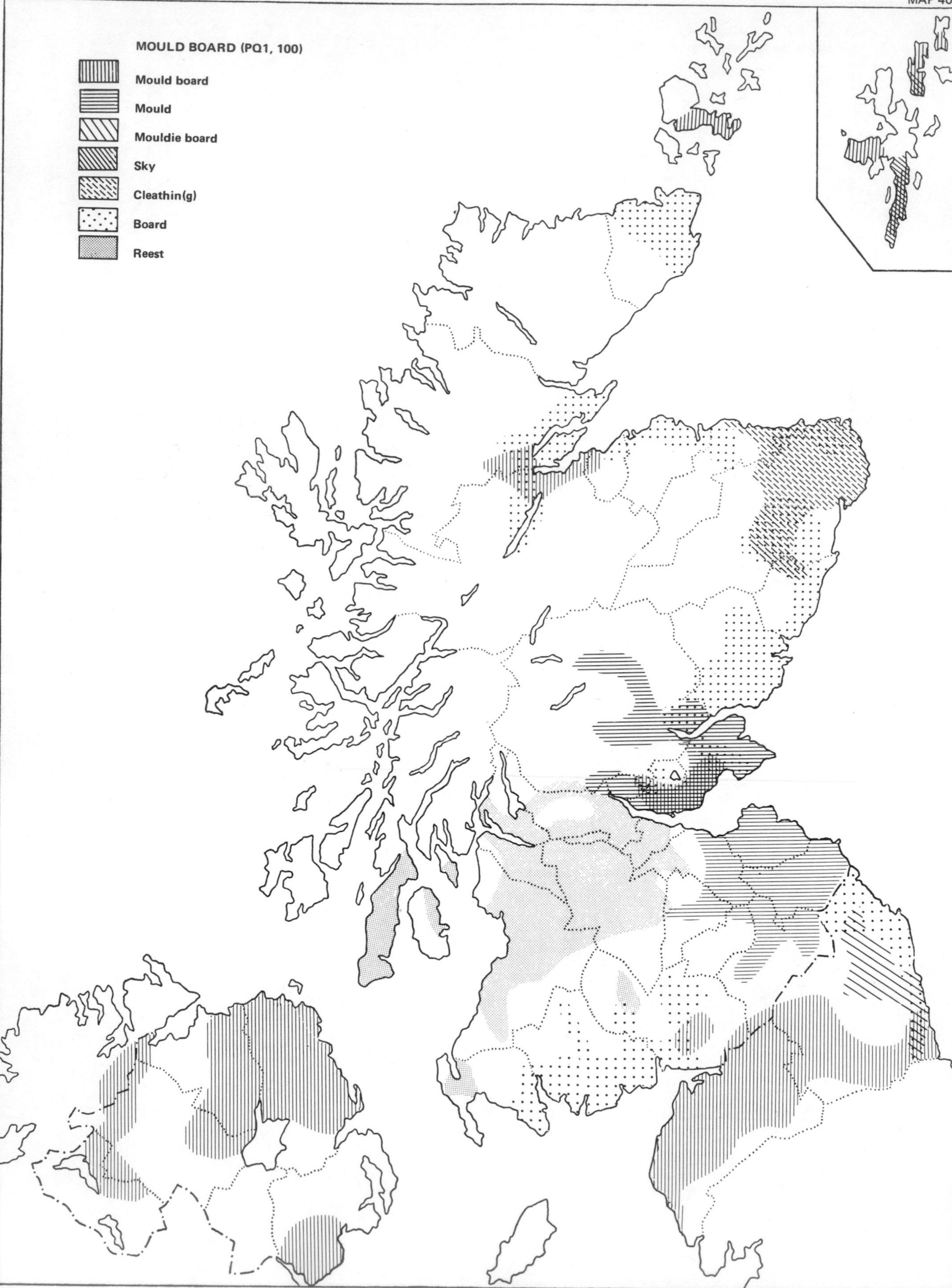
MOULD BOARD (PQ1, 100)
Mould board
Mould
Mouldie board
Sky
Cleathin(g)
Board
Reest

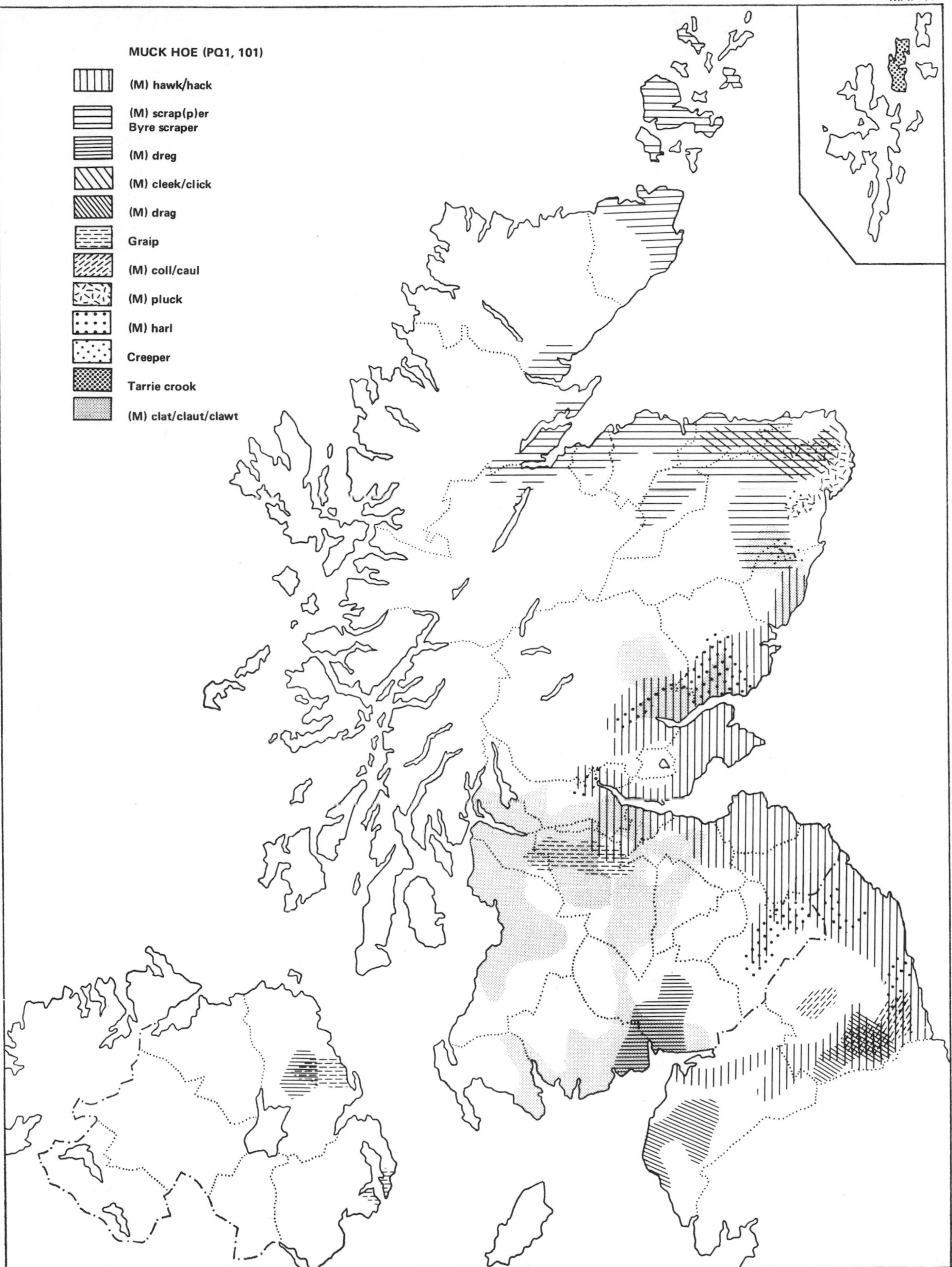
MUCK HOE (PQ1, 101)
(M) hawk/hack
(M) scrap(p)er
Byre scraper
(M) dreg
(M) cleek/click
(M) drag
Graip
(M) coll/caul
(M) pluck
(M) harl
Creeper
Tarrie crook
(M) clat/claut/clawt

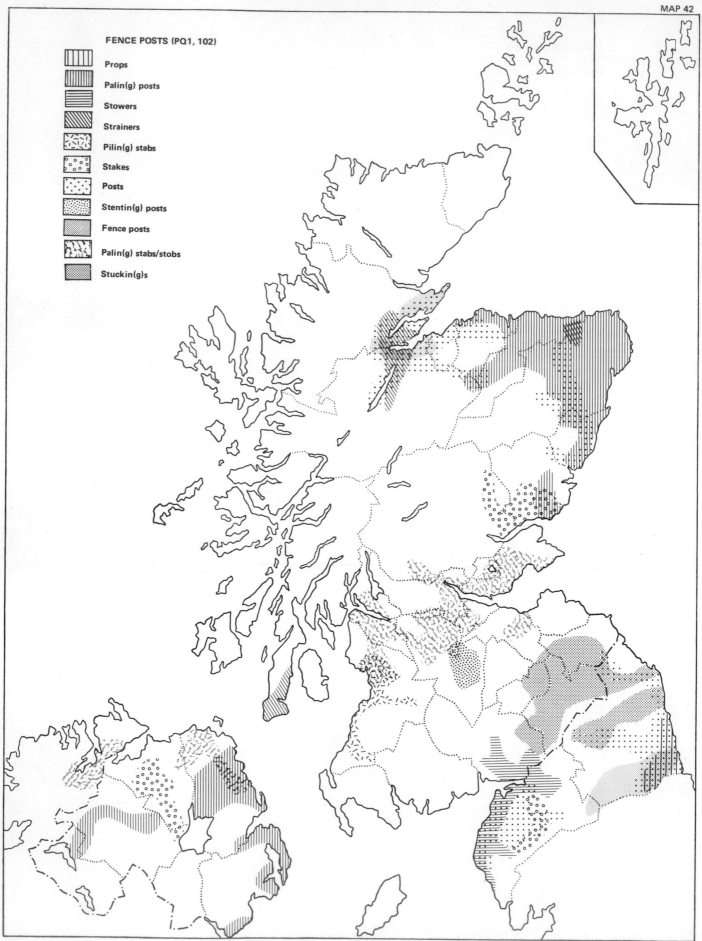

FENCE POSTS (PQ1, 102)

- Props
- Palin(g) posts
- Stowers
- Strainers
- Pilin(g) stabs
- Stakes
- Posts
- Stentin(g) posts
- Fence posts
- Palin(g) stabs/stobs
- Stuckin(g)s

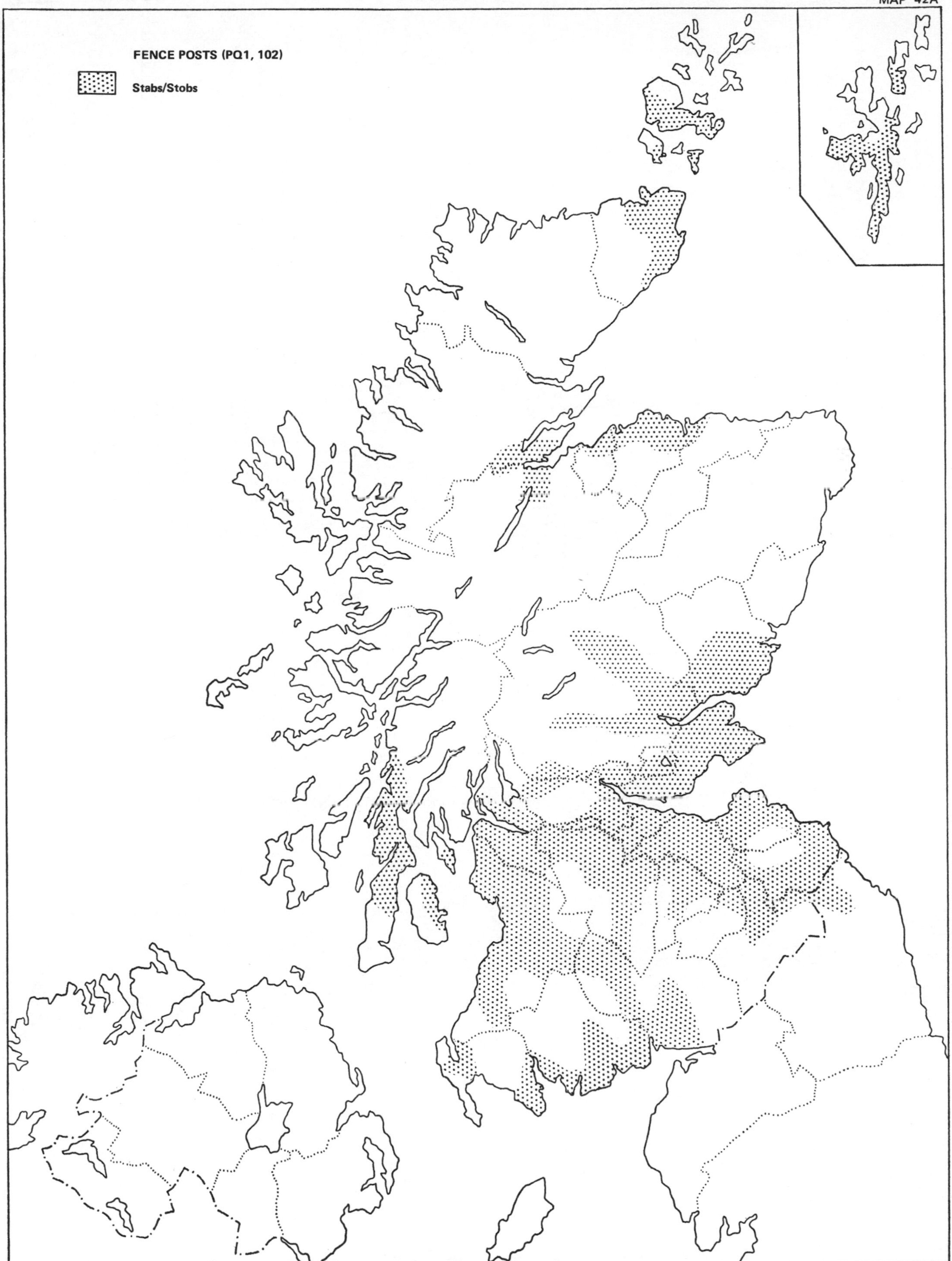
FENCE POSTS (PQ1, 102)
Stabs/Stobs

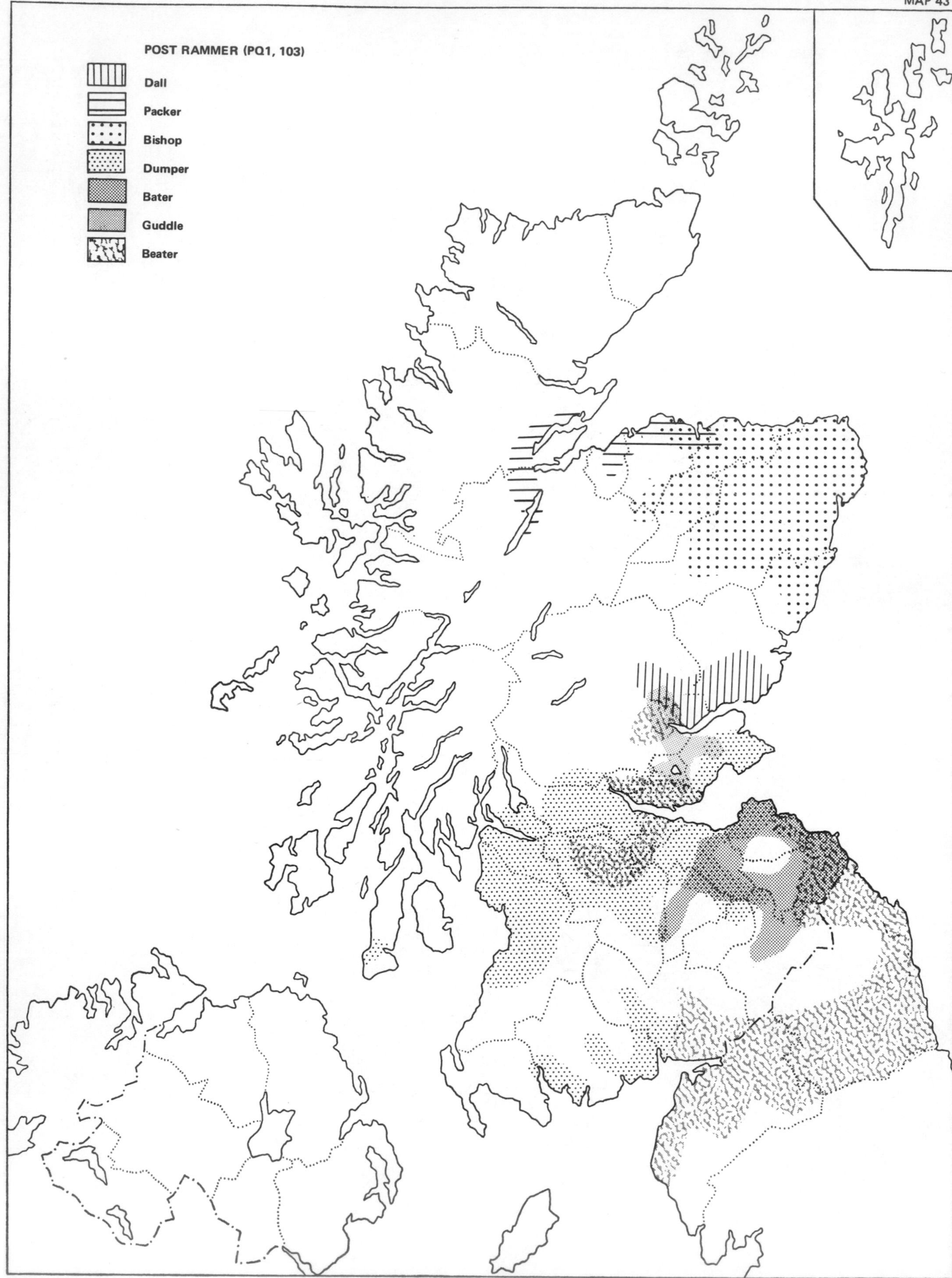
POST RAMMER (PQ1, 103)
Dall
Packer
Bishop
Dumper
Bater
Guddle
Beater

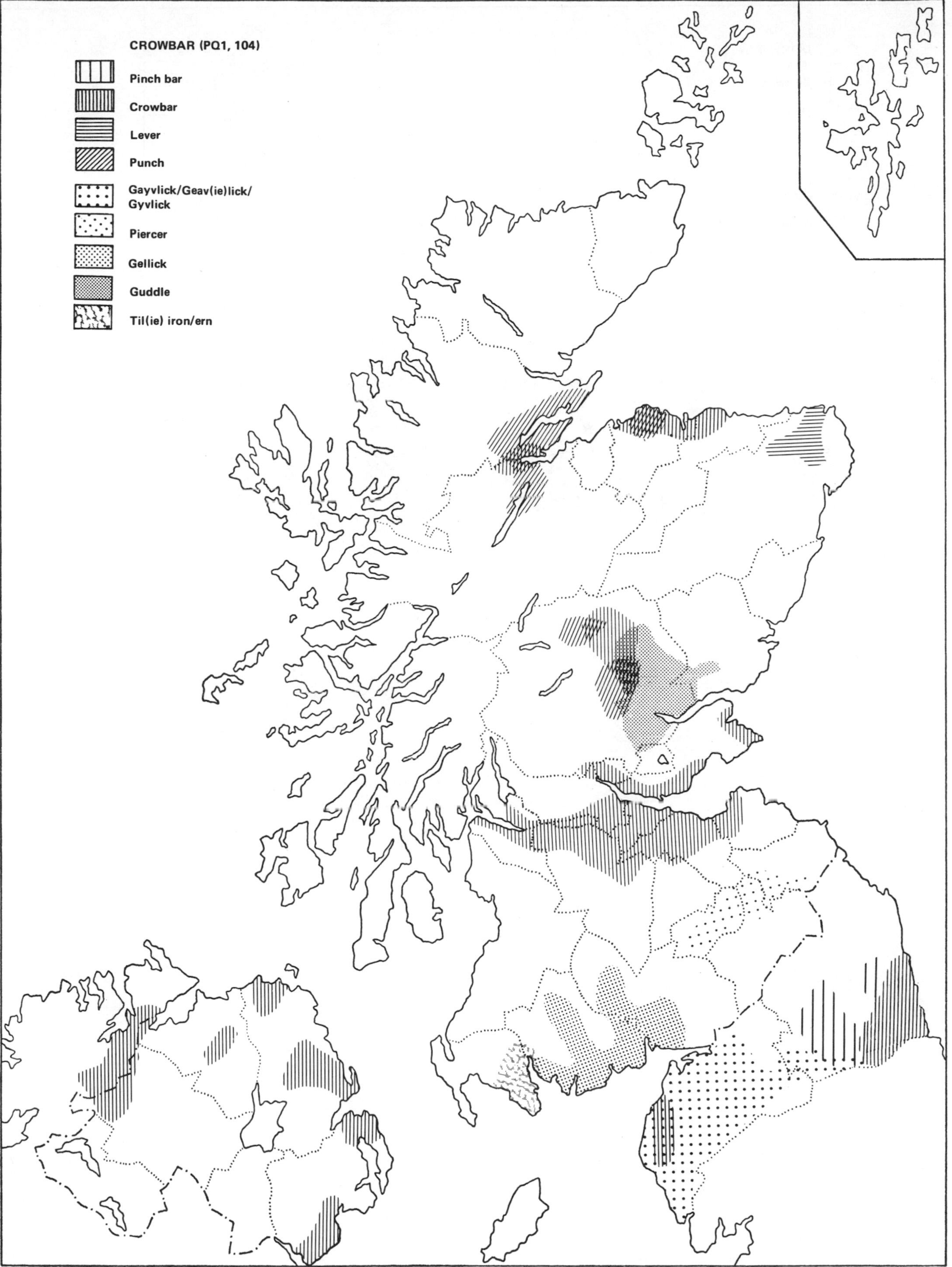
CROWBAR (PQ1, 104)
Pinch bar
Crowbar
Lever
Punch
Gayvlick/Geav(ie)lick/
Gyvlick
Piercer
Gellick
Guddle
Til(ie) iron/ern

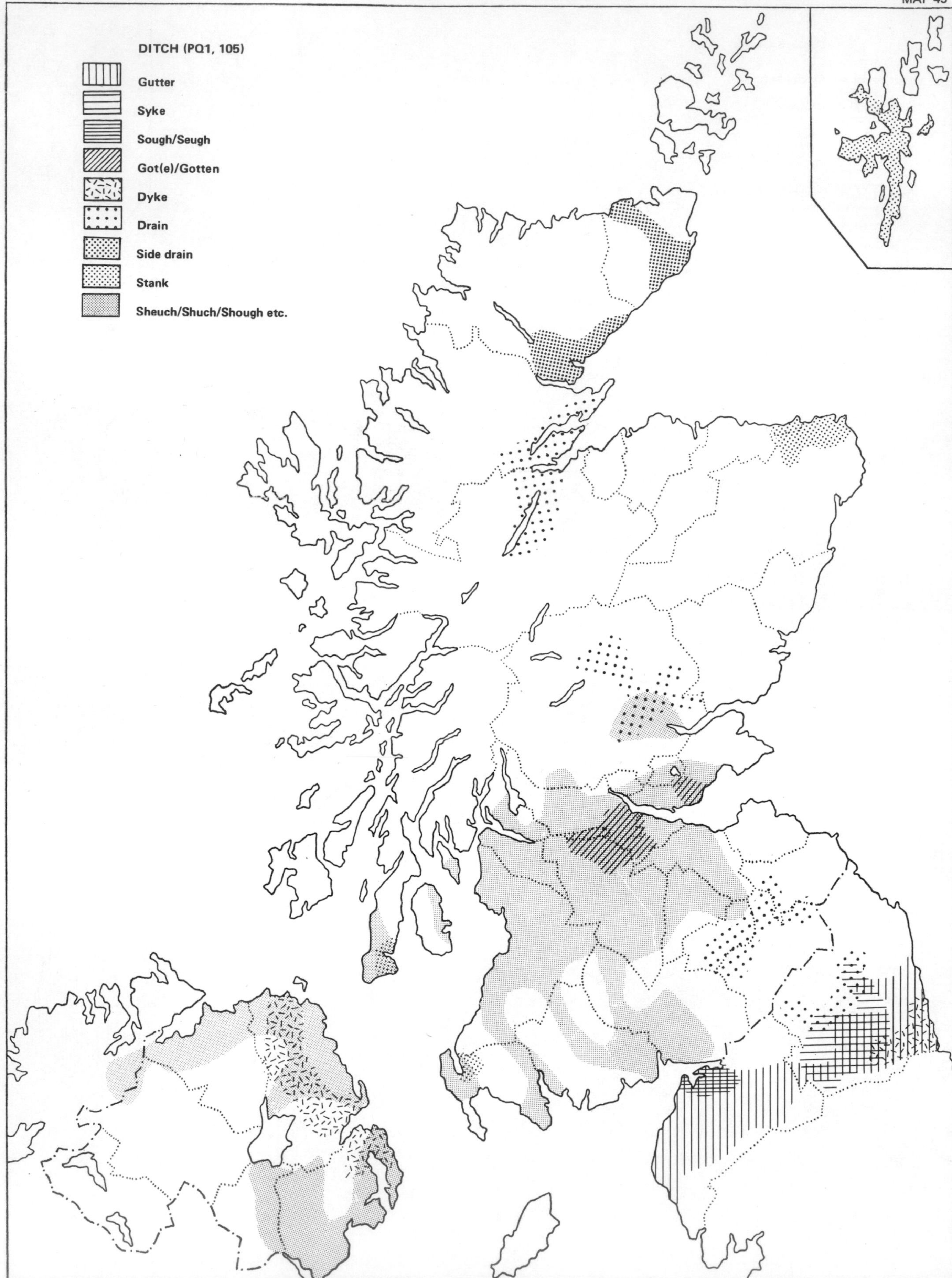
DITCH (PQ1, 105)
Gutter
Syke
Sough/Seugh
Got(e)/Gotten
Dyke
Drain
Side drain
Stank
Sheuch/Shuch/Shough etc.

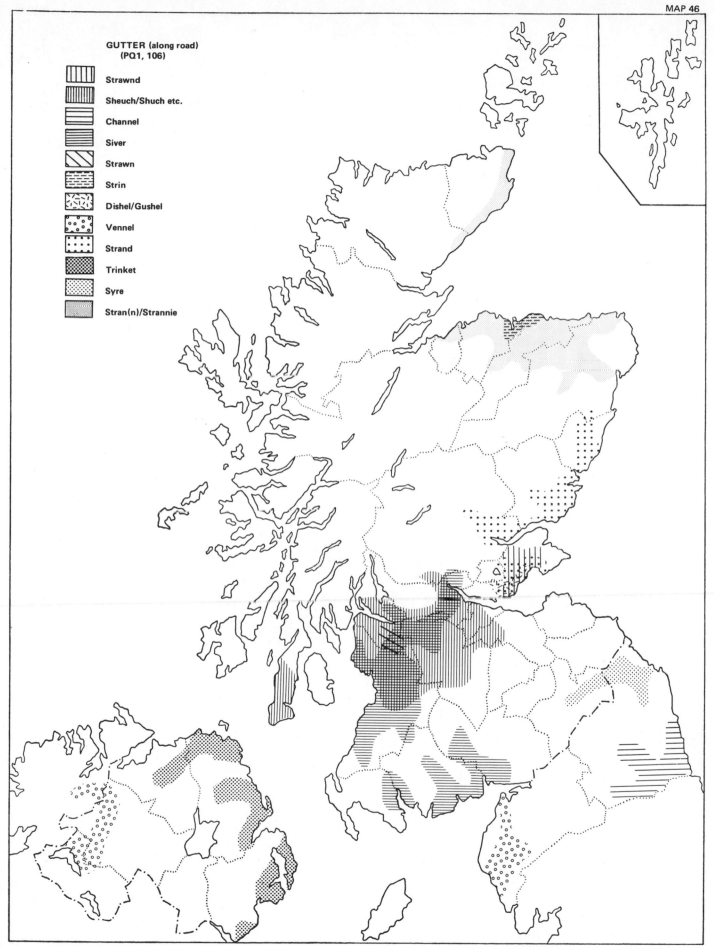

GUTTER (along road)
(PQ1, 106)

Strawnd
Sheuch/Shuch etc.
Channel
Siver
Strawn
Strin
Dishel/Gushel
Vennel
Strand
Trinket
Syre
Stran(n)/Strannie

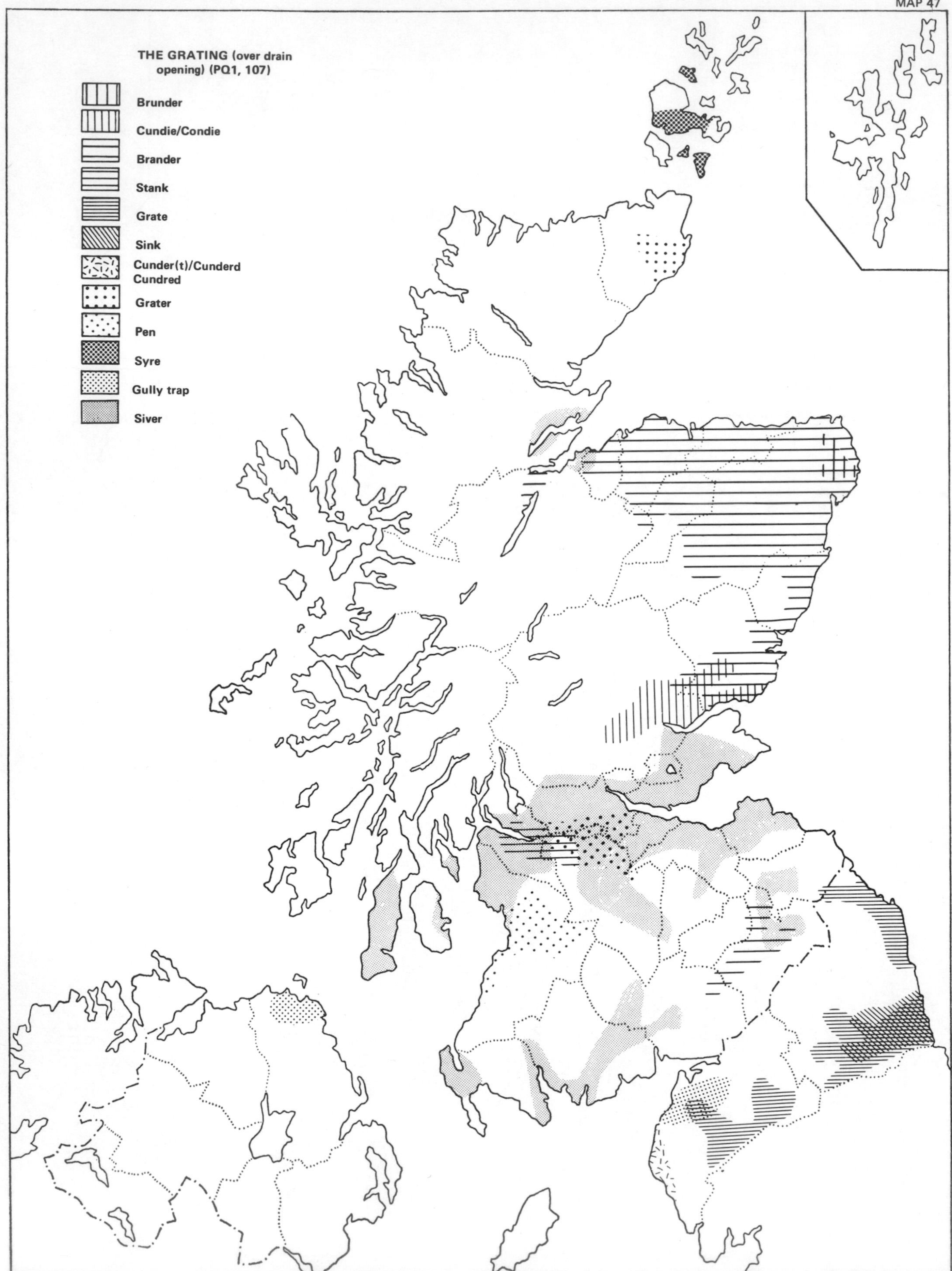
THE GRATING (over drain opening) (PQ1, 107)
Brunder
Cundie/Condie
Brander
Stank
Grate
Sink
Cunder(t)/Cunderd
Cundred
Grater
Pen
Syre
Gully trap
Siver

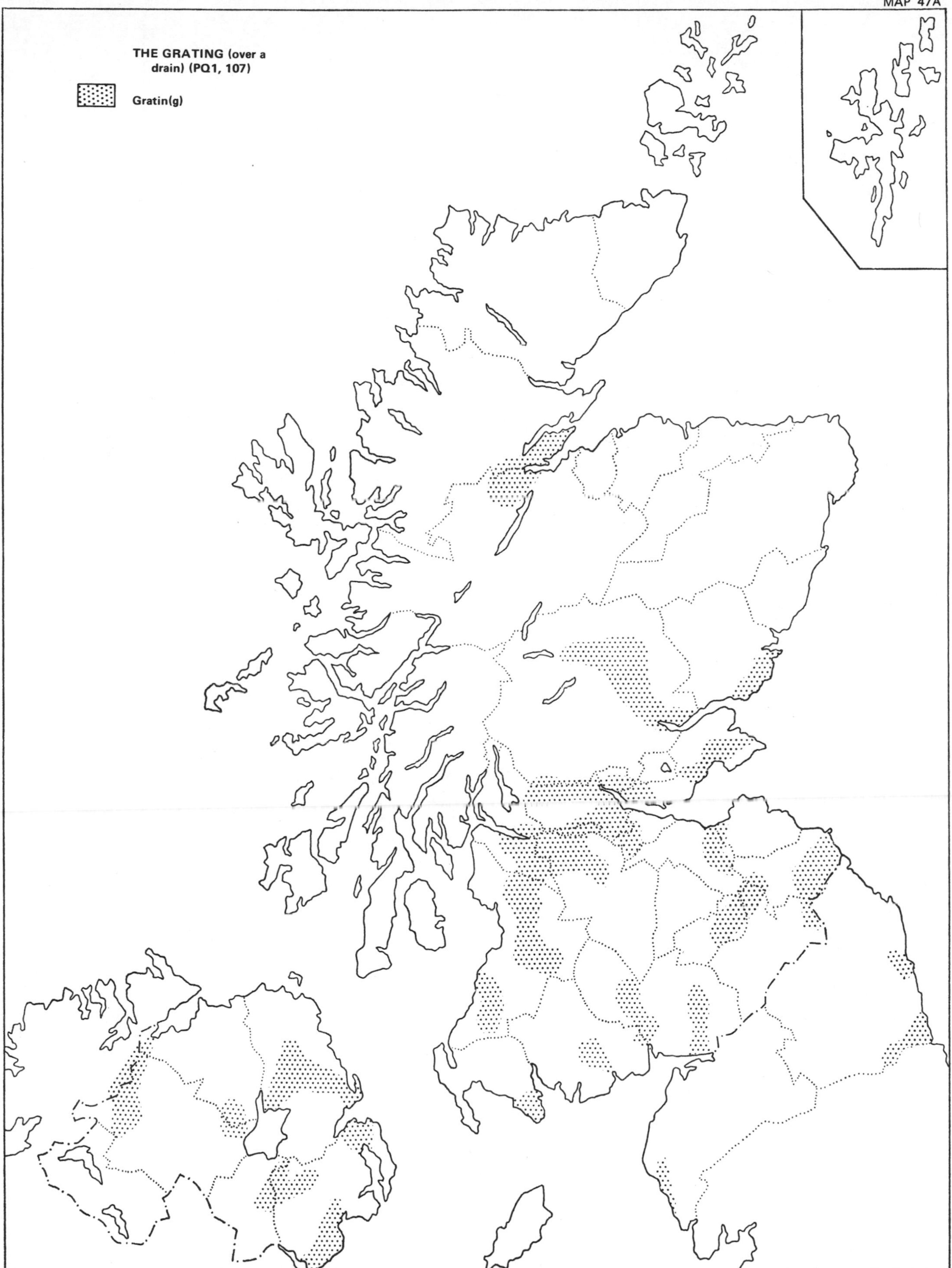
THE GRATING (over a drain) (PQ1, 107)
Gratin(g)

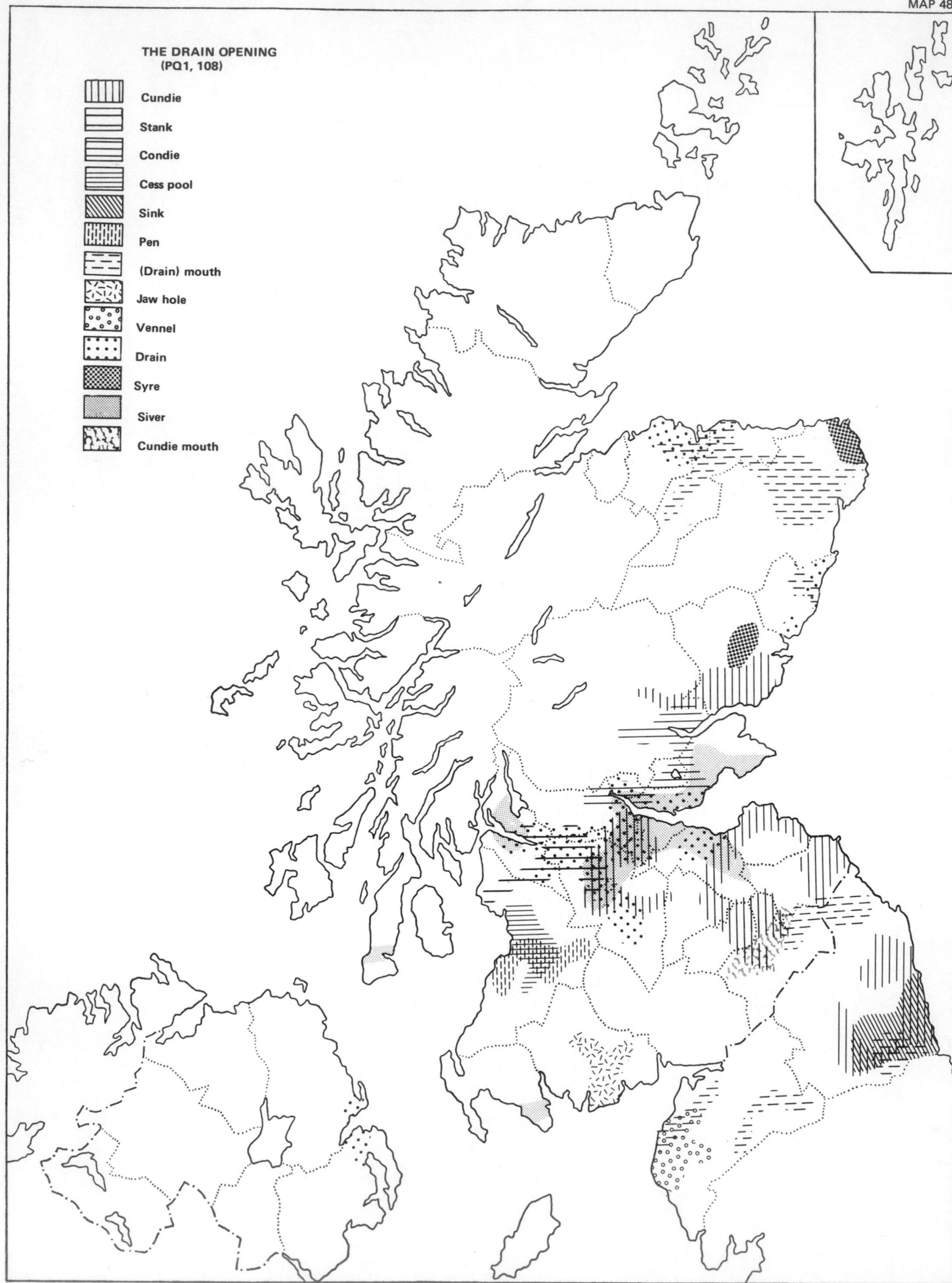
THE DRAIN OPENING
(PQ1, 108)
Cundie
Stank
Condie
Cess pool
Sink
Pen
(Drain) mouth
Jaw hole
Vennel
Drain
Syre
Siver
Cundie mouth

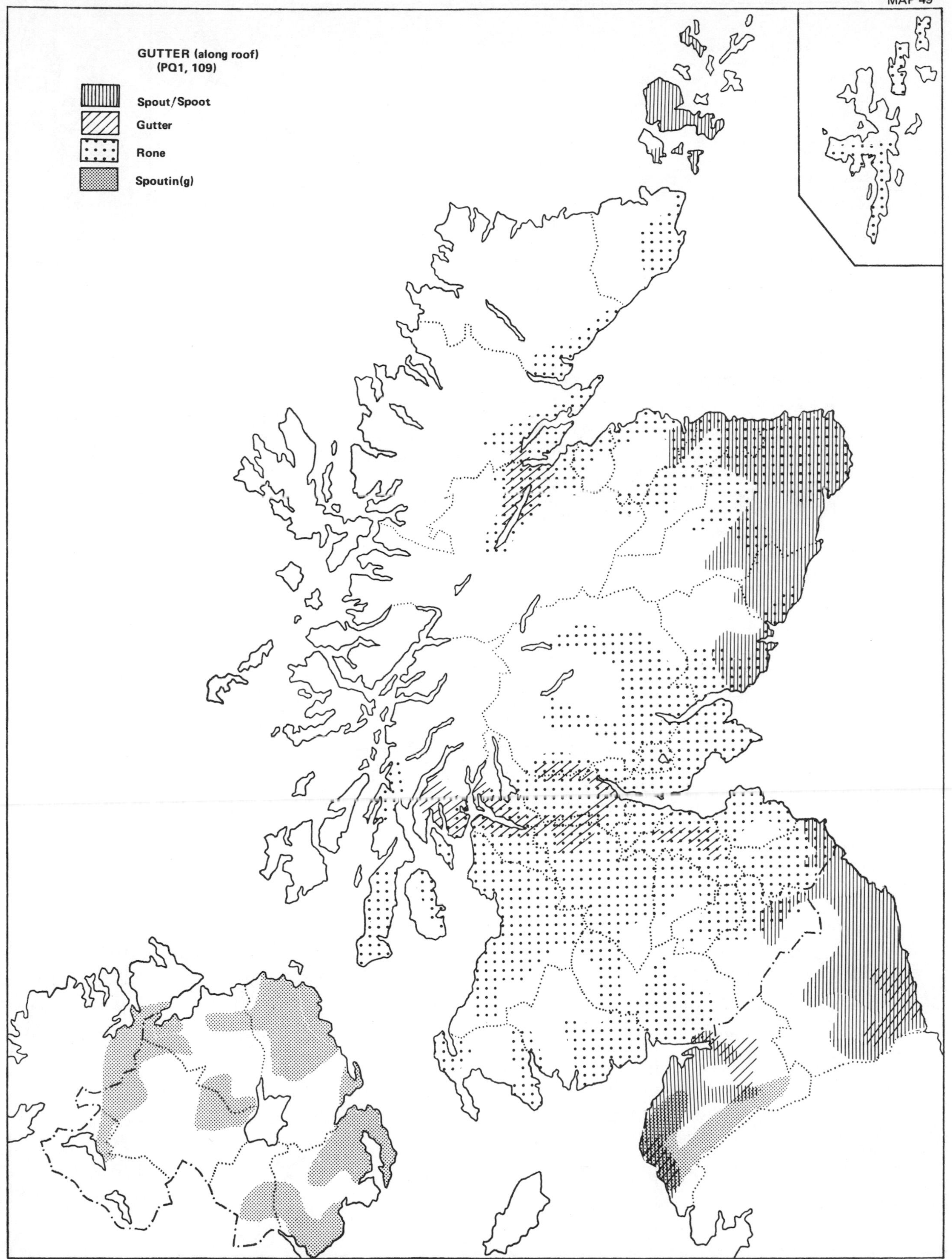
GUTTER (along roof)
(PQ1, 109)
Spout/Spoot
Gutter
Rone
Spoutin(g)

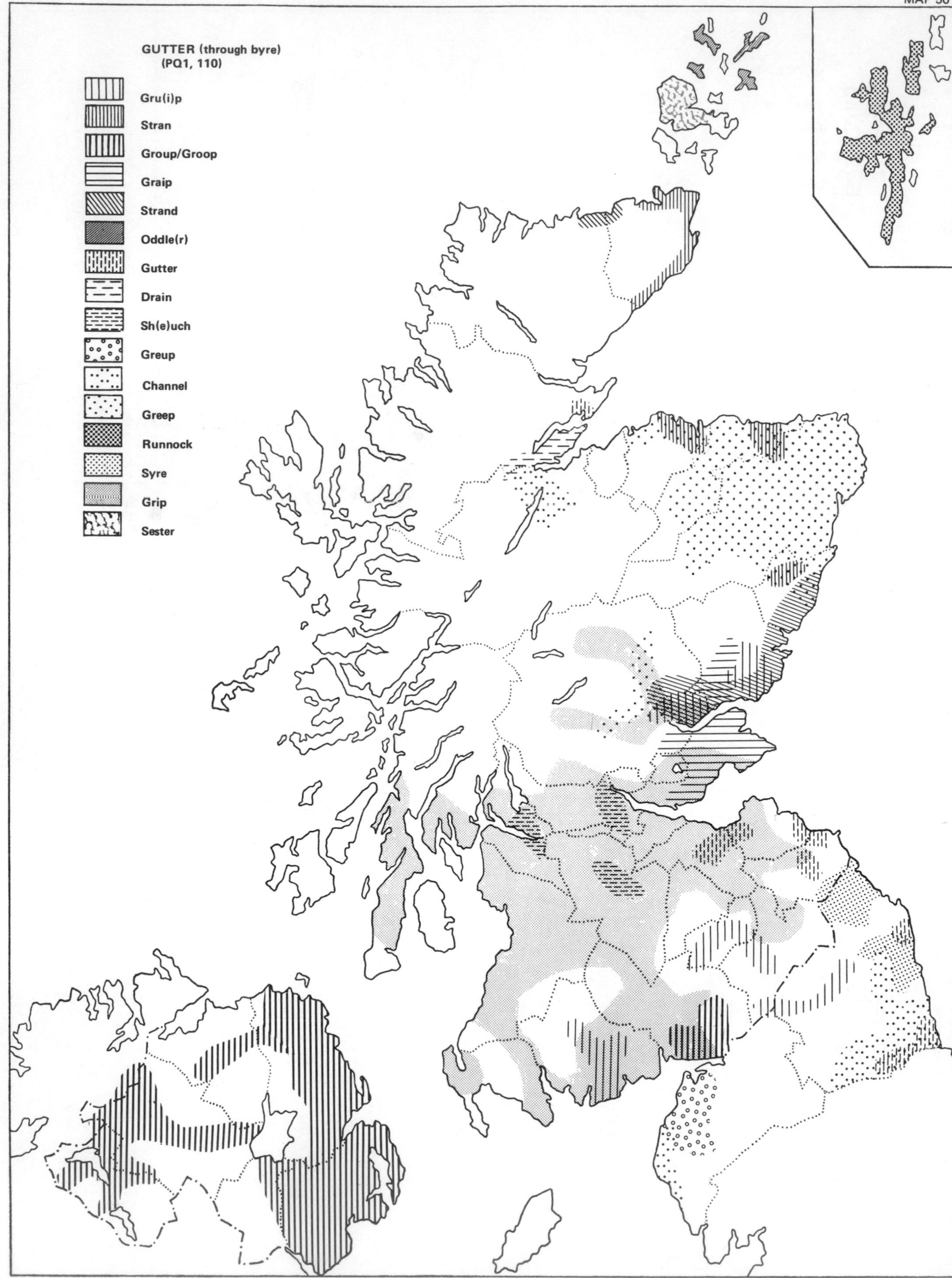
GUTTER (through byre)
(PQ1, 110)
Gru(i)p
Stran
Group/Groop
Graip
Strand
Oddle(r)
Gutter
Drain
Sh(e)uch
Greup
Channel
Greep
Runnock
Syre
Grip
Sester

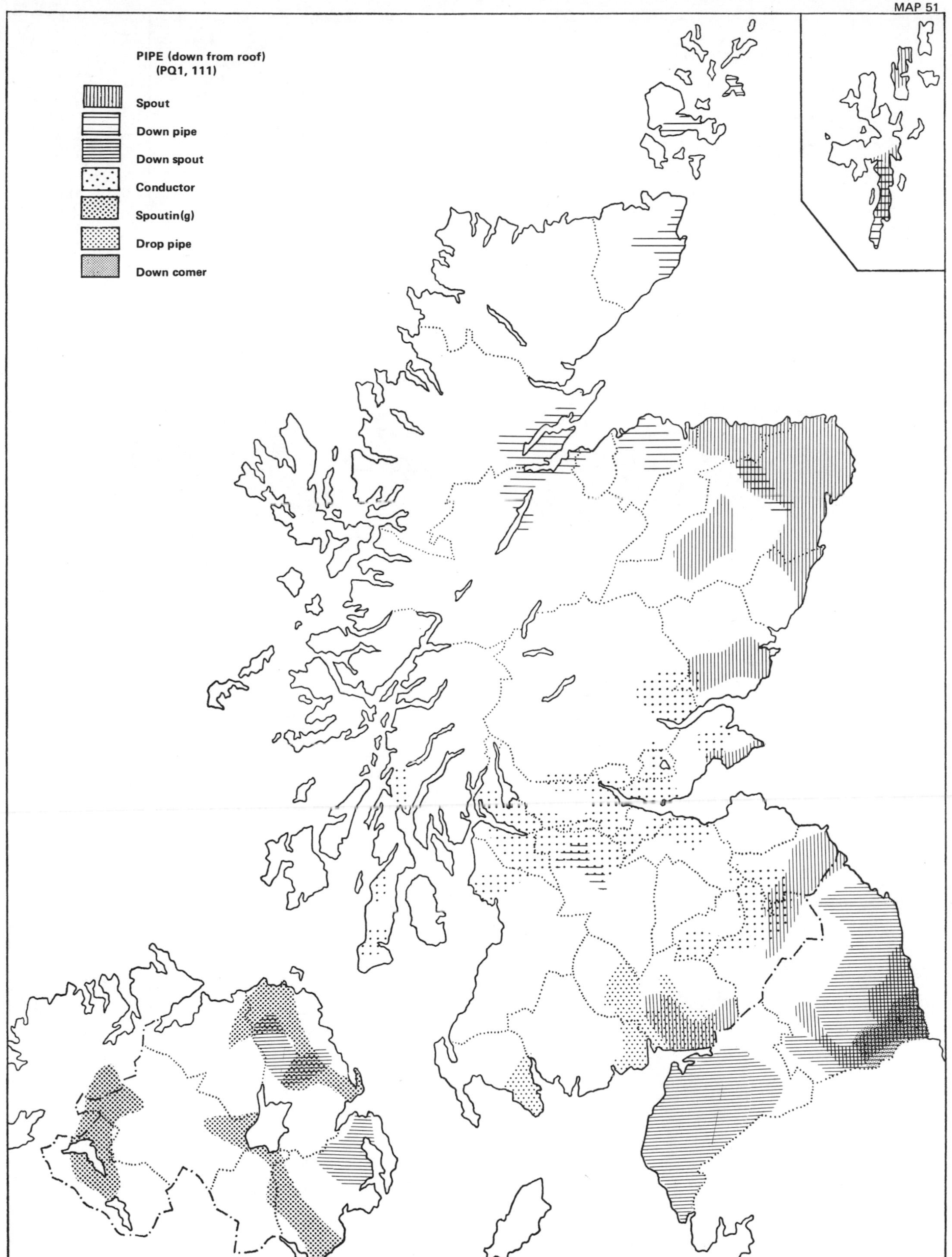
PIPE (down from roof)
(PQ1, 111)
Spout
Down pipe
Down spout
Conductor
Spoutin(g)
Drop pipe
Down comer

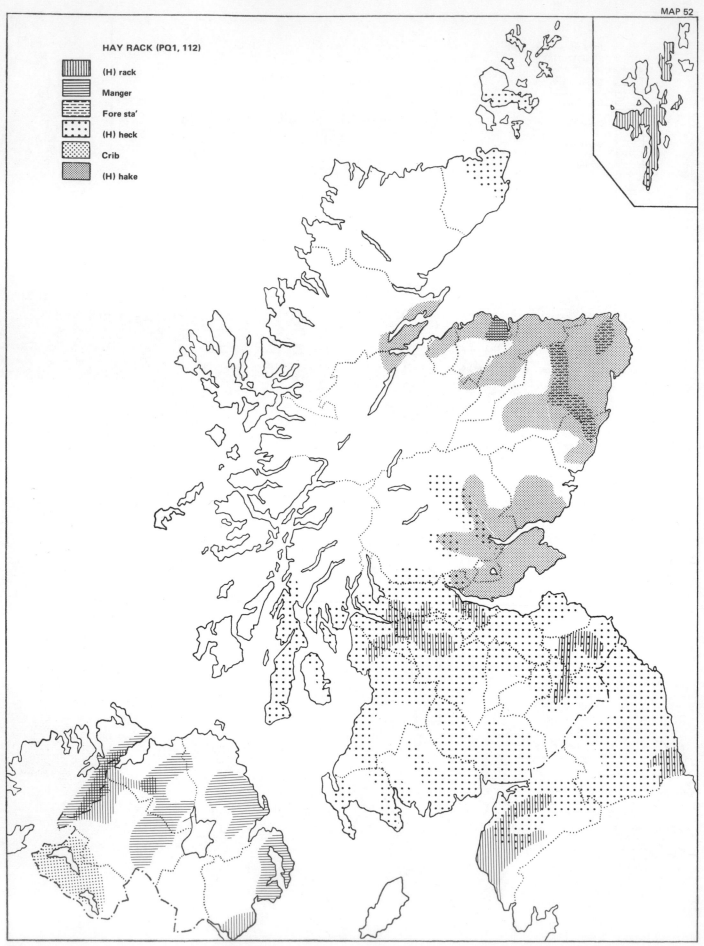

HAY RACK (PQ1, 112)

(H) rack
Manger
Fore sta'
(H) heck
Crib
(H) hake

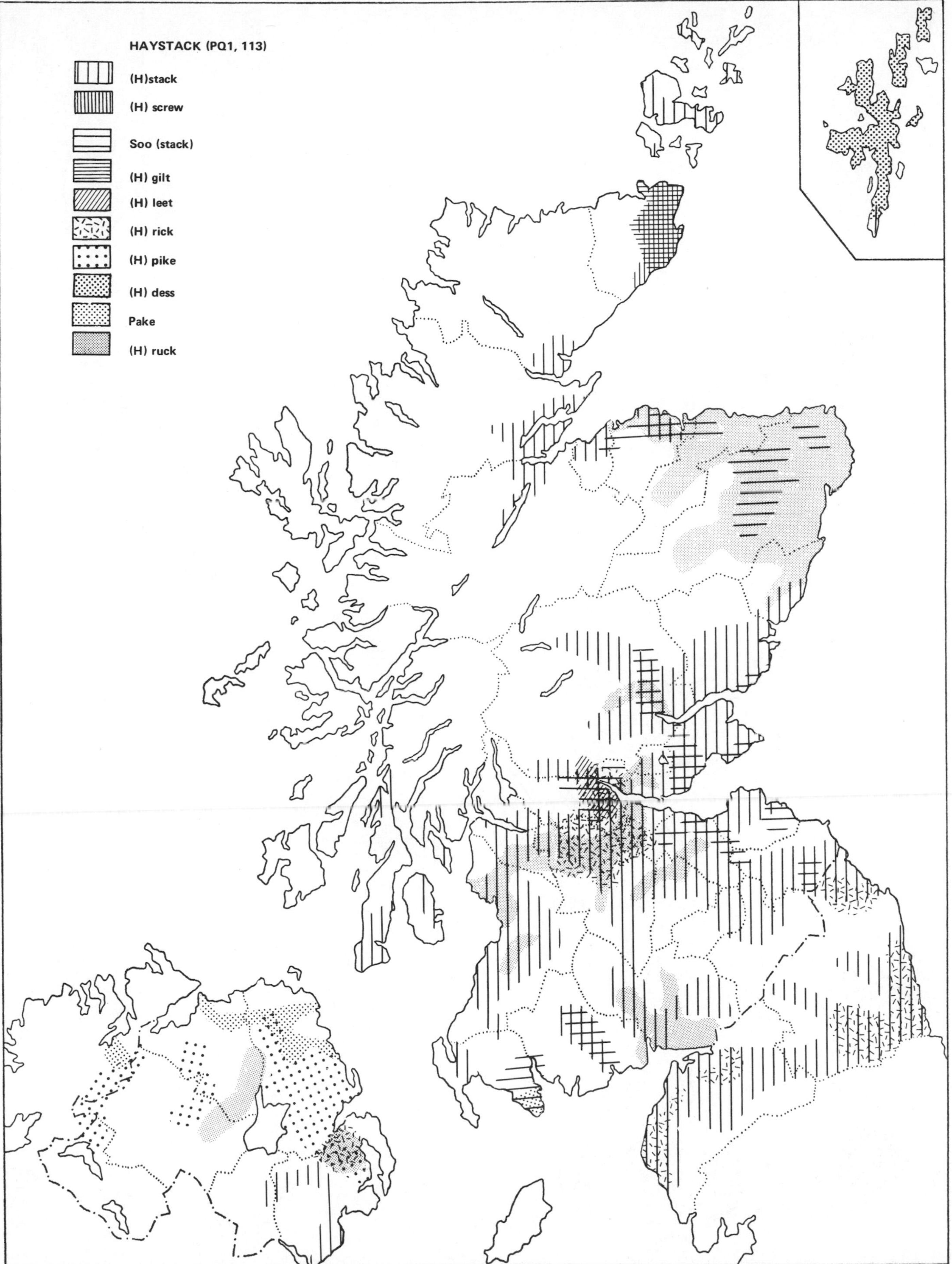
HAYSTACK (PQ1, 113)
(H)stack
(H) screw
Soo (stack)
(H) gilt
(H) leet
(H) rick
(H) pike
(H) dess
Pake
(H) ruck

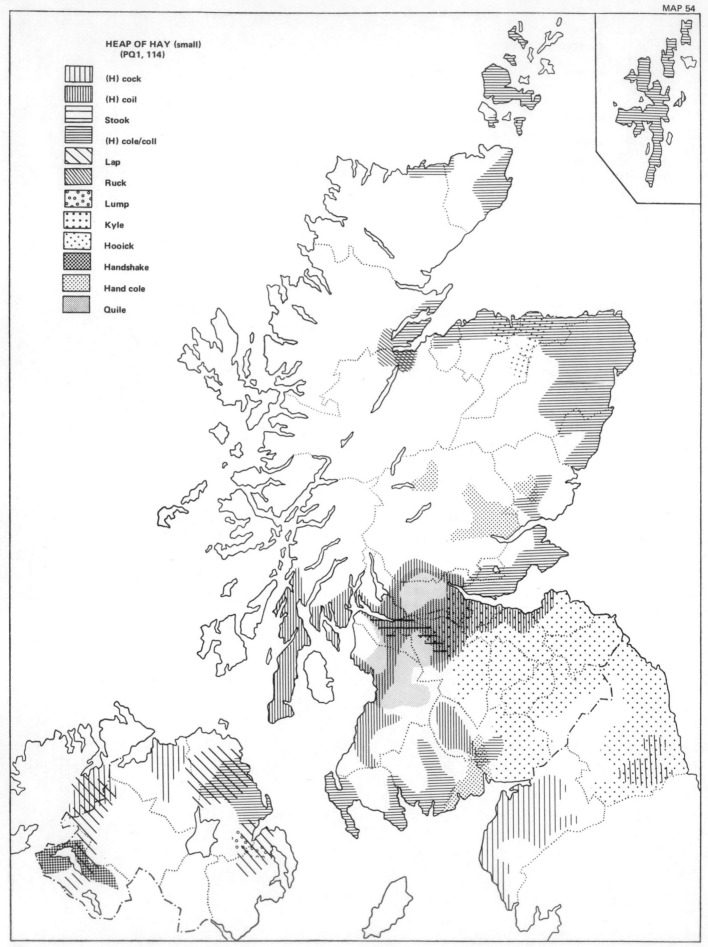

HEAP OF HAY (small)
(PQ1, 114)
(H) cock
(H) coil
Stook
(H) cole/coll
Lap
Ruck
Lump
Kyle
Hooick
Handshake
Hand cole
Quile

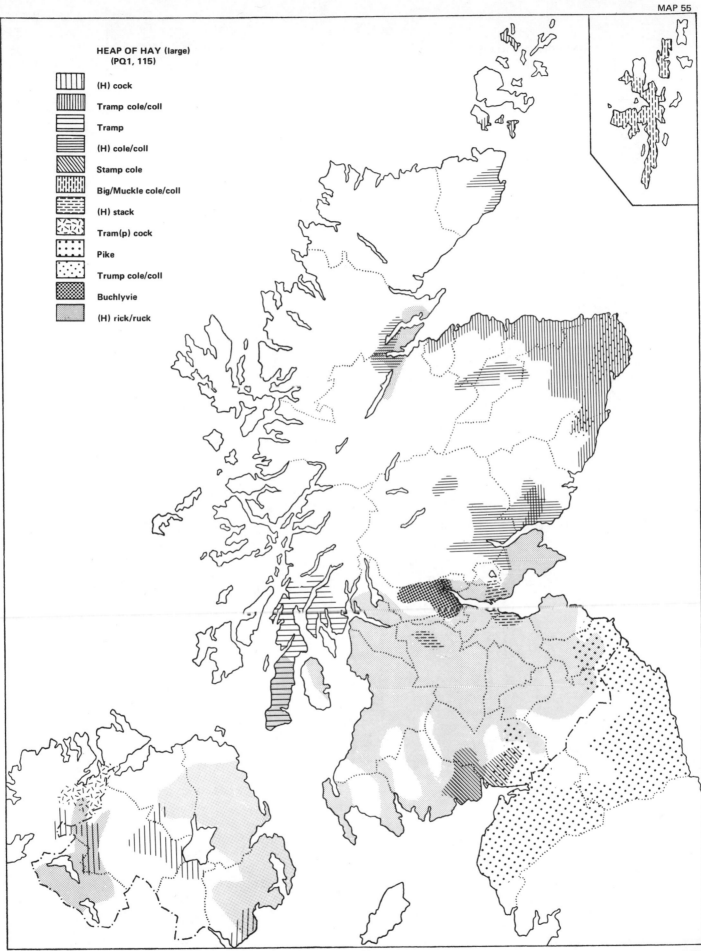

HEAP OF HAY (large)
(PQ1, 115)

(H) cock
Tramp cole/coll
Tramp
(H) cole/coll
Stamp cole
Big/Muckle cole/coll
(H) stack
Tram(p) cock
Pike
Trump cole/coll
Buchlyvie
(H) rick/ruck

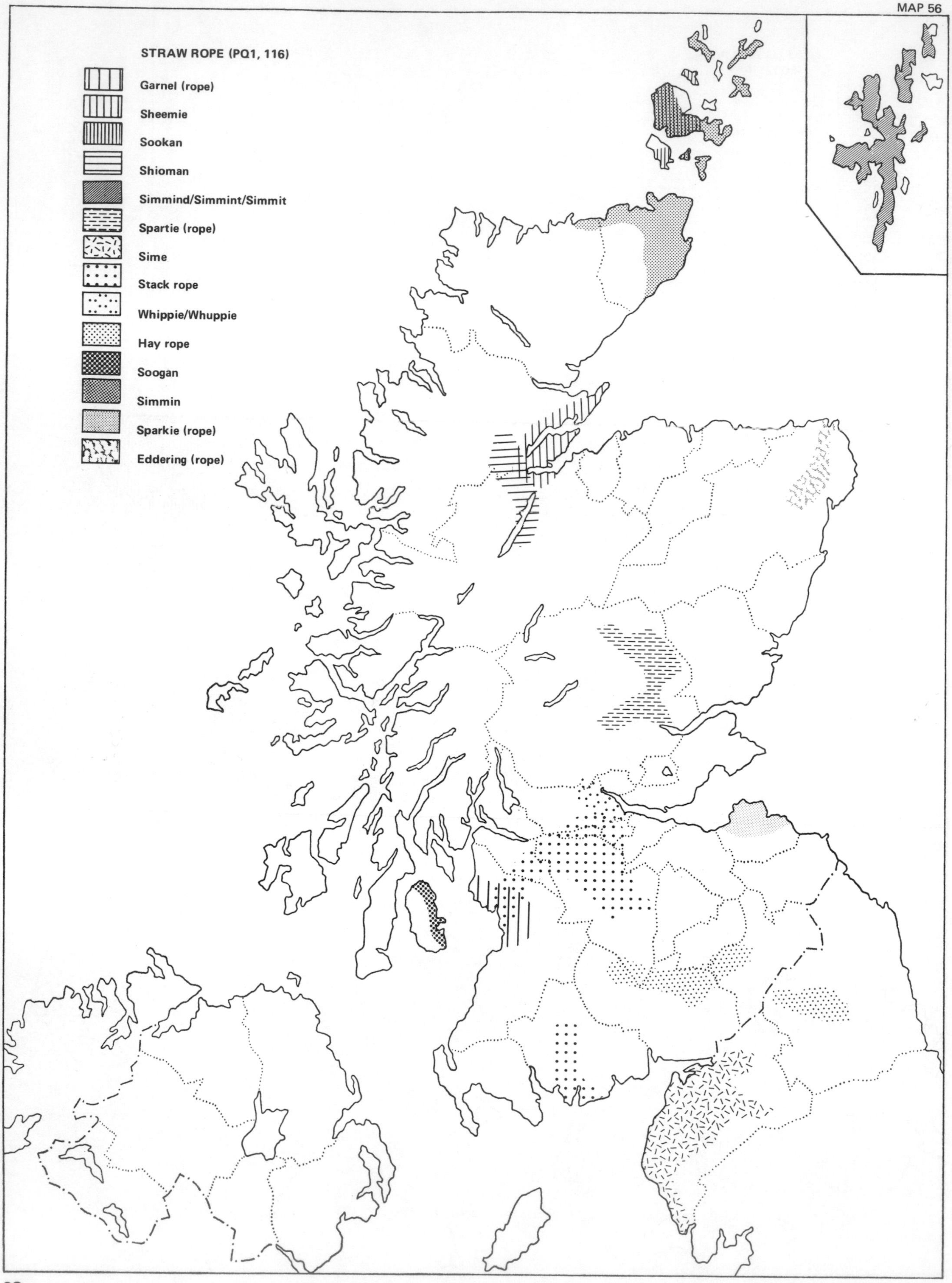

STRAW ROPE (PQ1, 116)

- Garnel (rope)
- Sheemie
- Sookan
- Shioman
- Simmind/Simmint/Simmit
- Spartie (rope)
- Sime
- Stack rope
- Whippie/Whuppie
- Hay rope
- Soogan
- Simmin
- Sparkie (rope)
- Eddering (rope)

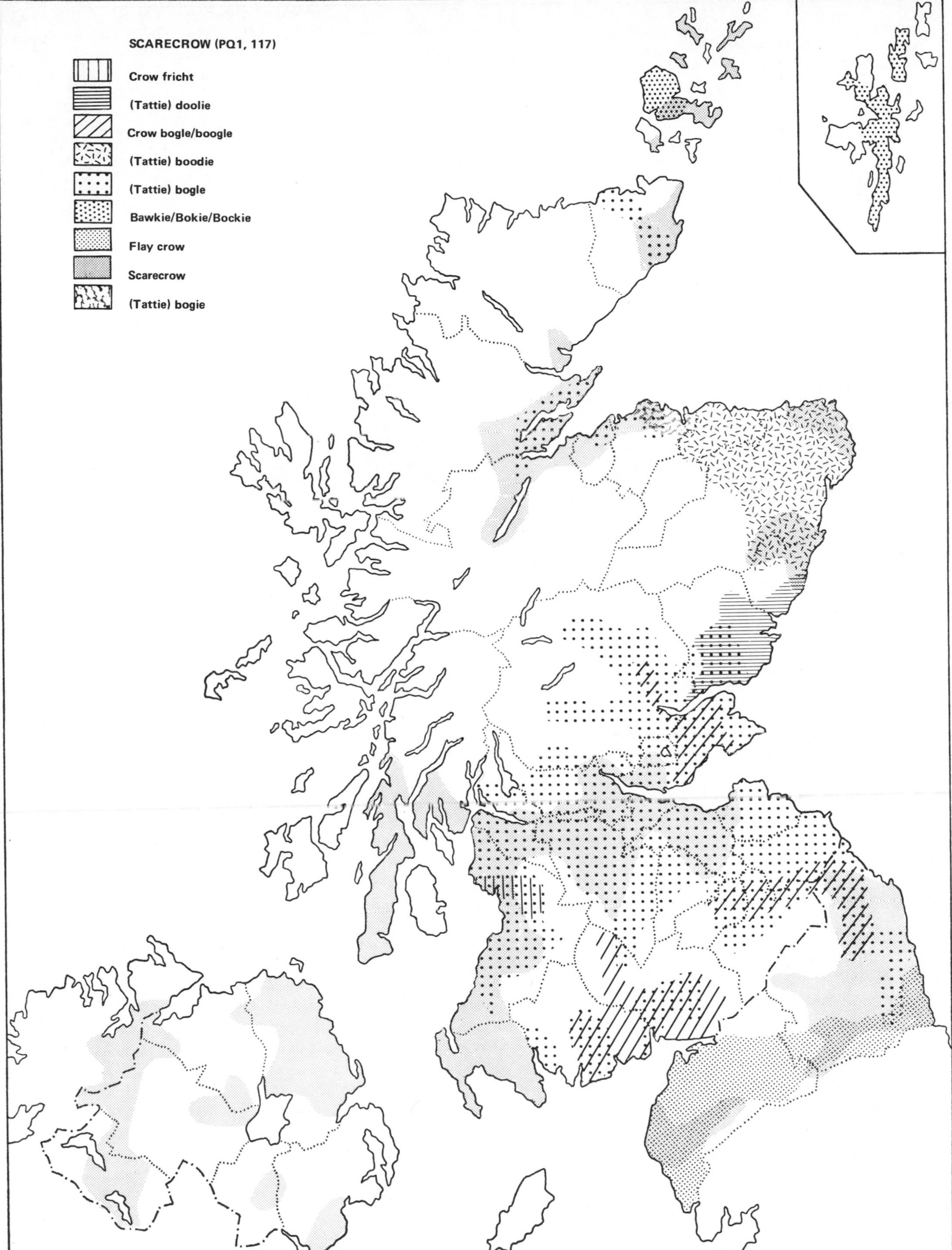
SCARECROW (PQ1, 117)
Crow fricht
(Tattie) doolie
Crow bogle/boogle
(Tattie) boodie
(Tattie) bogle
Bawkie/Bokie/Bockie
Flay crow
Scarecrow
(Tattie) bogie

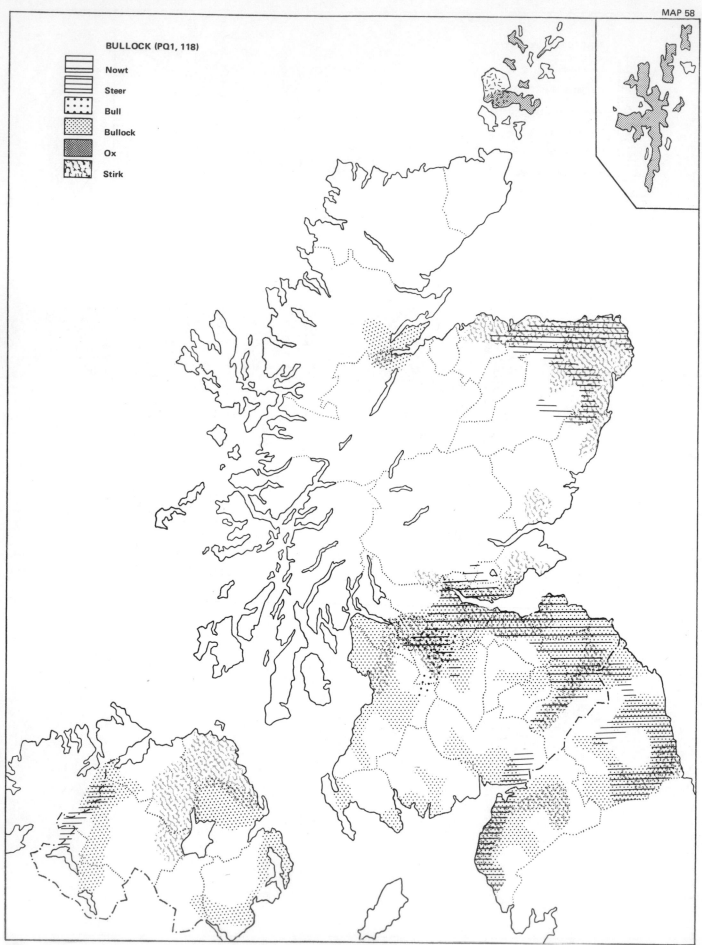

BULLOCK (PQ1, 118)

Nowt
Steer
Bull
Bullock
Ox
Stirk

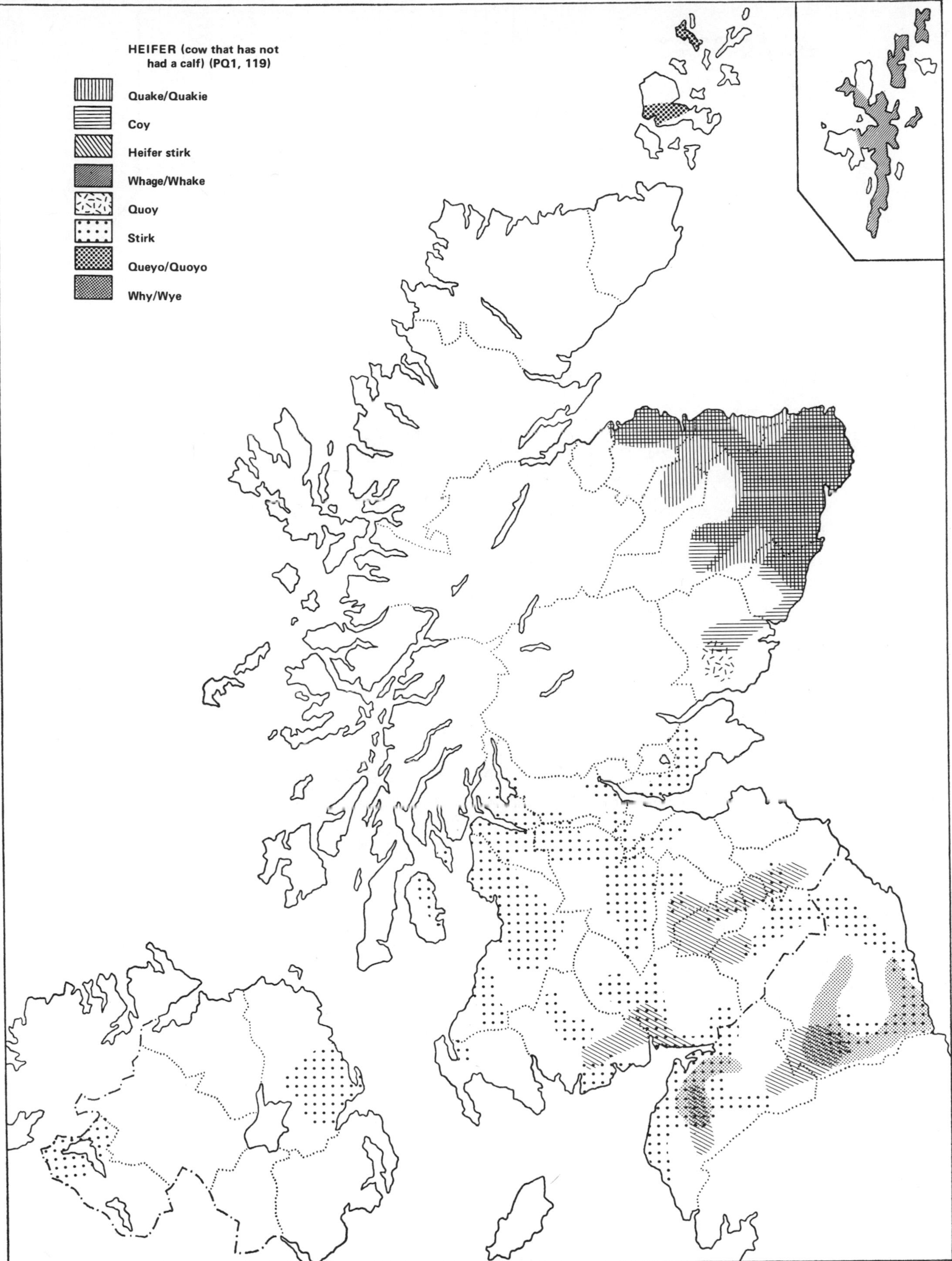
HEIFER (cow that has not had a calf) (PQ1, 119)
Quake/Quakie
Coy
Heifer stirk
Whage/Whake
Quoy
Stirk
Queyo/Quoyo
Why/Wye

HEIFER (cow that has not had a calf) (PQ1, 119)

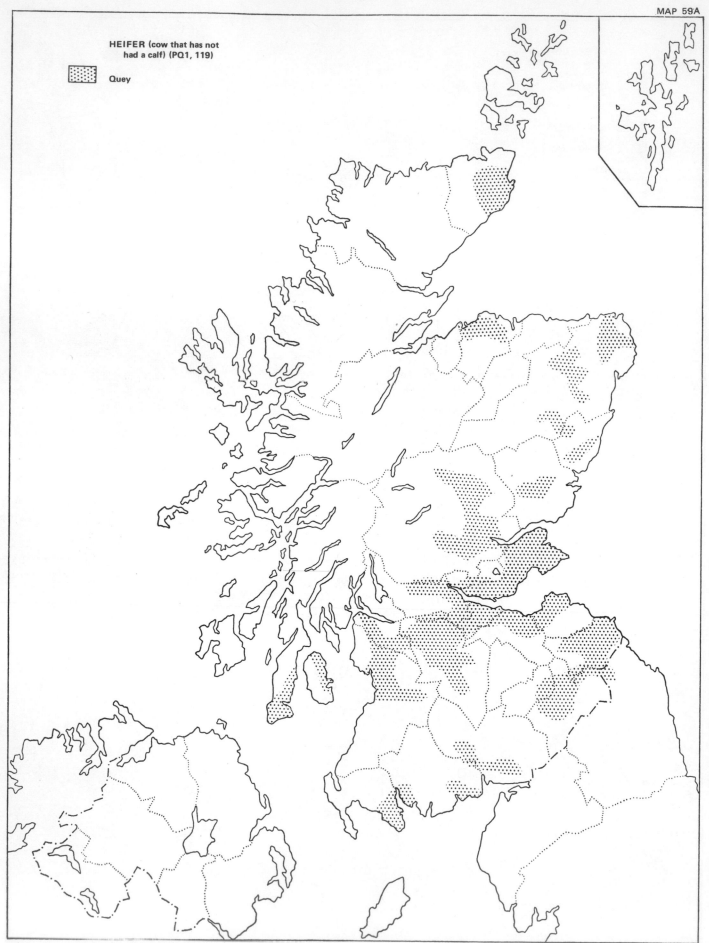

Quey

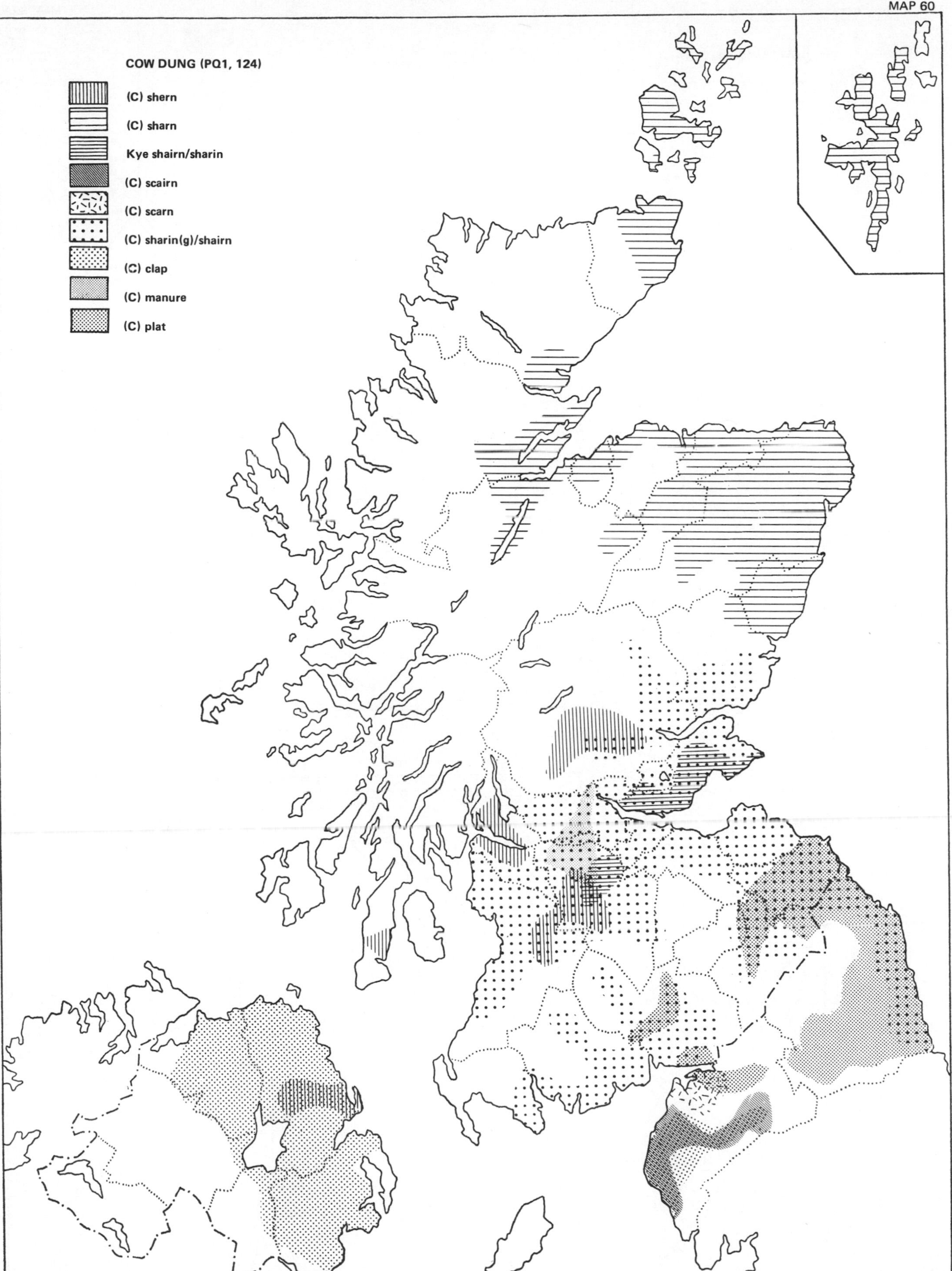
COW DUNG (PQ1, 124)
(C) shern
(C) sharn
Kye shairn/sharin
(C) scairn
(C) scarn
(C) sharin(g)/shairn
(C) clap
(C) manure
(C) plat

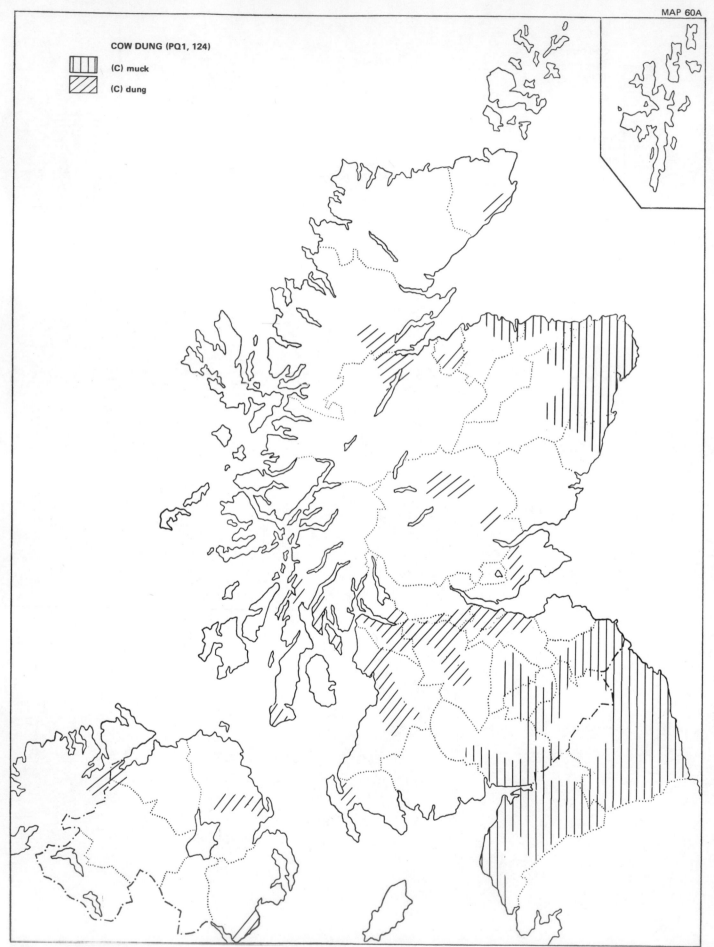

COW DUNG (PQ1, 124)
(C) muck
(C) dung

COLT (PQ1, 126)

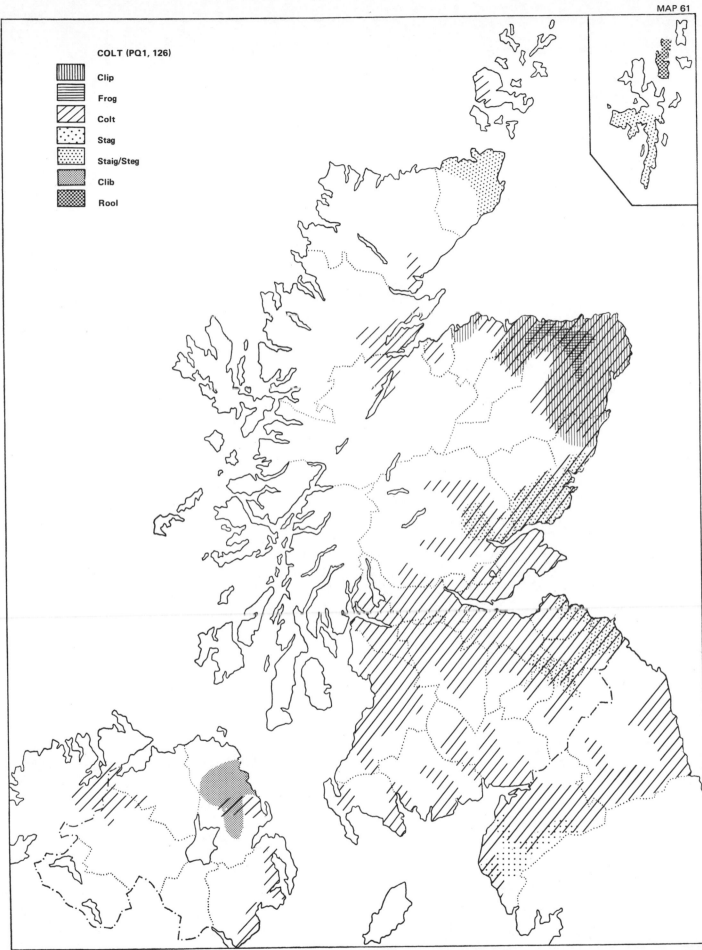

Clip
Frog
Colt
Stag
Staig/Steg
Clib
Rool

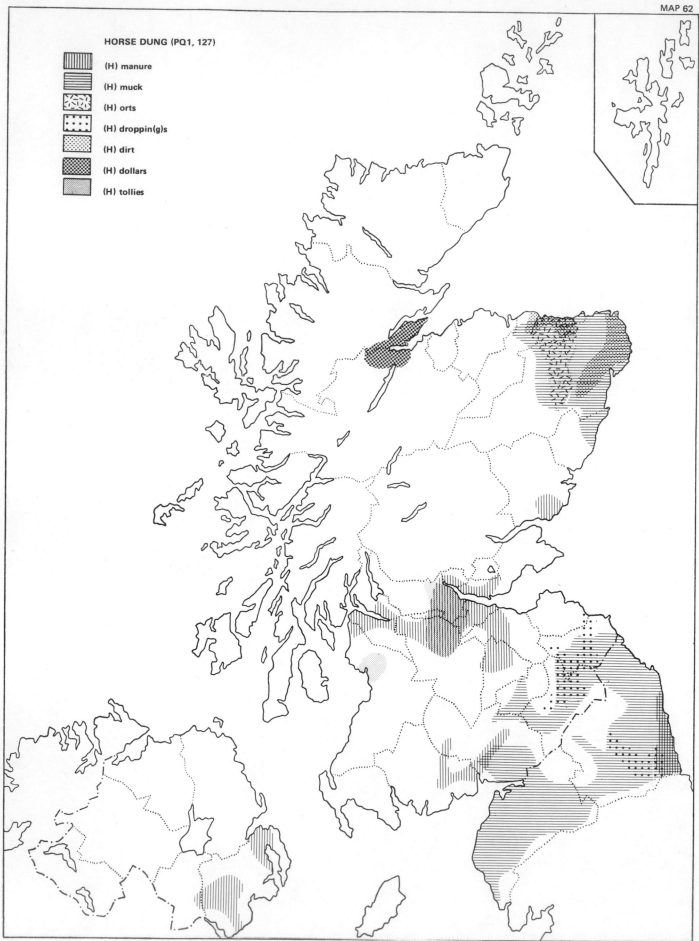

HORSE DUNG (PQ1, 127)

(H) manure

(H) muck

(H) orts

(H) droppin(g)s

(H) dirt

(H) dollars

(H) tollies

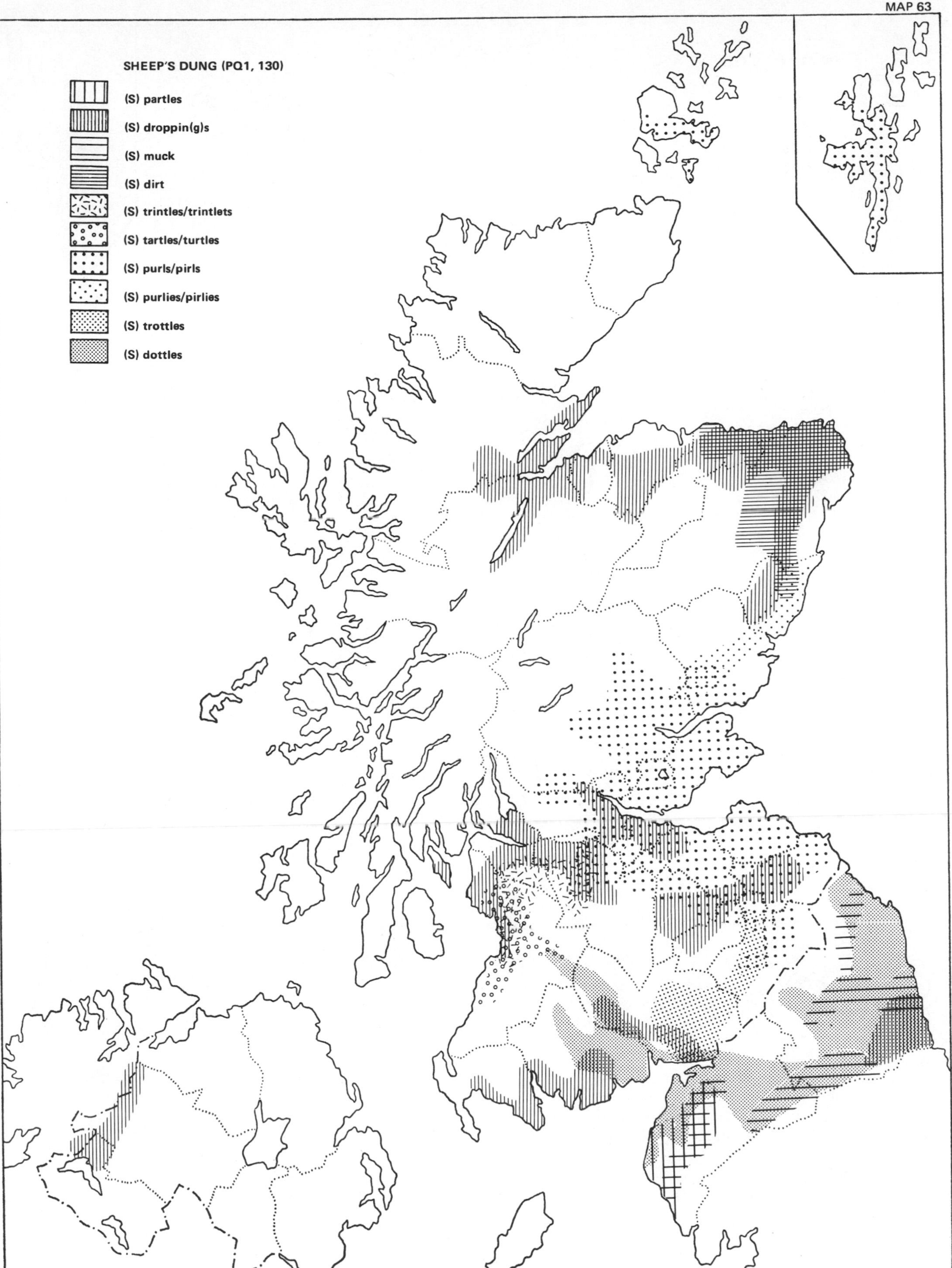
SHEEP'S DUNG (PQ1, 130)
(S) partles
(S) droppin(g)s
(S) muck
(S) dirt
(S) trintles/trintlets
(S) tartles/turtles
(S) purls/pirls
(S) purlies/pirlies
(S) trottles
(S) dottles

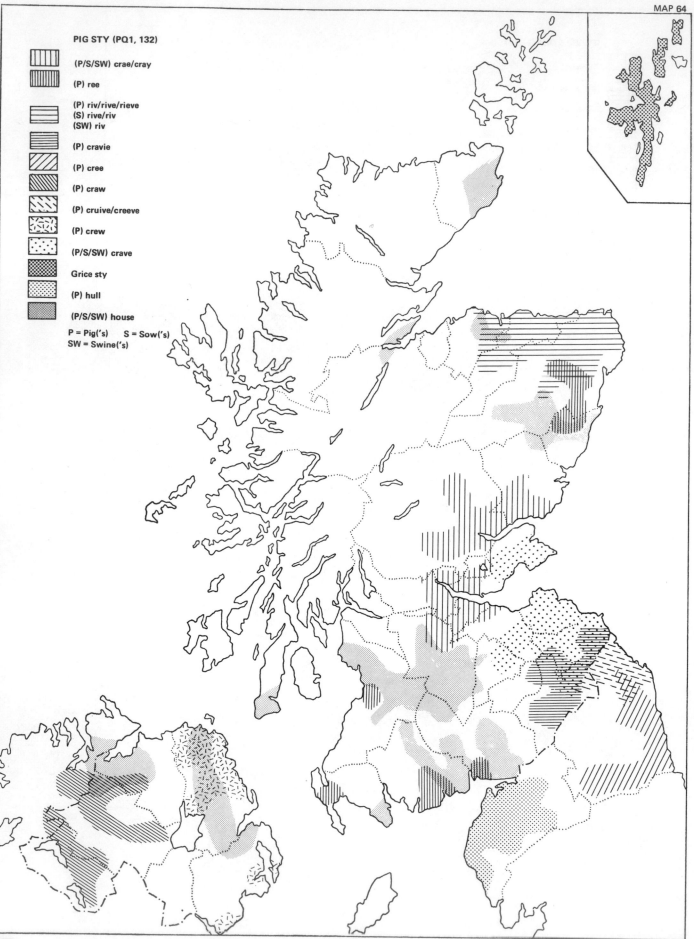

PIG STY (PQ1, 132)

(P/S/SW) crae/cray

(P) ree

(P) riv/rive/rieve
(S) rive/riv
(SW) riv

(P) cravie

(P) cree

(P) craw

(P) cruive/creeve

(P) crew

(P/S/SW) crave

Grice sty

(P) hull

(P/S/SW) house

P = Pig('s) S = Sow('s)
SW = Swine('s)

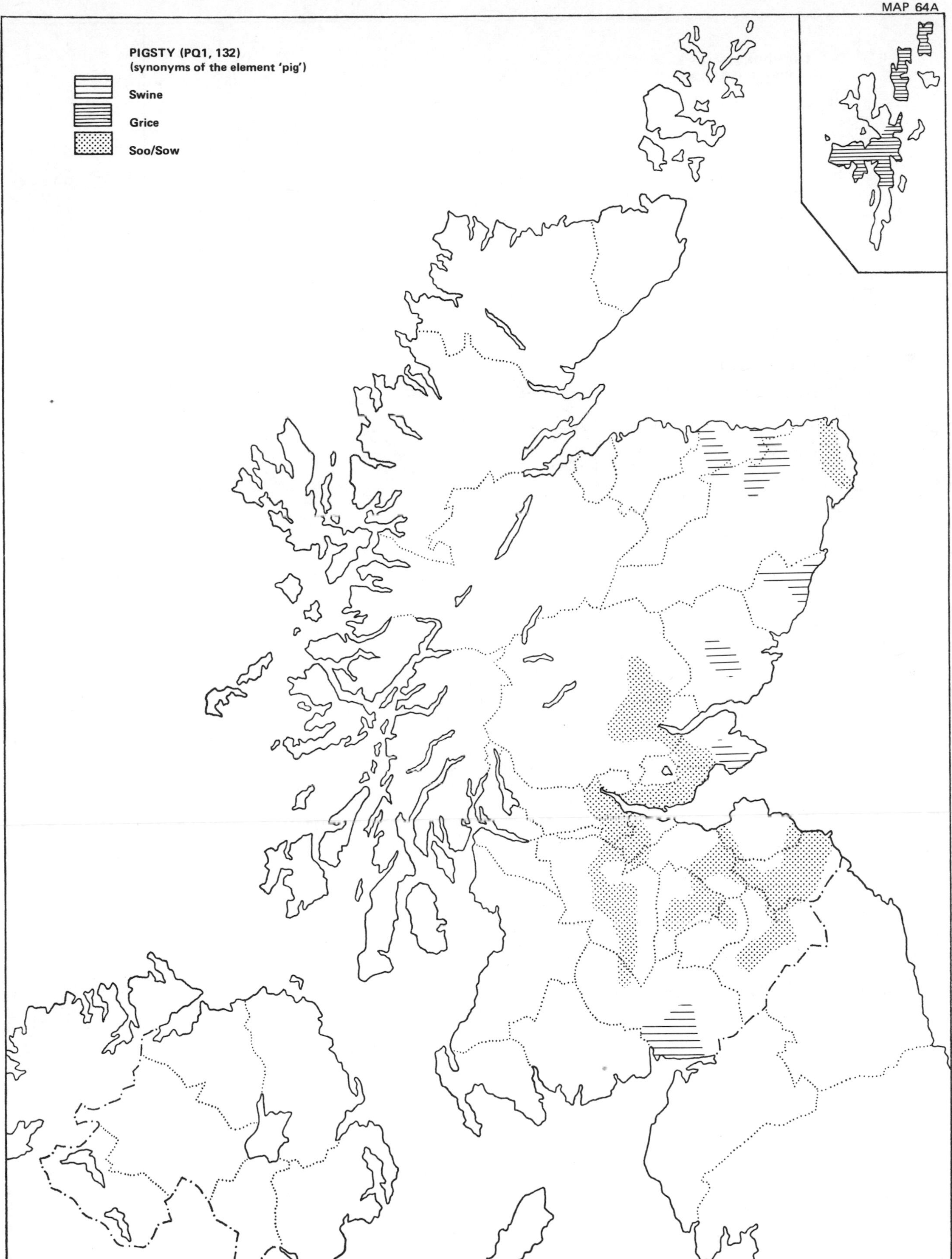
PIGSTY (PQ1, 132)
(synonyms of the element 'pig')
Swine
Grice
Soo/Sow

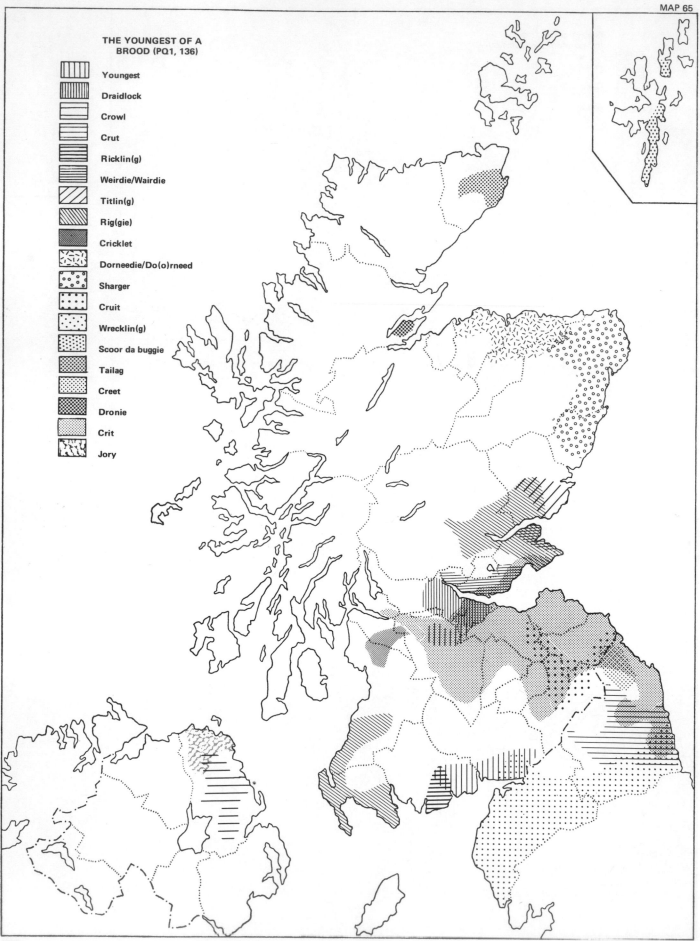

THE YOUNGEST OF A BROOD (PQ1, 136)

Youngest
Draidlock
Crowl
Crut
Ricklin(g)
Weirdie/Wairdie
Titlin(g)
Rig(gie)
Cricklet
Dorneedie/Do(o)rneed
Sharger
Cruit
Wrecklin(g)
Scoor da buggie
Tailag
Creet
Dronie
Crit
Jory

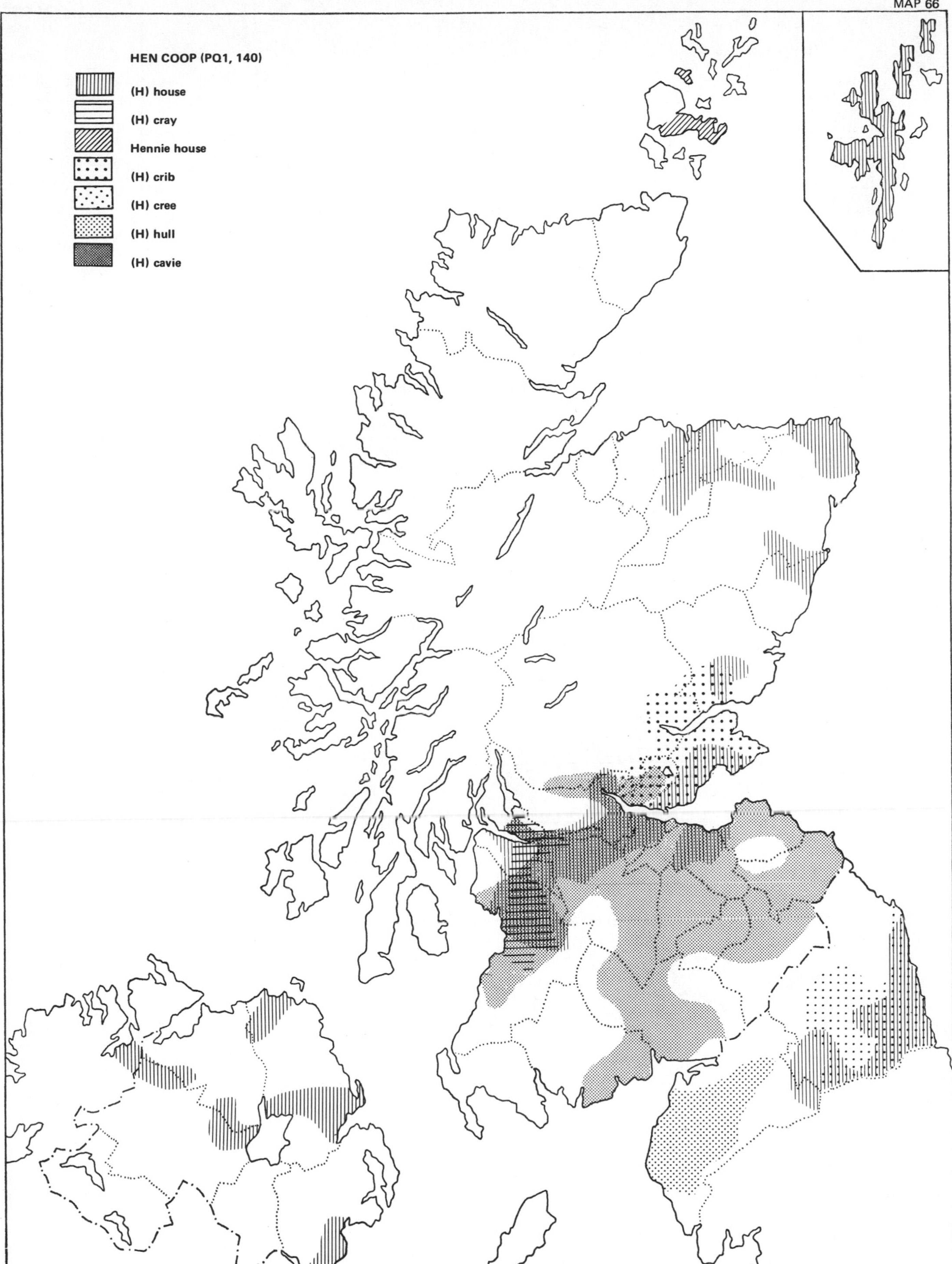
HEN COOP (PQ1, 140)
(H) house
(H) cray
Hennie house
(H) crib
(H) cree
(H) hull
(H) cavie

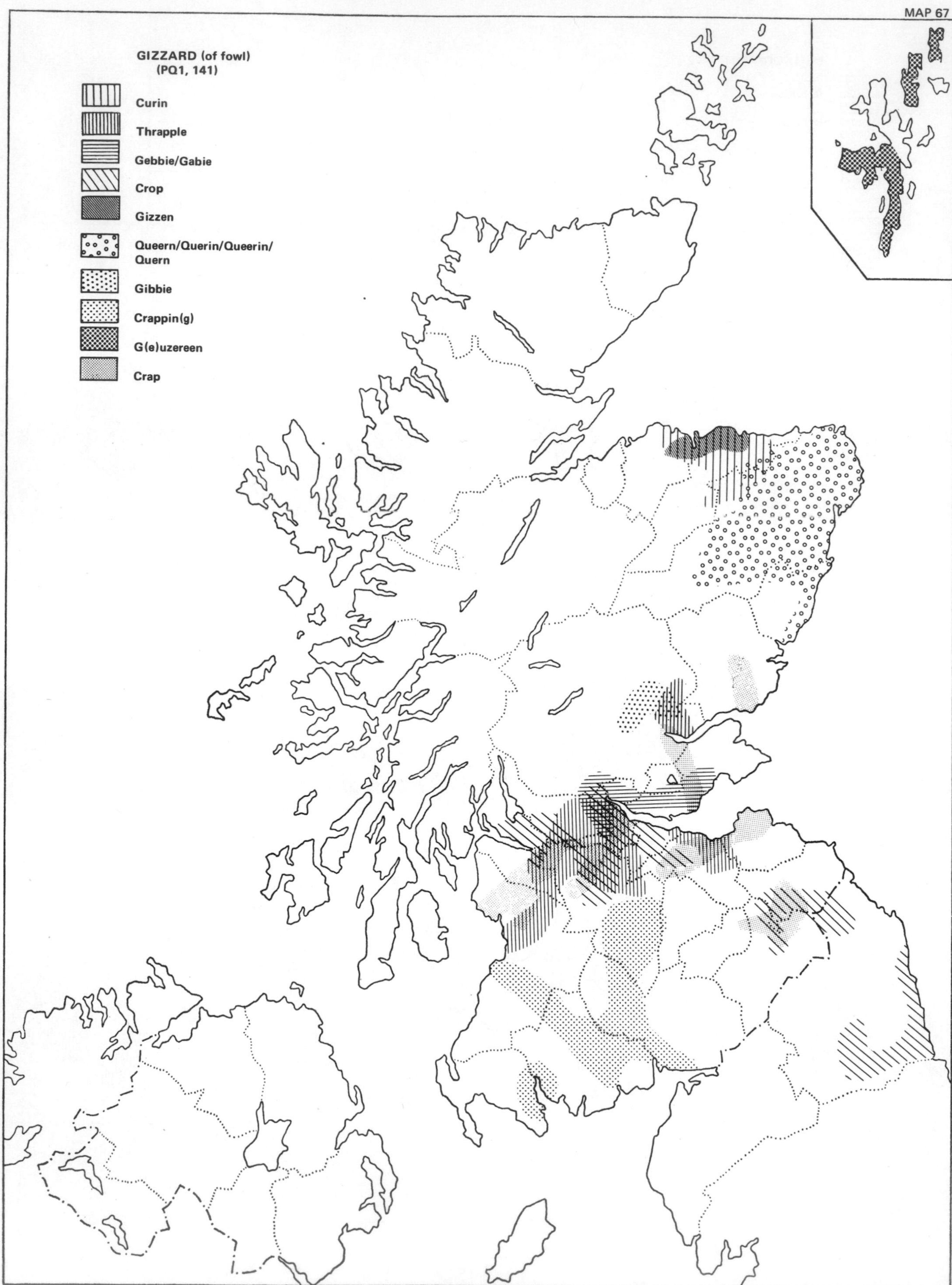
GIZZARD (of fowl)
(PQ1, 141)
Curin
Thrapple
Gebbie/Gabie
Crop
Gizzen
Queern/Querin/Queerin/Quern
Gibbie
Crappin(g)
G(e)uzereen
Crap

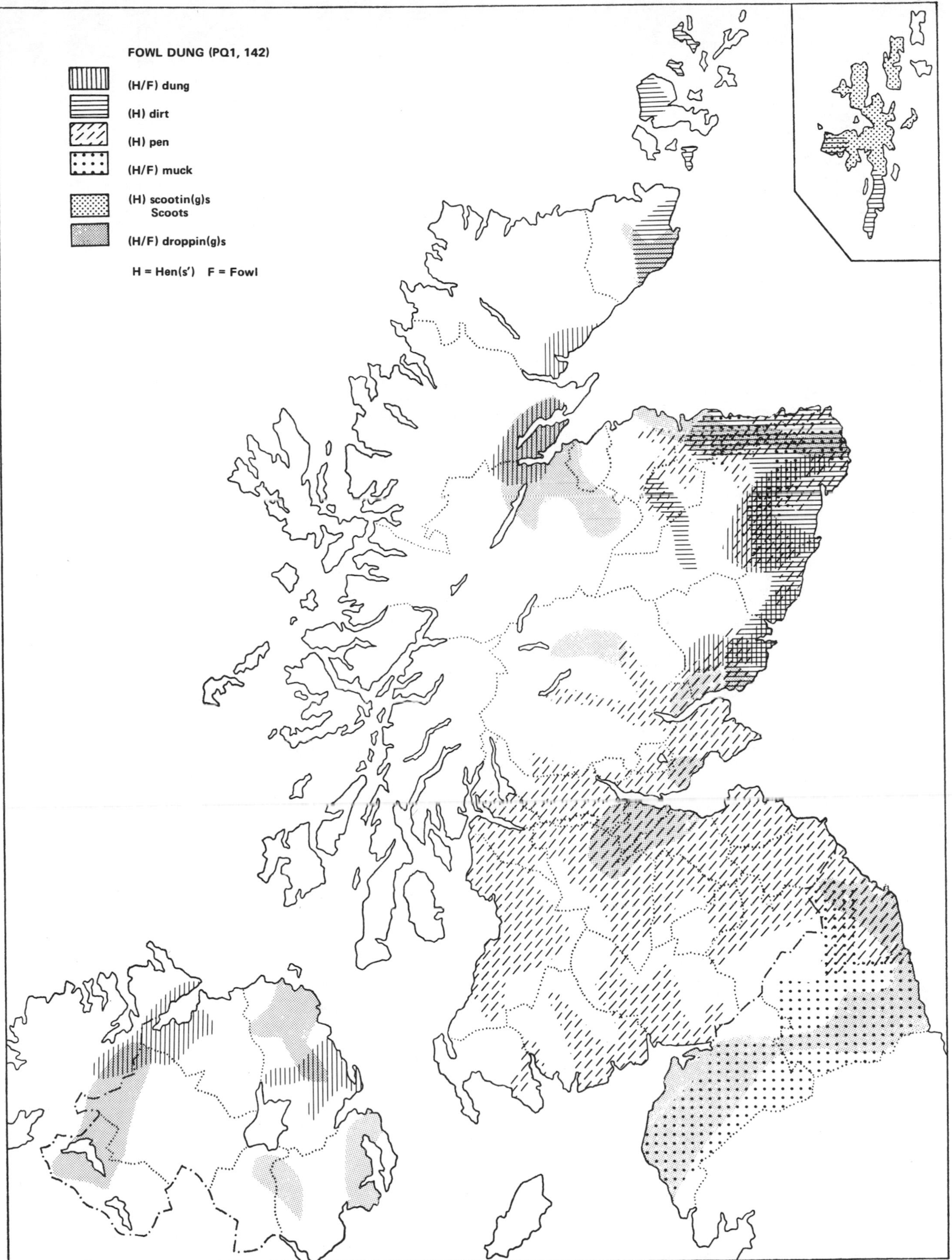
FOWL DUNG (PQ1, 142)
(H/F) dung
(H) dirt
(H) pen
(H/F) muck
(H) scootin(g)s
Scoots
(H/F) droppin(g)s
H = Hen(s') F = Fowl

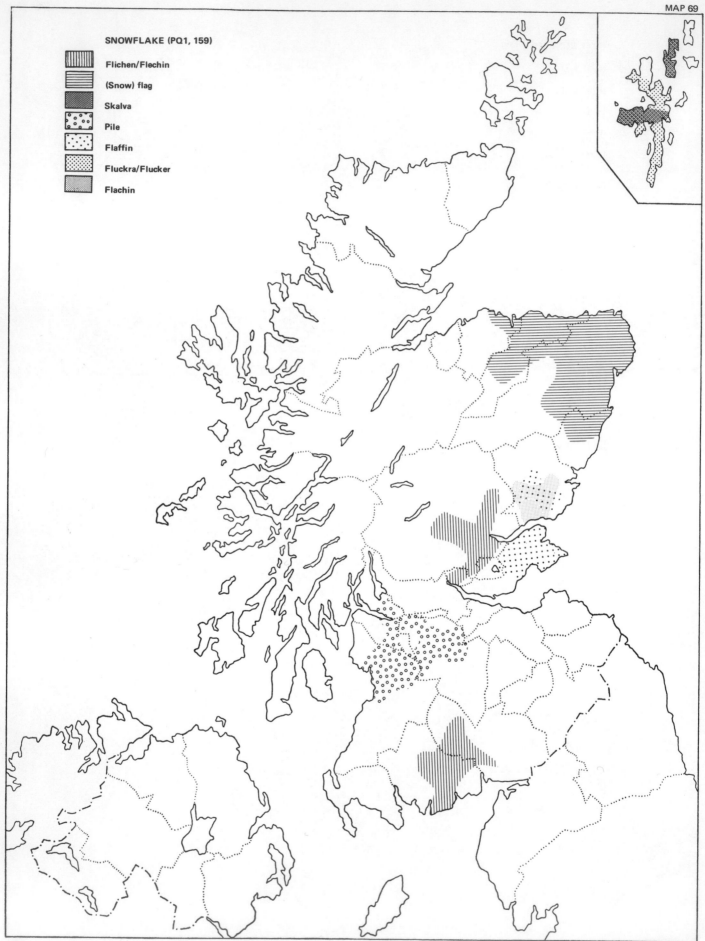

SNOWFLAKE (PQ1, 159)

Flichen/Flechin

(Snow) flag

Skalva

Pile

Flaffin

Fluckra/Flucker

Flachin

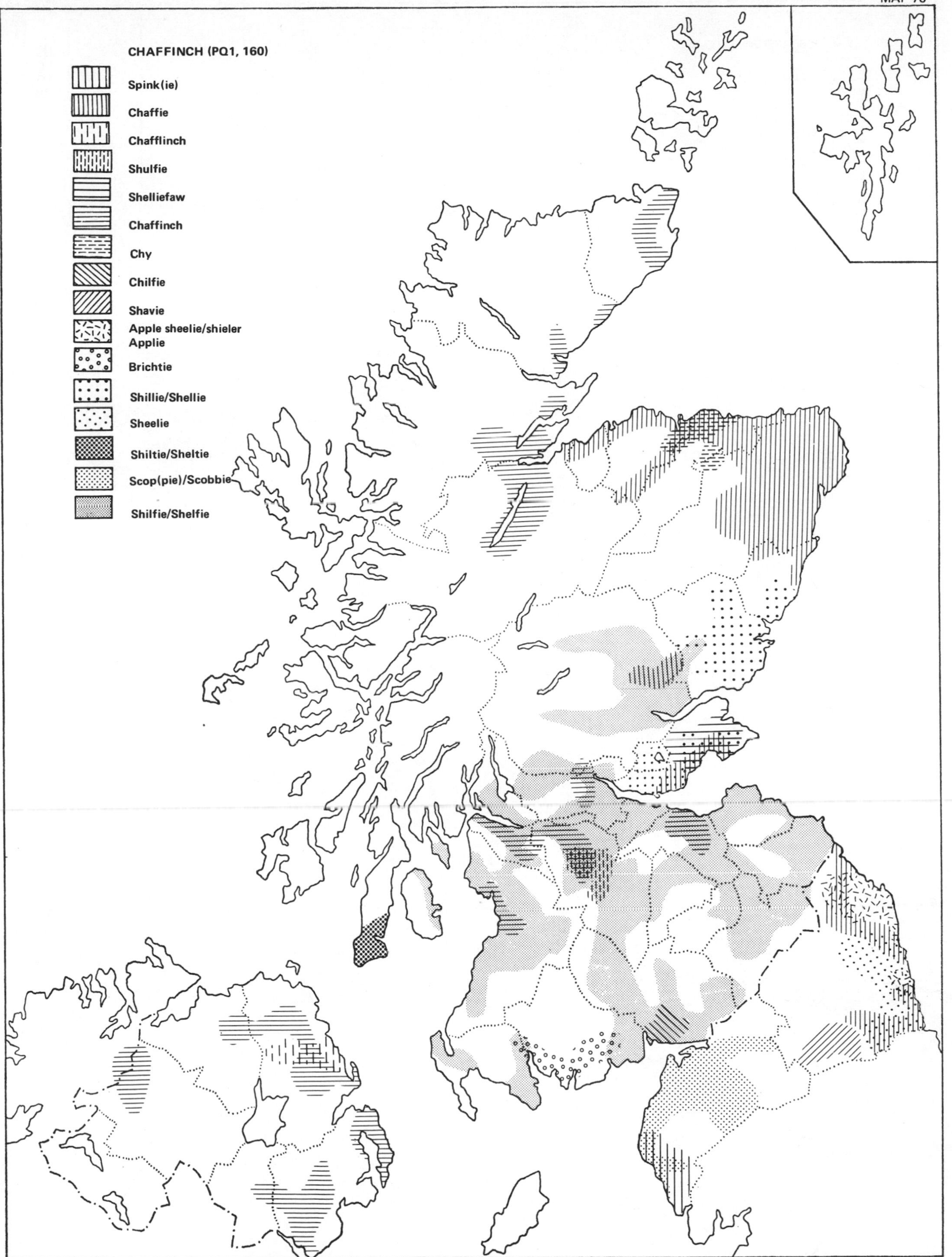
CHAFFINCH (PQ1, 160)
Spink(ie)
Chaffie
Chafflinch
Shulfie
Shelliefaw
Chaffinch
Chy
Chilfie
Shavie
Apple sheelie/shieler
Applie
Brichtie
Shillie/Shellie
Sheelie
Shiltie/Sheltie
Scop(pie)/Scobbie
Shilfie/Shelfie

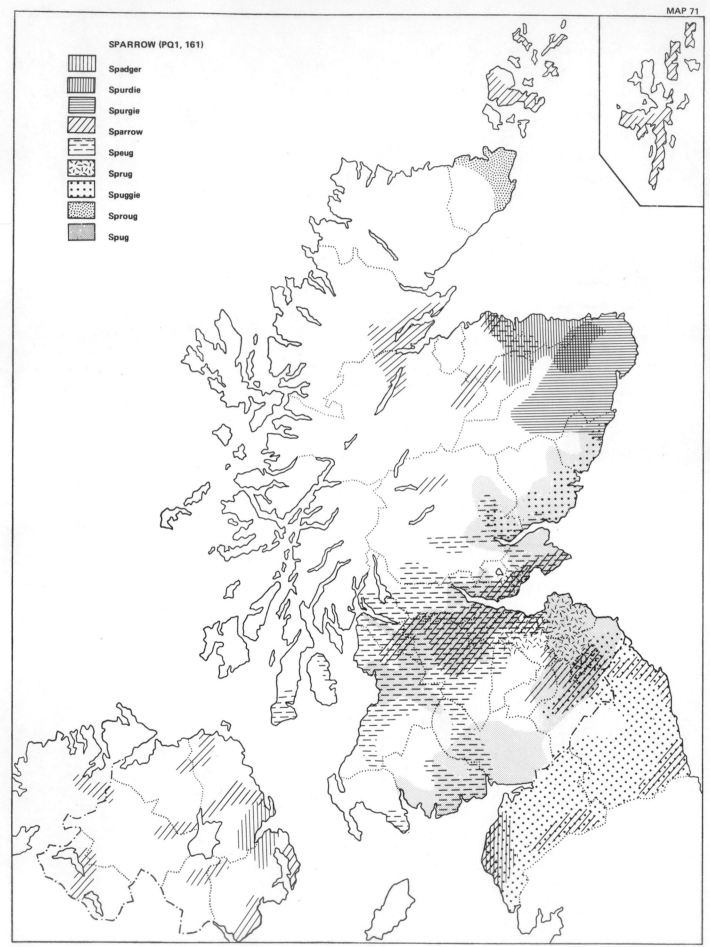

SPARROW (PQ1, 161)

Spadger
Spurdie
Spurgie
Sparrow
Speug
Sprug
Spuggie
Sproug
Spug

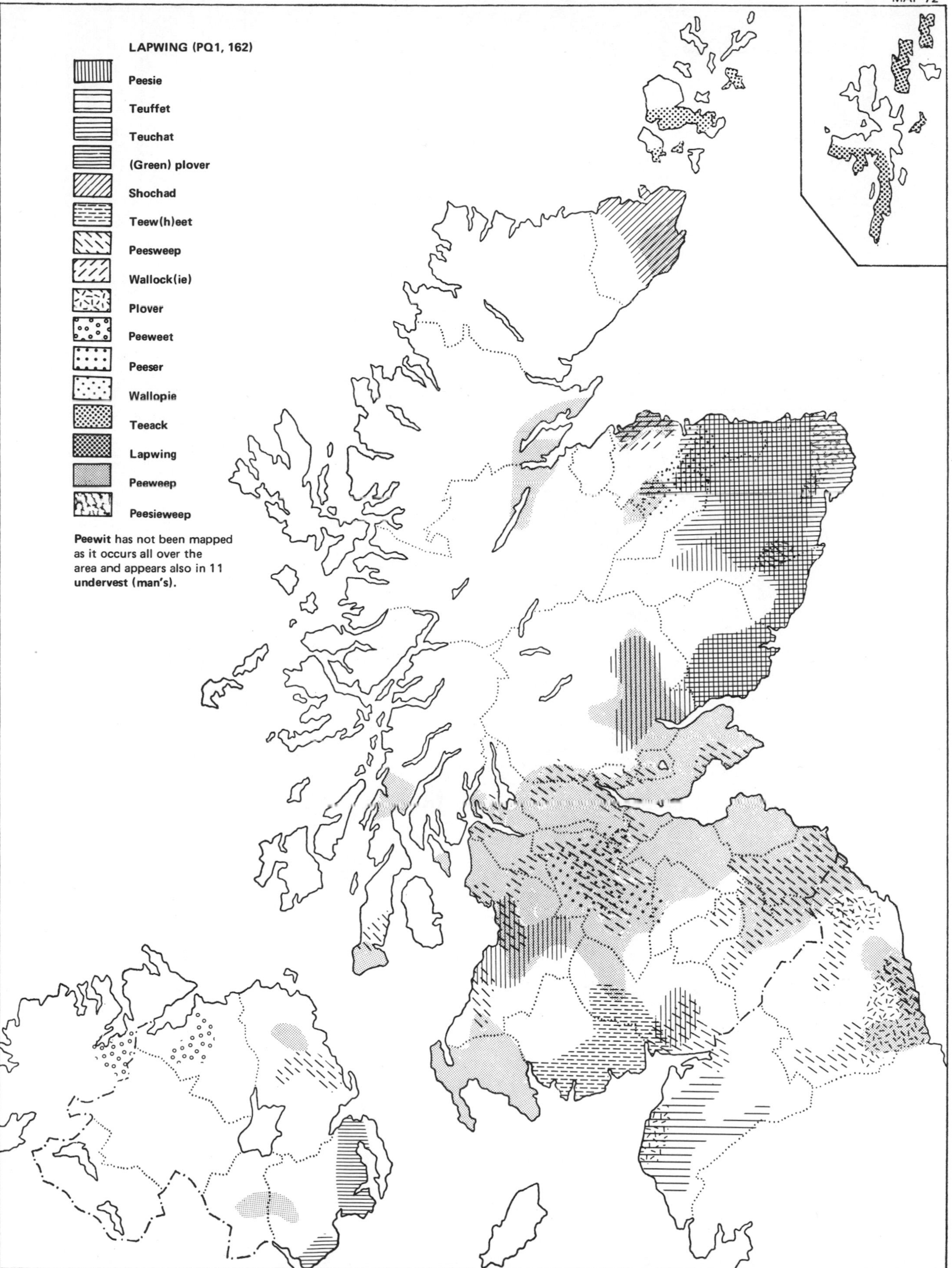

LAPWING (PQ1, 162)
Peesie
Teuffet
Teuchat
(Green) plover
Shochad
Teew(h)eet
Peesweep
Wallock(ie)
Plover
Peeweet
Peeser
Wallopie
Teeack
Lapwing
Peeweep
Peesieweep
Peewit has not been mapped as it occurs all over the area and appears also in 11 undervest (man's).

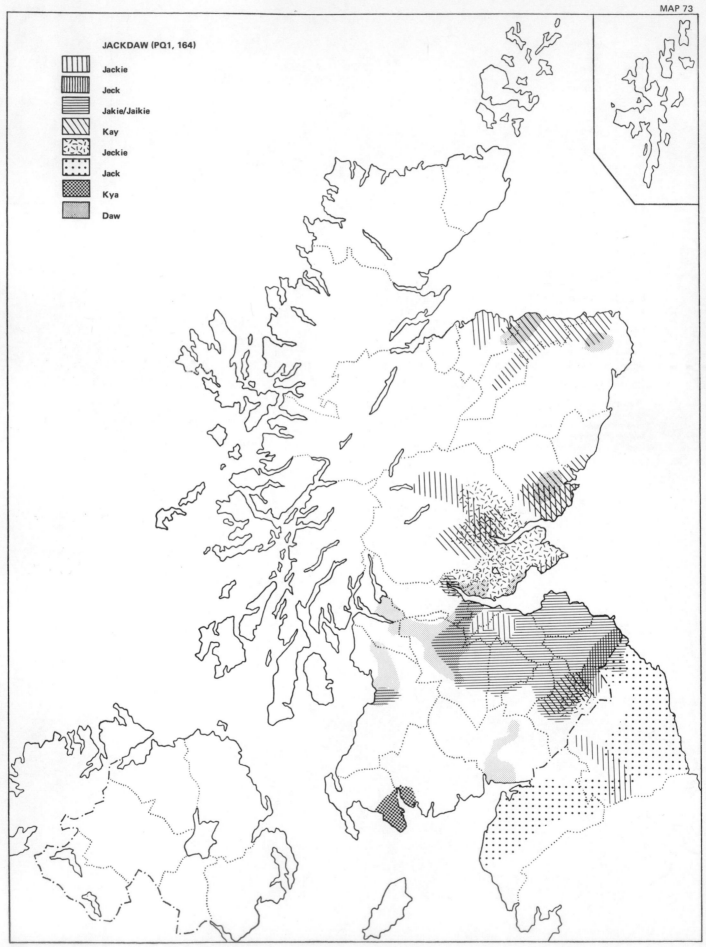

JACKDAW (PQ1, 164)

Jackie
Jeck
Jakie/Jaikie
Kay
Jeckie
Jack
Kya
Daw

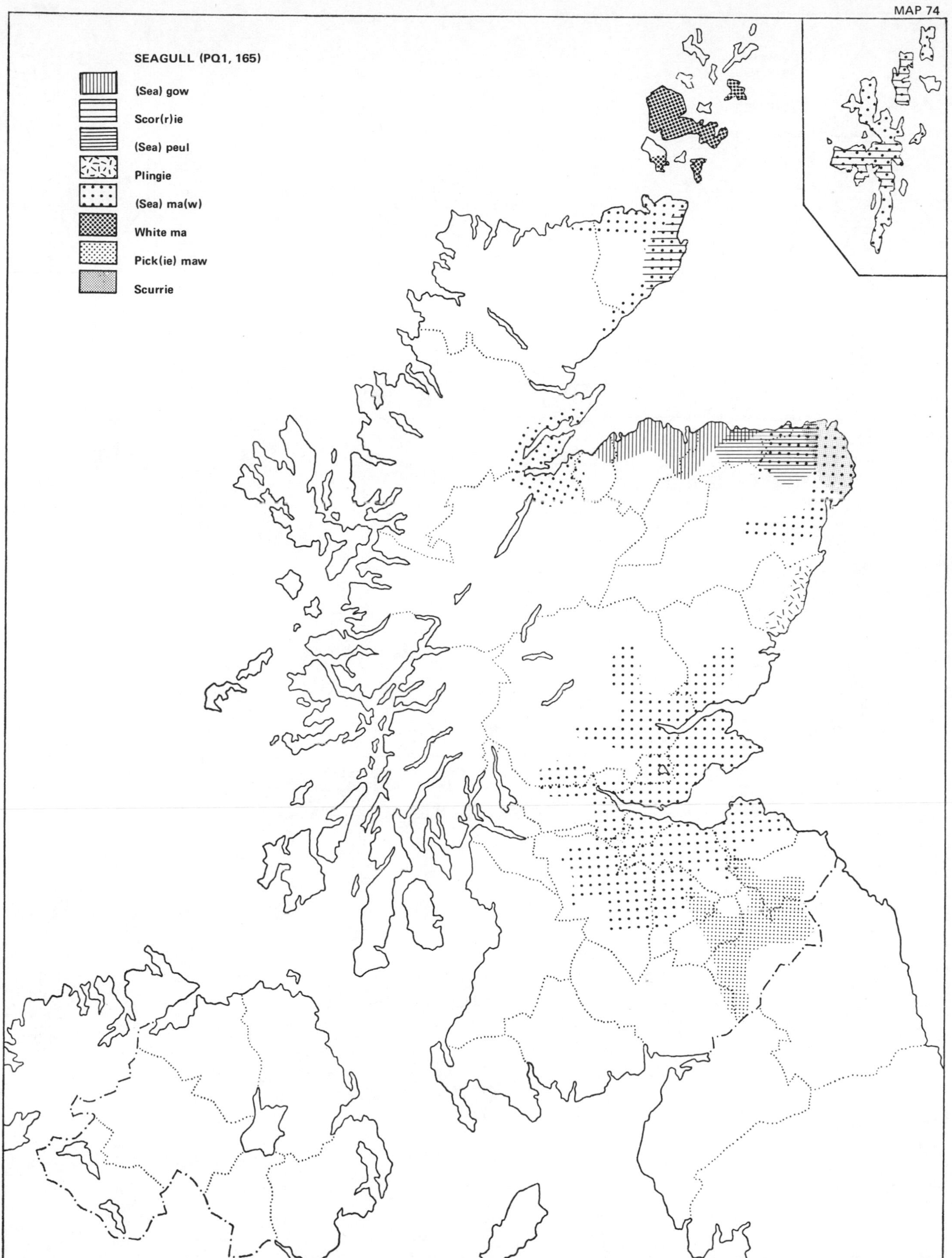
SEAGULL (PQ1, 165)
(Sea) gow
Scor(r)ie
(Sea) peul
Plingie
(Sea) ma(w)
White ma
Pick(ie) maw
Scurrie

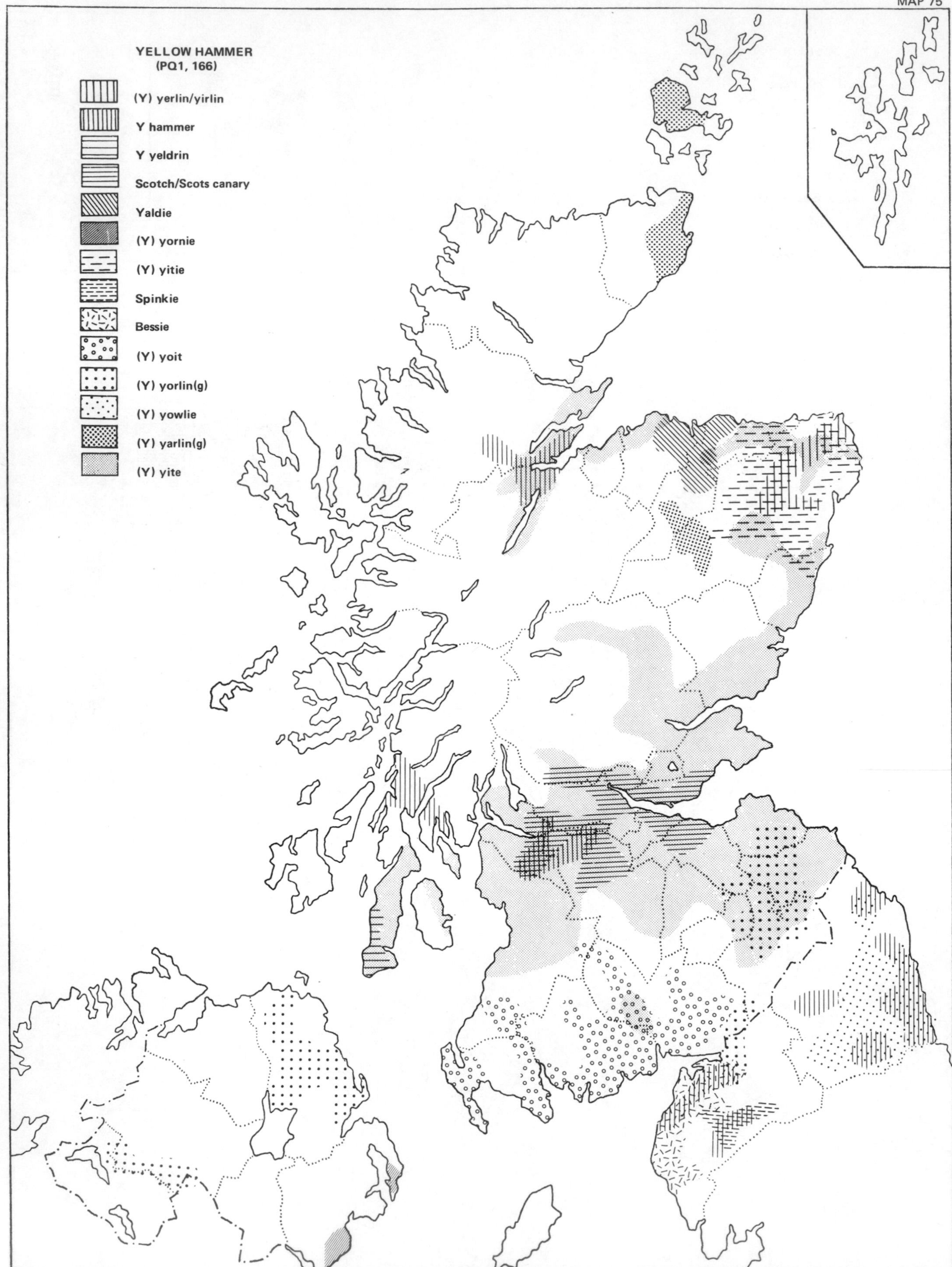
YELLOW HAMMER
(PQ1, 166)
(Y) yerlin/yirlin
Y hammer
Y yeldrin
Scotch/Scots canary
Yaldie
(Y) yornie
(Y) yitie
Spinkie
Bessie
(Y) yoit
(Y) yorlin(g)
(Y) yowlie
(Y) yarlin(g)
(Y) yite

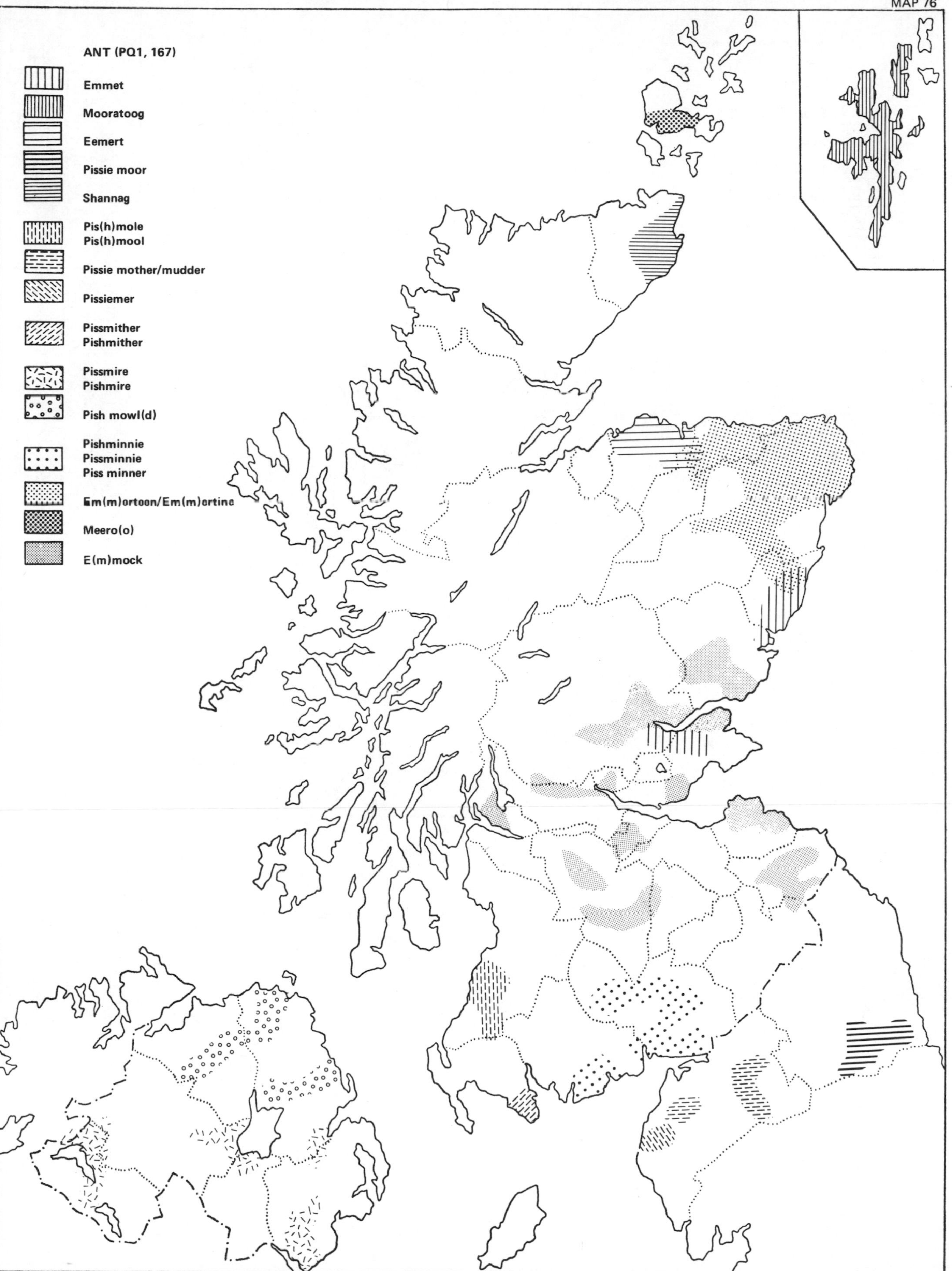

ANT (PQ1, 167)
Emmet
Mooratoog
Eemert
Pissie moor
Shannag
Pis(h)mole
Pis(h)mool
Pissie mother/mudder
Pissiemer
Pissmither
Pishmither
Pissmire
Pishmire
Pish mowl(d)
Pishminnie
Pissminnie
Piss minner
Em(m)ortoon/Em(m)ortino
Meero(o)
E(m)mock

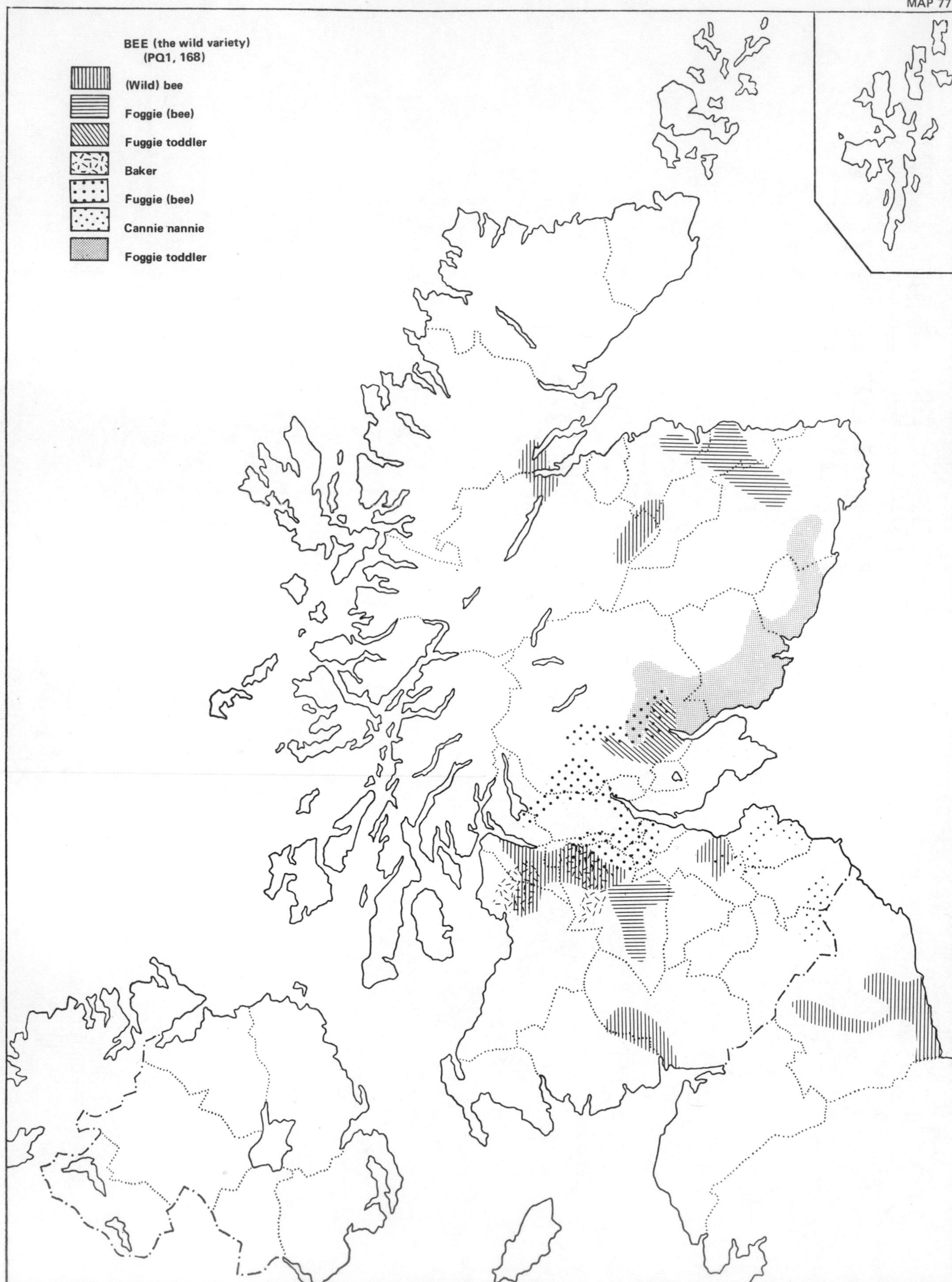

BEE (the wild variety)
(PQ1, 168)
(Wild) bee
Foggie (bee)
Fuggie toddler
Baker
Fuggie (bee)
Cannie nannie
Foggie toddler

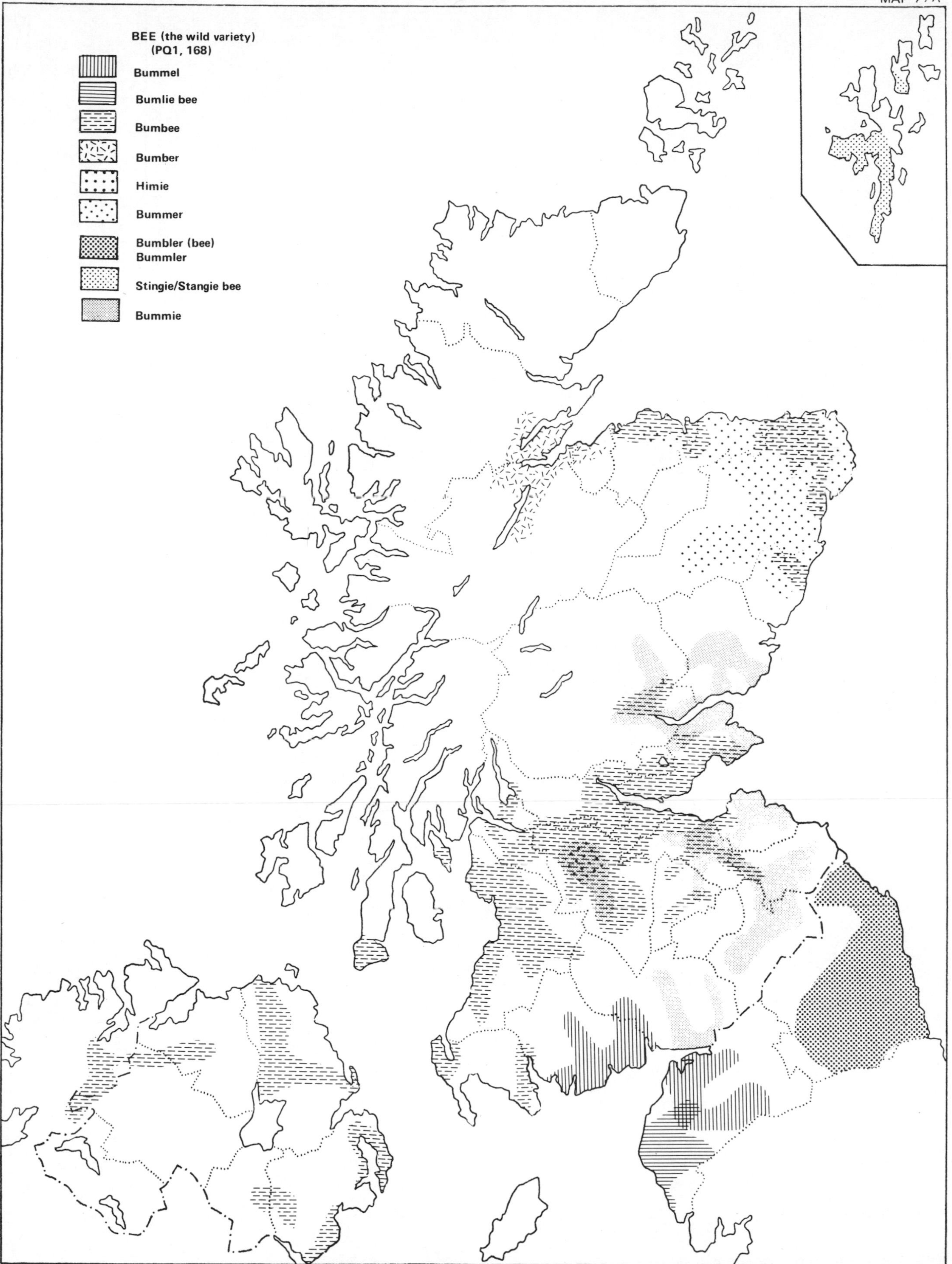
BEE (the wild variety)
(PQ1, 168)
Bummel
Bumlie bee
Bumbee
Bumber
Himie
Bummer
Bumbler (bee)
Bummler
Stingie/Stangie bee
Bummie

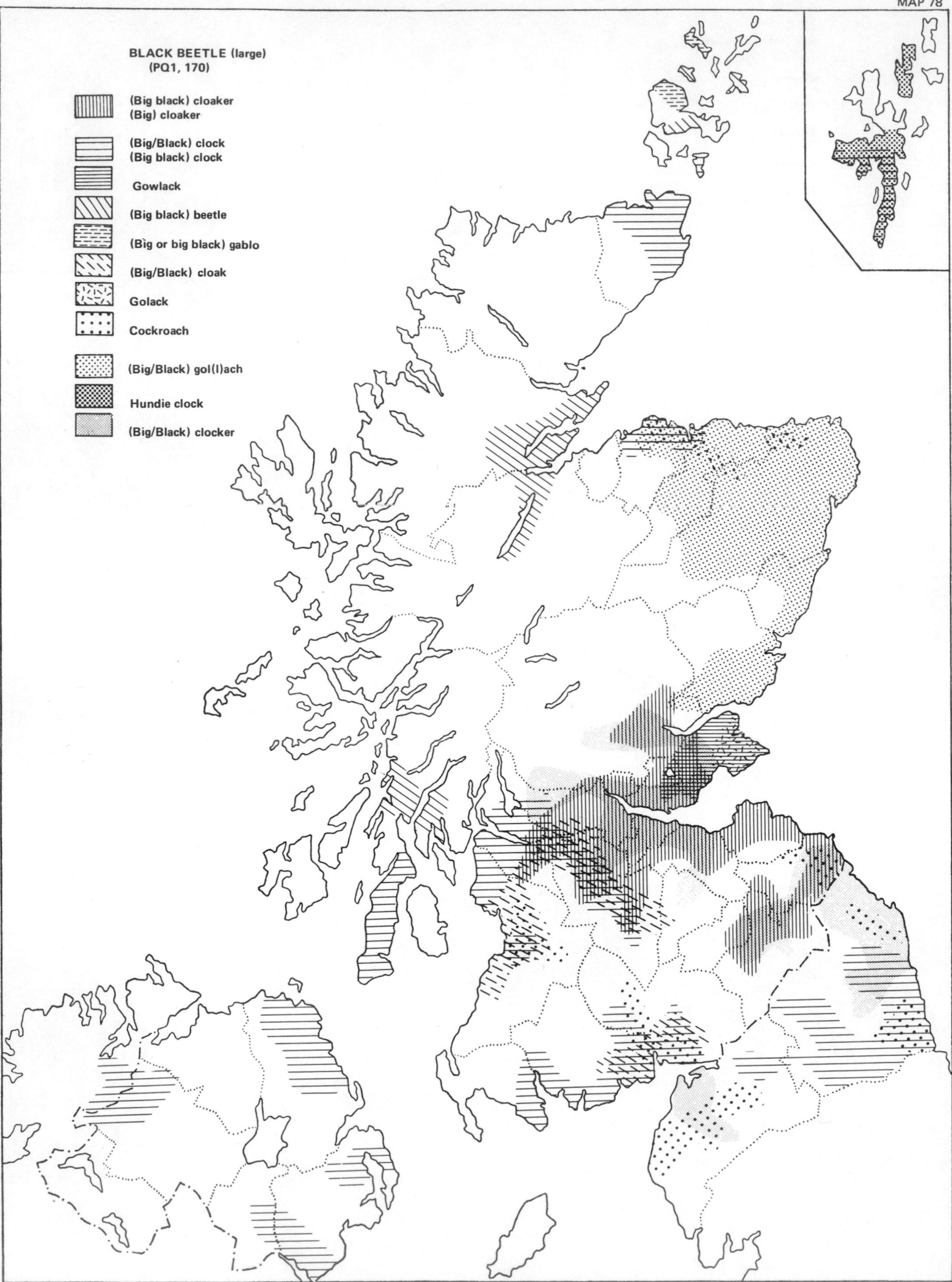
BLACK BEETLE (large)
(PQ1, 170)
(Big black) cloaker
(Big) cloaker
(Big/Black) clock
(Big black) clock
Gowlack
(Big black) beetle
(Big or big black) gablo
(Big/Black) cloak
Golack
Cockroach
(Big/Black) gol(l)ach
Hundie clock
(Big/Black) clocker

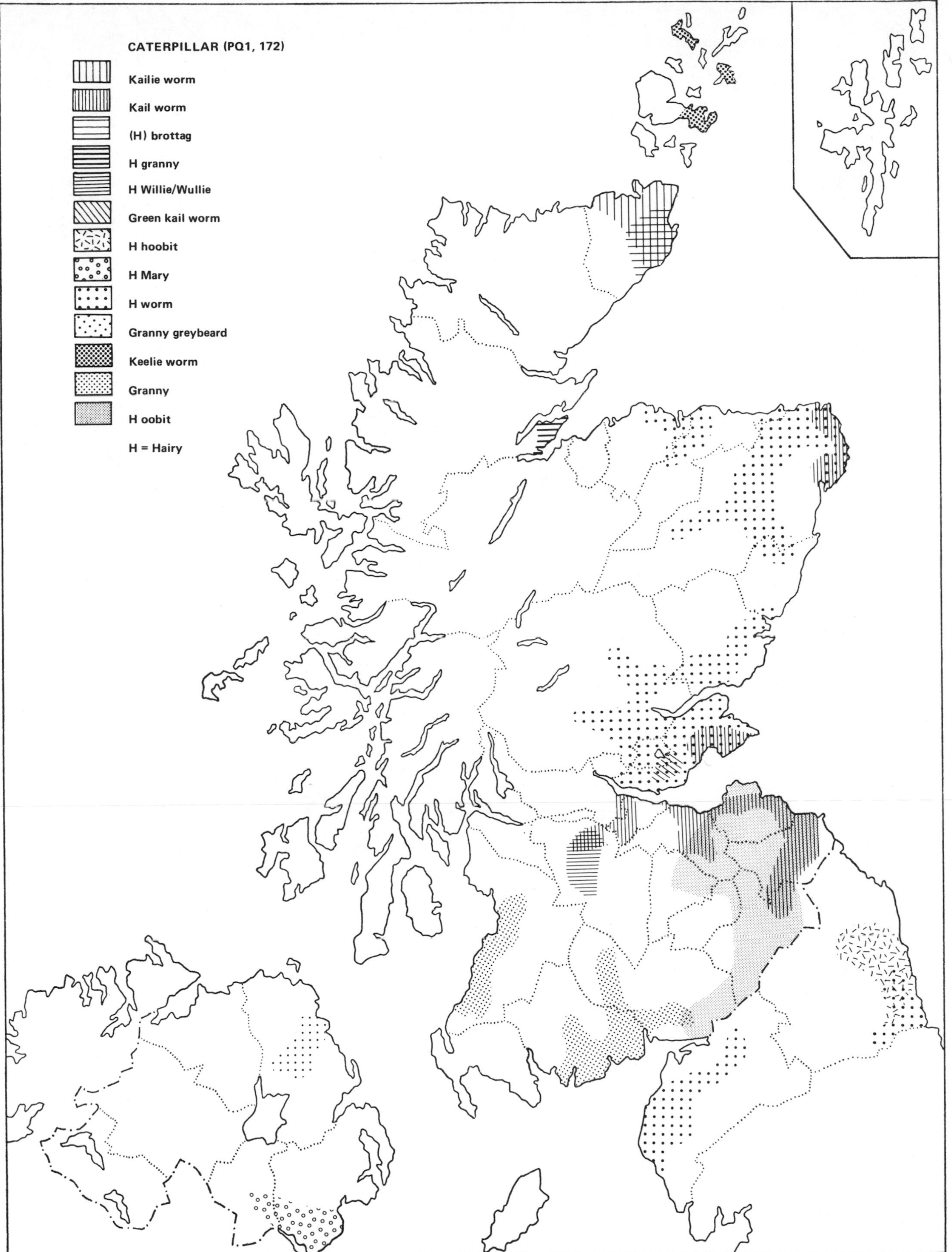
CATERPILLAR (PQ1, 172)
Kailie worm
Kail worm
(H) brottag
H granny
H Willie/Wullie
Green kail worm
H hoobit
H Mary
H worm
Granny greybeard
Keelie worm
Granny
H oobit
H = Hairy

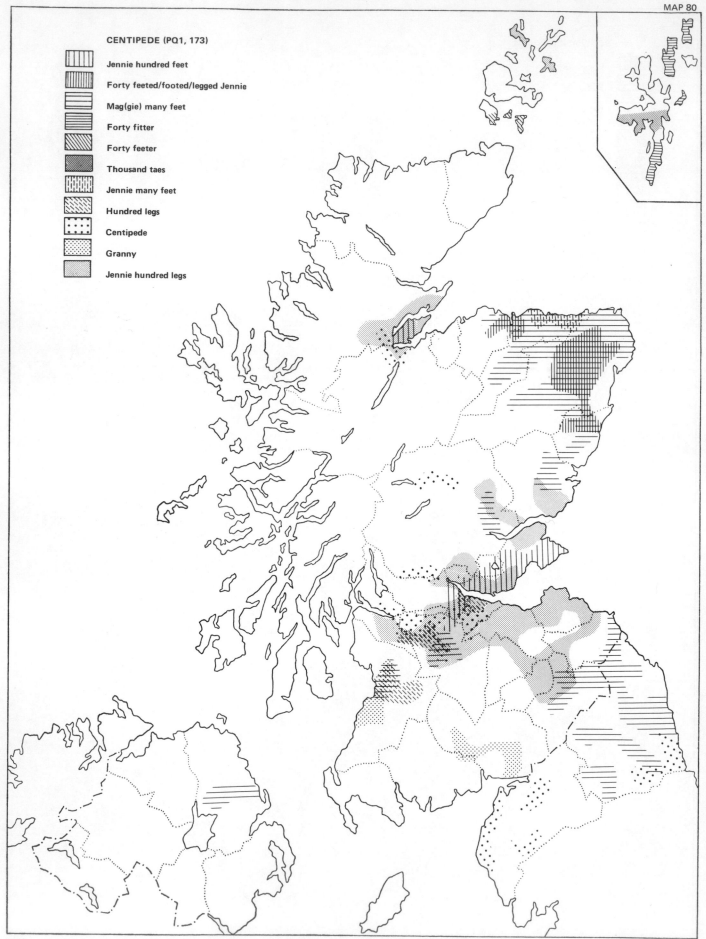

CENTIPEDE (PQ1, 173)

Jennie hundred feet

Forty feeted/footed/legged Jennie

Mag(gie) many feet

Forty fitter

Forty feeter

Thousand taes

Jennie many feet

Hundred legs

Centipede

Granny

Jennie hundred legs

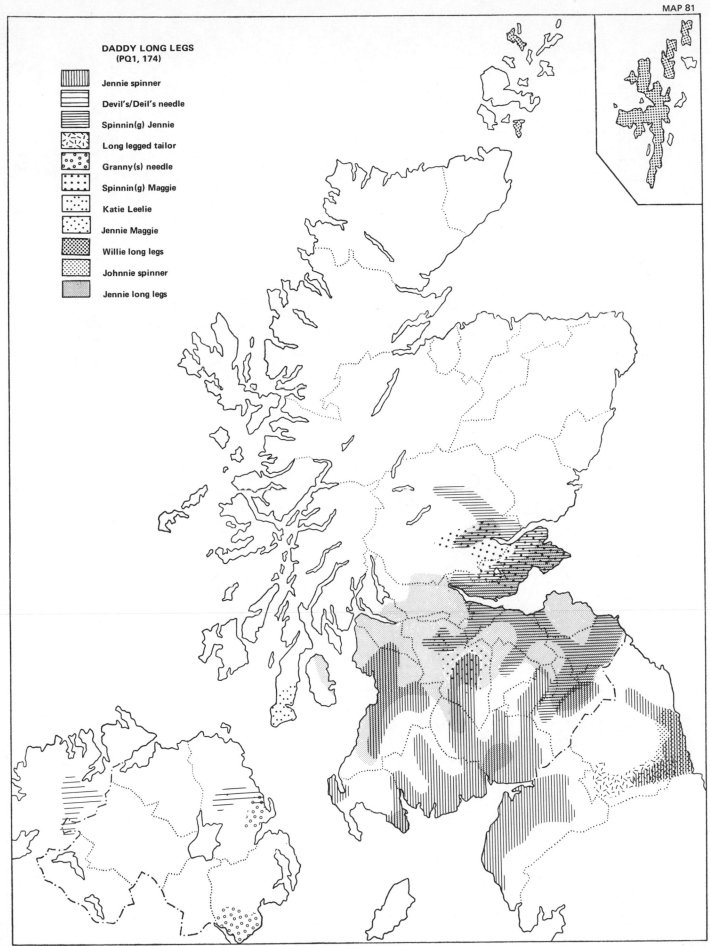

DADDY LONG LEGS
(PQ1, 174)
Jennie spinner
Devil's/Deil's needle
Spinnin(g) Jennie
Long legged tailor
Granny(s) needle
Spinnin(g) Maggie
Katie Leelie
Jennie Maggie
Willie long legs
Johnnie spinner
Jennie long legs

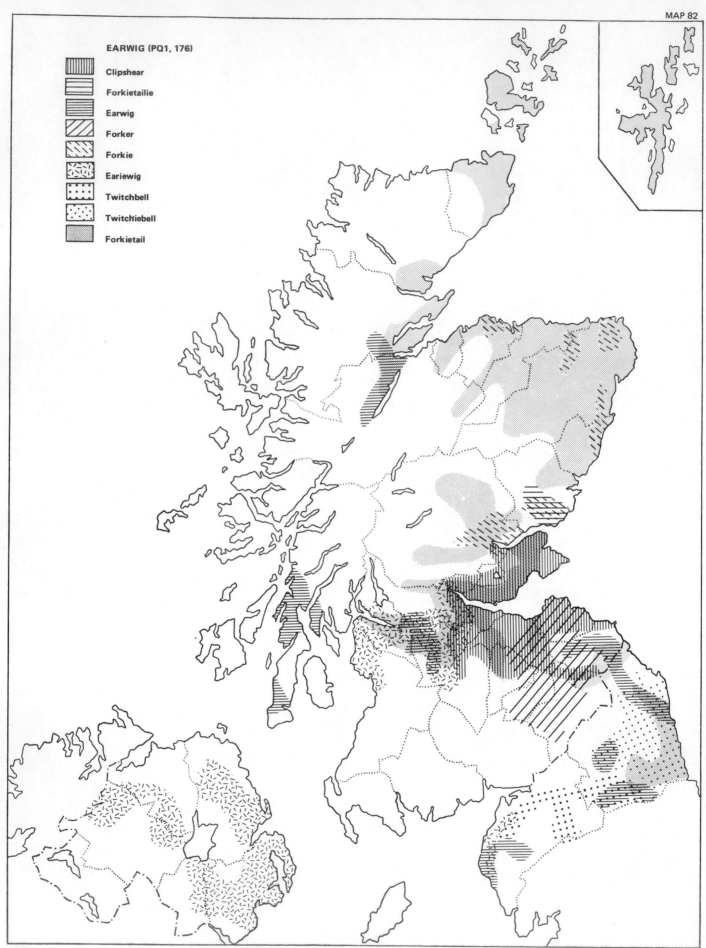

EARWIG (PQ1, 176)

Clipshear
Forkietailie
Earwig
Forker
Forkie
Eariewig
Twitchbell
Twitchiebell
Forkietail

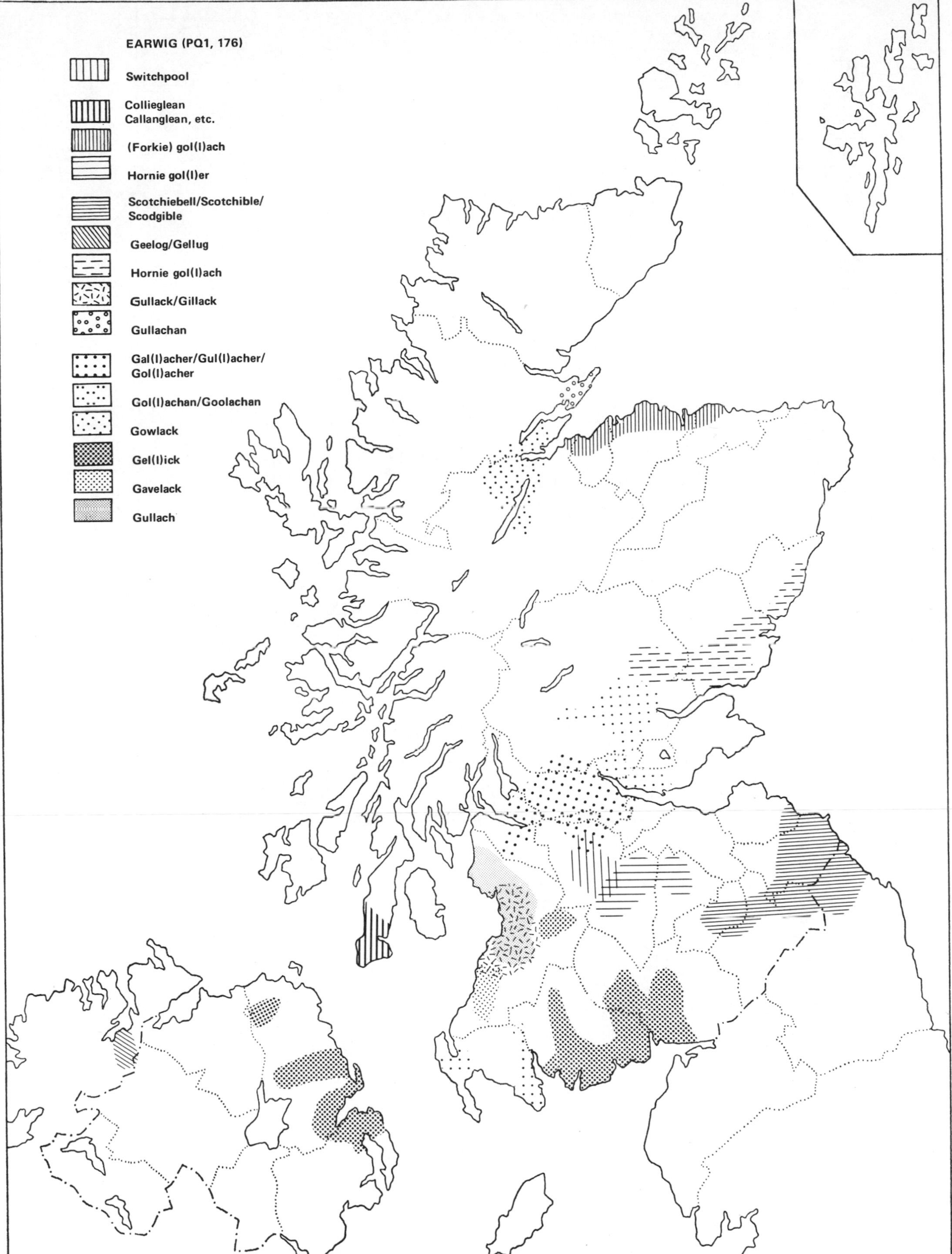
EARWIG (PQ1, 176)
Switchpool
Collieglean
Callanglean, etc.
(Forkie) gol(l)ach
Hornie gol(l)er
Scotchiebell/Scotchible/
Scodgible
Geelog/Gellug
Hornie gol(l)ach
Gullack/Gillack
Gullachan
Gal(l)acher/Gul(l)acher/
Gol(l)acher
Gol(l)achan/Goolachan
Gowlack
Gel(l)ick
Gavelack
Gullach

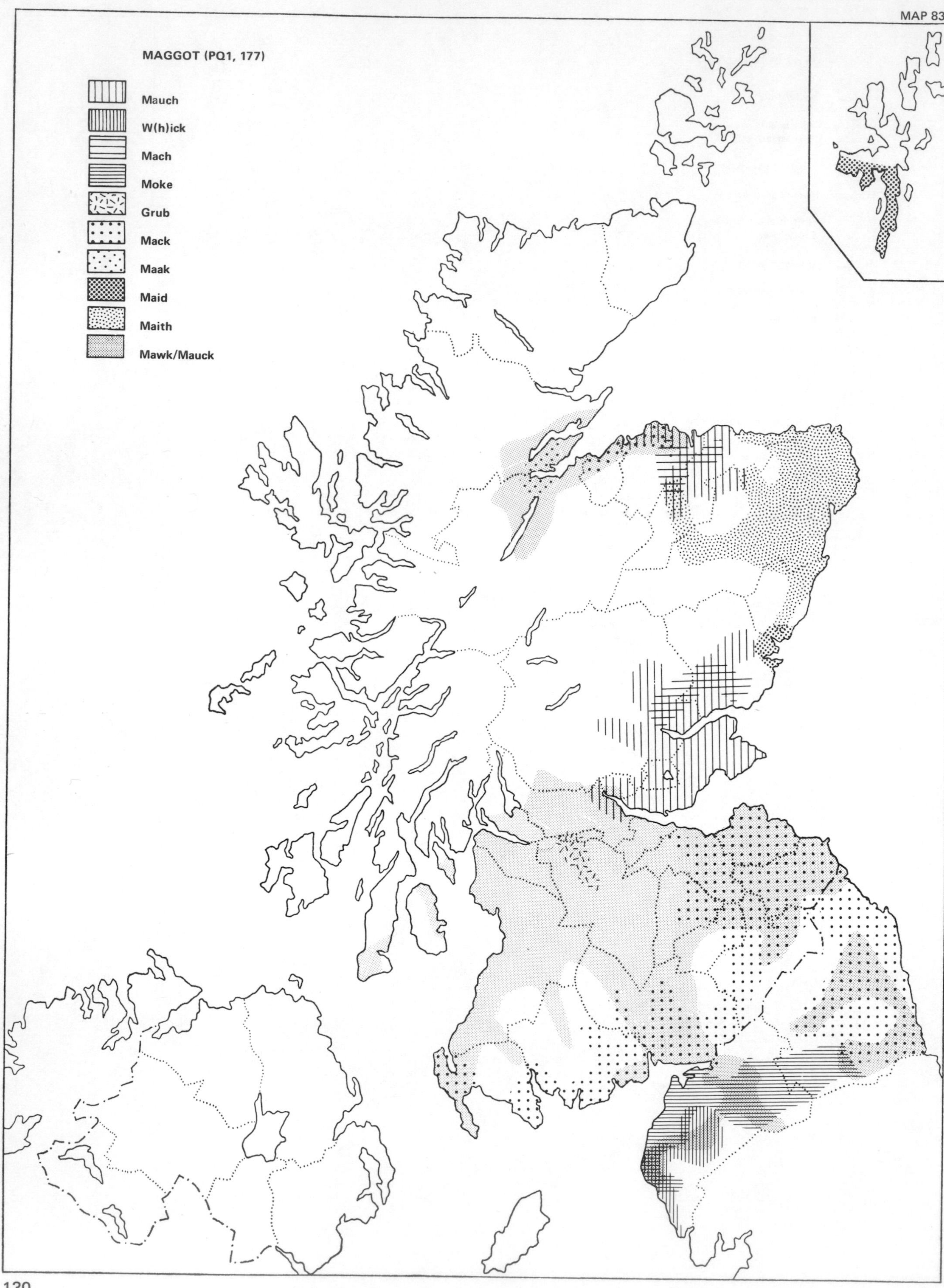
MAGGOT (PQ1, 177)
Mauch
W(h)ick
Mach
Moke
Grub
Mack
Maak
Maid
Maith
Mawk/Mauck

SPIDER (PQ1, 178)

Spider
Netterie
Nettercap/Nettercrap
Ettercap
Weiver/W(e)aver
Willie w(e)aver
Wiver/Wyver

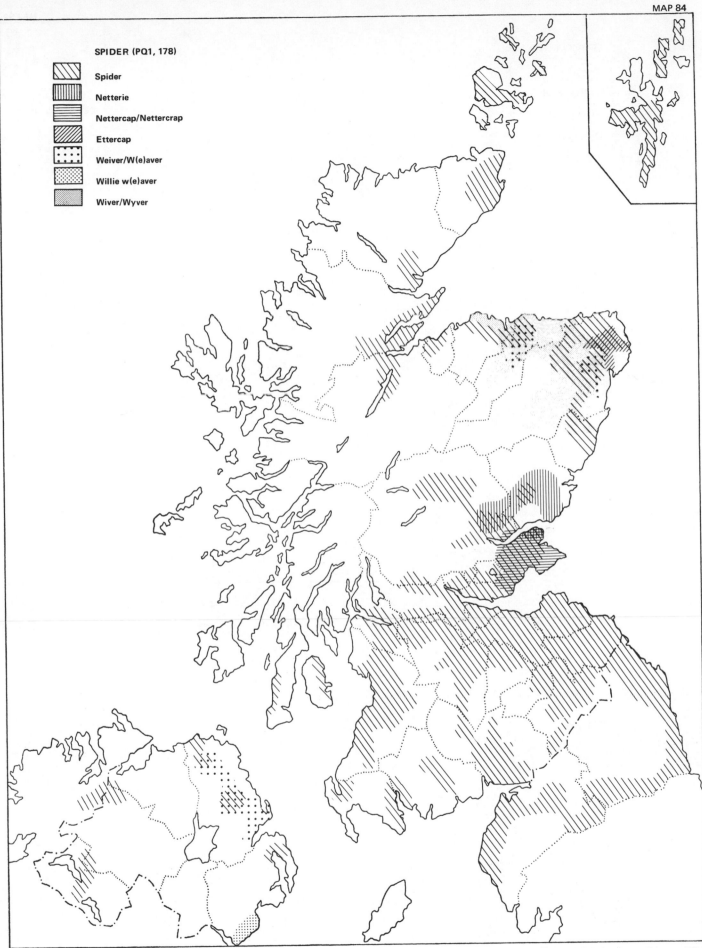

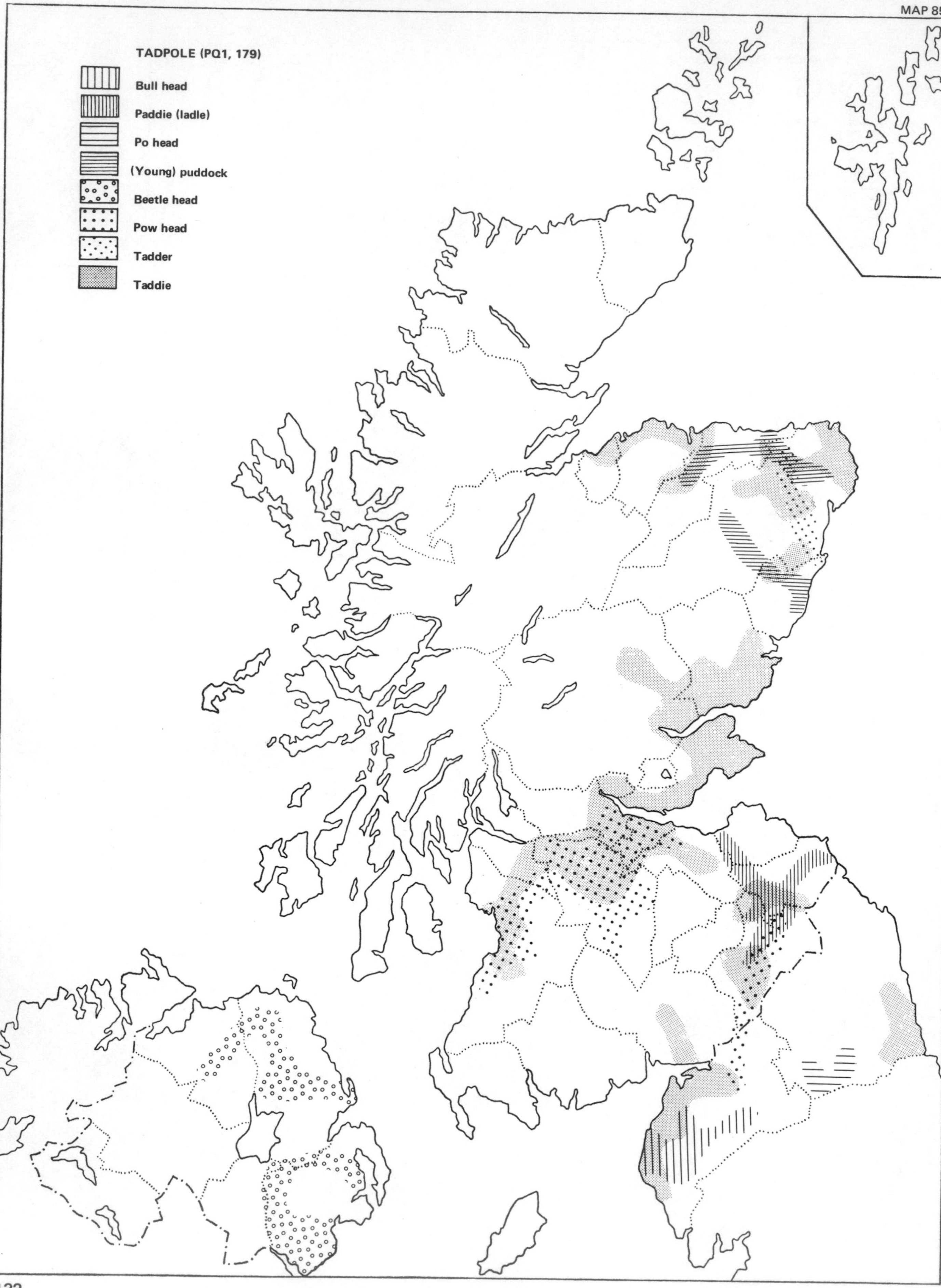
TADPOLE (PQ1, 179)
Bull head
Paddie (ladle)
Po head
(Young) puddock
Beetle head
Pow head
Tadder
Taddie

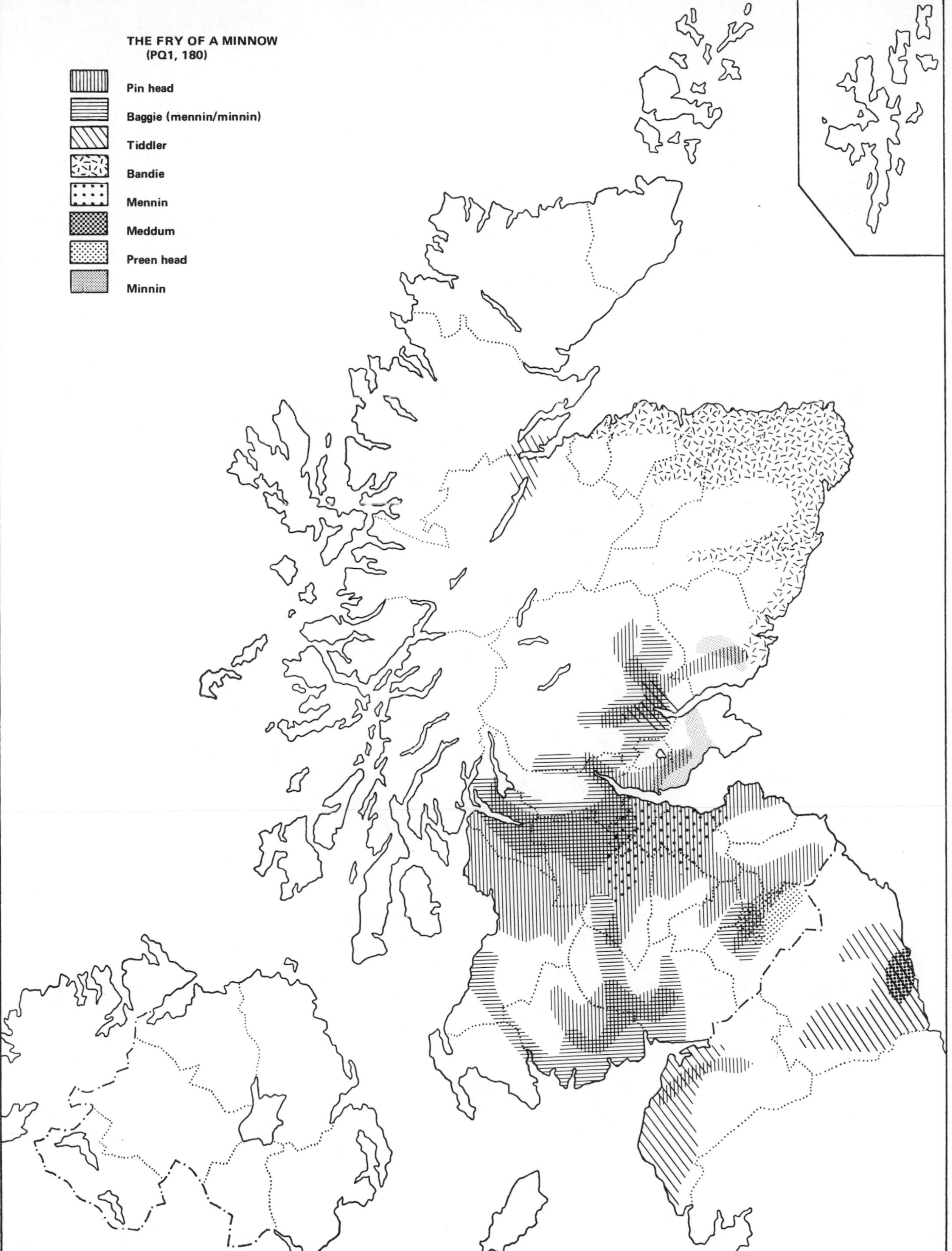
THE FRY OF A MINNOW
(PQ1, 180)
Pin head
Baggie (mennin/minnin)
Tiddler
Bandie
Mennin
Meddum
Preen head
Minnin

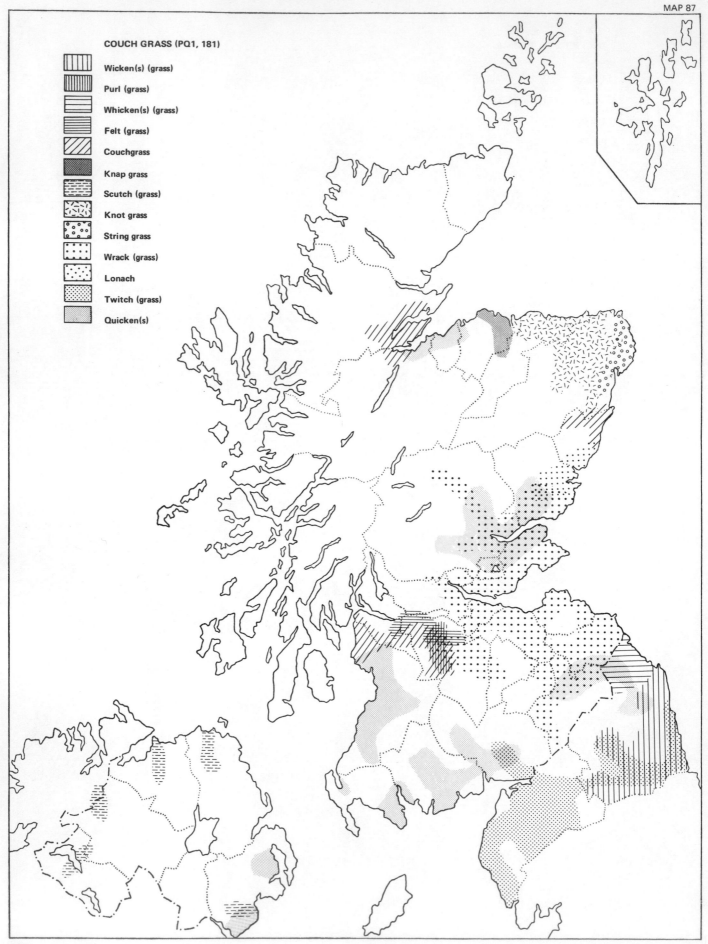

COUCH GRASS (PQ1, 181)

Wicken(s) (grass)

Purl (grass)

Whicken(s) (grass)

Felt (grass)

Couchgrass

Knap grass

Scutch (grass)

Knot grass

String grass

Wrack (grass)

Lonach

Twitch (grass)

Quicken(s)

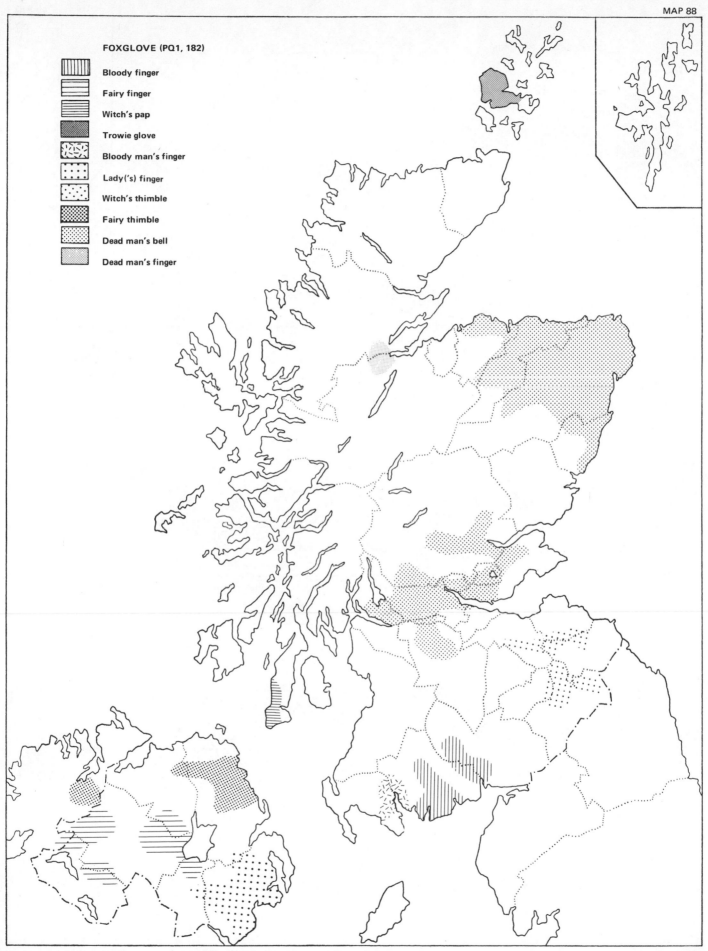

FOXGLOVE (PQ1, 182)

Bloody finger

Fairy finger

Witch's pap

Trowie glove

Bloody man's finger

Lady('s) finger

Witch's thimble

Fairy thimble

Dead man's bell

Dead man's finger

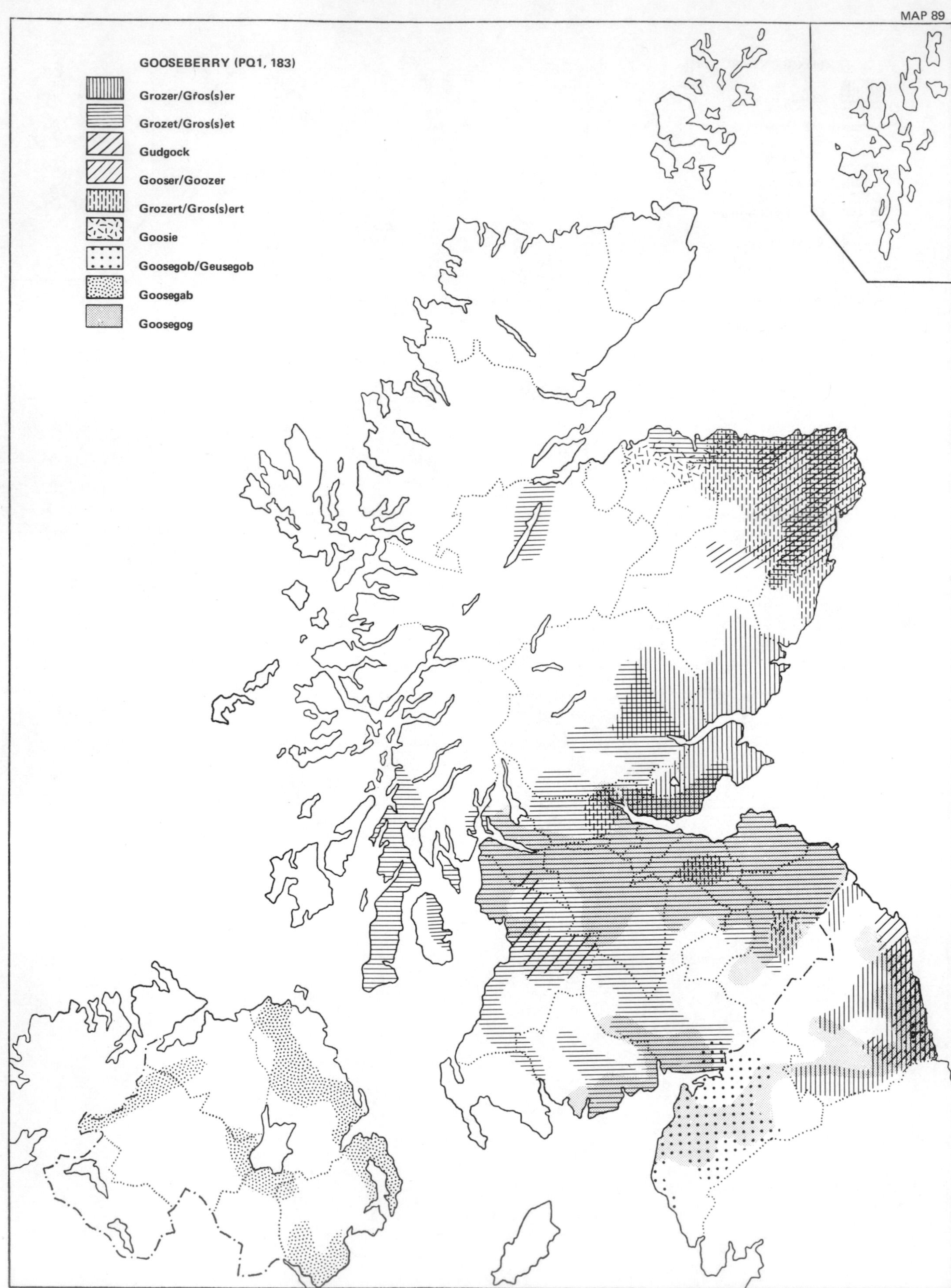
GOOSEBERRY (PQ1, 183)
Grozer/Grŏs(s)er
Grozet/Gros(s)et
Gudgock
Gooser/Goozer
Grozert/Gros(s)ert
Goosie
Goosegob/Geusegob
Goosegab
Goosegog

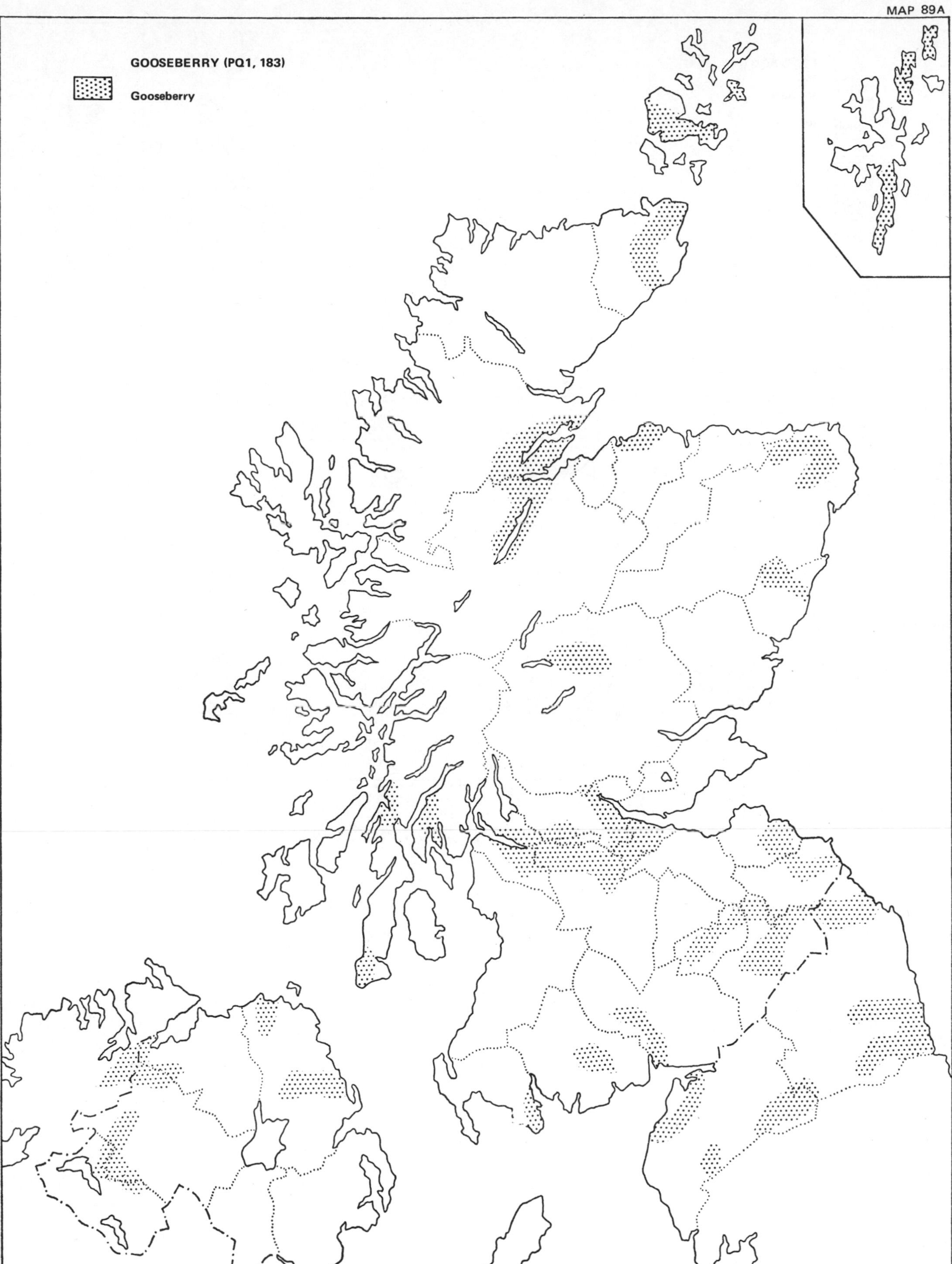
GOOSEBERRY (PQ1, 183)
Gooseberry

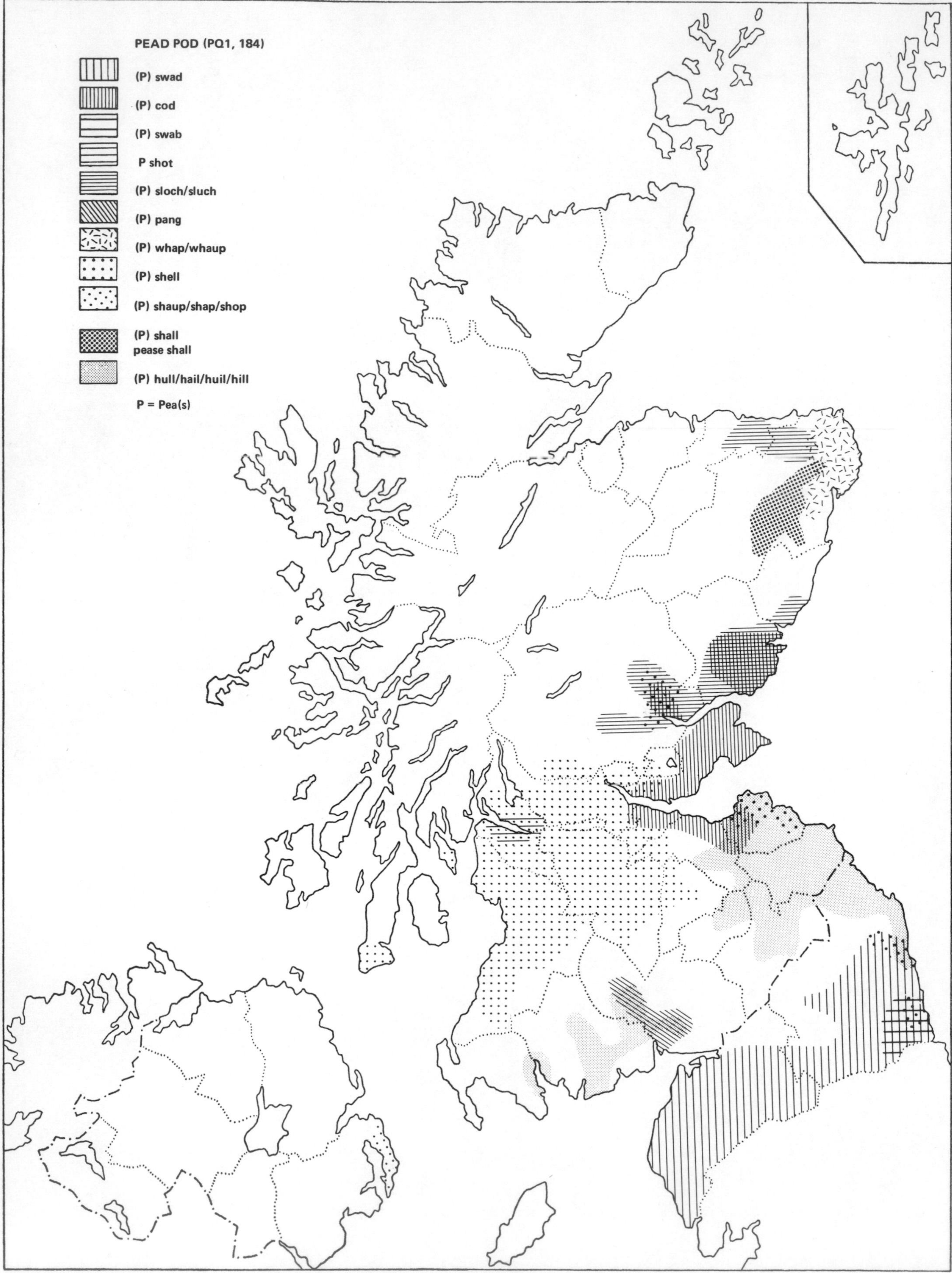
PEAD POD (PQ1, 184)
(P) swad
(P) cod
(P) swab
P shot
(P) sloch/sluch
(P) pang
(P) whap/whaup
(P) shell
(P) shaup/shap/shop
(P) shall
pease shall
(P) hull/hail/huil/hill
P = Pea(s)

ADDITIONAL MAPS WITHOUT LISTS

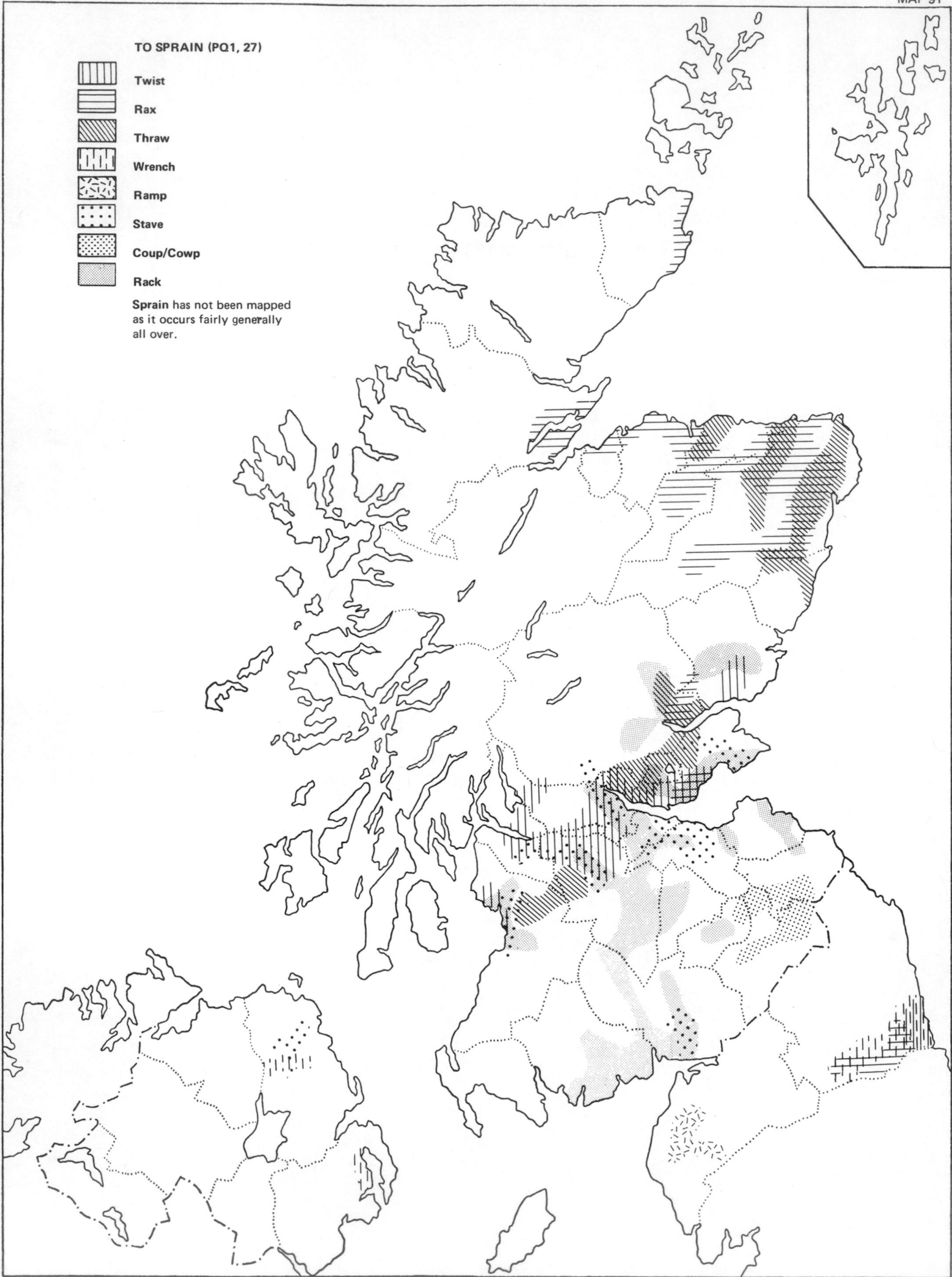
TO SPRAIN (PQ1, 27)
Twist
Rax
Thraw
Wrench
Ramp
Stave
Coup/Cowp
Rack
Sprain has not been mapped as it occurs fairly generally all over.

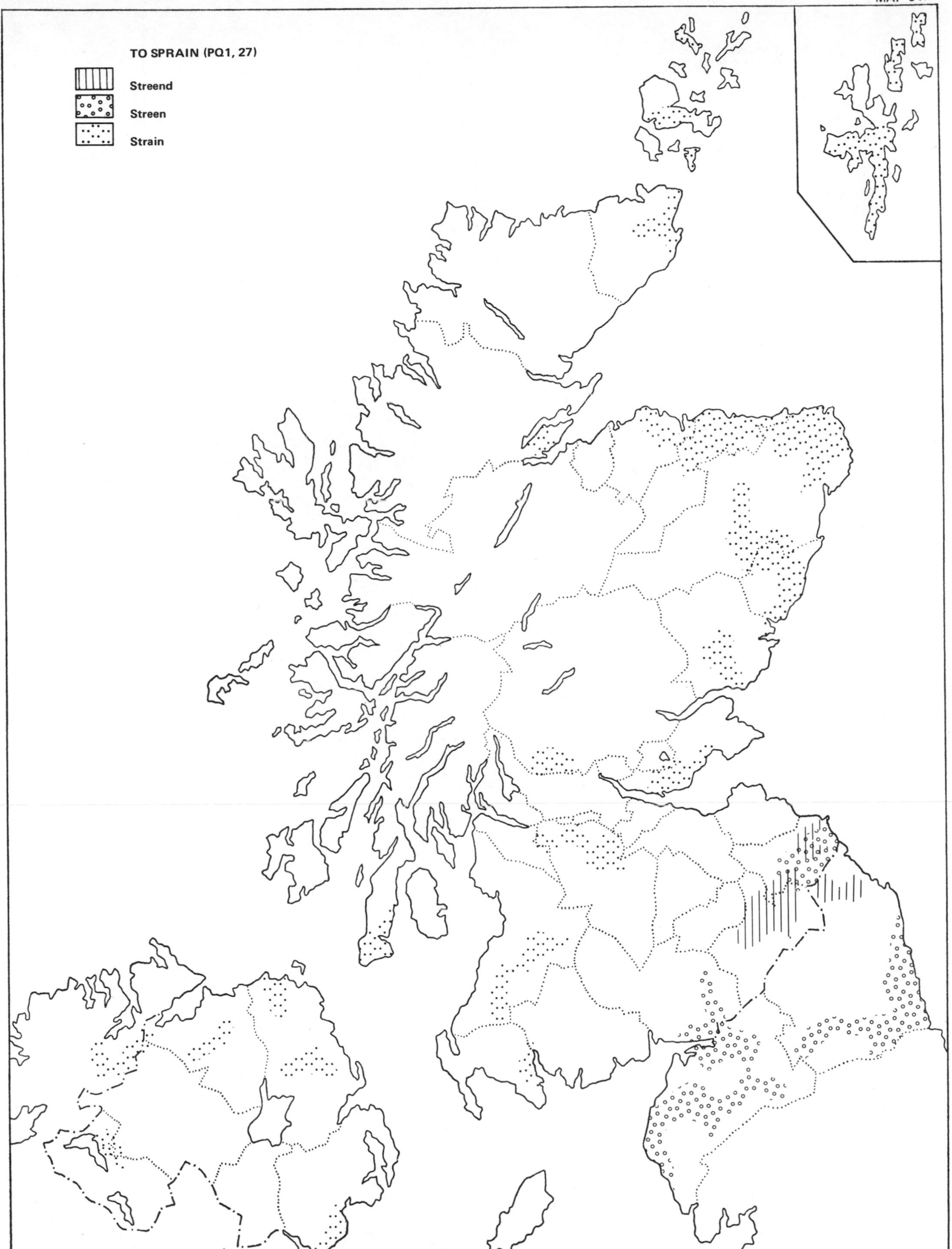
TO SPRAIN (PQ1, 27)
Streend
Streen
Strain

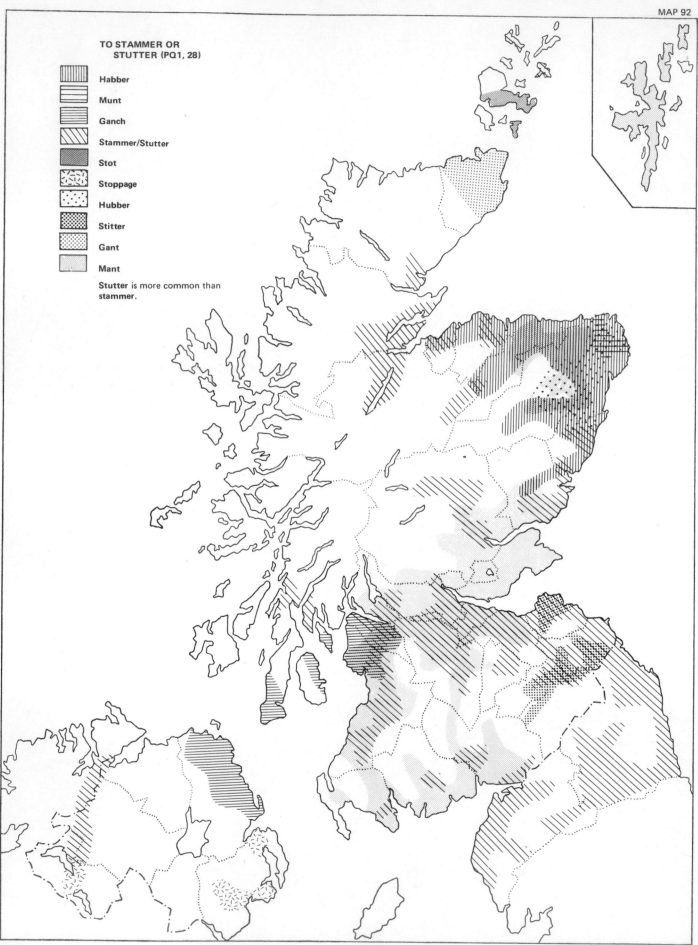

TO STAMMER OR
STUTTER (PQ1, 28)

Habber
Munt
Ganch
Stammer/Stutter
Stot
Stoppage
Hubber
Stitter
Gant
Mant

Stutter is more common than **stammer.**

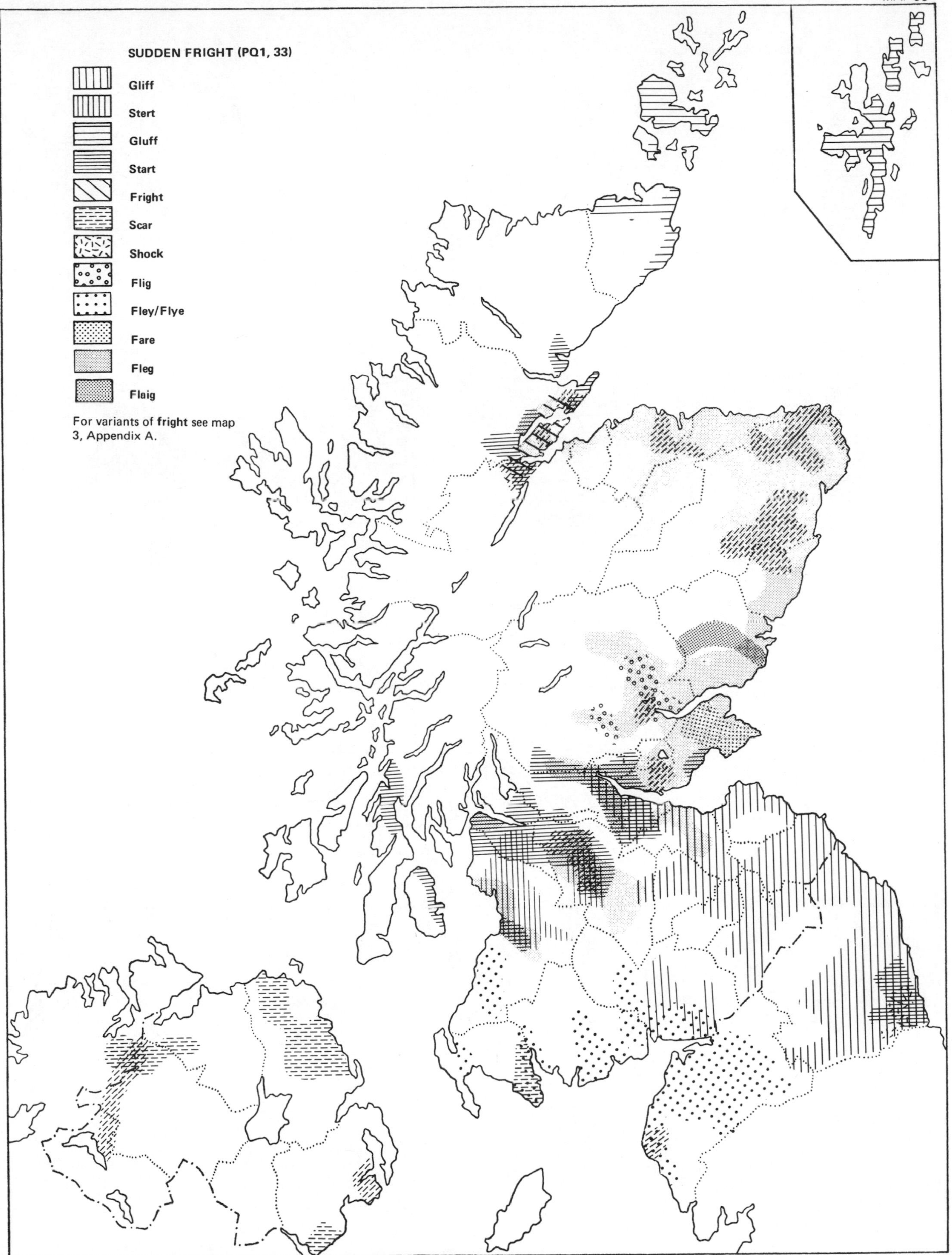
SUDDEN FRIGHT (PQ1, 33)
Gliff
Stert
Gluff
Start
Fright
Scar
Shock
Flig
Fley/Flye
Fare
Fleg
Flaig
For variants of fright see map 3, Appendix A.

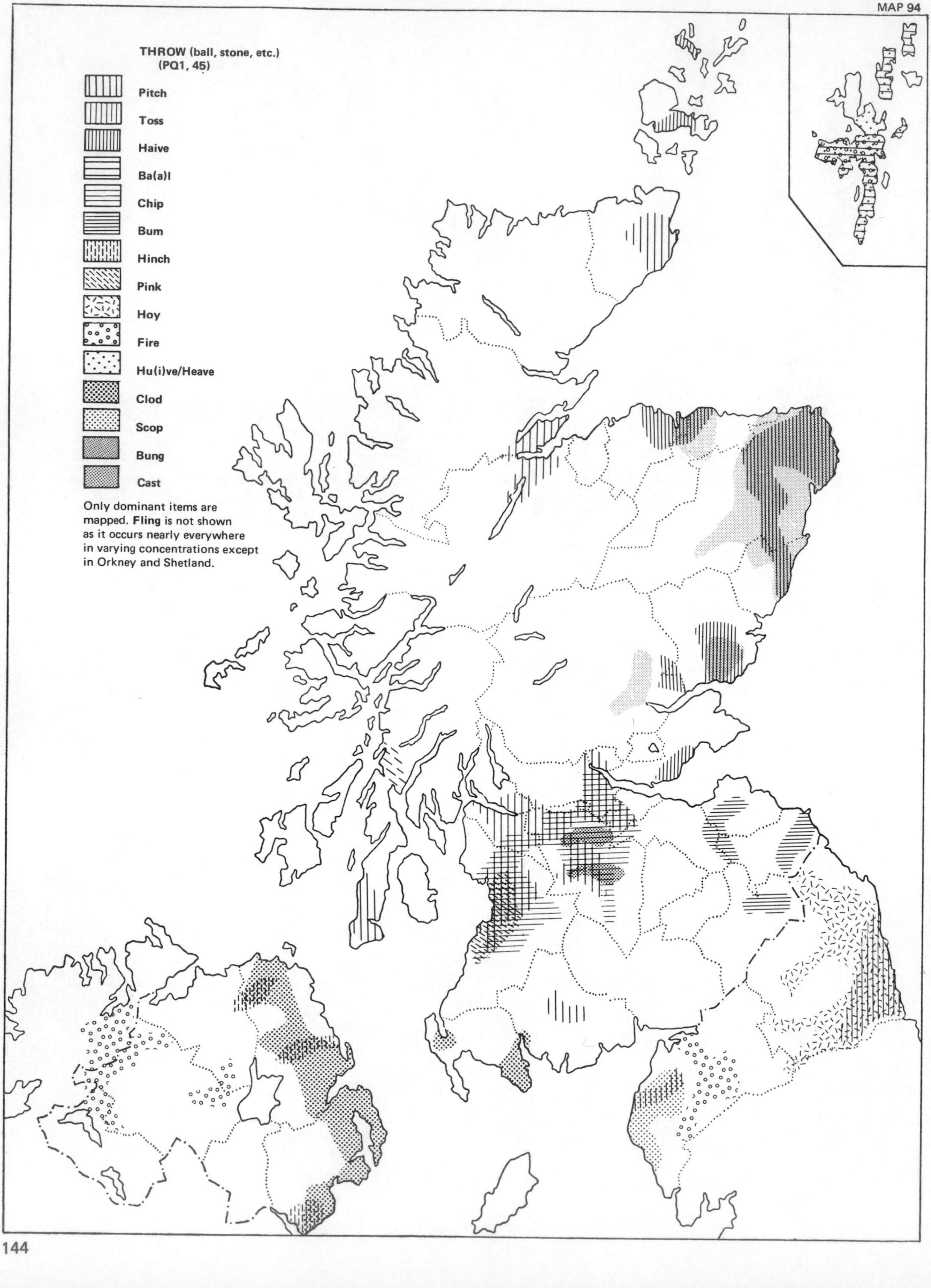

THROW (ball, stone, etc.)
(PQ1, 45)
Pitch
Toss
Haive
Ba(a)l
Chip
Bum
Hinch
Pink
Hoy
Fire
Hu(i)ve/Heave
Clod
Scop
Bung
Cast
Only dominant items are mapped. **Fling** is not shown as it occurs nearly everywhere in varying concentrations except in Orkney and Shetland.

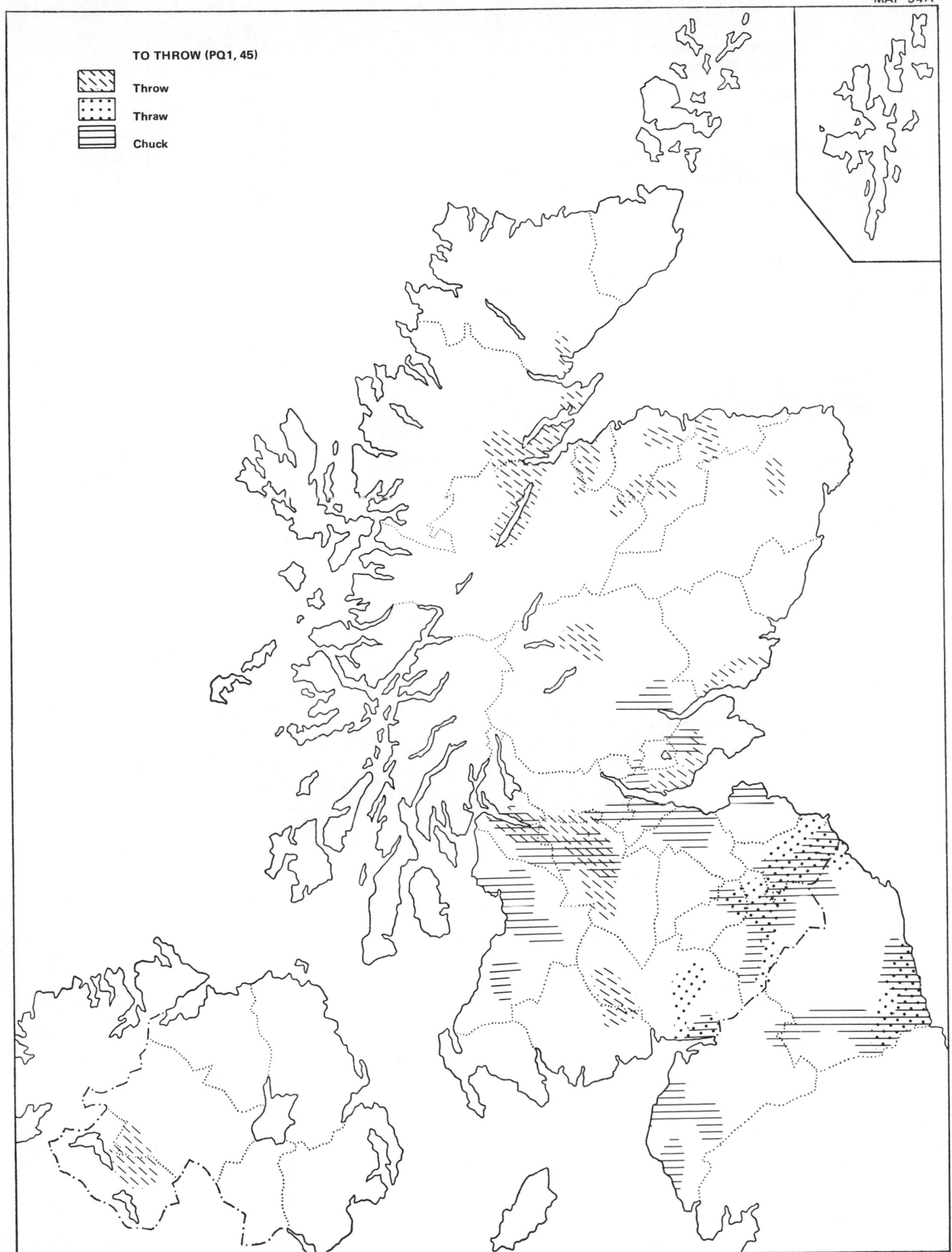
TO THROW (PQ1, 45)
Throw
Thraw
Chuck

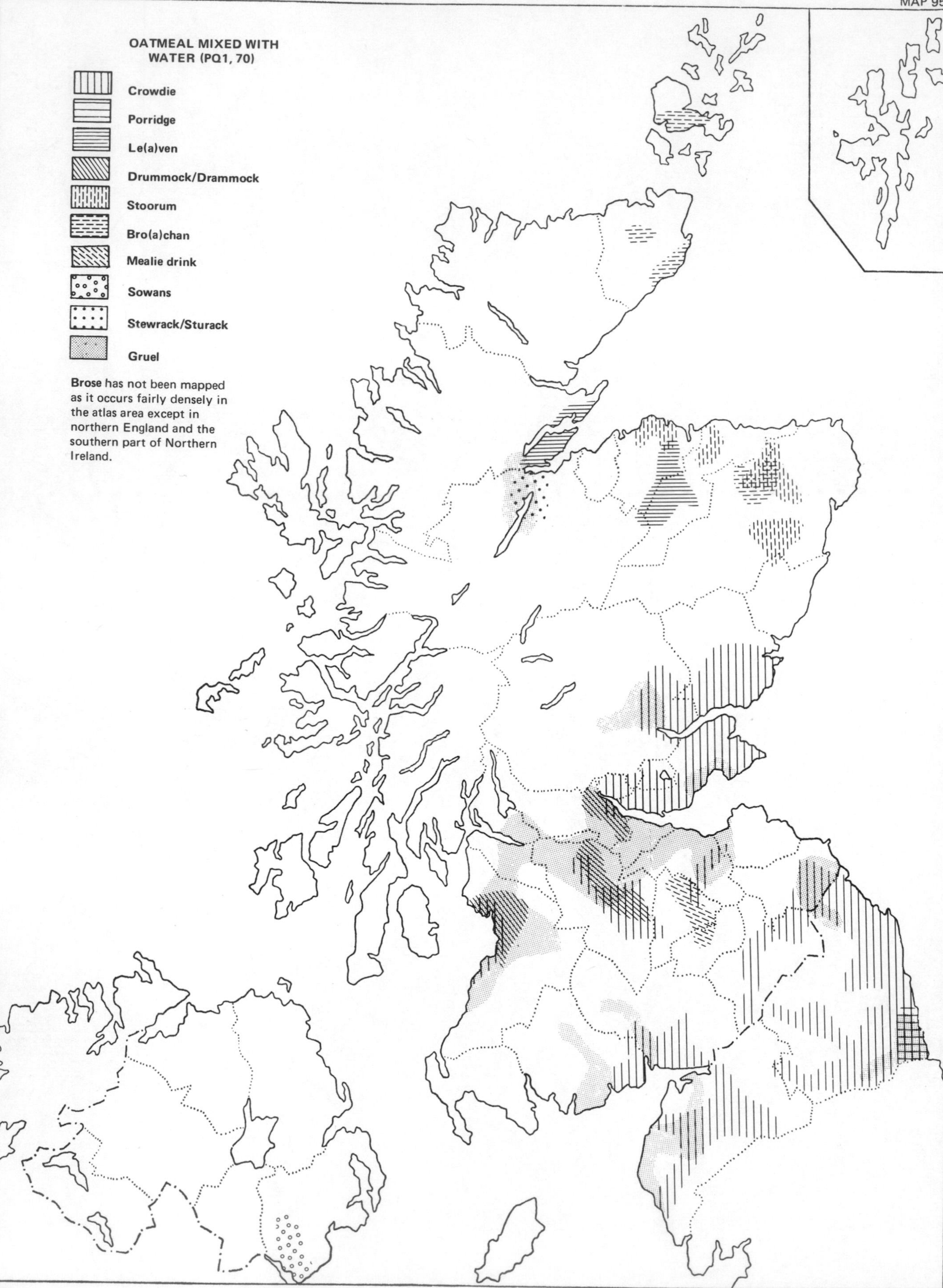
OATMEAL MIXED WITH WATER (PQ1, 70)
Crowdie
Porridge
Le(a)ven
Drummock/Drammock
Stoorum
Bro(a)chan
Mealie drink
Sowans
Stewrack/Sturack
Gruel
Brose has not been mapped as it occurs fairly densely in the atlas area except in northern England and the southern part of Northern Ireland.

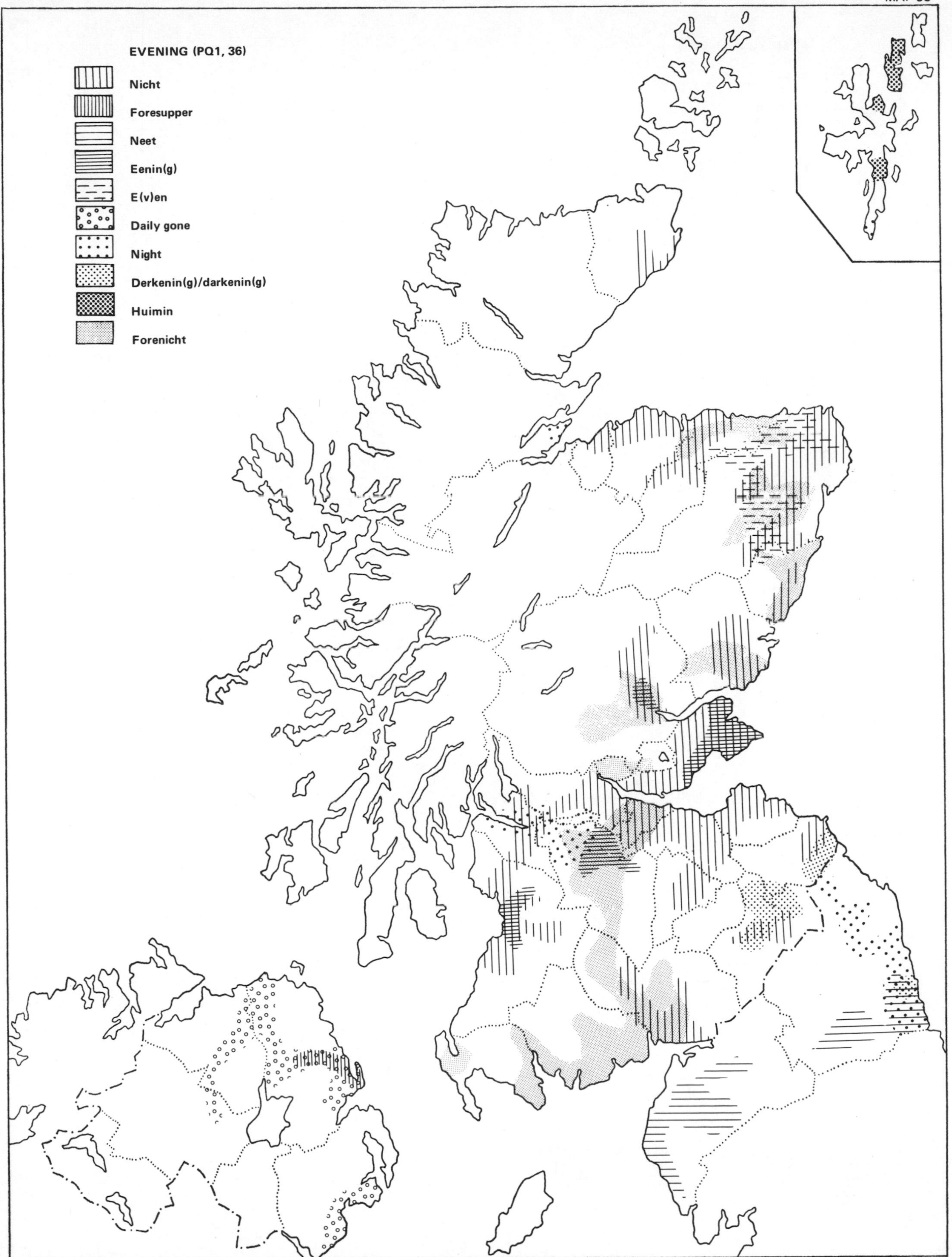

EVENING (PQ1, 36)
Nicht
Foresupper
Neet
Eenin(g)
E(v)en
Daily gone
Night
Derkenin(g)/darkenin(g)
Huimin
Forenicht

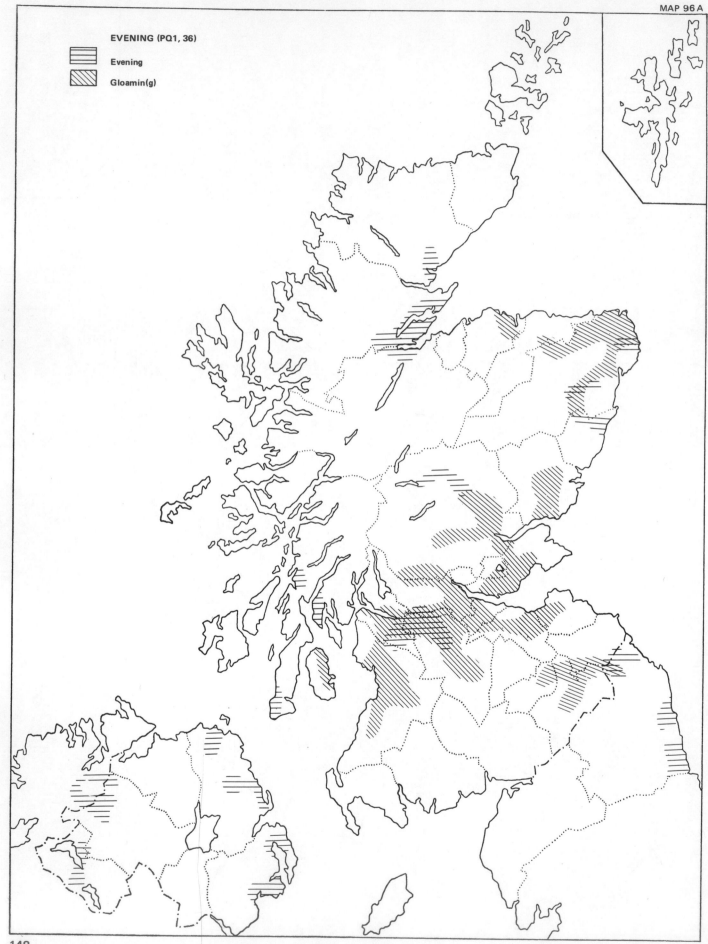

EVENING (PQ1, 36)

Evening

Gloamin(g)

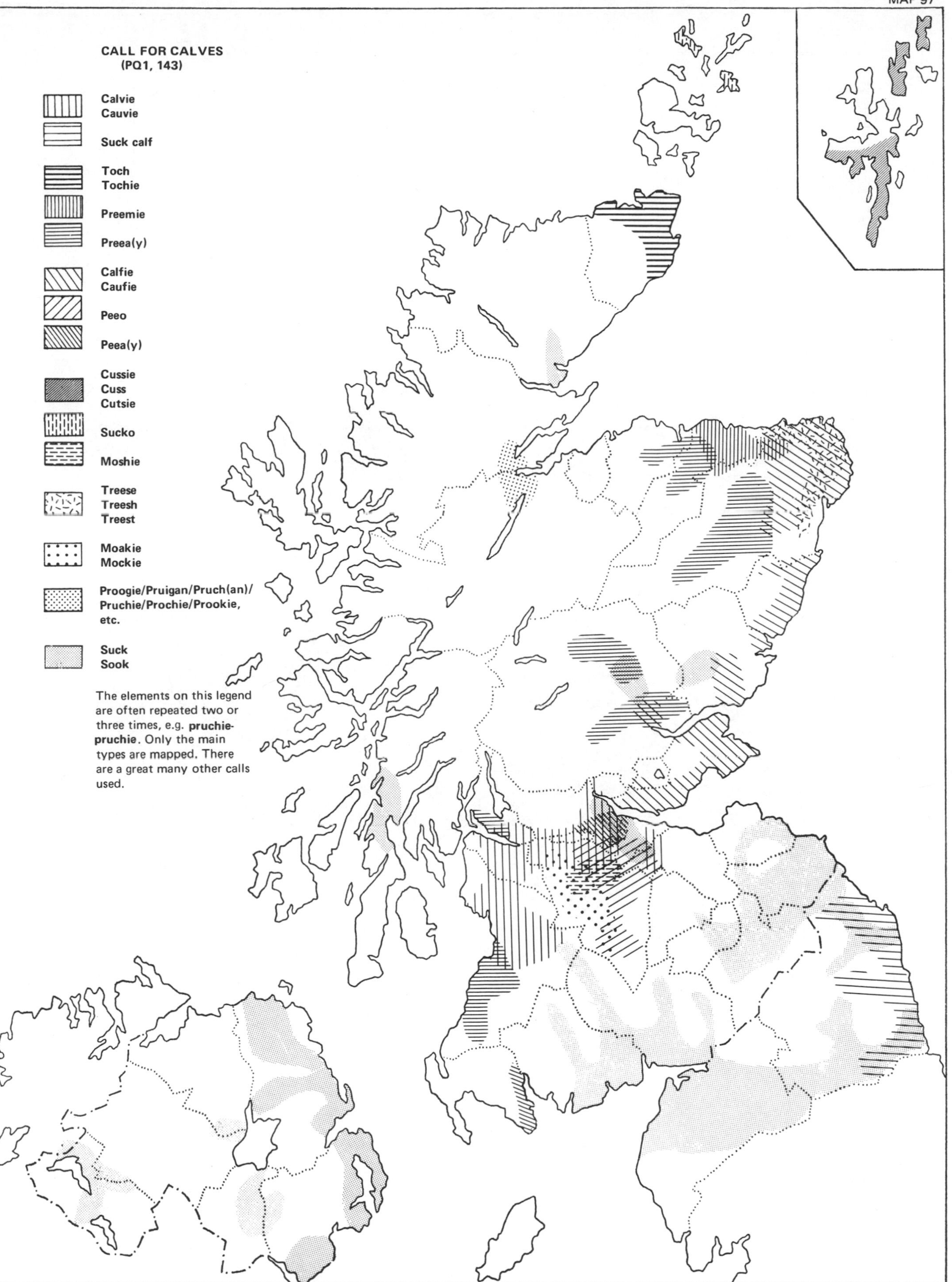
CALL FOR CALVES
(PQ1, 143)
Calvie
Cauvie
Suck calf
Toch
Tochie
Preemie
Preea(y)
Calfie
Caufie
Peeo
Peea(y)
Cussie
Cuss
Cutsie
Sucko
Moshie
Treese
Treesh
Treest
Moakie
Mockie
Proogie/Pruigan/Pruch(an)/
Pruchie/Prochie/Prookie,
etc.
Suck
Sook
The elements on this legend are often repeated two or three times, e.g. **pruchie-pruchie**. Only the main types are mapped. There are a great many other calls used.

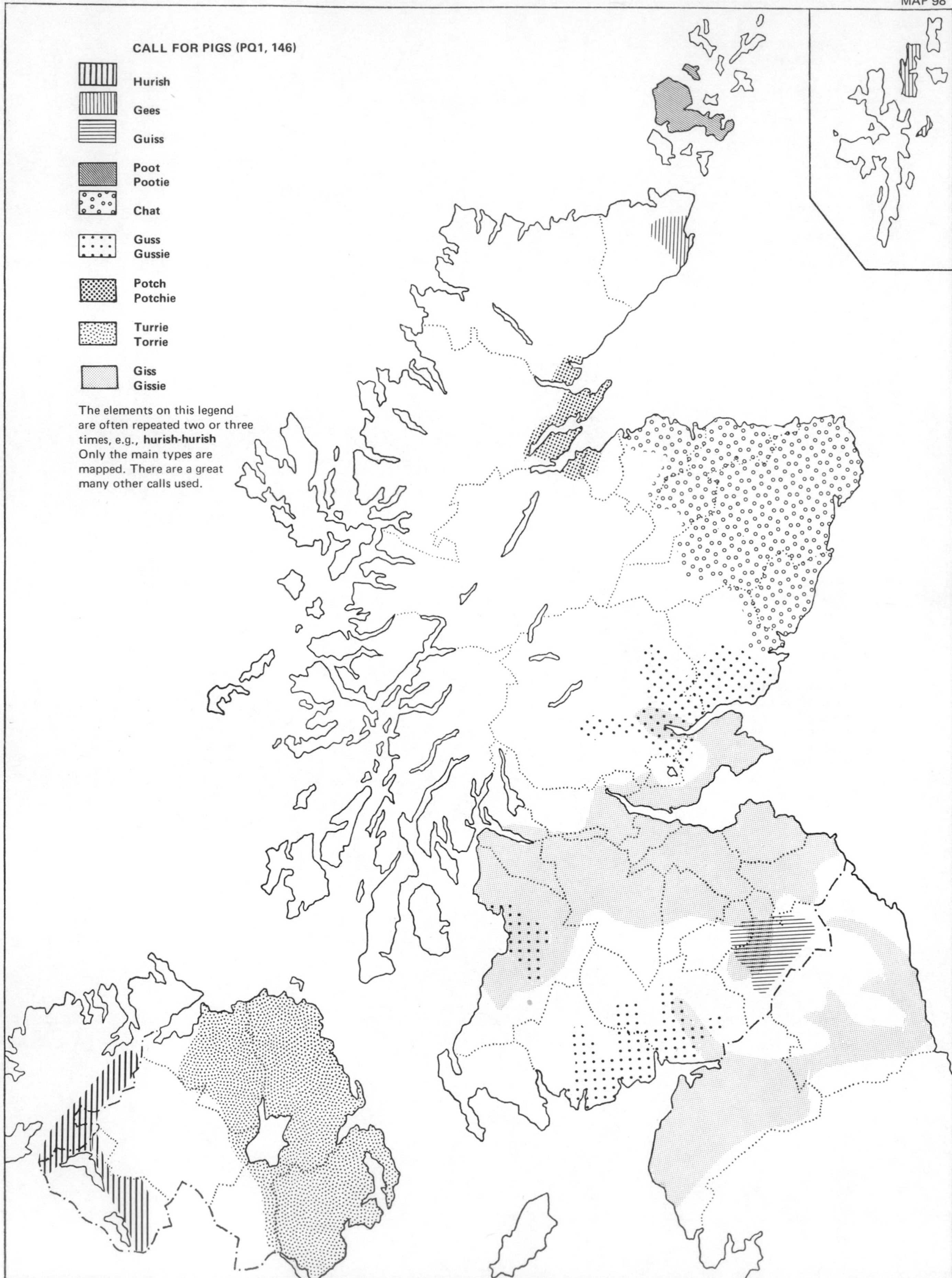
CALL FOR PIGS (PQ1, 146)
Hurish
Gees
Guiss
Poot
Pootie
Chat
Guss
Gussie
Potch
Potchie
Turrie
Torrie
Giss
Gissie
The elements on this legend are often repeated two or three times, e.g., **hurish-hurish**
Only the main types are mapped. There are a great many other calls used.

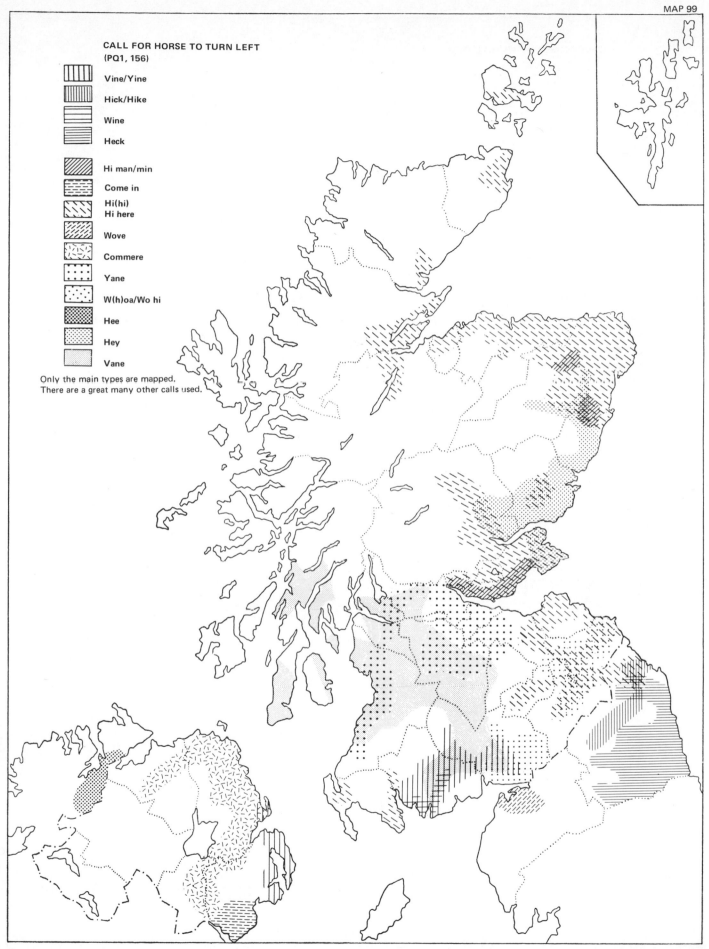

CALL FOR HORSE TO TURN LEFT
(PQ1, 156)

Vine/Yine
Hick/Hike
Wine
Heck
Hi man/min
Come in
Hi(hi)
Hi here
Wove
Commere
Yane
W(h)oa/Wo hi
Hee
Hey
Vane

Only the main types are mapped.
There are a great many other calls used.

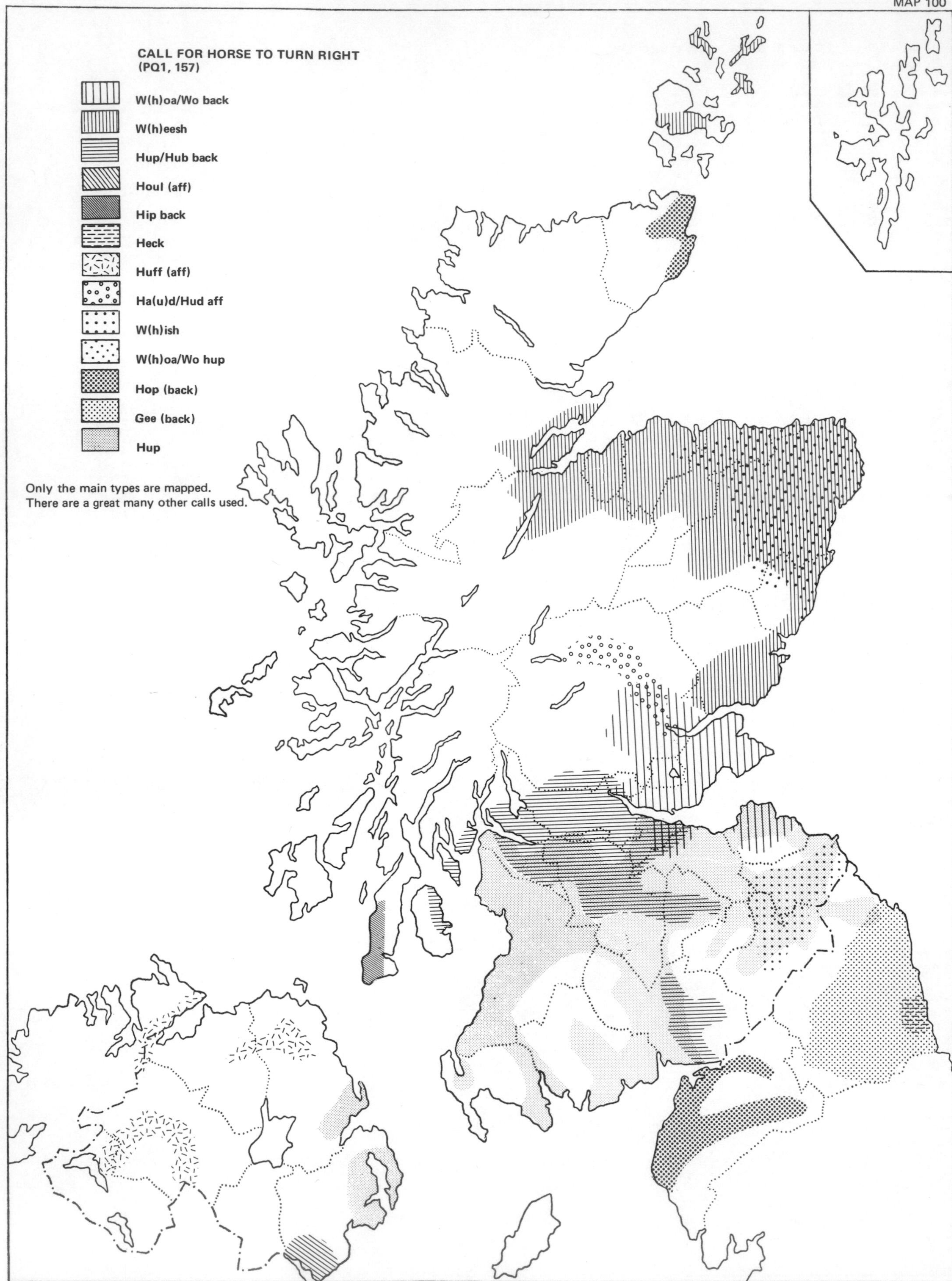
CALL FOR HORSE TO TURN RIGHT
(PQ1, 157)
W(h)oa/Wo back
W(h)eesh
Hup/Hub back
Houl (aff)
Hip back
Heck
Huff (aff)
Ha(u)d/Hud aff
W(h)ish
W(h)oa/Wo hup
Hop (back)
Gee (back)
Hup
Only the main types are mapped.
There are a great many other calls used.

1 ANKLE (PQ1, 17)

Ankle has not been mapped as it occurs fairly densely all over the area.

Shetland

Ankle — 1, 3-4, 7, 17, 20, 21a, 22, 25, 29-30, 33
Ankler — 2, 5, 7-8, 10-11, 14-16, 18-19, 21a, 22, 24, 26-28, 30
Ankler ben — 21b
Chut — 13
Funny bane — 23
Guit — 19
Inkler — 32
Kenit — 16
Keut — 13
Kuit — 6, 9-10, 12, 16, 21b, 22, 24, 26, 29
Shin — 32
Sma leg — 26
Wrist — 17
Nil — 31

Orkney

Ankle — 1-5, 7-9, 13ab, 15-21
Ankler — 6
Cuit — 1, 3-8, 10-12, 13ab, 14-16, 21

Caithness

Ankle — 2b, 5, 8-11, 12a, 13-14, 16b
Hankle — 2b, 6
Keet — 2a, 5, 11, 12b
Shank — 13
Nil — 1, 3-4, 7, 12c, 15, 16a, 17

Sutherland

Ankle — 1, 3-8, 9ab, 10-13. 17
Nil — 2, 14-16

Ross & Cromarty

Ankle — 1, 3-6, 8-9, 13-14, 16-20, 22-24, 25b, 26-27, 29-31, 32abc, 36, 39
Crockle — 31, 34, 37ab
Knockle — 25ab
Shin — 34
Nil — 2, 7, 10-12, 15, 21, 28, 33, 35, 38

Inverness

Ankle — 1-12, 13abcde, 16-17, 19-20, 21ab, 22-23, 25-26, 28-30, 32-40
Shin — 9, 18, 20, 27
Nil — 14-15, 24, 31

Nairn

Ankle — 1ab, 2, 4, 6
Queet — 1abc
Shin — 5
Nil — 3

Moray

Ankle — 5, 8bdf, 11, 15, 19-20, 23
Knockle — 2b, 3
Queet — 1, 2a, 3-4, 6ab, 7, 8abdef, 9ab, 10, 12-22
Shank — 8c
Shin — 6a, 7

Banff

Ankle — 3, 8, 16-17, 19, 21, 25
Cuit — 21
Knockle — 2b
Queet — 1, 2abc, 3-5, 6ab, 7-17, 18bcd, 20, 22-34
Shin — 16, 20-21, 27
Nil — 18a

Aberdeen

Ankle — 4, 8, 29, 34, 42, 51, 54, 59, 70, 71b, 73, 82, 84, 100, 102, 105, 108
Ankle bean — 29
Cuit — 10
Queet — 1-2, 3ab, 4, 5abcd, 6-9, 11-27, 28abc, 29-46, 47abcdef, 48-53, 55-67, 69, 71abc, 72-89, 91-109
Queet been — 68
Queetkin — 5b
Shank — 36
Shen — 73
Shinbane — 11
Nil — 90

Kincardine

Ankle — 8, 10, 12, 16, 17c, 19, 26-27
Coot — 20
Cuit — 15, 20-21
Kyit — 28
Kyuit — 25
Queet — 1-7, 9-14, 16, 17abcd, 18, 22-23, 27
Shin — 12, 24, 26

Kinross

Ankle — 2-3, 6
Cait — 2-4
Cuit — 5, 7
Kit — 1

Angus

Ankle — 8-10, 12-13, 14b, 17b, 18, 20, 24, 26, 28, 29ab, 32, 34, 36
Cate — 19-20
Coort — 28
Coot — 30
Cuit — 1, 4, 5ac, 7-8, 12-13, 14abcd, 17b, 21-23, 27, 31-32, 33b, 34, 36-37
Cut — 35
Cute — 15
Kit — 3, 5c, 6, 10-11, 18, 25, 29a
Leg bane — 33b
Queet — 17a
Quet — 5b
Shankle bone — 7
Shin — 5b, 22, 31, 33b, 36
Nil — 2, 16, 33a

Perth

Ankle — 1, 2a, 4-10, 12-15, 20, 25, 27-28, 29a, 32-33, 36, 40, 47, 51b, 52ae, 57, 60, 66-68, 71, 74
Ankle bane — 18, 41a
Clit — 56
Coite — 53
Cuit — 7, 13, 20, 23, 32-33, 37, 44, 46, 50, 51a, 52abc, 54, 58-60, 63-65, 69
Keet — 39-40, 45
Keit — 41b
Keut — 22, 25
Kit — 27-28, 29b, 31, 42, 44, 48, 52d, 62, 66, 68, 70, 72-73
Queet — 30, 43, 53, 64, 67
Shin — 21, 29b, 30, 41a, 48, 50
Nil — 2b, 3, 11, 16-17, 19, 24, 26, 34-35, 38, 49, 55, 61

Fife

Ankle — 1, 4, 6-8, 9a, 10-11, 13-14, 16, 19, 21-24, 28, 30, 36b, 37, 39, 41abd, 43a, 44bce, 46-47, 49-51, 55abdef, 56-57, 62-63
Cairt — 64b
Cate — 2, 5-6, 9ab, 10, 12-15, 17, 20, 23, 25-26, 28, 32-34, 38, 44df, 48
Clit — 12, 37
Cluit — 53
Coot — 64a
Cuit — 21, 27, 35, 40b
Cut — 40b
Cute — 8
Hogh — 4
Kit — 7, 11, 17, 29, 31, 33, 35, 36a, 39, 40a, 42, 44acd, 47-49, 51-52, 55bdfg, 56, 59, 61
Knucklebane — 55d
Queet — 12
Shinbane — 58
Nil - 3, 18, 41c, 43b, 45, 54, 55c, 60

Clackmannan

Ankle — 4bc, 6
Clit — 1, 4c
Cuit — 1-2
Kit — 3, 4ad, 5, 7

Stirling

Ankle — 4, 7abcef, 8, 11-13, 16, 18, 21ab, 23abc, 25cd, 26acd, 27a, 28, 30, 32, 34, 35a, 36, 37a, 40
Clit — 7b, 21b
Coot — 7d
Cuit — 2, 7de, 26c
Keet — 7d
Kit — 3, 7ade, 12, 17, 20, 21ab, 22ab, 25abd, 26d, 27a, 31-33, 35ab, 36, 37b, 38, 39b, 42a
Sclit — 7b
Shin — 25a
Shinbane — 26b
Sma' o' leg — 35b
Nil — 1, 5-6, 9-10, 14-15, 19, 24, 26ef, 27b, 29, 39a, 41, 42b

Dunbarton

Ankle — 1, 3, 6, 7bc, 8, 10-12, 13abc, 16b
Cuit — 7c
Kit — 3, 7c, 9, 14a, 16a
Kit shin — 16a
Shin — 2, 9
Shinbane — 5
Nil — 4ab, 7a, 14b, 15, 17-18

Argyll

Ankle — 1-12, 14-17, 19, 21-25, 27, 30, 33, 35-36, 38-39
Ankle joint — 33
Kit — 19, 34
Pastern — 34
Shin — 27, 29, 34
Nil — 13, 18, 20, 26, 28, 31-32, 37, 40

Bute

Ankle — 1cd, 2, 7, 8ab, 9
Coot — 1a
Cuit — 1a, 9
Kit — 1e
Shin — 1a
Nil — 1b, 3-6

Ayr

Ankle — 1b, 2ab, 3, 5-6, 8b, 10-11, 12ab, 15, 16a, 17, 20bc, 21, 24b, 25, 26ab, 27, 28cef, 30a, 31, 34, 35b, 42-43, 45, 48, 50-52, 53a, 54-57
Cleet — 7
Cuit — 8b, 26c, 41, 53a
Hough — 57
Kif — 35a
Kit — 3-5, 9, 12b, 13-15, 16ab, 20cgh, 24ab, 25, 26c, 28cd, 30ab, 33-34, 35b, 36, 42, 44-46, 57
Koot — 19
Shank — 41
Shin — 35b, 38, 43, 56
Shinbane — 20ae
Nil — 1a, 8a, 18a, 20df, 22-23, 28ab, 29, 32, 37, 39-40, 47, 49, 53b

Renfrew

Ankle — 1b, 2abchij, 4acde, 8, 11acel, 12ab, 13c, 14a, 15, 16abd, 18ab, 19, 20a
Ankle bane — 11l
Keet — 21
Kit — 5, 11f, 14b, 17, 19, 21
Shin — 2j, 16d
Shinbone — 2i
Nil — 1a, 2defg, 3, 4b, 6-7, 9-10, 11bdghijk, 13abd, 16c, 20b

Lanark

Ankle — 1-3, 5-6, 7ac, 8ab, 9a, 10b, 12, 14abd, 15ac, 16ab, 19-23, 25abc, 26ab, 27ab, 29cdf, 31ad, 32aef, 33a, 35acd, 37, 38c, 39, 45, 46ab, 48, 49ab, 51, 52b, 57a, 58, 59b, 60-61, 65
Ankle bane — 46b
Coot — 17
Cuit — 61
Keet — 67b
Kit — 9ab, 11, 13, 14d, 15ab, 19-20, 22-24, 27a, 29ag, 30, 31d, 32cdf, 33bcd, 35b, 37, 38abd, 39-45, 46ac, 47-48, 49b, 50, 52ab, 53, 55-56, 57abc, 58, 59ab, 61-63, 64ab, 65-66, 67a
Shakle bane — 67a
Shank — 29e
Shin — 17-18, 39, 62
Shin bane — 36, 46b
Nil — 4, 7b, 10a, 14c, 25d, 28, 29b, 31bc, 32b, 34, 38e, 54

West Lothian

Ankle — 1a, 2-3, 5-6, 8, 10-13, 15-16, 17a, 18, 20ab, 21b, 22
Ankle bane — 1d
Clit — 21a
Kip — 21b
Kit — 4, 11-12, 17a, 18, 20a, 21a
Kit bane — 19b
Shin — 4, 11
Shin bane — 15, 17a
Nil — 1bc, 7, 9ab, 14, 17b, 19a

Midlothian

Ankle — 2-3, 6ab, 7a, 8ab, 10-11, 14a, 15-16, 18-21, 23ab, 24, 25abd, 28-29, 32
Ankie — 12a
Cuit — 30
Kit — 2, 14b, 24, 26a, 32
Pastern — 14b
Queet — 4
Shank — 1
Nil — 5, 7b, 9, 12b, 13, 17, 22, 25c, 26b, 27, 31

East Lothian

Ankle — 1, 4b, 5, 6ab, 7, 9, 13, 15-16, 18-21
Cate — 17
Coot — 13
Cuit — 16
Cwet — 13
Hock — 14
Kit — 2, 4a, 7, 11
Shin — 4a, 15
Nil — 3, 8, 10, 12

Berwick

Ankle — 1-2, 6-10, 12-13, 15, 16abc, 24, 28-32
Cate — 4, 7, 14
Clit — 13
Cuit — 5, 8, 11, 16b, 17-18, 21-22, 30, 32
Keet — 7, 32
Kit — 16a, 23, 25, 27-28, 31-32

Berwick cont'd

Shin — 3. 20. 26-27
Shin bane — 19

Peebles

Ankle — 2-3, 4bc, 5, 6ab, 8
Cuif — 4a
Cuit — 2
Kit — 3, 4c, 5, 6a, 10
Shin — 1, 7
Nil — 9

Selkirk

Ankle — 2abcd, 8
Cuit — 2ab, 3-4, 7-8
Kit — 1, 2d, 6
Kite — 2e
Shin — 5

Roxburgh

Ankle — 1-2, 5, 13, 15b, 20, 21a, 25-28
Cate — 5-6
Cuit — 2, 3ab, 8, 9ab, 12-13, 15ab, 16-18, 20, 21acde, 24-26, 28
Cut — 23
Cute — 4, 21f
Kit — 1, 4, 8, 11, 15a, 19
Shin — 7
Nil — 10, 14, 21b, 22

Dumfries

Ankle — 1a, 4, 8a, 12, 15, 17ab, 18, 20, 21b, 22, 24, 26, 28-29, 31bde, 32-33, 35, 37, 39-40, 42-43, 45a, 46-47
Cate — 6
Cleat — 9
Cluit — 31a
Cowt — 29
Cuit — 4
Kit — 2, 5, 11, 29, 31b
Shin — 5-7, 8b, 13-14, 16, 18, 23, 27, 31ab, 32, 46
Shinbane — 44
Nil — 1b, 3, 10, 19, 21a, 25, 30, 31cf, 34, 36, 38, 41, 45b, 48-49

Kirkcudbright

Ankle — 1, 3-4, 6-7, 10, 12b, 15a, 16, 19-20, 21a, 22-23, 25, 27
Coot — 1, 17
Cuit — 1-2, 17
Cuitie — 17
Shin — 5, 7-8, 14, 21c
Nil — 9, 11, 12a, 13, 15b, 18, 21b, 24, 26

Wigtown

Ankle — 1, 3, 5a, 9, 11-12, 14, 16
Anklet — 10
Coot — 2
Shank — 2, 17
Shin — 2, 7, 17
Nil — 4, 5b, 6, 8, 13, 15, 18

Northumberland

Ankle — 1a, 2ab, 5-6, 13-14, 16, 18, 19a, 20b, 21-22, 26, 28, 29bd, 30-31, 34b, 35-38, 40ab, 41cd, 42-43, 45-46, 48, 52, 53ab, 54, 56-57, 59be, 60 62bg, 64ab, 65a, 69ch, 70, 71abcd, 72abcdgij, 73, 77-78, 80, 82-83, 85-87, 88ab, 89-93, 94b, 95b, 96, 98, 99bd, 100, 102, 103abc, 104ab, 107, 109, 111ab, 112, 118b, 119, 120abc, 121, 123, 124b, 126acf, 127acdg, 130bcdef, 132, 135, 137-138, 142-143
Ankler — 103a
Anklet — 1b, 7, 15, 17, 24a, 41c, 45, 48, 71ac, 124a, 127g, 134, 142,
Coot — 59b
Cuit — 29f
Hock — 70
Hunker — 126f
Joint — 127e
Kit — 12
Shank end — 86
Sheen — 69a
Shin — 13, 17, 56, 61, 62eh, 69abf, 75, 87, 108b, 114, 116, 118a, 129b, 130a
Shin bone — 69b, 110
Wrist o' the foot — 124a
Nil — 1c, 3-4, 8-11, 19b, 20a, 23, 24b, 25, 27, 29ace, 32, 33ab, 34a, 39, 41abd, 44, 47, 49-51, 55, 58, 59acdf, 62acdf, 63, 65b, 66-68, 69deg, 71e, 72efhkl, 74, 76, 79, 81, 84, 94a, 95a, 97, 99ac, 101ab, 105-106, 108ac, 113, 115, 117, 122ab, 125, 126bde, 127bfh, 128, 129ac, 131, 133, 136, 139-141

Cumberland

Ankle — 1a, 2-4, 7, 9, 12, 13c, 15ac, 21-26, 28, 31, 33, 38, 40, 42, 46-50, 52-53, 56-58, 62
Ankle bane — 16
Fetlock — 9, 54
Hock — 46
Joint — 15b
Knockle bean — 56
Shank — 46
Shin — 5a
Nil — 1b, 5b, 6, 8, 10-11, 13abd, 14, 17-20, 27, 29-30, 32, 34-36, 37ab, 39, 41, 43-45, 51, 55, 59-61, 63ab

Down

Ankle — 1, 2a, 3, 5-7, 9, 11-12, 15, 18-19, 24, 26, 28
Anklet — 2a, 3, 7, 11, 13-14, 25, 27, 30
Coot — 13
Hough — 19
Shin — 4, 15
Nil — 2b, 8, 10, 16-17, 20-23, 29

Tyrone

Ankle — 1, 6-8, 10-11
Ankler — 2, 5-6, 12
Shin — 1, 8, 11, 13
Nil — 3-4, 9, 14-16

Antrim

Ankle — 5b, 10, 13, 15, 17, 19-20, 22, 25-26, 28-29, 33
Ankler — 2-3, 4A, 5ab, 9, 16c
Anklet — 12
Shin — 1, 8a, 14
Nil — 4, 6-7, 8b, 11, 16ab, 18, 21, 23-24, 27, 30-32, 34

Donegal

Ankle — 1, 5, 5A, 6, 7A, 8, 10a, 12
Ankler — 7, 7A, 8, 10ab, 11
Pastern — 10a
Nil — 1A, 2-4, 9, 13

Fermanagh

Ankle — 2, 4-5, 7a, 9
Nil — 1, 3, 6, 7b, 8, 10

Armagh

Ankle — 3, 6a
Shin — 4
Nil — 1-2, 5, 6b

Londonderry

Ankle — 2, 3A, 6-7
Ankler — 1, 1B, 2-4, 6
Shin — 5
Nil — 1A

2 LITTLE FINGER (PQ1,18)

Pinkie has not been mapped as it occurs densely nearly everywhere.

Shetland

Little finger — 20
Peerie finger — 1-3, 6, 8-11, 15-19, 21ab, 22-27, 30-33
Peerie fjinner — 5
Peerie winkie — 23
Perrie finger — 4, 7, 14
Pinkie — 10, 17, 26, 33
Waenkie — 32
Nil — 12, 28-29

Orkney

Peedie finger — 1-3, 9, 12
Peedie winkie — 3
Peedie winko — 1-2, 6
Peerie finger — 5, 8, 13b, 15, 17, 21
Peerie winkie — 11, 13a
Pinkie — 7, 19
Winkie — 4-5, 8-10, 12, 13a, 14-21
Winko — 4, 13a

Caithness

Currag — 12c
Peedie finger — 5, 14
Peedie pinkie — 11, 12ac, 14
Peerie finger — 13
Peerie pinkie — 15
Pinkie — 1, 2ab, 3-11, 12bc, 13-15, 16ab, 17

Sutherland

Crannie — 15
Creenie — 14
Little finger — 3-4, 6-7, 9b, 11, 13, 17
Pinkie — 1-6, 8, 9ab, 10-12, 15-17
Wee finger — 1, 16

Ross & Cromarty

Creenack — 7, 11, 21, 23, 28, 31, 32c, 35
Creenie — 6, 8-10, 12-15, 18-24, 25ab, 26, 29-31, 32abc, 33-36
Creenuch — 33
Crenack — 17
Kittie conie — 37ab
Little finger — 3-5, 9, 16-17, 22, 26-27, 29, 36
Pinkie — 2-5, 9, 13, 15, 17, 20, 23, 25ab, 26-29, 34-36, 38-39
Wee finger — 25b, 39
Nil — 1

Inverness

Crannie — 27
Creenach — 13ace, 15, 25
Creenack — 9, 17, 21a
Creenie — 8, 10, 13abcde, 14, 19, 31
Crennack — 21b
Crinack — 7, 9
Crionag — 26
Little finger — 1, 4, 6, 11, 13ce, 21a, 23, 32-33, 35
Lutack — 24, 31
Pinkie — 2-3, 5-6, 8-9, 12, 13ab, 14, 16-20, 22, 24-29, 31-40
Wee finger — 3, 25
Nil — 30

Nairn

Crannie — 1c
Creenach — 6
Creenack — 1a, 5
Creenie — 1abc, 3-4
Crenock — 2
Little finger — 2

Moray

Crammie — 7, 10, 18
Crannie — 3-4, 6a, 7, 8bd, 9a, 13, 16, 18-21
Creemie — 1, 2a, 7, 8abcdef, 9b, 10, 14, 16, 18, 20-21
Creemie crammie — 8c, 15
Creenack — 22
Creenie — 2b, 3-5, 11-13, 17, 22-23
Creenie crannie — 4
Crinkie — 18
Little finger — 6b
Pinkie — 5, 6a, 7, 8bcf, 9a, 13, 15, 21-23

Banff

Crannie — 1, 2ac, 3-5, 6ab, 7-17, 18abd, 19-34
Crannie weekie — 2c
Creemie — 18c, 25
Creenie — 5
Granny fingerie — 2b
Little finger — 2b, 3
Peerie weerie — 2b
Pinkie — 1, 2a, 3, 5, 6b, 8-11, 13-17, 18bcd, 23-25, 27-29, 32, 34

Aberdeen

Crannie — 1-2, 3ab, 4, 5abcd, 6-27, 28abc, 29-46, 47abcdef, 48-70, 71abc, 72-109
Crunnie — 104
Little finger — 8, 29, 70, 106
Little fingerie — 47d
Pinkie — 2, 3a, 5b, 6, 9-10, 14, 16, 23, 27, 28ab, 33-34, 45, 47cdf, 48, 51, 53, 55-57, 65-66, 68, 74-75, 78, 80, 83, 86, 96, 98-99, 103, 105
Wee finger — 107

Kincardine

Crannie — 1-16, 17abcd, 18 20, 23, 28
Pinkie — 3, 7, 10, 12-16, 17abcd, 18-28

Kinross

Curnie — 3-5, 7
Pinkie — 1-4, 6-7
Wee finger — 7

Angus

Crannie — 5b, 17a, 26
Little finger — 17b
Pinkie — 1-4, 5abc, 6-13, 14abcd, 15-16, 17ab, 18-28, 29ab, 30-32, 33ab, 34-37

Perth

Crannie — 30
Creenie — 37
Curnie — 26, 33, 45, 52a, 65
Kirnie — 42
Little finger — 2a, 4, 14, 24-25, 36
Pinkie — 1, 2ab, 3-28, 29ab, 30-40, 41ab, 42-50, 51ab, 52abcde, 53-64, 66-74
Pirlie — 39
Wee finger — 16, 28, 29a, 52e

Fife
Carnie — 9b
Churnie — 64b
Crannie — 12
Curnie — 4, 6, 8, 9a, 10-14, 16, 18-22, 24-28, 30-31, 34, 36ab, 37-39, 40ab, 41abcd, 42, 43ab, 44bcdef, 45-52, 54, 55abcdef, 56, 58-61, 64ab
Currie — 23
Kirnie — 7, 12, 28, 33-34, 53
Penkie — 6
Pinkie — 1-5, 7-8, 10-27, 29-35, 36ab, 37-39, 40ab, 41abcd, 42, 43ab, 44abcef, 45-49, 51-54, 55abcdefg, 56-63, 64a
Pirlie — 33
Pirlie winkie — 21
Smaw finger — 50
Wee finger — 7, 41b, 43a, 45, 48

Clackmannan
Curnie — 6
Pinkie — 1-3, 4abcd, 5-7

Stirling
Curlie — 7ab
Curnie — 7d
Diggit — 21a
Little finger — 35a
Peerie — 2
Pinkie — 1-6, 7abcdef, 8-20, 21ab, 22ab, 23abc, 24, 25abcd, 26abcdef, 27ab, 28-34, 35ab, 36, 37ab, 38, 39ab, 40-41, 42ab
Pirlie winkie — 26e
Purlie — 12
Purlie wurlie — 21b, 26a
Wee finger — 7ce, 12-13, 16, 23a, 26d, 34, 35a, 39b

Dunbarton
Curnie — 14a
Little finger — 8, 13c
Pinkie — 1-3, 4ab, 5-6, 7abc, 8-12, 13abc, 14ab, 15, 16ab, 17-18
Wee finger — 1-2, 8, 16b

Argyll
Last finger — 34
Little finger — 2, 6, 9, 12, 17, 27
Pinkie — 1-12, 14-16, 18-40
Wee finger — 3, 10, 23, 32-33, 35
Nil — 13

Bute
Pinkie — 1abcde, 2-7, 8ab, 9
Wee finger — 7, 8b

Ayr
Birlie — 19
Little finger — 28e
Peerie — 16b
Peerie pinkie — 43
Pinkie — 1ab, 2ab, 3-7, 8ab, 9-11, 12ab, 13-15, 16ab, 17, 18ab, 20abcdefgh, 21-23, 24ab, 25, 26abc, 27, 28abcdef, 29, 30ab, 31-34, 35ab, 36-52, 53ab, 54-57
Pirlie winkie — 19
Tinker — 16b
Wee finger — 5, 25, 45, 53a, 57

Renfrew
Little finger — 2d, 8, 13a, 20a
Pinkie — 1ab, 2abcdefghij, 3, 4abcde, 5-10, 11abcdefghijkl, 12ab, 13abcd, 14ab, 15, 16abcd, 17, 18ab, 19, 20ab, 21
Small finger — 2d
Wee finger — 2gi, 4b, 11cel, 13d, 17

Lanark
Curnie — 38d
Little finger — 6, 26a, 29f
Peerie winkie — 15a, 30, 33cd, 38c, 65
Pinkie — 1-6, 7abc, 8ab, 9ab, 10ab, 11-13, 14abcd, 15abc, 16ab, 17-24, 25abcd, 26ab, 27ab, 28, 29abcdefg, 30, 31abcd, 32abcdef, 33abcd, 34, 35abcd, 36-37, 38abcde, 39-45, 46abc, 47-48, 49ab, 50-51, 52ab, 53-56, 57abc, 58, 59ab, 60-63, 64ab, 65-66, 67ab
Small finger — 14d
Wee finger — 6, 7a, 9a, 14d, 15c, 20, 25bc, 29e, 31ad, 33cd, 35d, 48, 61-62,
Wee Willie Winkie — 15b

West Lothian
Curnie — 1c, 6
Pinkie — 1abcd, 2-8, 9ab, 10-16, 17ab, 18, 19ab, 20ab, 21ab, 22
Wee finger — 2, 6, 8, 11, 13, 15-16, 17a

Midlothian
Pinkie — 1-5, 6ab, 7ab, 8ab, 9-11, 12ab, 13, 14ab, 15-22, 23ab, 24, 25abcd, 26ab, 27-32
Wee finger — 3, 8a, 10, 14a

East Lothian
Curnie — 2, 20
Pinkie — 1-3, 4ab, 5, 6ab, 7-19, 21
Purlie wurlie — 4a
Wee finger — 4b, 8-9

Berwick
Little finger — 10, 32
Pinkie — 1-15, 16abc, 17-32
Wee finger — 16b, 32

Peebles
Little finger — 6b
Pinkie — 1-3, 4abc, 5, 6ab, 7-10
Wee finger — 4c, 6a

Selkirk
Pinkie — 1, 2abcde, 3-8

Roxburgh
Little finger — 4, 9a, 15b, 20
Peerie winkie — 21c
Pinkie — 1-2, 3ab, 4-8, 9ab, 10-14, 15ab, 16-20, 21abcdef, 22-28
Pirlie winkie — 28
Wee finger — 1, 5, 21f

Dumfries
Pinkie — 1ab, 2-7, 8ab, 9-16, 17ab, 19-20, 21ab, 22-30, 31abcdef, 32-44, 45ab, 46-49
Wee finger — 12, 19, 21b, 26-27, 32, 37, 39, 43, 46
Nil — 18

Kirkcudbright
Peerie — 15a
Pinkie — 1-9, 11, 12ab, 13-14, 15ab, 16-20, 21abc, 22-27
Pirlie winkie — 17
Wee finger — 1, 7, 10, 16, 21a, 27

Wigtown
Peerie — 13
Peerie pinkie — 5a
Pinkie — 1-4, 5ab, 6-11, 13-18
Wee finger — 9, 11-13

Northumberland
Ear finger — 69ab
Finger — 7, 26, 111a
Fourth finger — 20b, 89
Granny — 59e, 127c
Kiddie finger — 56
Kittie — 56, 73-74, 76, 78-79, 104a, 106-107, 108a, 110, 111ab, 118ab, 124a, 136-140
Little Dick — 59d
Little finger — 2b, 5, 13-14, 17, 23, 28, 29bd, 30-31, 35-36, 40ab, 41cd, 42, 45, 48, 52, 53ab, 54, 59b, 62bg, 64ab, 65a, 68, 69dh, 70, 71abcd, 72abcdgijk, 77, 80, 82, 85-87, 88ab, 89-92, 94b, 95b, 96, 98, 99b, 100, 102, 103abc, 104b, 107, 109, 111b, 112, 118b, 119, 120ab, 121, 124b, 126cf, 127adg, 129c, 130bce, 132, 134, 140, 142-143
(Little) gannie — *64b, 69a, 90, 97 116*
Little man — 59e
Littlest finger — 99d
Littlie — 46
Piggie — 18, 69ab
Pinkie — 1abc, 2ab, 3, 5-6, 8-14, 16-18, 19ab, 20ab, 21-22, 28 29df, 32, 33b, 34b, 37, 39 41a, 43, 47, 49, 51, 53b, 57, 59abde, 60, 69c, 71c, 72ai, 75-76, 79, 108c, 120c, 122ab, 124b, 126e, 131
Skinny finger — 125
Smaal un — 83
Small finger — 24a, 93, 126c, 130c, 135
Tiny man — 59e
Titch finger — 38
Winkie — 46, 79
Nil — 4, 15, 24b, 25, 27, 29ace, 33a, 34a, 41b, 44, 50, 55, 58, 59cf, 61, 62acdefh, 63, 65b, 66-67, 69efg, 71e, 72efhl, 81, 84, 94a, 95a, 99ac, 101ab, 105, 108b, 113-115, 117, 123, 126abd, 127befh, 128, 129ab, 130adf, 133, 141

Cumberland
Fowth finger — 56
Laal finger — 1a, 2-3, 9, 12, 15abc, 16-20, 22, 24-28, 36, 37ab, 38-41, 44-52, 54, 56-59, 62
Lesser digit — 56
Leyl finger — 7-9, 11
Little finger — 4, 5a, 13c, 21, 23, 31, 33, 42, 46, 53
Pinkie — 7, 13ab, 14
Nil — 1b, 5b, 6, 10, 13d, 29-30, 32, 34-35, 43, 55, 60-61, 63ab

Down
Little finger — 2a, 12, 15, 19
Pinkie — 13, 24
Wee finger — 1, 2a, 3, 5-7, 9, 13-20, 23-24, 26-28
Wee pinkie — 11
Nil — 2b, 4, 8, 10, 21-22, 25, 29-30

Tyrone
Beggin mare — 9
Little finger — 11
Wee an — 1
Wee finger — 1, 5, 7-11, 13-16
Nil — 2-4, 6, 12

Antrim
Grub hook — 33
Little finger — 13, 22, 25
Pinkie — 5b, 8b, 11, 16c, 28, 31
Wee finger — 1-3, 4A, 5ab, 7, 9-10, 15, 16c, 17, 19-20, 23, 25-28
Wee stump — 34
Wee Willie Winkie — 16b
Willie Winkie — 17, 21
Nil — 4, 6, 8a, 12, 14, 16a, 18, 24, 29-30, 32

Donegal
Pinkie — 10b
Wee finger — 1, 4-5, 5A, 7A, 8, 10a, 11-12
Nil — 1A, 2-3, 6-7, 9, 13

Fermanagh
Little finger — 4-5
Wee finger — 2, 4-5, 7a, 8-10
Nil — 1, 3, 6, 7b

Armagh
Little finger — 6a
Wee finger — 3-4, 6a
Nil — 1-2, 5, 6b

Londonderry
Little finger — 2
Wee finger — 1, 1A, 3, 3A, 5, 7
Nil — 1B, 4, 6

3 BLISTER (on skin) (PQ1, 19)

Blister has not been mapped as it occurs all over the area. The concentration of some of the items mapped is not very high.

Shetland

Blaib – 26
Blemick – 4, 9, 12, 22
Blibe – 1-3, 5-6, 8, 10, 15, 19, 27
Blister – 1-2, 4, 7-8, 10-11, 13, 15-17, 20, 21ab, 25, 27, 29-30, 32-33
Sig – 24
Stane loopin – 13, 19
Steen loppin – 6
Sten loppin – 24
Watery bleb – 24
Watery blibe – 5, 21a, 22, 28
Nil – 14, 18, 23, 31

Orkney

Blab – 12, 20
Bladder – 8
Blaib – 10
Bleeb – 7
Blether – 4, 8, 11, 15
Blibe – 1-2, 4-6, 9, 12, 13a, 15-20
Blister – 1-5, 7-8, 11, 13ab, 15, 17-18, 21
Leepid – 14

Caithness

Breaking – 17
Bleb – 7, 11
Blibe – 2ab, 5-6
Blister – 2b, 6, 10, 13-14, 16b
Blob – 4, 8-11, 12ab, 13-15, 16b
Nil – 1, 3, 12c, 16a

Sutherland

Blister – 1, 3-8, 9ab, 10-13, 16-17
Blob – 2, 14
Boil – 3
Nil – 15

Ross & Cromarty

Beal – 37b
Billins – 2
Blads – 37a
Blister – 1, 3-6, 8-9, 16-20, 22-24, 25ab, 26-29, 31, 32abc, 33, 36, 37a, 39
Bloab – 9
Blob – 9, 13-14, 18-20, 25b, 28, 31, 34-36
Cuspach – 30
Gussie – 37b
Weal – 36
Nil – 7, 10-12, 15, 21, 38

Inverness

Blister – 1-12, 13abce, 16-20, 21ab, 22-23, 25, 27-30, 32-40
Blob – 9, 13ce, 17, 19, 26, 29
Plook – 13d
Nil – 14-15, 24, 31

Nairn

Blister – 1b, 2, 4-6
Blob – 1c
Nil – 1a, 3

Moray

Balin – 8d
Bleb – 6a, 8b, 9ab
Blibe – 1
Blister – 2a, 5, 6b, 7, 8bc, 11, 14, 18, 20, 23
Bloab – 4
Blob – 4, 8b, 12, 19, 22
Fire – 22
Fired hands or feet – 13
Nil – 2b, 3, 8aef, 10, 15-17, 21

Banff

Beelin fester – 2c
Blaaver – 3
Bleb – 10, 18c, 26
Bleesin – 8
Blibe – 5
Blister – 1, 2b, 3-4, 6b, 8-9, 13, 15-17, 18c, 19-21, 24-25, 30, 32, 34
Blob – 6b, 14, 18b, 28-30
Blowb – 2b
Plook – 27
Nil – 2a, 6a, 7, 11-12, 18ad, 22-23, 31, 33

Aberdeen

Beelin – 29, 47c
Blaver – 53
Blaw – 88
Bleb – 28b, 77
Bledder – 41
Blister – 1, 3b, 4, 5c, 6-9, 11-12, 14, 17, 20-23, 27, 28a, 31, 34-35, 44-46, 47e, 48-50, 53-54, 59, 66-67, 70, 71bc, 72-76, 81-85, 94-96, 98, 100, 104-106, 108
Blob – 2, 19, 27, 47f, 56, 62, 69, 77, 93, 97, 103, 107
Blobber – 51
Bloob – 84
Burn – 70
Festerin – 29, 47c
Fired – 101
Horn – 23
Poold – 10
Puddin – 63
Scam – 33
Scaumt – 36
Squile – 16
Watery beelin – 5a
Watery bleb – 28a
Watery bledder – 80
Watery blister – 3a, 44
Watery lump – 32
Weet blob – 104
Nil – 5bd, 13, 15, 18, 24-26, 28c, 30, 37-40, 42-43, 47abd, 52, 55, 57-58, 60-61, 64-65, 68, 71a, 78-79, 86-87, 89-92, 99, 102, 109

Kincardine

Blaib – 26
Bleb – 1, 12, 15, 17bcd, 20, 22
Blister – 3, 5-8, 10, 12, 16, 17bcd, 19, 21, 24, 27
Blob – 7, 15
Blub – 1
Watery blaib – 28
Nil – 2, 4, 9, 11, 13-14, 17a, 18, 23, 25

Kinross

Bleb – 2
Blister – 1-4
Blob – 3
Bubble – 6
Nil – 5,7

Angus

Blab – 29a, 33b
Blaib – 5a, 13, 14bc, 24, 30, 33b
Blaub – 17b
Bleab – 17b
Bleb – 1, 4, 5bc, 6-9, 12, 14ad, 16, 19-21, 23, 31, 33a, 34, 36-37
Blister – 1, 8, 10, 15, 17b, 18, 20, 22, 24-26, 28, 29b, 32, 34, 36
Postule – 33b
Scadded – 17a, 23
Watery bleb – 27, 35, 37
Nil – 2-3, 11

Perth

Blab – 73
Blaib – 31, 52c
Blaub – 47
Bleb – 15, 18, 20-21, 23, 25-26, 32-33, 41ab, 44, 48, 51a, 52bd, 53, 60, 62, 66
Blender – 44
Blib – 29b
Blibe – 7, 25, 27, 42, 48, 52d, 57, 65
Blister – 1, 2a, 3-4, 6, 8-10, 13-14, 20, 25, 27-28, 29a, 32-33, 35-36, 40, 43, 46, 50, 51b, 52ae, 57, 60, 62, 64, 67-71, 74
Blob – 5, 11-12, 17, 30, 66-67, 69
Blobst – 11
Pustule – 3
Watery bleeb – 56
Nil – 2b, 16, 19, 22, 24, 34, 37-39, 45, 49, 54-55, 58-59, 61, 63, 72

Fife

Blab – 53
Blaub – 33
Bleb – 3, 7, 12, 22, 27, 37, 40b, 42, 44a, 55d
Blister – 1, 4, 6, 8, 9a, 10-11 13-14, 16-17, 19-21, 23-25, 28, 30, 32, 36ab, 37, 39, 40b, 41abd, 43ab, 44bcde, 46-51, 53-54, 55abde, 56-57, 59, 62-63, 64b
Blob – 7, 13, 27, 55g
Burn – 15
Sair – 40
Shiver – 13
Watery blab – 18
Welt – 43b
Wind gell – 35
Nil – 2, 5, 9b, 26, 29, 31, 34, 38, 40a, 41c, 44f, 45, 52, 55cf, 58, 60-61, 64ab

Clackmannan

Blab – 5
Blaub – 5
Blister – 1-3, 4abc, 7
Blob – 6
Nil – 4d

Stirling

Blab – 17, 21b, 27a
Bleb – 6, 7e, 8, 18, 21b
Bleib – 26d
Blister – 2-4, 6, 7acef, 8-9, 11-13, 16-18, 20, 21ab, 22ab, 23bc, 25cd, 26acdf, 27a, 28, 30-34, 35a, 36, 37ab, 39b, 40-41, 42a
Bloab – 9
Blob – 25b
Bubble – 35b
Ootbrak – 7b
Plook – 12
Shiver – 21b, 25ad
Nil – 1, 5, 7d, 10, 14-15, 19, 23a, 24, 26be, 27b, 29, 38, 39a, 42b

Dunbarton

Blab – 2, 7c, 9
Bleb – 6, 15
Blister – 1, 3, 7abc, 8, 10-12, 13abc, 16ab
Blob – 5
Pimple – 8
Scad – 14a
Nil – 4ab, 14b, 17-18

Argyll

Abraison – 34
Balg – 12
Blab – 31, 33, 35
Bleb – 24, 35
Blister – 1-12, 14-17, 19, 21-27, 30, 32-33, 35-36, 38-39
Nil – 13, 18, 20, 28-29, 37, 40

Bute

Blab – 1a
Blister – 1cd, 2, 7, 8ab, 9
Dog blister – 8a
Nil – 1be, 3-6

Ayr

Birstle – 8a, 29
Birze – 38
Blab – 10, 16b, 37, 47
Blain – 41
Bleb – 52, 53a
Blipe – 18a
Blishen – 46
Blister – 1ab, 2ab, 3, 5-7, 8b, 10-11, 12a, 13-15, 16a, 20bch, 21, 24b, 25, 26abc, 28f, 30ab, 31-34, 35ab, 36, 38, 40, 42-45, 48-52, 53a, 54-57
Blob – 1a, 10, 35b
Blotch – 47
Burze – 14, 24b
Clour – 18b
Dog blushin – 51
Hive – 28a, 39
Plook – 15
Swallin – 28f
Water blab – 57
Water blister – 5
Water blob – 57
Welt – 7
Nil – 4, 9, 12b, 17, 19, 20adefg, 22-23, 24a, 27, 28bcde, 53b

Renfrew

Blab – 1b, 2ef, 4d, 11efjl, 20b, 21
Bleb – 6, 9, 11jl, 16a, 18b
Blister – 1b, 2achij, 4ace, 8, 11acdekl, 12a, 13c, 14a, 16abd, 18ab, 19, 20a
Blob – 14b
Blushin – 21
Plook – 8
Water blister – 17
Watery blab – 11l
Watery bubble – 2i
Nil – 1a, 2bdg, 3, 4b, 5, 7, 10, 11bghi, 12b, 13abd, 15, 16c

Lanark

Birse – 57a
Blab – 9b, 17, 20, 23, 30, 33cd, 35b, 36, 38d, 46b, 57b
Bleb – 32f, 48
Blister – 1-3, 5-6, 7ac, 8b, 9a, 10b, 11-12, 14bd, 15ac, 16ab, 19-22, 25abc, 26ab, 27b, 29cdf, 31ad, 32aef, 33a, 34, 35abcd, 38abc, 39-40, 44, 46abc, 48, 49ab, 51, 52ab, 53, 56, 57ab, 58, 59ab, 60, 62, 64b, 65
Bloatch – 29a
Blob – 17, 33cd, 38d, 47, 67a
Blotch – 47, 55
Check – 15c, 39
Fire – 13
Girn – 67b
Pimple – 8a
Plook – 25d, 29ef, 54
Poop – 31c
Scouther – 56
Water blab – 20, 36
Water blister – 18, 45
Nil – 4, 7b, 10a, 14ac, 15b, 24, 27a, 28, 29bg, 31b, 32bcd, 33b, 37, 38e, 41-43, 50, 57c, 61, 63, 64a, 66

West Lothian

Blab – 11
Blister – 1ab, 2-3, 5-8, 10-13,

West Lothian cont'd
15-16, 17a, 18, 20ab, 22
Blob — 4
Bull — 11
Burse — 19a
Check — 21a
Water blister — 17a
Water still — 1c
Watery bubble — 19b
Nil — 1d, 9ab, 14, 17b, 21b

Midlothian

Bleb — 4-5, 14b
Blister — 2-3, 6ab, 7a, 8a, 10-11, 12a, 14a, 15-16, 18-19, 21, 23b, 25b, 28-30
Blob — 7b, 24, 25a
Blotch — 20, 32
Blush — 30
Bubble — 25d
Check — 3
Pustle — 12a
Sair — 1
Weal — 6a
Nil — 8b, 9, 12b, 13, 17, 22, 23a, 25c, 26ab, 27, 31

East Lothian

Beeling — 6a
Blain — 16
Bleb — 2, 11, 13
Blipe — 10
Blister — 1, 4b, 5, 7-9, 13, 15-21
Blob — 17
Gleb — 2
Scuddie — 13
Shaeburn — 6b
Nil — 3, 4a, 12, 14

Berwick

Bile — 8
Blaub — 10
Bleb — 5, 7, 10, 16a, 27, 32
Blibe — 20, 32
Blister — 1-2, 6-10, 12-13, 15, 16bc, 19, 24, 28, 32
Blob — 17-18, 21, 23, 27-28, 30
Blossom — 32
Blotch — 31
Blush — 3, 11, 16a, 18, 22-23, 26-27, 29, 31-32
Water blob — 15, 24
Nil — 4, 14, 25

Peebles

Blain — 6a
Bleb — 4a, 8
Blister — 1-2, 4b, 5, 6ab, 9
Blob — 4c
Nil — 3, 7, 10

Selkirk

Blister — 2bcd, 8
Bloatch — 6
Blob — 2e, 3, 5
Blush — 1, 2ad, 4-8

Roxburgh

Blab — 3a
Blain — 13
Bleb — 15b, 19-20, 21c, 27
Bleeb — 4
Blister — 1, 13-14, 15b, 20, 21a, 25, 28
Blob — 9a, 13, 21ac, 28
Blush — 2, 3a, 4-8, 9b, 10-11, 15a, 16-18, 21adef, 22-26, 28
Brizzed — 12
Bubble — 19
Chuck — 1
Nil — 3b, 21b

Dumfries

Bleb — 10, 32, 37, 44, 47, 49
Blister — 1a, 4, 7, 8a, 12, 15-16, 17b, 18, 20, 22, 24, 26-27, 31bde, 32-33, 40, 43, 46
Bloab — 5-6, 35
Blob — 1b, 12, 17ab, 28-29, 32, 34, 37-39, 42, 45ab, 46
Blotchin — 31b
Blushin — 13
Scad — 42, 46
Scaud — 8b
Scauld — 25
Water blister — 21b
Nil — 2-3, 9, 11, 14, 19, 21a, 23, 30, 31acf, 36, 41, 48

Kirkcudbright

Bleb — 1, 12b
Blister — 1, 3-7, 10, 14, 15a, 18-20, 21bc, 22-23, 25, 27
Blob — 1-2, 15a, 17
Bloshin — 12a, 21c
Breeze — 16
Chack — 1, 8
Check — 8
Stane — 16
Water bleb — 26
Water bloab — 14
Water blob — 12b, 21a
Nil — 9, 11, 13, 15b, 24

Wigtown

Blab — 2
Blaub — 17
Bleb — 5b, 7-8, 17
Blister — 1, 3, 5a, 9, 11-12, 14, 16-17
Blob — 9, 13
Blughin — 5a
Blushin — 10
Scouder — 10
Nil — 4, 6, 15, 18

Northumberland

Blackman's pinch — 122b
Bleb — 1c, 2ab, 8-9, 14-16, 18, 22-23, 24ab, 28, 29abde, 32, 33a, 36-39, 40ab, 41b, 43-50, 53a, 54, 56-58, 59abcdef, 60-61, 62abcdefgh, 63, 64ab, 65ab, 66, 68, 69abcdefgh, 70, 71bce, 72acdfgijkl, 73-85, 87, 88ab, 89-92, 94b, 95b, 96-98 99abcd, 100, 101a, 102, 103a, 104ab, 105, 107, 108abc, 109, 111ab, 112-117, 118ab, 119, 120abc, 121, 122ab, 123, 124ab, 125, 126abdef, 127bcdfgh, 128, 129abc, 130acdf, 131-140, 142
Blemish — 21
Blibe — 1bc, 2ab, 3, 7-9, 11-13, 16-18, 19ab, 20b, 21, 24b, 25-28, 29bcdef, 31, 33b, 34ab, 35-36, 39, 40b, 41ad, 45, 48, 59d, 64b, 65b, 68, 83, 122a
Blish — 44, 47, 72d
Blister — 1a, 2b, 5-6, 8, 13-14, 28, 30, 35-36, 40a, 41cd, 42, 52, 53b, 54, 59b, 62b, 64b, 69b, 71acd, 72acgi, 78, 82, 86-87, 88a, 96, 103abc, 104a, 109-110, 111b, 112, 121, 126ac, 130c, 133, 139-140
Blob — 17, 56, 65b, 71ac, 72ik, 79, 95b, 121, 127eh, 129a, 130b, 131
Blotch — 56
Blush — 29ab, 33b, 34b, 37, 39, 40a, 41ac, 42, 44, 47, 49-50, 53b, 57-58, 59e, 60, 62eh, 64b, 65ab, 66, 68, 69g, 71bd, 72bdegi, 76, 79, 82, 85, 101b, 106-107, 108a, 112, 115,. 122b, 124b, 126f, 127abc, 129c, 130de, 133-138, 141-143
Brushburn — 86
Flush — 124b
Gather — 89
Plook — 20b
Sair please — 103bc, 106
Skinned — 93
Water bleb — 126b
Nil — 4, 10, 20a, 51, 55, 67, 72h, 94a, 95a

Cumberland

Blash — 8
Bleb — 1a, 2-4, 5a, 6-11, 13acd, 14, 15abc, 16-19, 21-22, 24-29, 31, 34, 37a, 38-43, 45-47, 49, 51-55, 57-58, 60, 62, 63ab
Blish — 8-9, 11-12, 22, 30-33, 35-36, 37b, 38-40, 47-48, 56, 62
Blister — 1a, 7, 9, 20, 23, 40, 46, 48, 50, 53, 56-59
Blush — 4
Hawk — 27
Plish — 22
Scadert — 56
Scawder — 44
Scoder — 61
Seg — 28, 37a, 46, 63a
Sore spot — 54
Water bleb — 56
Water jag — 28
Nil — 1b, 5b, 13b

Down

Blab — 4, 13, 27
Blister — 1, 2a, 5, 7, 9, 12, 18-19, 24, 26
Blushen — 18
Burn — 15
Nip — 5
Scald — 15
Sore spot — 17
Welt — 26
Nil — 2b, 3, 6, 8, 10-11, 14, 16, 20-23, 25, 28-30

Tyrone

Blab — 5
Bleb — 11
Blister — 1, 7-8, 10-11
Spot — 9
Water blob — 15
Nil — 2-4, 6, 12-14, 16

Antrim

Bleb — 7
Blister — 1, 3, 5b, 7, 9-10, 13, 16c, 17, 19-20, 22, 25-26, 28-29
Blue gan — 7
Bluggin — 16b
Boggin — 5a
Buggin — 16b, 33
Water blab — 11
Weal — 8b
Nil — 2, 4, 4A, 6, 8a, 12, 14-15, 16a, 18, 21, 23-24, 27, 30-32, 34

Donegal

Bile — 6
Blab — 5A, 10a, 12
Blister — 1, 4-5, 5A, 7A, 8
Blob — 10a, 12
Lump — 4
Nirls — 10a
Welt — 9
Nil — 1A, 2-3, 7, 10b, 11, 13

Fermanagh

Beal — 1
Beelding — 6
Blister — 2, 4-5, 7a, 9
Buggin — 5
Nil — 3, 7b, 8, 10

Armagh

Bile — 4
Blister — 3, 6a
Blushin — 1
Kibe — 1
Welt — 6a
Nil — 2, 5, 6b

Londonderry

Blister — 2, 3A
Bluggin — 4
Buggin — 1A
Scam — 3
Nil — 1, 1B, 5-7

4 SPLINTER (tiny fragment of wood driven into finger etc.) (PQ1, 25)

For the recurrence of **stab, stob,** see 5 to **prick,** 13 **three legged stool,** 26 **bradawl** and 42 **fence posts.**

Shetland

Bit o' wid – 20
Fliss – 2, 21b, 30
Peerie bit o' wid – 30
Peerie fliss – 30
Skelfen – 14
Skilf – 22
Something – 33
Spale – 11, 26
Speeger – 5
Speelick – 25
Spell – 17, 24
Spellick – 17, 24
Spjolk – 19
Spleet – 2, 6
Splint – 15
Splinter – I-2, 4, 7-8, 10, 15, 17, 21a, 22-23, 27
Spoilk – 3
Spolk – 12
Nil – 9, 13, 16, 18, 28-29, 31-32

Orkney

Bit of wid – 6
Bit of wood – 9
Jag – 5
Skliver – 15
Sliver – 7, 13a
Slivver – 17
Speel – 7-8
Spell – 16
Splint – 13b
Splinter – 2-5, 8, 11, 13ab, 15, 17-21
Sprack – 2, 4, 15
Nil – 1, 10, 12, 14

Caithness

Bit – 4
Pirk – 12b
Purr – 11, 13
Skelf – 2a, 12c, 15
Skelp – 16a
Spale – 1, 11, 13-14, 16b
Speeling – 12c
Spilk – 2b, 5-6, 8-9, 12abc, 14-15, 16b, 17
Splinter – 8, 16b
Nil – 3, 7, 10

Sutherland

Jag – 3
Skelf – 10
Spale – 8, 11, 14
Speal – 13
Spike – 8, 15
Splinter – 3, 5-8, 9a, 13, 16
Stab – 1-4, 6, 9b, 10, 15-17
Nil – 12

Ross & Cromarty

Bit wood – 9
Skelding – 31
Skelf – 5-6, 25a, 26-27, 38-39
Skelve – 23
Slipe – 25a
Sliver – 20
Spale – 9, 13-14, 18, 20-21, 25a 28, 32b, 33, 35-36
Spaleack – 20
Speel – 11, 25b, 34
Spellack – 29
Splinter – 1, 5-6, 8-9, 16-17, 20, 23-24, 26-27, 29-30, 32a, 36, 39
Stab – 3-4, 11-12, 15-17, 19, 22, 31, 32c, 34
Stick – 36
Stob – 22, 27, 31, 37ab
Thorn – 22
Whittle – 13
Nil – 2, 7, 20

Inverness

Chop – 1
Fire – 13a
Jag – 30
Skelf – 12, 13b, 19, 22, 24, 27, 35-38, 40
Sleeshack – 13d
Sliver – 13a
Spailach – 14, 20
Spale – 9, 13e, 26, 33
Spealg – 26
Spell – 31
Spellack – 24
Spirack – 18
Splinter – 1-8, 10, 13ce, 18-20, 21b, 23, 29, 33, 35
Split – 1
Stab – 6, 8-9, 11, 13abc, 16-17, 21ab, 22, 25, 27-28, 32, 34, 36, 38-40
Stob – 29, 33
Thorn – 6
Nil – 15

Nairn

Spalach – 4
Spale – 1b, 2-3
Splinter – 5-6
Stab – 1ac, 2

Moray

Bit stick – 7
Scob – 17
Skelb – 1, 2a, 6a, 8b, 10, 12-13, 16, 22
Skelf – 3, 13
Skelp – 5, 8bf
Spale – 2b, 9b, 18, 21-22
Spalin – 9a
Splinter – 6b, 8d, 9a, 11, 14
Stab – 3-4, 7, 8bc, 13, 15, 21-23
Steug – 9a
Stob – 5, 6a, 8ae, 9a, 19-20, 23
Stobe – 8d

Banff

Skelb – 4-5, 8, 15, 18bcd, 23, 26, 29, 31
Skelf – 2c, 6b, 18c, 28, 30, 32
Skilf – 20
Sliver – 34
Spale – 32-34
Speel – 22
Splinter – 15, 21, 34
Stab – 5, 9, 16, 25
Stick – 13, 19
Stob – 1, 2ac, 3, 5, 6ab, 7, 9-11, 13-14, 17, 18bd
Stowb – 2b, 3
Nil – 12, 18a, 20, 24, 27

Aberdeen

Bit (of) stick – 32, 44, 62, 86, 108
Bittie (of) stick – 10, 35
Brob – 16
Brod – 5c, 14
Jag – 39
Job – 1, 9, 40, 63, 74, 105
Jobbie – 9
Piece of stick – 70
Skelb – 3b, 5bd, 11-12, 20-21, 23, 26-27, 28abc, 42, 47a, 50-51, 53, 65, 77, 80-81, 88, 97-98, 103-104
Skelbie – 35
Skelf – 2, 14, 19, 28a, 51, 80, 96
Skelfin – 19
Skellie – 9
Skelp – 27
Skelve – 51
Skiff – 30
Skilf – 60
Slether – 71a
Sliver – 5b
Speel – 23
Spell – 69, 79
Spilk – 14
Splint – 59
Splinter – 6, 8, 22, 45-46, 72, 75, 83, 90, 94
Stab – 48, 74
Stick – 29, 47f, 79
Stob – 1, 3a, 4, 5ab, 7, 9, 14, 17, 19, 24-25, 28b, 31, 34, 36, 40-41, 47abcde, 48-49, 51-52, 54, 56, 60, 63-64, 66-67, 70, 71abc, 73-74, 76, 78, 82-84, 92-93, 95-97, 99-102, 104, 106-109
Stowb – 7, 47d
Nil – 13, 15, 18, 33, 37-38, 43, 55, 57-58, 61, 68, 85, 87, 89, 91

Kincardine

Bit stick – 11, 19, 26
Chip – 3, 8
Skelb – 14, 17a, 18, 21, 23, 28
Skelf – 7, 23, 25
Skelve – 1
Slither – 27
Sliver – 7, 22
Speil – 1
Spell – 2, 16
Splice – 17b
Splinter – 5-6, 8, 10, 17c, 21, 27
Stob – 4, 12, 15, 17abcd, 20, 22, 24
Stobe – 18
Nil – 9, 13

Kinross

Skelb – 1-5, 7
Skelf – 1, 6
Spale – 3, 7
Splinter – 1

Angus

Bit stick – 15
Bittie stick – 33b
Crum – 33b
Jobie – 5a, 8
Prickle – 33b
Scliff – 14a
Scroag – 10
Skelb – 4, 5c, 6, 8-10, 14abcd, 15, 19, 22, 32, 35-36
Skelf – 9, 12, 14b, 17a, 19, 23, 25-26, 29a, 30, 33a, 37
Skelp – 14d
Skelve – 14a, 28
Skiff – 34
Sliver – 27
Spale – 7, 13, 32, 34, 37
Speel – 5b, 31
Spelk – 29b
Splice – 17b
Splinter – 1, 3, 17b, 18, 20, 24-25, 29b, 34, 36
Stick – 2
Stob – 2, 5b, 14c, 21, 24, 35, 37
Stobbie – 24
Stobie – 5a
Stog – 21
Thorn – 33b
Nil – 11, 16

Perth

Drob – 41a
Jag – 26
Jobe – 20
Jug – 69
Scare – 47
Skale – 25
Skelb – 11, 15, 20-21, 23, 27-28, 29ab, 30-31, 39, 41b, 42, 44, 46, 48-50, 51b, 52abde, 53, 55-57, 59-60, 63-66, 72
Skelf – 1, 10, 13, 21, 29a, 34-35, 38, 42, 44, 48, 52b, 56, 62, 66-68, 70-71, 73-74
Skellock – 61
Skelp – 18, 45
Skelve – 3, 25, 52ae, 69, 73
Sliver – 24, 52e
Spale – 1, 2b, 3, 5, 7, 9, 12, 16-17, 25, 32-33, 37-40, 41ab, 42-46, 50, 51a, 52c, 54, 62, 69-70
Speel – 22
Spelf – 26
Spelk – 26
Splinter – 2a, 4, 8, 10, 12-13, 24-25, 33, 36, 60, 74
Stab – 2b, 14, 16, 25, 41a, 43
Steuog – 13
Stick – 6
Stob – 7, 15, 20, 25-26, 37, 40
Stub – 25
Thorn – 8
Nil – 19, 58

Fife

Brog – 58
Brug – 37
Bruggle – 51
Skel – 37
Skelb – 1-4, 6-8, 9ab, 10-35, 36ab, 37-39, 40ab, 41abcd, 42, 43ab, 44acdef, 45-54, 55abcdefg, 56-63, 64ab
Skelf – 21, 23, 28, 37-39, 42, 43a, 44be, 47, 52-53, 55abcg, 59, 62, 64a
Skellock – 37
Skelpe – 44f
Skelve – 2, 12, 34, 39, 41b, 44b, 48
Skelye – 33
Sliver – 43b, 53
Slivver – 55f
Spale – 37, 51, 55ab, 59
Speld – 43a
Speldron – 55d
Splinter – 5, 40a, 41a, 57, 63

Clackmannan

Skelb – 1-3, 4abd, 6-7
Skelf – 1, 4cd, 5-6
Skelve – 4a
Spale – 5
Spelk – 4b

Stirling

Risp – 27a
Sclif – 18
Skelb – 3, 7e, 8-10, 12, 20, 22a, 25abcd, 26de
Skelf – 5-6, 7abce, 8-9, 11-17, 19, 21b, 22ab, 23ab, 25acd, 26abcdef, 27ab, 28-33, 35ab, 36, 37b, 38, 39a, 40-41, 42ab
Skelp – 25d, 26a
Skelve – 4, 7df, 18, 21a, 22b, 23c, 24, 26af, 34, 37a, 39b
Sliver – 19
Spale – 7b, 8-9
Splinter – 4, 21b, 23a, 26d, 35a, 39b
Sprit – 2
Nil – 1

Dunbarton

Risp – 13a
Skelf – 1-3, 4ab, 5-6, 7abc, 8-12, 13abc, 14ab, 15, 16ab, 17-18
Splinter – 7c, 13c
Stab – 2

Argyll

Jag – 11, 18, 28, 35
Scliff – 40
Spealb – 27
Skelb – 5

Argyll cont'd

Skelf — 1-3, 7-13, 15-16, 18-21, 23-25, 30, 36-40
Skiff — 4
Skleef — 29, 32, 37-38
Spale — 1-2, 34-35
Spill — 8
Splinter — 1, 6, 9, 11-12, 14, 16-17, 22-23, 25, 27
Stab — 3, 8, 10, 24, 30, 33-35
Thorn — 3
Wood — 33
Nil — 26, 31

Bute

Skeef — 4
Skelf — 1abcd, 2-3, 5, 7, 8ab, 9
Sliver — 9
Spale — 6
Splinter — 8b
Nil — 1e

Ayr

Chip — 43
Skelf — 1ab, 2ab, 3-7, 8ab, 9-11, 12ab, 13-15, 16ab, 17, 18ab, 19, 20abcdefgh, 21-23, 24ab, 25, 26abc, 28abcdef, 29, 30ab, 31-34, 35ab, 36-52, 53ab, 54-57
Skilf — 27
Sklaff — 20g
Skliff — 9, 27
Sliver — 17, 57
Spale — 43
Spelk — 45
Splinter — 38, 43, 57

Renfrew

Skelf — 1ab, 2abcdefghij, 3, 4acde, 5-10, 11abcdefghijkl, 12ab, 13abcd, 14ab, 15, 16abcd, 17, 18ab, 19, 20ab, 21
Skelp — 21
Skliff — 16d
Spelk — 15
Splinter — 4e, 11c, 20a
Stob — 1b
Nil — 4b, 17

Lanark

Skale — 20
Skalf — 33cd
Skelf — 1-6, 7abc, 8ab, 9ab, 10ab, 11-13, 14abcd, 15abc, 16ab, 17-24, 25abcd, 26ab, 27ab, 28, 29abcdefg, 30, 31abcd, 32abcdef, 33abcd, 34, 35abcd, 36-37, 38abce, 39-45, 46abc, 47-48, 49ab, 50-51, 52ab, 53, 55-56, 57abc, 58, 59ab, 60-63, 64ab, 65-66, 67ab
Skelft — 32e
Skelp — 58
Skilf — 6
Skliff — 32d
Slivver — 2
Spale — 21, 38d, 49b
Speil — 36
Spelk — 46ac
Spell — 29f
Spilk — 38d
Splice — 7a, 54, 62, 66, 67ab
Splinter — 1, 6, 10b, 15c, 25a, 26a, 27b, 29f, 45

West Lothian

Skelf — 1abd, 2-8, 9ab, 10-16, 17ab, 18, 19ab, 20ab, 21ab, 22
Skelp — 1acd, 2, 8
Spale — 4, 9b, 11, 14-15, 20a, 21a, 22
Splice — 6
Stob — 11

Midlothian

Skelb — 2, 21
Skelf — 3, 5, 6b, 8a, 10-11, 12ab, 13, 14ab, 15, 18, 22, 23b, 25b, 26ab, 29-32
Skelp — 24
Skelve — 16
Skleff — 8b
Skliff — 10
Spale — 1-5, 6ab, 7ab, 8b, 9-11, 12b, 16, 18, 19-20, 23ab, 24, 25ac, 26a, 27-29, 31
Speal — 7b
Splice — 8ab, 9, 17-19, 21, 23a, 24, 25acd, 26ab, 27, 30-32
Splinter — 10, 15, 21, 23ab

East Lothian

Jag — 16
Skelf — 1-3, 4ab, 6ab, 7, 11, 13
Skliff — 14
Slice — 6b
Sliver — 15
Spale — 2, 5, 6a, 9-10, 13-15, 21
Speel — 11
Speld — 13
Spelk — 8, 19
Splice — 1, 4a, 5, 6ab, 8-13, 15-18, 20-21
Splint — 15
Splinter — 18, 21

Berwick

Prog — 7
Skelb — 8
Skelf — 16c, 24, 27
Skelp — 15
Spale — 1, 6
Spelk — 10, 16a, 18, 22, 32
Splice — 1, 3-5, 7-15, 16abc, 17-21, 23-27, 29-32
Splint — 31
Splinter — 2, 16c, 26, 28

Peebles

Jag — 6b, 6a
Skelf — 1-2, 4b, 5, 6a, 7-10
Spale — 3, 4c, 8
Spavin — 4a
Spelk — 3
Splice — 1, 3, 4ac, 5, 8-10
Splinter — 4b, 6ab

Selkirk

Skelf — 2b, 5
Spale — 1
Spelk — 3-4, 6
Splice — 2abcde, 3-8
Splinter — 8

Roxburgh

Jag — 3b, 22
Skelf — 9b, 12, 21af, 23
Skilp — 15b
Skilver — 15b
Slipe — 15b
Sliver — 9b, 15b, 28
Spale — 3a, 4, 8, 9a, 21c, 23, 26-27
Spelk — 8, 9b, 15b, 17, 20, 21c, 26
Splice — 1-2, 3ab, 5-8, 9ab, 10-11, 13-14, 15a, 16-20, 21abcdef, 23-26, 28
Splint — 9b
Splinter — 3a, 15b, 21a, 25

Dumfries

Bit — 32
Skelf — 1ab, 2-4, 14, 19, 21b, 22-23, 26, 29, 31abf, 32, 34-35, 38-39, 41
Skelp — 5, 19, 41-42
Skelth — 31d
Slither — 23
Sliver — 7
Spale — 17ab
Speel — 37
Spelk — 2, 4, 6-7, 8ab, 9-13, 15-16, 20, 21ab, 23-28, 30, 31cdef, 32-37, 39-44, 45ab, 46-47, 49
Splice — 2, 17b, 18, 29
Splint — 28, 46
Splinter — 12, 17b, 46
Nil — 48

Kirkcudbright

Skelf — 1, 3, 7-9, 11, 12a, 15a, 16, 18, 23-24
Skelp — 1, 14, 17, 19, 21c, 26
Spelk — 2-5, 7-10, 12ab, 13, 15ab, 16-18, 20, 21abc, 22-23, 25-27
Spelve — 11
Spike — 7
Splinter — 6-7

Wigtown

Geg — 5b
Purr — 5a
Skelf — 1-4, 5ab, 6-20, 12-18
Skelg — 11
Skelp — 5a
Skliff — 5b
Sliver — 17
Spale — 2, 11
Spelk — 12

Northumberland

Progle — 114
Sliver — 29e
Spelk — 1abc, 2ab, 6-8, 11-18, 19a, 20b, 21-23, 24ab, 25-28, 29abcdef, 30-32, 33ab, 34ab, 35-39, 40ab, 41abcd, 42-52, 53ab, 54-58, 59abcdef, 60-61 62abcdefgh, 63, 64ab, 65ab, 66-68, 69abcdefgh, 70, 71abcde, 72abcdefghijkl, 73-87, 88ab, 89-93, 94ab, 95ab, 96-98, 99abcd, 100, 101ab, 102, 103bc, 104ab, 105-107, 108abc, 109-110, 111ab, 112-117, 118ab, 119, 120abc, 121, 122ab, 123, 124ab, 125, 126abcdef, 127abcdefgh, 128, 129abc, 130abcdef, 131-143
Spell — 46, 63, 72i, 109, 118b, 121, 133, 137, 142
Spile — 71c
Spilk — 28
Splice — 2b, 3-5, 8-10, 16-17, 19ab, 20ab, 68, 71c
Splinter — 1a, 2b, 5-6, 13, 18, 28, 35-36, 40a, 42, 52, 59bd, 62b, 71a, 72c, 82-83, 85, 95b, 99b, 103a, 112, 121, 126cf, 127ah, 130c, 137, 140
Splint — 59b
Wedge — 13

Cumberland

Jag — 14
Prick — 61
Prickle — 58
Spale — 9, 32
Sparlin — 56
Speil — 2, 56
Spelk — 1ab, 2-3, 5a, 6-8, 11, 13abcd, 14, 15ab, 16-18, 20-23, 28, 31-32, 35, 37ab, 38-40, 45, 47-50, 56-57, 62, 63b
Spell — 1b, 2-4, 7-9, 12, 14, 15c, 17-19, 21, 24-31, 33-34, 36, 37a, 41-46, 51-58, 60-62
Spiel — 62
Spile — 60
Spilk — 57
Spill — 12
Splinter — 1a, 9, 24, 28, 37b, 46-47, 53, 56, 59
Nil — 5b, 10, 63a

Down

Chip — 17
Jag — 2a, 6, 15, 20, 26
Jeg — 20, 22, 24
Scalf — 1, 4, 6, 20
Scelf — 11
Shavin — 26
Skelf — 2b, 3, 7, 9-10, 12-13, 18, 24, 26-29
Skilf — 24, 30
Splinter — 2a, 5, 15, 19
Stab — 6, 19, 23
Nil — 8, 14, 16, 21, 25

Tyrone

Chip — 16
Jag — 15
Skelf — 1, 6, 8-13
Skelp — 5, 11
Spale — 3-4, 7
Splice — 5, 16
Splint — 6, 14
Splinter — 1, 11, 14
Stab — 2, 8, 14-15

Antrim

Jag — 6
Scalph — 10
Scelp — 1
Skelf — 1, 4, 5ab, 8ab, 9, 11-12, 14-15, 16abc, 17-23, 25-31, 33-34
Skiver — 25
Sliver — 25
Splint — 4A
Splinter — 13, 25
Stab — 7, 21, 29
Nil — 24, 32

Donegal

Scalp — 12
Scelp — 12
Skelf — 8
Skelp — 10a
Sliver — 10a
Spale — 2, 4, 6, 10b, 11
Splinter — 1, 1A, 5A, 8
Stab — 7
Nil — 3, 5, 9, 13

Fermanagh

Chip — 4, 9-10
Skelf — 5
Skelp — 3
Sliver — 1
Spale — 2
Splice — 8
Splinter — 4, 9
Nil — 6, 7ab

Armagh

Scalp — 1, 3
Skelf — 4-5
Skelp — 1-2, 6b
Splinter — 6a

Londonderry

Skelf — 1, 1B, 2, 4-7
Skilf — 3
Spale — 5
Splinter — 3A
Stab — 1A, 5

5 TO PRICK (one's finger) (PQ1, 29)

For the recurrence of **stab, stob,** see note in 4 **splinter.**

Shetland

Chob — 15-16
Jab — 3, 5, 7, 10, 14, 19, 22, 26
Jag — 6, 17, 21a, 22, 30
Job — 10, 13, 21b
Jaub — 9
Perse — 11
Prick — 1-2, 7-8, 13, 15, 20, 21ab, 25, 27, 30, 32-33
Skart — 24
Stab — 10, 19
Nil — 4, 12, 18, 23, 28-29 31

Orkney

Bogan — 6
Bore — 1-3, 6, 9, 11, 13a, 15, 17-18, 20
Brog — 12, 15
Brogue — 2, 9
Dob — 5-6, 13ab
Jab — 4, 8, 15, 17
Jag — 5, 21
Job — 19
Prick — 1, 4, 7-8, 13ab, 15, 17, 20-21
Prog — 12, 13a, 15-16, 19-20
Pur — 21
Nil — 10, 14

Caithness

Jag — 12b, 15, 16b
Prick — 13
Prong — 15
Proug — 14-15
Purr — 2ab, 4-6, 8-11, 12abc, 14, 17
Stab — 7, 13
Nil — 1, 3, 16a

Sutherland

Jab — 5
Jag — 1, 5, 10-11, 14-15
Prick — 1, 3-7, 13, 15-17
Progeg — 9b
Purr — 9a
Stab — 3, 6, 8, 11-13, 15, 17
Nil — 2

Ross & Cromarty

Dob — 37b
Jab — 18, 26
Jag — 9, 14, 25a, 26, 35
Job — 7
Prick — 1, 5-6, 8-9, 15-18, 22, 24, 26-27, 29-31, 32a 36, 39
Prike — 6
Prog — 15, 34
Scratch — 4, 24
Stab — 3, 8-11, 13, 17, 19-23, 25ab, 26, 28-29, 31, 32abc, 33-36, 37a
Stob — 25a, 31
Nil — 2, 12, 38

Inverness

Brog — 14
Jab — 13ab, 26
Jag — 1, 12, 13b, 16-18, 20, 21ab, 27, 30, 32, 35-38, 40,
Prick — 2-6, 8, 10-11, 13ce, 18, 21b, 23, 25, 28-29 32-35, 37 39
Prog — 24
Stab — 1, 3, 8-11, 13ce, 14-16, 19-20, 21b, 22, 25, 29, 31, 33
Nil — 7, 13d

Nairn

Dab — 1c
Jab — 1a
Stab — 1ab, 2, 4-6
Nil — 3

Moray

Dab — 1, 2a, 3-5, 6ab, 8bce, 9b, 10, 12-13, 15-16
Dob — 6a, 9a, 19
Jab — 2b, 5, 8cd, 9a, 12, 14, 19
Jag — 7, 17-18, 22
Job — 6a, 19
Jobe — 8d
Prick — 23
Stab — 6b, 7, 8ab, 11, 18, 20-21, 23
Stob — 22-23
Nil — 8f

Banff

Brod — 11
Dab — 5, 6b, 16-17, 18a, 19, 26, 31
Dawb — 4
Dob — 1, 2ac, 3, 5, 6a, 15, 29-31
Dowb — 2ab, 3
Jab — 6b, 7, 13, 15, 18ac, 20, 25
Jag — 7, 18c, 33-34
Job — 3, 6b, 8-11, 13-15, 18b, 21-24, 26-27, 29
Jobe — 12
Prob — 27
Stab — 5, 6b, 18c, 23, 25, 28, 32, 34
Stob — 5, 6b, 10, 17, 27, 29
Nil — 18d

Aberdeen

Brob — 2, 3a, 5b, 16-17, 33-34, 38-39, 43, 47a, 56, 66, 69, 74, 77
Brobbet — 18
Brobe — 55
Brod — 5b, 28a, 30-31, 57, 62, 64, 86, 103
Dab — 50, 53
Dob — 53
Dobbie — 27
Jab — 2, 14, 20, 23, 26-27, 29, 34, 50-52, 54, 67, 93-94, 96
Jag — 14, 65, 107
Jaub — 90
Job — 1, 3ab, 4, 5abcd, 6-17, 19, 21, 24, 27, 28abc, 29-30, 32-37, 40-46, 47abcdef, 49, 51, 53-54, 56-70, 71abc, 72-75, 77-83, 86-89, 95-102, 105-107, 108-109
Jowb — 7
Nip — 20
Prick — 14, 25, 70, 73
Prob — 9, 35, 40, 64, 103
Probe — 98, 104, 106
Prod — 62, 64
Stab — 6, 23, 25-26, 29, 48, 59, 79
Stob — 3b, 5b, 10, 16, 22, 28a, 39-40, 48, 57, 70, 71ac, 74, 78-79, 82, 84-87, 90-94, 96, 99-101, 103-104, 107, 109
Nil — 76

Kincardine

Dab — 19
Jab — 4, 8, 11
Jag — 15-16, 17a
Job — 1, 3, 5, 7, 9-10, 12-13, 15, 17ab, 23-24, 26-27
Jobe — 2, 18, 28
Prick — 8, 17c
Stob — 4, 6-7, 9, 11-15, 17bcd, 19-22, 25, 27-28
Stobe — 18

Kinross

Broque — 3
Broug — 7
Jag — 1-6
Joug — 2
Stab — 6

Angus

Jab — 3, 19-20, 29b, 32, 33a
Jag — 4, 13, 14a, 17a, 19, 22-24, 33a, 37
Jaub — 10, 18, 30
Job — 5abc, 7, 13, 14bcd, 17b, 19-21, 23, 25, 28, 29b, 32, 33ab, 34-37
Jobe — 6, 8, 12, 14a, 26-27, 29a
Jobbit — 15, 31
Pierce — 33b
Prick — 17b, 18, 34
Prog — 9
Scart — 14a
Stob — 1-2, 4, 5ac, 7, 11, 14c, 22, 24, 36
Stobe — 6, 14a
Stobit — 5b
Nil — 16

Perth

Broag — 20
Brob — 26
Doab — 62-63
Dob — 44
Drob — 26, 57, 65-66
Jab — 25-26, 30, 33, 48, 51b, 52abd, 62
Jag — 2b, 3, 5-11, 13 15-19, 22, 24-28, 29ab, 31, 33-35, 38-40, 41ab, 43-44, 46-48, 50, 51a, 52acde, 53-57, 59, 61-68, 70-71, 73-74
Joag — 48
Job — 27-28, 42, 45-46, 52c, 54, 57-58
Jobe — 20-21, 23, 32, 52e
Jog — 26, 53, 60
Jug — 69-72
Pierce — 8
Prick — 2a, 4, 8, 10, 24-25, 36, 57
Proag — 27, 32
Prog — 1
Skart — 50
Stab — 1, 12, 14, 16, 25, 37, 56, 62
Stob — 25
Nil — 49

Fife

Jab — 13, 43b, 53, 55de
Jag — 1, 4-8, 9ab, 10, 12-15, 19, 21-23, 25, 28, 30-31, 33-35, 36b, 37-39, 40b, 41abcd, 42, 43ab, 44bcdef, 45-46, 48-54, 55abcdf, 56-57, 59, 61-63, 64a
Jaub — 29, 53
Jawg — 44b, 47, 52
Joab — 2, 6, 21-22, 34, 44ae
Joag — 4, 8, 10-12, 25-26, 42, 44e, 49, 64b
Job — 3, 9b, 12, 15, 19, 27, 30, 32-33, 44f, 50
Jobbit — 16
Jog — 7, 17, 20-21, 24, 41c, 48
Joog — 18, 55g
Joug — 51, 57-58
Jug — 36a, 37, 39, 41c, 53, 55bcdefg, 59-60
Prick — 43a, 44c, 55e, 57, 63
Nil — 40a

Clackmannan

Jag — 1, 4bcd, 5-6
Joog — 2
Jug — 1-3, 4abc, 6-7

Stirling

Dob — 8
Jag — 1-6, 7abcde, 8-9, 11-19, 21ab, 22ab, 23abc, 24, 25abcd, 26abcdef, 27ab, 28-34, 35ab, 36, 37ab, 38, 39ab, 40, 42ab
Jaug — 20, 22b
Jug — 3, 7e, 9-10, 12, 32-33
Prick — 4, 7f, 21b, 26ad, 29-31, 39b
Prod — 10
Nil — 41

Dunbarton

Jag — 1-3, 4b, 5-6, 7abc, 8-12, 13abc, 14ab, 15, 16ab, 17-18
Prick — 7c, 8, 13bc
Stab — 1
Nil — 4a

Argyll

Jag — 1-3, 5, 7-10, 13-16, 19-26, 28-29, 31, 33-40
Nale — 18
Pick — 11
Prick — 1-2, 6, 12, 17, 19, 30
Puncture — 33
Stab — 3-4, 12, 26-27, 30, 32

Bute

Jag — 1abcde, 2-5, 7, 8ab, 9
Nil — 6

Ayr

Jag — 1ab, 2ab, 3-7, 8ab, 9-11, 12ab, 13-15, 16ab, 17, 18ab, 19, 20abcdefgh, 21-23, 24ab, 25, 26abc, 27, 28abcdf, 29, 30ab, 31-34, 35ab, 36-46, 48-52, 53ab, 54-57
Joeb — 7
Jug — 47
Pierce — 28e
Prick — 8a, 28e

Renfrew

Cut — 14a
Jab — 5
Jag — 1ab, 2abcdefghij, 3, 4abcde, 5-10, 11abcdefghijkl, 12ab, 13abcd, 14ab, 15, 16abcd, 17, 18ab, 19, 20ab, 21
Jog — 11l
Prick — 2adi, 4d, 8, 16a, 20a
Skart — 18a

Lanark

Jab — 58
Jag — 1-6, 7abc, 8ab, 9ab, 10ab, 11-13, 14abcd, 15abc, 16ab, 17-24, 25abcd, 26ab, 27ab, 28, 29abcdefg, 30,31abcd, 32abcdef, 33abcd, 34, 35abcd, 36-37, 38abcde, 39-45, 46abc, 47-48, 49ab, 50-51, 52ab, 53-56, 57abc, 58, 59ab, 60-63, 64ab, 65-66, 67ab
Prick — 1, 6, 10b, 14d, 20, 25c, 26a, 29f, 37
Prog — 57a
Scart — 36
Stab — 46c

West Lothian

Jab — 11
Jag — 1abcd, 2-8, 9ab, 10-16, 17ab, 18, 19ab, 20ab, 21ab, 22
Job — 11
Let oot — 1c
Prick — 16
Stab — 1a

Midlothian

Jab — 6a, 23a
Jag — 1-5, 6ab, 7ab, 8ab, 9-11, 12ab, 13, 14ab, 15-18, 21-22, 23ab, 24, 25abcd, 26ab, 27-32
Jog — 19
Prick — 11, 21
Prog — 20
Stab — 11

East Lothian

Jab – 8, 21
Jag – 1-3, 4ab, 5, 6ab, 7-21
Jaub – 10
Preck – 4b
Prick – 1, 13, 16
Progue – 14
Stob – 4a

Berwick

Brug – 8
Jab – 23
Jag – 1-4, 6-15, 16abc, 17-18, 20-28, 30-32
Jawg – 29
Prick – 26, 28
Prod – 27
Prog – 4, 7
Progue – 10
Nil – 5, 19

Peebles

Jag – 1, 3, 4abc, 5, 6a, 7-10
Jauk – 6b
Joab – 2
Prick – 4bc, 6ab
Prog – 10

Selkirk

Jag – 1, 2abcd, 3-7
Jaug – 2e, 8

Roxburgh

Jab – 7
Jag – 1-2, 3ab, 4-8, 9ab, 10-14, 15ab, 16-20, 21abcdef, 22-26, 28
Jawg – 8, 27
Prog – 9a, 15b, 25

Dumfries

Jaag – 31d
Jag – 1ab, 2-3, 5-7, 8ab, 9-16, 17ab, 18-20, 21ab, 22, 24-25, 27-30, 31abcef, 32, 34-42, 44, 45ab, 47-49
Jog – 43
Prick – 4, 12, 46
Prod – 26, 39, 42, 46
Scart – 6
Stab – 4, 23, 26, 33
Stob – 33

Kirkcudbright

Jag – 1-11, 12ab, 13-14, 15ab, 16-20, 21abc, 22-27
Prick – 6-7, 10
Prod – 7, 17
Stab – 27

Wigtown

Jab – 5b
Jag – 1-4, 5ab, 6-18
Porr – 5a
Prod – 9

Northumberland

Hurt – 126c
Jaab – 118b
Jab – 14, 46, 52, 53b, 64a, 72i, 77, 101b, 118a, 122b, 124b
Jag – 1c, 3-4, 8-13, 16, 18, 19ab, 27-28, 29f, 30, 42-43, 53a, 57, 59b, 76, 79
Jarp – 64a
Pierce – 52
Poke – 58
Powk – 84
Prick – 2b, 5, 18, 19a, 29a, 35-36, 40a, 41c, 42-43, 46, 52, 53ab, 54, 59b, 62b, 64b, 69c, 70, 72bcik, 77-78, 80, 82, 85-87, 96, 99d, 101b, 103abc, 104a, 106-107, 108b, 111b, 112, 119, 120bc, 121, 126cf, 127acfh, 130ce, 132, 137-138, 140, 142
Prickle – 20b, 69b, 82
Prod – 26, 28, 53b, 72l, 103b, 110, 135, 143
Prog – 1a, 2ab, 3-6, 9-11, 13-17, 20a, 21-23, 24ab, 25-27, 29abde, 30-32, 33b, 34ab, 36-39, 40ab, 41acd, 43, 45, 47-51, 55-58, 59cdef, 60, 62acdefgh, 63, 64b, 65ab, 66-68, 69abdeh, 70, 71abcde, 72acdeghijl, 74, 79-82, 84-86, 88ab, 89-93, 94ab, 95ab, 96-98, 99bc, 100, 101ab, 102, 107, 108ac, 109, 111ab, 112, 114-117, 118ab, 120a, 121, 122ab, 123, 124ab, 126abde, 127bdgh, 129abc, 130abcd, 131, 134, 137-138, 140
Proggle – 39, 53a, 60, 72ej, 73, 89, 108c
Progue – 1b, 2a, 7, 108c
Prowg – 100
Stab – 20b, 46, 62h, 77, 127e
Steek – 33b, 36
Stick – 33b, 75, 125
Stob – 103c, 142
Stuck – 46, 69c, 72k, 78, 80, 83, 91, 102, 104b, 111a, 123
Stuek – 62h
Nil – 29c, 33a, 41b, 44, 59a, 61, 69fg, 72f, 99a, 105, 113, 128, 130f, 133, 136, 139, 141

Cumberland

Jab – 15b, 37a, 42, 47
Jag – 2, 13b, 14
Powk – 43
Prick – 1a, 9, 13c, 21-26, 28, 33, 40, 42, 46-47, 49, 52-53, 56-58
Prod – 5a, 9, 11, 13a, 20, 37a, 40, 56, 62
Prowk – 32, 56
Ram – 46
Rov – 46
Stab – 2, 12, 18, 35, 46-47, 57
Stob – 2-4, 7-8, 12, 15abc, 16-19, 28-31, 34, 37ab, 38, 44, 46, 48, 51, 54, 58, 61
Stub – 46
Stuck – 50
Nil – 1b, 5b, 6, 10, 13d, 27, 36, 39, 41, 45, 55, 59, 60, 63ab

Down

Jag – 1, 2ab, 3-7, 9, 12-14, 20-31, 26-27
Jeg – 11, 17-18, 20, 22-24, 26, 28
Prick – 2a, 9, 15
Stab – 6, 11, 13, 16, 19, 27, 30
Stob – 29
Nil – 8, 10, 25

Tyrone

Dab – 15
Jag – 1, 3-9, 11, 13-15
Jeg – 9-10
Pick – 1
Poke – 1
Prick – 8, 11, 14
Stab – 2, 9-11, 14, 16
Nil – 12

Antrim

Jaag – 19-20, 23, 25
Jag – 1-4, 5b, 6, 8b, 9, 11-12, 14-15, 16bc, 17-18, 21-22, 26-28, 30-31, 33-34
Jaig – 5a
Jeg – 7, 8a, 29
Prick – 25
Prod – 13
Stab – 4A, 13, 19, 21
Nil – 10, 16a, 24, 32

Donegal

Dab – 8
Daub – 5A
Jag – 1-2, 5, 7, 7A, 11
Jeg – 4
Prick – 5A, 10a
Prod – 6
Stab – 3, 6, 10a, 12
Nil – 1A, 9, 10b, 13

Fermanagh

Jab – 1
Jag – 1-2, 5, 7a, 9-10
Jeg – 4
Prick – 4
Prod – 10
Stab – 2
Stob – 6
Nil – 3, 7b, 8

Armagh

Jag – 1, 6b
Jeg – 4
Prick – 6a
Stab – 4-5, 6a
Nil – 2-3

Londonderry

Dab – 2, 3A
Jag – 1A, 1B, 2, 4-6
Jeg – 3, 7
Prick – 2
Nil – 1

6 LEFT HANDED (PQ1, 30)

Map 6 shows the distribution of the elements meaning **left**, map 6A those of **handed.** The compound forms are not mapped because the picture is rather confusing.

On map 6A the SE form **handed** has not been shown as it occurs nearly everywhere.

The variants of HANDED (**hannit, hawndit, hant,** etc.) have been subsumed. The endings –it, –ed in **cleuked, cleukit, clucket, jookit, jooked** etc., have been subsumed under the majority spelling of such items in each county.

Shetland

Kag handed – 24
Left handed – 1-4, 6-8, 10, 13, 15-17, 19, 21ab, 25, 27, 30, 32-33
Left (maig) – *5*, 20
Maeg handed – 9
Squint handed – 23
Wrang handed – 14, 26
Nil – 11-12, 18, 22, 28-29, 31

Orkney

Left handed – 1-5, 7-9, 11, 13ab, 16-17, 19-21
Pardie pawed – 16
Nil – 6, 10, 12, 14-15, 18

Caithness

Carrie handed – 12b
Corrie fisted – 15
Corrie handed – 6, 12b, 16a
Left handed – 2ab, 8-9, 11, 13-14, 16b
Left mitted – 12a
Left spoke – 5
Left spound – 4
Left spung – 8
Wrong handed – 13
Nil – 1, 3, 7, 10, 12c, 17

Sutherland

Corrie fisted – 5
Corrie (handed) – 9*ab*
Corrie juked – 8
Karisbag – 12
Karispogue – 10, 15
Kerrack – 14
Kervack – 8
Left handed – 1, 3-4, 6-8, 10-13, 16-17
Leftie – 3, 16
Nil – 2

Ross & Cromarty

Carrie fisted – 34
Carrie handed – 11
Caurie fisted – 17
Corrie fisted – 20, 25a
Corrie handed – 24
Garvack – 8
Karavack – 17, 28, 31
Kearack – 3
Kearavack – 32b
Kearvack – 7, 23
Kerivack – 12, 27
Kervack – 35
Kervag – 14
Kervie – 13
Kiarvack – 10
Kippie – 18
Kyarvack – 18, 20
Left handed – 1, 3-5, 9-10, 16-17, 19, 24, 25b, 26-27, 29-31, 32ab, 36, 39
Left mellett – 37a
Left pawed – 25b
Nil – 2, 6, 15, 21-22, 32c, 33, 37b, 38

Inverness

Carie handed – 9, 22
Corrie fisted – 38, 40
Corrie handed – 24, 31, 33, 37
Kairack – 24
Karvack – 20
Kàarack – 31

Inverness cont'd

Kearag — 13d
Kerrack — 14
Kiarack — 13ace
Kiotach — 26
Kwarach — 13b
Left handed — 1-6, 8-9, 11-12, 13ce, 16-19, 21ab, 22-23, 25-30, 32-37, 39-40
Leftie — 14
Nil — 7, 10, 15

Nairn

Corrie fisted — 1b
Corrie handed — 2
Garroch — 1b
Guarrach — 1c
Kiarack — 1a
Left handed — 2, 6
Nil — 3-5

Moray

Carie fisted — 6a
Corbie — 22
Corrie fisted — 12, 22
Corrie handed — 18
Corvie fisted — 21
Kargarack — 22
Kiarrack — 8d
Left cleuched — 2b, 3, 5, 9a, 16, 18
(Left) cleukit — 1, *22*
Left clooched — 4, 6b, 15
Left clookit — 6a, 7, 8b, 9a, 10, 19-21
Left handed — 4, 6b, 7, 11, 14
Left spyogued — 13
Lett clouch — 8e
Nil — 2a, 8acf, 9b, 17, 23

Banff

Carrie handed — 33
Caurie handed — 27
Conter handed — 23
Corrie fisted — 11, 14-15
Currie fisted — 18d
Kair cuekit — 1, 2bc, 3
Left cleekit — 11
Left clewkit — 14-15, 20, 30
Left clookit — 3-5, 6ab, 7, 9-10, 12, 16-17, 18b, 19, 21-25, 27, 31-32, 34
Left handed — 8-9, 13, 16, 18c
Left hewkit — 2a, 4, 6a
Left kewkit — 2b
Left mitted — 18b
Left puttett — 17, 18b
Maukin — 33
Nil — 18a, 26, 28-29

Aberdeen

Cair cuikit — 53
Carrie handed — 34
Corrie fisted — 25, 47bd, 65, 107
Corrie (handed) — *3a,* 60
Currie handed — 28b, 47e
Flukie — 23, 25
Hanless — 10
Kippie han — 6
Left cleekit — 16, 53, 77
Left cleukit — 3b, 10, 29, 47c, 72, 79-80, 83, 89, 101, 104, 106
Left clinkit — 97
Left clookit — 1-2, 4, 5bd, 8-9, 14, 17-18, 21-22, 24, 26, 28a, 31, 34-35, 37, 39, 41-42, 44-45, 47abef, 49-52, 54-56, 61-67, 69-70, 71c, 74-75, 77, 81, 87, 90, 93, 96, 99, 102-103, 105
Left cloukit — 95
Left cluckit — 12, 16, 27, 71a
Left dibber — 88
Left dig — 77
Left flippit — 47df
Left flookit — 107
Left fluke — 51
Left handed — 4, 5bc, 6-8, 11, 14-16, 19-21, 28ac, 29, 32, 34-35, 44, 46, 47b, 48, 59, 66, 70, 71b, 75, 81-83, 86, 94-95, 98, 104, 108-109
Left Huikit — 53
Pallie handed — 47e
Nil — 5a, 13, 30, 33, 36, 38, 40, 43, 57-58, 68, 73, 76, 78, 84-85, 91-92, 100

Kincardine

Carie fisted — 22
Corrie fisted — 2
Corrie handed — 22
Kippie handed — 17b
Left cleukit — 17c
Left clookit — 3, 5, 7, 10-11, 13-14, 16, 17a, 18, 21, 23-24, 27
Left flooket — 9
Left handed — 1, 4, 6-8, 17bc, 18-19, 27
Pallie handed — 15, 17a, 21, 26-28
Nil — 12, 17d, 20, 25

Kinross

Carrie (fisted) — *1,* 5
Carrie handed — 6
Carrie paw — 6
Caurie fisted — 1, 7
Caurie (handed) — *2,* 3, *4, 7*
Kippie — 5

Angus

Carrie fisted — 17a
Corkie — 29a
Cor(r)ie fisted — 5b, 23
Corrie handed — 32
Kippie (handed) — 1, *7*
Left crookit — 18
Left handed — 17b, 18, 28, 29b
Left hooker — 21
Leftie — 6, 8, 14acd, 15
Palie fisted — 31
Palie (handed) — 5c, 14c, *22* 29a
Palie hander — 17b
Pallie euchered — 9
Pallie (handed) — *1-4,* 5abc, 6, *7, 9,* 10-11, *12,* 13, 14*bcd, 15,* 17b, *19-20, 24-26,* 27, *28,* 29b, 30, 32, 33a, 34-47
Pallie jookered — 32
Paulie (handed) — 8, *23, 33b*
Nil — 16

Perth

Carie handed — 24
Carrie fisted — 9, 15, 38, 40, 45, 52c, 66, 70, 73-74
Carrie (handed) — *11,* 28, *32,* 33, *39, 41a, 46, 69*
Caur handed — 25
Caurie handed — 62, 65
Cleutach — 39
Coir handed — 37
Corie handed — 64
Corrie (fisted) — *2a, 8, 10, 16,* 31, *34-35, 41a,* 42, *44, 53, 56, 61, 67-68, 71-72, 74*
Corrie handed — 59
Keppie — 41a, 63
Kippie fisted — 15, 43-44
Kippie (handed) — 1, *3,* 12, *17-18,* 19-20, *21,* 25-28, 29ab, 30-31, 39, 41b, 42, *45,* 47-49, *50,* 51ab, 52abcde, 53-55, 57, *58,* 59, 61-62
Left handed — 2a, 4, 7, 14, 24-25, 32, 36, 52e, 57, 74
Palie handed — 21
Pallie deuked — 20, 48
Pallie (handed) — 1, *5, 7, 9, 13, 22,* 23, 27, *29a,* 31, *32,* 33, 52a, 57, *59,* 60
Nil — 2b, 6

Fife

Car cleekit — 44f
Car handed — 44e
Carrie fisted — 12, 18, 23, 28
Carrie handed — 1, 10-11, 13, 21, 40b, 44ef, 46
Carrie (pawed) — *1, 4-5, 8,* 9b, *11-12, 14-18, 23, 25-26,* 27, *28, 30,* 31, *33-35, 40ab, 43a, 48, 61*
Carrie pout — 23
Carrie plunk — 48
Carrie wheech — 64a
Carrie wheeched — 44e, 45
Carrie wheeded — 21
Carrie wheeked — 2, 4-6, 12-13, 16, 19, 23-26, 33-34, 41d, 42, 43a, 44de, 45, 48-49
Car wheekit — 44a, 50
Car wipe — 48
Caurie deukit — 52
Caurie fisted — 7, 9a, 29, 42
Caurie (handed) — *7,* 41a*d, 43b, 44ab,* 47, *50-52,* 53-54, *55b, 57,* 58, *64b*
Caurie pawed — 2, 6-7, 41cd, 44f, 49, 52, 54, 55befg, 56, 60, 63
Caurie ploukit — 47
Caurie soupaw — 38
Caurie wheekit — 43b
Caur pawed — 32
Corra pawed — 36a
Corrie fisted — 44c, 55ac
Corrie handed — 37, 41b, 44c
Corrie kniffed — 39
Corrie (pawed) — *36b, 37, 39,* 41a*b, 55d,* 59, 62
Corrie wheeched — 14
Corrie wheeked — 37, 44c, 55c, 59
Currie wawpit — 20
Dirrie — 8
Gawkie — 41c
Left handed — 4, 40a, 43a, 50, 55dg, 57
Palie handed — 44a
Pallie handed — 3, 22-23, 37, 53
Pallie jookit — 37
Parrie handed — 23
Paulie (handed) — *8,* 44b
Sooth pawed — 55f

Clackmannan

Carrie (fisted) — 4a, *6*
Carrie handed — 2, 4b
Carrie pawed — 6
Cawrie fisted — 5, 7
Cawrie (handed) — *1,* 3, *7*
Cawrie pawed — 5
Corrie handed — 4cd
Fuddie — 1
Left handed — 1, 4c

Stirling

Carrie (fisted) — *2, 4, 7bd, 8, 25b,* 26ef, *39a, 40*
Carrie handed — 7bf, 18, 23b, 25c, 26a, 40
Cawr fisted — 26b
Cawrie fisted — 3, 6, 7ae, 9, 11-12, 14, 22ab, 23a, 25ad, 26a, 29-31, 34, 37ab
Cawrie (handed) — *7a, 9, 12, 20, 21a, 22ab, 23ab, 25d,* 26b, 30, *34,* 42ab
Cawrie pawed — 26ad
Corrie fisted — 7bc, 10, 13, 15, 17, 21b, 26c, 27ab, 28, 32-33, 36, 38, 39b, 41
Corrie (handed) — 1, 5, *7b, 10,* 15-16, *17, 19, 23c,* 24, 26e, *28, 35a,* 36, *41,* 42b
Corrie pawed — 35b
Fister — 4, 24, 30
Kippie — 6
Left handed — 7e, 13, 21b, 26d, 35a, 36
Skei handed — 7d

Dunbarton

Cawrie fisted — 13a
Cawrie handed — 13a, 15, 18
Corrie (fisted) — *1-3,* 4ab, *5-6, 7bc, 8-9, 11-12, 13bc, 14ab, 16ab, 17*
Corrie funkered — 6, 7a
Corrie handed — 2, 4b, 5, 7a, 10, 16ab
Honey pawed — 14a
Left handed — 1, 7c, 8, 13bc, 14b

Argyll

Carrie fisted — 35
Cawrie fisted — 23
Ciotach — 3, 10, 12, 27, 29, 39
Corrie (fisted) — *3, 5, 9-10, 12,* 13, *15-16,* 17, *18-21, 24-25, 30,* 36-38
Corrie handed — 7-8, 10-11, 22, 29, 40
Cutach — 13, 16, 20, 32
Kaetoch — 31, 40
Ke(e)tach — 24, 28, 30, 33-36, 38
Left handed — 1-2, 6, 9, 14, 16-17, 19, 23, 25, 27, 33
Nil — 4, 26

Bute

Carrie fisted — 5
Cawrie fisted — 1a
Cooter — 7
Corrie deuk — 1e
Corrie (fisted) — 1abcde, 2-3, *4, 6-7, 8ab, 9*
Corrie handed — 2
Fistie — 8b
Keetough — 8b
Left handed — 7, 8a

Ayr

Carrie fisted — 47, 49
Carrie handed — 26c, 45-46, 49, 52
Cawrie (fisted) — *4, 8a, 9,* 12a, 13, *14-15, 16a,* 20aegh, 24b, 25, *28d, 32,* 34, 35ab, *43, 50, 53a,* 55, *57*
Cawrie handed — 8a, 16a, 18a, 19, 20fg, 30a, 32, 36
Chuggie — 38
Corrie (fisted) — 1ab, 2*ab, 3,* 6, *7, 8b, 10,* 11, *12b, 16b, 17, 18b,* 20bcd, *21-23,* 24a, *26ab,* 27, 28abef, *29,* 30b, *33-34, 37,* 38, *39-41, 44, 48, 53b, 54, 56-57*
Corrie foostie — 8b
Corrie fusted — 26b
Corrie handed — 3, 5, 7, 12b, 18b, 21, 29, 31, 37, 42, 44, 48, 52
Currie (fisted) — 51, *53b*
Fyuggie — 54
Left fisted — 5
Left handed — 2b, 5, 28ce, 42, 45, 47, 53a, 57
Pallie handed — 7
Skibbie — 36
Soosie — 27, 28c
Sousie — 26b

Renfrew

Cair handed — 21
Cawrie (fisted) — 2ch, 5, 11ab, 13b, *20b,* 21
Cawrie handed — 2h, 17
Corrie (fisted) — *1a,* 2befgij, *3, 4ae, 6-8,* 9-10, 11cdefghijkl, *12ab,* 13acd, *14ab,* 15, *16abcd,* 18ab, 19, 20a, 21
Corrie handed — 1b, 2d, 4bcd
Fister — 11il, 15, 16b, 18b
Kerrie — 15
Kittie fisted — 2ej
Kittie handed — 3
Kittie (winded) — 1b, 2ai

Renfrew cont'd

Left handed — 2adi, 4e, 8, 20a
Mickie fisted — 4d

Lanark

Cack handed — 13
Carrie fisted — 39, 55, 62-63, 64a, 67a
Carrie (handed) — 9b, *13,* 24. *39, 60, 67ab*
Carrie micked — 59b
Cawrie fisted — 7c, 11, 15c, 16b, 17, 27b, 31d, 32af, 33bcd, 38b, 46c, 48, 49b, 56, 58, 61, 64b, 66
Cawrie (handed) — *13,* 14*ab, 16b,* 24, *26a, 27b,* 29d, *33cd, 36,* 41, *45, 46a,* 47, *48, 49a, 53, 58,* 59a, *65*
Cawrie jeuked — 14c
Cawrie micked — 40, 49a, 51, 65
Cawrie pawed — 20
Chorie fisted — 44
Cor fisted — 23
Corrie (fisted) — *1-6, 7ab, 8ab, 9a,* 10ab, *12,* 14d, *15ab, 16a, 18-19,* 21, *22, 25abcd, 26b, 27a, 28,* 29abcefg, *30* 31ab, 32b*cde, 33ab, 34,* 35a*cd,* 37, 38ade, 42-43, 46b, 50, 52ab, 57ac
Corrie handed — 4, 9a, 15b, 23, 28, 29f, 31c, 33a, 35bd, 38c, 57ab, 60
Corrie micked — 52b
Corrie mitted — 52a
Fister — 6, 14b, 15b
Kerr handed — 38d
Kipie — 38e
Left handed — 1, 5, 7c, 9a, 10b, 12, 14d, 15ac, 19, 25c, 26a, 31d, 32f, 35d, 44, 48, 49b, 58
Skibbie — 9b
Nil — 54

West Lothian

Cairie handed — 3
Carrie handed — 1c, 3
Carrie pawed — 3
Cawrie (fisted) — 1*abd,* 2, 4, *7,* 19a
Cawrie handed — 13, 18
Cock handed — 13
Corrie fisted — 5-6, 8, 10-11, 15-16, 20b, 22
Corrie (handed) — *6,* 9ab, *12, 14, 17ab, 19b,* 20ab, 21ab, *22*
Corrie pawed — 6, 8, 14-15
Corrie plugged — 11

Midlothian

Carra pawed — 23a
Carrie fisted — 18
Carrie handed — 8b, 17, 21, 26a, 27, 29-30, 32
Carrie pawed — 8b, 9, 17, 19-20, 25ac, 26a, 27, 29, 31
Cawrie fisted — 13, 14b, 22
Cawrie handed — 4, 7b, 11, 12ab, 14b, 22, 23b
Cawrie pawed — 23b, 25b, 28
Coarie fisted — 3
Coarie jooked — 3
Corrie dukit — 2
Corrie (fisted) — *1-3,* 5, *7a, 10, 12a,* 14a, *16, 24*
Corrie handed — 2, 6b, 7a, 10, 12a, 15, 26b
Corrie jukit — 2-3, 5, 7a
Corrie pawed — 2, 6b, 25d
Ker handed — 32
Left handed — 6a, 8a, 14a, 18-19, 23b, 24
Leftie — 10

East Lothian

Carra pawed — 17
Carrie (handed) — *1, 9,* 15-16
Carrie juked — 1, 9
Carrie pawed — 2, 4a, 6a, 7-9, 12-14, 16, 18, 21
Cawrie (pawed) — *4b, 5,* 6b, *11*
Corrie (pawed) — *3, 10, 19,* 20
Kerrie — 4a
Kippie — 13
Left handed — 4b, 5, 18
Pallie handed — 10
Skellie handed — 1

Berwick

Carrie handed — 3, 18, 20, 32
Carrie mitted — 32
Carrie pawed — 3-5, 7-9, 16ab, 17-18, 20-21, 23, 25, 27
Cawrie handed — 13, 16c
Cawrie pawed — 1, 10, 14, 31
Corrie fisted — 23, 29
Corrie pawed — 6, 19
Ker handed — 22
Kerrie fisted — 12, 31
Kerrie handed — 11-12, 15, 23-24, 26-27, 30
Kerrie pawed — 12
Left foosh — 32
Left handed — 2, 12, 15, 16bc, 26, 28-29
Left mitted — 14
Skeckie handed — 24
Skerrie handed — 23

Peebles

Carrie (fisted) — *1, 4b,* 5, 6b
Carrie handed — 1, 3, 4c, 6a, 10
Cawrie fisted — 7
Cawrie handed — 9
Cawrie mitted — 9
Coorie handed — 2
(Corrie) fisted — *4a,* 5, *8*
Corrie handed — 10
Kerrie handed — 4c
Left handed — 4bc, 6ab

Selkirk

Carie handed — 1
Carra handed — 8
Corrie fisted — 3
Corrie handed — 5
Ker handed — 2a
Kerrie handed — 4, 6-7
Left handed — 2c, 5, 8
Skeckie — 2bde
Skerrie (handed) — 2b*c, 6*

Roxburgh

Carrie fisted — 5
Carrie handed — 15a, 28
Carrie pawed — 10
Cawrie fisted — 23
Currie fisted — 14
Kar fisted — 8
Kar handed — 28
Ker (handed) — *15ab, 16,* 19, *26, 28*
Ker mitted — 17
Ker pawed — 6
Kerrie fisted — 13-14
Kerrie (handed) — *2, 3b, 4,* 12, *17, 20, 21cf, 23-25*
Kerrie mitted — 5, 7-8, 18
Kerrie pawed — 10
Left handed — 21a, 26
Lift haused — 21c
Skellie handed — 1, 21ace, 28
Sker handed — 3a, 9b, 21c
Skerrie handed — 21a
Skerrie (mitted) — *9ab,* 11, 21d
Nil — 21b, 22, 27

Dumfries

Cairie fisted — 23
Cairie handed — 23, 33
Carie — 7
Carrie fisted — 1a, 2, 4-5, 8a, 9-11, 22, 30, 31bde, 32, 34, 41
Carrie (handed) — *2, 4, 6, 12-13, 21b, 22, 24, 27, 31cde, 32,* 38, *41-42*
Carrie mitted — 14
Carrie pawed — 20
Cawrie fisted — 31f
Cawrie (handed) — *17a,* 31a
Corrie fisted — 3, 8b, 21a, 25, 31e, 47
Corrie (handed) — *1b, 17b, 31e,* 38
Kar handed — 32
Ker handed — 16, 29
Kerrie (handed) — 17b, 19, *26, 28, 35,* 48-49
Kerrie hanned — 39
Left handed — 4, 12, 17a, 18, 29
Skellie handed — 40, 45a, 46
Skerrie fisted — 25
Skerrie (handed) — *15-16,* 34, *36-37,* 43-44, *45b, 46*

Kirkcudbright

Back handed — 17
Carrie fisted — 2, 8, 11, 15a, 16, 21c, 22
Carrie (handed) — *4-5, 7, 9, 11,* 12a*b, 14, 21ab, 26,* 27
Corrie fisted — 1, 12a, 17, 20, 23, 26
Corrie handed — 6, 17
Currie fisted — 7
Currie handed — 25
Flog fisted — 18
Fluck fisted — 21c
Gummie fisted — 15b
Kar handed — 21b
Left handed — 7, 10, 15a, 19, 27
Muckle fisted — 15b
Skarrie — 24
Skellie handed — 18
Nil — 3, 13

Wigtown

Carrie fisted — 7
Carrie handed — 14
Cawrie fisted — 5b
Corrie (fisted) — *1, 10, 12, 15, 17,* 18
Feug fisted — 17
Fhug fisted — 14
Flug fisted — 2-3, 5a, 6, 9
Flugh fisted — 10
Gammie — 8
Kar fisted — 5a
Ker handed — 5a
Left handed — 11, 16
Speug fisted — 5b
Nil — 4, 13

Northumberland

Bang handed — 53a
Buck handed — 135
Caa handed — 12, 29ce, 31, 33b, 35, 39, 45, 69g, 124b, 134
Caa pawed — 24b
Cack handed — 59de, 60, 69d
Cad handed — 54
Caggie handed — 59e, 125
Ca handed — 8, 26, 29d, 34ab, 37-38, 46, 68, 107, 122a
Caow handed — 106
Carie pawed — 16
Car handed — 2b, 6, 13-14, 18, 19a, 20ab, 26-28, 29b, 30, 33a, 36, 41a, 59b, 79, 134
Car mitted — 5
Car pawed — 17
Carra pawed — 20a, 33a, 58
Carrie fisted — 1a
Carrie handed — 1a, 29f
Cat's pawed — 59b
Caw(ie) handed — 1b, 2a, 3, 8, 17-18, 29c, 134, 136-138
Caw meggeet — 7
Clack handed — 127g
Cloutie pawed — 10
Cooie handed — 59c, 87, 101b
Coo(ie) pawed — 124a, 127d, 129c, 131
Corrie pawed — 2a
Cow handed — 26, 59de, 60, 78, 98, 127cf
Cowie fisted — 47, 62g
Cowie (handed) — *22, 29abd, 37-38,* 39, *40ab, 41ab, 45, 47-52, 56-57,* 59abcdf, *61,* 62acdefh, *63, 64a, 65b,* 66-67, *69abcdefgh, 70,* 71*abcde*, 72*abcdefghjkl*, 74, *76-77, 80,* 81, *82,* 83-85, *86,* 88ab, 89-90, *91,* 92, *93,* 94ab, *95b,* 96, *97,* 98, 99b, *100,* 101b, 105, 109, *111ab,* 113-117, *118ab,* 119, *120abc,* 122ab, *123, 124b, 125,* 126*b*ef, *127abd, 129ab,* 130*abcd, 133, 139*
Cow(ie) pawed — *40a,* 41*cd,* 59de, 64*ab,* 65*a, 72i,* 79, *82,* 95*a,* 99*a,* 101a, 108*a,* 122b, 124a, 126*abcde,* 127cdeh, *128,* 130de
Cowpie — 121
Cubbie — 89
Cuddlie handed — 69b
Cuddy fisted — 25, 79, 108c, 124b, 127c, 143
Cuddy handed — 32, 68, 69g, 112, 126bf, 127bgh, 130f, 134, 141
Cuddy pawed — 10, 24a, 33a, 99d, 127c, 143
Cuddy whiffer — 129a
Cuffie — 116
Gammie — 63
Gley handed — 22
Gollie handed — 122b
Ham fisted — 79
Ham handed — 77
Keer handed — 39
Keggie — 72l
Ker handed — 10-11, 15, 29f, 34a, 41a, 51
Kerrie handed — 19b
Kie handed — 45
Kithogue — 72l
Left handed — 2b, 5, 13-14, 28, 29a, 35-36, 40a, 41c, 42-43, 52, 53b, 54, 60, 62b, 64b, 71c, 72aci, 82, 87, 99d, 102, 103ac, 104ab, 106, 108c, 110, 111b, 112, 119, 121, 123, 127agh, 130ce, 132, 142
Left jouked — 1b
Left neefed — 71c
Pallie juked — 127h
Port — 62h
Sooth pawed — 62h, 91
South pawed — 33b, 37, 62h, 130c
Wingie — 41c
Nil — 1c, 4, 9, 21, 23, 44, 55, 72h, 73, 75, 99c, 103b, 108b, 140

Cumberland

Bang handed — 12, 17, 20 37a, 38, 40, 46, 54, 56, 62
Coo handed — 2, 13d
Corrie fisted — 9
Cow handed — 13a
Cowie — 25
Cuddy flip — 40
Gammie handed — 40
Ham fisted — 15b
Left handed — 3-4, 5a, 9,13c, 15a, 21, 23, 40, 42, 46, 48-50, 56-57
Leftie — 22
Left neifed — 62
Left pawed — 7, 62
Left pawed kittie — 31
Left poted — 56
Numun — 2
Poddie handed — 54
Scarrie handed — 16
South pawed — 3

Cumberland cont'd
Wrang handed – 56
Nil – 1ab, 5b, 6, 8, 10-11, 13b, 14, 15c, 18-19, 24, 26-30, 32-36, 37b, 39, 41, 43-45, 47, 51, 53, 55, 58-61, 63ab

Down
Cauldie – 21
Clootie – 1, 3, 11, 21, 24, 28-30
Cloutie – 4, 8, 10
Cluttie – 5
Feughie – 2b
Feugie – 2a
Fuggie – 6-7, 21
Kiddher Paw – 14
Kitherplak – 22
Kitogue – 26
Kitter fisted – 20, 27
Kitter (pawed) – *18*-19, 23, *25*
Left cuttie – 11
Left handed – 2a, 9, 12, 15, 18, 24
Shovel handed – 17
South pawed – 1
Wrang hand – 13
Nil – 16

Tyrone
Clootie – 4
Couter fisted – 13
Couther fisted – 3
Fuggie fisted – 11
Kater – 6
Kitach – 5
Kitachan – 16
Kither fisted – 10
Kither handed – 7, 14
Kithogue – 2
Kitter fisted – 15
Kitter handed – 8-9, 14
Left handed – 1, 8, 11, 14
Ridyick – 2
Nil – 12

Antrim
Ciotach – 7
Clootie (handed) – 1-3, 8b, 10, 12, 14, 16ac, *21*, 22, 24, 28, 30-31, 34
Cloutie – 8a, 18, 22, 26, 34
Cluttie – 33
Crittie – 1
Doutie – 8a
Feeuggie – 16a, 24, 28
Fluggie – 20
Fueg – 25
Fuggie – 12, 27
Hyuggie handed – 23
Kettick – 6
Kit handed – 15
Kit mit – 14
Kitta handed – 1
Kittagh fisted – 5a
Kitter fisted – 8a
Kitter (handed) – 18, *19*
Kittugh handed – 4A
Left handed – 5b, 13, 17, 19, 25-26
Nil – 4, 9, 11, 16b, 29, 32

Donegal
Clouter pawed – 5
Khitter pawed – 10b
Kit-a – 8
Kiteog – 7A
Kithoge – 10a, 13
Kitog – 1A, 6
Kittach – 1
Kitter – 2
Kitter fisted – 9
Left handed – 5A, 7A, 8, 10a
Nil – 3-4, 7, 11-12

Fermanagh
Clootie – 5
Kithog – 6, 7a, 8
Kitter (fisted) – *5*, 7b, *10*
Kitther fisted – 2, 4, 8
Kittugh fisted – 1
Left handed – 4, 9
Nil – 3

Armagh
Clootie – 4
Kitterdie – 6b
Kitter fisted – 2
Kitter pawed – 1, 4
Left handed – 6a
Nil – 3, 5

Londonderry
Caldie – 4
Cauldie – 3A, 5
Clootie – 5
Corrie fisted – 3
Kithan – 3
Kithogue – 1B, 5
Kittoch fisted – 1A
Left handed – 2
Nil – 1, 6-7

7 ROUND SHOULDERED (PQ1, 31)

Round shouldered has not been mapped as it occurs all over the area. For variants of the elements ROUND and SHOULDER(ED) see maps 1 and 2, Appendix A. The informants do not seem to have been clear about the distinction between **round shouldered** and **humpbacked.**

Shetland
Booed – 9
Croiled shouldered – 17
Crooked (backed) – 19, *32*
Crool atween the shoulders – 23
Crool backed – 26
Crool shouldered – 13, 17, 26
Cruged shouldered – 21b
Hool shouldered – 18
Huilked – 31
Hump backed – 23-24
Humped – 7, 26
Humpie (backed) – *19, 22,* 33
Hunched – 8, 30
Hyulk backed – 27
Lood shouldered – 15
Lootin – 30
Loot shouldered – 5-6, 16, 18, 21b
Louted (shouldered) – *3,* 10
Round shouldered – 1-2, 4, 20, 21a, 22, 24-25, 30, 32-33
Sputcher shouldered – 13
Nil – 11-12, 14, 28-29

Orkney
Booed – 11, 13a, 15
Bottle shouldered – 20
Hookie – 20
Huldrie – 4
Humpie (backed) – *3-7, 9, 12, 13b, 15, 18-19,* 20, *21*
Humpie shouldered – 13a
Hunkie – 7
Roondie backed – 12
Round shouldered – 1-2, 5, 8, 13a, 14-17, 21
Wheel backed – 15
Nil – 10

Caithness
Booed – 6
Drooped – 4
Hounked – 11, 12b, 15, 17
Humped – 2a, 7-10, 14
Humphie – 16ab
Hunched – 8
Looted – 5
Round shouldered – 2b, 6, 11, 12a, 14
Skookin – 12c
Stooped – 15
Nil – 1, 3, 13

Sutherland
Bent – 5, 17
Clookach – 16
Croatch – 10
Crotchach – 14
Hump backed – 9b, 13
Humped – 6, 9a
Humpie – 5, 10
Hunched – 11
Round shouldered – 1, 3-8, 9b, 10-13, 16
Stoop shouldered – 3
To have a crotch – 8
Nil – 2, 15

Ross & Cromarty
Bent – 17, 19, 25b
Boo backed – 25b
Booed – 25b
Crotchach – 25b, 26, 28, 30
Hump backed – 28, 31
Humped (backed) – 4, *22*
Humphie (backed) – 12-13, *25a*
Humpie backed – 15, 24, 26
Round – 18
Round shouldered – 1-3, 5-6, 8-9, 14, 16-17, 19, 23, 26-27, 29, 31, 32abc, 34, 36, 37a, 39
Stooped – 25a, 36
Stooping – 22, 32c
Nil – 2, 7, 10-11, 20-21, 33, 35, 37b, 38

Inverness
Bent – 16
Bottle shouldered – 1
Crotchach – 15, 19, 24, 31
Hump backed – 11, 13e
Humped – 16, 22, 28, 32
Humphie (backed) – *9,* 13ab, 38
Humpie (backed) – 22, 26-*27,* 33, 39
Humptie – 14
Hunched – 12
Round shouldered – 2-6, 8-10, 13bce, 17, 21ab, 23, 25-26, 28-29, 32-38, 40
Stooped – 37
Nil – 7, 13d, 18, 20, 30

Nairn
Crouchie – 2
Croutchach – 1c
Humped – 5
Humpie – 1b
Hunchie – 1b
Rouch – 1a
Round shouldered – 1a, 2, 6
Nil – 3-4

Moray
Boo backed – 3-4, 19
Booed – 3, 19
Boolie backed – 9a
Bottle necked – 2a
Bow backed – 4
Bowie backed – 9a
Chairlie – 8c
Charlie – 8d
Hump backed – 8a
Humphie backed – 18
Humpie backed – 4, 6a, 8bd, 9b, 10, 13, 15, 20-22
Hunch backed – 22
Round shouldered – 4-5, 6ab, 7, 8ce, 9a, 10-11, 14, 20-21
Rowd (shouldered) – 1, *16-17*
Stooped – 8d
Nil – 2b, 8f, 12, 23

Banff
Boo backed – 13
Booed – 18d, 23
Hogged – 1, 6a
Hoogered – 32
Howged – 2b, 3
Hugged – 2c
Huggered – 5
Hump backed – 11
Humpie backed – 2a, 4, 6b, 8-9, 14, 19-20, 23, 25, 28-32
Hunchie (backed) – 4, *16*
In ower the shoulders – 21
Round shouldered – 2a, 6b, 7, 9-13, 15-17, 18c, 19, 21, 24-26, 29, 33-34
Row shouldered – 22, 27, 34
Up in the back – 15, 17
Nil – 18ab

Aberdeen
Bent (ower) – 29
Booed – 53, 62-63, 67, 78, 94
Bow shouldered – 67
Doon i' the shoulder – 6
Hog backed – 88
Hump backed – 15, 31, 59, 65, 71a, 80, 84-85, 94, 96
Humped backed – 10
Humphie (backed) – 5b, *7,* 24, *28b, 39,* 40, *47cdef, 49, 51, 60, 83, 90,* 93, *103, 105-106*
Humpie (backed) – 3ab, *5b, 8-9, 11-12, 19, 23, 26-27, 41, 47a,* 48, *51, 54, 56, 64, 67, 69, 71c, 73, 79-80, 86-87, 89, 92, 97, 99, 104, 108*
Hunchie (backed) – *49,* 102
In o'er – 13, 27
In ower – 9, 12, 28c, 36, 49, 51-52, 57-58, 66, 75, 77, 98
Roo backed – 61
Roud backed – 104
Roued shouldered – 95
Round shouldered – 1-2, 4, 5abcd, 8-9, 11-12, 16-17, 19-21, 23, 25, 28ch, 29-30, 32, 35, 43-46, 47abf, 53, 55, 57, 59, 62-64, 69-70, 71c, 73-74, 76-77, 81-82, 86, 95-98, 100-101, 104, 106-107, 109
Rou shouldered – 14, 22
Row backed – 47b, 61

Aberdeen cont'd

Rowed backed — 71a
Rowdie shouldered — 17
Rowed in the shoulders — 78
Rowed shouldered — 1, 34, 71b, 81, 91, 95, 109
Row shouldered — 14, 22, 39, 50, 59, 72, 77, 88
Shilped — 53
Stooped — 57
Up in the back — 28a, 49, 94, 105
Up in the shoulders — 35
Nil — 18, 33, 37-38, 42, 68

Kincardine

Bent — 20
Booed — 15
Hump backed — 3
Humphie backed — 3, 5, 15, 18, 26
Humpie backed — 1, 4, 9, 11, 14, 23, 27
In over — 8
Round shouldered — 2, 5-7, 10, 12, 16, 17abch, 19, 21, 27-28
Rowed — 8, 24
Row shouldered — 13, 21
Stooped — 26
Up in the back — 7
Nil — 17d, 22, 25

Kinross

Boolie backed — 7
Humphie (backed) — *1, 3,* 5, *6-7*
Humpie backed — 1, 6-7
Hunch back — 3
Round shouldered — 2-7
Stooped — 3

Angus

Boo backed — 17a
Booed — 23-24, 36
Boolie backed — 37
Bow backed — 17a
Creeged in — 14a
Heich i' the back — 8
High shouldered — 18
Humph backed — 3
Humphie (backed) — *1-2, 5a, 6, 9-10,* 13, *14bcd, 15, 17b, 18-19, 21-22, 24, 26, 30-32, 33ab, 35, 37*
Hunchie — 24
Round shouldered — 6, 10, 12, 14a, 17ab, 18, 20, 22, 25, 28, 29b, 32, 34, 36
Rowed shouldered — 7
Row shouldered — 4, 5bc, 14cd, 15, 27
Stooped — 8, 17b, 23, 32
Twa fa'd — 14b
Up in the back — 5b, 29a
Nil — 11, 16

Perth

Bent — 71
Boo backed — 17, 41b, 62
Booed — 41a, 52d, 53
Boolie backed — 7, 15, 17-19, 25, 27, 32, 42, 46, 48, 52bde, 53, 56-60
Bow backed — 22
Heich backed — 33
Hoolachie — 6
Hump backed — 25
Humph — 34
Humphie (backed) — *1, 2a, 5, 9-11,* 12, *13,* 14, *16,* 20-21, *25,* 26, 29b, *30,* 31, 32, *38-39,* 40, *41b,* 44, *45,* 46, *47,* 49, *52ad, 54,* 55, 57, 62-64, *72-73*
Humpie (backed) — *26,* 48, *53, 61, 65, 67*
Hunchie — 26, 31, 46, 51a
Round shouldered — 2a, 4, 8, 28, 29a, 32-33, 36, 42-43, 50, 51b, 52ce, 57, 66, 68-72, 74
Stooped — 26, 29b
Nil — 2b, 3, 23-24, 35, 37

Fife

Bent — 48, 53
Boo backed — 53
Booed — 51, 64a
Boo'ie backed — 44e
Boolie backed — 3, 14, 21, 26, 34, 38, 41d, 44f, 47, 49-50, 55f
Couchie necked — 32
Fair stooped — 50
Forrit — 34
Humph backed — 18
Humphie (backed) — *1, 4, 6-8, 9ab, 10-13, 15-16, 20-22, 25, 27, 29-30, 35, 36a, 37-39, 40ab, 41ab, 42, 44abcef, 47-52, 54, 55abcdeg, 56, 59, 61-63*
Humphie backik — 60
Humpie backed — 23, 33-34, 41c
Hunch backed — 31, 37, 55e
Montie backed — 64a
Round shouldered — 5-8, 13, 16-17, 19, 23-25, 28, 33, 36ab, 40a, 41ab, 43ab, 44df, 45-46, 49-52, 55bdg, 58-60, 62-63
Stooped — 12, 40b, 43a, 44f, 53, 57-58
Tanker backed — 52
Twa fawd — 60
Nil — 2, 64b

Clackmannan

Bent shouldered — 3
Boolie backed — 4a
Crookie — 1
Cruchach — 4c
Humphie (backed) — 1-*2, 4b*
Humph bawked — 7
Humpie backed — 1
Round shouldered — 3, 4cd, 5-7

Stirling

Bent — 21b, 22b
Bo'ed backed — 26d
Boo backed — 7e, 18, 26b, 31
Booed — 1, 26a
Boolie backed — 26c
Croochie — 7b
Crouchie (backed) — 7d, *26b*
Hog backed — 7d
Humphed — 17
Humphie (backed) — *4, 6, 7abe, 8-10, 12, 14, 17-18, 20, 21ab, 22a, 23ac,* 25abcd, *26acde, 27a,* 31, *32-34,* 35ab, *37ab, 38, 39b, 42a*
Humphie shouldered — 19
Humpie backed — 2, 7e, 11, 26b
Hump shouldered — 26b
Hunchie — 26f
Round shouldered — 3-4, 7ace, 8-9, 12-13, 15-16, 18, 21ab, 22a, 23b, 25cd, 26cd, 28, 30-31, 34, 36, 37a, 39b, 40-41, 42b
Sair bent — 16
Stooped — 15, 22ab, 26a, 27b, 40
To have a stoup — 7f
Nil — 5, 24, 29, 39a

Dunbarton

Booed — 16a
Bow backed — 5, 14a
Crauchie — 14a
Gathered up — 18
Humphie (backed) — *1-2,* 3, *4b, 7abc, 9,* 10-11, *12, 13abc, 14b 15, 16ab, 17,* 18
Hunch backed — 11
Hunchie backed — 3
Round shouldered — 1, 4b, 6, 7bc, 8, 13abc, 14b, 16b
Stooped — 2
Nil — 4a

Argyll

Bent — 13, 15
Boo backed — 18
Croochie — 34
Crootchach — 23, 28
Crotach — 3, 5
Croutach — 26
Cruitch — 12
Crutchie — 40
Drooped — 38
Humph backed — 9-10
Humphie (backed) — 16, *18, 20, 24,* 26, *30,* 31-32, *33, 39,* 40
Humpie (backed) — 3, *12, 19,* 34
Hunch backed — 34
Round in the back — 36
Round shouldered — 1-2, 6-7, 9-12, 14, 16-17, 22-23, 30, 35-36, 39
Stooped — 19
Nil — 4, 8, 21, 25, 27, 29, 37

Bute

Bowed — 1a, 8b
How backed — 9
Humphie (backed) — *1cde, 2-3,* 5, 7, *8a*
Humpie backed — 1a, 8b
Hunch backed — 8b
Hunched — 7
Round shouldered — 1ab, 4, 7, 8ab, 9
Stooped — 1a
Nil — 6

Ayr

Bent backed — 28e
Bo'ed backed — 18b, 41
Boo backed — 3, 7, 8a, 28b, 35b, 53ab
Booed — 7, 12b, 15, 20h, 25, 30a, 37, 44
Booed back — 18b
Bowed — 43
Crouchie — 41
Hog shouldered — 18b
Hump backed — 29
Humped — 6
Humphed — 43
Humphie (backed) — *1a, 2a, 3, 7, 8ab, 9, 13, 15, 16ab, 17, 18ab,* 20bfg, *23, 24ab, 25, 26b,* 27, 28abf, *30b,* 33, *34,* 35a, *37-39, 45, 47-48,* 50-51, *53a, 56,* 57
Humpie (backed) — *35b,* 41, *52*
Lout shouldered — 19
Round shouldered — 1b, 2b, 4-5, 7, 8b, 10-11, 12a, 14, 16a, 20cdgh, 21-22, 26abc, 28acdef, 29, 30a, 31, 35b, 36, 40, 42, 45, 47-49, 53b, 54-55, 57
Stooped — 14-15, 18b, 20d, 32
Stoop shouldered — 57
Up on the shoulders — 20ae
Nil — 46

Renfrew

Bent — 16a
Boo backed — 11l
Bow backed — 5, 12a, 14a
Bowlie backed — 21
Crootchach — 1b
Gathered at the shoulders — 1b
Hump backed — 13c
Humped — 2d
Humphie (backed) — 1ab, *2abcdegh, 3, 4bde, 6,* 7, *8-9,* 11*acdfgijk, 13ac,* 14b, 15, *16bcd,* 18a, 19, 21
Humpie (backed) — 2gi*j*, 4ac, 12b, *21*
Humptie — 16b
Hunch backed — 20b
Round shouldered — 2gij, 4de, 8, 11acdeghkl, 13d, 14a, 16a, 17, 19, 20a, 21
Shouldered run over head — 2i
Slope shouldered — 2i
Stooped — 11b, 14a, 16a, 18a
Stooping — 1b
Nil — 2f, 10, 13b, 18b

Lanark

Bent — 13, 35b
Boo backed — 7a, 15b, 27a, 31d, 32d, 33cd, 35b, 37, 38a
Booed — 3, 13, 35b
Bottle necked — 1
Bow backed — 11-12, 14c, 17, 29e, 33b
Crouchie — 9b, 17
Deformed — 29f
Gethered — 28, 36
Hump backed — 20, 29cf
Humph backed — 64b
Humphie (backed) — *4,* 5-6, *7ab, 8ab,* 10b, *11,* 14abcd, *15ab, 16a, 17-23, 25cd, 26ab, 27b, 28, 29befg, 30, 31ab,* 32ce, 33*ac, 35ad, 36-37, 38abc, 40, 42, 44, 46c, 50, 52a, 55-56,* 57ac, *58, 59b, 62-63, 64a, 65-66, 67b*
Humpie (backed) — *29cf, 31c,* 32bd, *38e, 67a*
Hunch backed — 25a, 29f
Hunched — 32d
Narrow chested — 25c
Out in the back — 5
Round shouldered — 1-2, 6, 7ac, 9a, 10ab, 12, 14d, 15c, 16b, 25bc, 26a, 27b, 29acd, 32af, 33acd, 34, 35c, 38cd, 39, 41, 44-45, 46ab, 47-48, 49ab, 51, 52b, 53, 57ab, 58, 59a, 61, 67a
Soo backed — 4bc
Stooped — 15c, 27a, 30, 31d, 35d
Stouped — 3, 39
Nil — 24, 43, 54, 60

West Lothian

Boo backed — 22
Booked — 4
Boolie backed — 2, 8
Humphie (backed) — *1a, 3-4, 6-7,* 9a, *10-12, 14, 16, 17a, 19ab, 20a, 22*
Humpie (backed) — *1b, 5, 15,* 21a
Hunch backed — 21a
Hunchie backed — 3
Leanin — 18
Round shouldered — 1c, 3, 8, 9b, 11, 15-16, 17a, 18, 20b
Stooped — 13, 18
Stoop shouldered — 13
Nil — 1d, 17b, 21b

Midlothian

Bent (furrit) — 17, 22, *25d,* 26b
Boolie backed — 2, 26a, 30, 32
Bowed — 22
Coorie shouldered — 10
Crooked — 26b
Humph a back — 23a
Humphie (backed) — *1, 3, 4, 5, 6b, 7b, 9,* 11, *12ab, 14a,* 15, 20, *23b, 24, 28-29, 31-32*
Humpie backed — 14b, 16, 21
Round backed — 22
Round shouldered — 1-3, 6a, 7a, 8a, 10-11, 12b, 13, 14a, 18-19, 23ab, 24, 25a, 30
Sair stooped — 25b
Stooped — 8b, 14b, 22, 27
Nil — 25c

East Lothian

Boolie backed — 2, 4a, 5, 6ab, 7
Bow backed — 14

East Lothian cont'd
Hump backed — 13
Humph backed — 4b
Humphie backed — 1-2, 4b, 6a, 8-12, 14-16, 18
Humpie backed — 1, 13
Round in the back — 2
Round in the shoulders — 8
Round shouldered — 2, 4b, 5, 6a, 8-10, 13, 16, 18-19, 21
Stooped — 17, 20
Nil — 3

Berwick
Boo backed — 18
Boolie backed — 5
Bowlie backed — 18
Hump backed — 2
Humph backed — 17
Humphie bawked — 29
Humphie (backed) — *3-4, 6-11,* 12, *16ab, 22, 24, 31-32*
Humpie (backed) — *1, 9, 15, 21, 23, 25, 27*
Hunched — 16c
Poo backed — 8
Round shouldered — 8, 10, 12-13, 16b, 18-20, 26-28, 30-32
Up in the back — 14
Up in the shoulders — 7

Peebles
Boo backed — 2
Boolie backed — 4a
Bowed — 6a
Humphie backed — 3, 10
Humphie backted — 8
Humpie backed — 4b, 6b
Round shouldered — 1-2, 4bc, 5, 6ab, 7, 9

Selkirk
Humphie backed — 1, 2abcd, 6-7
Humpie — 2e
Round shouldered — 2ac, 3-5, 8

Roxburgh
Booed — 14
Bowed backed — 15b
Droopie shouldered — 23
Gangs forrit — 12
Hirteg backed — 11
Humphie (backed) — *3ab,* 4, *5, 8, 9ab, 10, 15b, 17-18,* 20, *21abcdef, 26*
Humpie backed — 7, 19, 23
Hurkle backed — 21c, 28
Loor shouldered — 28
Round shouldered — 1-2, 4-5, 9a, 13, 15ab, 16-17, 20, 21ad, 25-28
Stooped — 25
Nil — 6, 22, 24

Dumfries
Bent — 42
Boo backed — 12, 22, 31c
Booed — 4
Bow backed — 10, 43
Bowed — 42
Crippenin — 2
Gans forrit — 36
Hinchie backed — 32
Hump backed — 28
Humph backed — 44
Humphie (backed) — *1ab, 3-7, 8b, 10,* 13, *14, 19, 21b, 23, 25-27, 31bdf, 34, 41*
Humpie backed — 11, 15-16, 22, 32-33, 39-40, 42
Round in the shoulder — 31f
Round shouldered — 2, 8a, 12, 15, 17ab, 18, 21b, 24, 29-30, 31ade, 32-33, 36-37, 39, 43, 45a, 46-47
Stooped — 20, 26, 37, 42, 45b
Up in the shouldered — 17b
Up i' the shoulder — 35
Nil — 9, 21a, 38, 48-49

Kirkcudbright
Bent — 3
Boo backed — 3
Boo shouldered — 8
Bow backed — 1
Doon i' the shoulders — 3
Hoodered — 21c
Humph backed — 2
Humped — 24
Humphie (backed) — *3-5, 7, 10, 14, 15ab, 16*-17, *21ab*
Humpie (backed) — *1, 12b,* 18, *25*
Hunch backed — 6
Hunchie — 11
Lout shouldered — 17
Round shouldered — 1, 7, 9-10, 12a, 15b, 18-20, 22, 26-27
Stoop — 19
Up in the shoulders — 23
Nil — 13

Wigtown
Bent — 17
Booed — 5b, 14, 17
Humphie (backed) — 2, *3, 5a, 6-7, 12, 15-16,* 18
Humpie backed — 13
Hunchie — 6
Round shouldered — 1, 5a, 8-9, 11, 13, 15, 17
Stooped — 8
Stooped shouldered — 5a
Up in the back — 10
Nil — 4

Northumberland
Bent — 32, 52, 79
Bow backed — 34a
Bowed — 12, 79
Bumpie — 12
Bunn shouldered — 140
Droopie — 105
Droopie shouldered — 26
Droop shoulders — 20b
Forrard — 42
Heart grown — 25
Hook backed — 6
Hump backed — 20b, 22, 24b, 41a, 56-57, 71d, 95a, 103a, 104a, 120c
Humped — 49, 77
Humph backed — 19a
Humphie backed — 2a, 3, 11, 19b, 21, 36, 61, 108c
Humpie shouldered — 64a
Humpie (backed) — *8-10, 13, 15-16, 18, 24a, 27-28, 29bf, 33b, 37-39, 40ab, 41bc, 44-50, 53b, 54, 59bcdef, 60, 62abcdegh, 63, 64b, 65b, 66-68, 69abceh, 71bd, 72adgik, 73-76, 82-86, 88ab, 89, 91-92, 94a, 96-97, 99d, 100, 101ab, 102, 104b, 107, 108c, 111b, 118a, 120a, 122b, 124ab, 126abd, 127bcdeg, 128, 129bc,* 130*acdef, 133, 135-136*
Humptie backed — 59d, 69d, 78, 87, 90, 93, 94b, 95b, 103b, 106, 108abc, 111a, 114-116, 118b, 119, 122a, 126f, 127ah, 130b, 138, 141
Hunch backed — 28, 29b, 58, 62a, 77, 81, 104a, 127b, 128h
Hunched — 39, 69b, 77
Hunchie (backed) — *108a,* 111a, *121, 127h*
Roach shouldered — 88b
Round shouldered — 1ab, 2b, 5-7, 13-14, 17-18, 23, 27-28, 29abd, 30-31, 34b, 35-37, 39, 40ab, 41acd, 42, 45, 53ab, 57, 59b, 62b, 64b, 65a, 69a, 71ac, 72bcgj, 80, 82-83, 87, 90, 98, 99b, 100, 103bc, 106, 109-110, 111ab, 112, 121, 126c, 127ah, 130c, 131-132, 134, 137-138, 140, 142-143
Stooped — 19a, 39, 56, 77
Stoopie — 52
Stooping — 89
Stoop shouldered — 41a
(To have) man on back — 76
(To have) monkey on back — 19b
Up at the shoulders — 111ab
Up in the back — 56
Nil — 1c, 4, 20a, 29ce, 33a, 43, 51, 55, 59a, 62f, 69fg, 70, 71e, 72efhl, 99ac, 113, 117, 120b, 123, 125, 126e, 127f, 129a, 139

Cumberland
Barrow backed — 30-31
Bow backed — 5a
Chicken breated — 44
Cobble back — 15b
Gaan bent — 11
Grundstun backed — 56
Hoodie shouldered — 63a
Hump backed — 4, 15c, 20, 36, 37b, 42, 46-48, 62, 63b
Humped backed — 28
Humpie backed — 3, 5a, 13abd, 29, 37a, 54
Humptie backed — 1b, 8-9, 15a, 16, 25-26, 33, 41, 45, 50-52
Hunch backed — 8, 39, 46-47
Hunched (up) — 43, 46
Hunchie backed — 2
Huttie backed — 57
Round shouldered — 1a, 5a, 7, 9, 13c, 15c, 16-18, 21-24, 28, 38, 40, 42, 46-47, 49, 56-59
Shoulder bund — 54
Stooped — 6, 61
Stooping — 44
Nil — 5b, 10, 12, 14, 19, 27, 32, 34-35, 53, 55, 60

Down
Gathered on shoulders — 30
Hooped — 30
Humphie (shouldered) — *15,* 21
Humpie (backed) — 2a, 3-6, 12-*13,* 17, 19, 21, 23-24, 26-27, 29
Hunch backed — 9, 16
Hunched — 9
Kruck — 22
Round shouldered — 2a, 5, 7, 12, 15, 18-19
Up in back — 4
Nil — 1, 2b, 8, 10-11, 14, 20, 25, 28

Tyrone
Bottle shouldered — 14
Capt — 13
Castor oil bottle — 14
Croochie — 5
Cruit on him — 5
Gathered — 15
Humpie — 3, 5-8, 11, 15-16
Hump on him — 9
Hunched — 8
Jucked — 1
Round — 8
Round shouldered — 1, 8, 10-11, 14
Stooped — 10
Nil — 2, 4, 12

Antrim
Barrow backed — 18
Bit crootched — 10
Booed doon — 28
Bottle necked — 34
Croochie — 1
Gathered in shoulders — 21
Hooped — 14
Humped — 5b, 6
Humpie (shouldered) — 2, 4A, 7, 9, *15,* 16b, 18, 21, 29, 33
Humpit — 8b
Humptie (backed) — *25,* 34
Hunched — 13, 25
Hunchie — 8a, 12
Round in the shoulder — 14
Round shouldered — 3, 5b, 17, 19-20, 22, 26
Shupit — 33
Spindle — 34
Stooped — 14, 25, 28
Up in shoulders — 23
Vinegar bottled — 16a
Nil — 4, 5a, 11, 16c, 24, 27, 30-32

Donegal
Bottle — 10b
Croochie — 2
Duked — 1
Gathered — 13
Githered — 11
Humped — 6, 13
Humpie (backed) — 4-5, *7,* 8, 10a, 11
Hunch backed — 12
Round at shoulders — 4
Round shouldered — 5A, 7A
Stooped — 4
Nil — 1A, 3, 9

Fermanagh
Bottle shouldered — 6, 10
Gathered — 4
Humpie (backed) — *1,* 2, *9*
Hunched — 10
Hurchin — 1
Round shouldered — 4-5, 9
Nil — 3, 7ab, 8

Armagh
Humpie (backed) — *1,* 4-5
Humpie Willie — 4
Hunch backed — 1
Round shouldered — 6a
Nil — 2-3, 6b

Londonderry
Gethered — 3
Humped — 3A
Humpie — 1A, 2, 5
Nil — 1, 1B, 4, 6-7

8 STARK NAKED (PQ1, 32)

Variants of STONE (**stean, styen** etc., Northumberland) and NAKED (**nya(c)kit, nyaked** Morayshire, Banffshire, Aberdeenshire; **nyecked** south-east Northumberland; **neeked, nyakkt, nea(c)ked, neeaked** etc., Cumberland) have been subsumed.

Shetland

Bare naked – 14, 18, 21a, 22, 30
Bare scud – 24
Bare skinned naked – 24
Born naked – 10
Midder naked – 1, 3-7, 9-12, 17-20, 21ab, 22, 24-25, 28, 30, 32-33
Midder needle naked – 8, 13-15, 23
Mother naked – 26
Needle naked – 2, 7, 17, 19, 22, 26, 30-31
(Stark) naked – *2*, 7, 13, *21a*, *27*, *29*
Nil – 16

Orkney

Bare naked – 3, 9, 13a, 16, 20
Fairly bare naked – 13a
Fairly naked – 13b
In his neterals – 13a
Mither naked – 4, 7-9, 11-12, 15, 17
Mother naked – 5
Needle naked – 15, 19, 21
Scuddie – 14
Stark naked – 1-2, 4-8, 11, 15, 17, 20-21
Nil – 6, 10, 18

Caithness

As bare as the day you were born – 17
As naked when born – 13
Bare – 4
Bare buff – 6
Bare naked – 2b, 8, 11, 12a
Needle naked – 2a, 3, 5-11, 12abc, 13-15, 16ab, 17
Stark naked – 10
Without a stitch – 14
Nil – 1

Sutherland

Bare – 1, 5
Bare buff – 9b
Bare naked – 8, 9ab
In the buff – 8
Nude – 3
(Stark) naked – 1, 3-4, *5*, 6, *7-8*, *10-13*, 16, *17*
Stripped naked – 12
Nil – 2, 14-15

Ross & Cromarty

Bare – 6
Bare naked – 4, 8-9, 16, 32b, 34-36
Bare to the skin/winds – 25b
(Having) not a thing on – 25b
Mother naked – 25b, 36, 37ab
Nude – 5, 16, 18, 22, 26
Quite naked – 5
Stark – 10
(Stark) naked – *1, 3, 9*, 14-15, 17, *20, 23-24, 25a, 26-27, 29-30*, 31, *32abc, 36, 39*
Starko – 11
Start naked – 28
Stripped – 13
Without a stitch – 10
Nil – 2, 7, 12, 19, 21, 33, 38

Inverness

Bare – 5, 13b, 16
Bare buff – 13a
Bare buffed – 13b
Bare naked – 9, 13b, 14, 22, 28, 37-38, 40
Nude – 13e, 18, 20, 21ab, 26
Rusht – 24
Stark – 13b
(Stark) naked – 1, *2*, 3-4, *6-12*, *13cde, 17*, 18, *19, 21ab, 23, 25*, 26, *27, 29*, 32, *33*, 34-36, 39
Stripped – 20, 21b
Stripped bare – 26
Stripped naked – 15, 38
Nil – 30-31

Nairn

Bare bluff – 1c
Bare naked – 1c, 6
Naked – 2, 5
Nude – 2
Nil – 1ab, 3-4

Moray

Bare – 7, 14, 23
Bare buff – 13
Bare naked – 2a, 4-5, 6b, 7, 8cdef, 17, 21-22
Mither naked – 9a
Moder naked – 22
Red naked – 1
(Stark) naked – 3-4, 6a, 7, 8*ab*, 10, *11*, 12, 15-16, 18-20, 23
Stripped – 7
Nil – 2b, 9b

Banff

Bare – 19-20
Bare naked – 2c, 11, 15, 17, 25-26, 28
Fair naked – 24
Gack naked – 13
In his birthday suit – 21
Mither naked – 15
(Stark) naked – 1, 2ab, 3, *4*, 5, 6ab, 7-10, *11*, 12-16, 18bcd, 21, 23-24, 27, 29, 31-33
Stripped – 14, 34
Tirred – 8
Turred – 34
Without a steek on – 18c
Nil – 18a, 22, 30

Aberdeen

Bare – 22, 109
Bare buff – 10, 23, 68
Bare naked – 1-2, 3ab, 4, 5abcd, 7-8, 14, 17, 19, 21, 24-27, 29, 32, 35, 40, 42-46, 47abcdef, 49, 54, 56-58, 63, 67, 69-70, 71b 72, 74-75, 77, 79, 83, 85-87, 89, 93, 95, 97-101, 104-106
Bare skin – 23
Clean naked – 53
Fair naked – 16, 28b, 77
In the nude – 70
Midder naked – 3a
Mither naked – 28a, 78
Na a cloot on – 1
Na a rag on – 59
Na a stitch on – 47d
Nae claes on – 70
Nae dressed at a' – 29
Naething on – 83
Reed naked – 62
Skirl naked – 71c
Skirlie naked – 31
Stark – 11
(Stark) naked – 6, 8, 10-12, 14-*15*, 20, 24, *25*, 26-27, 28abc, 29-31, 33-*34*, 37, 39, 44, 47ab, 48-49, 51, 53, 55, 59-61, 64, 71ab, 73-74, 80-82, 84-*85* 87-88, 96, 98, 100, 102-103 105, *107*, 108
Stripped – 5b, 23, 66-67
Stripped to the skin – 94
Tirred – 10
Tirred to the very skin – 9
Unclothed – 70
Withoot a steek – 65
Without a stitch – 65
Without ony claes – 32
Yacked – 50
Nil – 13, 18, 36, 38, 41, 52, 76, 90-92

Kincardine

Bare – 27
Bare naked – 2, 4, 7-13, 15, 17abd, 19, 21, 26-27
Nude – 20
Reed naked – 14, 17c
(Stark) naked – *1*, 5-*6*, 16, *17c*, 18, 24-25, *28*
Stripped – 3, 7, 13, 17c
Tirred – 7
Nil – 22-23

Kinross

Bare buff – 3
Bare naked – 1, 4, 6
Scuddie – 6
Skeer naked – 2
Stark naked – 1
Stripped – 3
Nil – 5, 7

Angus

As bare as birkie – 14c
As bare as buff – 14cd
As bare as when he was born – 31
Bare – 22, 30
Bare buff – 5c, 8, 14a, 19, 23-24, 29b, 30
Bare naked – 9, 14b, 17b, 24, 26, 29a, 32, 33a
Bare skin – 17a
Bare to the buff – 5a, 10, 33a
Birthday claes – 5b
Mither naked – 14a, 23, 37
Needle naked – 13
No' a steek o' claes on – 8
Not a russem on – 29a
Sarked – 17a
Sark naked – 14cd
Scuddie – 33b
Skin naked – 28
(Stark) naked – *1*, 4, 5ac, 6-8, *12, 14a, 15, 17b*, 25, *29b*, 33b, *34-35*, 36
Stripped – 14a, 37
Stripped to skin – 33b
Tirred – 14cd, 33b, 37
Tirred to skin – 14d
Withoot a steek on – 31
Nil – 2-3, 11, 16, 18, 20-21, 27

Perth

Bare – 8, 11-12, 34, 43
Bare buff – 1, 15, 27-28, 32-33, 44, 52e, 55, 64, 71
Bare naked – 13-14, 16, 21, 23, 25, 29a, 33, 37, 40, 41b, 52cde, 66-68, 74
Bare skin – 73
Bare skinned – 57
Birthday suit – 18, 24
In the buff – 52e
Mither naked – 66
No a steek on – 29b
Nude – 8, 12, 51a, 73
Red naked – 37
Scuddie – 29a, 62, 65, 68
Scurl naked – 29a
Skeer – 42, 46
Skeer naked – 27, 33, 41a, 47-48, 51b, 56, 62
(Stark) naked – 2a, *4-5, 9-10*, 14, 20, *25*, 30, *32*, 36, 50, *51b*, 57, *60*, 70, *72*
Stripped – 16, 38
Stripped to the skin – 39
Tail naked – 18
Without a steek – 15, 52c
Nil – 2b, 3, 6-7, 17, 19, 22, 26, 31, 35, 45, 49, 52ab, 53-54, 58-59, 61, 63, 69-70

Fife

Bare – 11, 33, 60
Bare buff – 1-2, 7, 12-13, 18-19, 23, 26, 34, 36a, 37, 39, 40b, 41acd, 42, 43ab, 44b, 45, 48-49, 51, 55bdf, 58-59, 62, 64b
Bare buffed – 8, 64a
Bare naked – 4, 6-7, 9ab, 10, 14, 16-17, 21-22, 24-25, 28, 30, 38, 43a, 44bcef, 46, 48-49, 51, 53-54, 55abdeg, 57, 61-62
Bare scud – 12, 37, 41b
Bare scuddie – 15, 55b
Bare skinned – 10
In birthday suit – 7
Kittle naked – 27
No a steek on – 51
Nude – 63
Scuddie – 35, 55cd
Skin naked – 9b, 28, 32, 44a
Skirl naked – 27, 43a
Stark – 48, 50
Starkie – 61
(Stark) naked – *15, 19*, 23, 41a, *47*, 50, 55d, *59*
Steekless – 43b
Stripped – 8, 21, 37, 44b
Stripped naked – 7
Stripped to the buff – 44d
Nil – 3, 5, 20, 29, 31, 36b, 40a, 52, 56

Clackmannan

Bare naked – 1, 4a, 5-7
Bare skin – 4c
Mither naked – 2
Skin naked – 4d
Stark naked – 2, 4b
Nil – 3

Stirling

Bare – 26a
Bare birket – 18
Bare buff – 4, 7ab, 8-9, 12, 18, 22a, 23b, 24, 25abd, 26b, 27ab, 28, 32-34, 35a, 37b, 39a, 42a
Bare buffed – 20, 26a
Bare naked – 3, 7c, 10-11, 13, 15-17, 20, 21ab, 22b, 25cd, 26de, 27a, 36, 37b, 39ab
Bare pelt – 23a
Bare scud – 5, 8, 26b
Bare scuddie – 7e, 13, 22b, 27a, 29
Bare skin – 7a, 23a
Bare skinned – 7e
Bare to the buff – 30
Birthday uniform – 26d
Buff naked – 30
In one's birthday suit – 7e
In the bare buff – 29
Mither naked – 7d
Nude – 4, 7e, 21a, 26d, 35b
Scuddie – 2, 7b, 9, 14-15, 25a, 26b, 31, 38
Skin naked – 21b
(Stark) naked – 4, *7f*, 18, *23c*, 26cd, *30-31*, 34
Stripped – 1, 37a
Without a steek on – 22b
Without a stitch – 7a, 26e
Nil – 6, 19, 26f, 40-41, 42b

Dunbarton

As bare as the pelt – 5
Bare – 10-11
Bare as birkie – 13bc
Bare buff – 3, 5, 14a, 16b, 17
Bare naked – 1-3, 6, 8, 12, 13b,

Dunbarton cont'd
16b, 18
Bare scud — 4b, 6, 7a
Bare scudded — 16a
Bare scuddie — 2, 4a, 7a, 9, 12, 14ab
Bare skin — 4b
Ber cuttie — 7b
Birthday suit — 2, 5
Naked — 13c
Nude — 7b
Scuddie — 10-11, 13a, 15
Scuddie bare — 7c
To the pelt — 5

Argyll
Bare — 16
Bare buff — 23, 27, 38
Bare naked — 2-3, 5-6, 9, 11, 15, 18, 20, 22, 24-25, 29-35, 39-40
Bare skinned — 10
Birthday suit — 19
Not a stitch on — 34
Nude — 12, 27, 33
Scuddie — 19
(Stark) naked — 2, *6*-7, 10, 14, *17-18,* 19, *24,* 37
Stripped — 28
Nil — 1, 4, 8, 13, 21, 26, 36

Bute
Bare buff — 8a
Bare naked — 1bcd, 3, 7, 8b
Bare scud — 4, 8ab
Bare scuddie — 1a, 2, 5, 9
Scuddie — 8ab
Scuddie bare — 7
Stark naked — 8ab
Stripped — 9
Nil — 1e, 6

Ayr
A' claes aff — 43
As bare as birkie — 20h, 24b
Bare — 55
Bare birkie — 8a, 20aeg
Bare buff — 1a, 2a, 7, 8ab, 9-10, 12ab, 14-15, 16ab, 18ab, 20bdgh, 21, 24ab, 26b, 27, 28d, 29, 30a, 31-34, 36-38, 41, 45-46, 49, 57
Bare burk — 35a
Bare naked — 1a, 2ab, 4-7, 8b, 11, 13, 15, 20cf, 22-23, 25, 26c, 28af, 29, 30b, 31, 35b, 40-41, 44-45, 56-57
Bare pelt — 6, 23, 32, 41-42, 47, 51
Bare scud — 2a, 3, 5-7, 8b, 9-10, 13-14, 18b, 20bg, 26b, 29, 32, 37, 46
Bare scuddie — 7, 8b, 10, 16a, 17, 24b, 26ac, 28bd, 50, 53a
Bare skinned — 28e
Bare to the buff — 28b
Birkie — 14
Birthday suit — 15
Buffed — 29
In a state of nature — 57
In his bare buff/pelt — 48
Mither naked — 53b
Mother naked — 8b
Nude — 6, 19, 57
Quite naked — 28e
Scud — 20d
Scuddie — 3, 20g, 29, 37
Scuddie bare — 1a, 4, 15, 30b
(Stark) naked — 6, *11, 28c,* 30a, 42, *47,* 52, *53a, 54, 57*
Stripped — 18b, 43
Stripped to the buff — 29
Nil — 1b, 39

Renfrew
Bare — 3
Bare buff — 2cgh, 8, 11ce, 14b, 15, 18a
Bare naked — 2dj, 4acd, 7-8, 11adghj, 13ad, 14a
Bare pelt — 11c
Bare scaldie — 4d
Bare scud — 11bdk, 13c, 14ab, 17
Bare scuddie — 2bf, 6, 11aefi, 12a, 13c, 18a, 20b, 21
Bare skelp — 11c
Bare skin — 2i
Bare skinned — 2ag
(In) birthday suit — 1b, 2i, 4d, 11j, 12b, 20a
Mither naked — 11l
Naething on — 2j
Not a shred of clothing — 8
Nude — 2di, 14a, 16ad, 20a
Scuddie — 2j, 4ac, 9, 11fl, 14b, 15, 16bcd, 18b, 19, 20a
Scuddie bare — 16bc
Scuddie buddie — 11k
Stark — 18b
(Stark) naked — *1b,* 2b, *4e,* 8, *13a,* 20a
Stripped to the buff — 1b, 16a
Stripped to the pelt — 5
Strippted to the skin — 2a
Withoot a stitch — 2g
Nil — 1a, 2e, 4b, 10, 13b

Lanark
Bare — 21, 29b, 32d
Bare as birkie — 46ac
Bare buff — 9b, 11, 14b, 22, 25b, 29c, 32cd, 33abcd, 35d, 38a, 39, 46a, 47-48, 50-51, 52ab, 53-55, 57abc, 59a, 61-62, 67a
Bare naked — 1, 3, 6, 9a, 10a, 16b, 20, 23, 25c, 26ab, 27b, 30, 32ad, 35abc, 37, 38cde, 39-40, 44-45, 48, 49ab, 51, 57b, 60, 63, 65-66, 67b
Bare pelt — 2, 12, 25b, 28
Bare scaddie — 31c
Bare scud — 4, 7a, 9a, 13, 25a, 28, 29e, 31b, 32f, 33cd, 39, 46b, 50, 52b, 57ac, 64b
Bare scuddie — 7ac, 8ab, 10b, 11-12, 14acd, 15ab, 16a, 17, 25c, 29acde, 31a, 34, 35b, 39, 43, 47, 50, 56, 65
Bare skin — 5, 33cd
Bare skinned — 31a
Bare to the buff — 15c
Birthday suit — 35d
Cleedless — 32d
In bare scud — 4, 26
In his bare skin — 4
In the buff — 19
In the nude — 14c
Modyr naked — 38d
Nae clathes — 27b
Nude — 14b, 29bf, 58
Scuddie — 4, 7b, 8a, 10a, 15b, 17, 21, 27a, 29g, 30, 31d, 32e, 35b, 38b, 42, 52a
Scuddie bare — 46a
Scudie — 23, 32b
Scud naked — 18
Skirl bare — 60
Stark — 26a, 29c, 32e
(Stark) naked — *1-2,* 4, 6, 7c, *10b,* 14d, *15a,* 16b, 26a, *29c,* 32d, *35c, 44,* 59ab
Stripped — 25b, 29f, 32d
(Stripped) to the buff — 31a
(Stripped) to the skin — 15c
Nil — 24, 25d, 36, 41, 64a

West Lothian
Bare buff — 1d, 4, 6-8, 13, 17a, 19b, 22
Bare buffed — 11
Bare naked — 1bc, 2-3, 5-6, 8, 9a, 10, 12-13, 18, 20ab, 22
Bare pelt — 16
Bare scud — 1a, 4
Bare scuddie — 17a
Bare skin — 16
Mither naked — 18
Nude — 16, 19a
Scuddie — 22
Scudelie bare — 14
Stark — 20a
Stripped — 11, 21a
Stripped naked — 15
Without a steek — 2
Nil — 9b, 17b, 21b

Midlothian
As naked as the day they were born — 13
Ballocks naked — 25c
Bare — 19-20
Bare buff — 7a, 10-11, 12ab, 23b, 25bc
Bare naked — 2, 4, 6a, 7a, 12ab, 14ab, 15, 17-18, 21, 24, 25a, 26ab, 27-28
Bare scuddie — 13
Bawlock naked — 7a
Nethin on — 1
Nude — 23b, 26b,
Scuddie bairdie — 14a
Skirl — 29, 32
Skirl naked — 25c, 30
Stark — 22
(Stark) naked — *8a,* 9, *11, 16-17,* 19, *23a, 29*
Stripped — 10
Struped — 7b
Nil — 3, 5, 6b, 8b, 25d, 31

East Lothian
As the Lord Almighty made ye — 8
Bare — 1
Bare buff — 1-2, 4a, 7, 10, 13
Bare buffed — 16
Bare naked — 4b, 5, 6a, 8-9, 12, 16-17, 21
Bare scud — 4b, 5
Buff — 1
Kittle naked — 8
Mither naked — 2
Same as you were born — 20
Scud — 8
Scuddie naked — 2
Skirl — 6b, 14
Skirl naked — 1, 4a, 6a, 10, 13
Stark naked — 18-19
Stripped bare — 8
Stripped to the buff/skin — 15
Nil — 3. 11

Berwick
Bare buff — 10, 24, 27, 32
Bare naked — 1, 6, 10, 13, 15, 20, 23-25, 29, 31
Kittle naked — 17-18, 28, 32
Skinle naked — 22
Skirl — 12, 15
Skirled — 5
Skirlie — 4
Skirl naked — 2-4, 7-9, 11, 13, 16abc, 17-21, 23, 26-27, 30-32
(Stark) naked — 8, 12, *26, 32*
Nil — 14

Peebles
Bare buff — 4c, 6a, 7-10
Bare naked — 2, 4b
Bare scuddie — 8
Mither naked — 10
Mother naked — 4b
Skirl naked — 1, 3, 6a, 10
Stark naked — 4c, 6ab
Stripped to the skin — 6b
Nil — 4a, 5

Selkirk
Bare naked — 2d, 4
Birthday suit — 8
Skirl — 3
Skirl bare — 5
Skirl naked — 1, 2abe, 4, 6-8
Stark naked — 2c

Roxburgh
Bare buff — 23
Bare naked — 1-2, 5, 9a, 10, 15b, 21ae, 25-28
Scuddie naked — 21c
Skirl — 12
Skirl naked — 3ab, 4-8, 9ab, 10-11, 13, 15ab, 16-20, 21abcdef, 23-24, 26, 28
Stark naked — 4, 21a
Stripped tae the skin — 13
Nil — 14, 22

Dumfries
As bare as a birkie — 9, 22, 34, 38, 41
Bare — 13, 42, 45b
Bare buff — 1a, 3, 14, 19, 26-28, 31ab, 43, 46
Bare naked — 1b, 2, 5, 8ab, 11-12, 17ab, 21b, 23-24, 30, 31def, 32, 35, 39-41, 44, 45a, 46
Bare scud — 46
Bare scuddie — 2
Bare skin — 46
Buff — 4, 45b
In his bare skin — 29
Mither naked — 39
Mother naked — 29
Naked as the day he was born — 16
Nowt on — 29
Nude — 15, 18
Scuddie — 25, 49
Skirl — 7
Skirl naked — 29
(Stark) naked — *4,* 33, 37, *42,* 47
Stripped — 31c, 32
Stripped to the buff — 3
Stripped to the skin — 4
Nil — 6, 10, 20, 21a, 36, 48

Kirkcudbright
Bare — 17
Bare as birkie — 2, 21a
Bare birkie — 3, 21c
Bare buff — 9, 12ab, 15ab, 16, 19, 21c, 23-25
Bare naked — 1, 3-8, 10, 13, 16, 18-20, 21ab, 22, 26
Bare pelt — 1
Bare scud — 6
Bare to the buff/pelt — 2
Birthday suit — 7
Mother naked — 7
Naw claes on — 18
Naked — 14, 15a
Nude — 6
Scuddie — 11
Start naked — 27

Wigtown
Bare buff — 6, 14-15, 18
Bare naked — 2, 5a, 7-9, 12, 16-17
Bare pelt — 1, 10, 13
Bare scuddie — 3
In yer skin — 13
Naked pelt — 11
Scud — 5a
(Stark) naked — *5a,* 14
Stripped — 15, 17
The first suit ma mither guin me — 1
Nil — 4, 5b

Northumberland
Aal bare — 72d
Adam's suit — 41a
As naked as they were born — 83
As you're born — 22
Bare — 12, 14, 32, 35, 46, 59b, 62h, 72l, 75, 92, 99d, 108c, 111b, 130b, 140
Bare buff — 1b, 22, 29de, 39, 40a, 50, 60, 62e, 63, 66, 69abcdfh, 70, 76, 86, 89, 118b, 124b

Northumberland cont'd

Bare buffed — 29b, 120a
Bare naked — 1ab, 5-6, 8-9, 13, 16, 18, 19b, 20b, 21, 27-28, 29b, 31, 36, 41c, 48, 53b, 62ah, 103b, 126f
Bare nude — 111a
Bare pelt — 29f, 39, 57, 118b
Bare skin — 52, 60, 74, 91, 105, 130c
Bare skinned — 40b, 114
Bare to the buff — 27, 33b, 40b, 118a
Bare to the pelt — 130f
Bare to the skin — 71a
Birthday suit — 5, 14, 22, 40b, 41a, 46, 69ab, 77, 79, 130c
Bone naked — 83
Borthday suit — 87, 131
Doffed — 79
Higgie shaggie — 126d
In his bare skin — 101b, 126a
In his pelt — 29e
In me nothings — 77
In the buff — 29c
Mother naked — 15, 46, 72b, 125, 126f
Nae claes on — 88a
Nakes as a robin — 141
Naked truth — 69b
Nakie — 98, 104a, 122b
Nakie shackie — 96, 124b
Nakie shaggie — 124b
Nakkie shackie — 95a
Nee claes on — 121
Nekkie shakie — 115
No clos on — 121
Not a stitch on — 53b
Nowt on — 16, 57, 64b, 71a, 72k, 90, 96, 101b, 109, 121, 126a, 127h, 130de
Nude — 69ab, 77, 123, 127e
Nudist — 140
Pelt — 130c
Scuddie — 18
Shaggie — 79
Skerl — 39
Skerl naked — 8, 22
Skirl — 59b, 77
Skirl bare — 29f
Skirl naked — 1a, 2ab, 3, 10-13, 17, 19ab, 23, 34ab, 37-38, 43, 51, 55, 62c, 77
Snekked — 39
Stark — 59b, 126f
(Stark) naked — *2b*, 7, *29a*, *30*, *35*, 39, *40a*, *41bcd*, *42*, *45-47*, *53ab*, 54, *56-57*, 59*d*e, 62a*bceg*h, 64ab, *65a*, 67-68, 69*c*d, *70*, 71*acde*, 72*acegij*k, *77*, *80-82*, 85, *87*, 88a*b*, *90*, 94ab, *95b*, 96-97, *99b*, *100*, 103a, *104ab*, *106*, 108b, *109*-110, *111a* *112*, 115, 117, 118b, *119*, *120bc*, 121, *122a*, 125, *126c*, *127afh*, *130abce*, *133*, 137-138, *142-143*
Starn naked — 26
Stone naked — 49, 56-57, 59c 65b, 71ab, 72j, 73, 78, 84. 89, 91, 93, 102, 103bc, 106-107, 108a, 110, 111b, 123, 124a, 126b, 127c, 129c, 132-133, 135, 141
Stripped — 72l, 89
Stripped naked — 69b, 83
Stripped to the buff — 40b, 82, 134
Withoot a stitch of clothing on — 20b
Without a stitch on — 45, 99d
Nil — 1c, 4, 20a, 24ab, 25, 33a, 44, 58, 59af, 61, 62df, 69eg, 72fh, 99ac, 101a, 113, 116, 126c, 127bdg, 128, 129ab, 136, 139

Cumberland

Bare as a badger — 58
Bare as a gorp — 30
Bare buff — 9, 28, 30
Bare pelt — 1b, 13a, 17, 24, 42, 45-46, 61-62
Bar scutie — 53
In the buff — 14
Mother naked — 35
Nowt on — 12, 25, 37a, 63a
Oa' bare — 56
Reet naked — 8
Showrn — 22
Skirl naked — 13b
Stafen naked — 4
(Stark) naked — *1ab*, 2-3, *5ab*, 7, 9, 13*c*d, *15ac*, *20-27*, 28, 37a, 38, *42*, 44, *46-47*, *50*, 51, *52-54*, *56-58*, 59
Stone naked — 11, 15b, 16, 18, 24-25, 27, 29-31, 33, 37b, 39-41, 43, 45-46, 48, 52, 54, 57, 62
Stripped — 6
Stripped to the buff — 15c, 28, 30
Widdoot a stitch — 56
Nil — 10, 19, 32, 34, 36, 55, 60, 63b

Down

As bare as birkie — 4
Bare — 6, 28
Bare pelt — 3, 13, 29
Birthday costume — 5
Birthday suit — 21
In one's pelt — 19, 26, 30
Like the hour he was born — 5
No a runion on — 13, 23-24
Not a stitch on — 15, 25
Nude — 21
Pelt — 21
(Stark) naked — 7, *12*, 15, *17*, 24
Stripped — 18, 26
Nil — 1, 2ab, 8-11, 14, 16, 20, 22, 27

Tyrone

As the night he was born — 14
Bare — 0
Bare buff — 4, 14
Bare pelt — 2, 5, 11, 16
In his buff — 3
In his skin — 6-7
In one's pelt — 6-7, 9-10, 15
Mother naked — 11
Naked — 8, 10-11
Pelt — 14
Stripped — 1, 15
Without a dollie on — 15
Without a dollion on — 6
Nil — 12-13

Antrim

Bare as birkie — 33
Bare pelt — 5a, 7, 16b, 19, 21, 28, 34
Bare to the world — 14
Birthday suit — 14
Buff — 21
Mother naked — 5a
Nae clathes on — 17
Not a dollie on — 11, 13, 19-20, 26
Not a dud on — 11, 29
Pelt — 6, 15, 16a, 18
Scuddie — 8b
(Stark) naked — 3, 5ab, *19*, *25*
Stripped — 1, 22, 25
Stript naked — 25
Without a doil-ay — 14
Nil — 2, 4, 4A, 8a, 9-10, 12, 16c, 23-24, 27, 30-32

Donegal

Bare — 5A, 12-13
Bare pelt — 1, 3-4, 6, 10ab
Birthday suit — 10a
Buff — 10a
Nude — 5, 5A
Pelt — 13
Scared — 7A
(Stark) naked — 4-5, *12*
Stripped — 3-4
Stripped naked — 2
Stripped to skin — 8
Undressed — 12
Nil — 1A, 7, 9, 11

Fermanagh

Bare buff — 8
Bare hide — 1
Bare pelt — 1-2, 4
Bare skin — 1, 9
Buff — 6
Pelt — 2, 6
Skin — 6
Nil — 3, 5, 7ab, 10

Armagh

Bare — 1, 4
Not a runyen — 2
Skinfits — 1
Stark naked — 6a
Nil — 3, 5, 6b

Londonderry

Bare — 1A, 5
Bare as birkie — 3
Bare pelt — 1B
Naked — 3A
Nyuht — 3
Without a dollie — 6
Without a tatter — 2
Nil — 1, 4, 7

9 The kind of GLOVES with one compartment for the thumb and another for all the fingers together (PQ1, 51)

(1) Note the recurrence of some items in 10 **socks without feet.**
(2) **Mitten** has not been mapped. It occurs in varying concentrations nearly everywhere.
The variants of the unstressed vowel in **mog(g)Ans, muggAns**, etc., have been subsumed.

Shetland

Dags — 9, 21b, 22, 24, 26, 30, 33
Degs — 16
Mittens — 1-16, 18-20, 21ab, 22-23, 25, 27-33
Mitts — 7, 26, 30
Muffs — 17

Orkney

Mittens — 1-5, 7-12, 13a, 14-21
Mitts — 7, 13a
Mogans — 15
Moggies — 5
Mogies — 13b
Moogies — 6

Caithness

Mittens — 4, 7, 11, 12ac
Moagans — 4
Mogans — 3, 8, 11, 12bc, 13-15
Moggans — 10, 16ab
Moogans — 12b, 14, 17
Muffles — 2b, 3-6, 8-11, 12ac, 14-15
Muffs — 2a, 5
Nil — 1

Sutherland

Mittens — 3, 5, 7, 12-13, 16
Mitts — 7, 9b, 15
Mogans — 4, 6, 9b, 14
Moggans — 1-3, 5, 8, 9a, 10, 13, 15-17
Muffles — 9a
Nil — 11

Ross & Cromarty

Maughan — 25b
Mittens — 1, 7, 15-16, 26-28, 32abc, 36, 38-39
Mitts — 2-4, 8, 14, 18-19, 23, 28, 32c, 36, 39
Mockans — 29
Mogans — 6, 9-15, 17-21, 24, 25a, 26, 31, 32b, 35
Moggans — 8, 22, 33, 36
Moogans — 30
Mowgans — 34
Muttens — 37ab
Pockies — 36
Nil — 5

Inverness

Gloves — 18
Mittens — 2-3, 7-9, 13a, 16-19, 21a, 22-23, 25, 27, 29, 32-35, 38-39
Mitts — 4-5, 8, 10, 12, 13bcd, 17, 20, 22-23, 30-32, 36-38, 40
Mochtach — 24
Mockans — 14, 38
Mogans — 13b, 15, 18, 20, 26-27
Moggans — 9-10, 13e, 21ab
Moogans — 16
Muffles — 28-29
Pawkies — 39
Nil — 1, 6, 11

Nairn

Hoomacks — 4
Mittens — 1c, 2

Nairn cont'd

Mitts — 1a, 2, 5
Moggans — 1b, 3, 6

Moray

Hoomacks — 1, 2b, 3-4, 6b, 8b, 13-14, 18
Hummle doddies — 6a, 8a, 9a, 20-22
Hummle dodies — 8b
Hummles — 6a, 9a, 19
Hummlies — 6a, 7, 8d, 9ab, 10, 16, 20, 22
Mittens — 3-4, 8ace, 19
Mitts — 2a, 5, 7, 8cd, 11, 13, 15, 21
Mogans — 13
Moochins — 17
Muffles — 1, 8bc, 16, 21-23
Thoomacks — 3-4, 12, 15-16
Nil — 8f

Banff

Doddie mittens — 13
Doddies — 13
Homilies — 18a
Hummels — 2c
Hummle dodies — 2c, 3
Hummle doddies — 1, 2c, 3, 6b, 7-12, 15-17, 18b, 20-23 26-29, 31-32
Hummlicks — 1
Hummlies — 2a, 3-5, 6ab, 7, 9-11, 14, 16-17, 18bcd, 19-21, 23-24, 26-27
Mittens — 2b, 3, 18c
Mitts — 2a
Moggans — 32
Muffles — 2c, 25, 29-30, 32-34
Muffles dodies — 2c

Aberdeen

Doddie mittens — 4, 14, 109
Doddies — 1, 3b, 13-14, 17, 21, 41, 48, 82, 96
Humblies — 91
Hummle doddies — 2, 3a, 4, 5abcd, 6-12, 14, 17-21, 24-27, 28bc, 29-39, 42-46, 47abcdef, 49, 51-62, 64-70, 71abc, 72-78, 80-90, 93, 95-97, 99-101, 103-105, 107-108
Hummle dodies — 50, 94, 98, 102, 106
Hummle dods — 40
Hummle mittens — 47d, 76
Hummlies — 9-10, 12-13, 15-17, 22-23, 25-27, 28a, 29-30, 47ac, 48-51, 53, 60, 63-64, 66-67, 77, 80-81, 83, 86, 89, 95-96, 98, 104
Hummocks — 77
Mittens — 5d, 7, 10, 21, 25, 27, 38, 70, 105
Mitts — 12, 47f, 70, 93
Metts — 73
Moggans — 3a, 6, 24
Muffles — 53, 78-80, 84, 86, 92-94, 96, 100, 107
Pawkies — 14

Kincardine

Doddie mittens — 5, 13, 15, 17bcd, 21, 25, 27-28
Doddies — 1-7, 10-12, 14, 16, 17ad, 18-28
Hummle doddies — 2-3, 5, 7, 9-10, 12-13, 17a, 18, 24
Hummlies — 4, 10, 17b
Mittens — 3, 17c
Muffles — 6, 8

Kinross

Dobbie mittens — 5
Doddies — 1
Mittens — 2
Mitts — 4, 6
Pawkies — 1-2

Pokies — 3, 6
Nil — 7

Angus

Doddie mittens — 1, 4, 5ac, 7, 13, 14ad, 17b, 20, 23, 25, 27, 29ab, 31, 36-37
Doddies — 2, 4, 5b, 7-9, 12, 14abcd, 15-16, 17a, 18, 21-24, 32, 33ab, 34-35
Dodies — 3, 6, 11, 19, 26, 30
Doodies — 10
Hummle doddies — 8
Mittens — 2, 5b, 12, 24, 28, 32, 33b
Mitts — 14ad, 17b, 18, 20, 22, 29b, 30
Mutts — 14b

Perth

Doadie mitts — 59
Doddie mittens — 7, 15-16, 31, 33, 45, 55, 57-58, 60 65
Doddie mitts — 26, 32
Doddies — 13, 21, 23, 27, 29b, 53-54, 64
Dodies — 5
Gloves — 71
Hedger's gloves — 68
Hummle doddies — 43, 45, 52ad
Mittens — 2a, 4, 8, 10, 14, 19-20, 29a, 30, 34, 36, 40, 42, 47, 50, 51a, 52bc, 56, 71-74
Mitts — 1, 2a, 8-10, 12, 14, 17, 19-20, 22, 25-28, 29ab, 32, 35, 38, 41a, 44, 48-49, 51b, 52ae, 56, 59, 63, 66-67, 69, 71, 73
Mockans — 18
Moggans — 1, 2b
Moochers — 52c
Muffies — 6
Muffles — 25, 39, 67
Muggans — 40, 41b
Mutts — 44, 46, 48
Pawkie muffities — 62
Pawkies — 10, 31, 41a, 61, 66, 68
Pokies — 41b, 45
Nil — 3, 11, 24, 37

Fife

Bags — 34
Dobbies — 1-2, 4, 9b, 11, 17, 27-28, 31, 35
Dobies — 5-6, 12, 14, 21, 25-26
Doddie mittens — 12, 53
Doddies — 3
Dodies — 13
Mittens — 7-8, 21, 32-34, 44f, 46-48, 55af, 56-57
Mitts — 7, 11, 16, 21-23, 30, 33-34, 36b, 37, 44bdf, 45, 49, 51, 55ae, 57, 63
Pawkies — 8, 9a, 12-13, 15, 18-21, 23-24, 26-29, 33, 36a, 37-39, 40ab, 41abcd, 42, 43ab, 44abcef, 45-50, 53-54, 55abcdefg, 58-63, 64ab
Paws — 9a
Pokies — 10, 12, 22, 44e
Scayvies — 35
Nil — 52

Clackmannan

Doddie mitts — 3
Mittens — 4b, 6-7
Mittings — 4b
Mitts — 1, 3, 4bc, 6
Pawkies — 2, 4ad, 5

Stirling

Doadies — 8
Doddies — 27a
Mawkies — 8
Mittens — 7d, 18, 23ab, 25abcd, 26abd, 28-29, 32-33, 35a, 36, 42b
Mitts — 1, 3-4, 6, 7abde, 9, 11-12, 14-17, 19-20, 21a, 22a, 23abc, 24, 25acd, 26abcde, 28 31-34, 35a, 36, 37a, 39ab, 40
Packies — 7bd
Pawkies — 6, 7ac, 8, 11, 13, 17-19, 21b, 22ab, 25ad, 26f, 27a, 31, 35b, 37a, 38, 40, 42a
Pawmies — 38
Pokies — 9, 27a, 30, 39a
Puckies — 10
Nil — 2, 5, 7f, 27b, 37b, 41

Dunbarton

Baby gloves — 14b
Mittens — 3, 4b, 7ac, 8-9, 16ab, 18
Mitts — 1, 3, 4ab, 6, 7bc, 8-12, 13abc, 14b, 15, 16ab, 17-18
Muffins — 10
Muggans — 2
Pankies — 14a
Pawkies — 4a, 5, 16a

Argyll

Gloves — 17
Mittens — 4, 7, 9, 11, 14, 16, 18, 22, 26-27, 33, 35, 39
Mitts — 1-3, 5, 8-10, 12-13, 15-16, 19-21, 23-28, 30, 32, 35, 37-40
Mutts — 31, 33
Pawkies — 24
Nil — 6, 29, 34, 36

Bute

Maugans — 8b
Mittens — 1c, 7, 8a, 9
Mitts — 1abcde, 2-5, 8b
Pawkies — 1a, 8b
Nil — 6

Ayr

Hummle dawdies — 37
Liffies — 54
Mittens — 1ab, 3, 5, 21, 27, 28cf, 38, 43, 47
Mitts — 1ab, 3, 5, 7, 8a, 9, 18b, 26a, 28cdf, 33, 48, 53a, 56
Packies — 47
Pawkies — 2ab, 4-7, 8ab, 9-11, 12ab, 13-15, 16ab, 17, 18ab, 19, 20abcefgh, 21-23, 24ab, 25, 26abc, 27, 28abcde, 29, 30ab, 31-32, 34, 35ab, 36, 38-46, 48-49, 51-52, 53b, 54, 56-57
Pokies — 28f, 50, 55
Nil — 20d

Renfrew

Fingerless — 2i
Gloves — 8
Mittens — 2aeh, 4abc, 11ehik, 12b, 13ac, 15, 16bc, 21
Mitts — 1ab, 2abcfghij, 3, 4bde, 5-7, 9-10, 11abcdegijkl, 12b 13bcd, 14ab, 16abcd, 18a, 19, 20b
Pawkies — 2e, 5, 7, 11dfgh, 14b, 17
Pokies — 4d
Nil — 2d, 12a, 18b, 20a

Lanark

Doddies — 56
Gloves — 16b
Mittens — 3-4, 6, 9b, 12, 25a, 26b, 27b, 29bcf, 31d, 32d, 35d, 59b, 67a
Mitts — 2, 4-6, 7abc, 10b, 12, 14a, 15c, 16a, 21, 25cd, 28, 29cg, 32c, 38cd, 45, 59ab, 64b
Packies — 23, 67ab
Pawkies — 2, 7abc, 8ab, 9a, 10ab, 11, 13, 14abcd, 15abc, 16ab, 17-20, 22, 24, 25abcd, 27ab, 28, 29adefg, 30, 31abcd, 32acdef, 33abcd, 34, 35abcd, 36-37, 38ace, 39-45, 46abc, 47-48, 49ab, 50-51, 52ab, 53-56, 57abc, 58, 59a, 60-63, 64ab, 65-66
Pokies — 3, 23, 26a, 29b
Pookies — 32b
Nil — 1, 38b

West Lothian

Mittens — 3, 5, 11, 16
Mitts — 1abd, 2-3, 6, 13, 16, 17a, 18, 20b
Pawkies — 1a, 2, 4, 6-8, 9ab, 10-16, 17ab, 18, 19ab, 20ab, 21ab, 22
Pokies — 1c, 12

Midlothian

Mittens — 3, 8a
Mitts — 1, 6a, 11, 12a, 13, 17-22
Packies — 4, 25c
Pawkies — 1-3, 5, 6ab, 7b, 8b, 9-11, 12ab, 13, 14ab, 15-19, 21-22, 23ab, 24, 25abd, 26ab, 27-32
Steering gloves — 22
Nil — 7a

East Lothian

Half mitts — 17
Mittens — 4ab, 6b, 9
Mitts — 2, 5, 9, 13
Packies — 7
Pawkies — 1-3, 4ab, 5, 6ab, 8, 10-13, 16, 18-21
Pokies — 14-15

Berwick

Mittens — 2, 7-8, 10-11, 13, 15, 24, 27
Mitts — 1, 6, 8-10, 15, 16c, 23, 25, 31-32
Moggies — 6
Noggies — 5
Pawkies — 9, 11-13, 24, 26-29, 31
Pokies — 1-5, 7, 14-15, 16bc, 17-23, 29-30, 32
Pookies — 16a

Peebles

Mittens — 2, 6a
Mitts — 4b, 6a, 8, 10
Packies — 4b
Pawkies — 1-3, 4ac, 5, 6ab, 7-10
Pockies — 10

Selkirk

Mittens — 1
Pawkies — 1, 2abcde, 3-6, 8
Pokies — 2d, 7

Roxburgh

Mittens — 4, 21c
Mitts — 4, 13, 15b, 20, 21ce
Moggums — 2
Pawkies — 3a, 4, 7, 9a, 14, 15ab, 16-17, 21f, 25
Poke mittens — 28
Pokies — 2, 3b, 5-6, 8, 9b, 10-13, 18-20, 21d, 23-26
Pookies — 1
Nil — 21ab, 22, 27

Dumfries

Baggies — 29
Gloves — 1a
Loofs — 21a
Luiffies — 23, 32
Mittens — 4, 12, 15, 19, 22, 24, 27-28, 30, 31cdf, 32, 41, 44, 45a, 48
Mitts — 4, 7, 8ab, 10-11, 21ab, 27, 29, 31abe, 33-35, 37, 39-43, 45ab, 46, 49
Muffies — 23
Packies — 6, 21a, 26
Palmies — 14
Pawkies — 1ab, 2-3, 5, 7, 10-13,

Dumfries cont'd

16, 20, 32, 36, 38, 41-42, 44
Pokies — 17ab, 29, 39
Powkies — 47
Nil — 9, 18, 25

Kirkcudbright

Liffies — 8
Loofies — 17
Mittens — 1-2, 6-7, 10-11, 15a, 19, 21abc, 22, 25-27
Mitts — 2-11, 12a, 14, 15b, 16, 18, 20, 23-24, 26
Muffetees — 23
Packies — 17
Pawkies — 1, 15a
Pokes — 12b
Pokies — 2
Nil — 13

Wigtown

Mags — 10-11, 13, 15, 17
Mittens — 1, 5ab, 6, 10, 14, 17-18
Mitts — 2-3, 7-8, 14, 16-17
Pawkies — 5a
Pokies — 9
Nil — 4, 12

Northumberland

Bags — 40b, 41a
Bobs — 59d
Driving gloves — 69a
Gauntlets — 69ab
Gloves — 28
Hand pads — 69ab
Mittens — 13-14, 20a, 24a, 25, 28, 29bce, 33ab, 35, 40ab, 41d, 44-45, 48-50, 53b, 57, 59bcf, 60, 62bh, 63, 64b, 66-67, 69abcfgh, 70, 71cd, 72bdegikl, 73, 75-78, 81, 83-85, 87, 88ab, 91, 94b, 95ab, 99bc, 101a, 103bc, 104ab, 106-107, 108b, 110, 111ab, 113, 115-117, 118a, 119, 120ac, 122a, 123, 124a, 125, 126bcde, 127adeh, 130cd, 131-135, 138-143
Mitts — 1ab, 12, 14-15, 19ab, 20b, 21-22, 26, 29abdef, 30, 32, 33ab, 35, 38-39, 40b, 41acd, 42-47, 49-52, 53b, 54-56, 58, 59abcde, 61, 62bcdegh, 63, 64ab, 65a, 66-67, 69abcdeg, 70, 71bce, 72abdgijkl, 76-82, 84-86, 88ab, 89-93, 94ab, 95b, 97, 98, 99bcd, 100, 101ab, 102, 103ab, 104ab, 105, 108ac, 109, 111ab, 112, 114, 116, 118ab 119, 120bc, 121, 122ab, 124ab, 126abef, 127abcgh, 128, 129ab, 130acdef, 131-133, 137, 140-141, 143
Muffaties — 103bc
Muffles — 7
Pawkies — 11, 13, 19a
Pokes — 34a, 43, 47, 96
Pokie gloves — 79, 136
Pokie mittens — 57, 68, 74
Pokies — 1abc, 2ab, 3-6, 8-10, 12, 16-18, 20ab, 22-23, 24b, 26-28, 29a, 31, 33b, 34b, 36-37, 39, 41c, 45-46, 53ab, 58, 59cde, 60, 65a, 68, 71c, 82, 89, 98, 102, 122b, 130b
Pookes — 42, 86
Satpokes — 25
Nil — 41b, 62af, 65b, 71a, 72cfh, 99a, 127f, 129c

Cumberland

Dykin mitts — 46
Hummle — 31
Hummle mittens — 27, 30
Mittens — 1ab, 2-4, 5b, 8-9, 12, 13ad, 15abc, 18, 20, 22, 24-26, 28-30, 38, 41, 44-45, 49-54, 56-58, 61, 63b
Mitts — 1a, 2-4, 5a, 6-7, 9, 11-12, 13abc, 14, 16-19, 21, 23-26, 28-29, 31-36, 37ab, 38-40, 43, 47-48, 51, 53-62
Muffatees — 4, 62
Pwok mittens — 46
Steering gloves — 42
Nil — 10, 63a

Down

Mittens — 2ab, 4-5, 7, 9, 11, 14-15, 17, 19, 22, 25
Mitts — 1, 2ab, 3, 6, 9, 11-14, 16, 18-21, 23-24, 26-30
Nil — 8, 10

Tyrone

Mittens — 5, 7-11, 15-16
Mitts — 5-6, 9-11, 13-14
Mutts — 1
Nil — 2-4, 12

Antrim

Mittens — 1-2, 5ab, 6-7, 9, 16b, 17-19, 21-22, 25, 28-31, 33
Mitts — 4A, 5b, 7, 8ab, 11-13, 15, 16b, 19-22, 25-27, 31
Pokes — 21
Pulse heaters — 14, 30
Nil — 3-4, 10, 16ac, 23-24, 32, 34

Donegal

Mittens — 1A, 5-8
Mitts — 1, 2, 4, 5A, 7, 7A, 10b, 12-13
Muffs — 13
Nil — 3, 9, 10a, 11

Fermanagh

Mittens — 1, 4-5, 7a, 8, 10
Mitts — 4-5, 9
Nil — 2-3, 6, 7b

Armagh

Mittens — 4-5, 6b
Mitts — 1-3
Nil — 6a

Londonderry

Mittens — 1B, 2, 4-5
Mitts — 1A, 2-3, 3A, 4-5
Nil — 1, 6-7

10 SOCKS WITHOUT FEET (PQ1, 52)

See note (1) and remark on **mog(g)Ans** etc., in 9 **gloves.**

Shetland

Fitties — 7
Kjuclikens — 19
Sock a leegs — 1, 4-5, 9, 33
Sock a legs — 2-3, 6, 10, 12, 14, 19-20, 21ab, 22-25, 27-28, 30-32
Sock legs — 7, 13, 16-17, 26
Suckle leigs — 8
Suckliks — 7
Sucklins — 18, 24
Tjutikins — 15
Nil — 11, 29

Orkney

Ceutikins — 10, 13ab, 21
Ceutkin hose — 13a
Ceuto(o)s — 10-11
Ceutties — 12
Cuitacks — 15
Hose tops — 14
Socklegs — 17
Sprettu — 7
Spurries — 7
Stockin(g) legs — 15, 19
Nil — 1-6, 8-9, 16, 18, 20

Caithness

Feetags — 4, 11
Gaiters — 13
Hose tops — 17
Moogans — 8-9, 12b, 14-15
Mougans — 7
Pads — 13
Snow legs — 16b
Socks without feet — 11, 12b
Stockin legs — 5
Nil — 1, 2ab, 3, 6, 10, 12ac, 14, 16a

Sutherland

Anklets — 3, 14
Hose tops — 8, 9b
Meulags — 10
Millags — 5
Moulags — 15
Snow legs — 7
Snow lugs — 4, 6
Stocking legs — 9a
Nil — 1-2, 11-13, 16-17

Ross & Cromarty

Ankle cloots — 24
Anklets — 27
Hose — 8
Hose tops — 13, 16, 19, 22, 32b
Leggings — 36
Mogans — 2, 28
Mougrans — 37a
Mowgrans — 25b
Mugrans — 37b
Socks without feet — 3
Spats — 34, 36
Nil — 1, 4-7, 9-12, 14-15, 17-18, 20-21, 23, 25a, 26, 29-31, 32ac, 33, 35, 38

Inverness

Anklets — 32, 35
Hose — 21a, 40
Hose tops — 16, 26, 39
Mackans — 24
Moccasins — 5
Mockans — 19, 22
Mockhans — 38
Moggans — 1, 3, 28
Moicans — 12
Socks feetless — 10
Socks without feet — 13ae, 37
Stocking legs — 13c
Nil — 2, 4, 6-9, 11, 13bd, 14-15, 17-18, 20, 21b, 23, 25, 27, 29-31, 33-34, 36

Nairn

Feetless socks — 6
Moggans — 1bc
Socks without feet — 1a
Nil — 2-5

Moray

Gardie moggans — 22
Ho tops — 8b, 10
Leggins — 14
Mauggans — 11
Mogans — 8d, 13, 21
Moggans — 1, 2a, 4, 6ab, 7, 8bf, 9a, 16, 19-20, 22
Muggans — 3
Queetigins — 6a, 17
Shanks — 12
Slip ons — 21
Nil — 2b, 5, 8ace, 9b, 15, 18, 23

Banff

Anklets — 20
Hose tops — 24
Mogans — 16, 34
Moggans — 9, 14, 18c, 19, 27, 29, 31-32
Moogans — 25
Queetikins — 2c, 5, 6b, 7, 10-11, 15, 18d, 31, 33
Socks — 8
Nil — 1, 2ab, 3-4, 6a, 12-13, 17, 18ab, 21-23, 26, 28, 30

Aberdeen

Anklets — 24, 27
Feetless (socks) — 5b, 60
Fettecks — 36
Fitticks — 1
Ho tops — 47f, 77
Leggins — 1, 6, 24, 51, 67, 107
Legs — 107
Mogans — 13, 23, 66, 75, 80, 106
Moggans — 2, 4, 9-10, 12, 21, 25, 28b, 29, 33-34, 39-41, 44, 47bdef, 48-49, 54-56, 62-65, 67, 71a, 73-74, 76, 84, 87, 90, 95, 97, 99, 101, 103-105
Mowgan legs — 5d
Mowgans — 7
Muggans — 78-79, 92-94, 106-107
Mutts — 96
Queeteens — 31
Queetikins — 5c, 10-11, 14-15, 17, 19, 25, 27, 28c, 30, 32, 37, 51-53, 64, 71bc, 76, 81, 83, 86, 88, 92, 98, 109
Queetpins — 31
Shanks — 22, 28a
Socks without feet — 17

Aberdeen cont'd

Spats — 48, 104
Walltams — 10
Nil — 3ab, 4, 5a, 8, 16, 18, 20, 26, 35, 38, 42-43, 45-46, 47ac, 50, 57-59, 61, 68-70, 72, 82, 85, 89, 91, 100, 102, 108

Kincardine

Hose tops — 17c
Huggers — 22
Legums — 3
Mogans — 8
Moggans — 9-10, 13-15, 17abd, 20
Muggans — 7
Queetikins — 4, 17ac
Shanks — 24, 27
Spats — 18, 26
Nil — 1-2, 5-6, 11-12, 16, 19, 21, 23, 25, 28

Kinross

Gaiters — 3
Hogers — 2
Ho tops — 3
Huggers — 1-2, 6-7
Leggins — 6
Spats — 3
Nil — 4-5

Angus

Anklets — 5b
Gaiters — 2
Hogers — 10
Hoggers — 7, 31, 34
Hose — 10
Ho tops — 14b, 29a
Huggers — 8, 17a, 19, 22, 35
Nickie tams — 14cd
Plough share — 33b
Sock legs — 36
Stockin(g) legs — 1, 4, 5ac, 14cd, 28, 33b, 34
Stockings with short legs — 33b
Nil — 3, 6, 9, 11-13, 14a, 15-16, 17b, 18, 20-21, 23-27, 29b, 30, 32, 33a, 37

Perth

Anklets — 8
Baffles — 61
Drab hose — 30
Feetless socks — 68
Gaiters — 26
Hoggers — 2b, 16, 18, 64
Hose — 15
Hose tops — 5, 8, 10, 29b, 52e
Ho tops — 28, 32-33, 41b, 50, 51b, 52e
Huggers — 7, 11, 13, 20, 25, 29a, 37, 39-40, 41a, 48, 52c, 54, 60, 62, 65-67, 69-71, 73-74
Hushions — 25
Leggings — 26
Legs — 44
Moccans — 14
Moggans — 52b
Nickie tams — 29b
Putties — 2a
Queeticks — 53
Sock legs — 57
Socks without feet — 4, 43
Spats — 26
Stockin huggers — 56
Stockin(g) legs — 27, 52ce
Stockin ligs — 72
Tops — 44
Nil — 1, 3, 6, 9, 12, 17, 19, 21-24, 31, 34-36, 38, 42, 45-47, 49, 51a, 52ad, 55, 58-59, 63

Fife

Anklets — 56
Bate hose — 35
Drawers — 21
Feetless socks — 10, 40b, 43b, 57
Gaiters — 13, 41a, 55d
Hagers — 47
Hogers — 64b
Hoggers — 18
Hose — 46, 52, 55a
Hose taps — 39
Hose tops — 9a, 23, 37
Ho taps — 39, 55f
Howgers — 64a
Huggers — 1, 28, 35, 36a, 51, 53, 55e, 57
Hushons — 49
Keerie kins — 8
Leggins — 57
Legs — 44b, 48
Moggans — 12, 36b, 54
Muggans — 36a, 61
Nickietams — 12
Socks wanting feet — 7
Socks without feet — 44c
Spatties — 55d
Stockin(g) legs — 4, 9b, 13, 16, 20, 24, 33, 39, 42, 44cf, 55f, 60
Whirlers — 23, 48
Woollen legs — 15
Nil — 2-3, 5-6, 11, 14, 17, 19, 22, 25-27, 29-32, 34, 38, 40a, 41bcd, 43a, 44ade, 45, 50, 55bcg, 58-59, 62-63

Clackmannan

Feetless — 7
Ho tops — 4c
Huggers — 2, 4a, 5
Moggans — 4d
Nil — 1, 3, 4b, 6

Stirling

Anklets — 22b, 25ad
Feetless socks — 13, 26a
Gaiters — 4, 16, 23b
Hoggers — 35b
Hose — 18
Hose taps — 9
Hose tops — 19, 26c
Ho taps — 7a, 42a
Ho tops — 7a, 8, 22a
Huggers — 2, 7bde, 10, 17, 20, 26aef, 32, 39b
Hushions — 7d, 26b
Leggin(g)s — 27a, 37a
Mocans — 6
Moggans — 1, 7d
Socks without feet — 23c
Stockin(g) legs — 17, 21b, 23a, 25b, 26d, 30-31, 35a
Stockin huggers — 26d
Wugs — 26b
Nil — 3, 5, 7cf, 11-12, 14-15, 21a, 24, 25c, 27b, 28-29, 33-34, 36, 37b, 38, 39a, 40-41, 42b

Dunbarton

Hogers — 9
Hose taps — 16a
Hose tops — 7a, 16b
Huggers — 2, 4b, 13ab, 17
Hushins — 10, 14a
Huskins — 14a
Osans — 5
Sock legs — 13bc
Socks without feet — 7b, 10
Soldier's socks — 1
Nil — 3, 4a, 6, 7c, 8, 11-12, 14b, 15, 18

Argyll

Anklets — 27
Feetless socks — 22, 33
Hoagers — 31, 35
Hoggers — 16, 35, 39
Hose — 3, 12
Huggers — 18
Legs — 19
Legs without hogers — 33
Maukans — 5
Mogans — 10, 29
Moggans — 24, 30, 37-38
Ossans — 12
Socks — 6, 17
Stockin legs — 35
Nil — 1-2, 4, 7-11, 13-15, 20-21, 23, 25-26, 28, 32, 34, 36, 40

Bute

Half hose — 7
Hoagers — 3
Hogans — 5
Hoggers — 1a
Huggers — 1e, 9
Mawgans — 8b
Mogans — 7
Moggans — 1b, 3, 8a, 9
Puttie — 2
Nil — 1cd, 4, 6

Ayr

Feetless socks — 30a, 32, 38, 47
Gaiters — 43
Gallow gaskins — 57
Hoggers — 57
Hooshions — 18b
Hose tops — 1a, 29
Hoshions — 41, 45
Ho taps — 17
Ho tops — 27
Huggans — 8a
Huggers — 1a, 2a, 7, 8b, 13-14, 18b, 19, 20cg, 24b, 28b
Hushions — 8b, 9, 16b, 20ae, 28f, 29, 31, 33, 36, 41, 43, 46-48, 52, 53ab, 54, 56
Leggins — 3
Leglins — 57
Moggans — 53a
Muggers — 6
Spatties — 29
Stockin legs — 24b, 28f, 48
Nil — 1b, 2b, 4-5, 10-11, 12ab, 15, 16a, 18a, 20bdfh, 21-23, 24a, 25, 26abc, 28acde, 30b, 34, 35ab, 37, 39-40, 42, 44, 49-51, 55

Renfrew

Anklets — 11e, 15
Feetless socks — 16b
Gaiters — 18a
Half hose — 13c
Hogers — 2i
Hoggers — 16a
Hose — 4ac
Hose tops — 14b
Ho tops — 2f, 11ck, 18a
Huggers — 2j, 4d, 11i, 12a, 14b, 16a, 17, 18b, 19, 20b, 21
Hushions — 5, 21
Leggings — 16d
Legs — 14a
Socks — 8
Socks without feet — 2a, 16b
Spats — 3
Stockin feet — 2i
Stockin legs — 17
Nil — 1ab, 2bcdegh, 4be, 6-7, 9-10, 11abdfghjl, 12b, 13abd, 16c, 20a

Lanark

Ankle socks — 6
Anklets — 22
Cufs — 20
Feetless socks — 26a, 45, 58, 66
Feetless stockings — 33c
Gaiters — 10b, 25d, 27b, 29a, 32d, 40
Higgins — 31c
Hoagers — 54, 57a
Hoeshins — 9b, 17
Hoggers — 38bd, 47, 49b, 52a, 55-56, 59a, 63
Hose — 59a
Hose tops — 35d
Ho taps — 58
Huggers — 7a, 10a, 12-13, 14bc, 18, 23, 25c, 29e, 30, 31a, 32cf, 33cd, 37, 38a, 42, 44, 46b, 65
Huggerts — 27b
Hushions — 10a, 15b, 46c
Hussins — 46c
Leggins — 4, 49a
Legs — 18, 45
Logs — 39
Mitts — 20
Moggans — 17, 30
Sock legs — 15b, 35b
Spats — 10b, 32d
Stockin(g) legs — 3, 25c, 26a, 28, 52b
Woollen gaiters — 29f
Nil — 1-2, 5, 7bc, 8ab, 9a, 11, 14ad, 15ac, 16ab, 19, 21, 24, 25ab, 26b, 27a, 29bcdg, 31bd, 32abe, 33ab, 34, 35ac, 36, 38ce, 41, 43, 46a, 48, 50-51, 53, 57bc, 59b, 60-62, 64ab, 67ab

West Lothian

Gaiters — 6, 16
Hose tops — 14
Huggers — 1c, 9a, 18
Noggans — 4
Patties — 19b
Shanks — 11
Sock legs — 20a
Socks without feet — 5
Spats — 16
Stockin(g) legs — 3, 6, 8, 11
Nil — 1abd, 2, 7, 9b, 10, 12-13, 15, 17ab, 19a, 20b, 21ab, 22

Midlothian

Gaiters — 1, 6b, 17
Hoggans — 32
Hose tops — 15
Ho taps — 11, 16
Huggans — 4
Leggin(g)s — 17, 26a
Snaw legs — 30
Socks without feet — 8a, 20
Spats — 17, 25d
Stockin(g) legs — 8b, 12a, 27
Nil — 2-3, 5, 6a, 7ab, 9-10, 12b, 13, 14ab, 18-19, 21-22, 23ab, 24, 25abc, 26b, 28-29, 31

East Lothian

Cutikins — 13
Gaiters — 17
Hoggers — 6a, 15
Hose tops — 15
Huggers — 7
Kittikins — 2
Leggings — 1, 13
Leggums — 9
Patties — 4a
Socks without feet — 4b
Spatter dashes — 13
Stockin legs — 6b, 14
Woollen gaiters — 4a
Nil — 3, 5, 8, 10-12, 16, 18-21

Berwick

Catikins — 23
Cuitikins — 17, 21
Gaiters — 31
Heelless — 16c
Hose tops — 32
Ho tops — 32
Hushions — 23
Leggins — 8, 27
Logs — 13
Mogans — 16a
Shoddies — 28
Snaw legs — 3
Socks without feet — 16b
Stockin(g) legs — 11, 31
Stockin(g) taps — 27
Nil — 1-2, 4-7, 9-10, 12, 14-15, 18-20, 22, 24-26, 29-30

Peebles

Hoe taps — 3
Hogers — 10
Hoggans — 1
Hoggers — 3
Hoshins — 4b, 6a
Huggers — 4b
Hushins — 7
Kittikins — 5
Snaw bits — 10
Snaw feet — 10
Snaw hogs — 1
Stockin(g) legs — 2, 4b, 8-9
Nil — 4ac, 6b

Selkirk

Foats — 5
Gaiters — 2e
Leggums — 2e
Sna buits — 8
Nil — 1, 2abcd, 3-4, 6-7

Roxburgh

Buskins — 9a
Caitikins — 13
Cuitikins — 3a, 13, 17
Foats — 20, 21ac, 28
Fot hoggers — 4
Hoggers — 8
Hose — 26
Hoshen — 8
Ho tops — 8
Leggins — 19
Logs — 3b, 21d, 26
Loogs — 21c
Lougs — 7, 28
Moggans — 21c
Sna logs — 2
Snaw logs — 21f, 23-26
Snaw lougs — 7
Stocking legs — 11
Nil — 1, 5-6, 9b, 10, 12, 14, 15ab, 16, 18, 21be, 22, 27

Dumfries

Anklets — 8b
Cuitikins — 29
Feetless socks — 4, 31a
Fotties — 10
Fots — 32, 35, 37-38, 45a
Gaiters — 1b, 15, 35
Haaf stocking legs — 31d
Hassies — 14
Hose — 28
Hosens — 6
Hoshens — 1a, 2-3, 5, 11, 19, 21ab, 22, 32
Hoskens — 7
Hossens — 26
Hushions — 10, 12, 41
Lakes — 35
Leggins — 33
Leggums — 13
Shoshans — 9
Sna bits — 16
Sna fots — 39
Socks without feet — 4, 12
Spats — 46
Stockin legs — 33
Nil — 8a, 17ab, 18, 20, 23-25, 27, 30, 31bcef, 34, 36, 40-44, 45b, 47-49

Kirkcudbright

Hawshins — 1
Hoschins — 6
Hose tops — 4, 18
Hoshens — 2, 7-8, 15a, 17, 21a, 26-27
Hushens — 21c
Snaw hushens — 1
Stocking legs — 12b
Nil — 3, 5, 9-11, 12a, 13-14, 15b, 16, 19-20, 21b, 22-25

Wigtown

Anklets — 5b
Feetless socks — 2
Haskins — 5a
Hosen — 13
Hoshens — 5a, 10, 15
Nil — 1, 3-4, 6-9, 11-12, 14, 16-18

Northumberland

Ankle socks — 40a
Anklets — 81, 111a
Cutikins — 124a
Feetless socks — 69a
Feetless stockins — 69b
Footlets — 20b
Fots — 132
Gaitens — 110
Gaiters — 26, 28, 29e, 41c, 59bde, 64b, 90, 114, 118b, 130ce
Hoggans — 53a, 73, 110
Hoggers — 33b, 45, 50, 55, 57, 59c, 62a, 71c, 73-75, 78, 86, 102, 104b, 106-107, 111ab, 127e, 130b, 131, 133-136, 138, 140, 142-143
Hose tops — 53b
Ho tops — 1a, 18
Loags — 25, 36-37, 43, 80, 124a
Loggings — 44
Loogs — 25, 44
Logs — 68
Lougs — 25, 124a
Lugs — 46
Moggans — 9, 62f
Over socks — 40a
Pattens — 103a
Patties — 52
Snae lugs — 53a, 68
Sna lags — 21
Sna legs — 15
Sna loags — 37
Snaw lugs — 26, 42, 56
Sock legs — 69b
Socks 41c
Socks with no feet — 99d
Socks without feet — 70, 94b, 103c, 127a
Spats — 59bd, 69h
Spiral socks — 29b
Spud feet 125
Stockin(g) legs — 16, 19a, 22, 31, 33b, 39, 41d, 48, 54, 62g, 68, 69a, 83, 101a, 120c, 126c, 137
Stockins — 54
Woolly leggins — 124a
Nil — 1bc, 2ab, 3-8, 10-24, 17, 19b, 20a, 23, 24ab, 27, 29acdf, 30, 32, 33a, 34ab, 35, 38, 40b, 41ab, 47, 49, 51, 58, 59af, 60-61, 62bcdeh, 63, 64a, 65ab, 66-67, 69cdefg, 71abde, 72abcdefghijkl, 76-77, 79, 82, 84-85, 87, 88ab, 89, 91-93, 94a, 95ab, 96-98, 99abc, 100, 101b, 103b, 104a, 105, 108abc, 109, 112-113, 115-117, 118a, 119, 120ab, 121, 122ab, 123, 124b, 126abdef, 127bcdfgh, 128, 129abc, 130adf, 139, 141

Cumberland

Ankle jacks — 18
Anklets — 3-4, 9, 57, 60, 62
Fots — 5ab, 13bc
Gaiters — 2, 9
Hoggers — 5a, 23, 38
Leggings — 24
Muffaties — 12, 16, 29, 37a
Mufferties — 12
Scoggers — 5a, 28, 38, 41, 46, 50, 54, 56
Slivers — 56
Socks wid ne feet — 15a
Spats — 7, 15b, 51
Splats — 47
Stocking legs — 52
Welts — 46
Nil — 1ab, 6, 8, 10-11, 13ad, 14, 15c, 17, 19-22, 25-27, 30-36, 37b, 39-40, 42-45, 48-49, 53, 55, 58-59, 61, 63ab

Down

Bed socks — 5
Feetless stockings — 15
Hushion — 13
Legs of socks — 15
Socks — 13
Nil — 1, 2ab, 3-4, 6-12, 14, 16-30

Tyrone

Ankle socks — 11
Markins — 9
Marteens — 5
Nil — 1-4, 6-8, 10, 12-16

Antrim

Hogarts - 4A
Hogers — 2, 10-11, 23, 25
Hoggers — 24, 31
Huggers — 13, 16b, 19
Hushans — 30
Huskins — 33
Moggans — 5b, 6
Puttens — 21
Nil — 1, 3-4, 5a, 7, 8ab, 9, 12, 14-15, 16ac, 17-18, 20, 22, 26-29, 32, 34

Donegal

Leggings — 5A
Legs — 13
Mairteens — 6, 12
Marteens — 10a
Martins 3
Martyeens — 11
Mart yins — 8
Tryheens — 13
Nil — 1, 1A, 2, 4-5, 7, 7A, 9, 10b

Fermanagh

Gaiters — 10
Leggins — 10
Nil — 1-6, 7ab, 8-9

Armagh

Leggins — 3-4
Nil — 1-2, 5, 6ab

Londonderry

Anklets — 2
Hogars — 3
Hosetops — 5
Marchins — 6
Markins — 1A, 7
Martyins — 1B
Nil — 1, 3A, 4

11 UNDERVEST (man's) (PQ1, 53)

(1) Note the recurrence of some of the items in 12 **undervest** (woman's).
(2) The form **semit** has been subsumed under **sEEmit.**
(3) The distributions of **semmit** from item 11 and **semmit** from item 12, which do not always coincide, are shown on map 11A.
(4) **Peweep** appears also in 72 **lapwing.**

Shetland

Flaneen slip — 21b
Froak — 21b
Frock — 19
Joop — 21b, 26, 33
Joopie — 3-4, 6, 8-11, 16-17, 19, 21b, 22, 25, 28-30, 32
Juppie — 12-14
Semmit — 13, 22, 31
Singlet — 10, 21a
Slip — 3, 5, 7-8, 15-17, 20, 21ab, 22-24, 26-32
Slippie — 1-2, 4
Swara — 32
Swara joopie — 17
Swara slip — 21b, 30
Upstanner — 23
Nil — 18

Orkney

Flanneen — 13a
Flannel — 9
Flannen — 6
Flannen sark — 13a
Next sark — 2
Next shirt — 2

Orkney cont'd

Saimet — 15
Sark — 3
Semmit — 4-6, 8-9, 12, 13b, 14, 16-18, 20-21
Shirt — 3
Simmit — 11, 19
Singlet — 7
Slip — 4-6, 10-12, 13a, 15, 17
(Under)vest — *1, 4,* 9, 13a, *15*

Caithness

Flannel — 17
Gansie — 12b
Sark — 2a, 14
Seemit — 8, 12a
Semmit — 1, 2b, 3-6, 9, 11, 12c, 13-15, 16ab, 17
Vest — 10, 13
Nil — 7

Sutherland

Flannel — 6
Seemit — 8
Semmit — 1-7, 9ab, 10-17
Singlet — 5
(Under)vest — 3, *7-8*

Ross & Cromarty

Flanneen — 25b, 29
Flannel — 10, 20, 22-23, 25b, 29, 35-36
Flannel sark — 37ab
Linder — 11, 13, 28, 30, 32c
Lunder — 22, 24, 28, 31, 36
Seemit — 18
Semmit — 2-10, 12-15, 17, 19-20, 22-24, 25ab, 26-29, 31, 32abc, 33-36, 37b, 38-39
Shift — 15
Singlet — 16, 20, 28, 36
(Under)vest — 1, 8-9, 16-17, 23, 25b, *27,* 29
Nil — 21

Inverness

Flannel — 13d
Linder — 7, 11-12, 13acde, 18-19, 21b, 24, 26, 28-29
Lunder — 8-9, 15-17, 19, 21a, 27
Sark — 20
Seemit — 36
Semmit — 1, 3-6, 8-11, 13abcde, 14, 17-19, 21ab, 22-24, 27-28, 30-35, 37-40
Singlet — 1, 13c, 33
(Under)vest — 1-*2, 13ce,* 18-20, 21b, 29, 32-34, *35*
Nil — 25

Nairn

Linder — 1abc, 4-6
Lunder — 2
Semmit — 1ac, 2-3

Moray

Flannel — 9b, 21
Inside sark — 3
Linder — 1, 2a, 7, 8bcd, 9a, 16-19, 23
Linner — 6a, 10, 15, 20-21
Lunder — 4, 6b, 8ae, 12-15, 22
Sark — 8cd
Seemit — 4, 8e
Semmit — 2ab, 3, 5, 7, 8ac, 9a, 10-13, 18, 20, 23
(Under)vest — 7, 8*bd*, 14, 23
Nil — 8f

Banff

Flannel — 25
Flannin — 34
Linder — 1, 10, 15, 18c, 23, 28-29, 31
Linner — 2abc, 3-5, 6ab, 7-9, 11-12, 15-17, 18bd, 20-27, 30-31, 33
Luner — 34
Maasie — 15
Mawsie — 18c
Sark — 18ad
Sarket — 11, 15
Seemit — 4, 6b, 13, 32
Semmit — 1, 2ab, 3, 5, 7, 9, 11-12, 14-16, 18c, 19, 23, 25, 28, 30, 34
Simmit — 17, 20

Aberdeen

Flannel — 2, 3a, 11, 15, 28b, 32, 61, 85
Flannen — 8, 12, 17, 32-33, 35, 47ac, 83, 101
Flannen sark — 16
Linder — 3b, 5ab, 9-15, 17-18, 20, 23, 25, 28b, 37, 53, 56-57, 59-61, 64-65, 71abc, 72, 76-77, 79, 86-89, 92-93, 95-96, 98, 101, 103, 105-107, 109
Linner — 3a, 4, 5d, 6-7, 16, 21-24, 27, 28abc, 30, 34-36, 40, 42, 44-46, 47abdef, 48-53, 55, 62, 64, 67-69, 74-75, 80-82, 85, 87, 99, 102, 104, 108
Maasie — 23, 28b, 47d, 64
Masie — 58, 91
Mawsie — 34, 66, 68, 71a, 78
Sark — 10, 73, 90
Sarkit — 3b, 5c, 6, 14, 16, 19, 21, 31-32, 36, 43-45, 58-59, 71c, 74-76, 82, 94, 108
Seemit — 1-2, 4, 6-7, 14-15, 17, 29, 40, 47ad, 49, 51, 63, 82, 95, 98, 102, 104
Semmit — 5d, 6, 8, 11, 16, 20, 24, 28c, 38, 41, 43, 53-55, 64-67, 69-70, 73-74, 77, 81, 83, 85-86, 93, 96, 100, 103, 105-107
Singlet — 21, 29, 70
Sirket — 92
Surkit — 64, 71b, 84, 97, 101, 104
Underduds — 25
(Under)vest — *16,* 68, 70, 84, 89, 94, 105, 107
Westkit — 39
Nil — 26

Kincardine

Flannel — 10, 17c, 27
Linder — 3, 6, 9-10, 12, 14-15, 17c, 23-24
Linner — 5, 13
Sark — 17c, 18, 22
Sarkit — 7
Seemit — 8, 11-12, 18, 21
Semmit — 2-4, 10, 13-14, 16, 17bcd, 19-20, 24-25, 27-28
Simmit — 1-2, 26
Sirkit — 15, 28
Surcoat — 13-14, 17b
Surkit — 5, 23
Vest — 17c, 18, 21
Nil — 17a

Kinross

Flannel sark — 5
Sark — 2
Semmit — 1, 3-4, 6
Singlet — 6
Vest — 6
Wursit sark — 2
Nil — 7

Angus

Circuit — 14d
Flannel sark — 23, 31
Inner sark — 5b
Inside sark — 5a, 11
Linder — 29b
Sark — 7, 12, 14acd, 15, 18, 21, 26-27, 33a, 37
Seemit — 17a, 24
Semmit — 1-4, 5ac, 6-10, 12-13, 14bcd, 17b, 18, 20-23, 25-26, 28, 29ab, 30, 32, 33ab, 34-36
Serk — 10
Simmit — 18-19
Surcoat — 33b
Under sark — 17a
Under shirt — 17b
(Under)vest — *12,* 25, 34
Nil — 16

Perth

Fecket — 72
Flannel — 32, 40, 55, 60
Flannel sark — 26, 50, 52c
Flannen — 62
Linder — 29b, 30, 67
Sark — 7, 21, 41a, 45, 54, 56, 59-60, 62
Seemit — 18, 37, 46
Semmit — 1, 2ab, 3, 5-6, 8-17, 19-28, 29a, 31-36, 38, 41ab, 42-45, 47-50, 51ab, 52acde, 55-57, 60, 63-65, 67-68, 71, 73-74
Simmit — 61, 66, 69-70, 72
Singlet — 2a, 16, 25, 52e, 73
Under sark — 52c, 53
(Under)vest — *2a, 4,* 9-10, 25, 32, 36, 52a*bc*, 67
Nil — 39, 58

Fife

Feckit — 53
Flannel — 6, 31
Flannel serk — 4, 13-14
Flannen sark — 27
Inmost serk — 48
Inner waistcoat — 32
Peeweep — 37, 39, 43a, 50, 59
Peeweet — 41c
Sark — 3, 6, 33
Seemit — 35
Semmit — 1-5, 7-8, 9a, 10, 12-14, 16-24, 26, 28, 30, 33-34, 36ab, 38, 40ab, 41abcd, 42, 43ab, 44bcdf, 45-51, 53-54, 55abcdfg, 56-63, 64ab,
Serk — 12, 25, 33-34, 44a, 49, 55e
Simmit — 11, 37, 39, 44ef, 52, 54, 55de, 60
Singlet — 13, 37, 43a, 44b
Under sark — 21
Vest — 6, 41a, 42, 43a, 50, 55d, 63
Nil — 9b, 15, 29

Clackmannan

Feckit — 2-3, 7
Feskit — 1
Linder — 4d
Semmit — 1-3, 4abc, 5
Simmit — 1, 4d, 6-7
Singlet — 4c
Vest — 4c

Stirling

Faickit — 42b
Feckit — 8, 20, 22b, 25a, 26e, 27a, 35b, 42b
Flannel — 7bd
Ganzie — 8
Kerseckie — 7a
Peeweep — 19
Peeweet — 32, 39b
Sark — 23b
Seckie — 17
Seemit — 1, 5, 16, 20, 22a, 24, 25c, 39a
Semmit — 2, 4, 7abcdef, 8-11, 13-15, 17-19, 21ab, 22b, 23ac, 25abd, 26abdef, 27ab, 29, 31, 33-34, 35b, 36, 37a, 39a, 40-41, 42a
Serk — 23b
Shift — 23b, 25c
Shirt — 38
Simmit — 3, 6, 7bc, 12, 16, 23ab, 26c, 27a, 28, 30, 32, 35a, 37b, 38, 39b, 40
Singlet — 7ac, 17, 19, 21ab, 25d, 26d, 30, 38, 42b
(Under)vest — 4, 7ce, 17, *21b,* 26ac, 31, 35a, 36

Dunbarton

Seckie — 14a
Seemit — 3
Semmit — 1-2, 4ab, 6, 7ac, 8-10, 13abc, 14b, 15, 17-18
Simmit — 5, 7b, 10-12, 16ab
Singlet — 10, 18
Vest — 1, 8, 13a, 17

Argyll

Carseckie — 9
Sark — 35
Seemit — 11
Semmit — 1, 3, 5, 7-8, 10, 12-17, 19-25, 28-31, 33, 35-40
Simmit — 18
Singlet — 12, 25, 27, 35
(Under)vest — 2, 6, 12 *17,* 19, 30
Westcoat — 32
Woollen vest — 33
Nil — 4, 26, 34

Bute

Seemit — 1d
Semmit — 1bce, 2-3, 5, 9
Simmit — 1a, 4, 7, 8ab
Vest — 1a, 7, 8b
Nil — 6

Ayr

Feckit — 46
Liner — 20g
Sark — 9
Seemit — 15, 24a
Semmit — 1a, 2ab, 3-6, 8a, 9, 11, 12ab, 13-14, 17, 18ab, 19, 20acefgh, 22-23, 24b, 25, 26abc, 28bcdef, 29, 30ab, 31-34, 35ab, 37-43, 45, 47-52, 53ab, 54-57
Simmit — 2a, 7, 8b, 10-11, 16ab, 18b, 20bdh, 21, 27, 28a, 29, 32, 34, 36-37, 44, 46, 48
Singlet — 1b, 6, 26a, 28e
(Under)vest — 2b, 26b, *28e, 49, 53a*

Renfrew

Carseekie — 15
Interlock vest — 2i
Sark — 2b
Seemit — 7, 9, 11k, 16d
Semmit — 1ab, 2abdefghij, 3, 4cde, 5-6, 8-10, 11defhij, 12ab, 13abc, 14ab, 16ab, 18b, 19, 20ab, 21
Shift — 12a
Simmit — 2ch, 11abcgkl, 13d, 16c, 17, 18a
Singlet — 1b, 2ghj, 4a, 5, 12b, 16a, 20a
Unders — 2i
(Under)vest — 1b, 2g, 4de, 8, 11d, 13c, 16d, 18a, *20a*
Nil — 4b

Lanark

Feckit — 31c, 38a, 59ab, 61, 63, 66, 67ab
Peeweep — 19
Sark — 7a, 10a, 25b, 32d, 37, 52b
Seemit — 39, 49a, 59b
Semmit — 1, 4-6, 7abc, 8b, 9b, 10b, 11-13, 14abcd, 15ab, 16b, 17-18, 21, 23-24, 25abcd, 26b, 27ab, 28, 29deg, 31c, 32abcdf, 33b, 34, 35c, 36-37, 38abcde, 40-45, 46c, 49b, 50-51, 52ab, 53, 55-56, 57ac, 58, 59a, 60-62, 64ab, 65-66, 67b

Lanark cont'd
Serk — 10a, 39
Shift — 15b
Simmit — 2-4, 6, 8a, 9a, 15c, 16a, 18-20, 22, 25c, 27b, 29abc, 31abd, 32cf, 33acd, 35ad, 46ab, 47-48, 52a, 57bc, 67b
Singlet — 4, 7c, 29f, 44, 52b, 58
Under shirt — 21
(Under)vest — *1, 6,* 7a, 14d, 15abc, 25ac, 29cf, 35ac, 45
Woollen vest — 35d
Wyecoat — 38d
Nil — 26a, 30, 54

West Lothian
Banyon — 11
Feckit — 18
Peeweep — 1a, 6, 16, 20a
Semmit — 1ab, 2-5, 7-8, 10, 14-16, 18, 19a, 20ab, 21a, 22
Simmit — 1d, 6, 8, 9ab, 11-13, 17ab, 19b, 20a, 21b
Singlet — 5, 10-11, 13, 15-16, 17a
Vest — 10-11, 15
Waistcoat — 1c

Midlothian
Carseckie — 30
Flannel — 1
Flannen serk — 32
Peeweep — 14a, 25c
Sark — 23a, 25c, 26a, 27
Seemit — 15-16, 18, 23a, 25d
Semmit — 2-5, 6ab, 7b, 8b, 12ab, 13, 14ab, 17-22, 23b, 25abc, 26ab, 27-32
Simmit — 2, 7a, 8a, 9-11, 12b, 22, 24
Singlet — 8a, 11, 12a, 17, 23b, 25c
(Under)vest — 12a, 15, 19, *21,* 26b

East Lothian
Flannel — 2, 15, 20
Flannel serk — 21
Peeweep — 4ab
Seemit — 6ab, 19
Semmit — 1-3, 4ab, 7-18, 20-21
Serk — 21
Simmit — 5
Singlet — 15
Under serk — 8
Vest — 13

Berwick
Flannel — 10, 14, 27
Flannel serk — 4, 10-11, 26
Flannen serk — 8, 32
Kerseckie — 24
Sark — 2, 23
Seemit — 1, 5, 18, 24, 26, 32
Semmit — 4, 6-9, 11-13, 15, 16abc, 17, 19-24, 26-32
Serk — 2, 15, 27
Simmit — 10, 12
Under serk — 3, 16b, 20, 32
(Under)vest — 9, 13, 15, 31-*32*
Nil — 25

Peebles
Flannel — 4b
Sark — 6a
Seemit — 9
Semmit — 1-3, 4bc, 5, 6ab, 8, 10
Serk — 4a
Simmit — 7
(Under)vest — 5, *6b*
Woollen sark — 6a

Selkirk
Flannel serk — 4
Semmit — 1, 2bcde, 4-6, 8
Serk — 7
Singlet — 2a
Under serk — 2a, 3
Vest — 2c

Roxburgh
Curseck — 21c
Flannel — 1, 20, 21e
Flannel semmit — 21e
Flannel serk — 16, 20, 21b, 25
Flannen serk — 3b, 17
Linder — 21c
Sairk — 25
Seemit — 22
Semmit — 2, 3a, 4-5, 8, 9a, 11-12, 14, 15a, 16, 18-19, 21ae, 23, 25-26, 28
Serk — 9b, 13, 21df, 24-25
Simmit — 10
Singlet — 7
Under serk — 5, 7, 9a, 15b, 17, 23, 28
Under shirt — 13
(Under)vest — *9a,* 21a
Yad — 21c
Nil — 6, 27

Dumfries
Curfeckit — 2
Feckit — 3-4, 6, 9, 12, 38
Flannel — 35
Flannen — 42
Flannen serk — 37, 39
Flennel — 26
Flennel serk — 37
Seemit — 13, 23, 31f, 37
Semmit — 1ab, 4-5, 7, 8ab, 9-12, 14-16, 17ab, 19, 21ab, 22, 24-30, 31abcdef, 32-36, 38-43, 45ab, 46-49
Serk — 44
Shift — 46
Under shirt — 29
(Under)vest — *1a, 4,* 33, 46
Nil — 18, 20

Kirkcudbright
Feckit — 2
Flannel — 12b
Sark — 12a, 16
Seemit — 7, 13, 15b, 22
Semmit — 1-6, 8-11, 12ab, 14, 15a, 16-20, 21abc, 23-27
Singlet — 15a, 18
Vest — 18, 25

Wigtown
Sark — 3, 5b, 7
Seemit — 9, 13
Semmit — 1-2, 4, 5ab, 6-8, 10-12, 14-18
Shift — 7
Singlet — 7, 12-13
Vest — 12

Northumberland
Body flannel — 22, 41c, 69a, 72dg, 77, 102, 130d, 134, 138, 140
Body flannen — 40b, 72g, 103bc, 119, 130d, 142
Body sark — 36, 38, 41d, 73, 106, 112, 124b, 126c
Body shairt — 81
Body shart — 38-39, 40a, 41d, 45, 48-49, 56, 59d, 62acdg, 63, 64a, 65ab, 69abe, 70, 71abcde, 72afgj, 76, 78-79, 82-85, 88ab, 89-91, 93, 94a, 95b, 98, 99abd, 100, 101b, 105, 111ab, 114, 116-117, 118ab, 119, 120ab, 122b, 124b, 125 126bcdf, 127acfg, 128, 129bc, 130bdef, 136
Body shirt — 29a, 37, 40a, 41bd, 43, 48, 50, 52, 53b, 58, 59d, 60-61, 62b, 64b, 66, 69fh, 71a, 72cdghikl, 74, 76-77, 86, 92, 95a, 96, 103a, 104a, 108a, 112, 114, 122b, 123, 126a, 127abefh, 130c, 134, 139, 143
Body short — 71a, 76, 101a, 109, 113, 126a, 127f
Body vest — 57, 131
Bottom sark — 142
Clootie — 101b
Flannel — 47
Flannen — 132, 135, 142
Flannen body — 121
Lining — 11, 110
Little sark — 16
Little shirt — 5
Sark — 1c, 5, 10, 12, 21-23, 24ab, 27-28, 29d, 30, 33b, 34a, 37, 39, 41b, 45-52, 53b, 58, 59e, 62afgh, 67, 69e, 75-76, 80, 84, 91, 103bc, 115-116, 119, 120a, 124a, 126f, 134
Seemit — 51, 98
Semmit — 1b, 2ab, 8, 14, 17, 20a, 22, 34b, 38, 41a, 45, 47, 55, 59bce, 62b, 64b, 71c, 73, 122a
Shart — 12, 62h, 97
Shift — 19a, 59be, 60, 72a, 81, 107, 108c, 126e
Shimmie — 104b
Shirt — 53b, 68
Shirtie — 94b
Simmit — 1ac, 7, 15, 18, 19a, 29e, 33b, 118a, 126d, 130a
Singlet — 20b, 29bf, 35, 38, 40b, 43, 50, 60, 62bg, 68, 69abfg, 71d, 72bcdi, 76, 79, 89, 92, 99cd, 103a, 108ac, 111a, 118b, 120c, 121, 127ac, 130de, 133
Skinfit — 122b
Summit — 44
Under breeks — 110
Under flannel — 18
Under sark — 6, 9, 16, 18, 21, 26, 39, 53a, 68
Under shart — 40a, 62c, 71c, 118a, 142
Under shert — 42
Under shirt — 13, 20b, 29b, 40a, 41c, 44, 54, 69c, 72b, 77, 87, 142
Under short — 18
(Under)vest — 2b, *4,* 16, 19a, 20b, 23, *28,* 29b, 30-*31, 35-36,* 37, 40a, 42, *46*-47, 52, 57-58, *59b,* 60, 62*b*eh, 63, *64b* 66, 69cd, 71b, 72*c*deil, 73, 76, 82, 86-87, *93, 99b,* 103bc, 104b, 106, 111ab, 120c, 121, 127*a*bd, 130c, *132,* 137, *140*
Undie — 31
Nil — 3, 19b, 25, 29c, 32, 33a, 59af, 108b, 129a, 141

Cumberland
Dickie — 15bc, 16, 26, 44, 50, 54
Flannel — 19
Flannen — 8-9, 20-21, 23, 38, 49
Pit dickie — 24
Sark — 14, 15a, 24, 36, 37a, 41, 45, 55, 57
Semmit — 1a, 13ab
Shift — 6, 11, 15b, 34, 54
Shimmie — 2
Singlet — 1ab, 2-3, 5a, 7-8, 12, 13d, 15ab, 16-19, 21-22, 24-26, 28, 31-33, 35, 37a, 38-40, 42-48, 50-54, 56-62, 63ab
Under sark — 13c, 38, 56
Under shirt — 13c, 46
(Under)vest — 4, 7, *9, 13c,* 18, 23-24, 40, 42, 46, *49,* 53, 56
Nil — 5b, 10, 27, 29-30, 37b

Down
Inside shirt — 5, 11, 15, 18, 21, 24, 27
Sark (unner) — 13
Semmit — 7, 10, 20
Shirt — 14
Simmit — 2ab, 3-4, 6, 9, 12-13, 17, 21-24, 27, 29
Singlet — 15, 19, 26, 30
Under shirt — 18
(Under)vest — 1, *2a,* 19, 24
Nil — 8, 16, 25

Tyrone
Chemise — 6
Ganzie — 14
Inside shirt — 1, 5, 8-10, 13
Inside vest — 7
Semmit — 11
Shift — 6, 15
Simmit — 1-2, 4-7, 10, 15
Under shirt — 11
Vest — 8, 15
Nil — 3, 12, 16

Antrim
Inside shirt — 11, 21, 31, 33
Onther shirt — 5b
Sark — 18, 25
Semmit — 8b, 16a, 23
Shift — 31
Shirt — 17
Simmit — 1-2, 4, 4A, 5a, 6-7, 8a, 9-15, 16b, 17, 19-22, 24-25, 28-31
Singlet — 27
Under shirt — 25
Vest — 25
Woollens — 26
Nil — 3, 16c, 32, 34

Donegal
Inside shirt — 5A, 10b
Semmit — 13
Shirt — 5A, 9
Simmit — 1, 1A, 2-6, 7A, 8, 10b, 12
Singlet — 10b
Under shirt — 13
(Under)vest — 5, *12*
Nil — 7, 10a, 11

Fermanagh
Inside shirt — 2, 8-9
Semmit — 1
Simmit — 4, 6
Vest — 9
Nil — 3, 5, 7ab, 10

Armagh
Inside shirt — 6a
Semmit — 6b
Simmit — 1-2, 4-5
Singlet — 4
Vest — 4
Nil — 3

Londonderry
Inside shirt — 1, 1A, 2, 3A, 4-5
Simmit — 3, 3A, 5, 7
Singlet — 3
Nil — 1B, 6

12 UNDERVEST (woman's) (PQ1, 54)

Some of the items occur also in 11 **undervest** (man's). **Semit** has been subsumed under **sEEmit.**
The distributions of **semmit** from item 11 and **semmit** from item 12, which do not always coincide, are shown on map 11A.

Shetland

Jupie — 10, 19, 22
Juppie — 12
Sark — 17, 26
Semmit — 13, 31, 33
Simmit — 33
Slip — 3-5, 8, 11, 15-17, 19-20, 21ab, 22-23, 27, 30, 32
Slippie — 1-2, 6
Slug — 14
Spencer — 10, 24
Swairai — 32
Upstaner — 23
Vest — 7, 13
Nil — 9, 18, 25, 28-29

Orkney

Next sark — 2
Next shirt — 2
Sark — 3, 13a, 15, 19-21
Semmit — 4, 6, 8, 18
Shirt — 3, 9, 15
Simmit — 11
Slip — 7, 10-11, 13a, 15-16
(Under)vest — *4*-5, 9, 12, 13a, 15, 17
Nil — 1, 13b, 14

Caithness

Chemise — 12ac, 13
Pettie — 12b
Sark — 2ab, 8-9, 12a, 14, 16a
Seemit — 8
Semmid — 14
Semmit — 1, 2b, 16b
Shift — 12b, 16a
Shirt — 11, 16a, 17
Vest — 4-5, 10-11, 13, 16b
Nil — 3, 6-7, 15

Sutherland

Chemise — 6
Seemit — 8
Semmit — 9a, 13, 15
Shift — 14
(Under)vest — 1, 4-8, 9b, 10-12, *13,* 16-17
Undies — 3
Nil — 2

Ross & Cromarty

Chemise — 2, 6, 9, 13, 18-19, 22, 26, 29, 31, 32b, 33
Linder — 25a
Sark — 25b, 37a
Semmit — 3, 7-11, 23, 25a, 28, 36
Shift — 15, 25b, 27
Shirt — 31, 34
Slip — 24
(Under)vest — 1, 4, 8-10, 16-17, 19-20, 23, 25b, 26-*27,* 28-29, *30,* 32a, 33-34, *36,* 37b, 39 — 5, 12, 14, 21, 32c, 35, 38

Inverness

Chemmie — 14
Chemise — 8-9, 12, 13ad, 21a, 24, 28, 32, 36
Chemist — 16
Linder — 18
Semmit — 9, 13e, 15, 18, 26-27
Shift — 22, 38
Spencer — 18
(Under)vest — 2-6, 10, 13*bc*e, 16, 18-20, 21ab, 22-23, 26, 29-30, 32-40
Nil — 1, 7, 11, 17, 25, 31

Nairn

Chemise — 1c, 2
Semmit — 1b, 5-6
Shift — 1b
Undervest — 2
Nil — 1a, 3-4

Moray

Chemer — 22
Chemise — 9a, 22
Linder — 1, 23
Lunder — 8ae
Sark — 6a, 8c, 10, 13, 21
Seemit — 15
Semmit — 2a, 4-5, 6b, 7, 8abde, 9ab, 10, 14, 17, 19-20, 23
Shift — 9a
(Under)vest — 7, *8b,* 11, 14, 18, 23
Nil — 2b, 3, 8f, 12, 16

Banff

Chemise — 9
Flannel — 21
Linner — 15
Mauzie — 14
Sark — 3-4, 6b, 9-10, 18bd, 23, 28, 30
Seemit — 6b, 13, 32
Semmit — 2ab, 3, 7-12, 15-16, 19, 23-24, 26-27, 31, 34
Shift — 8
Simmit — 17
(Under)vest — 2ab, 4-5, 9, 16, 18c, 20, 23, 25, 30, *34.*
Nil — 1, 2c, 6a, 18a, 22, 29, 33

Aberdeen

Camiknicks — 9
Chemise — 66, 79, 98, 107
Flannel — 14
Flannen — 14, 46, 80
Flannen surket — 104
Linder — 47b, 71b, 100
Linner — 31, 47b, 49, 75
Maasie — 47d
Mausie — 32
Sark - 3a, 9-10, 23, 30, 40, 45, 47e, 66, 73, 79, 93, 101, 104, 107
Sarkit — 35, 37, 47a, 62, 87
Seemit — 1-2, 4, 5ab, 14, 17, 19, 22, 28ab, 29, 31, 34, 47abde, 51, 63, 71b, 74-75, 81-82, 102, 108
Semmit — 3b, 8, 10-13, 21, 23-25, 27, 28bc, 36, 38, 42, 44, 47cf, 48, 52, 54, 56-57, 59, 61, 64, 66-67, 69-70, 71c, 73-74, 76-78, 84-86, 88-91, 94, 96-97, 100, 103-105, 109
Shemie — 78
Simmit — 49
Surket — 86-88
Vest — 3a, 15, 20-21, 28c, 29, 35, 50, 53, 66, 70, 73, 79, 95, 98, 100, 105-107
Nil — 5c, 6-7, 16, 18, 26, 33, 39, 41, 43, 55, 58, 60, 65, 68, 71a, 72, 83, 92, 99

Kincardine

Bodice — 10
Chemise — 2, 14, 20-21
Flannin — 13
Linder — 17abd, 22
Sark — 13, 18
Sarket — 12
Seemit — 18
Semmit — 2-7, 9, 11, 15-16, 17bcd, 27-28
Simmit — 12, 26
Sirket — 28
Vest — 1, 5, 8, 10, 15, 17c, 18-19, 24
Nil — 23, 25

Kinross

Sark — 1-2
Semmit — 3
Shift — 3
Vest — 6
Nil — 4-5, 7

Angus

Chemie — 14d
Chemise — 7, 14bd, 17ab, 30-31
Sark — 1-2, 5a, 12, 14d, 24, 26, 33b
Seemit — 5b
Semmit — 3-4, 5ac, 6-8, 10, 12-13, 14cd, 15, 18, 21-22, 25, 27-28, 29ab, 32, 33b, 34, 37
Shemie — 14a
Shift — 14a, 29b, 33ab
Shirt — 9, 33b
Simmit — 18-19
Sirkit — 35
Vest — 1-2, 8-9, 12-13, 17b, 20, 25, 33b, 34, 36
Nil — 11, 16, 23

Perth

Chemie — 41a
Chemise — 16, 18, 26, 33, 45-46, 50, 51a, 56, 68, 71-72
Chimmie — 52c
Sark — 18, 26, 29a, 38, 42-43, 45, 51ab, 53, 55, 60-61
Seemit — 27, 37
Semmit — 5-9, 13, 15-16, 20-21, 24-25, 31-33, 41b, 44, 48, 52a, 58, 64-65
Shemie — 51b
Shift — 5, 21, 32, 53, 62, 66, 68
Shimmie — 17, 70
Shirt — 16, 23, 26, 28, 29a, 68
Shor(t) goon — 70
Sim(m)et — 40, 69
Slip body — 29b
(Under)vest — 1, *2a,* 3-*4, 8,* 9-10, 12, 16, *24,* 25-26, 28, 29a, 32-33, 36, 47, 49, 52a*be*, 57, 63, 67-68, 73-74
Nil — 2b, 11, 14, 19, 22, 30, 34-35, 39, 52d, 54, 59

Fife

Bodice — 39
Camisole — 39
Chemise — 4, 13, 28, 33, 55bg, 59-60, 64a
Chimmie — 3
Sark — 7, 27, 31, 35, 37, 44a, 48, 51, 63
Seemit — 36a, 49
Semmit — 1-2, 5-6, 8, 9a, 10, 12-13, 17, 19, 21-23, 25-26, 33-34, 36b, 40b, 41d, 42, 43a, 44bcf, 45-48, 50, 55abdf, 57, 61-63
Serk — 34, 44ad, 55c, 59
Shem — 52
Shemmie — 37
Shimmie — 43a, 44de, 58
Shift — 12, 51, 53, 64a
Simmit — 11, 24, 40a, 52, 55d
Singlet — 44c
Slip — 33, 59
Slip body — 32
(Under)vest — *4,* 6-7, 9a, 13, 16, *21,* 28, 41a, 42, 43a, 44c, 48, 50, 53, 55bde, 63
Nil — 9b, 14-15, 18, 20, 29-30, 38, 41bc, 43b, 54, 56, 64b

Clackmannan

Chemmie — 5
Saark — 2
Semmit — 1, 4abc, 5
Shift — 4bd, 5
Shuft — 2
Simit — 6
Vest — 4c
Nil — 3, 7

Stirling

Bodice — 36
Chemise — 7ae, 10, 12, 19, 21ab, 23ab, 24, 25bd, 27b, 28, 30, 32-33, 39b, 41, 42b
Sark — 2, 7bde, 12, 19-20, 25ac, 26bef, 37a, 39b
Seemit — 25c
Semmit — 7b, 8, 13, 15, 17, 31, 34, 39a
Serk — 12
Shemmie — 21b, 26a
Shift — 5, 7abde, 19, 21b, 22b, 23a, 25d, 26e, 32, 39a
Shirt — 38
Short shirt — 26b
Simmit — 7b, 18, 23b, 26c, 27a, 37b, 38
Slip — 25ad, 36
Vest — 1, 4, 7cef, 11, 16-17, 21ab, 22a, 23c, 25c, 26acdf, 28-29, 31, 33, 35ab, 37a, 39b, 40-41, 42ab
Nil — 3, 6, 9, 14

Dunbarton

Chemise — 6, 7c, 10, 14b
Cutty sark — 14a
Sark — 6, 7c, 14b
Seemit — 3
Semmit — 4b, 5, 9-10, 14b, 15, 17
Shift — 4ab, 7a, 14a, 16b
Simmit — 16ab
Slip — 2
(Under)vest — 1, 7bc, 8, 10-12, 13abc, *14b* 17-18

Argyll

Chemise — 9, 13, 19, 21, 30, 32, 35, 39
Sark — 19, 24, 35, 37
Semmit — 1, 25, 33, 35
Shift — 13, 24, 35
Singlet — 27
(Under)vest — 1-3, 5-12, *14*-15, *17,* 19-23, 28, 30, 38
Woolen(sic) vest — 33
Nil — 4, 16, 18, 26, 29, 31, 34, 36, 40

Bute

Chemise — 1be, 8ab, 9
Chimmie — 1a
Sark — 1a
Semmit — 2-3
Shift — 4-5, 8ab, 9
Slip (bodice) — 9
Vest — 1cd, 7, 8ab
Nil — 6

Ayr

Bodice — 28f
Camisole — 28f
Chemie — 12b, 28f, 57
Chemise — 1a, 3, 7, 15, 18a 20fg, 23, 26b, 27, 28f, 31, 33-34, 43, 46-49, 57
Sark — 18b, 19, 20bgh, 21, 23, 24b, 28d, 31, 39, 48, 54
Seemit — 24a
Semmit — 2b, 13, 17, 20c, 22, 24b, 26ac, 29, 30b, 31-32 41, 47, 53b
Serk — 15, 16b, 25
Shamese — 38
Shift — 7, 8ab, 16a, 18b, 20abeh, 21, 28d, 31, 33, 35a, 41, 48, 50
Shimmie — 1a, 48
Shimmie shirt — 18b

Ayr cont'd
Simmit — 8b, 10, 16a, 28a, 32, 44
Singlet — 26a
Slip — 8a, 39
Slip body — 28f
(Under)vest — 1ab, 2b, 4-5, *6*, 8b, 9-11, 12a, 14-15, 17, 25, 28*ef*, 30a, 31, 35b, 36, 40, 42-43, 45, 48, 52, *53a*, 56
Nil — 2a, 20d, 28bc, 37, 51, 55

Renfrew
Chemie — 11i
Chemise — 2be, 5, 7-8, 11adg, 13c, 14a, 16bd, 20a
Cutty sark — 21
Flannel — 14b
Sark — 9, 16ad, 20b
Semmit — 1b, 2adj, 3, 4d, 6, 10, 11fl, 16a, 19
Serk — 13a, 21
Shift — 1a, 2b, 11adgj, 12a, 16acd, 18ab, 20b
Shimmie — 14a, 16c, 18a
Simmit — 11kl, 13d, 18a
Singlet — 1b
Slip — 2f
(Under)vest — 1b, 2ghj, 4de, 7-*8*, 11abcdeg, 12b, 13c, 14b, 16d, 17, 18a
Nil — 2ci, 4abc, 11h, 13b, 15

Lanark
Bodice — 45
Chemise — 7a, 9b, 10a, 18, 25a, 29df, 32bcd, 33c, 35a, 37, 38b, 53, 58, 59a, 67b
Napekin — 60
Sark — 9b, 14c, 29e, 32f, 33d, 38ae, 39, 42, 46c
Seemit — 59b
Semmit — 1, 7b, 8b, 10b, 13, 14ad, 15b, 16b, 28, 29eg, 32adf, 34, 35bc, 38c, 41, 51, 52a, 58, 61, 63, 65, 67a
Serk — 29e
Shemie — 9a, 10a, 27b, 37, 52b, 57c
Shift — 3, 9b, 16b, 17-18, 29f, 39, 46c, 57b, 62, 66
Shimie — 15a, 32e, 46b
Shirt — 58
Simmit — 8a, 20, 29ac, 32e, 33a, 35d, 47, 52a, 57b
Slip — 26a, 28
Slip body — 32d, 66
Spencer — 11
(Under)vest — *1*-2, 4, 6, 7c, 8a, 10b, 12, 14bd, 15abc, 16a, *17*-18, *21*-22, 25abcd, 26b, 29c, 31a, 33a, 35ac, 36, 38e, 44-45, 46ab, 49b, 52b, 56, 57a, 58, 60, 64*ab*
Woollen vest — 35d
Wylie/woolly coat — 17
Nil — 5, 19, 23-24, 27a, 29b, 30, 31bcd, 33b, 38d, 40, 43, 48, 49a, 50, 54-55

West Lothian
Chemise — 4-5, 8, 11, 14, 19a
Sark — 4, 12
Semmit — 1a, 2-3, 10-11, 18
Shift — 21b
Shimmie — 19b
Simmit — 1cd, 9ab, 13, 17b
(Under)vest — 6, *8*, 10-12, 15, 17a, 18, 20ab, 21ab, 22
Nil — 1b, 7, 16

Midlothian
Chemise — 1-2, 7a, 10, 12a, 16, 21-22, 23b, 26a, 29-32
Sark — 10, 23a, 24, 25c
Seemit — 6a, 23a, 25d
Semmit — 6b, 8b, 12b, 16-17, 23b, 31
Serk — 24
Shemie — 23a
Shift — 3-4, 7b, 11, 14a, 25a, 26a, 29
Shift sark — 23b
Shirt — 11
Simmit — 12b
Singlet — 7a
(Under)vest — 6a, *8a*, 9-11, 12a, 15, 18-20, *21*, 22, 25b, 26b, 27
Nil — 5, 13, 14b, 28

East Lothian
Chemise — 11, 13-15, 17, 19
Sark — 2, 9, 11
Semmit — 1-2, 4ab, 8-10, 13, 20-21
Serk — 6a
Shemie — 6b
Shift — 2, 15
Simmit — 5
Slip — 6b
Vest — 4b, 7, 13
Under serk — 8
Nil — 3, 12, 16, 18

Berwick
Chemise — 7, 10, 22-24, 27-28
Cosie — 10
Cutty sark — 27
Sark — 2, 7, 23
Seemit — 1, 5, 16a, 18, 26
Semmit — 3, 6, 8-9, 11-15, 16b, 17, 19, 21, 29
Serk — 2, 4, 8, 31
Shemie — 20
Shift — 2, 8-9, 18, 32
Shiftie — 4
Simmit — 10
Slip — 27
Vest — 9, 12-13, 15, 23, 30-32
Nil — 16c, 25

Peebles
Chemise — 9
Semmit — 2-3, 4ac, 5
Serk — 1
Shift — 10
Undersark — 6a
(Under)vest— 4b, 5, *6ab*, 8
Woollen goon — 6a
Woollen sark — 6a
Nil — 7

Selkirk
Chemise — 2d, 3, 5
Semmit — 1, 2abc, 3, 6-7
Serk — 2e
Shift — 2a
Vest — 2ce, 8
Nil — 4

Roxburgh
Baiglet — 21c
Baiklet — 21c
Becklet — 21c
Chemise — 2, 4, 18, 21e
Seemit — 7
Semmit — 3a, 5, 8, 9a, 11, 13, 15b, 16-17, 19-20, 24-28
Serk — 21d, 26
Shift — 3a, 4, 15ab
Simmit — 10
Under serk — 28
(Under)vest — 1-2, 5, 13, 21a*ef*, 23
Nil — 3b, 6, 9b, 12, 14, 21b, 22

Dumfries
Cheemie — 32
Chemise — 5, 16, 17a, 21ab, 27, 31e, 42, 44, 45a, 46-47
Sark — 8a, 13-14, 22, 32, 35, 38, 45a
Seemit — 31f
Semmit — 1ab, 2, 6, 8b, 11-12, 20, 22, 24, 29-30, 31bcef, 33, 46, 48
Serk — 3-4, 10, 31e, 38
Shift — 3, 9, 12, 17b, 19-20, 21a, 32, 42
Shimie — 31d
Shirt — 17b, 41
Singlet — 45b
(Under)vest — *1a*, *4*, 7, 15, 17ab, 21b, 23, 25-26, 28, 31ef, 33, 36-37, 40, 45a, 46
Nil — 18, 31a, 34, 39, 43, 49

Kirkcudbright
Chemise — 3, 13, 16, 22-23
Feckit — 1
Sark — 1, 6, 12a, 15b, 16-17, 23, 25-26
Sheft — 14
Semmit — 1, 4, 12a, 21ac, 27
Shift — 3, 17, 20
Shimmie — 24
Shirt — 11, 12b
Simmit — 15a
(Under)vest — 1-2, 5, 7, 9-10, 15a, 18-19, *21c*, 25
Wylicoat — 1
Nil — 8, 21b

Wigtown
Change — 5b
Chemise — 3-4, 7, 9
Sark — 5ab, 6, 8, 17
Semmit — 5a, 7-8, 13
Shift — 4, 8, 11-12, 14, 17
Shiftsark — 2
Singlet — 15
Vest — 11-12, 14
Nil — 1, 10, 16, 18

Northumberland
Body vest — 71a
Chemise — 11, 19a, 29abe, 30, 58, 59b, 62a, 68, 69b, 71a, 76, 82, 89, 91, 99b, 104b, 120c, 123, 124a, 127ag, 130d, 132, 140, 143
Chemmie — 52, 59d, 71a, 126a, 127a
Chimmie — 34a, 41c, 45, 69b, 126a
Sark — 1a, 12, 23, 24ab, 28, 29e, 39, 40b, 61, 62h, 69ae, 71b, 79-80, 89, 96, 103b, 127d, 130d, 143
Semmit — 2b, 3, 13, 18, 20ab, 45, 62g, 73, 112, 117
Shart — 69e, 72g, 97, 104b
Shemmie — 62g
Shift — 1bc, 2a, 4, 6-7, 10-11, 17-18, 22-23, 24a, 27, 29bd, 32, 33b, 34ab, 36-37, 39, 40ab, 41bcd, 43, 45-47, 49-50, 52, 55, 57, 59cdef, 60, 62cdegh, 64b, 65b, 67-68, 69abefgh, 70, 71abde, 72acfhijkl, 76-77, 80-82, 84-86, 88ab, 89-92, 94ab, 95b, 96, 99abc, 100, 101b, 103b, 105-106, 108ac, 111ab, 114-115, 118ab, 119, 120ac, 122ab, 124ab, 126abcdef, 127abcdg, 128, 129bc, 130abdef, 131, 135, 140, 143
Shimmet — 53b
Shimmie — 40b, 42-43, 46, 54, 56, 59b, 62h, 64b, 65a, 69a, 72beij, 74-77, 82-85, 90, 96, 98, 99b, 101b, 106-107, 108ac, 109-110, 111ab, 116, 120c, 122b, 124ab, 127c, 130ce, 132, 134, 136-138, 142-143
Shirt — 53b
Simmet — 72e, 96
Singlet — 103a
Slip — 72l, 127e
Under sark — 53a
(Under)vest — 1a, 2b, *4*, *8-9*, 16, 20b, 21, 23, 26, 28, *31*, *35-36*, 37-38, *40a*, 41d, 42-43, 45, 47-49, 52, 53b, *54*, 56, 58, *59b*, 60, 62bg, 63, 64ab, 68, 69cd, 70, 71*a*cd, 72cd*g*ik, 73, 76-78, 82, 86-87, 99*bd*, *102*, 103*bc*, 104a, 106, 111ab, *112*, 118a, 120ac, 121, 127d, 129c, 130c, 132-133, 139-140, 142
Undie — 31
Nil — 5, 14-15, 19b, 25, 29cf, 33a, 41a, 44, 51, 59a, 62f, 66, 93, 95a, 101a, 108b, 113, 120b, 125, 127fh, 129a, 141

Cumberland
Chemise — 14, 22, 43, 47, 57, 60
Chimmie — 54
Flannin — 49
Sark — 3, 15b, 16, 26, 45, 56-57, 60-62
Shift — 8-9, 11, 14, 16-18, 24, 26-27, 29, 31, 37a, 38-39, 41-44, 48, 51-52, 55-56, 62
Shimmie — 2-3, 6, 13ac, 15abc, 17, 21-22, 31, 36, 37a, 38, 40-42, 44-46, 56, 62
Singlet — 8, 13d, 24, 28, 33, 37b, 54, 60
(Under)vest — *1a*, 4, *5a*, *9*, 12, 13c, 18-19, 23-25, 28, 40, *47*, 48, *49*, 50-51, 53, 56-57, *58*, 59
Nil — 1b, 5b, 7, 10, 13b, 20, 30, 32, 34-35, 63ab

Down
Chemise — 11, 14-15
Sark — 5
Shift — 2a, 5, 7, 11, 13-15, 17-19, 21-24, 26-27
Shimmie — 2a, 10, 18, 23-24, 27
Shirt — 3
Vest — 1, 2a, 4-6, 9, 21, 27
Nil — 2b, 8, 12, 16, 20, 25, 28-30

Tyrone
Cammysole — 11
Chemise — 7, 11
Chimese — 10
Shift — 1-5, 7-10, 13
Shimmie — 1, 5, 9
Smock — 14
Vest — 1, 6-8, 10-11, 15
Nil — 12, 16

Antrim
Chemie — 11
Chemise — 11, 13, 15, 22, 25, 27-28, 31
Flashbag — 21
Sark — 1, 5ab, 9-11, 14-15, 16b, 17, 19
Shift — 1-2, 5ab, 6-7, 8a, 9-12, 14-15, 16b, 17-18, 21-23, 25-26, 28, 31, 33
Shimmie — 8b, 30
Shirt — 21
Sim(m)et — 8a, 29
Vest — 13, 20, 25, 27-28, 31
Nil — 3-4, 4A, 16ac, 24, 32, 34

Donegal
Chemise — 10b
Chimmie — 10b
Shemmie — 13
Shift — 1, 4, 6-7, 10b
Shimmie — 6, 12
Shirt — 9, 13
Sirk — 4
(Under)vest — 1, 5, *5A*, 8, 10b
Nil — 1A, 2-3, 7A, 10a, 11

Fermanagh
Chemise — 9
Shift — 1-2, 4, 6, 8
Shimmie — 1-2, 9-10
Vest — 4, 7a, 9

Fermanagh cont'd

Nil — 3, 5, 7b

Armagh

Chemise — 6a
Shift — 1, 4
Shimmie — 4-5
Nil — 2-3, 6b

Londonderry

Chemise — 2-4
Shift — 1, 1AB, 2-3, 3A, 4-5, 7
Shimmie — 3
Shirt — 2
Vest — 2
Nil — 6

13 THREE LEGGED STOOL (PQ1, 60)

For the distribution and variants of STOOL(IE), see map 4, Appendix A.

The areas for PQ1, 61 **four legged stool** coincide more or less with those of 13 **three legged stool** except for the addition of "four legged" in front of some items. Therefore PQ1, 61 has not been included.

For the recurrence of **stab**, see 4 **splinter**, 5 **to prick**, 26 **bradawl**, and 42 **fence posts.**

Shetland

Creepie — 3-6, 9-10, 13-14, 16-17, 21b, 23-25, 27, 31
Creepie stool — 26
Stab — 2, 8-9, 15, 19-20
Steb — 26
(Three legged) stool — *1,* 7, 11, 15, 19, *21a,* 30
Nil — 12, 18, 22, 28-29, 32-33

Orkney

Creepie — 2-3, 7, 10, 13b, 14, 16, 20-21
Milking stool — 15, 17
Peedie creepie — 4
(Three legged) stool — 6, *8*-9, *13a, 19*
Nil — 1, 5, 11-12, 18

Caithness

Creepie — 2b, 3, 6-9, 12ab, 13, 15, 16a
Stoolie — 1, 4-5, 13-14, 16b, 17
Three legged stool — 2a, 11
Nil — 10, 12c

Sutherland

Creepie — 10
Milking stool — 3
(Three legged) stool — 1, 3, 5, *6-8,* 9ab, 11-13, 16-*17*
Nil — 2, 4, 14-15

Ross & Cromarty

Cracket — 19
Crechpan — 29
Creepie — 10, 15, 20, 25ab, 26, 31, 35-36
Creepie stool — 11
Cuttie — 18
Cuttie stool — 36
Milking stool — 34
Steelac — 37ab
Stoolie — 16, 18, 24, 26, 36
(Three legged) stool — *1, 3,* 4-5, 8-*9,* 14, 16-17, *23, 26-27,* 28-*29, 32ab,* 36, 37b, 39
Nil — 2, 6-7, 12-13, 21-22, 30, 32c, 33, 38

Inverness

Byre stool — 38
Creepie — 6, 21a, 22, 26, 28-29, 33, 39
Creepie stool — 13a
Form — 5
Milking stool — 13a, 26
Stoolie — 15
(Three legged) stool — *1-8, 10*-11, *13abc,* 16-*17, 19,* 21ab, *23,* 25, 29-30, 32-35, 37, 39-40
Nil — 9, 12, 13de, 14, 18, 20, 24, 27, 31, 36

Nairn

Creepie — 1bc, 5
(Three legged) stool — 2, 4, *6*
Nil — 1a, 3

Moray

Courie — 8b
Crackie — 9a
Creepie — 1, 2b, 4, 6a, 8bd, 9a, 12-13, 17, 19-22
Creepie stool — 8f
Cuttie stool — 9a
Luggie — 18
Spinney — 8c
Stoolie — 4-5, 7, 8cd, 10, 14-16, 19
(Three legged) stool — *2a,* 3, 7, 8be, *9b, 11, 14*
Nil — 6b, 8a, 23

Banff

Creepie — 2bc, 3, 6b, 8-9, 11, 18d, 23, 26-27, 29, 33
Cuttie stool — 18cd
(Three fitted) stoolie — 2a, 14-*15,* 21, 25
(Three legged) stool — 1, 3-5, 9, 13, *17, 19*-20, 23, 25, *31*-32, *34*
Nil — 6a, 7, 10, 12, 16, 18ab, 22, 24, 28, 30

Aberdeen

Byre stool — 6
Cog — 63
Coggie — 105
Creepie — 3ab, 5d, 10-11, 14, 20, 23-24, 27, 28a, 34, 38, 40-41, 46, 47a, 53, 57, 60-61, 64, 71ac, 73-76, 78, 80, 84, 88, 91, 96, 98, 101, 104, 108
Cuttie — 71a, 92
Cuttie stool — 77, 97
Leglin — 1
Milkin(g) stool — 6, 21, 28a, 37, 56, 70, 100, 109
Milkin stoolie — 101
Peerie — 47e
Stoolie — 5d, 7, 10, 12, 14-15, 27, 47d, 49, 59, 62, 64-67, 70, 71b, 78, 88, 98
Stoup — 47b
(Three legged) stool — *2,* 3a, *5c, 8-9,* 14, *17, 21-22, 25, 29-32, 34-35, 44,* 47acde, 48, *50,* 54, 59, 64-65, 67, 71b, *75,* 78, 81-84, 86, 89, 92, *94*-95, 99, 102, *106-107,* 108
Nil — 4, 5ab, 13, 16, 18-19, 26, 28bc, 33, 36, 39, 42-43, 45, 47f, 51-52, 55, 58, 68-69, 72, 79, 85, 87, 90, 93, 103

Kincardine

Creepie — 4-5, 7, 12, 14-15, 17a, 23
Cuttie — 13, 17ad
Cuttie stool — 17b, 21
Stoolie — 7, 12, 23-24, 26
(Three legged) stool — *1-3,* 5-*6,* 10-12, 16, 17c, 19, *27*
Tri stool — 8
Nil — 9, 18, 20, 22, 25, 28

Kinross

Creepie — 6
Cuttie — 3, 5
Cuttie stool — 2
Stool — 3-4, 6
Nil — 1, 7

Angus

Creepie — 6, 14ab, 23, 29b, 32, 33a, 34-35, 37
Cuttie — 14cd
Cuttie stool — 2-3, 5a, 7, 15, 17b, 19, 25, 33b
Jennie Geddes — 18
Luggie — 17a
Milking stool — 17b
Stoolie — 8, 14a, 24, 29a
Three futted stool — 6
(Three legged) stool — 4, *9, 12,* 14b, 15, 18, 20-22, *24-27,* 28, 29b, 32, *33b,* 34, 36
Nil — 1, 5bc, 10-11, 13, 16, 30-31

Perth

Byre stool — 2a, 49
Coggie stool — 11
Cogie — 53
Creepie — 1, 5-6, 8, 10, 12, 18, 20, 24-25, 29b, 37-39, 41b, 45-48, 50, 52be, 56-57, 66, 69-71
Creepie stool — 68
Cuttie — 17, 40, 62, 73
Cuttie stool — 2a, 21, 32-33, 41a, 51b, 52d, 53, 55-56, 60
Dumpie — 26
Leglin — 53
Luggie — 64, 73
Milkin stool — 55
(Three legged) stool — *2a, 4,* 7, 9, 13, *15,* 23-*24,* 27-28, 29ab, 31, *32-33,* 36, 43, *46,* 50, 51a, *52c,* 59, 61, 67, 74
Nil — 2b, 3, 14, 16, 19, 22, 30, 34-35, 42, 44, 52a, 54, 58, 63, 65, 72

Fife

Creepie — 1-2, 4, 6, 8, 9ab, 10-14, 16-23, 25-29, 31-35, 36ab, 37, 39, 40ab, 41d, 42, 43a, 44abcdef, 45-53, 55defg, 59-61, 63, 64a
Creepie stool — 32
Cuttie — 17, 38, 64ab
Cuttie stool — 3, 12, 14, 29, 54, 55a, 56
Luggie — 30, 33
Milking stool — 20
Peerie — 12
(Three legged) stool — 6-*7,* 11, *13,* 19, *21, 24,* 28, 37, 39, 40a, *41ab, 43ab,* 44c, 50, *51-52,* 55bdef, *57,* 58-59, *62*
Nil — 5, 15, 30, 41c, 55c

Clackmannan

Creepie — 1-2, 4a, 6-7
Stool — 2-3, 4c, 5
Nil — 4bd

Stirling

Byre stool — 9
Coggie — 35a
Creepie — 2, 6, 7bd, 9, 17-18, 21b, 23b, 26a, 27a, 32, 35b, 39ab, 42a
Creepie stool — 25b, 26b
Crupie stool — 26b
Currie — 7a, 11, 32
Cuttie stool — 7bd, 8, 21a, 26d, 36, 42a
Kut — 12
Leggie — 7e
Milking stool — 42a
Stoupie — 40
Three fitted stool — 30-31
(Three legged) stool — 4, *7abc,* 12-*13, 15*-16, *20,* 21b, *22b, 23abc,* 25cd, 26ad, 27a, 28, 31, *34,* 37a
Tristil — 13
Wee stool — 26d
Nil — 1, 3, 5, 7f, 10, 14, 19, 22a, 24, 25a, 26cef, 27b, 29, 33, 37b, 38, 41, 42b

Dunbarton

Coggie — 13a
Creepie — 1, 3, 4b, 7c, 9, 14b
Creepie stool — 16b
Currie — 5, 7c
Cuttie — 14a, 17
Cuttie stool — 16a
Milkin(g) stool — 2, 11
(Three legged) stool — 6, *7b, 8*-9, *12,* 13abc, *14b, 16a,* 18
Nil — 4a, 7a, 10, 15

Argyll

Buffet stool — 40
Creepie — 9, 13, 21-22, 24, 31, 37
Milking stool — 23, 33, 35
(Three legged) stool — 1-3, 5, *6-7,* 10, *11-12,* 14-15, *16-18,* 19, *23,* 25, 27, 33
Nil — 4, 8, 12, 20, 26, 28-30, 32, 34, 36, 38-39

Bute

Creepie — 1abe
Creepie stool — 9
Cuttie — 1ab
Peerie — 6
Stool — 2, 7, 8ab, 9
Nil — 1cd, 3-5

Ayr

Coggie — 7, 16b, 18b
Cowpie — 37
Creepie — 1a, 3, 6-7, 8ab, 9, 11, 14, 20gh, 29, 30b, 31, 33, 35a, 49, 53ab, 56-57
Creepie stool — 16a
Crookie — 7
Crudie — 43
Cuttie — 13, 16b, 41, 47, 53a, 57
Cuttie stool — 7, 18b, 28d
Kittie — 24b
Leglin — 18b, 43
Luggie — 2b, 7, 18b
Milkin(g) stool — 27, 47
Stool — 1a, 2a, 3, 5-6, 9-10, 12ac, 13, 15, 16ab, 21, 28df, 32-34, 36, 42-45, 47-48, 52, 53a, 54-57
Nil — 1b, 4, 12b, 17, 18a, 19

Ayr cont'd

20abcdef, 22-23, 24a, 25, 26abc, 28abce, 30a, 35b, 38-40, 46, 50-51

Renfrew

Byre stool — 10
Cogie — 2i, 11i
Courie — 21
Cracket — 3
Crackie — 21
Creepie — 2ehi, 4d, 5-6, 11el, 12a, 13b, 16d
Creepie three leg — 2i
Crupie — 8
Cuttie — 2
Cuttie stool — 2j, 16a
Luggie — 18ab
Milking stool — 16d
Peepie — 2a
Peggie — 11h
(Three legged) stool — *1b, 2gj,* 8, 11*abcfl, 13c,* 14a, *16b,* 17, 18ab, *19,* 20a
Nil — 1a, 2bcdf, 4abce, 7, 9, 11dgjk, 12b, 13ad, 14b, 15, 16c, 20b

Lanark

Byre stool — 15a, 33a
Coggie — 1, 42
Crakie — 7b, 38d
Creeper — 67a
Creepie — 8ab, 9b, 10a, 11, 13, 14c, 15ab, 23, 25b, 27ab, 29eg, 30, 31b, 32df, 35d, 36, 38bd, 46ac, 47-48, 52a, 54, 56, 57a, 60
Creepie stool — 15c, 29e, 64b
Currie — 24, 34, 38ad, 39, 47-48, 51, 57b, 61, 66
Currie stool — 50, 63
Cuttie — 14d, 17, 33cd, 37, 38e, 41, 44-45, 47, 61, 67a
Cuttie stool — 13, 18, 30, 35b, 60, 62, 66
Hussock — 25d
Leglin — 11
Luggie — 39, 46b
Milking stool — 3
Three fitted stool — 15a
(Three legged) stool — 1-*2, 5-6,* 7ac, *9a, 10a, 12.* 14bd, *15c,* 16ab, 17-*20, 25c, 26a,* 29d, 35bc*d,* 38ac, *44*-45, 46ab, 48, 49a, 57ab, *58, 59ab, 65*
Wee stool — 53
Nil — 4, 10b, 14a, 21-22, 25a, 26b, 28, 29abcf, 31acd, 32abce, 33b, 35a, 40, 43, 49b, 52b, 55, 57c, 64a, 67b

West Lothian

Byre stool — 7
Cougie — 17a
Creepie — 1a, 2, 6, 9a, 18, 20a
Cuttie — 8, 11
Cuttie stool — 6
Honey — 21b
Luggie — 6
Milkin stool — 15
(Three legged) stool — *1c, 2-3, 6,* 11-*12,* 18, 19a, 20a, *22*
Tokie — 5
Nil — 1bd, 4, 9b, 10, 13-14, 16, 17b, 19b, 20b, 21a

Midlothian

Byre stool — 12b, 13
Crackie — 32
Creeper — 25c
Creepie — 3-5, 8b, 9, 11, 12b, 14a, 17-18, 21-22, 23ab, 25ad, 26ab, 27, 29
Creppie — 20
Cruikie — 30
Cuttie stool — 26a
Leglin — 7b
Milkin stool — 12a, 18
(Three legged) stool — *1,* 2-3, 6a, *8a, 10,* 13, 14a, 15, 18-19, 21-22, 23b, *24,* 32
Nil — 6b, 7a, 14b, 16, 25b, 28, 31

East Lothian

Coggie — 11-12
Cracket — 9
Creepie — 2, 4ab, 5, 6ab, 7, 15, 19, 21
Cribbie — 8
Cricket — 13
Crockie — 2, 11, 13, 16-17
Cruggie — 14
Currie — 13
Cuttie — 2
Cuttie stool — 10
(Three legged) stool — 1, 4b, 5, *8-9,* 15-16
Nil — 3, 18, 20

Berwick

Coggie — 16c
Crachet — 27
Crackie — 2, 12, 22, 24, 26-28, 30-31
Crackie stool — 32
Creepie — 9, 27, 31
Croakie — 3, 6, 16c, 18, 20
Crockie — 1, 4-5, 7-8, 10, 14-15, 16ab, 17, 19, 21, 25, 27, 31
Cuttie stool — 29
Leglin — 23
(Three legged) stool — 8, *12,* 16, 16*bc*
Nil — 11, 13, 17

Peebles

Byre stool — 6b
Coggie — 4a
Creepie — 3, 4c, 5, 8, 10
Cuttie — 1
Cuttie stool — 4b
Milking stool — 4b
(Three legged) stool — *2*-3, *4bc, 6ab,* 9
Nil — 7

Selkirk

Crackie — 2abd, 3, 5-7
Creepie — 2ae, 3, 7
Stoolie — 8
(Three legged) stool — 1, 2bcd, *4,* 8

Roxburgh

Cracket — 9a
Crackie — 3ab, 4, 6-8, 9ab, 10, 15a, 16, 18-19, 21ace, 23-24, 26, 28
Crackie stool — 12-13, 15b, 17
Creepie — 3a, 13
Cuttie — 20, 21d, 23
Cuttie stool — 15a
Milking stool — 17
(Three legged) stool — 1-2, 5, 8, 21*acef,* 23, 25, 27-*28*
Nil — 11, 14, 21b, 22

Dumfries

Buttie — 1a
Byre stool — 47
Coorie — 9
Coppie — 15, 34, 36, 40, 47
Coppie stool — 37
Cowpie — 29
Creepie — 3, 7, 8a, 10, 17ab, 23, 28-29, 31b, 41
Creepie stool — 19
Currie — 7
Cuttie — 2, 14, 28, 31a, 32, 35, 42
Cuttie stool — 10, 16, 22, 29
Jennie Geddes — 13, 31c
Luggie — 29
Stool of repentance — 10
(Three legged) stool — 1a, *4,* 8b, *11-12, 15, 17b, 18,* 21a*b,* 22, 26-27, *29,* 31e, 32-*33,* 41, 45a
Trevet — 46
Wee stool — 31d
Nil — 1b, 5-6, 20, 24-25, 30, 31f, 38-39, 43-44, 45b, 48-49

Kirkcudbright

Coppie — 24
Creepie — 12b, 15a, 17, 21c, 23
Cuttie — 20
Cuttie stool — 1, 7
Luggie stool — 7
(Three legged) stool — 2-3, 6, 8-*10,* 15a, *16,* 19, 21a, 23, 26-27
Tripos — 17
Nil — 4-5, 11, 12a, 13-14, 15b, 18, 21b, 22, 25

Wigtown

Creepie — 5ab, 7-8, 10, 12, 14, 16-17
Crockie — 5a
Cuttie — 15
Cuttie stool — 5a, 13
Peggie — 6
(Three legged) stool — 2, *11*-12, 16, *17*-18
Nil — 1, 3-4, 9

Northumberland

Coppie — 37, 44-45, 130d, 132
Cowpie — 39
Cracket — 1abc, 2ab, 4, 7-8, 10, 12, 14, 17-18, 20a, 22-23, 24ab, 26, 28, 29abcde, 30-31, 33b, 36, 38-39, 41c, 43, 45-46, 49-51, 55, 57-58, 59bce, 62ae, 64a, 65a, 67-68, 69abcdfgh, 71abcd, 72adegkl, 74, 76-78, 81-83, 87, 88a, 89, 93, 94b, 95a, 96, 98, 99c, 101a, 103abc, 105, 107, 108c, 110, 111b, 113, 120c, 124b, 125, 127bc, 128, 130bdf, 133-137, 140, 142
Cracketie stool — 12
Cracket stool — 40b, 59d, 62h
Crackie — 1b, 2b, 3, 6, 8-10, 13-14, 18, 19a, 20b, 22
Crackie stool — 11, 15, 27
Crackum — 15
Creepie — 41a
Cuddie stool — 59d
Depuddies cracket — 69ab
Dollie stool — 72d
Kicker — 134
Leggie — 100
Milkin(g) stool — 20b, 64b, 69ab, 71c, 76, 99d, 104b, 120c, 122b, 124ab, 130c
Mushroom stool — 122b
Peggie — 126d
(Three legged) stool — *2b,* 4-5, 13, 16, 21, 23, *28,* 29b, 34b, 35, 37, 40a, *41d, 42*-43, *48,* 52, *53ab, 54,* 56, 58, 59b, 60, 62bg, 65a, 69b, 70, 71bd, 72*cegij,* 78, 82-84, 86-87, 88b, 90-91, 93, 95b, 102, 103c, 104a, 106, *109,* 111a*b, 112,* 118a, *119,* 121, 122a, 126*cf,* 127*adgh,* 130e, 131, 133, 138, 140, 142-143
Tripod — 127e
Tuffet — 72i
Wobbler — 94b
Nil — 19b, 25, 29f, 32, 33a, 34a, 41b, 47, 59af, 61, 62cdf, 63, 65b, 66, 69e, 71e, 72bfh, 73, 75, 79-80, 85, 92, 94a, 97, 99ab, 101b, 108ab, 114-117, 118b, 120ab, 123, 126abe, 127f, 129abc, 130a, 139, 141

Cumberland

Byre stool — 3
Coppie — 1a, 2-4, 5a, 6-9, 11-12, 13bcd, 14, 15abc, 17-22, 24-26, 28-34, 36, 37ab, 38-41, 43-58, 60-62, 63ab
Coppie stool — 1b, 5b, 13a, 27
Cricket — 5a
Milkin(g) stool — 1a, 47, 49, 56
Stool — 4, 5a, 8, 13c, 15a, 16, 23-24, 28, 30, 38, 42, 46, 49, 53, 56-57, 59
Nil — 10, 35

Down

Bucket stool — 3
Creepie — 2a, 4, 7-8, 10, 13-15, 18, 21-30
Creepie stool — 14
Milk stool — 17
(Three legged) stool — *2a,* 5, *7, 9, 15,* 19
Nil — 1, 2b, 6, 11-12, 16, 20

Tyrone

Creepie — 2-3, 5, 9, 14-15
Creep stool — 10
Reel stool — 4
Sate — 1
(Three legged) stool — 1, *7,* 8-9, 15-16
Nil — 6, 11-13

Antrim

Creepie — 2, 4A, 6ab, 7, 8b, 11, 13-14, 16a, 17-19, 21-26, 30-31, 33
Creepie stool — 29
Milking stool — 9, 34
(Three legged) stool — 5a, 20, 25, *28*
Nil — 1, 3-4, 6, 8a, 10, 12, 15, 16bc, 27, 32

Donegal

Creepie — 2-3, 5-7, 10a, 12-13
Creepie stool — 4, 8
Creep stool — 8
Crummie — 13
(Three legged) stool — *1,* 5A
Nil — 1A, 7A, 9, 10b, 11

Fermanagh

Camp stool — 1
Creepie — 6, 8, 10
Creepie stool — 1-2, 5
Stool — 4, 9
Nil — 3, 7ab

Armagh

Creepie — 2, 4, 6ab
Creepie (stool) — *1,* 6a
Milkin stool — 4
Nil — 3, 5

Londonderry

Creepie — 1AB, 2-3, 3A, 5-6
Milking stool — 4
Nil — 1, 7

14 SOAP SUDS (PQ1, 64)

The variants of SOAP (**sop** Shetland; a few scattered **saip; seeap, seap** Cumberland) and SOAPY (a few **soppy** and **saipy**) have been subsumed (but not **sowp(y)**).

Shetland
Bloots – 13
Cubb – 12
Froad – 22
Froath – 32
Greth – 11
Scoom – 16
(Soap) blots – *1,* 2-4, 6-7, 9-10, 14-15, *18-19,* 20, 21ab, *22,* 23-31, 33
Soap suds – 21a
Soapy blots – 5, 8, 17
Suttles – 10
Swills – 10

Orkney
Bloats – 11
Blots – 2, 4, 7, 9, 12, 15, 19
Graith – 19
Soap suds – 1, 13b, 15
Soapy blots – 5-6, 8, 10, 13a, 14, 16-18, 20-21
Soapy suds – 8
Soapy water – 5
Nil – 3

Caithness
Froth – 2b, 10, 12a, 13
Graith – 1, 6-7, 9, 11, 12b, 14, 16a
Greath – 12a, 13
Greith – 12c, 17
Grith – 1
Lather – 16b
Soap suds – 2a, 5, 11, 16b
Soapy water – 5, 8
Nil – 3-4, 15

Sutherland
Foam – 16
Froth – 3, 5, 16
Graith – 9ab, 12-13
Lather – 1, 7, 16-17
(Soap) suds – *4,* 5, *6,* 8, 10-11, *13,* 16
Soapy water – 3
Nil – 2, 14-15

Ross & Cromarty
Froth – 8, 25b, 32b, 34
Graith – 9, 11-12, 14, 18, 20-22, 24, 25ab, 26, 28-29, 31, 35-36, 37ab, 38
Greath – 13
Lather – 4, 6, 9, 17, 19, 22-23, 27-29, 32a, 36, 37b
Soap bubbles – 26
Soap flakes – 15
Soap suds – 1, 3, 5, 8, 16, 26-27, 32b, 39
Soapy water – 9
Soapy watter – 33
Nil – 2, 7, 10, 30, 32c

Inverness
Bubbles – 13c
Foam – 1
Froth – 18
Graith – 8-9, 13cde, 14-16, 26
Grath – 10
Greth – 11
Lather – 13a, 15, 17-18, 21ab, 24, 29-30, 33, 37
Saplines – 24
Sapple – 9, 22, 32
(Soap) suds – *2-3,* 4-5, *6-7, 10-11,* 13abe, *17,* 19, *21b, 23, 29,* 32-36, 38-40
Soapy water – 13c, 23, 32
Nil – 12, 20, 25, 27-28, 31

Nairn
Graith – 1ac
Greth – 1b
Sapple – 1b
Soap suds – 2, 5-6
Nil – 3-4

Moray
Bubbles – 5, 11
Froth – 18-19
Graith – 1, 3-4, 8ab, 12-13, 15, 17, 22
Lather – 4, 7, 8b, 11, 14, 18, 23
Sapple – 2b, 6a, 9a, 22-23
Soap suds – 8d, 11, 21, 23
Soapy blobs – 10
Soapy suds – 8c
Soapy water – 6b, 9b, 21
Nil – 2a, 8ef, 16, 20

Banff
Bubbles – 5, 20
Fraithin – 8
Fro – 14
Froath – 21
Froth – 19
Graith – 2c, 4, 27, 32
Laither – 10
Lather – 30
Sapples – 18c
Soap suds – 1, 8, 15
Soapy water – 2b, 4, 6b, 9, 16, 24-25, 27, 29, 34
Nil – 2a, 3, 6a, 7, 11-13, 17, 18abd, 22-23, 25-26, 28, 31, 33

Aberdeen
Blowing bubbles – 48
Freith – 47b
Fro – 92
Froath – 1, 4, 9, 64, 75, 85, 101, 109
Froth – 2, 19, 35, 41, 47ab, 56, 62, 69-70, 73, 77, 83, 86, 103
Frothin – 47c
Frothy water – 23, 47e, 54, 104
Froze – 19
Laither – 5b, 10, 46, 59, 69, 75, 97
Lather – 14, 16, 47df, 63, 70, 73
Saft soap – 32
Sapples – 60, 78, 101
Sids – 38, 74
Soap – 71b
(Soap) bubbles – 5b, *35,* 47b, 104
(Soap) suds – 12, 14, *28a, 34, 45,* 47e, *50,* 53, *66, 70, 94-95*
Soapy bubbles – 44, 98, 106
Soapy water – 3ab, 5cd, 14, 17, 21-24, 27, 28c, 29, 31, 61, 67, 73, 81, 88, 98, 104-105, 107-108
Throve – 47a
Nil – 5a, 6-8, 11, 13, 15, 18, 20, 25-26, 28b, 30, 33, 36-37, 39-40, 42-43, 49, 51-52, 55, 57-58, 65, 68, 71ac, 72, 76, 79-80, 82, 84, 87, 89-91, 93, 96, 99-100, 102

Kincardine
Froth – 5, 8, 11, 15, 17bcd, 24
Lathe – 19
Lather – 24
Soap suds – 6, 16, 17c
Soapy bubbles – 3, 26
Soapy water – 7, 9
Soapy watter – 10, 12

Nil – 1-2, 4, 13-14, 17a, 18, 20-23, 25, 27-28

Kinross
Fro – 7
Graith – 1-3, 5-7
Sapples – 3-4
Soapy suds – 6

Angus
Bubbles – 5b, 9, 24
Froth – 24
Graith – 5b, 7, 11-12, 14acd, 17a, 18-19, 22-23, 27, 31-32, 33ab, 34-37
Greth – 21
Grith – 22
Laither – 24
Lather – 1, 13, 29b, 30, 32
Lether – 14a
Sapples – 17a, 18
Soap suds – 22, 24-25, 29b, 32, 34
Soapy suds – 5c, 10
Soapy water – 2, 25, 28
Soapy watter – 5a, 6, 12, 15, 26
Nil – 3-4, 8, 14b, 16, 17b, 20, 29a

Perth
Fro – 57
Froth – 26
Graith – 1, 2b, 5-7, 11-13, 15-16, 18, 20-21, 23-24, 26-28, 29b, 31, 33, 37, 39, 41b, 42, 44-45, 47-48, 51b, 52cde, 53-54, 56-57, 60-63, 65, 72-73
Greath – 8, 50, 59
Greff – 64
Greth – 25, 27, 32, 41a, 46, 53-55, 58
Grewth – 2a
Lather – 34, 71
Soap suds – 2a, 4, 8, 10, 14, 24-25, 29a, 32, 36, 43, 52b, 74
(Soapy) sapples – 16, *40,* 41b, 62, *66,* 67-70, 73, *74*
Soapy suds – 50, 57, 72, 74
Soapy water – 9, 33, 41a
Nil – 3, 17, 19, 22, 30, 35, 38, 49, 51a, 52a

Fife
Freeth – 53
Fro – 1, 55e
Froth – 55e, 63
Graith – 2-6, 8, 9ab, 10-14, 16-17, 19-21, 23-35, 36ab, 37-39, 40abd, 41bcd, 42, 43ab, 44abcdef, 45-53, 55abdefg, 56-59, 61-62, 64ab
Greath – 18
Laither – 23
Sapples – 44c, 53, 55b
Soap suds – 1, 37, 44b, 55de
Soapy bubbles – 39
Soapy suds – 41a, 63
Soapy waa'er – 50
Soapy water – 30
Soapy watter – 7
Nil – 15, 22, 54, 55c, 60

Clackmannan
Graith – 1-3, 4abd, 6-7
Sapple – 4cd, 5
Soap suds – 4c
Soapy suds – 2

Stirling
Graith – 7bdef, 8-9, 11, 17-18, 21b, 22ab, 25abd, 26adef, 31, 37a, 39ab, 40
Greth – 2, 21a
Lather – 7e, 12, 23b, 26a, 33-34, 35b, 37b, 39ab
Sappies – 7b, 27b
Sapples – 2-3, 5-6, 7bde, 9, 13-15, 17-19, 21ab, 23ac, 25a, 26bc, 27ab, 29-33, 35ab, 38, 42a
(Soap) suds – *4, 7ac,* 21a, 25c, 26bc*d, 28,* 30, *31-32, 35a, 36*
Soapy bubbles – 10, 21b
Soapy suds – 4, 7c, 20, 34, 36
Soapy watter – 7a, 16
Nil – 1, 24, 41, 42b

Dunbarton
Fraith – 2
Freeth – 6
Freith – 14a
Graith – 17
Greth – 1
Sapples – 1-3, 4ab, 5-6, 7abc, 9-10, 12, 13abc, 14a, 16ab, 17-18
(Soap) suds – 1, *8, 11,* 13ab*c, 14b*
Nil – 15

Argyll
Bubbles – 3-4, 33
Lather – 5, 8, 12, 19
Sapple – 5, 7, 9-10, 13-16, 18, 22,24-26, 29-40
(Soap) suds – 1, *2,* 3, *6, 14, 16-17, 19, 23,* 25, *27,* 30
Soapy water – 11
Sugie – 22
Nil – 20-21, 28

Bute
Freeth – 8b
Graith – 1e
Lather – 2, 8b
Sapple – 1abcde, 3-7, 8ab, 9
Soap suds – 1cd, 2, 7, 8b

Ayr
Bubbles – 16a
Freath – 41, 56
Graith – 8b, 15, 28f, 35b
Lather – 6, 28e, 29, 38
Sapples – 1ab, 2ab, 3-7, 8ab, 9-11, 12ab, 13-15, 16ab, 17, 18ab, 19, 20abcdefgh, 21-23, 24ab, 25, 26abc, 27, 28abcdf, 29, 30ab, 31-34, 35ab, 36-39, 40-50, 52, 53ab, 54-57
(Soap) suds – 5, 8a, *28e,* 45, *51*
Soapy suds – 7

Renfrew
Bubbles – 16b, 18a
Flakes – 2d
Foamie – 2i
Freeth – 4d
Froth – 2i
Graith – 4d
Lather – 1b, 2ij, 4e, 8, 11d, 12b, 16d
Sapples – 1ab, 2abcefghj, 3, 4abcde, 5-7, 9-10, 11abcdefghijkl, 12a, 13abcd, 14ab, 15, 16acd, 17, 18ab, 19, 20b, 21
Sapplings – 7
(Soap) suds – *2ai, 4e,* 8, 18b, *20a*
Soapy suds – 11b

Lanark
Bubbles – 6, 59b
Freeth – 27a, 65, 67b
Frothy water – 32a
Graith – 7a, 10a, 11, 13, 14c, 20, 28, 29dg, 30, 32cd, 36, 38a, 39, 45, 49b, 50-51, 52a, 54, 56, 62, 64a
Lather – 7c, 10b, 14d, 25acd, 27b, 29c, 32d, 35c, 49a, 58
Sapples – 1, 4-6, 7abc, 8ab, 9ab, 10ab, 11-13, 14abc, 15abc, 16ab, 17-18, 20-23, 25bcd, 26a, 28, 29afg, 31abd, 32bcef, 33abcd, 35ad, 36-37, 38abcde, 39, 42-45, 46abc,

Lanark cont'd

47-48, 50, 55-56, 57abc, 59a, 61-63, 65-66, 67a
(Soap) suds — 1, *2-3,* 6, *9b, 10b, 12,* 14d, 15a*c,* 29cf, 31d, 35bd, *44,* 45, 52b, *53, 58,* 59a, *60, 64b,* 65
Soapy sappers — 31c
Soapy suds — 26b, 27b, 35b, 40, 48
Soapy water — 4, 29e, 31d
Soodges — 28
Sowp — 65
Sowpie sapples — 30
Wraith — 65
Nil — 19, 24, 29b, 34, 41

West Lothian

Freeth — 17a
Graith — 1cd, 2- 4, 6-8, 11-13, 15-16, 17a, 19a, 20a, 21a
Lather — 5-6
Sappie — 19b
Sapples — 1ad, 9a, 12, 17a, 18, 19b, 20b, 21ab, 22
Soap suds — 10-11, 22
Soapy suds — 15
Nil — 1b, 9b, 14, 17b

Midlothian

Bubbles — 10
Graith — 3-4, 6ab, 7b, 8b, 9-11, 12a, 13, 14b, 16-18, 22, 23b 24, 25abd, 26ab, 27 32
Lather — 1, 6a, 23b, 25c
Saiples — 14b
Sapples — 9, 11, 12b, 14a, 23b
Soap suds — 8a, 10, 12a, 14a, 15, 18-21, 23ab
Soapy graith — 23a
Soapy suds — 2, 7a, 12b, 14b
Soapy water — 25c
Nil — 5

East Lothian

Graith — 1-3, 4ab, 5, 6a, 7-9, 11-15, 17-18, 20-21
Lather — 1, 4b, 10, 13
Soap suds — 5, 9, 16, 18-19
Soapy sapples — 13
Nil — 6b

Berwick

Graith — 1-2, 5-13, 15, 16abc, 17-24, 26-27, 29, 32
Lather — 2, 8
Soap bubbles — 14
Soap suds — 2, 4, 12, 16c, 19-20, 28, 31-32
Soapy suds — 30-31
Soapy waeter — 16b
Nil — 3, 25

Peebles

Graith — 1, 3, 4abc, 5, 8, 10
Grath — 9
Lather — 8
Sapples — 2, 7-8
Soap fro — 6a
Soap suds — 3, 4c, 5, 6ab, 7
Soapy suds — 2, 8

Selkirk

Graith — 1, 2be, 3, 5-7
Soap suds — 2ac, 4, 8
Sorplins — 2a
Supples — 2d

Roxburgh

Fro — 20
Graith — 2, 3ab, 4-5, 7-8, 9ab, 10, 12-13, 15ab, 16-17, 19-20, 21abcde, 23-26
Lather — 5, 18, 20, 25-26
Lether — 7
Sapple — 14
(Soap) suds — *1-2, 8, 11,* 15b *17, 21adf, 28*
Soapy suds — 20
Soapy waitter — 17
Nil — 6, 22, 27

Dumfries

Freeth — 4, 21a
Graith — 11, 15, 20, 31b
Lather — 15
Saplins — 9, 12
Sids — 31f
Sapples — 1a, 2-7, 8b, 11, 13-14, 19, 21b, 22, 25, 30, 31ae, 32, 34-35, 38, 41, 45b, 49
(Soap) suds — 1a, 4, *8a, 12,* 16, 24,28-*29, 32-33, 37,* 40, *42,* 43, 46
Soapy suds — 17ab, 18, 23-24, 27, 29, 31d, 37, 39, 46
Sowp — 4-5, 7, 14, 30, 31e, 32, 34, 38, 45a
Steep — 2
Washins — 26
Nil — 1b, 10, 31c, 36, 44, 47-48

Kirkcudbright

Froth — 11
Graith — 1
Lather — 3, 13, 16, 24
Lether — 19
Sapple — 1-5, 7, 9-10, 14, 15a, 17, 23
(Soap) suds — *6-7,* 8, 12ab, 18, *21c, 23, 27*
Soapy water — 2
Sowp — 3, 8-9, 15a, 20
Sowp suds — 22
Nil — 15b, 21ab, 25-26

Wigtown

Freith — 5b
Sapples — 1-3, 5ab, 6-14, 16-18
Suds — 16
Nil — 4, 15

Northumberland

Bubbles — 69b, 89, 104b, 126f, 136
Dish weshings — 11b
Froth — 16, 126f
Graith — 17, 29f
Lather — 3, 9-10, 12, 16-18, 22, 24a, 27, 29bde, 32, 33ab, 34b, 35-37, 39, 41ab, 42, 46-49, 53ab, 56, 59bcd, 60, 62bcdegh, 63, 64ab, 65a, 66, 68, 69abcdg, 70, 71cd, 72acei, 74, 76-77, 79-81, 83-84, 86-87, 88a, 89-92, 94b, 96, 99bd, 100, 101b, 103bc, 104ab, 107, 108ac, 109, 111a, 114, 117, 118ab, 119, 121, 122b, 123, 126bdf, 127bcdh, 129c, 130cf, 135, 140, 143
Lathery wetter — 71a
Lawther — 7
Slops — 45
(Soap) suds — 2ab, *5-6,* 8, 13, *14,* 15, 18, *19a,* 20b, *21, 26, 29b, 30, 35, 40a, 41cd,* 43, *45,* 46-47, *48,* 52, *54,* 57, 59*b*ef, *62b, 64b,* 68, *69ab, 70, 71a, 72cdegij,* 73, 77, 82, *83, 88b, 90, 93,* 99bdi, 102, 103a*c, 109-110, 111ab,* 112, 120b, *124ab, 126ac,* 127a*bc,* 130def, *132,* 134, 138, *140, 142*
Soapy suds — 38, 72b, 83, 91, 120c, 130a
Soapy water — 1a, 20b, 40b, 59b, 78, 98, 108a, 111b, 126a, 127e, 130bc, 132, 137
Soapy wetter — 40b, 62g, 69h, 95b
Soapy witter — 31
Washing water — 28, 41c
Weshing water — 15
Wrinsings — 111b
Nil — 1bc, 4, 11, 19b, 20a, 23, 24b, 25, 29ac, 34a, 44, 50-51, 55, 58, 59a, 61, 62af, 65b, 67, 69ef, 71be, 72fhkl, 75, 85, 94a, 95a, 97, 99ac, 101a, 105-106, 108b, 113, 115-116, 120a, 122a, 125, 126e, 127f, 128, 129ab, 131, 133, 139, 141

Cumberland

Blebs — 56
Blobs — 56
Ladder — 25-26
Lather — 3, 6, 13a, 17, 21, 25-26, 41-42, 47, 51-54, 57, 61
Lether — 61
Ludder — 16
(Soap) suds — 1ab, 2-3, *4, 5a, 8-9, 12,* 13cd, *14,* 15*abc*, *18, 22-24, 26-28, 31, 37b, 38, 40,* 42, *45-47,* 48, *49-50, 53, 56-58,* 60, *62*
Soapy watter — 43
Weshings — 13d
Nil — 5b, 7, 10-11, 13b, 19-20, 29-30, 32-36, 37a, 39, 44, 55, 59, 63ab

Down

Froath — 22
Lather — 1, 14
Leather — 17
(Soap) suds — *1, 2a,* 5, 7, *9,* 15, 18-19, 21, 24, 26, 28, 30
Soupe — 13
Sup — 3
Nil — 2b, 4, 6, 8, 10-12, 16, 20, 23, 25, 27, 29

Tyrone

Foam — 1
Froth — 1, 5-6
Froath — 8
Sap — 1
Sapple — 2-3
Suds — 6-8, 10-11, 15
Nil — 4, 9, 12-14, 16

Antrim

Froath — 21
Lather — 1, 6
Leather — 8a, 26
Sapple — 2, 7, 16b
(Soap) suds — 1, 3, *5b,* 13-14, *19,* 20, 22, 25, 28-29, 33
Sonsie water — 5a
Sup — 8b, 16a, 30
Nil — 4, 4A, 9-12, 15, 16c, 17-18, 23-24, 27, 31-32, 34

Donegal

Freethe — 7
Sapple — 6-7, 10b
Soap bubbler — 10a
(Soap) suds — *1,* 5, 5A, 7A, 8, *10a, 12*
Nil — 1A, 2-4, 9, 11, 13

Fermanagh

Lather — 7a, 8, 10
Suds — 2, 4-5, 7a, 9
Nil — 1, 3, 6, 7b

Armagh

Leather — 4
Suds — 4, 6a
Wobble — 6b
Nil — 1-3, 5

Londonderry

Lather — 1A, 2, 5
Sapple — 5
Suds — 3A
Nil — 1, 1B, 3-4, 6-7

15 DOWN DRAUGHT (in chimney) (PQ1, 65)

For the variants of DOWN, see map 14 (cow), Appendix A, (**doon** occurs nearly everywhere, where there is a variant of **COW** but fewer standard forms are reported).

Variants of BLOW(IN(G)) (**blaw** very common, see map 15 (snow), Appendix A, for a rough guide) and DRAUGHT (a few "-ch-" spellings) have been subsumed.

The concentration of some of the items mapped is not very high.

Shetland

Back draw – 33
Back flam – 1
Back flan – 4
Blowin' down – 17
Down flam – 2
Down sook – 33
Flam down – 10
Flan – 5, 15-16, 18-19, 21a, 22, 24, 28 30-31
Flan down – 14, 21b, 26-27, 29
Flannin – 20, 23
Flannin down – 3, 6, 8-9, 12-13, 17, 25, 32
Nil – 7, 11

Orkney

Back dra – 13a, 17
Blow down – 8-9, 18-19
Blowing down – 15-16
Blowin oot – 6
Down draught – 4, 8, 13b
Fannin – 11
Flan – 3, 7, 10, 12, 13b, 14, 20
Flan down – 5
Flannin – 2, 11
Flannin oot – 6
Lums reeking – 15
Nil – 1, 21

Caithness

Bad ventin lum – 14
Blow down – 2ab, 3-9, 11, 12abc, 14-15, 16b
Blowin down – 15
Smoke – 13
Smoky – 13
Smoky airt – 12b
Nil – 1, 10, 16a, 17

Sutherland

Blow back – 12, 15-16
Blow down – 1-6, 8, 9ab, 10, 13-14, 17
Chimney's smoking – 8
Down draught – 7
Flam – 16
Smoky chimney – 11
Sookie blow – 3
Vent – 11

Ross & Cromarty

Back draught – 9, 22, 29, 37b
Back draw – 24, 36
Back flan – 25a
Blow back – 13, 17-18, 20, 23, 27, 32c, 34
Blow down – 1-2, 4-6, 8-9, 12, 14-16, 20-21, 25ab, 26, 28-31, 32ab, 35-36, 37ab, 38-39
Down blow – 10
Down draught – 3, 27, 32b
Nil – 7, 11, 19, 33

Inverness

Back blow – 31
Black smoke – 5
Blow back – 8, 13abe, 16-17, 21b, 24, 39
Blow down – 1, 3, 6-7, 9-10, 13a, 14, 20, 22-23, 26, 28-29, 32-40
Down draught – 11, 13be, 18-19, 23
Draught – 2, 21a
Flam – 13e, 15, 29
Flan – 13d
Flaun – 27
Flum – 27
Nil – 4, 12, 13c, 25, 30

Nairn

Blow back – 1c
Blow down – 1ac, 2
Flam – 1bc, 2-4, 6
Flan – 5

Moray

Back draught – 2b
Blow back – 7
Blow down – 1, 4, 6a, 7, 8abd, 9b, 10-11, 13-16, 18-22
Down blow – 8e, 9a
Flan – 2a, 3-4, 6ab, 7, 8abf, 9a, 12-13, 17, 22-23
Flaw – 11
Flawn – 16
Gliff – 18
Reek – 4, 8b
Reekie chimney – 2a
Reekie lum – 21
Reekin lum – 8c
Nil – 5

Banff

Back draught – 17
Back flan – 13
Back reek – 15
Blow down – 2ac, 6b, 7-9, 12, 15-17, 18bcd, 19, 21-25, 27-32, 34
Bluffert – 27
Down draught – 34
Fla – 21
Flacht – 1
Flan – 2abc, 3-4, 6a, 8, 10-11, 14, 18c, 23-24, 26, 29, 31-34
Flane – 20
Flawn – 5, 6b, 9, 25
Gluff – 2c
Reek – 2b
Nil – 18a

Aberdeen

Awfa flawn – 32
Back draught – 8, 88
Blow back – 50, 77
Blow down – 1-2, 3a, 4, 5bcd, 6, 9-12, 14-16, 18, 21, 26-27, 28c, 33-34, 36, 45-46, 47acf, 49-51, 53, 55, 57-61, 64-69, 71c, 73, 75, 77-78, 80-82, 84-85, 88, 92, 96, 98, 103-109
Blow oot – 94
Coom o' reek – 71b
Down blow – 93
Down draught – 14, 83, 107
Draught – 70
Fla – 44
Flach – 2
Flan – 3ab, 4, 10, 12-14, 17, 20, 22-25, 27, 28abc, 29-30, 34-37, 40-43, 47abef, 48, 51-52, 56-58, 60, 62, 64, 66, 69, 71bc, 72-78, 80, 82-83, 89, 91, 95, 97, 99-102, 104-105
Flan down the lum – 5d
Flan o' rick – 7
Flaw – 5a, 46, 56, 67, 71a
Flawn – 6, 8-9, 16, 19, 24, 31, 45, 47d, 79, 81, 86-87, 98, 103, 109
Flaw o' rick – 17
Fooshim o' reek – 71b
Fuff – 10
Reek – 10, 29
Reekie flaw – 32
Reekie lum – 31
Rick – 66
Smucht – 71a
Sooch – 63
Wind – 70
Nil – 38-39, 54, 90

Kincardine

Blow back – 18, 26
Blow down – 1-8, 10-14, 16, 17abcd, 18-19, 21-24, 26
Down flaw – 18
Draught – 27
Flan – 5, 12, 15, 17ac, 21, 24
Flawn – 7, 25
Reekie lum – 28
Nil – 2, 9, 20

Kinross

Back draught – 4, 7
Blow down – 1-3, 5-6
Down draught – 6

Angus

Back draught – 5c, 12, 27-28, 29b
Back reek – 5b, 23, 29b
Back smoke – 2, 14cd
Blow back – 13
Blow down – 1, 3, 5ac, 6, 8-11, 14bd, 15, 17a, 18-27, 29a, 30, 33ab, 34-37
Blow down the lum – 33b
Down draught – 14a, 25, 32, 34
Draught – 17b, 18, 32
Flaw – 17b
Lum reekin – 7
Reek – 14cd
Winds blown down the lum – 31
Nil – 4, 16

Perth

Back draught – 13, 25, 65
Back reek – 20, 45, 60
Back smoke – 1, 17-18, 26, 52d, 56
Back waught – 20
Blow back – 5-6, 10, 15-16, 22, 26, 33, 52ce, 55, 64
Blow down – 1, 2a, 3, 7-9, 11-13, 16-17, 21, 23-25, 27-28, 29ab, 31-36, 38, 40, 41ab, 42, 44, 46, 48-49, 51ab, 52ade, 53-54, 56-57, 59, 61-63, 66-73
Blown back – 50
Down draught – 4, 39, 52b, 53, 74
Draught – 2a
Contre wind – 61
Flan – 43
Reekie – 18
Smeek – 66
Nil – 2b, 14, 19, 30, 37, 47, 58

Fife

Back draught – 4, 6, 12-13, 24-27, 43a, 44b, 45, 58, 64b
Back flan – 46
Back reek – 43b
Back smoke – 18, 49
Bensil – 35
Blow back – 5, 7, 13, 30, 39, 44b
Blow back down the lum – 39
Blow down – 2-4, 7, 9ab, 10-12, 14, 16-23, 25, 27, 29, 31, 33-34, 36ab, 37-38, 40ab, 40ab, 41abcd, 42, 43a, 44abcdef, 46-54, 55abcdefg, 56-59, 61-63, 64a
Down blow – 52
Down cast – 37
Down draught – 8, 13, 28, 43a, 45
Guft of reek – 1
Lum reekin – 32
Lum's reekin – 39
Reekie lum – 33
Tap reek – 12
Nil – 15, 60

Clackmannan

Back draught – 4d
Blow back – 6
Blow down – 1-3, 4ad, 5-7
Nil – 4bc

Stirling

Back come – 10
Back draught – 13, 21a
Back smoke – 7b
Blow back – 1, 4, 6, 7e, 25cd, 26a, 34, 38, 39b
Blow down – 2-6, 7abcdef, 8-13, 15-20, 21ab, 22ab, 23ac, 24, 25abcd, 26acdef, 27ab, 30-34, 35ab, 36, 37ab, 38, 39ab, 40, 42a
Down draught – 23b
Draw back – 12
Sooch – 25a
Nil – 14, 26b, 28-29, 41, 42b

Dunbarton

Back draught – 5, 7a
Back smoke – 17
Blow back – 7b, 8
Blow down – 1-3, 4b, 5-6, 7c, 8-12, 13abc, 14ab, 15, 16ab, 17-18
Down blow – 7a
Nil – 4a

Argyll

Blow down – 1-3, 5-16, 18-40
Chimney smoking – 19
Down draught – 6, 17
Smoky chimney – 33
Nil – 4

Bute

Blow down – 1abcde, 2-7, 8ab, 9
Reek – 1a
Smeek – 1a

Ayr

Back draught – 6, 57
Back reek – 12a, 20g
Back smoke – 20g, 37
Black reek – 17
Blow back – 8ab, 20h, 49, 57
Blow down – 1ab, 2ab, 3-7, 8ab, 9-11, 12b, 13-15, 16ab, 17, 18ab, 19, 20acdefgh, 21-23, 24ab, 25, 26ac, 27, 28abcdef, 30ab, 31-34, 35ab, 36, 38-39, 41-52, 53ab, 54, 56-57
Blow out – 43
Down draught – 55
Luntin – 19
Reek – 47
Reeked out – 43
Reekin(g) – 31, 40, 47
Reekin lum – 57
Smeekin – 19
Smeekit – 47
Smoking – 40
Sough – 26b
Nil – 20b

Renfrew

Back smoke – 7, 11c, 18a
Blow back – 4b, 17
Blow down – 1ab, 2abcefghi, 3,

Renfrew cont'd

4abcd, 5, 8, 10, 11abcefhijkl, 12ab, 13abd, 14ab, 16abcd, 17, 19, 20ab, 21
Down blow — 11i
Draught — 13c
Vent — 2j
Nil — 2d, 4e, 6, 9, 11dg, 15, 18b

Lanark

Back draught — 15c, 18, 31d
Back reek — 30, 32e
Back smoke — 14b, 16a, 27b, 31d, 44, 50
Blow back — 1, 8a, 21, 25c, 26b, 62
Blow down — 1-6, 7abc, 8a, 9ab, 10ab, 11-13, 14abcd, 15abc, 16b, 17-18, 20, 22-24, 25abcd, 26a, 27ab, 28, 29abcdefg, 30, 31a, 32abcdef, 33abcd, 34, 35abd, 36-37, 38abce, 39-45, 46abc, 47-48, 50-51, 52b, 53-56, 57bc, 58, 59ab, 60-63, 64ab, 65-66, 67ab
Blow oot — 35c
Dad back — 52a
Dad down — 32d, 49b, 57a
Daud down — 49a
Down blow — 31c
Down draught — 8b, 49b
Draught — 3
Reek — 25d
Smoking — 29f
Vent — 38bd
Nil — 19, 31b

West Lothian

Back draught — 1c, 14
Blow back — 6, 16, 19b
Blow down — 1abcd, 2-8, 9ab, 10-13, 15-16, 17ab, 18, 19a, 20ab, 22
Daddin' down — 21a
Dad down — 13
Down blow — 3
Nil — 21b

Midlothian

Back draught — 23b
Blow back — 5, 10, 12a, 22, 23a
Blow down — 1, 3-5, 6ab, 7ab, 8-11, 12ab, 13, 14ab, 15-16, 18, 20-22, 23ab, 24, 25bcd, 26ab, 27-30, 32
Blow goon — 17
Blow oot — 1
Dad down — 15, 24
Daud down — 3, 26a, 27-29, 31
Down blow — 25a
Down draught — 2, 18, 23b
Draught — 19
Gust — 17

East Lothian

Back castin — 6a
Back draught — 7
Back draw — 16
Back smoke — 13
Blow back — 1, 5, 9
Blow down — 1-2, 4ab, 6b, 8, 11, 13-15, 18, 20-21
Dad down — 14, 17
Daud — 16
Daud down — 12, 16
Sough — 2, 6a
Soughing — 10
Stife — 19
Nil — 3

Berwick

Back dad — 4
Back daud — 21
Back draught — 10
Back reek — 11
Blow back — 6, 18, 32
Blow down — 3, 12-13, 16c, 17-18, 26-28, 31
Blow oot — 12, 23
Borrit reek — 10
Borrowed reek — 8
Dad — 25
Dad down — 2, 4, 8, 15, 16a, 18, 23, 25, 30
Daud — 5, 14, 16b, 17, 19, 21
Daud down — 2, 7-9, 11, 16b, 24, 27, 29, 32
Down dad — 20
Puff down the chumley — 10
Reek — 27
Whuff — 31
Nil — 1, 22

Peebles

Back reek — 2
Back smoke — 6b
Blow back — 1, 5, 9
Blow down — 1-2, 4bc, 5, 6b, 7-10
Dad down — 3
Down fa' — 4a
Down reekin lum — 6a
Ill reekin lum — 6a

Selkirk

Blow down — 1, 2abcd, 3-6, 8
Dad down — 2d, 7
Daud down — 2ae

Roxburgh

Back reek — 9a, 20
Blow down — 2, 3b, 4, 11, 13-14, 15ab, 17, 19-20, 21abcdef, 23, 25-26, 28
Dad — 1
Dad down — 3a, 4, 6-8, 9b, 12, 24
Daud down — 2, 5, 10, 13, 15a, 16-18
Owre blast — 28
Smeek — 9a
Nil — 22, 27

Dumfries

Back draught — 15, 17b
Blow back — 31c
Blow down — 1ab, 2-3, 5-7, 8ab, 9, 11-14, 16, 17ab, 18-20, 21ab, 23-30, 31def, 32-43, 45a, 46-49
Blown down — 44
Down blast — 12, 32
Down blow — 22, 31ab
Draught — 4
Reekin — 10, 29, 32
Spew o' reek — 42
Nil — 45b

Kirkcudbright

Blow down — 1, 4-5, 9-11, 12ab, 15b, 16, 18, 21c, 22-23, 25-26
Down blast — 12b, 18
Down blow — 1-4, 6-8, 10, 13-14, 15a, 17, 19-20, 21ab, 26-27
Down draught — 7-8
Reekin — 12a
Reekin lum — 24

Wigtown

Back draught — 6
Back draw — 14
Blow down — 1-4, 5ab, 6-7, 9-12, 14-18
Down blow — 8, 13
Lum's reekin — 2

Northumberland

Back blaaing in — 62h
Back draught — 47, 79, 83, 86, 100, 103b, 107
Back smoke — 47
Blow back — 14
Blow down — 12, 14, 21, 42, 44, 53a, 54
Blowing down — 31
Borrowed smoke — 41a
Chimley's smoking — 130e
Chimney (is) smoking — 15, 121
Daddin down — 2a, 16
Dad down — 2a, 8, 11, 16, 20a, 22, 34b
Daud down — 1a, 29f
Down blow — 18, 20b
Down cast — 64b, 69a, 72i
Down come — 13, 71d
Down dad — 25, 27, 62f, 124a, 134
Down draught — 1b, 6-7, 10, 14, 17, 26, 29bd, 30, 33b, 36-38, 40ab, 41bcd, 45-46, 48-50, 52, 53ab, 56, 59bcdef, 60, 62bh, 64a, 69abc, 71abcd, 72bcdj, 82, 85, 87, 88ab, 89-90, 93, 94b, 99d, 103c, 104a, 106, 109-110, 111a, 112, 120abc, 126c, 127ach, 129b, 130cef, 131-132, 135, 137, 140, 142-143
Down fla — 101b
Down snook — 138
Down sook — 140
Draught — 78, 83, 124b
Draughtie — 13
Fire reekin — 68
Flume — 105
Puff — 59b
Puff down — 104b
Puffie — 126d
Puffin' down — 111b, 142
Reek — 108a, 124a
Reeked oot — 9
Reeking — 16, 59d, 62g, 77, 99a, 102, 111b, 129b
Reeking lum — 19a
Smeeked oot — 9
Smokin(g) — 16, 65a, 77, 87, 92
Smoky — 69c, 111b
Smoky chimbley — 101b
Sook — 55
Stife — 73, 81, 108a
Stoor — 95b
Swirl — 127e
Sworl — 69e
Whiff — 59b
Nil — 1c, 2b, 3-5, 19b, 23, 24ab, 28, 29ace, 32, 33a, 34a, 35, 39, 43, 51, 57-58, 59a, 61, 62acde, 63, 65b, 66-67, 69dfgh, 70, 71e, 72aefghkl, 74-76, 80, 84 91, 94a, 95a, 96-98, 99bc, 101a, 103a, 113-117, 118ab, 119, 122ab, 123, 125, 126abef, 127bdfg, 128, 129ac, 130abd, 133, 136, 139, 141

Cumberland

Back blow — 30
Back caist — 15a, 16
Back draught — 3, 5a
Back reek — 9
Blow back — 60
Blow down — 3, 5a, 9, 13a, 33, 37a, 46
Blown down — 2, 16, 48
Blow out — 31
Chimney's reekin — 17
Down draught — 1a, 9, 13c, 14, 38, 41, 47, 49-50, 56-58, 62
Gush — 60
Puff down — 54
Puffin down — 23
Puffing — 46
Reek — 4, 13d, 15b, 19, 36, 42
Reekin — 28
Reekin back — 20
Reekin chimney — 21
Rek — 15b
Smoky chimney — 6
Smookin back — 57
Sweel — 37b
Waff — 4
Waff down — 44
Waft — 12
Whiffle — 12
Whuff — 29
Whuffle — 12, 15c
Wind has changed — 22
Nil — 1b, 5b, 7-8, 10-11, 13b, 14, 18, 24-27, 32, 34-35, 39-40, 43, 45, 51-53, 55, 59, 61, 63ab

Down

Blow down — 1, 2ab, 3-6, 8-13, 15-30
Blowin' oot — 7
Down draught — 2a
Swirl — 14

Tyrone

Back draught — 11
Blow down — 1, 3, 5-11, 14-16
Down draught — 14
Down smoke — 11
Reek — 7
Reekin' chimney — 1
Smoke — 8
Nil — 2, 4, 12-13

Antrim

Blow down — 1, 3, 4A, 5ab, 6-7, 8b, 9-13, 15, 16b, 17-19, 21-23, 25-28, 30-31, 33
Blow oot — 20
Down blast — 2, 19
Down blow — 19
Reek — 5ab, 7, 29
Sough — 14
Suck — 14
Nil — 4, 8a, 16ac, 24, 32, 34

Donegal

Blow down — 1, 1A, 2-5, 5A, 6-7, 7A, 8-9, 10ab, 11-13
Down blow — 10a
Ert win in chimne — 6
Reek — 4, 13
Smoke — 4, 13

Fermanagh

Blow down — 1-2, 4-5, 7b, 8, 10
Draught — 9
Nil — 3, 6, 7a

Armagh

Blow down — 1-5
Nil — 6ab

Londonderry

Blow down — 1, 1AB, 2-3, 3A, 4-7
Reek — 3

16 PAIL (PQ1, 66)

Pail and **bucket** have not been mapped as they occur all over the area (very few **bucket** in Northern Ireland). Some of the other items mapped do not appear in high concentrations.
Informants' responses to '. . . specify names for different types, according to shape, material and purpose' have been classified and indicated by small raised letters :

c	=	cross-bar handle	s	=	small
f	=	for feeding	sh	=	one side-handle
h	=	one handle	t	=	tapering
i	=	for milk	u	=	one upright/straight handle
l	=	with lid	w	=	wood
m	=	metal	y	=	straight sides
p	=	with spout	z	=	for coal

Note also the recurrence of **cog, cog(g)ie** in 18 **porridge bowl.**

Shetland

Bucket — 1, 5, 7, 10, 13-14, 16, 18, 21a^{w}, 29, 33^{w}
Daffick — 3, 4^{w}-6^{w}, 9^{w}-10^{w}, 12, 14, 17, 20, 21ab^{w}, 22^{w}, 23^{w}-24, 25^{w}, 28, 29^{w}-31^{w}, 33^{w}
Daffil — 19
Davock — 23, 26
Feddick — 16
Feddig — 16
Fiddick — 9, 12, 15, 24
Flaggine — 16
Haivel daffick — 30^{w,c}
Kit — 31
Pail — 1-2^{m}, 4^{m}-6^{w}, 7-8, 10^{m}, 11, 15, 17-18, 21ab, 22, 25, 27-30, 32-33
Pitcher — 4, 21a
Pitcherd — 15
Stoop — 26
Tinnie — 22^{m}

Orkney

Bucket — 4-6, 13ab, 14^{w}, 15, 16^{m}, 17, 19, 21
Cog — 16^{w}
Pail — 1-4, 5^{m}, 8-9, 11-12, 13a^{m}b, 15, 17, 20-21
Pitcher — 5^{m}-6
Tinnie — 7
Nil — 10, 18

Caithness

Bucket — 4, 13, 15, 17
Coug(ie) — 7-8^{w}
Pail — 2ab, 5, 8-11, 12ab, 14, 16b
Pailie — 16b, 17
Pitcher — 13
Nil — 1, 3, 6, 12c, 16a

Sutherland

Bucket — 2-3, 5, 7-8, 9b, 10, 11^{w}, 12, 14-16
Pail — 1, 3-8, 9ab, 10-13, 16-17
Rake — 16

Ross & Cromarty

Bucket — 3^{w}, 5, 7, 10, 12, 14, 16-18, 20, 22, 25ab, 26-29, 31, 32ab, 34, 36^{w}
Can — 14, 29
Coggie — 22^{w,sh}
Flag(g)on — 30-31, 32a, 35-36^{s,m}
Pail — 1, 3-9, 13-14, 16, 18-20 22-23, 25b, 26-29, 31, 32ab, 36, 37ab, 39
Pailie — 24, 25b
Pitcher — 7-8, 10-15, 17, 25b, 29, 33, 36
Rooser — 37b
Roosher — 37b
Skalat — 32c
Water jug — 32c
Nil — 2, 21, 38

Inverness

Bucket — 1^{w}, 6, 9^{w}-11^{w}, 13bce, 14, 16, 18, 21a, 22, 24-26^{w}, 28, 32-33, 35, 39-40
Can — 40
Cog — 15^{w}
Coggan — 31^{f}
Cuman — 26
Flag(g)on — 9^{s,i}, 13e, 15^{s,i}, 19
Pail — 1-6, 8, 10-11, 13abce, 16-20, 21ab, 23, 25-27, 29, 32-40
Nil — 7, 12, 13d, 30

Nairn

Bucket — 1c, 2
Cog — 1b^{w}, 3
Flaggon — 6
Pail — 1a, 2, 5
Nil — 4

Moray

Backet — 9a
Bucket — 2a, 3-4, 7, 8ab^{w}cde^{w}, 11, 13-16, 18-20, 22-23
Cog — 1^{w}, 6a, 7^{w}, 8b^{w}d, 20^{w}
Coggie — 6a, 9a^{w}, 22
Luggie — 7^{m,sh}, 22
Pail — 5, 6b, 7, 8d^{w}e^{w}f, 10-11, 14, 19-21, 23
Slop pail — 8b
Stoup — 21
Nil — 2b, 9b, 12, 17

Banff

Backet — 18c^{w}
Bucket — 2abc, 3-4^{w}, 5, 6b, 9^{w}-10, 13, 14^{w}, 15, 18b, 19, 24-25, 29, 33-34
Cog — 5, 8^{sh,f}, 9^{w,i}, 25, 31
Coggie — 2c, 5^{sh,f}, 7, 31^{w,i}
Cogie — 12, 18d^{sh,i}, 27
Cogue — 7
Dirler — 13
Flagon — 9^{i}, 24
Leglen — 14^{m}
Pail — 1, 2ab, 3-4, 6b, 7-9, 15, 17, 18c, 19, 21, 25^{sh,i}, 26-27, 30, 32, 34
Pellie — 18c
Pitcher — 20
Nil — 6a, 11, 16, 18a, 22-23, 28

Aberdeen

Backet — 73, 77^{w}
Bucket — 2, 3a, 5ad^{w}, 6, 9-10, 13-14, 19-21, 23^{w}, 25, 28a, 31^{w}-32^{w}, 33, 37, 46, 47acdef, 48, 53^{w}, 59, 61-63, 67, 69-70, 71b^{w}c^{w}, 75-76, 77^{w}, 80-81^{w}, 84, 89, 96^{w}-97^{w}, 98, 100^{w}-101, 103-105, 107, 109
Can — 1, 48, 64
Chappin flaggon — 80
Cog — 5d, 23^{w}, 27^{w}, 28b, 29, 52, 55, 64, 71b^{i}, 77^{w,f}, 79, 85, 88
Coggie — 5d, 11, 17, 28b, 47a^{w}, 56^{w,f}, 85^{w}
Cogie — 32, 53^{f}, 82^{w}
Cougie — 84
Flag(g)on — 8, 21, 29-30, 32^{m,s,l}, 34, 48, 56^{l,s}, 59, 64, 67, 70, 71c^{s}, 72, 74, 78, 80^{m,s,i}, 86, 88^{m,s}, 89, 93-95, 104, 107
Fluggon — 17, 40, 47a, 75, 99
Log — 79^{w,i}
Pail — 3ab, 4, 5c, 6, 8-12, 14, 16-17, 21-22, 23^{m}, 24, 28ac, 32^{m}, 34-35, 44-45, 47b, 48-50, 53, 56, 59, 63, 66, 70, 71b^{m}, 73, 81^{m}, 83-86, 94-95, 98, 100-101, 104, 106, 108
Troch — 14
Vessel — 70
Nil — 5b, 7, 15, 18, 26, 36, 38-39, 41-43, 51, 54, 57-58, 60, 65, 68, 71a, 87, 90-92, 102

Kincardine

Boggie — 12
Bucket — 3^{w}, 6^{w}-7, 9-10, 14-15^{w}, 17b^{w}cd, 18, 21, 23-24, 27-28^{w},
Cog — 2-3^{w,m,h}, 6-7, 21^{w}
Cogue — 17c
Flag(g)on — 6, 8, 10, 15^{m}, 17b^{s,m}d^{w}, 24^{i}, 27
Pail — 1, 5-8, 12, 14, 16, 17bcd, 19, 26-27
Pan — 20, 23, 27-28
Pitcher — 15
Rooser — 23-24
Stable pail — 21^{m}
Nil — 4, 11, 13, 17a, 22, 25

Kinross

Bucket — 4, 6
Luggie — 1, 2^{w,u}, 3
Pail — 2^{m}-3, 6
Pitcher — 3^{m,i}
Stoup — 2^{w,c}, 3^{sh}
Nil — 5, 7

Angus

Backet — 10, 14d
Bucket — 1, 3, 6-9, 12-13^{x}, 14bcd, 15-16, 17ab^{w}, 18, 20^{w}, 21^{w}-26, 29a^{m}b^{w}, 31-32, 33ab^{x}, 34, 36^{w}-37
Cog — 5c, 37
Coggie — 4^{s,i}, 5bc^{w,f,i}, 14a^{w}
Cogie — 5a^{m}
Flag(g)on — 5a^{s}, 13^{i}, 14a^{i}, 32^{i}, 34-35^{i}
Luggie — 23^{w,i,u}, 30, 34^{w,f}
Pail — 1, 4, 6, 12, 14a^{m}b, 17b^{m}, 20, 24, 28^{m}, 29b^{m}, 32, 34-36^{m}
Pan — 5ac^{x}, 14a^{x}, 18^{x}, 22, 24-25, 28^{m}, 29a^{m}
Pitcher — 3, 6-7, 11, 14a^{p}, 18^{i}, 32^{i}, 33b, 34
Scuttle — 18^{z}
Nil — 2, 19, 27

Perth

Broke pail — 62
Bucket — 1, 2a, 5-10, 12, 16, 21, 23-24, 25^{w}-26^{m}, 27, 29a, 30, 32, 33^{m,w}, 34, 36^{w}, 38, 40, 41ab, 43-46, 48-50, 51b, 52acde, 53, 55-60, 62-63, 65, 67-68, 71-72
Can — 9
Coag — 6-7^{s,f}, 13^{i,u}
Cog — 20^{i}, 21^{w,sh}, 25, 53
Coggie — 41b^{w}, 42
Cogie — 5^{w,h,i}, 6, 16, 26^{w,i,sh}, 39, 69^{w}
Flag(g)on — 2b, 7^{i}, 16, 30, 50^{s,i}
Handie — 62^{i}
Luggie — 13, 20^{s}-21^{w,sh}, 26^{m,i}, 29b, 30, 31^{s,h}, 32^{i,u}, 33-39^{i,u}, 46^{w,sh}, 52a^{w,u}, 62^{i}
Pail — 2a, 4, 8-10, 13, 14^{m,z}, 15-16, 21, 24^{x}-25^{x,i}, 28, 29a, 32, 36, 39, 46-47, 52be, 55, 57, 64, 66, 68-69, 71-74
Pan — 18, 66
Pitcher — 2b, 3, 5^{i}-6, 13^{i,p,h}, 16, 18, 25, 26^{i}, 27^{i}, 30, 33, 45^{i,x}, 50, 51a, 52cd, 57, 64-65
Stoop — 16
Stoup — 24^{w}, 29b, 45, 62, 68^{w,c,x}, 70^{x}
Nil — 11, 17, 19, 22, 35, 37, 54, 61

Fife

Backet — 49
Bin — 37
Bucket — 2, 4-5^{w}, 7, 9a, 11, 13, 17, 19^{w}-20^{w}, 21, 23-24^{w}, 29, 31-35, 36a, 37, 39^{w}, 40b, 41acd, 42, 43a, 44abce, 47^{w}, 50, 52, 53^{w}-54^{w}, 55abdeg^{w}, 57-59, 62^{z}, 63
Can — 49
Coag — 23, 55b
Coggie — 28^{i}, 35^{w}, 53
Cogie — 21^{w}
Flagon — 3, 6^{i}, 35^{l}
Leglen — 55f
Luggie — 18, 20^{i}-21^{w,u}, 23, 28^{h}, 32, 37-38, 40b, 42^{i,h}, 44a^{i,s}, 48, 51^{w}, 53, 55bf, 62^{i}, 64a
Pail — 1, 4-6^{x}, 8, 9a, 10-11^{x}, 14, 16^{m}, 19, 21, 24-25, 28, 30, 32^{i,x}, 34, 36b, 39, 40b^{x,z}, 41abd, 43a, 44def, 45-50^{m,x}, 51, 53^{m}-54, 55abdeg^{m}, 56-57, 59, 61, 62^{x}, 63
Petcher — 6^{i}
Pitcher — 21, 23, 26, 33, 38, 44bf, 48, 51^{x}
Scuttle — 48
Stoop — 64a
Stoup — 12^{w}, 36a^{w,c}, 44f^{x}, 45^{w}-48, 50^{w,m}, 55a^{x,w}, 64b
Nil — 9b, 15, 22, 27, 40a, 43b, 55c, 60

Clackmannan

Bouay — 2^{w,i}
Bucket — 2, 4bcd, 7
Hannie — 5^{m,i}
Luggie — 5^{w,i}
Pail — 1-3, 4c, 6-7
Pitcher — 1
Stoup — 1, 4ad^{w,t}

Stirling

Bakie — 7b, 9, 19, 25ad
Bine — 26b
Bowie — 7d
Boyne — 7b^{i}d
Bucket — 1-2, 4, 7ef, 8, 10^{w,x}, 11-12, 17-18, 20, 21ab, 22ab, 23bc, 25bd^{m}, 26acde, 27a 30^{w}, 33, 35b, 36^{w}, 37b, 39b
Can — 35a
Cob — 26b
Cog — 8^{w,i}, 9^{i}, 21b^{w}, 25c^{i,u}, 39b^{i}
Coggie — 25a^{w,f}, 31^{i}
Cowgie — 26b
Cowie — 7b^{i}
Leglen — 7d, 26b
Luggie — 7be^{i}, 9, 12^{i,u}, 18^{w,u}, 21b^{m,i}, 25c^{i,u}, 26b, 27a^{w}, 31^{i}, 35a, 39a^{i}b^{i}
Pail — 2, 4, 7ace, 8-10^{m}, 12-13, 16-17, 21ab, 23bc, 25bcd^{m}, 26acd, 27a^{m}, 28, 30^{m}-32, 34, 35a, 36, 40, 42a
Pitcher — 18^{s,i}, 37b, 39a^{i}, 42a
Scuttle — 8^{z}
Stoup — 7bd, 9^{w,t,x}, 17^{w}, 18^{w,c}, 19^{w,i}, 22a^{w,x},b^{w,x}, 25c^{x,t}d, 26b^{f}f^{w,x}, 27a, 32^{w}, 39b
Nil — 3, 5-6, 14-15, 23a, 24, 27b, 29, 37a, 38, 41, 42b

Dunbarton

Bakie — 4b^{w,z}
Bucket — 1, 4b^{i}, 6^{x}, 7c, 8^{z}, 10-11, 13bc, 16ab, 17-18
Can — 3^{i}
Cog — 13a^{i}
Coggie — 5^{i,h}, 7c^{i}
Cuggie — 5^{i,h}
Luggie — 4b, 7c^{i}
Pail — 1, 3^{x}, 6^{z}, 7bc^{w,u}, 8-10, 12, 13abc, 14b, 16ab
Staup — 2
Stoup — 5^{x,c}, 6^{w,x,c}, 7ac^{t,c}, 9, 13a^{w,x,c}, 14a^{w}
Nil — 4a, 15

Argyll

Bucket — 5, 8, 10-13, 15-16^{m}, 18-19, 21, 22^{w}, 23, 27^{m}-31^{x}, 34, 35^{w}, 36-39
Can — 17
Coag — 32^{i}, 35^{i}
Luggie — 24^{i}, 31^{i}-33^{i}, 35^{i,w,u}, 37, 40
Pail — 1-3, 5-7, 9-10, 14, 16^{m}-19, 21-23, 25, 27^{w}, 33, 35^{m}, 39^{i}
Pitcher — 17
Scuttle — 16
Stoup — 9, 35^{t,h}
Nil — 4, 20, 26

Bute

Bucket — 1e, 3, 5, 7, 8ab, 9
Coggie — 1a
Luggie — 1a^{i}, 4^{i}, 7^{i,u}, 8b^{i}
Pail — 1cde, 2, 7, 8ab^{i}, 9^{m}
Sputcher — 8b^{sh}
Stoop — 8b
Stoup — 1a^{x}, 8b^{w,l}, 9^{w}
Nil — 1b, 6

Ayr

Bakie — 18b, 54^{w,z}
Bine — 24a
Bowie — 8b^{i}
Bucket — 1ab, 2a^{w}b, 3^{m}, 5-7, 8a^{w,m}b, 9, 15, 16b, 17, 21-22, 24b, 26ab, 28df, 29, 30ab, 32, 35b, 38, 41, 43, 45, 47-49^{m}, 53a^{w}, 56-57^{w}
Can — 47, 49^{m}-50, 55
Chappin can — 53a
Laiglen — 19^{i}
Luddie — 18b
Luggie — 2a^{i}, 5^{i,u,w}, 6^{i}, 7^{i}, 8a^{i,u}b^{i}, 9^{i}, 11^{i,u}, 12a^{i,u}, 16b, 17^{i}, 18a^{i}b, 19, 20h, 24a^{i,w}b^{i}, 27, 28f^{i}, 30a, 31^{i}, 35a^{i,w}b, 37^{u,i}, 40, 41^{i}, 42^{i}, 43, 47^{i}, 48, 51^{i}, 53a^{i}b^{i}, 54^{i}
Pail — 1a, 2b, 3^{m}-6, 9-11, 12a, 13-14, 16a, 20bcg, 21, 24b, 25, 26abc, 27, 28ef^{m}, 30a, 31, 32^{m}-33^{m}, 34, 35ab, 36-37, 40-42, 44-45, 48^{i}, 52, 53a^{m}, 54, 57
Pitcher — 53a^{i}
Scuttle — 28f^{m,z}, 45^{z}
Stoop — 18b
Stoopie — 19
Stoup — 3^{w,x}, 6, 8ab^{x}, 15^{w}, 16b^{w}, 18b, 20gh, 24b^{w,x}, 25^{w}, 27^{w,x}, 31^{w,c}, 33, 35b^{w,x}, 42^{w}, 46^{w}, 49^{w}, 51^{w,x}, 53b^{w}, 57^{w,t}
Nil — 12b, 20adef, 23, 28abc, 39

Renfrew

Bakie — 16d
Bucket — 1ab, 2abcefghij, 3, 4a^{w}c^{w}de, 5, 7-8, 11ac^{w}de, 12ab, 13c, 14a, 16acd, 17, 20ab
Can — 17
Cog — 11a^{w,i}
Coggie — 2d^{w}j^{i}
Cogie — 2e^{i}
Hankie — 21^{t}
Luggie — 2e^{i}g^{i}, 9, 11a^{i}f^{i}j^{w,i}, 14b^{w,i,u}, 18ab^{i}
Pail — 1b, 2ad^{m}hi, 4a^{m}c^{m}e, 8, 11abcdehjl, 12a, 13c, 14a, 16abc, 17, 18ab, 19, 20a
Stoup — 2g, 11b^{w}f^{x}, 21^{w}
Unit — 11a
Nil — 4b, 6, 10, 11gik, 13abd, 15

Lanark

Bakie — 11^{z}, 22, 25d, 36^{z}
Bin — 25d
Bucket — 1^{m,w}, 3^{x}-6, 7a^{x,z,c}c, 9a, 11^{w}, 13^{w}, 14bd, 15ab, 17-18, 20-22, 25acd, 26a, 28, 29a^{w}bcfg, 30, 31c, 32abce^{z}, 33ac^{w,m,c}, 35d^{w,m}, 36-37, 38c^{w}e, 39, 42, 44-45, 46b, 49ab, 51, 52b, 56, 57ac^{w}, 58, 64a
Can — 11^{s,i}, 63, 67b^{x}
Cog — 8a
Coggie — 52a^{i,h}, 56^{i}
Cogie — 30, 35d
Handie — 54^{i}, 56^{i}
Hannie — 7a^{i,h}, 15b, 33c^{i}, 38c^{i}, 45^{i}, 59a^{i,u}, 64b^{i}, 65^{i}
Haunie — 46ab^{i}, 49b^{w,i}, 52a^{i,h}b^{sh,i}, 57b^{i,u}
Honie — 30^{i}
Leglin — 38d
Luggie — 7a^{i,h}, 9b, 11, 15bc^{i}, 23, 30, 36, 38ad, 45^{i}, 49b^{w,i}, 52b^{sh,i}, 54^{i}, 56^{i}, 57c^{i}, 59a^{i}, 64b^{i,u}
Pail — 1^{m}-3^{z}, 6, 7c, 8ab, 9a, 10b, 12-13^{m}, 14ad, 15ac, 16ab, 17^{m,x,i}, 19-20, 23, 25bcd, 26ab, 27b, 29acdf, 31ad, 32e^{x}, 33acd, 35abcd, 38ac, 39, 45, 46a^{m}c, 47-48, 49ab, 52b, 53, 56, 58, 59b, 60, 62, 64b, 65^{x}
Pitcher — 29e^{i,x}, 32d, 38c, 66^{x}
Scuttle — 7c, 32e^{z}
Stoup — 1^{w}, 9b, 13^{t,w,x}, 15a^{w}c^{w}, 17-18, 20^{w}, 23, 27b^{w}, 29a^{w}g, 30^{x}, 32f, 33cd^{w,i}, 35d, 46c, 47^{w,x}, 52b, 57a^{w,x}, 64b
Nil — 7b, 10a, 14c, 24, 27a, 31b, 33b, 34, 38b, 40-41, 43, 50, 55, 61, 67a

West Lothian

Bakie — 2
Bucket — 1acd, 2-3^{w}, 6, 8, 11, 13, 15-16^{x}, 17a, 19a, 20a, 21b
Can — 16
Luggie — 1a^{i}, 4^{i}, 17a
Pail — 1a^{w}, 2^{i,x}, 3^{m}, 5, 7, 9a, 10-11, 15-16^{z}, 17a, 18^{m}, 20a^{x}b, 21a, 22
Pitcher — 20a^{s}
Scuttle — 6, 11
Stoup — 1c, 5^{x}-6^{w}, 9a^{w}, 12^{t,x}, 18^{w}, 19b
Nil — 1b, 9b, 14, 17b

Midlothian

Bucket — 3, 6ab^{w}, 7a, 8b, 10-11, 12ab, 15-20, 22, 23a^{w}b, 24, 25c, 26b, 29, 30^{w,h}, 31
Hannie — 11^{i}, 27
Kit — 30^{w}
Luggie — 11^{i}, 27, 30
Pail — 1-3, 8a, 9-11, 12b, 13, 14a, 15-16, 18-19, 21-22, 23b, 25a, 27-29
Pitcher — 6b, 14a^{x}b, 17^{i}, 28, 30^{m}-32
Scuttle — 29^{z}
Stoup — 10
Nil — 4-5, 7b, 25bd, 26a

East Lothian

Bauket — 4a
Baukie — 4a^{z}
Bucket — 2, 4ab, 6ab, 7^{z}-9, 11, 13-15^{w}, 17
Cog — 16^{w}
Coggie — 14^{s,i}, 15^{w,i,u}, 16^{w}
Keggie — 15^{w,i,u}
Luggie — 14^{i}
Pail — 1, 4b, 5, 6a, 7^{x}-9, 14-16^{m}, 19-21
Pitcher — 7^{i}, 12^{i}, 14^{x}, 16^{m}-17^{i}
Nil — 3, 10, 18

Berwick

Bowie — 22^{w}
Bucket — 1-2, 6, 8-10, 12, 15, 16c, 17-18, 20, 23-24, 27, 28^{m,w}, 29-30, 31^{x}, 32
Coggie — 22^{w}, 27
Kit — 8
Luggie — 11^{i}, 22^{s,w,h}, 32^{i}
Pail — 1-2, 7-8, 10, 12, 15, 16bc, 21, 28, 32
Pitcher — 3^{i}-4, 8, 11, 13, 23, 26-28^{m}, 31^{x}-32^{i}
Tin — 10
Nil — 5, 14, 16a, 19, 25

Peebles

Bowie — 4a
Bucket — 2, 4bc, 6ab, 8
Handie — 5^{i}
Hannie — 10^{i}
Luggie — 9^{u}-10^{i}
Pail — 4abc, 5, 6ab, 7
Pitcher — 1, 3, 5^{x}, 10
Scuttle — 4b

Selkirk

Bucket — 2d, 8
Handie — 4^{w,h}
Luggie — 3^{i}-4
Pail — 1, 2abcde, 3-4, 8
Nil — 5-7

Roxburgh

Bowie — 13^{w}
Bucket — 2, 7-8, 9a, 11, 15ab, 20, 21ce, 25-26, 28
Can — 8, 15b^{m,y}, 20^{i}, 23
Coggie — 4, 21a^{w}, 28
Kit — 21a
Luggie — 13^{w}
Pail — 1-2, 3a, 4-5, 8, 9a, 13, 15b, 17-19, 21af, 23, 28
Pan — 10
Pitcher — 5^{i,y}, 7, 10^{i}, 13^{s,i}, 16-17^{y,i}
Stoup — 4, 28
Nil — 3b, 6, 9b, 12, 14, 21bd, 22, 24, 27

Dumfries

Bucket — 1b, 2, 4-7, 8ab, 12^{x,c}-15, 17ab, 19-20, 21a, 24-26, 27^{w,m}, 28-30, 31bcdef, 32-40, 42^{x}-44, 45a, 46-48
Can — 3-4, 9-12^{x,c}, 17ab, 18-19, 21b, 24, 26-27, 31a^{i,x}c, 32, 37^{i}, 42-43, 45a^{m}, 46^{i}
Cog — 12
Handie — 42^{i}
Hanna — 15^{i}
Hannie — 3^{i}-4^{i}, 21b^{i,u}, 23^{i}, 32^{w}-33^{i}, 35^{i}, 41^{i}, 45a, 46^{i}
Lippie — 35^{i}
Luggie — 1a^{i}, 3^{i}, 12, 22^{i}-23^{i}, 31a^{w,u}, 32^{i,u}, 34^{i}-35^{i}, 39^{i}, 46
Pail — 1a, 4, 8a, 15-16, 17a, 22, 27^{m}, 29, 31c^{i}e, 46
Pitcher — 6
Sloppie — 35
Stoup — 49
Nil — 45b

Kirkcudbright

Bucket — 1, 3, 4^{m,w}-11, 12b 13-14, 15b, 17, 19, 21bc, 22-23, 25, 27
Can — 1-2, 4^{m}, 6, 8, 10-11, 12a, 13, 16, 18, 21a, 22, 24, 26
Coggie — 1^{i}
Handie — 6
Hannie — 3^{i}, 15a, 16, 21b, 26-27
Laiglen — 17
Luggie — 1^{i}, 3^{i}-4^{i,h}, 6, 11, 15a, 26-27
Pail — 1, 7-8, 21b
Stoup — 1^{w}-2, 26
Nil — 20

Wigtown

Bucket — 5a, 7-9, 11-13, 17
Can — 1-4, 5ab, 6-7, 9, 11-12^{x}, 13-18
Cog — 5b^{w}
Cogie — 17^{i}
Handie — 6^{i}
Hannie — 12^{i}
Loggie — 5a
Luggie — 1^{i}-2, 4^{i}, 5ab, 6^{i}-7^{i}, 10^{w,h}, 13, 16^{i}
Pail — 4, 5a, 7, 11-13
Stope — 17

Northumberland

Bucket — 1abc, 2b, 4-5, 8-12, 14^{w}, 16-18, 19a, 20b, 21-22, 24b, 26-28, 29abcde, 32, 33ab, 34ab, 35, 37-39, 40a^{w}b, 41acd, 42-47, 49-52, 53a^{w}b, 54-58, 59abcdef, 60-61, 62abdefgh, 63, 64ab^{w}, 65a, 66, 68, 69abcd, 70, 71abcd, 72abcdegijk, 73-77, 79-87, 88b, 89-93, 94b, 95ab, 96, 99bd, 100, 101ab, 102, 103abc, 104ab, 105, 107, 108abc, 109-110, 111ab, 112-114, 116, 118ab, 119, 120ac, 121, 122ab, 123, 124b, 125, 126abcdef, 127abcdegh, 129b, 130abcdef, 131-134, 136-137, 139-140
Can — 13, 33b, 35, 41d, 73
Coggie — 29f
Flag(g)on — 111b, 133-135, 138, 142
Kit — 117^{w}, 142
Luggie — 29c, 41a^{w,u}
Pail — 1a, 2ab, 4-8, 13-14^{m}, 16-17, 19a, 20b, 21, 29b, 30-31, 35-38, 40ab, 41d, 42, 45-46, 48, 52, 53a^{m}b, 56-57, 59bd, 62bg, 64b^{m}, 65a, 68, 69bdh, 70, 71ad, 72bcgijk, 73, 77-78, 81-82, 86-87, 88ab, 89-92, 96, 98, 99bd, 100, 102, 103bc, 104b, 106, 109, 111ab, 112, 119, 120bc, 121, 126bc, 127ag, 130ce, 132, 135, 139-143
Pitcher — 28, 59b
Scuttle — 35, 39, 47, 56, 62a, 64b^{m}, 65a, 66, 69abh, 71ad, 72d, 91-93, 97, 100, 122b, 127a, 130ce
Swill — 142
Nil — 3, 15, 19b, 20a, 23, 24a, 25, 41b, 62c, 65b, 67, 69efg, 71e, 72fhl, 94a, 99ac, 115, 124a, 127f, 128, 129ac

Cumberland

Booket — 41
Bucket — 1ab, 2-4, 5a, 6-9, 11-12, 13acd, 14, 15abc, 16-19, 21-25, 28, 31-34, 36, 37ab, 38-40, 42-60, 62, 63b
Can — 15a
Geggin — 44^{w}, 46
Keg — 61
Kit — 30-31
Pad — 30
Pail — 1a, 3, 12, 23, 31, 37b, 38,

Cumberland cont'd
42, 53, 58
Nil — 5b, 10, 13b, 20, 26-27, 29, 35, 63a

Down
Bucket — 1, 2a, 3-9, 11-13, 14[m]-15[f], 16-19[m], 20-21 22[m,f], 23-30
Can — 6, 8, 14[m]-15[m,i], 19
Ken — 22[m,i]
Pail — 2a
Nil — 2b, 10

Tyrone
Bucket — 1-2, 5-11, 13-16
Can — 8, 10-11, 15
Ken — 13[m]
Pail — 1[m]
Swinger — 2
Nil — 3-4, 12

Antrim
Bucket — 1-3[m], 4A, 5a[m]b, 7, 8b, 9-15, 16b, 17-23, 25-31, 33
Can — 5b, 15, 16b, 17[m], 21, 26, 31
Pail — 25
Piggin — 4[w,i], 8b, 24[w,i], 28
Pitcher — 11
Nil — 6, 8a, 16ac, 32, 34

Donegal
Bucket — 1, 3-5, 5A, 6-7, 7A, 8[m], 10ab, 11-13
Can — 8[m]
Pail — 2
Pan — 4, 13
Stoap — 1A, 6[w], 12[w]
Stoop — 6
Timmer bucket — 10b
Nil — 9

Fermanagh
Bucket — 1-2, 4[m]-5, 7a, 8-10
Pail — 4
Nil — 3, 6, 7b

Armagh
Bucket — 3, 4[m], 5, 6ab,[m]
Pail — 3
Nil — 1-2

Londonderry
Bucket — 1A, 2-3, 3A, 4-5, 7
Can — 4[i], 6
Nil — 1, 1B

17 TWO PAILFULS OF WATER CARRIED TOGETHER (PQ1, 67)

The variants of the elements TWO (**twa(y), twae, twee**) and -FUL(S) (**fu', fie** etc.) have been subsumed.

Shetland
Fraat — 26
Fracht — 15, 17, 20, 21ab, 22-25, 28, 30-33
Fraught — 2, 10, 12-13, 19
Frecht — 22, 27
Freicht — 3, 6
Freight — 1-2, 4-5, 7-9, 14, 18, 29
Nil — 11, 16

Orkney
Fracht — 20
Fraught — 10
Freight — 1-5, 8-9, 11, 13a, 15, 17, 21
Frite — 6, 16, 18-20
Run — 4
Two pails — 5
Nil — 7, 12, 13b, 14

Caithness
Fracht — 2b, 3, 5, 9, 11, 12bc, 13-15, 16ab
Fraucht — 6-7, 12a, 15
Fraught — 2a
Freicht — 17
Rake — 8, 11
Nil — 1, 4, 10

Sutherland
Double Pails — 3
Draught — 14
Frachk — 10
Fracht — 9a, 15
Rake — 9b, 16
Two pailfuls — 16
Two pails — 13
Nil — 1-2, 4-8, 11-12, 17

Ross & Cromarty
Craft — 36
Fracht — 6, 12, 15, 21-22, 33, 35
Frak — 14
Fraucht — 23-24, 31
Fraught — 10, 17, 21, 30, 37ab
Gird — 18-19, 25b, 34
Two pailfuls — 1, 5, 28
Two pails — 9, 39
Nil — 2-4, 7-8, 11, 13, 16, 20, 25a, 26-27, 29, 32abc, 38

Inverness
Draught — 15, 21b
Fracht — 29
Fraucht — 9, 21a, 26
Fraught — 29
Gird — 9
Pailful — 21a
Rake — 21b
Stoup — 22
Two buckets — 39
Two pailfuls — 5, 18, 23, 37
Two pails — 25
Nil — 1-4, 6-8, 10-12, 13abcde, 14, 16-17, 19-20, 24, 27-28, 30-36, 38, 40

Nairn
Fracht — 1b, 5
Fraucht — 4
Fraught — 1c, 2
Gird — 1b
Two flagons — 6
Nil — 1a, 3

Moray
Fracht — 1, 2a, 3-4, 6ab, 7, 8abd, 9a, 12, 14, 18, 20-23
Fraucht — 5, 8e, 9b, 10, 15-16, 19
Fraught — 2b, 4, 13, 17
Frucht — 7
Two pailfuls — 8b
Nil — 8cf, 11

Banff
Draught — 20
Fracht — 2b, 3-4, 6ab, 8-9, 12-17, 18bcd, 19, 21-22, 25, 29, 31-34
Fraucht — 2ac, 5, 7, 10-11, 23, 26, 28, 30
Fraught — 24
Vraucht — 27
Nil — 1, 18a

Aberdeen
Dracht — 102
Draucht — 95
Flacht — 47a
Fracht — 1-2, 4, 5ab, 7, 9-11, 13-17, 19, 21, 25-26, 28ab, 31-32, 34, 40, 43-44, 46, 47abce, 49-50, 53, 55, 57-58, 61-63, 65-67, 69, 71c, 73-75, 78-79, 83-86, 88, 91-92, 94, 100-101, 106
Fraucht — 3ab, 5bcd, 11, 20, 23, 28c, 29-30, 35-37, 42, 45, 47d, 51, 53, 56, 60, 64, 68, 71bc, 72, 80, 87, 89, 93, 97, 99, 103-105, 107-109
Fraught — 5c, 6, 12, 22, 24, 27, 29, 39-41, 48, 52, 59, 71a, 76-77, 81, 96, 98
Thracht — 16
Vracht — 8, 33
Yoke — 47d, 70
Nil — 18, 38, 47f, 54, 82, 90

Kincardine
Doket — 20
Dracht — 28
Draught — 8
Fracht — 5, 7, 9-11, 13, 16, 18, 23
Fraucht — 4, 6, 12, 17bc, 21
Fraught — 3, 14, 17a, 19, 24-25
Two pailfuls — 27
Two pails — 1, 26
Nil — 2, 15, 17d, 22

Kinross
Couple of pails — 6
Race — 2-3, 5
Rake — 2
Stoups — 4
Two pails — 3
Two pitchers — 3
Nil — 1, 7

Angus
Dracht — 27, 35
Fracht — 5a, 10, 14cd, 20, 23, 29b
Fract — 13
Fraucht — 1, 8, 22, 31
Fraught — 7, 13
Gine — 29b
Ging — 14c, 20, 34
Rake — 10
Swingle tree — 17a
Two buckets — 26
Two pails — 34
Two panfu — 24, 28
Twosum — 33b
Yoke — 2, 17b
Nil — 3-4, 5bc, 6, 9, 11-12, 14ab, 15-16, 18-19, 21, 25, 29a, 30, 32, 33a, 36-37

Perth
Double rake — 29a
Fracht — 16-17, 26, 28, 31
Fraucht — 11, 29a, 39, 52c, 65
Fraught — 7, 21, 45
Gang — 44-47, 55, 62, 68
Gine — 59
Ging — 31
Gird — 66
Load — 52d
Race — 25, 45-46, 65
Rake — 66, 68
Stoop — 20
Stoup(s) — 41b, 61, 71
Stowps — 71
Stroup — 41a
Two buckets — 5, 67
Two can — 52c
Two pailfuls — 4, 52b
Two pails — 1, 50
Two stoops — 40
Yoke — 2a, 15, 25, 29b, 38, 53
Nil — 2b, 3, 6, 8-10, 12-14, 18-19, 22-24, 27, 30, 32-37, 42-43, 48-49, 51ab, 52ae, 54, 56-58, 60, 63-64, 69-70, 72-74

Fife
Brace(s) — 55e, 56
Fraucht — 27
Gallases — 36a, 37, 41a, 55e, 57, 60-61
Gang — 17, 51, 53
Gird — 60
Race — 4, 6, 8, 9ab, 10, 12-14, 18, 20-21, 23, 25, 27, 31-32, 34, 36a, 39, 40b, 43b, 46, 48, 50, 52, 56
Rake — 53-54
Reath — 12
Span — 44e
Stoop — 37
Stoup — 12, 40a, 49, 51, 55b, 61
Stoupts — 58
Stowp(s) — 19, 44b, 45
Trace — 22
Two pailfuls — 11, 24, 62
Two pails — 50
Two stowps — 50
Yawk — 37
Yoke — 1, 55ef
Nil — 2-3, 5, 7, 15-16, 26, 28-30, 33, 35, 36b, 38, 41bcd, 42, 43a, 44acdf, 47, 55acdg,

Fife cont'd

59, 63, 64ab

Clackmannan

Bal — 4d
Gang — 4a, 5
Rake — 1
Stoop — 3, 7
Stoup — 4d, 7
Two bucketsful — 4b
Nil — 2, 4c, 6

Stirling

Couple of pails — 4
Dracht — 26f
Fracht — 8
Galluses — 18-19, 25a
Gang — 6, 7bd, 23b, 30, 33
Gird — 25a
Pannier pails — 13
Rake — 2, 7a, 9, 12, 17, 20, 21ab, 22a, 25bc, 35ab, 37a, 39ab, 42a
Stoops — 36
Stoup(s) — 7b, 10-11, 23c, 26e, 36
Two buckets — 4
Two pailfuls — 23b
Two stoups — 21b, 26d, 31-32
Yang — 7b
Yock — 26b
Yoke — 7e, 8, 23b, 24, 25d, 27a, 31
Nil — 1, 3, 6, 7cf, 14-16, 22b, 23a, 26ac, 27b, 28-29, 34, 37b, 38, 40-41, 42b

Dunbarton

Gallus — 13a
Gang — 6, 7c, 16a
Rake — 2, 5, 7c, 10, 18
Two pailfuls — 6, 7b
Nil — 1, 3, 4ab, 7a, 8-9, 11-12; 13bc, 14ab, 15, 16b, 17

Argyll

Cans — 17
Couple of buckets — 29
Gang — 23, 27, 35
Lawt — 12
Luggies — 24
Pails — 1
Pitchers — 17, 33
Rake — 26, 35
Stoups — 33
Two pailfuls — 6, 12
Two pails — 11, 17
Yang — 26
Nil — 2-5, 7-10, 13-16, 18-22, 25, 28, 30-32, 34, 36-40

Bute

Galluses — 1a
Gang — 1e, 7, 8a
Rake — 3, 8a
Slipe — 2
Two pailfuls — 1a
Nil — 1bcd, 4-6, 8b, 9

Ayr

Brace of stoups — 15
Gallon — 48
Gang — 8a, 13, 23, 24b, 35b, 36, 42, 49
Rake — 13, 19, 27, 28f, 30ab, 33-34, 35b, 36, 38, 40, 42, 46, 49, 52
Stoup and bearises — 20g
Stoup(s) — 1a, 2a, 10, 30b, 41, 45, 54, 56
Stowps — 9, 18b, 50
Two buckets — 43
Two pailfuls — 20g
Two pitchers — 1a
Two stoups — 47
Yoke — 2b, 8b, 20h, 28e
Nil — 1b, 3-7, 11, 12ab, 14, 16ab, 17, 18a, 20abcdef, 21-22, 24a, 25, 26abc, 28abcd, 29, 31-32, 35a, 37, 39, 44, 51, 53ab, 55, 57

Renfrew

Couple of buckets — 2g, 5
Gang — 2g, 12a, 17
Rake — 2e, 11e, 17, 21
Stoop — 11k
Stoups — 1b, 4d, 7-8, 11bj
Two pailfuls — 2a, 16b
Two pails — 11e
Two stoupfuls — 11f
Two stoups — 4ac
Yoke — 2h, 15, 16a, 20b
Nil — 1a, 2bcdfij, 3, 4be, 6, 9-10, 11acdghil, 12b, 13abcd, 14ab, 16cd, 18ab, 19, 20a

Lanark

Brace of stoups — 9b
Braces — 38e
Gallus(es) — 5, 11, 32d, 33b, 37, 52ab
Galluses and stoups — 15a
Gang — 30, 46c
Gird — 38d
Rake — 2-3, 9ab, 12-13, 15b, 17-18, 20, 23, 27ab, 29afg, 30, 32d, 33d, 35b, 36, 38a, 39-40, 42, 44, 46ab, 47-48, 49b, 50, 52a, 56, 57ac, 59a, 61, 63, 64ab, 65, 67a
Ring — 52b
Stoots — 7a
Stoup(s) — 6, 22, 29e, 31c, 32cf, 33b, 38b, 41, 43, 57b
Trestle — 38d
Two pailfuls — 16b, 59b
Two pails — 16b
Two stoups — 33cd
Yoke — 7c, 29df, 31b, 38c
Yoke and stoups — 15a
Nil — 1, 4, 7b, 8ab, 10ab, 14abd, 15c, 16a, 19, 21, 24, 25abcd, 26ab, 28, 29c, 31ad, 32abe, 33a, 34, 35acd, 45, 49a, 51, 53-55, 58, 60, 62, 66, 67b

West Lothian

Gallus(es) — 19a, 20b
Rake — 1abcd, 2-4, 6-8, 9b, 10-11, 16, 17a, 19b, 20a, 21a, 22
Stoup — 5
Two pails — 18
Yoke — 11, 13
Nil — 9a, 12, 14-15, 17b, 21b

Midlothian

Couple of buckets — 19
Galluses — 17
Girr — 23a
Gulluses — 23b
Load — 23a
Rake — 11, 14b, 16, 20, 23a, 24, 26b, 27, 29-30
Stoop — 14a
Stoup — 12ab, 25d
Two pails — 1
Yoke — 6a, 11, 25c
Nil — 2-5, 6b, 7ab, 8ab, 9-10, 13, 15, 18, 21-22, 25ab, 26a, 28, 31-32

East Lothian

Rake — 4a, 6ab, 7, 10-11, 14-15, 17
Two pailfuls — 1, 4b, 8
Yoke — 2
Yoker — 21
Nil — 3, 5, 9, 12-13, 16, 18-20

Berwick

Burthen — 27
Gird — 8, 15, 22-23
Nake — 5
Rake — 1, 3, 13, 16a, 18-19, 21, 28, 31-32
Two pailfuls — 16b
Yoke — 23
Nil — 2, 4, 6-7, 9-12, 14, 16c, 17, 20, 24-26, 29-30

Peebles

Buckets — 2
Gang — 2
Rake — 7
Stoops — 10
Two pailfuls — 1
Yoking — 6a
Nil — 3, 4abc, 5, 6b, 8-9

Selkirk

Heck — 2e
Rake — 2a, 8
Nil — 1, 2bcd, 3-7

Roxburgh

Gird — 7
Girnel — 13
Rake — 4, 9a, 10, 17, 28
Two pailfuls — 1, 21f
Yoke — 3a, 25
Yokin — 2
Nil — 3b, 5-6, 8, 9b, 11-12, 14, 15ab, 16, 18-20, 21abcde, 22-24, 26-27

Dumfries

Buckets — 13
Hoop — 45b
Hoopie — 29
Rack — 48
Rake — 2, 7, 12, 28, 32, 42
Reck — 16
Two buckets — 30, 31d, 40
Two canfuls — 18-19
Two pails — 29
Two pail stoups — 1a
Yokel — 29
Nil — 1b, 3-6, 8ab, 9-11, 14-15, 17ab, 20, 21ab, 22-27, 31abcef, 33-39, 41, 43-44, 45a, 46-47, 49

Kirkcudbright

Gang — 1, 17
Rake — 2-3, 5, 7, 12b, 15ab, 17, 20
Reck — 12a
Stoups — 21c
Two buckets — 26
Two canfuls — 4
Two cans — 10, 18
Yoke — 12a, 14, 24
Yokin — 15a
Nil — 6, 8-9, 11, 13, 16, 19, 21ab, 22-23, 25, 27

Wigtown

Couple of cans — 2
Fraught — 5a
Gang — 5a, 6, 8, 17
Rake — 7, 11-12, 16
Stretch — 7
Nil — 1, 3-4, 5b, 9-10, 13-15, 18

Northumberland

Couple of pailfuls — 83
Couple of pails — 31, 111b, 126c
Couple pailfuls — 42
Couplin(g) — 69ab
Frame — 20b
Gaird — 26, 33b, 34a, 37, 138
Garedle — 142
Gird — 24a, 41a, 60, 77, 89, 108a, 114, 118b
Girdle — 12, 108c
Girth — 108a
Gite — 117
Gord — 59d, 62g, 64a, 120c
Gorth — 120c
Guard — 53b, 56, 59c, 81
Hoop — 59c
Pailsful — 46
Pair — 83
Pannier — 69b
Rails — 57
Rake — 1a, 2ab, 3-5, 9-11, 15-17, 19ab, 25, 27, 39, 45, 47, 50, 53a, 54, 57, 59b, 62ac, 67-68, 69g, 71ad, 72b, 73, 76, 78-79, 94b, 104a, 109, 116-117, 134
Scale — 64b
Skeel — 38, 64b, 69ab, 115
Square — 52, 55, 59c, 69ce, 81
Two bucketfuls — 56, 110
Two buckets — 130c
Two pailfuls — 30, 40a, 59b, 109, 137
Two pails — 6-7, 13, 41d, 78
Yoke — 22, 32, 33b, 41a, 52, 72i, 74, 77, 89, 100, 122b, 134-135
Nil — 1bc, 8, 14, 18, 20a, 21, 23, 24b, 28, 29abcdef, 33a, 34b, 35-36, 40b, 41bc, 43-44, 48-49, 51, 58, 59aef, 61, 62bdefh, 63, 65ab, 66, 69dfh, 70, 71bce, 72acdefghjkl, 75, 80, 82, 84-87, 88ab, 90-93, 94a, 95ab, 96-98, 99abcd, 101ab, 102, 103abc, 104b, 105-107, 108b, 111a, 112-113, 118a, 119, 120ab, 121, 122a, 123, 124ab, 125, 126abdef, 127abcdefgh, 128, 129abc, 130abdef, 131-133, 136, 139-141, 143

Cumberland

Buckets — 54
Couple of buckets — 48
Rake — 3, 5a, 11, 13a, 15bc, 18, 28, 33
Two bookets — 41
Two booketsful — 41
Two buckets — 4, 12, 57, 59
Two bucketsful — 19, 23, 50
Yoke — 16, 42, 46-47, 60
Nil — 1ab, 2, 5b, 6-10, 13bcd, 14, 15a, 17, 20-22, 24-27, 29-32, 34-36, 37ab, 38-40, 43-45, 49, 51-53, 55-56, 58, 61-62, 63ab

Down

Couple of bucketfuls — 2a
Go — 2a, 3, 5, 8, 10, 13-14, 17, 21, 24, 27, 29
Two pailfuls — 7, 19
Nil — 1, 2b, 4, 6, 9, 11-12, 15-16, 18, 20, 22-23, 25-26, 28, 30

Tyrone

Go — 1-5, 7-10, 14-16
Goin — 13
Gopen — 1
Hoopin — 11
Rake — 16
Nil — 6, 12

Antrim

Brace — 34
Draw — 11
Go — 1-2, 4, 5a, 6-7, 8a, 10-13, 15, 16ab, 17, 19, 21, 24-25, 27-28, 30, 34
Pull — 11
Yoke — 4A, 34
Nil — 3, 5b, 8b, 9, 14, 16c, 18, 20, 22-23, 26, 29, 31-33

Donegal

Go — 1A, 3, 5A, 6-7, 7A, 8, 10ab, 11
Two pailfuls — 12
Nil — 1-2, 4-5, 9, 13

Fermanagh

Couple of buckets — 8
Go — 1-2, 4-5
Two buckets — 8

Fermanagh cont'd

Nil — 3, 6, 7ab, 9-10

Armagh

Couple of buckets — 4
Go — 1-2, 5, 6b
Two buckets — 4
Nil — 3, 6a

Londonderry

Go — 1, 1AB, 3, 3A, 4-7
Two buckets — 2

18 PORRIDGE BOWL (PQ1, 71)

Porridge bowl has not been mapped as it occurs nearly everywhere in some degree of concentration except in Shetland. Some of the other items mapped do not appear in high concentrations.
For the variants of BOWL , see map 6, Appendix A. The variants of the stressed vowel and the final consonant cluster of PORRIDGE are shown on map 5, Appendix A. (Variants with different central consonants (**poddish, pottage**) are retained in the list.) For **cog, cog(g)ie,** see also 16 **pail.**

Shetland

Cap — 15, 21a, 26, 29
Gruel bowl — 1-2, 5-6, 13-14, 16, 18, 31-33
Gruellie bowl — 19, 22
Gruel plate — 17
Gruel truncher — 10
(Porridge) bowl — *2,* 15, 25, 27
Porridge plate — 17, 30
Porringer — 23
Nil — 3-4, 7-9, 11-12, 20, 21b, 24, 28

Orkney

Bummie — 12
Cap — 15, 18
Caup — 7
Cog — 7
Grole bowl — 2-3
Gruel bowl — 13a
Gruel cog — 13a
(Porridge) bowl — *1, 4-6, 8-9, 11,* 13ab, *15-17,* 19
Nil — 10, 14, 20-21

Caithness

Bowlie — 7, 12a, 16a
Brose bowl — 13
Cougie — 12b, 15
(Porridge) bowl — *2ab,* 4, 8, *9-11, 14, 16b*
Porridge plate — 13
Nil — 1, 3, 5-6, 12c, 17

Sutherland

Bowlie — 15
Breakfast bowl — 3
(Porridge) bowl — 1, 3, 5, *6-8, 9ab, 10,* 11, *12*-13, 15
Porringer plate — 3
Nil — 2, 4, 14, 16-17

Ross & Cromarty

Bowlie — 19, 25b, 26, 37b
(Porridge) bowl — *1, 3*-4, *5-6, 8-9,* 14, 16-17, *18*-19, 22-23, *24,* 25a, 26, *27-29, 31,* 34, *39*
Porridge bowlack — 31
Porridge plate — 36
Porringer — 29, 32a
Nil — 2, 7, 10-13, 15, 20-21, 30, 32bc, 33, 35, 37a, 38

Inverness

Bowlie — 13c
Caup — 26
Cogie — 26
Cuach — 26
(Porridge) bowl — *1-3,* 4, *5-6, 8, 10*-11, 13*bce,* 15, 18, 21ab, *22-23, 29, 32*-33, 35-36, *38-39*
(Porridge) plate — *13a,* 40
Porringer — 20, 21a, 37
Nil — 7, 9, 12, 13d, 14, 16-17, 19, 24-25, 27-28, 30-31, 34

Nairn

(Porridge) bowl — 1ac, *5-6*
Porringer — 1b, 2
Nil — 3-4

Moray

Bowlack — 8e
Bowlie — 3, 8be, 9a, 14, 18
Brose cap — 7, 11
Cap — 13, 21
Cappie — 3-4, 18-20, 22
Caup — 1, 6ab, 8bd, 9a
Coggie — 8a, 9a
(Porridge) bowl — 2a, 8*b*cd, 10-11, 14, 16, 23
Porringer — 2b, 21
Timmer bowlie — 8b
Nil — 5, 8f, 9b, 12, 15, 17

Banff

Bowlie — 2b
Brose bowl — 5
Brose cap — 5, 22, 25
(Porridge) bowl — 1, 2a, 6b, *9, 15,* 17, 18c, *19,* 21, 23-*24,* 31, *34*
(Porridge) cap — 3-4, 9-10, 17, 18d, *26,* 31
(Porridge) caup — 2c, 6b, 7-8, 11, 13-*14,* 16, 18c, 27-30, 32-33
Porringer — 2b
Timmer cap — 20
Nil — 6a, 12, 18ab

Aberdeen

Bicker — 73
Boolie — 90
Bossie — 27
Bowlie — 10, 21, 28b, 47bd, 60, 78, 83
Brose bowl — 8, 106
Brose cap — 2, 6, 22, 32, 47c, 49, 85, 103, 106
Brose caup — 3a, 9, 57, 64, 71c, 72, 78, 80, 82, 93, 104, 107
Cap — 2, 5b, 7, 9, 13, 15, 26, 31, 41, 44-45, 47a, 54, 58, 63, 67, 69, 100
Cappie — 24, 47b, 67, 81
Caup — 4, 5ad, 9, 11, 17, 19-20, 23, 25, 27, 28bc, 30, 34, 36, 42, 46, 47e, 48, 55-56, 60, 62, 68, 71a, 76-79, 84, 88, 92, 95, 97, 105, 109
Coggie — 11
Luggie — 61
Plate — 53, 106
(Porridge) bowl — 1, 6, 8, 12, 17, 20, 28a, 29, *35,* 38, 46, 50, *59,* 71c, 73, *94,* 98, 101, 104-*105,* 108
Porridge plate — 100
Porringer — 23, 70, 71c
Pottage bowl — 3b, 21, 26, 40, 47f, 65, 75
Pottage cap — 26
Nil — 5c, 14, 16, 18, 33, 37, 39, 43, 51-52, 66, 71b, 74, 86-87, 89, 91, 96, 99, 102

Kincardine

Bowlie — 7, 10, 17c
Brose bowl — 3, 26
Brose cap — 3, 7, 13, 15, 18, 20, 23, 27
Brose caup — 12, 22
Caup — 2, 17b, 25
(Porridge) bowl — 1, *6,* 8, *16,* 17bc, 19, *21,* 24
(Porridge) cap — *7,* 9-10, 14, 17c, 23, 28
Nil — 4-5, 11, 17ad

Kinross

Cog — 2-3
Kep — 1
Luggie — 5, 7
(Porridge) bowl — *1,* 3, *6*
(Porridge) cap — 2-3, *4*

Angus

Brose cap — 7-9, 11, 20, 25, 34, 36
Caup — 1, 5bc, 10, 13, 14acd, 17ab, 21, 31-32, 33b, 37
Caupie — 14d
Coggie — 19, 33b, 37
Cogie — 32
(Porridge) bowl — *2, 8,* 10, 12, 15, 17b, 18, 24-*25, 28,* 29b, 30, 32, 33b, *34*
(Porridge) cap — 5a, 6, 12, 14b, 15, 22-23, 27-*28,* 29ab, 30, 33a, 35
Porridge keppie — 4
Porridger — 18
Pottinger — 3
Nil — 16, 26

Perth

Brochan bowl — 67
Brose cap — 5, 13, 26, 33, 44, 49, 64
Brose cup — 17
Cap — 1, 16, 21-23, 25, 31, 42, 46, 60, 64
Cappie — 29b, 54-55
Caup — 20, 27, 32, 39, 45, 50, 52cd, 56-57, 62, 65-66
Caupie — 27
Coag — 51b, 70
Cog — 18, 41b
Coggie — 1, 11, 40, 41b, 44-46, 51be, 52e, 56, 65-66
Cogie — 8, 12, 14, 24, 37, 41a, 52bd, 53, 62
Coppie — 53
Kep — 20, 48
Luggie — 61, 71
Mealie brose — 72
(Porridge) bowl — *2a, 4,* 7, *8-10, 13, 15*-16, *20,* 24-27, 29a, *32, 36, 46, 52abc,* 57, *59, 67-69,* 74
Porringer — 2a, 17, 41a, 42-43, 61, 68, 73
Quaigh — 3
Wooden coggie — 55
Nil — 2b, 6, 19, 28, 30, 34-35, 38, 47, 51a, 58, 63

Fife

Bicker — 27
Brose bowl — 49
Brose cap — 2, 14, 25, 30, 48
Brose caup — 2, 6
Cap — 1, 3, 5, 7, 9b, 10, 12, 21, 26, 31, 35, 38, 44a, 48, 53, 55b, 61, 64b
Caup — 7, 18, 21, 23, 27, 51-52, 55f
Coag — 55b, 64a
Cog — 4, 17, 23, 51, 64b
Coggie — 11, 18, 23, 40b, 43ab, 44a, 49, 53, 55df, 58-59, 61
Cogie — 8, 12-13, 29, 36a, 44be, 55g, 64a
Coogie — 33
Cougie — 49
Cowg — 50
Logie — 45
Luggie — 37, 39, 44f, 47, 50, 55dg, 56-57
(Porridge) bowl — 6-8, *9a, 11,* 13-*14, 16, 19*-20, *22, 24, 28, 34, 37, 39,* 41abc, 43a, *44ce, 46*-47, *49-50, 52, 55abf, 56*-57, 59, *61-62,* 63
(Porridge) cappie — 10, 12, *32,* 36b, 40b, 44df, 64a
(Porridge) plate — *42,* 55d
Porringer — 9a, 21, 37, 39, 53-54, 55bde, 63
Quaich — 12
Nil — 15, 40a, 41d, 55c, 60

Clackmannan

Coggie — 1, 4b
Porridge bowl — 1-2, 4cd, 5-6
Porridge coag — 2
(Porridge) luggie — *3,* 4a, 7
Porringer — 4c
Stoup — 4b

Stirling

Bicker — 22a
Bowlie — 25a
Cappie — 9
Cog — 3, 10, 21b
Coggie — 21b, 26d, 27a, 38
Cogie — 6, 7e, 26e, 32
Luggie — 7abd, 9, 18, 20, 27a
(Porridge) bowl — 7*ace, 8-9,* 11-12, *13,* 15-18, 21ab, *22b, 23abc,* 25acd, *26acd, 27a, 28,* 30-*31,* 34, *36,* 37a, 39b, 42a
Porringer — 4, 10, 24, 25ab, 27a, 35a, 39a, 40
Nil — 1-2, 5, 7f, 14, 19, 26bf, 27b, 29, 33, 35b, 37b, 41, 42b

Dunbarton

Cog — 14a
Coggie — 2, 14a, 16a, 17
Cogie — 1, 5
Luggie — 16a, 17
(Porridge) bowl — *1-3,* 6, *7bc,* 10, 13*abc,* 16b
Porringer — 4b, 7a, 9, 14b
Nil — 4a, 8, 11-12, 15, 18

Argyll

Basin — 34
Brochan bowl — 40
Brose bowl — 37
Cap — 35
Caup — 35
Cogie — 35
(Porridge) bowl — *1-3, 6-7, 10,* 11,

Argyll cont'd

12, 14, 15, *16-19,* 22-24, *27, 29*-30, *33, 35, 38-39*
Porridge dish — 6
Porringer — 3-4, 9, 33
Nil — 5, 8, 13, 20-21, 25-26, 28, 31-32, 36

Bute

Cap — 8b
Coggie — 1a
(Porridge) bowl — 1a, 2, 4, 7, *8a, 9*
Porringer — 1b, 6
Nil — 1cde, 3, 5

Ayr

Dish of porridge — 38
Coag — 28d
Cog — 2b, 13, 24b, 48, 57
Coggie — 1a, 7, 8b, 20h, 28b, 35b, 49, 57
Cogie — 20g
Luggie — 19
Nappie — 19
Platter — 41
(Porridge) bowl — 2a*b, 3, 5*-6, *8b, 10-11, 12a, 13-15, 16a,* 20cg*h,* 21, *23, 24b, 25, 26a,* 28ace, *29, 30ab, 31-34, 35ab, 36,* 38, *41-42,* 43, *44, 46-48,* 49, *51-52, 53ab,* 54-55, *57*
Porridge pat — 19
Porridge plate — 2b
Porringer — 1a, 15, 18b, 22, 28e, 56-57
Punch bowl — 28f
Quaich — 16b
Wallie bowl — 41
Nil — 1b, 4, 8a, 9, 12b, 17, 18a, 20abdef, 24a, 26bc, 27, 37, 39-40, 45, 50

Renfrew

Basin — 16a
Cog — 12a, 21
Coggie — 11j, 21
Coggle — 15
Cogie — 5, 16d
Luggie — 4d, 12a, 15, 16a, 17
Porridge — 2j
(Porridge) bowl — 1ab, 2agh*i*, 4a*c*de, 5, *7-8,* 11a*bdefhikl,* 13ac, *14a,* 15, *16bd, 17,* 18ab, 20a*b*
Porringer — 2be, 3, 11d
Skillie — 18a
Nil — 2cdf, 4b, 6, 9-10, 11cg, 12b, 13bd, 14b, 16c, 19

Lanark

Backie — 32d, 38e
Basin — 6, 29f
Bicker — 17, 39, 46c, 64b
Bowie — 42
Cappie — 56
Caup — 1, 38a, 43
Cog — 9b, 50
Cogie — 30, 38d, 49b, 57a
Cootie — 8a
Luggie — 8b, 14c, 18, 27b, 30, 32f, 34, 35d, 46c, 47-48, 52a, 57ab, 67a
Plate of porridge — 25c
(Porridge) bowl — *2, 5-6,* 7ac, 8a, *9a, 11-13,* 14d, 15a, 16a*b,* 17-18, *20, 22,* 25b*c, 26a,* 27b, 29cdef, *30,* 31ad, *32e, 33cd,* 35bc*d,* 36-*37,* 38c, *39-40, 44-45, 46ab,* 49ab, *51, 53,* 57a, *58, 59b,* 60, *62,* 64a*b,* 65
(Porridge) coggie — 9b, *15a,* 29g, 32d, 47, 57c, 65
Porridgie — 3, 10a, 33a
Porringer — 1, 3-4, 7c, 12, 15c, 17, 22, 32bf, 36, 44, 67a
Skillet — 29f

Nil — 7b, 10b, 14ab, 15b, 19, 21, 23-24, 25ad, 26b, 27a, 28, 29ab, 31bc, 32ac, 33b, 35a, 38b, 41, 52b, 54-55, 59a, 61, 63, 66, 67b

West Lothian

Bicker — 9a, 16
Coggie — 1a, 4, 6-7, 19a
Cogie — 11
Keggie — 10
Luggie — 1d, 5-6, 8, 9b, 18, 19b
(Porridge) bowl — *3, 9a,* 11-13, *15*-16, *17ab, 18,* 20a, 22
Porridge cog — 1c
Porringer — 2, 4, 8, 16
Nil — 1b, 14, 20b, 21ab

Midlothian

Bicker — 8b, 20, 22, 24, 30-31
Caup — 14b
Coggie — 6b, 7b, 10, 12a, 22, 26ab, 32
Cogie — 13
Luggie — 1, 4, 7b, 14b, 17, 22, 26a
Porridge basin — 9
(Porridge) bowl — *1, 3,* 6a*b,* 7a, *8a, 10-11,* 12ab, *14ab, 15*-16, 18-19, 23ab, 25ac, *28-29*
Porridge plate — 2, 21
Porringer — 17, 22, 24, 25d, 27
Stoup — 11
Nil — 5, 25b

East Lothian

Bakie — 3
Bicker — 2, 4b, 6a, 8, 11-17, 20
Biggie — 2
Caup — 4a, 10
Coggie — 4a, 6a, 8, 13
Cogie — 10
Luggie — 4a, 6ab, 7, 13
(Porridge) bowl — *1,* 4b, 5, 6b, 7, *9,* 16, 19, *21*
Porringer — 9, 13
Stoup — 4a
Nil — 18

Berwick

Basin — 9
Bicker — 3-6, 10, 14-15, 16a, 18, 21, 23-27, 30-32
Bowie — 6, 17, 23
Brose bowl — 8
Coggie — 7-8, 17
(Porridge) bowl — *1, 8,* 9, *10-13, 16bc, 20, 27,* 29, *32*
Porringer — 2, 23, 28, 31
Nil — 19, 22

Peebles

Bicker — 6a, 10
Coggie — 6a, 8, 10
Cogie — 5
Luggie — 4a, 10
Plate — 6a
(Porridge) bowl — *1-2,* 3, *4bc,* 6a*b, 7, 9*
(Porridge) cog — *2,* 6a
Porringer — 4c

Selkirk

Bakie — 1
Bicker — 2d, 4, 7
Cap — 2a
Caup — 8
Cog — 2a
(Porridge) bowl — 2abc*e, 8*
Nil — 3, 5-6

Roxburgh

Backie — 21ac
Bicker — 1-2, 3a, 4, 6-7, 9b, 10, 13, 16-17, 22, 24, 28
Bowie — 9b, 17, 21c, 26
Coggie — 2, 17

Cogie — 10
Crib — 21c
Luggie — 15a
(Porridge) bowl — 1-*2, 4,* 5, *6, 8, 13, 15b, 17, 21f, 25,* 27-*28*
Porringer — 9a, 21a
Nil — 3b, 11-12, 14, 18-20, 21bde, 23

Dumfries

Basin — 47
Bicker — 17ab, 28-29, 42
Broos bowl — 37
Cogie — 2, 31b, 37
(Porridge) bowl — *1a,* 2, 4-*5,* 7, *8b,* 12, 15-*16,* 17b, *18,* 19-20, 21b, 22, 24, *26,* 28, 30, *31def, 37,* 39-40, *45ab, 46*
Porringer — 6, 12-13, 23, 29, 35
Nil — 1b, 3, 8a, 9-11, 14, 21a, 25, 27, 31ac, 32-34, 36, 38, 41, 43-44, 48-49

Kirkcudbright

Coggie — 11, 17, 24
Cogie — 1, 12b
(Porridge) bowl — *1-2, 4-7, 9,* 10-11, 14, *15a,* 16, 18-*19,* 21c, 22-23, 26-*27*
Porringer — 12b, 15a, 21a
Nil — 3, 8, 12a, 13, 15b, 20, 21b, 25

Wigtown

Bicker — 5b
Cog — 5ab
Coggie — 5a, 10
Cogie — 17
(Porridge) bowl — 1, *2-3, 5a, 6,* 7-8, *11,* 12, *13-17*
Porringer — 17
Nil — 4, 9, 18

Northumberland

Beeasin — 42, 132
Beersin — 142
Bicker — 29af, 38
Bowlie — 17
Croodie bowl — 62h
Crowder — 9
Crowdie basin — 62h, 71b, 104b
Crowdie beasin — 135
Crowdie bowl — 39, 71d, 81
Crowdie dish — 39, 124a
Crowdie pot — 130c
Hollow plate — 69a
Luggie — 124a
Platter — 20b, 110
Platter bowl — 89
Porridge — 1b
(Porridge) basin — *7, 13,* 16, 19a, *21,* 23, 24b, 26, 29e, 34ab, 36, 38, *41d, 45,* 46-47, 53b, 54, 56-57, 59c, 62a, 65a, 69c*h,* 71d, *72cdg,* 76, 78, 83-84, *85*-86, 88a*b,* 94b, *98,* 99bd, 104a, *109,* 111a*b, 112,* 118a, 125, 126a, 127bc, 129b, 130*bc,* 132-133, *136*
(Porridge) bowl — *2b,* 8, 19a, *28, 29bd,* 30, *34a,* 46, 52, 59b*d, 64a, 69d, 89, 99b, 100, 102, 103c, 106-107, 109, 120a, 124b, 126f,* 130f
(Porridge) dish — *64b, 71c,* 83, *87, 90,* 118b, 130e, *138*
Porridge pan — 77
(Porridge) plate — 24a, 38, *40a, 62g, 64b, 69be,* 82, *90, 103a,* 130e, *143*
Porringer — 1ac, 2b, 10, 14, 16, 19b, 22, 28, 31, 33a, 37, 40b, 41ac, 44-45, 47-49, 52, 59bc, 60-61, 68, 69ab, 71c, 72bc, 75, 77, 79, 84, 86, 106, 108a, 120c, 122ab, 126be, 127bde, 131, 134
Porringer basin — 7, 59b
Soup plate — 87

Nil — 2a, 3-6, 11-12, 15, 18, 20a, 25, 27, 29c, 32, 33b, 35, 41b, 43, 50-51, 53a, 55, 58, 59aef, 62bcdef, 63, 65b, 66-67, 69fg, 70, 71ae, 72aefhijkl, 73-74, 80, 91-93, 94a, 95ab, 96-97, 99ac, 101ab, 103b, 105, 108bc, 113-117, 119, 120b, 121, 123, 126cd, 127afgh, 128, 129ac, 130ad, 137, 139-141

Cumberland

Beasin — 2
Crowdie beasin — 6
Hannie — 30
Piggin — 30-31
Plate — 14
Platter — 42
Poddish basin — 1a, 13d, 15ac, 16-18, 24-26, 28, 32, 40-41, 49, 52, 57, 59-60, 62
Poddish bassin — 56
Poddish bowl — 5a, 7-9, 12, 13a, 22, 31, 38, 40, 46-47, 56, 58
Poddish dish — 11, 37b, 45, 61
Poddish plate — 28
(Porridge) basin — 2-3, 14, *18-19,* 20, 23, *24-25,* 33, 36, 40, *44, 46, 50*-51, 53, *57, 60*-61
(Porridge) bowl — *1a,* 2, *7, 13c, 24, 48, 54*
Porringer — 4, 38, 47, 57
Porrin — 21
Nil — 1b, 5b, 10, 13b, 15b, 27, 29, 34-35, 37a, 39, 43, 55, 63ab

Down

Bicker — 13
Bowl — 5, 15, 18, 23, 26
Cap — 2a
Noggin — 23
(Porridge) bowl — *2a,* 5-6, *7, 9, 11, 13,* 15, 17-18, *19,* 21, 23-24, 26
Nil — 1, 2b, 3-4, 8, 10, 12, 14, 16, 20, 22, 25, 27-30

Tyrone

Brochen bowl — 1-2
Noggin — 3, 5
(Porridge) bowl — *1,* 5, 7-10, 14
Porridge dish — 11
Porringer — 5, 11, 14, 16
Nil — 4, 6, 12-13, 15

Antrim

Brochen bowl — 8a
Brose bowl — 8b
Noggin — 5a, 16b, 30
Piggin — 16b
(Porridge) bowl — 1-2, *5ab,* 7, 9, 12-13, 15, *17,* 18, *19-20,* 21, *22, 25-26,* 28-29
Porringer — 11, 13, 21
Stirabout bowl — 17
Nil — 1A, 3-4, 6, 10, 14, 16ac, 23-24, 27, 31-34

Donegal

Bowl — 5A, 12
Brachan dish — 6
Brochan bowl — 1, 4
Brohan bowl — 8
Brohan dish — 8
Dish — 5, 5A
Stirabout dish — 6, 8
Nil — 1A, 2-3, 7, 7A, 9, 10ab, 11, 13

Fermanagh

Bowl — 2, 4-6, 9
Stir about bowl — 1
Nil — 3, 7ab, 8, 10

Armagh

(Porridge) bowl — *3,* 4, 6a

Armagh cont'd

Stir about bowl — 1
Nil — 2, 5, 6b

Londonderry

Bowl — 2
Braughan bowl — 6
Brochan bowl — 1A
Broughen bowl — 1
Porringer — 5
Nil — 1B, 3, 3A, 4, 7

19 PORRIDGE STICK (PQ1, 72)

For variants of PORRIDGE, see map 5, Appendix A, and note on PORRIDGE in 18 **porridge bowl.** Variants of the unstressed vowel before final '-l' in **theevIl, theedIl,** have been subsumed (**-el, -al,** etc.).

Shetland

Gruel tree — 1-10, 12-20, 21ab, 22-33
Sportle — 26
Spurtle — 3, 10-11

Orkney

Groll tree — 5
Groal tree — 6
Gruel tree — 12, 13a
Porridge stick — 8-9, 11, 13ab, 15, 17, 19
Porridge tree — 5, 19, 21
Pot tree — 1-4, 7, 12
Spirtle — 14
Spurtle — 10, 15-16
Nil — 18, 20

Caithness

Chapper — 2b
Porridge spindle — 13
Porridge stick — 2ab, 7, 9-11, 12c, 14, 16b
Porridger — 12a
Spirtle — 8, 12c
Spurtle — 5-7, 12b, 15, 16a
Nil — 1, 3-4, 17

Sutherland

Porridge stick — 4, 6-7, 10
Pot stick — 3
Spirtle — 5-7, 9b, 13
Spurtle — 1-3, 8, 9a, 10-12, 14-17

Ross & Cromarty

Keltrie — 37ab
Porridge stick — 1, 4-6, 9, 24, 39
Spindle — 19
Spirtle — 3, 5, 11, 13-14, 17-18, 20-22, 26-28, 31, 35, 37b, 38-39
Spurtle — 7-10, 12, 15-16, 19, 23-24, 25ab, 29-30, 32abc, 33-34, 36
Nil — 2

Inverness

Porridge stick — 2-6, 13e, 23, 36
Spirkle — 13a
Spirtle — 3, 6-8, 10, 12, 13abe, 16, 19, 21a, 22-26, 28-29, 31, 33, 35
Spurkle — 27, 37
Spurtle — 9, 11, 13cd, 14-15, 17018, 20, 21b, 27, 30, 32, 34, 36, 38-40
Stirrer — 18
Nil — 1

Nairn

Spirtle — 2-3
Spurtle — 1abc, 4-6

Moray

Spirk — 18
Spirkle — 5, 20
Spirtle — 8a, 14, 20
Spurkle — 1, 2a, 3-4, 6a, 7, 8be, 10, 15-17, 19, 22
Spurtle — 2b, 4, 6b, 7, 8bcdf, 9ab, 11-13, 18, 21, 23
Steerer — 21
Theevle — 8d

Banff

Spirtle — 23
Spurkle — 1, 2ac, 3, 5, 6b, 7, 9-11, 13-14, 16, 18bcd, 21, 23-26, 29-30
Spurtle — 1, 2b, 3-4, 6ab, 8, 10-13, 15, 17, 18ac, 19-20, 22-24, 27-29, 31-34
Theevil — 11, 25

Aberdeen

Drootlin — 69
Spirtle — 92
Spurkle — 1, 5b, 8-9, 12, 14-15, 17-18, 21-24, 26-27, 28abc, 29-30, 32-35, 37, 39, 42, 45-46, 47af, 48, 51-53, 59, 62-64, 66, 72, 75, 77, 80, 82, 86, 91, 104-105
Spurtle — 2, 3ab, 4, 5acd, 6-7, 9-14, 16-17, 19-20, 24-25, 27, 28a, 30-34, 36, 38, 40-41, 44, 47bcde, 49-51, 53-58, 60-62, 64-65, 67-70, 71abc, 72-90, 93-109
Theevil — 14, 28a, 41, 64
Wooden spoon — 70
Nil — 43

Kincardine

Spurkle — 2
Spurtle — 1, 3-16, 17abcd, 18-20, 23-25, 27
Theevil — 3-4, 7, 12-13, 15, 17abcd, 18-19, 21-22, 24-28

Kinross

Spirtle — 3
Spurkle — 1-2, 7
Spurtle — 1, 6-7
Theedle — 2, 4-5, 7

Angus

Hadle — 28
Porridge stick — 17b, 18
Spirtle — 2, 5c, 8, 19, 30
Spurtle — 5b, 7, 14a, 17a, 18, 22-24, 29b, 32
Stirple — 5c
Theebil — 24
Theedil — 17b, 23, 27, 29a, 34-35, 37
Theevil — 1, 3-4, 5abc, 6, 8-13, 14abcd, 15-16, 17ab, 18-23, 25-26, 29b, 30-32, 33ab, 34, 36
Thevil — 2, 7

Perth

Porridge stick — 2a, 4, 8, 24, 57
Spindle — 20
Spirkle — 8, 56
Spirtle — 11, 13-14, 19, 21, 24-25, 39, 41b, 50, 52cd, 53, 57, 63, 67
Spurkle — 30, 69, 72
Spurtle — 1, 2b, 3, 5-6, 9-10, 12, 15-16, 18, 20, 23-26, 28, 29ab, 31-32, 34-38, 40, 41ab, 42, 44, 46-49, 51ab, 52abe, 53-55, 61-62, 66, 68-71, 73-74
Tamoy — 20
Theedil — 26
Theevil — 2a, 5-7, 11, 13, 15-18, 20-23, 25-28, 29a, 31-33, 39, 41a, 42-46, 49-50, 51b, 52acde, 53-55, 57-60, 62, 64-66
Thevil — 12, 29b, 30, 40, 47, 51a, 56
Threevil — 48

Fife

Porridge keel — 37
Porridge stick — 40b, 41a, 43a, 54, 55d
Spertle — 22
Spirkle — 52, 55abg
Spirtle — 5, 13-14, 18, 23, 28, 38, 41acd, 44a, 49, 53, 55abg, 62
Spurkle — 36a, 39, 41b, 53-54, 55bcdef, 56-61, 63
Spurtle — 1, 4, 7-8, 12, 19-21, 26-27, 29, 33, 35, 36b, 37, 39, 40ab, 41ad, 42, 43ab, 44acef, 45-52, 54, 55d, 63, 64a
Steck — 50
Thale — 45
Theedil — 3, 16, 20, 38-39, 40b, 43b, 44e, 55f, 60-61, 64b
Theel — 1-2, 4, 6-8, 9ab, 10-14, 16-21, 23-35, 40a, 41d, 42, 43a, 44abcdef, 45-50, 52, 55f, 56
Theetle — 43a
Theevil — 1, 3-5, 7, 11-12, 18, 23, 37, 43a, 52, 64b
Thevil — 2, 21
Nil — 15

Clackmannan

Spirkle — 3
Spurkle — 1, 4acd, 5-7
Spurtle — 2, 4bc, 5-6

Stirling

Gruel tree — 7d
Gruet tree — 7b
Pat stick — 23a
Porridge stick — 29
Pote stick — 23a
Spirkle — 2, 12, 38
Spirtle — 1, 7b, 11, 29, 37a, 38
Spurkle — 3, 6, 7c, 8-10, 16-18, 20, 21a, 22ab, 23bc, 24 25abcd, 26abcef, 27a, 28, 30-31, 33, 35a, 36, 37b, 39ab, 40, 42a
Spurtle — 3-6, 7abdef, 8-9, 12-15, 18, 21b, 22ab, 25acd, 26abde, 27b, 31-32, 34, 35b, 36, 37b, 39ab, 42ab
Swevel — 7e
Theedil — 10
Theevil — 6
Widden spin — 31
Nil — 19, 41

Dunbarton

Pot stick — 1, 18
Spirkle — 7a
Spirtle — 7a, 16b
Spurkle — 2, 4ab, 5, 7b, 9, 13ac, 16ab
Spurtle — 1-3, 4b, 6, 7c, 8, 10-12, 13abc, 14ab, 16ab, 17
Stir about — 18
Theivil — 15

Argyll

Porridge stick — 6, 17, 19, 30, 35
Porridge stirrer — 33
Pot stick — 14
Spirkle — 33
Spirtle — 2, 4, 8-9, 12-13, 15, 20-23, 32, 35, 40
Spurtle — 1, 3, 5, 7-8, 10-11, 14, 16, 18-19, 23-31, 34, 36-39

Bute

Spirtle — 6
Spurkle — 1ce, 4-5
Spurtle — 1abd, 2-3, 7, 8ab, 9
Theevil — 9

Ayr

Spirkle — 12b, 22, 48
Spirtle — 12b, 18b, 28d, 48, 57
Spurkle — 6-7, 8b, 15, 16b, 17, 18b, 20bgh, 23, 25, 26a, 27, 28bef, 31-32, 37, 40, 42-44, 57
Spurtle — 1ab, 2ab, 3-7, 8ab, 9-11, 12a, 13-15, 16ab, 17, 18ab, 19, 20abcdefg, 21, 24ab, 26abc, 28abce, 29, 30ab, 31, 33-34, 35ab, 36-39, 41-43, 45-47, 49-52, 53ab, 54-57

Renfrew

Poat stick — 11d
Porridge spoon — 2a
Pot stick — 2eij, 4e, 20a
Spirtle — 2g, 4ac, 14a
Spurkle — 1b, 2bfg, 8, 10, 11abcdefghjk, 13ac, 16cd, 17, 18b, 21
Spurtle — 1ab, 2abcdefhj, 3, 4bde, 5-9, 11abdefghikl, 12a, 13bcd, 14b, 15, 16abcd, 18ab, 19, 20ab, 21
Nil — 12b

Lanark

Porridge spin — 20
Porridge stick — 6, 14ad, 60
Pot stick — 7c, 15c, 29b, 35a, 38d
Spirkle — 13, 25d, 33a, 38c
Spirtle — 14c, 25cd, 29f, 32de, 38c, 45, 48, 55-56
Spurkle — 2-6, 7abc, 8a, 10b, 13, 14ab, 15abc, 16ab, 17-20, 23-24, 25abd, 26ab, 27ab, 28, 29ac, 30, 31ab, 32c, 33bcd, 35bcd, 36-37, 38ab, 39-41, 44-45, 46ac, 47, 49b, 50, 52b, 57c, 58, 59ab, 60, 62, 64ab
Spune — 32d
Spurtle — 1, 4-5, 7abc, 8ab, 9ab, 10ab, 11-12, 14cd, 15bc, 16b, 17, 21-22, 25ac, 26a, 29cdeg, 30, 31abcd, 32abdef, 33bd, 34, 35d, 37, 38de, 39, 42-43, 46bc, 48, 49a, 51, 52ab, 53-54, 57abc, 58, 61, 63, 65-66, 67ab
Theevil — 4
Thevil — 36

West Lothian

Porridge stick — 8, 13
Spirkle — 4, 9a
Spirtle — 1b, 3, 8, 19a, 20a
Spurkle — 1acd, 2-3, 5-7, 9b,

West Lothian cont'd
10-11, 17ab, 18, 19b, 20ab, 21a, 22
Spurtle — 12, 14-16, 20b, 22
Theel — 4
Theevil — 11
Nil — 21b

Midlothian

Porridge stick — 2, 8a, 12b, 15, 19, 23a, 29, 32
Spirkle — 24
Spirtle — 1, 6ab, 11, 24, 27-29
Spoon — 17
Spurkle — 10-11, 12b, 14b, 25b
Spurtle — 2-5, 7ab, 8b, 9-10, 12ab, 13, 14a, 15-18, 20-22, 23ab, 25abcd, 26ab, 30-31
Stirrie — 5

East Lothian

Pirtle — 14
Porridge stick — 1-2, 6b, 8-9, 15-16, 18
Spirkle — 4a
Spirtle — 4a, 5, 7, 10
Spurtle — 2-3, 4b, 6a, 7-8, 11-13, 15-19, 21
Steerer — 20

Berwick

Coggie stick — 8
Porridge stick — 1-3, 6, 8-10, 12, 16abc, 17-18, 21, 31-32
Spirkle — 15
Spirtle — 1, 8, 16a, 29
Spurkle — 8, 16c
Spurtle — 4-5, 7-8, 11-14, 17-18, 20-23, 25-28, 30, 32
Theedil — 17
Theevil — 21
Theevil stick — 20
Nil — 19, 24

Peebles

Porridge purdle — 4c
Porridge stick — 3, 4bc, 6ab
Spirkle — 4b
Spurkle — 7-8
Spurtle — 1-3, 4abc, 5, 6ab, 8-10

Selkirk

Porridge stick — 2bc, 8
Spirtle — 2d
Spurtle — 2abce, 3-5, 7
Theevil — 2a
Nil — 1, 6

Roxburgh

Kale stick — 28
Pintle — 12
Porridge stick — 1-2, 4, 6, 8, 10, 15b, 16-17, 21acf, 25
Spurkle — 26
Spurtle — 3ab, 4-5, 8, 9ab, 11, 13, 16, 19, 21a, 24, 26, 28
Nil — 7, 14, 15a, 18, 20, 21bde, 22-23, 27

Dumfries

Kale stick — 15, 18, 29, 37, 43, 45a, 48
Keel stick — 38, 44, 45b, 46
Porridge spin — 31d
Pot stick — 1a, 8b, 12, 17ab, 19-20, 21b, 24, 27-28, 31e, 32, 36, 40, 42
Spirkle — 47
Spirtle — 23, 25, 31bd
Spurtle — 1ab, 2-7, 8ab, 9-14, 16, 17ab, 19-20, 21a, 22, 26-30, 31acdef, 32-37, 41-42, 44, 46, 49
Theevil — 15, 46-47

Kirkcudbright

Porridge steerer — 1
Porridge stick — 9
Pot stick — 1, 3-4, 6-8, 10, 12ab, 14, 18, 20, 21ac, 22, 26
Spirtle — 16
Spurkle — 18, 26
Spurtle — 1-2, 4-9, 11, 12ab, 15ab, 17, 19, 21abc, 23-27
Nil — 13

Wigtown

Porridge tree — 5a
Pot stick — 2, 7, 17
Spurkle — 15
Spurtle — 1-4, 5ab, 6-18
Wudden spin — 14

Northumberland

Crowdie stick — 1c, 24b, 62h, 69b, 71b, 78, 111b, 130f, 135
Fivel — 28
Keel stick — 42, 132
Ladle — 14, 69a
Meal stick — 46
Plunger — 29c
Porridge pirtle — 124a
Porridge spoon — 2b, 13, 22
Porridge stick — 1a, 2b, 29b, 30, 40b, 41cd, 46, 52, 53b, 54, 56, 59b, 64a, 71c, 83, 104a, 106, 109, 111ab, 120a
Porridge storrer — 71c
Spirtle — 79, 124b, 134
Sportle — 26
Spurtle — 22, 41a, 62f, 111a, 127b
Stirrer — 94b
Thibel — 31, 39, 62a, 69ab, 110, 117, 138
Thievil — 114
Thiling stick — 9
Thi-oal — 38
Thivel (stick) — 2b, 7, *10, 15-16,* 17-18, *19a,* 20ab, 21, 25, 27, 33b, 34ab, 35-37, 39, 40b, 41ad, 43-45, 51, 53ab, 54, 57, 59bde, 60, 62g, 64b, 68, 72d, 73, 75, 77, 79, 81, 86, 102, 103abc, 104b, 105-107, 108a, 117, 124a, 127d, 132-133, 135, 138, 142-143
Thrivel (stick) — *8, 11,* 122b
Tivel — 28
Torner — 101b
Trivel — 122a
Wooden spoon — 68, 130c
Wooden stirring rod — 130c
Wood spoon — 40a, 69b
Wudden spune — 69b
Nil — 1b, 2a, 3-6, 12, 19b, 23, 24a, 29adef, 32, 33a, 41b, 47-50, 55, 58, 59acf, 61, 62bcde, 63, 65ab, 66-67, 69cdefgh, 70, 71ade, 72abcefghijkl, 74, 76, 80, 82, 84-85, 87, 88ab, 89-93, 94a, 95ab, 96-98, 99abcd, 100, 101a, 108bc, 112-113, 115-116, 118ab, 119, 120bc, 121, 123, 125, 126abcdef, 127acefgh, 128, 129abc, 130abde, 131, 136-137, 139-141

Cumberland

Crowdie stick — 6
Kail stick — 13b, 37a
Keel stick — 1b
Poddish spoon — 40, 56
Poddish stick — 13a, 26-27, 46, 56-58, 62
Poddish thivel — 9, 24, 40
Porridge spoon — 57
Porridge stick — 13c, 23-24, 27, 46, 50, 54
Thaval — 23
Thibel — 14, 59-61, 63ab
Thievel — 5a
Thivel — 1ab, 2-4, 5ab, 7-8, 10-12, 13abd, 14, 15abc, 16-22, 25-36, 37ab, 38-39, 41-49, 51-52, 54, 56, 60-61
Thrivel — 2, 53
Nil — 55

Down

Porridge stick — 2a, 7, 15
Pot stick — 2a, 3, 5, 8-11, 13-14, 17-19, 21-24, 26-29
Spurtle — 13
Nil — 1, 2b, 4, 6, 12, 16, 20, 25, 30

Tyrone

Beetle — 8
Pot stick — 1-3, 5-11, 13-16
Sturrer — 11
Sturrin stick — 11
Nil — 4, 12

Antrim

Beetle — 14
Porridge stick — 26, 28
Pot stick — 1-2, 4A, 5ab, 6-7, 8b, 9-13, 15, 16ab, 17, 19-21, 23-25, 27-31, 33-34
Spurtle — 16b
Stirrer — 15
Nil — 3-4, 8a, 16c, 18, 22, 32

Donegal

Porridge stick — 10a
Pot stick — 1-3, 5, 5A, 6-8, 10b, 11-13
Spurtle — 11
Stirrer — 13
Theeval — 10a
Nil — 1A, 4, 7A, 9

Fermanagh

Pot stick — 1-2, 4-6, 8-10
Nil — 3, 7ab

Armagh

Pot stick — 1, 4-5, 6ab
Nil — 2-3

Londonderry

Pot stick — 1, 1A, 2, 3A, 4-7
Nil — 1B. 3

20 MEAL BIN (PQ1, 74)

The following variants have been subsumed :MEAL (a few **mael, male**), the unstressed vowel in items ending in -l, as e.g., **girnEl** etc., (**-al, -ol** etc.)

Shetland

Box — 7
Floer barrel — 33
Girn — 7
Girner — 9
Meal barrel — 1, 15
(Meal) bin — *2,* 7
Meal bunker — 15
(Meal) girnel — 4-*6, 8,* 10-13, 19, 22-23, *25, 28,* 30, 33
Meal kist — 3, 16-20, 21a, 27, 30-31
Meal kyist — 21b, 24, 32
Nil — 14, 26, 29

Orkney

(Meal) girnel — *1-2,* 3-12, 13ab, 14-21
Meal girrel — 5
Meal kist — 4

Caithness

Box — 13
Meal barrel — 5, 12a
(Meal) girnel — 2ab, *5-6,* 8, *10,* 12bc, 13-15, 16ab, 17
Meal gurnel — 9, 11
(Meal) kist — *2b, 3,* 4, *5, 7-8, 10, 12a,* 13, *14, 17*
Nil — 1

Sutherland

Bin — 1
Gurnel — 8
Kirn — 15
Meal barrel — 10
(Meal) chest — *3, 5, 7, 12-13,* 15-16
(Meal) girnel — 2-4, 6, 9a*b,* 10-11, 14-15
Meal guirnel — 13
(Meal) kist — 1-*2, 4-6, 8, 13,* 14-17

Ross & Cromarty

Boatie — 10, 18
Bunk — 8
Guernel — 11
(Meal) barrel — *7, 9, 19,* 25b, *26*-27, 29
(Meal) bin — *1, 3,* 17-*18, 27, 29, 32c*
Meal box — 5
Meal cask — 9
(Meal) chest — *2, 4,* 7-8, *16, 20,* 29, *39*

Ross & Cromarty cont'd

(Meal) girnel — 7, 10, 13, 15, 17-18, 20-24, *28,* 29-30, *31,* 32a, 34-*36,* 37ab, 38
(Meal) gurnel — 25ab, *27,* 32bc, 33
(Meal) kist — 10-*11, 16*-17, 25ab, 29, *31, 32b,* 33, *35,* 37ab
Nil — 6, 12, 14

Inverness

Bunk — 27
Girder — 13a
Girnler — 31
Gurnel — 10, 14, 27, 33
Meal ark — 35
Meal barrel — 2, 13e
(Meal) bin — *2, 13b,* 18, *23, 26, 32, 34,* 36
(Meal) chest — *1, 3-5, 7,* 13a*de, 16-18, 21a, 26, 37,* 40
(Meal) girnel — 3, 6, 8, 11, 13ce, 15, 21b, 22, 26, 28-30, 35, *39*
(Meal) kist — *8-9, 12, 13c,* 14, 19-20, *21a,* 24-*25, 31, 38*

Nairn

Bowie — 1b
Girnel — 1abc, 3-4
Meal bunk — 6
Meal girner — 2
Meal kist — 5

Moray

Bunker — 18
(Meal) bowie — *2b, 7,* 8*bc*d, 23
Meal barrel — 15
Meal bin — 21
Meal bunk — 7, 11, 15, 20
(Meal) girnel — 1, 2a, 3, 5, 6ab, *7,* 8*b*d, 9ab, 10, 12-14, 16-18, *19,* 20-23
(Meal) gurnel — 4, 8e, *15*
(Meal) kist — *3, 5,* 8bc, *13, 22*
Nil — 8af

Banff

Gernel — 19
Gyirnel — 16
(Meal) bowie — *2ac, 9-10, 13, 19,* 28, *30,* 32
(Meal) girnel — 1, 2bc, 3-5, 6ab, 7-8, 9, 10-12, 14-15, *17,* 18bcd, 20, *21,* 22-34
(Meal) kist — 23, 25, *34*
Nil — 18a

Aberdeen

Bassie — 62, 71b
Bunk — 75
Gernel — 7, 47d, 49
Meal barrel — 5d
Meal bin — 70
(Meal) bowie — *1, 6-8,* 10-11, 14, 16, 21, *25, 28a, 38, 44,* 47*a*d, 48, 56, 63, 67, 69, 81, 83-84, 87, 90, 104-105
Meal chest — 70, 105
(Meal) girnel — 1-2, 3ab, 4, 5abcd, 6, 8-27, 28abc, 29-46, 47abcef, 48, 50-61, 63-64, *65-66,* 67-69, *70,* 71abc, 72-80, *81-82,* 83, *84,* 85-91, *92,* 93-94, *95,* 96-102, *103,* 104-105, *106,* 107-109
(Meal) kist — 10, 27, *70*

Kincardine

Gernel — 2
Meal bin — 17c
(Meal) bowie — *13,* 15, 17bd
Meal bunk — 4, 17c, 28
Mealer — 28
(Meal) girnel — 1, *3,* 4, *5-7,* 8-15, *16,* 17abcd, 18-21, 23-28
Meal kist — 3, 26
Nil — 22

Kinross

Girnel — 1-3, 5-7
Kist — 1
Meal barrel — 3
Meal bin — 6
Meal bing — 4

Angus

Bowie — 5c, 37
Bunk — 9
Corn kist — 5a
Crock — 18
Girnel — 1-4, 5abc, 7-8, 10-12, 14abcd, 15, 17a, 19, 21-24, 27-28, 29b, 30-32, 33ab, 34-37
Giurnel — 13
Gurnel — 6, 20
Meal bin — 17b, 34
Meal box — 29b
Mealer — 5a
(Meal) kist — *8-9,* 10, 14cd, *17b,* 20, 22, *25,* 29ab, *30,* 32, 33a, 36
Pig — 5c
Nil — 16, 26

Perth

Box — 57
Gernel — 72
Kest — 42
(Meal) barrel — 46-47, *51a*
(Meal) bin — *2a, 4, 24*-25, *67, 74*
Meal chest — 3, 36
(Meal) girnel — 1, *2ab,* 3, 5-13, 15-25, 28, 29ab, 30-33, 38-40, 41ab, 42, *43-44,* 45-46, 48-50, 51ab, 52abcde, 53-54, 56-*57,* 59-60, 62, 64-65, *66,* 67, *68,* 69-71, 73
(Meal) gurnel — 26, *37*
(Meal) kist — *2b, 14, 16, 26-27, 33,* 41a, 49-*50, 51b, 52ac,* 58, *61*-62, *68-69*
Nil — 34-35, 55, 63

Fife

Corn kist — 26, 37, 39, 64a
Gurnel — 55d
Meal backet — 27
(Meal) barrel — *10, 48, 55a,* 56-57
Meal ben — 50
(Meal) bin — *11, 13,* 16, *24,* 39, *46, 50, 56*-57, *62*
Meal bist — 9b
(Meal) box — *44b,* 56
Meal buist — 23
Meal can — 43a, 44e, 58
(Meal) crock — *9a,* 12, 49, 55g
Meal garnel — 41a
(Meal) girnel — 1-4, 6-7, 10-12, 14, 17-18, 20-*21,* 23, 25, 27, 29-31, 33, 35, 36ab, 38-39, 40b, 43ab, 44a, 47, 49, 51-54, 55bef, *59,* 64ab
Meal kest — 50
(Meal) kist — *5, 8, 12, 14, 18, 20, 28, 32, 41c, 45,* 48, *52,* 57
Meal poke — 6, 47
Stoup — 63
Nil — 15, 19, 22, 34, 40a, 41bd, 42, 44df, 55c, 60-61

Clackmannan

Gaurnel — 4d
Girnel — 1, 5-7
Gurnel — 2
Meal bist — 4a
(Meal) kist — 1, *3*
Nil — 4bc

Stirling

Ark — 26b
Baurrel — 20
Chest — 25d
Gernel — 15
Gurnel — 7e, 22b, 26d
Kirnel — 34
Meal bakie — 4
Meal barrel — 21b, 25ad
(Meal) bin — *4, 16, 23b,* 25cd, *26d,* 28, *34, 36*
(Meal) crock — 7c, 12, 17, 23c, 25b, 26d, *31*-32
Meal garnel — 36
(Meal) girnel — 1-3, 6, 7bd*ef,* 8-10, 12, 14, 17-*18,* 21ab, 22a, 24, 25a*b*d, 26cd*ef,* 27a*b,* *29-33,* 35ab, *36,* 37*ab,* 39ab, 42a
(Meal) kist — *2,* 6, 7*abd, 11,* 13, *21b,* 25ac, *26a, 36, 39a*
Meal poke — 9
Nil — 5, 19, 23a, 38, 40-41, 42b

Dunbarton

Girnel — 1-3, 4ab, 5-6, 7c, 9, 13a, 14a, 16a
Gurnel — 17
Meal barrel — 6
(Meal) bin — *7b,* 10, *13c, 16b*
Meal chest — 16b
(Meal) crock — 4a, *6,* 14a
(Meal) garnel — 9, *15*
(Meal) kist — 4a, 13c, *14b*
Nil — 7a, 8, 11-12, 13b, 18

Argyll

Gardner — 24
Gernel — 1, 10, 34
Kirnel — 32
Meal barrel — 19, 23, 35
(Meal) bin — *6,* 10, 12, *17, 27*
Meal chest — 14, 30, 33
(Meal) garnel — 19, 30 *33, 38*
(Meal) girnel — 3, 5, *7, 9,* 11-15, 18, 24-25, *35,* 37
(Meal) kist — 8, *13,* 18, 21-*22, 28-29, 31*-32, *34, 37, 39-40*
Meal pin — 36
Nil — 2, 4, 16, 20, 26

Bute

Barrel — 3
Crock — 1b
Garnel — 1a, 3, 6-7, 8ab
Girnel — 1ae, 4, 9
Meal ark — 9
(Meal) kist — 1ace, *2, 5*
Nil — 1d

Ayr

Corn kist — 41
Croak — 11
Crock — 26b, 53b
Grist girnel — 28d
Gurnel — 7, 27
Killer — 18b
Kirnel — 53a
Meal ark — 32, 41, 45, 47, 49, 53a, 54, 56-57
Meal barrel — 57
Meal bin — 5, 43
Meal chest — 28e
(Meal) garnel — 4, 8ab, 10-11, 12ab, 13-14, 16b, 17, 18b, 20abdefgh, 21-23, 26a, 28abdf, 29, 30ab, *31,* 32-34, 35b, 36, 38-39, *40,* 41-46, *47,* 50-52, 54
(Meal) gaurnel — 2ab, *3,* 8b, 15, 20c, 24b, 25
(Meal) girnel — 6, 8ab, 9, 12a, 15, 16a, *18ab,* 19, 20h, 28abcde, 30a, 41, 48, 52, 56-57
(Meal) gornel — 1a, *7,* 24a
(Meal) kist — *1a, 5, 7, 8a,* 12a, *16ab,* 18b, 20bg*h,* 28b, 32, 45-46, 51, *53a,* 55
Meal pock — 57
Poke — 57
Nil — 1b, 26c, 35a, 37

Renfrew

Barrel — 15
Bing — 3
Croak — 11gk
Garnel — 7-9, 11b
Gornel — 11a
Gurnel — 11f, 12a, 13c, 18a
Kernel — 1b
Kirnel — 11l
(Meal) bin — *2i, 4e,* 5, *8, 11e,* 13c, *16b,* 18b, *20a*
Meal box — 2a
Meal chest — 2d
(Meal) crock — 1a, *2g,* 3, 4b, 11adghj, 16a*c,* 19
Meal dish — 2i
(Meal) girnel — 2befh*j,* 4d, 5-6, 11bejl, 13a, 14b, 15, 17, 19, 21
(Meal) kist — 1b, *2a, 11i,* 13c, 16d, *17, 20b,* 21
Meal poke — 16a
Meal tin — 2a
Stock bin — 2i
Nil — 2c, 4ac, 10, 11c, 12b, 13bd, 14a

Lanark

Aumrie — 38d
Bakie — 38a
Broke barrel — 25b
Creel — 9b
Hog yett — 11
Kest — 37
Killer — 31b
Kirnel — 57c
(Meal) ark — *15bc,* 38bd, *39, 46b, 48, 49b, 53-56, 57a, 59b, 61, 63, 64b, 65-66, 67ab*
Meal barrel — 3, 27b, 29af, 30, 46a
(Meal) bin — 6, *15c, 26a, 27b, 29c, 33d, 35d, 45, 48*
(Meal) crock — 7ab, *8a,* 18, 25d, 31d
Meal croke — 15a, 18
(Meal) garnel — *22, 33cd, 38c, 42, 44, 46c, 53, 56, 57c, 60-61*
(Meal) girn — *14c,* 27a
(Meal) girnel — 1-*2,* 5, 7ac, 9a, 11-*12,* 15abc, 17, 23, 30, 31ac, 32bcdf, 33bcd, 34, 35bd, 38e, 40-42, 46ac, 47-48, 52a, 57a, 62
(Meal) kist — *8b, 9a,* 10a, *13, 15ab, 20*-21, 29def, 31d, *35d, 39*-40, 42, *45,* 49ab, *51,* 52ab, 57*ab, 58, 59a,* 64ab, 65
Meal poke — 16b
(Meal) tin — 6, *14d,* 33a
Nil — 4, 10b, 14ab, 16a, 19, 24, 25ac, 26b, 28, 29bg, 32ae, 35ac, 36, 43, 50

West Lothian

Corn bin — 6
Croak — 16
Crock — 1d, 13, 16
Girnel — 1a, 3, 8, 11, 18, 19b, 20a, 21a, 22
Gurnel — 17a
Kernel — 10
Meal ark — 6-7
Meal barrel — 1bc
Meal bin — 2, 5, 7, 11
(Meal) kist — 4, 9b, 11-12, *15*
Nil — 9a, 14, 17b, 19a, 20b, 21b

Midlothian

Bing — 25c
Brock — 18
Bunker — 27
Crock — 17-18
Garnel — 16
Guern — 1
Guernel — 1, 15
Meal airk — 7b, 30

Midlothian cont'd

(Meal) ark – *12a, 24,* 27, *32*
Meal barrel – 17
Meal bin – 8a, 15-16, 19, 21, 23b
(Meal) girnel – 3, 6b, 7ab, 8b, *9*-11, *12b,* 14ab, 24, 25a, 26a, 27
Meal jar – 2
(Meal) kist – *3-4,* 11, 15, *18,* 20, 22, *23b,* 29
Poke – 25a
Nil – 5, 6a, 13, 23a, 25bd, 26b, 28, 31

East Lothian

Corn kist – 13
Croak – 5, 6a
Crock – 4a, 12
Girnel – 8, 10, 15
Meal airg – 11
(Meal) ark – *2,* 6a, *8, 13*-14, *16*
Meal barrel – 4b, 7
Meal bin – 19
Meal box – 17
Meal bunker – 6b
Meal eark – 16
(Meal) kist – 3, *4b,* 9, 14, *20*
Meal tin – 1
Tun – 13
Nil – 18, 21

Berwick

Crock – 10
Girnel – 1, 13, 16b, 21-23
Gurnel – 8
(Meal) ark – 3, *5-6, 11-14, 16b, 17-19,* 22-23, *25-27, 29-30, 32*
Meal barrel – 31-32
(Meal) bin – 2, *9, 15, 16c,* 28, *32*
Meal box – 8
Meal bunker – 8
Meal can – 8
Meal chest – 27
Meal erk – 16a
(Meal) kist – *1*-2, *4, 6,* 10, 15, *16b,* 23, *27,* 31-32
Meal poke – 16c, 32
Tun – 10, 18
Nil – 7, 20, 24

Peebles

Crock – 2
Girdle – 5
Girnel – 2-3, 4a, 7, 10
(Meal) ark – *1-3, 5,* 6ab, *7-10*
Meal bin – 4c, 6a
Meal kist – 4bc, 6b

Selkirk

Bunker – 2e
Meal ark – 1, 2a, 3-5, 7-8
Meal bin – 2bcd
Meal erk – 2b
Meal girnel – 2a, 6
(Meal) kist – 5, *8*

Roxburgh

Bine – 21c
Corn kist – 5
Girnel – 4, 13, 28
Kill – 8
Meal airk – 3b, 15a, 16-17, 20, 21a, 25-26
(Meal) ark – *1-2, 4-7, 9ab,* 13, *19, 23-24, 28*
Meal bin – 21a
Meal box – 15b
Meal croak – 11
Meal erk – 10, 21d
(Meal) kist – 1-*2,* 3a, *4,* 7-*8,* 12-13, 17, *19,* 21af, 22-23, *28*
Nil – 14, 18, 21be, 27

Dumfries

Booat – 37
Garnel – 1a, 10, 12
Gaurnel – 5
(Meal) ark – *2, 4-6,* 7, 8ab, 9, *10-14, 16, 17b, 18-19,* 20, 21ab, *22-27, 30, 31abcdef, 32-36,* 37-38, *39, 41*-42, *45ab, 46, 48*
(Meal) bin – *15,* 46
(Meal) girnel – 2-3, 9, *22-23, 25,* 28-29, 45a
Meal jar – 29
(Meal) kist – 2, *6*-7, *17ab,* 25, *26-27,* 28, *29, 31d, 32,* 34, 37-38, *39-40,* 41-42, *43,* 44, *46*-47, 49
Nil – 1b

Kirkcudbright

Gairnel – 17
Girnel – 2-3, 11, 24
(Meal) ark – *1-10,* 11, 12ab, *13-14, 15ab, 16,* 17, *18-20, 21abc, 22-23, 25-27*
Meal bin – 26
Meal garnel – 1, 6
(Meal) kist – *1, 8,* 18, 24

Wigtown

Aumrie – 5b
Gernel – 14
Girnel – 5b
Meal ark – 1-4, 5a, 6-13, 15-18
(Meal) kist – *5b, 10,* 14

Northumberland

Bran tub – 40a, 69ab
Corn bin – 108a, 130b
Crock – 2a
Crowdie tin – 62h
Floor bin – 41b, 83, 88a, 111ab, 127d, 130e
Floor kist – 117
Flour barrel – 95a
Flour bin – 28, 40a, 41a, 59b, 69c, 72i, 87, 100, 120c, 126c, 127c
Flour kit – 126b
Girnel – 29f, 127b
Hopper – 60, 130c
Kest – 8
Kit – 40b
Meal ark – 29f, 38, 62f, 124a
Meal barrel – 21
(Meal) bin – *1a,* 4, *6,* 16, *20b,* 26, *28,* 29b, *30-31, 35-36,* 38, 41*ad, 46-47,* 51, *53a,* 57, *59b, 64ab,* 65a, 68, *69d,* 71ad, *72cg, 73,* 77, 82, *86,* 88b, *89-90,* 92, *94b, 99bd,* 103*bc, 104a, 106, 109-110, 112, 120a,* 127g, *130c, 132-133, 140*
(Meal) bing – 29a, 52, 57, 78-79, *103*b, *106*-107, *110, 142*
Meal box – 42
(Meal) chest – *41ac,* 53b, *81, 103a, 124a,* 137-*138*
Meal gonnel – 134
(Meal) kist – 2a, *10*-11, 14, 16, 19a, *20a, 22,* 34ab, 35, 37, 42-43, 44-45, 49, *51, 53ab, 54,* 56, 59cd, 60, 69eg, *72b, 73,* 75, 77, *78-81, 98,* 102, 103abc, *104ab, 105-106,* 108*ac,* 109, *111b,* 114, *118b,* 119, 124b, 125, 127e, *132-136, 139-143*
Meal tin – 7
Meal tub – 13, 40a, 71c, 105
(Meal) tun – 2a, 3-4, 9, 12, 14, 16-18, 19a, *22*-23, 24a, 25, 27, 29ac, 33b, 36, 38-39, 41a, 48, 62a, *64b,* 68, 69ab, 77, 122a
Nil – 1bc, 2b, 5, 15, 19b, 24b, 29de, 32, 33a, 50, 55, 58, 59aef, 61, 62bcdeg, 63, 65b, 66-67, 69fh, 70, 71be, 72adefhjkl, 74, 76, 84-85, 91, 93, 94a, 95b, 96-97, 99ac, 101ab, 108b, 113, 115-116, 118a, 120b, 121, 122b, 123, 126adef, 127afh, 128, 129abc, 130adf, 131

Cumberland

Bunker – 51, 57, 59, 61
Corn kist – 1a, 16
Cworn kist – 45
Floor bin – 24
(Meal) ark – *1b, 15c,* 22, 30-31, 38, 41, *60*
(Meal) bin – *1a, 23,* 40, *50, 56-57*
Meal chest – 18, 46
(Meal) chist – *24,* 28
(Meal) kist – 2-4, 5ab, 7-11, 12, 13*abcd,* 14, 15abc, 17, *18,* 19-21, *22, 24-25,* 26-29, *30,* 31-34, 36, 37ab, *38-44, 46,* 47-48, *49,* 52, 54-56, *57-58, 60,* 61, *62,* 63a
Nil – 6, 35, 53, 63b

Down

Bing – 23
Keev – 4
(Meal) ark – 2a, *3,* 5, 11, *13,* 14, 17-18, 21, 23-24, *25,* 27-29
(Meal) bin – *2a, 7, 9,* 14-*15, 19*
Trough – 4
Nil – 1, 2b, 6, 8, 10, 12, 16, 20, 22, 26, 30

Tyrone

Chest – 5, 8
Meal ark – 5, 10, 14
Meal barrel – 9
(Meal) bin – *1, 6,* 7-8. *9,* 10, *11,* 14
Nil – 2-4, 12-13, 15-16

Antrim

Corn bin – 16b
Feed box – 34
Hogan – 11
Kist – 4A, 5a, 10, 24
(Meal) ark – 5a, 6-7, 8b, 12, 16ab, 18-19, 21-22, *23,* 24-33
Meal barrel – 5a, 17
(Meal) bin – 1, *5b,* 9, 13-14, *19-20,* 28, *31*
(Meal) tub – *26,* 34
Nil – 2-4, 8a, 15, 16c, 29-30, 32

Donegal

Chest – 10b
Hogget – 6
Meal ark – 7-8
(Meal) bin – 1, 5, 5A, *8, 12*
Meal box – 8
Meal kist – 11
Nil – 1A, 2-4, 7A, 9, 10a, 13

Fermanagh

Barrel – 9
Chest – 6
Meal ark – 1, 5
(Meal) bin – *2,* 4-5, 9
(Meal) chist – *2,* 6, 10
Nil – 3, 7ab, 8

Armagh

(Meal) ark – *1,* 5, 6ab
Meal bin – 4
Meal tub – 4
Nil – 2-3

Londonderry

Barrel – 5
Chist – 1A
Hogsit – 6
(Meal) ark – 3, *5*
Meal bin – 3A
Meal box – 2
Nil – 1, 1B, 4, 7

21 CRUMBS (PQ1, 75)

Crumbs has not been mapped as it appears all over the area. The variants of CRUMBLES have been subsumed (**crummels** is much more common everywhere than the SE form).
Variants of the unstressed vowels in items ending in **-ick, -ock** etc., have been subsumed under the majority spelling in each county.

Shetland

Ackers – 2
Aff fains – 23
Brucks – 1-2, 5-6, 8-10, 12-13, 15-16, 18, 22, 29-30
Coombs – 7
Crumbles – 19
Crumbs – 3, 14-16, 20, 21a, 25, 30, 32-33
Crummicks – 33
Dumba – 2
Herda – 2
Millin(g)s – 2, 31
Muilders – 22, 27
Muillins – 3, 17, 21b
Mullders – 12, 17, 30
Nirts – 2
Oarmills – 24
Sids – 2
Soe – 2
Truss – 5
Nil – 4, 11, 26, 28

Orkney

Breed crumbs – 2
Corns – 13a
Crumbs – 1, 4-5, 7-9, 13ab, 15-17, 19-20
Mellins – 13b
Meteens – 4
Moolders – 6
Mulderings – 8
Mulders – 1, 3, 12, 13a, 15-16
Muldrins – 12
Muldroos – 10-11
Muldros – 7
Nil – 14, 18, 21

Caithness

Brakins – 6
Crumbs – 2ab, 8-11, 13, 16b
Gnop – 12b
Male corns – 5
Malings – 10
Mealin(g)s – 6-7, 10, 14, 17
Meals – 10
Millings – 12a
Nil – 1, 3-4, 12c, 15, 16a

Sutherland

Crumbs – 1, 3-8, 9ab, 10-13, 16
Nil – 2, 14-15, 17

Ross & Cromarty

Bitties – 14, 25b
Bits – 16
Crumbacks – 31
Crumbles – 37b
Crumbs – 1, 3-5, 8-9, 14, 16-19, 22, 24, 25a, 26-29, 31, 32ab, 34, 36, 39
Murrlacks – 36
Pickings – 19
Prinels – 37a
Nil – 2, 6-7, 10-13, 15, 20-21, 23, 30, 32c, 33, 35, 38

Inverness

Crumbs – 1-6, 8, 10-11, 13abce, 16-20, 21ab, 22-23, 26, 29-30, 32-40
Meelicks – 13c
Pronn – 26
Smoorach – 14, 24
Nil – 7, 9, 12, 13d, 15, 25, 27-28, 31

Nairn

Crumbs – 1a, 2, 5-6
Merls – 1bc
Murls – 1c
Nil – 3-4

Moray

Broke – 21
Crumbles – 4, 12
Crumblicks – 1, 18
Crumbs – 2a, 8bde, 14, 16
Crummies – 8c
Grummets – 9a
Mealicks – 20
Mirlacks – 3, 7, 8b, 22
Mirls – 3, 8b
Moolichs – 21
Murlicks – 1, 5, 6a, 9a, 10, 16-17, 21
Murrlins – 9a
Murrels – 2b, 4, 8a, 12-13, 23
Orels – 18
Orts – 18
Pron – 22
Smurlacks – 23
Smurls – 23
Nil – 6b, 8f, 9b, 11, 15, 19

Banff

Chads – 23
Crumblicks – 1, 2a, 9, 34
Crumblies – 14
Crumbs – 4-5, 9, 15, 18c, 19, 21, 24
Dramlachs – 27
Mealicks – 1, 6ab, 11, 13, 15, 23, 30-31
Mellocks – 33
Merlicks – 8, 10, 29
Mirls – 28
Murlichs – 17
Murlicks – 2abc, 3, 5, 7, 9, 12, 14-15, 18cd, 25-26, 30-32, 34
Orrals – 16
Smush – 25
Nil – 18ab, 20, 22

Aberdeen

Crumbles – 14, 80, 99
Crumblicks – 8, 10, 17, 28a, 51, 64-65, 71b, 84, 107
Crumbs – 3a, 6, 8-9, 20, 28ac, 29, 32, 44, 48-50, 53, 66, 69-70, 71b, 73, 81, 85, 94-95, 98, 100, 104-106
Crumlies – 73
Crumocks – 83
Dramlicks – 14
Grated bread – 70
Leavins – 47c
Mealicks – 1, 3a, 4, 5acd, 6-8, 10-14, 16, 18-27, 28abc, 30, 33-35, 37, 39-42, 44-45, 47abdef, 51-52, 54-57, 59-62, 64, 67-68, 71ac, 72-78, 80, 82-83, 86, 88, 92-95, 97-99, 101-105, 108-109
Mealochs – 3b, 58
Mealsicks – 46
Mellicks – 31
Merlicks – 77, 100
Millicks – 78
Mirlicks – 77, 87, 107
Murlicks – 10, 12, 14-15, 22, 27, 28abc, 51, 53, 63, 80, 83, 85-86, 88, 96
Murlies – 100
Murlochs – 34, 49, 51, 64, 75
Pickings – 56
Purlocks – 10
Scraps – 48
Smush – 81
Wee bitties – 29
Nil – 2, 5b, 36, 38, 43, 79, 89-91

Kincardine

Crumbs – 1, 3, 5-6, 8, 10-12, 16, 17c, 18-19, 24, 26
Mealicks – 4-7, 10-13, 16, 17abcd, 23
Mealins – 15
Moolins – 15, 22-23, 27-28
Moulichs – 14
Moulins – 20, 25
Murlins – 2, 17b
Nil – 9, 21

Kinross

Crumbs – 3, 6
Mailins – 4
Mealins – 5
Muilins – 7
Murls – 1-2
Murrlins – 3

Angus

Crumbies – 14a
Crumblins – 14a
Crumbs – 2, 8-10, 12-13, 17b, 22, 24-25, 28, 29b, 32, 34, 36
Mailins – 14d
Mealin(g)s – 5c, 13, 18, 20, 29a, 31
Mealocks – 17a
Millins – 14abc, 20, 22, 29b
Moolicks – 32
Moolins – 4, 5c, 37
Moulins – 1, 14a, 33a
Mowlins – 6, 13
Muilins – 7-8, 10, 12, 27
Muillicks – 7
Mullicks – 33a
Mullins – 15, 17b, 25, 35
Murlins – 4, 14acd, 21, 29b, 31
Murls – 30
Murrlies – 19
Nil – 3, 5b, 11, 16, 23, 26

Perth

Bittocks – 16
Crimacks – 16
Crumbies – 25
Crumble – 68
Crumbs – 1, 2a, 4-5, 7-10, 12, 14-15, 20, 24-25, 28, 29a, 32-33, 36, 46, 48, 52ab, 57, 60, 66-67, 71-72, 74
Fragments – 43
Mealachs – 45
Mealicks – 16, 20, 25, 27, 33, 51b, 58, 62
Mealies – 44
Mealins – 60
Mellocks – 41b
Millicks – 26, 31, 33, 54
Millins – 52d
Mirles – 39
Mirlins – 50
Mirlocks – 70
Muillicks – 22, 32
Muluckies – 61
Murlies – 52d, 73
Murrles – 21, 32, 53, 62
Murrlicks – 30, 69
Murrlin(g)s – 19-20, 27, 32, 37, 40, 41a, 45-48, 52cd, 56-57, 62, 65-66
Nil – 2b, 3, 6, 11, 13, 17-18, 23, 29b, 34-35, 38, 42, 49, 51a, 52e, 55, 59, 63-64

Fife

Bits – 55e
Crowdie – 39
Crumbies – 33
Crumbs – 1, 7-8, 11, 13, 16-17, 19, 24-25, 36b, 37, 40ab, 41ab, 43a, 44bcde, 50, 53, 55bde, 57, 62
Mailins – 13, 32, 44d, 48, 51
Maurles – 64a
Mealins – 12, 31, 35
Merrles – 50
Millins – 40a, 54, 55fg
Mirlins – 55ag, 59, 61
Mirrles – 7, 36a, 58
Moolins – 21, 55d
Mouls – 12
Murrles – 10, 16, 19, 25-28, 43b, 44aef, 45-49, 55d, 56, 63
Murrlins – 3, 9ab, 10, 18, 21, 23, 28, 40b, 42, 48, 52, 55d, 64a
Mylins – 12
Orts – 53
Scraps – 37
Thrums – 53
Nil – 2, 4-6, 14-15, 20, 22, 29-30, 34, 38, 41cd, 55c, 60, 64b

Clackmannan

Chirls – 5
Crockles – 5
Crumbs – 4c
Mealins – 4d, 6
Millins – 3, 4ab, 7
Millocks – 7
Mirls – 6
Moulachs – 1
Mullins – 2
Murlins – 2
Murls – 4c

Stirling

Crumbles – 2, 23a
Crumbs – 4, 7acef, 8-9, 11-12, 15-16, 18, 21b, 23bc, 25cd, 26abcd, 27a, 28-29, 31-32, 34, 35a, 36, 39b
Mealin(g)s – 17, 26b
Mealocks – 3, 7e, 33
Millins – 7b, 9, 12-13, 18, 20, 25abc, 26c, 27a, 39b, 42a
Millocks – 7a, 9, 15, 21a, 24, 27a, 29, 32
Mirlins – 22b
Mirls – 9, 18
Moolicks – 6, 7b
Moolins – 26d, 30, 39a
Mulins – 26d
Mullins – 17, 25ad, 31, 35b
Mullocks – 18, 23b, 35a
Mulls – 25d
Murls – 7abd, 10, 21b, 22a, 25d, 26e, 34, 39a
Nil – 1, 5, 14, 19, 27b, 37ab, 38, 40-41, 42b

Dunbarton

Crumbles – 10, 12, 16b
Crumbs – 1, 3, 6, 7bc, 8-11, 13abc, 14b, 16b
Millings – 2, 6, 7c, 9, 13bc, 14a, 16a, 17
Millocks – 5, 16a
Moulins – 1
Murrels – 17
Nil – 4ab, 7a, 15, 18

Argyll

Bits – 4
Broken bread – 33
Crumbles – 38
Crumbs – 1-3, 5-7, 9-12, 14-17, 19, 22-25, 27, 35, 37
Leavings – 33
Mealins – 31, 35, 37, 39-40
Scraps – 18, 35
Nil – 8, 13, 20-21, 26, 28-30, 32, 34, 36

Bute

Crumbs — 1acd, 7, 8ab
Mealins — 1a, 9
Mildrens — 8b
Millins — 8ab
Nil — 1be, 3-6

Ayr

Crotals — 41
Crotlins — 41
Crumbles — 15, 17, 20bgh, 25, 27, 28d, 31, 34, 48-49, 51, 53a, 56-57
Crumbs — 2ab, 3-5, 8b, 9, 11, 12a, 20c, 21, 26b, 28cdef, 30a, 31-32, 34, 35b, 36, 42-45, 49, 52, 53a, 54-57
Mealins — 16a
Meals — 1a
Millin(g)s — 1a, 2a, 3-7, 8b, 10, 13-15, 16b, 18b, 20acdefh, 21, 23, 25, 26ac, 28bc, 30ab. 33-34, 35b, 36, 38, 40-42, 46-47, 57
Mills — 1a
Moolies — 53b
Moolins — 16a, 18ab, 19, 53a
Morsels — 26b
Mouls — 1a
Mullins — 18b, 20fg, 22, 24ab, 30ab
Mummles — 24b, 27
Murrels — 19
Nyimlins — 8b
Nil — 1b, 8a, 12b, 28a, 29, 35a, 37, 39, 50

Renfrew

Crimbles — 5
Crottles — 13a
Crumbles — 1a, 4d, 11ac, 13b, 14a, 16d, 17
Crumblins — 11a
Crumbs — 1b, 2ahij, 4acde, 5, 8, 11abdel, 13c, 16ab, 18b, 19, 20a
Mealins — 12a
Millins — 2fg, 4d, 11abefikl, 13c, 14b, 17, 18ab, 19, 21
Mimmles — 15
Moolins — 20b
Murrels — 20b
Scraps — 16a
Tiny portions — 16a
Nil — 2bcde, 3, 4b, 6-7, 9-10, 11ghj, 12b, 13d, 16c

Lanark

Broke — 20
Crumbles — 3-4, 9a, 14a, 22, 25c, 29f, 31bd, 32e, 38a, 45, 46b, 57b
Crumbs — 1-3, 5-6, 7ac, 8a, 10ab, 12, 14bd, 15ac, 16ab, 18-19, 21, 25bc, 26ab, 27b, 29cf, 31ad, 32be, 33a, 35bcd, 38c, 44-45, 46ab, 48, 49a, 52b, 53, 58, 59b, 60, 64b
Mealin(g)s — 13, 47, 61, 63, 66, 67a
Mealocks — 13
Merrels — 32f
Millin(g)s — 7a, 8b, 11, 13, 14c, 15abc, 20, 23, 27a, 29adeg, 30, 31cd, 32cd, 33cd, 35b, 37, 38b, 40-44, 46c, 48, 49b, 52a, 55-56, 57ac, 62, 65
Millocks — 11
Mills — 67b
Mirrels — 38d
Moolins — 17
Moulins — 33b
Mules — 9b
Mulins — 38d
Mullins — 7a, 27b, 48, 59a
Murlins — 13
Nirrels — 32b
Scraps — 39

Wee bits — 29e
Nil — 7b, 24, 25ad, 28, 29b, 32a, 34, 35a, 36, 38e, 50-51, 54, 64a

West Lothian

Breed crumbs — 1c
Crumbers — 17a
Crumbles — 2
Crumblins — 15
Crumbs — 3, 5-7, 9a, 10-13, 15-16, 22
Millin(g)s — 1d, 4, 7-8, 9b, 19b, 21a
Millocks — 11
Muckles — 4
Mullins — 1d
Murlins — 3
Nil — 1ab, 14, 17b, 18, 19a, 20ab, 21b

Midlothian

Crumbs — 1-2, 7a, 8a, 10-11, 12a, 14a, 15-16, 18-21, 23b, 24, 25c, 27, 29, 32
Mailins — 30
Mealin(g)s — 9-10, 16, 32
Millins — 12a, 13, 14ab, 23a, 24, 26a
Mullins — 23b
Nil — 3-5, 6ab, 7b, 8b, 12b, 17, 22, 25abd, 26b, 28, 31

East Lothian

Crumbs — 1-2, 4b, 5, 6b, 8-9, 13, 15-16, 19-21
Mealins — 4a, 10, 13-14, 16-17
Millin(g)s — 2, 6a, 7-9, 21
Mirrels — 13
Moulins — 9
Mullins — 4a
Wee bits — 2
Nil — 3, 11-12, 18

Berwick

Breed mealins — 26
Crumblies — 31
Crumbs — 1-2, 6-9, 12-13, 15, 16bc, 19, 21, 23, 27, 29, 31-32
Mailins — 6, 11
Mealins — 7-8, 10, 23, 32
Millins — 16abc, 18, 28
Moolins — 5
Mullin(g)s — 21, 23
Murlings — 21
Rumples — 27
Snippets — 17
Nil — 3-4, 14, 20, 22, 24-25, 30

Peebles

Crumbs — 3, 4bc, 5, 6b, 8
Mealins — 2, 4b
Millins — 1, 3, 4c, 8, 10
Nil — 4a, 6a, 7, 9

Selkirk

Crumbs — 2bc, 3, 8
Mailings — 2e
Mealin(g)s — 2ad, 6
Muilins — 4, 7
Nil — 1, 5

Roxburgh

Crumbles — 21c
Crumbs — 1-2, 3a, 8, 13, 15b, 17, 21aef, 25-26, 28
Frush — 21c
Mailin(g)s — 5, 13, 24
Mealin(g)s — 2, 7, 9a, 15b, 16, 18, 21d
Millin(g)s — 8, 19, 21e
Moolins — 4, 6
Muilers — 17
Muillins — 15b, 17, 21a, 26, 28
Nil — 3b, 9b, 10-12, 14, 15a, 20, 21b, 22-23, 27

Dumfries

Crumbles — 9
Crumbs — 1a, 4-5, 8ab, 10, 12-13, 15, 17a, 18-20, 21b, 22-24, 26-29, 31bdef, 33, 37, 40, 45a, 46-47
Emil jooks — 2
Fragments — 42
Leavings — 42
Mailins — 22
Mallins — 12
Mealin(g)s — 6, 14, 17b, 22, 24-25, 31b, 32, 35, 38, 44
Meulins — 2, 37
Millins — 11, 16, 17b, 21b, 25, 32
Molings — 7
Moolins — 17a, 29, 38
Mools — 4
Nil — 1b, 3, 21a, 30, 31ac, 34, 36, 39, 41, 43, 45b, 48-49

Kirkcudbright

Affains — 15a
Critlans — 7
Crumbles — 14, 21a
Crumbs — 1, 3, 6-7, 10, 15a, 16, 18-19, 21c, 22-23, 27
Leavins — 1
Mealins — 12ab, 15a, 21c
Millins — 5, 7
Moels — 24
Moulins — 1
Muilins — 2, 7
Mullins — 1-2
Murls — 17
Pyles — 17
Nil — 4, 8-9, 11, 13, 15b, 20, 21b, 25-26

Wigtown

Crumbles — 6
Crumblins — 17
Crumbs — 1, 4, 5a, 11-12, 14, 16
Lavins — 2
Mealins — 7
Mimoles — 10
Nil — 3, 5b, 8-9, 13, 15, 18

Northumberland

Bits and pieces — 118b, 130b
Breed crumbs — 13, 69b, 72b
Crottles — 134, 142
Crottlies — 142
Crottlings — 111b
Crumbles — 3, 15, 19a, 27, 62a, 65b, 69abh, 72j, 90, 98, 122a, 130e
Crumblies — 69a
Crumbs — 1a, 2ab, 5-6, 8, 12, 14-16, 18, 19a, 20b, 21, 26, 28, 29b, 30-31, 34b, 35-38, 40a, 41cd, 42, 45-48, 52, 53ab, 54, 56, 59bd, 60, 62bg, 64ab, 65a, 68, 69bcd, 71abcd, 72bcdgij, 77-78, 82-83, 86-87, 88b, 89-91, 93, 94b, 95b, 99bd, 100, 101b, 102, 103ac, 104ab, 106-107, 109-110, 111ab, 112, 117, 119, 120abc, 121, 124b, 126cf, 127acdg, 130cf, 132, 135, 137, 142-143
Morsels — 127e
Particles — 127e
Raspings — 17
Scraps — 125, 138
Nil — 1bc, 4, 7, 9-11, 19b, 20a, 22-23, 24ab, 25, 29acdef, 32, 33ab, 34a, 39, 40b, 41ab, 43-44, 49-51, 55, 57-58, 59acef, 61, 62cdefh, 63, 66-67, 69efg, 70, 71e, 72aefhkl, 73-76, 79-81, 84-85, 88a, 92, 94a, 95a, 96, 97, 99ac, 101a, 103b, 105, 108abc, 113-116, 118a, 122b, 123, 124a, 126abde, 127bfh, 128 129abc, 130ad, 131, 133, 136, 139-141

Cumberland

Bread scraps — 57
Crottles — 30
Crottlins — 5b
Crowkins — 46
Crumbles — 41
Crumblins — 56
Crumbs — 1a, 2-4, 5a, 7, 9, 12, 13c, 15ac, 21-25, 28, 37b, 38, 40, 42, 46-50, 52-54, 56-60, 62
Cruttlins — 30
Grain — 16
Merrlins — 56
Murrlins — 30-31, 56
Pickle — 16
Nil — 1b, 6, 8, 10-11, 13abd, 14, 15b, 17-20, 26-27, 29, 32-36, 37a, 39, 43-45, 51, 55, 61, 63ab

Down

Crumbles — 8, 10, 13, 22, 24, 28
Crumbs — 2a, 5, 7, 9, 15, 18-19, 24, 26
Crumlins — 27
Waste — 17
Nil — 1, 2b, 3-4, 6, 11-12, 14, 16, 20-21, 23, 25, 29-30

Tyrone

Crumbleens — 5
Crumbles — 2, 7, 9-10
Crumbs — 1, 6-8, 10-11
Kibbles — 1
Nil — 3-4, 12-16

Antrim

Coom — 16b
Crumbles — 2, 4A, 5b, 8a, 10-11, 13, 16b, 17, 19-21, 25, 33
Crumbs — 1, 3, 5a, 13, 22, 25-26, 28-31
Grell — 33
Grummels — 5b, 8b
Nyms — 16b
Picks — 17
Nil — 4, 6-7, 9, 12, 14-15, 16ac, 18, 23-24, 27, 32, 34

Donegal

Brioscar — 12
Brock — 13
Crumlins — 6, 8
Crumbs — 1, 5, 5A, 7-8, 12
Cunamar — 12
Fragments — 5A
Scrap — 13
Nil — 1A, 2-4, 7A, 9, 10ab, 11

Fermanagh

Crumbs — 4-5, 7a, 9
Crumlins — 1, 3
Grummel — 5
Nil — 2, 6, 7b, 8, 10

Armagh

Crumbles — 1-2
Crumbs — 3-4, 6a
Lavins — 4
Nil — 5, 6b

Londonderry

Crumbles — 1, 3, 3A, 7
Crumbs — 2
Grout — 3
Nil — 1AB, 4-6

22 QUARTER OF A PECK (PQ1, 76)

The concentration of some of the items mapped is rather low.

Shetland

Half a leespin — 14
Leisbin — 16
Lespon — 13
Twa po — 5
Wharter of a peck — 6, 32
Nil — 1-4, 7-12, 15, 17-20, 21ab, 22-31, 33

Orkney

Half a gallon — 17
Pint — 17, 20
Quarter of peck — 4
Two gallons — 11
Nil — 1-3, 5-10, 12, 13ab, 14-16, 18-19, 21

Caithness

Bushel — 8
Forpit — 12b
Furlid — 12a
Leepie — 12b
Mutchkin — 7
Point — 5, 17
Nil — 1, 2ab, 3-4, 6, 9-11, 12c, 13-15, 16ab

Sutherland

Puckle — 17
Quarter of a peck — 5
Nil — 1-4, 6-8, 9ab, 10-16

Ross & Cromarty

Firlet — 20
Half gallon — 5, 16, 39
Leepie — 12, 22, 27, 31, 36, 37a
Lippie — 25b
Quart — 27
Quarter (of a) peck — 3, 27-28, 34
Nil — 1-2, 4, 6-11, 13-15, 17-19, 21, 23-24, 25a, 26, 29-30, 32abc, 33, 35, 37b, 38

Inverness

Forpit — 33
Half gallon — 23, 37
Leepie — 26
One gallon — 36
Quarter (of a) peck — 4, 21b, 22-23
Quarter stane — 13a
Nil — 1-3, 5-12, 13bcde, 14-20, 21a, 24-25, 27-32, 34-35, 38-40

Nairn

Leepie — 1bc
Lippie — 1c
Quarter of a peck — 6
Nil — 1a, 2-5

Moray

Bushel — 21
Firlot — 19
Furlet — 18
Half a gallon — 23
Leepie — 4, 8ef, 17
Lippie — 8b, 9a, 22
Quarter of a peck — 8b
Nil — 1, 2ab, 3, 5, 6ab, 7, 8acd, 9b, 10-16, 20

Banff

Cog — 14
Firlot — 7, 30
Fortie — 19
Furlin — 2b
Half a bowe — 30
Leepie — 9-12
Lippie — 18c, 20, 27
Quarter (of a) peck — 4, 8
Nil — 1, 2ac, 3, 5, 6ab, 13, 15-17, 18abd, 21-26, 28-29, 31-34

Aberdeen

Bottle — 6
Chapan — 78
Coggie — 106
Fardle — 62
Feed — 51
Feedie — 75
Firlot — 3a, 10, 15, 18, 40, 47ae, 56-57, 68, 104
Flagon — 101, 108
Forpit — 47c, 91
Fowr pints — 109
Gowpen — 47d
Gowpen fu' — 88
Half gallon — 48, 59, 86
Leepie — 11, 17, 21, 28b, 31-32, 47d, 55, 61, 65, 75
Lippie — 23-25, 28ab, 47c, 64, 76, 80
Quart — 6
Quarter of a peck — 96, 98
Quarter of a stane — 29
Scoop — 51
Teedie — 46
Three gowpenfas — 25
Twa pints — 3a
Two neive fu's 88
Nil — 1-2, 3b, 4, 5abcd, 7-9, 12-14, 16, 19-20, 22, 26-27, 28c, 30, 33-39, 41-45, 47bf, 49-50, 52-54, 58, 60, 63, 66-67, 69-70, 71abc, 72-74, 77, 79, 81-85, 87, 89-90, 92-94, 96-97, 99-100, 102-103, 105, 107

Kincardine

Bushel — 6
Cog — 27
Cogie — 14, 17abcd, 27
Firlet — 3
Forpit — 20
Half a gallon — 26
Leepie — 10
Lippie — 13, 17ab, 28
Quarter (of a peck) — 8, 12
Nil — 1-2, 4-5, 7, 9, 11, 15-16, 18-19, 21-25

Kinross

Bowel — 3
Forpit — 5
Lippie — 1-3, 5
Quarter of a peck — 3, 6
Nil — 4, 7

Angus

Bowl — 1
Forpit — 33b
Half a seck — 28
Half gallon — 24
Half lippie — 17a
Lippie — 6, 14abcd, 18, 21, 23, 29b, 33ab, 34, 36-37
Quarter of a peck — 35
Two lippies — 13
Nil — 2-4, 5abc, 7-12, 15-16, 17b, 19-20, 22, 25-27, 29a, 30-32

Perth

Bou — 23
Firkin — 41b
Firlot — 13, 18
Forpit — 54, 67
Gowpen — 26, 52c
Half lippie — 52d
Leepie — 40, 52e
Lippie — 12, 15-16, 18, 25, 29ab, 32-33, 39, 41a, 44-46, 48, 50, 51b, 52be, 53, 55-56, 59-60, 62, 65-66, 69
Peck quarter — 2a
Puckle — 52c
Quarter (of a) peck — 4-5, 25, 57, 67, 73
Nil — 1, 2b, 3, 6-11, 14, 17, 19-22, 24, 27-28, 30-31, 34-38, 42-43, 47, 49, 51a, 52a, 58, 61, 63-64, 68, 70-72, 74

Fife

Forpit — 33, 51, 55f, 57, 61, 63, 64a
Leepie — 12-13, 17, 19-21, 24, 26, 28, 30, 33-35, 40a, 43a, 44acef, 47-50, 64ab
Lippie — 2-3, 10, 12-13, 18, 23, 27, 32-33, 36ab, 37-39, 40b, 41abd, 42, 43b, 51, 53-54, 55abcdefg, 56-61, 64ab
Forpeck — 28
Fourpit — 49, 60
Fowerpit — 43a
Gowpen — 3
Half a leepie — 9b
Half a lippie — 7
Hawf a gallon — 62
Leppie — 31
Quarter lippie — 42
Quarter of a peck — 11, 16, 25
Seeven pun — 50
Nil — 1, 4-6, 8, 9a, 14-15, 22, 29, 41c, 44bd, 45-46, 52

Clackmannan

Forpit — 4d, 5
Lippie — 1, 3, 4acd, 7
Luppie — 2, 4b
Nil — 6

Stirling

Firkin — 21a
Forpit — 2, 7b, 17-18, 25acd, 26adf, 31, 36, 39a, 42a
Four peck — 5, 33
Fourpit — 9, 20, 21b, 23bc, 26e, 27ab, 30, 32-33, 35ab
Fower pit — 22b
Half a gallon — 4
Leepie — 11
Liffie — 7a
Lippie — 7bef, 8, 10, 12, 18, 25b, 26d, 31, 39a
Luppie — 7d
Quarter of a peck — 23b, 34, 35a
Stimpart — 26b
Nil — 1, 3, 6, 7c, 13-16, 19, 22a, 23a, 24, 26c, 28-29, 37ab, 38, 39b, 40-41, 42b

Dunbarton

Four peck — 7c
Four pints — 7c
Fourpit — 7c, 16ab, 17-18
Goupen — 9
Half a gallon — 7c
Lippie — 1
Part of a lippie — 15
Quarter of a peck — 7b, 16a
Nil — 2-3, 4ab, 5-6, 7a, 8, 10-12, 13abc, 14ab

Argyll

Bushel — 18
Feorlan — 12
Forpit — 9
Fourpit — 24
Half gallon — 33
Quarter (of a) peck — 6, 17, 22
Two quarts — 7, 33
Nil — 1-5, 8, 10-11, 13-16, 19-21, 23, 25-32, 34-40

Bute

Bushel — 9
Lippie — 5
Nil — 1abcde, 2-4, 6-7, 8ab

Ayr

Chappen — 41-42
Feed dish — 28f
Forpit — 2a, 3, 6-7, 12b, 19, 28c
Fourpit — 8b, 20g, 35b, 53a
Half a gallon — 56
Half mutchkin — 18b
Lippie — 7, 19
Pun — 45
Quart — 43
Quarter a stane — 4, 47
Quartern — 28e
Quarter (of a) peck — 8b, 28e, 35b
Quarter of a stone — 38
Stimpart — 9, 14, 16b, 19, 20a, 23, 24a, 43
Stimpit — 8b, 9, 12b, 15, 16b, 17, 20abd, 21, 24b, 25, 33
Stumper — 28d
Three and a half pun — 47
Twa chappins — 57
Two chopins — 57
Nil — 1ab, 2b, 5, 8a, 10-11, 12a, 13, 16a, 18a, 20cefh, 22, 26abc, 27, 28ab, 29, 30ab, 31-32, 34, 35a, 36-37, 39-40, 44, 46, 48-52, 53b, 54-55

Renfrew

Cogill — 21
Forpit — 2j, 21
Fourpit — 17
Half a gallon — 7
Lippie — 11f, 16a
Measure — 21
Muttie — 21
Quarter — 8
Quarter a stone — 11l
Quartern — 11a
Quarter of a peck — 2aj, 13c, 19
Stimpart — 14b, 21
Two quarts — 2i
Nil — 1ab, 2bcdefgh, 3, 4abcde, 5-6, 9-10, 11bcdeghijk. 12ab, 13abd, 14a, 15, 16bcd, 18ab, 20ab

Lanark

Bushel — 64b
Chappin — 31d, 39, 57b
Cog — 42
Faurpit — 43
Firlot — 38bd
Forpeck — 46c, 47
Forpit — 3, 10b, 12-13, 15b, 17, 25d, 27b, 29g, 30, 32bf, 33bcd, 46a
Four peck — 32d, 37, 45
Fourpit — 15a, 16b, 18, 32c, 35d, 36, 56, 59b, 63
Fower peck — 11
Gill — 67b
Gowpen — 60
Lippie — 31d, 36, 38cd
Mutchkin — 9b
Pottle — 57a
Quart — 58
Quarter — 29f
Quarter o' a stane — 33d
Quarter (of a) peck — 6, 7a, 35d, 44
Twa or three haunfas — 29e
Nil — 1-2, 4-5, 7bc, 8ab, 9a, 10a, 14abcd, 15c, 16a, 19-24, 25abc, 26ab, 27a, 28, 29abcd, 31abc, 32ae, 33a, 34, 35abc, 38ae, 40-41, 46b, 48, 49ab, 50-51, 52ab, 53-55, 57c, 59a, 61-62, 64a, 65-66, 67a

West Lothian

Ferpit — 14
Firkin — 22
Forpeck — 21b
Forpit — 1ac, 2, 4-6, 8, 9b, 13-14, 16, 17a, 19b, 20a, 21b

West Lothian cont'd

Fourpit — 9a, 11, 15, 18, 19a
Fropit — 1d
Lippie — 21b
Quarter — 11
Nil — 1b, 3, 7, 10, 12, 17b, 20b, 21a

Midlothian

Chappin — 10
Forpit — 1-2, 4-5, 6b, 7b, 8b, 11, 12a, 13, 14b, 16, 18, 22, 23b, 25a, 26a, 30
Four peck — 25b
Fourpit — 3, 6a, 7a, 9, 12b, 14a, 15, 17, 20-21, 23a, 26b, 27
Quarter o' a stane — 25d
Stimpart — 23b
Nil — 8a, 19, 24, 25c, 28-29, 31-32

East Lothian

Forpit — 2, 5, 6ab, 7, 12-16, 18-19, 21
Fourpit — 1, 4ab
Fowerpit — 15
Lippie — 8
Quarter of a peck — 17
Nil — 3, 9-11, 20

Berwick

Dab — 27
Firpit — 18
Forpit — 8, 10-11, 18, 21
Fourpit — 27-28
Gowpen — 23
Gowpen fi' — 12
Half a stone — 8
Quarter bushel — 26
Quarter o' a stane — 31
Nil — 1-7, 9, 13-15, 16abc, 17, 19-20, 22, 24-25, 29-30, 32

Peebles

Forpit — 4ab, 10
Lippie — 2
Quarter o' a bushel — 6a
Twae gallons — 6a
Nil — 1, 3, 4c, 5, 6b, 7-9

Selkirk

Pottle — 2a
Nil — 1, 2bcde, 3-8

Roxburgh

Capfu — 21c
Firlot — 4
Forpit — 3a, 13, 28
Fourpit — 2
Gowpen — 12
Nil — 1, 3b, 5-8, 9ab, 10-11, 14, 15ab, 16-20, 21abdef, 22-27

Dumfries

Bushel — 13
Chappin — 19
Chopin — 1a
Forpit — 2
Hauf gallon — 4
Mutchkin — 1a
Quarter bushel — 6
Quarter of a peck — 12, 31de
Stimpart — 42
Nil — 1b, 3, 5, 7, 8ab, 9-11, 14-16, 17ab, 18, 20, 21ab, 22-30, 31abcf, 32-41, 43-44, 45ab, 46-49

Kirkcudbright

Half gallon — 4
Half stane — 16
Lippie — 17
Noggin — 12b
Quartern — 12b
Nil — 1-3, 5-11, 12a, 13-14, 15ab, 18-20, 21abc 22-27

Wigtown

Chappin — 11, 17
Lippie — 5a
Nil — 1-4, 5b, 6-10, 12-16, 18

Northumberland

Beak — 107
Beakment — 107
Beatment — 69ab, 108c, 124a
Bushel — 12
Dram — 102
Five punds — 118b
Forpit — 17, 20a, 29f, 134
Fower pints — 118b, 130e
Garter — 22
Gill measure — 52
Half (a) gallon — 15-16, 20b, 40a, 41d, 59f, 64b, 71d, 72b, 76, 83, 86, 127ac, 130ce
Heup — 124a
Quart — 24a, 41c, 58
Quarter — 46
Quarter full — 69b
Quarter of a boll — 110
Quarter (of a) peck — 30-31, 42, 52, 54, 59b, 60, 72g, 82, 94b, 103c, 109
Quarter stone — 13
Two quarts — 56, 83, 127c, 130e, 138
Nil — 1abc, 2ab, 3-11, 14, 18, 19ab, 21, 23, 24b, 25-28, 29abcde, 32, 33ab, 34ab, 35-39, 40b, 41ab, 43-45, 47-51, 53ab, 55, 57, 59acde, 61, 62abcdefgh, 63, 64a, 65ab, 66-68, 69cdefgh, 70, 71abce, 72acdefhijkl. 73-75, 77-81, 84-85, 87, 88ab, 89-93, 94a, 95ab, 96-98, 99abcd, 100, 101ab, 103ab, 104ab, 105-106, 108ab, 111ab, 112-117, 118a, 119, 120abc, 121, 122ab, 123, 124b, 125, 126abcdef, 127bdefgh, 128, 129abc, 130abdf, 131-133, 135-137, 139-143

Cumberland

Four gallons — 22
Half a gallon — 3, 14
Hauf a gallon — 46, 58
Lifterful — 9
Oaf gallon — 42
Quartern — 56
Quarter of a peck — 4, 38, 48, 59
Scoup — 16
Two quarts — 51, 60
Nil — 1ab, 2, 5ab, 6-8, 10-12, 13abcd, 15abc, 17-21, 23-36, 37ab, 39-41, 43-45, 47, 49-50, 52-55, 57, 61-62, 63ab

Down

Bushel — 6
Fourpit — 18, 26
Pinch — 28
Stimpart — 13
Nil — 1, 2ab, 3-5, 7-12, 14-17, 19-25, 27, 29-30

Tyrone

Goupan — 1
Peck — 7
Nil — 2-6, 8-16

Antrim

Bushel — 27
Half gallon — 6
Quartern — 25
Quarter of peck — 13, 19, 28
Nil — 1-4, 4A, 5ab, 7, 8ab, 9-12, 14-15, 16abc, 17-18, 20-24, 26, 29-34

Donegal

Half gallon — 12
Misure — 6
Nil — 1, 1A, 2-5, 5A, 7, 7A, 8-9, 10ab, 11, 13

Fermanagh

Nil — 1-6, 7ab, 8-10

Armagh

Nil — 1-5, 6ab

Londonderry

Cob — 6
Nil — 1, 1AB, 2-3, 3A, 4-5, 7

23 CINDER (black) (PQ1, 78)

For variants of CINDER, see map 7, Appendix A. The variants of COLD (**cald, cauld** Shetland) and COAL (**coll** Shetland, but **quile** remains in the list) have been subsumed.
Map 23A shows **cinder (glowing)** (PQ1, 77). The list has not been included as it is not very interesting.

Shetland

Aamer — 33
(Black) braand — 15, *21a,* 28
Black coal — 1, 17
Braas — 26
Brunt — 1
Cinder — 27, 32
Cold coal — 3-4, 6, 8, 12, 14, 16, 20, 21b, 22 23, 26, 30
Emer — 7
Ess — 2, 9, 11, 13, 29
Slokked coal — 19
Nil — 5, 10, 18, 24, 31

Orkney

Ashes — 14
Coal — 15
Dead ammer — 17
(Dead) cinder — 1, *2-3,* 4-5, *6,* 8-*9,* 11, 13ab, 15, 19-21
Dead coal — 15-18
Peece o' cramp — 13a
Nil — 7, 10, 12

Caithness

Ase — 5
Black coal — 3
Coke — 13
Dander — 12c, 14
(Dead) cinder — *2b,* 9, 11, *12a,* 14, 16b
Dead coal — 8
Nil — 1, 2a, 4, 6-7, 10, 12b, 15, 16a, 17

Sutherland

Ash — 10
Clinker — 9b, 15
(Dead) cinder — 1, *3,* 5, 7-8, 9a, 10-12, *13,* 16
Nil — 2, 4, 6, 14, 17

Ross & Cromarty

Ailack — 20
Ash — 20, 25a, 32a, 39
(Black) cinder — 1, 3, *4,* 5, 9, 14, 16-17, 19-20, 22-24, 26-27, 29, 31, 36, 37a, 39
Burnt cinder — 16
Clinker — 18, 25a, 28, 34
Coke — 26
Dander — 25a
Dead amber — 25b
Nil — 2, 6-8, 10-13, 15, 21, 30, 32bc, 33, 35, 37b, 38

Inverness

Ash — 5, 18, 32, 34
(Black) cinder — 1-4, 6, *7,* 8, 10-11, 13abce, 16-17, 21ab, 22-23, 28-30, 32-33, 35, 37-38, 40
Clinker — 26
Coal — 26
Coal cinder — 39
Nil — 9, 12, 13d, 14-15, 19-20, 24-25, 27, 31, 36

Nairn

(Black) cinder — 1a, 2, 5-*6*
Dander — 1bc
Nil — 3-4

Moray

Ace — 19
Aise — 9a
Ash — 14, 22
(Black) cinder — 4, 6b, 7, 8*be*, 18-22-23
Burnt oot cinder — 15
Clinker — 8c, 9b, 21-22
Dander — 2a, 4, 6a, 7, 8bd, 16-17, 22
Izel — 13
Nil — 1, 2b, 3, 5, 8af, 10-12, 20

Banff

Aise — 23, 27
Aizel — 2c, 14
Ash — 32
Black coal — 15
Black quile — 15
Cinder — 1, 2ab, 3-4, 6a, 9-13, 16-17, 18d, 19, 21, 24, 27, 29
Clinker — 6b, 8
Coke — 30
Cold coal — 34
Coom — 18c
Dander — 4-5, 6b, 8-9, 11, 16, 18b, 26, 33
Dandie — 19
Daunder — 25
Easel — 11
Izel — 31
Nil — 7, 18a, 20, 22, 28

Aberdeen

Ace — 63
Aizle — 78, 94
Ash — 15, 70, 106
(Black) aise — 15, 23, 28a, 32, *97*
Black cinder — 5c, 83
Black izle — 92, 97
Black quile — 26
Brunt cinder — 33
Burnt cinder — 85
Clinker — 20, 25, 70, 108
Cold aisil — 79
Dander — 5a, 6, 9, 25, 51, 57, 68, 70, 71b, 74-75, 80-81, 89, 103-104

Aberdeen cont'd

Daunder — 6, 88
(Dead) cinder — 2, 3ab, 4, 5bd, 6-7, 9-12, 14-22, 24, 28abc, 29-31, 34-35, 37, 39-42, 44-45, *46*, 47abcdef, 48-58, 60-61, 64-70, 71abc, 72-77, 80, 82, 86, 89, 95-96, 98, 101, 104, 107-109
Dead quile — 62
Ember — 40
Emmer — 59
Isie — 93
Smiddie coom — 9
Nil — 1, 8, 13, 27, 36, 38, 43, 84, 87, 90-91, 99-100, 102, 105

Kincardine

Ace — 11
Aise — 25
Aisel — 4
Black cinder — 18
Coke — 8
Cold cinder — 24
Dander — 5, 10, 12, 17abcd, 20, 26-28
(Dead) cinder — 1, 3, 6-*7*, 12-14, 16, 17c, 18-19, 21
Nil — 2, 9, 15, 22-23

Kinross

Ash — 6
Black cinder — 4
Dander — 3, 5
Daunder — 1-2
Nil — 7

Angus

Aisil — 29b
Ase — 7, 12, 33b
Ash — 9, 17a, 33b
(Black) cinder — 2-3, 17b, 18, 20, 24-*25*, 28, 29b, 34, 36
Burned coal — 33b
Clinker — 4, 5c, 17b, 22, 34
Dander — 5a, 6-8, 13, 14bcd, 15, 17b, 19, 22-23, 29a, 30-32, 33a, 35-37
Dead cinder — 34
Ess — 14a
Nil — 1, 5b, 10-11, 16, 21, 26-27

Perth

Ace — 7, 50, 52d, 53
Aise — 20, 33, 52a, 66
Ash — 8, 12, 20, 33, 48, 52a, 71
(Black) cinder — 1, *2a*, 3-5, *9*-10, 11, *14*, 16, 25, 28, 32-33, 36, 39, 52e, 57, 62, 67, 71-72, 74
Char — 71
Clinker — 21, 26, 41b, 46, 64
Dander — 2b, 15-16, 18, 21, 23, 25-27, 29a, 31, 42-44, 48, 50, 51b, 52bcd, 54, 56-57, 59-60
Daunder — 39, 49, 65
Dead cinder — 2a, 29a, 68
Dour cinder — 29b
Dross — 41a
Ess — 52c, 62
Gas coke — 51a
Nil — 6, 13, 17, 19, 22, 24, 30, 34-35, 37-38, 45, 47, 55, 58, 61, 63, 69-70, 73

Fife

Ace — 37, 55g
Ase — 6
Ash — 4, 13, 24, 41b, 43a, 55beg, 59
Black coal — 7
Clinker — 3, 12, 20-21, 49, 52, 55c, 58, 63
Coke — 46
Dander — 18, 26, 31, 36ab, 37-38, 47, 51, 54, 59
Daunder — 8, 9a, 10, 12, 14, 21, 25, 28, 30, 33-35, 39, 42, 46, 50, 55adf, 58, 60-61, 64a
(Dead) cinder — 11, 14, 16, 19, 21, 23, 25, 36b, 37, 39, 40b, 41a, 43a, 44cef, 50, *53*, 55bd, 57, 62
Half burnt coal — 44b
Oot fire — 7
Yad — 32-34, 49-50
Nil — 1-2, 5, 9b, 15, 17, 22, 27, 29, 40a, 41cd, 43b, 44ad, 45, 48, 56, 64b

Clackmannan

Ase — 4a, 5
Cinder — 2, 4c, 6
Clinker — 7
Dander — 2, 4bd
Nil — 1, 3

Stirling

Aizle — 26b
Ase — 7bd, 17
Ash — 4, 7f, 17, 19, 25c, 31, 33-34, 35a, 36, 37ab, 39a, 41
Ashie — 21a, 27a, 28, 30, 38
Big ash — 11
(Black) cinder — 7ce, 8-9, 13, 15-16, 21b, 22a, 23bc, 26acd, *29*, 36, 39b, 40
Chaur — 22b
Clinker — 7a, 8-9, 12, 21a, 25bc
Cold ash — 25d
Cold cinder — 20, 25ad
Dander — 6, 8, 12, 15, 18, 21b, 25bc, 26adf, 35b, 36
Daunder — 7a, 27ab, 30, 32, 35a, 42a
Dornar — 31
Nil — 1-3, 5, 10, 14, 23a, 24, 26e, 42b

Dunbarton

Ash — 7c, 8, 10-12, 13b, 18
Ause — 9, 16a
Cinder — 1, 3, 4a, 6, 7b, 13c, 16a
Clinker — 14a, 16ab
Dander — 17
Daunder — 2, 7c, 9, 13a, 14a
Nil — 4b, 5, 7a, 14b, 15

Argyll

Ash — 10, 15, 19, 23, 33
Black cinder — 29
Charred coal — 33
Clinker — 12, 35
Dander — 35
Daunder — 31
(Dead) cinder — 1-3, 6-*7*, 9-11, 14, 16-19, 22, 24-25, 27, *30*, 36, 38-39
Dead — 18
Nil — 4-8, 13, 20-21, 26, 28, 32, 34, 37, 40

Bute

Ash — 5
Awes — 8b
Char — 1cd
Cinder — 1a, 2, 7, 8a
Coke — 1d
Dander — 9
Dead ember — 9
Nil — 1be, 3-4, 6

Ayr

Aizle — 7
Ash — 2a, 6, 10, 13, 18a, 24b, 27, 33, 35b, 38-39, 43, 47, 52, 56
Ashie — 5, 16b, 17, 31, 44-45
Ause — 3-4, 16a, 33
Aw — 2a
Burnt (out) cinder — 21, *28e*
Char — 18b
Chaur — 15, 25
Cinder — 1a, 2b, 5-6, 8ab, 9-11, 12ab, 14-15, 16b, 18b, 20cdh, 22, 24a, 26abc, 28abcdf, 29, 30ab, 31-32, 34, 35b, 36-38, 40-43, 48-49, 53ab, 54
Clinker — 2a, 3, 8b, 15, 18b, 26b, 28e
Cold cinder — 20g, 49, 57
Dander — 7, 41, 47, 50, 56-57
Darkling — 19
Daunder — 2a, 3, 8b, 20adegh, 23, 24b, 26b, 28e, 33, 35b, 46, 51, 54, 57
Glum — 16b
Isle — 19
Shimmer — 10
Nil — 1b, 20bf, 35a, 55

Renfrew

Ash — 1b, 2bdfij, 3, 5, 11chj, 12b, 13c, 14a, 15, 16a, 18a, 20a
Ashie — 11k, 18a
Awse — 19
Cha(u)r — 11d
Cinder — 1a, 2ahij, 4e, 8, 11abegikl, 13d, 14a, 16b, 17, 18b, 19, 20a, 21
Clinker — 2j, 4e, 7, 13ac, 16a, 20b, 21
Coal cinder — 2g
Dander — 2j, 11e
(Dead) daunder — 2b, 4d, 7, 11cdf, 12a, 13c, 14b, 15, 16c, *18a*, 20b, 21
Dross — 16a
Konker — 8
Nil — 2ce, 4abc, 6, 9-10, 13b, 16d

Lanark

Aise — 9b, 29g, 32f
Aish — 32f
Ass — 31c, 32d, 38d, 49b
Aus — 25c
(Black) ash — 7a, 13, 15ac, 16a, 22-23, 25bc, 26b, 29ac, 31c, 32ae, 35ac, 39, 44-*45*, 51, 58
(Black) cinder — 1-3, 7c, 8a, 9a, 10ab, 11-12, 14b, 15b, 16ab, 18-19, 26a, 27b, 31ad, 33b*d*, 35bcd, 38acd, 40, 46b, 48, 52b, 55, 57ab, 59ab, 60-61, 63, 64a*b*, 65
Chaur — 7b
Clinker — 8b, 15b, 18, 29e, 30, 42, 56
Conker — 7a
Dander — 17, 29d, 30, 38e, 52b, 56, 57c
Daunder — 7a, 9a, 12-13, 15a, 17-18, 31bd, 32c, 38b, 46c, 47
Dead ash — 33c
(Dead) ashie — 20, 25d, 29c, 30, 33a*d*, 34, 57c
Dead cinder — 5, 67b
(Dead) coal — *18*, 23
Greeshoch — 9b
Remains of burnt coal — 29f
Skinner — 46b
Spent coal — 29f
Nil — 4, 6, 14acd, 21, 24, 25a, 27a, 28, 29b, 32b, 36-37, 41, 43, 46a, 49a, 50, 52a, 53-54, 62, 66, 67a

West Lothian

Ace — 11
Ash — 1b, 4, 13, 15, 19a, 20a, 21a
Char — 14
Cinder — 2-3, 5-6, 11-12, 18, 20b, 22
Clinker — 1a, 3
Cold cinder — 16
Dander — 1ad, 3, 9b, 19b
Daunder — 1c
Green cinder — 8
Nil — 7, 9a, 10, 17ab, 21b

Midlothian

Ase — 14b
Ash — 2, 15, 17, 19, 22, 25c
Ass — 24
Cinder — 2, 7a, 8ab, 10, 12a, 14a, 16, 18, 20-22, 23ab, 27, 32
Clinker — 7b, 10, 14b, 22, 23a, 26a
Dander — 4, 10-11, 12a, 26a
Daunder — 23b
Dead coal — 1
Ember — 6a
Nil — 3, 5, 6b, 9, 12b, 13, 25abd, 26b, 29-31

East Lothian

Ash — 1, 19
Ass — 6a
Burnt coal — 17
Cinder — 6b, 15-17, 21
Clinker — 8-9, 13
Coke — 13
Dander — 3, 4a, 7, 10, 14-16
Daunder — 4b, 11
Nil — 2, 5, 12, 18, 20

Berwick

Ase — 32
Ash — 2, 12, 30
Black oot cinder — 7
Burnt cinder — 8
Cinder — 6, 9-10, 12-13, 16b, 21, 23, 27-28, 31
Clinker — 5, 16a, 17, 32
Dander — 8, 11, 15, 17-18, 20, 23, 26-27, 31-32
Nil — 1, 3-4, 14, 16c, 19, 22, 24-25, 29

Peebles

Ase — 2
Ash — 1, 4c
Clinker — 4a
(Dead) cinder — *1*-2, *4b*, 5, 6b, 7-10
Nil — 3, 6a

Selkirk

Ass — 2e
Cinder — 2abcd, 4, 6, 8
Nil — 1, 3, 5, 7,

Roxburgh

Ace — 19
Ase — 9a
Ass — 5, 21de
Clinker — 24-25
Cold cinder — 13
Dander — 1, 7, 17
Daunder — 10
(Dead) cinder — 2, 3a, 4, *8*, 9ab, 12, 15b, 16-17, 19-20, 21abcef, 23, 25-26, 28
Nil — 3b, 6, 11, 14, 15a, 18, 22, 27

Dumfries

Ase — 42
Ash — 5, 15, 29, 31f, 43, 45b
Ass — 23, 29, 41
Black oot — 17b
Cinder — 1a, 2, 4-5, 7, 8ab, 9-12, 14, 16-20, 21b, 22, 24, 26, 28-30, 31abcdef, 32-33, 35, 38, 40-41, 47
Cinder dead oot — 37
Clinker — 4, 21a, 22, 27, 46
Cold cinder — 6, 13
Dead oot — 17b
Dead yin — 17b
Guest — 45a
Nil — 1b, 3, 25, 34, 36, 39, 44, 48-49

Kirkcudbright

Aizle — 1
Ash — 7
Ass — 1, 4
Awse — 24
(Black) cinder — 1-4, *5*-6, *8*-11, 12a, 13-14, 15ab, 16-20, 21abc, *22*-23, 25-27
Clinker — 12b

Wigtown
Ase – 5b
Ash – 5b, 14
Cinder – 2-4, 5ab, 6, 8-13, 15-16, 18
Dander – 7, 10, 14, 17
Nil – 1

Northumberland
Ash – 29ad, 35, 41d, 42, 46, 53b, 59c, 64a, 69abh, 71ab, 76, 80, 82-83, 87, 88a, 89, 91-93, 94b, 99b, 111ab, 118a, 122b, 126a, 127d, 130a, 134, 139
Black oot – 13
Breeze – 130c
Clinker – 10, 12, 14, 29e, 41a, 42, 45, 52, 53a, 60, 62dg, 69cdefh, 71bcd, 73, 76-77, 81, 84, 95a, 99bd, 102, 108b, 109, 111b, 113, 122ab, 124a, 126ef, 127b, 130e, 131, 138
Coke – 29e, 69ab, 127e
Cold cinder – 6, 49, 62a
Cool cinder – 75
Dander – 1a, 3, 8-11, 17, 19a, 22, 29f
Dead ash – 100
(Dead) cinder – 2ab, 5, 8, 16, 18, 20b, 21, 26, 29b, 30-31, 34b, 35-38, 40a, *41c,* 42, 46, 52, *56,* 59b, 60, 62ab, 64b, 65a, 70, 71d, 72abcdgi, 73, 77-78, 86-87, 91, 95b, 103abc, 104ab, 106-*107, 109-110,* 112, 119, 120ac, 121, 124b, 126c, 127ac, 130bef, 132, 137, 143
Dead coal – 59d, 135
Ember – 72i
Scar – 69e, 90, 96, 98, 111b, 124a, 130e
Sleck – 50
Nil – 1bc, 4, 7, 15, 19b, 20a, 23, 24ab, 25, 27-28, 29c, 32, 33ab, 34a, 39, 40b, 41b, 43-44, 47-48, 51, 54-55, 57-58, 59aef, 61, 62cefh, 63, 65b, 66-68, 69g, 71e, 72efhjkl, 74, 79, 85, 88b, 94a, 97, 99ac, 101ab, 105, 108ac, 114-117, 118b, 120b, 123, 125, 126bd, 127fgh, 128, 129abc, 130d, 133, 136, 140-142

Cumberland
Ash – 11, 14, 18, 57
Ass – 15c, 54
Bad coal – 22
Black het – 56
Clinker – 13b, 15b, 40, 46, 57
Cold cinder – 12
(Dead) cinder – 2-4, 7, 9, 13c, 15a, *17,* 21, *24*-26, 28, *33,* 42, 46-50, 52-53, *57*-58, 60, 62
Gowk – 37a
Lowe – 31
Nil – 1ab, 5ab, 6, 8, 10, 13ad, 16, 19-20, 23, 27, 29-30, 32, 34-36, 37b, 38-39, 41, 43-45, 51, 55, 59, 61, 63ab

Down
Ashes – 7, 20-21, 27
Clinker – 4, 12, 17
(Dead) cinder – *2a,* 5-6, 8-10, 13, 15, 18-19, 24, 26, 28-30
Greishie – 23
Nil – 1, 2b, 3, 11, 14, 16, 22, 25

Tyrone
Ashes – 1, 5, 8, 11
Cinder – 1, 6-8, 11
Embers – 5
Griosaig – 16
Nil – 2-4, 9-10, 12-15

Antrim
(Black) cinder – 3, 5ab, 10-12, 15, 16ab, 17-20, 22-26, *28*-29, 33
Clinker – 11
Coal – 2, 13
Greeshig – 1
Shuns – 16a
Nil – 4, 4A, 6-7, 8ab, 9, 14, 16c, 21, 27, 30-32, 34

Donegal
(Black) cinder – 2, 4-5, 5A, 6, 7A, *8,* 12
Black coal – 12
Clod – 13
Coke – 6
Dead – 10a
Slag – 13
Nil – 1, 1A, 3, 7, 9, 10b, 11

Fermanagh
Cinder – 4-5, 8-9
Greeshug – 1
Nil – 2-3, 6, 7ab, 10

Armagh
Ash – 3
Cinder – 6a
Clinker – 4
Nil – 1-2, 5, 6b

Londonderry
Cinder – 1-2, 3A, 5
Clinker – 4
Coal – 1A, 6
Nil – 1B, 3, 7

24 FORKED STICK (e.g., for making a catapult) (PQ1, 79)

GowlAck (with variant unstressed vowel) also appears in 78 **black beetle** and 82 **earwig.**

Shetland
Branch – 7
Crotch – 2
Twig – 7
Nil – 1, 3-6, 8-20, 21ab, 22-33

Orkney
Forked stick – 19
Plushnie – 6, 13b, 15
Nil – 1-5, 7-12, 13a, 14, 16-18, 20-21

Caithness
Cattag – 7
Han'el – 12b
Shotter – 12a
Tweeg – 14
Nil – 1, 2ab, 3-6, 8-11, 12c, 13, 15, 16ab, 17

Sutherland
Catapult stick – 9a
Fork – 10
Forked stick – 6, 13
Forkie stick – 3, 11
Two pronted stick – 1
Y stick – 3
Nil – 2, 4-5, 7-8, 9b, 12, 14-17

Ross & Cromarty
Catapult (stick) – 16, *26*
Cattie stick – 18, 29
Fork – 22, 33b
Forked stick – 3, 23, 28, 31, 32b 34
Golag – 39
Holder – 5
Sling stick – 1, 16, 26
Spake – 33
Twig – 17, 22
Y stick – 8, 14
Nil – 2, 4, 6-7, 9-13, 15, 19-21, 24, 25ab, 27, 30, 32ac, 35-36, 37ab, 38

Inverness
Catapult stick – 10
Fork – 11, 35
Forked stick – 2-3, 13e, 21ab, 22-23, 29, 37
Haimes – 21a
Handle – 20
Sling – 1, 30
Stick – 13b
Stopan – 9
Thumb stick – 13a
Y – 20
Nil – 4-8, 12, 13cd, 14-19, 21ab, 24-28, 31-34, 36, 38-40

Nairn
Nil – 1abc, 2-6

Moray
Catapult (stick) – *7,* 23
Cattie stick – 11, 13
Fork – 20
Forked stick – 8b
Guttie – 22
Twa legged – 21
Tweak (stick) – 6a, 8bcd, 9a, *14*
Yattie (stick) – *10,* 22
Y stick – 7
Nil – 1, 2ab, 3-5, 6b, 8aef, 9b, 12, 15-19

Banff
Breem cow – 16
Cattie stick – 10
Fork – 5
Forked stick – 4, 8, 15
Shangin – 14
Tweck – 6b
Nil – 1, 2abc, 3, 6a, 7, 9, 11-13, 17, 18abcd, 19-34

Aberdeen
Breem cow – 23, 104
Catapole – 6, 20, 25
Catapult (stick) *2,* 12, *29, 54, 70, 106*
Catie stick – 47b
Cattie (stick) – *5b,* 90
Cleft – 24
Crutch – 47b, 61
Crutchie – 47ae
Forket stick – 5c, 17, 28a, 29, 44, 73, 81, 86, 93-95, 105, 107-108
Forkie – 74
Glack – 71c, 98, 101
Haimes – 14, 27
Hems – 14, 75
Pronged stick – 47c, 67, 105
Pultie stick – 32
Quiver – 75
Scrog – 3a
Teeser – 10
Y – 7
Nil – 1, 3b, 4, 5ad, 8-9, 11, 13, 15-16, 18-19, 21-22, 26, 28bc, 30-31, 33-43, 45-46, 47df, 48-53, 55-60, 62-66, 68-69, 71ab, 72, 76-80, 82-85, 87-89, 91-92, 96-97, 99-100, 102-103, 109

Kincardine
Brechum – 28
Catapult stick – 26
Cattie stick – 24
Forket stick – 3, 5-6, 8
Forket twig – 10
Sling – 11
Nil – 1-2, 4, 7, 9, 12-16, 17abcd, 18-23, 25, 27

Kinross
Breek – 5
Breeked stick – 2, 7

Kinross cont'd

Crutch — 6
Forket stick — 4
Guttie — 6
Nil — 1, 3

Angus

Beek — 35
Breek — 5b, 14a, 23-24, 34
Breekie — 14b
Breeked stick — 10, 20, 22, 28
Catapult (stick) — *2,* 33b
Cattie (stick) — 18, *24, 36*
Crook — 14d
Fork — 25
Forkit (stick) — *9,* 17a, *29b*
Shangan — 29b
Sling — 17a, 19
Twa legged stick — 34
Twa pronged stick — 31
Nil — 1, 3-4, 5ac, 6-8, 11-13, 14c, 15-16, 17b, 21, 26-27, 29a, 30, 32, 33a, 37

Perth

Breek — 10, 26, 55
Breeked stick — 7, 23, 25, 27, 33, 42, 45, 50, 52c, 56, 65
Buch — 71
Catapult (stick) — 2a, *24*
Cattie (stick) — *15, 24,* 40, 41a*b*, 44, *62*
Cloven stick — 20
Doobler — 60
Fork — 9-10
Forked stick — 1, 4-5, 8, 28, 43, 74
Forkit stick — 32
Glack — 39
Goulet — 73
Gowlack — 16, 26, 37, 39, 66-67, 69-70
Gowrack — 68
Guttie (stick) — *13,* 30, 48, 53, *59*
Pringed stick — 68
Pronged stick — 12
Sling (stick) — 53, *72*
Twigger — 44
Nil — 2b, 3, 6, 11, 14, 17-19, 21-22, 29ab, 31, 34-36, 38, 46-47, 49, 51ab, 52abde, 54, 57-58, 61, 63-64

Fife

Breech — 12, 37-38, 41c, 43b
Breechie — 41d
Breek — 10, 19-20, 26, 39, 40b, 41bc, 42, 44bd, 45, 47, 55b, 64a
Breeked stick — 1, 3, 6, 14, 17, 21, 43a, 55b, 61, 64b
Breek end — 12
Breekie — 41d
Clove stick — 51
Fire away — 35
Forked stick — 11, 44c, 50, 55b, 62
Gutt breech — 12
Guttie paw — 31, 36a
Guttie pelt — 41a
Guttie pole — 12-13, 36b, 55ef
Guttie polt — 24, 36a, 37
Guttie (stick) — 5, 7, 9a, *12,* 18, 23, *25, 42,* 43a, 44e, 46, 48-*49,* 51, 52, 53, 55adg, 56-57, *58-59,* 63
Guttie Y — 45
Haundel for a fire awa — 32
Pold — 44b
Stick — 9b, 21
Y — 50
Nil — 2, 4, 8, 15-16, 22, 27-30, 33-34, 40a, 44acf, 54, 55c, 60

Clackmannan

Catapult — 4c
Cattie (stick) — *5,* 7
Guttie pole — 3
Guttie stick — 4d
Sling — 4c
Nil — 1-2, 4ab, 6

Stirling

Buggie — 8
Cuttie — 25b
Forked stick — 4, 7c, 16, 23b, 26a, 34
Forkie — 7abd
Gauluck — 1
Guttie — 7e, 26b
Guttie crutch — 8
Guttie paw — 18, 26df, 37b
Sling haunle — 12
Sling (stick) — 7f, *8,* 23*bc,* *25abd,* 26c, 27a, 28, *30-32,* 33, 36, 37a, 39b
Slung (stick) — *12, 17, 19,* 39b, *42a*
Strider — 17, 20
Stridie — 22ab
Thumb stick — 7b
Nil — 2-3, 5-6, 9-11, 13-15, 21ab, 23a, 24, 25c, 26e, 27b, 29, 35ab, 38, 39a, 40-41, 42b

Dunbarton

Cattie — 16b
Cleft stick — 6, 7c
Fork — 5
Forked stick — 6, 7b
Gowleg — 2
Guttie pole — 16a
Sling stalk — 11
Sling (stick) — 3, *4b, 7bc; 9, 16ab, 18*
Slung — 18
Nil — 1, 4a, 7a, 8, 10, 12, 13abc, 14ab, 15, 17

Argyll

Forked stick — 2, 11-12, 15, 17, 22
Fork stick — 33
Gabbed stick — 34
Golack — 35
Sling (stick) — 3, *9, 16, 18*-19, 21, *23-24,* 29, 32-33, 37-38
Thumb stick — 16
Nil — 1, 4-8, 10, 13-14, 20, 25-28, 30-31, 36, 39-40

Bute

Knee — 9
Sling handle — 9
Sling (stick) — 1a, 3, *7, 8b*
Nil — 1bcde, 2, 4-6, 8a

Ayr

Bucht stick — 24b
Catapult — 16b, 57
Cattie — 7
Changan — 41
Cuttie stick — 53a
Forked stick — 5
Forked wid — 20g
Gab — 1a
Gabbed stick — 4
Pea stick — 47
Shangan — 43
Sling (stick) — *7, 8ab, 10, 12b, 14*-15, 16*a*b, *18b, 19,* 20bcg, *21, 24a,* 25, 28d, *29, 30a, 33-34,* 35a, *36, 38, 40, 45,* 53b, 54, *56-57*
Slung fork — 49
Slung (stick) — *9,* 17, 27, 28acf, *31-32,* 41, *42-43, 47-48,* 49, *51*
Nil — 1b, 2ab, 3, 6, 11, 12a, 13, 18a, 20adefh, 22-23, 26abc, 28be, 30b, 35b, 37, 39, 44, 46, 50, 52, 55

Renfrew

Claevie — 11a
Forked stick — 2a, 8, 13c
Forkie — 15
Frame — 4be
Sling (stick) — 2ghj, *4ac, 5,* 11bdg, 12a, 15, 16a*b, 17, 18a,* 20b, 21
Y stick — 2i
Nil — 1ab, 2bcdef, 3, 4d, 6-7, 9-10, 11cdefhijkl, 12b, 13abd, 14ab, 16cd, 18b, 19, 20a

Lanark

Aish stick — 33c
Cattie — 7c
Cleft — 49b
Cloft — 38d
Crooked stick — 17
Crotch — 17
Crutch — 17
Fork — 59b
Forked stick — 3, 26a, 35d
Puggie (stick) — 31b, 33*ad, 34*
Sling (stick) — *6,* 7*ac,* 8b, 10a*b, 12-13, 16a,* 18-*19, 22*-23, 27a, 29fg, 30, 31c, 32f, 37, 39, *45, 46c, 47, 49a, 52b, 55, 57b, 58, 61,* 64b, 67ab
Slug — 29g
Slung (stick) — *2-3, 9a,* 18, *19-20,* 23, *25d,* 26b, 27b, 28, 30, *31d, 33ad, 34, 35a,* 36, *38a, 41, 44, 46b, 48*
Stick — 25c
Tattie bogle — 29e
V stick — 33c
Y stick — 56
Nil — 1, 4-5, 7b, 8a, 9b, 11, 14abcd, 15abc, 16b, 21, 24, 25ab, 29abcd, 31a, 32abcde, 33b, 35bc, 38bce, 40, 42-43, 46a, 50-51, 52a, 53-54, 57ac, 59a, 60, 62-63, 64a, 65-66

West Lothian

Catapult stick — 11
Fork — 8
Forked stick — 5-6
Guttie pole — 13
Guttie (stick) — *2,* 11, *15*
Prong — 15
Sling — 1d, 4, 21ab
Slung (stick) — *17a, 18, 19b,* 21b, 22
Y — 9a
Nil — 1abc, 3, 7, 9b, 10, 12, 14, 16, 17b, 19a, 20ab

Midlothian

Cattie — 5
Cuttie stick — 32
Forked stick — 23b
Guttie (stick) — 15, 17, *19,* 21, 25a*c*
Prong — 8ab, 23b
Sling — 1, 6a, 12a, 15-18, 20
Slung stick — 23a
Y — 31
Nil — 2-4, 6b, 7ab, 9-11, 12b, 13, 14ab, 22, 24, 25bd, 26ab, 27-30

East Lothian

Catapult stick — 17
Cattie stick — 13
Cuttie stick — 8, 12, 14
Guttie (stick) — *1*-2, 5, *6a, 13*
Prong — 4b
Slung stick — 4b, 7
Nil — 3, 4a, 6b, 9-11, 15-16, 18-21

Berwick

Catapult stick — 7, 10
Cattie (stick) — 8, *15, 19, 31-32*
Cleft stick — 3
Cuttie stick — 13, 23-24, 29, 31
Forked stick — 1-2, 16b
Guttie stick — 4, 16a
Shank — 27
Nil — 5-6, 9, 11-12, 14, 16c, 17-18, 20-22, 25-26, 28, 30

Peebles

Catapult stick — 1
Cattie stick — 4b, 6ab
Forked stick — 2, 8
Shanghai — 6a
Nil — 3, 4ac, 5, 7, 9-10

Selkirk

Cattie — 2e
Cuttie — 2b
Nil — 1, 2acd, 3-8

Roxburgh

Catapult stick — 16
Cattie stick — 5, 9a, 17
Cleft stick — 12, 21f
Cloft — 21c
Crotchie stick — 15b
Cuttie stick — 7-8
Guttie stick — 25
Y (stick) — *23,* 26
Nil — 1-2, 3ab, 4, 6, 9b, 10-11, 13-14, 15a, 18-20, 21abde, 22, 24, 27-28

Dumfries

Ash sling — 35
Cattie (stick) — *6,* 28-*29, 38-40*
Cleft stick — 1a
Clofted (stick) — *21b,* 29, *32*
Forked stick — 4-5, 21b, 22
Shangan — 42
Shangie — 42
Sling (stick) — *12*-13, 16, *27, 29,* 31*ce*
V stick — 15
Y — 19, 32
Nil — 1b, 2-3, 7, 8ab, 9-11, 14, 17ab, 18, 20, 21a, 23-26, 30, 31abdf, 33-34, 36-37, 41, 43-44, 45ab, 46-49

Kirkcudbright

Caster — 14
Cattie stick — 11
Cleft stick — 4, 16
Forked stick — 10
Shangan — 1, 17
Shank — 17
Sling (stick) — 1-*2, 7, 12b, 18, 21, 26*
V stick — 4
Nil — 3, 5-6, 8-9, 12a, 13, 15ab, 19-20, 21bc, 22-25, 27

Wigtown

Catapult stick — 11
Cattie (stick) — 2, *8, 14*
Forked stick — 7
Prong — 5a
Y stick — 7
Nil — 1, 3-4, 5b, 6, 9-10, 12-13, 15-18

Northumberland

Catapult — 46, 100
Catapult Y — 62e
Catie stick — 13
Catiwye — 78, 122b
Cattie (stick) — *1c, 6-7,* 9, *15, 20b, 31, 38, 72d,* 104b
Cattie wee — 130d
Cattie why — 17, 22, 46, 65a, 70, 76, 105, 107, 110, 111a, 118b
Cattie Y — 1b, 2a, 3, 5, 12, 16-18, 20a, 21-22, 24a, 27, 29acde, 34a, 36-37, 39, 41b, 43, 45, 48, 52, 53a, 57, 59b, 60, 63, 68, 69c, 71d, 72j, 78-80, 82, 87, 92, 102, 104a, 106, 108c, 109, 112-113, 116-117, 120abc, 124b, 125, 127b,

Northumberland Cont'd

129a, 130a, 133, 135-137, 139
Cleft (stick) — *19a, 28,* 53a, *71c*
Clofted stick — 140
Forked stick — 28, 41c, 54, 59b, 72d, 103c, 126c, 132
Forkie stick — 99d
Gattie — 94b
Gattie Y — 118a
Jemmy — 83
Jimmer — 124a
Pult stick — 40a, 69ab
Pult Y — 71b
Sling stick — 23, 24b
Striddle — 122a
Striddler — 41d
Wand — 130f
Why stick — 8, 64a, 65b, 69de, 70, 72g, 90, 97, 103c, 111a
Y (stick) — 8, 10, *13,* 26, 30, 33b, 34b, *37*-38, 40a, *41bc,* 42, 44, 47-49, *50,* 53b, 55-56, 58, 59acde, 61, 62adh, 64b, 66, 68, 69abfg, 72g, 74-75, 77, *81*-82, *84, 86-87, 88b,* 89, 94b, 95ab, *96,* 98, 103bc, *108a,* 111b, 114, 116, *119,* 122b, 124b, 127e, 128, 129b, *130c,* 134, 138, *140-141, 142*
Nil — 1a, 2b, 4, 11, 14, 19b, 25, 29bf, 32, 33a, 35, 40b, 41a, 51, 59f, 62bcfg, 67, 69h, 71ae, 72abcefhikl, 73, 85, 88a, 91, 93, 94a, 99abc, 101ab, 103a, 108b, 115, 121, 123, 126abdef, 127acdfgh, 129c, 130be, 131, 143

Cumberland

Catapult stick — 9, 56,
Cate stick — 15b
Cattie fang — 26
Cattie (stick) — *2, 8-9, 11-12, 14, 15c, 17-18,* 22, *24-25, 27-28, 30-32, 37b, 38, 40-41, 42, 45-46, 48, 51, 54-55, 57, 59*
Cattie Y — 6, 13c
Cettie stick — 51
Cleft stick — 5a, 50
Clofted stick — 4
Cloft stick — 3
Cluft stick — 38
Crotched stick — 57
Crutch — 18
Fork — 30
Forked stick — 16, 46, 53, 57
Pronged stick — 46, 62
Y stick — 23
Nil — 1ab, 5b, 7, 10, 13abd, 15a, 19-21, 29, 33-36, 37a, 39, 43-44, 47, 49, 52, 58, 60-61, 63ab

Down

Facing stick — 17
Forked stick — 15, 19
Forkie stick — 4
Forks — 20, 24, 28
Golog — 22
Pair of forks — 7, 26
Sputle — 22
Stick — 9
Whin fork — 3, 13, 18-19, 21
Whun fork — 3
Nil — 1, 2ab, 5-6, 8, 10-12, 14, 16, 23, 25, 27, 29-30

Tyrone

Forked stick — 7, 9, 11
Forkie stick — 13
Prong — 1
Nil — 2-6, 8, 10, 12, 14-16

Antrim

Catapult — 13, 26
Crotch — 25
Crutch — 25
Forked stick —5a, 5A, 19-20, 22
Forkie — 21
Forks — 11, 27-28
Golach — 7
High o scute — 16a
Pair of forks — 15, 17
Pronged stick — 4A, 6, 9, 33
Shielden — 34
Nil — 1, 1A, 2-4, 5b, 7A, 8ab, 10, 12, 14, 16bc, 18, 23-24, 29-32

Donegal

Fork — 1
Forked stick — 5, 5A, 8
Knee — 5
Prong — 6
Nil — 1A, 2-4, 7, 7A, 9, 10ab, 11-13

Fermanagh

Forked stick — 4
Two pronged stick — 4
Nil — 1-3, 5-6, 7ab, 8-10

Armagh

Fork — 3
Pair of forks — 4
Nil — 1-2, 5, 6ab

Londonderry

Cleft stick — 4
Forked stick — 2, 3A
Pronged stick — 1A
Prongs — 1B, 6
Stilts — 3
Nil — 1, 5, 7

25 PASSAGE BETWEEN HOUSES (PQ1, 80)

Close has not been mapped as it occurs fairly densely nearly everywhere except in Cumberland, Northern Ireland, and parts of Northumberland. Variants of CLOSE, CLOSIE have been subsumed (**closs,** Shetland, Orkney, Aberdeenshire, Kincardineshire; a few scattered **clossie**).
The additional request: 'State if a different word is used when the passage is arched', did not yield many answers. Therefore responses have not been included.

Shetland

Alley way — 23
Alley wye — 32
Close — 6, 10, 17, 21a, 22, 24, 26-28, 30
Gate — 19
Gjet — 4
Nosamil — 9
Opening — 21a
Orrie — 1
Staggie — 20
Stiggie — 13-16
Stroadie — 8, 24
Trance — 3, 5, 10, 12, 17, 19, 23, 28, 30
Trenkie — 21b
Trinkie — 2, 6, 10, 26, 31
Yat — 25
Nil — 7, 11, 18, 29, 33

Orkney

Brigstanes — 8, 15
Brigstones — 8
Close — 1-12, 13ab, 14-21
Passage — 8, 21
Trance — 10, 13a
Trowgang — 12
Walk — 15

Caithness

Close — 1, 2ab, 3, 5-8, 12a, 14-15
Entry — 2b, 5-6, 8-11, 12a, 13, 16ab, 17
Lane — 4
Space — 13
Vennel — 2b, 11
Nil — 12bc

Sutherland

Alley — 3
Close — 7-8, 9b, 14, 16
Entry — 9a
Lane — 10, 17
Pass — 1, 3, 13
Passage — 5, 7, 12-13
Pathway — 3
Nil — 2, 4, 6, 11, 15

Ross & Cromarty

Bennel — 14
Close — 3, 7-8, 10, 16, 21, 23, 25ab, 28-29, 31, 32abc, 33-36, 39
Closie — 25b, 37ab
Lane — 2, 10, 17, 20, 27, 32a
Passage — 4-5, 24, 26-27
Path — 26
Vennel — 6, 8-15, 18-20, 23, 28
Nil — 1, 22, 30, 38

Inverness

Alley — 13c, 18-19
Close — 3, 6, 10, 13bce, 14, 17, 19, 21ab, 26-28, 30, 32-33, 35-36, 38-40
Closie — 26
Lane — 11, 19-20, 22-23, 25, 37
Passage — 1, 3, 11, 13a, 34
Path — 7, 16, 29
Roadie — 9, 29
Vennel — 13a
Walk — 5
Nil — 2, 4, 8, 12, 13d, 15, 24, 31

Nairn

Close — 1a, 2, 4
Lane — 2
Lanie — 5
Pen — 1b
Roadie — 6
Scuttle — 1c
Vennel — 1b
Nil — 3

Moray

Close — 2a, 3-5, 7, 8abcd, 9a, 10-15, 17-18, 20-23
Closie — 1, 6af, 8f, 16
Entry — 4
Lane — 7, 8be, 14-15, 20-21
Lanie — 3-5, 8a, 16
Loanie — 9a
Slap — 16
Slappie — 6b, 8d, 13
Stripie — 2b
Trochie — 2a, 8d, 9ab, 19
Wynd — 7, 18, 20
Wynnie — 9a

Banff

Bole — 18b
Bollie — 17
Close — 1, 2abc, 3-5, 6a, 7, 10-11, 13, 15, 18c, 20, 25-26, 28-29, 31-32
Closie — 2c, 6b, 7, 21
Drain — 12
Gap — 16
Lane — 15, 21, 23, 29-30, 33
Lanie — 6b, 9, 21, 23, 32
Pass — 22-25
Pen — 11-12, 23-24, 27
Pend — 15
Posie — 2abc, 6ab
Pozzie — 3
Slap — 5, 16, 19, 34
Slappie — 8-9
Slattie — 7
Trance — 14
Nil — 18ad

Aberdeen

Alley — 5b
Close — 1, 4, 5ab, 6-7, 9-10, 12, 14, 19-22, 26, 28ac, 40, 42, 44, 46, 47abcdef, 49, 53, 55-56, 58, 60, 62-63, 66-67, 69-70, 71bc, 74-79, 81-83, 85-88, 93-97, 99-100, 102 104-105, 107-108
Closie — 5d, 25, 41, 47d, 73, 75, 98
Gangway — 70
Lane — 2, 5d, 12, 14, 17, 20, 31-32, 35, 45, 64, 70, 71c, 81-82, 96, 103, 105
Lanie — 25, 27, 47f, 50-51, 64, 80, 90, 106
Lennie — 7
Loan — 10, 71a
Lobby — 109
Opening — 101
Pass — 84
Passage — 14, 54
Path — 38, 59
Pathie — 29
Pen — 3ab, 5ab, 6, 9-10, 15, 17, 20, 25-27, 28b, 30, 32, 36, 39, 47ad, 48, 51-52, 56, 65 73, 77, 98, 108
Pend — 47c, 68, 76, 105

Aberdeen cont'd

Roadie — 14, 24, 90
Roddie — 1
Slap — 16, 49, 62, 72
Slappie — 14-16, 24, 34, 61, 67, 72-73
Trance — 23
Trochie — 6-7
Vent — 23
Walkie — 29, 90
Wynd — 47c
Nil — 5c, 8, 11, 13, 18, 33, 37, 43, 57, 89, 91-92

Kincardine

Alley — 17c
Close — 1-3, 5, 7, 10-13, 15-16, 17abcd, 18, 24, 27-28
Closie — 2, 14, 17c, 21-22, 25-27
Lane — 5, 8-9, 16, 17c
Loan — 15
Passage — 6
Pen — 13, 17b, 28
Pend — 15, 17c, 20, 23, 28
Roadie — 19
Slap — 25
Nil — 4

Kinross

Close — 1-7
Entry — 2-3
Pend — 6
Vennel — 1

Angus

Causeway — 22
Close — 1-2, 4, 5abc, 6-8, 10-13, 14ad, 15, 17b, 18, 20-28, 29b, 30, 32, 33ab, 34-37
Closie — 3, 9, 12-13, 14bcd, 19, 22, 29a, 32
Cundie — 17a
Entry — 17b, 29b
Lane — 9, 17a, 33b
Pen — 31
Pend — 4, 5ac, 7-8, 14a, 17b, 20-24, 30, 33b
Slap — 20
Trance — 6, 14acd
Vennel — 14a, 33b, 37
Wynd — 14a
Nil — 16

Perth

Alley — 10, 12, 25, 32, 47, 56, 74
Close — 3, 5-7, 9, 12-13, 16, 19, 21-25, 27-28, 29ab, 30-33, 35-36, 38, 41ab, 43, 46, 48-50, 51ab, 52ade, 53, 55-63, 66-73
Closie — 45
Entry — 14-15, 20, 25, 29b, 37, 39-40, 41b, 61-62
Gate — 25
Lane — 2a, 3, 18, 48, 52e
Loan — 10
Lobby — 73
Passage — 4, 8, 10, 24
Pen — 5-6, 17, 24, 26, 50, 69
Pend — 12-13, 16, 20-21, 26-27, 32-33, 39-40, 41a, 44, 46-48, 51a, 52bcd, 53, 57-59, 63-64, 66
Row — 25
Vennel — 16, 18, 25, 41a, 52e, 55, 68, 70
Wynd — 16, 18, 25, 41a, 45, 52d, 62
Nil — 1, 2b, 11, 34, 42, 54, 65

Fife

Close — 1-4, 6-8, 9ab, 10-14, 16-21, 23-24, 27-28, 30, 32-33, 35, 36b, 37-39, 40ab, 41abcd, 42, 43ab, 44bcdef, 45-54, 55abcdefg, 56-63, 64ab
Entry — 7, 9b, 10-11, 20, 44f, 48, 54
Gile — 23, 28
Lane — 29
Peand — 6
Pen — 18
Pend — 2, 5, 8, 12, 18-20, 22-23, 25, 27-28, 31-35, 41d, 43a, 44abef, 46-49, 55b, 64a
Trance — 29, 32
Vennel — 14, 21, 23, 26-27, 35, 36a, 37-38, 40b, 41ac, 44c, 49-51, 53, 55ef, 57-58, 62
Wynd — 33, 44ac, 53
Nil — 15

Clackmannan

Close — 1-3, 4abcd, 5-7
Entry — 1
Near — 2
Pen — 6
Pend — 1
Vennel — 4bd
Wynd — 3

Stirling

Ben — 19
Cat's walk — 7abd
Close — 1-6, 7abf, 8-13, 15-20, 21ab, 22b, 23abc, 24, 25abcd, 26abcdef, 27ab, 28, 30-34, 35ab, 36, 37ab, 38, 39ab, 40-41, 42a
Entry — 7e, 8, 25ad, 30, 36
Lane — 7e
Loan — 39a
Pen — 3, 5, 7abcf, 9, 15, 17-18, 23a, 25c, 26abe, 31, 33
Pen close — 27a
Pend — 7bce, 9, 14-15, 22ab, 25c, 26abde
Pend close — 14
Vennel — 4-5, 7abe, 8-10, 12, 21a
Wynd — 2, 7b, 25acd
Nil — 29, 42b

Dunbarton

Alley — 11
Alleyway — 5
Close — 1-2, 4ab, 5-6, 7abc, 8-12, 13a, 14ab, 15, 16ab, 17-18
Dunnie — 14b
Entry — 7c
Lane — 13bc, 18
Lobby — 4b
Passage — 11
Pathway — 11
Pen — 3, 4b, 7a, 12, 13a, 16b
Pend — 1, 8, 10
Pend close — 7c
Trance — 16a
Vennel — 9, 14a

Argyll

Alley — 24
Close — 3, 5-7, 9, 20-21, 24, 26-28, 30-33, 35-37, 39-40
Entry — 26
Lane — 3, 12, 14-15, 19, 23, 29, 33
Loan — 35
Opening — 19
Passage — 2, 6, 11-12, 16-17, 23
Path — 15
Pen — 18, 36
Road — 22
Walk — 22
Nil — 1, 4, 8, 10, 13, 25, 34, 38

Bute

Alley — 1a
Close — 2ab, 2-7, 8ab, 9
Entry — 8b, 9
Peind — 8b
Pen — 1e
Pend — 1a
Pend close — 1e
Nil — 1cd

Ayr

Aisle — 41
Alley — 57
Back — 50
Bole — 13
Close — 1a, 2b, 3-7, 8ab, 9, 11, 12ab, 15, 16ab, 18ab, 20abefgh, 21-23, 24b, 25, 26bc, 27, 28bcdef, 29, 30a, 31-34, 35ab, 36-39, 41, 45, 47-49, 52, 53ab, 55-57
Drive — 28e
Entry — 1a, 5, 7, 8a, 9, 11, 16ab, 18ab, 20g, 21-22, 24ab, 25, 26b, 27, 28e, 29, 30b, 32-34, 35b, 42, 44-46, 49-51, 54, 56
Foley — 2b
Gavel — 7
Gavel end — 35a
Ginnel — 28a
Lane — 17, 26a
Loanin — 9
Lobby — 5
Pen — 3, 6-7, 8ab, 13, 16ab, 18a, 20b, 33, 38
Pend — 3, 18b, 21, 41, 48, 57
Through gang — 19
Through gaun — 35b
Trance — 38
Vennel — 28b, 36, 41-42
Vernel — 38
Vowt — 30b, 35b
Walk — 28e
Want — 20g
Wide pen — 15
Wynd — 28b, 41
Nil — 1b, 2a, 10, 14, 20cd, 40, 43

Renfrew

Alley — 2e, 4ace, 16a
Close — 2bfghij, 3, 4be, 5-6, 8, 10, 11j, 12a, 13c, 14b, 15, 16cd, 17, 18a, 19, 21
Entry — 17
Lane — 1b, 2abdi, 4bd, 11l, 12b, 16abd
Lobby — 11j
Opening — 4b
Passage — 8, 20a
Passage way — 2i
Path — 2g, 4b, 16a
Pen — 5, 8-9, 11abdefijk, 12a, 16cd, 18a, 20b
Pen close — 11f
Pend — 2ef, 11adij, 14b, 16cd, 21
Through gaun — 18b, 20a
Vennel — 11h, 16abcd
Wynd — 11ael
Nil — 1a, 2c, 7, 11cg, 13abd, 14a

Lanark

Alley — 15b, 26a, 29f
Causeway — 37
Close — 1-5, 7a, 8a, 9ab, 10a, 11-13, 14abcd, 15bc, 16ab, 17-21, 23-24, 25abcd, 26ab, 27ab, 28, 29abcdfg, 30, 31abcd, 32abcdef, 33abcd, 34, 35ab, 36-37, 38abc, 39, 41-42, 44-45, 46abc, 47-48, 49ab, 50-51, 52ab, 53, 55, 57abc, 58, 59a, 60-61, 64ab, 67b
Cundie — 49b
Entry — 9a, 15a, 17-18, 27ab, 29e, 32df, 33cd, 35d, 40, 46a, 47, 50, 52a, 56, 62-63, 65-66
Gable end — 15a
Gushet — 38d
Lane — 7c, 20, 23, 25d, 29f, 35cd, 50
Lobby — 30
Opening — 6, 59b
Passage — 29f
Pen — 3, 6, 7ab, 8a, 10a, 11, 15b, 16b, 22, 25abd, 29bc, 30, 31d, 32c, 36, 38a, 44, 48, 57a
Pen close — 15b, 29c, 33cd
Pend — 6, 7c, 10a, 14c, 16b, 32be
Road — 59b
Through gate — 59a
Throught gate — 38b
Vennel — 7a, 8b, 13, 14c, 32df, 38e, 49b, 54, 65
Wicket — 67ab
Wynd — 15b, 32bd
Nil — 10b, 43

West Lothian

Alley — 1a
Close — 1abcd, 2-8, 9ab, 10-13, 15-16, 17ab, 19b, 20ab, 21ab, 22
Entry — 7, 18, 21a
Gale — 11
Lobby — 19a
Pen — 1c, 4, 17a, 19b, 22
Pen close — 2
Pend — 1a, 5, 11, 16, 22
Through gate — 4
Through gaun — 18
Vennel — 6, 10, 14, 16

Midlothian

Close — 1, 3-5, 6a, 7ab, 8ab, 9-11, 12ab, 13, 14ab, 16-18, 21-22, 23ab, 24, 26ab, 27-29, 31-32
Entry — 7b, 22, 23b, 27
Lane — 2, 6b, 17
Lobby — 11
Passage — 8a, 10, 12b
Pen — 18, 23b
Pend — 5, 6b, 7b, 8b, 10, 12a, 22, 26a, 29
Tunnel — 17
Vennel — 3, 9-11, 12b, 15, 17-20, 23ab, 24, 25abcd, 26ab, 27-32
Wynd — 8b, 26a

East Lothian

Close — 1-2, 4ab, 5, 6ab, 9-15, 18
Entry — 1, 4a
Pend — 4a, 9-10, 13-14
Vennel — 1-3, 4ab, 5, 6ab, 7-9, 11-17, 19-21
Wynd — 5, 9, 13
Yett — 4a

Berwick

Close — 2, 16c, 17, 23-24, 27, 29
Cundie — 21
Entry — 8, 16c
Lane — 2
Passage — 8
Pen — 27
Pend — 9
Vennel — 1, 3-15, 16abc, 17-23, 25-28, 30-32
Vowt — 8, 10

Peebles

Close — 1-3, 4abc, 5, 6ab, 7-8
Entry — 4b, 10
Pen — 9
Vennel — 2-3, 6b, 8, 10
Wynd — 2, 4ab, 6a

Selkirk

Close — 1, 2abcde, 3-8
Pen — 7
Pend — 2b
Vennel — 1, 3, 7-8

Roxburgh

Alla — 19
Alley — 26
Close — 2, 3ab, 8, 9b, 13, 15ab, 19-20, 21abcdef, 23, 25-26, 28
Entry — 3a, 13, 15a, 17, 21ac, 26, 28
Mean — 21c
Pen — 1, 9b
Pend — 12, 15b, 20, 21d, 26
Vennel — 1, 3a, 4-8, 9ab, 10-11, 13, 15ab, 16-18, 20, 21a, 23-28

Roxburgh cont'd
Wynd – 9b
Nil – 14, 22

Dumfries
Alley – 27-28, 46-47
Awlleyway – 37
Causie – 23
Close – 1a, 4, 6-7, 8ab, 10, 12, 14, 17ab, 20, 21ab, 25-28, 30, 31acef, 32-35, 40-44, 45b
Cundie – 31c
Entry – 1b, 3-7, 8b, 9, 11-13, 15-16, 17b, 19, 22, 24-26, 29, 31f, 32, 34-39, 41-42, 45a
Ginnel – 34
Nick – 31bdf
Passage – 46
Pen – 20, 33, 46
Poorch – 46
Vennel – 25
Nil – 2, 18, 48-49

Kirkcudbright
Alley – 6, 24
Close – 1-3, 5-7, 9, 11, 12b, 15a, 16, 21abc, 25-26
Entry – 1-4, 7-11, 12ab, 14, 15ab, 16-20, 21c, 22-23, 26-27
Pangen – 3
Pangent – 1
Pen – 17, 21ac
Slap – 21b
Trance – 17
Vennel – 1
Nil – 13

Wigtown
Big slap – 14
Close – 1, 3, 5ab, 7-11, 15-17
Entry – 5a, 7-8, 10, 12-15, 18
Lanin – 6
Lobby – 8
Pad – 2
Passage – 17
Slap – 18
Nil – 4

Northumberland
Alley – 1b, 2b, 14, 18, 19a, 20b, 26, 28, 29abef, 30, 32, 33a, 35, 37-39, 40b, 41b, 42-43, 46-50, 53a, 55, 59def, 60, 62bcefh, 63, 64ab, 66, 68, 69ceh, 70, 71bd, 72acik, 77-79, 81-82, 86-87, 89-90, 92, 95ab, 97, 99bcd, 101b, 103ac, 104b, 107, 108b, 110, 111a, 113-114, 116, 118ab, 121, 122ab, 123, 124b, 125, 126adef, 127bceh, 128, 129a, 130d, 132, 134, 137, 139
Alley way – 2b, 3, 5, 12, 16, 21, 31, 34a, 36, 40b, 52, 53ab, 54, 56-58, 59bc, 71d, 72bci, 74-76, 84-85, 88b, 100, 101b, 102, 103b, 104b, 106, 108ac, 109, 112, 126c, 127ad, 130e, 136, 138, 141-142
Arcade – 69b
Arch – 1c, 69b, 85
Back lane – 121, 126f, 130a
Bennel – 19b, 24a
Cassie – 41d, 54
Causie – 41d, 46, 51, 79
Chare – 62f, 71c, 99c, 100, 108a 121, 122a, 124a, 126ef, 127h, 130d, 133
Close – 1c, 32, 33a, 34b, 39, 40b, 69c, 72ik, 79, 117, 124a, 127bch, 130d
Corner end – 111b
Court – 29be, 82
Cundie – 72fl, 83
Cut – 37, 40a, 69f, 71c, 72k, 94b, 99d
Entrance – 33b
Entry – 1c, 5, 7, 11-12, 18, 20b, 24a, 27, 29b, 40b, 41ac, 44, 47, 56, 59b, 69ab, 71c, 72e, 73, 117, 126af, 127e, 143
Gangway – 140
Gantry – 49
Gap – 69a
Garth – 126f
Gully – 12
Hatch – 130d
Hoose end – 111b
Lane – 6, 29bf, 40a, 71d, 82, 135
Lobby – 130f
Lone chare – 127b
Neuk – 69a
Nick – 17-18, 37, 46, 60, 69d, 130d, 134
Open – 89
Opening – 41ab, 62acg, 65a, 66-67, 69abe, 72el, 76, 88a, 90, 98, 111ab
Opens – 1b, 10, 19a, 59b
Passage – 1a, 20b, 24a, 30, 36, 40a, 41d, 42, 46, 59bef, 64b, 65a, 71a, 72dgi, 82, 87, 99b, 103bc, 104a, 105, 120c, 126ab, 127c, 130be, 140
Passage way – 59d, 62h, 126c
Path – 82
Road – 127h
Snecket – 20b
Snicket – 124b
Street – 127h
Vennel – 1abc, 2a, 8-10, 13-15, 19ab, 20a, 24b
Wynd – 1c, 33a
Yard – 45
Nil – 4, 22-23, 25, 29cd, 59a, 61, 62d, 65b, 69g, 71e, 72hj, 80, 91, 93, 94a, 96, 99a, 101a, 115, 119, 120ab, 127fg, 129bc, 130c, 131

Cumberland
Alley – 1a, 2, 6-7, 9, 11, 14, 15ab, 16-19, 34-36, 37b, 38, 42, 46, 57
Alley way – 1b, 4, 15c, 31, 38, 40, 44, 47-48, 54, 58
Arch – 24
Back lane – 24
Bane passage – 56
Court – 46
Entry – 3, 13c, 23, 47,51-53, 63b
Gangway – 16-17, 54, 56, 59
Gantry – 63a
Ginnel – 15b, 38, 56, 63ab
Gollick – 15b
Lane – 13a, 14, 39
Lobby – 62
Lonnin – 13a
Opening – 41, 44
Passage – 1a, 12, 13c, 16, 24, 28, 40, 42, 50, 56, 58
Rwoard oot – 22
Seams – 46
Shoot – 9
Slip whol – 46
Slit – 20
Slit whol – 46
Slype – 60
Smoot – 44
Snicket – 30, 38
Trod – 8
Vennel – 5a, 32-33
Vent – 61
Went – 7, 25, 30-31, 41, 45-46, 57, 60-61
Wynd – 60
Yard – 30-31
Nil – 5b, 10, 13bd, 21, 26-27, 29, 37a, 43, 49, 55

Down
Alley – 6, 9
Archway – 19
Close – 10, 13
Corridor – 9
Entry – 1, 2ab, 3-4, 11, 15, 17-21, 23, 25-27, 30
Lane – 20
Lonan – 22
Pad – 29
Passage – 2a, 5, 19
Path – 5
Vennel – 7
Nil – 8, 12, 14, 16, 24, 28

Tyrone
Alley – 11
Archway – 1
Cassie – 5
Entry – 3, 7-8, 10-14
Gateway – 6, 10-11
Gut – 14
Pad – 1, 9, 15
Passage – 8
Nil – 2, 4, 16

Antrim
Alley – 8a, 11, 13, 33
By street – 11
Casie – 5a
Cassie – 7, 14, 16b
Close – 4A, 34
Coort – 25
Entry – 1-3, 6-7, 10, 15, 17-19, 21-22, 24-25, 27, 29, 34
Gavel of house – 28
Lane – 19, 25
Lonan – 19
Pad – 19, 30, 33
Pass – 5a
Passage – 25-26
Path – 28
Thong – 1
Nil – 4, 5b, 8b, 9, 12, 16ac, 20, 23, 31-32

Donegal
Alley – 5
Alleyway – 1
Arch – 2
Close – 1A
Entry – 5A, 10b
Gateway – 5A
Gep – 7A
Lane – 6
Lonan – 6
Open – 8
Opening – 10a
Pass – 12
Passage between – 10a
Right of way – 5A
Vennel – 10b
Nil – 3-4, 7, 9, 11, 13

Fermanagh
Alley – 7a
Entry – 2, 4, 7a, 8, 10
Pass – 9
Nil – 1, 3, 5-6, 7b

Armagh
Alley – 3-4, 6a
Entry – 1, 3-4, 6b
Nil – 2, 5

Londonderry
Alley(way) – 5
Entry – 1A, 3-7
Gap – 1A
Lane – 2
Nil – 1, 1B, 3A

26 BRADAWL (PQ1, 83)

Bradawl and **awl** have not been mapped as they occur nearly everywhere (although not very densely) except in Shetland.
Stob also occurs in 4 **splinter**, 5 **to prick**, 13 **three legged stool** and 42 **fence posts.**

Shetland
Ailison — 28
Allishon — 21a
Allison — 13
Awl — 19, 29
Borer — 33
Borie — 22
Borie stob — 21a
Brog — 25
Brogue — 1, 3-10, 13-14, 16, 21a, 22, 24, 27, 30, 32
Broog — 15
Ellishon — 2-3, 5, 7, 9, 11-12, 19-20, 21b, 25-26, 29
Ellison — 16
Stobbie — 23
Nil — 17-18, 31

Orkney
Awl — 11, 15
Borag — 18
Borick — 13a, 19-20
Borawl — 6, 21
Borie — 7, 11
Borro — 5
Bradawl — 1, 8, 13b, 15-16
Brog — 13a, 21
Brogue — 2, 4-5, 9-10, 12, 13b
Pluggie — 17
Prog — 13a, 17, 20-21
Nil — 3, 14

Caithness
Awl — 10, 13-14
Borag — 12b
Brad — 3
Brog — 7, 17
Brogue — 14
Broig — 5
Browg — 2b, 6, 8-9, 11, 12abc, 14-15, 16ab
Brugue — 2a
Nil — 1, 4

Sutherland
Awl — 3, 7-8, 11
Brad — 13
Bradawl — 1, 7, 10, 12
Brog — 5-6, 9ab, 11, 13-15
Brogue — 16
Punch — 5
Shoemaker's awl — 3
Slicking awl — 3
Nil — 2, 4, 17

Ross & Cromarty
Awl — 4-5, 14, 16, 23, 32ac
Bradawl — 1, 8, 17, 27, 34, 39
Braddie — 25b
Brag — 33
Brog — 5, 7, 9, 11-13, 15, 17-18, 20, 27-30, 32b, 36
Brogie — 21, 25b
Brogue — 21, 23, 25ab
Gimlet — 26
Meenie — 10, 12, 18, 28
Pinch — 37b
Prog — 36
Shaving spoke — 31
Stabbing awl — 36
Nil — 2-3, 6, 19, 22, 24, 35, 37a, 38

Inverness
Awl — 3, 6, 8, 13ac, 19, 21b 28
Brad — 22, 26
Bradawl — 2, 4-6, 10-11, 13b, 18, 23, 26, 36, 39
Brog — 8-9, 17, 20, 23-24, 26, 29-31, 38
Brogue — 1, 13e, 19
Ellsin — 26
Gimlet — 33
Meenie — 31
Mennie — 24
Pegnal — 11
Prog — 37
Nil — 7, 12, 13d, 14-16, 21a, 25, 27, 32, 34-35, 40

Nairn
Brogue — 1abc, 4
Nil — 2-3, 5-6

Moray
Auger — 8c, 22
Awl — 11, 22
Borer — 4
Bradawl — 23
Brod — 21, 23
Brodder — 21
Brog — 3, 8b, 14, 22-23
Brogue — 4, 7, 8e
Gimlet — 3
Stob — 1, 2a, 6a, 8ab, 9a, 13, 15-16, 18-20
Stobing aal — 8d
Nil — 2b, 5, 6b, 8f, 9b, 10, 12, 17

Banff
Awl — 6b, 15, 18c, 20, 25
Brod — 31-32
Brogue — 23
Ellisser — 18d
Gimlet — 29
Gimlick — 2b
Stob — 1, 2c 3-5, 6b, 7-11, 17, 18d, 19, 22-24, 26-29, 31-34
Stoub — 2b
Nil — 2a, 6a, 12-14, 16, 18ab, 21, 30

Aberdeen
Allison — 95
Awl — 18, 28b, 29, 59-60, 76, 86, 100
Beetle — 50
Bore — 89
Boring brace — 70
Boring stob — 16, 19, 27, 71b, 72, 80-81, 87, 92, 97-99, 107
Bradawl — 95, 104, 106
Braddle — 19
Brod — 101
Brogue — 3a
Cobbler's stob — 57
Ellison — 31
Ellshin — 28ab, 101
Gimlet — 47f, 48, 61
Nail — 105
Piercer — 109
Stabawl — 5b
Stob — 2, 3ab, 4, 5abd, 6, 8-12, 14, 17-18, 20-27, 28abc, 30-35, 39-45, 47be, 48-49, 51-54, 56, 58, 61, 63-65, 67-69, 71ac, 72-75, 77-78, 82, 85, 93-94, 96, 103, 105, 108
Stobe — 102
Souter's awl — 10, 88, 97
Wummle — 79, 92
Nil — 1, 5c, 7, 13, 15, 36 38, 46, 47acd, 55, 62, 66, 83-84, 90-91

Kincardine
Borin(g) stob — 7, 13, 17bcd, 25
Bradawl — 19
Brogue — 18, 20, 26-27
Broug — 27
Gimlet — 24
Progue — 18
Punch — 11
Stob — 1-4, 10, 12, 14, 16, 23, 28
Stobe — 18, 21
Nil — 5-6, 8-9, 15, 17a, 22

Kinross
Awl — 3
Brog — 2
Brogue — 3
Broug — 7
Brug — 2
Ellsin — 7
Gimlet — 3
Nil — 1, 4-6

Angus
Awl — 14cd, 17b, 24, 32
Brad — 30
Bradawl — 12
Brog — 7, 17b, 21, 31, 35, 37
Brogue — 1-4, 5ac, 9, 13, 14ab, 15, 20, 22-23, 26, 28, 29ab, 32, 33b, 34-36
Piercer — 33b
Stob — 5b, 25
Nil — 6, 8, 10-11, 16, 17a, 18-19, 27, 33a

Perth
Awl — 24-25, 34, 46, 51a, 65, 73
Borer — 43
Brad — 5, 51b
Bradawl — 2a, 9-10, 12, 36, 48, 52b, 74
Brag — 8
Broch — 18
Brod — 25
Brog — 1, 7, 11, 13, 15-18, 20, 22, 24, 26, 29a, 50, 52bd, 53, 56, 73
Brogue — 19, 21, 23, 25, 28, 29b, 31-33, 35, 41a, 42, 44, 49, 52e, 57, 59, 64, 66, 68
Brug — 27, 29b, 37, 39, 48, 52c, 53, 56, 62-63, 68-72
Drill — 57
Gimlet — 25-26, 41ab, 52e, 60
Nogger — 68
Nil — 2b, 3-4, 6, 14, 30, 40, 45, 47, 52a, 54-55, 58, 61, 67

Fife
Auger — 8, 36b
Awl — 9a, 21, 28, 30, 44d, 49, 53, 57
Bradawl — 7-8, 24, 36a, 37, 44c
Brod — 56
Brog — 9b, 10, 17, 20-21, 55f, 64a
Brogie — 31
Brogue — 1-2, 4, 6-7, 12-14, 19, 23, 25-26, 33, 35, 40b, 41c, 42, 43a, 44abef, 46, 48, 54, 59, 61- 62, 64b
Broug — 58
Brug — 7, 37, 39, 41bc, 43b, 47-48, 51-53, 55adefg 56-57, 60, 62, 64a
Ellshin — 27
Ellsin — 27
Gaimlet — 3
Nil — 5, 11, 15-16, 18, 22, 29, 32, 34, 38, 40a, 41ad, 45, 50, 55bc, 63

Clackmannan
Brog — 4d, 5
Brogue — 1
Brug — 1-2, 4acd, 5-7
Nil — 3, 4b

Stirling
Awl — 13, 18, 23b, 26d, 34, 35ab, 37b
Bradawl — 21a, 26a
Brode — 27a
Brog — 10, 14, 25cd, 26bd, 42a
Brogue — 5, 7ae, 11, 13, 15-17, 25a, 26a, 27ab, 29-32, 39a
Brug — 2-4, 7abde, 8-9, 16-18, 20, 21b, 22a, 23c, 25abcd, 26acef, 33, 36, 37b
Brugue — 12, 40
Ellshin — 7b, 35a
Gimlet — 15, 22b, 28
Nil — 1, 6, 7cf, 19, 23a, 24, 37a, 38, 39b, 41, 42b

Dunbarton
Awl — 3, 6, 9, 13c
Borer — 10
Brad — 10
Bradawl — 7b, 13c
Brog — 14a, 17
Brogue — 1-2, 7c, 9, 13b, 14b
Gimlet — 7ac, 16a
Nil — 4ab, 5, 8, 11-12, 13a, 15, 16b, 18

Argyll
Awl — 1-2, 5, 10, 15, 24, 27
Bradawl — 6, 12, 16-17, 22
Brog — 1, 10, 12, 23, 25, 27, 35, 39
Brogue — 11, 16, 18, 23, 26, 28, 33, 40
Ellsin — 35
Gimlet — 33
Marlin spike — 37
Mennie — 7, 9
Progue — 26
Nil — 3-4, 8, 13-14, 19-21, 29-32, 34, 36, 38

Bute
Bradawl — 1a, 8b
Brogue — 1cd, 7, 8ab, 9
Nil — 1be, 2-6

Ayr
Awl — 7, 15, 28ef, 41, 43, 48, 51-52, 57
Bodkin — 43
Brad — 2b
Bradawl — 54
Brog — 3, 8a, 20fh, 27, 28c, 30a, 53a
Brogue — 1ab, 2ab, 5-7, 8b, 9-10, 13-14, 16b, 18ab, 19, 20bcdeg, 21, 23, 24ab, 26b, 27, 28bc, 29, 30a, 32-34, 35b, 36, 41, 44-47, 49-50, 52, 56-57
Ellshin — 36
Gimlet — 20a, 28be, 29, 30b, 40
Ogg — 28d
Ogre — 18b
Piercer — 38
Punch — 28d
Wummle — 44
Nil — 4, 11, 12ab, 16a, 17, 22, 25, 26ac, 28a, 31, 35a, 37, 39, 42, 53b, 55

Renfrew
Awl — 4de, 11e, 14a, 20a
Borer — 11j, 15
Bradawl — 2a, 4e, 13c, 17
Brog — 11l 12a, 16a, 21
Brogue — 1ab, 2bfghij, 4ac, 6-8, 11afj, 12a, 13a, 15, 18a, 19, 21
Ellchion — 20b
Gimlet — 16ab
Percer — 2i
Row — 9
Nil — 2cde, 3, 4b, 5, 10, 11bcdghik, 12b, 13bd, 14b, 16cd, 18b

Lanark
Awl — 7a, 15a, 16a, 18, 27b, 35d, 38c, 44, 57a, 61, 63, 67b

Lanark cont'd
Borag — 17
Bore awl — 17
Borer — 5, 29f
Brad — 25c
Bradawl — 3, 6, 8b, 26a, 29c, 31a, 32e, 45
Brod — 15c, 57a
Brog — 7c, 9b, 12, 32ef, 33cd, 35d, 38d, 39, 45, 46a, 47-48, 49b
Brogue — 6, 9a, 10a, 13, 14b, 15abc, 20, 22, 25a, 29e, 30, 31bcd, 32abc, 34, 35b, 38ab, 40, 46c, 50, 53, 55-56, 57ab, 58, 60, 65, 67a
Brug — 33b, 44
Ellshin — 17
Ellsin — 17, 29d
Gimlet — 2, 15b, 20, 33c, 36, 59a
Lingelen — 59b
Ogre — 27b, 29e, 46c
Punch — 29f
Nil — 1, 4, 7b, 8a, 10b, 11, 14acd, 16b, 19, 21, 23-24, 25bd, 26b, 27a, 28, 29abg, 32d, 33a, 35ac, 37, 38e, 41-43, 46b, 49a, 51, 52ab, 54, 57c, 62, 64ab, 66

West Lothian
Awl — 6, 16, 18, 22
Borker — 8, 18
Brad — 8
Bradawl — 11, 17a, 19b
Brod — 1c
Brog — 1a, 8
Brogue — 1b, 4-5, 8, 11, 13-15, 17a, 21a
Brooge — 19a
Brug — 1c, 2-3, 8, 9b
Nil — 1d, 7, 9a, 10, 12, 17b, 20ab, 21b

Midlothian
Awl — 10, 18, 23a
Brace — 6a
Brad — 12a
Bradawl — 15, 18
Brawl — 31
Brog — 11, 25c, 26a, 32
Brogue — 1, 3, 6b, 8b, 12ab, 14a, 15-16, 18-19, 21, 23ab, 24, 25d, 27, 29-30
Gimlet — 7b
Nail — 20
Nil — 2, 4-5, 7a, 8a, 9, 13, 14b, 17, 22, 25ab, 26b, 28

East Lothian
Augre — 4b
Awl — 4ab, 9, 15-17
Borker — 6ab
Bradawl — 1
Brod — 2
Brog — 13
Brogue — 2, 4a, 8, 11-12, 14
Ellshin — 8, 10, 15-16, 21
Ellshin brod — 7
Gimlet — 6a
Nil — 3, 5, 18-20

Berwick
Awl — 8, 10, 16b
Bodkin — 8
Borer — 8
Boring brass — 15
Brog — 3, 7, 16a, 25-26, 32
Brogue — 1, 6, 9, 14, 19-20, 22-24, 27-28, 31
Ellchin — 16a, 23, 26
Ellshin — 5, 11, 13, 16b, 18, 21, 30, 32
Ellsin — 11, 31-32
Gimlet — 4
Nellshin — 12
Nil — 2, 16c, 17, 29

Peebles
Awl — 2, 4c, 8
Bradawl — 1
Brog — 4b, 6a, 10
Brogue — 2-3, 5, 7, 9
Nil — 4a, 6b

Selkirk
Awl — 2d
Bradawl — 2cd
Brog — 2a, 3, 8
Brogue — 2be, 7
Nil — 1, 4-6

Roxburgh
Awl — 9a
Brod — 3b
Brog — 1, 6, 15b, 17, 21ae, 25, 28
Brogue — 2, 3a, 5, 13, 15a, 16, 18, 20, 21d, 24
Ellshin — 9a, 17
Ellshin brogue — 10
Ellsin — 21c, 28
Ellsing — 15b
Gimlet — 4, 10, 13
Nil — 7-8, 9b, 11-12, 14, 19, 21bf, 22-23, 26-27

Dumfries
Allson — 42
Augre — 31c, 42
Awl — 13, 31e, 42, 46
Boorer — 37
Bradawl — 4
Bredawl — 16
Brog — 6-7, 9, 12, 20, 29, 31a, 36, 45a
Brogue — 1a, 2, 8a, 10-11, 17b, 18-19, 21b, 25-27, 31d, 34-35, 42, 44
Ellshin — 4
Feght — 28
Gemerel — 22
Gemlet — 15
Gimble — 31c
Gimlet — 31b, 37, 42, 46
Ogre — 15
Pricker — 39
Shoemaker's brogue — 16
Wummle — 8b
Nil — 1b, 3, 5, 14, 17a, 21a, 23-24, 30, 31f, 32-33, 38, 40-41, 43, 45b, 47-49

Kirkcudbright
Augre — 12a
Awl — 10, 16, 21a
Borer — 11
Brad — 12b, 17
Bradawl — 21c
Brog — 5, 7, 23, 27
Brogue — 1-4, 6-8, 14, 15ab, 17, 24, 26
Ellsin — 17
Neich — 9
Ogre — 19
Stobe — 18
Nil — 13, 20, 21b, 22, 25

Wigtown
Awl — 8
Brad — 5a
Bradawl — 1, 11
Brogue — 4, 6-7, 12, 14-15, 17-18
Gimlet — 10, 12
Gimmer — 6
Twang — 7
Nil — 2-3, 5b, 9, 13, 16

Northumberland
Aage — 17
Aggre — 80
Augre — 42
Awl — 1ab, 9, 19a, 29b, 46-47, 52, 56, 59bc, 60, 64a, 70, 79, 81, 83, 94b, 95b, 106, 111a, 126f, 130b, 134
Brace and bit — 69a
Bradawl — 1a, 5, 14, 18, 28, 31, 37, 42, 53b, 64b, 86-87, 99d, 102, 112, 124b, 126c, 131, 135
Braddie — 124b
Brog — 59b
Brogger — 17
Brogue — 17
Broog — 4
Cobbler's awl — 41a, 109
Cobbler's pricker — 136
Cobbler's spike — 120c
Drill — 138
Ellchin — 24b, 51
Ellshin — 2a, 5, 8, 11-12, 15-16, 19a, 20b, 21, 25, 28, 29f, 36, 39, 45
Ellsin — 62f
Gimlet — 41d, 43, 52, 59bf, 62g, 89, 103b, 122b, 123
Gimlick — 41d, 43, 62g, 80
Leather pricker — 90
Pricker — 4, 6, 13, 18, 20b, 22, 26, 28, 29b, 30, 33b, 38-39, 41c, 44-46, 48-50, 54-55, 57, 59e, 62aeh, 64ab, 65a, 69abde, 71bcd, 72bcdfjl, 75, 81, 88ab, 96, 98, 101a, 103bc, 104ab, 105-107, 111ab, 113, 116-117, 118, 120ab, 121, 122ab, 124a, 126af, 127acde, 129b, 130ace, 135, 142-143
Prickie — 130f
Prigger — 126c
Prodder — 48, 107
Progger — 23, 29bd, 38, 46, 48, 51, 69abe, 71cd, 72c, 79, 101b, 114, 118a, 122b, 129ab, 137
Nil — 1c, 2b, 3, 7, 10, 19b, 20a, 24a, 27, 29ace, 32, 33a, 34ab, 35, 40ab, 41b, 53a, 58, 59ad, 61, 62bcd, 63, 65b, 66-68, 69cfgh, 71ae, 72aeghik, 73-74, 76-78, 82, 84-85, 91-93, 94a, 95a, 97, 99abc, 100, 103a, 108abc, 110, 115, 119, 125, 126bde, 127bfgh, 128, 129c, 130d, 132-133, 139-141

Cumberland
Augre — 37b
Awl — 27, 51, 56
Bradawl — 1a, 4, 23, 46, 48, 57-58, 60
Brawl — 60
Brod — 27
Ellsin — 13b, 37a, 56
Gimlick — 15b
Leather pricker — 7
Pricker — 2-3, 5a, 6, 8-9, 15ac, 16, 18, 20, 22, 25-28, 30-31, 34, 40-42, 46-47, 50, 54, 56-57, 62
Prod — 38
Prodder — 17
Prowker — 56
Stobber — 38
Whummle — 37b
Nil — 1b, 5b, 10-12, 13acd, 14, 19, 21, 24, 29, 32-33, 35-36, 39, 43-45, 49, 52-53, 55, 59, 61, 63ab

Down
Awl — 11, 13-14, 28
Bradawl — 2a, 7, 15, 20
Elshin — 13
Elson — 10, 24
Fight — 17
Percer — 10, 17
Piercer — 2ab, 4, 10-11, 17, 20
Punch — 18
Screw driver — 3
Nil — 1, 5-6, 8-9, 12, 16, 19, 21-23, 25-27, 29-30

Tyrone
Awl — 9, 11
Brad — 7
Bradawl — 1, 5, 7
Percer — 14
Piercer — 11, 14
Nil — 2-4, 6, 8, 10, 12-13, 15-16

Antrim
Aal — 19
Bradawl — 22, 26, 28
Elshin — 4A, 7, 10, 18
Elson — 16b, 33
Gimlet — 27
Percer — 15, 19
Piercer — 4, 6, 9, 12-13, 15, 16b, 20-21, 23, 25
Punch — 21
Sprig bit — 25
Stubbin' aal — 16b
Nil — 1-3, 5ab, 8ab, 11, 14, 16ac, 17, 24, 29-32, 34

Donegal
Awl — 2, 4, 5A, 10a, 12
Brad — 6
Woodawl — 5, 8, 12
Nil — 1, 1A, 3, 7, 7A, 9, 10b, 11, 13

Fermanagh
Awl — 2, 5
Bradawl — 4
Percer — 2
Nil — 1, 3, 6, 7ab, 8-10

Armagh
Awl — 4
Nil — 1-3, 5, 6ab

Londonderry
Aal — 1A
Elchin — 4
Elshin — 3, 6
Woodawl — 4-5
Nil — 1, 1B, 2, 3A, 7

27 LEAD PENCIL (PQ1, 84)

(Lead) pencil has not been mapped as it occurs nearly everywhere in the area.
For variants of LEAD, see map 8, Appendix A.
Variants of PENCIL (**pincil** fairly densely from Morayshire and Banffshire southward including the central belt but not the border counties and Northern Ireland) have been subsumed.

Shetland
Califeen — 1, 4, 21b, 22
Califin — 5, 9, 12, 20, 23, 26, 31
Califine — 2, 8, 14, 17-18, 22, 25, 29-30, 33
Caliveen — 6, 21a
Calivine — 3, 7, 13, 15, 19, 28, 32
Callifine — 16, 24, 27
(Lead) pencil — *1,* 15, 17, 21a, *29*-30, *32*
Nil — 10-11

Orkney
Black lead (pencil) — 2-3, *16*
(Lead) pencil — *1,* 4-5, *7-8,* 9, *13ab, 15, 17, 19-20*
Nil — 6, 10-12, 14, 18, 21

Caithness
Lead — 11
(Lead) pencil — 2ab, 4, 8-*9,* 10, *11,* 12a, 13-*14,* 16b
Scrawler — 7
Scribbler — 7
Writing timber — 3
Nil — 1, 5-6, 12bc, 15, 16a, 17

Sutherland
(Lead) pencil — 1, *3-5,* 6, *7,* 8, 9ab, 10, *11-13,* 16
Nil — 2, 14-15, 17

Ross & Cromarty
Lead — 17, 28-29, 35
(Lead) pencil — *1, 3-6, 8-10, 14, 16,* 17, *18,* 19-20, *22-24,* 25ab, 26, *27, 29, 31,* 32abc, *34, 36,* 39
Rulin(g) — 10-11, 13, 37a
Scalie — 19
Nil — 2, 7, 12, 15, 21, 30, 33, 37b, 38

Inverness
Gillivine — 11, 13e
Keelivine — 26
Lead — 3, 15
Leadack — 13a, 14
Leader — 9
(Lead) pencil — *1,* 2-3, *4,* 5, *6-7,* 8, *10-11,* 13abce, *16-17,* 18-20, 21ab, *22-23, 26,* 27-28, *29-30,* 32, *33,* 34-36, *37-40*
Nil — 12, 13d, 24-25, 31

Nairn
Lead — 2
Leadie — 1b
(Lead) pencil — 1a, *2, 5-6*
Nil — 1c, 3-4

Moray
Kailivin — 8f
Keelivine — 9a
Keelivine pen — 8a
Leadie — 5, 8b, 9b, 15-16, 18
(Lead) pencil — 2a, *4,* 6b, 7, 8*bcdef,* 14, *15,* 16, *21-23*
Nil — 1, 2b, 3, 6a, 10-13, 17, 19-20

Banff
Culliveen — 18d
Lead — 11, 20
Leadie — 5, 30, 32
(Lead) pencil — 1, 2ab, 4, 6b, 7, *8,* 9-10, 13-17, 18cd, *19,* 21, 24, 31, 33-34
Nil — 2c, 3, 6a, 12, 18ab, 22-23, 25-29

Aberdeen
Leadie — 27, 53
(Lead) pencil — 1, 3ab, 4, *5a,* 6-8, 10, 12, 14, 16-17, *20,* 21, *22-23,* 24, *25,* 28abc, *29-30,* 31-32, 34-*35, 38*-39, *44-46,* 47*bcdef, 48-49,* 50, 53-*54,* 56, 59, *62,* 63, *64-66,* 67, *69*-70, 71b, *73-75, 81, 84*-85, *94-95, 97*-98, *100-101,* 103, *104-107,* 108
Peck — 96
Pinkie — 71a
Timmer pencil — 80
Nil — 2, 5bcd, 9, 11, 13, 15, 18-19, 26, 33, 36-37, 40-43, 47a, 51-52, 55, 57-58, 60-61, 68, 71c, 72, 76-79, 82-83, 86-93, 99, 102, 109

Kincardine
Leadie — 6, 9
(Lead) pencil — 1-2, *3, 5-7,* 8, *10-11,* 12, *13-15,* 16, 17cd, *18-19,* 21, *26,* 27-28
Nil — 4, 17ab, 20, 22-25

Kinross
(Lead) pencil — 1-4, *6*
Nil — 5, 7

Angus
Black lead — 18
Leadie — 5b, 26
(Lead) pencil — 1-2, 4, 6-*10,* 12-13, 14ab, 15, 17ab, *18,* 19-20, 22, 24-26, *28,* 29b, 32, *33b, 34-35,* 36-37
Scalie — 33b
Nil — 3, 5ac, 11, 14cd, 16, 21, 23, 27, 29a, 30-31, 33a

Perth
Keelivine — 69
(Lead) pencil — *1,* 2a, *4*-5, 7-9, *10,* 11-12, 14-15, *16, 20*-21, 23, 25, 27-28, 29a, 32, *33,* 34, *36, 39-40,* 41a, *43, 46, 48,* 50, *51b,* 52abc, *56*-57, 59-*60,* 64, 66-*67,* 71, *72-74*
Pint — 40, 51a
Scalie — 67
Vine — 68
Nil — 2b, 3, 6, 13, 17-19, 22, 24, 26, 29b, 30-31, 35, 37-38, 41b, 42, 44-45, 47, 49, 52de, 53-55, 58, 61-63, 65, 70

Fife
Lead — 7
Leadie — 33
(Lead) pencil — *1, 4,* 7-*8,* 9a, 10-11, 13, 16-17, *19, 21,* 23, *25,* 28, 30, *32,* 36ab, *37,* 39, 40b, 41abc, 43a, 44*bcde,* 45, *46,* 47, *48,* 49-53, 55abdeg, 57, *58,* 59, 61, *62,* 63
Pokum — 39
Nil — 2-3, 5-6, 9b, 12, 14-15, 18, 20, 22, 24, 26-27, 29 31, 34-35, 38, 40a, 41d, 42, 43b, 44af, 54, 55cf, 56, 60, 64ab

Clackmannan
(Lead) pencil — 1, 3, 4ac, *5-6,* 7
Nil — 2, 4bd

Stirling
Cullivan — 25b
Keelie — 7e
Keelie pencil — 26e
Keelivine — 39ab
(Lead) pencil — 3-4, 7abcef, *8-9,* 11-12, *13, 15*-16, *17,* 18, *20,* 21ab, *22b, 23abc,* 25*abcd,* 26*acd, 27a, 28,* 30, *31-33,* 34, *35a,* 36, 37*ab,* 38, 39*ab,* 42a
Skeelie — 22a
Nil — 1-2, 5-6, 7d, 10, 14, 19, 24, 26bf, 27b, 29, 35b, 40-41, 42b

Dunbarton
Black lead — 2
Keelivine — 14a
(Lead) pencil — *1-3,* 5-*6, 7bc,* 8-9, *10-11, 13abc, 14b, 16a*
Nil — 4ab, 7a, 12, 15, 16b, 17-18

Argyll
Keelivine — 35
(Lead) pencil — 1-3, *5-7,* 9-11, *12, 14,* 15-16, *17-19, 22-23,* 24, *25, 27,* 30, *32-33, 35,* 37, *38-39*
Nil — 4, 8, 13, 20-21, 26, 28-29, 31, 34, 36, 40

Bute
Cullivine — 8b
Culvine — 7
Kilivine — 9
Killivine — 8a
(Lead) pencil — 1acd, 2, *3-4,* 5, *7,* 8a*b,* 9
Nil — 1be, 6

Ayr
Culivin — 41, 53b
Cullivin — 10, 20g, 47, 49-51, 54
Cullivine — 48, 53a, 56-57
Kalivin — 21
Keelie — 16b
Keelivin — 20ace, 26a, 28f, 29, 52
Keelivine — 8b, 19, 20h, 27, 28abc, 31, 42-43
Keelvine — 57
Keevlin — 29
Leadie — 7
(Lead) pencil — 1b, 2ab, *3, 5,* 6-7, 8b, *9,* 10-11, 12a, *15,* 16ab, 17, *18ab, 20bcg, 21-23, 24b, 25,* 26abc, *28def, 30a, 31-34,* 35ab, *36,* 38, *41-45,* 46, *47-48,* 51, *52, 53a, 54-55*
Wad pencil — 13
Nil — 1a, 4, 8a, 12b, 14, 20df, 24a, 30b, 37, 39-40

Renfrew
Keelivine — 21
Kelivine — 14b
(Lead) pencil — 1a*b,* 2acg*hij,* 4*acde,* 5, 11acdef*hjkl, 12b,* 13cd, *16abd, 17,* 18ab, *19, 20a*
Nil — 2bdef, 3, 4b, 6-10, 11bgi, 12a, 13ab, 14a, 15, 16c, 20b

Lanark
Keelivine — 9b, 17, 38d
Lead — 15b, 35d
Leadie — 15b, 16b, 28, 29cef, 31d, 32c, 33abcd, 36, 39, 44, 57c
(Lead) pencil — 2, *3,* 4, *5-6,* 7ac, 8*ab, 9a, 10ab, 12*-13, 14bd, 15*ac,* 16*ab,* 18-19, *20,* 21, *22, 25bc,* 26ab, *27b,* 28, 29acdef, *30, 31abd,* 32ae, 33a, *34,* 35*abcd,* 38ac, *39-41,* 42, *44*-45, 46*abc, 47-48,* 49ab, 53, *56,* 57ab, 58, 59b, *60, 62*-63, *64ab, 65*
Wad — 11
Nil — 1, 7b, 14ac, 23-24, 25ad, 27a, 29bg, 31c, 32bdf, 37, 38be, 43, 50-51, 52ab, 54-55, 59a, 61, 66, 67ab

West Lothian
Lead — 16
Leadie — 14
(Lead) pencil — *1c, 3,* 5, *6-8, 9ab, 10,* 11, *12,* 13, *15-16,* 17a, 18, 20a, *22*
Marker — 19b
Skillie — 14
Nil — 1abd, 2, 4, 17b, 19a, 20b, 21ab

Midlothian
Black lead pencil — 1
Keelie pencil — 30
Keelivine — 4
Kylivine — 26a
Leadie — 5, 6b, 10, 31
(Lead) pencil — *2-3, 6a, 7a,* 8ab, 10-*11,* 12a*b, 13, 14ab,* 15, *18,* 19, *20,* 21-22, *23ab,* 24, 25ab*c, 26b,* 27, *28,* 29, 32
Nil — 7b, 9, 16-17, 25d

East Lothian
Keelie — 13, 16
Keelivin — 15
Keelivine — 11-12, 14, 16-17
Leadie — 4b, 21
(Lead) pencil — *1, 4b,* 5, *6ab, 7-9, 15, 19*
Skeelie — 2
Skeelivin — 15
Skeelivine — 8, 14
Nil — 3, 4a, 10, 18, 20

Berwick
Keelie — 1-2, 4, 6-9, 11-12, 14-15, 16abc, 17-20, 22-23, 25-27, 28, 30
Keelifine — 4
Keelivin — 23, 31
Keelivine — 3, 7-10, 13, 16b, 17-18, 20-22, 29, 32
Kellie — 5, 27
Leadie — 31
(Lead) pencil — 2, *8,* 10, *12,* 15, 16*abc,* 24, *29*
Steekie — 24
Wad — 16c

Peebles
(Lead) pencil — 1-2, *3, 4bc, 5,* 6*ab,* 8, *9*
Wud pencil — 10
Nil — 4a, 7

Selkirk
Keelie — 2d, 6-7
Keelivin — 7
Keillie — 2d
(Lead) pencil — 2abcd*e,* 8
Nil — 1, 3-5

Roxburgh
Keelie — 1, 3ab, 5, 8, 9a, 11, 13, 17-20, 21c, 23-26
Keelifin — 3b
Keelivin — 2, 7, 13, 26
Keelivine — 3a, 4, 6, 8, 9ab, 15ab, 16-17, 23
Lead — 13
(Lead) pencil — 1-*2,* 4, *10,* 13, *17, 20,* 21a*f, 26, 28*
Skeelifin — 21d
Wad — 21c, 27-28
Nil — 12, 14, 21be 22

Dumfries
Caliveen — 9

Dumfries cont'd

Calivin — 11, 13, 19, 21ab, 22, 24, 26, 30, 31d
Calivine — 31bef, 42
Callivin — 27, 31a, 32, 41-42
Cillivin — 32
Culivin — 8a
Lead — 28
(Lead) pencil — 1a, *4,* 9-10, *12, 16,* 17ab, *18*-19, *20,* 21b, 22 24, *28-29,* 31*de*, *33,* 45*ab*
Wad — 5, 7, 12, 27, 29, 34-35, 37-39, 42, 44, 45a, 48-49
Wad pencil — 6, 15, 17ab, 25-26, 40, 46
Waud — 8b
Wod — 35
Nil — 1b, 2-3, 14, 23, 31c, 36, 43, 47

Kirkcudbright

Caliveen — 7, 24
Calivin — 7-9, 15ab, 17, 19-20, 23, 26
Calivine — 1-2
Culivin — 6
Kallivin — 16, 21b
Keelivine — 5, 27
Kelivin — 11, 14
Kellinine — 3
Kellvin — 18
Kiliveen — 15a
Kilivin — 6, 10, 22
Killie — 12b
Killivin — 4, 12ab, 13, 21a, 26
(Lead) pencil — *1,* 3-4, 6, 10, 14, 19, 21bc
Wad — 1, 17
Nil — 25

Wigtown

Calivin — 1, 13-14
Calivine — 10-12, 15
Calliveen — 18
Callivine — 12
Collivin — 6
Culivin — 2, 9
Culivine — 4, 5a, 8
Cullivine — 3, 5b, 7, 17
Keelivine — 5a
Kellivine — 5a
Kylivine — 5a
(Lead) pencil — 7, *11,* 12-13, 16-17

Northumberland

Bit vine — 101b
Black lead pencil — 69b, 72d
Crayon — 46
Keel — 122a
Keelie — 1a, 2a, 19b
Keelivane — 29f
Keelivine — 1ac, 8, 11, 19a, 51
Lead — 93
(Lead) pencil — *1a,* 2b, 4, *5-6, 13-14,* 15, 18, 21, 23, 26, 28, 29ab, 33b, *35*-36, 40a, *41cd, 42,* 46, *47,* 48, 52, 53ab, *54,* 56-57, 59*be*, 60, *62b, 64b,* 68, 69c, *70,* 71*acd,* 72abcd*g*ik, 82, 86-87, 88b, 90-91, 95b, 96, 99d, *100,* 102, *103bc,* 104ab, *106, 109, 111ab, 112, 119,* 121, 127adf*g, 132, 140, 142*
(Lead) vine — *1ab,* 2ab, 3-5, 7, 9, 12-13, 15-18, 20ab, 22-23, 24ab, 25-28, 29abcde, 30-32, 33ab, 34ab, 35-36, 38-39, 40ab, 41abcd, 43, 46, 48-52, 55-58, 59abcdef, 60, 62abcdegh, 64ab, 65ab, 66-68, 69abcdefgh, 71abde, 72bcdef-ghijkl, 76-87, 88ab, 89-93, 94ab, 95ab, 96-98, 99abcd, 100, 101ab, 104b, 106-107, 108abc, 110, 111ab, 112-117, 118ab, 119, 120abc, 121, 122ab, 123, 124ab, 125, 126abcdef, 127acdefgh, 128, 129abc, 130abdef, 131, 134, 136-141, 143
Pencil for paper — 138
Piece vine — 101a
Propelling pencil — 69b
Veyen — 23
Vine pencil — 6, 10, 37, 41ad, 43-45, 62f, 71c, 74-75, 78, 83, 99c, 103abc, 109, 120c, 127a, 130c, 133, 135, 143
Wad — 111b, 127c
Waird pencil — 142
Nil — 61, 63, 73, 105, 127b

Cumberland

Black lead — 60
Lead — 8, 51
(Lead) pencil — 1a, 7, *9, 13c, 15a, 23-24, 40, 42, 46, 53, 56-57, 59*
Scrat — 31
Vine — 30
Wad — 5b, 8, 39, 41, 43, 47, 51-52
Wad pencil — 1a, 2-4, 5a, 11-12, 13abc, 15abc, 16, 18-19, 22, 24-33, 38, 40-42, 44-50, 53-54, 56-58, 61-62
Ward (pencil) — *8-9, 17, 20,* 37ab, *58*
Nil — 1b, 6, 10, 13d, 14, 21, 34-36, 55, 59, 63ab

Down

Lead — 20
(Lead) pencil — 1, *2a, 3,* 5, 7, 9, *13,* 15, *18-19,* 24, *26,* 28
Nil — 2b, 4, 6, 8, 10-12, 14, 16-17, 21-23, 25, 27, 29-30

Tyrone

(Lead) pencil — *1, 5,* 6-8, *10*-11, *13,* 16
Nil — 2-4, 9, 12, 14-15

Antrim

Lead — 8a, 21, 25
(Lead) pencil — 1, *3, 4A, 5a, 9,* 13, *15, 17, 19*-20, *22, 25*-26, 28-29, 31
Marker — 25
Scrawler — 16b
Nil — 2, 4, 5b, 6-7, 8b, 10-12, 14, 16ac, 18, 23-24, 27, 30, 32-34

Donegal

(Lead) pencil — 1, 5, 5A, *6,* 8, *10a, 12*
Nil — 1A, 2-4, 7, 7A, 9, 10b, 11, 13

Fermanagh

(Lead) pencil — 2, 4-*5,* 9
Nil — 1, 3, 6, 7ab, 8, 10

Armagh

(Lead) pencil — 3-4, *6a*
Nil — 1-2, 5, 6b

Londonderry

(Lead) pencil — *1, 1A, 2,* 3A
Nil — 1B, 3-7

28 SLATE PENCIL (PQ1, 85)

For variants of PENCIL, see note in 27 **lead pencil**. Variants of SLATE have been subsumed (**sleeat, sleat,** Cumberland) except **sclate.**

Shetland

Sclate pencil — 3, 6-7, 11, 21b, 24
Scet pencil — 15, 22
(Slate) pencil — *1, 7, 13, 16-17,* 19, *20, 21a, 25, 30, 32-33*
Nil — 2, 4-5, 8-10, 12, 14, 18, 23, 26-29, 31

Orkney

Slate pen — 4-5, 13a
Slate pencil — 1-3, 5, 7-9, 13ab, 15-17, 19-20
Nil — 6, 10-12, 14, 18, 21

Caithness

Slate pin — 12b
Scratcher — 7
Slate pen — 9, 12b, 17
Slate pencil — 2ab, 4, 8, 10-11, 13-14, 16b
Slate pin — 6
Slay pencil — 11
Nil — 1, 3, 5, 12ac, 15, 16a

Sutherland

Scaalie — 8
Slate pencil — 1, 3-8, 9ab, 10-13, 16
Nil — 2, 14-15, 17

Ross & Cromarty

Slate pen — 36
(Slate) pencil — *1, 3-6, 8-9, 14, 16-20, 22-24, 25ab, 27-31, 32ab, 34,* 37a, *39*
Two bits — 31
Nil — 2, 7, 10-13, 15, 21, 26, 32c, 33, 35, 37b, 38

Inverness

Slate ack — 13a, 14
(Slate) pencil — *1-6, 8, 10-11, 13abce, 17-18, 20, 21ab, 22-23, 26-27,* 28, *29-30, 32-40*
Slatie — 15
Nil — 7, 9, 12, 13d, 16, 19, 24-25, 31

Nairn

Skeelack — 5
Skellach — 4
Slate pencil — 1a, 2, 4, 6
Slatie — 1b
Nil — 1c, 3

Moray

Sclate pencil — 3
Sclatie pen — 9a
Skaalie — 10
Skalie — 1, 3-4, 6a, 7, 8abef, 14, 16-19, 21
Skallie — 22
Skeelie — 2a, 4, 8ab, 11-13
Skellie — 20
Skylie — 9a
Slate pencil — 7, 8df, 15, 19, 23
Slate pin — 8e
Slatie — 5, 6b, 8bc, 9b, 11, 14-15, 21
Nil — 2b

Banff

Sclate — 2c
Skalie — 1, 3-4, 6ab, 7-10, 15-17, 18cd, 20-21, 23-32
Skallie — 7, 12-13, 19, 22, 27
Skawlie — 11
Skeelie — 5
Skellie — 18b, 33
Skylie — 2abc, 6b, 14-15
Slate pen — 34
Slate pencil — 6b
Slatie — 14, 18b, 25, 30, 32
Nil — 18a

Aberdeen

Sclate pencil — 21, 97
Skaalie — 3a, 5a, 11, 25, 28ab, 29-30, 34, 56, 72, 95, 101
Skalie — 1, 5bd, 6, 8, 10, 12-16, 19, 21-24, 26, 28c, 29, 31, 33, 37, 40-43, 45, 52-54, 58-59, 62-63, 65-70, 71abc, 72, 77, 83, 87, 89, 91, 96, 99, 103-105
Skallie — 2, 3b, 5c, 7, 9, 17, 19, 27, 32, 35, 38-39, 44, 46, 47abcdef, 49-51, 55, 57, 60-61, 64, 74-75, 78-79, 81-82, 85,

Aberdeen cont'd

92, 102
Skawlie — 4, 18, 48, 53, 65
Skeelie — 20
Skellie — 108
Skylie — 5b, 10, 73, 76, 80, 84, 86, 93-94, 97-98, 100, 106-107, 109
Slate pencil — 70, 105, 108
Slatie — 79
Nil — 36, 90

Kincardine

Pake — 22
Peek — 19, 22
Skalie — 3-4, 8, 10, 12, 17abd
Skallie — 16
Skeelie — 17a, 19, 26
Skellie — 2, 17a, 20
Skylie — 1, 3, 5-7, 9, 11-15, 17cd, 18, 21, 23-24, 27-28
Slate pencil — 1, 8, 12, 17c
Slatie — 19-22, 26
Slattie — 27
Nil — 25

Kinross

Skeelie — 1-3, 5, 7
(Slate) caum — 2, *3,* 4-5, *6,* 7
Slate pencil — 3

Angus

Pike — 1, 4, 5c
Schillie — 11
Sclatie — 14b
Skalie — 1-3, 5a, 10, 13, 14acd, 17b, 20, 25, 28, 29b, 33ab, 34
Skeelie — 4, 9, 31, 35
Skellie — 16, 18-19, 21, 23, 30
Skillie — 5b, 7, 14bd, 17a, 22, 29a, 31
Skitie — 5a, 22-24, 26
Skulie — 8
Skylie — 5c, 6, 12, 14cd, 15, 24, 27, 31-32, 36-37
Slate pen — 32, 34
Slate pencil — 17b, 18, 29b
Slatie — 8, 20, 22, 32

Perth

Cam — 16, 37, 40, 44, 68-71
Campain — 39
Campen — 56
Caum — 62-63, 65, 73
Coam — 72
Keelivan — 66
Skalie — 5, 13, 23, 25, 39, 43, 45, 67, 73
Skallie — 18, 30
Skeelie — 11-12, 15, 17, 19-22, 25-28, 29ab, 37-38, 40, 41ab, 42, 44, 46, 49-50, 51b, 52abcde, 54-58, 61-62
Skeelievine — 53
Skellie — 2a, 7, 16, 48, 64
Skillie — 18, 31, 42
Skylie — 3, 32-33, 51a, 59-60, 65
Slate pen — 33, 61
Slate pencil — 1, 2a, 4, 8-10, 14, 16, 25, 29a, 32, 36, 66-67, 72, 74
Slatie — 13
Stelpan — 14
Nil — 2b, 6, 24, 34-35, 47

Fife

Caum — 2, 7-8, 9b, 10-12, 16-17, 19-23, 25, 29, 37, 39, 40ab, 41bcd, 42, 44abef, 46-48, 50-51, 53, 55be, 59-61, 64b
Caum pen — 13, 23
Caum stick — 49
Skalie — 3-4, 12, 28
Skallie — 18, 34
Skeelie — 2, 6-7, 12, 14, 21, 27, 32-33, 35, 36ab, 37-39, 40a, 43b, 49, 51-54, 55abcdeg, 56-61, 64a

Skellia — 31
Skellie — 34
Skillie — 5, 12, 23, 26, 44d, 55f, 62
Slate caum — 9a, 18, 36b, 43ab, 44cf, 45, 49, 52
Slate coam — 41a
Slate pen — 4, 44e, 63
Slate pencil — 11, 16-17, 21, 30, 37, 39, 40b, 43a, 46, 50, 55bc, 57
Slatie — 3, 8
Nil — 1, 15, 24

Clackmannan

Cam — 2, 4ad, 7
Caum — 1-3, 4cd, 5-6
Skailie — 4d
Slate pencil — 4c
Nil — 4b

Stirling

Cam — 7abd, 17, 22a, 39b
Camstane — 7e
Caum — 2-4, 7f, 9-10, 12, 19-20, 21b, 22b, 23c, 25ad, 26d, 32, 35ab, 36, 42a
Caumstane — 7e
Crome — 34
Keelievine — 26f
Piece of cam — 25b
Sclate pencil — 9
Skallie — 25a
Skeelie — 26f, 39b
Skellie — 10
Skillie — 6, 12, 26b
Skillie pin — 12
Slate cam — 16, 26ac
Slate caum — 8, 31, 33
Slate caun — 23b
Slate coam — 16, 21a, 42b
Slate column — 23b
(Slate) pencil — *4, 7acf, 11, 13, 15, 21b, 22b, 23a, 25cd, 26acd, 27a, 28, 30, 32, 35a, 36, 37b, 42a*
Slatie — 26a
Nil — 1, 5, 14, 18, 24, 26e, 27b, 29, 37a, 38, 39a, 40-41

Dunbarton

Bit o'caum — 7c
Cam — 17
Caum — 7c, 14a
Skalie — 2
Slate pen — 14a
Slate pencil — 1, 6, 7bc, 9-11, 13abc, 14b, 16a
Nil — 3, 4ab, 5, 7a, 8, 12, 15, 16b, 18

Argyll

Keelievine — 35
Sclate pencil — 35
Skeelie — 16
Slate pencil — 1, 3, 5-7, 9-12, 14-17, 19, 22-25, 27, 30, 33, 37, 39
Nil — 2, 4, 8, 13, 18, 20-21, 26, 28-29, 31-32, 34, 36, 38, 40

Bute

Skeelie — 7
Slate pencil — 2-4, 7, 8ab, 9
Slatie — 9
Nil — 1abcde, 5-6

Ayr

Bit linn — 24b
Callifan — 30b
Cam — 18b, 35b, 41, 44, 46, 52
Caum — 7, 18b, 33-34, 35a, 36-38, 45, 57
Caumstane — 24b
Cleffie — 57
Keelivin — 26c
Keelivine — 29
Keevlin — 29

Linn — 13-14, 20abefh, 22-23
Lint — 20b
Sclate pen — 8b
Sclate pencil — 8b, 15, 28f, 54
Scraper — 18b
Scriever — 12b
Skallie — 18b
Skeelie — 1a, 19, 29
Skellie — 7
Skillie — 50, 53a
Slate caum — 15
Slate coam — 9
Slate leed — 44
Slate linn — 15, 20cg, 25
Slate lint — 21
Slate pen — 8a, 12a, 16ab
Slate pencil — 1b, 2ab, 5, 20cg, 24b, 26b, 27, 28e, 30a, 31-32, 34, 41-43, 45, 47-49, 51, 53a, 56-57
Slatie — 18b
Stack o'linn — 19
Nil — 3-4, 6, 10-11, 17, 18a, 20d, 24a, 26, 28abcd, 39-40, 53b, 55

Renfrew

Caum — 21
Common slate — 2i
French chalk — 2i
Hone — 19
Hone pen — 14b
Sclate pencil — 2h
Skallie — 5
Skeelie pen — 20b
Slate pencil — 1b, 2acfgj, 4cde, 11acehkl, 13cd, 15d, 16ab, 17, 19, 20a
Slatie — 5, 12b
Nil — 1a, 2bdef, 3, 4ab, 6-10, 11bdfgij, 12a, 13ab, 14a, 15, 16c, 18ab

Lanark

Bit o'caum — 29e
Cam — 9b, 63, 67ab
Campen — 45
Campin — 30, 33c
Camskelie — 39
Caum — 3, 8b, 10b, 11-13, 14ac, 15abc, 17-19, 24, 27ab, 29d, 30, 35bd, 38abcde, 42, 44, 46a, 47-48, 49b, 51, 52a, 53, 55, 57abc, 59ab, 61, 64a, 65
Caum pen — 43, 46c
Caum skelie — 39
Leed pencil — 18
Scartie — 57b
Skalie — 4, 9b
Skallie — 38d
Skeelie — 7a, 11, 14b, 15b, 17, 23, 26a, 27ab, 29ag, 32bdf, 36-37, 53-56, 59b, 60, 62-63, 65
Skeelie pen — 35b
Skellie — 32c, 35d
Skillie — 33bcd, 40, 50
Skullie — 33b
Slate cam — 56
Slate caum — 19-20, 35ac, 49a, 52b, 58
Slate coam — 34
Sl ate pen — 46ab
Slate pencil — 2, 5-6, 7ac, 8ab, 9a, 10b, 12, 14d, 15ac, 16ab, 21-22, 25bc, 26a, 29cf, 31ad, 35abd, 37, 39, 48, 60, 64b, 65
Slatie — 14d, 16b, 21, 25d, 31d, 33a
Nil — 1, 7b, 10a, 25a, 26b, 28, 29b, 31bc, 32ae, 41, 66

West Lothian

Cam — 3, 7
Cauk — 11
Caum — 1bd, 8, 9b, 10, 16, 17a, 18, 19b, 21a
Coam — 19a
Keelie — 4
Skeelie — 1a, 3, 6-8, 9b, 22
Skellie — 17a
Skillie — 14-15, 20a
Slate cam — 4
Slate caum — 1c, 5, 9a, 11-12, 17b, 20a, 21b
Slate coam — 1a, 4, 22
Slate pencil — 1c, 2-3, 10, 13, 15-16, 18
Slatie — 6-7, 14
Nil — 20b

Midlothian

Bit skeelie — 24
Caum — 4, 10-11, 12ab, 13, 14b, 16
Skeelie — 1, 6b, 7b, 10, 12b, 17-18, 21, 23ab, 25acd, 26a, 27-28, 30-32
Skellie — 15, 18, 20
Skillie — 2-5, 6b, 7a, 8b, 12a, 16, 26b, 29
Slate caum — 14a
Slate pen — 2, 7a
(Slate) pencil — *6a, 8a, 10-11, 14a,* 19, *23b*
Slatie — 25a
Nil — 9, 22, 25b

East Lothian

Keelie — 15
Keelivine — 10
Skalie — 9
Skeelie — 4ab, 6a, 10-13, 15, 21
Skeelivine — 2
Slate pencil — 1, 5, 8, 14, 16-17, 19-20
Slatie — 4b, 5, 6a, 7, 13
Nil — 3, 6b, 18

Berwick

Keelie — 31-32
Keelivine — 1
Sclate — 30
Skailie — 17
Skeelie — 7-8, 17, 23
Skillie — 24
Slate keelie — 15
(Slate) pencil — *2,* 6-7, *9-10, 12-13, 15, 16bc, 19, 21, 26, 28*
Slatie — 10, 27
Nil — 3-5, 11, 14, 16a, 18, 20, 22, 25, 29

Peebles

Cam — 7
Skeelie — 1, 3, 4abc, 6b, 10
Skillie — 4b, 6a, 7-8
Slate pencil — 2, 4c, 5, 6b
Nil — 9

Selkirk

Keelie — 1, 6
Skalie — 2e
Skeelie — 2abd, 3-5, 7-8
Skeelie pen — 2a
Skillie — 2c
Slate pencil — 2c, 8

Roxburgh

Keelie — 3a, 17
Sclatie — 9a
Skalie — 10, 13, 21c
Skeelie — 3b, 4, 8, 19-20, 21acde, 25-26, 28
Sklate pencil — 4, 15b, 26
Skulie — 21b
Slate keelie — 5
Slate pencil — 1-2, 4, 9a, 13, 15b, 16-17, 21af
Slatie — 9a
Nil — 6-7, 9b, 11-12, 14, 15a, 18, 22-24, 27

Dumfries
Callivant — 20
Callum — 23
Cam — 1b, 5, 8a, 9, 11-13, 19, 22, 27, 32, 38, 41-42
Cammie — 31e
Caum — 1a, 2-3, 8b, 35
Kevin — 45a
Markin — 40
Sailor's pencil — 31e
(Sclate) pencil — 24, *28, 31ab*
Screevie — 35
Skalie — 6, 17ab, 18, 39
Skallie — 10
Skeelie — 16, 29, 38, 46
Slate pencil — 1a, 4, 12, 18-19, 21b, 24, 28-29, 31e, 32-33, 37, 46
Nil — 7, 14-15, 21a, 25-26, 30, 31cdf, 34, 36, 43-44, 45b, 47-49

Kirkcudbright
Cam — 2, 12b, 17
Cam stane — 8
Caum — 1
Sclate pencil — 1
Scorin pencil — 14
Shallie — 17
Skeelie — 15a
Skillie — 12a
(Slate) pencil — *1, 4, 6, 10, 16,* 18, *21c, 22, 27*
Nil — 3, 5, 7, 9, 11, 13, 15b, 19-20, 21ab, 23-26

Wigtown
Cleffie — 5a
Slate calavine — 10
(Slate) pencil — *5a, 10-11,* 14, *16-17*
Slatie — 2
Nil — 1, 3-4, 5b, 6-9, 12-13, 15, 18

Northumberland
Calm (pencil) — *25, 37,* 59b, 62f, 77, 96, *124a, 134*
Cam (pencil) — *59c,* 62f, *69h,* 96-97, 107, 111b, 122b, *124a, 134*
Coamie pencil — 133, 140
Coam pencil — 75
Crawstone — 79
Dent — 2a
Keelie — 1c, 2a
Ladies' pencil — 47
Lead — 118b, 124b
Pencil — 69ab
Scratcher — 124b
Skeelie — 43
Slag — 58
(Slate) pencil — *1a, 2b, 5-6, 13-14,* 15, *16-18, 19a,* 20b, *29ab, 30-31, 34b, 35-36, 40a, 41acd, 42, 45, 48, 52, 53ab, 54, 56-57, 59bd, 60, 62bg,* 64ab, *65a, 69abc, 70, 71acd, 72bcdgi, 77-79,* 83, *86-87, 88ab, 89-90, 93, 94b,* 95ab, *96, 98, 99d, 100, 102, 103bc, 104ab, 106, 109-110, 111ab, 112, 119, 120ac, 121,* 126a, *127ag, 130cef, 132-133, 135, 137-138, 140, 142-143*
Slatie — 13, 22, 41a, 52, 99a
Squeaker — 125
Nil — 1b, 3-4, 7-12, 19b, 20a, 21, 23, 24ab, 26-28, 29cdef, 32, 33ab, 34a, 38-39, 40b, 41b, 44, 46, 49-51, 55, 59aef, 61, 62acdeh, 63, 65b, 66-68, 69defg, 71be, 72aefhjkl, 73-74, 76, 80-82, 84-85, 91-92, 94a, 99bc, 101ab, 103a, 105, 108abc, 113-117, 118a, 120b, 122a, 123, 126bcdef, 127bcdefh, 128, 129abc, 130abd, 131, 136, 139, 141

Cumberland
Cam pencil — 13b
Kennal — 60
Scrat — 30-31
Sill (pencil) — 18, *27, 54, 61*
Slate pencil — 1a, 2-4, 5a, 7-9, 12, 13c, 15ac, 16-18, 22-26, 28, 30-31, 40, 42, 45-50, 52-54, 56-59, 62
Steean pencil — 38
Nil — 1b, 5b, 6, 10-11, 13ad, 14, 15b, 19-21, 29, 32-36, 37ab, 39, 41, 43-44, 51, 55, 63ab

Down
Chalk — 1
Slate pencil — 5, 9, 15, 18-19, 24, 26
Stane pencil — 13
Stone pencil — 15
Nil — 2ab, 3-4, 6-8, 10-12, 14, 16-17, 20-23, 25, 27-30

Tyrone
Scraper — 1
Slate pencil — 7, 11
Nil — 2-6, 8-10, 12-16

Antrim
(Slate) pencil — 13, *17, 19-20, 22, 25-26, 28*
Slater — 11
Nil — 1-4, 4A, 5ab, 6-7, 8ab, 9-10, 12, 14-15, 16abc, 18, 21, 23-24, 27, 29-34

Donegal
Cutter — 10a
Slate pencil — 5, 5A, 6, 12
Nil — 1, 1A, 2-4, 7, 7A, 8-9, 10b, 11, 13

Fermanagh
Slate pencil — 2, 4-5, 9
Nil — 1, 3, 6, 7ab, 8, 10

Armagh
Cutter — 2
Slate pencil — 4, 6a
Nil — 1, 3, 5, 6b

Londonderry
Slate pencil — 3A
Nil — 1, 1AB, 2-7

29 TO PLAY TRUANT (from school) (PQ1, 86)

Shetland
Bedd fae — 17
Bide awa — 14, 21b
Biding hame — 20
Hoyde thee — 26
Pipsie lills — 24
(Play) truant — *16, 21a,* 27
Run away — 13
Nil — 1-12, 15, 18-19, 22-23, 25, 28-33

Orkney
Bide away — 6
Play plunkie — 7
(Play) truant — *1-5, 7-9, 11, 13b,* 15, *17, 19-20*
Skin — 13a, 15-16
Skin awa — 10
Skin fae — 13a
Nil — 12, 14, 18, 21

Caithness
Pedle — 3
Skip — 16b
Trot — 12b
Trottin — 12a, 16a
Trow — 2ab, 3, 5-11, 12bc, 14-15, 16b, 17
Trowin — 12a, 16a
Truant — 4
Nil — 1, 13

Sutherland
Jink — 6, 8
(Play) truant — *1, 5,* 12
Skip — 11, 15
Skulk — 15
Slip — 2-4, 6, 8, 9b, 10, 13-14, 16
Trou — 9b
Trow — 9a
Nil — 7, 17

Ross & Cromarty
Foodge — 25ab
Jink — 2, 8, 14, 25a, 37b
Mitch(ing) — 27
(Play) truant — *9, 16,* 26, *31, 39*
Plunk — 24
Skip — 4, 6, 9, 16, 19-20, 32b, 34
Skulk — 1, 38
Slip — 3, 7-12, 14-15, 17-23, 26, 28-29, 31, 32ac, 33, 35-36, 37ab
Stay away — 5
Nil — 13, 30

Inverness
Dodge — 31
Dupe — 10, 13abc, 19, 21a, 31
Flee — 13ae, 26
Flood — 13abce
Flunk — 26
Jink — 27, 31, 38, 40
Jook — 13a, 19-20
Jouk — 26
Joup — 13d
Play truant — 1-2, 4-6, 13c, 18, 23, 29-30, 34-35, 37
Plunk — 22, 37
Skip — 9, 20, 32, 39
Slink — 16
Slip — 6-11, 14-15, 17-18, 21b, 25, 27-29, 33, 38
Nil — 3, 12, 24, 36

Nairn
Foodge — 2
Foodgie — 1abc, 3-4
Hookie — 5
Jink — 5
Jook — 6
Slip — 2

Moray
Foodgie — 6a
Forhooie — 16
Jink — 8b, 21-23
Jook — 2ab, 3-5, 6b, 7, 8abcdef, 9ab, 10, 12-22
Jouk — 1, 11
Play the kip — 8a
Quack — 8ef
Slip — 23
Troo — 8f

Banff
Dodge — 18a
Flee — 23
Foodge — 1, 2ac, 3-5, 6a, 29-30
Foodgie — 6b, 7-9, 12, 14-17, 18bcd, 19, 22-28, 31, 33
Forhooie — 11
Jink — 2a, 9, 21, 25, 31-32, 34
Jook — 2abc, 3-5, 6a, 10-13, 20-21, 25, 28, 32
Jouk 6b, 15, 18c, 34
Plunk — 10, 18d
True — 6b

Aberdeen
Dodge — 2, 5d, 7, 14
Duck — 31
Foodge — 63
Foodgie — 9-10, 12, 22-24, 26-27, 28abc, 29-30, 34, 40, 48, 50-53, 65, 96
Forhooie — 80, 109
Fuggie — 25
Fuggin — 31
Hooie — 16, 77, 98
Jink — 2, 5b, 14, 25, 36-37, 71a, 87, 105
Jook — 1-2, 4, 8, 11, 13-15, 17, 28a, 30, 32, 41, 46, 75, 79, 92, 97
Pervoo — 14
(Play) truant — 3b, 5cd, *6-7,* 20, *59, 70,* 71c, 94, 98, 106, 109
Plunk — 47a, 73
Privoo — 21
Ruint — 5b
Scoff — 5b, 19, 41, 44-45, 47abdef, 102
Skiff — 47d
Skip — 5b, 7
Skulk — 28c, 47bc, 70, 74, 90,

Aberdeen cont'd

103, 106
True — 3a, 5b, 10, 12, 16-17, 19, 21, 24, 28b, 29, 33-35, 38-39, 43, 55-57, 60-62, 64, 66-67, 69, 71ab, 72-86, 88-89, 95, 99-101, 104-105, 107-108
Nil — 18, 42, 49, 54, 58, 68, 91, 93

Kincardine

Kip — 20
(Play) truant — *15, 24,* 26
Skulk — 10, 13, 15, 17c
True — 2-14, 16, 17abcd, 19, 21, 23
Nil — 1, 18, 22, 25, 27-28

Kinross

Kip — 5
Play the pug — 2
Play truant — 2
Plug — 1
Plunk — 3, 6
Skip — 3
Nil — 4, 7

Angus

Bide awa — 1
Bunk — 14bcd, 25
Chuck — 8
Jink — 15
Jook — 13, 21
(Play) hookie — *14d,* 22-*23, 30, 32, 37*
Play kit — 33a, 35, 37
(Play) plunk — 19, 32, 33b, *34*
(Play *or* play the) kip — *4, 17ab,* 18
(Play *or* play the) tip — 5*abc*
Play poke — 15, 26-27, 29b
Play the diddler — 13
Play troon — 21
(Play) truant — *2*-3, *6,* 7-8, *9-10, 12, 14a,* 17b, 24, *28, 32, 34, 36*
Play yite — 34
Poke — 29a
Skip — 18
Yite — 19, 33a
Nil — 11, 16, 20, 31

Perth

Bunk — 26, 28
Dodge — 16, 48
Foodgie — 30
Jink — 27, 73
Jook — 1, 9, 25, 27, 61
Kip — 3, 25, 45
Nick — 26
(Play) hookie — 23, *27,* 33, *39,* 41a, 64
Play kick — 21
Play kippie — 12
(Play *or* play the) kip — *1,* 3, *15,* 25, 27, *41ab,* 45
(Play) truant — *2a, 4-5, 7-8, 10, 16, 20, 24*-25, *27, 34,* 36, *46, 57,* 65, *74*
Play trunk — 48, 51a, 52ce, 53, 64
Plug — 71
Plunk — 10, 26, 29b, 32, 38, 40, 41ab, 44, 50, 52abe, 53, 56, 62, 66-72
Skip — 24, 73
Slink — 14
Slip — 24
True — 43
Trunk — 29a, 42, 51b, 52ade, 53-55
Yite — 33, 60
Nil — 2b, 6, 11, 13, 17-19, 22, 31, 35, 37, 47, 49, 58-59, 63

Fife

Ditch — 37
Dodge — 37
Dog — 37-38
Funk — 8
Hop — 37
Jink — 48
(Play) hookie — *12, 41c,* 46, *49, 52*-53, *55a, 63*
(Play) kip — *3*-4, 17, 23, 33, *35,* 36a, 40b, 42, 44a, 55d, 59, 61, 64b
(Play *or* play the) tick — *12, 16,* 19-*20, 22-23, 43a,* 44*abcde, 45, 47-49, 64b*
(Play *or* play the) troon — 5, *6-7, 9a, 11-13, 21, 25, 27-28, 44f, 47-48, 50*
(Play the) ech — *55bdefg,* 59
Play the plug — 43a
Play the teck — 50
(Play the) plunk — 2, 20, 23, 29, 36a, 39, 45-47, *48,* 51, 54, 55b, 61
(Play) truant — 4, 30, 32, 41a, *45, 55de, 57*
Play yight — 14
Plog — 53
Plug — 36ab, 37-39, 40ab, 41abcd, 43ab, 44f, 52, 55c, 59-60, 63
Plump — 34
Skip — 28, 34, 37, 41a, 43a, 44f, 51, 53-54, 55abg, 58, 62
Stay aff — 50
Trick — 24
Tunt — 64a
Yite — 2
Nil — 1, 9b, 10, 15, 18, 26, 31, 56

Clackmannan

Hookie — 3
Kip — 2, 5
(Play) puggie — 4*abd*
Play the pug — 1-2
Play truant — 6
Plug — 4cd
Plunk — 2-3, 4a, 7
Trow — 1

Stirling

Fob — 7f
(Play) hookie — *7a,* 19
(Play *or* play the) fab — *4, 7e,* 9-10, *12*
(Play *or* play the) truff — *24,* 25b, 26a, *39ab*
Play the trounie — 12
(Play the) plug — 5, 7*be,* 8-9, 11-12, 17, 19-20, 21ab, 22ab, 23b, 24, 25abcd, 26ace, 33-34, 35ab, 36, 37*ab,* 38, 39ab, 40, 42ab
(Play) truant — *4, 21b,* 26d
Plunk — 2-4, 6, 7abcde, 8-10, 12-18, 21b, 23abc, 25abcd, 26abdef, 27ab, 29-33, 39ab
Run about — 18
Skame — 27a, 29
Skip — 21b, 26a, 28
Skirt — 7a, 23a, 28, 32
Nil — 1, 41

Dunbarton

Dodge — 1
Dog — 13bc, 16b
Jink — 1
Jouket — 2
Play hookie — 4b
Plunk — 1-3, 4ab, 5-6, 7abc, 8-12, 13abc, 14ab, 15, 16ab, 17-18
Skip — 16a, 18
Skirt — 16a
Skulk — 5, 10
Slope — 1
Tron — 14a
Truant — 11, 13bc

Argyll

Jook — 8, 24
Kip — 24
(Play) truant — *2,* 6, *16-17, 32-33*
Plunk — 9-16, 18-23, 28-30, 33-40
Skip — 1
Skulk — 1, 3, 7, 17, 25
Nil — 4-5, 26-27, 31

Bute

Plunk — 1abcde, 2-7, 8ab, 9
Skip — 8b
Skulk — 9

Ayr

Cut — 8ab
Dog — 12b, 20b
Fooge — 9
Fugie — 16a
Kip — 19
Leg bail — 43
Miskip — 57
Plank — 47
(Play) hookie — 16a, *20h*
Play (the) plug — 27
Play truant — 3, 28e
Plug — 7, 9, 17, 31, 35a, 36-37, 44, 46
Plunk — 1ab, 2ab, 3-7, 8ab, 9-11, 12ab, 13-15, 16ab, 17, 18ab, 19, 20abcdefgh, 21-23, 24ab, 25, 26abc, 27, 28abcdef, 29, 30ab, 31-34, 35ab, 36-43, 47-52, 53ab, 54-55, 57
Skip — 1a, 36, 38, 45, 56-57
Skirt — 24ab
Skulk — 56
Trant — 51
Tron — 6, 42, 47
Trone — 18b, 26a, 28bc, 29, 30a, 33, 35b, 36, 41, 44-46, 48-50, 52, 53ab, 54

Renfrew

Dodge — 14a, 20b
Dog — 8, 11ik, 12b, 13c, 15, 20b
Jouk — 2d
Midge — 2cg, 4b
Play hookie — 2a, 7, 11d, 16c
(Play the) plug — 1ab, 2abcdefghij, 3, 4b, 8, *17*
(Play) truant — 2i, 4e, *20a*
Plunk — 1b, 2bcfgh, 4cd, 5-10, 11abcdefghijkl, 12ab, 13abcd, 14ab, 15, 16abcd, 17, 18ab, 19, 20ab, 21
Skidge — 1a, 2eg, 4abcde, 5
Skip — 18a, 20b

Lanark

Bide aff — 64b
Dodge — 14b, 29f
Dog — 7a, 10b, 15a, 25cd, 26a, 29f, 30, 31b, 32e, 36
Gadgie — 7b
Jick — 49ab, 51, 52a, 59ab
Jink — 38c
Jook — 52a, 65
Play hookie — 28, 29b
Play plunkie — 29e
(Play the) plug — 2-3 9a, 10b, 11-*13,* 14abcd, 15ab*c,* 16ab, 17-18, *19-20,* 22-23, 25abcd, 26ab, 27ab, 28, 29ab*c*efg, 30, 31ab, 32abcde, 33abc*d,* 34, 35*abcd,* 37, 38*ace* 39-45, *47*-48, 50, 52ab, *53,* 55-56, 57abc, 58, 59a, 60-61, 64a
Plunk — 1, 4-6, 7abc, 8ab, 9ab, 10a, 11-12, 14c, 15bc, 16a, 21-22, 24, 25acd, 26b, 29cd, 30, 31abcd, 32def, 33cd, 35abd, 36-37, 38abcd, 39, 43, 46ac, 47, 49b, 50, 52b, 55, 57ab, 58, 59a, 61-63, 65-66, 67a
Shineevie — 7b
Skip — 6, 25c, 27b
Slip — 53
Trone — 67b
Nil — 54

West Lothian

Bag — 3
(Play the) kip — 1c, 8, *10,* 11, 13-14, *15*
(Play the) plug — 1ac, *2,* 4-8, 9a*b,* 12-14, 16, 17ab, *18,* 19ab, 20ab, 21ab, 22
(Play the) plunk — 1b*d,* 7, 9b, 11, 17a, 20ab
(Play) truant — *3, 15,* 18
Skip — 3, 11, 13, 22
Tip — 16
True — 11

Midlothian

Play hookie — 18
(Play *or* play the) kip — 1, *2,* 3-5, 6a*b,* 7ab, 8ab, 9-*11, 12ab,* 13, 14a, 15-16, *17-18,* 20-*21,* 23ab, *24, 25abcd,* 26ab, *27-28,* 29-31
(Play the) plug — 4, *11,* 12a, 14a, 16, 26b
(Play the) plunk — *11,* 14b, 23b
Play the tip — 14b
(Play the) truant — *13,* 15, 23b
Pug — 31-32
Skip — 6a, 10, 19, 22

East Lothian

Dodge — 13
Jig — 17
Play hookie — 1
Play the kep — 10
Play (the) kip — 1, 3, 4ab, 5, 6a, 7-9, 11-12, 13-16, 19, 21
Play the kippie — 2
Play the pug — 10
Play truant — 16
Plunkie — 14
Skip — 4b, 6ab, 7, 9
Nil — 18, 20

Berwick

Bide away — 8
Dodge — 19
Gie it the slip — 12
Go to the rabbit school — 23
Hookie — 27
(Play *or* play the) kip — 17, *20, 23, 31-32*
(Play *or* play the) truant — *2, 6-7,* 8, *9-10, 12*-13, *15, 16b, 21,* 25, 32
Play the nick — 3
Play the pug — 23-24
Plunk — 16c
Plunkie — 27
Skip — 29
Nil — 1, 4-5, 11, 14, 16a, 18, 22, 26, 30

Peebles

Play hookie — 4c
Play pug — 3
Play (the) kip — 3, 4abc, 6ab, 8
Play truant — 4b, 6b
Plug — 7
Plunk — 2, 5, 8, 10
Skip — 1-2, 7, 9

Selkirk

Play puggie — 4
Play (the) pug — 1, 2abcde, 3-7
Play truant — 8
Stay away — 2c

Roxburgh

Hornie — 5
Jook — 9a
(Play *or* play the) truant — *15b,* 16-*17, 20,* 21acd*ef, 25, 28*
(Play the) kip — 2, *3a,* 4-5, 7-*8,* 9a*b, 13, 17*-18, 20, 21c
(Play the) pug — 1-2, *10*
Plunk — 3b, 14, 21c
Skip — 9a, 15a, 26
Nil — 6, 11-12, 19, 21b, 22-24, 27

Dumfries

Bag — 4-5, 19, 31bcdef, 32
Jink — 31f

Dumfries cont'd

Jouker — 42
Kippen — 10
(Play) hookie — *43-44*
Play the kip — 20
Play (the) truant — 1a, 4, 8a, 18, 22, 29, 33, 37, 39-40
(Play) trownie — 7, 14-16, *23,* 26-28, 34-35, 49
Plunk — 4-7, 10, 25, 31a
Skip — 5, 32
Skirt — 3
Trogue — 31b
Tron — 1b, 9-10, 12-13, 21a, 24, 41-42
Trone — 2-4, 8b, 11, 19, 21b, 22, 30, 31a, 32, 38
Trotch — 36, 44, 45b, 46
Trou — 1a
Trounce — 45a
Trown — 5, 17ab, 38
Nil — 47-48

Kirkcudbright

Bag — 9
Misskip — 17
Plunk — 1
Rin away — 1
Skip — 15a, 19
Strushin — 20
Throosh — 21abc
Tron — 2, 12b, 17, 27
Trone — 1, 3-11, 12ab, 13-14, 15ab, 16, 19-20, 21b, 22-24, 26
Truant — 18
Nil — 25

Wigtown

Misskip — 5a, 7-8, 10-12, 15
Plunk — 6, 15, 17-18
Skip — 1, 5b, 7-8, 10-14, 16, 18
Skulk — 2, 4, 5a, 6, 9, 14, 17
Skunk — 3

Northumberland

Chore away — 29d
Do a mick(ie) — 46, *109*
Dodge the column — 69b
Doging — 110
Hide awa — 9, 135
Gawdie — 44
Kip — 29f
Lie off — 111b
Mizzle — 69ab
Play buck — 102
(Play) hookie — *1ab, 18, 40b,* 55, 59*ace*, 60, *62e, 63, 66,* 69ab, *72adi, 79,* 81, *83, 89, 101b, 111a,* 122b, 124b, 125, *126ef,* 127bdg
Play kittie — 105
(Play *or* play the) dollie — *65b, 72bdeghijk, 93,* 95b
(Play *or* play the) truant — *2b, 6-7,* 12-14, *15-16, 17-18,* 20b, *21, 23,* 29ab, *30-31,* 34b 35-36, *37, 40a, 41c, 42,* 46, *53b,* 54, 59b*d*, *62bh, 64b, 65b, 66,* 68, *70, 71a, 72c,* 77-78, 82, *87, 88a,* 91, 95b, *99b, 103bc, 104ab, 108c, 111ab, 112, 121, 127a, 132, 138,* 142
Play stickie — 83
(Play) the dodge — 39, *72i*
(Play the) doll — 69abe, *72al, 79,* 81, 95b, *96*
Play the dot — 41abd, 66, 69d
Play the mickie — 124b
Play (the) nick — 1c, 47, 57, 69g
Play the niggie — 130d
Play the trot — 41c
Play (the) trown — 5, 11, 69g
(Play the) wag — *12, 18, 22, 24b, 25, 27, 29bde,* 30, *32, 33b, 35, 37-39, 40ab, 41ab, 45,* 46, *47-50, 52, 53ab, 56-58,* 59abcdef, *60, 62acefgh,* 63, *64ab, 65ab, 66, 69abde, 71abcde, 72abcdefij, 74,* 75, *76-77, 79-80,* 81-82, *85-87, 88ab, 89-93,* 95a, *96, 98, 99abcd, 100,* 101ab, *103abc, 104a, 106-107, 108abc,* 110, *111a,* 113-114, *115-117, 118ab, 119, 120abc,* 121, 122ab, 123, *124ab,* 125, *126abdef, 127abcdfgh,* 128, 129abc, 130abcdef, *131, 134-137, 139, 141*
(Play the) wig — *101b,* 130e
(Play the) wiggie — 126b, 130ab
Pug — 29f
Stop away — 10
Stop off — 127b
Swing the lead — 77
Take the kittle — 47
Troon — 94b, 109
Whag — 127e
Nil — 2a, 3-4, 8, 19ab, 20a, 24a, 26, 28, 29c, 33a, 34a, 43, 51, 61, 62d, 67, 69cfh, 73, 84, 94a, 97, 133, 140 143

Cumberland

Bide away — 56
Bide off — 30
Hookie — 15b
Jigger — 41, 50-51, 54-55, 57, 59, 61-62
Laala truin — 48
Lak tick — 26
Mike — 14
Nick off — 34, 40
Play bush — 11
Play jigger — 63b
Play the buck — 9, 13ad, 14, 20
Play the wag — 12
(Play) tick — *15ac,* 16, *18, 24, 28, 40, 42-43,* 45, *60*
(Play) truant — *1a,* 2, *3-4,* 5ab, *7,* 8-9, *13ac,* 22-23, *25,* 28, *37b, 38, 40, 46-49, 53,* 56-57, *58*
Play tuck — 60
Skip — 27
Slip — 30-31
Slype off — 46
Stop off — 55
Wander aboot — 17
Nil — 1b, 6, 10, 13b, 19, 21, 29, 32-33, 35-36, 37a, 39, 44, 52, 63a

Down

Absent — 15
Mitch — 1, 2ab, 3-30
Schame — 12
Scheme — 9, 21

Tyrone

Bunch — 1
Lie out — 9, 16
Mitch — 1-6, 8, 10-15
Schame — 2-3, 6-7
Scheme — 1, 5-6, 8-10, 12-13, 15

Antrim

Dodge — 11
Duke — 11
Hookie — 1
Juke — 16b
Lie out — 11
Mitch — 1-3, 5b, 6-7, 8ab, 10-15, 16ab, 17-31, 33-34
Mootch — 4A, 9
Pogey — 18
Schame — 14
Scheme — 4, 8a, 9, 22
Nil — 5a, 16c, 32

Donegal

Hedge — 13
Lie oot — 6
Mitch — 3, 6, 10ab, 13
Renage — 12
Schame — 5, 10b, 11
Scheme — 1, 3, 5A, 7, 7A, 8-9, 10a
Sconce — 4
Slope — 12
Nil — 1A, 2

Fermanagh

Hide — 1
Lie out — 3
Mitch — 2-6, 7a, 8, 10
Schame — 1-2, 4
Scheme — 1, 7ab, 9-10
Sconce — 7b

Armagh

Mitch — 2-5, 6ab
Nil — 1

Londonderry

Mitch — 1, 5, 7
Schame — 3A, 4, 7
Scheme — 1, 1AB, 2-7
Sconce — 5

30 A STROKE with the tawse (PQ1, 88)

Variants of PALMIE have been subsumed (**pawmie** Fife, the Lothians, Lanarkshire; **pammie** Central Scotland).
Where an item was followed by phrases like **with the tawse/belt**, etc., (e.g. **belt** with the tawse) these have not been included in the list, but preceding ONE WITH (variants subsumed) as in **one with the belt**, etc., has been retained.

Shetland

Lash — 17
Lauber — 9
Ledder — 9
Leesh — 20
Lick — 2, 7, 10, 14, 21a, 22, 30, 32
Palmie — 5-6, 11, 19, 24, 30-31
Pandie — 13, 33
Straik — 21b
Strap — 18, 23, 27, 33
Tawse — 24
Wallop — 10
Whip — 10
Nil — 1, 3-4, 8, 12, 15-16, 25-26, 28-29

Orkney

Beltin(g) — 4-5
Leathering — 15
One of the clip — 13a
One of the strap — 13a, 17
One of the tawse — 13a
Palm — 1-3, 5-7, 10-12, 13b, 14-21
Skelp — 4
Slerp — 4
Strap — 8-9

Caithness

Lick — 10-11
One of the strap — 11
Palmie — 1
Pandie — 3, 5, 7, 11, 12abc, 13, 15, 16ab, 17
Scud — 2b
Shot — 12c, 16b
Skelp — 4
Strap — 4, 13
Tip — 2ab, 5-6, 8-9, 12a, 14
Whack — 8

Sutherland

Belt — 16
One of the strap — 8, 10-11, 15
One of the tawse — 11
Palmie — 3
Pandie — 2-8, 9ab, 10-17
Sonker — 10
Strap — 1, 5

Ross & Cromarty

Belting — 36
Blow — 39
Docker — 25a
One of the strap — 23, 29
Pandie — 2-4, 6-15, 17-18, 20-24, 25ab, 26-31, 32abc, 33-34, 36, 37ab, 38
Slash — 1
Strap — 11, 19, 35
Stroke — 5, 16

Inverness

Belt — 13c, 38
One of the belt — 27, 35, 39
One of the strap — 34-35
Pake — 13cde
Palmie — 5, 17
Pandie — 8-12, 13abcde, 14-18, 20, 21ab, 24-26, 29-31, 33, 38, 40
Strap — 3, 23, 29, 32
Strapping — 19
Stroke — 1-2, 7, 13a, 39
Thrash — 5
Wallop — 22
Nil — 4, 6, 28, 36-37

Nairn

Pandie — 1abc, 2-5
Whack — 1a, 6

Moray

Lick — 11, 22
One of the belt — 7
Pandie — 2b, 3-5, 6ab, 7, 8abcdef, 9ab, 10, 12-13, 15-19, 21-23
Pap — 1, 3, 8def, 17
Paup — 2a
Smack — 10

Moray cont'd
Strap — 14
Wallop — 20

Banff
Dole — 12-13
Doll — 10-11
Lick — 9, 15, 18d, 23-24, 32-33
One of the strap — 21
One of the tag — 21
Pake — 18c, 29
Palmie — 2c, 6b
Pandie — 1, 2abc, 3-5, 6ab, 7-9, 11-17, 18cd, 20, 22-25, 27-31, 34
Pap — 17, 18b
Skelp — 18b
Skilp — 16
Slap — 34
Smack — 7, 19, 24, 26
Strap — 1
Tag — 4, 18a

Aberdeen
Belt — 42, 86
Beltin — 3a
Birchin — 47c
Crack — 39
Dirl — 2
Lash — 104
Leather — 24
Leatherin — 76
Leck — 61
Leerip — 69
Lick — 5b, 9-11, 16, 21, 28b, 33, 51, 62, 71b, 72, 75-77, 79-81, 84, 86-87, 97, 107
Lickin — 47c
Liffie — 71a
One of the tag — 34-35
Pake — 55
Palmie — 28a, 31, 53, 60, 89, 100
Pandie — 1, 4, 5bd, 7-10, 12, 14, 16-17, 21, 23, 28abc, 29-30, 32-34, 36, 44-46, 47abe, 51-53, 56-58, 60, 64, 67, 71bc, 73-77, 81, 83-85, 87-90, 92-94, 96, 98-100, 103-106, 108
Pandie smack — 68
Pap — 29
Scolt — 41, 44, 47af, 102
Scringe — 27
Scud — 13, 28a, 50, 53, 64, 67, 86, 101, 103, 105-106
Serrip — 27
Skelp — 3a, 5ab, 9, 18-19, 24-25, 27, 33, 40-41, 47d, 49-50, 53, 64-67, 71a, 79
Skelpin — 47c
Smack — 3b, 4, 6, 8, 12, 15, 18, 22, 30, 32, 59
Strap — 5c, 7, 47f, 70, 94
Strappin — 3a
Stroke — 73
Swipe — 2
Tag — 20, 38
Tagged — 10
Taggin — 95
Wallop — 5b, 26, 37, 48-49, 63, 66, 69, 73
Wap — 101, 105
Whack — 62, 109
Nil — 43, 54, 78, 82, 91

Kincardine
Lick — 4, 11, 16
One of the tug — 10
Palmie — 17abd, 20, 22, 25, 27-28
Pandie — 2, 4-7, 10, 12-15, 17abcd, 23-24
Scud — 1, 10 13
Skelp — 5, 9
Smack — 8, 19
Tag — 15, 26-27
Taggit — 21
Tan — 3
Wullop — 26
Nil — 18

Kinross
Belting — 4
Lick — 1, 6-7
One of the strap — 3
Palmie — 2-3, 5
Swipe — 6

Angus
Belt — 17a, 29b, 34
Knacker — 17b
Lick — 1, 24
One of the belt — 9, 13
One of the scud — 20
Palmie — 4, 5bc, 8, 13, 14a, 17b, 18, 22, 31, 33b, 35
Pambie — 23, 25, 33a
Pandie — 1, 5a, 6-8, 10, 12-13, 14a, 21-23, 27, 29ab, 30-32, 33b, 34-37
Scud — 3, 7-13, 14abcd, 18-19, 21-23, 25-26, 32, 33b, 34, 36
Scuddin — 15
Skelp — 20, 28
Strap — 2
Whack — 17a
Yark — 17b
Nil — 16

Perth
Belt — 32, 64, 73
Caker — 60
Lick — 12, 24, 61, 74
Luiffie — 52d
One o' the belt — 52a, 72
One o' the strap — 72
Pake — 53
Palmie — 1, 15-16, 22, 24-27, 29b, 36-40, 41a, 42-45, 48, 50, 51ab, 52abde, 53-54, 56, 59, 61-63, 65, 68-69, 71, 73
Pambie — 33, 44, 50, 52c
Pandie — 1, 2a, 3, 5-9, 11, 13-14, 16-18, 20-21, 23-24, 26, 29a, 31-33, 39-40, 41ab, 42-43, 48, 52bd, 57, 59, 62
Scoult — 24
Scud — 5, 24
Scult — 70
Skelp — 46, 66
Souff — 30
Strap — 8
Stroke — 4, 10, 25, 67
Wallop — 30, 49
Whack — 46
Whackie — 28, 52c
Whauckie — 52e
Nil — 2b, 19, 34-35, 47, 55, 58

Fife
Belt — 6, 24, 37, 41b, 46, 53, 55ae
Draw — 45
Lick — 41a, 51, 63
Liffie — 55b
One of the tawse — 25, 36b
One of/with the belt — 7, 20, 22, 36b, 41c, 43a, 50, 54, 55b, 62,
Palmie — 1-2, 5-6, 8, 9ab, 10-14, 16-23, 26-35, 36a, 37, 39, 40ab, 41ad, 42, 43b, 44abcdef, 45, 47-50, 51ab, 52abde, 53-54, 55fg, 56, 59-61, 63, 64ab, 65, 68-69, 71, 73
Palmie stendie — 59
Pambie — 3
Pandie — 12, 22-23, 44a, 55d
Skelp — 4
Stendie — 55g, 59
Strap — 37, 40b, 46, 55e
Tawse — 21
Wallop — 52, 63
Nil — 15, 38, 55c

Clackmannan
Belt — 3
Palmie — 1-3, 4abc, 5-7
Pandie — 4bd
Scud — 7
Scult — 2, 5
Skelp — 6
Slap — 4c

Stirling
Belt — 7f, 10, 21b, 26b, 31, 37a, 38, 40
Belting — 12
Hutten — 28
Liffie — 9, 12, 17, 19, 21a, 25d, 27a, 30-32
One — 34
One of the stinger — 23b
One of the strap — 23b
One of the tawse — 23b
One of/with the belt — 7c, 8, 11, 17-18, 21b, 23b, 25a, 26a, 27a
Palmie — 2, 4-6, 7bcde, 9, 12-15, 17-18, 21ab, 25abcd, 26adef, 27a, 30-34, 35b, 36, 38, 39ab, 42a
Pandie — 15
Scoult — 26d
Scud — 7a, 32
Scult — 3, 6, 8-9, 20, 22b, 23c, 25bc, 26ce, 33, 35ab, 37b, 39b, 41, 42a
Skelp — 22a, 41
Slap — 23a
Strap — 27ab, 33, 40
Tawse — 7f
Whack — 16
Nil — 1, 24, 29, 42b

Dunbarton
Belt — 5, 11, 13bc
Liffie — 2, 5, 7ac, 14b
Loofie — 14b
One of/with the belt — 8, 15, 16ab
One of/with the strap — 1, 7c, 8, 16a
Palmie — 2-3, 4b, 6, 7abc, 8-10, 12, 13ab, 14ab, 16a, 17
Pake — 14a
Pandie — 5, 13a, 14a
Scud — 18
Skelp — 5
Slap — 11, 16b, 18
Smack — 6
Strap — 11
Stroke — 14a
Nil — 4a

Argyll
Lick — 5, 25
One — 1
Palmie — 4-5, 12, 19, 24, 35
Pandie — 4, 17, 20, 24
Scud — 11-12, 14-16, 19-20, 23
Skelp — 9
Squett — 26
Squite — 26-28, 30, 32-35, 37, 39-40
Squoit — 29
Strap — 2, 10, 21
Stroke — 6, 22
Tawse — 17
Wallop — 3, 7
Walt — 40
Whack — 18
Whelt — 18
Nil — 8, 13, 31, 36, 38

Bute
Belt — 1a
Beltin — 4
Liffie — 8b
One of the belt — 1cd
One of the strap — 1c
Palmie — 1abcd, 2-3, 5, 7, 8b, 9
Scud — 3
Squite — 7
Strap — 8b
Nil — 1e, 6, 8a

Ayr
Beltin — 16a
Biff — 12a, 36, 42-43
Crack — 20b
Laldie — 6
Lick — 16a, 49
Liffie — 2a, 6, 8b, 15, 16a, 18ab, 20fgh, 24ab, 26c, 27, 28bc, 29, 30a, 31-32, 35b, 36-38, 46, 48, 52, 53b, 54, 57
Loofie — 25, 57
One of the best with the strap — 26b
One of/with the belt — 9, 20b, 21
One of/with the strap — 5, 37, 43
One with the tawse — 44
Palm — 57
Palmie — 1a, 2ab, 3-4, 6-7, 8ab, 9, 11, 12b, 15, 16ab, 17, 18b, 19, 20cdgh, 22, 24b, 26ac, 27, 28abcdef, 29, 30b, 31-34, 35ab, 36, 39-41, 43, 45-48, 50-52, 53ab, 54, 56-57
Pandie — 1a, 2b, 3, 6, 8b, 9-11, 12ab, 13-15, 16ab, 17, 18a, 20acefgh, 25, 29, 32, 50
Scud — 8a, 47
Skelp — 28d
Slap — 28d
Strap — 17, 31, 47-48
Stroke — 28e, 48
Swipe — 20ef, 23, 24b
Nil — 1b, 55

Renfrew
Belt — 1a, 11a
Beltin — 11dh
Biff — 5
Cut — 11j
Lash — 2i
Liffie — 2dfghj, 5, 8, 11abefil, 12a, 13b, 14b, 16d, 17, 18a, 19, 20b
One of the belt — 13c, 18b
One of the strap — 11a
Palmie — 1b, 2abcdefghij, 4d, 6-8, 11abefhikl, 12a, 13acd, 14b, 15, 16abcd, 17, 18ab, 20ab, 21
Pandie — 16c
Punished — 2i
Rap — 11j
Scud — 2c, 4acd, 11j
Skelp — 3, 10, 11j, 12b
Slap — 2eg, 4be, 11cdg, 13b
Sooker — 11e
Strap — 2ag, 4e, 14a, 16a
Stroke — 2i
Nil — 9

Lanark
Belt — 7c, 11-12, 26a, 27b, 32e, 35c, 58
Belting — 36
Leathering — 39, 67b
Leftie/richtie — 15b
Lick — 28, 30, 33c
Liffie — 9b, 12-13, 14cd, 15abc, 17-18, 21, 29g, 30, 31ad, 33c, 35b, 38ac, 41, 43, 47, 56, 59a, 63, 65
Loofie — 32f
Luffie — 9b
Luiffie — 17, 33d
One of the tawse — 52b
One of/with the belt — 3, 7ab, 8a, 10b, 14d, 16b, 25c, 26b, 37, 46b, 49b, 52b, 60
One of/with the strap — 3-4, 14d, 19, 33a, 45, 46b
Pake — 33c
Palmie — 1-2, 5, 7ac, 8b, 9ab, 10ab, 11-13, 14acd, 15abc, 17-18, 20-24, 25abc, 26a, 27ab, 29acdefg, 30, 31abcd, 32abcde, 33bcd, 34, 35abcd, 37, 38abd, 39-45, 46ac, 47-48, 49ab, 51, 52ab, 53, 55-56, 57abc, 58, 59ab, 61-62, 64ab, 65, 67a

Lanark cont'd
Pandie — 4, 38d
Pauk — 38d
Scud — 11
Scult — 20
Skelp — 11, 32d, 40, 48, 60
Slap — 6, 16a, 25d, 28, 35a
Strap — 1, 7c, 23, 25d, 26a, 29f, 35c, 39
Stripe — 38d
Stroke — 6, 29f
Welt — 29f
Whack — 38c, 48
Whalin — 11
Nil — 14b, 29b, 38e, 50, 54, 66

West Lothian
Belt — 11, 22
Crack — 1a
Liffie — 16, 17a
One — 2
One of/with the belt — 6, 9a, 13
Palmie — 1abd, 3-8, 9ab, 10, 12-16, 17a, 18, 19ab, 20a, 21a, 22
Scud — 2, 11, 20a
Scult — 6, 19b
Skelp — 2, 8, 18
Slap — 21b
Whack — 15
Nil — 1c, 17b, 20b

Midlothian
Belt — 8a
One — 19
One of the belt — 10, 18, 22
One of the strap — 10
One with the tawse — 15
Paik — 5
Palmie — 1-5, 6ab, 7ab, 8b, 9-11, 12ab, 13, 14ab, 16-18, 20-22, 23ab, 24, 25abcd, 26ab, 27, 30, 32
Pandie — 5, 11, 23b
Puck — 3, 7a, 10
Scud — 12a, 14a
Skelp — 14a
Slap — 26b
Smack — 6a
Strap — 26b
Nil — 28-29, 31

East Lothian
Belt — 16
Belting — 16
Lounderin — 4a
One of the belt — 1, 4b, 5, 9
Palmie — 2, 4ab, 5, 6ab, 7-9, 11-21
Pandie — 10
Wallop — 13
Nil — 3

Berwick
Belt — 12, 29
Lick — 19
Palmbie — 8
Palmie — 1-13, 15, 16abc, 17-21, 23, 25-28, 31-32
Pandie — 14, 17, 22, 24, 30-32
Pawndie — 29
Punished — 8
Scult — 32
Tawse — 12

Peebles
Liffie — 3, 8
One of the belt — 9
One of the tawse — 7
One with the strap — 4c
Palmie — 1-3, 4abc, 5, 6ab, 7-8, 10
Skelp — 6a
Wallop — 2

Selkirk
Palmie — 2a, 7
Pandie — 1, 2abcde, 3-4, 6-8
Stroke — 2c
Nil — 5

Roxburgh
Belt — 18
Bleacher — 12
Liffie — 14
One with the belt — 20
Paddie whack — 21c
Palmie — 2, 4-5, 7-8, 9a, 20
Pandie — 2, 3ab, 4, 8, 9ab, 10-11, 13, 15ab, 16-20, 21abcde, 23-26, 28
Skelp — 1, 21f
Swabble — 21c
Welt — 23
Whank — 21c
Nil — 22, 27

Dumfries
Belt — 8a, 10, 23, 25, 31f
Belting — 46
Leathering — 31be, 46
Lick — 7, 8b, 9, 12, 19, 31a
Liffie — 1a, 5, 19
One of the belt — 31cd, 33-34, 44
One of the strap — 31c
One of the tawse — 4
Paik — 31a
Palmie — 1a, 2-3, 5-7, 9-11, 20, 22, 26-27, 31af, 32, 41-42, 45a, 49
Pandie — 17ab, 18, 21b, 29, 41
Pannie — 39
Peasie — 9
Scud — 5
Scult — 2, 42
Skelp — 13, 32
Slap — 31f
Straip — 37
Strap — 5, 30, 31e, 36
Stripe — 7, 15-16, 25-28, 35, 38, 47
Strop — 46
Wallop — 14, 33
Walt — 8b
Whack — 12
Wiggin — 31b
Nil — 1b, 21a, 24, 40, 43, 45b, 48

Kirkcudbright
Belt — 1
Belting — 9, 25
Leatherin — 24
Lick — 4, 12a, 18, 21c
Liffie — 1
Luiffie — 21a
One of the belt — 3, 12b
One of the strap — 18, 26
One of the tawse — 22
Paik — 17
Palmie — 1-2, 5-8, 11, 15a, 17, 20, 21abc, 27
Scud — 17, 19, 21c, 23
Strap — 1, 10
Swipe — 18
Tawse — 9
Whack — 11, 16
Nil — 13-14, 15b

Wigtown
Belting — 10
Leathering — 5b
Lick — 7, 16
Lunnering — 10
Palmie — 6-7, 15, 17
Scud — 1-4, 5a, 6, 8-9, 11, 13-14, 17-18
Skelp — 7
Spank — 5b
Spankie — 5b
Whack — 9
Nil — 12

Northumberland
Bat — 33a
Belch — 81
Belt — 1b, 8, 15, 38, 46, 48, 52, 59b, 60, 62g, 66-67, 69eg, 71bc, 72a, 88a, 89, 108a, 111b, 118a, 123, 125, 126f, 127bcd, 130ace, 135
Beltin(g) — 18, 71d, 72k, 73, 92, 100, 103a, 109, 111a, 118b, 127h
Bray — 62h
Cane — 53b
Clip — 101b
Cloot — 62h, 95b
Clout — 33a, 53a, 62h, 63, 81, 118a, 122b
Dad — 97
Flap — 69ab
Flick — 69b
Flip — 69ab
Flogged — 58
Georgie knock — 125
Hide — 60
Hiding — 9, 59c, 71d, 78, 109, 127h
Hit — 24a, 99d
Lash — 124b, 127e, 134, 138
Lashing — 28
Leatherin(g) — 41a, 71c
Leish — 7
Lick — 6, 8-9, 20a, 45, 120a
Licking — 59c
One belt — 18, 65a
Paik — 62f
Palmie — 1a, 3
Pandie — 2ab, 10-11, 13-14, 16, 19a, 20b, 25-28, 29bf, 34ab, 36-37, 41a, 44-45, 53a, 59b, 75, 124b
Rang — 93
Skelp — 10, 40a, 71d, 72d, 101b, 102, 104b, 120b, 137
Slap — 17, 33a, 39, 59d, 69ab, 72a, 82-83, 88b, 95a, 111b, 126a
Smack — 33a, 69ab, 72g, 81, 111b, 120c
Strap — 13, 26, 29bd, 39, 55, 59b, 62e, 66, 83, 122b, 126cf, 127f, 129b, 130b
Strapping — 73
Stripe — 77
Stroke — 30, 36, 42, 46, 54, 59b, 62b, 72c, 82, 87, 103c, 104a, 127ag
Tan — 22
Tannin — 59c
Tan the hide — 82
Tawse — 69a, 92-93
Thrashing — 62d
Threshing — 78
Twelt — 41c
Twelting — 41c
Wack — 40a
Wallop — 8, 21, 31, 60, 64ab, 110, 130f
Walloping — 28
Welt — 30, 35, 40ab, 41d, 47, 49-50, 56, 79, 83, 90, 97, 99b, 101a, 108a, 110, 111b, 114, 118b, 124a, 126b, 129b, 130c
Welting — 111a
Whack — 12, 56, 59d, 63, 64a, 72bd, 79, 94b, 98
Whacking — 28
Whelt — 64b, 107, 108b
Yark — 12, 69d
Nil — 1c, 4-5, 19b, 23, 24b, 29ace, 32, 33b, 41b, 43, 51, 57, 59aef, 61, 62ac, 65b, 68, 69cfh, 70, 71ae, 72efhijl, 74, 76, 80, 84-86, 91, 94a, 96, 99ac, 103b, 105-106, 108c, 112-113, 115-117, 119, 121, 122a, 126de, 128, 129ac, 130d, 131-133, 136, 139-143

Cumberland
Bat — 15c
Belt — 2, 15c
Belting — 39, 42
Cane — 4, 14, 28, 33
Dander — 44
Frap — 56
Lam — 30-31
Larrup — 30-31
Lash — 27
Leathering — 54
Ledder — 56
Panie — 5a
Scop — 44
Shot at marbles — 47
Skelp — 3, 13d, 20, 41, 46, 56
Slash — 42
Smack — 46, 52
Stick — 35
Strap — 9, 14, 57
Strappin — 56
Stripe — 31
Stroke — 4, 9, 49
Swish — 54
Wallop — 2
Welt — 9, 16, 26, 57, 60
Whang — 9
Whap — 30
Whong — 9
Nil — 1ab, 5b, 6-8, 10-12, 13abc, 15ab, 17-19, 21-25, 29, 32, 34, 36, 37ab, 38, 40, 43, 45, 48, 50-51, 53, 55, 58-59, 61-62, 63ab

Down
Lick — 24
Skalp — 11
Skelp — 8
Slap — 5, 7
Slashin — 17
Smack — 11
Stroke — 2a, 13
Tanning — 4
Welt — 4
Nil — 1, 2b, 3, 6, 9-10, 12, 14-16, 18-23, 25-30

Tyrone
Batin — 2
Skelp — 1
Slap — 11
Nil — 1, 3-10, 12-16

Antrim
Belt — 7
Flail — 31
Fleechin — 26
Hidin — 12
Lash — 28
Lick — 7, 21, 25
Screeng with the succour — 16b
Skelp — 22
Slap — 4A, 9, 17, 25
Slash — 21
Smack — 28
Sthrap — 25
Stroke of the cat — 11
Wallop with a thong — 1
Welt — 8a, 16, 21, 25, 33
Whack — 16b, 31
Whahin' — 25
Whang — 8b
Nil — 2-4, 5ab, 6, 10, 13-15, 16c, 18-20, 23-24, 27, 29-30, 32, 34

Donegal
Leathering — 8
Skelp — 10a
Slap — 2, 10a
Threshing — 8
Nil — 1, 1A, 3-5, 5A, 6-7, 7A, 9, 10b, 11-13

Fermanagh
Nil — 1-6, 7ab, 8-10

Armagh
Slap — 6a

Armagh cont'd
Whack — 4
Nil — 1-3, 5, 6b

Londonderry
Slap — 6
Nil — 1, 1AB, 2-3, 3A, 4-5, 7

31 BROKEN PIECES OF CHINA (used as playthings) (PQ1, 89)

Shetland
Bits o' lame — 21a, 30, 32
Bits o' leem — 1, 5
Bits o' lem — 21b, 28
Broken lame — 3, 27, 31
Broken leem — 2
Broken lem — 22, 24
Lallies — 7, 10, 14, 20, 23, 25
Lame — 13, 17
Lame Lallies — 17
Lawlies — 4, 6
Leem — 4, 9, 16
Lem lallies — 17, 19
Lemm — 18
Shal millings — 12
Nil — 8, 11, 15, 26, 29, 33

Orkney
Bits o' lame — 11, 13a, 16, 18-19
Bits o' leem — 4
(Broken) pieces of leem — *1*, 9
Laimags — 17
Lame — 7, 12, 14-15
Leem — 2, 4-5
Splenders o' lame — 13a
Nil — 3, 6, 8, 10, 13b, 20-21

Caithness
Delf — 5
Dishes — 13
Gless — 2b
Lames — 4-6, 9-11, 12b, 14
Lamies — 2b, 7-8, 11, 12ac, 14, 16a
Leems — 15
Pengies — 12b, 15
Pingies — 17
Pinkies — 16a
Nil — 1, 2a, 3, 16b

Sutherland
Broken dishes — 13
Chippies — 3
Chips — 3
Dishes — 1, 8, 17
Dishies — 15
Gleeshans — 16
Lame — 9a
Little housie — 7
Ornaments — 1
Piggans — 2, 4-6, 13
Nil — 9b, 10-12, 14

Ross & Cromarty
Boychans — 6
Broken bits of china — 5
Broken bits of dishes — 5
Broken dishes — 4, 9
Broken plates — 39
Dishes — 7-8, 14, 17, 20, 26, 31, 32bc, 34, 36
Dishies — 24, 25b
Housies — 11, 15, 37a
Leemies — 25a
Lim — 25a
Piggans — 2-3, 17, 28-30, 32a, 38
Shallies — 37b
Skits — 27
Wee housies — 16
Nil — 1, 10, 12-13, 18-19, 21-23, 33, 35

Inverness
Bits — 30, 40
Broken dishes — 23
Broken pieces — 5, 22
Chipa — 13e
Crocks — 10
Dishes — 1, 8-9, 16, 26, 36-38
Dishies — 15, 29, 31
Houses — 39
Pickies — 11, 14, 21b, 31
Piggans — 6, 9-10, 17, 22, 25
Wee houses — 3
Nil — 2, 4, 7, 12, 13abcd, 18-20, 21a, 24, 27-28, 32-35

Nairn
Housies — 2
Pitchers — 1c
Skeetchies — 1c
Wallies — 1b
Wee dishes — 5
Nil — 1a, 3-4, 6

Moray
Broken dishes — 8b
Chuckies — 2b
Dishes — 7, 9b, 15
Lames — 8f, 10, 16-22
Lamies — 4, 9a, 14, 21
Leemies — 1, 8d
Leems — 3
Lemmies — 8b
Lems — 6a
Pickies — 22
Piggies — 22
Pitchies — 5, 8d
Playacks — 8e
Skeetchies — 12-13
Nil — 2a, 6b, 8ac, 11, 23

Banff
Delf — 32
Lames — 1, 2ac, 5, 6b, 8, 11, 13, 16, 18bc, 19, 22-24, 26-29, 31-32
Lamies — 1, 2abc, 3-4, 6ab, 7, 9-11, 14, 17, 21, 23, 27
Leem — 30, 34
Leeman — 34
Lemmies — 15, 31, 33
Lems — 12, 18cd, 20, 25
Piggies — 32
Nil — 18a

Aberdeen
Bitties o' gosh — 7
Broken bits o' pig — 106
Broken pigs — 105
Lames — 1-2, 4, 5abcd, 6, 8-10, 12, 14-19, 21, 24, 26-27, 28abc, 29-30, 33-46, 47ac, 49-52, 54-55, 57-59, 61-70, 71ac, 72-78, 80-85, 87-88, 91, 93-95, 98, 100-103, 108
Lamies — 7, 9, 13-14, 22, 47abde, 48-49, 51, 63, 79-80, 96, 100
Leems — 31
Lemmies — 3b, 11, 23, 32, 47f, 53, 60
Lems — 3a, 11, 25, 32, 53, 56, 71b, 74, 86, 89, 97, 99, 104
Limies — 20
Piggies — 10, 98, 101, 104
Pigs — 76, 86
Plaiks — 3b
Playacks — 83
Nil — 90, 92, 107, 109

Kincardine
Broken pigs — 10
Crocks — 14
Lames — 1-2, 4, 7-8, 10, 12-13, 16, 17ab, 24
Lamies — 9
Leems — 17a
Lemmies — 26
Lems — 11, 17a
Piggies — 15, 17c
Pigs — 3-4, 6, 11-13, 17b, 20, 22-23, 28
Nil — 5, 17d, 18-19, 21, 25, 27

Kinross
Bits o' pig — 3, 6
China — 6
Pigs — 2, 5
Wallies — 2, 4
Nil — 1, 7

Angus
Bits o' pig — 5c, 20
Bitties o' pig — 29b
Broken china — 12
Broken pigs — 31
Chuckies — 17b
Dishes — 13
Dishies — 34
Hoosies — 19, 25, 29a
Paigs — 18
Palallies — 9
Pallies — 22
Peggies — 18
Piggies — 6-7, 10-11, 14acd, 21-22, 26, 28, 30-32, 33b, 34-35, 37,
Pigs — 1, 3-4, 5a, 14d, 15, 27, 33a, 37
Sciffies — 8
Wallies — 17a
Nil — 2, 5b, 14b, 16, 23-24, 36

Perth
Bits — 29a
Broken cheenie — 32
Broken china — 4, 52b
Broken dishes — 5, 7-8
Broken pigs — 56
Cheenie — 41a, 46
Cheenie dishes — 56
Chips — 29a, 52c
Chuckies — 52d
Chucks — 67
Crocks — 53
Lems — 43
Peakies — 16, 18
Peevers — 27
Peevies — 27
Peugs — 25
Piggies — 16, 23, 29b, 31, 33, 40, 56-58, 60
Pigs — 13, 18, 25-26, 39, 41ab, 44, 50, 52c, 62, 65-66, 70
Shard — 25
Shoppies — 29b
Skeetchies — 59
Wallie money — 68
Wallies — 55, 61, 64, 73
Wee housies — 67
Nil — 1, 2ab, 3, 6, 9-12, 14-15, 17, 19-22, 24, 28, 30, 34-38, 42, 45, 47-49, 51ab, 52ae, 54, 63, 69, 71-72, 74

Fife
Bit deeshay — 50
Bits of cheenie — 16
Bits o(f) pig — 8, 29-30, 42
Bits of piggie — 41b
Broken pigs — 9b, 36a, 55f
Cheenie — 8, 33-34
Cheenie chips — 55d
Chuckies — 23, 40b, 48, 55dg
Chucks — 55d
Crocks — 12, 35
Deeshes — 6
Delf — 41a
Dishes — 5
Paigs — 48
Paldies — 48, 55e
Pauldies — 9a, 38, 44b, 64a
Pennies — 44a
Penny money — 44a
Piggie bits — 49
Piggies — 2, 14, 26, 28, 31, 36b, 37, 39, 41cd, 43ab, 44c, 45-47, 52, 54, 55b, 59-60, 63, 64a
Piggie wigs — 62
Pig money — 36a
Pigs — 6-7, 10, 13, 17, 20-21, 27, 32-33, 40ab, 44e, 51, 53-54, 55ac, 56-57, 59, 61
Pillallies — 3
Prall — 4
Sketches — 48
Wallies — 37, 53
Nil — 1, 11, 15, 18-19, 22, 24-25, 44df, 58, 64b

Clackmannan
Bits o' pig — 1, 5
Piggies — 4cd, 6
Pigs — 2-3, 4a, 7
Nil — 4b

Stirling
Bits o' piggie — 25b
Broken pigs — 20
Cheenie — 26d
China — 26d
Chuckies — 36
Chucks — 7d
Crocks — 18
Delf — 9
Dishie wallies — 7a, 28, 32
Peevers — 4, 36
Pegs — 7c
Piggies — 5, 7be, 8, 10-11, 17, 19-20, 21ab, 22b, 25acd, 26ae, 31, 33-34, 35ab, 37ab, 38, 39b, 40, 42ab
Piggie wallies — 23b, 33
Pigs — 7de, 9, 16, 25cd, 26ad
Shaird — 7a
Shard — 7a
Wallie money — 25a
Wallies — 2, 5, 7a, 9, 11-13, 15, 17-19, 21b, 23ac, 25a, 27ab, 29-31, 35b, 38
Nil — 1, 3, 6, 7f, 14, 22a, 24, 26bcf, 39a, 41

Dunbarton
Bits of china — 8
Broken delf — 5
Chuckies — 15
Chucks — 9
Lamies — 10
Pigs — 17
Wallie money — 6, 16a
Wallies — 1-2, 4b, 7bc, 8-10, 12, 13b, 14ab, 16ab, 17-18
Walshies — 11
Nil — 3, 4a, 7a, 13ac

Argyll
Bits o' delf — 35
Bits o' lallie — 35
Bits of wallie — 9
Broken china — 33
Broken delf — 22, 29, 33
Broken dishes — 10, 19
Broken pieces — 17
Broken to splinters — 34
Crockery — 27
Delf — 27, 31
Dishes — 3
Glessocks — 23
Lallies — 37, 39-40
Peevers — 18
Splinters — 14
Wallies — 24
Nil — 1-2, 4-8, 11-13, 15-16,

Argyll cont'd
20-21, 25-26, 28, 30, 32, 36, 38

Bute
Cheenie — 3
Dishes — 8b, 9
Playacks — 8b
Wallies — 1abde
Nil — 1c, 2, 4-7, 8a

Ayr
Bits o' pig — 41
Broken cheenie — 8b, 54
Broken chenyie — 47
Broken delf — 47
Broken wallies — 20g
Cheenie — 20c, 25, 30b
Cheenie money — 10, 12b, 15, 20b, 21
China money — 10
Chuckies — 1a, 56
Chucks — 44
Delf — 4, 20ae, 28f
Dish wallies — 7
Hoosies — 43
Limers — 24ab
Peevers — 18b, 26b, 28f
Piggins — 22, 29, 35ab, 36-38, 40, 42, 45-46, 53a
Pigs — 1a
Playacks — 16a
Plenage — 16b
Shards — 57
Wallie dishes — 19
Wallie money — 2a, 18c
Wallie pigs — 28e
Wallies — 1a, 7, 8a, 9, 17, 18b, 20h, 24b, 25, 27, 28abcde, 29, 31, 37, 41, 43, 48, 53b, 57
Nil — 1b, 2b, 3, 5-6, 11, 12a, 13-14, 18a, 20df, 23, 26ac, 30a, 32-34, 39, 49-52, 55

Renfrew
Bits o' cheenie — 18a
Bits of china — 2a, 8
Bits o' delf — 17
Bits o' wallie — 11l
Broken delf — 2i
Cheenie — 11d
China — 11e
Chips — 16a
Chuckies — 5
Crocks — 5
Delf — 4e
Delft — 4d
Lames — 2ej
Lamies — 2fi, 8
Peggie wallies — 8
Plenish — 4acd
Plunish — 4d
Wallie money — 20b
Wallies — 2gh, 8-10, 11acdefghijkl, 12ab, 13abd, 14b, 15, 16abcd, 17, 18ab, 19, 21
Nil — 1ab, 2bcd, 3, 4b, 6-7, 11b, 13c, 14a, 20a

Lanark
Auld crock — 52a
Bits o' cheenie — 5
Bits o' delf — 20
Bits of pig — 49b
Broken cheenie — 44
Broken delf — 40, 51, 62
Cheenie — 46c
Cheenie wallies — 46a
Chips — 22, 32d
Chuckies — 11, 32e
Crocks — 65
Delf — 44
Grit — 59b, 67b
Lames — 14d, 38d
Minkies — 57b
Peevers — 49a
Piggies — 3, 15c, 20, 27a, 32bdf, 33a, 35ac, 38ac, 39, 41, 46a, 49a, 52b, 55, 57b, 58, 59a, 61
Pigs — 14d, 38b, 48, 51, 56, 57a
Plaiks — 38d
Smithereens — 32d
Wallies — 2, 6, 7abc, 8b, 9ab, 10ab, 11-13, 14ac, 15abc, 16ab, 17-18, 21, 23, 25bcd, 26a, 27ab, 28, 29abcdefg, 30, 31abcd, 32abcdf, 33abcd, 35ad, 36-37, 38ace, 39, 41-43, 45, 46c, 47, 56, 57c, 60, 63, 64b
Nil — 1, 4, 8a, 14b, 19, 24, 25a, 26b, 34, 35b, 46b, 50, 53-54, 64a, 66, 67a

West Lothian
Broken delf — 18
Chucks — 1d, 16
Delf — 1c, 7
Goldies — 20a
Piggies — 1bc, 2, 4, 6-8, 9ab, 11-16, 17ab, 19b, 20a, 21ab, 22
Pigs — 3, 20a
Wallies — 18, 20ab, 22
Nil — 1a, 5, 10, 19a

Midlothian
Bits o' cheenie — 18
Bits of china — 8a
Bits of pig — 8b
Cheenie — 10, 26a
Chuckies — 2, 18, 22
Lames — 26a
Peevers — 2
Piggies — 3, 9-11, 12ab, 14ab, 17, 20-21, 23ab, 24, 25ac
Piggie wiggies — 5
Pigs — 4-5, 7b, 13, 23a, 30
Smithereens — 1
Wallies — 14a, 17
Nil — 6ab, 7a, 15-16, 19, 25bd, 26b, 27-29, 31-32

East Lothian
Chips — 13
Chuckies — 2
Crocks — 16
Palalls — 4a
Peevers — 1, 9, 21
Piggies — 4b, 6ab, 7
Pigs — 4a, 16
Pilalls — 21
Playgins — 10-11, 17
Prawls — 1, 9
Wee dishes — 14
Nil — 3, 5, 8, 12, 15, 18-20

Berwick
Bits of pig — 8
Broken dishes — 2, 31
Dies — 7-8, 10
Dishes — 4, 15, 22
Flinders — 23
Pe(e)vers — 16c
Pigs — 24
Plafens — 5
Playgins — 3, 6, 14, 16ab, 18, 20-21, 23, 26-28, 30-32
Pligins — 12
Nil — 1, 9, 11, 13, 17, 19, 25, 29

Peebles
Bits o' delf — 7
Broken Playgins — 9
Chuckies — 2
Crocks — 8
Dishies — 1
Piggies — 4b
Pigs — 3, 10
Pitchers — 4a
Wallies — 2, 8
Wean's playthings — 6b
Nil — 4c, 5, 6a

Selkirk
Cheenie — 2c
Peevers — 2e
Piggie pieces — 2d
Piggies — 2b
Pigs — 2a, 4
Playgins — 7
Nil — 1, 3, 5-6, 8

Roxburgh
Bits — 1
Bits o' pig — 15b, 28
Boodies — 27
Brock — 13
Broken deeshes — 10
Bullies — 4, 28
Chuckies — 3b, 21a, 22
Chuckie stanes — 21a
Dishies — 26
Hoosie dishes — 25
Hoosies — 26
Pigs — 3a, 21d
Playgins — 2, 4-8, 9ab, 15a, 16-19, 21c, 24
Nil — 11-12, 14, 20, 21bef, 23

Dumfries
Beds — 31e
Bits o(f) cheenie — 4, 31f
Bits o'pig — 31f
Broken cheenie — 31d
Broken delf — 13
Broken dishes — 18, 33
Chuckies — 9, 12, 31bd
Clinkies — 23, 35
Crocks — 8a
Delf — 6
Dishes — 1a, 8b, 14, 17b, 31c, 33, 40
Dishies — 20
Hoosies — 49
Peevers — 49
Piggies — 34
Pigs — 2, 11, 21b
Plakes — 15-16, 28-29, 35, 37-39, 49
Nil — 1b, 3, 5, 7, 10, 17a, 19, 21a, 22, 24-27, 30, 31a, 32, 36, 41-44, 45ab, 47-48

Kirkcudbright
Broken cheenie — 1
Broken delf — 4
Broken dishes — 5, 8, 22
Chuckies — 1
Chucks — 23
Clinkies — 15a
Crocks — 1
Dishes — 13, 18
Flinners — 17
Jecks — 15a
Peevers — 12b
Peevies — 12a
Piggies — 1
Pitchers — 15b
Potties — 24
Scraps — 14
Smithereens — 17
Splinners — 21c
Wee hooses — 7
Nil — 2-3, 6, 9-11, 16, 19-20, 21ab, 25-27

Wigtown
Bits o' delf — 2
Bits o' dish — 16
Broken cheenie — 17
China bits — 14
Dishes — 5a, 9
Wee hooses — 5a, 7
Nil — 1, 3-4, 5b, 6, 8, 10-13, 15, 18

Northumberland
Bodies — 89
Bollies — 136
Boodies — 22, 25, 29abc, 33a, 37, 39, 40b, 41a, 43, 49, 51, 57-58, 59acde, 62efgh, 64ab, 65b, 69be, 70, 71cde, 72acdgi, 73-74, 76-77, 79-80, 84-87, 88ab, 90-92, 94b, 95a, 96-98, 99bc, 100, 101b, 105-106, 108ac, 111a, 112-114, 116-117, 118ab, 119, 120abc, 121, 122ab, 123, 124ab, 125, 126abcdf, 127abcdfgh, 128, 129abc, 130abcdef, 131, 134, 139, 141
Boolies — 25, 34a, 37, 43-44, 46, 51, 53b, 55-56, 59c, 60, 62d, 70, 73-75, 77-78, 80-81, 86, 102, 103abc, 104ab, 106-107, 108a, 109-110, 111ab, 132-135, 137-138, 140-142
Boullies — 53a
Bowdies — 69g
Broken cheenie — 69ab
Broken china — 13, 30, 54
Broken pieces — 28, 72c
Buddies — 81
Cheenie — 20b, 69f, 83
China — 59b
Chucks — 29b, 31, 37, 45, 47, 124b, 126e
Crocks — 14, 65a, 99c, 101a, 114, 127e, 140
Dabbers — 47, 63, 72f, 99d
Dobbers — 99d
Goodies — 29b, 37, 39, 41b, 47, 49-50, 57, 59abdf, 62abce, 63, 64a, 65b, 66-67, 69abdefgh, 71ab, 72abcdeghijkl, 83, 93, 95b, 96, 99c, 124b
Gowdies — 29d, 82
Hitchie dabbers — 47, 59e, 108b
Hoosies — 42
Pieces — 46
Pigs — 15
Plaggans — 9, 18, 38, 41a
Plaugans — 36
Playgins — 1abc, 2ab, 3, 6-8, 10-17, 19a, 20ab, 21-23, 24b, 27-28, 29b, 30, 33b, 34b, 35, 37, 39, 40ab, 41abcd, 50, 52, 59bf, 60, 68, 69g, 82, 122a
Playkins — 34a, 48
Nil — 4-5, 19b, 24a, 26, 29ef, 32, 61, 69c, 94a, 99a, 115, 143

Cumberland
Babbie hooses — 54
Babbie lakings — 46, 56
Bits — 50
Bits o' pot — 24, 42, 46
Boodies — 30
Boolies — 5ab, 13c, 23
Boulies — 13b
Broken pots — 18, 24, 48, 56-57, 62
Chards — 57
Chuckies — 15a
Chucks — 28, 50
Clinkies — 2
Clinks — 38
Crocks — 42, 47
Dabbers — 15b
Doll house pots — 33
Doll pots — 8
Doll's houses — 16
Hitchie beds — 17
Hitchie pots — 2, 13a
Hitchie stones — 37a
Jacks — 41
Jocks — 45
Lakins — 31, 40
Pots — 16, 20, 25
Nil — 1ab, 3-4, 6-7, 9-12, 13d, 14, 15c, 19, 21-22, 26-27, 29, 32, 34-36, 37b, 39, 43-44, 49, 51-53, 55, 58-61, 63ab

Down
Babbies — 4, 17
Bobbie dishes — 10
Broken pieces of china — 7
Crocks — 10
Dies — 8, 11, 13, 15, 28
Flinders — 13
Gies — 18, 22, 24, 29-30
Guys — 27
Jies — 14
Jigs — 23
Joys — 23
Rattlies — 25
Nil — 1, 2ab, 3, 5-6, 9, 12, 16, 19-21, 26

Tyrone
Baby dishes — 11
Bits o' delph — 8
Chainies — 5
Delph — 7
Dies — 11
Gee gaws — 1
Rattlies — 1
Smithereens — 9
Nil — 2-4, 6, 10, 12-16

Antrim
Babbie dishes — 10, 27-28, 31
Chainies — 26
Crockery — 25
Crocks — 16b
Delph — 25
Delph money — 2
Dies — 5b, 6-7, 13, 16b
Dise — 17
Giys — 27
Rubbidge — 21
Shards — 8b
Nil — 1, 3-4, 4A, 5a, 8a, 9, 11-12, 14-15, 16ac, 18-20, 22-24, 29-30, 32-34

Donegal
Broken delph — 5A, 6
Delph — 5
Dies — 3, 10a
Nimlins — 8
Nil — 1, 1A, 2, 4, 7, 7A, 9, 10b, 11-13

Fermanagh
Delph — 4
Smithereens — 3
Nil — 1-2, 5-6, 7ab, 8-10

Armagh
Babbie dishes — 1-2
Baby dishes — 3
Delph — 4
Nil — 5, 6ab

Londonderry
Babbie dishes — 2
Crockery — 1A
Dies — 1A, 6
Nil — 1, 1B, 3A, 4-5, 7

32 HOLE (in playing marbles) (PQ1, 91)

Shetland
Hole — 15-18, 22, 27, 32
Mug — 30
Nil — 1-14, 19-20, 21ab, 23-26, 28-29, 31, 33

Orkney
Hole — 13b, 16-17
Mallie hole — 5
Marble hole — 2
Pungie — 18-19
Nil — 1, 3-4, 6-12, 13a, 14-15, 20-21

Caithness
Hole — 2a
Holie — 12a
Pit — 8
Nil — 1, 2b, 3-7, 9-11, 12bc, 13-15, 16ab, 17

Sutherland
Chukie hole — 3
Hole — 1, 13, 16
Pittie — 10
Punkie — 14
Nil — 2, 4, 5-8, 9ab, 11-12, 15, 17

Ross & Cromarty
Bonnetie — 21
Hole — 3, 5-6, 8-9, 16, 30
Holie — 24, 25b
Marble hole — 12
Nookie — 36
Punkie — 23, 25a, 32c
Ringie — 34
Toadie's hole — 29
Nil — 1-2, 4, 7, 10-11, 13-15, 17-20, 22, 26-28, 31, 32ab, 33, 35, 37ab, 38-39

Inverness
Base — 6
Hole — 2, 5, 13b, 20, 21a, 29, 35, 37
Holie — 29
Home — 6
Mooshie — 26
Plunkie — 16
Punkie — 9-10, 13abcde, 14-15, 18, 21b, 23, 25, 33
Nil — 1, 3-4, 7-8, 11-12, 17, 19, 22, 24, 27-28, 30-32, 34, 36, 38-40

Nairn
Boulie hole — 1b
Hole — 2
Holie — 5-6
Nil — 1ac, 3-4

Moray
Cappie — 8a
Doolie hole — 8b
Hame — 12
Hole — 1, 7, 18
Holie — 6b, 7, 8c, 10-11, 14, 18
Kipie — 6a, 8def, 9a, 16, 22
Kite — 8b
Pit — 20
Punkie — 8c
Tattie pit — 20-21
Nil — 2ab, 3-5, 9b, 13, 15, 17, 19, 23

Banff
Beddie — 14
Cud — 17
Cuppie — 2a
Holdie — 1
Holie — 3, 5, 6b
Kipe — 11, 15, 18d, 22
Kipie — 5, 6ab, 7, 9-13, 15, 17, 20-21, 23-27
Kite — 8, 29-31, 33-34
Kitie — 5, 10, 16, 28, 31-32
Kittie — 19
Kivie — 4
Rowin' holie — 2b
Nil — 2c, 18abc

Aberdeen
Caipie — 38
Caupie — 97
Cuype — 5c, 24
Kipe — 5c, 6, 8, 11, 14, 19, 23, 25, 39-41, 43, 52, 62, 64-65, 69-70, 71ac, 75, 78, 92-93, 102
Kipie — 1-2, 3ab, 4, 5abd, 8-22, 24-27, 28abc, 29-30, 32-37, 42, 44-46, 47abcef, 48-51, 53-64, 66-68, 71abc, 72-91, 94-96, 98-100, 103-108
Kippie — 12, 31, 101
Kite — 23, 92
Kitie — 4, 109
Kyptie — 47d
Rannie — 47c
Nil — 7

Kincardine
Caipie — 3, 27
Dirt holie — 17a
Hole — 19
Kipe — 6, 16
Kipie — 1-2, 4-5, 7-15, 17ab, 18, 21-24, 26
Kitie — 17c
Pottie — 26, 28
Ringie — 19
Nil — 17d, 20, 25

Kinross
Den — 4
Hole — 6
Holie — 3
Moshie — 3
Punk — 1
Nil — 2, 5, 7

Angus
Capie — 23
Cappie — 12, 35
Coupie — 19
Cundie — 27
Dockie whack — 34
Doupie — 14d
Dumpie — 6, 14ab, 23, 32
Dumps — 14cd, 33b
Hole — 13, 18, 34
Holie — 5bc, 17b, 18, 28, 29a
Kipe — 26
Kipie — 20
Kittie — 30
Lakie — 37
Moshie — 17a
Nest — 14a
Plunk hole — 17b
Pot — 5b
Potlie — 31
Potter — 10
Pottie — 3, 24
Puggie — 24
Puttie — 32
Ringie — 7
Steesh — 9
Trinkie — 24
Nil — 1-2, 4, 5a, 8, 11, 15-16, 21-22, 25, 29b, 33a, 36

Perth
Basin — 15
Beddie — 21-22
Bool hole — 11
Cleash — 25
Croon — 43
Den — 8, 20
Hastie holie — 53
Hole — 4, 9-10, 12, 25, 27-28, 29a, 48, 52b, 57, 66, 72
Holie — 13-14, 16, 32, 40, 51b, 62
Kipe — 39
Kippie — 30, 52a
Kittie — 55
Laig — 27
Lake — 46
Moshie — 71-72
Mouchie — 73
Mug — 69
Plunk hole — 26
Plunkie — 56
Ring — 7, 67
Taw — 41a
Towf — 60
Nil — 1, 2ab, 3, 5-6, 17-19, 23-24, 29b, 31, 33-38, 41b, 42, 44-45, 47, 49-50, 51a, 52cde, 54, 58-59, 61, 63-65, 68, 70, 74

Fife
Daggie tam — 23
Demin — 29
Den — 11, 28, 33, 35
Dennie — 33
Dykie — 27
Hole — 4, 7, 11, 16, 21, 41ab, 42, 44ce, 55be
Holie — 3, 8, 9ab, 36a, 38, 40b, 47, 50, 55a, 56-58, 62
Hollie — 32
Kellie (hole) — *12, 37,* 43ab 44a

Fife cont'd

Kipe – 63
Knuklie – 43b
Moash – 52
Mooch – 55d
Mosh – 23, 36b, 45, 47-49, 55d
Moshie – 22, 47-48, 52-53
Plunkie – 2
Pout hole – 39
Ring – 20
Ringie – 1, 27
Saikie hole – 37
Smout – 64a
Tammie hole – 14, 25
Taw – 12-13
Nil – 5-6, 10, 15, 17-19, 24, 26, 30-31, 34, 40a, 41cd, 44bf, 46, 51, 54, 55cfg, 59-61, 64b

Clackmannan

Bowlie – 3
Moshie – 4c
Moss – 4d
Muggie – 6
Smout – 7
Nil – 1-2, 4ab, 5

Stirling

Bool – 26f
Cap – 26d
Cup – 22a
Den – 21b, 23b
Hashie bashie – 4
Hole – 34, 39b
Holie – 10, 26a
Hollie – 18
Keelie hole – 7e, 8
Killie – 7bd
Kype – 7d, 26b
Moash – 28
Moashie – 9, 28, 30
Mosh – 6, 7b, 12, 17, 19
Moshie (hole) 10-11, 13-*15*, 18, 23a, 25ab, 27ab, 29, 31-32
Mosie – 23a
Mosp – 7b
Moss – 7a
Mug – 3, 7a, 8, 22a, 25abc, 35ab, 37b, 40, 42ab
Muggie – 2, 9, 17, 20, 21b, 23abc, 25cd, 26e, 33
Piggie – 12
Pit – 21a
Pluggie – 22b
Pussie hole – 4
Pussie knuckle – 8
Ring – 12, 25b, 31
Ringie – 8, 23b
Square – 21b
Nil – 1, 5, 7cf, 16, 24, 26c, 36, 37a, 38, 39a, 41

Dunbarton

Dull – 9
Kweep – 5
Mashie – 15
Mooshie – 7b
Mosh – 1-2, 13c, 14ab
Moshie (hole) – 4b, *5*, *7a*c, 16a*b*
Mossie – 18
Mowsh – 6
Mug – 13bc
Ring – 11
Nil – 3, 4a, 8, 10, 12, 13a, 17

Argyll

Brook – 35, 37
Den – 7
Hole – 2, 12, 14-15, 17, 22-23, 30
Jarie – 24
Moash – 9, 32
Mosh – 18
Moshie – 19
Mug – 16
Three holes – 33
Nil – 1, 3-6, 8, 10-11, 13, 20-21, 25-29, 31, 34, 36, 38-40

Bute

Din – 1e
Mooshie – 8a
Mosh – 7
Moshie hole – 1ab, 3
Mosie hole – 1c
Mouchie – 1a
Ring – 8b
Score – 8b
Nil – 1d, 2, 4-6, 9

Ayr

Bruch – 45
Cullie – 18b, 47, 53b
Cuppie – 18b
Den – 6
Gug – 26bc
Hole – 24b, 49
Holie – 16b, 48, 52
Kipie hole – 53a
Kittie – 6
Knuckle hole – 53a
Moashie hole – 8b
Mooshie – 41
Mosh – 7
Moshie (hole) – 2a, 7, 20h, 29, 47, *57*
Mouchie – 19
Mug – 3, 8a, 11, 12a, 13-15, 16b, 18a, 20aef, 23, 25, 27, 29, 31-34, 35ab, 36-38, 40, 44, 46, 50, 56
Muggie – 24b, 26a, 29, 32, 42-43, 53a
Mushie – 54
Plunkie hole – 54
Pot – 28f
Puggie – 16b, 20f
Ring – 30a, 45
Shirrie – 18b
Tee – 51
Yake – 7
Nil – 1ab, 2b, 4-5, 9-10, 12b, 16a, 17, 20bcdg, 21-22, 24a, 28abcde, 30b, 39, 55

Renfrew

Bools – 16a
Hole – 2ij, 4ae
Home – 20b
Jug – 11k
Moash – 7, 11k
Moashie hole – 17
Mooshie – 2f
Mosh – 6, 8-9, 18a
Moshie – 1b, 11e, 14b, 15, 16ac, 21
Moush – 16b
Muckie – 2a
Mug – 1a, 2g, 4d, 5, 8-10, 11abcdefghijkl, 12ab, 13bc, 14ab, 16a, 17, 18b, 19
Muggie – 2af, 12b, 13a
Nest – 16d
Owe – 4c
Plug – 2i
Ringie – 2e
Smout – 11b, 15
Nil – 2bcdh, 3, 4b, 13d, 20a

Lanark

Dill – 15c
Hole – 12, 27b, 45
Kittie – 53
Mashie – 32d
Moash – 4, 16b, 29f, 31b, 32e, 57b
Moashie – 7c, 18, 27b, 32b
Moe – 7b
Moosh – 6
Mooshie – 26a
Mosh – 6, 25bd, 30, 31ad, 33b, 34, 35ac
Moshie (hole) – 1-2, 5-6, *7a*b, 8ab, 9a, 10a, *14a*, 15b, 17, 22-23, *25c*, 28, 29ceg, 31c, 32aef, 33acd, *36*, 37, 38*ac*, 41-42, 44, *46abc*, 49a, 52b, 57ac, 58, 63
Mossie – 55-56
Mowsh – 16a
Mug – 12-13, 15a, 19-20, 23, 27b, 29ad, 34, 35d, 39, 47-48, 59a, 61
Muggie – 3, 19, 32c
Naggie – 9b
Pat lid – 15a
Pattie – 42
Pot – 40, 49b, 54, 56
Ring – 59b
Trollie – 67a
Nil – 10b, 11, 14bcd, 21, 24, 25a, 26b, 27a, 29b, 35b, 38bde, 43, 50-51, 52a, 60, 62, 64ab, 65-66, 67b

West Lothian

Den – 11
Hole – 15
Mash hole – 3
Moggie hole – 21a
Mogie – 21b
Mosh ring – 17a
Mossie – 1d
Mug (hole) – 1c, 8, 9a, 12, 16, 18, *19a*, 20a
Muggie – 1c, 2, 4-6, 11, 19b
Ring – 17b
Troo – 13
Nil – 1ab, 7, 9b, 10, 14, 20b, 22

Midlothian

Bunker – 20
Den – 12b, 32
Dill – 13
Hole – 2, 6a, 8a, 23b
Holie – 5, 18, 23b
Howkie – 14a
Kip – 27
Kittie – 12a, 14b
Kuipie – 7b
Mosh – 24
Mug – 10, 12a, 14a
Muggie – 10, 12b
Mush – 8b, 19
Plunket – 1
Puggie – 30-31
Ring – 25b
Ringie – 25bc
Nil – 3-4, 6b, 7a, 9, 11, 15-17, 21-22, 23a, 25ad, 26ab, 28-29

East Lothian

Geggie – 1
Hole – 7, 15, 18-20
Holie – 6a, 17, 21
Kellie – 6b
Mushie – 4b, 21
Pug – 14
Puggie – 2, 13
Nil – 3, 4a, 5, 8-12, 16

Berwick

Dump – 22
Hole – 10, 13, 16b
Holie – 6, 8
Pottie – 32
Puggie – 1-4, 7-9, 11-12, 14-15, 16abc, 17-20, 23-24, 27-28, 30-32
Punt – 29
Nil – 5, 21, 25-26

Peebles

End – 1
Holie – 10
Kittie – 6b
Moshie – 2
Pot – 4b, 6a, 8-9
Pottie – 3, 10
Tee – 3
Nil – 4ac, 5, 7

Selkirk

Den – 2a
Hole – 2d
Pottie – 3-4
Puggie hole – 2b, 7
Nil – 1, 2ce, 5-6, 8

Roxburgh

Dubbie – 17
Dump – 15a, 21ac
Kittie – 3a
Muggie – 15b, 17, 21c
Puggie (hole) – 3ab, 4-7, *8*, 9*ab*, 12, 16-18, 23-24, 26
Whull – 21c
Nil – 1-2, 10-11, 13-14, 19-20, 21bdef, 22, 25, 27-28

Dumfries

Duggie – 35
Geg hole – 29
Hame – 42
Hole – 1a, 4-5, 16, 28, 31e
Holie – 12, 21a, 38, 44
Hoolie – 15, 37, 46
Kipie – 14
Kittie – 10
Pan – 21b
Pluggie – 11
Pot (hole) – 29, *40*
Pottie – 6
Smout (hole) – 8b, 12-13, 26, *27*, 30, *31cf*, 32, 41
Smut – 45b
Tee – 17b
Wee hole – 2
Nil – 1b, 3, 7, 8a, 9, 17a, 18-20, 22-25, 31abd, 33-34, 36, 39, 43, 45a, 47-49

Kirkcudbright

Hole – 5, 15a, 17
Holie – 4
Lunkie – 1
Moshie – 15a
Mushie hole – 10
Pin – 21c
Plunkie – 2
Ring – 12ab
Smout – 7-9, 15b, 16
Tee – 1-2, 11, 12a
Nil – 3, 6, 13-14, 18-20, 21ab, 22-27

Wigtown

Bulkie – 2
Hole – 16
Holie – 5a, 7-9, 11
Moshie – 5b
Plunkie – 3
Putt hole – 14
Ringie – 5a
Nil – 1, 4, 6, 10, 12-13, 15, 17-18

Northumberland

Billie (hole) – *29ad, 37, 39, 40a, 41bc, 51, 55, 59cf, 62a, 64b,* 69d*g*, 72b, *78-79, 86, 115-116, 120ac, 122a, 123, 124ab, 127e, 130e, 134, 142*
Billie hole teaser – 71c
Billie holie – 14, 36, 38, 45, 52, 60, 65a, 68, 72d, 74, 104b, 108a, 127h
Billie hoolie – 56, 135
Bolie hole – 130c
Boolie (hole) – 31, 34b, *62g*
Boorie hole – 23, 29b, 35, 41a, 44, 47, 51, 56, 59d, 62cgh, 71ae, 72ik, 75, 77, 79, 97, 117
Borie – 33b
Bowdie hole – 57
Bowlie (hole) – 28, *112*
Bown – 28
Bowrie (hole) – *45*, 89
Boxie – 41c
Bullie hole – 14

Northumberland cont'd
Chancie hole – 126c
Chuckie hole – 17
Dibble – 22
Ditch – 60
Dump – 124b
Gootch – 125
Hill or hole – 130d
Hole – 26, 30, 48, 56, 59b, 70, 72ad, 82, 87, 101b, 103b, 104a, 105-106, 109-110, 111ab, 119, 127a, 130b, 132, 137, 143
Holie – 7, 13, 20b, 24ab, 28, 46, 59b
Killer hole – 129a
Marble hole – 21, 37
Mott – 40a
Muggie hole – 29cd, 45, 62g, 69c
Muggle hole – 130af
Paulie – 94b, 95b, 97
Penker hole – 139
Penkie boorie – 111b
Penkie hole – 118a
Penkie three hole – 118b
Pit – 5
Pitch – 59b
Poggie hole – 18
Pot (hole) – 14, 41a, 42, *64b, 72d, 76, 89,* 90, *92, 100,* 111b
Potseye – 76
Potsie (hole) – 38, 41ab, 59d, 62def, 63, 66, 71d, 84-85, 91-92, 97, *98*
Potsh – 72hi
Potshie (hole – 39, *49*-50, 57 62aeh, 64b, 65b, 66-67, 69abd*e*h, 71be, 72*c*fgl, 82, 90, 93, 95a, 96, 99b, 107, 114-115, 122ab, 124b, 126f
Pottie (hole) – 17, 47, *62g, 83*
Puggie (hole) – 1b, 3-4, 8, *9,* 12, 16-*17,* 19a, 26
Purlie hole – 98, 99d
Rap – 129a
Ring – 71a
Three hole teaser – 126c
Thribbler – 141
Nil – 1ac, 2ab, 6, 10-11, 15, 19b, 20a, 25, 27, 29ef, 32, 33a, 34a, 40b, 41d, 43, 53ab, 54, 58, 59ae, 61, 62b, 64a, 69f, 72ej, 73, 80-81, 88ab, 94a, 99ac, 101a, 102, 103ac, 108bc, 113, 120b, 121, 126abde, 127bcdfg, 128, 129bc, 131, 133, 136, 138, 140

Cumberland
Boolen whol – 45
Boolie whol – 30-31
Den – 46
Dennie – 54
Hole – 3-4, 9, 20-22, 24, 47, 57-58
Holie – 60
Laggie hole – 50-51, 54
Marble whoal – 22
Marlie hole – 61
Mott – 14
Oilie catcher – 2
Pot – 20
Pottie – 33
Pot whoal – 20
Ringie – 7
Whoal – 21, 27
Whol(l) – 1b, 12, 13d, 15c, 21, 25, 28, 33, 37ab, 38, 40-41, 43, 46-47, 49, 52, 56-58, 62
Whollie – 16, 48
Wole – 9, 11, 19
Wol(l) – 8, 15b, 17-19, 24, 26, 29, 34-36, 37a, 42, 55, 57
Nil – 1a, 5ab, 6, 10, 13abc, 15a, 23, 32, 39, 44, 53, 59, 63ab

Down
Gug – 2b
Hole – 2a, 5, 15, 19, 24, 28
Mug (hole) – 9, *18,* 22-23, *24, 29*
Pogie hole – 13
Pots – 26
Pug – 21
Puggie – 8
Puggs – 3
Pug hole – 7
Nil – 1, 4, 6, 10-12, 14, 16-17, 20, 25, 27, 30

Tyrone
Alley – 5
Hole – 1, 6-7, 11
Ring – 5
Nil – 2-4, 8-10, 12-16

Antrim
Bull's eye – 34
Butts – 20-21
Den – 28
Kings – 19
(Mug) hole – 13, 25-26, *27,* 31, 33
Ring – 7, 25
Nil – 1-4, 4A, 5ab, 6, 8ab, 9-12, 14-15, 16abc, 17-18, 22-24, 29-30, 32

Donegal
Den – 6
(Marble) hole – 5A, *8*
Mug – 5A, 7
Puddlie – 10b
Square – 6
Nil – 1, 1A, 2-5, 7A, 9, 10a, 11-13

Fermanagh
Hole – 2, 4, 7a
Nil – 1, 3, 5-6, 7b, 8-10

Armagh
Hole – 4
Muggie hole – 1
Nil – 2-3, 5, 6ab

Londonderry
Hole – 3A
Pollie – 5
Pot – 1B, 6
Ring – 2
Nil – 1, 1A, 3-4, 7

Nil – 2, 4-8, 9ab, 11-12, 15-16

Ross & Cromarty
Drop – 19
Fleckie – 22
Flirt – 3
Forgie – 25b
Knuckle – 12, 18, 23, 28
Knuckle set – 32b
Pitch – 17, 20, 34
Play – 24
Plunk – 28
Shoot – 25a
Spin – 36
Thumb – 8
Nil – 1-2, 4-7, 9-11, 13-16, 21, 26-27, 29-31, 32ac, 33, 35, 37ab, 38-39

Inverness
Flick – 21b, 26
Knuckle – 29, 31
List – 13a
Plunk – 38-39
Plunkie – 23
Shoot – 5, 26
Skittle – 16
Nil – 1-4, 6-12, 13bcde, 14-15, 17-20, 21a, 22, 24-25, 27-28, 30, 32-37, 40

Nairn
Knicklie – 4
Knuckle – 5-6
Peek – 2
Skeetie – 1c
Thumbock – 1b
Nil – 1a, 3

Moray
Chuck – 4
Knickle – 3, 7, 8aef, 9a, 10, 17-18
Knicklie – 8d
Knuckle – 2b, 6b, 13, 20, 22
Knuckler – 21
Peek – 3
Pick – 11
Skite – 1, 8bc, 16
Nil – 2a, 5, 6a, 9b, 12, 14-15, 19, 23

Banff
Chuck – 4, 14, 25
Flick – 14
Flype – 31
Hannig – 2c
Knickle – 6b, 11, 13, 18d, 29, 31, 33-34
Knuckle – 1, 6b, 9, 18c, 20, 26, 28-29, 32
Knucklie – 2c
Nick – 7, 29
Pick – 2b
Ping – 2a
Pirk – 16
Pirkie – 12
Pitch – 2a, 19
Plunk – 8
Putt – 2a, 3
Skite – 2b, 5, 10, 15, 18b, 21, 24-25, 30
Thoom – 2b
Nil – 6a, 17, 18a, 22-23, 27

33 The word used of the action of SHOOTING A MARBLE by flicking the thumb over the forefinger (PQ1, 92)

We have changed -in(g) forms of words (**knuckling, knickling** etc.) to the infinitive, as informants gave this form in preference to the former in most parts of the area.

Shetland
Click – 13
Pleenk – 6
Plink – 25
Plumb – 3
Skeet – 24
Snick – 17, 21b, 22, 24-25
Snickum – 12
Snit – 5, 19, 27-30
Spang – 14
Nil – 1-2, 4, 7-11, 15-16, 18, 20-21a, 23, 26, 31-33

Orkney
Knuckler – 19
Nick – 14
Snick – 17
Span – 9
Spoot aff – 6
Spootan – 2
Stot – 16
Nil – 1, 3-5, 7-8, 10-12, 13ab, 15, 18, 20-21

Caithness
Flick – 8
Knuckle – 12c
Nil – 1, 2ab, 3-7, 9-11, 12ab, 13-15, 16ab, 17

Sutherland
Chuck – 3
Click – 3
Fire – 17
Flick – 7
Knuckle – 10, 14
Shoot – 1
Throw – 13

Aberdeen
Cock knuckle – 3a
Fire – 27, 82
Flick – 25, 67
Flipe – 47f, 108
Hard knickle – 73
Hielan sweetie – 29
Knickle – 4, 5c, 6-7, 27, 28a, 64, 78, 92-93, 95
Knuckle – 3b, 5b, 9-11, 24-25, 30, 37, 40, 48, 56, 60-61, 65, 71ac, 73, 79-81, 85, 101, 104-105

Aberdeen cont'd

Knucklie — 11, 41, 90
Laggie lag — 47ae
Nick — 5b, 43
Pin — 71b, 95
Ping — 13, 51, 104
Pirk — 8, 10
Pitch — 9, 12, 17, 21, 31, 59, 75, 77, 79, 89, 94
Skite — 2, 5ad, 8-10, 14, 18-19, 22-23, 28b, 32-34, 39, 47adf, 49-50, 53-54, 56, 66, 69, 74, 77, 83-84, 86, 88, 97-99, 102-104, 107
Skoot — 96
Snipe — 44
Thoom — 51, 87
Thoomie — 14
Twirl — 47c
Nil — 1, 15-16, 20, 26, 28c, 35-36, 38, 42, 45-46, 47b, 52, 55, 57-58, 62-63, 68, 70, 72, 76, 91, 100, 106, 109

Kincardine

Feef — 2
Hard knuckle — 4
Knickle — 6
Knuckle — 1, 5, 9, 13-14, 17bd
Knucklie — 3, 11, 17c
Ping — 27
Pitch — 8
Plunk — 17c
Skite — 2, 4, 7, 12, 15-16, 17ab, 18, 24, 20-28
Nil — 10, 19-23, 25

Kinross

Knickle — 2, 4, 7
Knuckle — 1-3, 5-6

Angus

Cushie knuckle — 13
Fire — 28
Flick — 17a
Knucklie — 5b, 22, 33a
Nick — 3
Pitch — 24, 32
Plunk — 7, 17b, 19-20, 23, 31, 33b, 36-37
Plunkie — 29a
Putt — 10
Skite — 4, 5ac, 9, 14bcd, 18, 21-22, 27, 30, 35, 37
Spunge — 5a
Stinch — 23, 34
Thoombie — 12, 23
Throw — 24
Nil — 1-2, 6, 8, 11, 14a, 15-16, 25-26, 29b

Perth

Fire — 16, 48
Flipe — 55
Keist — 52de, 53-54
Kiste — 42
Knicket — 41b
Knickie — 29b, 40
Knickle doon — 56
Knickle laigh — 73
Knuckie — 15, 50, 51b
Knuckle — 3, 14, 25, 27-28, 39, 44, 46, 48-49, 52c, 62, 66-67, 71
Nick — 41a, 42
Nickle — 70
Ping — 7
Pitch — 34
Plonkie — 41b
Plunk — 13, 15, 20-21, 23, 31-33, 44, 51a, 57, 65, 67-71
Pussie knickle — 71-72
Pussie knuckle — 26
Scunch — 60
Shoot — 8, 29a
Skit — 30
Skite — 7
Snipe — 59
Spung — 13
Twick — 6
Nil — 1, 2ab, 4-5, 9-12, 17-19, 22, 24, 35-38, 43, 45, 47, 52ab, 58, 61, 63-64, 74

Fife

Boolie — 4
Fire — 48
Flick — 21
Funny knuckle — 57
Kneckle — 31
Kneyckle — 44d, 64b
Knickle — 7, 19-20, 32-34, 36b, 39, 40a, 41d, 44bce, 45-46, 49-51, 55bde, 56, 59-60, 64a
Knicklie — 7, 25, 41a, 44e, 55fg
Knieckie — 17
Knuckle — 9a, 10-11, 16, 21, 23-24, 26, 30, 34, 38, 41cd, 42, 43ab, 44a, 47, 52-54, 55abcd, 59, 61-62
Knuckle deid — 63
Knucklie — 2, 5, 8, 13, 27-28, 36a, 55g
Navie — 37
Nivvie — 14
Pitch — 33
Pitch pussie — 47
Plonk — 37
Plonkie dabbie — 37
Plunk — 6, 12, 21, 29, 41b, 48, 52-53
Punt — 52
Pushie knuckle — 37
Pussie knickle — 49
Pussie knuckle — 22, 40b, 58
Scoot — 1
Skite — 3, 23
Snaffle — 35
Sneevle — 35
Snib — 44f
Stavie — 18
Taw — 44f
Nil — 9b, 15

Clackmannan

Knickle — 2, 4c, 6-7
Knuckle — 2
Knucklie — 3
Play smouts — 4b
Plunk — 2, 4cd, 5-6
Nil — 1, 4a

Stirling

Knickle — 3, 6, 9-10
Knuckle — 2-3, 26a, 33
Nickle doon — 9
Plunk — 4-6, 7abcdef, 8-20, 21ab, 22ab, 23abc, 24, 25abcd, 26abcdef, 27ab, 28-34, 35ab, 36, 37ab, 38, 39ab, 40, 42ab
Poofie knuckle — 26d
Pooshie knickle — 9
Pussie knickle — 18
Pussie knuckle — 36
Nil — 1, 41

Dunbarton

Knuckle doon — 14a
Mochie — 9
Plunk — 1-3, 4b, 5-6, 7abc, 8, 10-11, 13abc, 15, 16ab, 17-18
Pussie knuckle — 16b
Sheevie — 18
Nil — 4a, 12, 14b

Argyll

Knuckle — 2, 8-9, 32
Knuckle doon at evens — 8
Pink — 20
Plunk — 7, 13-16, 18-19, 21, 23, 30-31, 33-35, 37-40
Snipe — 22
Nil — 1, 3-6, 10-12, 17, 24-29, 36

Bute

Plunk — 1abe, 2-5, 7, 8ab, 9
Nil — 1cd, 6

Ayr

Flick — 19
Knickle — 8a, 34, 45-46
Knuckle — 8a, 16b, 28e, 32
Knucklie — 53a
Neavie — 31
Plunk — 1a, 2ab, 3-7, 8ab, 9-11, 12ab, 13-15, 16ab, 17, 18ab, 20abcdefgh, 21-23, 24ab, 25, 26b, 27, 28bcdef, 29, 30a, 31-34, 35ab, 36-38, 40-52, 53b, 54-57
Pussie knuckle — 51
Shillie — 8b
Strunk — 18a
Swinge — 28c
Nil — 1b, 26ac, 28a, 30b, 39

Renfrew

Fire — 2h
Hosie — 7, 11c
Knickle — 2c, 11i
Knickle deid — 2j
Knickle doon — 21
Knickle stinch — 2j
Knuckle — 2fgi, 11adk, 12b, 13c, 14ab
Knucklie — 4d
Moochie — 2e
Moshie — 5
Play — 20a
Plonk — 4e
Plunk — 1b, 2e, 4ac, 7-10, 11befhjkl, 12a, 13abd, 14b, 15, 16abcd, 17, 18ab, 19, 20b, 21
Putt — 11f
Scop — 11k
Shoot — 20a
Stinch — 2f
Nil — 1a, 2abd, 3, 4b, 6, 11g

Lanark

Hunk — 4
Knickle — 61
Knuckle — 7a, 59b, 67ab
Knuckle doon — 7b
Plunk — 1-6, 7abc, 8ab, 9ab, 10ab, 11-13, 14abcd, 15abc, 16ab, 17-20, 22-24, 25abcd, 26ab, 27ab, 28, 29abcdefg, 30, 31abcde, 32abcdef, 33abcd, 34, 35abcd, 36-37, 38abcde, 39-45, 46abc, 47-48, 49ab, 50-51, 52ab, 53-56, 57abc, 58, 59a, 60-61, 63, 64ab, 65-66
Sheeve — 22
Shoot — 37
Nil — 21, 62

West Lothian

Knickle — 8
Knuckle — 1a, 7, 11
Play poofie — 3
Plug — 14, 21b
Plunk — 1bcd, 2, 4-6, 8, 9ab, 11-16, 17ab, 18, 19ab, 20ab, 21ab, 22
Pushie knickle — 15
Pussie knucklie — 22
Nil — 10

Midlothian

Bools — 20
Cushie knuckle — 25b
Knick — 17
Knickie — 17
Knickle — 3-5, 6b, 17, 21, 23ab, 26a
Knickle deid — 9
Knuckle — 1, 7a, 8a, 10, 12ab, 18-19, 21-22, 24, 25ac, 26a, 32
Knuckle dean — 15
Knuckle deid — 7b, 25c, 26b, 27
Ping — 17
Plonk — 5
Plunk — 2, 7b, 8b, 10-11, 12a, 13, 14ab, 16, 18, 23b, 25c, 28
Punt — 30
Skite — 29
Spin — 6a
Thoomie — 4
Thummie — 25d
Nil — 31

East Lothian

Cushie knuckle — 2
Knickle — 4a, 5, 7, 12, 19
Knickle deid — 8
Knuckle — 4b, 6ab, 9-11, 13-14, 17
Knuckle deid — 1
Pentle — 4a
Play — 15
Plunk — 5, 11, 14, 20
Plunkie — 2, 21
Shoot — 15
Nil — 3, 16, 18

Berwick

Funk — 23
Kneave — 8
Knickle — 12
Knuckle — 1-15, 16ab, 17-18, 20-24, 26-29, 32
Knucklie — 31
Pitch — 16c
Plunk — 16c, 28
Plunkie — 27
Punt — 15, 17-19, 28, 30, 32
Sling — 16c
Nil — 25

Peebles

Funk fall — 4c
Funk full — 4b
Knuckle — 6b, 8-10
Knuckle dead — 4b
Knuckle deid — 4c
Nickie — 10
Plunk — 2-3, 5, 6a, 7-8, 10
Pussie knuckle — 1
Shoot — 9
Nil — 4a

Selkirk

Knuck — 2bc
Knuckle — 1, 2acde, 4, 6-8
Plunk — 5
Punt — 2d
Nil — 3

Roxburgh

Click — 19
Knuckle — 3ab, 4-5, 7, 9a, 10, 13, 15ab, 16-18, 20, 21abde, 23-26, 28
Knucklie — 8, 9b
Picket — 21c
Punt — 1, 17, 23
Nil — 2, 6, 11-12, 14, 21f, 22, 27

Dumfries

Fire — 43
Jubilee — 31b
Kneave — 23, 25, 38
Knickle — 2, 7, 22
Knockle — 49
Knuckle — 1b, 4-6, 8b, 9-11, 13, 15-16, 20, 21ab, 26-30, 31ac, 32-38, 41-42, 45b, 46
Knuckle stinch — 31bd
Knuckle up an foorcie — 39
Knucklie — 12, 24, 44
Pirl — 32
Play — 17b
Plunk — 1a, 4-5, 17a, 19, 22, 28
Scoot — 14
Skite — 14, 40

Dumfries cont'd
Smout — 3, 31e
Nil — 8a, 18, 31f, 45a, 47-48

Kirkcudbright
Boit — 17
Flick — 12a
Goit — 4
Knuckie — 14
Knuckle — 1-2, 5, 7, 10, 12ab, 16-19, 21c, 23, 25
Knucklie — 4, 10, 22
Nievie — 27
Plonk — 15a
Plunk — 1, 11, 21a, 24
Scoot — 7
Shoot — 16
Smout — 9
Thoom — 1
Thoomie — 26-27
Nil — 3, 6, 8, 13, 15b, 20, 21b

Wigtown
Dribble — 2
Goit — 10
Knuckle — 3, 5ab, 6-7, 10-12, 14, 16-17
Knucklie — 8
Plunk — 18
Poofie — 6
Scoot — 13
Thoomie — 8
Nil — 1, 4, 9, 15

Northumberland
Bleese — 110
Bore — 29b
Bull — 62h, 126b
Bulleek — 106
Bullock — 38-39, 41b, 50, 69g, 72j, 75, 78-79, 99d, 111a, 129b
Fire — 21, 40a, 48, 72i, 77, 82, 87, 89, 92, 111b, 126c, 127d,
Flick — 13, 22, 29d, 52, 56, 66, 70, 72dk, 94b, 104a, 112, 122b,
Flip — 62dh, 72di, 83-84, 97, 99b, 138
Follick — 32, 84, 124b
Fuddick — 111b
Fulliake — 76
Fullock — 39, 41a, 44, 51, 54, 62f, 64ab, 69h, 72j, 74, 79, 85, 95a, 99a, 101b, 107, 111ab, 112, 127f, 130cdf, 131, 140
Knack — 33b
Knockle — 24a, 127h, 130ef, 135
Knockle down — 136
Knockle tight — 136
Knocklie — 135
Knuckle — 1bc, 4, 6, 8, 11-12, 14, 20b, 23, 24b, 28, 34b, 42, 55, 59ce, 71c, 72d, 82, 95b, 96, 99a, 101b, 118a, 124b, 126f, 127c, 130ab, 134
Knuckle doon — 81, 111b
Knucklie — 1a, 10, 18, 19ab, 41c, 71c, 118a
Pantin — 1c
Pawl — 142
Penk — 62a, 71d, 118b, 129b
Penker — 40a
Pick — 127f
Ping — 46, 116
Plonk — 29e, 72i, 92, 126a, 129a
Plonkie — 97
Plunk — 64b
Pot — 62eh, 122b
Pushie knuckle — 41a
Pussie knuckle — 15
Scon — 71a, 99b
Scoot — 69a, 114
Shoot — 30, 36, 41d, 45, 62g, 69d, 72gij, 82-83, 87, 90, 93, 98, 104b, 108ac, 109, 111ab, 116, 122b, 126b, 127ad, 130d, 132
Shootie — 69c
Shootie boorie — 127e
Shuttie — 67, 69abg, 72b, 86, 88a, 120ab, 137, 141
Snick — 52
Stiff fingering — 118b
Stiffie knuckle — 129b
Tak aim — 31
Thump — 120c
Tip — 124a
Tipsie — 45
Nil — 2ab, 3, 5, 7, 9, 16-17, 20a, 25-27, 29acf, 33a, 34a, 35, 37, 40b, 43, 47, 49, 53ab, 57-58, 59abdf, 60-61, 62bc, 63, 65ab, 68, 69ef, 71be, 72acefhl, 73, 80, 88b, 91, 94a, 99c, 100, 101a, 102, 103abc, 105, 108b, 113, 115, 117, 119, 121, 122a, 123, 125, 126de, 127bg, 128, 129c, 133, 139, 143

Cumberland
Bool — 37a
Double duck — 22
Fillick — 19, 48
Fillip — 3, 8, 15abc, 16, 24-25, 28-34, 42, 45, 51, 60
Flap — 17
Flick — 12, 36, 37a, 43, 50
Flip — 4, 18-19, 24, 30, 40, 57, 59
Flurt — 30
Foter — 56
Fullick — 7, 9, 18, 27-28, 30-31, 40-41, 43, 46, 48, 52, 54, 61-62
Futer — 56
Knuckle — 26
Knucklie — 2
Liftie — 33
Rack up — 44
Scop — 14, 17, 20
Shoot — 46-47, 49
Shuttie — 38
Thomie — 23
Thumbie — 54
Nil — 1ab, 5ab, 6, 10-11, 13abcd, 21, 35, 37b, 39, 53, 55, 58, 63ab

Down
Bulk — 2b, 3, 8, 10
Dribble — 2b
Flinch — 23
Funk — 6
Knuckle — 4, 13, 15
Knuckle down — 1
Pug — 7
Scoot — 9
Shoot — 1, 4-5, 18-20, 22, 24, 26, 28-29
Thumb it — 17
Nil — 2a, 11-12, 14, 16, 21, 25, 27, 30

Tyrone
Knuckle — 14
Pink — 9
Roul — 1
Shoot — 8, 13
Nil — 2-7, 10-12, 15-16

Antrim
Baulk — 16b
Bulk — 10, 12, 16a, 34
Dougie — 18
Dribble — 16b
Drootle — 13
Filtch — 21
Flick — 34
Hinch — 21, 27
Knuckle — 7, 8a, 9, 11, 14, 18, 31, 33-34
Punt — 34
Scoot — 1, 11, 16b, 26
Shoot — 7, 15, 17, 19-20, 22, 25-26
Thumb — 34
Nil — 2-4, 4A, 5ab, 6, 8b, 16c, 23-24, 28-30, 32

Donegal
Knuckle — 1, 5A, 6, 10a
Scoot — 8
Shoot — 5, 5A, 7, 11
Pink — 7
Nil — 1A, 2-4, 7A, 9, 10b, 12-13

Fermanagh
Shoot — 2, 4-5
Nil — 1, 3, 6, 7ab, 8-10

Armagh
Shoot — 3-4
Nil — 1-2, 5, 6ab

Londonderry
Knuckle — 3
Knuckle down — 5
Pink — 1A
Prabe — 1
Scoot — 3
Shoot — 2-3, 3A
Nil — 1B, 4, 6-7

34 HOME (in the sense of the 'base' used in playing certain games) (PQ1, 93)

Variants of HOME (a good number of **hame** from Aberdeenshire southwards) have been subsumed except where they begin with '(h)y', like e.g., **yam, (h)yem.**.
Note **bases** in 37 **rounders.**

Shetland
Block — 15, 22, 25
Den — 22, 24, 26
Doors — 2
Dule — 17
Haad — 33
Home — 1, 4, 6, 8, 10, 27, 32-33
Hoose — 15, 33
In (bye) — 14, *30*
Nil — 3, 5, 7, 9, 11-13, 16, 18-20, 21ab, 23, 28-29, 31

Orkney
Blocking stone — 9
Den — 14, 16, 20
Dol — 15
Doule — 15
Dull — 1-2
Hail — 5
Haud — 4
Hel — 13b
Home — 1-3, 7-8, 17, 19
In barrel(s) — 11-12
Mark — 6
Stage — 17
Nil — 10, 13a, 18, 21

Caithness
Base — 16b
Den — 1, 11, 15
Free hoosie — 11
Goal — 15
Home — 2b, 5, 10, 14
Hoosie — 7
Housie — 8
In — 2b
Stand — 12a
Nil — 2a, 3-4, 6, 9, 12bc, 13, 16a, 17

Sutherland
Base — 14, 16
Den — 1, 8, 10, 15-17
Goal — 3
Hail — 3
Home — 1, 3, 5, 7, 9b, 16
House — 9a
Housie — 8, 13
Stance — 5, 8, 11
Nil — 2, 4, 6, 12

Ross & Cromarty
Den — 1-2, 4, 9, 12, 21, 23, 25ab, 26, 28, 31, 32ab, 33-36, 39.
Din — 20
Gameack — 37a
Goal — 18
Hail — 18
Home — 5, 8, 16-17, 24, 31, 32ab
Hoosie — 21
House — 1, 32b, 35
Housie — 22, 36
Stam — 6, 14
Stance — 7-9, 13, 19-20, 27-29, 32a, 38
Station — 12
Nil — 3, 10-11, 15, 30, 32c, 37b

Inverness
Base — 32
Den — 3-4, 9-10, 13ab, 14-18, 20, 21a, 22-24, 27, 29, 34-40
Home — 2-3, 5-6, 8-10, 13c, 19, 21ab, 26, 28, 30, 33
Hut — 1
Parlie — 13e
Stage — 8
Staint — 27
Stance — 10, 14, 23
Nil — 7, 11-12, 13d, 25, 31

Nairn
Den — 1ac, 3-4
Dennie — 1abc, 4
Home — 2
Hoosie — 5

Nairn cont'd

In — 2
Nil — 6

Moray

Den — 1, 3-4, 6ab, 7, 8bde, 9ab, 10-19, 21-23
Dennie — 5, 8c, 11, 20
Home — 2b, 7, 21
Hoosie — 6a, 7
Pot — 8ad
Pottie — 8c
Nil — 2a, 8f

Banff

Basie — 11, 21, 24
Beddie — 14
Dale — 6b, 19
Dell — 6b, 10, 12-13, 15-16, 24, 26-27, 30
Dellie — 15
Den — 1, 2abc, 3-5, 6ab, 7, 9-10, 15, 18b, 21, 25, 28, 30-34
Dennie — 2b, 7-8, 17
Hell — 11
Home — 2a, 6b
Hoose — 18d, 34
Hoosie — 9, 18c, 21, 29
Housie — 20
Parlie — 13, 23
Ringie — 16
Stance — 34
Nil — 18a, 22

Aberdeen

Barlie — 19, 47abcf
Base — 11, 78
Basie — 19-20, 29-30, 32, 35, 41, 47a, 54, 71a, 72, 102
Bed — 77
Beddie — 11
Biel — 25
Blockie — 8
Dale — 8, 29, 41, 96
Dalie — 29, 34, 51, 71c
Dell — 2, 3a, 10, 12-14, 16-17, 19, 21-22, 26-27, 28a, 31, 39, 41-42, 44-46, 47ae, 48, 50, 52-53, 56-60, 62, 64, 66-67, 69-70, 71b, 73-75, 77, 79-80, 83, 86, 89, 94-95, 98, 100-101, 104-106, 108-109
Dell free — 12
Dellie — 19, 47c, 79, 93
Den — 46, 47b, 53, 77, 85, 87, 93, 107
Dennie — 5d
Ha — 25
Hauled — 25
Home — 1-2, 3a, 7, 9, 15, 18, 23, 25, 27, 47ab, 54, 56, 61-62, 65-66, 70, 71c, 73, 79, 81-82, 87, 95, 104
Hoosie — 3b, 4, 5d, 6, 14, 23, 28b, 31, 35, 47d, 49, 55, 73, 75, 84-85, 88, 90, 92, 97, 103, 105, 107
Housie — 24, 36-38, 74
In — 7
In dell — 76
In den — 40
Kale pot — 10
Nil — 5abc, 28c, 33, 43, 63, 68, 91, 99

Kincardine

Block — 19
Dale — 15, 17cd
Dalie — 27
Dell — 1-2, 4, 6-7, 9-14, 16, 17abcd, 18-19, 21-24
Dellie — 20-21, 28
Den — 13, 15, 22
Home — 3, 5, 8, 24, 26
Hoosie — 11
Nil — 25

Kinross

Base — 5
Den — 1-4, 6-7
Home — 1
Housie — 5

Angus

Base — 34-36
Beeze — 8, 10
Beise — 7
Bike — 3
Block — 25
Boxie — 18
Dale — 5ab, 17b, 24, 29b
Dalie — 4, 24, 29b
Dealie — 5c
Dell — 10, 17b
Den — 1, 4, 6, 9-10, 13, 14abcd, 15, 17b, 18-24, 26, 29b, 30-31, 33ab, 34-35, 37
Dennie — 12, 14acd, 18, 24, 32
Dennie block — 34
Dillie — 15, 27, 29ab
Dull — 10
Home — 2, 14d, 17b, 19, 28, 32
Hoose — 17a
Hoosie — 9
Housie — 15
Stachie — 22
Steech — 5b
Steesh — 13
Steeshie — 9
Stishie — 24
Nil — 11, 16

Perth

Base — 8, 33, 57
Beesie — 46, 52a
Block — 23, 33
Boons — 62
Den — 1, 3, 5-13, 15-18, 20-22, 25-28, 29a, 31-32, 34-37, 39-40, 41ab, 42-48, 50, 51ab, 52abcde, 53, 55-56, 59, 61-62, 64, 67-68, 70-71
Home — 2a, 4, 8, 30, 36, 46, 53, 60, 66-67, 72, 74
Hoose — 69
Hoosie — 51b, 52de, 53
Housie — 50
Kirk — 29b
Pin — 29b
Stance — 73
Stent — 14
Taw — 41a
Nil — 2b, 19, 24, 38, 49, 54, 58, 63, 65

Fife

Dale — 12
Dell — 53
Den — 1-8, 9ab, 10-14, 16-23, 25-30, 33-35, 36ab, 37-39, 40ab, 41abcd, 42, 43ab, 44abcdef, 45-54, 55abcdefg, 56-63, 64a
Doll — 45
Dull — 33, 51
Dult — 23, 36b, 37, 41d, 47, 52
Home — 32
Mug — 53
Nil — 15, 24, 31, 64b

Clackmannan

Den — 1-3, 4abcd, 5-7

Stirling

Base — 25d
Bulk — 7d
Bunk — 24
Crown — 4
Den — 2-6, 7abcdef, 8-12, 14-20, 21ab, 22ab, 23b, 25abcd, 26abcdef, 27ab, 28-34, 35ab, 37ab, 38, 39ab, 40, 42ab
Dollie — 8
Dool — 7bd
Dule — 7bd
Dull — 6, 26a, 27a, 31
Dullie — 22a
Dult — 3, 23ac, 27a, 42a
Home — 2, 25ad, 27a, 36, 37b
Nil — 1, 13, 41

Dunbarton

Base — 8
Den — 1-3, 4b, 5-6, 7abc, 9-12, 13abc, 14a, 15, 16ab, 17-18
Dene — 5
Dull — 2, 14ab
Dulse — 9
Dult — 8-9, 11
Home — 8, 14a
Toddie's ground — 14a
Nil — 4a

Argyll

Base — 11, 34
Box — 19
Castle — 6
Dale — 30
Den — 1-3, 5, 7-10, 15-16, 19-25, 28-29, 32, 35-40
Garrison — 6
Goal — 17
Home — 6, 18-20, 22
Hoose — 35
Nil — 4, 12-14, 26-27, 31, 33

Bute

Den — 1acd, 2-7, 8ab, 9
Dult — 1bcde
Home — 7

Ayr

Boonie — 37
Cosh — 24a
Dale — 49, 57
Dell — 7, 10, 16ab, 18ab, 26b, 47-48
Den — 1a, 2a, 5-6, 8ab, 11, 12ab, 15, 16b, 17, 18b, 20g, 22, 26abc, 27, 28abcdef, 29, 30b, 31-32, 35b, 36-37, 42, 44-48, 52, 53ab, 54, 57
Dill — 2a, 7, 34, 41, 50-51, 56
Dilt — 31
Dirlie — 19
Dull — 2b, 3-5, 7, 8ab, 9-10, 13, 15, 16ab, 17, 20acefgh, 21, 23, 24ab, 25, 26ab, 28bc, 29, 30a, 32-34, 35ab, 38, 41-42, 44, 48, 52
Dult — 8b, 11, 12a, 18b, 20h, 29, 39, 48
Dunnel — 20g, 32
Durl — 12ab, 14, 20bd, 24b, 29, 37
Goal — 38
Home — 16a, 28e, 41, 43
In — 43
Pitch — 18b
Stump — 16b
Winning post — 38
Nil — 1b, 40, 55

Renfrew

Base — 15, 20a
Dale — 8, 11acdfgik. 12b, 16a, 18b, 21
Dell — 12b, 18b
Den — 1ab, 2abcdfghj, 4abcd, 5, 8-9, 11abcdefghjl, 12a, 13acd, 14ab, 15, 16abcd, 17, 18ab, 19, 20ab, 21
Dill — 21
Dool — 21
Dull — 4de, 13b, 14b, 15, 17
Dult — 14b, 18a
Goal — 16a
Home — 1a, 2bei, 8, 20a
Hoose — 2i
Hut — 2j, 4acd, 8
Mug — 17
Pot — 4d
Nil — 3, 6-7, 10

Lanark

Base — 1
Bed — 15b
Creash — 15b
Dall — 34, 45, 48
Dell — 15c, 53, 57b
Den — 2-6, 7bc, 8ab, 9ab, 10b, 11-13, 14acd, 15ab, 16ab, 17-23, 25abcd, 26ab, 27ab, 28, 29abdfg, 30, 31acd, 32acde, 33abcd, 34, 35abc, 36-37, 38abce, 39-40, 42 44-45, 46abc, 47, 49ab, 50, 52ab, 54-56, 57abc, 58, 59ab, 60-61, 63, 64b, 65, 67b
Dill — 15c, 35d, 62
Dule — 9b
Dull — 2, 7c, 10ab, 11-12, 14ac, 15abc, 18, 25c, 29ce, 34, 35d, 38ac, 41, 43, 57ab, 58, 61
Dult — 7abc, 10b, 22, 26b, 31b, 39, 52b
Home — 1, 6, 14d, 27b, 28, 31d, 32bdf, 35b, 51, 57a, 58, 64b
Home den — 7a
Home dult — 7a
In — 8a
Trigger — 15b
Nil — 14b, 24, 38d, 64a, 66, 67a

West Lothian

Base — 11, 15
Den — 1cd, 2, 4-8, 9ab, 12-13, 16, 17ab, 19ab, 20ab, 21ab
Dilt — 1a
Dull — 1d, 2-4, 6, 14-15, 18, 22
Dult — 4, 6, 8, 11-12, 15, 17a
Goals — 18
Home — 1b, 10
House — 4

Midlothian

Base — 23b
Bed — 14a
Dall — 12a
Den — 1-5, 6ab, 7ab, 8ab, 10-11, 12ab, 13, 14b, 15-19, 21-22, 23ab, 24, 25abc, 26a, 27-32
Dull — 14a, 15, 22, 24
Dullie — 4
Dult — 10
Home — 17, 23b
Hoose — 31
Ludo — 20
Nil — 9, 25d, 26b

East Lothian

Base — 4a
Den — 1-3, 4ab, 5, 6ab, 7-15, 17-21
Home — 4b
Nil — 16

Berwick

Base — 5, 10
Bay — 3, 15, 16b, 18-21, 27, 31-32
Beesie — 7
Den — 1-2, 4, 8-9, 11-15, 16abc, 17-20, 22-24, 27-31
Home — 9-10, 23, 26-27
Hoosie — 8
Presin base — 6
Ring — 10
Tars — 7
Nil — 25

Peebles

Den — 1-3, 4abc, 5, 7-9
Home — 6ab
In — 10
Pottie — 4b

Selkirk

Den — 2abce, 3, 5, 7-8

Selkirk cont'd

Home — 1, 2d, 4
Nil — 6

Roxburgh

Den — 1-2, 3ab, 4-8, 9ab, 10, 13-14, 15a, 16-20, 21abcde, 23, 25-26
Hail — 20
Home — 13, 28
Hoose — 5
Huim — 12
Hyim — 15b
Kittie — 24
Nil — 11, 21f, 22, 27

Dumfries

Corner — 43
Dale — 11
Den — 1ab, 2-7, 8ab, 9-10, 12-15, 19, 21ab, 24, 26-29, 31abcdef, 32, 34-44, 45b, 46
Home — 1a, 12, 16, 17a, 20, 22, 31def, 33, 43-44, 45a, 46-47, 49
Hoose — 2
In — 1a, 17a
Stawkie — 30
Stinkin hole — 26
Tee — 7, 37
Nil — 17b, 18, 23, 25, 48

Kirkcudbright

Base — 3
Dale — 7-8, 11, 12a, 14, 17
Dell — 14
Den — 1, 3-5, 8-9, 11, 12ab, 14, 15ab, 17-19, 21a, 22-27
Dill — 1
Dult — 10
Goal — 7
Hale — 17
Home — 2, 6-7, 16, 21b
Pin — 21c
Post — 3
Prisoners' base — 21c
Strannie — 7
Nil — 13, 20

Wigtown

Dale — 5b, 17
Den — 1, 3-4, 5a, 6-18
Home — 2

Northumberland

Bandie — 69a
Barlie — 62c
Base — 2b, 15, 19a, 28, 31, 46, 69c, 111b, 130c
Bay — 1abc, 6-7, 10, 14, 16-17, 19a, 20b, 24ab, 25-28, 29bcde, 30, 32, 33b, 34a, 36-39, 40ab, 41acd, 42-43, 47-51, 53ab, 54-55, 57-58, 59bce, 60, 62aeh, 63, 66, 68, 69cdegh, 70, 71cd, 72cdegik, 73, 77-80, 82, 85-86, 89, 91-92, 95a, 96-98, 99bc, 101b, 102, 104ab, 105-107, 108ac, 110, 111ab, 112-115, 118ab, 120ac, 121, 122ab, 124ab, 125, 126abcef, 127bcdh, 129abc, 130acdef, 131, 133-137
Block — 34a, 40b, 41a, 46-47, 59cd, 62b, 71bd, 72a, 76, 90, 92, 96, 99d, 101b, 122b, 124b, 126b, 127cg, 132
Blockie — 96
Boorie — 62h, 69d, 71b, 77, 109
Butt — 56
Bye — 51, 134
Daddie — 69h, 72a
Den — 1b, 3, 9, 21, 68, 94b, 125, 127b, 132
Duckstone — 69b
Game — 123, 127ae
Goal — 138
Home — 6, 8, 12-13, 18, 20b, 22-23, 29a, 41c, 46, 52, 56, 59b, 62bg, 64b, 72cdg, 81, 83-84, 103c, 111b, 117, 119, 120b, 130cd, 135, 142-143
Home bay — 72l
House — 1c, 34b
Hyem — 45, 67, 69a, 71a, 72bi
Paa — 41b
Pot — 38, 96, 126d
Pottie — 96
Round the stone — 11
Stanch — 110
Station — 104b
Stinkie — 11
Tip the block — 69ab
Yame — 100
Yem — 45, 64a, 72j, 93, 118a, 130b
Yum — 129b
Nil — 2a, 4-5, 19b, 20a, 29f, 33a, 35, 44, 59af, 61, 62df, 65ab, 69f, 71e, 72fh, 74-75, 87, 88ab, 94a, 95b, 99a, 101a, 103ab, 108b, 116, 127f, 128, 139-141

Cumberland

Bay — 3, 15b, 21, 37b, 63b
Block — 13c
Den — 1a, 2-4, 5a, 6-7, 9, 11, 13ad, 14, 15c, 16, 18-20, 22, 24-27, 29, 33-34, 37ab, 39, 42-48, 50-57, 60-62, 63b
Dennie — 42, 53
Home — 4, 9, 13c, 28, 31, 38, 44, 58-59, 62
Home be home — 15b
Jack stand — 30
Kittie — 9
Stannie — 30
Tennie — 35, 41
Yam — 12, 15b, 17, 24, 33, 37a, 40, 56, 63a
Yem — 7-8
Nil — 1b, 5b, 10, 13b, 15a, 23, 32, 36, 49

Down

Den — 2ab, 3-4, 7-8, 11, 13-14, 16-18, 23-24, 26-29
Dool — 24, 29
Home — 5, 9, 13, 15, 19-20
Stump — 30
Nil — 1, 6, 10, 12, 21-22, 25

Tyrone

Back — 8
Butt — 11
Den — 1-3, 5-7, 10, 12-13
Granny — 6
Home — 1, 8, 12
In — 8
Nil — 4, 9, 14-16

Antrim

Butt — 1, 16b
Den — 3, 5b, 7, 9, 14-15, 16ab, 17, 20, 22, 24-25, 30-31, 33-34
Home — 10, 12-13, 21, 26, 28, 31
House — 34
Landed — 21
Parley — 19
Target — 34
Nil — 2, 4, 4A, 5a, 6, 8ab, 11, 16c, 18, 23, 27, 29, 32

Donegal

Den — 5-9, 10ab
Granny — 6, 12
Home — 5A, 12
Nil — 1, 1A, 2-4, 7A, 11, 13

Fermanagh

Den — 2, 4, 9-10
Home — 7a
Nil — 1, 3, 5-6, 7b, 8

Armagh

Den — 1, 4-5, 6b
Home — 3, 6a
Nil — 2

Londonderry

Den — 1, 3-4, 6-7
Home — 1A, 2
Nil — 1B, 3A, 5

35 HOP SCOTCH (PQ1, 94)

Shetland

Hoppie — 24
Hop scotch — 15, 22, 25, 32
Tusie busie — 19
Nil — 1-14, 16-18, 20, 21ab, 23, 26-31, 33

Orkney

Boxes — 7, 15
Hipple scotch — 2, 13a
Hop scotch — 1, 15, 17, 19
Peevers — 14
Nil — 3-6, 8-12, 13b, 16, 18, 20-21

Caithness

Hap beds — 5
Hoppie scotch — 9, 12a
Hoppie scottie — 11
Hoppie stonie — 8, 12a
Hop scotch — 2ab, 16b
Nil — 1, 3-4, 6-7, 10, 12bc, 13-15, 16a, 17

Sutherland

Hop scotch — 1, 7, 9a, 11, 13, 16
Sceetchie — 10
Scotchie — 9b
Nil — 2-6, 8, 12, 14-15, 17

Ross & Cromarty

Beddie(s) — 35
Beddock(s) — 37ab
Hoppie — 35
Hoppitie — 24
Hop scotch — 5, 8-9, 16-18, 26-27, 30, 39
Kettle — 11
Kettlie — 19, 21-22, 28-29, 32a, 36
Kettlock — 18, 20
Kittlack — 22
Lakie — 13
Peetlie pot — 15
Peever(s) — 6, 19, 32b
Port — 14
Pot — 11-12
Skeetchie — 14, 19, 34
Sketchie — 31
Skitchie — 20, 23
Sklitchie — 25ab
Nil — 1-4, 7, 10, 32c, 33, 38

Inverness

Beddies — 13ab
Beds — 20
Boxes — 29
Boxies — 35
Hop scotch — 2, 4-6, 21ab, 33, 36, 39
Kettle — 13e, 26
Peever(s) — 8, 16, 20, 26, 28, 34, 37-38, 40
Skeetcher — 13a
Skeetchie — 9-10, 13bcd, 14, 17, 19-20, 21a, 24
Sketcher(s) — 13a, 23
Sketchie — 8, 32
Nil — 1, 3, 7, 11-12, 15, 18, 22, 25, 27, 30-31

Nairn

Beddies — 1abc
Hoosie — 4
Hop scotch — 2
Pitcher — 1a, 3
Sketchie — 2, 5
Nil — 6

Moray

Beddies — 2ab, 3-5, 6b, 7, 8bcdf, 9ab, 11, 13-16, 20-22
Beds — 8b, 17
Hippin beds — 6a, 19
Hipplin beds — 1, 9b
Hoppies — 3
Hoppin beds — 10, 18, 21
Peever(s) — 8a, 23
Pitchers — 18
Pitchies — 8abe, 9a
Skeetchies — 11-12

Banff

Beddies — 6b, 11, 13, 15-17, 18b, 23, 25, 28, 32
Beds — 18d, 34
Bladies — 3
Blockies — 15
Happin beds — 29
Hap the beds — 14
Hippin badies — 22
Hippin beddies — 10
Hippin bed(s) — 8-9, 15, 26
Hipplicks — 1, 2b, 3, 6a, 23
Hipplin blades — 2a
Hoplicks — 4-5, 6b, 10
Hoppin(g) beddies — 6b, 7, 12, 21, 24, 27
Hoppin beds — 11, 18c
Hopplin beddies — 6b
Houps — 20
Hupplicks — 2ac
Hupplin bladies — 2c
Scuscle the bladie — 6b
Sketchie — 21
Skippin beds — 11
Nil — 18a, 19, 30-31, 33

Aberdeen

Basies — 4, 5abd, 6
Beadies — 90, 94, 107
Beddies — 3a, 9-10, 12, 14, 16-25, 29, 34-35, 40-46, 47abdef, 49, 51-58, 60-69, 71bc, 72-85, 87-90, 93, 95-101, 103, 105, 108
Beds — 71c
Bedsies — 3b
Bides — 7
Hippin beddies — 10, 12, 15, 24, 28b, 51, 53
Hippins — 53
Hopie — 104
Hoppin basies — 29
Hoppin beddies — 8, 11, 26-27, 30, 49, 63
Hoppin beds — 9, 28a
Hopplicks — 53
Hotch potch — 59
Slaitie beds — 48
Nil — 1-2, 5c, 13, 28c, 31-33, 36-39, 47c, 50, 70, 71a, 86, 91-92, 102, 106, 109

Kincardine

Baidies — 25
Beddies — 1-2, 4-5, 7, 9-16, 17abcd, 19, 21-24, 27
Blockies — 28
Hoppie — 26
Hop scotch — 8
Mixter maxter — 3
Slatie — 18
Nil — 6, 20

Kinross

Beds — 6
Paldies — 3
Pallies — 3
Peever(s) — 1-6
Poldie beds — 1
Nil — 7

Angus

Baidies — 18
Beddies — 14a, 37
Blockie — 17b, 24
Boxies — 23, 33a
Half loaf — 22
Hap stap — 17a
Hap stap and loup — 25
Hoppie crispie — 6
Hoppin — 18
Hop scotch — 12, 17b, 18, 29b
Hop step and jump/loup — 33b
Loup back — 5b
Palallies — 5c, 7-8, 10, 12-13, 19-20, 30, 34-37
Palawlies — 23
Palies — 14c, 17b, 29a
Pallies — 10-11, 14acd, 15, 17b, 19, 21-22, 24, 26-27, 29ab, 34
Pawlie — 14b, 23, 28
Pee allies — 4
Peever(s) — 3, 30, 34
Pilallies — 5a
Nil — 1-2, 9, 16, 31-32

Perth

Baadies — 28
Baidies — 32
Beddies — 11, 26, 44, 47-48, 52ab, 62
Beds — 39, 68
Blockie — 12, 33
Boxies — 1, 25
Cockie duntie — 64
Faldies — 21
Hoppie — 56
Hop scotch — 4-5, 7-8, 25, 36
Pakies — 2a
Palallie(s) — 23, 33, 45, 60
Peever(s) — 11, 17-18, 20, 25-28, 29ab, 31-32, 34-35, 37-39, 41a, 43, 45-46, 48, 50, 51ab, 52abde, 53, 55-57, 62, 66-69, 71-73
Peevies — 15, 27, 52a
Poachie — 41ab, 61
Potchie — 40
Skeetchie(s) — 50, 54, 59
Skivvies — 13
Tookies — 62
Nil — 2b, 3, 6, 9-10, 14, 16, 19, 22, 24, 30, 42, 49, 52c, 58, 63, 65, 70, 74

Fife

Ba beds — 40a
Baw beds — 37
Bebs — 53, 55abd, 57, 63
Beddies — 2, 17, 33-34
Beds — 9a, 34, 63
Happin beds — 51
Hoppie — 7, 11
Hoppin bebs — 55dfg
Hoppin beds — 36a
Hop scotch — 58
Padlies — 50
Palalls — 2, 10, 21, 27, 33, 35
Paldie beds — 52, 55be
Paldies — 1-2, 7, 11-12, 14, 16, 20, 23, 30, 42, 44a
Paralies — 6
Pauldie beds — 38, 40a, 41ab, 43a, 44b, 60
Pauldies — 5-6, 8, 12-13, 19, 21-22, 25-28, 36b, 37, 39, 40b, 41acd, 43ab, 44cdef, 45-50, 55c
Peeverie beds — 61
Peever(s) — 1, 9a, 17-18, 23, 27-28, 33, 35, 36a, 40b, 43a, 44acf, 47-48, 51-54, 55bfg, 62-63
Prauldies — 4
Sketches — 12, 23, 48, 64a
Skippie — 3
Skitches — 47, 64a
Tig — 33
Nil — 9b, 15, 24, 29, 31-32, 56, 59, 64b

Clackmannan

Beds — 4c
Paldie — 4d
Peevers — 1-3, 4abcd, 5-7

Stirling

Beds — 7a, 8-9, 18, 22a, 23bc, 25c, 26abcdf, 39ab
Cockie rooster — 17
Dunchie — 21b
Happin Chairlie — 23a
Hap the beds — 2
Haupie — 20
Hop scotch — 28
Pal — 21b, 23b, 33
Peebs — 22b, 25c
Peever(s) — 2, 4-6, 7abcdef, 8-9, 11-12, 15-16, 18-19, 21b, 22ab, 23b, 25abcd, 26abdf, 27ab, 29-34, 35ab, 36, 37ab, 39ab, 40, 42a
Tak what's gaun — 10
Tig — 21a
Nil — 1, 3, 13-14, 24, 26e, 38, 41, 42b

Dunbarton

Beds — 10-11, 14a, 16ab
Hop scotch — 13a
Hop step and jump — 16a
Jump the humplicks — 2
Peever(s) — 1, 3, 5-6, 7abc, 8-12, 14ab, 15, 16ab, 17
Nil — 4ab, 13bc, 18

Argyll

Beds — 30, 35-36
Hop scotch — 5, 17, 22, 33
Peever(s) — 1-2, 5, 7, 9, 14-16, 19, 21, 23-25, 30-32, 35-38
Nil — 3-4, 6, 8, 10-13, 18, 20, 26-29, 34, 39-40

Bute

Hop scotch — 1a
Hunchie dunchie — 1e
Peever(s) — 1abcd, 2-3, 6-7, 8ab, 9
Nil — 4-5

Ayr

Baw beds — 24a
Beds — 1a, 3, 5-7, 8ab, 9-11, 12b, 14, 16b, 18b, 20abcdeg, 21, 27, 28ad, 29, 31, 36-37, 41-42, 44-45, 50, 52, 55
Cocker ootchie — 28f
Hap step and loup — 46
Hap the beds — 57
Hippin jump — 17
Hop scotch — 28e
Hop the beds — 57
Kite — 16a
Peever beds — 18b
Peevers — 1ab, 2ab, 3, 5-7, 8ab, 9-11, 12ab, 14, 16ab, 17, 18ab, 19, 20abcdegh, 22-23, 24ab, 25, 26ac, 27, 28abcd, 30b, 31-34, 35ab, 36-39, 41-45, 47-50, 52, 53ab, 54, 56-57

Renfrew

Beds — 2bceh, 4bde, 7, 11cg, 13c, 15, 17
Heppitie hornie — 14b
Hip step and jump — 2i, 16b
Hop — 2i
Hop scotch — 2a, 8
Leap frog — 12b
Palal — 15
Peever(s) — 1b, 2bcefghj, 3, 4acde, 6-7, 9-10, 11abcdefgh-ijkl 13abcd, 15, 16ad, 17, 18ab, 19, 20b, 21
Silly cuddie — 12a
Skip — 2i
Skipping — 4e
Nil — 1a, 2d, 5, 14a, 16c, 20a

Lanark

Beds — 7abc, 13, 15b, 16b, 22, 25d, 29c, 30, 31b, 35a, 38e, 43, 49a, 52b, 67b
Cuddie loup the dyke — 59b
Dunshie — 31d
Hap step and loup — 9b
Hap the beds — 33d, 38d
Hop and carry — 27a
Hop scotch — 1, 3, 14b, 23, 38c
Hop step jump — 32c
Hotchie potchie — 36
Lang Jack — 32e
Lang Tam — 32e
Leap frog — 45
Palalls — 50
Peever(s) — 4-6, 7abc, 8ab, 9a, 10ab, 11-13, 14ac, 15ab, 16ab, 17-22, 24, 25abcd, 28, 29abcdefg, 30, 31abc, 32abdf, 33abcd, 34, 35abcd, 36-37, 38abde, 39, 41-44, 46abc, 47-48, 49ab, 50, 52ab, 53-56, 57abc, 59a, 60-63, 64ab, 65, 67a
Peeveral — 29e
Peever beds — 58
Pickie — 13
Nil — 2, 14d, 15c, 26ab, 27b, 40, 51, 66

West Lothian

Ball beds — 8
Baw beds — 9a
Beds — 1a, 8, 11-13, 17ab, 21ab
Hop cock a rooster — 20a
Hop scotch — 16
Labbers — 2
Peever(s) — 1a, 2, 5-6, 9ab, 11-13, 15, 17ab, 20b, 21ab, 22
To hap — 19b
Nil — 1bcd, 3-4, 7, 10, 14, 18, 19a

Midlothian

Beds — 10-11, 22, 32
Hap step and loup — 14b
Hop scotch — 10, 15, 20
Jig — 25d
Kick the can — 30
Kippies — 15-16
Keap frog — 4
Palall — 23a
Peeverie beds — 2, 5, 6b
Peever(s) — 1-3, 5, 6ab, 7ab, 8b, 9-11, 12ab, 13, 14ab, 16-19, 22, 23b, 24, 25a, 26a, 27, 29-30, 32
Pickie beds — 17, 21, 23a, 24, 26a, 27
Pickies — 8a, 18, 24, 25abc, 26b, 28-29
Pigies — 19
Nil — 31

East Lothian

Beds — 1, 4b, 5, 6ab, 7, 9
Cuddie loup the dyke — 16
Hop beddies — 17
Palallie — 13
Palalls — 2, 4b, 5, 6a, 7-8, 11, 14-15
Peever(s) — 1-3, 4ab, 5, 6a, 7-15, 18-20
Piawls — 20
Pickies — 6b, 8-9
Pippielaws — 2
Plaws — 13
Prawls — 1, 9
Nil — 21

Berwick

Bebs — 14
Beddies — 8, 20
Beds — 1-2, 4-7, 9, 11, 13, 15, 16b, 17-18, 21-22, 24, 26-27, 29-32
Bedsie — 23
Happin — 10
Hap stap and jump — 10
Peevers — 1, 7-8, 11-12, 17-18, 23, 27-28
Pitchie — 16a, 19
Nil — 3, 16c, 25

Peebles

Beds — 9
Hap step and loup — 6b
Hippie beds — 3
Hop scotch — 1, 6a
Jumping — 5
Peever(s) — 2-3, 4abc, 7-8
Peevies — 9-10
Pickie beds — 3
Pitcher beds — 4bc

Selkirk

Babittie beds — 2d
Beds — 2abcde, 3-4, 6-7
Hop scotch — 8
Peevers — 2b, 7
Squares — 1
Nil — 5

Roxburgh

Ba' beds — 23
Beddie — 4
Bedgels — 8
Beds — 1-2, 3ab, 5, 7-8, 9a, 10-11, 13-14, 15ab, 16-20, 21acd, 24-26
Bedzel — 7
Hip beds — 9a
Hippie beds — 21e
Peevers — 19, 23
Stovies — 15a
Nil — 6, 9b, 12, 21bf, 22, 27-28

Dumfries

Beds — 1b, 2, 5-7, 8a, 9-12, 14-16, 19-20, 21ab, 23, 26-30, 31acdef, 32-34, 37-38, 40-42, 46
Boxes and beds — 39
Corsie — 35
Haftie — 12
Hitchie den — 48
Hop carry caroostie — 22
Hoppie beds — 16, 17b, 29
Hop the beds — 8b
Peever beds — 46
Peeverie beds — 29
Peever(s) — 1ab, 4, 7, 9, 13, 17a, 19, 21ab, 23, 25, 29, 31bcd, 32, 38, 41-42, 45b, 48
Peevie — 41, 45a
Nil — 3, 18, 24, 36, 43-44, 47, 49

Kirkcudbright

Beddies — 14, 16
Beds — 2-3, 6, 8-9, 11, 12a, 13, 15ab, 16, 21c, 22, 24-25
Hap the beds — 1, 17
Hop beds — 19
Hop scotch — 7
Hop the beds — 5-7, 12a, 18, 20, 27

Kirkcudbright cont'd
Loup the beds — 27
P beds — 7
Peever(s) — 1, 4, 7, 12b, 15a, 24
Skip the beds — 23
Nil — 10, 21ab, 26

Wigtown
Beds — 5a
Hap tae — 1
Hap the bed(s) — 5a, 10-17
Hops — 9
Hop the beds — 6, 8-9
Peever(s) — 2, 4, 5ab, 7, 12, 17-18
Pitchers — 7-8, 10
Nil — 3

Northumberland
Bays — 1a, 2a, 8, 10, 12, 15-16, 18, 23, 24a, 29cde, 33a, 46, 49, 52, 62bg, 64a, 65b, 66, 69ah, 72ai, 76, 80, 82-84, 90-92, 94b, 99bd, 106, 118b, 121, 123, 124b, 126e, 127h, 129ac, 130ab, 139
Bed(s) — 10, 28
Bedsies — 1b, 10
Chucks — 40b
Dabbers — 29d, 127b
High e dabber — 100
Hippie — 33b, 121
Hippie bays — 37, 39, 46, 53b, 68
Hippie beds — 2b, 3, 11, 25, 36
Hippie pennets — 56
Hippie ring — 28
Hippin — 34b, 75, 78
Hitch — 9
Hitchie — 27, 45, 62d, 63, 126b, 127f
Hitchie bays — 17, 45, 71d, 72c, 74, 107, 124b, 127bf
Hitchie bed — 133
Hitchie dabber(s) — 7, 25, 29b, 33a, 34a, 38-39, 40b, 41ab, 47, 49-50, 56, 58, 59bcdf, 60, 62abcefgh, 64ab, 65b, 66, 69abdgh, 71abd, 72cdegijkl, 76, 82, 84, 86, 88ab, 89-93, 95a, 96-98, 99b, 101b, 103c, 104a, 105, 109, 111ab, 112, 114-117, 118b, 119, 120ac, 122ab, 124ab, 126acef, 127cdegh, 129bc, 130def, 131, 134-135, 137-138, 142-143
Hitchie dobber — 51-52, 57, 70, 71c, 72di, 77-79, 81, 95b, 99ac, 101b, 102, 104ab, 108a, 122b, 125, 126d, 127a, 129a, 130c
Hitchie hoppie — 40a
Hitchie pellet — 136, 138
Hitchie pot — 44
Hitchin — 78
Hitch tin — 22
Hop and step — 69c
Hoppie — 83
Hoppie beds— 132
Hop scotch — 2b, 14, 30-31, 40a, 42, 48, 53a, 55, 71a, 72c, 109-110
Kicking the square — 13
Lowpie lang lonnen — 72b
Pitcher — 1b, 19a, 20b
Polka — 41c
Scotchie — 126d
Skippie bays — 57
Squares — 132
Nil — 1c, 4-6, 19b, 20a, 21, 24b, 26, 29af, 32, 35, 41d, 43, 54, 59ae, 61, 65a, 67, 69ef, 71e, 72fh, 73, 85, 87, 94a, 101a, 103ab, 108bc, 113, 118a, 120b, 128, 140-141

Cumberland
Hitchie — 9, 13a
Hitchie bed — 1a, 7-8, 14, 17, 33, 37a
Hitchie post — 22
Hitchie pot — 1a, 2-3, 5ab, 11, 13cd, 14, 19, 21, 36, 37b, 38-40
Hoppie — 53
Hoppie bed(s) — 4, 15bc, 16-18, 24-26, 29, 31, 34, 40-45, 50-57, 61-62
Hoppie dens — 4
Hop scotch — 1a, 9, 13c, 46-48, 50, 57-58, 60
Itchie bed — 28
Lowpies — 15b
Nil — 1b, 6, 10, 12, 13b, 15a, 20, 23, 27, 30, 32, 35, 49, 59, 63ab

Down
Haabeds — 27
Hop scotch — 1, 2a, 5, 7, 9, 18-20, 26, 28
Scotch hop — 13, 23-24, 30
Scotch up — 22
Nil — 2b, 3-4, 6, 8, 10-12, 14-17, 21, 25, 29

Tyrone
Hop scotch — 1, 6, 11
Scotch — 7
Nil — 2-5, 8-10, 12-16

Antrim
Foot and a half — 16b
Hop says — 14
Hop scotch — 3, 19, 25-26, 28-29, 31
Hopsies — 17
Kippie — 34
Pique — 34
Scotchup — 12
Step and hop — 34
Nil — 1, 1A, 2, 4, 5ab, 6-7, 8ab, 9-11, 13, 15, 16ac, 18, 20-24, 27, 30, 32-33

Donegal
Diamonds — 12
Hop scotch — 5A, 6, 10b
Nil — 1, 1A, 2-5, 7, 7A, 8-9, 10a, 11, 13

Fermanagh
Hop scotch — 4, 7a
Nil — 1-3, 5-6, 7b, 8-10

Armagh
Hop scotch — 4
Scotch hop — 1-2, 5
Nil — 3, 6ab

Londonderry
Hop scotch — 2-3, 3A, 4
Nil — 1, 1AB, 5-7

36 LEAP FROG (PQ1, 95)

Leap frog has not been mapped as it occurs fairly densely everywhere except in Wigtownshire and Selkirkshire. Some of the other items mapped are not strongly concentrated.
Variants of the item FOOT AND A HALF have been subsumed.
Puddock appears also in 85 **tadpole.**

Shetland
Cuddie leap the daek — 24
Dirl back — 19
Hedder kin dunk — 31
Leap frog — 1, 3-4, 7, 10, 15-17, 21a, 32-33
Nil — 2, 5-6, 8-9, 11-14, 18, 20, 21b, 22-23, 25-30

Orkney
Huppidie cra — 15
Leap frog — 1-5, 7-9, 11, 13b, 15-17, 19-20
Nil — 6, 10, 12, 13a, 14, 18, 21

Caithness
Hulchie — 12b
Jump a backie — 12a
Leap frog — 2ab, 8-11, 13-14, 16b, 17
Loup e' backie — 14
Nil — 1, 3-7, 12c, 15, 16a

Sutherland
Leap frog — 1, 3-8, 9ab, 10-13, 16
Puddock leap — 9b
Nil — 2, 14-15, 17

Ross & Cromarty
Cockie headie — 37b
Hop step and leap — 31
Humpie backie — 34
Leap frog — 1, 3-6, 8-9, 13-14, 16-18, 20, 23-24, 25ab, 26-31, 32ab, 36,.39
Paddockie — 29
Paddock jump — 22
Twopenny halfpenny — 31
Nil — 2, 7, 10-12, 15, 19, 21, 32c, 33, 35, 37a, 38

Inverness
Frog leap — 30
Leap frog — 1-8, 10-11, 13abce, 17-18, 20, 21ab, 22-23, 26-29, 32-40
Lime a crachin — 24
Nil — 9, 12, 13d, 14-16, 19, 25, 31

Nairn
Fitna — 1c, 3
Froggie — 1b
Frog leap — 2
Leap frog — 4-5
Twopenny nip — 1a
Nil — 6

Moray
Backies — 8c, 13
Bull the cuddie — 11
Foot and a half — 1, 8e
Hump backie — 2a
Leap frog — 3, 8bde, 14, 19-20, 22
Loup the cattie — 9a
Loup the cuddie — 4, 6a
Paddocks' loup — 5
Puddock('s) loup — 8b, 18
Skin the donkey — 16
Turn the cat — 21
Nil — 2b, 6b, 7, 8af, 9b, 10, 12, 15, 17, 23

Banff
Backie(s) — 9, 11, 14
Bousters — 13
Hinch currie hinch — 34
Jumping backie — 29
Jump the *or* jumpie backie — 2abc, 3-5, 6b, 10
Jump the puddock — 16
Leap frog — 1, 2a, 8, 15, 17, 19, 24-25
Leapie — 18c
Louping the frog — 30
Loup the cuddie — 7, 32
Loup the froggie — 21-22
Loup the puddock — 24
Pallying — 13
Puddock loup — 28
Nil — 6a, 12, 18abd, 20, 23, 26-27, 31, 33

Aberdeen
Backie(s) — 5b, 28a, 44, 47abcdef, 63, 102, 105
Balla cuddie — 5d
Jump/leap the puddock — 101, 104
Leap (the) frog — 3a, 6, 8-9, 16, 22, 28c, 36, 53, 59, 67, 70, 73-74, 82, 94-95, 97, 100, 104, 107
Loup frog — 65
Loup/jump the cuddie — 3a, 10,

Aberdeen cont'd

12, 17, 19, 28ab, 42, 45, 47a, 64, 76-77, 88, 106
Loup puddock – 34
Loup the frog(gie) – 29, 50-51, 66, 81
Loup the paddock – 55, 77
Loup the poddock – 8, 32
Loup the pudd – 49
Loup (the) puddock – 11, 23, 27, 28a, 34, 46, 47a, 52-53, 56, 62, 69, 74-75, 94, 103, 108
Loup the salmon – 49
Puddock jump – 48
Puddock loup – 45, 57, 71c, 73, 80, 97
Skin the cuddie – 5b, 10, 12, 14, 24-25, 37, 71c, 74, 83, 87, 98-99
Strining/string the inguns – 3b, 5a, 21, 61, 105
Tummle the cat – 31
Nil – 1-2, 4, 5c, 7, 13, 15, 18, 20, 26, 30, 33, 35, 38-41, 43, 54, 58, 60, 68, 71ab, 72, 78-79, 84-86, 89-93, 96, 109

Kincardine

Bobit the bowster – 20, 28
Coup the cuddie – 3
Coup the ladle – 24
Frog leap – 7
Lang inguns – 12
Leap frog – 1, 6, 8, 10-12, 16, 17c, 19, 28
Loup the back – 17c
Loup the cuddie – 7, 15
Loup the puddock – 2, 13, 15
Puddock(ie) loup – 5, 10, 12, 17b, 26
Salmon loup – 11
Skin the cuddie – 4
Stringing enions – 9
Stringin ingins – 4, 14
Nil – 17ad, 18, 21-23, 25, 27

Kinross

Cuddie loup – 5
Hunch cuddie hunch – 5
Leap frog – 1, 3, 6
Puddock loup – 2, 4, 7

Angus

Backies – 17b
Cat ma – 18
Cuddie loup the dyke – 19-20, 37
Hackie duck – 37
Hippie dip – 8
Hockie dock – 29b
Hokie duck – 2
Huck a duck – 33a
Huckie duck – 7, 14abcd, 21-22, 30, 33b, 34-35
Humph the cuddie – 32
Jumpin backie – 17a
Leap frog – 9-10, 13, 17b, 18, 24, 29b, 32, 33b, 34, 36
Loup/jump the cuddie – 5c, 14a, 15, 25, 27-28, 29a, 30-31
Loup the backie – 5c
Loup the frog – 6
Loup the puddie – 23
Mount the cuddie – 34
Nerde coffie – 1
Paddockie – 5b
Puddock loup loup – 22
Nil – 3-4, 5a, 11-12, 16, 26

Perth

Backies – 26, 62
Backits – 62
Bull (the) cuddie – 7, 11, 28
Cat maw – 18
Cuddie loup (the dyke) – 38, 41b, 42-43, *45, 52a*
Foot and a half – 41a
Hackie duck – 50, 57, 60
Hunch cuddie – 21
(Jump ma) cuddie – 41a, *56*
Leap frog – 1, 2a, 4-5, 8-10, 13, 15, 25, 32-33, 36, 46, 48, 51b, 52b, 57, 66-67, 71, 74
Loup/jump the cuddie – 12, 17, 20, 25, 27, 29ab, 30-32, 41b, 45, 48, 50, 52ce, 53, 64-65, 69-70, 73
Loup the puddock – 68
Paddock loup – 21
Puddock loup – 40
Nil – 2b, 3, 6, 14, 16, 19, 22-24, 34-35, 37, 39, 44, 47, 49, 51a, 52d, 54-55, 58-59, 61, 63, 72

Fife

Backie – 16, 41a, 55e
Backs – 55b
Bunks – 19
Cuddie back(s) – 40b, 55d
Cuddie loup(s) – 12, 41d, 47-49, 53, 61
Cuddie loup the dyke – 34, 55b, 64a
Cuddie(s) – 23, 63
Foot and a half – 38, 43a, 55g
Funkin cuddies – 13
Hop step and a loup – 41a
Huckie duckie – 35
Jump for doon – 44f
Jumpin ower backs – 32, 44e
Jump the bogie – 43b
Leap frog – 4, 7-8, 9a, 11, 13, 21, 23, 36a, 37, 39, 42, 43a, 50, 53, 55ade, 57-58, 62
Long ingin(g)s – 41ab
Loupers – 33
Loup/jump the cuddie – 4, 9a, 12, 20-21, 24-28, 30, 36b, 39, 40c, 41ad, 44bc, 45, 48, 51, 55
Loup the coudie – 17
Puddock leap the dyke – 21
Puddocks – 7
Puddock's loup – 10, 46, 60
Round the world – 43b
Teypnie – 44d
Tippenie nippenie – 54
Nil – 1-3, 5-6, 9b, 14-15, 18, 22, 29, 31, 40a, 41c, 44a, 52, 55c, 56, 59, 64b

Clackmannan

Cuddie loup – 2, 4ab
Funk the cuddie – 4bc
Jump/loup the cuddie – 1, 4c, 6-7
Loup the dyke – 7
Loup the puddock – 5
Nil – 3, 4d

Stirling

Backie – 7c, 25b
Bowster and rider – 12
Cow the cuddie – 9
Cuddie loup (the dyke) – 18, *25a,* 26b, 34, 39b
Cuddies – 20
Cuddie's houp – 37a
Foot and a half – 22a, 26a, 35a
Fusk the cuddie – 7b
Hap ower – 12
Hotch cuddie hotch – 35b
Hunch cuddie hunch – 15, 25b
Joup the cuddie – 10
Jumpin ower backs – 7a
Jump/loup the cuddie – 2, 7bf, 8-10, 16, 22ab, 25acd, 37b, 39a, 41, 42a
Jump/loup the puddock – 13, 27a, 36
Leap frog – 4, 7ade, 8, 11-12, 16-17, 21ab, 23bc, 25c, 26acd, 27a, 28, 30-31, 34, 36, 40
Loupitie back – 27a, 29
Loup the bullocks – 26b
Puddock's loup – 31
Tippnie nippnie – 32
Nil – 1, 3, 5-6, 14, 19, 23a, 24, 26ef, 27b, 33, 38, 42b

Dunbarton

Backie – 13c
Coorie doon – 18
Foot and a half – 9
Hinch cuddies hinch – 14a
Humpie backie – 7c
Hunch cuddie hunch – 2
Leap frog – 1, 6, 7bc, 8, 11, 13abc, 14b, 16b
Loupitie back – 16ab
Loup the back – 17
Loup the cuddie – 3, 7c
Loup the puddock – 13bc
Nil – 4ab, 5, 7a, 10, 12, 15

Argyll

Foot and a half – 35
Hot pies – 23, 37, 39-40
Hump back – 9
Hunch carry hunch – 28
Hunch ma cuddie – 23
Leap frog – 1-2, 5-7, 9-11, 15-17, 19, 22, 24-25, 33, 35
Loup the cuddie – 18
Nil – 3-4, 8, 12-14, 20-21, 26-27, 29-32, 34-36, 38

Bute

Hunch cuddie – 1a
Leap frog – 1cd, 2, 7, 8ab, 9
Loup (the) cuddie – 1a, 8ab, 9
Loup the puddock – 9
Nil – 1be, 3-6

Ayr

Backie – 16b, 28b, 43
Cuddie loup (the dyke) – *8b, 18b,* 20e, *22,* 28f, 41, *53a*
Foot and a half – 8a, 20e
Hap step and loup – 41
Hoch ma gandie – 18b
Hot pies – 8a 20ae
Hunch cuddie – 24b
Leap frog – 1a, 2a, 5-6, 8b, 10-11, 12a, 20c, 26b, 28e, 34, 36, 43, 45, 54-55, 57
Leap the cuddie – 18b
Loupie – 16b
Loup the bullock – 35a, 36, 50, 53ab, 54, 57
Loup the cuddie – 16b, 20ag, 26b, 27, 28abc, 29, 30ab, 31-33, 35b, 36, 39-40, 42, 46-49, 53a, 56
Loup the frog – 26c
Loup the pig – 2a
Loup the puddock – 1b, 4, 7, 20e, 33-34, 36-38, 44, 51-52
Owr loup – 19
Puddocks – 9
Puddock('s) loup – 10, 13, 15, 21, 24a, 25
Skin the cuddie – 20ae
Sullie cuddies – 16a
Nil – 2b, 3, 12b, 14, 17, 18a, 20bdfh, 23, 26a, 28d

Renfrew

Backies – 15
Cockie back – 13a
Cuddie cap – 11k
Cuddie leap – 11k
Cuddie loup (the dyke) – *2gi, 6,* 11*k*l, 19
Cuddie's lupe – 2i
Foot and a half – 13c, 17, 20a
Hot pies – 1b, 2df, 12a
Hunch cuddie – 21
Hunch cuddie hunch – 11ai, 16a
Jump the cuddie – 11h, 13c
Keep the pudden hot – 4d
Leap frog – 2adhi, 4ace, 5, 8, 11abe, 12b, 14a, 19, 20a
Loup the cud – 11c
Loup the cuddie – 2be, 8, 11bfj, 13c, 14b, 16d, 17
Loup the dyke – 18b
Loup the puddock – 13bd, 18a, 20b
Lup the puddock – 11e
Pickie – 21
Silly cuddies – 2j, 16b
Turn the pie – 11a
Nil – 1a, 2c, 3, 4b, 9-10, 11dg, 16c

Lanark

Backie – 12, 33cd, 38d
Buckie tae buckie – 37
Cuddie loup (the dyke) – *7a,* 30, *49a,* 56, 59a, 63, 66
Cuddie lupe – 25b
Foot and a half – 7a, 15a, 16b, 18-20, 25c, 29d, 38a, 40, 46c, 47, 52b, 55, 57bc, 58
Hands up – 37
Hap step and jump – 10a
Hap step and loup – 30
Hinch cuddie – 8b
Hop step and jump – 46a
Hunch cuddie hunch – 9a, 16b, 25d, 28, 32a, 46c, 56
Hunchie cuddie – 49b
Hunchin cuddie – 47
Hunch (ma) cuddie – 7ab, 8a, 22, 27a, 32e, 49b
Leap frog – 1-3, 6, 7ac, 8a, 10b, 12, 14bd, 15c, 16a, 21, 25a, 26ab, 27b, 29cf, 31a, 35d, 38ac, 44-45, 46b, 48, 49ab, 56, 58, 60, 64b
Louping – 33b
Loup/jump the cuddie – 11, 30, 32c, 35bd, 38ad, 39
Loup the back – 6
Loup the bullock(s) – 32df, 35ac, 36
Loup the puddock – 7c, 9b, 13, 14ac, 15b, 17, 29ae, 30 31cd, 32f, 35d, 42, 61
Puddock('s) loup – 31a, 33d, 38b, 39, 44, 53, 59b
Roon the world – 57b
Round the world – 10b
Silly cuddies – 46c
Silly cuds – 27b
Stringing ingins – 12-13
Sullie cuds – 14c
Whites – 57b
Nil – 4-5, 23-24, 29bg, 31b, 32b, 33a, 34, 38e, 41, 43, 50-51, 52a, 54, 57a, 62, 64a, 65, 67ab

West Lothian

Backie – 3
Crooch cuddie – 18
Cuddie laup – 7
Cuddie loup – 1abd, 3-4, 13, 15, 19a, 22
Foot and a half – 1c, 9ab, 16, 18
Hunch cuddie hunch – 7, 16, 17a
Hurdies – 8
Leap frog – 5, 8, 11-12, 17a, 22
Loup – 19b
Loup/jump the cuddie – 6, 10, 21b
Puddocks – 1c
Puddock's loup – 2
Round the world for a ha'penny – 14
Silly cuddies – 8, 21a
Nil – 17b, 20ab

Midlothian

Cuddie leap – 19
Cuddie loup (the dyke) – 2, 5, 8b, 15-16, 18, 21, 23ab, 24, 25abcd, 26ab, 29, 31-32
Cutter – 14a

Midlothian cont'd
Foot and a half – 11, 14a
Hennie – 5
Hop step loup – 20
Hunch cuddie hunch – 10-11
Leap frog – 3, 6a, 7a, 8a, 10, 12a, 15, 17-18, 23b, 30
Loup the cuddie – 1
Puddocks – 27
Puddock's loup – 14b
Skin the cuddie – 14b
Tipennie nipennie – 4, 7b, 30
Tipping – 28
Tuppennie – 5
Tuppennie nuppennie – 6b
Nil – 9, 12b, 13, 22

East Lothian
Cockie duntie – 14
Cuddie hunch – 13
Cuddie loup (the dyke) – 2, 4a*b*, 5, 6a, 7-8, 10, 12-13, 18
Foot and a half – 4a
Leap frog – 1, 4b, 5, 6b, 18-20
Quaker – 4a
Tipennie nip – 11, 15-16
Tipnie nipnie – 2, 6b
Twopenny nip – 13, 17, 21
Twopenny nippenie – 4a
Nil – 3, 9

Berwick
Auntie Katie – 8
Cuddie loup (the dyke) – *4*, 7, 11-*13,* 16a*b*, 18-20, 22-24, 26-27, *30,* 31-32
Froggie – 14
Leap frog – 2, 12, 15, 16c, 29
Loupie – 9
Loup the cuddie – 17, 32
Paddie – 31
Paddie hop – 16c
Paddie loup – 23, 25
Tip an a nip – 18
Tipennie nip – 1, 6, 16ab, 21
Tippin nip – 5
Nil – 3, 10, 28

Peebles
Backie – 10
Cuddie loup – 1, 3, 4c, 6a, 7-9
Leap frog – 4bc, 5, 6b
Loup the cuddie – 2
Loup the puddock – 6a
Paddie loup – 4b
Nil – 4a

Selkirk
Cuddie loup (the dyke) – 1, 2abcde, 3, *4,* 5, 7-8
Paddie loup – 6

Roxburgh
Bonnettie – 21ac, 28
Cuddie loup (the dyke) – 1-2, 3ab, *4-5, 7-8,* 9a*b,* 10, *12*-13, *15ab, 16-18,* 19-20, 21abcd*ef, 23-26,* 28
Foot and a half – 17, 21a
Leap frog – 9a, 10, 21a
Tippennie nippennie – 21c
Nil – 6, 11, 14, 22, 27

Dumfries
Backie – 35
Buck a back – 46
Cuddie loup (the dyke) – *3,* 7, 11-12, 16, 27-29, 34, *42,* 44
Foot and a half – 8b
French flea – 6
French fly – 25
Froggie – 15
Hotch and skipper – 29
Hotch potch – 29
Leap frog – 1a, 4, 8b, 12, 15-16, 17ab, 18, 20, 21b, 22, 24, 30, 31bde, 38, 40, 47
Leap the cuddie – 1a
Loup the cuddie – 1a, 5, 9, 21b, 31a, 32, 35
Loup the dyke – 19, 31a
Muntie kittie – 39
Paddock loup – 13
Tippennie nip – 26
Nil – 1b, 2, 8a, 10, 14, 21a, 23, 31cf, 33, 36-37, 41, 43, 45ab, 48-49

Kirkcudbright
Backie – 5, 12b
Cuddie loup (the dyke) – *1-3, 12a,* 15a, 27
Cuddies – 8
Foot and a half – 21a
Jump/loup the bullock – 12a, 14, 17, 21c
Leap frog – 1-3, 7-8, 10, 16, 19, 21bc, 23
Leap the cuddie – 22
Loup backs – 4
Loup the cuddie – 9, 12a
Paddock loup – 6
Nil – 11, 13, 15b, 18, 20, 24-26

Wigtown
Cuddie leap the dyke – 16
Loup/lope the bullock(s) – 1-3, 5ab, 6-9, 10-15, 17-18
Nil – 4

Northumberland
Bounders – 59b
Cuddie jump/loup the lang dyke – 1a, 6, 9, 19a
Cuddie loup – 8, 29f, 122b
Cuddie loup (the) dyke– 16, 34b
Cuddie loup the lang loaning – 11
Cuddie loup the (lang) lonning – *16*-17, *41c*
Foot and a half – 132
Frog loup – 105
Glory taffie – 51
Hunchies – 1b, 16
Jumpie – 31
Jumpie back – 50, 83, 127e
Jumpie lang lonning – 74, 76, 88b
Jumpie lang run – 79
Jumpie ower(back) – 101b, *122b, 126bc, 129b*
Jumping the backs – 130c
Jump/loup the kittie – 36, 143
Leap frog – 1a, 2b, 8, 13-14, 17-18, 21-22, 26, 29d, 30, 36-37, 40a, 41cd, 42, 45, 48, 52, 53ab, 54-55, 59bde, 60, 62b, 64a, 66, 68, 69cdh, 70, 71d, 72acdgi, 77, 79, 82-83, 85-87, 89-91, 94b, 95b, 99bd, 100, 102, 104a, 106, 111a, 112, 120a, 121, 124b, 126f, 127acdg, 130ef, 132-133
Lop a kittie – 131
Loupie – 12
Loupie dyke – 62c, 65b, 72i, 108a
Loupie lang lonning – 62a, 72b, 95a
Loupie (ower) back – 25, 71d, 85, *98,* 124a, 129a
Loup(in) – 56, 78, 93
Loup(ing) the frog – 105
Loup/jump the cuddie – 1c, 2a, 10, 24a, 27, 29bd, 33b, 45-46, 49, 53a, 62eh, 65a, 68, 69ab, 72e, 79, 107, 138, 143
Loup ower – 127c, 131
Loup the dyke – 72e, 122a, 127a
Loup the lang lonnen – 38, 43
Montie kittie – 90, 106, 126d
Moontie bank – 126a
Moontie kittie – 109, 111b, 130c, 135, 142
Moont the cuddie – 29b, 40b, 41b, 59bd, 62h, 71a, 72fl
Moont the kittie – 20b, 71c, 115, 117, 124a, 130b
Mountie bank – 37
Mountie kiddie – 99b
Mountie kittie – 104b, 108b, 119, 127b, 133-134, 141
Mount the/a kittie – 62f, 89, 103abc, 110, 122a
Mount the cuddie – 29a, 35, 41a, 51, 69g, 72c, 136
Muntie kittie – 130cd, 135
Off off off – 46
Ower the back – 120c
Paddock jump/loup – 57, 64b, 75, 78
Pick a back – 114
Skeel the water – 59e
Nil – 3-5, 7, 15, 19b, 20a, 23, 24b, 28, 29ce, 32, 33a, 34a 39, 44, 47, 58, 59acf, 61, 62dg, 63, 67, 69ef, 71be, 72hjk, 73, 80-81, 84, 88a, 92, 94a, 96-97, 99ac, 101a, 108c, 113, 116, 118ab, 120b, 123, 125, 126e, 127fh, 128, 129c, 130a, 137, 139-140

Cumberland
Bull jump/loup – 13a, 15bc, 16, 18, 25, 30-31, 40, 57
Bull truss – 33
Footie – 41
Frog jump/leap/loup – 8, 16, 26, 28, 41, 49, 51, 53, 59, 61
Harie cockalorum – 44
Hoppie beds – 54
Lantie loup – 38, 40
Leap frog – 1a, 2-4 7, 13c, 14, 22-24, 26, 42, 46-48, 50, 53, 56-58
Loppies – 15b
Loup back – 19
Loup frog – 45, 62
Loupie(back) – *13a,* 16, 24, *27-28,* 43
Montie kittie – 5a
Moontie kittie – 15a, 23
Mountie back – 5b, 40
Mountie kittie – 1b, 11, 39
Mount the kittie – 6
Mum – 42
Muntie kittie – 13d
Ower back – 56
Paddock loup – 60
Sam – 37b
Spanish fly – 37a
Trustie bum – 41
Twopenny nipennie – 33
Nil – 9-10, 12, 13b, 17, 20-21, 29, 32, 34-36, 52, 55, 63ab

Down
Jump the bullock – 10-11, 13, 17
Leap at the bullock – 8
Leap frog – 1, 2a, 5, 7, 9, 15, 18-19, 24, 26, 28
Lept the bullock – 2a
Nil – 2b, 3-4, 6, 12, 14, 16, 20-23, 25, 27, 29-30

Tyrone
Bull jump – 8
Leap frog – 1, 6-8, 11
Nil – 2-5, 9-10, 12-16

Antrim
Bullet jump – 21
Cope carlie – 1
Hoope the barrel – 28
Jump the bullock – 5b, 6, 15, 16b, 17, 19-20, 23, 33
Leap frog – 1, 3, 13, 19-20, 22, 25-26, 28, 31
Nil – 2, 4, 4A, 5a, 7, 8ab, 9-12, 14, 16ac, 18, 24, 27, 29-30, 32, 34

Donegal
Hop – 2
Jump the bullock – 5-6 11
Leap frog – 1, 5, 5A, 8, 12
Nil – 1A, 3-4, 7, 7A, 9, 10ab, 13

Fermanagh
Jump the bullock – 4
Leap frog – 4, 7a, 9
Nil – 1-3, 5-6, 7b, 8, 10

Armagh
Leap frog – 3, 6a
Nil – 1-2, 4-5, 6b

Londonderry
Jump the bullock – 1A, 5
Leap frog – 2-3,3A
Nil – 1, 1B, 4, 6-7

37 ROUNDERS (PQ1, 96)

Rounders has not been mapped as it occurs fairly densely nearly everywhere.
For variants of ROUNDERS, see map 9, Appendix A.
The form **basies** has been subsumed under **basEs**.
See also 34 **home**.

Shetland
Bat an' ba' — 21ab
Rounders — 3-4, 6-10, 15-17, 19, 21a, 22, 24-25, 27, 30, 32-33
Nil — 1-2, 5, 11-14, 18, 20, 23, 26, 28-29, 31

Orkney
Bat an' ba' — 11,13a
Bullie — 8-9
Rounders — 1-5, 7-8, 13b, 14-17, 19-20
Nil — 6, 10, 12, 18, 21

Caithness
Ba' — 12b
Dead ba' — 5
Deid ba' — 2b
Glesga hoosie — 3
Hoosie meetie — 12a
Rounders — 8-11, 16b, 17
Nil — 1, 2a, 4, 6-7, 12c, 13-15, 16a

Sutherland
Housie meetie — 8
Rounders — 1, 3-8, 9ab, 10-13, 16
Nil — 2, 14-15, 17

Ross & Cromarty
Bases — 18-19
Bonnetie — 31
Bowlers — 6, 15, 18-20, 23, 33-34
House ball — 21-22, 24, 25b, 35-36
Loonie — 31
Rounders — 3-5, 8-10, 13-14, 16-18, 20, 25ab, 26-31, 32ab, 39
Service — 1
Nil — 2, 7, 11-12, 32c, 37ab, 38

Inverness
Bowlers — 9, 14-15, 18, 20, 21b
Fielders — 13d
Rouders — 22
Rounders — 1-8, 10-11, 13abce, 16-17, 19-20, 21ab, 23, 26-30, 32-40
Nil — 12, 24-25, 31

Nairn
Bowlers — 1bc
Rounders — 1ab, 4-5
Nil — 3, 6

Moray
Bases — 6a
Bat an' ba' — 21
Bowlers — 3, 5, 9a, 11, 18, 22
Glesgow hoosies — 21
Hoose — 3
Hoosie — 23
Rounders — 2a, 3-4, 6b, 7, 8bcde, 9b, 12, 14, 19-21, 23
Nil — 1, 2b, 8af, 10, 13, 15-17

Banff
Bases — 1, 6b, 8-9, 18cd, 22, 25, 28
Basie ba' — 1, 2abc, 3-4
Bats and bases — 10-13, 16-17, 19, 23-24, 26-27
Bessie ba' — 5
Glasgow hoosie — 29
Hoose ba' — 32, 34
Rounders — 2a, 4, 13-15, 18c, 21, 23, 25
Nil — 6a, 7, 18ab, 20, 30-31, 33

Aberdeen
Ba' — 3a
Ba' an' the bases — 12, 15
Baller — 71c, 73
Ba' 'n bases — 28b
Base(s) — 3b, 23-24, 40, 47b, 50-53, 58, 62, 64, 66, 84-85, 91
Bases ba' — 92
Bats and ba' — 79
Bats and bases — 2, 4, 5abd, 6-7, 9-11, 14, 16-17, 19-22, 26-27, 28ac, 29-32, 34-35, 37, 39, 41, 44-46, 47acef, 48-49, 51, 53, 55-57, 59, 61, 67, 69, 71c, 72, 74-75, 77, 104, 106
Batsers — 13, 74
Bess — 84, 108
Bools — 25
Burn hell — 76
Glesca hoosies — 71b, 74, 80, 97, 99, 104-105
Hoosie — 42, 60, 107
Rounders — 3a, 21, 28c, 44, 47b, 50, 70, 71b, 73, 78, 80-83, 94-95, 98-101, 105, 108
Nil — 1, 5c, 8, 18, 33, 36, 38, 43, 47d, 54, 63, 65, 68, 71a, 86-90, 93, 96, 102-103, 109

Kincardine
Beyie — 20
Bools — 25
Bowler — 19
Buller — 12
Corners — 3
Glesga hoosies — 1, 4-5, 9, 11, 13-14, 17abd
Glesga ringies — 17c, 18
Rounders — 1, 5-8, 10, 12, 15-16, 17c, 19, 24, 26-28
Nil — 2, 21-23

Kinross
Rounders — 1-4, 6-7
Nil — 5

Angus
Base ball — 33b
Beesie — 2-4, 5abc, 6-13, 14abcd, 15, 17b, 19-25, 27, 29ab, 30-32, 33ab, 34-37
Cattie and doggie — 17a
Dullie — 34
Hand ball — 17b
Peesie — 26
Rounders — 1-2, 9, 15, 17ab, 18, 25, 28, 29b, 34
Nil — 16, 20

Perth
Baw in the hods — 62
Beesie — 13, 15-17, 20-21, 23, 25, 27-28, 31-33, 44, 49, 52b, 54, 57-58, 60
Burnie ba' — 40, 41b
Catchie — 61
Docks — 14
Hoosie — 52d
Hoosie ba' — 51b
Housie — 56
Housie ba' — 20
Peesie — 29a
Rounders — 1, 2a, 4-5, 7-13, 25, 29ab, 32, 36, 39, 41a, 42-43, 46, 48, 50, 51b, 52ace, 53, 59-60, 62, 65-69, 71-74
Nil — 2b, 3, 6, 18-19, 22, 24, 26, 30, 34-35, 37-38, 45, 47, 51a, 55, 63-64, 70

Fife
Ba' — 52
Ball o — 55d
Bangalow — 33
Bases — 64a
Beesie — 2-3, 12, 18, 21, 23, 26, 45, 48-49
Beesie ba' — 6, 14, 21
Beesie baw — 4
Chreeshon — 35
Dooble dolls — 44e
Dulls — 44e
Hoosie baw — 25
Keppies — 37
Rounders — 1, 5-8, 9a, 10-11, 13, 16-17, 19-21, 23-24, 28, 30, 33-34, 36ab, 37-39, 40b, 41abd, 43ab, 44bcef, 45-51, 53, 55abde, 56-58, 62-63
Saft ba' — 37
Scúdgies — 55cd
Scuggies — 52
Nil — 9b, 15, 22, 27, 29, 31-32, 40a, 41c, 42, 44ad, 54, 55fg, 59-61, 64b

Clackmannan
Burnie toon — 1-2
Rounders — 1, 4bc, 5-7
Nil — 3, 4ad

Stirling
Basie — 7d
Beesie — 8
Burlie toon — 7b
Dulls — 25c
Prisoner's base — 7d, 26b
Rounders — 4, 7abcdef, 8, 11-13, 15-18, 20, 21ab, 22ab, 23bc, 25abcd, 26acd, 27a, 28-34, 35a, 36, 37a, 39b, 40-41, 42a
Nil — 1-3, 5-6, 9-10, 14, 19, 23a, 24, 26ef, 27b, 35b, 37b, 38, 39a, 42b

Dunbarton
Bat and ball — 5
Rounders — 1, 3, 6, 7bc, 8-11, 13abc, 14ab, 16ab, 17
Nil — 2, 4ab, 7a, 12, 15, 18

Argyll
Rounders — 1-3, 5-7, 9-11, 14-19, 22, 25, 27, 30, 33-40
Service — 23-24
Nil — 4, 8, 12-13, 20-21, 26, 28-29, 31-32

Bute
Beezie — 1a
Moshie — 7
Rounders — 1acd, 2-3, 7, 8ab, 9
Nil — 1be, 4-6

Ayr
Bat and ball — 57
Battins — 50
Homers — 6
Rounders — 1b, 2ab, 5-6, 8ab, 9-11, 12a, 13, 15, 16ab, 18b, 20bc, 21, 24b, 25, 26b, 27, 28bcef, 29, 30a, 31-34,35ab, 36, 38, 41-45, 48, 49, 51-52, 53a, 54-57
Nil — 1a, 3-4, 7, 12b, 14, 17, 18a, 19, 20adefgh, 22-23, 24a, 26ac, 28ad, 30b, 37, 39-40, 46-47, 53b

Renfrew
Bat and baw — 2j
Coolers — 16a
Rounders — 1b, 2abchij, 4acde, 5, 8, 11abefhl, 12ab, 13c, 14a, 16bd, 17, 18ab, 19, 20a, 21
Service — 1b
Nil — 1a, 2defg, 3, 4b, 6-7, 9-10, 11cdgijk, 13abd, 14b, 15, 16c, 20b

Lanark
Bat and ball — 31c, 67a
Bat the ball — 23
Roon dulls — 46c
Rounders — 1-3, 6, 7ac, 8ab, 9a, 10b, 12-13, 14bd, 15abc, 16ab, 17-21, 25abcd, 26ab, 27b, 29cdf, 30, 31ad, 32ae, 33acd, 35bcd, 37, 38acd, 39-40, 44-45, 46ab, 47-48, 49ab, 51, 52ab, 53, 56, 57ab, 58, 59b, 60, 62-63, 64b, 65-66, 67a
Nil — 4-5, 7b, 9b, 10a, 11, 14ac, 22, 24, 27a, 28, 29abeg, 31b, 32bcdf, 33b, 34, 35a, 36, 38be, 41-43, 50, 54-55, 57c, 59a, 61, 64a, 67b

West Lothian
Ba' bases — 14
Bat and baw — 19b
Rounders — 1abcd, 2-3, 5-6, 8, 9ab, 10-13, 15-16, 17a, 18, 20b, 21a, 22
Nil — 4, 7, 17b, 19a, 20a, 21b

Midlothian
Babbisses — 29
Bat and ball — 10
Dollie — 3
Dullie — 4-5, 6b, 7a, 8b, 18, 26ab, 27
Hoose ba' — 31
Hoosie ba' — 32
Rounders — 1-2, 6a, 8a, 10-11, 12a, 13, 14a, 15-21, 23b, 24, 25abc, 28, 30
Nil — 7b, 9, 12b, 14b, 22, 23a, 25d

East Lothian
Ba' bases — 2, 12, 15
Ba' basie — 11
Backits — 6a
Base baw — 16
Hoosie — 14
Rounders — 1, 4b, 5, 6ab, 7-8, 10, 13, 16-19, 21
Nil — 3, 4a, 9, 20

Berwick
Ba' basie — 4
Base ba' — 16a
Bat — 7
Bowler — 16b, 31
Hoose ba' — 2
Hoosie — 8
Hoosie ba' — 10, 13, 16b, 17-19, 21, 23, 27
Housie ball — 2
Rounders — 1, 6, 8-9, 12-13, 15, 16bc, 19-20, 22-23, 26-27, 29-32
Tie — 5
Nil — 3, 11, 14, 24-25, 28

Peebles
Rounders — 1-3, 4bc, 5, 6ab, 7-9
Nil — 4a, 10

Selkirk
Beesie — 3
Hoose ba' — 2abcde, 4, 7
Rounders — 2c, 3, 8
Nil — 1, 5-6

Roxburgh
Boandie — 5
Boondie — 8
Buknie — 2
Burn ma toor — 15a
Burn the house empie — 21d
Hoose ba' — 2, 3ab, 4-5, 9b, 17-18, 24
Hoose baw — 26
Rounders — 1-2, 4, 7, 9a, 10, 13, 16, 20, 21ae, 25-28
Tig — 15b
Nil — 6, 11-12, 14, 19, 21bcf, 22-23

Dumfries
Ba' — 35
Beezie — 12, 44
Cats — 23, 33
Dools — 29, 39, 45a
Fower cats — 36
Hand ba' — 38
Lob — 37
Rounders — 1a, 4-5, 7, 8ab, 9, 12-13, 15-16, 17ab, 19-20, 21b, 22, 24, 26-28, 30, 31abde, 32-33, 40, 45ab, 46
Nil — 1b, 2-3, 6, 10-11, 14, 18, 21a, 25, 31cf, 34, 41-43, 47-49

Kirkcudbright
Bat and ball — 1
Box and kid — 21a
Pitch ba' — 7
Rounders — 1, 3-8, 10, 12b, 15a, 16, 18-19, 21bc, 22-23, 26-27
Sketchers — 2
Nil — 9, 11, 12a, 13-14, 15b, 17, 20, 24-25

Wigtown
Gem o' ba' — 18
Heck — 10
Pout the ba' — 7
Rounders — 1-3, 5a, 9, 11-14, 16-17
Nil — 4, 5b, 6, 8, 15

Northumberland
Answers — 29b
Ball — 103a
Bat and ball — 75
Battie oot — 95b
Bays — 7, 11, 19a, 33b, 35, 45-47, 55, 59bd, 62b, 72f, 80, 89, 108a, 122b, 127b
Buck stick — 114
Burnie bay — 36
Burn the bay — 29a
Cannon — 69ab
Corners — 129a
Feeder — 59b
Fielders — 90
Flinch — 69g
Flincher(s) — 69g, 107
Fours — 64b
Fower bays — 62e
Hoosie ba' — 3, 8
Hoosie bad — 9
Hoosie ball — 16
Hot rice — 59e, 65b, 69ab, 86, 92, 99d, 129b, 130d
Housie ba' — 10
Jack baal — 69a
Parliament — 134-135
Pie ball — 143
Pie sers — 56
Puttie oot gans in — 41d
Relieve oh — 93
Rollicks — 83-84
Rollies — 38, 41bd
Roodie — 138
Rounders — 1ab, 2b, 6, 8-9, 12-14, 17-18, 19a, 20b, 21-23, 26, 29bcd, 30-31, 34b, 36-39, 40ab, 41cd, 42-43, 45-48, 50, 52, 53ab, 54, 56, 59bcd, 60, 62abegh, 63, 64ab, 65a, 66-68, 69cd, 70, 71bcd, 72acdgikl, 77-79, 82, 86-87, 88ab, 89-90, 94b, 97-98, 99b, 100, 101b, 102, 103bc, 104ab, 105-107, 108ac, 109-110, 111ab, 112, 117, 118b, 119, 120abc, 121, 124b, 126abcf, 127acdg, 129c, 130abcef, 131-134, 141-142
Sargeen — 40ab, 41a
Sarras — 17
Sassage — 90
Savage — 69e, 72bgj, 88a, 91, 94a, 95a, 96, 99b, 122a
Stra'ball rallie — 69a
Three big uns — 69ab
Tiggie — 59f
Tradgie — 123
Tragie — 123
Tredgie — 74, 122ab, 124ab, 127f, 129b
Try ball — 41b
Try ball a rollie — 69h
Try ball the rollie(s) — 62g, 64b, 69abeg
Nil — 1c, 2a, 4-5, 15, 19b, 20a, 24ab, 25, 27-28, 29ef, 32, 33a, 34a, 44, 49, 51, 57-58, 59a, 61, 62cdf, 69f, 71ae, 72eh, 73, 76, 81, 85, 99ac, 101a, 108b, 113, 115-116, 118a, 125, 126de, 127eh, 128, 136-137, 139-140

Cumberland
Bantrie hap — 5a
Bat and ball — 19
Battie baw — 38
Clottie — 56
Corners — 31
Dennie — 9, 11, 13ad, 15bc, 34, 45, 54, 60
Dennis — 60
Rounders — 1a, 2-4, 6-9, 13c, 14, 15a, 16-17, 22-28, 37b, 40-42, 46-49, 53, 55-60, 62
Stannie ronds — 30
Tennie — 13d, 33, 50
Tennie ba' — 18
Tennis — 45
Nil — 1b, 5b, 10, 12, 13b, 20-21, 29, 32, 35-36, 37a, 39, 43-44, 51-52, 61, 63ab

Down
Ball — 17
Boundary — 28
Bullets — 15
Rounderies — 8
Rounders — 1, 2a, 5, 7, 9, 15, 19, 24, 26, 28
Town ball — 11
Town tot — 21
Nil — 2b, 3-4, 6, 10, 12-14, 16, 18, 20, 22-23, 25, 27, 29-30

Tyrone
Rounders — 6-8, 11
Time tot — 1
Touch and run — 1
Town tot — 1
Nil — 2-5, 9-10, 12-16

Antrim
Corners — 34
Duck at the table — 23
Geeragh — 7
Pussy in the four corners — 25
Pussy wants a corner — 16b
Rounders — 1, 3, 13, 17, 25-26, 28-29, 31
Town ball — 33
Nil — 2, 4, 4A, 5ab, 6, 8ab, 9-12, 14-15, 16ac, 18-22, 24, 27, 30, 32

Donegal
Base ball — 8
Hand ball — 1
Rounders — 5, 5A, 10b, 12
Town tot — 10b
Nil — 1A, 2-4, 6-7, 7A, 9, 10a, 11, 13

Fermanagh
Dens — 2
Rounders — 4, 7a, 9
Nil — 1, 3, 5-6, 7b, 8, 10

Armagh
Rounders — 3
Nil — 1-2, 4-5, 6ab

Londonderry
Hand ball — 1A
Rounders — 2-3, 3A
Town ball — 4
Nil — 1, 1B, 5-7

38 (A child's) SWING (PQ1, 97)

Swing has not been mapped as it occurs densely all over the area. The variants of SWING have been subsumed (negligible except **sweeng** in Angus).

Shetland
Sway — 5, 14
Swei — 16
Swing — 1-3, 6-7, 10, 13, 17, 20, 21ab, 22, 24-25, 32-33
Swye — 15, 17, 30, 32
Nil — 4, 8-9, 11-12, 18-19, 23, 26-29, 31

Orkney
Sweengo — 4
Swing — 2-3, 5, 7-9, 11, 13ab, 14-17, 19-20
Swingie — 17
Nil — 1, 6, 10, 12, 18, 21

Caithness
Showrie — 12b
Sway — 6, 12b
Swing — 2b, 6, 8, 10-11, 13-14, 16b, 17
Swye — 2a
Nil — 1, 3-5, 7, 9, 12ac, 15, 16a

Sutherland
Swing — 1, 3-8, 9a, 10-11, 13, 16
Nil — 2, 9b, 12, 14-15, 17

Ross & Cromarty
Shoag — 22
Shogle — 6
Shoogle — 20, 25b
Shoud — 36
Shoudie — 37b
Shudie — 31, 37a
Swing — 1, 3-6, 8-9, 13-14, 16-20, 23-24, 25ab, 26-29, 32ab, 34, 36, 39
Nil — 2, 7, 10-12, 15, 21, 30, 32c, 33, 35, 38

Inverness
Greallag — 26
Swing — 1-6, 8, 10-11, 13abce, 16-17, 19-20, 21ab, 22-23, 26-30, 32-40
Nil — 7, 9, 12, 13d, 14-15, 18, 24-25, 31

Nairn
Shougie — 1bc
Showg — 1b
Swing — 1ab, 2, 4-5
Nil — 3, 6

Moray
Drollack — 23
Drowlack — 1
Shoag — 4, 9a, 13, 16, 18-19
Shoagie — 5
Shoagin boat — 9a
Shog — 1, 2a, 8be, 9b, 10, 12, 17, 22
Shoggie — 3, 8b, 21
Showd — 6a, 9a
Showdie — 3
Showg — 4, 15
Swing — 3-4, 6b, 7, 8bd, 14, 20-21, 23
Swingie — 8c
Nil — 2b, 8af, 11

Banff
Drowlack — 32-33
Shoag — 2a, 5
Shog — 2c, 3
Shogie — 15
Shoggie — 14
Shoud — 1, 8, 11, 15, 23, 29, 31
Shoudie — 1, 15, 31
Showd — 6ab, 7, 10, 13, 18c, 26
Showdie — 7, 9, 17, 33
Showg — 2ab, 10
Swing — 4, 9, 15, 18c, 19, 21, 24-25, 34
Nil — 12, 16, 18abd, 20, 22, 27-28, 30

Aberdeen
Shoggie — 53
Shoud — 3ab, 5abd, 6, 11, 15-16, 19-21, 25, 29-30, 33-34, 37, 39-40, 42, 45-46, 47bef, 51, 56-57, 62, 75-78, 80-81, 83, 86, 91, 97, 100-101, 104-107
Shoudie — 32, 48, 61
Showd — 4, 7, 9-12, 14, 17, 22, 28ab, 35, 44, 47ad, 55, 58, 65, 67, 69-70, 71c, 72-74, 79, 84-85, 88, 98, 102, 108
Showdie — 31-32, 34, 47ac, 48, 53, 61, 67
Showdin tow — 9
Shuid — 1
Swing — 8, 14, 20-21, 23, 28c, 34, 44-45, 48, 50, 53, 59, 66, 70, 71b, 73, 79, 82, 94-95, 99-100, 104-105, 107
Swingie — 29, 90
Nil — 2, 5c, 13, 18, 24, 26-27, 36, 38, 41, 43, 49, 52, 54, 60, 63-64, 68, 71a, 87, 89, 92-93

Aberdeen cont'd

96, 103, 109

Kincardine

Glesga' ringie — 17a
Shoag — 15, 28
Shog — 22, 26-27
Shoud — 1, 3, 5, 7, 11, 13, 16, 24
Showd — 4, 10, 12, 14-15, 17bcd, 18
Swing — 1, 5-6, 8, 10, 12, 16, 17c, 19, 26
Nil — 2, 9, 20-21, 23, 25

Kinross

Jow — 5
Shoogie — 4
Shoogie shoo — 2
Shuggie — 5
Swey — 2
Swing — 2-3, 6
Nil — 1, 7

Angus

Shoag — 3, 5a, 6, 8, 11-12, 14abc, 15, 17b, 21, 25, 27-28, 29ab, 31, 33a, 34, 36
Shoagen — 18
Shog — 10, 13, 14d, 22-24, 33b, 35, 37
Shoggie — 5b
Shogie — 5ac, 19
Showd — 25
Showg — 30
Sway — 23
Swee — 10
Swing — 1-2, 4, 7-9, 12, 14a, 17b, 23, 29b, 32, 34, 36
Swingie — 18
Nil — 16, 17a, 20, 26

Perth

Scleid — 62
Shoag — 15, 18, 20, 25, 32-33, 50, 57, 65
Shog — 13, 17, 31, 44, 52c, 56, 58, 60
Shoggie — 46
Shogie — 16, 21, 25, 29b, 39, 62
Shoogie — 45, 66, 69-72
Shoogie shoo — 73
Shoud — 67
Showed — 67
Shuggie — 40, 44
Shuggie boat — 41b
Suggie — 67
Swee — 51a
Swey — 53
Swing — 1, 2a, 4-5, 7-13, 21, 25, 27-28, 29a, 32-33, 36, 41a, 43, 46, 48, 51b, 52abe, 57, 68, 71, 74
Nil — 2b, 3, 6, 14, 19, 22-24, 26, 30, 34-35, 37-38, 42, 47, 49, 52d, 54-55, 59, 61, 63-64

Fife

Chow — 35
Gow — 9b
Jow — 1-2, 4, 6, 9a, 12-14, 20-21, 23, 25-28, 31, 35, 46-48
Shog — 23, 37
Shoge — 3
Shoog — 21
Shoogie — 36a, 51, 53-54, 55f
Shou — 32
Show — 33-34, 47
Shuggie shoo — 40b
Sough — 31
Sway — 7, 12, 17, 19, 38, 40b, 41d, 42, 44acdf, 47, 49, 52, 55dfg, 56, 59-60
Swee — 9a, 33, 61, 64a
Swei — 43a, 55e
Sweiy — 64b
Swing — 6-8, 10-11, 13, 16, 19, 21, 24, 30, 36b, 37, 39, 41a, 43a, 44b, 50, 53, 55abde, 57-58, 62-63
Swye — 17, 39, 44e, 48, 50-51, 55d, 57, 64a
Traipse — 37
Trapeze — 37
Nil — 5, 15, 18, 22, 29, 40a, 41bc, 43b, 45, 55c

Clackmannan

Shoogie — 1, 6
Shuggie — 1
Shuggie shoo — 4ad
Sway — 4d, 7
Swing — 1
Swye — 5
Nil — 2-3, 4bc

Stirling

See saw — 26d
Shoggie shoo — 26b
Shoo — 27a, 39a
Shoogie — 2-3, 7a, 8, 11, 14, 17-20, 21b, 23ac, 24, 25acd, 26acde, 30, 32-33, 36, 37b, 38, 39ab, 42ab
Shoogie shoo — 7b, 25a, 27a
Shougie — 35ab
Shuggie — 4, 6, 7bd, 10, 25b, 27b, 34, 37a
Shuggie shaggie — 22a
Snee gee — 7d
Swee — 15, 30
Swing — 4, 7abce, 12-13, 15-16, 21ab, 23b, 26acd, 27a, 28, 30-31, 34, 35a, 36, 40-41
Nil — 1, 5, 7f, 9, 22b, 26f, 29

Dunbarton

Shoo — 2, 6
Shoogie — 18
Shoogie shoo — 14a
Shoo shoogie — 7c, 14b
Shoo shuggie — 9-10
Swee — 14a
Swing — 1, 3, 6, 7abc, 8-11, 13abc, 14b, 16a
Nil — 4ab, 5, 12, 15, 16b, 17

Argyll

Shoggie — 40
Shoogie — 30-31, 37
Shoogie shoo — 9, 30, 35-36
Shoo shaggie — 24
Swing — 1-3, 5-7, 9-11, 14-17, 19, 22-23, 25, 30, 35, 39
Nil — 4, 8, 12-13, 18, 20-21, 26-29, 32-34, 38

Bute

Shaggie — 1a
Shoo — 8b
Shougie — 1a
Shugie — 5
Swing — 1acd, 2, 7, 8ab, 9
Nil — 1be, 3-4, 6

Ayr

Doodle — 41
Heezie — 19
See saw — 8a
Shoo — 30a
Shoogie — 36, 53a
Shoo shaggie — 16b, 20ae, 24b, 25, 35b, 41
Shoo shuggie ower the waggie — 8a
Sway — 53b
Swee — 18b, 28c, 41
Swing — 1b, 2ab, 5-6, 8b, 9-11 12a, 13, 15, 16a, 20bc, 21, 24b, 25, 26b, 27, 28ef, 29, 30ab, 31-34, 35a, 36, 38, 42-45, 48-49, 51-52, 54-57
Nil — 1a, 3-4, 7, 12b, 14, 17, 18a, 20dfgh, 22-23, 24a, 26ac, 28abd, 37, 39-40, 46-47, 50

Renfrew

Birlie — 8
Shaggie — 16a
Shoo — 1b, 2i, 9, 15, 21
Shoogie — 17, 18a, 21
Shoogie shoo — 1b, 2e
Shooin — 4d
Shoo shaggie — 11fj, 17
Shoo shuggie — 6, 20b
Swee — 16d
Swing — 1b, 2abchij, 4ace, 5, 8, 11aehl, 12ab, 13c, 14a, 15, 16bd, 19, 20a
Nil — 1a, 2dfg, 3, 4b, 7, 10, 11bcdgik, 13abd, 14b, 16c, 18b

Lanark

Punt — 25d
See saw — 29ef
Shoggie shoo — 32f
Shoo — 8a, 9b, 29a, 31d, 33cd, 37, 42, 46c
Shoogie — 9a, 13, 15ac, 19-20, 27a, 29d, 32adf, 36, 38ae, 39, 47-48, 54-56, 59ab
Shoogie shaggie — 10b
Shoogie shoggie shoo — 32f
Shoogie shoo — 30
Shoo shaggie — 8b, 10a, 17, 29fg, 36
Shougie — 38e
Shuggie — 29d, 32d, 38bc, 50, 63
Shugie — 61
Suggie — 53
Sway — 29e
Swee — 29e
Swing — 1-3, 6, 7ac, 8a, 9a, 10b, 12, 14bd, 15ac, 16ab, 18-19, 21, 25bc, 26ab, 27b, 29c, 31a, 32e, 35bcd, 38d, 39, 44-45, 46ab, 49ab, 51, 52b, 58, 59a, 60-61, 64b, 65-66
Nil — 4-5, 7b, 11, 14ac, 15b, 22-24, 25a, 28, 29b, 31bc, 32bc, 33ab, 34, 35a, 40-41, 43, 52a, 57abc, 62, 64a, 67ab

West Lothian

Shoggie — 19a
Shoogie — 1a, 2-3, 6, 9a, 17a, 20a, 21ab, 22
Shoogie shoo — 1d
Shuggie — 11
Suggie — 19b
Swee — 2, 13, 15
Sweezie — 8, 16
Sweezie boat — 12
Swing — 1c, 2-3, 5, 8, 9b, 10-11, 13, 15-16, 17a, 18, 20b, 22
Nil — 1b, 4, 7, 14, 17b

Midlothian

Shogie — 5
Shoo — 13
Shoogie — 12ab, 13, 14ab, 24, 31-32
Shuggie — 11
Swee — 1-2, 4-5, 7b, 8b, 9, 21, 23b, 26ab, 27, 30
Swee heezie — 6b
Sweezie — 12b, 23a, 25ad
Swing — 2, 6a, 7a, 8a, 10-11, 12ab, 15-21, 23b, 24, 25bc, 28-29
Nil — 3, 22

East Lothian

Sheugie — 17
Shoogie — 4b, 13-14
Shuggie — 15-16
Swee — 2, 4a, 6a, 7, 15, 18
Sweegie — 2, 4b, 8, 15, 21,
Swey — 11
Sweezie — 4a
Sweggie — 16
Swing — 1, 4b, 5, 6ab, 13, 15, 18-21

Nil — 3, 9-10, 12

Berwick

Shoogie — 1-6, 9, 12-14, 16abc, 17-18, 21-25, 27, 31-32
Shougie — 26
Shug — 8, 10
Shuggie — 11, 20, 29-30
Swee — 7, 32
Sweegie — 23
Swing — 2, 7-8, 12, 15, 29, 31
Nil — 19, 28

Peebles

Shoogie — 1, 3, 4c, 7, 9-10
Shoogie shoo — 6a
Shougie — 4b
Shuggie — 4a, 5
Swing — 2-3, 4bc, 5, 6b, 8

Selkirk

Shoogie — 2bcde, 3-4, 6-7
Shuggie — 1, 2ac
Swing — 8
Nil — 5

Roxburgh

Shoogie — 3b, 4-8, 9a, 10, 13, 17-18, 20, 21e, 22, 24, 26
Shuggie — 2, 3a, 6, 8, 9ab, 11, 15b, 16-17, 19-20, 21abcde, 23, 25-26, 28
Suggie — 15a
Swing — 1, 9a, 21a
Nil — 12, 14, 21f, 27

Dumfries

Shoggie shoo — 42
Shoogie — 2, 16
Shuggie — 6, 17ab, 18, 29, 39, 49
Swing — 1a, 4-5, 8ab, 9, 12-13, 15-16, 18, 20, 21b, 22, 24, 28, 31bde, 32-33, 35, 37, 40, 45a, 46-47
Nil — 1b, 3, 7, 10-11, 14, 19, 21a, 23, 25-27, 30, 31acf, 34, 36, 38, 41, 43-44, 45b, 48

Kirkcudbright

Birlie — 1
See saw — 1
Shoogie shoo — 21a
Shuggie — 12b, 15a, 18, 20, 22
Shuggie shoo — 5, 7, 11, 15b, 17
Swing — 1-4, 6-7, 10, 15a, 16, 19, 21bc, 23, 27
Nil — 8-9, 12a, 13-14, 24-26

Wigtown

Swing — 1-3, 5a, 9, 11-14, 16-17
Nil — 4, 5b, 6-8, 10, 15, 18

Northumberland

Hickie — 118b
Higher and higher — 138
Hikie — 51, 64a, 71cd, 72d, 79, 87, 101a, 111ab, 117, 118a, 119, 120ab, 126abcdef, 127abcgh, 128, 129ab, 130abe, 131, 133-135
See saa — 24b
See Saw — 72i, 76, 121
Shogie — 23
Shoogie — 55, 99d
Shug — 142
Shuggie — 1a, 2ab, 3, 6, 8, 10-14, 16-17, 19b, 20ab, 22, 24a, 26-28, 29abd, 30-31, 33ab, 34ab, 35-39, 40ab, 41abcd, 45, 48-52, 53a, 56-57, 59bdef, 60-61, 62abcdefgh, 63, 64ab, 65b, 66-68, 69abcdegh, 70, 71abcde, 72abcdefgijkl, 73-86, 88ab, 89-93, 94ab, 95ab, 96-98, 99b, 100, 103a,

Northumberland cont'd

104b, 105, 107, 108ac, 109, 112, 114-117, 118ab, 120ac, 122ab, 123, 124ab, 125, 126ef, 127cdeh, 128, 129bc, 130cd, 133, 136, 140-141, 143
Shuggie boat — 62h, 69ab, 77, 82, 84, 108a, 118a, 129c, 130e
Shuggie shaw — 98
Shuggie shoo — 81, 113, 121, 127g, 129c, 130de, 143
Suggie — 123
Swee — 142
Swiggie — 1a, 2b, 15, 19a
Swing — 2b, 5, 7, 12-14, 18, 21, 23, 26, 28, 29b, 30, 35-36, 40a, 41cd, 42-43, 46-48, 52, 53b, 54, 59bd, 60, 62ab, 64b, 65a, 68, 69c, 71ad, 72ck, 77, 82, 86-87, 89, 102, 103c, 104ab, 110, 112, 120c, 121, 126c, 127a, 132-133, 135, 140
Swingie — 109-110
Swuggie — 1a
Nil — 1bc, 4, 9, 25, 29cef, 32, 44, 58, 59ac, 69f, 72h, 99ac, 101b, 103b, 106, 108b, 127f, 130f, 137, 139

Cumberland

See saw — 46
Shaggie — 30
Shuggie — 5a, 14
Sway — 8-9, 11, 15ab, 16-18, 24-25, 27, 29-31, 33, 35, 40, 56
Sway boat — 20
Swee — 15c
Sweigh — 19, 22, 38
Swing — 1a, 2-4, 7, 13c, 14, 23-24, 28, 37b, 40, 42, 46-50, 53, 56-59, 62
Swye — 39
Nil — 1b, 5b, 6, 10, 12, 13abd, 21, 26, 32, 34, 36, 37a, 41, 43-45, 51-52, 54-55, 60-61, 63ab

Down

Swing — 1, 2a, 5, 7, 9, 15, 18-19, 24, 26, 28
Nil — 2b, 3-4, 6, 8, 10-14, 16-17, 20-23, 25, 27, 29-30

Tyrone

Hobbeltie cuttie — 5
See saw — 5
Swing — 1, 6-8, 11, 16
Nil — 2-4, 9-10, 12-15

Antrim

Hobblie currie — 16b
See saw — 25
Shuggelie shoo — 15, 16a, 25
Swing — 1, 13, 17, 19-20, 25-26, 28-29, 31
Nil — 2-4, 4A, 5ab, 6-7, 8ab, 9-12, 14, 16c, 18, 21-24, 27, 30, 32-34

Donegal

Swing — 1, 5, 5A, 6, 8, 10a, 12
Nil — 1A, 2-4, 7, 7A, 9, 10b, 11, 13

Fermanagh

Swing — 2, 4-5, 7a, 9
Nil — 1, 3, 6, 7b, 8, 10

Armagh

Swing — 6a
Nil — 1-5, 6b

Londonderry

Swing — 2-3, 3A, 4
Nil — 1, 1AB, 5-7

39 The name for the STRIP OF ICE children slide on (PQ1, 98)

Slide has not been mapped as it occurs densely all over the area. Some of the other items mapped are not very densely concentrated.
Rone also appears in 49 **gutter** and 51 **pipe.**

Shetland

Gaet — 6
Glerl — 26
Skeet — 4
Skeetie — 9
Skitch — 8
Slidderie — 3, 6, 21ab, 22
Slidderie bed — 15
Slide — 1-2, 4-5, 10, 17-19, 21a, 23-25, 28, 30-33
Slidie — 7, 16
Nil — 11-14, 20, 27, 29

Orkney

Skeet — 4, 19
Slide — 7-9, 13ab, 14-21
Slidie — 4
Slido — 1-3, 5-6, 12
Slidoo — 10-11

Caithness

Skeel — 12c
Sklide — 12b, 15
Slide — 2b, 3-6, 8-11, 12ac, 13-15, 16ab, 17
Slider — 13
Slidie — 7
Nil — 1, 2a,

Sutherland

Shute slide — 3
Slide — 1-8, 9ab, 10-11, 13-17
Nil — 12

Ross & Cromarty

Slide — 1-24, 25ab, 26-31, 32abc, 33-36, 38-39
Slidie — 37ab

Inverness

Slide — 1, 3-6, 8-12, 13abcde, 14-20, 21ab, 22-40
Nil — 2, 7

Nairn

Slide — 1abc, 2-6

Moray

Rone — 6a, 8b
Skite — 8b
Sleyd — 7
Slide — 2ab, 3, 6b, 8bcde, 9ab, 10-11, 13-16, 18-23
Slidie — 4-5, 22
Nil — 1, 8af, 12, 17

Banff

Hushle — 13
Rone — 8-9, 11-12, 14-15, 18cd, 20-27, 29, 31
Ronie — 8, 10, 15, 17, 18ab
Skip — 33-34
Sledge — 6a
Slide — 1, 2a, 3-5, 6b, 7, 9, 13, 16, 19, 24-25, 28, 30-31, 33-34
Slidie — 2b, 27, 31-32
Nil — 2c

Aberdeen

Rone — 3b, 5bd, 8-12, 14-15, 22-25, 27, 28abc, 30-32, 39, 42, 45, 48, 50-53, 55, 58, 64, 66-67, 69, 71ac, 72, 75, 77, 79-82, 85, 94-95, 100
Ronie — 9, 11, 25, 96
Rowin — 5b
Scutch — 5b, 25
Scutchie — 26
Skiddie — 29, 71c
Slide — 1-2, 3ab, 4, 5abcd, 6-7, 10, 12-14, 16-17, 19-21, 23, 28abc, 29-31, 33-40, 42, 44-46, 47abcdf, 49, 56-57, 59-62, 65-67, 69-70, 71b, 72-77, 82-86, 88, 97-100, 102-106, 108-109
Skidie — 63
Skip — 78, 92-93, 107
Skite — 82, 95
Skitie — 67, 96
Skurr — 8, 11, 15, 25, 28a
Skurrie — 8
Slid — 29
Slidder — 3a
Slidderie — 29
Slidie — 19, 24, 29, 47ae, 51, 53-54, 63, 87-88, 90, 96, 101, 104
Nil — 18, 41, 43, 68, 89, 91

Kincardine

Rone — 11, 23
Ronie — 10
Skiddie — 24
Slide — 1-9, 11-12, 14-16, 17abcd, 19-23, 25-28
Slidie — 10, 18
Nil — 13

Kinross

Skite — 2
Slide — 1-4, 6-7
Nil — 5

Angus

Nairrie slide — 31
Sclide — 15
Skite — 29b
Slide — 1-4, 5abc, 6-10, 12-13, 14abcd, 15, 17ab, 18-28, 29ab, 30, 32, 33ab, 34-37
Slidie — 18, 34
Slipperie — 33b
Nil — 11, 16

Perth

Rone — 67
Sclide — 29b
Skite — 25
Skutch — 30
Slide — 1, 2a, 4-16, 18, 20-28, 29ab, 31-34, 36, 39-40, 41ab, 42-44, 46-50, 51ab, 52abcde, 53, 55-68, 70-74
Nil — 2b, 3, 17, 19, 35, 37-38, 45, 54, 69

Fife

Scoorie — 43b
Skite — 7, 33-34, 51
Slide — 1-5, 7-8, 9ab, 10-14, 16-26, 28, 30, 32-35, 36ab, 37-39, 40ab, 41abcd, 42, 43ab, 44abcdef, 45-54, 55abcdefg, 56-63, 64a
Slidz — 6
Nil — 15, 27, 29, 31, 64b

Clackmannan

Slide — 1-3, 4abcd, 5-7

Stirling

Sklidder — 7d
Slide — 1-4, 6, 7abcdef, 8, 11-20, 21ab, 22ab, 23abc, 24, 25abcd, 26abcdef, 27ab, 28-34, 35ab, 36, 37ab, 38, 39ab, 40-41, 42ab
Nil — 5, 9-10

Dunbarton

Slide — 1-3, 4ab, 5-6, 7abc, 8-12, 13abc, 14b, 15, 16ab, 17-18
Nil — 14a

Argyll

Ice — 17
Ice run — 22
Slide — 1-3, 5, 7-16, 18-21, 23-27, 29-33, 35, 37-39
Nil — 4, 6, 28, 34, 36, 40

Bute

Slide — 1abcd, 2-5, 7, 8ab, 9
Nil — 1e, 6

Ayr

Raik — 28b
Skid — 20g
Sklide — 54
Slide — 1ab, 2ab, 3-7, 8ab, 9-11, 12ab, 13-15, 16ab, 17, 18ab, 19, 20abcdefgh, 21-23, 24ab, 25, 26ab, 27 28bcdef, 29, 30ab, 31-34, 35ab, 36-52, 53ab, 54-57
Nil — 26c, 28a

Renfrew

Sklide — 11l, 21
Slick — 2b
Slide — 1ab, 2abcdefghj, 3, 4abcde, 5-9, 11abcdefghijkl, 12ab, 13abcd, 14ab, 15, 16abcd, 17, 18ab, 19, 20ab
Slider — 2i
Nil — 10

Lanark

Scloy — 9b, 50, 65
Sklide — 20
Slide — 1-6, 7abc, 8ab, 9a, 10ab, 11-13, 14abd, 15abc, 16ab, 17-24, 25abcd, 26ab, 27ab, 28, 29acdefg, 30, 31acd, 32abde, 33abcd, 34, 35abcd, 36-37, 38ace, 39-40, 42-45, 46abc, 47-48, 49ab, 51, 52ab, 53, 55, 57abc, 58, 59ab, 60-62, 64ab, 65
Slire — 11, 38d
Slowie — 52a, 56
Sloy — 60, 63, 67ab
Spiel — 61
Nil — 14c, 29b, 31b, 32cf, 38b, 41, 54, 66

West Lothian

Slide — 1abcd, 2-8, 9ab, 10-16, 17ab, 18, 19a, 20ab, 21ab, 22
Slipe — 11
Nil — 19b

Midlothian

Howkie slide — 16
Scud — 32
Skid — 30
Slide — 1-5, 6ab, 7a, 8ab, 9-11, 12ab, 13, 14ab, 15, 17-22, 23ab, 24, 25abcd, 26ab, 27-30, 32
Slipperie — 5
Sly — 31
Nil — 7b

East Lothian

Scud — 4a
Skid — 4b, 8, 10-11, 14, 16-17
Skide — 2, 13
Slide — 1-3, 4ab, 5, 6ab, 7-9, 12-13, 15, 18-21

Berwick

Block — 27

Berwick Cont'd

Skid – 2-11, 13-15, 16abc, 17-23, 26-27, 31-32
Skide – 11
Sklie – 30
Slide – 1-2, 8, 12, 16c, 17, 23-26, 29, 31-32
Sly – 4, 24, 30
Swea – 27
Nil – 28

Peebles

Scloy – 5, 6a, 9
Slide – 1-3, 4abc, 5, 6b, 7-8
Sloy – 4bc, 7, 10
Sly – 3

Selkirk

Scly – 2a
Slide – 8
Sly – 1, 2abcde, 3-8

Roxburgh

Skid – 6, 10
Sklidder – 21c
Sklide – 15b
Skly – 15b, 17, 21a, 26, 28
Slay – 4
Slide – 1, 5-6, 10, 12, 14, 15ab, 19, 22, 26, 28
Sly – 2, 3ab, 5, 7-8, 9ab, 11, 13, 15ab, 16-20, 21abcdef, 23-28

Dumfries

Sclay – 1a
Sclide – 8a, 31a
Scloy – 11
Scly – 23-24, 26
Slade – 42
Slay – 41
Slide – 1a, 3-4, 7, 8b, 12, 15, 17ab, 19, 21a, 22-24, 28, 30, 31abcdef, 41, 43, 45b, 46
Slire – 6-7, 15, 27-28, 33-38, 40, 43-44, 45ab, 46-49
Sloy – 2, 5, 9-13
Sly – 14, 16, 17ab, 18-20, 21b, 22, 26, 29, 32, 39, 42
Nil – 1b 25

Kirkcudbright

Sclide – 1
Scly – 1
Skide – 11
Slay – 21b
Slide – 1-3, 5, 7-9, 11, 15b, 18-19, 25, 27
Sloy – 4, 6, 12a, 17-19, 21ac, 22-23
Sly – 3-4, 7-8, 10, 12ab, 13-14, 15a, 16-17, 21b, 24, 26
Nil – 20

Wigtown

Slide – 1-4, 5ab, 6-8, 10-18
Nil – 9

Northumberland

Glide – 75
Shordle – 142
Shurl – 133
Slappie place – 103b
Sleyd – 7, 142
Slide – 1ab, 2ab, 3-6, 8-18, 19ab, 20ab, 21-23, 24a, 26-28, 29abde, 30-31, 33ab, 34ab, 35-39, 40ab, 41acd, 42-44, 46-52, 53ab, 54-56, 58, 59bcdef, 60-61, 62bcdegh, 64ab, 65ab, 66-68, 69abcdefgh, 70, 71abde, 72abcegijkl, 73, 75-76, 78, 82, 84-87, 88a, 89-93, 94b, 95b, 96-97, 99bd, 101b, 102, 103ac, 104ab, 105-107, 108a, 110, 111b, 112, 116, 118ab, 120c, 121, 122a, 124b, 125, 126ae, 127abcdfh, 129c, 130b, 132-133, 135-140, 142
Slidie – 24b, 45, 51, 57, 59cd, 62f, 69abe, 71cd, 72abd, 74, 76-77, 79-81, 83, 87, 88b, 93, 95a, 98, 99b, 100, 101ab, 108c, 109, 111ab, 113-114, 117, 118ab, 119, 120abc, 121, 122ab, 123, 124a, 126bcdef, 127abcefgh, 128, 129ab, 130acdef, 131, 134, 139-141, 143
Slippie place – 103b
Slither – 124a
Slurrie – 79
Sly – 29f
Nil – 1c, 25, 29c, 32, 41b, 59a, 62a, 63, 72fh, 94a, 99ac, 108b, 115

Cumberland

Screw – 62, 63ab
Scuddle – 41, 53
Scurl – 3-4, 8, 11, 15bc, 16-19, 24-33, 42-45, 47, 50-62
Shurl – 23, 33, 37a, 38-39, 46-47, 56
Sleyd – 7, 9, 12
Slidder – 56
Slide – 1ab, 2-3, 5a, 6, 12, 13acd, 14, 17, 20-24, 28, 36, 37ab, 38, 40, 42, 44, 46-49, 53, 55-58, 60
Slire – 3
Nil – 5b, 10, 13b, 15a, 34-35

Down

Boor – 22
Sheet – 22
Slide – 1, 2ab, 3-12, 14-15, 17-21, 23-24, 26, 28-29
Slip – 4
Slipe – 13
Strip of ice – 2a
Nil – 16, 25, 27, 30

Tyrone

Slide – 1-2, 5-14, 16
Nil – 3-4, 15

Antrim

Slide – 1-3, 5ab, 6-7, 8a, 9, 11-13, 15, 16b, 17-22, 25-28, 30-34
Nil – 4, 4A, 8b, 10, 14, 16ac, 23-24, 29

Donegal

Slide – 1-3, 5, 5A, 6-9, 10ab, 11-12
Nil – 1A, 4, 7A, 13

Fermanagh

Slide – 2-6, 7ab, 8-10
Nil – 1

Armagh

Slide – 2-4, 6a
Nil – 1, 5, 6b

Londonderry

Slide – 1AB, 2-3, 3A, 4, 6-7
Nil – 1, 5

40 MOULD BOARD (of a plough) (PQ1, 100)

For variants of the elements MOULD(IE) and BOARD, see maps 10, 11, Appendix A.

Shetland

Board – 33
Mould board – 1-2, 4, 7, 10, 15, 17-18, 21ab, 22, 25, 29-30, 33
Sky – 6, 9, 22, 24, 29, 32
Nil – 3, 5, 8, 11-14, 16, 19-20, 23, 26-28, 31

Orkney

Board – 2-4, 19-21
Mould board – 1, 6-7, 11, 13ab, 16-18
Plough board – 5, 9
Nil – 8, 10, 12, 14-15

Caithness

Board – 2b, 3, 5-6, 8-11, 14, 17
Maw wing – 7
Mould board – 2a, 12b, 16b
Mould stilt – 7
Sorn – 7
Nil – 1, 4, 11, 12ac, 13, 15, 16a

Sutherland

Board – 5-6, 8, 9a, 13, 16
Mould board – 1, 3-4, 7, 10-12
Plough mould – 11
Nil – 2, 9b, 14-15, 17

Ross & Cromarty

Blade – 1
Board – 5, 7-10, 17, 21, 23, 28, 31, 32abc, 33, 37a
Bord tionndaidh – 16
Breist – 7
Mould – 36
Mould board – 3-4, 22, 26-27, 29-30, 32b, 39
Mounting – 18
Ploughshare – 34
Wing – 1
Nil – 2, 6, 11-15, 19-20, 24, 25ab, 35, 37b, 38

Inverness

Board – 8, 11, 17, 19, 21b, 23, 25, 27, 29, 34
Cladding – 20
Mould – 18
Mould board – 4, 6-7, 10, 13e, 21a, 26, 28, 32, 36-37
Packer – 14
Presser – 14
Sock – 16
Wing – 30, 38
Nil – 1-3, 5, 9, 12, 13abcd, 15, 22, 24, 31, 33, 35, 39-40

Nairn

Board – 1c
Drill plough – 2
Mould board – 1b, 6
Ploo board – 5
Nil – 1a, 3-4

Moray

Board – 2a, 3-5, 6a, 7, 8be, 11, 14, 16, 22
Briest – 8d
Cleddin – 10
Cooter – 9b, 18
Drill plo – 21
Fur side – 8b
Lanside – 9a
Mould – 6b, 13
Mould board – 7, 9a, 20, 23
Moulder – 21
Ploo board – 12
Skimmer – 8c
Soo's lug – 16
Nil – 1, 2b, 8af, 15, 17, 19

Banff

Board – 4-5, 9, 11, 15, 18d, 23, 34
Breest – 32
Cladin – 31, 33
Claithin – 31
Cleasing – 20
Cleathin(g) – 2c, 3, 6b, 8-12, 22, 24, 27
Cleather – 23
Cleaving – 18b
Feather – 19
Mould – 25
Mould board – 21
Moulder – 16
Pattle – 14
Ploo board – 17
Nil – 1, 2ab, 6a, 7, 13, 18ac, 26, 28-30

Aberdeen

Beam — 89
Board — 2, 6, 9, 16, 20, 22-23, 46, 52-53, 64, 66, 68-69, 79, 82, 88, 92, 94, 98, 100, 104, 106
Claithing — 15, 25, 78
Cleanthe — 31
Cleathin(g) — 3a, 5acd, 9-12, 14, 17-21, 24, 26-27, 28a, 29-30, 32, 34, 37, 39-45, 47abde, 48, 50-51, 55, 57-58, 61, 65-68, 70, 71ab, 72-77, 80-81, 85-86, 94-95, 97, 99, 101, 104-105
Cleavin — 3b, 8, 28b, 42, 59, 83
Cleavlin(g) — 9, 47a, 63
Clething — 6, 33, 71c
Couter — 103
Double moulder — 28c
Metal — 57
Mould board — 65, 108
Moulder — 107-108
Ploo board — 105
Side board — 104
Sock — 56
Splash board — 64
Suck 90
Nil — 1, 4, 5b, 7, 13, 35-36, 38, 47cf, 49, 54, 60, 62, 84, 87, 91, 93, 96, 102, 109

Kincardine

Board — 1, 4-5, 11, 13, 15, 17bcd, 19, 23-24, 26-28
Cleathin — 5, 8-9, 12, 17a
Cleavin — 10
Cooter — 3
Mould board — 2, 12
Moulder — 7
Ploo board — 6
Plough board — 8
Sheer — 14
Nil — 16, 18, 20-22, 25

Kinross

Mould — 1-2, 7
Mould board — 3, 6
Wreest — 4
Nil — 5

Angus

Board — 1-3, 5c, 7-8, 10, 13, 14b, 15, 17a, 20-22, 24, 28, 29ab, 30, 34, 36-37
Cleathin — 23
Firin board — 14d
Mould board — 6, 17b, 37
Plate — 14a
Ploo board — 9, 35
Share — 19
Wing — 31
Wooden board — 33b
Nil — 4, 5ab, 11-12, 14c, 16, 18, 25-27, 32, 33a

Perth

Board — 5, 7, 15, 23, 27, 48, 50, 52c, 59-60
Coulter — 41a
Couter — 35, 37
Face — 29a
Flauchter board — 39
Furrie — 48
Mould — 8-12, 16-17, 25, 28, 29a, 31-32, 39, 42, 46, 56-58, 62, 64-65, 72
Mould board — 1, 4, 20-21, 24, 33, 52b, 66
Plough board — 13
Plough wing — 24
Recest — 67
Reest — 24, 29b, 41b, 68, 70, 73
Share — 25, 71
Shear — 40
Sock — 45
Nil — 2ab, 3, 6, 14, 18-19, 22, 26, 30, 34, 36, 38, 43-44, 47, 49, 51ab, 52ade, 53-55, 61, 63, 69, 74

Fife

Board — 7-8, 21, 26-27, 53
Breast — 12
Breist — 23
Cleedin — 14, 17, 27, 32
Cooter — 61
Coulter — 49
Mould — 1-2, 4-6, 9ab, 14, 17-18, 20, 23-24, 28, 30, 36a, 37, 40b, 41d, 43a, 44e, 45, 48, 53, 55bd
Mould board — 21, 25, 43a, 44c, 55f
Reest — 22, 36b, 37, 41a, 42, 44ac, 51-52, 55e, 57, 59
Share — 35
Side — 38
Side plate — 56
Wing — 43b
Nil — 3, 5, 10-11, 13, 15-16, 19, 29, 31, 33-34, 39, 40a, 41bc, 44bdf, 46-47, 50, 54, 55acg, 58, 60, 62-63, 64ab

Clackmannan

Board — 2
Cooter — 4d
Mould — 5-7
Reest — 1, 3, 7
Nil — 4abc

Stirling

Board — 7b
Breist — 15, 27a, 31
Cooter — 39b
Coulter — 40
Mould — 4, 7b, 8
Mould board — 7cf, 34
Plough sock — 35b
Reest — 1-3, 7abcde, 8-13, 17-18, 20, 21ab, 22b, 23bc, 24, 25bc, 26acd, 27b, 28-33, 35a, 36, 37ab, 39b, 42a
Share — 22a, 26b
Nil — 5-6, 14, 16, 19, 23a, 25ad, 26ef, 38, 39a, 41, 42b

Dunbarton

Pattle — 14a
Pettle — 14a
Reenst — 9
Reest — 1, 3, 4ab, 5-6, 7c, 13abc, 14a, 15, 16b
Share — 18
Nil — 2, 7ab, 8, 10-12, 14b, 16a, 17

Argyll

Breast — 33
Reest — 3, 10-11, 18-19, 23-24, 29-33, 35, 37-40
Reisht — 26
Mould board — 6, 14, 17, 25
Share — 9
Straight edge — 27
Wing — 1, 6-7, 12, 15
Wrest — 22
Nil — 2, 4-5, 8, 13, 16, 20-21, 28, 34, 36

Bute

Breest — 1b
Reest — 1ac, 3-5, 7, 8a, 9
Nil — 1de, 2, 6, 8b

Ayr

Board — 45
Coulter — 28c, 29
Couter — 35b, 40
Cutter — 18b
Mould board — 34
Reesht — 44
Reest — 1a, 2ab, 3-5, 7, 8ab, 9-11, 12a, 13-15, 16a, 17, 18a, 19, 20abcdeg, 23, 26a, 27, 28bdf, 30a, 31-34, 36-37, 41-44, 46-52, 53a, 54, 56-57
Sole shea — 22
Nil — 1b, 6, 12b, 16b, 20fh, 21, 24ab, 25, 26bc, 28ae, 30b, 35a, 38-39, 53b, 55

Renfrew

Breast — 20b
Breet — 16d
Coulter — 16a
Couter — 2e, 17, 21
Double reest — 11a
Mizzle — 12a
Mould board — 2a, 11e, 16b, 20a
Mouldie board — 21
Plough — 8
Plough share — 2i, 12b
Reest — 1b, 2bg, 5, 7, 9, 11abef, 13ac, 19, 21
Reester — 15
Nil — 1a, 2cdfhj, 3, 4abcde, 6, 10, 11cdghijkl, 13bd, 14ab, 16c, 18ab

Lanark

Board — 52a
Breest — 59a
Cheeck — 57b
Couter — 9b, 32f, 62
Lug — 57a
Mouldie board — 30
Mould — 56, 60
Mould board — 17, 33cd, 44
Plough staff — 18
Priest — 57c
Reese — 33a
Reest — 1-2, 7a, 10a, 12-13, 14b, 15abc, 16b, 17, 20-23, 27b, 29d, 30, 31b, 32c, 33cd, 35d, 38abcde, 39, 41-42, 44-45, 46bc, 47-48, 49b, 50-51, 53-56, 57a, 58, 59a, 63, 64b
Rest — 3, 37
Rusk — 29e
Share — 32a
Sock — 15b, 59b, 62
Socket — 15b
Stilt — 49a
Wreath — 46a
Nil — 4-6, 7bc, 8ab, 9a, 10b, 11, 14acd, 16a, 19, 24, 25abcd, 26ab, 27a, 28, 29abcfg, 31acd, 32bde, 33b, 34, 35abc, 36, 40, 43, 52b, 61, 64a, 65-66, 67ab

West Lothian

Birler — 11
Board — 7-8
Coulter — 19a
Knead broad — 19b
Mould board — 12, 15
Reest — 1ad, 5, 8, 9a, 10, 14-15, 17a, 21a
Share — 18
Shear — 16, 18
Sock — 11, 19a
Solshie — 6
Nil — 1bc, 2-4, 9b, 13, 17b, 20ab, 21b, 22

Midlothian

Breest — 32
Cheeks — 20
Coulter — 9
Couter — 9
Mould Board — 10, 27
Mould — 6b, 14b, 18, 21, 23b, 24, 29-32
Plooshear — 7b
Reest — 10, 12a, 14a, 16, 18, 32
Share — 19, 25c
Shoo — 6a
Sock — 1, 17
Sook — 1
Nil — 2-5, 7a, 8ab, 11, 12b, 13, 15, 22, 23a, 25abd, 26ab, 28

East Lothian

Board — 3
Breist — 7
Couter — 6a
Mouldie board — 15
Mould — 2, 10-11, 13-15, 21
Mould board — 4b, 17, 20
Ploo mould board — 6b
Ploo mould — 8, 16
Reist — 2
Nil — 1, 4a, 5, 9, 12, 18-19

Berwick

Coulter — 27
Couter — 9
Mould — 1, 3-4, 6, 8, 10-13, 15, 16ab, 18-23, 25-27, 32
Ploo mould — 31
Share — 23
Sheer — 8
Soaket — 29
Sock — 24
Turner — 27
Nil — 2, 5, 7, 14, 16c, 17, 28, 30

Peebles

Coulter — 2
Mould — 3, 5, 6b, 8-9
Mould board — 6a
Reest — 6a, 7
Sokle — 5
Nil — 1, 4abc, 10

Selkirk

Mould — 1, 2d, 6
Mould board — 8
Mouldie board — 2a
Reest — 3, 5
Nil — 2bce, 4, 7

Roxburgh

Couter — 13, 15a
Fur side — 21c
Mould — 1-2, 3b, 4-8, 9a, 10, 16-17, 20, 21f, 24-25
Mould board — 15b, 28
Nil — 3a, 9b, 11-12, 14, 18-19, 21abde, 22-23, 26-27

Dumfries

Board — 6-7, 8b, 11-14, 17a, 19-20, 21ab, 26, 29-30, 31acd, 32-35, 37 41-42 44
Breist — 45a
Couter — 2
Mould — 32, 36, 40
Mould board — 4, 16, 18, 21b, 24, 27-28, 33, 39, 43
Ploo board — 22
Ploo mould — 46-47
Reest — 3, 5, 9-10, 12, 17ab, 25-26, 32
Share — 7
Sock — 15
Weist — 1a
Wing — 38
Nil — 1b, 8a, 23, 31bef, 45b, 48-49

Kirkcudbright

Board — 1, 4-9, 12b, 13, 15a, 16-18, 21ac, 24-27
Coulter — 3
Couter — 14
Plate — 14
Reest — 2, 10, 12a, 13
Sock — 23
Wing — 19
Nil — 11, 15b, 20, 21b, 22

Wigtown

Board — 5ab, 8, 10-16
Breest — 5b, 6
Ploo reest — 17
Reest — 1, 3-4, 5a, 6, 9, 11, 16
Nil — 2, 7, 18

Northumberland

Board — 1b, 2a, 3-6, 8-11, 13, 16-18, 19ab, 20a, 22-23, 29abcd, 33b, 34b, 39, 40a, 41cd, 45-46, 48, 50, 68, 92, 124a
Board share — 39
Breast — 9, 77, 143
Colter — 69ab
Coulter — 59d, 69ab, 114
Heck board — 83
Mould board — 8, 20b, 29a, 31, 35, 42-43, 51-52, 53ab, 54-57, 59bd, 60, 62g, 65a, 69c, 71cd, 77, 79, 86, 88b, 98, 106-107, 108a, 109-110, 111ab, 112, 117, 120ac, 127d, 129b, 130c, 132-134, 138-139, 141
Mouldie board — 6, 14-15, 26, 29a, 30, 34a, 36-38, 41a, 51, 62ab, 64b, 69ab, 90, 102, 122a
Mowin board — 76
Plate — 127e
Plough share — 41b, 89, 130d, 136
Share — 72b, 127c
Sheer — 33b, 58
Shield — 72k
Wing — 21
Nil — 1ac, 2b, 7, 12, 24ab, 25, 27, 29ef, 32, 33a, 40b, 44, 47, 49, 59acef, 61, 62cdefh, 63, 64a, 65b, 66-67, 69defgh, 70, 71abe, 72acdefghijl, 73-75, 80-82, 84-85, 87, 88a, 91, 93, 94ab, 95ab, 96-97, 99abcd, 100, 101ab, 103abc, 104ab, 105, 108bc, 113, 115-116, 118ab, 119, 120b, 121, 122b, 123, 124b, 125, 126abcdef, 127abfgh, 128, 129ac, 130abef, 131, 135, 137, 140, 142

Cumberland

Breast — 5a
Breist — 44
Mould — 63b
Mould board — 2-4, 7-9, 12, 13c, 15ac, 16-19, 22, 25-26, 28, 30-31, 33, 36, 37ab, 38, 40-42, 45-53, 56-59, 62
Plough breest — 11
Ridger — 54
Share — 60-61
Nil — 1ab, 5b, 6, 10, 13abd, 14, 15b, 20-21, 23-24, 27, 29, 32, 34-35, 39, 43, 55, 63a

Down

Board — 2a, 15
Breast — 4
Mould board — 9, 11, 18-19, 22-26, 29
Recest — 3
Reece — 12
Reest — 13, 21, 27
Wing — 28
Nil — 1, 2b, 5-8, 10, 14, 16-17, 20, 30

Tyrone

Board — 1, 11
Mould board — 6-13, 15
Shoot — 5
Nil 2-4, 14, 16

Antrim

Beam — 15
Furrow break — 34
Mould board — 1, 5a, 7, 9-14, 16b, 17, 19-22, 25, 31, 33
Ploo shar — 25
Shear — 26
Wing — 34
Nil 2-4, 4A, 5b, 6, 8ab, 16ac, 18, 23-24, 27-30, 32

Donegal

Board — 5, 7
Coulter — 10a
Mould board — 5, 5A, 7A, 8, 10b, 12
Mould wing — 5A
Reath — 1
Reest — 1
Nil — 1A, 2-4, 6, 9, 11, 13

Fermanagh

Mould board — 1-2, 4-5, 8
Swing — 1
Nil — 3, 6, 7ab, 9-10

Armagh

Mould board — 4
Nil — 1-3, 5, 6ab

Londonderry

Breaker — 5
Breast — 5
Mould board — 1-3, 6-7
Mowl board — 1B, 3A
Mowlding board — 1A
Plough board — 5
Plough share — 4

41 MUCK HOE (PQ1, 101)

For variants of HOE, see map 12, Appendix A.

Shetland

Byre hoe — 19
Klurrie — 12
(Muck) hoe — *1-2, 6,* 15-16, *21a,* 22, *25, 30,* 33
Scraper — 32
Sharnie hoe — 19
Shuil — 17, 21ab, 26
Tarrie crook — 3, 5, 8, 14, 23, 30
Terrie fork — 21b
Nil — 4, 7, 9-11, 13, 18, 20, 24, 27-29, 31

Orkney

Byre scraper — 1-2, 4, 6, 8, 10-11, 17
Dung scraper — 5
Graip — 13a
Hack — 19
Muck pick — 15
Muck rake — 4
Oot haler — 16
Scraper — 7, 9, 12, 14, 18, 20-21
Ware pick — 15
Nil — 3, 13b

Caithness

Hoe — 4, 13, 16a
(Muck) hack — *2b,* 15
Muck rake — 15
Scraper — 2a, 3-4, 6-11, 12ab, 14, 16b, 17
Screeper — 12c
Nil — 1, 5

Sutherland

Byre hoe — 5
Byre scrapper — 2
Dirt hoe — 3
(Muck) hoe — 6-7, 10-*12,* 16-17
(Muck) scraper — 1, *3*-4, 6, 8, 9ab, 13-16
Screeban — 5

Ross & Cromarty

Clart — 13
Clot — 25b
Draw hoe — 4
Hack — 23, 32c, 37a
(Muck) hoe — 2, *3,* 4-5, 8, 16-18, 20-21, 25a, 26-*27,* 29, 31, 32a, 33, 36, 39
Scraper — 6, 9-10, 12, 15, 22, 24, 25b, 27-28, 31, 33-34
Nil — 1, 7, 11, 14, 19, 30, 32b, 35, 37b, 38

Inverness

Draw hoe — 32
Dung rake — 26
Hack — 9, 19
Hower — 31
(Muck) hoe — 1-4, 6, 8, 11, 16, 18, *22*-23, 27, 30, 33, 35-36, *37,* 38-39
Muck rake — 13a, 26
Muck roe — 5
(Muck) scraper — *7,* 10, 13e, 14-15, 17, 21ab, 29, 31-32
Scrapper — 20, 28
Nil — 12, 13bcd, 24-25, 34, 40

Nairn

Graip — 1c
Muck hoe — 1a
Scraper — 1b, 2, 4, 6
Nil — 3, 5

Moray

Cleek — 6a
Draw hoe — 21
Graip — 8b, 19, 21
Midden — 5
(Muck) hack — *6a,* 8d
Muck hawk — 7
(Muck) hoe — 3-4, 7, *8c,* 9b, 14, *18*
Scraper — 2a, 10-11, 16, 20-21, 23
Scrapper — 7, 8b, 9a, 11, 13, 15, 22
Nil — 1, 2b, 6b, 8aef, 12, 17

Banff

Graip — 2c
Hack — 34
Hag — 32
Muck — 34
(Muck) cleek — 6b, *9, 12,* 17
(Muck) click — 20-*21,* 24
(Muck) drag — *3,* 6a, 16, 19, 29
(Muck) hoe — 1, 2ab, *9,* 29
Scraper — 4, 10-11, 15, 18d, 22-23, 25, 27, 33
Scrapper — 5, 8, 14, 17, 30-32
Nil — 7, 13, 18abc, 26, 28

Aberdeen

Byre rake — 97
Clait — 99
Clapt — 59
Clat — 47b, 69, 71c, 74, 86, 89, 94, 97-98, 101, 105, 109
Clook — 29
Creeper — 16, 26, 51-52, 69, 71b, 72-73, 77, 79, 88, 100, 104, 108
Creepie — 71a
Creepin — 58
Drag — 23, 25-26
Dung clat — 106
Graip — 3a, 9, 47c, 50, 54, 60, 70, 103
Midden — 27
(Muck) cleek — 10, *11-12,* 30
(Muck) click — *15,* 17, 19, *32-33,* 47ae
Muck Datter — 96
Muck hawk — 66
(Muck) hoe — 5d, 7, 28a, *44, 65,* 75, 84, 100, *105,* 107,
(Muck) pluck — 12, 17, 34, 37, 40, *46,* 47e, 61, 73-77, 85
Muck rake — 4, 5c
(Muck) scraper — 1-2, 3b, 5a, 6, 8, 14, 18, 21-*22,* 24-25, 28a, 31, 35-36, 39, 41, 45, 47d, 48, 53, 59, 63-64, 67-69, 71c, 77-78, 80-83, 85-86, 95, 99, 101
Muck spreader — 104
Plug grape — 62
Scrapper — 92, 105
Scrawper — 53
Nil — 5b, 13, 20, 28bc, 38, 42-43, 47f, 49, 55-57, 87, 90-91, 93, 102

Kincardine

Clat — 3-7, 9, 11, 17abd, 21-23, 28
Creeper — 5, 10, 12
Dung creeper — 14
Dung hack — 13, 24
Gutter clat — 26
(Muck) hack — *10,* 12, *15,* 19-20, 25-27
(Muck) hawk — 17c, *18*
Muck hoe — 1, 6
Pluck — 10, 14
Scraper — 8, 16
Nil — 2

Kinross

Clat — 5, 7
Clawt — 3
Haurl — 2, 4, 7
Hoe — 6
(Muck) hawk — *1,* 5

Angus

Clat — 5b, 10, 13, 14bcd, 17ab, 19, 22-23, 33ab, 35, 37
Draw hoe — 17a
Dung hack — 9, 24
Graip — 5a, 6, 14b, 25
Hack — 3, 5ac, 9, 11-12, 15, 17b, 21-22, 26-28, 32, 35-37
Hake — 14a
Harl — 1-3, 6-8, 13, 14bd, 15, 20, 22-23, 29a, 30-31, 34, 36
Hawk — 14a, 34
Hoe — 17b
Midden clat — 14a
Midden rakie — 18
Nil — 4, 16, 29b

Perth

Bitter hoe — 66
Clat — 5-8, 10-13, 15, 17-18, 21,

Perth cont'd
29b, 33, 41b, 45-46, 51a, 52c, 53, 55, 57, 64
Claut — 69, 73
Cloat — 67
Draw hoe — 9
Dung clot — 70
Dung hack — 28, 30
Dung hawk — 26, 58
Hake — 22, 54
Harl — 20-21, 25-26, 29a, 33, 37-38, 44-46, 52c, 56, 68
Horl — 39
Howk — 48
Midden — 59
(Muck) clot — 49, *72*
(Muck) hack — 20, 22-23, 26, *29a, 31*-32, 40, *42-43,* 50, 56, 60, *65*
(Muck) hawk — 25, *27, 47-48, 55, 61-62, 71-72*
(Muck) hoe — *1,* 2ab, *4,* 8, 16, 19, 24-*25,* 36, 41a, 52d, 56, 74
Paidle — 8, 16-17
Scrapper — 3
Nil — 14, 34-35, 51b, 52abe, 63

Fife
Clack — 22
Clat — 53, 64a
Clawt — 27, 36b, 44c
Cleet — 61
Drag hawk — 44e
Dung hoe — 60
Dung tem — 18, 54
Graip — 12, 37, 55d
Harl — 36a
Haurl — 51-52
Howk — 45
(Muck) hawk — *1-2, 4-6,* 9a, *12-14, 17-18, 20-22, 25-28, 30-32, 35, 39, 40b, 41a,* 42, *43a, 44e, 48, 55bcde, 59, 62, 64b*
(Muck) hoe — 7-8, *11-12, 19, 24, 26,* 36*a*b, *38,* 41b, *43b,* 52, *55ef*
Muck hoop — 23
Muck rake — 32, 43b, 55g, 57, 63
Scraper — 51
Tae hoe — 23
Tamma hawk — 9b
Nil — 3, 10, 15-16, 29, 33-34, 40a, 41cd, 44abdf, 46-47, 49-50, 55a, 56, 58

Clackmannan
Clawt — 5
Dung huck — 7
Harl — 2
Hoe — 4ad
Muck clat — 1
Muck hawk — 3, 6
Muck huck — 7
Muck rake — 4d
Nil — 4bc

Stirling
Clat — 1, 7abd
Clatch — 7a
Draw hoe — 6
Dung clot — 23b
Dung hack — 26a
Dung halt — 27b
Dung hawk — 37b
Dung hoe — 14, 25a
Harl — 7b, 9-10, 23c, 26c, 39b
Haurl — 3, 11, 26a
Lawk — 22a
Midden — 26d
(Muck) clawt — 2, 8-9, *13,* 25abd, 27a, *28,* 30-33, 36, 39b, 42a
(Muck) clot — 15, 21a, 24, *26b, 28*-29, 36, 39b
(Muck) hawk — *4, 7cef, 12, 17-18, 20, 21b, 22b,* 23b, *25c, 26cf,* 27a, *33, 35a, 37a,* 39b
(Muck) hock — *4, 12,* 23b, 26f
(Muck) hoe — 7a*c, 9, 25abd, 34, 36,* 40
Muck rake — 35b, 36
Nil — 5, 16, 19, 23a, 26e, 38, 39a, 41, 42b

Dunbarton
Clat — 17
Clawt — 3, 4a, 7ac, 10, 13a, 14a, 15, 16a
Clot — 1, 5, 9
Dung clot — 4b, 6
Hock — 16b
Horl — 13a
Manure grab — 16b
(Muck) hoe — 2-*3,* 13abc
Rake — 18
Nil — 7b, 8, 11-12, 14b

Argyll
Clah — 9
Clat — 10, 21
Claud — 3
Clautter — 34
Clawt — 18, 23, 26, 29, 32, 35
Clot — 11, 19
Draw hoe — 27
Dung hock — 24
Hack — 19
Hawk — 31, 33
(Muck) clatter — 33, *37,* 38-40
(Muck) hoe — 1-2, 5-8, *12-17, 22,* 25
Nil — 4, 20, 28, 30, 36

Bute
Clawt — 4, 8b, 9
Clot — 1a, 3, 7, 8a
Glaur hoe — 8b
Graip a crom — 9
Hawk — 1c
Hoe — 1e, 2, 5
Nil — 1bd, 6

Ayr
Clat — 7, 18b, 21, 41, 45, 48-49, 53b, 56-57
Clawt — 3, 8ab, 9, 12ab, 13-15, 16ab, 18ab, 19, 20acdeh, 22-23, 25, 26c, 28bcf, 29, 30b, 31-34, 35ab, 36, 40-43, 46-48, 50-52, 55
Clot — 1ab, 2a, 5-7, 17, 20b, 22, 26b, 38, 44, 54
Cluat — 27
Dreg — 57
Dung drag — 2b
Dung graip — 20f
Dung hawk — 4, 53a
Dung hock — 5
Dung hoe — 57
Glaur hoe — 28d
Glaurie hoe — 37
Graip — 20g, 24b
(Muck) hawk — 8*a*b, *11,* 20c*g, 30a, 36*
(Muck) hoe — *10,* 18b, *51*
(Muck) rake — 27, *57*
Shovel — 16b
Tammie hack — 24b
Tammie hock — 24b
Nil — 24a, 26a, 28ae, 39

Renfrew
Clart — 11i
Dung hawk — 1b
Dutch hoe — 1b
Graip — 2i. 11j, 14b, 15
Hawk — 2b, 7
Ladle — 11a
Muck clawt — 2g, 8, 10, 11bf, 12a, 13a, 16b, 17, 19, 20b, 21
(Muck) clot — *2b,* 5, 10, 11l, 13c, 16a, 18a, 21
(Muck) hoe — *2a,* 11e, *18b, 20a*
Muck rake — 12b
Nil — 1a, 2cdefhj, 3, 4abcde, 6, 9, 11cdghk, 13bd, 14a, 16cd

Lanark
Clat — 7c, 15b, 19, 22, 24, 32df, 38bcd, 39-40, 50-51, 55-56, 57ab, 59ab, 60, 62-63, 64ab, 66, 67a
Dreg — 35a
Dung hack — 20, 46c, 53
Dung midden — 36
Dutch hoe — 49a
Glammer hoe — 42
Glaur hoe — 58
Graip — 8b, 10a, 17-18, 27b, 35b, 37, 46c
Hack — 1, 5, 23, 32c, 54, 63
Hoer — 29f
Howk — 27b
Midden — 32c
Midden hoe — 8b, 33cd, 47
(Muck) Clawt — 9ab, 11, 15*a*b, 29d, 31*a*c*d*, 32f, 33cd, 44-45, 46ab, 47, 49b, 52a, 57b, 65
Muck clot — 7a, 12, 15c, 21, 27a, 30, 32a, 42, 57c
(Muck) hawk — 13, 15*a*b, 27b, *35d, 48*
(Muck) hock — *2,* 35a
(Muck) hoe — 2-*3,* 6, 15c, *16b,* 25bc, *26a,* 29ce, *31b,* 33ab, 35c*d, 44-45,* 60-61, 67b
Rake — 29f, 38a
Scraper — 29f
Nil — 4, 7b, 8a, 10b, 14abcd, 16a, 25ad, 26b, 28, 29abg, 32be, 34, 38e, 41, 43, 52b

West Lothian
Clat — 3, 9a, 19b
Clawt — 10, 18
Clot — 3, 7, 12, 21a
Dung hack — 17a
Dung hawk — 6
Dung heck — 1a
Glaur hoe — 4
Graip — 16
Hoe — 1b, 5, 9b, 11-13, 15, 20a
(Muck) Hawk — *1d, 8, 11,* 14-16, 17a
Nil — 1c, 2, 17b, 19a, 20b, 21b, 22

Midlothian
Clat — 3, 9, 13, 14b, 20-21, 26a, 27, 32
Claur — 12a
Dung hoe — 8a, 23a
Graip — 7b, 23b
Hack — 30-31
Hake — 23b
Muck claut — 3, 10, 12b, 16
(Muck) clot — 14a, 16, *18*
(Muck) hawk — 6b, *17-18, 24,* 29
(Muck) hoe — 1, 11, 18, *23ab, 25c,* 26b, 28
Muck rake — 4, 15, 19
Paidle — 32
Nil — 2, 5, 6a, 7a, 8b, 22, 25abd

East Lothian
Clat — 4a
Claut — 2-3, 13
Dutch hoe — 4b
Glar hoe — 17
Graip — 6a
Hack — 3, 6a, 14, 16
Harl — 8, 13, 21
(Muck) hawk — *2, 6a, 7, 10-12,* 13, *15, 19-21*
(Muck) hoe — *6a, 9*-10
Muck rake — 6b
Pedal — 13
Shit hoe — 1
Slat — 13
Nil — 5, 18

Berwick
Graip — 16c, 32
Harl — 18, 20
Hoe — 2, 25, 30-32
(Muck) hack— 1, 6, *9-10,* 12, 14-15, *17, 19,* 21, *23, 31*
(Muck) hawk — *3-4,* 5, *8, 11, 13,* 16a*bc, 18-19,* 22, *24, 26,* 29
Muck rake — 9
Paidle — 30
Nil — 7, 27-28

Peebles
Clat — 5, 6ab, 7, 9-10
Clot — 8
Dung hoe — 1
Hoe — 3, 5, 10
Muck hawk — 4b
Muck rake — 2, 4b, 6a
Nil — 4ac

Selkirk
Clat — 2e, 3, 7
Clawt — 5
Harl — 7
Muck Hack — 4, 8
Muck hawk — 1, 2ad, 6
Muck huck — 2b
Nil — 2c

Roxburgh
Clat — 28
Graip — 15a
Hoe — 5, 13
(Muck) hack — *3b, 6*-8, 9b, *12, 18,* 22
(Muck) harl — 5, 7-8, 15b, 16-*17,* 20, 21c, 22-23, 26, 28
(Muck) hawk — *1-2, 3a,* 9a, 10, *17, 21f, 24,* 26
Muck rake — 4
Paidle — 20, 21ad, 25-26, 28
Nil — 11, 14, 19, 21be, 27

Dumfries
Byre clawt — 42
Clart — 16
Clat — 1a, 2-7, 10, 12, 17ab, 18, 21a, 22, 24-25, 27, 29-30, 31abde, 32-35, 37-38, 40-41, 45a, 46, 49
Clawt — 9, 11, 13, 19, 21b, 26
Dreg — 7, 14, 20, 23, 28, 31c, 44
Hack — 7, 15, 31c, 36, 47
Harl — 39, 45a
(Muck) hawk — 1a, 28, 31c, 35, *43, 45b*
(Muck) hoe — 5, 8b, *12*
Nil — 1b, 8a, 31f, 48

Kirkcudbright
Clat — 3-11, 12ab, 13-14, 15b, 16, 18-19, 21a, 22, 27
Clawt — 1-2, 17, 21c
Dreg — 9, 15a, 24
Glar hoe — 26
Greg — 23
Muck hack — 25
Nil — 20,21b

Wigtown
Clat — 1, 5a, 6-8, 10, 13-18
Clawt — 5b, 11-12
Dreg — 3, 5b, 17
Hoe — 7, 12
Midden — 2
Scraper — 5a
Shovel — 9
Nil — 4

Northumberland
Cal — 106
Clart hoe — 82
Clat — 77
Cole — 42
Drag coll — 56
Drag hack — 43

Northumberland cont'd

Drag hoe — 52
Draw hoe — 69b, 71c
Filling hawk — 37
Graip — 14, 21, 28, 64b, 99d, 122b, 123, 126f
Gripe — 64b, 69b, 118b, 122b, 126df
Hack col — 76
Hack rake — 114
Harl — 2a, 10, 16-17, 20a, 27, 29bf, 34ab, 36, 38, 41c, 45, 51, 60, 62a, 79, 102
Hurl — 102
(Muck) caul — 52, 53a, 79, 92, *104b*, 108a, *111b*, 112, 124a
(Muck) coll — 29ab, 38, 44, 54, 56, 60, 77, *80*, 82, 104a, 139-141
(Muck) drag — 29b, 56, *59d*, 68, 69abf, 74, 76, 78, 88b, 90, *103bc*, 107, 109-110, 112, 129b, 130d, 134-136, *142*
Muck filler — 29b
(Muck) fork — *69c*, 97, 99d
(Muck) hack — 3, *8*-11, 13, 15, 17-18, 19a, 20*ab*, 21, 23, *25*-26, 29*bd*, *33b*, *34a*, 35, *39*, 40a*b*, *41d*, *44*-48, *49*;50, 55, *57-58*, 59*ce*, 62*g*, 64b, 65a, *68*, 69abef, 72e*i*, 75, *78*-79, 81, 86, 88ab, 98, 99a, *103bc*, *105*, *108a*, *109*, 111b, 117, 118b, 120a, *122a*, 124a, 125, *129b*, 130cd, *132-133*, *138*-139, *142*-143
Muck hacker — 76
Muck hake — 90
(Muck) hawk — 24a, *28*, *50*, 59b
(Muck) hoe — 1b, 12, 30-*31*, 37, 41bc, *42-43*, *45*, 51-*52*, 53b, *54*, *59b*, 64a, *66*, 71b, 72fgl, 73, 84, *93*, 94b, *108a*, 111ab, 112, 120*bc*, *124b*, 126*c* 127b, *129b*, *135*
(Muck) rake — *1a*, *33a*, *56*, *59b*, *61*, *62h*, 71d, 72e, 76, 83, *103a*, 114, *117*, *124a*, 126a, 127e, 130e
Mud hoe — 89
Plate hoe — 29c
Scraper — 140
Teeming hack — 34a
Teeming hawk — 37
Nil — 1c, 2b, 4-7, 19b, 24b, 29e, 32, 41a, 59af, 62bcdef, 63, 65b, 67, 69dgh, 70, 71ae, 72abcdhjk, 85, 87, 91, 94a, 95ab, 96, 99bc, 100, 101ab, 108bc, 113, 115-116, 118a, 119, 121, 126be, 127acdfgh, 128, 129ac, 130abf, 131, 137

Cumberland

Clat — 12, 14
Col — 13c
Collar rake — 2, 12, 15a, 33, 37b
Collar reak — 9, 38, 48
Collar rock — 22
Collar yak — 15c
Coll rake — 3, 59
Coll ruck — 39
Cooreak — 49
Corrack — 56, 60, 62
Cowl rake — 12, 31, 40, 56
Gowp — 31
Gripe — 54
Harl — 13b
Muck ack — 8
(Muck) drag — *7-8*, *12*, *15b* *16-17*, *23*, *25-26*, *28*-29, *34*, *36*, *37a*, *41-42*, *44-45*, 46, *47*, 51-52, *53-54*, 56, *57*, 58, 61, 63a
(Muck) hack — 4, *5ab*, *6-7*, *9*, *11*, 13a*d*, *20-21*, *23*, *27-28*, *32*, *47*
(Muck) hoe — 15c, *24*, 30, *40*, 43, *48*
Muck pick — 19

Muck rake — 41, 46, 50, 56
Muck reak — 18, 30-31, 63b
Muck ryak — 46
Scrappel — 44
Scrat — 62
Nil — 1ab, 10, 35, 55

Down

Grape — 12-13, 15
Gutter — 3
Hoe — 2a, 6
Muck rake — 9
Scuffle — 7
Nil — 1, 2b, 4-5, 8, 10-11, 14, 16-30

Tyrone

Clatter — 7
Grape — 9, 12
Hoe — 1
Nil — 2-6, 8, 10-11, 13-16

Antrim

Clabber hoe — 31
Drag — 11, 15, 16b
Dreg — 7, 13, 16b, 17, 19
Grape — 6, 8a, 17, 21, 25
Hoe — 1, 9, 13, 26
Muck rake — 14
Navvie — 21
Nil — 2-4, 4A, 5ab, 8b, 10, 12, 16ac, 18, 20, 22-24, 27-30, 32-34

Donegal

Clatter — 10b
Draw hoe — 5
Hoe — 6, 12
Nil — 1, 1A, 2-4, 5A, 7, 7A, 8-9, 10a, 11, 13

Fermanagh

Hoe — 2, 4, 9
Nil — 1, 3, 5-6, 7ab, 8, 10

Armagh

Drag — 1
Nil — 2-5, 6ab

Londonderry

Hoe — 2
Scraper — 1A
Nil — 1, 1B, 3, 3A, 4-7

42 FENCE POSTS (PQ1, 102)

Stob and **stab** have been mapped in 42A. They appear also in 4 **splinter**, 5 **to prick**, 13 **three legged stool** and 26 **bradawl.**

Shetland

Fence posts — 20
Fencing stakes — 25
Fencin posts — 17, 21ab, 30-31
Fencin stabs — 33
Posts — 15-16, 22, 33
Railin(g) stabs — 13
Railing stakes — 17, 27
Railin posts — 17
Stabs — 5, 7, 9, 14-16, 19, 21a, 23-25, 28-30, 32-33
Stakes — 1-3, 8
Steks — 4
Stobs — 6, 10, 21b
Nil — 11-12, 18, 26

Orkney

Fence posts — 13a, 17
Fencin(g) posts — 5, 8, 15
Fencin(g) stabs — 5-6, 8, 10-11
Fencing stobs — 8
Stabs — 1-4, 7, 9, 12, 13ab, 14-21
Stobs — 7, 13a

Caithness

Posts — 3, 13
Stabs — 2ab, 3-11, 12abc, 13-15, 16ab, 17
Stays — 16b
Stobs — 12b, 16b
Strainers — 16b
Nil — 1

Sutherland

Fence posts — 4-7, 11-13, 16
Fencing stabs — 3
Posts — 11
Stabs — 2, 4, 6, 9ab, 10
Stickin(g) — 1-8, 13-15
Stob — 6-8, 9b, 10, 12-13, 16
Strainers — 17

Ross & Cromarty

Fence posts — 1, 3-6, 8, 10, 19-20, 25a, 27, 29, 32b
Palin(g) (posts) — *23*, 37*ab*
Posties — 37b
Posts — 7, 9, 14, 16-18, 22, 24, 26, 28, 31, 32a, 33, 36
Stabs — 25b, 34
Stobs — 7, 10, 22, 24, 27-29, 31, 33, 39
Strainers — 15, 20, 30, 35-36
Nil — 2, 11-13, 21, 32c, 38

Inverness

Droppers — 19
Fence posts — 1-2, 4-5, 10, 13abce, 21a, 23, 33, 39
Fence stobs — 1
Fencing posts — 13e
Fence posts — 13e
Paling posts — 11, 21b
Posts — 8, 16-20, 21b, 26-29, 32, 35, 37
Stabs — 3, 6, 9, 13c, 22, 36
Stakes — 9
Staves — 38
Stobs — 3, 6, 13a, 14, 18, 20, 24, 27-28, 30-35, 37-40
Strainers — 13c, 19, 26, 33
Nil — 7, 12, 13d, 15, 25

Nairn

Fence posts — 2, 6
Paling posts — 1a
Posts — 5
Stabs — 1a
Stobs — 1ab
Strainers — 1b
Nil — 1c, 3-4

Moray

Fence posts — 2a
Palin(g) (posts) — *1*, *2b*, *4-5*, *6b*, *7*, *8bd*, 9*ab*, *10*, *16*, *18-19*, *23*
Pellin posts — 20
Posts — 3, 11, 14, 21, 23
Stabs — 4, 11, 18
Stays — 7
Stobs — 6a, 11, 13-14, 21-22
Strainers — 7
Nil — 8acef, 12, 15, 17

Banff

Fence posts — 1, 19
Palin(g) (posts) — *2ab*, *4-5*, *6ab*, *7-10*, *12-17*, 18b*cd*, *21-26*, *28-31*, *34*
Posts — 15, 27, 32, 34
Stabs — 3
Stobs — 2c, 5, 27, 31
Strainers — 11, 33
Nil — 18a, 20

Aberdeen

Bailing posts — 41
Deels — 80
Paling fences — 105
Palin(g) posts — 2, 3ab, 4, 5abcd, 6-10, 12, 14-19, 21-23, 26-27, 28bc, 30-32, 34-37, 43-46, 47bcdef, 48-49, 51, 53, 56-59, 61, 63-65, 67, 70, 71c, 72-75, 77, 81-82, 87-89, 94, 96-100, 102-106, 109
Palin stabs — 28a, 107
Pam posts — 69
Pellin(g) posts — 1, 29, 54, 62, 101
Posts — 8, 11, 20-21, 28a, 39, 50, 53, 66, 71b, 79, 83, 85-86, 95, 104
Stabs — 73, 90, 107-108
Stakes — 1, 11
Stobs — 4, 20, 23-25, 30, 33, 39-40, 64, 80, 95, 104, 108
Strainers — 8-9, 12, 53, 77
Straining posts — 40
Nil — 13, 38, 42, 47a, 52, 55, 60, 68, 71a, 76, 78, 84, 91-93

Kincardine

Palin(g) posts — 1-2, 4, 6-8, 10-16, 17bcd, 18-19, 22-25, 27

Kincardine cont'd
Pellin posts — 3
Posts — 5, 17c, 21, 26, 28
Stabs — 7, 11, 18
Stobs — 17c, 27
Strainers — 12, 20-21
Nil — 9, 17a

Kinross
Paling stabs — 3
Palin posts — 2
Stabs — 1-2, 4-7
Stobs — 5
Strainers — 1

Angus
Fence posts — 17b
Palin(g) (posts) — *4, 5c, 13, 14abcd, 22,* 28, *31*-32, 33b, *37*
Paling stobs — 17a
Posts — 1-2, 24, 29b, 32, 34-36
Stabs — 3, 9, 13, 14b, 17b, 21-22, 30, 34, 37
Stakes — 6-8, 12, 14cd, 15, 19-22, 25, 29b, 31-32, 33b, 34
Steeks — 18
Steks — 10
Stobes — 27
Stobs — 5ab, 7-9, 11, 15, 18-19, 22-24, 29b, 31-32, 33ab, 34, 36-37
Strainers — 5a, 14a, 22
Nil — 16, 26, 29a

Perth
Fence posts — 4, 8, 24
Fence stabs — 36
Paling (posts) — *1, 24, 33, 46, 52c,* 53
Palin(g) stabs — 37, 40, 41a, 69-70, 72
Paling stobs — 45, 52b
Palin stakes — 32
Posts — 10, 16-17, 25, 28, 48, 57
Rances — 25
Spars — 25
Stabs — 1, 6, 11, 13, 20-21, 26-27, 29ab, 30-31, 34, 38-39, 41a, 46, 50, 51a, 52ce, 55, 59, 62, 65, 67-68, 71
Stakes — 7, 13, 20, 22-23, 29a, 58, 60
Stobes — 59, 62
Stobs — 2b, 5, 9-10, 12, 14-16, 18, 20, 25, 27-28, 29ab, 32, 34-35, 39, 41b, 42-44, 48-49, 51b, 52ade, 53-54, 56-57, 60-61, 63-64, 66-67, 71, 74
Strainers — 16, 25, 48, 73
Straining — 2a
Uprights — 2a
Nil — 3, 19, 47

Fife
Fence stabs — 38
Palin(g) stabs — 2, 7, 9b, 12-13, 20-21, 24, 27, 29, 32-33, 36a, 37, 40b, 41c, 42, 43a, 44ac, 45-46, 48-49, 51-52, 55abcdfg, 56, 59, 62-63
Palin(g) stobs) 55bd, 64a
Paling stubs — 55d
Palins — 8
Poles — 57
Posts — 24, 57
Stabs — 1, 4-5, 7, 9a, 10-12, 14, 16-19, 23, 25-26, 28, 30-31, 34-35, 36ab, 39, 40a, 41abd, 43b, 44bdef, 47, 49, 53-54, 55e, 57-58, 60-61, 64ab
Stakes — 50
Staves — 44b, 48, 50
Stobs — 3, 6, 8, 11-12, 16, 22-23, 37, 39, 43b, 44f, 47, 52, 54, 55d, 58
Strain posts — 64b
Nil — 15

Clackmannan
Palin stabs — 2-3, 5, 7
Stabs — 1, 4abd, 6
Stobs — 1, 4bd, 6
Nil — 4c

Stirling
Corner posts — 7c
Fence posts — 21b
Fence stabs — 28
Paling posts — 4, 15
Palin(g) stabs — 7abd, 20, 21b, 23abc, 24, 25abc, 26a, 27a, 32, 34, 36, 39b, 40
Paling stobs — 19, 22b, 23b, 26d
Stabs — 1, 3, 6, 8, 10, 12-13, 15-18, 21a, 22a, 25d, 26abce, 27b, 29-31, 33, 35a, 37a, 39a, 42ab
Stanchions — 35b
Standards — 3
Staves — 38
Stays — 35b
Stenting posts — 35a
Stobs — 4, 6, 7bcf, 14, 18, 21ab, 25ad, 26ef, 29, 31, 36, 39a
Stopper posts — 25b
Strainers — 7e, 9, 37b
Strainin(g) posts — 3, 7c, 11, 25b, 33, 35a
Nil — 2, 5, 41

Dunbarton
Fencing stabs — 5
Palin(g) stabs — 2, 4b, 7ab, 9, 12, 16b, 18
Palin(g) stobs — 7c, 8, 12, 17
Stabs — 1, 3, 5, 10-11, 13abc, 14a, 16a
Stobs — 3, 4a, 6, 13bc, 14ab
Strainers — 7c
Straining posts — 7c
Nil — 15

Argyll
Fence posts — 2, 6, 17, 22
Palings — 12
Palin stabs — 30, 35, 39
Palin stobs — 35
Posts — 5, 19
Stabs — 1, 3, 7-9, 11, 13, 16, 20-21, 24-26, 28-29, 37-38
Stobs — 1, 3, 6, 8, 10, 12, 14-16, 19-20, 23-24
Strainers — 5, 18, 26, 31-33, 38, 40
Strainin(g) posts — 27, 33-35, 39
Nil — 4, 36

Bute
Droppers — 7
Paling stobs — 1e
Stabs — 1abcd, 2-4, 7, 8ab
Stobs — 1a, 5-6, 8b, 9
Straining post — 9
Strains — 1a

Ayr
Fence posts — 42
Palings — 8a
Palin(g) stabs — 3, 7, 17, 19, 21, 25, 28ce
Palin(g) stobs — 28e, 52
Pilin(g)s — 20b, 28d
Pilin(g) stabs — 5, 11, 14, 16a, 18b, 20ade, 24b, 25, 26c, 28c, 31, 35b, 45, 47, 53b, 56-57
Piling stobs — 26c
Posts — 12a
Stabs — 1ab, 2a, 7, 8ab, 9-10, 12b, 13, 15, 16b, 18a, 20bcf, 22, 24a, 26b, 27, 28adf, 29, 30ab, 33-34, 35a, 37-38, 40-44, 46-50, 52, 53a, 54-55, 57
Stenting posts — 38, 57
Stobs — 1a, 2ab, 6, 8a, 9, 12a, 16b, 18b, 20h, 26a, 28b, 29, 34, 36, 39, 41, 43, 48-49, 56-57
Strainers — 23, 51
Straining posts — 4, 10, 20g, 32, 36, 57

Renfrew
Fence posts — 2a
Fencing stabs — 2h
Gate posts — 2i
Palings — 1ab, 2j, 11h, 13c
Palin(g) stabs — 2egj, 4d, 11bel, 13a, 14b, 16bc, 17, 18a
Paling stobs — 3, 6, 11i
Poles — 12b
Posts — 3c, 20a
Stabs — 2bfh, 4ac, 5, 7-10, 11acfk, 12a, 16ad, 18b, 19, 21
Stobbings — 15
Stobs — 2b, 7-8, 11aij, 13cd, 16ad, 19, 20b
Straining posts — 11a
Nil — 2cd, 4be, 11dg, 13b, 14a

Lanark
End posts — 47
Fence — 7c
Fence posts — 35d
Merch posts — 29e
Pale stabs — 46c
Palings — 7c, 14d, 25bd, 28, 29f, 31b, 32d
Palin(g) stabs — 2, 7a, 10a, 14c, 15ac, 17, 19, 25c, 29f, 30, 32a, 33b, 35b, 36-37, 46c, 51
Paling stobs — 7a, 10a, 14c, 15c, 32e
Posts — 25ac
Rances — 57b
Stabs — 3, 5-6, 9ab, 10b, 11-12, 15bc, 16b, 20, 22-24, 25bc, 26ab, 27ab, 29dg, 31abcd, 32bdf, 33acd, 34, 35acd, 38abcde, 39, 41-44, 46ab, 47-48, 49b, 50-51, 52ab, 53, 55, 57abc, 58, 59ab, 61-62, 64ab, 65-66, 67ab
Stays — 63
Stenters — 50
Stentin(g) posts — 2, 39-40, 42, 52b, 56, 59a, 63
Stobs — 1, 6, 7b, 8ab, 10b, 12-13, 14b, 15bc, 18, 21, 23-24, 25a, 26a, 29cg, 32df, 43, 49a, 50
Strainers — 32c, 60
Strainin(g) posts — 45, 49b, 57b, 58
Strain posts — 47
Nil — 4, 14a, 16a, 29ab, 54

West Lothian
Fencing stabs — 17a
Palin — 11
Palin(g) stabs — 3, 6, 9b, 10, 17a, 21b
Stabs — 1bd, 4-5, 7-8, 9a, 10, 12-16, 17b, 18, 20ab, 21a, 22
Stoabs — 8
Stobs — 1a, 4, 8, 12, 15-16, 20a, 21b, 22
Strainers — 19b
Strainin posts — 11
Nil — 1c, 2, 19a

Midlothian
Fence posts — 6a, 23b
Palin(g) stabs — 9-10, 13, 14ab, 18, 21, 24, 25a
Palins — 1
Posts — 19
Stabs — 3, 6a, 8a, 10-11, 12ab, 14a, 17-20, 23ab, 25c, 26a, 30-32
Stakes — 17
Stobs — 6ab, 7b, 8b, 11, 15-16, 23a, 24, 26b, 27, 29-30
Stuckins — 30
Nil — 2, 4-5, 7a, 22, 25bd, 28

East Lothian
Fence posts — 8, 20
Net stabs — 16
Palins — 6b
Palin stabs — 4b
Stabs — 1-2, 4ab, 5, 6a, 7-13, 15-17, 21
Stakes — 15
Stobs — 1, 3, 4a, 5, 7-9, 14-15, 18-19
Strainers — 2, 14

Berwick
Fences — 8
Palins — 16a
Posts — 8
Stabs — 2-10, 12-13, 15, 16abc, 17-23, 25-27, 30, 32
Stobs — 1-2, 16c, 17, 23, 25, 29, 31-32
Streendin posts — 16b
Stuckin(g)s — 11, 13, 15, 16a, 18, 24, 31-32
Nil — 14, 28

Peebles
Fencing posts — 6a
Stabs — 1-3, 4b, 5, 6ab, 7-8
Stenting posts — 5
Stobs — 4b, 6ab, 9-10
Strainers — 10
Strainin posts — 7
Stuckins — 4b, 9
Stuggings — 10
Nil — 4ac

Selkirk
Fence posts — 4
Fence stabs — 1
Stabs — 2abd, 5
Stobs — 6
Strainin posts — 8
Stuckins — 2abde, 3, 6
Nil — 2c, 7

Roxburgh
Net stabs — 5
Posts — 15b
Stabs — 1-2, 4-5, 7-8, 9b, 12, 17
Stakes — 28
Stobs — 3a, 4-5, 10-11, 20, 21abf, 28
Stowers — 28
Strainers — 25
Stuckin(g)s — 2, 3ab, 4-5, 7-8, 9ab, 13, 15ab, 17-20, 21acdef, 22-24, 26, 28
Streending posts — 16
Nil — 6, 14, 27

Dumfries
Net stakes — 46
Nogs — 6-7
Paling stobs — 1b
Palin stabs — 31b
Pilin stabs — 24
Posts — 46
Sign posts — 28
Stabs — 2-3, 5, 8ab, 9-11, 13-14, 19-20, 21b, 26-28, 30, 31acd, 32, 34, 41-42, 46
Stakes — 17b, 18, 46
Stenters — 1a
Stobs — 1a, 4, 7, 11, 18, 21a, 22-23, 25-26, 31cef, 32, 34-36, 41, 43, 45a, 46, 49
Stowers — 15, 26-27, 29, 32-40, 43-44, 45ab, 46-47
Strainers — 34
Strainin(g) posts — 12, 16, 18
Stuckin(g)s — 17ab, 29, 32
Nil — 48

Kirkcudbright
Piling stabs — 4
Stabs — 1, 5-11, 12ab, 13-14, 15b, 16-17, 21c, 22-27
Stobs — 3, 6-7, 11, 12b, 15a, 17-20, 21abc, 25-27
Straining posts — 2

Wigtown
Paling stabs — 5a
Pilin stabs — 7
Stabs — 2-4, 5ab, 6-10, 14, 17
Stenters — 6, 17
Stobs — 1, 5ab, 8, 12-16, 18
Stouters — 5b
Strainers — 5b
Straining posts — 5a, 11

Northumberland
Baffs — 77
Brattish — 126f
Creeps — 22
Draw posts — 71c
Droppers — 68
Dyke posts — 45, 62a, 76, 120c
Dykin(g) posts — 104b, 110, 140
Dyking stoors — 136
Fence poles — 83
Fence posts — 5-6, 14, 18, 30-31, 35, 41c, 53b, 59bd, 66, 71d, 72cg, 86, 88b, 94b, 103bc, 106, 112, 124b, 126c, 138, 140, 143
Fence props — 59d
Fencin(g) posts — 18, 65a, 66, 69abc, 109
Nest stakes — 29c
Palings — 118a, 130f
Pointed props — 41c
Posts — 2b, 3, 15-16, 20b, 23, 36, 38, 40a, 41d, 42-43, 46, 48, 52, 53a, 54-57, 59e, 60, 64a, 68, 69d, 72d, 77, 87, 91, 99d, 104a, 111ab, 120a, 130e, 132, 135
Powels — 76
Props — 41a, 62eh, 64b, 66, 69c, 70, 71bd, 72bgl, 81, 83 88a, 89-91, 95a, 97-98, 100, 111ab, 114, 116
Railing props — 71b
Railin(g)s — 29d, 72adi, 78, 99b, 117, 118a, 126af, 127b, 130f
Railin posts — 78
Rails — 76, 117
Spars — 41a, 126d
Spiked fencin posts — 69a
Spiked props — 69b
Sprags — 33b
Stabs — 1a, 2a, 8-9, 13, 16, 19ab, 26, 29f, 34b, 43
Stakes — 16, 25-26, 28, 38, 46, 59b, 77, 79, 92, 105, 107, 122a, 129b, 130cd, 134
Stanchions — 40b
Stays — 46, 122b
Stobs — 1b, 2a, 10, 12, 15, 28, 29a, 36-37, 39, 40a, 43-44, 51, 53a, 60, 79, 81, 108c, 124ab, 127a, 128, 134-135, 142
Stocking posts — 76
Stokins — 26
Stoockins — 23
Stoops — 62f, 73
Stoors — 111b, 139
Stowers — 75, 103bc, 133
Strainers — 27, 68
Straining posts — 76
Streenders — 8, 68
Streendin posts — 27
Stuckin(g)s — 2b, 10-12, 17-18, 19a, 21, 24a, 27, 29b, 37, 42-44, 53a, 59b, 122a
Stumps — 124a
Styakes — 108a
Uprights — 71d, 87, 127a
Nil — 1c, 4, 7, 20a, 24b, 29e, 32, 33a, 34a, 41b, 47, 49-50, 58, 59acf, 61, 62bcdg, 63, 65b, 67, 69efgh, 71ae, 72efhjk, 74, 80, 82, 84-85, 93, 94a, 95b, 96, 99ac, 101ab, 102, 103a, 108b, 113, 115, 118b, 119, 120b, 121, 123, 125, 126be, 127cdefgh, 129ac, 130ab, 131, 137, 141

Cumberland
Dyke posts — 15c, 17, 27, 37a
Dyke stakes — 22, 37a
Dyke stower — 33-34, 37a, 38
Dykin(g) posts — 2, 18, 24, 37b, 53
Dyking steeks — 38
Fence — 4, 13c, 23, 47, 53
Piles — 60
Posts — 2, 6-7, 9, 14, 15a, 21, 25, 28, 31, 40, 46, 48, 50-51, 56-59
Railing posts — 16, 23
Rail posts — 30
Staaks — 16
Stakes — 11, 13b, 20, 28-29, 31, 39-40, 42, 46
Stobs — 2, 7, 13b, 30-31, 41, 52, 57
Stoops — 1b, 13c
Stoors — 44
Stowers — 2-4, 5ab, 8-9, 12, 15a, 26-28, 44, 54, 56, 61-62
Stuckings — 13b
Styaks — 18, 42-43, 45, 49, 54, 56
Nil — 1a, 10, 13ad, 15b, 19, 32, 35-36, 55, 63ab

Down
Fence — 9
Fence posts — 6, 15
Palin(g) posts — 2a, 7, 11, 13, 15, 18, 24, 27
Paling stabs — 21
Posts — 5, 19, 28
Stabs — 22, 24, 28
Stakes — 14, 17
Nil — 1, 2b, 3-4, 8, 10, 12, 16, 20, 23, 25-26, 29-30

Tyrone
Fence posts — 11
Paling posts — 7-11, 14
Palin stabs — 2, 7
Pallin posts — 1
Pallins — 1
Pallin stabs — 1
Stabs — 5, 16
Stakes — 6, 12
Nil — 3-4, 13, 15

Antrim
Palin(g) posts — 6-7, 12, 14-15, 17, 19, 21, 24-27, 33-34
Palin(g) stabs — 2-4, 5ab, 13, 20, 22, 34
Paling stobs — 5a
Palins — 8a, 28
Palin stumps — 16b
Posts — 31-32
Stabs — 1, 11, 29
Stakes — 11
Stobs — 7, 10
Nil — 4A, 8b, 9, 16ac, 18, 23, 30

Donegal
Fence posts — 12
Palin(g) posts — 1-2, 5, 5A, 7A, 8, 10ab
Palin(g) stabs — 3-5, 5A, 6, 8, 10b
Stabs — 1, 11
Stakes — 12
Nil — 1A, 7, 9, 13

Fermanagh
Palings — 1
Palin posts — 2, 4
Posts — 2, 9
Stabs — 2
Nil — 3, 5-6, 7ab, 8, 10

Armagh
Paling stabs — 2, 6b
Palin posts — 4
Posts — 6a
Stabs — 1
Stakes — 4
Nil — 3, 5

Londonderry
Palin(g) posts — 2, 4,
Palin stabs — 3
Powls — 6
Stabs — 5
Stakes — 1B, 3A, 5-7
Nil — 1, 1A

43 POST RAMMER (for firming earth round fence posts etc.) (PQ1, 103)

Mell has not been mapped. It occurs fairly generally in the area in varying concentrations.

Shetland
Bishop — 17
Packer — 5, 9
Rammer — 2, 30
Nil — 1, 3-4, 6-8, 10-16, 18-20, 21ab, 22-29, 31-33

Orkney
Beater — 15
Mall — 14, 16
Packer — 9, 19
(Post) rammer — *4,* 8, 17, 21
Pounder — 19
Nil — 1-3, 5-7, 10-12, 13ab, 18, 20

Caithness
Beater — 2a, 3, 7-8, 10, 15
Beyter — 14
Bishop — 5
Crowbar — 13
Mall — 12b
Mell — 4, 11, 12c
Packer — 8
Pinch — 13
Rammer — 5
Nil — 1, 2b, 6, 9, 12a, 16ab, 17

Sutherland
Beater — 1, 9ab
Dumper — 7
Firmer — 3
Mall — 11
Mell — 5, 17
Packer — 10, 13, 15
(Post) rammer — 3, 6, *8*
Ram — 11
Nil — 2, 4, 12, 14, 16

Ross & Cromarty
Beater — 5, 12, 20, 27, 32ac, 39
Mail — 37a
Mall — 3
Mallet — 29
Mell — 2-3, 11, 14, 18, 23-24, 25a, 28, 31, 36
Packer — 8-10, 13, 20, 22, 25b, 29
(Post) rammer — *4, 16,* 32b, 34
Punch — 17, 26
Stumper — 37a
Nil — 1, 6-7, 15, 19, 21, 30, 33, 35, 37b, 38

Inverness
Beater — 9, 13e, 14, 20, 32, 37-38
Bishop — 27, 29
Dumper — 8, 20
Mail — 30
Mall — 26
Mallet — 6
Mell — 6, 14, 19, 21a, 26, 33, 40
Packer — 7, 9, 19, 24-25, 31, 39
Pummer — 1
Punch — 16
Rammer — 3, 10, 19, 23, 34-36
Stemmer — 11
Nil — 2, 4-5, 12, 13abcd, 15, 17-18, 21b, 22, 28

Nairn
Beater — 1c
Mall — 2
Mell — 1b
Packer — 1ac, 6
Tamp — 4
Nil — 3, 5

Moray
Beetle — 9a
Bishop — 4-5, 6a, 8be, 10-11, 16-17, 19, 21-23
Chapper — 8b
Dumper — 8c
Jumper — 20
Maiden — 20
Mattock — 8d
Mell — 2b
Packer — 1, 2a, 3, 5, 6b, 7, 9a, 11-15, 18, 22
Plumper — 3
Nil — 8af, 9b

Banff
Beetle — 14
Bishop — 1, 2bc, 3-5, 6ab, 7-13, 15-17, 18bcd, 20-29, 31, 33-34
Bushop — 32
Mell — 1, 30-31
Packer — 5
Pinch — 19
Nil — 2a, 18a

Aberdeen
Beetle — 15-16, 19, 55, 57, 73
Bishop — 2, 3ab, 5bc, 6, 8, 10-12, 14-18, 20-27, 28a,

Aberdeen cont'd

30-37, 39-46, 47abdef, 48, 50-53, 55-56, 58-59, 61, 63-70, 71abc, 72-83, 85-86 91-95, 97-101, 103-108
Haimmer — 5d
Mail — 5a, 9-10, 28b, 53, 84, 90
Mall — 47c
Mell — 5d, 53, 89, 96, 108
Pinch — 62
Plumper — 29
Priest — 103
Punch — 54
Stay — 88
Strainer — 28c
Nil — 1, 4, 7, 13, 38, 49, 60, 87, 102, 109

Kincardine

Beetle — 11, 28
Bishop — 2-10, 13-15, 17abcd, 18-19, 21, 23-25, 27
Deeple — 18
Dimple — 18
Mell — 12, 20, 26
Nil — 1, 16, 22

Kinross

Beater — 7
Dall — 5
Dumper — 1
Guddle — 2-3
Nil — 4, 6

Angus

Beadle — 2
Beater — 17a
Bishop — 1, 4, 5c
Dall — 3, 5a, 6-11, 13, 14b, 15, 19-24, 27-28, 30-31, 33a, 34, 36
Doo — 8
Dull — 37
Mallet — 14a, 26
Mattock — 5b
Mell — 14a, 17b, 29a, 35
Ram — 33b
Tamper — 21
Trampick — 32
Nil — 12, 14cd, 16, 18, 25, 29b

Perth

Bater — 27, 40
Beater — 2b, 12, 16, 24, 48-49, 51a, 55, 63-65, 68
Beetle — 18
Bishop — 30
Dall — 7, 15, 21-22, 25, 32-33, 51a, 52c, 60, 66
Daul — 30, 50 59
Dumper — 9, 16, 19, 25, 54, 67, 69, 72
Dunter — 41a, 46
Fencin beetle — 70
Girdle — 1
Guddle — 26, 29ab, 31, 38, 52c, 55, 62, 73
Mall — 34
Mallet — 42-43
Maul — 48
Mell — 8, 12, 18, 31, 34, 37, 52a, 57, 61, 71-72
Packin mell — 20
Pinch — 56
(Post) rammer — *4,* 11, 24-25, 44, 74
Punch — 13
Ram — 28
Ramming mell — 39
Stab mell — 39
Stemmer — 3, 10
Stob hammer — 34
Nil — 2a, 5-6, 14, 17, 23, 35-36, 41b, 45, 47, 51b, 52bde, 53, 58

Fife

Bate — 55f
Beater — 3, 11, 21, 29, 40b, 43a, 44b, 53, 55bef, 57, 59, 62, 64a
Beetle — 35, 43a, 44f, 48
Bettle — 9b
Bishop — 53
Bugger — 58
Clod hammer — 55d
Deeple — 60
Doll — 18
Dowfin post — 47
Dumper — 11-12, 14, 20, 22-23, 30, 39, 40b, 41ac, 42, 44c, 48, 51, 55d, 56-57, 61, 63, 64b
Dunter — 31
Guddle — 8, 9a, 10, 12, 23, 41b
Jumper — 5
Mash — 37
Mell — 3, 12-13, 18, 37, 41d, 44a
Mole — 53
Packer — 1-2, 6, 25, 43b
Pinch — 42, 43b, 54
(Post) bater — 4, 7, 26, *28,* 44e
Post rammer — 36a, 58
Putter — 9a
Ram — 19
Stab mell — 32
Nil — 15-17, 24, 27, 33-34, 36b, 38, 40a, 44d, 45-46, 49-50, 52, 55acg

Clackmannan

Bater — 5
Beater — 7
Beetle — 7
Mell — 4a
Stab beater — 6
Nil — 1-3, 4bcd

Stirling

Beater — 4, 10, 18
Beetle — 3, 7e, 25ad, 26a, 39b
Bugger — 10
Dump — 13
Dumper — 3, 7ab, 9, 11, 15, 17-18, 23b, 25cd, 26ac, 27b, 30-34, 35a, 36, 37b, 39b, 40, 42a
Guddle — 1
Jemmy — 23b
Mall — 25b
Mash — 17, 39b
Mell — 7de, 8, 12, 23c, 26b, 27a, 35b, 39a
Mollit — 20
Packer — 7b
Pounder — 22a, 24, 25ad, 26c, 30
Rammer — 7ab, 16, 25cd
Stamper — 28
Thumper — 21a
Wooden beater — 7d
Nil — 2, 5-6, 7cf, 14, 19, 21b, 22b, 26def, 29, 37a, 38, 41, 42b

Dunbarton

Bater — 6
Beater — 4a, 17
Dump — 7a
Dumper — 2, 4b, 7c, 9, 13c, 16a, 18
Dumplin — 5
Gell(ick) — 14a
Jumper — 16b
Mallet — 10
Mell — 10-11, 14a
Pommer — 3
(Post) rammer — 7b, *9*
Reemer — 7c
Stamper — 11
Nil — 1, 8, 12, 13ab, 14b, 15

Argyll

Beater — 23
Beetle — 18, 27
Dumper — 16, 19, 33-35, 37
Dunt — 30
Dunter — 18
Jammer — 33
Mallet — 24
Mell — 3, 9, 24
Pinch — 38
Plock — 31
(Post) rammer — 3, *6, 14,* 17, 22
Stamper — 7
Stemmer — 11
Stob mell — 15
Nil — 1-2, 4-5, 8, 10, 12-13, 20-21, 25-26, 28-29, 32, 36, 39-40

Bute

Beater — 8ab
Beetle — 2
Dollie — 1b
Dumper — 7, 9
Masher — 8b
Mell — 3
Plump — 1a
Punch — 1c
Ram — 1a
Stamper — 1e
Nil — 1d, 4-6

Ayr

Bater — 12a, 30a
Beater — 19, 20f, 33
Beetle — 4, 8a
Beetler — 14, 35a
Champer — 20h, 32
Dumper — 2ab, 3-4, 8b, 13, 15, 17, 18a, 20cef, 21-23, 24ab, 27, 28bdef, 33-34, 35ab, 36, 38, 41, 43-45, 49, 51-52, 53b, 54
Mall — 43
Mallet — 43
Mash — 32
Maul — 43
Pinch — 40, 47
(Post) mell 1a, 2a, 6, *8b,* 9, 16ab, 18b, 20ag, 30b, 31, 45, 48
(Post) rammer — 9, 19, 20c, 28e, *42, 56*
Stab mell — 7, 18b, 53a
Stumper — 55
Tamper — 43
Nil — 1b, 5, 10-11, 12b, 20bd, 25, 26abc, 28ac, 29, 37, 39, 46, 50, 57

Renfrew

Beater — 11e, 18b
Beedle — 13c
Beetle — 8, 11j
Champer — 2i
Dumper — 2h, 9, 11cl, 14a, 15, 16ab, 17, 19, 20b, 21
Jumper — 8
Maul — 16a
Mell — 5, 8, 11bf, 18a
Mundie hammer — 11a
Pinch — 12a
Post rammer — 2a, 11e
Shamfer — 2i
Stamper — 4ac
Stob mell — 3
Nil — 1ab, 2bcdefgj, 4bde, 6-7, 10, 11dghik, 12b, 13abd, 14b, 16cd, 20a

Lanark

Bater — 5, 40, 46b, 47
Beater — 6, 10a, 15a, 29de, 31c, 34, 38e, 47
Beetler — 18
Champer — 38c
Dump — 59b
Dumper — 2-3, 7a, 9ab, 11-13, 14bc, 15ab, 20, 25c, 26a, 31d, 32abc, 33acd, 35acd, 36-37, 39, 42, 44-45, 46c, 48, 49b, 51, 52ab, 53, 56, 57ac, 58, 60, 63, 66
Duncher — 57b
Hoarding — 29f
Mall — 67b
Mash — 27b, 31b, 32f
Mell — 21, 23, 27b, 30, 31bd, 38ad, 39, 57c
Pinch — 32f
Podger — 13
Rammer — 15c, 17, 38b, 64b
Stake — 29f
Thumper — 6
Nil — 1, 4, 7bc, 8ab, 10b, 14ad, 16ab, 19, 22, 24, 25abd, 26b, 27a, 28, 29abcg, 31a, 32de, 33b, 35b, 41, 43, 46a, 49a, 50, 54-55, 59a, 61-62, 64a, 65, 67a

West Lothian

Beater — 5, 7, 14-15, 18
Beetle — 1a, 13
Beetler — 4
Dumper — 1bc, 3-4, 8, 9a, 12, 15-16, 17a, 19ab, 22
Fencin mell — 16
Mallet — 17a
Mell — 17a, 21a
Piercer — 11
Pounder — 2
Ram — 11
Rammer — 13, 22
Stab mell — 6
Stamper — 20a
Nil — 1d, 9b, 10, 17b, 20b, 21b

Midlothian

Bater — 15, 18, 24, 29, 32
Beater — 6b
Bittle — 23a
Bumper — 8ab
Dumper — 1, 4, 6b, 8a, 10-11, 12ab, 14ab, 17, 19, 21, 23b, 26a, 27, 30-31
Mell — 9, 20
Rammer — 23b
Tamper — 25c
Thumper — 8b
Nil — 2-3, 5, 6a, 7ab, 13, 16, 22, 25abd, 26b, 28

East Lothian

Bater — 6b, 8, 15-16
Beater — 4a, 11, 15, 17, 21
Beetle — 10
Dump — 14
Dumper — 2, 4b, 7, 11, 13, 20
Dumpie — 3
Lazy man — 12
Mash — 6a
Mell — 6a
Rammer — 16
Spile — 2
Thumper — 13
Nil — 1, 5, 9, 18-19

Berwick

Bater — 3-4, 6, 10, 13-15, 17-19, 21, 23-24, 26, 30-31
Bawter — 29
Beater — 1, 16ab, 26, 32
Beetle — 22
Dumper — 5, 8, 23, 25, 27, 31
Mell — 8, 12, 27
Piercer — 11, 16c
Pinch — 17
Pounder — 26
Rammer — 2, 32
Stamper — 20
Streendin post — 27
Nil — 7, 9, 28

Peebles

Bater — 3, 7-8, 10
Beater — 4b, 5, 6b
Dumper — 2-3, 9-10
Pinch — 1
Pinch bar — 6a
Ram — 8
Rammer — 6a

Peebles cont'd
Nil — 4ac

Selkirk
Bater — 1
Beater — 6
Dumper — 2b, 5
Iron bar — 2e
Mell — 2ad, 4
Poss — 8
Post rammer — 8
Nil — 2c, 3, 7

Roxburgh
Bater — 1, 3a, 5, 8, 10, 12, 15b, 16-17, 20, 21d
Beater — 2, 6-7, 9a, 15ab, 28
Bishop — 21a, 28
Mell — 3b, 13, 22
Pinch — 13, 26
Plunger — 9a
Podger — 9a
Poss — 21f
Posser — 23-25
(Post) rammer — 4, *26*
Punner — 15b
Nil — 9b, 11, 14, 18-19, 21bce, 27

Dumfries
Beater — 6, 15-16, 18, 27, 29, 32, 34, 36-40, 45a
Beetle — 2, 31c
Dabber — 22
Dumper — 3-4, 17b, 21a, 24, 28, 32, 42
Dunter — 29
Gellick — 8b, 13
Mell — 25, 32, 35, 37, 41, 45b
Pinch — 8a, 19, 33
Plunger — 11
Posser — 46
(Post) Bater — *12,* 26, 35, 44
Post rammer — 1a
Post thumper — 12, 31d
Ram — 1a, 26, 43
Stinchle — 31a
Nil — 1b, 5, 7, 9-10, 14, 17a, 20, 21b, 23, 30, 31bef, 47-49

Kirkcudbright
Bater — 8, 17-18
Beetle — 2, 26
Bumper — 10
Champer — 15a
Clamp — 22
Dumper — 4-5, 14, 19, 21c
Mell — 7, 9, 12b, 23-24
Mell hammer — 12a
Pinch — 16
Pounder — 18
Stamper — 1
Tamper — 12b
Nil — 3, 6, 11, 13, 15b, 20, 21ab, 25, 27

Wigtown
Champin stab — 14
Dumper — 1, 5a, 6, 10-11
Dunt — 5a
Mell — 2, 6-7, 14
Ram — 18
Stemmer — 8
Nil — 3-4, 5b, 9, 12-13, 15-17

Northumberland
Banjo — 69b
Batter — 52
Beater — 2a, 4, 6, 9-11, 13-16, 18, 19ab, 20b, 22-23, 24ab, 28, 29b, 32, 33b, 35-39, 40a, 41abcd, 44-45, 47-51, 53a, 54-55, 57-58, 59cf, 61, 62aeh, 64b, 65a, 68, 69abdf, 72i, 75-77, 79-82, 88ab, 89-90, 94b, 95a, 102, 104b, 109, 111ab, 112, 114, 117, 118b, 125, 129b, 130de, 134, 136-138, 140-142
Beetle — 101a, 127e
Bittle — 17
Bittler — 31
Boater — 77
But — 68
Damper — 130c
Dollie — 56
Dumper — 10, 42, 64a, 70, 129b
Duncher — 105
Earth rammer — 72g
Hydrolic ram — 69b
Jumper — 79
Mallet — 99d
Mell — 26, 30, 37, 46, 57, 59bcd, 64a, 68, 69e, 71e, 72bd, 74, 76-78, 83, 92, 104a, 108ac, 110, 116, 118a, 120a, 122ab, 124a, 126d, 132-133
Paddie — 126c
Pavior's rammer — 69b
Pile driver — 69ab
Pinch bar — 78, 125
Plunger — 12, 57
Posser — 120c
Post — 52
Prodder — 135
Punner — 127c, 143
Ram — 69ab, 73, 100
Rammer — 30, 53a, 60, 62g, 64b, 69c, 71cd, 72i, 79, 81, 86, 111ab, 120b, 126b, 129b, 130b, 140
Ram rod — 127a
Stamper — 34b, 84, 111ab
Stemmer — 93, 96, 98
Tamper — 39, 59e, 69a, 127c
Nil — 1abc, 2b, 3, 5, 7-8, 20a, 21, 25, 27, 29acdef, 33a, 34a, 40b, 43, 53b, 59a, 62bcdf, 63, 65b, 66-67, 69gh, 71ab, 72acefhjkl, 85, 87, 91, 94a, 95b, 97, 99abc, 101b, 103abc, 106-107, 108b, 113, 115, 119, 121, 123, 124b. 126aef, 127bdfgh, 128, 129ac, 130af, 131, 139

Cumberland
Beater — 2-3, 7, 11, 13cd, 16-18, 20, 23, 25-26, 32-33 39, 44, 47, 50, 62
Beetle — 25
Bumper — 40, 63a
Champer — 13b
Dumper — 16, 24, 41, 59, 62
Geublick — 37a
Gyavlick — 24
Maul — 31
Mell — 1a, 2, 4, 5a, 14, 15b, 31, 36, 40, 42, 51, 59
Peter — 63b
Pinch bar — 37a
Plunger — 54
Poonder — 9, 24
Posser — 57
Post thumper — 57
Pum — 63b
Punner — 41
Rammer — 9, 38, 48, 56-58, 60
Stamper — 37b, 46
Stemmer — 7, 22
Stob ram — 30
Truncher — 56
Nil — 1b, 5b, 6, 8, 10, 12, 13a, 15ac, 19, 21, 27-29, 34-35, 43, 45, 49, 52-53, 55, 61

Down
Butt — 17
Dumper — 4
Mell — 13
Rammer — 5, 7, 15, 19, 29
Thumper — 2a
Nil — 1, 2b, 3, 6, 8-12, 14, 16, 18, 20-28, 30

Tyrone
Crowbar — 13
Earth rammer — 11
Mallet — 1, 5
Rammer — 11
Ramming pole — 11
Sledge — 1, 5-6
Sledge hammer — 7, 12
Nil — 2-4, 8-10, 14-16

Antrim
Battering ram — 33
Crowbar — 21
Crow iron — 21
Mallet — 7, 12
Mell — 1-2, 5b, 7, 14, 20
Ram — 25, 28-29
Rammer — 25
Sledge — 7, 11
Sledge hammer — 32
Nil — 3-4, 4A, 5a, 6, 8ab, 9-10, 13, 15, 16abc, 17-19, 22-24, 26-27, 30-31, 34

Donegal
Crowbar — 5A
Mall — 1, 10b
Mallet — 5
Mell — 2, 5
Pounder — 6, 10b
Ram — 10b
Rammer — 8, 10a, 12
Sledge (hemmer) — *4,* 7A
Nil — 1A, 3, 7, 9, 11, 13

Fermanagh
Rammer — 4
Sledge — 9-10
Nil — 1-3, 5-6, 7ab, 8

Armagh
Pounder — 4
Nil — 1-3, 5, 6ab

Londonderry
Mell — 1, 3, 5
Post rammer — 2
Rammer — 3A
Sledge hammer — 7
Stake — 6
Nil — 1AB, 4

44 CROWBAR (PQ1, 104)

Pinch has not been mapped. It occurs in considerable density all over the area except in Cumberland and Northern Ireland.

A small raised + symbol given after a locality number marks responses to the request: 'Say whether you have separate word for kind with a forked end.' The variants of unstressed vowels in the ending **-Ick** have been subsumed.
Note the recurrence of some items in 78 **black beetle** and 82 **earwig.**

Shetland
Claw bar — 14+
Crowbar — 30, 32-33
Crow iron — 30
Hand iron — 16
Hands pick — 13
Pinch (bar) — 1-3, *4,* 5, *6,* 7, *8,* 9-10, 13, 17, 19-20, 21ab, 22, 24, *25,* 27-30, 32
Punch — 22
Swey — 9
Swy — 15-16, 27
Nil — 11-12, 18, 23, 26, 31

Orkney
Bar — 21
Crowbar — 1, 8, 17, 21
Crow iron — 2
Nail bar — 21+
Pick — 7, 16
Pinch (bar) — 1-2, 4-*5,* 8-12, 13ab, 15, *17,* 18-21
Quarry iron — 3
Quarry pinch — 6
Swey — 2
Nil — 14

Caithness
Crowbar — 13, 16b
Lever — 7
Pinch — 2a, 3-9, 11, 12bc, 13-15, 17
Pincher — 12a
Nil — 1, 2b, 10, 16a

Sutherland
Bar — 16
Crowbar — 1, 3, 6-8, 10, 12-13, 16
Fencing hole bar — 3

Sutherland cont'd

Iron lever — 11
Lever — 2
Pinch — 4, 9ab
Punch — 5-7, 11, 14-15
Nil — 17

Ross & Cromarty

Bar — 28
Claw punch — 32c$^+$
Crowbar — 1, 3-5, 8-9$^+$, 16-17, 22, 25a, 26-27, 29, 32a, 39
Lever — 8$^+$, 10
Pinch (bar) — 4, *5*, 12-13, 18, 26, 30
Punch — 7, 9, 12, 14, 20-21, 23, 25b, 27-29, 31, 32c, 34-36, 38
Trampike — 31$^+$
Nil — 2, 6, 11, 15, 19, 24, 32b, 33, 37ab

Inverness

Bar — 38
Crowbar — 1-5, 7-8, 10-11, 13abe, 21b, 22-23, 30, 33-39
Gailick — 18
Gailag — 28$^+$
Lever — 7
Pinch — 7, 10, 13c, 17-18, 24, 28-29
Punch — 6, 9, 11, 14, 19-20, 21a, 23, 26-27, 31, 38
Nil — 12, 13d, 15-16, 25, 32, 40

Nairn

Crowbar — 2
Pinch — 3, 6
Punch — 1abc
Trampick — 4
Nil — 5

Moray

Crowbar — 1$^+$, 2a, 6b, 7$^+$, 14, 18, 23
Jimmie — 18
Lever — 5, 8c
Lowther — 21
Pinch — 3-4, 6a, 8be, 9ab, 13-14, 17, 19, 22-23
Punch — 1, 4, 7, 8d, 15, 20
Trampick — 15$^+$
Nil — 2b, 8af, 10-12, 16

Banff

Bar — 6b, 7, 23
Crowbar — 2b, 5, 13, 16
Jumper — 11
Lever — 4, 20
Lowder — 25
Pinch (bar) — 1, 2c, 3, 6a, 8-9, 11-12, 14-15, 17, 18cd, *19*, 21-24, 26-29, 31, 34
Punch — 29-30, 33
Trampick — 10
Wa eyron — 32
Nil — 2a, 18ab

Aberdeen

Bar — 53
Binch — 19
Crowbar — 12, 32, 47b, 64$^+$, 71b, 94-95, 105, 108$^+$
Fork — 9$^+$
Howder — 101
Laver — 22, 49, 86
Lever — 5c, 12, 14, 16, 35, 49, 63, 66, 70, 78, 101
Louder — 97-98, 104-105
Lumphanan auger — 108
Pick — 14, 27, 35, 48, 70$^+$, 101$^+$
Pinch (bar) — 3ab, *5d*, 6, 9-11, *16*, 17-19, 21, 23-27, 28a, 29-35, 37, 39-42, *43*, 44, *46*, 47abcde, 50-53, 55-56, 58-59, *60*, 61, 64-65, 67-69, 71c, 72-75, 77, 79-81, 83, 85, 87, 93, 95-99, 101, 103, 105-107, *108*
Pitch bar — 90
Staple picker — 67$^+$
Trampick — 48$^+$, 76, 88-89, 100
Wa iron — 30, 74
Nil — 1-2, 4, 5ab, 7-8, 13, 15, 20, 28bc, 36, 38, 45, 47f, 54, 57, 62, 71a, 82, 84, 91-92, 102, 109

Kincardine

Bar of iron — 8
Big pinch — 9
Breem dog — 4$^+$
Crowbar — 6, 10, 14, 17c$^+$
Jimmie — 16
Lever — 17bd, 19, 26
Lowder — 3, 5-6
Pick — 12, 24
Pinch (bar) — 1, 4, 6$^+$-7, 10-14, 17bc, 18, *21*, 27
Pincher — 12
Sock bar — 15
Nil — 2, 17a, 20, 22-23, 25, 28

Kinross

Borker — 7
Guddle — 2
Pinch — 1-7

Angus

Bar — 13
Beakin — 20
Bykin — 13
Crowbar — 6, 17b, 34
Guddle — 20, 22
Jumper — 5a, 37
Lever — 14a
Mannie — 5b
Mell — 14b
Pench — 9
Pick — 1
Pinch — 4, 5c, 6-7, 11-13, 14a, 15, 17a, 20, 22-24, 29a, 31-32, 33ab, 34-37
Punch — 8, 17b, 28, 33b
Trampick — 22
Nil — 2-3, 10, 14cd, 16, 18-19, 21, 25-27, 29b, 30

Perth

Bar — 28
Claw — 73$^+$
Crowbar — 2a, 4-5, 9-10, 12, 17, 24-25, 41a, 71, 74
Deel — 37
Gellick — 3
Gibble — 52c
Gorrel — 49
Guddle — 7, 10-12, 20-21, 25, 27, 29a, 32, 40, 43-44, 46, 49, 52de, 54, 58, 60, 62-63
Gunnel — 57
Janker — 33
Lever — 8$^+$, 30, 50, 56
Levering iron — 26
Lowther — 39
Mell — 41b
Peunch — 25
Pick — 41b
Pike — 71
Pinch (bar) — *9*, 10-13, 15, 19-22, 24-25, 29b, 31-33, 39-40, 44, 46, 48, 51b, 52bce, 53, *55*, 57, 59, 62-65, *66*, 67-69, 73
Poker — 16
Punch — 1, 2b, 3, 7-8, 16, 18, 24, 29a, 45, 72
Spoke — 20
Twa taed — 52c$^+$
Nil — 6, 14, 23, 34-36, 38, 42, 47, 51a, 52a, 61, 70

Fife

Bar — 63
Crowbar — 1, 4, 6, 11, 16-17, 24, 32, 36a, 44c, 50, 55abe, 57
Guddle — 8, 18, 27, 43a
Jemmy — 13, 55d
Jumper — 54
Lever — 43b, 44e
Nail drawer — 9b$^+$
Peever — 43b
Pinch (bar) — 1-2, 4, 7-8, 9ab, 10-12, 14, 19-30, 33, 35, 36b, 37-39, 40b, 41abcd, 42, 43ab, 44abcef, *45*-48, *49*, 51-53, 55*bcdef*, 56, 58-61, *62*, 63, 64ab
Pincher — 55b
Spoke — 3
Spoogel — 24$^+$
Stench — 55b
Nil — 5, 15, 31, 34, 40a, 44d, 55g

Clackmannan

Crowbar — 3
Jimper — 4b
Jumper — 4b
Pinch (bar) — 1-*2*, 5-7
Nil — 4acd

Stirling

Claw lever — 40$^+$
Claw pinch — 30$^+$
Crowbar — 4, 21ab, 26ab, 31, 36
Guddle — 3, 7e
Jemmy — 16, 23b, 35a$^+$
Lever — 35a$^+$, 40
Pinch (bar) — 1-3, 6, 7abdef, 8-13, 15, 17-20, 21ab$^+$, 22a, 23b$^+$c, 24, 25abcd, 26acd, 27ab, 28-*34*, 35ab, 36, 37ab, 39ab, 42a
Punch — 6, 7d, 39b
Nil — 5, 7c, 14, 22b, 23a, 26ef, 38, 41, 42b

Dunbarton

Crowbar — 3, 7c$^+$, 11, 13bc, 14b
Jemmy — 13c$^+$
Peevie — 7b
Pinch — 1-2, 4ab, 5-6, 7ac, 8-10, 13bc, 14a, 15, 16a, 17-18
Nil — 12, 13a, 16b

Argyll

Bar — 5
Claw pinch — 22$^+$
Crowbar — 2, 6-7, 10, 12, 14, 16-17, 22, 25, 27, 35, 37, 39$^+$
Jemmy — 35
Jumper — 6, 33
Lever — 10, 23
Pench — 12, 23
Pinch (bar) — *5*, 8-9, 11, 14-16, 18-19, 22-24, 26-27, 31-32, 35, 38, 40
Punch — 3, 29, 33-34, 39
Nil — 1, 4, 13, 20-21, 28, 30, 36

Bute

Crowbar — 1a, 2
Gemalick — 7
Lever — 8b
Pinch — 1ce, 4, 7, 8ab, 9
Punch — 1a
Nil — 1bd, 3, 5-6

Ayr

Corbie pinch — 18b
Crowbar — 5, 26b, 28e, 56
Dumper — 20b
Flake iron — 28f
Gellick — 45
Lever — 38
Pike — 41
Pinch (bar) — 1a, 2ab, 3-7, 8*a*b, 9-11, 12a, 13-15, 16ab, 17, 18ab, 19, 20acdefgh, 21, 23, 24ab, 26b, 27, 28bdf, 29, 30a, 31-34, 35ab, 36-38, 40-41, 43-52, 53a, 54-57
Winch — 30b
Wire strainer — 42
Nil — 1b, 12b, 22, 25, 26ac, 28ac, 39, 53b

Renfrew

Crowbar — 1b, 2adhi, 11e, 13a, 14a, 18b, 20a
Jemmy — 12b
Lever — 2d
Lever iron — 2i
Pinch (bar) — 1b, 2*b*fgh*j*, 4ac, 5, 7-10, 11abcefijkl, 13abc, 14ab, 15, 16*a*b, 17, 18ab, †19, 20b, 21
Podger — 16b
Purchaser — 15
Nil — 1a, 2ce, 3, 4bde, 6, 11dgh, 12a, 13d, †16cd

Lanark

Claw — 2$^+$
Crookie — 6$^+$
Crossbar — 29g
Crowbar — 1, 6$^+$, 7c, 8a, 29cf, 31a, 35b$^+$cd, 53
Drawbar — 47$^+$
Gellick — 17, 60
Iron — 25c
Iron pinch — 37
Jemmy — 17, 22, 36
Jimmie — 6$^+$, 32f
Lever — 15bc, 20, 29cf, 47, 58
Mell — 38d
Piercer — 60
Pinch (bar) — 1-3, 5-6, 7a, 8b, 9ab, 10a, 11-13, 14bc, 15abc, 16b, 17-21, 23-24, 25ab*c*, 26a*b*, 27b, 29de, 30, 31acd, 32bce, 33acd, 34, 35abd, 38*abcde*, 39-45, 46*ab*c, 47-48, 49b, 50-51, 52b, 55-56, 57ab, 58, 59ab, 60-63, 64b, 65-66, 67ab
Punch — 32e
Swinger — 46b$^+$
Taed pinch — 11$^+$
Toggle baur — 31d
Winch — 32a
Wreckin bar — 6$^+$
Nil — 4, 7b, 10b, 14ad, 16a, 25d, 27a, 28, 29ab, 31b, 32d, 33b, 49a, 52a, 54, 57c, 64a

West Lothian

Bar — 18
Crowbar — 3, 11, 13, 16, 20a
Dug drawer — 6$^+$
Jemmy — 1d, 17a
Jumper — 3
Pinch (bar) — 1ab, *2*, 3-8, 9a, 11-16, 17a, 18, 19ab, 20ab, 21a, 22
Nil — 1c, 9b, 10, 17b, 21b

Midlothian

Clat — 23b$^+$
Claw bar — 14a$^+$
Claw end — 8a$^+$
Crowbar — 1, 6b, 14b, 15, 23b
Fish tail — 8a$^+$
Heel bar — 30
Lever — 4, 18
Pinch (bar) — 1, 3, 6b, 8ab, 10-11, 12ab, 13, 14a, 15-18, 20, 23ab, 24, 25bc, 26a, 27, 29-31, *32*
Punch — 7a
Wedge — †
Nil — 2, 5, 6a, 7b, 9, 19, 21-22, 25ad, 26b, 28

East Lothian

Bar — 6a, 17
Crowbar — 1, 9, 13, 19-21
Heel — 17
Lever — 8, 15-16
Pench — 2, 4b
Pinch (bar) — 3, 4a, 6*b*, 7-8, 11-16, 18

East Lothian cont'd

Nil — 5, 10

Berwick

Bar — 26
Crowbar — 2, 10, 15
Draw pinch — 16c+
Heel bar — 24+, 26
Jimmie — 32
Lever — 1
Piercer — 20, 23, 29, 32
Pinch (bar) — *1,* 3-4, 8-11, 13-14, 16abc, 17-27, 30-32
Punch — 7
Wrecker — 16c+
Nil — 5-6, 12, 28

Peebles

Crowbar — 1
Pinch (bar) — 3, 4b, 5, 6*a*b, 7-8, 10
Pincher — 9
Lever — 2, 4b
Nil — 4ac

Selkirk

Piercer — 4-5, 8
Pinch — 1, 2abde, 3, 6, 8
Nil — 2c, 7

Roxburgh

Crowbar — 21a
Gaylick — 21c
Gylick — 28
Iron lever — 21c
Jemmy — 4
Kinch — 21a
Lever — 9a
Mell — 13
Pick — 14
Piercer — 10
Pinch (bar) — 1-2, 3a, *5,* 6-8, 9a, 12, *15b,* 16-18, 21*d*f, 22-26, 28
Nil — 3b, 9b, 11, 15a, 19-20, 21be, 27

Dumfries

Crowbar — 4, 15, 46
Gaylick — 18, 29
Gelich — 21a
Gellick — 4-5, 8ab, 9, 11-12, 16, 19, 21b, 22-24, 26-27, 29-30, 31ac, 32, 34-35, 42
Gylick — 39
Jemmy — 12+
Jumper — 31c
Peevie — 31b
Pinch (bar) — 1a, 2-7, 8b, 10, 12-14, *16,* 17ab, *18,* 19-20, 21ab, 22-30, 31cde, 32-34, *35-36,* 37-38, 40-43, *44,* 45a, *46* 47, 49
Nil — 1b, 31f, 45b, 48

Kirkcudbright

Gelick — 15b
Gellick — 1-8, 10-11, 12ab, 13-14, 15a, 16-19, 21abc, 22-24, 26-27
Pinch — 1-2, 8-9, 14, 15ab, 17, 19, 26-27
Till ern — 17
Till iron — 6
Nil — 20, 25

Wigtown

Gellick — 1
Gillick — 7
Pinch — 1-4, 5ab, 6, 8-11, 14-15, 17
Straining bar — 9+
Till ern — 12-13
Tillie ern — 10, 12, 14, 16, 18
Tillie iron — 3
Till iron — 5ab, 8, 11, 15

Northumberland

Bar — 30
Case opener — 69a+b+
Claw crowbar — 41c+
Claw ended pinch — 139+
Claw hammer — 76+
Crow — 16+, 57, 95a, 126f
Crowbar — 2b, 5, 28, 30, 35, 40a, 41c, 42+, 45+, 53b, 59b, 61, 69b, 71b, 72cg, 77, 86-87, 95b, 99d, 101b, 103ac, 124b, 127ag, 130b
Gavelick — 44, 62f, 69a, 74, 77, 103b, 127c, 141
Geerielick — 142
Geevalick — 134
Geevlick — 107, 132-133, 136
Gylick — 53a
Gyvlick — 69a
Handspike — 95b
Jemmy — 69c, 72e, 76, 117, 126ad
Jimmie — 130e
Jumper — 142
Lever — 81, 87, 92, 111a
Lick — 127c
Nail drawer — 69b+, 109+, 141+
Neavlick — 140
Paise — 124a
Pench — 8
Piercer — 51
Pig's foot — 72j+
Pinch (bar) — 1ab, 2a, 3-4, *6,* 7, 9-11, 13-18, 19ab, 20ab, 21-22, 24ab, 25-28, 29abcdef, 31, 33ab, 34ab, 35-36, *37,* 38-*39, 40a,* 41abc*d, 43,* 42-47, *48,* 49, *50-52, 53a, 54,* 55, *56-57,* 58, 59bcdef, 60, 62a*g,* 64ab, 65a, 66, 68, 69*abd*egh, 70, 71bc*d,* 72b*dgij,* 73, *74,* 75, *76,* 77, *78,* 79-80, *81,* 82-84, 86, 88ab, 89-91, 93, 94b, 96, 98, *100, 101a,* 103abc, 104*a*b, 106-107, 108*a*c, *109*-110, 111*ab,* 112, 114, *118b,* 120*abc,* 122a, 124a, *125,* 126ce, 127eg, *128, 129b, 130c,* 132-133, *134-135,* 136-140, *141,* 142, *143*
Pinch and drawer — 13+
Pitch bar — 105
Post hadder — 76+
Priser — 79+
Split pinch — 135+
Wrecking bar — 76
Wrencher — 126c+
Nil — 1c, 12, 23, 32, 40b, 59a, 62bcdeh, 63, 65b, 67, 69f, 71ae, 72afhkl, 85, 94a, 97, 99abc, 102, 108b, 113, 115-116, 118a, 119, 121, 122b, 123, 126b, 127bdfh, 129ac, 130adf, 131

Cumberland

Bar — 57
Claw — 44+
Claw ended (crow) bar — 57+
Clinch bar — 2+
Crowbar — 7, 9, 12, 23-24, 26, 46, 53, 56-58
Dog bar — 56
Gaovelick — 16
Gavelet — 47
Gaviller — 54
Gaylick — 13c
Gayvlick — 1a, 2-3, 7, 10, 13d, 17, 19, 22, 25, 31-32, 34-36, 39-41, 48, 55, 59-61, 63ab
Gearlick — 18
Geavelick — 20, 30, 37b, 40, 44, 52, 56, 62
Geavlick — 3, 5ab, 9, 12, 13a, 15ab, 21, 27-28, 33, 38+, 45, 56
Gellick — 14
Gevlick — 23, 42
Givlick — 4, 13c
Gyavlick — 11, 15c, 24, 26, 46, 49, 53, 57
Gyelick — 3, 13b
Gyvlick — 8
Heelbar — 56
Javelick — 25
Javelin — 47
Jimmie — 43
Pinch (bar) — *4, 5a,* 6, *12,* 13a, *24, 26, 31+, 46+, 54+, 61-62+*
Pincher — 50
Podger — 41
Prowk bar — 56
Ring bar — 56
Tommie bar — 41
Nil — 1b, 29, 37a, 51

Down

Bar — 2a, 4, 15+
Crowbar — 2a, 5, 7, 9, 15, 18-19, 24, 26, 28
Jimmie — 21
Pinch bar — 2b, 10+, 22
Sheriff — 24+
Small bar — 10+
Till bar — 12
Till iron — 13
Nil — 1, 3, 6, 8, 11, 14, 16-17, 20, 23, 25, 27, 29-30

Tyrone

Bar — 1
Crowbar — 1, 6-8, 10-11, 15
Jack — 6
Pinch (bar) — 1, *11+, 15*
Sheriff — 5
Nil — 2-4, 9, 12-14, 16

Antrim

Bar — 9
Craw iron — 23, 28, 33
Crow — 8b
Crowbar — 1, 3, 5a, 13, 17, 19-20, 22, 25-26, 31
Crow iron — 1, 4A, 5b, 16b
Pinch bar — 7, 23+
Shifter — 34
Shifting bar — 34
Shirif — 5b+
Nil — 2, 4, 6, 8a, 10-12, 14-15, 16ac, 18, 21, 24, 27, 29-30, 32

Donegal

Bar — 3, 7
Crow — 6
Crowbar — 1, 3-5, 5A, 8, 10a, 12
Iron crow — 6
Lifter — 10a
Pinch (bar) — 3, *11+*
Nil — 1A, 2, 7A, 9, 10b, 13

Fermanagh

Crow — 2
Crowbar — 2, 4-5, 7a, 9
Forked crowbar — 9+
Pinch bar — 5
Nil — 1, 3, 6, 7b, 8, 10

Armagh

Crowbar — 6a
Nil — 1-5, 6b

Londonderry

Crowbar — 2, 3A, 6
Nail puller — 3A+
Pinch (bar) — 6
Nil — 1, 1Ab, 3-5, 7

45 DITCH (e.g., alongside a country road) (PQ1, 105)

(1) Note the recurrence of similar or identical target items in 46-50. Where they occur in these items, Variants of sheuCH and shuCH (some spellings with "-gh") have been subsumed.
(2) **Ditch** has not been mapped as it occurs in considerable concentration nearly everywhere.

Some variants of DITCH have been subsumed (**dutch** Caithness, Aberdeenshire, Kincardineshire, Angus, East Lothian; a few **detch** in Aberdeenshire and Fife).

A raised + symbol after a locality number in Northern Ireland means that the informant pointed out that 45 **ditch** referred to a (stone) wall or fence.

Shetland
Ditch — 15-17, 29-30, 32
Drain — 1, 7, 10, 17, 21a, 22
Side ditch — 20
Side drain — 32
Stank — 2-11, 13-15, 17-19, 21ab, 22-31, 33
Stripe — 15
Trench — 23
Nil — 12

Orkney
Ditch — 2-5, 7, 9, 11, 13ab, 17, 19-20
Drain — 4, 12, 15
Grip — 10, 13b
Road ditch — 16
Side ditch — 8, 15
Side drain — 1-2, 8, 21
Nil — 6, 14, 18

Caithness
Ditch — 2ab, 5-6, 8, 10-11, 12abc, 13-14, 16b, 17
Drain — 7
Side drain — 3, 8-9, 11, 12b, 13, 15
Nil — 1, 4, 16a

Sutherland
Ditch — 1, 4-5, 8, 11, 13, 16
Drain — 1, 4, 15, 17
Side drain — 2-3, 5-8, 9ab, 10-13, 15
Nil — 14

Ross & Cromarty
Ditch — 1, 3-6, 8-9, 11, 13-14, 16-17, 19, 22-24, 25a, 26-29, 32b, 33, 36, 37b
Drain — 11-12, 16-18, 20, 25b, 26-27, 29, 32bc, 33-34, 37a, 38-39
Drainer — 20
Side drain — 2, 5, 10, 12, 21, 24, 32a
Side dren — 31
Nil — 7, 15, 30, 35

Inverness
Ditch — 1-5, 7-8, 10-11, 13abce, 19-20, 21b, 22-23, 26-29, 32-35, 37-38, 40
Drain — 1, 3, 6, 8-9, 11, 13cd, 14, 16-18, 20, 21a, 24, 26, 30-31, 33, 36, 39
Side ditch — 13e
Side drain — 25, 38
Nil — 12, 15

Nairn
Birnie — 4
Ditch — 1a, 2
Drain — 5
Drainie — 1c
Side drain — 6
Nil — 1b, 3

Moray
Burn — 16
Ditch — 2a, 4-5, 6b, 7, 8bcde, 9b, 14, 18-23
Runnel — 6a
Sheuch — 1
Stran — 8d
Stripe — 18
Trenkie — 9a
Nil — 2b, 3, 8af, 10-13, 15, 17

Banff
Burn — 30
Burnie — 6b
Ditch — 1, 2ab, 3-5, 6b, 7-9, 13, 15-17, 18c, 19-21, 23-26, 30, 32, 34
Shauch — 10
Sheuck — 14
Stank — 6b, 11
Stripie — 14
Trink — 31
Trinkie — 31
Nil — 2c, 6a, 12, 18abd, 22, 27-29, 33

Aberdeen
Burn — 51, 59
Ditch — 1-2, 3ab, 4, 5bcd, 6, 8-10, 12-14, 16-21, 26, 28ac, 29-31, 33-39, 41-46, 47abdef, 48-50, 53, 56, 58, 61-63, 66-67, 69-70, 71bc, 72-75, 77, 79-84, 88-89, 91, 94-95, 97-108
Fell dyke — 47c
Roadside ditch — 22-23, 32
Stank — 5d, 6-7, 14, 28a, 42, 46, 71abc, 76, 97
Stankie — 14, 101
Stran — 75
Stripe — 23, 28b, 53
Stripie — 14, 75
Stunk — 27, 105
Wa' lat — 25
Wee burnie — 29
Nil — 5a, 11, 15, 24, 40, 52, 54-55, 57, 60, 64-65, 68, 78, 85-87, 90, 92-93, 96, 109

Kincardine
Burn — 16, 18
Burnie — 23
Conduit — 24
Ditch — 1, 3-8, 10-16, 17abcd, 18-19, 21, 24, 26-28
Nil — 2, 9, 20, 22, 25

Kinross
Ditch — 2-3, 6
Pow — 2
Sheuch — 1, 3-4,
Shuch — 5
Stank — 2
Nil — 7

Angus
Burn — 22, 28, 30
Ditch — 1-4, 5a, 6-10, 12-13, 14ac, 15, 17ab, 18, 20, 24-25, 29a, 31-32, 33b, 34-37
Drain — 15, 17b
Dren — 19
Nil — 5bc, 11, 14bd, 16, 21, 23, 26-27, 29b, 33a

Perth
Afflet — 73
Burn — 30
Ditch — 1, 2a, 4-5, 7-10, 12-13, 15, 17, 20-21, 25, 27-28, 29a, 31-33, 36, 39-40, 41a, 45-46, 48, 50, 51ab, 52ace, 57, 60, 64-65, 67, 71-74
Drain — 2b, 8-9, 13-14, 18, 25, 29b, 36, 41b, 67
Open drain — 43, 55
Pow — 25, 57, 59
Sheuch — 25, 37, 50, 52b, 56, 66, 69
Shooch — 16
Shuch — 40, 44, 62, 68
Shuck — 12
Side ditch — 24
Side drain — 3, 16, 24
Nil — 6, 11, 19, 22-23, 26, 34-35, 38, 42, 47, 49, 52d, 53-54, 58, 61, 63, 70

Fife
Burn — 3, 13
Dishel — 39, 55d, 60
Ditch — 1, 4, 6-8, 9a, 11, 14, 16-17, 19, 21, 23-25, 28, 30, 32-33, 36b, 37-38, 40b, 41abd, 42, 43a, 44ace, 46-50, 53-54, 55abe, 56-57, 62-63, 64a
Dyke — 10, 47
Gotten — 37, 39, 41b, 50
Gully — 59
Heuch — 37, 58
Sheuch — 7, 12, 23, 29, 39, 44a, 51, 53, 55f, 61, 64b
Shoogh — 55b
Shuch — 41a, 44e, 55b
Stank — 20
Trench — 36a, 44b, 56
Trink — 27
Trinket — 36a
Nil — 2, 5, 9b, 15, 18, 22, 26, 31, 34-35, 40a, 41c, 43b, 44df, 45, 52, 55cg

Clackmannan
Burn — 4b
Ditch — 1-3, 4c, 6-7
Drain — 4d
Sheuch — 4d, 6
Shuch — 5, 7
Shuck — 7
Nil — 4a

Stirling
Burn — 7f, 17
Ditch — 4, 7ce, 11, 13, 16, 18, 21ab, 26acd, 28-31, 34, 35a, 36, 40-41
Drain — 7b
Dyke — 20, 25c, 26ad
Gote — 21b, 29-31
Gotten — 17, 19
Gutter — 26f
Pow — 23c
Sheoch — 7b
Sheuch — 3, 6, 7abde, 8-9, 12-14, 17-18, 22ab, 23ab, 25ad, 26ace, 27a, 30-33, 35ab, 37ab, 39a, 40, 42ab
Shuch — 2, 15, 25bc, 26bd, 27b, 30, 38, 39b
Stank — 7d
Trench — 27b
Nil — 1, 5, 10, 24

Dunbarton
Ditch — 1, 7bc, 8, 10-11, 13abc, 16b
Drain — 5, 18
Dyke — 5, 13b
Gotten — 13c
Sheuch — 1, 4ab, 5-6, 10, 13abc, 14ab, 15, 16ab
Shough — 3
Shuch — 2, 4a, 8-9
Nil — 7a, 12, 17

Argyll
Ditch — 1-3, 5, 8, 10-12, 14-17, 19, 22-25, 27, 30, 34-35, 38
Drain — 8, 10, 38
Gutter — 12
Road ditch — 6
Sheuch — 12, 18-19, 32-33, 39-40
Shuch — 26, 28, 30, 36-37
Side drain — 3, 5, 7, 9, 11, 14
Stank — 31-33, 35, 40
Strand — 11
Nil — 4, 13, 20-21, 29

Bute
Burn — 1b
Ditch — 1a, 2, 7, 8b
Dyke — 7
Schuch — 1e
Sheuch — 1acd, 3-4, 8a, 9
Shuch — 7, 8b
Shuck — 5
Nil — 6

Ayr
Cundie — 1b, 9
Ditch — 8b, 11, 15, 21, 26b, 28e, 43, 45, 57
Drain — 45
Glaur hole — 38
Gotten — 54
Heuch — 53b
Open drain — 43
Puddle hole — 38
Scheuch — 28e
Sheuch — 1a, 2ab, 3-6, 8ab, 9-11, 12ab, 13-15, 16ab, 17, 18ab, 19, 20abcdefgh, 22, 24ab, 26c, 28abcdf, 29, 30ab, 31-34, 35ab, 36, 39-42, 44-52, 53ab, 54-57
Shuch — 7, 14, 21, 23, 27, 30b, 48
Siver — 1b
Stank — 32
Trench — 43
Nil — 25, 26a, 37

Renfrew
Burn — 11i, 16a
Ditch — 2adhij, 4ac, 11abce, 13c, 16b, 18b, 20a
Drain — 1b
Gully — 16a
Gutter — 4d
Open drain — 11j
Schuch — 10
Sheuch — 2befg, 3, 4d, 7-9, 11efil, 12a, 13ab, 14a, 16c, 17, 18ab, 19, 20b, 21
Shough — 15
Shuch — 2a, 5, 9, 11abl
Nil — 1a, 2c, 4be, 6, 11dghk, 12b, 13d, 14b, 16d

Lanark
Burn — 6
Cundie — 15c
Ditch — 1-2, 7ac, 12, 14bd, 15ac, 16ab, 18, 24, 25bc, 26b, 29cf, 31d, 35cd, 36, 39-40, 44-45, 47, 49ab, 51, 52b, 53, 60-61
Drain — 15a
Dyke — 32e
Dykeside — 46c
Got — 6
Gote — 5-6
Gotten — 13, 27b
Gutter — 29f

Lanark cont'd

Hopen drain — 37
Sheuch — 1, 7ac, 8b, 9ab, 10ab, 11-12, 14c, 15b, 16b, 17-22, 24, 25ac, 26a, 27ab, 29cde, 30, 31abcd, 32cdf, 33a, 35abd, 38acde, 39-41, 43, 46abc, 47, 49b, 50, 52a, 55-56, 57c, 58, 59ab, 63, 65-66, 67a
Shooch — 42
Shough — 67b
Shuch — 3, 8a, 23, 31c, 32ag, 38b, 44, 48, 49a, 54, 57ab, 62, 64ab
Shuck — 3
Stank — 13, 17
Trench — 29f
Nil — 4, 7b, 14a, 25d, 28, 29abg, 32b, 33b, 34

West Lothian

Burn — 10
Ditch — 1c, 3, 6-8, 9ab, 10-11, 13, 15-16, 17a, 22
Drain — 13
Dyke — 3, 16
Gotten — 11
Heuch — 1d
Lead — 6
Sheuch — 1abc, 2, 5, 7, 12, 17a, 18, 19b, 20ab, 21a
Shuch — 4, 14-15
Syke — 8
Nil — 17b, 19a, 21b

Midlothian

Burn — 20
Ditch — 6a, 7a, 8a, 9-11, 12b, 14ab, 15, 17-19, 21-22, 23ab, 24, 25b, 27-29, 32
Drain — 25c
Dyke — 23a, 26b
Gundie — 31
Gutter — 17
Open drain — 1, 10
Seuch — 7b
Sheuch — 8b, 10, 12a, 14a, 18, 24, 26a, 30
Shooch — 3
Shuch — 4, 13, 16, 21, 23b, 32
Nil — 2, 5, 6b, 25ad

East Lothian

Cundie — 4a, 13, 15
Ditch — 1, 4b, 5, 6b, 7-9, 11, 15-16, 18-21
Dyke — 6a
Gutter — 17
Runnel — 21
Sheuch — 2-3, 4ab
Shuch — 14
Nil — 10, 12

Berwick

Cundie — 11, 17
Ditch — 1-2, 6-10, 13, 15, 16abc, 19, 21, 23, 26, 29, 31-32
Drain — 2, 12, 22, 31
Dry burn — 8
Dyke — 23
Dyke back — 8
Open drain — 23
Runner — 27
Sheuch — 17
Shough — 21
Shuch — 16a, 18
Siver — 27
Nil — 3-5, 14, 20, 24-25, 28, 30

Peebles

Ditch — 2-3, 4b, 6b
Drain — 10
Runnel — 2
Sheuch — 6a, 8
Shuch — 1, 3, 5, 7, 9-10
Nil — 4ac

Selkirk

Ditch — 2bcde, 6, 8
Drain — 2a, 4, 8
Shough — 5
Nil — 1, 3, 7

Roxburgh

Burn — 6, 9b
Cundie — 4, 26
Ditch — 1-2, 3a, 4-5, 7, 9a, 10, 13, 15b, 16, 21acf, 23
Drain — 4, 8, 19, 25
Dyke seuch — 28
Seuch — 28
Shuch — 1
Syke — 3b, 9b, 17, 21d
Nil — 11-12, 14, 15a, 18, 20, 21be, 22, 24, 27

Dumfries

Culvert — 42
Ditch — 1a, 4, 8a, 15, 17ab, 18, 22, 24, 27-28, 31bd, 32-33, 37, 40, 45a, 46-47
Drain — 4, 8b, 12
Dyke — 38
Got — 31b
Grip — 4
Open drain — 46
Roadside ditch — 43
Seugh — 29
Sheuch — 1a, 3-4, 6, 9-12, 16, 19, 23, 26, 28, 34-35, 39, 41-42, 46
Shooch — 5, 25
Shoogh — 20
Shough — 13
Shuch — 21a, 26, 31e, 45b
Shuech — 7
Siver — 2
Syke — 5
Syre — 22
Nil — 1b, 14, 30, 31acf, 36, 44, 48-49

Kirkcudbright

Ditch — 10, 12b, 18-20, 21abc, 22-23, 27
Drain — 1, 6, 18, 26
Sheuch — 1-8, 12a, 15a, 16-17, 21c, 24, 26
Shuch — 13
Stank — 16
Nil — 9, 11, 14, 15b, 25

Wigtown

Ditch — 3, 5a, 12
Drain — 7
Gullion hole — 5b
Heugh — 7
Road heugh — 13
Road Sheuch — 11
Sheuch — 1-2, 4, 5b, 7-10, 14, 16-18
Shuch — 6
Stank — 2-3, 6, 17
Water table — 6
Nil — 15

Northumberland

Back ditch — 75, 103bc, 104b, 142
Beck — 29c, 140
Borne — 83, 101b
Burn — 11, 58, 72i, 116
Cundie — 45-46, 53b, 57, 59d, 99a, 135
Ditch — 1a, 2ab, 3, 5-6, 8-9, 13, 16-18, 19a, 20b, 22, 26, 29ab, 30-31, 35-37, 40a, 41cd, 43, 45, 52, 53a, 56, 59b, 62b, 64b, 65a, 66, 68, 69bcdeh, 70, 71ad, 72abcdegi, 73, 77, 86-87, 88b, 91, 93, 101b, 106, 111b, 112, 119, 120bc, 121, 126cf, 127a, 129b, 130bce.
Drain — 21, 26, 30, 34b, 42, 44, 46, 54-56, 59c, 68, 69c, 104b
Dyke — 12, 14, 25, 29d, 33b, 47-48, 59acef, 62eh, 64a, 65b, 67, 71bce, 72bcikl, 76, 79, 83, 89, 94ab, 98, 99bcd, 111a, 117, 120c, 122b, 124ab, 125, 126def, 127abc, 128, 129bc, 130ef
Dyke back — 111b
Dyke bottom — 82
Dyke side — 38, 50, 92, 97, 126e
Gully — 87, 130c
Gut — 126b
Gutter — 9, 29ab, 30, 33b, 34a, 35, 37, 39, 41d, 45-46, 49, 53a, 54, 57-58, 59bc, 60, 62a, 64ab, 69abe, 72deg, 73-74, 76-78, 80-84, 88a, 89-90, 93, 95ab, 96, 99a, 100, 102, 104a, 105, 108c, 109, 111b, 113-114, 117, 118ab, 120a, 122ab, 123, 126a, 127h, 130cd, 132, 137-141, 143
Hedge — 91
Let — 69a
Letch — 69a, 124a
Open ditch — 140
Open drain — 28
Road seyde — 111ab
Runner — 47, 77, 103b
Seauch — 103c
Seeaf — 132-133, 135
See erf — 142
Seugh — 51
Stream — 58
Syke — 25, 37, 52, 53b, 56-57, 61, 74, 79, 103abc, 104b, 105, 107, 108a, 110 112, 133-134, 136, 142
Syre — 10
Nil — 1bc, 4, 7, 15, 19b, 20a, 23, 24ab, 27, 29ef, 32, 33a, 40b, 41ab, 62cdfg, 63, 69fg, 72fhj, 85, 101a, 108b, 115, 127defg, 129a, 130a, 131

Cumberland

Beck — 58
Chennel — 37b
Ditch — 3, 9, 23-26, 40, 46, 52-53, 56-58
Dyke — 14, 35, 42, 60
Dyke boddom — 63b
Dyke bottom — 12
Dyke gutter — 27
Dyke side — 63b
Greup — 17
Gully — 38
Gutter — 1b, 2, 4, 5ab, 6-9, 12, 13cd, 15abc, 16-20, 22, 24, 26, 28-29, 31-34, 36, 37ab, 39-40, 43-45, 47-50, 52-54, 56-59, 61-62
Runnel — 30, 42
Seeof — 3
Seugh — 1b, 3, 13b
Sough — 1a, 7, 9, 11, 35, 44, 47, 56
Sow — 1ab, 11, 29-30, 60
Storm water ditch — 46
Syke — 21, 30, 37a, 38, 41
Syre — 30
Nil — 10, 13a, 51, 55, 63a

Down

Ditch — 2a, 8^{+}, 12^{+}, 15
Dyke — 2a, 3, 5, 7-8^{+}, 10, 13
Road — 28
Sheogh — 25
Sheuch — 2b, 6-7, 12-14, 18, 21, 23-25, 27, 29
Shouch — 19
Shough — 9, 16-17, 28
Shuch — 14, 24^{+}, 26, 30^{+}
Nil — 1, 4, 11, 20, 22

Tyrone

Bank — 11
Dake — 5, 7
Deek — 1-2
Ditch — 7-8, 11^{+}, 14, 16^{+}
Dyke — 7
Fence — 9
Hedge — 8
Sheuch — 3-4, 6^{+}, 12^{+}, 14
Shough — 2, 15
Nil — 10, 13

Antrim

Bunker — 13, 19^{+}, 21
Dake — 3-4, 9
Deck — 5b
Ditch — 1, 25^{+}, 29
Dyke — 1, 10-11, 14, 17, 25^{+}, 26, 28, 31, 33
Gatten — 7
Sheuch — 2, 7, 8ab, 15, 16ab, 18, 27-28
Shough — 5b, 6, 12, 18-19^{+}, 22, 32
Shuch — 20, 23
Shuck — 34
Sod dyke — 19^{+}
Trinket — 5a
Nil — 4A, 16c, 24, 30

Donegal

Broad — 2
Dake — 8
Dake merin — 6
Deek — 4, 7
Ditch — 1, 3, 5, 8
Dyke — 3, 12
Hedge — 5A
Sheuch — 5, 10a^{+}
Shough — 3, 11, 13^{+}
Shuch — 9, 12
Sod ditch — 10b
Stone ditch — 10b
Thorn ditch — 10b
Water table — 7A, 13^{+}
Nil — 1A

Fermanagh

Drain — 4, 9-10
Hedge — 1
Road drain — 4^{+}
Sheuch — 3, 5-6, 10
Shough — 2
Shuck — 7a
Trinket — 2
Water channel — 2
Water table — 4^{+}
Nil — 7b, 8

Armagh

Sheuch — 1, 4 5^{+}, 6b
Shough — 2, 6a
Shuck — 3

Londonderry

Deek — 1
Ditch — 3A
Drain — 5
Dyke — 1A
Sheuch — 1, 1B, 2, 4, 6^{+}-7^{+}
Shough — 5
Shuch — 3

46 GUTTER (the kind running along the side of a paved street) (PQ1, 106)

Gutter has not been mapped as it occurs in some concentration nearly everywhere except in Shetland. Variants of GUTTER have been subsumed (**guitter** Roxburghshire; a few **gitter, gaetter** Fife). See also note (1) on 45 **ditch.**

Shetland

Drain — 2, 5, 17, 21b, 22
Gutter — 10, 32
Runnock — 12, 21a, 22
Stank — 20
Stripe — 14
Nil — 1, 3-4, 6-9, 11, 13, 15-16, 18-19, 23-31, 33

Orkney

Ditch — 19
Drain — 9, 19
Gutter — 2-5, 8, 11, 13a, 15, 20-21
Rinnel — 13a
Rinnick — 16
Rinnie — 2
Rino — 7
Runnack — 18
Runnel — 7
Runner hole — 6
Vennel — 13a
Nil — 1, 10, 12, 13b, 14, 17

Caithness

Cundie — 12c
Drain — 13
Gutter — 2a, 8, 13-14
Muck — 4
Stran — 6, 12abc, 15, 17
Strand — 3
Strannie — 2ab, 16ab
Nil — 1, 5, 7, 9-11, 15

Sutherland

Drain — 10, 15-16
Drainer — 15
Gutter — 1, 3-4, 12-13, 16
Stran — 9ab, 10, 16
Nil — 2, 5-8, 11, 14, 17

Ross & Cromarty

Drain — 18-19, 36
Drainer — 9, 14
Gut ridge — 37a
Gutter — 1, 3-5, 8-9, 16-17, 20, 23-24, 25ab, 27, 29, 32ab, 34, 39
Side drain — 2, 13, 24, 36
Stripe — 25b
Trink — 15
Trinkie — 37b
Nil — 6-7, 10-12, 21-22, 26, 28, 30-31, 32c, 33, 35, 38

Inverness

Channel — 13e
Dirt — 5
Drain — 6, 13e, 20, 29, 32, 35
Gutter — 2-4, 7-10, 13abc, 16-19, 21ab, 22-23, 28, 30, 34, 37-40
Kennel — 26
Sewer — 26
Strawn — 27
Nil — 1, 11-12, 13d, 14-15, 24-25, 31, 33, 36

Nairn

Drainie — 5
Gutter — 1a, 6
Kerb — 2
Strannie — 1abc
Nil — 3-4

Moray

Channel — 6a
Cuddie — 9a, 22
Cundie — 9a
Dreep — 18
Greep — 18
Gutter — 2a, 5, 7, 14, 20, 23
Stran — 2a, 3-4, 8cde, 13, 17-18
Strand — 8a
Strannie — 6a, 8b, 12-13, 21-22
Strawn — 8a
Strin — 9b, 10, 19
Strun — 1, 7, 16
Strunnie — 3-4
Nil — 2b, 6b, 8f, 11, 15

Banff

Cassie — 10
Drain — 9
Dreep — 14
Greep — 4
Gutter — 2a, 6b, 21, 30, 34
Rhone — 33
Stran — 1, 4, 6b, 8, 15-16, 18bd, 23-24, 29, 31
Strand — 18c, 23, 25
Strannie — 2c, 6a, 7, 9, 11, 15, 17, 28, 32
Strawn — 5, 26
Strawnie — 11
Strin — 2b, 3, 6b, 13
Stripie — 3
Nil — 12, 18a, 19-20, 22, 27

Aberdeen

Channon — 56
Chunnel — 106
Drain — 70
Dreep — 75
Greep — 25
Gutter — 2, 3ab, 6, 9, 14, 20-21, 23, 26, 28ac, 31-32, 34, 36, 43-46, 47abef, 50, 53, 59, 66, 69-70, 71b, 73, 81-83, 88, 94-95, 98, 100, 103-105, 107
Sewer — 47c
Stran — 5d, 11, 16, 28ab, 29, 51, 65, 73, 75, 80, 105, 108
Strand — 67, 101
Strannie — 5b, 12, 22, 48, 106
Strawn — 71a, 85
Strawnie — 85, 96
Strin — 4
Stripe — 5c, 11, 18
Stripie — 62
Trinkie — 17
Nil — 1, 5a, 7-8, 10, 13, 15, 19, 24, 27, 30, 33, 35, 37-42, 47d, 49, 52, 54-55, 57-58, 60-61, 63-64, 68, 71c, 72, 74, 76-79, 84, 86-87, 89-93, 97, 99, 102, 109

Kincardine

Alley — 8
Culvert — 20
Gutter — 1, 3, 5-7, 10-12, 16, 17bcd, 19, 21, 24, 26, 28
Stank — 14
Stran — 17a
Strand — 6, 15, 17bd, 18, 22
Strandie — 25
Trank — 14
Trink — 12
Trinkie — 23
Nil — 2, 4, 9, 13, 27

Kinross

Channel — 4
Gutter — 1-3, 5-6
Sheuch — 7
Siver — 7
Strand — 5
Strawnd — 3

Angus

Channel — 14ad, 22, 34
Cribbie — 19, 29a
Cundie — 1, 22, 25, 34
Curb — 12
Ditch — 1
Grape — 5b
Gutter — 2, 4, 6-10, 13, 14abc, 15, 17b, 18, 23-24, 30, 32, 33b, 34, 36-37
Kerb — 24
Kirb and channel — 33b
Siever — 17a
Strand — 5c, 8, 14a, 17b, 18, 22, 28, 31, 33b, 35, 37
Syre — 5a
Trinkie — 10
Nil — 3, 11, 16, 20-21, 26-27, 29b, 33a

Perth

Channel — 25, 52e, 60
Condie — 62
Cundie — 57
Drain — 9
Dub — 25
Glaur — 29b
Gully — 12, 48, 51b
Gutter — 1, 2a, 4-5, 8, 10, 12-13, 15-16, 20-21, 25, 27-28, 29a, 32-33, 39-40, 41a, 46, 50, 52ae, 53, 57, 64, 74
Runnel — 25
Sheuch — 10, 71
Shochie — 65
Shuch — 55, 70, 72
Sifer — 66, 69
Siver — 52b, 68
Sivver — 71
Skew — 73
Stank — 62-63
Stran — 43
Strand — 16, 25, 32-33, 48, 50, 52d, 62, 67, 69
Stripe — 41b
Nil — 2b, 3, 6-7, 11, 14, 17-19, 22-24, 26, 30-31, 34-38, 42, 44-45, 47, 49, 51a, 52c, 54, 56, 58-59, 61

Fife

Channel — 3, 40b, 44cf
Condie — 8, 12
Cribbie — 12
Cundie — 12
Dishel — 38-39, 40a, 41ad, 43a, 44cf, 46-47, 49, 59
Dishet — 64a
Dushel — 43b
Gawten — 12, 43a, 45-46
Gully — 6
Gushel — 36a, 39, 45-49, 55adef, 59-60
Gutter — 1, 4, 6-8, 9a, 10-11, 13, 16-21, 24-25, 28, 32, 36ab, 37-38, 41ab, 42, 44abcdef, 47-50, 52-53, 55abdeg, 56-58, 62-63
Runnel — 23, 55c
Sheuch — 44f, 53
Shuch — 46, 55c
Siver — 51, 56
Strand — 12, 18, 21, 23, 33, 40b, 44b, 61
Strawn — 35
Strawnd — 9b, 12, 14, 19, 21, 33, 40a, 46, 49-50, 64b
Trinket — 54, 55f
Water shed — 18
Nil — 2, 5, 15, 22, 26-27, 29-31, 34, 41c

Clackmannan

Gully — 6
Gutter — 3, 4c, 6
Run channel — 1, 4bc, 7
Runnel — 4b
Sheuch — 4ad
Siver — 1-2, 4a, 5

Stirling

Channel — 6, 25b
Condie — 7a
Crib — 9
Cribbie — 26c
Cundie — 7a
Gutter — 2, 4, 7c, 11-13, 16, 21ab, 23b, 25c, 26ad, 29-31, 34, 35a, 36, 37ab, 38, 40
Kerb — 26c
Run channel — 4, 7f
Seuch — 10
Sheaugh — 10
Sheuch — 17-18, 20, 21a, 22b, 25a, 26e, 33, 42a
Shuch — 16, 23c, 24, 27b, 38, 39b
Siver — 7abcde, 8-9, 12, 18-19, 22ab, 25abd, 26bd, 27ab, 28-29, 32, 34, 39b
Nil — 1, 3, 5, 14-15, 23a, 26f, 35b, 41, 42b

Dunbarton

Drain — 11
Gotten — 13b
Gully — 7b
Gush — 15
Gutter — 3, 6, 7c, 8-11, 13abc, 16b, 18
Runnel — 2, 5
Sheuch — 4b, 6, 7ac, 12, 13c, 16a, 18
Shuch — 7b
Siver — 1, 5, 9, 14ab, 16a, 17
Nil — 4a

Argyll

Channel — 33
Drain — 2, 18, 24
Grip — 18
Gutter — 1-3, 6-7, 10, 12, 14, 16-19, 22-23, 27, 30, 33-35, 37
Sheuch — 32, 34-35
Shuch — 26, 28, 30-31, 36
Side drain — 11
Nil — 4-5, 8-9, 13, 15, 20-21, 25, 29, 38-40

Bute

Gutter — 1acde, 7, 8a
Sheuch — 1cd
Siver — 2-3
Nil — 1b, 4-6, 8b, 9

Ayr

Channel — 57
Conduit — 57
Gutter — 1a, 5-7, 8ab, 9, 11, 12a, 13-14, 17, 21, 26b, 28e, 43, 57
Sheuch — 1b, 2a, 8b, 9, 15, 16a, 20g, 25, 31, 35ab, 36-37, 40, 43
Shouch — 37
Shuch — 14, 21, 38
Sipher — 32
Siver — 1a, 2ab, 3-4, 7, 8ab, 9,

Ayr cont'd
12b, 15, 16ab, 18ab, 19, 20abcdefgh, 21-22, 24ab, 25, 26abc, 27, 28abcdef, 29, 30ab, 31, 33-34, 35b, 36, 39, 41-52, 53ab, 54, 56-57
Strand — 1a, 19
Nil — 10, 23, 55

Renfrew
Crib — 11i
Cundie — 14b
Drain — 12b
Goat — 17
Gutter — 1b, 2adhi, 4ace, 5, 10, 11abde, 13c, 16b, 18ab, 19, 20a
Runnel — 2e, 21
Sheuch — 1b, 2fj, 3, 4d, 11i, 13bc, 14ab, 17, 18b
Shough — 2i
Shuch — 2d, 13d, 16d
Siver — 2b, 9, 11adej, 13a, 14b, 15, 16c, 18b, 20ab, 21
Strand — 16a
Straw — 16a
Strawn — 8, 11abcfkl, 12a, 13c, 14b, 18b
Trench — 16a
Nil — 1a, 2cg, 4b, 6-7, 11gh

Lanark
Channel — 10b, 16b, 29e, 35b, 45
Cribbing — 23
Cundie — 32c, 54, 57a
Drain — 25d, 59b, 67b
Gatten — 67a
Gully — 12-13, 48
Gundie — 39
Gutter — 1, 5-6, 7c, 14bd, 15bc, 17, 20-21, 26b, 29c, 31ad, 35bd, 39, 45, 46a, 48, 49ab, 53, 56, 58, 59b, 65
Kerb — 14d
Open pen — 46b
Sheuch — 6, 7a, 12-13, 14ad, 15abc, 16ab, 17-18, 23, 25cd, 26a, 27ab, 28, 29cfg, 30, 31bd, 32bd, 33abcd, 34, 35abd, 36-37, 38ac, 40, 43, 45, 46ac, 47, 51, 52b, 57c, 63
Shuch — 2-3, 8a, 25b, 29ad, 31c, 32ae, 35c, 44, 59b, 60
Siver — 1, 4, 6, 7abc, 8ab, 9ab, 10ab, 12, 14ac, 15a, 17-18, 22, 25ac, 32f, 42, 61-62, 64b, 66
Strawn — 9b
Syre — 38d
Nil — 11, 19, 24, 29b, 38be, 41, 50, 52a, 55, 59a, 64a

West Lothian
Cundie — 1b, 15
Gundie — 1c, 21a
Gutter — 1a, 3, 11-13, 15-16, 17a, 18, 22
Rannie — 15
Schuch — 9b
Sheuch — 1ac, 2-3, 5, 8, 17ab, 18, 19b, 20ab, 21b, 22
Shuch — 6, 9a, 10-11
Shuck — 19a
Nil — 1d, 4, 7, 14

Midlothian
Channel — 7b, 26a
Cundie — 25a
Gundie — 12a
Gunnel — 25b
Gutter — 1-3, 6a, 7a, 8a, 9, 11, 15-22, 23ab, 24, 25bc, 26b, 27-32
Sheuch — 10-11, 12ab, 14ab, 15, 26b
Siver — 1, 10, 23b
Stank — 7b
Strand — 30
Stripe — 7b
Nil — 4-5, 6b, 8b, 13, 25d

East Lothian
Brander — 1
Cundie — 1
Ditch — 6b
Drain — 1
Gutter — 1-2, 4b, 5, 6a, 7-9, 13-21
Runnel — 16
Sheuch — 3, 5, 11
Siver — 4a
Stripe — 4a, 6b, 8
Nil — 10, 12

Berwick
Channel — 22
Drain — 23
Gutter — 1-2, 6, 8-13, 15, 16bc, 19, 21, 23-24, 26, 29, 31-32
Rinner — 16ab, 18, 31
Runner — 27
Seever — 12
Siver — 16c
Strand — 7-8
Nil — 3-5, 14, 17, 20, 25, 28, 30

Peebles
Channel — 4b
Cundie — 4a
Gutter — 1-3, 4bc, 5, 6ab, 8-9
Open drain — 6a
Shuch — 4c, 7
Sipher — 2
Siver — 2, 8
Nil — 10

Selkirk
Grip — 1
Gutter — 2abcde, 4, 6-8
Nil — 3, 5

Roxburgh
Channel — 15a, 20
Chennel — 21ac, 26
Cuddie — 4, 21c
Cundie — 13
Grip — 15b
Gutter — 1-2, 3a, 4-5, 7-8, 9a, 13, 15b, 16-17, 19, 21abdef, 25-27
Rinner — 5
Runnel — 17
Strand — 9a
Syre — 8, 17, 20, 28
Nil — 3b, 6, 9b, 10-12, 14, 18, 22-24

Dumfries
Conduit — 42
Cundie — 22
Drain — 41
Dyke sheuch — 38
Group — 45a
Gully — 46
Gutter — 1a, 6, 8b, 16, 17ab, 18-20, 21b, 22-23, 26-28, 31de, 32-33, 35, 37, 39, 46-48
Rib — 5
Sewer — 42
Sheuch — 3, 24, 27, 31f
Siver — 1ab, 4, 6, 8a, 9, 11-13, 19, 25, 31abe, 34, 41
Syre — 8a, 14-15, 29, 41, 45a
Nil — 2, 7, 10, 21a, 30, 31c, 36, 40, 43-44, 45b, 49

Kirkcudbright
Channeling — 15a
Gutter — 1, 6-7, 10, 18-19, 21b, 23
Pen — 27
Shuch — 11
Sipher — 21c
Siver — 1, 3-4, 12ab, 14, 15ab, 17, 19, 21ab, 22, 26
Syre — 2, 7, 16
Nil — 5, 8-9, 13, 20, 24-25

Wigtown
Drain — 14
Gutter — 1-2, 5a, 12-13, 16
Siver — 3, 5ab, 7-8, 10-11
Water table — 17
Nil — 4, 6, 9, 15, 18

Northumberland
Borne — 83
Cassie — 17, 37
Causie — 130a
Cazzie — 17
Channel — 40b, 41ad, 47, 49-50, 57, 59bf, 62ac, 64b, 69abe, 72e, 77, 79-81, 83-84, 87, 88a, 89-91, 93, 94ab, 103a, 109-110, 111ab, 112, 114, 123, 127e, 129c, 134, 138, 141
Chunnel — 10
Cundie — 29d, 45, 56
Ditch — 46
Drain — 104a
Grip — 77
Grup — 77
Gully — 56, 58, 59e, 92, 95b, 122b
Gutter — 1a, 2b, 3, 5-6, 8, 11, 13-14, 16-18, 20b, 21-22, 26, 28, 29b, 30-31, 34ab, 36, 38, 40a, 41ad, 42, 45-46, 48, 52, 53ab, 54-57, 59bcd, 60-61, 62bg, 64ab, 65ab, 66, 69bcdh, 70, 71abcd, 72abcdegik, 77-80, 82, 86-87, 88b, 89, 91, 93, 96, 98, 99bd, 100, 101b, 102, 103bc, 104ab, 105, 107, 108a, 111ab, 112, 117, 118b, 119, 120abc, 121, 124b, 126abcf, 127acg, 129b, 130bcdef, 132, 135, 137, 142-143
Lander — 124a
Open sewer — 41c
Runnel — 2a, 51, 72b
Runner — 7, 19a, 47, 60, 79
Safe — 104b
Sewerage — 12
Sike — 75
Syre — 2a, 9, 12-13, 15, 17-18, 19a, 27
Nil — 1bc, 4, 19b, 20a, 23, 24ab, 25, 29acef, 32, 33ab, 35, 39, 41b, 43-44, 59a, 62defh, 63, 67-68, 69fg, 71e, 72fhjl, 73-74, 76, 85, 95a, 97, 99ac, 101a, 106, 108bc, 113, 115-116, 118a, 122a, 125, 126de, 127bdfhj, 128, 129a, 131, 133, 136, 139-140

Cumberland
Channel — 11, 13c, 22, 40, 52
Chennel — 8, 38, 62
Chenneling — 38
Cunderd — 52
Cundreth — 46
Drain — 53
Gully — 15c, 29
Gutter — 2, 4, 7, 9, 12, 13c, 14, 15c, 16-18, 20, 23-26, 28, 31, 33, 36, 40, 42, 46, 48-50, 53, 56-58, 60, 62
Street channel — 9
Street chennel — 9
Vennel — 7, 15b, 30-31, 44, 47, 54, 56-57, 59-61
Nil — 1ab, 3, 5ab, 6, 10, 13abd, 15a, 19, 21, 27, 32, 34-35, 37ab, 39, 41, 43, 45, 51, 55, 63ab

Down
Channel — 2a, 18, 23
Drain — 19-20, 24
Gutter — 2a, 5, 9, 15, 19
Kennel — 2b
Runner — 7
Shouch — 19
Shuck — 20, 22
Trinket — 3, 7, 10-16, 21, 23, 26-27, 29
Water table — 17
Watter channel — 11, 14, 21
Nil — 1, 4, 6, 8, 25, 28, 30

Tyrone
Channel — 10
Clabber — 5
Gutter — 8, 11
Sheuch — 1
Side trench — 10
Trinket — 14
Trinnel — 12
Vannel — 16
Vennel — 2-3, 7-9, 14
Water channel — 11
Water table — 10
Nil — 4, 6, 13, 15

Antrim
Channel — 34
Cribbin — 8a
Drain — 17, 32
Gully — 2
Gutter — 1, 13, 15, 19-20, 25-26, 28-29
Runnel — 16b
Shough — 30
Trinket — 2, 4, 5b, 7, 9-10, 16b, 18, 21-22, 24, 31, 33
Vennel — 34
Water course — 6
Water table — 21
Nil — 3, 4A, 5a, 8b, 11-12, 14, 16ac, 23, 27

Donegal
Channel — 10b, 13
Drain — 4
Gully — 10b
Gutter — 1, 5, 5A
Shough — 4, 6, 10a
Vannel — 12
Vennel — 1A, 2, 7A, 8, 10a, 13
Water table — 5
Nil — 3, 7, 9, 11

Fermanagh
Gutter — 5, 9
Runnel — 7a
Sink — 3
Trinket — 2
Vennel — 4-5
Water channel — 1
Water coorse — 1
Water table — 6
Nil — 7b, 8, 10

Armagh
Channel — 1, 3-4
Trinket — 1
Water table — 6ab
Nil — 2, 5

Londonderry
Bucket — 3
Gutter — 2, 3A
Muck — 1A
Trinket — 1B, 3, 5-6
Vennel — 5
Water course — 4
Water vennel — 4
Nil — 1, 7

47 The GRATING over a drain-opening in such a gutter (PQ1, 107)

See note (1) on 45 **ditch.**

Shetland

Gratin(g) — 5, 7, 21b, 30, 32-33
Nil — 1-4, 6, 8-20, 21a, 22-29, 31

Orkney

Grating — 3-4, 7-8
Gutter — 16
Syre — 1, 5, 9-12, 13a, 14-15, 17-21
Nil — 2, 6, 13b

Caithness

Brander — 7
Grate — 13
Grater — 8-9, 12ac, 13-14, 17
Grating — 2ab, 11, 15
Siver — 1
Nil — 3-6, 10, 12b, 16ab

Sutherland

Brander — 15
Cover — 7
Grating — 1, 3, 7-8, 9ab, 10, 12-13, 16
Grid — 5
Gutter — 3
Nil — 2, 4, 6, 11, 14, 17

Ross & Cromarty

Brander — 7, 11, 27
Culvert — 23, 26
Drain — 25b
Grater — 33
Grating — 1, 3-5, 8, 16-17, 23, 27-29, 31, 32abc, 34, 37a, 39
Gully grid — 36
Sewer — 35
Siver — 9, 12-13, 18, 20, 24, 33
Nil — 2, 6, 10, 14-15, 19, 21-22, 25a, 30, 37b, 38

Inverness

Brander — 7, 9, 14, 17, 27, 29-30
Drainer — 36
Grater — 26
Grating — 1-5, 7-8, 10, 13abce, 16-17, 21ab, 22-23, 26, 28, 32, 34-35, 37-39
Grid — 24
Siver — 6, 15, 20
Nil — 11-12, 13d, 18-19, 25, 31, 33, 40

Nairn

Brander — 1bc, 2-4, 6
Seever — 1a
Siver — 1c, 3
Nil — 5

Moray

Brander — 1, 2a, 3-5, 6ab, 7, 8abcde, 9a, 10-11, 13, 15-22
Gratin(g) — 7, 11, 14, 23
Siver — 4
Nil — 2b, 8f, 9b, 12

Banff

Brander — 1, 2abc, 3-5, 6ab, 7-13, 15-17, 18bc, 20-34
Grating — 15
Siber — 18d
Nil — 14, 18a, 19

Aberdeen

Brander — 2, 3b, 4, 5ab, 9-17, 20-27, 28ab, 29-37, 40, 43-46, 47bcdef, 48-56, 58-68, 70, 71abc, 72, 74-83, 85-93, 95-101, 103, 105-109
Brunder — 6, 17-19, 21, 39, 42, 45, 47ad, 69, 73, 104
Buchan trap — 28c
Drain — 3a
Mou — 105
Soir — 5c
Syre — 10, 14, 41, 47a, 81, 84, 92, 94, 107
Syre brander — 5d
Nil — 1, 7-8, 38, 57, 102

Kincardine

Brander — 1-16, 17abcd, 18-28
Siever — 17b

Kinross

Condie — 5
Gratin(g) — 3, 6
Sipher — 2
Siver — 1, 3-4, 6
Nil — 7

Angus

Brander — 2-4, 5ab, 6-8, 11-13, 14acd, 15, 17ab, 18, 20, 22-24, 27, 31, 35-37
Brandie — 17b
Cundie — 8, 11, 19, 21, 29a, 32, 33a
Gratin(g) — 1-2, 9, 17b, 18, 28, 29a, 34-35
Siver — 34
Syre — 5c, 14bcd, 25, 33b
Nil — 10, 16, 26, 29b, 30

Perth

Brander — 15, 22, 60
Condie — 1, 3, 18, 25, 27, 29b, 41a, 42, 52e, 53
Conduit — 25, 44, 52d
Cundie — 21, 23, 31-32, 51a, 59
Gottin — 70
Gratin(g) — 4-5, 8-10, 12-13, 20, 24-25, 27-28, 29a, 33, 36, 46, 48, 50 51a, 52bc, 57, 60, 67-68, 71-72, 74
Hake — 29a
Heck — 62
Man hole — 2a
Siver — 40, 41b, 52e, 64-65, 67-68, 70, 73
Stank — 8
Trap — 66
Nil — 2b, 6-7, 11, 14, 16-17, 19, 26, 30, 34-35, 37-39, 43, 45, 47, 49, 51b, 52a, 54-56, 58, 61, 63, 69

Fife

Brander — 24, 53
Condie — 8, 19
Cover — 33
Cundie — 3
Gratin(g) — 1, 4, 13, 16-17, 21, 24-25, 36a, 37-38, 43a, 45, 50-51, 53, 55b, 57-58, 62
Grid — 33
Gully (box) — 55e, *56*
Gundie — 28
Sipher (lid) — 9b, 52, 54, 55dfg
Sipher tap — 55f
Siver — 7-8, 9a, 10-12, 18-20, 22-23, 26-27, 30, 32, 34, 36b, 37, 39, 40ab, 41abc, 42, 43b, 44abcdef, 46, 48, 50, 52-53, 55ae, 59, 63, 64ab
Nil — 2, 5-6, 14-15, 29, 31, 35, 41d, 47, 49, 55c, 60-61

Clackmannan

Brander — 2
Grate — 5
Grating — 5
Gully gratin — 6
Siver — 4cd, 7
Nil — 1, 3, 4ab

Stirling

Brander — 8
Cess pool — 35a
Condie — 9
Cran — 7ac
Drain — 25c
Grate — 26b
Grater — 21a, 23a, 25abd, 27a, 28, 30, 32, 39ab, 41
Gratin(g) — 3-4, 7abef, 12-13, 15, 18, 20, 21b, 23b, 25c, 26cd, 27a, 31, 34, 36, 37ab, 40, 42a
Grid — 22a
Gully (box) — 10, *17*
Lid — 20
Siver — 2, 6, 8, 10-13, 16-17, 23c, 26acef, 31, 33, 37b
Stank — 25a
Trap — 7d
Nil — 1, 5, 14, 19, 22b, 24, 27b, 29, 35b, 38, 42b

Dunbarton

Brander — 7b
Drain — 11
Grater — 15, 16b, 18
Gratin(g) — 3, 10, 13bc, 16a, 17
Heck — 2
Siber — 7a
Siver — 4ab, 6, 7ac, 12, 13ac, 16a, 18
Stank — 7a, 9, 13c, 14b, 17
Nil — 1, 5, 8, 14a

Argyll

Drain cover — 33
Goocher — 24
Grater — 14, 23
Grating — 2-3, 6-7, 10-11, 15, 17, 19, 22, 27, 34-35
Grid — 12
Ootlet — 18
Sipher — 40
Siver — 13, 16, 19, 24-26, 28, 30-31, 36-39
Siver grating — 33
Strainer — 12
Nil — 1, 4-5, 8-9, 20-21, 29, 32

Bute

Grating — 1acd, 2, 7
Sink — 9
Siver — 1abe, 3, 5, 8a, 9
Stank — 6
Trap — 1a
Nil — 4, 8b

Ayr

Cess pool — 33
Cess pool cover — 8a, 38
Cess pool lid — 17
Conduit cover — 57
Cundie — 57
Drain — 5, 28e
Grate — 8b, 16a
Gratin(g) — 2a, 3, 5, 9, 12a, 15, 20c, 21, 28f, 30a, 31-32, 34, 35b, 43, 45, 47, 49, 54-57
Grating grid — 8a
Grill — 8a
Gully cover — 18a, 53a
Gutter — 42
Lid — 13, 36, 41
Pen — 12b, 14, 16b, 20abdefg, 24b, 26c, 27, 28abd, 29, 35a, 36-37, 39, 44, 48, 53b
Pen cover — 27
Pen lid — 20g, 29
Siver — 1a, 2b, 6, 11, 14, 18b, 37, 53b
Siver cover — 5
Stank — 18b, 28de, 53a
Sump — 24a, 30b
Sump grater — 33
Sump lid — 24b
Tap — 41
Nil — 1b, 4, 7, 10, 19, 20h, 22-23, 25, 26ab, 28c, 40, 46, 50-52

Renfrew

Bars — 2h
Brander — 9
Cess pool cover — 4a
Cran — 1b, 2abcefgj
Cundie — 16a
Grate — 2i
Grater — 11a
Gratin(g) — 4e, 5, 11af, 13c, 17, 18a, 20b
Gully grating — 10
Sink — 11cek, 12b
Sipher — 11i
Siver — 2behi, 3, 4d, 8, 11bkl, 14a, 16abc, 18b, 19, 21
Stank — 2e, 6, 11a, 12b, 18b, 19, 20a
Nil — 1a, 2d, 4bc, 7, 11dghj, 12a, 13abd, 14b, 15, 16d

Lanark

Brander — 13
Cover — 29e, 37
Cundie — 32f, 38a, 57b
Drain — 26b, 29c, 32e, 49a
Drainer — 16ab, 25c
Grater — 10b, 12, 14d, 15bc, 16a, 18, 20, 40
Gratin(g) — 1-3, 6, 7ac, 12, 15bc, 17, 20, 25b, 29a, 53, 57a, 59b, 60, 64b
Gully — 16b, 35d
Gully grating — 29d
Sand trap — 38c
Seeve — 67a
Sipher — 51
Siver — 5, 11, 13, 14b, 16b, 23, 25bd, 26a, 27a, 28, 29bcfg, 30, 31abcd, 32cd, 33abcd, 34, 35abd, 36, 38bde, 41, 44-45, 46bc, 47-48, 49b, 52ab, 59a, 63
Siver gratin — 58
Siver jawbox — 39
Sivie — 62
Stank — 1, 4, 6, 7ab, 8ab, 9ab, 22, 25ad, 31b
Stank cover — 15a
Tobie — 27b
Water grating — 27b
Nil — 10a, 14ac, 19, 21, 24, 32ab, 35c, 42-43, 46a, 50, 54-56, 57c, 61, 64a, 65-66, 67b

West Lothian

Brander — 11
Cundie — 4, 20b
Drain — 21b
Drain cover — 16
Grater — 17a
Gratin(g) — 6, 17a, 18, 20ab
Gully — 1a
Gundie — 1cd, 4, 17ab
Gutter cover — 19a
Siver — 1a, 2, 4-5, 7-8, 9b, 10-15, 19b, 20a, 21a, 22
Nil — 1b, 3, 9a

Midlothian

Cundie — 17, 26b
Drain — 8a
Grater — 25d
Gratin(g) — 1, 9-10, 15, 23b, 25c, 30, 32
Gully — 26a
Siver — 2-4, 7ab, 10-11, 12a, 13, 14ab, 15-22, 23a, 24, 25ab, 26a, 27-28
Siver cover — 29
Siver grating — 24
Siver lid — 6a
Nil — 5, 6b, 8b, 12b, 31

East Lothian

Brander — 1
Cundie — 1, 6ab, 14

East Lothian cont'd
Drain – 4b
Grater – 3
Gratin(g) – 5, 6b, 7, 11, 13, 16, 19-20
Grid – 4a, 17
Seizer – 2
Siver – 2, 4b, 5, 9-10, 13, 15-16, 18, 21
Siver grid – 4a
Nil – 8, 12

Berwick
Brander – 28
Cundie – 2, 8
Cundie grating – 16c
Drain – 29
Gratin(g) – 1, 6-7, 9-10, 12, 15, 16a, 18, 21, 31-32
Grid – 31
Gundie – 24
Sink – 3, 8, 16b
Siver – 13, 21, 23, 26
Siver grid – 18
Stank – 16c
Tobie – 24
Nil – 4-5, 11, 14, 17, 19-20, 22, 25, 27, 30

Peebles
Cundie – 4c
Grating – 1, 6b, 8
Jawbox – 6a
Sieve – 6a
Sipher (gratin) – 2, 9
Siver – 3, 4bc, 5, 7, 10
Nil – 4a

Selkirk
Brander – 2a
Cundie – 2cd, 6
Gratin(g) – 1, 2e, 3-4, 8
Gundie – 2b
Nil – 5, 7

Roxburgh
Brander – 2, 4, 11-12, 17, 19-20, 21abcdef, 23, 25-26
Brawnder – 27
Cundie – 15a
Grate – 15b
Gratin(g) – 1, 4, 8, 9a, 16, 18
Sink – 3a
Siver – 2, 9a, 13, 15a, 17, 20
Sump – 9b
Nil – 3b, 5-7, 10, 14, 22, 24, 28

Dumfries
Brander – 17a
Cess pool covering – 15
Cundie – 15, 28-29, 35
Gratin(g) – 1a, 4, 6-7, 8a, 12-13, 16, 17b, 18, 22, 24, 31bd, 33, 37, 45a, 46-47
Heck – 2
Pen – 31ef
Siver – 5, 8b, 10, 20, 21a, 26, 28, 32
Syre – 30
Trap – 37
Nil – 1b, 3, 9, 11, 14, 19, 21b, 23, 25, 27, 31ac, 34, 36, 38-44, 45b, 48-49

Kirkcudbright
Cundie – 15a
Gratin(g) – 1, 5-6, 10, 16, 22-23
Grid – 3, 17, 24
Heck – 17
Jaa hole – 15b
Jaw hole gratin – 4
Pen – 12b, 15a
Siver – 6-7, 9-11, 12a, 14, 18, 21c, 27
Syre – 7
Nil – 2, 8, 13, 19-20, 21ab, 25-26

Wigtown
Grat – 5a
Gratin(g) – 11-14, 16-17
Hack – 5a
Pen – 7
Siver – 1-2, 4, 5a, 6, 8-9, 15, 18
Siver cover – 13
Nil – 3, 5b, 10

Northumberland
Beetle drive – 48
Cover – 28, 40a, 59b, 69f, 110
Cundie – 7, 13
Cundie cover – 135
Cundie opening – 33b
Dinkie – 125
Grailin – 71c
Grate – 2a, 5, 16-17, 19a, 28, 29bd, 31, 36, 40a, 49, 54, 56, 59d, 62e, 65a, 69d, 70, 71d, 72adek, 74, 77-79, 81-82, 88a, 89, 98, 101b, 104a, 106-107, 111ab, 112, 120abc, 126f, 127abdh, 129b, 130e, 137-138, 142
Grate cover – 41c
Gratin(g) – 1a, 6, 8, 18, 20b, 29b, 30, 38, 40a, 42, 45-46, 52, 53b, 59b, 69ch, 72cgi, 86, 88b, 90, 99d, 103ac, 109, 111a, 119, 124b, 126c, 127ac, 132, 134
Grid – 25, 34b, 53a, 69a, 71a, 72k, 130f
Grill – 69f
Gully – 17, 61, 75
Gully grate – 104b
Gully grate and frame – 69b
Gutter – 66
Hatch lid – 59b
Lid – 91, 118b
Man hole cover – 76, 130c
Mesh – 29d
Runnel – 51
Screen – 83
Sink – 1b, 9, 21, 30, 40a, 57-58, 59bde, 60, 62abg, 65a, 68, 69e, 71c, 72cl, 76-77, 88a, 94b, 97, 99b, 100, 105, 118ab, 123, 124a, 127b, 129a, 130ab
Sink cover – 62h, 143
Sink grating – 64b, 69b
Sink lid – 87, 93
Sink top – 50, 69c, 71b, 91, 95b
Siver – 29f
Storm grate – 41d
Wummel – 77
Nil – 1c, 2b, 3-4, 10-12, 14-15, 19b, 20a, 22-23, 24ab, 26-27, 29ace, 32, 33a, 34a, 35, 37, 39, 40b, 41ab, 43-44, 47, 55, 59acf, 62cdf, 63, 64a, 65b, 67, 69g, 71e, 72bfhj, 73, 80, 84-85, 92, 94a, 95a, 96, 99ac, 101a, 102, 103b, 108abc, 113-117, 121, 122ab, 126abde, 127efg, 128, 129c, 130d, 131, 133, 136, 139-141

Cumberland
Colvert – 61
Cundath – 19
Cunderd – 42, 54
Cundert – 33, 41, 61
Cundred – 42, 50, 55
Drain trap – 44
Gob cover – 56
Grate – 2, 15c, 17, 20, 22, 40, 46, 48, 56
Gratin(g) – 3-4, 9, 14, 16, 23, 28, 46, 53, 57-58, 62
Grid – 7, 31, 38, 46-47, 60, 62, 63b
Guard – 30
Gully – 16
Gully trap – 8, 13c, 18, 26, 29, 33, 57
Gunderd – 24, 43

Rack – 30
Sink – 4, 5a
Sink cover – 57
Trap – 30
Vennel – 18, 25, 43-44
Nil – 1ab, 5b, 6, 10-12, 13abd, 15ab, 21, 27, 32, 34-36, 37ab, 39, 45, 49, 51-52, 59, 63a

Down
Drain pipe – 19
Gratin(g) – 1, 2a, 5, 7, 9, 15, 17-19, 21, 24, 26, 29
Grid – 6, 22
Jaw trough – 13
Nil – 2b, 3-4, 8, 10-12, 14, 16, 20, 23, 25, 27-28, 30

Tyrone
Gratin(g) – 6-8, 10-12, 16
Grid – 5
Gully cover – 11
Gully trap – 1
Man hole – 12
Vennel – 6
Nil – 2-4, 9, 13-15

Antrim
Grate – 10
Gratin(g) – 12-13, 15, 17, 19-20, 22, 25-26, 28, 31, 33
Grid – 7, 8b
Gully trap – 1, 4, 5b, 6, 15, 34
Trinket – 3
Nil – 2, 4A, 5a, 8a, 9, 11, 14, 16abc, 18, 21, 23-24, 27, 29-30, 32

Donegal
Grate – 12
Grating – 5, 5A, 8, 10ab
Gutter trap – 6
Nil – 1, 1A, 2-4, 7, 7A, 9, 11, 13

Fermanagh
Gratin(g) – 2, 4, 9
Gully – 2
Sink – 5
Nil – 1, 3, 6, 7ab, 8, 10

Armagh
Grate – 3-4
Grating – 6a
Gully trap – 2
Nil – 1, 5, 6b

Londonderry
Gratin(g) – 2, 3A, 5, 7
Grid – 5
Shore – 1B
Stank – 3
Nil – 1, 1A, 4, 6

48 The DRAIN OPENING itself (PQ1, 108)

The concentration in some of the mapped areas is not very strong.
Variants of MOUTH have been subsumed (some **mooth; moo, mou** Aberdeenshire).
See also note (1) on 45 **ditch.**

Shetland
Daeye id da runnick – 4
Drain – 25
Inlet – 5
Mouth – 6-7, 15, 21b, 30
Runnock – 12
Wirlie – 15
Nil – 1-3, 8-11, 13-14, 16-20, 21a, 22-24, 26-29, 31-33

Orkney
Ditch – 21
(Drain) mouth – *3*, 5, *11*, *16*, *19*
End – 8
Eye – 4
Ootlet – 8
Runnie – 6
Syre – 9, 13a
Nil – 1-2, 7, 10, 12, 13b, 14-15, 17-18, 20

Caithness
Culvert – 7
Cundie – 7, 12a
Ditch – 13
Drain – 8

Caithness cont'd
Drain opening — 16b
Mouth — 11, 16b
Sink — 3, 6
Nil — 1, 2ab, 4-5, 9-10, 12bc, 14-15, 16a, 17

Sutherland
Culvert — 9ab
Drain — 17
Drain inlet — 13
Intake — 13
Man hole — 15
Mouth — 12
Outlet — 4
Spout hole — 5
Trap — 1
Nil — 2-3, 6-8, 10-11, 14, 16

Ross & Cromarty
Channel — 32a
Ditch — 18
(Drain) mouth — 9, *27*-28, 31, *39*
Drain (opening) — 1, *8*, 16, 25a, 26
Gully — 11
Man hole — 17
Opening — 9
Sink — 25b
Şinkie — 37b
Siver — 19, 23, 29
Nil — 2-7, 10, 12-15, 20-22, 24, 30, 32bc, 33-36, 37a, 38

Inverness
Culvert — 16
Drain head — 4
Drain hole — 3
Drain (opening) — 5, 13a, *21b*, 23, *27*, *29*, 37
Drain pipe — 22
Eye — 11
Mouth — 34
Opening — 10
Sewer mouth — 26
Trap — 38
Nil — 1-2, 6-9, 12, 13bcde, 14-15, 17-20, 21a, 24-25, 28, 30-33, 35-36, 39-40

Nairn
Calvert — 2
Gully — 1c
Nil — 1ab, 3-6

Moray
Cess pool — 5
Cundie — 11
Drain — 4, 7, 11, 14, 21
Gullet — 19
Gully — 7, 19
Gully hole — 8b
Gully trap — 22
Man hole — 23
Mouth — 6a, 7, 9a, 16
Ootfa — 1
Sump — 22
Trap — 8e, 13
Nil — 2ab, 3, 6b, 8acdf, 9b, 10, 12, 15, 17-18, 20

Banff
Brander — 19
Cundie — 10
Drain — 3-4, 13, 23
(Drain) mouth — 5, *6b*, *14*-15, *17*, 22, 24-25, 32
Eye — 34
Gully — 7, 23
Jaw hole — 9
Man hole — 30
Ootlet — 31
Sewer — 20
Stripe — 33
Syre — 3, 8
Trap — 29
Nil — 1, 2abc, 6a, 11-12, 16, 18abcd, 21, 26-28

Aberdeen
Culvert — 6, 27
Cundie — 40
Drain — 3a, 9, 20, 34, 50, 98, 108
(Drain) mouth — *5c*, *10*-11, *17*, 21, *23*-24, *26*, *31*-*33*, *35*, 41, 46, 47a, *48*, *53*, 59-*60*, *62*, *66*, 69, 71b, *73*-*74*, 75, *78*, 80-81, *82*-*83*, *86*, *88*, *94*-*95*, *97*, *100*, *104*-*106*
Gully — 3b, 28a, 39, 51, 73
Gully trap — 14
Jaw hole — 64, 71a, 80
Leader — 67
Ootlet — 25
Pot hole — 96
Sewer — 71c
Stran hole — 101
Syre — 5d, 7, 19, 44, 47bcef, 102, 109
Tay — 67
Track — 29
Vent — 70
Nil — 1-2, 4, 5ab, 8, 12-13, 15-16, 18, 22, 28bc, 30, 36-38, 42-43, 45, 47d, 49, 52, 54-58, 61, 63, 65, 68, 72, 76-77, 79, 84-85, 87, 89-93, 99, 103, 107

Kincardine
Brander hole — 3
Cess — 7
Channel — 24
Conduit — 6
Culvert — 28
Ditch — 20
Drain — 19, 26, 28
(Drain) mouth — *7*, 8-9, *10*, 11, 17a, 21
Dren — 1
Gutter — 22
Sand trap — 5
Spoot — 22
Sump — 14
Syre — 6, 17c
Track — 24
Nil — 2, 4, 12-13, 15-16, 17bd, 18, 23, 25, 27

Kinross
Condie — 1, 3, 6
Jawbox — 5
Mouth — 4
Siver — 3
Nil — 2, 7

Angus
Afflet — 22
Brander — 8, 12
Cleaner — 28
Cundie — 5a, 6-8, 11, 14acd, 21, 23, 27, 29a, 30-32, 34-37
Drain — 2, 19, 24
Gully — 18
Mouth — 5b, 20, 22
Mouth o'cundie — 10
Ootfa — 14b, 33b
Sewer — 17b
Syre — 4, 5c, 13, 14a
Trap — 9
Nil — 1, 3, 15-16, 17a, 25-26, 29b, 33a

Perth
Afflet — 33
Condie — 1, 15, 27, 40, 41ab, 45, 47-48, 50, 51b, 52d, 54-55, 64, 72
Conduit — 35, 44, 52d
Cundie — 7, 16, 20, 31-34, 52a, 60, 66
Ditch — 67
Drain (hole) — 13, *29a*, 41a, 46, 71, 74
(Drain) opening — *4*, 8, *12*, 57
Duct — 25
Gullet — 24
Man hole — 2a, 9
Mouth — 10, 28, 52c, 56, 62
Offlet — 18, 25
Ootlet — 65-66
Outlet — 51a
Sink — 23
Siver — 24
Stank — 52b
Strand — 21
Sump — 53
Sumph — 29b
Tail run — 68
Tail rush — 68
Track — 21
Trench — 21, 73
Nil — 2b, 3, 5-6, 11, 14, 17, 19, 22, 26, 30, 36-39, 42-43, 49, 52e, 58-59, 61, 63, 69-70

Fife
Cess pool — 55e
Common shore — 53
Condie — 7, 11, 19-20, 55e, 64a
Cundie — 2, 7, 23, 39, 53
Dishel — 40b
(Drain) mouth — *4*, 11, 62
Drain (opening) — 7, 11, 13, 37, 42, *44c*, 50, 55e, 56, 63
Gillie trap — 25
Gollet — 53
Gully — 9b, 18, 30
Gully hole — 43b
Gundie — 23, 53
Gutter hole — 51
Jaw box — 41b, 43a, 57
Jaw hole — 26, 31
Main hole — 48
Man hole — 44b
Sipher — 55df
Siver — 8, 9a, 10, 12, 16, 20-21, 33-35, 36a, 38-39, 41ad, 43a, 44ef, 45-47, 49, 55bc, 59, 61-62
Stank — 44a
Tobbie — 52
Trap — 4
Nil — 1, 3, 5-6, 14-15, 17, 22, 24, 27-29, 32, 36b, 40a, 41c, 44d, 54, 55ag, 58, 60, 64b

Clackmannan
Cess pool — 4d
Condie — 2
Cundie — 5
Drain — 1, 4c
Gully box — 2, 6
Mouth — 7
Siver — 3, 4ab

Stirling
Baring pipe — 27b
Cess pool — 7b
Condie — 3, 7abe, 8-9, 22b, 25abd
Conductor — 21b
Culvert — 10
Culvie — 19
Cundie — 21b, 26e, 33, 37b, 38, 42ab
Drain — 4, 7c, 11-12, 16, 21b, 23b, 25c, 26ac, 29, 31, 36, 40
Drain trap — 36
Gotten — 23c, 32
Grating — 27a
Grease box — 18
Gully — 9, 12-13, 23c, 25ad
Gully hole — 2
Gully pot — 28
Gully trap — 18
Gundie — 26a
Maun hole — 20
Mouth — 25c
Sand box — 27a
Sipher — 15
Siver — 7c, 17, 21b, 26df, 39a
Stank — 18, 21b, 25c, 29-31, 34
Sump — 7d, 22a
Swiver — 7f
Tobie — 24
Trap — 8, 12, 39b
Nil — 1, 5-6, 14, 21a, 23a, 26b, 35ab, 37a, 41

Dunbarton
Cess pool — 3, 5
Cundie — 9
Drain — 7c, 11-12, 13c, 16b
Siver — 2, 4b, 10
Stank — 7abc, 12, 13c, 14a, 16ab
Nil — 1, 4a, 6, 8, 13ab, 14b, 15, 17-18

Argyll
Drain — 2, 7, 27, 30
(Drain) mouth — *17*, 19, *22*, *24*, *29*, *31*
Gully trap — 3
Gutter — 33
Hole — 13
Offlet — 1
Ootlet — 38
Sheep drain — 6
Sheuch — 18, 37
Siver — 33, 35-36
Trap — 23, 35
Nil — 4-5, 8-12, 14-16, 20-21, 25-26, 28, 32, 34, 39-40

Bute
Cundie — 1ae, 9
Drain (opening) — 2-3, *7*
Siver — 1cd, 5, 8b
Stank — 3, 6
Nil — 1b, 4, 8a

Ayr
Cess pool — 2a, 8a, 9, 12a, 14, 16a, 17, 20cd, 22-23, 27, 28f, 30b, 32, 34, 35b, 42-43, 51, 57
Cundie — 1a, 7, 8b, 18b, 41, 54
Drain — 1a, 2ab, 8b, 14, 20b, 48
(Drain) mouth — *5*, 15, *44*, 56
Grating — 16b
Gully — 1b, 8a, 18a, 20f, 29, 53a
Gundie — 7
Jawbox — 18b
Pen — 12b, 20bgh, 28bc, 29, 31-32, 36-38, 41, 45-46, 49, 52
Pend — 10, 21
Pen hole — 28d
Pen mouth — 33, 35a
Sewer — 6
Siver — 2b, 12a, 13, 55
Stank — 2a, 3, 7, 8b, 21, 24b, 36
Sump — 8a, 20ae, 24ab, 25, 30a
Sumph — 9
Trap — 57
Wallie — 53b
Nil — 4, 11, 19, 26abc, 28ae, 39-40, 47, 50

Renfrew
Cess pool — 4a
Cran — 2j
Culvert — 2i
Cundie — 20b, 21
Drain (opening) — *2a*, 4e, 11ace, 18b, 19
Gully — 10, 13ac
Outlet — 8
Sewer — 11j
Sink — 4e, 5
Sipher — 11i
Siver — 2fh, 4a, 11cfhl, 17
Sluice — 16a
Stank — 2b, 4d, 9, 11ad, 12a, 13a, 15, 16ab, 18a, 20a, 21
Tobie hole — 16d
Trap — 1b, 2i, 13c
Nil — 1a, 2cdeg, 3, 4bc, 6-7, 11bghk, 12b, 13bd, 14ab, 16c

Lanark

Buchan Trap — 36
Cess pool — 3, 36, 39
Cundie — 11, 15c, 17, 25d, 30, 33cd, 38cd, 46c, 47-48, 52ab, 55-56, 57c
Cundie hole — 33d
Drainer — 16b
Drain hole — 26b
(Drain) mouth — *20,* 40, *47,* 57a
Drain (opening) — 2, 7c, 12, 14b, 25ac, *27b,* 29c, 31a, 49a, 51, 59b, 64b
Gully — 12, 35b
Gully hole — 17
Gundie — 52b
Gutter — 5, 32f
Gutter box — 53
Hole — 27a, 60
Jaw hole — 20, 50
Man hole — 18, 29e
Open drain — 44
Sheuch — 44
Siver — 7ac, 12, 15b, 16b, 26a, 27a, 29cde, 33cd, 37, 38a, 43, 45, 48, 54, 56, 58
Stank — 2, 7abc, 8a, 10ab, 13, 15ab, 17, 29f, 30, 31cd, 32e, 46b, 52a, 56, 57b
Stank heid — 9a
Trap — 49b, 58
Nil — 1, 4, 6, 8b, 9b, 14acd, 16a, 19, 21-24, 25b, 28, 29abg, 31b, 32abcd, 33ab, 34, 35acd, 38be, 41-42, 46a, 59a, 61-63, 64a, 65-66, 67ab

West Lothian

Cundie — 3, 11, 21a
Drain — 11, 20a, 21b, 22
Gundie — 1ad, 2-3, 17a
Hopper — 11
Jaw box — 8
Jaw hole — 8
Man hole — 5
Mouth — 12, 15, 19b
Sifer — 6
Siver — 3, 5, 9a, 16, 17a, 18
Trap — 16
Nil — 1bc, 4, 7, 9b, 10, 13-14, 17b, 19a, 20b

Midlothian

Cess — 25b, 30
Cess pool — 16
Cundie — 3, 8b, 9, 14a, 21, 23a, 28
Dirty hole — 1
Drain — 8a, 15, 22, 23b
Grease box — 27
Gully — 15, 32
Mouth — 10
Sink — 30
Siver — 2-3, 5, 6ab, 7a, 8b, 9, 12ab, 16-19, 22, 24, 25c, 29, 32
Trap — 11
Trench — 20
Vent — 10
Nil — 4, 7b, 13, 14b, 25ad, 26ab, 31

East Lothian

Condie — 2
Cundie — 4a, 6b, 9, 11, 16
Drain (opening) — *1,* 4b, *7*
Grease box — 15
Gully — 13
Mouth — 17, 20
Sink — 14, 16
Sither — 6a
Siver — 3, 6a, 14
Nil — 5, 8, 10, 12, 18-19, 21

Berwick

Burst trap — 3
Cundie — 2, 4-5, 7-9, 15, 16ac 23, 27
(Drain) mouth — 6, *10, 16b, 32*
Drain (opening) — *1,* 8, 12, 29-30
Gully — 13, 31
Gully box — 23
Gutter hole — 29
Jaw box — 11
Jaw hole — 12
Sink — 21
Siver — 7-8, 11, 18
Slap — 27
Stank — 16c
Tail — 10
Track — 26
Trap — 20
Nil — 14, 17, 19, 22, 24-25, 28

Peebles

Cundie — 3, 4b, 8-9
Doon the dran — 4c
Drain — 5
Drain mouth — 6b
Open drain — 6a
Sewer — 6a
Sipher — 2
Siver — 4a
Stank — 2, 7
Nil — 1, 10

Selkirk

Cundie — 2abe, 4, 6-7
Cundie hole — 2d
Cundie mouth — 3
Nil — 1, 2c, 5, 8

Roxburgh

Culvert mouth — 5
Cundie — 2, 3b, 7, 9b, 13, 19, 21ace, 23, 28
Cundie hole — 26
Cundie mouth — 5, 8, 12, 15b, 25-26
Drain — 13, 21a
(Drain) mouth — 1, 3a, *9a, 15b, 16-17, 25*
Drip — 4
Gully — 21d
Tile mouth — 17
Nil — 6, 10-11, 14, 15a, 18, 20, 21bf, 22, 24, 27

Dumfries

Burst — 47
Burst drain — 6
Cess pool — 15, 42
Culver — 2, 34
Cundie — 1b, 2, 7, 16, 26, 37, 42
Cundie hole — 29
Cundie mouth — 35
Ditch — 17b
Drain — 4
Drain hole — 22
(Drain) mouth — *1a, 18,* 28, 45a
Gully hole — 46
Gully trap — 46
Inlet — 5, 38
Lunkie — 8b
Man hole — 13
Pen — 7, 8ab, 31ce, 37
Sewer — 17b
Sewie — 43
Sink — 9, 27
Siver — 10, 17a, 21b, 31cd
Spoot — 12
Stank — 4, 31a
Syre — 21b
Nil — 3, 11, 14, 19-20, 21a, 23-25, 30, 31bf, 32-33, 36, 39-41, 44, 45b, 48-49

Kirkcudbright

Cess pool — 1, 15a, 16
Drain hole — 18
(Drain) mouth — *2,* 17, *24, 27*
Drain opening — 15b
Heid o the drain — 10
Ja hole — 22
Jaw hole — 3-4, 7-8, 15a, 20, 23
Pen — 14, 21c
Sewer — 21c
Stank — 26
Syre — 25
Trap — 12b
Nil — 5-6, 9, 11, 12a, 13, 19, 21ab

Wigtown

Burst — 2
Cess pool — 11, 17
Gully — 7, 9
Jaw hole — 5a, 15
Pen — 9, 18
Pend — 1
Siver — 12-14, 16-17
Stank — 7
Trap — 8
Nil — 3-4, 5b, 6, 10

Northumberland

Culvert — 68
Cundie — 7, 22, 24a, 25, 31, 33b, 37-38, 41c, 44, 50, 56, 59c, 68, 76, 78, 89, 96, 106, 108c, 110, 122a, 124a
Cundie gob — 133
Cundie mouth — 36, 103c, 114, 138
Cundie opening — 34a
Dinkie — 124b
Ditch — 59b
Drain — 1a, 40a, 59b, 60, 71c, 82, 99d, 120c, 124b, 126c
Drain hole — 31
(Drain) mouth — 5, 12-13, *16, 28, 41c, 51, 53a, 76-77, 103c,* 107, *111ab, 120a, 124a,* 130c, *140, 142*
(Drain) openin(g) — *17,* 45, *53b, 69a, 94b*
Effluent — 77
Grate — 18
Grating — 46
Gully — 6, 8-9, 59f, 69abd, 73, 81, 95b, 104b, 118b, 122b, 126f, 129b, 134
Gully hole — 98
Gundie — 34b, 59b, 135
Gut — 61
Gutter — 11, 69a
Inspection chamber — 76
Manhole — 20b, 52, 71a, 76, 89, 100, 117
Offset — 141
Ootlet — 41d, 93
Outlet — 35, 74-75
Runnel — 111a
Sewer — 76, 127b
Sink — 1b, 18, 19a, 40a, 41ab, 42, 49-50, 54, 57, 62begh, 63, 64ab, 65a, 66-67, 69cdh, 71bd, 72abceij, 76, 79, 86-87, 88a, 90-91, 97, 99b, 101b, 104a, 108a, 109, 118b, 126ad, 127d, 128, 129ac, 130bde, 143
Sink openin(g) — 69b
Sump — 79
Trap — 130c
Nil — 1c, 2ab, 3-4, 10, 14-15, 19b, 20a, 21, 23, 24b, 26-27, 29abcdef, 30, 32, 33a, 39, 40b, 43, 47-48, 55, 58, 59ade, 62acdf, 65b, 69efg, 70, 71e, 72dfghkl, 80, 83-85, 88b, 92, 94a, 95a, 99ac, 101a, 102, 103ab, 105, 108b, 112-113, 115-116, 118a, 119, 120b, 121, 123, 125, 126be, 127acefgh, 130af, 131-132, 136-137, 139

Cumberland

Burst — 4
Catch pit — 26
Culvert — 34
Cundert — 18, 38, 54, 62
Cundeth — 28, 37b
Cundred — 50-51
Drain (gob) — 15c, 53, *56*
(Drain) mouth — *3,* 9, 17, *20, 22-23, 25,* 30, *33, 40, 42, 44, 48*
Drain opening — 48, 57
Drop — 30
Gully — 2, 13c, 14, 30-31, 37a
Outlet — 21
Sink — 24
Sump — 47
Track — 61
Vennel — 16, 24, 26, 41, 45-46, 53, 57
Vent — 40
Nil — 1ab, 5ab, 6-8, 10-12, 13abd, 15ab, 19, 27, 29, 32, 35-36, 39, 43, 49, 52, 55, 58-60, 63ab

Down

Burn — 2a
Drain — 1, 2a, 5, 9, 15
(Drain) mouth — 18, *21,* 26
Grating — 6, 19
Gully hole — 22
Jaw hole — 13
Sewer — 17
Shuch — 30
Sink — 29
Slough — 11
Nil — 2b, 3-4, 7-8, 10, 12, 14, 16, 20, 23-25, 27-28

Tyrone

Gully — 11
Mouth — 9, 14
Sheuch — 1
Shuch — 5
Nil — 2-4, 6-8, 10, 12-13, 15-16

Antrim

Brust — 21
Drain — 28, 31
Drain hole — 26
(Drain) mouth — 1, 5b, 12, *20*
Gully — 15, 33
Gully hole — 25
Gully trap — 10, 19
Sheuch — 21-22
Trinket — 17
Nil — 2-4, 4A, 5a, 6-7, 8ab, 9, 11, 13-14, 16abc, 18, 23-24, 27, 29-30, 32, 34

Donegal

Drain (mouth) — 5, 5A, *8, 10b*
Pipe — 2, 12
Nil — 1, 1A, 3-4, 6-7, 7A, 9, 10a, 11, 13

Fermanagh

Gully — 4
Gully hole — 1
Nil — 2-3, 5-6, 7ab, 8-10

Armagh

Gully trap — 3
Mouth — 4
Outlet — 4
Nil — 1-2, 5, 6ab

Londonderry

Drain — 2, 3A
Trinket — 1A
Nil — 1, 1B, 3-7

49 GUTTER (the kind running along the edge of a roof) (PQ1, 109)

Variants of SPOUT, SPOUTIN(G) have been subsumed (**spoot** everywhere except in Northumberland, where **spout** is concentrated. There are only a few **spoutin(g)**, the prodominant variant is **spootin(g)**). See note (1) on 45 **ditch.**

Spout and **rone** occur in 51 **pipe;** note **rone, ronie** in 39 **strip of ice.**

Shetland
Gutter – 10
Rone – 1-9, 15-16, 19-20, 21ab, 24, 26-28, 30, 32-33
Rone pipe – 22
Spout – 13, 18, 24-25
Water rone – 17
Nil – 11-12, 14, 23, 29, 31

Orkney
Eave gutter – 8
Eave spout – 8
Gutter – 3
Rone – 4-6, 8, 15, 17, 19, 21
Rone pipe – 5
Spout – 2, 4-5, 7, 9, 11-12, 13a, 14-20
Nil – 1, 10, 13b

Caithness
Gutter – 2a, 11
Raggle – 8
Rone – 2b, 6, 9, 12ac, 13-15, 16ab, 17
Stroop – 6
Nil – 1, 3-5, 7, 10, 12b

Sutherland
Gutter – 3, 6
Rain gutter – 11
Rone – 1, 3-5, 7-8, 9ab, 10, 13-17
Nil – 2, 12

Ross & Cromarty
Gutter – 5, 16-17, 24, 30, 32b, 39
Rain gutter – 27
Rone – 1, 3, 5-15, 18-23, 25ab, 26-29, 31, 32ab, 33-36, 37b
Valley – 28
Nil – 2, 4, 32c, 37a, 38

Inverness
Dirt – 5
Gutter – 2, 6, 10-11, 13c, 17, 23, 28, 33, 40
House rone – 7
Rond – 13a
Rone – 3, 8-9, 11-12, 13abcde, 14, 16, 18, 20, 21ab, 22, 26-27, 29-32, 34-39
Valley – 1
Nil – 4, 15, 19, 24-25

Nairn
Gutter – 6
Rhon – 1a
Rone – 1abc, 2, 4-5
Nil – 3

Moray
Gutter – 2a, 11
Rone – 4-5, 6ab, 8abcd, 9ab, 10, 12-15, 17-20, 22-23
Rone pipe – 7
Spout – 8e, 9b, 16, 21
Nil – 1, 2b, 3, 8f

Banff
Gutter – 18c
Ron – 30
Rone – 1, 2abc, 5, 7-10, 14-17, 19, 23, 25, 27-29, 31-34
Rone pipe – 21
Spout – 3-4, 6b, 9, 11, 13, 17, 18b, 21-24
Nil – 6a, 12, 18ad, 20, 26

Aberdeen
Gutter – 2, 9, 12, 14, 25
Pipe – 59
Rone – 4, 5ad, 14, 20, 23-24, 31, 37, 40, 45, 47bcdef, 48, 50, 55, 60, 63-65, 75-78, 81, 84, 95, 98, 100, 107
Rone pipe – 63, 71ac
Spout – 1, 3ab, 4, 5bcd, 6-8, 10-11, 13-22, 26-27, 28a, 29-32, 34-35, 39-42, 44-46, 47a, 49, 51, 53-54, 56, 58-59, 61, 66-70, 71b, 72-75, 79-83, 85-88, 90, 93-94, 97, 99, 101, 103-106, 108-109
Spoutin – 98
Water spout – 8, 21
Nil – 28bc, 33, 36, 38, 43, 52, 57, 62, 89, 91-92, 96, 102

Kincardine
Gutter – 5, 8, 16, 21
Rone – 4, 17bd, 19-20, 24
Spout – 1, 3, 7, 9-16, 17ac, 18, 23, 25-28
Spoutin – 6
Nil – 2, 22

Kinross
Rone – 1-7

Angus
Dreep pipe – 17a
Gutter – 6-7, 15, 18, 35
Quey – 19
Ren pipe – 19
Rone – 2, 7-10, 18, 20-22, 24-25, 29a, 30-32, 33ab, 36-37
Spout – 1, 3-4, 5abc, 12-13, 14abcd, 15, 17b, 18, 21-28, 32, 33a, 34, 36-37
Nil – 11, 16, 29b

Perth
Condie – 56
Flank – 73
Gutter – 4, 8, 21, 25, 33, 64, 67, 74
Ron – 39
Rone – 1, 2a, 3, 5-13, 15-21, 23-28, 29ab, 31-32, 34-35, 37-38, 40, 41ab, 42-50, 51ab, 52abcde, 53-55, 57-58, 60-62, 64-66, 68-72
Spout – 43, 60
Valley – 73
Nil – 2b, 14, 22, 30, 36, 59, 63

Fife
Dub – 60
Gutter – 17, 24-25, 44c, 57
Rone – 1, 3-8, 9ab, 10, 12-14, 16, 18-23, 26-30, 33-35, 36ab, 37-39, 40ab, 41abcd, 42, 43ab, 44abdef, 45-54, 55abcdefg, 56-60, 62-63, 64ab
Rone pipe – 2
Runnel – 44c
Spout – 12, 32, 50
Spout o'rone – 11
Nil – 15, 31, 61

Clackmannan
Rone – 1-3, 4abcd, 5-7

Stirling
Gutter – 4, 7bc, 11, 16, 20, 25d, 34
Gutter rone – 7f
Half roond gutter – 7d
Ron – 9
Rone – 1-3, 6, 7abce, 8, 10, 12, 15-20, 21ab, 22ab, 23bc, 24, 25abcd, 26abcde, 27ab, 28-34, 35ab, 36, 37ab, 38, 39ab, 40, 42ab
Rone pipe – 22b
Nil – 5, 13-14, 23a, 41

Dunbarton
Gutter – 1, 8, 11, 13bc, 17
Riggin – 5, 9
Rone – 2-3, 4b, 6, 7abc, 9-10, 12, 13ac, 14b, 15, 16ab, 17
Rone pipe – 11, 18
Nil – 4a, 14a

Argyll
Gutter – 6, 14, 17, 19, 22, 30, 33-34
Lead gutter – 27
Rone – 1-3, 5, 7-10, 12-13, 15-16, 18-19, 21, 23-26, 28-30, 32-33, 35-37, 39-40
Rone pipe – 11
Rowan – 24
Nil – 4, 20, 31, 38

Bute
Gutter – 1cd, 7
Rone – 1abcde, 2-3, 5-7, 8ab, 9
Nil – 4

Ayr
Gutter – 1a, 2b, 15, 20c, 25, 41, 45, 49, 54-55, 57
Rone – 1ab, 2ab, 3-7, 8ab, 9-11, 12ab, 13-14, 16ab, 17, 18ab, 20abdefgh, 21-22, 24ab, 26abc, 27, 28abcdef, 29, 30ab, 31-34, 35ab, 36-39, 42-43, 46-48, 50-52, 53ab, 54, 56-57
Rone pipe – 44
Nil – 19, 23, 40

Renfrew
Gutter – 1b, 2h, 4d, 5, 11hl
Rone – 1b, 2abefghij, 4ace, 6-10, 11abcefikl, 12a, 13abcd, 14a, 15, 16abcd, 17, 18ab, 19, 20ab, 21
Rone pipe – 12b
Roof gutter – 2i
Sough – 16a
Nil – 1a, 2cd, 3, 4b, 11dgj, 14b

Lanark
Gutter – 1, 6, 8b, 14bd, 15a, 17, 58, 67a
Rain gutter – 18
Ron – 38e
Rone – 1-6, 7ac, 8a, 9ab, 10ab, 11-13, 14ac, 15abc, 16ab, 17-24, 25abcd, 26ab, 27ab, 29acdefg, 30, 31abcd, 32acdef, 33acd, 34, 35abcd, 36-37, 38abcd, 39-42, 44-45, 46abc, 47-48, 49ab, 50-51, 52ab, 53-56, 57abc, 58, 59ab, 60-63, 64b, 65-66, 67b
Valley – 56
Nil – 7b, 28, 29b, 32b, 33b, 43, 64a

West Lothian
Gautten – 19b
Rone – 1acd, 2-3, 5-8, 9a, 10-16, 17ab, 18, 19a, 20ab, 21ab, 22
Nil – 1b, 4, 9b

Midlothian
Gutter – 10, 15, 19-20, 23b, 30
Lead gutter – 11
Rone – 1-5, 6b, 7ab, 8a, 9-11, 12ab, 13, 14ab, 15-18, 21-22, 23ab, 24, 25bc, 26ab, 27-29, 31-32
Rone pipe – 6a, 25a
Nil – 8b, 25d

East Lothian
Channel – 17
Gutter – 13, 16
Rone – 1-3, 4b, 5, 6ab, 7, 9-12, 14-16, 18-21
Spout – 4a, 6a, 8
Valley – 13

Berwick
Gutter – 16c, 31
Gutter spout – 6
Rain spout – 32
Rone – 1-5, 8-9, 11-13, 15, 16ac, 17-20, 22-25, 27, 29, 32
Roon – 26
Spout – 1, 4, 7-8, 10, 16ab, 19-21, 27
Nil – 14, 28, 30

Peebles
Gutter pipe – 2
Rone – 1-3, 4abc, 5, 6ab, 7-10

Selkirk
Rone – 1, 2abcde, 3-8

Roxburgh
Gutter – 21a
Rone – 1-2, 3ab, 4-5, 8, 9a, 10-14, 15a, 16-20, 21abcdef, 22-28
Spout – 7, 9b, 10, 15b, 23
Nil – 6

Dumfries
Gutter – 1a, 5, 17b, 22, 31bd, 42, 46-47
Rone – 1ab, 2-4, 6-7, 8ab, 9-14, 16, 17a, 19-20, 21b, 23-24, 26-29, 31cde, 32-34, 36, 38-39, 41, 45ab, 46
Rone pipe – 35, 40, 43-44
Spout – 37, 46, 49
Spoutin(g) – 15, 38
Nil – 18, 21a, 25, 30, 31af, 48

Kirkcudbright
Gutter – 10
Ron – 15a
Rone – 1-9, 12ab, 13-14, 15b, 16-20, 21abc, 22-23, 25-27
Nil – 11, 24

Wigtown
Heck – 10
Rone – 1-2, 4, 5ab, 6-8, 11-17
Nil – 3, 9, 18

Northumberland
Channel – 59b
Culvert – 75
Drain – 22
Easing box – 142
Eaves gutter – 41d, 77, 91
Eaves spouting – 103a
Gully – 17, 122b
Gutter – 6, 18, 29d, 31, 35, 41ac, 46, 59bc, 61, 70, 72acdi, 87, 88b, 101b, 109-110, 111a, 120b, 121, 127a, 139
Guttering – 18, 89, 92, 103c, 130b
Rainwater spout – 69b
Rainwetter spout – 69ab
Rone – 1c, 2a, 4, 13, 26, 29f
Roof gutter – 126f, 137
Roof spouting – 103a

Northumberland cont'd

Roof wetter spout – 126c
Rowan – 21
Runner – 1c
Spout – 1ab, 2b, 4-5, 7-11, 13, 15-16, 18, 19a, 20b, 23, 25-28, 29abcdf, 30, 33b, 34a, 36-39, 40ab, 41bd, 42, 44-45, 47-50, 52, 53b, 55-58, 59bcdef, 60-61, 62abcegh, 63, 64ab 65a, 66-68, 69abcdeh, 71abcde, 72bcdefgikl, 74, 77-84, 86-87, 88a, 89-90, 93, 94ab, 95ab, 96-98, 100, 102, 105-107, 108ab, 109-110, 111ab, 112-114, 116, 118ab, 119, 120ac, 122ab, 123, 124ab, 125, 126abd, 127bce, 128, 129abc, 130def, 136, 139, 141, 143
Spouting – 1b, 14, 43, 51, 53a, 54, 69g, 73, 75-76, 103bc, 104a, 111ab, 114, 121, 127dg, 130c, 132-135, 138, 141-142
Valley gutter – 20b, 104b
Water way – 41c
Nil – 3, 12, 19b, 20a, 24ab, 29e, 32, 33a, 34b, 59a, 62df, 65b, 69f, 72hj, 85, 99abc, 101a, 108c, 115, 117, 126e, 127fh, 130a, 131, 140

Cumberland

Cross spout – 24
Down spout – 48
Drain piping – 5a
Easing gutter – 22
Easins gutter – 56
Eaves gutter – 50
Eaves spout – 62
Gutter – 4, 9, 12, 13c, 16, 19, 24, 47, 52-53, 57-59
Guttering – 53
Lander – 55
Spout – 2, 6, 8-9, 11, 13c, 14, 15bc, 16-18, 21, 25-26, 29, 31-34, 36, 37b, 39-42, 44-45, 54, 57-59, 61, 63b
Spout easing – 46
Spoutin(g) – 3, 7, 13d, 23, 28, 37a, 38, 43, 48-49, 51, 57, 60
Nil – 1ab, 5b, 10, 13ab, 15a, 20, 27, 30, 35, 63a

Down

Easen – 22
Eave spouting – 21
Gutter – 2a, 15, 19
Spout – 13
Spoutin(g) – 1, 2a, 3-11, 17-18, 20, 23-24, 26-27, 29
Water spout – 28
Nil – 2b, 4a, 12, 14, 16, 25, 30

Tyrone

Easen – 5
Eave spout – 11
Gutter – 10
Spoutin(g) – 1-2, 6-13, 16
Nil – 3-4, 14-15

Antrim

Easen – 5b, 17
Eave spoutin – 23
Gully – 21
Gutter – 22, 29
Rone – 25
Spoutin(g) – 1-3, 5ab, 7, 8ab, 11-13, 15, 16b, 18-21, 26-28, 31-33
Trinket – 9
Nil – 4, 4A, 6, 10, 14, 16ac, 24, 30, 34

Donegal

Eave pipe – 6
Eaves – 5
Ridge pipe – 13
Shuch – 5A
Side spout – 10a
Spout – 1
Spoutin(g) – 2-5, 7, 7A, 8, 10b, 11-13
Nil – 1A, 9

Fermanagh

Easen – 6
Eave run – 10
Lead valley – 1
Spout – 2
Spoutin(g) – 2, 4, 7a, 9-10
Nil – 3, 5, 7b, 8

Armagh

Roof gutter – 4
Spout – 1-3
Spoutin(g) – 4-5, 6ab

Londonderry

Spout – 6
Spoutin(g) – 1, 1AB, 2-3, 3A, 4-7

50 GUTTER (the kind running through a byre) (PQ1, 110)

Shetland

Drain – 1
Gutter – 21a
Odler – 30
Oiler – 18, 21ab, 24, 27, 33
Oilick – 21a, 25-26
Runnock – 2-10, 12-20, 22, 24-26, 29-30, 32
Nil – 11, 23, 28, 31

Orkney

Channel – 8
Greup – 13a
Groop – 19-21
Gruep – 17
Grup – 16
Gutter – 8, 15
Oddle – 4, 8-9, 12, 21
Oddler – 1-4, 6, 13b
Rinnag – 17
Rinnick – 15
Runnag – 18
Runnick – 19
Sester – 5, 7, 10-12, 13a, 15, 20
Sister – 14
Uddler – 5, 16

Caithness

Drain – 13
Graip – 6
Greep – 8, 14
Muck hole – 13
Stran – 2ab, 4-5, 11, 12c, 14-15, 16a, 17
Strand – 3, 9-10, 16b
Strang – 5, 8
Strannie – 12a
Nil – 1, 7, 12b

Sutherland

Chink – 14
Gutter – 8, 11, 16
Stran – 1, 3-6, 9ab, 10, 16
Strand – 2, 4, 7-8, 13, 15
Nil – 12, 17

Ross & Cromarty

Carcar – 28
Channel – 23, 29, 31
Clohan – 33
Drain – 5, 18-19, 29, 32a, 34, 39
Grip – 4, 25b
Gutter – 1, 3, 8-9, 13, 16, 20, 22, 26-27
Runnel – 21
Stran – 17, 20
Strang – 8, 11
Trench – 36
Trink – 24
Trinkie – 37b
Wash – 15
Nil – 2, 6-7, 10, 12, 14, 25a, 30, 32bc, 35, 37a, 38

Inverness

Brander – 13e
Carcre – 31
Channel – 8-9, 12, 17, 20, 21a, 26
Clash – 22
Drain – 1, 3, 13a, 16, 32, 38
Greep – 27
Grip – 37-38
Gutter – 2, 5, 7, 13c, 17, 21a, 23, 28-30, 33-35, 37, 39
Sewer – 14
Stran – 21b
Strand – 10, 28
Strang – 15
Strawnie – 27
Syver – 13e
Nil – 4, 6, 11, 13bd, 18-19, 24-25, 31, 36, 40

Nairn

Channel – 2
Greep – 4
Gutter – 1a, 6
Strang – 1c, 2-3
Strang channel – 1b
Strangie – 1b
Nil – 5

Moray

Dreep – 14, 18
Greep – 4-5, 6a, 8bd, 10-11, 16, 19, 21
Gutter – 14
Stran – 2a, 6b, 8de, 9a, 12-13, 17, 20, 22
Stranie – 23
Strannie – 8b, 9a
Strin – 15
Strun – 1, 7, 16, 18
Nil – 2b, 3, 8acf, 9b

Banff

Dreep – 18b
Greep – 1, 2c, 3-5, 6ab, 7-11, 13-17, 18cd, 19, 22-23, 25-34
Gutter – 8
Stran – 9, 12, 18b, 21, 23-24
Strand – 30
Stranie – 20
Strin – 13
Nil – 2ab, 18a

Aberdeen

Channel – 6, 20, 47b, 59, 69, 73-74, 77, 86
Chunnel – 106
Drain – 21, 47c, 70
Dreep – 108
Greep – 2, 3ab, 5bcd, 7-16, 19, 22-27, 28bc, 29-32, 34-36, 39-40, 42, 44-46, 47abd, 48-58, 60-61, 63, 65-66, 68-69, 71abc, 72-76, 78-80, 82-84, 87-93, 95-101, 103-104, 107, 109
Gutter – 17, 34, 70, 105
Sheuch – 5a
Spoot – 92, 105
Stank – 37
Stran – 28a, 47e, 51, 81, 86, 88, 105
Strand – 67-68
Strang – 20-21, 34
Strang rin – 32
Strannie – 12, 27, 64, 69
Strawn – 85, 94
Stripe – 20
Stripie – 47e, 62
Trink – 40
Nil – 1, 4, 18, 33, 38, 41, 43, 47f, 102

Kincardine

Channel – 5,8
Graip – 23
Greep – 1-4, 6-7, 10-11, 14-16, 17abc, 18, 23
Gripe – 25
Groop – 21, 25-27
Gruip – 19
Stran – 5, 9, 12, 24
Strand – 4, 13, 17bd, 20, 27-28
Trink – 12
Nil – 22

Kinross

Graup – 5
Grip – 1-6
Gruip – 7

Angus

Channel – 14a
Drain – 15
Graip – 3, 8, 11, 14a, 17b, 20-21, 23, 30, 32
Graith – 33b
Greep – 13, 17a
Grip – 6, 9, 20, 36
Groop – 7, 14a, 34
Gruip – 1, 4, 5a, 14cd, 22, 27, 31, 35
Grup – 33a
Gundie – 5b
Gutter – 10, 17b, 18, 23, 33b
Sheuch – 5c
Strand – 18, 22, 24, 28, 37
Strang – 23
Trink – 24
Wash – 15, 24
Wash channel – 19
Nil – 2, 12, 14b, 16, 25-26, 29ab

Perth

Channel – 60
Creep – 17
Drain – 13
Dub – 25
Graip – 23, 37, 63-65
Greep – 5-6, 12-13, 17-18, 20, 25-26, 29b, 30, 39-40, 42, 45, 56
Grep – 67
Greup – 22
Grip – 1, 3, 8-11, 15-16, 24, 26, 28, 29a, 33-35, 38, 41ab,

Perth cont'd
42-45, 47-49, 51a, 52c, 56, 59, 60-62, 67-74
Grit — 27
Gruip — 7, 31-32, 46, 58
Grup — 50, 66
Guthe — 4
Gutter — 36
Sheuch — 24
Strand — 21, 25, 33, 56-57
Wash channel — 32
Wash hole — 45
Nil — 2ab, 14, 19, 51b, 52abde, 53-55

Fife
Channel — 44e
Dishel — 55d
Gaulen — 49
Gitter — 52
Graip — 1-2, 4-6, 8, 9b, 11-14, 17, 20-21, 23, 25-26, 28, 30, 39, 40b, 45, 55f, 64b
Graip run — 32
Greep — 54d, 59
Grip — 7, 10, 18, 21, 23, 33-35, 36ab, 38, 41ab, 42, 43a, 46, 51-53, 55bdefg, 56-57, 61-62, 64a
Gripe — 37, 64a
Grit — 41d, 54
Gruip — 27
Gutter — 9a, 11, 16, 38, 44c
Shuch — 44e, 55c
Strand — 3, 5, 23, 26-27
Trap — 12
Trough — 29
Wash run — 43b
Nil — 15, 19, 22, 24, 31, 40a, 41c, 44abdf, 47-48, 50, 55a, 58, 60, 63

Clackmannan
Grip — 1, 3, 4d, 5-7
Grup — 5
Gutter — 2
Nil — 4abc

Stirling
Channel — 7c, 36
Drain — 26a
Grip — 1-3, 7abdef, 9, 11-15, 17-18, 20, 21ab, 22b, 23bc, 24, 25abcd, 26abcdf, 27ab, 28-34, 35ab, 37ab, 38, 39b, 40, 42ab
Gripe — 6, 10
Grup — 8, 25d
Gully — 22a
Gutter — 4, 31, 36
Sheuch — 7b, 19, 36
Syver — 19
Nil — 5, 16, 23a, 26e, 39a, 41, 42b

Dunbarton
Channel — 5
Grip — 1-3, 4ab, 5-6, 7c, 13abc, 15, 16ab
Gripe — 14a
Grit — 7a
Grup — 9
Sheuch — 5, 11, 14a
Shuch — 7b
Shuck — 14a
Nil — 8, 10, 12, 14b, 17-18

Argyll
Crib — 27
Drain — 1
Greep — 33, 35, 37-40
Grip — 3, 5, 7-8, 10, 12, 14-15, 19-24, 26, 28-33
Gripe — 11
Grup — 18
Gutter — 5-6, 17
Sheuch — 10, 13
Nil — 2, 4, 9, 16, 25, 34, 36

Bute
Grip — 1abce, 2-7, 8ab, 9
Nil — 1d

Ayr
Channel — 57
Dreep — 43
Greep — 18b
Grip — 1ab, 2ab, 3-7, 8ab, 9-11, 12ab, 13-15, 16ab, 17, 18ab, 19, 20abcdefgh, 22-23, 24b, 26abc, 27, 28abcdf, 29, 30ab, 31-34, 35b, 36-52, 53ab, 54-57
Gripe — 21
Grit — 27
Groop — 4
Grup — 12a, 28b, 48
Syver — 30b
Nil — 24a, 25, 28e, 35a

Renfrew
Channel — 2b, 11j
Cullis — 16a
Grip — 2befgi, 4acd, 5, 7-10, 11abfl, 12a, 13abc, 14b, 15, 16abd, 18a, 19, 20b, 21
Grup — 1b, 17
Gutter — 2ai, 4e, 11e, 20a
Sheuch — 11c
Shuch — 1a
Nil — 2cdhj, 3, 4b, 6, 11dghik, 12b, 13d, 14a, 16c, 18b

Lanark
Aidle rin — 9b
Channel — 2
Drain — 15a, 25c
Gotten — 6
Grip — 2-3, 7a, 9ab, 10a, 12-13, 14bc, 15abc, 16b, 17, 19-22, 24, 27ab, 29def, 30, 31abcd, 32acf, 33cd, 34, 35abd, 37, 38abcde, 39-41, 45, 46ab, 47-48, 49ab, 50-51, 52ab, 54-56, 57abc, 58, 59ab, 60-63, 64ab, 65-66, 67ab
Grit — 7c
Gruip — 1, 53
Grup — 5, 23, 42-44, 46ac
Gutter — 26b, 35d, 44
Sheuch — 26b, 36, 38a, 52a
Wash run — 18
Nil — 4, 7b, 8ab, 10b, 11, 14ad, 16a, 25abd, 26a, 28, 29abcg, 32bde, 33ab, 35c

West Lothian
Channel — 21b
Crib — 22
Drain — 1a
Dung channel — 17a
Gang — 4
Grip — 1ad, 2-8, 9ab, 10, 12, 14-16, 17a, 18, 19b, 21a
Grit — 19a
Gunnel — 15
Gutter — 11, 13
Sheuch — 1c
Shuch — 13
Nil — 1b, 17b, 20ab

Midlothian
Grip — 3, 6b, 9-11, 12ab, 13, 14ab, 15-19, 21-22, 23b, 24, 26a, 27, 29, 32
Grit — 20
Gruip — 30
Grup — 4
Gutter — 8a, 15, 23b, 25c
Shuch — 1
Nil — 2, 5, 6a, 7ab, 8b, 23a, 25abd, 26b, 28, 31

East Lothian
Causey — 21
Channel — 6b, 13
Drain — 6a
Graip — 4b
Greep — 10, 17
Greet — 13
Grep — 4b
Grip — 3, 6ab, 7-8, 13, 15, 20
Grit — 20
Grith — 11
Grup — 15
Gutter — 5, 9, 14, 16, 21
Sheuch — 13
Nil — 1-2, 4a, 12, 18-19

Berwick
Drain — 2
Gater — 4
Geeter — 8
Getter — 32
Graip — 11
Grip — 3, 8, 12, 16ac, 17, 22-23, 29
Grit — 14
Gutter — 1, 10, 15, 16b, 25
Rinner — 16b, 31
Runnel — 21
Runner — 6
Strand — 32
Syre — 8, 32
Wash — 8
Nil — 5, 7, 9, 13, 18-20, 24, 26-28, 30

Peebles
Greep — 2
Grip — 2-3, 4b, 5, 6ab, 7-10
Grup — 1
Shuch — 4b
Slip — 2
Nil — 4ac

Selkirk
Grip — 1, 2be, 5, 7
Gruip — 3-4, 8
Guitter — 2ad
Nil — 2c, 6

Roxburgh
Gaetter — 5
Greup — 21df
Grip — 1, 4, 8, 12, 15b, 21a, 22
Gripe — 2, 10, 24
Griup — 21f
Groop — 25-26
Gruip — 17, 20, 21a, 26, 28
Grup — 7,23
Guddian — 21c
Gutter — 2, 4, 13, 21e
Rinner — 5
Strand — 3b, 24
Syre — 15a, 17
Nil — 3a, 6, 9ab, 11, 14, 16, 18-19, 21b, 27

Dumfries
Greep — 2, 9
Grip — 1ab, 2-3, 5-7, 8ab, 10-14, 17ab, 19-20, 21ab, 23-28, 30, 31cd, 32, 34, 36-38, 41-44, 46-47
Gripe — 16, 34-35
Groop — 18, 29, 33-34, 39-40, 45a, 46, 49
Gruip — 16, 45b
Gutter — 1a
Shuch — 31e
Syre — 15, 22, 35
Nil — 4, 31abf, 48

Kirkcudbright
Grip — 4-6, 9-10, 12b, 13-14, 15ab, 16, 18-19, 21c, 22-24, 26
Gripe — 17
Grit — 14
Gruip — 2-3, 7-8, 12a, 27
Grup — 1, 21a
Nil — 11, 20 21b, 25

Wigtown
Grip — 1-2, 4, 5ab, 6-11, 13-18
Gruip — 3, 12

Northumberland
Byre — 126c
Cassie — 41d, 52, 124a
Causie — 107, 124a
Causway — 110
Channel — 28, 34a, 37-39, 44, 46, 48-50, 53b, 54-55, 60-61, 62b, 65a, 68, 69abef, 71d, 72i, 76-83, 87, 88a, 93, 100, 104a, 108a, 109, 111b, 112, 118ab, 120a, 129b, 130d, 137-140, 142
Cundie — 29d, 56
Drain — 56, 69abd, 71c, 122b
Drain run away — 130c
Drip — 75
Graip — 123, 134, 140
Greate — 136
Greeap — 132, 135
Greep — 103bc, 124a, 133, 142
Grip — 26, 29cf, 40a, 44, 47, 59c, 60,74, 77, 89, 141
Gripe — 104b
Groop — 51, 62g
Growp — 38
Grup — 21, 34b, 36, 42, 44, 53a, 77, 79, 124a
Gully — 69c, 98, 111a
Gutter — 1a, 29b, 30-31, 35, 41c, 43, 46, 52, 59b, 64a, 70, 80-81, 87, 94b, 95b, 103b, 108c, 111b, 120b, 124b, 127a, 130e, 139
Muck run — 41c
Runaway — 99d
Runnel — 72bi, 114
Runner — 59be
Syke — 39
Syre — 1b, 2a, 3-6, 8-11, 13-18, 19a, 20b, 22, 25, 27, 29a, 33b, 39, 40a, 45, 60, 73, 122a
Trough — 72l
Wash away — 120c
Yeddle — 108c
Nil — 1c, 2b, 7, 12, 19b, 20a, 23, 24ab, 29e, 32, 33a, 40b, 41ab, 57-58, 59adf, 62acdefh, 63, 64b, 65b, 66-67, 69gh, 71abe, 72acdefghjk, 84-86, 88b, 90-92, 94a, 95a, 96-97, 99abc, 101ab, 102, 103a, 105-106, 108b, 113, 115-117, 119, 121, 125, 126abdef, 127bcdefgh, 128, 129ac, 130abf, 131, 143

Cumberland
Channel — 2-3, 9, 21-22, 24, 37a, 42, 48, 51, 53, 57-59
Chennel — 20
Drain — 14, 47
Graip — 13d, 37a
Greap — 31, 37b, 40, 47
Greuf — 8, 29
Greup — 5ab, 6, 8-9, 16-18, 25, 28, 33, 38, 44-46, 49, 62
Greup watter — 27
Grip — 12, 30, 36, 37a, 63b
Gripe — 63a
Groop — 4, 7, 11, 17, 32, 47
Grubstone — 51
Grufe — 15b
Grup — 3, 13bc, 26, 41, 57, 61
Gruve — 34
Gult — 37a
Gutter — 17, 19, 23-24, 46, 50, 53, 58
Stell — 30
Sump way — 57
Syke — 46
Vennel — 7, 18, 30, 54, 56, 59-60
Yeadle — 23

Cumberland cont'd

Nil — 1ab, 10, 13a, 15ac, 35, 39, 43, 52, 55

Down

Grip — 3, 8
Group — 2ab, 4-6, 8-11, 13, 15, 17-19, 21-28
Gutter — 2a
Trinket — 29
Nil — 1, 7, 12, 14, 16, 20, 30

Tyrone

Channel — 14
Grape — 1-2
Grip — 2, 11
Gripe — 11
Group — 3-16
Shern — 5
Water channel — 14

Antrim

Grape — 8b
Grip — 26, 30
Group — 1-2, 4, 5ab, 6-7, 8a, 9-13, 15, 16b, 17-25, 27-34
Nil — 3, 4A, 14, 16ac

Donegal

Drain — 10a
Grape — 1, 4, 5A, 7, 7A, 11
Group — 5, 10ab, 13
Sink — 2-3, 6, 12-13
Nil — 1A, 8-9

Fermanagh

Group — 1-6, 8-10
Nil — 7ab

Armagh

Group — 1, 3-5, 6ab
Nil — 2

Londonderry

Grape — 5
Groop — 1B, 2-3, 3A, 4-7
Grup — 1
Shire — 5
Nil — 1A

51 PIPE down the side of a house to drain water from the roof (PQ1, 111)

Rone pipe has not been mapped as it occurs rather densely everywhere in Scotland (but not in England and Northern Ireland).
Variants of DOWN have been subsumed (see note on DOWN in item 15 **Down Draught** and map 14 (cow), Appendix A).
Variants of SPOUT, SPOUTIN(G) (see note on 49 **gutter**) and DROP (some **drap**) have also been subsumed.
For **rone** cf. also 49 **gutter** and 39 **strip of ice.**

Shetland

Down pipe — 1, 3, 7, 17, 22, 27, 29, 32
Drain pipe — 8, 17
Rone pipe — 2, 10, 16, 19, 21ab, 23-24, 26, 33
Spout — 4-6, 13, 15, 20, 25, 28, 30
Water pipe — 30
Nil — 9, 11-12, 14, 18, 31

Orkney

Conductor — 2
Down pipe — 1, 5, 8-9, 12, 13a, 15, 19, 21
Down run — 18
Drop — 11
Rone (pipe) — *4,* 7, *13a, 14,* 16, *17, 19*-20
Spout (pipe) — 6, *16*
Nil — 3, 10, 13b

Caithness

Down led — 5
Down pipe — 2a, 6, 8, 10-11, 14, 16b
Rone (pipe) — *2b, 4,* 9, 12ab, 13-15, *16a, 17*
Stroop — 12c
Up and down rone — 3
Nil — 1, 7

Sutherland

Down pipe — 2, 11
Drop pipe — 1
Rone (pipe) — *3-8,* 9ab, *10, 13, 15-17*
Roof pipe — 3
Nil — 12, 14

Ross & Cromarty

Conductor — 32a
(Down) pipe— 1, *6-7, 9-10, 12-13, 15, 17-18, 21-23, 27-29,* 30, *32b, 33, 36*
Rhond — 32c
Rone (pipe) — 2, *3,* 4-5, *7-9, 11,* 14-17, *19-20,* 24, *25ab, 26, 29, 32b, 34, 37ab,* 39
Water conductor — 27
Water pipe — 31
Nil — 35, 38

Inverness

Conductor — 1, 3, 36, 38
(Down) pipe — 2, *4,* 8, *11,* 13ae, *14-15, 17, 21b, 23, 26, 28, 30-31, 34*
Get away — 22
Rone (pipe) — *3, 5-7,* 9-10, *12,* 13*bcd*, *16, 18,* 20, *21a, 25,* 27, *29, 32,* 33, *35, 37-39,* 40
Nil — 19, 24

Nairn

Down pipe — 1c, 2
Rhon — 1a
Rone (pipe) — 1a*b*, 3, 5-6
Nil — 4

Moray

Down pipe — 3, 5, 6a, 7, 8cde, 12-13, 15-16, 18, 20-22
Ron — 21
Rone (pipe) — 2b, *6b, 7, 8bc, 9a,* 11, 14, *17, 20, 23*
Spout — 1, 4, 9a, 10, 19
Stroop — 3-4
Nil — 2a, 8af, 9b

Banff

Down pipe — 7, 9, 24-25, 33-34
Down spout — 29
Down stoup — 2c
Ron — 30
Rone (pipe) — *4, 8,* 9, *10,* 11, *14-15,* 17, 18bc, 22-24, *27-29,* 31, *32*
Rone spout — 16, 19
Spout — 1, 2ab, 3, 5, 6ab, 8-9, 12-13, 17, 19-21, 23
Nil — 18ad, 26

Aberdeen

Down drap — 60
(Down) pipe — *6, 20, 24-25, 27,* 28c, *39, 45,* 49, *53, 71b, 73, 75, 81, 101*
Down spout — 5c, 65, 69, 80, 86
Gutter spout — 47c
Rain water pipe — 19
Rone (pipe) — 3ab, 6, 10-11, *12,* 13, *14,* 15, *18, 21,* 22, *23,* 28a, *30, 32,* 34, *38,* 40-41, 44, 47*ab*, 49-51, *55,* 56, 59, *61-62, 66*-67, 73-74, *78, 80, 82,* 83, *84,* 85, 88-89, 94, *95-98, 100,* 105-106, *108-109*
Spout — 1-2, 4, 5abd, 7, 9, 11, 13-14, 16-17, 19, 26-27, 29, 31, 35, 37, 46, 47adef, 48, 51-54, 59-60, 63, 69-70, 71c, 75-77, 79, 87, 92-93, 99, 103-104, 107-108
Water spout — 70
Watter spout — 32
Nil — 8, 28b, 33, 36, 42-43, 57-58, 64, 68, 71a, 72, 90-91, 102

Kincardine

Conductor — 27
Down (pipe) — 10, 19, *21*
Down spout — 10, 14, 17b
Drop — 18
Rone (pipe) — 3, *4,* 5, *6-8,* 10, *12,* 15, 17b*cd*, 18, *20,* 23, *26, 28*
Spout — 1-2, 10-11, 13, 16, 17ac, 18, 24-25
Nil — 9, 22

Kinross

Conductor — 1, 4
Rone pipe — 2-3, 6
Nil — 5, 7

Angus

Conductor — 2, 6, 36
Pipie — 18
Ren pipe — 19
Rin awa — 14a
Rone (pipe) — 1, 3-4, 5ac, *10, 13,* 14acd, *15,* 17b, *20-22,* 23-24, 26, *27,* 28, *30-31,* 33b, 34-35, 37
Spout — 5b, 7-9, 12, 14b, 18, 24-25, 29a, 30
Spoutie — 19
Tail pipe — 17a
Water spout — 33b
Nil — 11, 16, 29b, 32, 33a

Perth

Conductor — 3, 9, 19-21, 23-24, 29b, 31, 39, 56-57, 63, 71, 73
Conveyor — 24
Cundie — 30
Down fa pipe — 25
Down gae — 66
(Down) pipe — 4, *16, 21, 51a,* 52b, 57, *71*
Down spoot — 15
Drain pipe — 8, 25, 74
Gutter — 36, 50, 58
Rain pipe — 25, 41a, 65
Rone (pipe) — *1, 2a, 3, 5-6, 10-13,* 14, *16-17, 26-28, 29a, 32-35, 37, 40, 41b,* 43, *44-49, 51b, 52ace, 53, 55,* 60, *62,* 64, 67-*68, 72*-73
Shoot — 49
Spout — 7, 50, 51a, 52cd
Nil — 2b, 18, 22, 38, 42, 54, 59, 61, 69-70

Fife

Conductor — 4, 11, 13, 25, 28, 40a, 41b, 53, 55abf, 56, 62
Descending pipe — 21
Down pipe — 18, 43b, 45, 57
Drain pipe — 6, 9a, 36b, 40b, 50, 55bg, 60
Gutter — 54
Rone (pipe) — *1, 7-8, 9ab,* 10, *12-14, 16, 19-22, 24, 26-27, 29-30, 34,* 36ab, *37-39, 41acd, 42, 43a, 44abcdef, 45, 47-50, 52, 55bcd, 57, 59, 62-63, 64a*
Sile pipe — 47
Spout — 11, 23, 32-33, 35, 46, 61
Stack pipe — 58
Water pipe — 43a, 55e
Nil — 2-3, 5, 15, 17, 31, 51, 64b

Clackmannan

Conductor — 4cd, 6
Cundie — 4a
Down come — 2
Down pipe — 4b
Rone (pipe) — 1, *2-3, 5,* 7

Stirling

Conductor — 3-4, 6, 7cf, 9-10, 13, 18, 21b, 23c, 24, 26d, 27b, 30, 32, 34, 37b
Cunductor — 7a
Down lead — 31
Down pipe — 22ab
Drain pipe — 23a, 26c
Drop pipe — 39b
Gunnie pipe — 9

Stirling cont'd
Rain water pipe — 25ad
Rone (pipe) — *1-2*, 7*abcde*, 8, *10-12, 15-18, 20, 21ab, 22a,* 23ab, *25abc, 26abef, 27ab, 28-31, 34, 35a, 36, 37a, 38, 39ab, 40-41, 42a*
Soil pipe — 35b
Nil — 5, 14, 19, 33, 42b

Dunbarton
Conductor — 5, 7c, 8, 13c, 14b, 17
Down pipe — 16a
(Down) spout — *4b*, 9
Drain pipe — 8
Rone (pipe) — 1, *2*, 3, *6*, *7ab, 10-12*, 13abc, 14*ab*, *15, 16ab, 17-18*
Nil — 4a

Argyll
Conductor — 3, 10, 12, 14, 16, 19, 24, 26-28, 32-34, 37
(Down) pipe — *5, 10*, 17, *18-19*
Drain pipe — 24
Rone conductor — 35
Rone (pipe) — *1-2*, 6, *7-9*, 11, 13, *15-16*, 17, 20, *21*, 22, *23*, 25, 26, *29-31*, 33, *35-39*
Nil — 4, 40

Bute
Conductor — 1a
Down pipe — 8b
Rone pipe — 1cd, 2-3, 6-7, 8ab, 9
Rone pipe conductor — 1e
Nil — 1b, 4-5

Ayr
Conductor — 4, 6, 8a, 26b, 28e, 32, 57
Down pipe — 26b, 28f, 47, 57
Down spout — 55
Drop pipe — 6, 33, 44, 48
Rone (pipe) — *1ab, 2ab, 3, 5, 7, 8ab, 9*, 10-11, *12ab, 13-15, 16ab, 17, 18ab*, 19, *20abcdefgh, 21-23, 24ab*, 25, *27*, 28*bcd*, *29, 30ab, 31-32, 34, 35ab, 36-38, 40-43, 45*-46, *48*-49, *51, 53a, 54, 56-57*
Spout — 39, 53b
Nil — 26ac, 28a, 50, 52

Renfrew
Conductor — 2e, 4ac, 5, 8-9, 13b, 15, 20b, 21
(Down) pipe — *7*, 11e*j*
Drain pipe — 12b, 18a, 20a
Drop — 18a
Pipe — 11e
Rone (pipe) — 1ab, 2*abfgh*ij, 3, *4de, 6, 8, 10*, 11*abcd*f*hikl*, *13acd, 14ab, 16abcd, 17*, 18ab, *19*
Roof gutter pipe — 2i
Nil — 2cd, 4b, 11g, 12a

Lanark
Conductor (pipe) — *1*, 3, *12*-13, 14d, 15abc, 17, 26a, 30, 38c, 48, 56
Down drop — 20
Downer — 20
Down pipe — 8a, 15a, 29d, 32f, 39, 44, 47-48
Down rone — 48
Down water pipe — 58
Drain (pipe) — *25d, 26b*, 64a
Drop pipe — 53, 67a
Gutter — 5
Lead — 9b
Rain conductor — 58
Rain pipe — 16a, 18
Rain water pipe — 58
Rhon pipe — 38e
Rone (pipe) — *1-3*, 4, *6*, *7abc, 8ab, 10b, 11-13, 14ac, 15b, 16b, 17, 19, 21, 23-24, 25abcd, 26a, 27ab*, 28, 29acefg, *30, 31acd, 32abcdef*, 33acd, 34, *35abd, 36-37, 38ac, 40-42*, 43, *44-45, 46abc, 49ab, 50-51, 52ab*, 54, *57ab, 59ab, 60*, 61, *62, 64b, 65-66, 67b*
Ro pipe — 14b
Soil pipe — 22
Stack — 15a
Nil — 9a, 10a, 29b, 31b, 33b, 35c, 38bd, 55, 57c, 63

West Lothian
Conductor — 5, 10, 14-15, 19a, 21a
Conduit — 21a
Down comer — 12
Gutter pipe — 11
Rain water conductor — 16
Rain water pipe — 2
Rone (pipe) — 1a*bcd*, *3*, 5, *6-8*, 9ab, *11, 13*, 17a, *19b*, 20ab, *21ab, 22*
Water conductor — 17a
Water pipe — 18
Nil — 4, 17b

Midlothian
Conductor — 8b, 11, 12a, 15, 26a, 29, 32
Down pipe — 3, 16, 29, 32
Drain pipe — 2, 6a, 22
Drop pipe — 12b
Gutter pipe — 10
Rain pipe — 18
Rone (pipe) — *1, 3, 6b, 7ab, 8a, 9-10, 12a, 13, 14ab, 17-19*, 20, *21, 23ab*, 24, *25bc, 26b, 27-28, 31*
Sile pipe — 23a
Soil pipe — 15
Water conductor — 4
Nil — 5, 25ad, 30

East Lothian
Conductor — 13, 15
Down fa pipe — 8
Down pipe — 13
Pipe — 19
Rain pipe — 1
Rone pipe — 2, 4ab, 5, 6a, 7, 9-11, 14, 17-18, 20-21
Sile pipe — 6b
Soil pipe — 16
Spout — 21
Nil — 3, 12

Berwick
Conductor — 14, 23, 27
Down pipe — 16c, 20, 22, 32
Down spout — 20
Drop pipe — 27
Rone (pipe) — *1-2*, 6, *8-10*, 11, *12-13, 15, 16ac*, 19, 21, *23-24, 29, 31-32*
Spout — 3-4, 7-8, 10, 16b, 17-19, 25-26, 30-32
Nil — 5, 28

Peebles
Conductor — 4b
Overflow of rone's pipe — 6a
Rain water pipe — 4b
Rone conductor — 2
Rone pipe — 1, 3, 4c, 5, 6b, 7-9
Nil — 4a, 10

Selkirk
Conductor — 3, 8
(Down) pipe — *1*, 2a
Rone pipe — 2c, 4
Spout — 2bde
Nil — 5-7

Roxburgh
Conductor — 1-2, 9a, 12, 15a, 17, 21cd
Cundie — 13
Down pipe — 21f, 22, 28
Down spout — 15b
Rain spout — 21a
Rone (pipe) — *2, 3ab, 5, 7-8*, 9ab, *10, 18*, 19-20, *21b, 24-25, 28*
Spout — 4, 6, 16-17, 23, 28
Nil — 11, 14, 21e, 26-27

Dumfries
Chop pipe — 10
Down pipe — 9, 13, 43
Draa pipe — 2
Drop pipe — 1a, 5-7, 8b, 11-12, 16, 18, 21ab, 26-27, 30, 31abcde, 32-33, 36-37, 40-42, 44, 45ab, 46-47
Drop spout — 35, 46
Fa pipe — 12
Gitr — 37
Rone (pipe) — *1b*, 3-4, *8a, 14, 17ab, 19-20, 21b, 22, 24*, 31aef, *38, 46*
Spout — 15, 28-29, 37, 39, 46
Nil — 23, 25, 34, 48-49

Kirkcudbright
Down pipe — 21a
Drain pipe — 9-10
Drop pipe — 1, 5, 8-9, 12b, 15a, 16, 18, 21a, 24-25
Rhon pipe — 15a
Rone drop — 11
Rone pipe — 1-4, 6, 10, 12b, 13-14, 15b, 18-19, 21b, 22-23, 26-27
Rone spout — 12a, 21c
Spout — 7, 17, 19
Nil — 20

Wigtown
Down pipe — 1
Drop pipe — 5a, 6, 8, 10-12, 14-15, 17
Drop rone — 13
Rone (pipe) — *2, 4, 5b, 6-7*, 9, *16*
Spout — 18
Nil — 3

Northumberland
Cuttie — 22
Down comer — 3, 12-13, 23, 29d, 34a, 41abd, 50, 57, 59e, 60, 62cgh, 69abdh, 71d, 72dg, 76, 79, 81-84, 86, 89, 91, 95ab, 96, 98, 99c, 103a, 104b, 108c, 112, 116, 118b, 120abc, 124ab, 126cde, 127abcd, 129ab, 130acd, 140-141, 143
Down commer — 34a, 62a, 65b, 111a, 116, 124a, 126b, 127e, 136
Down dropper — 63
(Down) pipe — *2a, 4, 20b*, 40a, *41d, 42-43, 51*, 57-58, 59b, *61, 62b, 64b, 69bc, 72j, 75-76, 87, 93, 99d, 103b, 104b, 106, 111b, 114, 121, 140, 142*
Down pour — 33a, 134
Down pourer — 59c
Down runner — 29b, 62e, 72e, 111b
Down spout — 5-6, 9-10, 14-18, 20a, 22, 24a, 26-28, 29af, 30, 33b, 34b, 35-39, 41bcd, 44-45, 48, 53a, 54, 56-57, 59cd, 60, 62g, 63, 68, 69e, 71bh, 73, 77-81, 83, 90, 99b, 102, 103c, 104a, 107, 108a, 109, 111b, 116, 122a, 130f, 133, 135, 137-138, 142
Drain (pipe) — *41c*, 46, *49*, 62g, 70, 76, *83, 86, 92, 94b, 111a, 118a, 122b, 127d*
Fall pipe — 96, 104b, 130c
Ootside spout — 101b
Rain pipe — 40a, 72d, 76, 127f, 130e
Rone down comer — 13
Rone (pipe) — *1a*, 8, 11, *47, 91*
Rowan — 21
Runner — 100
Soil pipe — 20b
Spout — 1b, 2b, 7-8, 29b, 32, 40b, 46, 48, 52, 53b, 59abf, 62de, 64a, 66, 69af, 71acd, 72abcehik, 76, 87, 88ab, 91, 93, 95b, 97, 99c, 101b, 105, 108c, 110, 113, 117, 122b, 123, 124b, 125, 126adef, 128, 129a, 130b, 131-132, 140
Spout down comer — 19a
Stand pipe — 24b
Water spout — 99a, 111a
Witter pipe — 31
Nil — 1c, 19b, 25, 29ce, 55, 62f, 65a, 67, 69g, 71e, 72fl, 74, 85, 94a, 101a, 108b, 115, 119, 129c, 139

Cumberland
Down drain pipe — 9
Down pipe — 4, 19, 23-24
Down spout — 2-3, 6, 8, 11, 13cd, 14, 15abc, 16-18, 20-21, 24-27, 29, 33-34, 36, 37a, 38-42, 45-48, 51-52, 54, 56-62, 63b
Drain pipe — 7, 9, 53
Drop pipe — 31
Drop spout — 44
Faa pipe — 57
Fall pipe — 13a, 50
Faw pipe — 49
Piping — 28
Spout — 5a, 12, 37b, 43, 50, 53-54
Spouting — 22, 28
Nil — 1ab, 5b, 10, 13b, 30, 32, 35, 55, 63a

Down
(Down) pipe — 2ab, *6, 9, 14-15, 17*, 19, *21*
Down spout — 2a, 4-5, 10-11, 23
Drain pipe — 1, 8-9, 19-20, 26
Gutter pipe — 3
Rone pipe — 12
Spoutin(g) — 6-7, 13, 18, 22, 24, 27-29
Water spout — 27
Nil — 16, 25, 30

Tyrone
(Down) pipe — 1, 8-9, *14*
Down spout — 14
Down spoutin(g) — 1, 10-11
Drain pipe — 6, 12
Spoutin(g) — 5-7, 9, 11-13, 16
Nil — 2-4, 15

Antrim
Down pipe — 3, 5b, 19, 25, 32
Down spout — 8b, 12, 14, 16b, 21, 33-34
Drain pipe — 2
Gutter pipe — 29
Rone (pipe) — *7, 20-21*, 22, *23*, 24
Spout — 8a, 10, 26-27, 31, 34
Spoutin(g) — 3, 5ab, 9-11, 13, 15, 17-18, 25, 28, 34
Nil — 1, 4, 4A, 6, 16ac, 30

Donegal
Down pipe — 3, 5A, 6, 7A, 10ab, 12-13
Down pour — 5
Down spout — 1-2
Drain pipe — 13

Donegal cont 'd

Spoutin(g) – 4-5, 8
Nil – 1A, 7, 9, 11

Fermanagh

Down pipe – 2, 9
Drain pipe – 4
Spout – 1, 5, 7a
Spoutin(g) – 3-4, 9-10
Nil – 6, 7b, 8

Armagh

Down pipe – 6b
Down spout – 2, 4
Spout – 1, 3
Spoutin(g) – 4, 6a
Nil – 5

Londonderry

Down pipe – 3A, 4
Down spouting – 5
Drain pipe – 1B, 2, 4, 7
Rone pipe – 3
Spoutin(g) – 1A, 3, 6
Nil – 1, 8

52 HAY RACK (in byre etc.) (PQ1, 112)

Comments in response to the questions 'Are there different words according to the animal it is for?' and 'Is there a different word if it is in the fields?' have been classified. The following symbols have been used:

- c for cows, cattle
- h for horses
- s for sheep
- x outdoors
- + indoors

Shetland

Cow rack – 5
Crib – 25
Diss – 33^{x}
Hake – 28
(Hay) rack – 3-4, 6-*7*, 14-16, *17, 19-20, 21a, 29-30*
Heck – 9, 29, 32
Lamb's crib – 21b^{+}
Lamb's rack – 5, 7^{x}
Manger – 1
Meenger – 6
Menger – 22
Sheep's crib – 17^{+}
Sheep's trough – 17^{x}
Troch – 24
Trough – 5^{x}
Nil – 2, 8, 10-13, 18, 23, 26-27, 31

Orkney

Hake – 5, 11, 15
(Hay) heck – 1-4, 6, 8-10, 12, 13a, *16,* 19-21
Hay rack – 17
Heak – 11
Rick – 7
Trevis – 15
Nil – 13b, 14, 18

Caithness

Feeding place – 13
Hake – 12b
(Hay) rack – 2a, *5, 10-11*^{x}, 14, *16b*
Heck – 2b, 4-5, 7-8, 12ab, 14-15
Manger – 11, 12c
Rackie – 7
Trough – 13
Nil – 1, 3, 6, 9, 16a, 17

Sutherland

Crib – 3-5
Feed box – 5^{x}
Flake – 5^{x}
Hake – 1, 6, 8, 9b, 10-11, 13-15
(Hay) rack – *6*-7, 10, 15-16
Heck – 2^{x}, 9a
Manger – 13^{h}
Menger – 9b^{h}
Straw bracket – 3
Nil – 12, 17

Ross & Cromarty

Flake – 29^{x}
(Hay) hake – 7-13, 15, 18-*19,* 21-24, 25ab, 26-31^{s}, 32a, 33-36, 37a
(Hay) rack – *1, 3-5,* 9, 16-*17, 27,* 32c^{x}
Manger – 18, 32c, 39
Menger – 31^{h}
Nil – 2, 6, 14, 20, 32b, 37b, 38

Inverness

Hake – 8-10, 11^{c}, 12, 13e, 14-15, 17, 20, 21ab, 26-29, 31
(Hay) rack – 4, *5-7,* 13ac, *22-23, 25*^{x}, 32, *35,* 36-*37, 39*
Heck – 37-38
Loft – 16
Manger – 11^{h}, 34
Menger – 25
Nil – 1-3, 13bd, 18-19, 24, 30, 33, 40

Nairn

Hake – 1abc, 2-6

Moray

Hake – 1, 2ab, 3-5, 6ab, 7^{x,c}, 8ab^{x}c^{s}de, 9a, 10-23
Manger – 7^{h}, 15^{h}, 18^{h}, 20^{h}-21^{h}
Rack – 17^{s}
Trevis – 9b
Nil – 8f

Banff

Fore sta' – 16, 27
Hake – 1, 2c, 3, 4^{c}, 5, 6ab, 8-13, 15-17^{x,s}, 18bcd, 20-21, 23-34
Hay rack – 27^{+}
Heck – 19, 22, 29
Manger – 4^{h}
Sta' – 2a
Trankle – 14
Nil – 2b, 7, 18a

Aberdeen

Fore sta' – 5d^{h}, 14, 27^{+}, 22^{+}, 25, 28a^{+c}b^{+h}, 39^{h}, 48^{h}, 65-66^{+h}, 74^{h}-75, 81^{+h}, 98^{+h}, 104^{h}
Fore stall – 53^{h}, 77^{+}
(Hay) hake – 1^{+c}, 3ab, 5abcd^{c}, 6, 8-24, 26-27, 28abc, 29-35, 37, 39-40, 42-46, 47abe, 48-52. 53^{c}, 54-62, 64-69, *70,* 71abc, 72-76, 77^{x}, 78-83, 85-89 91-93, 94^{c,s}, 95-101, 103-105, 107-109
(Hay) rack – *6*^{x}, 77^{x}
Heck – 2, 63, 106
Hike – 41
Manger – 60^{+}, 70^{+h}, 71b^{+h}, 94
Ruck – 90
Straw hake – 70
Trevis – 38
Nil – 4, 7, 36, 47cdf, 84, 102

Kincardine

Fleck – 12
Fore sta' – 6^{+}, 11^{h}, 13
Fore stall – 17b^{h}d^{h}
Fore straw – 10^{h}
Hake – 1-7, 8^{c}, 9-10, 12-16, 17abcd, 18-21, 23-24, 26-28
Manger – 6^{+}, 8, 10^{h}, 17b^{h}
Rack – 8
Trevis – 11
Nil – 22, 25

Kinross

Hake – 1, 2^{s}, 3^{s}, 4^{s}, 5, 7
Heck – 6

Angus

Cole – 17b
Hay barra' – 24^{s}
(Hay) hake – 1-4, 5abc, 6-9, 11-13, 14abc*d,* 15, 19-24^{c}, 26, *27,* 28, 29a, 30-32, 33ab, 34-37
Hay rack – 17b, 25
Hay rick – 17b, 33b
Heck – 10, 13, 14a, 37
Manger – 17a, 22^{h}, 24^{h}
Sheep hake – 22^{s,x}, 31^{x}
Nil – 16, 18, 29b

Perth

Crup – 2a
Hake – 1, 5-7, 10, 13, 15, 17-18, 20-23, 25-28, 29ab, 30-34, 37, 39, 41a, 42-50, 51a, 52ac, 56-66
Hay rack – 4, 8, 24, 36, 67, 74
Heck – 1, 2b, 3^{x}, 9-12, 16$^{xs, +c}$, 24, 26-27, 38, 40, 41b, 52b, 56, 61, 68-73
Manger – 16, 20^{h}, 29b, 39^{h}, 41a
Pipe – 43
Trevis – 16
Nil – 14, 19, 35, 51b, 52de, 53-55

Fife

Cole – 44b
Hake – 1-8, 9ab, 10-12, 14, 17-32, 35, 36ab, 38-39, 40b, 41d, 42, 43ab, 44acde^{c}f, 45, 47-48, 50-54, 55bcf, 56-57, 59-63^{c}, 64ab
Hakie – 33
(Hay) rack – *13,* 16, *19,* 37, *39, 44bc,* 55de
Heck – 36b, 41a, 43b, 55e
Mange – 48
Manger – 14^{h}, 44e^{c}, 63^{h}
Ruck – 37
Nil – 15, 34, 40a, 41bc, 46, 49, 55ag, 58

Clackmannan

Hake – 2-3, 6-7
Heck – 1, 4d, 5-7
Nil – 4abc

Stirling

Hack – 7b
Hake – 26d, 37a, 39b
(Hay) rack – *4,* 8, *15, 22b,* 27a, 28, *31, 36*
Heck – 1-3, 6, 7abcdef, 9-14, 17-20, 21ab, 22a, 23bc, 24, 25abcd, 26abcf, 27ab, 29-34, 35ab, 36, 37b, 39b, 40, 42ab
Manger – 8
Trough – 16, 26b, 40^{x}
Nil – 5, 23a, 26e, 38, 39a, 41

Dunbarton

Hake – 1
Hay rack – 7b, 10, 13c
Heck – 1-3, 4ab, 5-6, 7ac, 9-10, 13a, 14a, 15, 16ab, 17
Sheep rack – 6^{x}
Trough – 2^{x}
Nil – 8, 11-12, 13b, 14b, 18

Argyll

Cruach – 6^{x}
Dash – 6
Hake – 8, 21
(Hay) rack – 1, *17,* 33
Heck – 5, 7, 9-15, 18-19^{x,c,s}, 22-24, 26-35^{h}, 37-40
Manger – 19^{+h}, 35^{h}
Trough – 35^{c}
Nil – 2-4, 16, 20, 25, 36

Bute

(Hay) rack – 1a, *2*
Heck – 1abce, 3-5, 7^{h}, 8b, 9
Nil – 1d, 6, 8a

Ayr

Bakie – 37
Biss – 20h, 22, 32^{c}
Feeding rack – 15
Hake – 11
(Hay) heck – 1a, 2a, 3-4, *5,* 6-7, 8ab, 9-11, 12ab, 13-14, 16a, 17, 18ab, 19, 20abceg; 21-23, 24b, 26a, 28bcf, 29, 30ab, 32-34, 35ab, 36-*37,* 40-45, *46,* 47-50, 51^{+x}, 52, 53ab, 54-57
Hay neuk – 51^{+}
(Hay) rack – 2b, *3, 5, 15, 43, 45, 57*
Heak – 27
Hecket – 20f
Hick – 31
Hodder – 20g
Manger – 16b, 20bc^{h}, 30b, 38
Nil – 1b, 20d, 24a, 25, 26bc, 28ade, 39

Renfrew

(Hay) heck – 1b, 2bg, 4acd, 5, 7-10, 11abl^{+}, 13abc, 14b, 15, 16ad, 17, 18a, 19, 20ab, 21
(Hay) rack – *2i, 11e, 16b,* 18b
Hay rick – 11h
Haystack – 2a, 11dh, 12b
Heak – 11f
Heap – 2d
Manger – 18b
Trough – 11l^{c}
Nil – 1a, 2cefhj, 3, 4be, 6, 11cgijk, 12a, 13d, 14a, 16c

Lanark

Bakie – 52a^{x}
Crib – 45
Fodder – 17

Lanark cont'd

Hack — 3^{c}
Hake — 13, 50
(Hay) heck — 1, *2,* 3^{h}, 6, 7a^{h}c, 9ab, 10a, 12-13, 15a^{+}bc, 16b, 18-24, 26a, 27ab 29de, 30, 31abcd, 32cf, 33cd, 35abd, 38abcde, 39-43, 46abc, 47-48, 49ab, 51, 52a, 53-56, 57abc, 58, 59ab, 60-63, 64ab, 65-66, 67*a*^{x,s}b
Hay loft — 44
Hay neuk — 63, 67a
(Hay) rack — 7a^{x,s}, *8b, 14b,* 15bc, *25c, 26a, 29e*^{c}*, 32a, 35d,* 52b, *57b,* 60, 66
Haystack — 49a
Heak — 37
Loft — 29f
Manger — 15a, 29e^{x+}, 35a, 64b^{h}
Ruck — 5
Trevis — 39
Trivis — 35b
Trough — 15a^{+}
Nil — 4, 7b, 8a, 10b, 11, 14acd, 16a, 25abd, 26b, 28, 29abcg, 32bde, 33ab, 34, 35c, 36

West Lothian

Hake — 11
(Hay) rack — *3*$^{+h}$, 11, 13, 22
Heck — 1abd, 2-8, 9ab, 10, 12, 14-16, 17a, 18, 19b, 21a
Manger — 6^{h}
Net — 11^{x}
Ruck — 15
Nil — 1c, 17b, 19a, 20ab, 21b

Midlothian

Dass — 11
Hake — 11, 16
(Hay) heck — 3^{h}-4, 6b, 7ab, 8b, 9-10, 12ab, 13, 14*ab*$^{+h}$, 15-21, 23ab, 24, 25c, 26a, 27, 29-*30,* 32
Hay rack — 8a, 23b
Hemmel — 29-30
Manger — 31
Nil — 1-2, 5, 6a, 22, 25abd, 26b, 28

East Lothian

Hake — 17
(Hay) heck — 3, 6ab, 7, *8,* 9-13, 14^{h}, 15-*16,* 20-21
Hay lick — 2
Hay rick — 4b
Hick — 2
Trevis rack — 6a^{+h}
Nil — 1, 4a, 5, 18-19

Berwick

Daise — 1
(Hay) heck — 4-14, 16ab*c,* 17-19, *20,* 21-25, *26,* 27, 29-*32*
Hay moe — 27
(Hay) rack — 2, 12, 15, 17, *29*
Hemmel — 22^{c}
Hep — 27
Manger — 31
Peck — 3
Nil — 28

Peebles

Hake — 2^{x}
(Hay) heck — 1, 2^{+}, 3, 4b, *5,* 6ab, 7-10
Hay rack — 2^{x}, 6a
Manger — 4b, 8^{+}
Nil — 4ac

Selkirk

(Hay) heck — 1, 2abde, 3, *4,* 5-7, *8*
Hemmel — 1^{x}
Nil — 2c

Roxburgh

Crib — 5
(Hay) heck — 1-2, 3ab, 4, *5,* 6, *7,* 8, 9ab, *10, 12*-13, 15b, *16-17,* 18-20, 21a^{x}cdf, 22-*26,* 28
Hay rack — 21a
Hemmel — 1$^{c,x,h+}$, 6^{x,c}, 9b, 17^{x+}, 20, 24^{x}
Manger — 25^{h}
Sheep heck — 22^{x,s}, 28^{x}
Nil — 11, 14, 15a, 21be, 27

Dumfries

Crib — 2^{c}, 32
(Hay) heck — 1a, 2^{h,s}, 4-7, 8b, 9-11, *12,* 13-16, 17ab, 18-20, 21ab, 22-25, *26,* 27-30, 31acd, 32-44, 45ab, *46*-47, 49
Hay neuk — 3
Hay nook — 16
Hay rack — 12
Manger — 7^{h}, 12^{h}, 40^{h}
Peck — 1b
Wheel heck — 12^{x}
Nil — 8a, 31bef, 48

Kirkcudbright

Hake — 11
Hay hack — 6
(Hay) heck — 1-*2,* 3-*6,* 7$^{+,x,s}$ 8-10, 12ab, 13-14, 15a, 16-19, 21ac, 22-24, 26-27
Rack — 7^{+}
Nil — 15b, 20, 21b, 25

Wigtown

Crae — 5b
Crib — 5b, 10^{h,c}
(Hay) heck — *1,* 2-3, 5ab, 6-7, 9-10, *11,* 12-18
Hecket — 5a
Rack — 8
Nil — 4

Northumberland

Beers heed — 108c, 142
Crib — 40a^{h}, 60, 68^{+}, 73^{h}, 90, 110, 141^{+}
Cribbage — 31
Fodder beers — 132
Hack — 69b
Hatch — 69b
Hay box — 69a^{x}
Hay cuddie — 47
(Hay) heck — 1b, 2ab, 3-4, *5-6,* 7-11, 13-15, *16-18,* 19a, 20*ab, 21-22,* 23, 24ab, 25, *26-27,* 28, 29*ab*cdf, 30, 33b, 34ab, 35, *36,* 37, *38,* 39, 40*a*^{c}b, 41*ab*cd, 42-46, 48-49, *50,* 51-52, *53ab*^{x}*, 54,* 55-57, *58,* 59abcde, *60,* 61, 62*a*g, 64b, 65ab, 66, *68*$^{+}$, 69*c*ef, 71cd^{s}, 72bi, 73^{x}, 74-76, 77^{+}, 78-82, 88ab, 89-90, 92, 95ab, *98,* 102, *103bc,* 104*ab,* 105-107, 108*ab,* 109-110, *111ab,* 112, 114, 117, 118a, 122a, 124*ab,* 127d, 130cd, 133, *134-135,* 136-138, *139-140,* 141, 143
Hay hole — 72i, 125
(Hay) rack — *1a,* 19a, *30, 40a, 41c, 53b, 57, 69c, 70, 72cg,* 79^{+h}, *82*-83, *86*-87, *94b,* 99d, *100,* 103c, *111ab, 120ab, 126c, 127a,* 129b, 134
Hay rick — 118b, 120c
Hay trough — 130c
Horse heck — 98
Manger — 44, 53a, 69abf, 72l, 77^{+}, 83, 118a, 122b, 123, 127c, 130c
Rack trough — 71d
Sheep heck — 98^{x}
Tumbler — 79^{x}
Tumblin heck — 33b
Nil — 1c, 12, 19b, 29e, 32, 33a, 59f, 62bcdefh, 63, 64a, 67, 69dgh, 71abe, 72adefhjk, 84-85, 91, 93, 94a, 96-97, 99abc, 101ab, 103a, 113, 115-116, 119, 121, 126abdef, 127befgh, 128, 129ac, 130abef, 131

Cumberland

Cawf rack — 48
Crib — 4^{h}, 31^{+}, 40, 54, 57^{h}
Fodder rack — 26
Fother gang — 37b
(Hay) rack — *1a,* 3-*4*^{x}, 12, *14, 17*^{x}*, 24-25, 30, 40, 42*-43, *46*-47, *48, 50,* 51-52, 56^{h}, 57^{c}, 58, *60,* 62
Heck — 1a, 2-4, 5ab, 6-9, 11, 13abcd, 14, 15ab, 16-19, 21-23, 28-29, 32-33, 37b, 38-39, 44-45, 47, 56^{h}, 58
Manger — 37a, 46, 55, 57^{h}
Sheep rack — 15a^{x}, 31^{x}, 37b, 46^{x}, 57^{c,x}
Nil — 1b, 10, 15c, 20, 27, 34-36, 41, 49, 53, 59, 61, 63ab

Down

Crib — 11, 14, 21
Hay rack — 2a, 5, 26
Manger — 3-4, 6-7, 11, 15^{h}, 17-19, 21, 23^{h}-24
Rack — 2a, 7, 15$^{+,x,c}$, 23^{x,c}, 24, 29
Stall — 22
Nil — 1, 2b, 8-10, 12-13, 16, 20, 25, 27-28, 30

Tyrone

Crib — 14
Hay rack — 1, 7
Manger — 1, 5, 9-10, 11^{h}-12, 15
Rack — 10^{x}-11
Trough — 12
Nil — 2-4, 6, 8, 13, 16

Antrim

Crib — 12, 16b, 25, 27-28, 33
Fodder rack — 34
Hay box — 34
Hay rack — 19-20
Head stall — 16b
Laft — 2
Manger — 1, 8b, 13, 15^{h}, 16b, 17, 21, 25^{+}, 28, 31-32
Rack — 31^{x}
Reek — 9
Stall — 5ab, 15^{c}, 26
Nil — 3-4, 4A, 6-7, 8a, 10-11, 14, 16ac, 18, 22-24, 29-30

Donegal

Fodder rack — 5A
Hay rack — 5, 7, 12
Head stall — 10a
Manger — 1-2, 4^{+}, 5-6^{h}, 12^{+}-13
Rack — 2, 10b, 13
Rakie — 5A
Reck — 7A, 8
Nil — 1A, 3, 9, 11

Fermangh

Crib — 1-2, 4, 6, 9-10
Loft — 7a
Manger — 1^{h}-2, 4, 8
Rack — 1^{x}
Nil — 3, 5, 7b

Armagh

Boose — 1
Manger — 3-4^{+}
Rack — 4^{x}, 6a
Nil — 2, 5, 6b

Londonderry

Bracket — 5
Hay feeder — 5^{x}
Hay rack — 4-5^{x}
Loft — 1A
Manger — 2-3, 5, 6^{+h}, 7
Reck — 3A
Nil — 1, 1B

53 HAYSTACK (PQ1, 113)

(1) Note the recurrence of similar or identical target items in items 54-55.

(2) Comments in answer to the request: 'If there is more than one word, say how they differ in meaning', have been classified. The following symbols have been used:

c = conical
f = in fields
g = green grass
l = large
lg = long
o = oblong
ov = oval
r = round
s = small
sq = square
sw = straight walls
y = in yard
z = made under bad conditions

Shetland

Coll — 10^{s}, 26^{s}
(Hay) dess — 1-10, 12-16, *17*, 18-20, 21ab, 22-25, 26^{l}, *27*, 28-29
Haystack — 29-30, 32-33
Nil — 11, 31

Orkney

Cole — 16^{r}
Gilt — 15^{lg}, 17-18^{lg}, 19-20, 21°
Haystack — 1-5, 7-9, 11, 13ab, 14-15, 16^{sq}, 17, 18^{r}, 20-21
Screw — 19, 21
Nil — 6, 10, 12

Caithness

Coalie — 17
Gilt screw — 12a
(Hay) gilt — 1, 2a^{o}, *5*^{sq,c}, 6°, 8°, 11, 12b^{o,sq}c, *13*, 14°-15, 16b
Hay rick — 15
(Hay) screw — 2a^{o}*b*, *3*^{r}, 4, *5*^{r}, 6^{r}, 7, *8-9*, 10-11, 12bc, 14^{r}, 15
Haystack — 3^{c}, 10
Nil — 16a

Sutherland

Gilt — 2, 4, 6^{l}, 9b^{sq}, 14
Haystack — 1, 3, 5-8, 9ab^{sw}, 10-16
Rack — 15
Rick — 15
Ruck — 5, 12
Screw — 4, 9ab^{sq,o}
Soo — 14
Nil — 17

Ross & Cromarty

(Hay) rick — 7^{s}, 22, *25b*, 37a
(Hay) stack — *1*, *3-9*, 14, *16-17*, 18, *19-20*, *23-24*, *25a*, *26-29*, *31*, *32ab*, *33-34*, 39
Ruck — 7^{s}
Ruckan — 7^{s}
Soo — 8^{sq}, 13, 18, 22^{sq}, 28
Nil — 2, 10-12, 15, 21, 30, 32c, 35-36, 37b, 38

Inverness

Hay rick — 1, 6, 9, 20
(Hay) stack — *1-8*, *10-11*, 13abce^{r}, 16, *17-19*, 20, *21ab*, *22-23*, *28-30*, *32-33*, 34, *35-39*, 40
Soo — 8, 11, 26^{sq}
Sow — 13e^{o}
Nil — 12, 13d, 14-15, 24-25, 27, 31

Nairn

Hay cole — 1b
(Hay) stack — 1a, *2*, *5-6*
Rick — 1b
Soo — 3^{l,o}, 4
Nil — 1c

Moray

Cole — 5
(Hay) ruck — 2a, 3-4, 6a^{r}*b*^{s}, 8d, 9a, *10*, 15-16, 19^{r}, 20, *21*
Hay screw — 22^{s}
(Hay) soo — *1*, 6a^{l}, 7^{sq}, *8b*, *9a*, 13, 17, *18*, 19^{sq}, *22*^{lg,o}
Haystack — 3, 6b, 7^{r}, 8be, 11, 14, 18, 20, 23
Rick — 12, 14, 18, 22
Nil — 2b, 8acf, 9b

Banff

(Hay) ruck — 1, 2ac, *3-5*, *6ab*, 7, *8-9*, 10, *11-15*, *16-17*, 18bd, 19-20, *21*, 22-23, *24*, 25, *26-27*^{r}, 30-34
(Hay) soo — *9*^{l}, 18c^{o}, 27^{sq}, 29, 31^{l,o}
Hooick — 4^{z}
Rick — 1, 18c, 30
Ruckie — 2b
Tochienealer — 6b
Nil — 18a, 28

Aberdeen

Cock — 24
Cole — 24, 47b
(Hay) rick — *6*, 11, 37, *47c*, 50, 53, *59*, *77*, 89
(Hay) ruck — 1-2, *3ab*, 4, 5abcd, *6*, 7, *8*, 9-11, *12*, 13, *14-15*, 16^{r}, 17-18, *19*, 20, *21*^{l} 22-24, *25-26*, 27, *28a*^{r}*bc*, *29*, 30^{r}-31, *32*^{r}*-33*, 34, *35*, 39, *40-41*, *44-46*, 47*abde*, 48^{r}, 50-53^{r}, 54-55, *56-57*, 58, *60*-62, *63*, 64, *65-66*, 67-69, *70*, 71a*bc*, 72, *73*, 74, *75*, *77*, 78-80^{r}, *81-83*, 84-85, *86*, 87, *88*, 92^{r} 93-94, *95-98*, 99, *100-101*, 103-109
(Hay) soo — 2, *21*, *25*, 28a^{lg}b^{lg}, 30^{lg}, *32*^{o}, 48°, 64°, 67°, 74^{lg} *76*, 80^{lg}, *84*, 92°, 94, *107*^{lg}
Haystack — 70
Huick — 21^{s}
Tramp cole — 85
Nil — 36, 38, 42-43, 47f, 49, 90-91, 102

Kincardine

(Hay) ruck — *1-10*, 11-12, *13*, 14-16, 17abcd, 18, 20, 23-24
(Hay) stack — 17c, *19*, *21-22*, 24, *26-28*
Rick — 18
Soo — 17b^{lg}d^{lg}
Stook — 25

Kinross

Hay ruck — 4, 7^{r}
(Hay) soo — *3*, 5, 7^{ov}
(Hay) stack — *1-2*, 3
Rick — 3
Nil — 6

Angus

Frandie — 23^{s}
Hay cole — 25
Hay ruck — 1, 17a
(Hay) soo — 2^{sq}, *4*, 5c, *14cd*, 18-*19*, 22, *29a*, 35, *37*
Hay sow — 33b
(Hay) stack — 2^{r}, *3*, 5a, *6-10*, *12*-13, 14ab, *15*, *17b*, *18*, *20-21*, *24*, *27*, 28, *31-32*, *34*, *36*
Rick — 5b, 33a
Nil — 11, 16, 26, 29b, 30

Perth

Coil — 41a
Cole — 40-41a
Corn ricks — 36
(Hay) rick — 5, *11*, 18, 20^{r}-21, *25*^{r}, 29a, 34, 39, 41ab, 45, 59, 64, *66*, 73
(Hay) soo — *7*, *13*^{o}, 18, 20^{sq}, 25-26^{sq}, 29b, 37^{lg}, *46*^{lg}, 52b, *56*, 62°
Hay sow — 8°, 57°
(Hay) stack — 1, *2a*, 3^{sq,r}, *4*, 8, *9*, 10, *12-13*^{r}, *15*, *16*^{r}, *17*, *21*, *23-25*, 26^{r}, *27-28*, *29a*, 31, *32-33*, *36*, *41b*, 44, *46*, 49-*50*, 51a, *52c*, *57*, 60, 62, *64*-65, 67-68^{r}, 72^{r}, 74
Lut — 72^{sq}
Ruck — 29a, 30, 34, 43-44, 52a, 59, 62^{l}, 70
Soo stack — 16^{r}, 66^{sq}
Sow stack — 68°, 71^{sq}
Tramp coil — 48
Tramp cole — 48
Nil — 2b, 6, 14, 19, 22, 35, 38, 42, 47, 51b, 52de, 53-55, 58, 61, 63, 69

Fife

Beg ruck — 44d
Cole — 2
(Hay) rick — 3, 8, 11-13, *49*, 51, *54*, 55f
(Hay) ruck — 2, *36b*, *41a*, 52, 55f
(Hay) soo — 5^{lg}, *6-7*, 8^{l}, *9b*, *21*, *24*^{o}, 26, *33*, *35*^{o}, 44a^{o}, *45*^{sq}, 47-*48*^{sq}, *55d*^{o}, *64a*
(Hay) stack — *4-5*^{r}, *7*, *9a*, *11*, 12-13, *14*, *16-17*, *19-20*, 23-*24*^{r}, *25*-26, *28*, 30, *36a*, 37, *39*, *40b*, *41a*, *42*, *43a*, *44bce*, *46-47*, *48*^{r}-49, *50*, *52-53*^{r}, *55ab*^{r}*d*^{r}*eg*, *56-57*, *59*, *61-62*, 63
Hay stal — 43a
Reck — 50
Soo stack — 53°-54^{sq}, 55b^{lg}c, 60
Sow — 10, 38
Staithel — 39
Tramp ruck — 45
Nil — 1, 15, 18, 22, 27, 29, 31-32, 34, 40a, 41bcd, 43b, 44f, 58, 64b

Clackmannan

Haystack — 2^{r}, 4bc, 6
Rick — 4d
Soo stack — 2°, 5°
Nil — 1, 3, 4a

Stirling

Big rick — 27b
(Hay) leet — 6^{sq}, 7a^{sq}e^{o}, 10°, 12°, *17*^{sq}-18^{lg}, 21b^{sq}, 22b, *24*, 26c, 30°, 35a^{lg}
(Hay) rick — 7*bde*^{r}, 9-10, 13-14, *16*, *21b*^{r}, 23c, 24, 25b*c*, 26be, 31, *39b*, 42b
(Hay) ruck — 2-3^{r}, 7ae^{r}, 11, *20*, *21b*, 22a, 25a, 26b, 29, *33*, 40, 42a
Hay sow — 35b
(Hay) stack — 4, 6^{r}, 7c, 15, 19, 23ab, 25c, 26acde, *27a* *28-29*, 30^{r}, *31-34*, 35a, *36*, 37ab^{r}, *38*, 39a, *40-41*
Round stack — 12^{r}, 36^{r}
Soo (stack) — *3*^{sq}, 7a^{sq}*df*, 8^{lg}, *10*^{o}, *16*^{l}, *18*^{sq}, *21ab*^{sq}, *25a*^{sq}*d*^{sq}, 26f, 33^{sq}, 35a^{lg}, *36*, *37b*^{o}
Sow stack — 6^{sq}, 7f, 26f
Nil — 1,5

Dunbarton

Big ruck — 5, 7c, 15^{r}
(Hay) rick — 4b, *13b*
(Hay)stack — *1*, 5, 7*abc*, *10-11*, *13abc*, *14b*, *16ab*
Leet — 9
Ruck — 2-3, 6, 9, 17
Soo — 10^{lg}, 15^{sq}
Soo stack — 3^{lg}, 9
Sow stack — 4a
Nil — 8, 12, 14a, 18

Argyll

Big rick — 33
Coil — 17
(Hay) rick — 4, 13, 19, 24-25, 31, 37, *40*
(Hay) ruck — *3*, 5, 13, 32
(Hay)stack — *1-3*, *6-8*, 9, *10*, 11, *12-14*, *17*, 18^{r}, 19, *22*-23, *25*, *27*, 29-31, 33, *34-35*, *38-39*
Sow — 18^{lg}
Nil — 20-21, 26, 28, 36

Bute

Haystack — 1a, 2, 4, 7, 8ab, 9
Rick — 1bc^{r}d, 3, 5
Ruck — 1bc^{r}e
Soo — 1c^{o}
Soo stack — 1a
Sow stack — 9^{lg}
Nil — 6

Ayr

Big ruck — 12a^{g}
Biss — 18b
Field ruck — 5^{f}, 26a^{f}
Hayrack — 35a
(Hay) ruck — 4, 5^{y}, 6-7, *10*, *17*, 18b, 20h, 26a, 28f^{r}, *34*, *36*, *43*, 51
(Hay)stack — 1a, 2a, 3, *5*, *8ab*, *9*, 11, 12ab, 13-14, *15*, 16b, 18a, *20abce*, *21-22*, *24b*, *25*, 26b, 28*bcef*, 29, 30ab, *31*, 32, *33-34*, *38*^{r}, 39, *40-45*, *48-49*, 50-51, *52*, *53a*^{r}, *54*, *56-57*
Heck — 35a
Rick — 2b, 7, 15, 18b, 19, 26a, 27, 35b, 43, 53b
Roon stack — 47
Soo — 28f^{o}, 38^{o,sq}, 41
Soo stack — 47^{sq}-48^{sq}, 53a^{o}
Sow — 1a^{o}
Yard ruck — 26a^{y}
Nil — 1b, 16a, 20dfg, 23, 24a, 26c, 28ad, 37, 46, 55

Renfrew

Big ruck — 20b
Big stack — 10
(Hay) rick — 2f, *8*, *16a*, 18b, *20a*
(Hay) ruck — 7, 11j, 16a, 17, 18ab, 19, 21
(Hay) stack — *1b*, *2acdfghi*, *4acde*, *5-6*, *8*, 11*abcehkl*, 12ab, *13c*, 14b, 16*bd*, *17*, *18a*, *20a*
Leet — 2b
Mow — 11f
Nil — 1a, 2ej, 3, 4b, 9, 11dgi, 13abd, 14a, 15, 16c

Lanark

Big rick — 15b
Big ruck — 46c
(Hay) rick — 7b, *8a*, 9b^{f}, 10a, *11*, *13*, *14d*, 15b, 18-19, 21,

Lanark cont'd

25c, 29e, 32d, *33cd*, 35a, 37, 38d, *57a*, 66[r]
(Hay) ruck – 6, 12, 15b, 20, 23-24, 27b, 32f, *36*, 38a, 41, *54*, *58*, 60, 62, 67b
(Hay)stack – *1-2*[r], *3*, *5*-6, 7a[r]*c*, *8b*, *9a*, *12*, 14bd, 15ac, *16ab*, *19*, *22*-23, *25abc*, *26a*, *29cdf*, *30*, 31*acd*, *32ad*[y], 34, *35bcd*, *38c*, 39-40, *44-45*, 46ab, *48*, 49ab, *51*, 52b, *53*, *56*, 57b[o], *59b*, 60-61, *64b*, 65-66[sq], *67a*
Leet – 7a[sq], 32c, 42, 47
Pike – 3, 32c
Soo stack – 2[o,sq], 7a[lg], 17[y], 38b, 49b[o], 51[o], 63
Sow stack – 50[sq]
Winter ruck – 67a
Nil – 4, 10b, 14ac, 25d, 26b, 27a, 28, 29abg, 31b, 32be, 33ab, 38e, 43, 52a, 55, 57c, 59a, 64a

West Lothian

Clamp – 19b
(Hay) rick – *1d*, *11*-12, 19a, 21b, *22*[f]
(Hay) ruck – 1c, 4-6, 9a, *17a*, 21a
(Hay)stack – 1ac, *2-3*, 6[l], 8, *9ab*, *10-13*, *15-16*, *17a*, *18*, 20ab, *22*[y]
Leet – 16[l]
Soo – 10-11[lg]
Sow – 10[lg]
Nil – 1b, 7, 14, 17b

Midlothian

Hay mow – 11
(Hay) ruck – *10*, *14b*, 18, 23a, 25c
(Hay) soo – 3[o], *9*
(Hay)stack – *1*, *3*[r], 6ab, 7a, 8ab, *11*, 12ab, *14a*, *15*, 16-17, *18-21*, *23b*, *24*, *25d*, 26b, 27, *29*, 30-31, *32*
Rick – 7b, 10, 23a, 26a,
Round stack – 4
Soo stack – 4[sq], 12b, 17[sq] 23b, 31
Sou back – 26a
Sow – 23a
Nil – 2, 5, 13, 22, 25ab, 28

East Lothian

Hay moo – 16[o]
(Hay) rick – *4b*, 12
(Hay)stack – *1-2*, 4ab, 6ab, *7-9*, *11*, 14, *15*[r], *16*[r], *18-21*
Soo stack – 4b[lg], 13-14[l,o], 15[l], 17
Nil – 3, 5, 10

Berwick

Hay mow – 18
(Hay) rick – 8, *20*
(Hay) ruck – *1*, *4*, 29
(Hay)stack – *2-3*, *6-7*, 8, *9-10*, 12, *15*, *16abc*[r], *17-18*, *21-23*[r], *25-27*, 30, *31-32*[r]
Prop – 19
Rance – 19
Soo – 8[o], 21[sq], 27
Soo stack – 12, 16c[o], 17[o,sq], 23[o], 32[o]
Sow stack – 16c[o], 32
Nil – 5, 11, 13-14, 24, 28

Peebles

Biggit stack – 6a
Built stack – 6a
Hay rick – 5
(Hay) ruck – 1, *3*, *5*, *8*
(Hay)stack – *1-2*, *4b*, 6ab[r], *7*, 9
Round stack – 6b
Soo stack – 4b, 10[lg]
Sow stack – 6b[o]
Wunter ruck – 10[r]
Nil – 4ac

Selkirk

Hay cock – 2d
(Hay) rick – 2b, *8*
Haystack – 1, 2a[c], 4, 8
Ruck – 2e
Soo stack – 2a[o]
Nil – 3, 5-7

Roxburgh

(Hay) ruck – 9a, 19, *21c*
(Hay)stack – *1-2*, 3ab, *4-6*, *8*, 9a, *10*, *13*, *15b*, *16-17*, *19-20*, *21af*, *22*-23, *28*
Hummel – 4
Kiles – 14
Rick – 11, 14, 17
Soo stack – 10[sq], 26
Sow stack – 22[o], 25[o,sq]-26
Winter stack – 20, 25[r]
Wunter ruck – 21ad, 28
Nil – 7, 9b, 12, 15a, 18, 21be, 24, 27

Dumfries

(Hay) rick – 1b, 8a, 19, 23, 25, 31bc, 34, 38, *43*, *46*
(Hay) ruck – 7, 10, 13, 15-16, 22, *24*, 26[r], *27*, 28, *31cd*, 32[r], 33, 34, *35-36*, 37, 39-40, 42, *43*, 44, 45a, *46*-47
(Hay)stack – *1a*, 2, 4-5, *8b*, *12*, *16*, *17a*, *18*, *20*, *21b*, 26[sq], 29, *31f*, 32-33, 41, *45b*, *46*
Soo stack – 1a[lg], 5[o], 12, 21ab[o]
Sow ruck – 46
Sow stack – 15[sq]-16, 32[sq]
Winter rick – 6, 17b
Winter ruck – 17b
Nil – 3, 9, 11, 14, 30, 31ae, 48-49

Kirkcudbright

Big ruck – 21c
Cole – 11
(Hay)stack – *1-2*[r], 3, *4*-5, *6-7*, 8, *10*, *12a*, 14[r], 15b, *18-19*, *22*-23, *27*
Moo – 4
Rick – 15a[r]
Roon stack – 10
Round stack – 2
Ruck – 11, 16, 25
Soo – 14[o], 15a[o], 17, 24
Soo stack – 2, 4[lg], 10, 12b, 19[sq]
Sow – 17
Nil – 9, 13, 20, 21ab, 26

Wigtown

(Hay) ruck – 1[r,y], *6*[r]
(Hay)stack – 1, *2*, 3, *5a*, *6*[o], *7-9*, *12-13*[l], *17*
Pake (stack) 11[r], 12[s,r], 14[r], 16, *18*[r]
Pike (stack) 3, *10*[r]
Rick – 1f
Soo (stack) – *1*, 5*ab*[o], *10*[lg], 11[o], 12[o], *14*[o], 18[o]
Nil – 4, 15

Northumberland

Eek – 79
(Hay) cock – 72l[i], *124b*
(Hay) mow – 3, 11, *17*, 26, 29c, 76, 79, 107, 134
(Hay) rick – 1b, 10, *13*-14, *16*-17, 19a, *20b*, 26, 28, 29ab, 33a, 38, 40a, 41*ac*, 45[lg], *53b*, 55, 57, 59*be*, 61, 62ef, *64b*, 66, *69ef*, 71ade, *73*, 75, *76*, 77, 79[ov], 81, *88b*, 91, *95a*, *101b*, 107, *108c*, 110, 111b, 112, 114, 118*ab*, 120a, 125, 126f, 127*adef*, 129b, 130bc, 135-137, 141
(Hay)stack – *1a*, *2ab*, *5-6*, *8-9*, *13*-14, *16*, *18*, 19a, *21*, *28*, 29bd, 30-*31*, 33a, *34ab*, *35-36*, 37-38, *40a*, 41acd, 42-43, *44*, 45-46, *48*, 52, *53ab*, *54*, 56-57, 59*bcd*, 60, *62bg*, 64ab, *65a*, *66*, 69cdh, *70*, 71acd, 72abc*d*gikl, *73*, 77-*78*, *80*, 82, *86-87*, *88ab*, *89*, 90-92, *94b*, *95ab*, *96*, *98*, *99bd*, 100, *101b*, 102, *103abc*, 104ab, 105-*106*, 108a, *109*, 111*ab*, 113, *117*, 118a, *119*, 120bc, *126c*, *127ac*, 130ade, 132, 135, 138, 142-*143*
Hick – 22
Pike – 62h, 83
Roond stack – 33b[r], 69ab
Ruck – 142
(Sow) stack – 18[lg], 23[lg], 33b[o], *41a*[o], *69a*[sq]*b*
Square stack – 69b
Stamp – 79
Stook – 122a
Nil – 1c, 4, 7, 15, 19b, 20a, 24ab, 25, 27, 29ef, 32, 39, 40b, 41b, 47, 49-51, 58, 59af, 62acd, 63, 65b, 67-68, 69g, 71be, 72efhj, 74, 84-85, 93, 94a, 97, 99ac, 101a, 108b, 115-116, 121, 122b, 123, 124a, 126abde, 127bgh, 128, 129ac, 130f, 131, 133, 139-140

Cumberland

Hay moo – 54
Hay myow – 54
(Hay) rick – 2, *9*, *12*, 13a, 14[o], 15b, 16, 22, 27, 41[s], 42-43, 47, 51, 53, 56-57, 61, 63a
(Hay)stack – *1a*, *2*[y], 3, *4*, *5a*, *7-9*, *12*, 13*acd*, 14[r], *15ac*, 16, 19, *22-23*, *24-26*, *27*[r], *28*, 31, 37b, *38*, 40, *46-49*, 51-52, *53*, 56, *57-58*, *60-62*
Nil – 1b, 5b, 6, 10-11, 13b, 17-18, 20-21, 29-30, 32-36, 37a, 39, 44-45, 50, 55, 59, 63b

Down

Havel – 11[sq], 24[sq], 29
Hay cock – 8
(Hay) pike – 3, 10-11[r], 17, *21*, *24*[r]
(Hay) rick – 1, 2b, 4, 6, *8*, 21, 24
Haystack – 2a, 5, 9, 12, 14-15, 18-19, 24, 26, 28
Peck – 28
Reek – 22
Ruck – 2b, 4, 6, 8, 21
Nil – 7, 13, 16, 20, 23, 25, 27, 30

Tyrone

Hay cock – 10-11
Hay pake – 1, 7
(Hay) rick – 1, *11-12*
Haystack – 8, 11
Pake – 5, 9
Peak – 5, 8
Peck – 15
Pike – 6, 9-10[l]
Ruck – 10[s], 13
Nil – 2-4, 14, 16

Antrim

Havel – 5b, 7[o], 33
Haypek – 5b
(Hay) pike – *1*, 9, *10*, 11-12, 15[c], *16b*, 18-19, 21-23, 25[c]-27, 29-34
(Hay) ruck – 14-15, 21, *28*-29
Haystack – 3[c], 5a, 17, 20
Hovel – 34
Pake – 7[c], 9, 11, 13, 16b, 22
Rick – 3[o], 9, 14, 34
Shig – 8a
Tramp cock – 1
Nil – 2, 4, 4A, 6, 8b, 16ac, 24

Donegal

(Hay) cock – 5[s], 6, *9*
Hay pake – 7A
Hay reek – 3
Hay sheek – 8[o]
(Hay)stack – 2-*3*, 4-5, 5A, *12*
Pake – 10b, 11[r]
Pike – 5[s]-6, 10a[r], 13
Rick – 6, 12-13
Sheeg – 10a[o], 11[o]
Shig – 1
Nil – 1A, 7

Fermanagh

(Hay)stack – *1*[l], 2[o], *3*[o], *4*[o], *5*[o], *9*
Peak – 2
Peck – 2, 6
Pike – 1[r,c], 2[r,c], 3[r], 4[r], 5[r], 6[s]
Rick – 10
Ruck – 7a
Nil – 7b, 8

Armagh

(Hay)stack – *3-4*, *6a*
Hovel – 1[lg]
Pack – 1[r]
Rick – 6a
Nil – 2, 5, 6b

Londonderry

(Hay) pike – *4*-5, 7
Pake – 1[r], 3, 5
Peek – 1A, 6
Rick – 2
Sheag – 1[lg]
Steck – 3A
Nil – 1B

54 HEAP OF HAY (the first small heap, usually three feet high, made by haymakers) (PQ1, 114)

See note (1) on 53 **haystack**.
Where comments of informants did not fit the description of the heading, the items concerned have not been included.

Shetland
Cole — 1-5, 13, 15-17, 21a, 23-28, 30-32
Coll — 6-7, 11, 18-19
Coorsmelt — 23
Diss — 33
First cole — 22, 29
Peerie — 3, 6
Peerie cole — 16, 21b, 30
Peerie coll — 8, 10, 14
Perrie coll — 20
Rick — 33
Scruvlick — 9
Nil — 12

Orkney
Coll — 6, 13a
Diss — 13a
First gathering — 9
(Hay) cole — 1-4, *5,* 7, 10-12, 14-21
Heap of hay — 13a
Peerie cole — 8
Small cole — 8
Nil — 13b

Caithness
Colag — 14
Cole — 2ab, 3, 5-11, 13
Collie — 15, 16ab, 17
Heapie of hay — 13
Hillag — 14
Rick — 15
Small cole — 12b
Small colie — 4
Nil — 1, 12ac

Sutherland
Cock — 5
Coil — 2-4, 6, 8, 12, 15
Coilie — 5
Cole — 1, 4, 6, 8, 9b, 10-11, 14-15, 17
Colie — 16
Gorag — 3-4, 6
Rick — 9a
Small coil — 7
Small coll — 13

Ross & Cromarty
Coil — 2-5, 8-10, 17, 26, 32bc, 37a, 38-39
Coilie — 28
Cole — 5-7, 9-19, 21-24, 25ab, 27, 31, 32a, 33-36, 37a
Coll — 24
(Hay) rick — 17, 21, 29, *30,* 36
Little cole — 20
Rookan — 29
Ruck — 32c, 39
Ruckie — 31
Nil — 1, 37b

Inverness
Cockie — 13e
Coilie — 31
Cole — 3, 7, 10, 13c, 14-16, 19-20, 21ab, 26-29, 35
Colie — 11
Coll — 33
Golack — 21b
Hay cock — 6
(Hay) coil — *5,* 13d, 15-19, 22-23, 36-40
Rick — 15, 30
Rickie — 19
Rouchan — 24, 31
Rouchkan — 8
Roukan — 8
Ruck — 8, 13c, 14, 32
Ruckie — 12, 13c, 19
Small coil — 25, 34
Small cole — 9
Stook — 13a
Nil — 1-2, 4, 13b

Nairn
Cole — 1ac, 2-4
Colie — 6
Small cole — 1b
Wee hay ruck — 5

Moray
Coil — 11
Cole — 2ab, 3-5, 6ab, 7, 8abcde, 9a, 10, 12-16, 19, 22
Colie — 23
Coll — 11, 20
Hooick — 1, 10, 18, 21
Hoomack — 8b
Little cole — 23
Rick — 9b
Nil — 8f, 17

Banff
Cole — 1, 2c, 3-5, 6a, 7-9, 11-12, 15-16, 18bc, 19-27, 32, 34
Coll — 13-14, 17
Heap — 6b
Hooick — 6b, 9-10, 16, 29-31, 33
Ruckie — 2a
Small cole — 30
Stook — 2b
Nil — 18ad, 28

Aberdeen
Cole — 2, 3ab, 5abc, 6, 9-12, 14-15, 17-18, 21-27, 28ac, 29-32, 34-37, 39-46, 47abcde, 48-55, 58-59, 61-62, 64-66, 68-70, 71ab, 72, 74-82, 84-96, 99-109
Colie — 8, 98
Coll — 1, 5d, 13, 16, 19-20, 33, 56-57, 60, 67, 71c, 73, 83, 97
Gipe — 84
Hooick — 22, 28a, 42, 76
Hooickie — 106
Little cole — 8
Pushlie — 63
Rick — 38
Stook — 47f
Nil — 4, 7, 28b

Kincardine
Hand cole — 21
(Hay) cole — 1-13, 15-16, 17abcd, 19, *21,* 22-28
Small cole — 20
Nil — 14, 18

Kinross
Coil — 6
Cole — 1-5, 7

Angus
Cock — 22
Coil — 36
Colie — 28, 34
Collie — 34
Hand cole — 7, 10, 13, 22, 31
(Hay) cole — 1-2, 4, 5abc, 8, *14a,* 15, 20-21, 23, 25, 32, 33b, 37
(Hay) rick — 7-9, *14a,* 19, 27
Hut — 11
Kyle — 33a
Little cole — 14cd
Mole heap — 12
Quile — 14b
Reck — 35
Ruck — 34
Stookie — 18
Wee cole — 3
Wisp — 17a
Nil — 6, 16, 17b, 24, 26, 29ab, 30

Perth
Coil — 10, 14, 24-25, 33-36, 66-68, 70-74
Colack — 1
Cole — 1, 3, 5, 7, 10, 12-13, 17, 19, 27, 29b, 30, 37-38, 41ab, 43, 45, 47, 51a, 52bd, 54-56, 60, 64, 70
Colie — 6
Hand coil — 16
Hand cole — 2b, 3-4, 8-9, 12, 15, 20-21, 28, 31-32, 39-40, 42, 46, 48, 51a, 52c, 57, 62
Hand coll — 33
Haund cole — 50
(Hay) cock — *24,* 44
Heap (of hay) — *4,* 18
Kyle — 56
Quile — 29a, 59, 70, 72-74
Rick — 29b, 49
Shandie — 49
Small cole — 2a, 3
Wee cole — 11, 45, 62
Nil — 22-23, 26, 51b, 52ae, 53, 58, 61, 63, 65, 69

Fife
Baffle — 18
Clou — 1
Cock — 12, 55d
Coil — 17, 21, 29, 44a, 51, 55df
Coilie — 30
Cole — 3-4, 6, 9ab, 11, 13, 17, 20-28, 31-32, 34-35, 36ab, 37-39, 40b, 41ab, 42, 43ab, 44abcef, 47-48, 53-54, 55abcdefg, 56, 58-62, 64a
Coll — 44e, 51
Coul — 12
Frandie — 10
Frondie — 4, 8, 18
Hand cole — 5, 7, 13
Haund cole — 14
Haund kyle — 39
Heap — 8, 50, 55e
Keyle — 44d
Kyle — 2, 29, 64b
Pile — 37
Prandie — 7
Quile — 37, 59
Quiling — 41a
Rick — 33, 52, 57
Ruck — 33
Stook — 12, 50
Stookie — 55a
Wee cole — 45
Nil — 15-16, 19, 40a, 41cd, 46, 49, 63

Clackmannan
Bowrach — 5
Buchlyvie — 1
Coil — 4d
Cole — 1, 4ad, 5-7
Frandie — 4d
Quail — 7
Quile — 1, 5
Quillie — 2
Quoil — 7
Stook — 4bc
Nil — 3

Stirling
Coil — 1, 4, 7bcdef, 12-13, 20, 21a, 26bcd, 27b, 32, 34, 35b, 42ab
Cole — 10, 39a
Coll — 11, 38
Donnellie — 7b
Hay cock — 26a, 30
(Hay) rick — 19, 23a, *26f*
Kyle — 17-18, 21ab, 22b, 24, 25ad, 26a, 36, 37ab, 39b, 40-41, 42a
Quahil — 9
Quile — 2-3, 6, 7abe, 8, 13-18, 21b, 22a, 23b, 24, 25abc, 26e, 27a, 28, 30, 33, 35a, 36
Quoil — 23c, 27b, 29
Rickle — 26b
Sheaf — 31
Stook — 7b
Truss — 26b
Nil — 5

Dunbarton
Coil — 1, 3, 4ab, 5-6, 10, 13abc, 17
Cole — 4a
Kyle — 15
Quile — 1-2, 5-6, 7abc, 9, 13abc, 16ab, 17-18
Quoil — 14a
Nil — 8, 11-12, 14b

Argyll
Coil — 1, 4, 7-16, 18-19, 21-24, 26-35, 37, 39-40
Coilie — 6
Cole — 2, 33, 38
Hand coil — 5
Hay cock — 25, 35
Heap — 17, 25
Prapack — 3, 5-6
Quile — 19
Ruck — 26
Nil — 20, 36

Bute
Coil — 1abce, 2-6, 8b
Cole — 1a
Hut — 6
Quile — 7, 8ab
Quoile — 9
Nil — 1d

Ayr
Cock — 1a, 57
Coil — 1ab, 6, 8a, 12b, 14-15, 18ab, 19, 20h, 26a, 27, 28b, 39, 41, 45, 47-52, 53ab, 54, 56-57
Cole — 28b
Coll — 51, 57
Kyle — 2b, 5, 15, 25
Quile — 1a, 2ab, 3-5, 7, 8ab, 9-11, 13, 16ab, 17, 18ab, 20abcdeg, 21-23, 24b, 26a, 28acdf, 29, 30ab, 31-34, 35ab, 36-40, 42-46, 49
Quoile—7, 17, 18b, 20f, 43
Rickle — 18b, 20h, 53a, 57
Ricklet — 18b
Ruck — 24a
Stook — 26b, 28e
Nil — 26c, 55

Renfrew
Coil — 2def, 4ac, 8, 12a, 16bd, 19, 20b
Cole — 4ac, 16a
Cowl — 15
Hay cock — 13b
Hay rick — 2a
Haystack — 2a
Humplock — 11j
Kyle — 14b
Mound — 11e
Ovale — 10
Queyle — 2h
Quile — 1b, 2bdeg, 4d, 5, 7-9, 11abefkl, 12a, 13ac, 14b, 17, 18ab, 20a, 21
Quill — 15
Quoil — 3, 7, 11i
Stook — 2ci, 4e, 11dg, 16a
Swaithe — 11j

Renfrew cont'd

Wee cock — 2i
Wisp — 16c
Nil — 1a, 2j, 4b, 6, 11ch, 12b, 13d, 14a

Lanark

Bunch — 18
Bundle — 18, 29b
Coil — 2, 7c, 9b, 10a, 11-13, 14c, 25ac, 29e. 32f, 35d, 38bc, 45, 46a, 47, 52a, 53, 56, 57c
Cole — 25c, 38d, 45, 55
Coop — 29f
Hay cock — 29f
Hummock — 26a
Humphlock — 23
Kyle — 3, 8b, 9a, 14c, 15abc, 19-20, 24, 27ab, 29cd, 30, 32df, 35b, 36, 38abcde, 39-40, 44, 47-48, 49ab, 50-51, 52ab, 54, 57abc, 58, 59ab, 60, 62-63, 64ab, 65-66
Kylin — 32f
Pile — 18
Quile — 1-2, 5-6, 7a, 10a, 12-13, 14b, 15b, 16ab, 23, 25a, 29e, 31abd, 33cd, 34, 35a, 37, 42-43, 46bc, 61, 67a
Quill — 1, 31b, 33a
Quoch — 33b
Quoil — 7a, 17, 21, 31c, 32ac, 41, 48
Rick — 29b
Rickle — 7a
Ruck — 60
Sheaf — 8a
Stook — 7c, 8a, 14d, 22, 25bd, 29a, 32b
Nil — 4, 7b, 10b, 14a, 26b, 28, 29g, 32e, 35c, 67b

West Lothian

Coil — 1bc, 3, 7-8, 11, 13-14, 17a, 19a, 21a, 22
Kyle — 1acd, 2-6, 8, 9ab, 10-12, 14-16, 17ab, 18, 19b, 20a
Quile — 17a, 21b
Stook — 21a
Nil — 20b

Midlothian

Cole — 4, 7ab, 11, 24
(Hay) cock — 7b, *26b*
(Hay) coil — 6b, 7a, 8b, 9-11, 16, 22, 23a, *26a*
Heap — 8a
Kailie — 28
Kyle — 1, 3, 7b, 10-11, 12ab, 13, 14ab, 15, 17-18, 20-22, 23ab, 25c, 27, 29-32
Pile — 6a
Quile — 4, 14b
Rick — 22, 23b
Rickle — 22
Ruck — 19
Stook — 23a
Nil — 2, 5, 25abd

East Lothian

Coil — 3, 6b, 7, 9-10, 14
Grip — 6a
Hot — 15
Hut — 15
Kylan — 10
Kyle — 1-2, 4b, 9, 11, 13, 15-17, 19-21
Kylie — 4a
Ruck — 6a
Wee hay ruck — 8
Nil — 5, 12, 18

Berwick

Cock — 16c
Coil — 7, 27
Hobbler — 18
Kyle — 1-6, 8, 10-15, 16ab, 17-23, 25-26, 29-32
Kylie — 24

Pike — 9, 27
Nil — 28

Peebles

Cock — 6a
Coil — 4b, 5, 6ab
Kyle — 1-3, 4b, 5, 7-10
Stook — 4ab
Nil — 4c

Selkirk

Cock — 8
Coil — 5
Kyle — 1, 2abde, 3-4, 6-8
Nil — 2c

Roxburgh

Cock — 21c
Coil — 6, 21c
Fit cock — 28
Hoddle — 21c
Kyle — 1-2, 3ab, 4-8, 9ab, 10-13, 15ab, 16-20, 21acdf, 22-26, 28
Nellie wud — 28
Pike — 4
Nil — 14, 21be, 27

Dumfries

Cock — 35, 46
Coil — 1ab, 3-4, 8b, 11, 13, 15, 17b, 21a, 22, 34, 43, 46
Cole — 3, 8a, 9, 21b, 23, 25-26, 30, 31ae, 32, 34
Coll — 10, 19
Han coil — 5, 20
Han coll — 12
Hand cole — 22, 24, 31c, 32, 41-42
Haun(d) cole — 21b, 33
Hot — 35
Keyle — 37
Kyle — 2, 6-7, 14, 16, 17ab, 18, 26-29, 32-36, 38-40, 43-44, 45ab, 46-47, 49
Kylie — 29
Quile — 1a, 22
Quoil — 26
Rick — 31f
Rickle — 46
Stamp cole — 25, 46
Stan cole — 22, 31bd
Nil — 48

Kirkcudbright

Bottom of ruck — 2
Cock — 24
Coil — 12b, 25
Cole — 1-7, 10, 12ab, 13-14, 17-20, 21abc, 22, 26-27
Colie — 1
Coll — 23
Hand cole — 8-9, 15a, 16, 24
Hillock — 15b
Quile — 1
Rickle — 11
Stan cole — 10
Wee dot — 18

Wigtown

Coil — 1, 5ab, 6-7, 12
Cole — 1-3, 5ab, 6, 8-18
Rickle — 5a
Stand cole — 3
Nil — 4

Northumberland

Cock foot — 111a
Coil — 77, 91
Cowlie — 71b
Foot cock — 29f, 102, 103ab, 110, 111b, 132, 135, 140
Half rick — 134
Half ruck — 132-133, 135, 142
(Hay) cock — 14, *18,* 20a, 29aef, *33a,* 41a, 44-45, 56, *59bd,* 60, *72e, 76,* 77, *78,* 79, *104b,* 106, 109, *111a,* 121, *122a,* 126adef, 127*ch,* 130de
Heap — 30, 72k
Keyle — 111a
Kyle — 1ab, 2ab, 3-18, 19ab, 20ab, 21-23, 24ab, 25-28, 29abcde, 30-32, 33b, 34ab, 35-39, 40ab, 41abcd, 42-52, 53ab, 54-58, 59abcdef, 60-61 62abcfg, 64b, 65ab, 68, 69abcdefgh, 70, 71bcd, 72bcdefgijl, 73-86, 88ab, 89-93, 95ab, 96, 98, 99acd, 100, 102, 103abc, 104ab, 105-107, 108abc, 109-110, 112-117, 118ab, 119, 120abc, 122ab, 123, 124ab, 125, 126ef, 127bde, 129b, 130abcd, 132-143
Kylie — 64a, 98
Pike — 1c, 40b, 46, 59a, 71e, 87, 126d
Pikie — 72h
Pile — 59b, 72l, 127a
Rick — 59b, 72j
Stook — 62h, 66, 71a, 130f
Tod — 62e
Whinraa — 46
Nil — 62d, 63, 67, 72a, 94ab, 97, 99b, 101ab, 126bc, 127fg, 128, 129ac, 131

Cumberland

Billie cock — 44
Bundle — 27
Feut cock — 12, 27, 46, 56
Fit cock — 8
Foot cock — 9, 16, 20, 37ab, 42, 44
Half ruck — 23
(Hay) cock — 1*ab*, 2-4, 5ab, 7, 9, 11, *12,* 13abcd, 14, 15*abc*, *16,* 17, *18-19,* 20-22, *24-26,* 28, *29-30,* 31-33, *34,* 35-36, 37ab, *38,* 39, *40,* 41, 43, 45-48, *49,* 50-51, *52,* 53, *54,* 55, 57-59, *60,* 61, 62, 63*ab*
Heap — 12
Kyle — 4, 6, 13b
Wap — 27
Woat — 27
Nil — 10

Down

Cock — 17, 23, 25
Cole — 6, 10
Forked ruck — 11
Hand cock — 11, 21, 24
Heap of hay — 2a
Hud — 13
Lap — 1, 2b, 4, 10, 14, 27-29
Lump — 4-6, 18-19, 26
Rick — 2a, 8, 15
Rickle — 13
Ruck — 15
Shak cole — 21
Shig — 22
Wee lock — 23
Nil — 3, 7, 9, 12, 16, 20, 30

Tyrone

Car cock — 13
Cock — 1-2, 14
Hand cock — 12
Handshaken — 14
Lap — 1, 3, 5-9, 11, 14
Purlie — 9
Ruck — 15-16
Shay cock — 10
Nil — 4

Antrim

Butt — 34
Cock — 2, 8b, 9
Cole — 11-12, 14-15, 16b, 17-18, 22, 24-25, 27, 29, 31
Cone — 1
Hand cock — 1, 5b
Hand cole — 7, 13, 17, 19-21

Hand rick — 10
Hand ruck — 18
Hump — 34
Lap — 4, 5ab, 6, 13-15, 21-22, 26, 30, 34
Lump — 8a, 21, 31-32, 34
Pile — 34
Rickle — 16b
Rule — 18
Shake cole — 23, 26, 28, 33
Nil — 3, 4A, 16ac

Donegal

Grainneog — 6
Hand cock — 3, 6-9, 11-13
Hand shakin(g) — 8, 13
(Hay) cock — 1-2, 4-*5,* 5A
Humplock — 10b
Lap (cock) 6, *8,* 10a
Lump — 5A, 10ab
Small cock — 5A
Nil — 1A, 7A

Fermangh

Cock — 10
Handshake — 1-3, 5-6, 10
Lap — 2, 4, 7a, 9-10
Ruck — 10
Nil — 7b, 8

Armagh

Lap (cock) — *4*-5
Lump — 3
Quill — 2
Rickle — 6b
Sheer cock — 1
Nil — 6a

Londonderry

Cock — 1, 1B
Hand cock — 1A, 2-3, 3A, 4-5, 7
Jockey — 6
Lap — 3A, 5

55 HEAP OF HAY (the big one, usually about six feet high, made afterwards, which stands about in the fields before stacking) (PQ1, 115)

See note (1) on 53 **haystack**.
Where comments of informants did not fit the description in the heading, the items concerned have not been included.

Shetland
Big cole – 17, 23, 27
Big coll – 8, 10, 21a
Biggit cole – 2
Cole – 1, 3, 19, 30
Coll – 9
Dess – 25
Diss – 33
Dush – 22
Duss – 22
Fit cole – 28
Fit coll – 7, 18
Muckle cole – 3, 16, 21b, 30-32
Muckle coll – 6, 10, 14, 20
Packed cole – 4
Second cole – 22, 29
Stack – 33
Tramp cole – 29
Nil – 5, 11-13, 15, 24, 26

Orkney
Cole – 13b
Coll – 13a
Diss – 7, 12, 14
Good big cole – 8
Hay screw – 9
Land cole – 16
Muckle diss – 13a
Tramp cole – 2-5, 10-11, 17-21
Tramp coll – 6
Nil – 1, 15

Caithness
Big coal – 2a, 3
Big coalie – 4
Cole – 5-6, 8-9, 12abc, 14, 16b
(Hay) gilt – 2b, 7, *13*, 15
(Hay) rick – *10*, 12a
Screw – 2b, 15, 16a
Tramp cole – 3
Nil – 1, 11, 17

Sutherland
Big cole – 10
Coil – 5, 8
Cole – 8, 9a, 16
Hand rick – 6
Hay cock – 3
Large coil – 7
Large cole – 13
Pike – 12
Rick – 2, 4, 6, 9b, 11, 14, 16-17
Rickie – 3
Ruck – 1, 11
Second cole – 15
Stackie – 10

Ross & Cromarty
Big coil – 4
Big cole – 7, 16
Cock – 27
Coil – 32c, 39
Cole – 20, 22, 28, 30-31
Dash – 5
Haystack – 36
Rick – 9, 17-18, 24, 25a, 29, 32ab, 35
Ruck – 8, 12, 23, 27, 32c, 33, 39
Ruckie – 34
Stamp cole – 19
Tramp coil – 3, 29
Tramp cole – 10, 13-15, 21, 25a, 29
Tramped cole – 23, 25b
Two coils – 26
Nil – 1-2, 6, 11, 37ab, 38

Inverness
Big coil – 18, 25
Big cole – 7, 9
Big ruck – 13c
Cairn – 6
Cole – 8, 11, 13e, 24, 28-29
Hay cock – 3, 22
(Hay) coil – *5*, 12, 30-32, 34
(Hay) rick – 10, 19, 21ab, 23, 26, 29, 31, 33, 36-37, *39*
Rook – 40
Ruck – 16, 38
Ruckie – 20
Stack – 1
Stook – 13a
Tramp cole – 27
Nil – 2, 4, 13bd, 14-15, 17, 35

Nairn
Big cole – 1a
Hay ruck – 5
Ruckie – 6
Soo – 1b
Tramp cole – 1bc, 2-4

Moray
Cole – 1, 17-18, 23
Coll – 21
Hooick – 12, 16, 22
Rick – 8e
Ruck – 7
Screw – 16
Tram cole – 8c
Tramp cole – 2a, 3-5, 6ab, 7, 8bd, 9a, 10-11, 13-15, 19
Tramp coll – 11, 20
Trampie – 20
Nil – 2b, 8af, 9b

Banff
Cole – 6b, 10, 18d, 28-33
Hooick – 11, 14, 18c, 25-26, 34
Hullock – 20
Tramp – 2c
Tramp cole – 1, 3-5, 6a, 7-9, 12, 18bc, 19-21, 23-24, 26-27
Tramp coll – 13, 17
Tramped cole – 15-16, 22
Nil – 2ab, 18a

Aberdeen
Big cole – 11, 15, 31
Clamp – 25
Cole – 4, 7-8, 19, 42, 63
Coll – 13, 73
Double cole – 103
(Hay) ruck – 47f, *90*, 108
Hay soo – 47bc
Hooick – 14, 28c, 33, 53, 60, 63-64, 69, 71c, 79, 87, 89, 95, 108
Rick – 10, 38
Screw – 6, 30, 47a, 74
Second cole – 5c, 21, 36, 39, 88, 104
Stack – 10
Tramp – 47d
Tramp cole – 2, 6, 9-12, 14, 19, 21-24, 26, 28a, 29, 32, 37, 41, 43, 47ade, 48-49, 51-54, 58, 64-66, 68, 71ab, 72, 76-78, 80, 82, 86, 88, 91-93, 96, 98-99, 106-107
Tramp coll – 5d, 6, 16, 20, 67, 97
Tramped cole – 104
Trunk cole – 46, 50
Trump cole – 3ab, 5ab, 17-18, 27, 34-35, 39-40, 44-45, 55, 59, 61-62, 69-70, 74-75, 79, 81, 94, 101, 105
Trump coll – 56-57
Nil – 1, 28b, 83-85, 100, 102, 109

Kincardine
Aff-cole – 17ad
(Hay) cole – 1, 14, 18, 20-*21*, 27
Rickle – 3
Tramp cole – 4, 6-8, 12-14, 17abc, 19, 21, 23, 25, 28
Trimp cole – 26
Trump cole – 2, 5, 9-11, 15, 18, 24
Nil – 16, 22

Kinross
Buchlyvie – 7
Rick – 2-3, 5
Ruck – 1-2
Tramped cole – 7
Wee ruck – 4
Nil – 6

Angus
Big cole – 37
Coll – 33b
(Hay) cole – 2-3, 6, 8-9, 11, 13, 14b*cd*, 15, 17ab, 18-20, 24-27, 29a, 30, 32, 33ab, 34-36
Haystack – 14a
Little cole – 37
Ramp – 14a
Rick – 23, 31-32
Tramp cole – 1, 5bc, 7, 10, 12, 14d, 20-23, 28, 31, 37
Nil – 4, 5a, 16, 29b

Perth
Big cole – 45, 55
Buchlyvie – 68, 70-74
Coil – 48
Coll – 25, 33
(Hay) cole – 1, 2a, 3, 5-6, 11, 18, 20-23, 26, 28, 29a, 32, 37, 41a, 44-45, 47-*50*, 51a, 52a*c*, 54-55, 58-59, 61, 63, 65
(Hay) rick – 9-10, 12, *24*-25, 29b, 36, 41ab, 60, 66-67, 72
Heap of hay – 4, 52b
Pile – 18
Ruck – 3, 12, 16, 35-36, 38, 43, 65, 68, 72
Stack – 6, 52d
Tramp – 29b
Tramp coil – 14, 16
Tramp cole – 2b, 4, 7-9, 13, 15, 17, 21, 27, 39-40, 42, 46, 50, 56-57, 62, 64
Tramped cole – 31
Tramp quile – 70
Nil – 19, 30, 34, 51b, 52e, 53, 69

Fife
Big cole – 45
Big heap – 50
Big stook – 50
Bucklyvie – 51
Cole – 5-8, 10, 12, 18-19, 64b
Coll – 12
Field rick – 59
Frandie – 51, 55d
Hape – 8
(Hay) rick – 3, 11, 13, *21*-24, 27, *29*-30 34-35, 36a, 38, 40b, 41c, 42, 44*ef*, 47, 53-54, 55*a*bde, 56, 60-61, 64a
(Hay) ruck – 1, 4, 6, 9ab, 12, 17, 20, 22, 25-28, 31, 34-35, 36b, 37-*39*, 41ad, 43ab, 44ce, 52, 55c, 62, 64a
(Hay) soo – *32*, 50
(Hay) stack – 33, 37, 41b, 42, 44f, 55g, *57*
Kyle – 12

Pig – 44b
Puckle – 63
Sow – 44b
Stook – 13
Tramp cole – 44a, 55f
Tramp ruck – 14, 48
Wee ruck – 44d
Winlin – 36a
Nil – 2, 15-16, 40a, 46, 49, 58

Clackmannan
Buchlyvie – 4d, 7
Cole – 2
Rick – 1, 4bc, 5
Ruck – 5-6
Tramp cole – 2
Nil – 3, 4a

Stirling
Buchlyvie – 2-3, 6, 7abcdef, 8-12, 14, 16-20, 21b, 22ab, 23bc, 24, 25b, 26acdef, 34, 36, 37b, 39b
Bucklyvie – 10, 26b
Coil – 4
Cole – 17
Donel – 13
Field rick – 25c
Field ruck – 21b, 25b
(Hay) rick – 7c, 8, 21a, 30-31, 35b, 36, *38*, 39a, 42b
(Hay) ruck – 1, 7be, 10, 12, 15, 21a, 25d, 26ab, 27a, 28-29, 31-33, 35a, 36, 37ab, 39a, 40-41, 42a
(Hay)stack – 26b, *30*
Lyvie – 22a
Quile – 31
Rickle – 35b
Stook – 26a
Tramp – 25a
Tramped rick – 24
Wee rick – 27b
Nil – 5, 23a

Dunbarton
Buchlyvie – 9
Cole – 3
Field ruck – 7c
(Hay) rick – 1, 4a, 7a, 9-*11*, 13bc, 14a*b*, 17-18
Haystack – 9, 18
Hut – 16a
Quile – 16a
Ruck – 2, 4b, 5-6, 7b, 14a, 15
Tramp – 3
Wee rick – 13a
Wee ruck – 9, 16b
Nil – 8, 12

Argyll
Coil – 5
Field rick – 19
(Hay) rick – *6*, 8-9, 14-15, 21-23, 26, 28, 31, 33-*35*, 37, 39-40
(Hay) ruck – 3, 7-8, 10, 12, 16, 18, 24, 29-30, 32, *35*, 38
Rook – 3
Stack – 1, 17
Tramp – 6-8, 11, 14-16, 19, 22-28, 31, 33, *35*, 39-40
Nil – 2, 4, 13, 20, 36

Bute
Rick – 1ab, 3, 6, 8ab, 9
Ruck – 1ab, 2, 4-5, 7, 8b
Stamp – 1e
Tramp – 1ac, 4, 8a
Nil – 1d

Ayr
Field rick – 19
Field ruck – 4-5, 13, 36
(Hay) rick – 1ab, 2ab, 3, 6, 8a, 12a, 15, 16b, 18b, 20bfh, 22, 25, *26b*, 28abcef, *29*, 30b, 39, 43, 45, 47, 49, 52,

Ayr cont'd

54, 56-57
(Hay) ruck — 1a, 5-6, 8ab, 9-11, 12ab, 14, 16ab, 17, 18a, 20abcdefg, 21, 23, 24b, 26a, 27, 28abd, 30a, 31-34, 35ab, 37-*38,* 39-46, 48-52, 53a, 56-57
Haystack — 7
Hook — 18b
Pike — 28b
Rickle — 28b, 41, 47
Rigg — 25
Stook — 53b
Nil — 24a, 26c, 55

Renfrew

Field rick — 11a
(Hay) rick — *1b,* 2defhi, 4ac, 6-8, 10, *11i,* 12a, 13c, 14b, 15, 16d, 20b
(Hay) ruck — 2bg, 3, *4d,* 5, 7, 9, 11*bef*i*kl*, 13a, 16abd, 17 18b, 19
(Hay)stack — 16a, *20a*
Hut — 15
Mow — 21
Quile — 16c, 18a
Pig — 21
Stook — 11j
Nil — 1a, 2acj, 4be, 11cdgh, 12b, 13bd, 14a

Lanark

Bigger ruck — 67b
Cole — 32f
(Hay) rick — 1-3, 7a, 8ab, 9ab, 12, 15abc, 17, 21-23, 25a, 26a, 29cdf, *30,* 31a*c,* 32abcd, 33bcd, 35ab*d,* 37, 38bce, *39,* 44-*45,* 46a, 47-48, *49a,* 52ab, 55-56, 57ac, 64a, 65
(Hay) ruck — 2, 5-6, 7a, 9a, 12, 14b, 15b, 16ab, *17,* 19-20, 27b, 31bcd, 33abd, 34, 38ab, *39*-44, 46bc, 48, 49b, 50-51, 52ab, 57ab, 58, 59ab, 61-63, 64b, 65-66, 67a
(Hay)stack — 7a, *14c,* 18, 21, *25bc,* 27a, 29c, *32d,* 35d, 36
Leat — 32f
Pike — 11, 38d
Rickle — 9b, 57b
Sow — 32f
Stook — 7c, 8a, 29e, 35c, 36
Summer ruck — 60
Wee rick — 53
Nil — 4, 7b, 10ab, 13, 14ad, 24, 25d, 26b, 28, 29abg, 32e, 54

West Lothian

Buchlyvie — 1a
(Hay) rick — *3*-4, 8, 11-12, 16, *22*
(Hay) ruck — 1abcd, 5-8, 9ab, 10, 12, 14-16, *17a,* 18, 19b, 20a, 21ab
(Hay)stack — 11, 13, *17a*
Hucklyvie — 1ad, 18
Lyvie — 18
Pike — 1c
Stook — 17b
Tramp ruck — 17a
Wee ruck — 2
Nil — 19a, 20b

Midlothian

Field ruck — 10, 18
(Hay) rick — 4, 6ab, 7a, 8b, 9, 12b, 16-17, *21,* 23ab, 24, 26ab, 27-28, 31
(Hay)stack— 3, *8a, 18, 25c*
Hut — 10
Kyle — 19
Pike — 32
Rickle — 7b, 14b
Ruck — 1, 3, 11, 12ab, 13, 14a, 15, 18, 20, 23b, 25c, 26a, 29-30, 32
Nil — 2, 5, 22, 25abd

East Lothian

Big ruck — 1, 19
(Hay) rick — 1, 3, *4ab,* 6b, 7, 10-11, 13, 15-16, 18
(Hay) ruck — 1, 6a, 9, 14-15, *17,* 20-21
Hay sow — 2
Pike — 16
Stook — 6a
Tramped kyle — 8
Nil — 5, 12

Berwick

Cock — 18
(Hay) ruck — 2-4, 11-12, 14, 18-19, 22-23, *24,* 25-27, 29-32
Kyle — 22
Pike — 1, 3-8, 10, 15, 16abc, 17-21, 23, 25-27, 32
Rick — 9, 12-13, 17, 27
Stawk — 29
Nil — 28

Peebles

Forked ruck — 6a
(Hay) ruck — *1,* 2-3, 4b, 5, *6b,* 7-10
Rick — 10
Stook — 4a
Tramp — 6a
Nil — 4c

Selkirk

Coil — 2e
Haystack — 2c
Nellie wud — 8
Pike — 4-6, 8
Rick — 5
Ruck — 1, 2ad, 3-4, 6-8
Nil — 2b

Roxburgh

(Hay) ruck — 1-2, 3ab, 5-6, 8, 9ab, 10, 12-13, 15b, 16-18, 20, 21adf, 22-24, 26, *28*
Hodlack — 21c
Pike — 6-7, 9a, 15b, 16, 18, 20, 23, 25, 28
Rick — 4-5, 7, 13, 15a, 19, 21a, 26
Tramp cole — 21c
Nil — 11, 14, 21be, 27

Dumfries

Pike — 5, 7, 10, 15-16, 17b, 25-26, 28-29, 32-40, 42-44, 45ab, 46-47, 49
Rick — 1ab, 3, 6, 8a, 11, 17a, 21b, 23, 31d
Ricklin — 31d
Ruck — 1a, 2, 4-5, 7, 10-12, 14, 17b, 18, 21a, 29-30, 32, 41
Stack — 8a, 49
Stamcole — 22, 24, 27
Stamkyle — 7
Stampcoil — 8b, 13
Stampcole — 12, 19, 21b, 26-30, 31ac, 32, 42
Stancoil — 20
Stancole — 19, 33, 44
Nil — 9, 31bef, 48

Kirkcudbright

Cole — 11
(Hay) cock — *7*
(Hay) ruck — 1-5, 7-10, 12ab, 13-14, 15b, 17, *18,* 19-20, 21a*c,* 22-23, 26-27
Pike — 24
Rick — 6
Rickle — 26
Stamcole — 7
Stamp cole — 2, 4, 8-9, 12b, 13-14, 15a, 18, 24
Stancole — 16
Nil — 21b, 25

Wigtown

Pake — 15
Rick — 4, 5b, 7
Rickle — 9
Ruck — 1-3, 5ab, 6, 8, 10-18

Northumberland

(Hay) cock — *58,* 72l, 79
(Hay) pike — 1ab, 2ab, 3-4, 6-18, 19ab, 20ab, 21-23, 24ab, 25-28, 29abcdef, 30-32, 33ab, 34ab, 35-39, 40ab, 41abcd, 42-52, 53ab, 54-56, *57,* 58, 59bcdef, 60-61, 62abcdfg, 63, 64ab, 65ab, 66-68, 69abcdefgh, 71bd, 72bcdefghijk, 73-87, 88ab, 89-93, 94b, 95ab, 96-98, 99abcd, 100, 102, 103abc, 104ab, 105-107, 108abc, 109-110, 112-117, 118ab, 119 120abc, 121, 122ab, 123, 124ab, 125, 126abcdef, 127abcdef, 129b, 130abcd, 132-143
(Hay) rick — 62h, 71c, 127c, 130e*f*
(Hay)stack — 69a, *71a,* 76
Kyles — 1c, 79
Peyke — 70, 111ab
Rack — 12
Reek — 72l
Ruck — 29c, 34b, 37, 42, 51
Teick — 76
Nil — 5, 59a, 62e, 71e, 72a, 94a, 101ab, 127gh, 128, 129ac, 131

Cumberland

Hay cock — 27
Peyke — 8-9, 27
Pike — 1ab, 2-4, 5ab, 6-7, 9, 11-12, 13abcd, 14, 15abc, 16-34, 36, 37ab, 38-49, 51-62, 63ab
Pykle — 56
Pyklin — 27
Rick — 13a
Nil — 10, 35, 50

Down

Bart — 27
Clump — 11
Cock — 1, 2a, 14, 18, 22, 24-25, 29
Hand cock — 27
Haystack — 8
Heap of hay — 2a
Lapcock — 26
Rick — 12, 21, 24
Ruck — 3-5, 10, 13, 17, 19, 21, 27-28
Shig — 9, 23
Tramped ruck — 11
Nil — 2b, 6-7, 15-16, 20, 30

Tyrone

Hand cock — 11
Handshaken — 9
(Hay) cock — *1,* 3, 5-*10,* 12, 14
(Hay) peck — 15-*16*
(Hay) rick — *8,* 14
Hay ruck — 10
Pake — 2
Peak of hay — 8
Ruck — 3, 8-9, 12-14
Nil — 4

Antrim

Fork cock — 1
Havel — 5b
(Hay) cock — 3, 5a, 8b, 10, 16b, *34*
(Hay) rick — 6, 19, 24, 26-27, *30*-32
(Hay) ruck — 7, 8a, 11-13, 15, 16b, 17-23, *25,* 27-29, 31-34
Haystack — 2, 34
Hut — 9
Tramp cock — 1, 5b
Nil — 4, 4A, 14, 16ac

Donegal

Big cock — 4
Big handcock — 10a
Clamp — 5A
Cock — 1, 5A, 8, 13
Fork cock — 10b
Hut — 5
Pike — 5
Ruck — 2, 9, 13
Stack — 9
Tram cock — 7A
Tramp cock — 3, 5-8, 10ab, 11-12
Nil — 1A

Fermanagh

Cock — 9
Handshake — 4
(Hay) rick — 1, 4-*5,* 7b, 8-9
Lap — 6
Ruck — 1-4, 6, 7b, 8
Shig — 10
Nil — 7a

Armagh

(Hay) cock — 1, 3-*4*
Hut — 4-5
Pack — 6b
Peck — 6b
Pike — 6b
Nil — 2, 6a

Londonderry

Cock — 7
Forked cock — 1, 5
Hand cock — 6
Hut — 5
Jinker cock — 1A
Large cock — 2
Lump — 3A
Pake — 3
Ruck — 3, 6-7
Tramped cock — 1, 4-5
Nil — 1B

56 STRAW ROPE (especially the kind used in thatching ricks) (PQ1, 116)

Straw rope has not been mapped as it occurs everywhere except north of Ross and Cromarty. Variants of ROPE are shown on map 13, Appendix A. Variants of STRAW have been subsumed (**strae** nearly everywhere in Scotland from Banffshire southwards and in the north-eastern part of Northern Ireland; **straa** eastern Northumberland; **stree** a few in Cumberland and the west of Northumberland). The density of some of the mapped items is not very high.

Shetland

Gossing simmit – 7
Simmin – 2
Simmind – 1-3, 6, 11-13, 15-16, 18-19, 22-24, 28, 30, 32
Simmint – 4-5, 8, 10, 14, 21ab, 27, 29, 33
Simmit – 9, 17, 19, 22-23, 31
Straein simmits – 17
Strain – 4
Straw simmit – 20

Orkney

Rope – 5, 10, 13a, 16, 20
Semmin – 20
Simmin – 1-4, 6-7, 9-12, 13ab, 14-19
Sookan – 4-8, 10-11, 13a, 15, 17, 20-21
Summin – 8, 21
Teck – 4

Caithness

Seimin – 12a
Simmin – 2ab, 3-9, 11, 12c, 14-15, 16ab, 17
Straw rope – 13
Straw simmens – 12b
Summin – 13
Nil – 1, 10

Sutherland

Hay simmind – 5
Sheemack – 15
Sheeman – 11
Sheemie – 16
Shimmie – 8, 12, 14
Shimmin – 3
Simmin – 2, 4, 9a
Stack rope – 15
Straw rope – 6-7, 13
Summin – 1, 9b, 10
Thumb – 1
Twister rope – 3
Nil – 17

Ross & Cromarty

Grass rope – 25a
Sheemie – 6, 9-13, 15, 20-23, 25a, 31, 32b, 33, 36, 37a
Sheenie – 19
Shemmie – 35
Shimmie – 8, 18, 24
Shioman – 3, 28-29, 32b
Slack rope – 28
Stack rope – 17, 19, 27, 34, 39
(Straw) rope – *3-5, 16, 26-27, 30,* 32a
Thatching rope – 29
Winch – 18
Wisp – 36
Nil – 1-2, 7, 14, 25b, 32c, 37b, 38

Inverness

Hay rope – 32, 38
Sheemie – 13e, 17
Shimmie – 20
Shioman – 8-9, 14, 21ab, 24, 26, 31
Stack rope – 8, 18, 33, 36
Straw rope – 3-5, 7, 9-11, 13c, 21b, 22-23, 29, 37
Nil – 1-2, 6, 12, 13abd, 15-16, 19, 25, 27-28, 30, 34-35, 39-40

Nairn

Glasgow jock – 1a
Straw rope – 1a, 2, 6
Nil – 1bc, 3-5

Moray

Glesga jock – 7, 9a
Straw rope – 1, 2a, 3-5, 6ab, 7, 8bcde, 10-11, 13-17, *18,* 19, *20,* 21-23
Thummack – 22
Nil – 2b, 8af, 9b, 12

Banff

Aitherin – 22
Edderin – 23
Ethrin rope – 16
Rickle – 5
(Straw) rope – 1, *2c,* 3-5, 6*ab, 7,* 8-14, *15,* 17, 18bcd, 19-21, 23-*24*
Thraip – 30
Nil – 2ab, 18a

Aberdeen

Clew – 25
Clew edderin – 11
Coil yarn – 61
Edderin(g) (rope) – *5b,* 17, 36, 39, 47e, 56, 71a, 72-73, 78
Eithrin – 25
Etherin – 85
Soderin – 10
(Straw) rope – 2, *3ab,* 5abcd, *6, 8,* 9-12, *14-17,* 18-20, *21,* 22-27, 28abc, *29,* 30-31, *32-34,* 35, 37, *38,* 39-40, *41,* 42-43, *44-45,* 46, *47*abcdf, 48-56, *57-58,* 59-60, 62-69, *70,* 71*abc*, 72-75, *76-78,* 79, *80,* 81, *82-84,* 85, *86,* 87-90, *91,* 92-93, *94,* 95-96, *97-98,* 99 *100,* 101, 103, *104,* 105, *106-107,* 108, *109*
Straw tow – 7
Tow – 13
Nil – 1, 4, 102

Kincardine

Edderin – 13
Stay rope – 25
Strain rope – 14
(Straw) rope – 1-2, *3,* 4-7, *8,* 9-13, 15-16, 17*abcd, 18-19,* 20, *21,* 22-23, *24, 26*-27, *28*

Kinross

Grass rope – 1
Shangie – 3
Sparta – 1
Stack rope – 3
Straw rope – 2, 5, 7
Thoomb rope – 7
Nil – 6

Angus

Stack rope – 13
(Straw) rope – *1-2,* 3, *4,* 5*abc,* 6-7, *8,* 9, *10, 12*-13, *14*acd, 15, 17*ab, 18,* 19, *20,* 21, *22-23,* 24, *25,* 26, *27-28, 29a,* 30, *31,* 32, 33*ab*, *34-37*
Twine rope – 14d
Nil – 11, 14b, 16, 18, 29b

Perth

Binder – 41a
Garlan – 70
Gress rope – 68
Rack rope – 73
Shiaman – 14
Sparkie – 26
Spartie (rope) – *2b, 5-6,* 11, *13,* 18, *21,* 25-26, 40, *41a,* 48, *52a*
Stack rope – 8, 24
(Straw) rope – *3-4, 7*-8, *9, 12*-13, *15-17, 20, 22-23, 25, 27-28, 29a, 31-33, 39, 45-46, 48,* 50, *51a, 52abcd, 55-56,* 57, *58-59,* 60, *62, 65*-67, *74*
Tarrie rope – 2a
Thack rope – 52c
Thrape rope – 6
Thraw rope – 71
Thumb rope – 30
Whirlin – 46
Wisp – 29b
Nil – 1, 10, 19, 34-38, 41b, 42-44, 47, 49, 51b, 52e, 53-54, 61, 63-64, 69, 72

Fife

Binder – 57
Cruck – 44e
Etherin – 56
Glesga' jock – 34
Grass rope – 9a, 44f, 53-54, 55g
Gressie rope – 8, 61
Gress rope – 18, 36b
Sparkie (rope) – *11,* 26
Sparrie rope – 39
Spartie rope – 42, 43a
Stack rope – 37, 41a
(Straw) rope – *1-4,* 5, *7, 9b,* 12-*13, 16-17, 20-21, 24-25, 27,* 31-32, *36a, 37, 40b, 44bce, 47-48, 51, 53, 55def, 57, 59, 61-62, 64a*
Straw waupie – 14
Straw wuppie – 28
Thack – 33
Thraw crit – 20
Wappie – 23, 48
Wawpie – 55b
Whippie – 51
Whuppie – 55c
Wuppie – 6, 35
Nil – 10, 15, 19, 22, 29-30, 38, 40a, 41bcd, 43b, 44ad, 45-46, 49-50, 52, 55a, 58, 60, 63, 64b

Clackmannan

(Straw) rope – *1,* 4d, *5-6*
Thumb rope – 7
Whuppie – 7
Nil – 2-3, 4abc

Stirling

Band rope – 26b
Binder – 30
Coir yarn – 30
Garland – 3-4, 7ce, 18, 25abcd, 36
Gorland – 11
Grass rope – 34
Gress rope – 39b
Owerrope – 3-4, 36
Side rope – 18
Sonk – 7d
Sparta – 8
Stack rope – 7e, 23b, 27b, 33, 40
Staple – 15
(Straw) rope – *2-3,* 7*abd*e, 8, *11, 15, 21a, 22a,* 23c, *25d,* 26d, *28, 31, 36, 37a*
Straw tow – 9
Straw whauppie – 23c
Thackit rope – 26d
Theakin rope – 32
Thoomie – 25c
Thoom rope – 9
Thrawin rope – 26f
Thumb rope – 7f, 12, 42a
Torrie rope – 9
Whippie – 17, 21b, 25c, 26c
Whoorlie – 10
Whoppie – 21b
Whuppie – 12, 20, 37b, 39b
Wuppie – 7b
Nil – 1, 5-6, 13-14, 16, 19, 22b, 23a, 24, 26ae, 27a, 29, 35ab, 38, 39a, 41, 42b

Dunbarton

Garland – 9
Grass rope – 16b
Stack rope – 7a, 17
Straw rope – 2-3, 5, 11, 13bc
Tarrie nettle – 1
Thraw – 14a, 15
Thrawkrit – 9
Nil – 4ab, 6, 7bc, 8, 10, 12, 13a, 14b, 16a, 18

Argyll

Brown rope – 7
Coir – 9
Grass rope – 11
Hay rope – 1, 38
Marneala twine – 30
Owergaun rope – 35
Soogan – 23
Stack rope – 3, 10, 21, 24, 33
Straw rope – 6, 14-15, 17-19, 22, 33, 35-36, 39-40
Threock – 37
Nil – 2, 4-5, 8, 12-13, 16, 20, 25-29, 31-32, 34

Bute

Burroch – 1a
Grass rope – 8b, 9
Soogan – 7, 8a, 9
Stack rope – 1b, 3
Straw rope – 1a, 8a
Nil – 1cde, 2, 4-6

Ayr

Band – 8b
Bindin rope – 38
Coir rope – 57
Garnel (rope) – 7, *17, 19,* 20c, 22, 28b, *36*
Glake rope – 35b
Glicks – 35b
Grass rope – 52, 57
Hecheled rope – 8b
Owergaun rope – 53a
Quire – 28d
Rape for theakin – 20b
Stack (rope) – 1ab, *2a, 3, 7, 8a, 16b, 17, 18b, 20g,* 40, *43, 56-57*
Stapple – 46
(Straw) rope – 1a, *2ab, 3, 5, 9-10, 12a, 13, 15, 18a, 20gh, 21, 24b, 26b, 28f,* 29, *30a,* 31, 34, *37,* 39, *41, 44-45, 47-48,* 49, *51, 54, 57*
Tar nettle – 43
Theaking – 27
Thrawclit rope – 14
Thrawcrop rope – 20d
Thraw cruck – 20e
Thrawn rope – 35a
Thraw rope – 1a
Nil – 4, 6, 11, 12b, 16a, 20af, 23, 24a, 25, 26ac, 28ace, 30b, 32-33, 42, 50, 53b, 55

Renfrew

Bindin — 16d
Binding twine — 11j
Pleat — 16a
Sheet rope — 12a
Stack rope — 10, 11a, 13a
Stack twine — 2b, 18b
Strap — 14b
Straw rope — 2agi, 3, 7, 11cel, 13c, 16b, 17, 20a
Thraw cruck — 20b
Tow rope — 21
Yarn — 5
Nil — 1ab, 2cdefhj, 4abcde, 6, 8-9, 11bdfghik, 12b, 13bd, 14a, 15, 16c, 18a, 19

Lanark

Bag rope — 17
Binder — 18
Bond — 27b
Brathins — 17
Dra'in straw rope — 38d
Glasgow jock — 25c
Hay rope — 61, 67b
Nowt — 33b
Rick rope — 44
Spartie — 57c
Spirkie rope — 51
Stack rope — 1, 15b, 21, 23, 27a, 31ad, 35a, 38ac, 39-40, 45, 46b, 48, 51, 52b, 53, 57c, 58, 59b
Straw band — 35d
Straw bond — 37
(Straw) rope — *2, 7a, 8a, 9ab, 11-13, 14b, 15ab, 16b, 18, 20, 22, 25c,* 29cd, *33d, 46c, 49b, 57a, 59a, 60, 67a*
Tar rope — 3
Taur nettle — 17
Thackin rope — 8a, 30
Thack rope — 33cd
Thatch cord — 29e
Thatching rope — 15c
Thatch rope — 29e
Theaking — 19
Thrawchlet — 5
Thrawcruck — 42
Thrawn — 47
Thrawn rope — 12
Thraw rope — 63
Throughle rope — 39
Wasp — 36
Whuppie — 32f
Wisp — 36
Nil — 4, 6, 7bc, 8b, 10ab, 14acd, 16a, 24, 25abd, 26ab, 28, 29abfg, 31bc, 32abcde, 33ab, 34, 35bc, 38be, 41, 43, 46a, 49a, 50, 52a, 54-56, 57b, 62, 64ab, 65-66

West Lothian

Garland — 16
Stack rope — 8, 15
Straw bond — 16
(Straw) rope — 1c, *5-6, 8, 9a, 10-11,* 14, *17a,* 19b, 21a, 22
Taper — 21a
Thatch rope — 21b
Thoomb rope — 1d
Thraw thruck — 2
Thumb rope — 7, 11
Whuppie — 18
Nil — 1ab, 3-4, 9b, 12-13, 17b, 19a, 20ab

Midlothian

Band — 23b, 28
Sparkie — 25c
Stack rope — 12b, 15
(Straw) rope — *8a, 10, 12b, 14b, 18, 21, 23a, 24, 25a,* 27, *29-30, 32*
Thack rope — 17
Thraw crook — 10
Whippie — 16
Whuppie — 23b, 24
Wisp — 20
Nil — 1-5, 6ab, 7ab, 8b, 9, 11, 12a, 13, 14a, 19, 22, 25bd, 26ab, 31

East Lothian

Band — 6a
Buncle — 13
Sparkie (rope) — 2, *7, 9,* 13
(Straw) rope — *4ab, 6ab, 8, 11,* 12-14, *16-17, 20-21*
Thack rope — 6a
Thauck — 4b
Thraip — 13
Wheepie — 15
Whippie — 16
Whoppie — 10
Whuppie — 2, 15
Nil — 1, 3, 5, 18-19

Berwick

Bunker — 27
Bunkle rope — 31
Simmin — 7
Stack rope — 16c
(Straw) rope — 1-*2, 4,* 5-6, *8,* 9, *10,* 11, *12-13,* 14, *15, 16abc 17-20,* 21, *22-24, 26-27, 29, 31-32*
Whuppie — 30
Nil — 3, 25, 28

Peebles

Stack rope — 5
Straw rope — 1, 3, 4b, 6ab, 8-9
Straw twine — 2
Nil — 4ac, 7, 10

Selkirk

Owergaun rope — 2a
(Straw) rope — *1, 2bde,* 3-4, *8*
Whuppie — 6
Nil — 2c, 5, 7

Roxburgh

Band — 11
Bunkle rope — 23
Hay rope — 19-20, 25
(Straw) rope — 1-*2, 3ab, 4-8, 9ab, 10, 12-13, 15a, 16-20, 21bdef, 22, 25*-26, *28*
Straw whuppie — 6
Thack rope — 15b
Waist rope — 21d
Whippie — 21c
Whuppie — 13, 21c
Nil — 14, 21a, 24, 27

Dumfries

Bridle — 5
Bridler — 30
Garnel — 5
Hame made rope — 17b
Hay rope — 2-3, 6, 17a, 27, 31d
Owergaun rope — 46
Owerrope — 38-39
(Straw) rope — *1a, 8b,* 10-11, *12-13, 16, 18-20, 21b, 22, 24, 26-27,* 28, *33, 37, 40,* 41, *42-43,* 45a, *47*
Swirl rope — 29, 38-39, 46
Theakin rope — 35
Thraw — 19
Thumbie — 32
Tirl rope — 45a
Waist rope — 38, 45a
Wattler — 21a
Weest rope — 46
Whammle — 15
Winlie — 25
Wunnel rope — 37
Whylie — 35
Whylie rope — 7, 12, 34
Nil — 1b, 4, 8a, 9, 14, 23, 31abcef, 36, 44, 45b, 48-49

Kirkcudbright

Bridle — 21a
Bridting rope — 11
Grass rope — 6, 22, 26
Hay rope — 1
Owergaun rope — 15a
Pike — 11
Rung — 9
Stack rope — 2, 4, 10, 18, 23
(Straw) rope — *5, 7-9,* 11, *12ab, 21c, 27*
Thoomb rope — 17
Whuppie — 24
Wylie rope — 12a
Nil — 3, 13-14, 15b, 16, 19-20, 21b, 25

Wigtown

Grass rope — 1-2
Ower gang — 13
Stack rope — 7
Strap — 9
(Straw) rope — *5, 7-9,* 11, *12ab, 21c, 27*
Thoomb rope — 3
Thraw rope — 5b
Twister — 12
Wattler — 13-14
Nil — 4, 10

Northumberland

Band rope — 59c
Bang — 57
Belly rope — 78
Binder — 86, 122b
Binder twine — 53b
Coir rope — 109
Collie twist — 64b
Dollie — 124b
Guy rope — 59c
Hay band — 69ab
Hay rope — 42, 44, 56-57
Hemp — 12
John Robert — 132
Michael — 132
Pike rope — 21, 46, 55, 104b
Plet band — 71c, 124a
Sign — 123
Sime — 106
Stack rope — 138
Stack toppin — 124a
Straw — 52, 93
Straw band — 25, 59b, 72b, 98, 125
(Straw) rope — *1a, 2b, 3, 5-11, 13, 15-16, 18, 19a, 20b, 26, 28, 29bdf,* 30, *31, 33b, 34ab, 35-36,* 37, *38, 40a, 41cd,* 43, *45,* 46, *53a, 59bd, 62a, 64ab, 65a, 66, 68, 69c, 71d,* 72c, *77, 83, 88b, 90, 95b, 99d,* 100, *103bc, 106-107, 110, 120c, 126f, 130be, 133,* 137, *140-143*
Tarrie tout — 62g
Thack rope — 104b, 134
Thatch — 54
Thumb rope — 16
Thraw crook — 60
Tie — 137
Twine — 72k
Twined straw rope — 130d
Twist — 105
Wappie — 24a
Whippie — 2a, 22, 41d, 68, 77
Whup — 45
Whuppie — 16, 45, 122a, 124a
Win rope — 111b
Wisp rope — 130c
Wuppie — 17
Wylie — 37
Nil — 1bc, 4, 14, 19b, 20a, 23, 24b, 27, 29ace, 32, 33a, 39, 40b, 41ab, 47-51, 58, 59aef, 61, 62bcdefh, 63, 65b, 67, 69defgh, 70, 71abe, 72adefghijl, 73-76, 79-82, 84-85, 87, 88a, 89, 91-92, 94ab, 95a, 96-97, 99abc, 101ab, 102, 103a, 104a, 108abc, 111a, 112-117, 118ab, 119, 120ab, 121, 126abcde, 127abcdefgh, 128, 129abc, 130af, 131, 135-136, 139

Cumberland

Binder twine — 51
John Robert — 43
Kepple — 61
Michael — 60
Seyme — 5a, 8-9, 13c
Sime — 1a, 2-4, 7, 9, 11, 13d, 15abc, 16-18, 20-22, 25-34, 37ab, 38, 40-42, 44-45, 47-48, 51-54, 56, 58-59, 61-62, 63a
Stack rope — 37a, 39, 56
Straw — 60
(Straw) rope — *4, 12, 13c, 24,* 28, *38, 46, 49, 57*
Thoumsine — 63b
Thumb sime — 60
Twine rope — 19
Nil — 1b, 5b, 6, 10, 13ab, 14, 23, 35-36, 50, 55

Down

Belter — 17
Currie rope — 11
Straw rope — 2a, 5, 9, 13, 15, 18-19, 24, 26, 29
Sugan — 2b, 14
Wap — 21
Nil — 1, 3-4, 6-8, 10, 12, 16, 20, 22-23, 25, 27-28, 30

Tyrone

Grass rope — 12
Gress rope — 1
Hay rope — 9, 11, 16
Straw rope — 1, 7, 9-11
Sugan — 5
Suggan — 14
Thatch rope — 11
Thumb rope — 5
Twist rope — 11
Nil — 2-4, 6, 8, 13, 15

Antrim

Grass rope — 21, 26, 31
Gress rope — 13
Hay rope — 29
Stack rope — 17, 34
Straw rope — 1, 5b, 9, 16b, 19-23, 25, 28, 33
Straw binder — 34
Sugan — 2, 7
Nil — 3-4, 4A, 5a, 6, 8ab, 10-12, 14-15, 16ac, 18, 24, 27, 30, 32

Donegal

Clue — 13
Grass rope — 1
Hag — 13
Sprittie — 2
Straw rope — 5, 5A, 8, 10ab
Sugan — 6, 10a, 12
Nil — 1A, 3-4, 7, 7A, 9, 11

Fermanagh

Hay rope — 2, 9
Rope — 4
Straw rope — 5
Sugan — 3, 7a
Nil — 1, 6, 7b, 8, 10

Armagh

Grass rope — 4
Hay rope — 3
Straw rope — 4
Suggan — 6b
Nil — 1-2, 5, 6a

Londonderry

Clue — 5
Grass rope — 1A, 2-3
Rope — 5

Londonderry cont'd
Straw rope — 3A
Nil — 1, 1B, 4, 6-7

57 SCARCROW (PQ1, 117)

The distribution of the variants of CROW is quite similar to that of map 15 (snow), Appendix A. Variants of SCARE (**scar, scaur** Argyllshire, Ayrshire, Lanarkshire, Kirkcudbrightshire, Wigtownshire) and TATTIE (**tawtie, tatie, tettie** etc.) have been subsumed.

Shetland
Bawkie — 1, 4-6, 8-9
Bogie — 24
Bokie — 3, 7, 10, 12-13, 18-20, 25, 27-30, 32
Bookie — 31
Faerie — 21ab
Gluff — 14, 22-23, 29
Gluffie — 19
Neep gluff — 21a, 24
Ro — 23, 26
Rorie — 17, 22
Scarecrow — 15, 33
Nil — 2, 11, 16

Orkney
Bawkie — 13b, 15
Bokie — 7, 15
Fly guest — 5
Scarecrow — 1-2, 4-5, 9, 11, 13ab, 15-17, 19, 21
(Tattie) bockie — 3, 8, 12, 15, *16*, 17
Tattie bogle — 20
Nil — 6, 10, 14, 18

Caithness
Scarecrow — 2ab, 6, 8-11, 13-15, 16b
(Tattie) bogle — *3-4, 7-8, 11, 12ab*, 15, *16ab*
Nil — 1, 5, 12c, 17

Sutherland
Bodach (rokish) *8*, 10, *15-16*
Bodach shnep — 5
Scarecrow — 1, 3, 6-8, 9a, 10, 12-13, 16
Tattie bogie — 11
(Tattie) bogle — *3*, 6, *8, 14-15, 17*
Nil — 2, 4, 9b

Ross & Cromarty
Bodach (rokish) — 10, 19, *28, 31*
Bodach rookish — 30
Crow bogle — 13
Scarecrow — 1, 3-6, 8-10, 14, 16-20, 22-23, 25ab, 26-29, 31, 32a, 34, 36, 39
Tattie bogie — 36
(Tattie) bogle — *11, 18-19, 22*, 27, *32b, 35*
Tattie man — 24
Nil — 2, 7, 12, 15, 21, 32c, 33, 37ab, 38

Inverness
Bodach rokish — 24, 26
Bogie — 29
Bottach — 31
(Crow) bodach — *8*, 11-*12*, 15
Crow mannie — 9
Scarecrow — 1-11, 13abce, 17, 19, 21ab, 22-23, 26, 30, 32-38
(Tattie) bogle — *13e, 14, 16, 26*, 28, *33, 37*, 39
Nil — 13d, 18, 20, 25, 27, 40

Nairn
Scarecrow — 1a, 2, 4, 6
Tattie bogle — 1abc, 4
Nil — 3, 5

Moray
Scarecrow — 3, 6b, 7, 8bdf, 9a, 11, 14
Tattie boggie — 5
Tattie boggle — 9a
(Tattie) bogie — *3-4, 7, 8b, 9b*, 12, *18*
Tattie bogle — 1, 2b, 6b, 8ce, 15
(Tattie) bokie — *2a, 8bf*, 14, 16, *22-23*
Tattie boodie — 6a, 8d, 10, 18-21
Nil — 8a, 13, 17

Banff
Scarecrow — 9, 13
Tattie bogie — 32-33
Tattie bogle — 6b, 15, 30
(Tattie) bokie — 28-*29*, 34
(Tattie) boodie — *1, 2abc, 3-5, 6ab, 7-17*, 18cd, *19*, 20, *21-27*, 29, *31*
Tattie buddie — 18b
Nil — 18a

Aberdeen
Scarecrow — 1-2, 6-7, 21, 29, 47bd, 54, 82, 98, 102, 104, 106, 108
Tatie boogle -- 37
Tattie bockie — 92
Tattie boddie — 86
Tattie bodie — 11, 31, 58
(Tattie) bogie — *16, 51, 55*, 93-*94, 102, 107*
(Tattie) bogle — *47f*, 62, *93*, 105
Tattie bokie — 78-79, 84, 95
(Tattie) boodie — *1-2, 3ab, 4*, 5*abcd, 6, 8-10, 12-15, 17-22*, 23, *24-27, 28abc, 29-30, 32-36*, 39, *40*, 41-42, *43-46, 47abcde, 48-53, 56-57, 59-70, 71abc, 72-78, 80-85, 87-89, 96-101, 103-106, 108-109*
Tattie boogie — 90
Nil — 38, 91

Kincardine
Bogie — 8
Crowfairer — 25
Scarecrow — 1, 3, 5-6, 17c, 18-19
Tattie bockie — 6
Tattie bodie — 9
Tattie bogle — 15, 17a, 24
(Tattie) boodie — *2-7, 10-14*, 16, *23*
Tattie doolie — 13, 15, 17abcd, 18, 20-24, 26-28

Kinross
Crow bogle — 7
Scarecrow — 1
(Tattie) bogle — *1*, 2, *3-5, 7*
Nil — 6

Angus
(Crow) bogle — 7, 11, *13*, 14c, *19-20*
Crow doodie — 26
Crow doolie — 22-24, 34
Dolie — 28
Scarecrow — 17b, 18, 34, 36
Tattie bogle — 4, 8-9, 14abd, 17b, 18, 22-23, 25, 31-32, 33a, 34-35, 37
Tattie boodie — 17a
(Tattie) doolie — *1*, 2, *3-4*, 5abc, *6-7, 9*, 10-11, *12-13, 14abcd, 15, 20-24, 27, 29a, 30, 33b, 36-37*
Nil — 16, 29b

Perth
Boggle — 73
(Crow) bogle — 8, *16*, 18, 22, *26*, 29ab, 32, 47, *48*, 51a, 52b, *55-56*, 60, 62, *65*
Guy — 25
Scarecrow — 4, 8, 10, 24-25, 28, 29a, 33, 36, 57, 66
Tattie bogle — 1, 2ab, 3, 5-7, 9-21, 23-27, 31-37, 39-40, 41ab, 42-46, 48-49, 51ab, 52acde, 53-54, 57-59, 61-62, 64, 66-72, 74
Tattie bollie — 50
Tattie doolie — 7, 11, 46, 57, 60
Nil — 30, 38, 63

Fife
Crow boggle — 7
Crow bogle — 1-2, 8, 12, 14, 18, 21, 23, 25, 28, 31, 33, 43a, 61
Dummie — 44b
Scarecrow — 4, 11, 39, 41a, 50, 52, 55bd, 57-58, 62-63
Tattie boggle — 7, 16
(Tattie)bogle — *2-3, 5-6, 9ab, 10-13, 17, 19-20, 22-24, 26-28*, 30, *32-35, 36ab, 37, 38-39, 40b, 41abd, 42*, 43b, *44abcf, 46-48, 51-53*, 54, *55abcdefg, 56, 59-63, 64ab*
Tattie boogle — 49
Tattie bowgle — 44de
Tattie doolie — 40b
Nil — 15, 29, 40a, 41c

Clackmannan
Scarecrow — 4c
Tattie boggle — 4c
Tattie bogle — 1-3, 4abd, 5-7

Stirling
Crow frichter — 25c
Scarecrow — 4, 7ac, 8, 21ab, 23a 26abcd, 27a, 28-30, 36, 41
(Tattie) bogle — *2-4, 6, 7abcdef, 8-9, 11 12*, 13, *14-16*, 17, *18*, 19-20, *21ab, 22ab*, 23abc, *24*, 25*abcd, 26abcdef, 27ab*, 29-30, *31-34, 35ab, 36, 37a, 39ab, 40*, 42ab
Tattie boglie — 37b
Nil — 1, 5, 10, 38

Dunbarton
Crow bogle — 11
Scarecrow — 1, 3, 7b, 10, 13abc, 16ab
Scart crow — 18
(Tattie) bogle — *1-2, 4ab*, 5-*6, 7ac, 9*, 11-12, 13abc, *14ab, 15, 16ab, 17*
Nil — 8

Argyll
Bawkan — 32
Crow bogle — 6
Frightener — 33
Scarecrow — 1-3, 5-7, 9-12, 14-17, 19, 22-23, 25, 27, 30-31, 33-35, 38-39
(Tattie) bogle — *5, 8-10, 12, 16, 18, 21, 24*, 29-30, *35, 37-38*
Nil — 4, 13, 20, 26, 28, 36, 40

Bute
Scarecrow — 1cd, 2, 7, 8ab
Scarrie — 1a, 4
(Tattie) bogle — *1abe, 2*-3, *5, 8ab, 9*
Nil — 6

Ayr
Boggle — 38
Bowdie — 18b
Crow bogle — 18b, 33, 39, 45
Crow fricht — 8a, 14-15, 16a, 17, 20adef, 23, 24b, 25, 30a, 32, 53b
Gowk — 35a
Scarecrow — 1a, 2b, 3, 5, 9-11, 16a, 18a, 20bcg, 21, 26b, 28ce, 30a, 31, 34, 35b, 42-44, 48-50, 52, 54, 56-57
Stookie — 18b
(Tattie) bogle — *1ab, 2ab, 3-4, 6-7, 8ab, 9, 11, 12ab, 13, 16ab, 17*, 18ab, 19, 20*abcdefgh, 21, 24b, 26ab, 27, 28abcdef, 29, 30b, 32, 36, 39, 41, 44-48*, 49, *51-52, 53ab, 54, 57*
Nil — 22, 24a, 26c, 37, 40, 55

Renfrew
Effigy — 2g
Scarecrow — 1b, 2ahi, 4e, 11aceijk, 12b, 13c, 14ab, 16d, 18a, 20a
(Tattie) bogle — *1b, 2befghj, 4acd, 5-9*, 11*abefijl, 12a, 13a*, 14ab, *15, 16abcd, 17, 18ab, 19, 20b, 21*
Tattie boogle — 1b
Nil — 1a, 2cd, 3, 4b, 10, 11dgh, 13bd

Lanark
Crow bogle — 67a
Crow fricht — 15b, 33cd, 43
Effigy — 37
Scarecrow — 1-3, 6, 7ac, 10a, 12, 14d, 15ac, 16ab, 21, 23, 25bc, 26b, 27b, 29cef, 31a, 35cd, 37, 38c, 39, 44, 47, 58, 60
Tattie boggle — 46b
(Tattie) bogle — *1-2, 4-5, 7abc, 8ab, 9ab, 10ab, 11, 13, 14abcd, 15abc, 16b, 17-20, 22-24, 25abcd, 26a, 27ab, 28, 29abcdefg, 30, 31bcd, 32abcdef, 33abcd, 34, 35abcd, 36, 38abcd, 39-42*, 45, *46ac, 47-48, 49ab, 50-51, 52ab, 53-54, 55-56, 57abc, 58, 59ab, 61-63, 64ab, 65-66, 67ab*
Wooden man — 45
Nil — 38e

West Lothian
Scarecrow — 1ac, 6, 8, 10-13, 15, 18, 20a, 21b, 22
Scarie crow — 2, 8
Tattie boggle — 1c
(Tattie) bogle — 1abd, *2-7, 9ab, 10-11, 13, 16, 17ab, 19b, 20ab, 21ab*
Nil — 14, 19a

Midlothian
Boggle — 20
Crow bogle — 3
Dummie — 17
Frichtie Jock — 18

Midlothian cont'd
Mawkin — 18
Scarecrow — 1, 3, 6ab, 8a, 10, 12b, 14a, 15, 19, 23ab, 30
Tattie bogle — 3-4, 6b, 7ab, 8b, 9-11, 12ab, 13, 14ab, 16-19, 21-22, 23ab, 24, 25a, 26ab, 27-32
Tattie boogle — 25c
Nil — 2, 5, 25bd

East Lothian
Crow doolie — 3
Pease bogle — 6a
Scarecrow — 1, 4b, 6a, 9, 18-19
(Tattie) bogle — *1-2, 4ab, 6ab, 7-9,* 10, *11, 13-14,* 15, *16-17, 20-21*
Nil — 5, 12

Berwick
Bougie — 27
Crow boggle — 27
Scarecrow — 8
Tattie bogle — 1-15, 16abc, 17-26, 29-32
Nil — 28

Peebles
Scarecrow — 1, 4bc
Tattie boggle — 2
(Tattie) bogle — *1, 3, 4abc, 5,* 6ab, 7-10

Selkirk
Crow bogle — 3, 7
Scarecrow — 4
Tattie bogle — 1, 2abcde, 3-8

Roxburgh
Crow bogle — 4-6, 16-17, 20
Scarecrow — 21a, 27-28
(Tattie) bogle — *1-2, 3ab, 5, 7-8, 9ab, 10-13,* 15b, *17-18, 20, 21acf, 22-23,* 24
(Tattie) boogle — *15a, 19,* 21*bcde,* 25-*26, 28*
Nil — 14

Dumfries
Crow boggle — 12
(Crow) bogle — 1ab, *2,* 5-6, 8a, *9-11, 13, 15, 18-20, 21ab, 22,* 23, *24-26, 28, 30,* 31*abcdef, 32, 38, 40-42, 45a, 48*
Crow boogle — 14, 27, 29, 33-34, 36-37, 39, 43-44, 45b, 46-47, 49
Flay crow — 46
Scarecrow — 1a, 4, 12, 22
Straw bogle — 35
(Tattie) bogle — 1a, *2-4,* 6-7, 8ab, *15-16, 17ab, 21ab,* 22-23, *28,* 31abce, *32, 38, 41-42*
Tattie boogle — 34, 47

Kirkcudbright
Crow boggle — 23
Crow bogle — 3-8, 10-11, 12b, 13-14, 15ab, 16, 20, 21a, 22, 26-27
Scarecrow — 1, 7, 19
(Tattie) bogle — *1,* 2, *3, 7,* 9, *11, 12a, 17-19, 21bc,* 24-25, *27*
Worrie cow — 17

Wigtown
Crow bogie — 5b
Scarecrow — 1-3, 5a, 6-9, 11-14, 16-18
Tattie boggle — 10
Tattie bogle — 6-8, 15
Nil — 4

Northumberland
Bird scarer — 69b
Bogie — 22, 81
Boodie — 127b
Clobber heed — 62h
Crow boggle — 19a, 44
Crow bogle — 2a, 5, 8-10, 12, 16, 20b, 27-28, 45, 56-57, 130d
(Crow) boogle — *53a,* 127b
Crow craw — 7
Dummie — 64b
Effigy — 127e
Fla crow — 76, 79, 126d
Flair crow — 95a
Flay crow — 28, 39, 49, 62af, 69e, 72j, 73, 77-78, 80, 89, 102, 103abc, 104a, 106, 111ab, 116-117, 118b, 124a, 130a, 131-134, 138-142
Guy — 69ab, 105
Guyser — 69ab
Hay crow — 62a, 125
Scare — 46
Scarecrow — 2b, 5-6, 14-16, 18, 20b, 21, 24b, 26, 29bd, 30-31, 33b, 35-36, 38-39, 40ab, 41acd, 42-43, 45, 48, 52, 53ab, 54, 56, 59bd, 60-61, 62ab, 63, 64ab, 65a, 66, 69cdeh, 70, 71abd, 72abcdgi, 77-78, 80, 83-84, 86-87, 89-91, 93, 94b, 95b, 98, 99b, 100, 101b, 104ab, 105, 109-110, 111b, 112, 119, 120abc, 121, 124b, 126cf, 127acdh, 130bce, 135, 137, 140
Shoo crow — 99d
Tattie boggle — 19b, 44, 75, 107, 117
(Tattie) bogle — *1ab, 2b, 3-4, 8, 10-11, 13, 15, 17-18,* 20a, *25, 27,* 29af, *32,* 34ab, *37, 40b, 41a, 46, 51, 56,* 58, 59b, 68, *71c, 72b, 81-82,* 112
Tubie bogle — 41c
Nil — 1c, 23, 24a, 29ce, 33a, 41b, 47, 50, 55, 59acef, 62cdeg, 65b, 67, 69fg, 71e, 72efhkl, 74, 85, 92, 94a, 96-97, 99ac, 101a, 108abc, 113-115, 118a, 122ab, 123, 126abe, 127fg, 128, 129abc, 130f, 136, 143

Cumberland
Crow bogle — 60
Crow boogle — 13b
Dummie man — 54
Fla crow — 21, 61
Flair crow — 15b, 39
Flay crat — 30
Flay crow — 1a, 2-4, 5ab, 7-9, 11-12, 13abcd, 15ac, 16-22, 24-33, 37ab, 38, 40-41, 44-45, 47-49, 51-52, 54, 56-60, 62, 63a
Flay scarl — 9
Scarecrow — 7, 9, 12, 23-24, 40, 42, 46, 53, 56-58
Tattie boggle — 47
Nil — 1b, 6, 10, 14, 34-36, 43, 50, 55, 63b

Down
Scarecrow — 2a, 5, 9, 12-15, 18-19, 24, 26, 28, 30
Nil — 1, 2b, 3-4, 6-8, 10-11, 16-17, 20-23, 25, 27, 29

Tyrone
Boogie man — 2
Scarecrow — 1, 5-12
Nil — 3-4, 13-16

Antrim
Carscra — 19
Farmer's friend — 34
Scarecrow — 1, 3, 5ab, 7, 12-13, 15, 17, 19-23, 25-26, 28-29, 31, 33
Silent land steward — 34
Tattie bogle — 24
Nil — 2, 4, 4A, 6, 8ab, 9-11, 14, 16abc, 18, 27, 30, 32

Donegal
Scarecrow — 1, 4-5, 5A, 6, 8, 10b, 12
Nil — 1A, 2-3, 7, 7A, 9, 10a, 11, 13

Fermanagh
Scarecrow — 2, 4-6, 7a, 8-10
Nil — 1, 3, 7b

Armagh
Barley boogle — 1
Scarecrow — 4-5, 6a
Nil — 2-3, 6b

Londonderry
Scarecrow — 2-3, 3A, 4, 7
Tattie bogie — 3
Nil — 1, 1AB, 5-6

58 BULLOCK (PQ1, 118)

Stot has not been mapped as it occurs fairly densely all over the area except in Cumberland and Northern Ireland.

Shetland
Bull — 13, 33
Ox — 1, 3-8, 10, 12, 14-15, 19-20, 21ab, 23, 25-27, 29, 32
Stot — 1, 11, 16, 19, 21a, 24, 30, 32
Young bull — 17, 22
Young ox — 30
Nil — 2, 9, 18, 28, 31

Orkney
Bull — 9
Bullock — 1, 8
Nout — 15
Ouzen — 3
Ox — 1-3, 5-6, 11-12, 15-19, 21
Oxie — 4
Stirk — 4, 7, 10-11, 13a, 15, 19-20
Stot — 2, 4-5, 10-12, 14, 17, 19-21
Strik — 13b

Caithness
Bull — 10, 13
Feeder — 5
Steer — 13
Stirk — 1, 6, 12ab
Stirkie — 12b
Stot — 1, 2ab, 3-6, 8-9, 11, 12abc, 14-15, 16ab, 17
Stotie — 17
Nil — 7

Sutherland
Bullock — 3, 7, 11, 16
Stirk — 3, 10, 13, 15
Stot — 1-2, 4-6, 8, 9a, 11, 13-16
Stote — 9b
Nil — 12, 17

Ross & Cromarty
Big stirk — 24
Bullock — 1, 3-5, 9, 16-17, 20, 23, 27, 29, 31, 32a, 39
Steer — 13, 22
Stirk — 18, 20, 25ab, 26, 28, 32bc, 37a, 39
Stot — 6, 8-13, 15, 17-19, 21, 25b, 27-30, 32bc, 33-36, 37a, 38
Nil — 2, 7, 14, 37b

Inverness
Bullock — 1-7, 10-11, 13abce, 16-17, 19, 21ab, 23, 30, 33-34, 36-37, 39
Steer — 19, 27, 29
Stirk — 9, 11, 19-20, 22, 27, 31-32, 35
Stoat — 8
Stot — 7, 9, 11, 13ace, 14-16, 19-20, 24, 26-29, 32, 37-38
Nil — 12, 13d, 18, 25, 40

Nairn
Bullock — 2
Stirk — 1bc, 2
Stot — 1abc, 3-4, 6
Stot stirk — 3
Nil — 5

Moray
Bull — 7, 8f
Caafie — 7
Steer — 13, 15-16, 20
Stirk — 1, 6a, 7, 12, 15, 19, 21, 23
Stirkie — 9a
Stot — 1, 2ab, 3-5, 6ab, 7, 8bcde, 9a, 10-18, 20-23
Sturk — 8c
Nil — 8af, 9b

Banff
Leiper — 2c
Ous — 18d
Steer — 5, 8, 10, 14, 16, 20, 29, 33
Stirk — 1, 2bc, 6b, 7-11, 13-15, 17, 18cd, 19, 23, 28
Stot — 1, 2c, 3-5, 6ab, 7, 9-17, 18cd, 19-27, 29-32, 34
Nil — 2a, 18ab

Aberdeen
Bull — 61, 108
Bullock — 5c, 6, 16, 44, 73, 105
Nout — 40, 102
Ous — 11, 28a, 76
Ox — 62, 86, 100
Steer — 3b, 6, 11, 17-24, 27, 28abc, 29, 31-32, 47a, 49, 65, 71ac, 73, 79, 87-89, 94
Stirk — 3a, 4, 5bd, 8-10, 19-21, 23, 28ab, 29-30, 34, 40, 46, 47abcd, 48, 53, 56-58, 60, 62, 64, 67, 70, 71c, 72, 76-78, 80, 85, 92, 100, 102-106
Stirkie — 90
Stoat — 44, 46, 49, 85
Stot — 2, 3ab, 4, 5abd, 6, 8, 10-21, 23-27, 28abc, 29-37, 39-42, 45, 47abde, 48, 50-60, 63-70, 71abc, 73-83, 85-89, 93-101, 104-109
Nil — 1, 7, 38, 43, 47f, 84, 91

Kincardine

Steer — 5, 8, 12
Stirk — 1, 3-4, 12, 14, 17c, 22-23
Stoat — 10, 26
Stot — 2-9, 11-15, 17abcd, 18-25, 27-28
Nil — 16

Kinross

Nowt — 2
Stot — 1-5, 7
Stot stirk — 2
Nil — 6

Angus

Bull — 18
Bullock — 4, 17b, 25, 34
Bullock stirk — 5c
Cattle beast — 24
Gelded bull — 33b
Nowt — 5b, 6, 17a, 29a
Steer — 1, 7, 14a, 22
Stirk — 2, 12-13, 14a, 15, 22-23, 32, 33a, 37
Stot — 1, 3, 5abc, 7-13, 14abcd, 15, 17ab, 19-24, 26, 30-32, 33ab, 34-37
Stote — 6, 27-28, 29a, 35
Nil — 16, 29b

Perth

Bull — 36
Bullock — 2a, 4-5, 9, 28, 46, 51a, 57
Cattle beast — 63
Nowt — 25, 44, 52c, 55, 66
Ox — 60
Steer — 12, 18, 24, 26, 43, 46
Stirk — 1, 3, 6, 8, 13, 25, 29ab, 31, 35, 38, 41b, 44, 51a, 52d, 55, 69, 72
Stoat — 47, 57, 62, 71-72
Stot — 1, 2b, 3, 7-11, 15-17, 20-28, 29ab, 30-33, 37, 39-40, 41ab, 42-45, 48-50, 52abcd, 54, 56, 58-59, 61, 64-70, 73-74
Nil — 14, 19, 34, 51b, 52e, 53

Fife

Bull — 8, 10, 33, 43a, 50, 63
Bullock — 7, 16, 20, 36a, 41a, 47, 55ae, 62
Coo — 43a
Nowt — 12, 19, 21, 36a, 53, 55df, 56, 58-59, 61
Steer — 32, 55b
Stirk — 3, 11, 23, 26, 30, 40b, 43b, 44af, 47, 52, 54, 55bf, 56, 64a
Stirkie — 44a
Stoat — 38, 41c
Stoot — 31
Stot — 1-7, 9ab, 11-14, 17-18, 21-28, 30, 33-35, 36b, 37, 39, 40b, 41ad, 42, 43ab, 44abcdef, 46, 48, 51-54, 55cef, 56, 58-61, 64ab
Sturk — 41b
Young bull — 52, 57
Nil — 15, 29, 40a, 45, 49, 55g

Clackmannan

Bull — 3
Bullock — 1, 6
Nowt — 1-2, 4ad, 5, 7
Stirk — 4d, 5
Stot — 1, 4abd, 5
Stut — 2
Nil — 4c

Stirling

Bull — 26d, 27b, 35b, 38
Bullock — 4, 8, 11-12, 16, 21b, 26a, 27a, 28, 31, 36, 37ab, 40
Bullock stirk — 18
Cut bull — 26b
Dressed bull — 7f
Feeder — 28
Noat — 31
Nowt — 7bd, 9, 22b, 25abd, 26cdf, 30, 34
Steer — 7b, 9, 26a
Stirk — 6, 7be, 10, 12, 26be
Stoat — 7e, 9-10, 21a, 23b, 26c, 32-33, 35a, 39b
Stot — 2-4, 6, 7abc, 8, 13-15, 17, 20, 21ab, 22ab, 23c, 24, 25abcd, 26adef, 27ab, 30-31, 34, 36, 37ab, 39a, 42ab
Stot calf — 18
Wattie — 26a
Nil — 1, 5, 19, 23a, 29, 41

Dunbarton

Bullock — 7b, 11, 13abc
Bull stoat — 16b
Nowt — 15
Steer — 4a, 5
Stirk — 2, 13b, 14b, 16a
Stoat — 17
Stot — 1-3, 4ab, 5-6, 7abc, 9-10, 13ac, 14a, 18
Nil — 8, 12

Argyll

Bullock — 2-3, 5-6, 10-12, 14-17, 19, 22-23, 27, 34
Bullock stot — 35
Nowt — 35
Steer — 33, 38
Stirk — 5, 7-8, 25
Stot — 3, 5-6, 9, 12-15, 18-19, 21-22, 24, 26, 29-34, 37, 39-40
Sturk — 1
Young bull — 2
Nil — 4, 20, 28, 36

Bute

Bullock — 8a
Nowt — 8b
Stirk — 1b, 2
Stot — 1ace, 3-7, 8ab, 9
Nil — 1d

Ayr

Bull — 1b, 16a, 25, 37-38
Bullock — 2b, 5-6, 8a, 10-11, 12a, 14-15, 16b, 18a, 20b, 21, 28e, 30a, 31, 34, 35b, 39, 42, 44-45, 47, 49, 52, 53b, 56-57
Bull stirk — 12b, 43
Bull stot — 43
Feeder — 1b
Nowt — 28f, 29, 34
Steer — 8b, 57
Stirk — 1a, 12b, 18b, 20f, 26b, 28de, 53a
Stoat — 7, 8b, 12a, 13, 18b, 20aceh, 35ab, 37, 46
Stot — 1a, 2ab, 3-4, 6, 8a, 9, 14, 17, 19, 20fg, 22, 24b, 26c, 27, 28abcf, 29, 30ab, 32-34, 36, 41, 48-51, 53a, 54, 56-57
Young bull — 28e
Nil — 20d, 23, 24a, 26a, 40, 55

Renfrew

Beast — 2a
Bowl — 1a
Bull — 1a, 2a, 11cjl, 18a
Bullock — 2hi, 5, 8, 11a, 13c, 16b, 17, 18b, 20a
Steer — 4d, 13c, 15
Stirk — 6, 9, 13b, 14b, 15, 16cd
Stoat — 4d, 7
Stot — 1b, 2bf, 4ac, 8-9, 11efjl, 12a, 13c, 15, 16a, 18a, 19, 20b, 21
Nil — 2cdegj, 3, 4be, 10, 11bdghik, 12b, 13ad, 14a

Lanark

Bull — 6, 7c, 14b, 18-19, 23-24, 25abc, 27a, 29ce, 33acd, 35b, 44, 46b
Bullock — 1-3, 5-6, 9a, 14d, 15bc, 16b, 22, 25c, 26a, 27b, 29c, 31ad, 35cd, 38ac, 39, 47-48, 49b, 52b, 53, 58, 61
Dressed bull — 32f
Nowt — 13, 24, 32c, 33b, 38e, 45, 48, 56, 57a, 59a, 61
Steer — 2, 21, 29de, 32cd, 33d, 37, 38a, 64ab
Sterk — 38d
Stirk — 7a, 8b, 9b, 10a, 15a, 18, 30, 32de, 46ab, 59a
Stirk stot — 11
Stoat — 15b, 29f, 35a, 40, 51, 52a, 57b, 58
Stot — 1, 3, 7c, 9ab, 10a, 12-13, 15ac, 17, 20, 29e, 30, 31d, 32ef, 33d, 38bd, 41-42, 45, 46ac, 48, 53, 56, 57c, 59ab, 60, 62-63, 65
Young bull dressed — 27b
Nil — 4, 7b, 8a, 10b, 14ac, 16a, 25d, 26b, 28, 29abg, 31bc, 32ab, 34, 36, 43, 49a, 50, 54-55, 66, 67ab

West Lothian

Bull — 21a
Bullock — 1ac, 5, 8, 10, 12-13, 18, 20a, 21b, 22
Heifer — 21a
Nowt — 1cd, 8, 17a, 18, 19b
Stirk — 1b, 3-4, 6, 11, 15
Steer — 1a, 21a
Stoat — 16
Stot — 1ad, 2-3, 5-6, 9a, 11, 18, 19b
Nil — 7, 9b, 14, 17b, 19a, 20b

Midlothian

Beast — 11
Bull — 8a, 18, 23a, 25a
Bullock — 9, 11, 14a, 15, 18-19, 21, 23b, 29, 31
Full grown steer — 1
Nowt — 8b, 10, 12a, 23b, 24, 26a, 27-28, 30
Steer — 7b, 27, 32
Stirk — 7b, 11, 17, 20, 22, 25c
Stoat — 3, 14a, 18
Stot — 4, 6b, 7b, 10, 12ab, 13, 14b, 16, 22, 25c, 26a, 27, 32
Nil — 2, 5, 6a, 7a, 25bd, 26b

East Lothian

Beast — 9
Bullock — 1, 4b, 6a, 8, 11, 15-21
Nowt — 2, 4a, 6ab, 7-8, 10, 14, 16
Steer — 13
Stirk — 2, 13, 15, 20
Stot — 2, 7, 13, 15
Nil — 3, 5, 12

Berwick

Bull — 8
Bullock — 1-4, 6, 9-10, 12, 15, 16bc, 19 20, 22-23, 25, 29, 31-32
Nowt — 1, 5, 10-13, 15, 16ac, 18, 21-22, 24, 26, 29, 31
Steer — 23, 27, 32
Stick — 8
Stirk — 3, 7, 17, 27, 32
Stot — 14, 17, 27, 32
Nil — 28, 30

Peebles

Bullock — 1, 4b, 6ab, 7, 9
Cattle beast — 2
Nowt — 6a
Steer — 3
Stirk — 8
Stot — 2-3, 4b, 5, 6a, 7, 10
Nil — 4ac

Selkirk

Bulock — 2c, 4, 8
Nowt — 2ad
Stirk — 2ab
Stoat — 6
Stot — 1, 2ae, 3, 5, 7

Roxburgh

Bease — 16, 22
Beast — 2
Bullock — 1-2, 3b, 5-6, 8, 9ab, 10, 13, 17, 20, 21adf, 28
Nowt — 1-2, 4, 9ab, 10, 13, 15a, 16-19, 25
Steer — 3a, 7, 25-26
Stirk — 8, 15b, 22, 25-26
Stot — 4, 12-13, 15b, 20, 22-23, 26, 28
Nil — 11, 14, 21bce, 24, 27

Dumfries

Bull — 6
Bullock — 4, 8a, 12, 15-16, 17ab, 18-20, 21b, 24, 26-27, 31bcd, 33, 37, 40, 43, 45ab, 46-47
Nowt — 7
Ox — 42
Steer — 7, 29, 32, 37, 39, 42, 46
Stoat — 3, 5, 22-23
Stot — 1a, 6-7, 8b, 10, 12-13, 16, 19, 25-28, 30, 32, 35, 38-39, 41-42, 44, 45a, 49
Nil — 1b, 2, 9, 11, 14, 21a, 31aef, 34, 36, 48

Kirkcudbright

Bull — 23
Bullock — 1, 4, 6-7, 9-10, 18-19, 21ab, 22, 27
Nowt — 3, 7-8, 13-14, 18, 21b
Ox — 11
Steer — 10, 12b, 15a, 17
Stirk — 1, 5, 17
Stot — 1-3, 5, 7-8, 11, 12a, 15a, 16-17, 21c, 24
Nil — 15b, 20, 25-26

Wigtown

Baist — 18
Beast — 7
Bullock — 1, 3, 5a, 6, 8-9, 11-12, 16-17
Nowt — 2, 18
Stores — 11
Stot — 1, 5ab, 7, 10, 12-15, 18
Nil — 4

Northumberland

Bease — 9, 26
Beast — 10, 18, 19a, 24b, 27, 40b, 46, 48, 59e, 64b, 68, 69ad, 71d, 88a, 95b, 98, 99d, 109, 118a, 124b, 130d, 139
Bull — 72dk, 83, 93, 121, 126ac
Bull calf — 69b
Bullock — 1ab, 2ab, 3, 5-7, 13-14, 16-18, 21, 26, 28, 29ad, 30-31, 35-36, 38, 40a, 41c, 42, 45-46, 52, 53ab, 54, 56, 59bc, 61, 62b, 64a, 65a, 69ch, 70, 71d, 72cg, 73, 77-78, 82, 87, 88b, 89-90, 94b, 98, 99b, 100, 102, 103c, 104ab, 106, 108c, 109, 111b, 119, 120abc, 123, 124b, 127ad, 130be, 132-133, 137, 140, 142-143
Cow — 72ad
Gelding — 69f
Kine — 110
Nowt — 11, 17, 19a, 29f, 41c
Ox — 59b, 69b
Stairk — 106
Stalk — 29c
Steer — 5, 14, 16, 20b, 22, 25, 28, 29ab, 30, 33b, 34ab, 35-38, 41ad, 42-44, 47, 51, 59bd, 60, 62a, 65b, 69b, 71c,

Northumberland cont'd

72bi, 73-82, 95a, 102, 105-107, 108a, 110, 111ab, 112, 117, 122a, 124a, 127e, 130cd, 134, 138, 140-141, 143
Steer bull — 127d
Stirk — 12, 14, 29b, 39, 46, 59bcd, 69a, 71d, 72b, 73, 81, 86, 108ac, 114, 116, 125, 129b, 130a, 133-135
Stirkie — 118b
Stot — 39, 41a, 43-44, 51, 57, 59b, 77, 107, 108c, 124a, 133-136, 140, 142
Why — 76
Young bull — 69b
Nil — 1c, 4, 8, 15, 19b, 20a, 23, 24a, 29e, 32, 33a, 41b, 49-50, 55, 58, 59af, 62cdefgh, 63, 66-67, 69eg, 71abe, 72efhjl, 84-85, 91-92, 94a, 96-97, 99ac, 101ab, 103ab, 108b, 113, 115, 122b, 126bdef, 127bcfgh, 128, 129ac, 130f, 131

Cumberland

Bullock — 2-4, 7-9, 12, 13c, 14, 15ac, 16-17, 21, 23, 25-26, 28, 38, 40, 45-46, 48, 53, 56-58, 61-62
Bullock stirk — 3, 31, 56
Bull stirk — 63b
Steer — 4, 7, 9, 13a, 15a, 26-27, 37b, 45, 47, 53-54, 59-61
Stirk — 5ab, 13d, 14, 15b, 19, 22, 28, 30, 39, 41-43, 52, 60
Stot — 13b, 38
Strick — 30
Nil — 1ab, 6, 10-11, 18, 20, 24, 29, 32-36, 37a, 44, 49-51, 55, 63a

Down

Baste — 22-23
Bullock — 2a, 5-6, 9, 12, 15, 18-19, 23-24, 26, 28
Steer — 3, 17, 21
Stirk — 11, 13, 27, 29
Nil — 1, 2b, 4, 7-8, 10, 14, 16, 20, 25, 30

Tyrone

Baste — 1
Bullock — 1, 7-8, 10-11, 14
Steer — 1-2, 5, 9, 14
Stirk — 2, 10-13, 15
Nil — 3-4, 6, 16

Antrim

Baste — 7
Beast — 7
Bull calf — 16b
Bullock — 1, 3, 13-14, 17, 19, 22, 25-26, 28-29, 31
Steer — 16b, 20, 33
Stirk — 2, 5b, 7, 8b, 10-11, 14, 19, 22, 25
Stoat — 16b
Store steer — 21
Nil — 4, 4A, 5a, 6, 8a, 9, 12, 15, 16ac, 18, 23-24, 27, 30, 32, 34

Donegal

Beast — 4
Bullock — 5, 5A, 8, 12-13
Statu — 8
Steer — 1, 10a, 13
Stirk — 4-6, 10ab, 13
Stot — 10a
Nil — 1A, 2-3, 7, 7A, 9, 11

Fermanagh

Bullock — 2, 4-5, 9
Steer — 1, 10
Stirk — 2-3, 8-10
Stirruck — 4
Nil — 6, 7ab

Armagh

Bullock — 3-4, 6a
Steer — 6a
Stirk — 1, 5
Nil — 2, 6b

Londonderry

Baste — 4-5
Bullock — 2, 3A, 7
Steer — 1A, 3, 5
Stirk — 2-3, 5-7
Nil — 1, 1B

59 HEIFER (young cow that has not had a calf) (PQ1, 119)

Heifer has not been mapped as it occurs fairly densely everywhere except in Orkney and Shetland. Variant spellings have been subsumed under HEIFER.

Some of the items mapped are not strongly concentrated. PQ1 also contains **heifer** (in sense beast in first calf) (PQ1, 120) which is not included in this atlas, as the areas of target items coincide widely with 59. The main differences are: PQ1, 120 did not produce **stirk** and **heifer stirk; heifer** was often qualified: **heifer in calf, heifer in first calf, calving heifer, springing heifer** (Northern Ireland). Northern Ireland also has **springer.**

Cow after her first calf (PQ1, 121) and **cow** after her second calf (PQ1, 122) were excluded here for similar reasons. Moreover, they are not particularly interesting cartographically but items PQ1, 119-122 might deserve a separate study as a word-field.

Shetland

Heifer — 16
Quage — 7, 30
Quak — 20
Quake — 17, 21b, 22
Quey — 11, 29
Stirk — 33
Strick — 12, 21a, 23, 26, 30
Whage — 2-6, 24-25, 27, 30-33
Whake — 1, 8, 10, 14-16, 19, 21a, 24
Nil — 9, 13, 18, 28

Orkney

Heifer — 5
Quaig — 16
Queg — 17-20
Quey — 1, 5-7, 9-10, 12, 13a, 16, 19, 21
Queyack — 13b, 21
Queyie — 14
Queyo — 2, 6-7, 13ab
Quoy — 4, 11, 15, 20
Quoyo — 3-4, 11, 14
Young quey — 8

Caithness

Heifer — 3, 8-9, 13
Quey — 3, 5-6, 8, 10, 12abc, 14-15, 16b, 17
Queyag — 12b, 14
Quoy — 2b, 4
Quoyag — 2b
Stirk — 2a, 3, 5, 16a
Nil — 1, 7, 11

Sutherland

Farrow cow — 5
Heifer — 3-8, 9b, 10-12, 14, 16
Quey — 8, 9a
Stirk — 1, 4-5
Young heifer — 13
Nil — 2, 15, 17

Ross & Cromarty

Cow heifer — 3, 15
Heifer — 1, 4-6, 8-10, 16-23, 25b, 26-29, 31, 32ab, 33, 39
Quey — 24, 36, 38
Quighie — 34
Stirk — 12, 21-22, 29, 38
Nil — 2, 7, 11, 13-14, 25a, 30, 32c, 35, 37ab

Inverness

Heifer — 1-5, 7, 10-11, 13ace, 15-19, 21ab, 22-23, 26, 28-30, 34-39
Quey — 19, 27, 29, 38
Quey stirk — 38
Stirk — 6, 8, 31-32
Stirkie — 8
Yearling heifer — 9
Nil — 12, 13bd, 14, 20, 24-25, 33, 40

Nairn

Heifer — 1abc, 2, 4-6
Heifer stirk — 3

Moray

Calf — 21
Coy — 2a, 6b, 8d, 9a, 10, 13, 15, 18
Heifer — 3-5, 7, 8cde, 11, 14, 19-20, 22-23
Quake — 2a, 3-4, 8b, 9a, 10, 13, 15-16, 20
Quakie — 6b
Quey — 2b, 4, 6a, 8b, 12, 17
Queyie — 3
Quoy — 13
Stirk — 21
Nil — 1, 8af, 9b

Banff

Clean heifer — 21
Coo stirk — 34
Coy — 2c, 3, 5, 16, 23
Heifer — 1, 4, 7, 9-10, 14-15, 18bc, 32
Heifer stirk — 21
Quake — 1, 2c, 3-4, 6ab, 8-9, 11, 13, 15, 17, 19-28, 31, 34
Quakie — 6b, 15-16
Quey — 18c, 20-21, 26, 34
Quoy — 1, 24, 29
Stirk — 29-30, 33
Nil — 2ab, 12, 18ad

Aberdeen

Calf — 8, 20
Calfie — 8, 20
Cooie — 53
Coy — 5b, 6, 9, 14, 24, 26, 28b, 30, 32, 47f, 51, 56, 64, 67, 71b, 75, 77-80, 83, 88, 98, 104, 106, 108
Heifer — 3b, 6, 10, 16-17, 21, 23, 28a, 32, 36, 38, 46, 54, 63-64, 66, 69-70, 71b, 73-74, 79, 82, 95, 97-98, 100, 105
Heifer calf — 107
Quake — 2, 5abcd, 6, 8-9, 11-14, 17, 19, 22, 24-26, 28abc, 29-30, 32-34, 39, 42, 44-45, 47abef, 49, 51, 53, 55-59, 62, 64-65, 68-69, 71bc, 72-73, 75, 77-81, 83-86, 88-89, 93-94, 100, 103, 108
Quakie — 29, 35, 47c, 52, 71b, 72, 87
Queck — 101, 104
Queckie — 18
Queek — 27
Quey — 4, 5a, 6, 12, 14, 29-30, 37, 39, 41-42, 47abd, 50, 52-53, 57, 59, 68, 78, 86, 89, 93, 96, 105, 109
Quick — 31
Quoy — 5b, 30, 75, 85, 94, 100
Spent calf — 3a
Stirk — 5b, 17, 60, 92
Whey — 28a
Yearlin — 48, 69
Nil — 1, 7, 15, 40, 43, 61, 71a, 76, 90-91, 99, 102

Kincardine

Coy — 1, 6, 9-10, 12, 14, 25, 27, 28
Coy calf — 3
Heifer — 5-8, 11, 17c, 18-19, 24, 26, 28
Quake — 2, 5, 10, 13, 23
Queck — 12
Quey — 4-5, 17c, 20-22
Quoy — 9, 13, 17abd
Yearlin — 14
Nil — 15-16

Kinross

Heifer — 1-3
Heifer stirk — 2
Quey — 2-7
Quey stirk — 2
Young heifer — 4

Angus

Cawfie — 33b
Coy — 5bc, 11-12, 14acd, 15, 22, 30
Female calf — 33b
Heifer — 2-3, 5a, 8-9, 13, 14b, 17b, 18-21, 23-24, 26, 28, 32, 34, 36
Heifer stirk — 23, 31
Quey — 1, 5c, 6-7, 14ad, 15, 17a, 21, 32, 35, 37
Quoy — 10, 14d, 22, 34
Slot stirk — 31
Stirk — 33b
Nil — 4, 16, 25, 27, 29ab, 33a

Perth

Clean heifer — 20
Coy — 7

Perth cont'd
Heifer — 2a, 4, 9-11, 13, 21-22, 24-25, 27-28, 31-33, 40, 43, 46, 48, 50, 51a, 57, 60, 68, 72, 74
Heifer stirk — 20, 64
Maiden heifer — 12
Maiden quey — 8
Quey — 1, 2b, 3, 5, 10, 12-13, 15-17, 24, 26-27, 29ab, 30-31, 37-39, 41ab, 42, 44-47, 49, 51a, 52bcd, 62, 65, 67-68, 70-71, 73-74
Quiy — 25, 56, 62
Quoy — 23
Stirk — 5-6, 33, 36, 63, 66
Nil — 14, 18-19, 34-35, 51b, 52ae, 53-55, 58-59, 61, 69

Fife
Cow — 42
Heifer — 4, 7-8, 11, 17, 19, 30, 32, 36ab, 37-38, 40b, 41ab, 44ce, 46-47, 53-54, 55eg, 56, 62-63
Heifer quey — 23
Heifer stirk — 55b
Quate — 6
Quenie — 44f
Quey — 1-3, 6, 9a, 12-14, 18, 20-22, 25-31, 35, 42, 43ab, 44af, 46, 48, 51-53, 55cf, 59, 61, 63, 64ab
Quye — 41c, 55d
Stirk — 4, 9b, 10, 22, 39, 49, 57, 60
Young quey — 45
Nil — 5, 15-16, 24, 33-34, 40a, 41d, 44bd, 50, 55a, 58

Clackmannan
Bulling heifer — 4c
Heifer — 4d, 7
Heifer quey — 1
Quey — 3, 5-7
Quye — 2, 4d
Nil — 4ab

Stirling
Farra cow — 7f
Heifer — 4, 7bd, 12, 23c, 26d, 27a, 31, 37a, 42b
Heifer stirk — 10, 26c
Maiden heifer — 26c
One/two year old heifer — 11
Quee stirk — 15
Quey — 2-3, 7ac, 9, 14, 16-20, 21ab, 22ab, 24, 25acd, 26bc, 27b, 32-34, 35ab, 36, 37a, 40
Quey stirk — 26a, 31, 37b
Quie — 38
Quoy — 28
Stirk — 1, 7e, 8, 13, 25b, 26f, 27a, 30-31, 37a, 42a
Stirk quie — 39b
Sturk — 23b
Nil — 5-6, 23a, 26e, 29, 39a, 41

Dunbarton
Cow — 18
Heifer — 5, 7b, 10-11, 13bc, 14a, 17
Heifer stirk — 16b
Quey — 1, 3, 4a, 6, 13a, 14b, 16a
Quye — 7c
Stirk — 2, 4b, 6, 7ac, 9, 14a
Yeld — 13a
Nil — 8, 12, 15

Argyll
Heifer — 1-3, 6, 10-11, 14-17, 24-25, 30, 33, 35
Quey — 5, 7-9, 12-14, 22-23, 26, 29, 31-32, 34-35, 37, 40
Quey old — 24
Quey stirk — 39
Stirk — 18, 21, 28, 35, 38
Yeld heifer — 19, 22
Yeld quey — 19, 33
Yell heifer — 34
Young cow — 2
Nil — 4, 20, 36

Bute
Heifer — 1a, 7
Quey — 1be, 4, 7, 8ab, 9
Quey yeld — 1ac
Quye — 2
Stirk — 3, 5, 7, 8b, 9
Nil — 1d, 6

Ayr
Cauf quey — 43
Heifer — 6, 8a, 10-11, 20ce, 21, 26b, 28cf, 36, 39, 44-45, 49, 53a, 54, 56
Heifer calf — 57
Merk — 41
Nowt stirk — 51
Quey — 2a, 4, 9, 12ab, 13, 16b, 18b, 19, 20cfh, 28ce, 30b, 33, 35a, 50
Quey stirk — 2a, 57
Quye — 34, 36-37, 47-48
Quye stirk — 18a
Stirk — 1a, 2b, 3-7, 8ab, 14-15, 16ab, 20abg, 24b, 27, 28abcde, 29, 30b, 31-32, 34, 37, 40, 42-44, 46-47, 52, 53b, 55-57
Stot — 17
Sturk — 23, 38
Twyearal — 50
Yearal — 50
Yeld quey — 42
Yell quey — 37
Nil — 1b, 20d, 22, 24a, 25, 26ac, 30a, 35b

Renfrew
Coo sturk — 17
Heifer — 2ai, 11acjl, 12b, 16b, 20a
Maiden — 16a
Quey — 2bg, 4ac, 6-8, 10, 13ac, 14b, 16d, 18b, 19, 20ab, 21
Quye — 4d, 16d, 18a
Stirk — 1b, 2be, 4d, 5, 11bef, 12a, 13c, 16a
Yeld quey — 9
Young coo — 2a
Nil — 1a, 2cdfhj, 3, 4be, 11dghik, 13bd, 14a, 15, 16c

Lanark
Calf — 6
Coo — 25b, 33a
Cow — 6
Cow heifer — 35a
Heifer — 1, 3, 6, 8b, 14b, 15ac, 16a, 18-19, 22, 26a, 27b, 29cd, 31ab, 35c, 38c, 44, 46b, 49a, 51, 52b, 53, 56, 58, 59b
Quey — 6, 7a, 8a, 9b, 10a, 11-12, 15b, 16b, 20, 26a, 27a, 29ce, 30, 31c, 33d, 35ad, 36, 38bde, 41-43, 45, 46a, 48, 51, 52ab, 57c, 58, 59a, 60, 65-66
Quey stirk — 32c
Quye — 2, 23, 31d, 46c, 57b, 59b
Stirk — 1-2, 5, 7a, 9a, 13, 15bc, 17, 20-21, 29f, 31b, 32a, 33bc, 35d, 37, 38a, 39-40, 47, 49ab, 54-55, 57ab, 58, 59a, 62-63, 64ab, 67a
Stirk heifer — 32e
Stirk quey — 32f
Stot — 32e
Yeld heifer — 45
Yell heifer — 7a
Young beast — 16b, 59b
Nil — 4, 7bc, 10b, 14acd, 24, 25acd, 26b, 28, 29abg, 32bd, 34, 35b, 50, 61, 67b

West Lothian
Eild quey — 21a
Heifer — 1ac, 2-3, 7-8, 11-13, 18
Maiden — 11
Quey — 1ab, 2, 4-6, 8, 9ab, 10-11, 15, 17a, 18, 20a, 22
Quye — 1c, 12
Stirk — 1d, 16, 19a, 21b
Strik — 19b
Nil — 14, 17b, 20b

Midlothian
Cauve — 18
Heifer — 6ab, 8a, 10-11, 12ab, 14a, 17, 19-21, 23ab, 24, 25c, 28, 31-32
Heifer cauve — 18
Heifer stirk — 30
Quey — 3-4, 10-11, 12a, 13, 14b, 16, 22, 26a, 27, 29
Quye — 19
Stirk — 1, 7b, 14a
Nil — 2, 5, 7a, 8b, 9, 15, 25abd, 26b

East Lothian
Calf — 16
Cow — 16
Eild heifer — 6a
Heifer — 1, 7, 9-10, 13-14, 16-21
Moakie — 13
Quey — 2-3, 6b, 7, 10, 13, 15-16
Quye — 4b, 8
Nil — 4a, 5, 11-12

Berwick
Heifer — 1-2, 6, 12, 15, 16c, 18, 21, 24, 26-27, 30-32
Heifer stirk — 16a, 22-23, 29
Quey — 3-4, 6-14, 16c, 17, 20, 25, 27
Quye — 16b
Stirk — 14
Nil — 5, 19, 28

Peebles
Free of the bull — 6a
Heifer — 2-3, 4b, 6a, 8, 10
Heifer stirk — 6b, 9-10
Quey — 4b, 6a
Quey stirk — 7
Quye — 3
Stirk — 1, 3, 4b, 5, 10
Suckler — 2
Young beast — 10
Nil — 4ac

Selkirk
Heifer — 2ad, 4
Heifer stirk — 1, 8
Quey — 2ae, 5, 7
Stirk — 2e, 3
Nil — 2bc, 6

Roxburgh
Calf — 23
Eild quey — 15b
Heifer — 3ab, 4, 9a, 10, 13, 20, 26
Heifer calf — 8, 21a
Heifer quey — 25
Heifer stirk — 17-18, 21af, 25
Quey — 2, 5, 7, 12-13, 16, 19, 21c, 22-24, 28
Quye — 1
Stirk — 4, 15b, 21d, 26
Nil — 6, 9b, 11, 14, 15a, 21be, 27

Dumfries
Bullin(g) heifer — 26, 43, 46
Bulling quey — 26, 43
Heifer — 1a, 12, 15-16, 18, 20, 21b, 22-23, 30, 31cd, 37
Heifer calf — 45a
Heifer stirk — 27, 41, 46
Quey — 7, 8b, 10-11, 17a, 19, 28, 30, 31c, 32-35, 38-39
Quey heifer — 42
Quye — 3, 40
Stirk — 5-7, 8ab, 10, 13-14, 21a, 24-25, 29, 41, 44, 45a, 47, 49
Yeld quey — 1a
Young quey — 17b
Nil — 1b, 2, 4, 9, 31abef, 36, 45b, 48

Kirkcudbright
Calving quey — 16
Eild — 15a
Heifer — 1, 3, 7-8, 10, 18, 19, 21b, 27
Heifer stirk — 10, 14, 22
Quey — 6, 9, 12ab, 15a, 17-18, 21abc, 23, 25-26
Quey stirk — 2
Stirk — 1, 4-5, 11, 21a, 24, 27
Yell heifer — 8
Nil — 13, 15b, 20

Wigtown
Cuddock — 8
Heifer — 1, 5b, 6, 9, 11, 13
Heifer stirk — 1, 5b
Quey — 11, 13, 15-18
Quey stirk — 5a, 14
Quie — 12
Stirk — 2-3, 10, 17
Nil — 4, 7

Northumberland
Bullin heifer — 53a, 108a, 142
Coo — 101b
Cow — 72ad, 87, 101b
Eild heifer — 20a, 43
Geld (heifer) — *43-44,* 69f
Geld why — 75
Geld wye — 75
Heifer — 1a, 2ab, 5-7, 11, 14-18, 28, 29abd, 30-31, 34ab, 35-37, 39, 41cd, 45-46, 48, 52, 56-57, 59e, 61, 62bg, 64ab, 66, 69bc, 72b, 73, 77, 80, 83, 86-87, 88ab, 89-90, 92, 94b, 95b, 98, 102, 104a, 106, 109, 111a, 112, 117, 120ac, 123, 124b, 127a, 130b, 132-133, 135, 137, 139
Heifer calf — 99d, 104a
Heifer coo — 111b
Heifer quey — 59b
Heifer stirk — 59c, 103c, 104a, 130d, 133, 136, 142
Hofle hofle — 119
Maiden heifer — 19a, 22, 29a, 78-79, 110, 127d, 141, 143
Poddie — 129b
Quey — 9, 15, 22, 29c, 33b, 51, 60, 65ab, 68, 69g, 75, 107, 111a, 132, 134
Quey stirk — 29f
Quiy — 1b, 20b, 39, 45, 59d, 72f
Stairk — 53b
Stirk — 13, 21, 26, 29e, 38, 40a, 42, 50, 55, 58, 59b, 69a, 70, 71c, 73, 107, 114, 124a, 134
Stirkie — 73, 76, 104b
Stork — 70, 124a
Wey — 79, 106
Whey — 76, 79
Why — 36, 44, 49, 54, 65a, 103b, 110, 143
Why coaf — 142
Wye — 39, 68, 69e, 71d, 81, 95a, 103c, 106, 111b, 112, 130c, 138
Young heifer — 13
Nil — 1c, 3-4, 8, 10, 12, 19b, 23, 24ab, 25, 27, 32, 33a, 40b, 41ab, 47, 59af, 62acdefh, 63, 67, 69dh, 71abe, 72aceghijkl, 74, 82, 84-85, 91, 93, 94a, 96-97, 99abc, 100, 101a, 103a, 105, 108bc, 113, 115-116, 118ab, 120b,

Northumberland cont'd

121, 122ab, 125, 126abcdef, 127bcefgh, 128, 129ac, 130aef, 131, 140

Cumberland

Barren heifer – 9
Bulling heifer – 46, 56
Bullock calf – 38
Cawf – 56
Gel(d) (heifer) – 6, *9, 15c*
Heifer – 3-4, 7, 12, 13acd, 14, 15a, 16, 19, 23-26, 28, 40, 43, 45, 47-50, 53, 57-60, 62
Heifer stirk – 16-18, 21-22, 29, 31, 46, 56, 63b
Quey – 2, 5ab, 13b
Risen' two – 56
Stirk – 3, 7, 13d, 28, 34, 37a, 38, 40, 42, 44, 47, 51, 53-54, 61, 63a
Stot – 38
Sturk – 8
Two year old heifer – 44, 56
Whey – 8
Why – 13c, 15b, 38
Wye – 8, 13c, 15b, 31-32
Wye cawf – 56
Yearling – 44
Nil – 1ab, 10-11, 20, 27, 30, 33, 35-36, 37b, 39, 41, 52, 55

Down

Heifer – 2a, 5-6, 14-15, 17-19, 24, 26, 28-29
Maiden heifer – 3-4
Quey – 10, 13, 21
Stirk – 28
Yeld heifer – 24
Nil – 1, 2b, 7-9, 11-12, 16, 20, 22-23, 25, 27, 30

Tyrone

Heifer – 1, 7-11, 15-16
Quy – 2
Springin heifer – 12
Stirk – 5, 9
Nil – 3-4, 6, 13-14

Antrim

Bulling heifer – 15
Heifer – 1, 5b, 10, 13, 22, 26-29
Quee – 24
Quey – 8b, 24
Quey calf – 30
Quy – 22
Quy stirk – 6
Stirk – 4A, 9, 15, 16b, 17-21, 23-24, 27-28, 31, 33
Yearling – 25
Yell heifer – 5b, 7, 23, 25, 33
Nil – 2-4, 5a, 8a, 11-12, 14, 16ac, 32, 34

Donegal

Bearrach cirim – 6
Heifer – 1-3, 5, 5A, 8, 12
Heifer calf – 10a
Heifer quey – 10b
Heifer stirk – 13
Quy – 1
Stirk – 3, 5, 5A, 13
Nil – 1A, 4, 7, 7A, 9, 11

Fermanagh

Heifer – 2, 4-5, 8-9
Stirk – 1, 3, 6
Nil – 7ab, 10

Armagh

Heifer – 4, 6a
Maiden heifer – 3
Stirk – 4
Nil – 1-2, 5, 6b

Londonderry

Heifer – 2, 3A
Quy – 3, 5
Springer – 1A
Stirk – 3A
Nil – 1, 1B, 4, 6-7

60 COW DUNG (PQ1, 124)

(1) Some second elements of target items appear repeatedly in items concerning animal dung, cf. 62 **horse dung,** 63 **sheep's dung,** and 68 **fowl dung.**
(2) For variants of COW see map 14, Appendix A.

Shetland

Byre muck – 30
Kuck – 10
Kye's dung – 14
Muck – 1, 17, 22, 27, 31, 33
Sharin – 18, 29
Sharn – 2-3, 7, 9-13, 15-17, 19-20, 21ab, 22-26, 28, 30-33
Shaurn – 1, 4-6, 8

Orkney

Blout – 19
Cow dirt – 2
Cow dung – 5, 8, 15, 17
Cow mallow – 3
Cow muck – 16
Cow plirts – 15
Cow scone – 4
Cow sharn – 1-4, 6-12, 13ab, 14-21
Iper – 4
Kye dung – 5
May scone – 3

Caithness

(Cow('s) dung – *8,* 13-14, 17
Muck – 14
Sharn – 2ab, 4-5, 7-11, 12abc, 13-15, 16ab
Nil – 1, 3, 6

Sutherland

Byre manure – 3
(Cow(s'))dung – 1, *3,* 4-5, *6-7,* 8, 11, *12-13,* 15-16
Cow shit – 9a
Manure – 11, 15, 17
Muck – 15
Sharn – 5, 8, 9b, 10, 13-16
Nil – 2

Ross & Cromarty

Byre dung – 3
(Cow) dung – *1, 3-5,* 8-*9,* 16-17, 23, *27, 29,* 32abc, *36, 39*
(Cow(s'))sharn – 2-3, 7-15, 17-22, 24, 25ab, 27-*28,* 29-31, 32abc, 33-36, 37ab, *39*
Manure – 18, 25b, 26, 29
Muck – 23, 36
Nil – 6, 38

Inverness

Camboo – 22
(Cow) dung – *1,* 2-3, *4-5,* 6-*7, 10-11,* 13bce, 18-19, 21b, *23, 27,* 29, *34*
(Cow) manure – *1, 23,* 32, 35-39
Cows' shairn – 26
(Cow(s')) sharn – *7*-9, 11-12, 13acd, 14-19, 21*ab, 22,* 24-26, 28-33, 37
Farm manure – 13e
Nil – 20, 40

Nairn

(Cow) dung – 2, *6*
Sharn – 1abc, 2-5

Moray

(Cow) dung – 2a, 8e, 11, *21*
Cow kips – 8b
Cow shards – 9a
(Cow) sharn – 1, 2ab, 3-5, 6ab, *7,* 8bcdf, 9a, 10, 12-13, 15-19, 21-23
Kyup – 8e
Muck – 4, 14-15, 20-22
Muck oot of the fal – 7
Strang – 8b
Nil – 8a, 9b

Banff

Dung – 2ab, 7, 34
Muck – 2c, 7, 15-16, 19, 21, 27, 33-34
Sharn – 1, 2a, 3-5, 6ab, 7-17, 18bcd, 20, 23-34
Sharrin – 22
Nil – 18a

Aberdeen

Dung – 4, 10, 24, 95-96, 98
(Cow) muck – *2,* 3ab, 8, 10-11, 14-17, 19-20, 24-25, 27, 28c, 29, 38, 47a, 48-49, 51, 54-55, 59, 62, 66-67, 69-70, 73, 75, 79, 81, 87, 96, 98-99, 101, 104, 108
Cows' dirt – 8
Cow shit – 73
Cyack – 47c
Kye's dirt – 8
Manure – 14
Shairn – 91
Sharn – 1-2, 3a, 4, 5abcd, 6-10, 12-15, 17-27, 28abc, 30-37, 39-42, 44-46, 47abcdef, 49-53, 56-65, 67-69, 71abc, 72-89, 92-94, 97, 100-101, 103-109
Shite – 73
Skitter – 8
Nil – 43, 90, 102

Kincardine

Cow manure – 8
(Cow) sharn – 2-5, *6,* 7, 10-16, 17abcd, 18, 20-24, 26, 28
Dung – 1, 21, 27
Kye sharn – 25
Muck – 2, 7, 9, 12, 17c, 19
Sharrin – 1

Kinross

(Cow) shairn – *2,* 6
(Cow) sharin – 1, *3*-4
Cow tuird – 7
Kye's shairn – 7
Sharn – 5

Angus

Cow dung – 17b, 18
(Cows') sharin – 5a, 6-*8,* 11-12, 14a, 19, 21, 24-25, 30, *31,* 32, 33b, 35
Kye shairn – 5c
Kye sharin – 8, 28
Muck – 1, 3, 8, 15, 32
Shairn – 9-10, 14bcd, 20, 22-23, 26, 33a, 34, 36-37
Sharn – 1-2, 4, 5b, 13, 17ab, 20, 29a
Shern – 27
Nil – 16, 29b

Perth

Byre manure – 3, 63
(Cow) dung – *2a,* 3-*4,* 5, 9-10, 14, 22, *24*-25, 28, 29a, 74
(Cow) manure – *2ab,* 8, *24,* 30, 36
(Cow) shairn – 1, 5, *8,* 15-*17,* 23, *24,* 25, 27, 29a, 31-*33,* 42, 45-*46, 48,* 51ab, 52abcde, 54, 56, 62, 65, 68
(Cow) sharn – 1, 6, 9, 42, 44, 50, *53, 55,* 64, *66*-67, 70
(Cow) shearn – *53,* 73
(Cow(s')) sharin – 7, 11-13, *18,* 20-22, 26, 29b, 39, 41a, 57, *58-59,* 60-61, 72
Kye shairin – 71
Muck – 44
Shearin – 14
Sherin – 40
Shern – 38, 41b, 43, 47, 49, 61, 69
Nil – 19, 34-35, 37

Fife

(Cow) dung – 8, *11,* 16, 20-21, 28, 37, *44bc,* 57, 63
Cow pats – 44a
Cow pie – 39
Cow plowters – 13
Cow shearin – 29
Cow shearn – 44b
Cow slip – 16, 55e
Cows' pancake – 13
(Cow(s')) shairn – 4, 7-8, *19-21,* 25-27, *30*-31, 35, *39,* 40a, 41bcd, *43a,* 44e, *45,* 53, 55f, *62*-63, 64ab
(Cow(s')) sharin – 2-3, 5-6, 11-*12,* 14, 17-18, 22, 25, 36b, *41a,* 44ae, *54,* 55c*d, 56, 58*
(Cow(s')) sharn – 1, *9b,* 23, *59,* 61
Kye shairn – 9a, 12-13, 36a, 40a, 41c, 42, 43ab, 55deg, 57
Kye sharin – 10, 20, 32-33, 40b, 44df, 46, 48, 51, 60
Manure – 37, 55b
Muck – 20, 38, 44c
Purlocks – 58
Shern – 52
Nil – 15, 24, 34, 49-50, 55a

Clackmannan

(Cow(s')) shairn – 1-*2,* 4*a*b*c*d, 5, *6,* 7
Cows' sharn – 3
Dub – 4b

Stirling

Bachrim – 26b
Cow clat – 26c
(Cow) manure – 4, 7f, 12, 23b, *36*
Cow patch – 7e
Cows' clap – 28
(Cow(s')) dung – 4, 7f, 12, 23ab, *25d,* 26c, *28, 30, 36,* 40-*41*
(Cow) sharn – 2, *7b, 17,* 22b, 26bf, 30, 33, 39a
Cow shern – 16, 27b
(Cow) skitters – 7d, *26a*
(Cow(s')) shairn – 1, *6, 7ae, 8,* 10, 14-*15, 18, 21b,* 25abcd, *26ad, 29, 31, 34, 35b, 36,* 37b, 38, 42ab
(Cow(s')) sharin(g) – 3, *6, 7cd, 11, 17, 19,* 21a, 22a, *24,* 26ce, *32, 35a, 37a, 39b,* 42b
Kahy sharin – 9
Kye dung – 25d
Kye shairn – 20, 25d, 27a
Muck – 22ab, 23c
Shearn – 2, 13
Sherin – 4
Shirn – 7b
Nil – 5

Dunbarton

Cow clap — 10
(Cow) dung — 7b, 11, *13bc, 16b*
(Cow) manure — *10, 16a,* 18
Cow shit — 7b
(Cows')) shairn — *1, 5,* 13a, 14b, *16ab*
(Cows')) shern — 2-3, *4b, 6,* 7a, 10
Kay shairn — 16a
Muck — 3, 7c
Sharin — 4a, 15
Sharn — 9, 14a
Shearn — 7c
Nil — 8, 12, 17

Argyll

(Cow) manure — *2-4*, 7, *15,* 23, *27, 33*-34
(Cow(s')) dung — 1, 5-*6*, 9, *10,* 11, *12,* 14, 16, *17,* 18-19, 21, *22-23,* 24-25, 30, *35, 37-39*
(Cow) sharn — 24-25, *35*
(Cow(s')) shern — *9, 16,* 30, *31,* 32, *35*
Farm yard manure — 19
Muck — 33-34
Shairn — 29
Sharin — 5, 19
Nil — 8, 13, 20, 26, 28, 36, 40

Bute

(Cow) dung — 1a, 2, *4, 7, 8ab*
(Cow) sharin — *3,* 6
(Cow) sharn — *5,* 8b, 9
(Cow) shern — 1a, *3,* 7, 8ab, 9
Muck — 7
Shairn — 1acde
Shearn — 1b

Ayr

Blitter — 15
Cow clabber — 57
Cow clap — 7, 9, 20ae, 41, 48, 53b
(Cow) dung — 2ab, *5-6,* 8b, *11, 12a, 18a, 20b,* 21, *26b, 30a, 31, 34,* 39, *42-46,* 49, *51*-52, 55, *56-57*
Cow glabber — 20b
Cow pancakes — 12b, 18b, 24a
(Cow) shairn — 1a, 2a, 3, *7, 8a,* 14-*15,* 16*ab*, 19, 20*dg*, 22, *27, 28f,* 29, 30a, *32, 34, 36,* 39, *40-41, 47*-50, *53ab,* 54
(Cow) sharin — 11, *12a,* 13, *18a,* 20*aceh*, *23,* 35a, 37-38, *42, 46, 51*
(Cow) sharn — 2b, *4,* 8b, 26a, 28*ab*, *57*
(Cow) shern — 9, 24b, 30b, *35b, 56*
Cow shit — 10, 15
Cow shurn — 18b
Cow taird — 26c
Cow turd — 57
Droppings — 28d
Glaur — 20b
Manure — 17, 21, 26b
Muck — 2b, 28f
Shearn — 18b, 20f, 33
Shite — 32
Nil — 1b, 25, 28ce

Renfrew

Clushan — 21
Cow clap — 2h, 11de
(Cow) manure — 2ad*i*, 10
Cow pat — 6
(Cow(s')) dung — 1a, *2a,* 4acd, *11ace,* 12ab, *13acd, 16b, 20a*
Cow sharn — 2fh
(Cow(s')) pancakes — *2h,* 11aj*kl*
(Cow(s')) shairn — 1b, 9, 11abj*k*, *13a, 16d,* 17, *20b*
(Cow(s')) sharin(g) — 2g, 3, 7-*8,* 11e*j*, 13c, 15, *16bc, 18a,* 21
(Cow(s')) shern — 2*bdfi*, *4d,* 5, *11l*
Muck — 4d
Plab — 14b
Sheirn — 16a
Sherrin — 2e, 19
Shit — 11j
Nil — 2cj, 4be, 11gh, 13b, 14a, 18b

Lanark

Charn — 29f
Cow clap — 28, 36
Cow clappins — 16b
Cow dirt — 20
Cow droppings — 28
(Cow) manure — 3, 7c, 14b, 17-18, *25b,* 27a, 29f, 32bd, *37*
Cow pancake — 7a
(Cow) plat — 11, *38d*
(Cow(s')) dung — *1-3, 9a, 12, 14d,* 16a, 29*cf*, 32d, *35d, 48,* 49ab, 59b, 60, 64a
(Cow) sharin — *2,* 5, *7a,* 11-12, *14c, 15bc, 18, 28, 29d,* 31a, 32ae, *34,* 38b, *39, 52b,* 54, 64b
Cow sherin — 6
(Cow) shern — *23,* 25c, *29e,* 31a*d*, 33b, 38e, 42-43, *47,* 53, *57ab, 58, 59a*
(Cow(s')) shairn — 4, 7b, 8b, *9ab,* 10a, *12*-13, *15a,* 16b, *17, 19-20,* 22, *25b, 26a,* 29*cg*, *30,* 31*bc*, *32f, 35bc,* 36, *38ad, 39*-40, 46ab, 48, *49b, 50-51,* 52a, 55-56, *57c, 61*-63, 65
(Cow(s')) sharn — *7c,* 16b, 21, 25c, *29e,* 32c, 67b
Cow turd — 33c
Farm yard manure — 38c
K'shairn — 27b
Kye shairn — 14d, 27b, 33c, 35d, 37, 45, 46c
Kye sharin — 33a
Kye shern — 29e, 33d, 35a
Kye sherrin — 44
Muck — 15b, 32f, 49b, 52b, 67a
Sheerin — 6, 36
Nil — 8a, 10b, 14a, 24, 25ad, 26b, 29ab, 41, 66

West Lothian

Blitter — 11
Cow clap — 17a
(Cow) dung — 5, *10,* 12, *15*
(Cow) muck — 4, *8,* 21ab
Cow shearin — 1d
Cow slips — 22
(Cow(s')) shairn — 1a, *3,* 7, *9b,* 12-13, 16, *17ab,* 20a, *21a*
(Cow(s')) sharin — *1b,* 2, 4, *6, 9a,* 11, *19ab, 22*
Keech — 11
Kye shairn — 18
Kye sharin — 1b
Pancake — 11
Sharn — 5
Skitter — 11
Nil — 1c, 14, 20b, 26b

Midlothian

(Cow) dung — 6ab, *8a, 12b, 14a,* 19, *23b*
Cow pancakes — 7a
Cow plat — 32
Cow shern — 28
(Cow(s')) shairn — *1-2,* 3, 6b, 8b, *10-11, 12b, 13,* 14b, *17,* 20, 23a, *25ab, 29*-30, *32*
(Cow) sharin(g) — 12a, *14a,* 15, *18, 21,* 23b, 24, 25cd, 26ab, 31
Green dung — 15
Manure — 6a
Muck — 16, 24
Plat — 27
Plet — 25c
Share — 25c
Sharn — 4, 9, 22
Nil — 5, 7b

East Lothian

Byre dung — 8
(Cow) dung — 1, *5, 19*
(Cow) muck — 1, 17, *21*
Cow plat — 16
(Cow) shairn — 4a, *6a,* 9-10, 15-*16,* 20
(Cow) sharin — *2-3, 4b, 8, 11, 13*
Grip — 4a
Manure — 1
Sharn — 5, 7
Shearn — 12
Shern — 6b, 7, 14
Nil — 18

Berwick

Cow dung — 8
(Cow) muck — 6, *10*-11, 15, *26*-27, *29-30,* 31
(Cow) plat — 1-*2,* 4, *8*-9, *17, 22-23,* 26, *32*
(Cow) shairn — 2, 7-9, *11,* 13, 16c, 18, 21, 23, 27, *32*
(Cow) sharin — 1, 4, 6, 10, 12, *16b,* 22, *26,* 31
Cow sharrin — 20
Jingalore — 32
Plaister — 8
Sharn — 3, 14, 16a, 17, 29
Nil — 5, 19, 24-25, 28

Peebles

Cow dung — 4b, 6ab
Cow pancake — 5
(Cow) shairn — 4ab*c*, 7, *10*
Cow shearn — 6a
Muck — 2, 4a, 8-10
Plat — 10
Sharin — 1, 3, 5
Sharn — 4b

Selkirk

(Cow) dung — *1,* 8
Cow plat — 2ace
(Cow) shairn — 2a*b*d, 3, 6-7
Muck — 4-5, 8
Sharin — 1
Sharn — 5

Roxburgh

(Cow) muck — 9ab, 11, *15ab,* 19, 21bdf, 25, 28
Cow plat — 4-5, 13, 17, 20, 21ae, 22, 26
(Cow) shairn — *2, 8,* 9ab, 10, 13, 15b, 16, *17,* 18-20, 21ace, 23, 26, 28
(Cow) sharin — 3b, *5*-7, 24
Dung — 1, 14
Sharn — 4
Shearn — 3a
Shern — 1
Nil — 12, 27

Dumfries

Byre muck — 43
(Cow) dung — 1a, *4, 12, 20,* 46
(Cow) muck — 1a, 8b, 17a, *18,* 22-23, *26,* 28-30, 31c, 37-38, 40-41, 44, 45a, 46
(Cow) plat — *3, 7, 15, 17ab,* 25, *31bd, 32, 36, 47-49*
Cow platter — 31f
(Cow) shairn — 1a, 2, 4, 10-11, 17ab, 19, *21b, 24,* 25-26, *27,* 28-29, 31a*df*, 32, *37*-38, 41, *46*
(Cow) sharin — 3, *5,* 7, 16, 21a, 22, *33,* 39
(Cow) sharn — 6, 10, *12*-14, *35,* 38-42
Cow shern — 31b
Shearn — 9
Nil — 1b, 8a, 31e, 34, 45b

Kirkcudbright

(Cow) dung — 1, *6, 19, 27*
Cow flop — 15b
(Cow) shairn — *1,* 2-3, *4, 7*-9, *12ab, 15a,* 17, 21abc, 24, 26-27,
Cow sharin — 18, 22
(Cow) sharn — 2, 5, *16,* 20
Cowslip — 1
Muck — 10, 21bc, 25
Shearn — 23
Shern — 14
Shite — 11
Skitter — 11
Nil — 13

Wigtown

(Cow) dung — *2-3, 5a, 13,* 15
(Cow) muck — 5a, *6-7*
(Cow) shairn — *8,* 10, 12, *14,* 16
Cow sharn — 7
Cow shearn — 5a, 11
(Cow) sherin — *2,* 9
Cow shern — 4, 6, 17
Cow shite — 1
Cow slip — 5a
Pad — 5b
Sharin — 15, 18

Northumberland

Byre muck — 135
Cow blakes — 134
Cow clap — 29f, 116, 130e
(Cow) dirt — 59c, *72d*
Cow droppings — 41c
(Cow) dung — 2b, 29b, *30, 35, 59b, 69b,* 82, 130e
(Cow) manner — *111ab,* 118a, 140
(Cow) manure — *69b,* 71d, 72b, 76, 123, 127d*e*, *130b,* 140
(Cow) muck — 2b, 5, 8, 10, 12-*13,* 16, *21*-22, 24ab, 26, 29ace, *31,* 34b, 36-37, *38-39,* 40a, *41d,* 42-44, *46-47, 53ab, 54,* 59*cd*, 60, 62a*e*h, *63, 64ab, 65a,* 68, *69abcdh, 70,* 71ad, 72bdegik, *73-74,* 75, *76,* 77-79, *81*-83, *87,* 89, *90-91,* 93, *94b, 98, 99bcd,* 100, 102, *103b,* 104ab, 105-106, 108ab, 109-110, 111ab, 112-113, 118ab, 120abc, 122a*b*, *123, 124b,* 126abef, 127abcd, *129c,* 130*cdf*, *132-133, 135,* 136-138, *139*-140, *142*
Cow plack — 118b
Cow plait — 62bg
(Cow) shairn — 1b, 10, *15, 20b,* 36, 44, 51, *53b, 56,* 61, 69g, 73, 102, *103b, 106,* 114, 133
Cow share — 1c, 64b, 76, 81, 95a, 111b
(Cow) sharin(g) — 2ab, *6-8, 17-18,* 22-23, *24a, 27*-28, 29ef, *33b, 41bcd, 47,* 59be, 61, *65b,* 68, *72bj, 79, 84, 88a, 95b, 99b,* 107, 122a, *124a, 127dh, 131*
Cow shearing — 76
Cow shearn — 52
Cow shern — 59c, 89, 110, 134, 142-143
Cow sherrin — 59f
(Cow) shirn — 73-*74, 103a*
(Cow) shit — 82, 108b, *128,* 130e
Cow slip — 33a, 40b, 126d
(Cow(s')) pancake — *72a,* 125
(Cows') plat — *1a, 9, 11, 13-14,* 16-*18, 20b, 22, 24b, 25-26,* 29bde, *32, 33a, 34a, 35, 38, 40b, 41ac,* 45, *46-50, 52, 53a, 55-58, 59c, 61, 62aceh, 64b,* 66, *68, 69aefgh, 71bc, 72a, 73, 76, 79,* 80-82, 85-*86,*

Northumberland cont'd

88b, *90*, 92, *95ab*, 96-97, *99bd*, *102*, *103abc*, *104a*, *107*, *110*, *111ab*, 114, *115*, 116, *117*, *119*, *122b*, *124ab*, 125, *126a*, 127c, *129b*, 130ae, *133-134*, *140*, *142*
(Cows') platter — 29d, 61, *71c*, 72ai, 122a, 125, *126d*, 127h, 130c
(Cow(s')) sharn — 19a, 34b, *35*, *117*, *130b*, *143*
Cuddie claps — 72i
Litter — 102
Manishment — 77
Shard — 114
Sharrin — 3, 38
Shawn — 62f
Shirin — 20a
Nil — 4, 19b, 59a, 62d, 67, 71e, 72cfhl, 94a, 99a, 101ab, 108c, 121, 126c, 127fg, 129a, 141

Cumberland

Clat — 27, 30
(Cow) clap — *8-9*, 15bc, *16*, *22*, *24-28*, 30, *32*, *36*, *37ab*, *38*, *40-46*, *48*, *51*, 56, *57-58*, *60-62*
(Cow) dung — *16*, *23*, 56-57
(Cow) muck — *1a*, 2-4, 6, *7-9*, *12*, 13bcd, *15a*, *17-18*, 19-20, *21*, *23*, *29*, *32-34*, 35, *36*, *39*, 41, *43-44*, *46*, 47, *48*, 50-51, *53*, 54, *55*, 56, *57*, *59*, *63b*
(Cow) plat — *1b*, *5a*, *8*, *13a*, 14
(Cow) scairn — *7*, 8, *9*, *11*, *13a*, 17
(Cow) scarn — 15c, *20-21*, 28, 30-31, 33, 37b, *38*, 40, 49, *52*, 54, *59*, 61-*62*
Cow shit — 9
(Cow) skitter — 8-*9*, 37a, 56
Fan kyak — 41
Manishment — 15c
Manure — 47, 50, 57
Scane — 19
Scare — 34
Sharin — 13b
Sharn — 5b
Skite — 46
Swat — 14, 27, 30
Nil — 10, 63a

Down

Bacle — 13
Baughran — 14
Clabber — 24
Clart — 27
(Cow) clap — *2a*, *3-5*, *10-11*, *17*, *19*, *21-22*, 28
Cow dung — 5, 14-15, 19, 22, 24, 26, 29
(Cow) manure — *2a*, 4, 6, 9, 28
Pachle — 18, 26
Plap — 15
Nil — 1, 2b, 7-8, 12, 16, 20, 23, 25, 30

Tyrone

Cow cherin — 1
Cow clabber — 7
Cow clap — 3-4, 6, 11-15
Cow dung — 1, 7-10, 15
Manure — 2, 8, 16
Sheerin — 7
Sherin — 5

Antrim

(Cow) clap — 1, 3, *4A*, *5a*, *7*, *9-12*, *16b*, *17-18*, *21*, *23-25*, 26, 29-31, *33*
(Cow) dung — *5a*, *10*, *15*, *19-20*, *22*, 25, 28
(Cow) shairin — *24*-25
(Cow) sheerin — 16b, *28*
(Cow) shern — 11, *15*, 16b, 26

Cow sherrin — 23
Manure — 13, 17, 25, 31
Muck — 25
Pat — 8b
Nil — 2, 4, 5b, 6, 8a, 14, 16ac, 27, 32, 34

Donegal

Cow clap — 4, 10a
Cow droppings — 10a
Cow dung — 1-2, 5, 5A, 8, 12
Cow manure — 5A, 8
Cow sheerin — 6
Cow t(h)urd — 6, 10a, 13
Farmyard manure — 5
Pancake — 13
Sharin — 10b
Shern — 11
Nil — 1A, 3, 7, 7A, 9

Fermanagh

(Cow) clap — *6*, 7b, *10*
Cow dung — 2, 4, 9
(Cow) manure — 2, 4, 8-*9*
Cow platt — 5
Cow sherin — 1, 5
Turd — 1
Nil — 3, 7a

Armagh

(Cow) clap — 1, *2-5*
Cow manure — 4, 6a
Nil — 6b

Londonderry

(Cow) clap — *1AB*, *2-3*, 5-6, *7*
Cow shern — 4-5
Dong — 3A
Nil — 1

61 COLT (PQ1, 126)

Variants of COLT (**cult** Banffshire, north-west Aberdeenshire; **cowt, cout** nearly everywhere from Aberdeenshire soutwards all over the area except in Ireland and parts of Northumberland; **coult, cault** a few in N. Ireland; **cowlt** a few in Northumberland) have been subsumed.
A raised + symbol after a locality indicates that the informant commented 'female'.

Shetland

Colt — 27
Foal — 15^{+}
Horse foal — 1, 7, 17
Kjussick — 3
Rool — 4-6, 8, 19, 30
Royl — 30
Staig — 6, 17, 19-20, 21ab, 26, 29-30
Steg — 12, 22, 33
Yearald horse — 22
Young horse — 7
Nil — 2, 9-11, 13-14, 16, 18, 23-25, 28, 31-32

Orkney

Colt — 1, 4, 6-7, 11, 15, 19-21
Powny — 21
Young horse — 2, 9, 13ab, 16-17, 19
Nil — 3, 5, 8, 10, 12, 14, 18

Caithness

Colt — 2a, 8, 10, 14, 16b
Horse — 13
Staig — 2b, 3, 5-7, 9, 11, 12abc, 15, 17
Staigie — 15, 17
Nil — 1, 4, 16a

Sutherland

Colt — 1, 3-8, 10-13, 16
Horse foal — 9b
Sholtie — 6
Staig — 9ab
Nil — 2, 14-15, 17

Ross & Cromarty

Cob — 33
Colt — 1, 3-5, 8-9, 16-20, 22-24, 25a, 26-31, 32abc, 33, 36
Coltie — 6
Filly — 18, 25b, 27^{+}, 32b^{+}c^{+}, 34
Foal — 39
Gelding — 25b, 27
Pony — 5
Nil — 2, 7, 10-15, 21, 35, 37ab, 38

Inverness

Colt — 2-11, 13ace, 16-19, 21ab, 22-23, 26-29, 32-35, 37-38
Garron — 9
Gelding — 30
Sheltie — 12
Nil — 1, 13bd, 14-15, 20, 24-25, 31, 36, 39-40

Nairn

Clip — 4
Colt — 1b, 2, 5-6
Nil — 1ac, 3

Moray

Clip — 2a, 3, 6a, 8b, 21
Colt — 1, 4-5, 6b, 7, 8e, 9a, 10, 14, 18-20, 23
Coltie — 8c, 9a
Cultie — 6b
Shelt — 3
Nil — 2b, 8adf, 9b, 11-13, 15-17, 22

Banff

Clip — 3, 5, 6b, 10-11, 13-15, 20-24, 29, 31
Colt — 1, 3-5, 6ab, 7, 9-10, 14-17, 18cd, 25-27, 29, 31-34
Cultie — 15, 29
Filly — 33^{+}
Frog — 6b, 8, 18d, 20, 22-23, 27
Froggie — 8, 27
Frogie — 4
Geldin — 19
Nil — 2abc, 12, 18ab, 28, 30

Aberdeen

Clep — 5b, 59, 73
Clip — 3ab, 4, 5acd, 9-21, 23, 27, 28abc, 30, 32-33, 35-42, 45-46, 47ade, 51, 53-54, 56, 58, 62, 64-66, 69, 72-75, 77, 80-81, 83, 85-86, 88-89, 92, 94-95, 100, 104, 106
Clipe — 1
CLippie — 55
Colt — 2, 6, 8-9, 16, 20, 22, 24-27, 28a, 31, 34, 44, 47a, 49-50, 53, 59, 64-65, 67, 69-70, 71bc, 77-79, 81-84, 86-87, 93-101, 103-109
Coutie — 52
Cultie — 29
Cuttie — 27, 71a
Filly — 22^{+}, 53^{+}, 73, 105
Frog — 9-10, 12-13, 28a, 30, 67
Froggie — 11
Geldin(g) — 48, 61
Shelt — 90
Yearling — 63
Yearling clip — 57
Nil — 7, 43, 47bcf, 60, 68, 76, 91, 102

Kincardine

Clip — 1, 3-4, 7-10, 12-14, 16, 17abd
Colt — 5-11, 15, 17c, 19, 26-28
Filly — 6^{+}, 18
Gelding — 6
Staig — 21-22, 24
Staigie — 17c, 23
Yearling — 20
Nil — 2, 25

Kinross

Colt — 1-7
Staig — 2, 5

Angus

Colt — 5c, 7-10, 14a, 15, 17b, 19, 22-24, 31, 34, 36-37
Coltie — 18
Foalie — 25
Gildin — 22
Horse foal — 34
Stag — 17a
Staig — 1, 3, 5ab, 6-7, 12-13, 14b, 17b, 19, 21-23, 30-31, 33a, 35-37
Yearlin — 28, 37
Young horse — 2
Young male horse — 33b
Nil — 4, 11, 14cd, 16, 20, 26-27, 29ab, 32

Perth

Colt — 1, 4-5, 7-11, 13-16, 18, 20, 23-28, 29a, 31-33, 36-37, 39-40, 41a, 42, 44-50.

Perth cont'd

52bcde, 56-57, 59-62, 64-74
Filly — 26[+]
Gildin — 30
Staig — 7, 12-13, 15-16, 20, 25, 31, 48, 50, 58
Shaltie — 57
Twa year auld — 51a
Young gelding — 43
Young horse — 24, 57
Nil — 2ab, 3, 6, 17, 19, 21-22, 29b, 34-35, 38, 41b, 51b, 52a, 53-55, 63

Fife

Colt — 1, 3-8, 9ab, 10-14, 17-23, 25, 27-28, 32, 36ab, 37-39, 40b, 41a, 42, 43ab, 44acde, 47, 51-53, 55beg, 56-58, 61-62, 64ab
Filly — 44e[+]
Foal — 23, 30, 44e, 55e
Gelding — 37
Horse — 63
Powny — 43a
Staig — 7, 13, 21, 27, 55f
Yearling male — 59
Young horse — 41a
Nil — 2, 15-16, 24, 26, 29, 31, 33-35, 40a, 41bcd, 44bf, 45-46, 48-50, 54, 55acd, 60

Clackmannan

Colt — 1-2, 4ad, 5-7
Nil — 3, 4bc

Stirling

Colt — 1-4, 6, 7abcde, 8-18, 21ab, 22ab, 23bc, 25abcd, 26acd, 27a, 28-29, 31-34, 35ab, 36, 37ab, 39b, 40, 42ab
Filly — 25d[+], 36[+]
Foal — 13, 38
Fully — 25a
Gelding — 26a, 30
Staig — 26a
Three year old — 26b
Year old — 7b
Young horse — 20
Nil — 5, 7f, 19, 23a, 24, 26ef, 27b, 39a, 41

Dunbarton

Colt — 1-3, 4ab, 5-6, 7bc, 9-10, 13abc, 14a, 15, 16ab, 17
Hogget — 14a
Young horse — 10
Nil — 7a, 8, 11-12, 14b, 18

Argyll

Colt — 1, 3, 5-7, 9-12, 14-15, 17-19, 21-24, 26-27, 30-35, 37-39
Young horse — 2, 33
Nil — 4, 8, 13, 16, 20, 25, 28-29, 36, 40

Bute

Colt — 1abce, 4, 8ab, 9
Filly — 7[+]
Foal — 2
Nil — 1d, 3, 5-6

Ayr

Colt — 2ab, 3-7, 8ab, 9-11, 12ab, 13-15, 16ab, 17, 18ab, 19, 20abcdefgh, 21, 23, 24b, 26bc, 27, 28abcdef, 29, 30ab, 31-34, 35ab, 36, 39-52, 53ab, 54-57
Colt foal — 1a, 26a
Filly — 15[+]
Foal — 42
Staig — 18b
Stallion — 42, 57
Unbacked filly — 19[+]
Yearling — 38
Nil — 1b, 22, 24a, 25, 37

Renfrew

Colt — 1b, 2abgi, 4acd, 5, 7-9, 11abcefil 12a, 13ac, 14b, 16abd, 17, 18ab, 19, 20ab, 21
Filly — 11a[+]
Young horse — 16a
Nil — 1a, 2cdefhj, 3, 4be, 6, 10, 11dghjk, 12b, 13bd, 14a, 15, 16c

Lanark

Colt — 1-3, 5-6, 7ac, 8b, 9ab, 11-13, 14c, 15abc, 16b, 17, 19-20, 22, 24, 26a, 27b, 29cdf, 30, 31ad, 32acdf, 33abcd, 35abd, 38abcd, 39-45, 46abc, 47-48, 49ab, 50-51, 52ab, 53-56, 57abc, 58, 59ab, 60-63, 64a, 65
Filly — 31c[+]
Foal — 29c
Gelding — 29f, 37
Male — 21, 44, 67a
Male horse — 23
Naig — 38d
Powny — 25b
Quennie — 18
Quite — 29e
Staig — 11, 38d
Yearling — 15a, 64b
Young horse — 14b, 29f, 35c
Nil — 4, 7b, 8a, 10ab, 14ad, 16a, 25acd, 26b, 27a, 28, 29abg, 31b, 32be, 34, 36, 38e, 66, 67b

West Lothian

Colt — 1abd, 2-8, 9a, 11-13, 15-16, 17a, 18, 19b, 20a, 21ab, 22
Filly —16[+]
Foal — 21a
Geldin — 1a
Nil — 1c, 9b, 10, 14, 17b, 19a, 20b

Midlothian

Colt — 3-4, 6b, 8a, 10-11, 12ab, 13, 14ab, 15-20, 23ab, 24, 25c, 26a, 27, 29, 32
Gelding — 11
Staig — 30, 32
Young male horse — 1
Nil — 2, 5, 6a, 7ab, 8b, 9, 21-22, 25abd, 26b, 28, 31

East Lothian

Colt — 1-2, 4b, 6a, 7-8, 13-18, 20-21
Cowtie — 6a
Gelding — 9
Male foal — 6b
Staig — 3, 9, 16
Nil — 4a, 5, 10-12, 19

Berwick

Colt — 1-4, 6, 8, 10, 12, 14-15, 16ac, 17-18, 21-24, 26-27, 29-32
Filly — 1[+], 29[+]
Horse — 9
Staig — 10, 13, 16ac, 17, 20-21
Young horse — 8, 16b, 31
Nil — 5, 7, 11, 19, 25, 28

Peebles

Colt — 1, 3, 4b, 5, 6ab, 7-10
Young horse — 2
Nil — 4ac

Selkirk

Colt — 1, 2ac, 3-4, 8
Staig — 2ad
Nil — 2be, 5-7

Roxburgh

Colt — 2, 3ab, 4-6, 8, 9a, 10, 15b, 17-18, 20, 21a df, 22, 25, 28
Colt foal — 13
Filly — 15b
Filly foal — 13
Naig — 6
Staig — 1, 17
Steg — 3a, 4
Yearlin(g) — 12, 23
Nil — 7, 9b, 11, 14, 15a, 16, 19, 21be, 24, 26-27

Dumfries

Colt — 1a, 2, 4-7, 8ab, 9-13, 15-16, 18-20, 21b, 22-30, 31abcd, 32-34, 37-44, 45ab, 46-47, 49
Gelding — 5
Male — 3
Yearling — 31c
Young horse — 17ab
Nil — 1b, 14, 21a, 31ef, 35-36, 48

Kirkcudbright

Colt — 3-10, 12ab, 15a, 17-19, 21abc, 22-23, 27
Filly — 18
Geldon — 16
Male foal — 10
Year auld horse — 1
Young male horse — 2
Nil — 11, 13-14, 15b, 20, 24-26

Wigtown

Colt — 1, 3, 5ab, 6, 8-17
Staig — 5b
Young horse — 2
Nil — 4, 7, 18

Northumberland

Cob — 114
Colt — 1a, 2a, 3, 5-6, 8, 10-12, 14, 16-18, 19a, 20b, 21, 23, 25-26, 28, 29abf, 30-31, 35-38, 40a, 41cd, 45-46, 48, 51-52, 53ab, 54, 56-57, 59be, 60, 62bfg, 64ab, 65a, 66, 68, 69bcd, 70, 71cd, 72bgi, 73, 76-79, 81-83, 86-87, 88b, 91, 98, 99d, 101b, 102, 103abc, 104a, 106-107, 108a, 109, 112, 117, 120ac, 124b, 126c, 127a, 132-133, 135, 137-139, 141-143
Colt foal — 69ab, 78, 111b
Cuddie — 130e
Filly — 23, 52, 59e, 108a
Filly foal — 68
Foal — 2b, 46, 94b, 111a
Galloway — 124a
Gelding — 34b, 41a, 42, 59b, 90, 127d, 140
Gout — 127d
Horse — 72d, 95b, 104b
Longtail — 53a, 110
Male foal — 69f, 130cd
Nag — 75, 140
Naig — 140
Powny — 67, 124a, 130e
Stag — 134
Yearling — 33b, 42, 136
Young entire — 57
Young horse — 13, 16, 22, 26, 41ac, 123, 125
Nil — 1bc, 4, 7, 9, 15, 19b, 20a, 24ab, 27, 29cde, 32, 33a, 34a, 39, 40b, 41b, 43-44, 47, 49-50, 55, 58, 59acdf, 61, 62acdeh, 63, 65b, 69egh, 71abe, 72acefhjkl, 74, 80, 84-85, 88a, 89, 92-93, 94a, 95a, 96-97, 99abc, 100, 101a, 105, 108bc, 113, 115-116, 118ab, 119, 120b, 121, 122ab, 126abdef, 127bcefgh, 128, 129abc, 130abf, 131

Cumberland

Colt — 2-4, 5a, 7-12, 13bcd, 14, 15ac, 16-18, 20-26, 28, 30, 33-34, 36, 37ab, 38, 40, 42, 44-50, 53, 56-58, 62
Galloway — 56
Gelding — 4, 15b, 39, 43, 45
Male (foal) — *47*, 54
Stag — 4, 15a, 31, 37a, 38, 46, 54, 56, 60
Stott — 37a
Two year old — 32
Yearling — 19, 32-33, 46
Young horse — 26
Nil — 1ab, 5b, 6, 13a, 27, 29, 35, 41, 51-52, 55, 59, 61, 63ab

Down

Clib — 23
Colt — 2a, 5, 11, 13, 15, 17-19, 24-26
Young horse — 2a
Nil — 1, 2b, 3-4, 6-10, 12, 14, 16, 20-22, 27-30

Tyrone

Clib — 9
Colt — 1-2, 7, 9-11, 14, 16
Six month — 12
Six quarter old — 14
Young horse — 11
Nil — 3-6, 8, 13, 15

Antrim

Clib — 6-7, 10-11, 13-15, 16b, 17-18, 21-23, 25-26, 33
Colt — 1, 4A, 5b, 9, 16b, 17, 19-20, 23, 25, 29, 31
Coult — 4A
Filly — 21
Six quarter old — 7
Yearling — 7
Young horse — 27
Nil — 2-4, 5a, 8ab, 12, 16ac, 24, 28, 30, 32, 34

Donegal

Clib — 2
Colt — 4-5, 5A, 6, 7A, 8, 11-12
Coult — 7A
Foal — 5
Young horse — 1, 5A
Nil — 1A, 3, 7, 9, 10ab, 13

Fermanagh

Clib — 1
Colt — 2, 4, 8-9
Nil — 3, 5-6, 7ab, 10

Armagh

Clib — 5
Colt — 2, 4-5
Six quarter — 5
Nil — 1, 3, 6ab

Londonderry

Colt — 1, 3A
Filly — 2, 6
Six quarter old — 4, 7
Young horse — 1A
Nil — 1B, 3, 5

62 HORSE DUNG (PQ1, 127)

Horse dung has not been mapped as it occurs fairly densely nearly everywhere except in Cumberland and Northumberland. Some of the items mapped do not show a high density. See note (1) on 60 **cow dung**.

Shetland

Horse cucks – 6
Horse dirt – 21b, 22-23, 33
(Horse) dung – *1-3, 7, 10, 14,* 20, *21a, 22*
Horse muck – 16, 24, 30, 32
Horse sharin – 18
Horse sharn – 15, 17
Stable muck – 30
Nil – 4-5, 8-9, 11-13, 19, 25-29, 31

Orkney

Horse cookies – 15
Horse dirt – 2, 4-5
Horse dung – 1, 3, 5, 8-9, 11, 13ab, 15-17, 19-21
(Horse) muck – 6-*7*
Horse sharn – 16
Horse shit – 3
Nil – 10, 12, 14, 18

Caithness

(Horse) dalls – 12c, *15*
Horse dirt – 11
(Horse) dung – *2ab, 5, 8,* 9, *10,* 13-*14, 16b*
Manure – 13
Muck – 8
Nil – 1, 3-4, 6-7, 12ab, 16a, 17

Sutherland

Droppings – 15
(Horse) dung – 1, *4-8, 9ab,* 10-11, *12-13, 16*
Manure – 17
Stable manure – 3, 11, 16
Nil – 2, 14

Ross & Cromarty

Dolders – 35
Dolts – 35
Droppings – 27
(Horse) dung – *1, 3-5, 8-9,* 14, 16-17, 19, 22-23, 25b, *27-29,* 31, 32abc, 34, *39*
(Horse) manure – *2, 18-19,* 25ab, 26, *29,* 38
Horse's dollars – 10, 24, 37a
Stable dung – 3
Nil – 6-7, 11-13, 15, 20-21, 30, 33, 36, 37b

Inverness

Dollars – 13a, 14, 16
Droppings – 14
Horse dolders – 9
(Horse) dung – *1-2, 3-7, 10,* 13abc, *19,* 21a*b*, 22, *26-27,* 28, *29-30,* 33-34
(Horse) manure – 13e, 26, 29, 32, 35, *37,* 38, *39*
Stable dung – 13e
Stable manure – 6, 23, 36
Nil – 8, 11-12, 13d, 15, 17-18, 20, 24-25, 31, 40

Nairn

Horse dung – 2, 4, 6
Stable manure – 5
Nil – 1abc, 3

Moray

Dollars – 8b
Dollops – 21
Droppins – 21
Horse dirt – 8b
(Horse) dung – *4-*5, 6b, *7,* 8ce, 9a 19-20, *21, 23*
(Horse) orts – 22-*23*
Horse tolls – 8b
Manure – 14
Muck – 6a, 16
Stable dung – 18
Toaldies – 4
Toalds – 4
Nil – 1, 2ab, 3, 8adf, 9b, 10-13, 15, 17

Banff

Dollacks – 32
Horse balls – 29
Horse dirt – 6b, 10, 17
(Horse) droppings – *17,* 23
(Horse) dung – *1,* 2a, 3-*4, 9, 15-16, 18c,* 19, *21, 23, 34*
(Horse) muck – *5, 9,* 13, *15-16,* 18b, *24, 26,* 32
(Horse) orts – *8, 10,* 18d, 23, 27, 33
(Horse) sharn – 2abc, *6b*
Orps – 14
Stable dung – 7
Turds – 14
Nil – 6a, 11-12, 18a, 20, 22, 25, 28, 30-31

Aberdeen

(Horse) dirt – *4, 5d, 8, 19, 28a, 36,* 41, *46,* 62, *71a, 73, 83*
(Horse) dung – *10, 20*-21, 44, 47bf, *53*-54, *59, 70, 74, 82, 94,* 98, *103, 106,* 108
Horse manure – 105
(Horse) muck – *1-2, 3a,* 5bc, *6,* 8-*9, 11*-12, 14, *15,* 16, *17,* 19-20, *21, 23, 25-26, 28c, 29,* 31, *32-35,* 37-38, 40, *45, 47ae, 49-51, 58, 62*-63, *65-67,* 69-*70, 71b,* 75, 77, 79, *81, 85-86, 88, 95,* 98-99, 101, *104*
(Horse) oranges – *9, 14,* 27, 32, *71c, 73*-74
(Horse) orts – *9, 25,* 48, 64, 68, *80, 97,* 101
Horse shit – 73
(Horse) tolls – 3a, *28a*
Oarts – 52, 67
Orse – 67
Sharn – 19
Stable manure – 22, 82
Stable muck – 3b
Strang – 47c
Nil – 5a, 7, 13, 18, 24, 28b, 30, 39, 42-43, 47d, 55-57, 60-61, 72, 76, 78, 84, 87, 89-93, 96, 100, 102, 107, 109

Kincardine

(Horse) dung – *1, 5-6, 10, 12, 14*-15, 17c, *19, 21, 26-28*
Horse dirt – 7, 11
Horse dovers – 4
(Horse) manure – *8,* 17c
(Horse) muck – *7, 9-10, 12,* 16, 17a, 20
Oranges – 24
Stable dung – 3
Nil – 2, 13, 17bd, 18, 22-23, 25

Kinross

(Horse) dung – *2,* 3, *4*
Horse toalies – 2
Nil – 1, 5-7

Angus

(Horse) dirt – 5ab, *35*
(Horse) droppings – *14a,* 17b
(Horse) dung – *1, 5c, 6-9,* 10, 12-*13,* 14a*b*cd, 17b, 20, *22, 25, 28, 31, 34-36,* 37
(Horse) manure – 22, 26, *28*
Oranges – 24
Stable manure – 33b
Stable mucking – 22
Stadung – 17a
Tollies – 23
Nil – 2-4, 11, 15-16, 18-19, 21, 27, 29ab, 30, 32, 33a

Perth

Doalies – 29a
Dovers – 64
Horse cackie – 52c
(Horse) droppin(g)s – 12, 29b, 41b, *56,* 68
(Horse) dung – *1, 4*-5, 7, 9-10, *15, 24-25, 27-28,* 29a, *32*-33, *39,* 43, *46, 49-50, 51a,* 52*ab, 57, 60, 62, 65-66, 71*-72, 73-74
(Horse) manure – 2a*b*, 24, *36,* 67
Horse oranges – 57
Kieck – 52c
Muckins – 20
Stable dung – 8, 16, 23
Stable manure – 3, 26, 39, 63
Toalies – 41a
Nil – 6, 11, 13-14, 17-19, 21-22, 30-31, 34-35, 37-38, 40, 42, 44-45, 47-48, 51b, 52de, 53-55, 58-59, 61, 69-70

Fife

Dachies – 27
Droppin(g)s – 9a, 33, 35
Duchies – 27
Horse dirt – 48
Horse's dovers – 55b
(Horse) dung – 3, *7-8,* 9a, *11,* 13-*14,* 16-*17, 19,* 20, *21,* 23, *25, 28,* 30, *32, 36ab, 37,* 39, 40*ab, 41a, 42,* 43a, *44e, 46-47, 51,* 55a, *56-57,* 62-63, *64a*
(Horse) manure – 38, *41a,* 55b, *57*
Horse's oranges – 39
Horse sharin – 58
(Horse) tollies – *33,* 45
Manure dung – 55e
Punks – 6
Stable dung – 4, 53
Turds – 39
Nil – 1-2, 5, 9b, 10, 12, 15, 18, 22, 24, 26, 29, 31, 34, 41bcd, 43b, 44abcdf, 49-50, 52, 54, 55cdfg, 59-61, 64b

Clackmannan

Horse droppin(g)s – 6
(Horse) dung – 4c, *7*
Horse manure – 3
Muck – 3
Posel – 4b
Toalies – 4d
Tollies – 5
Nil – 1-2, 4a

Stirling

Drappings – 7b
Dry muck – 7b
(Horse) droppin(g)s – 7d, 22b, *32*
(Horse) dung – 4, 7*cef, 8,* 11-*12,* 16-18, *20,* 21*ab*, 23bc, 25bc, 26abcd, 27a, *28, 30-32, 34, 35a, 36, 37ab,* 39b, 49-*41, 42a*
Horse manule – 21b
(Horse) manure – 7f, 18, 23b, 26d, *36*
(Horse) toalies – 8, *25d*
(Horse) tollie(s) – 9, 12, 22a, *33, 37a*
(Horse) turds – 7b*d*
Oranges – 7d
Short dung – 7a
Stable dung – 12, 21b
Stable manure – 7e, 36
Trots – 2
Nil – 1, 3, 5-6, 10, 13-15, 19, 23a, 24, 25a, 26ef, 27b, 29, 35b, 38, 39a, 42b

Dunbarton

Droppings – 14a
(Horse) dung – *1,* 3, *6, 7b,* 9, *13abc, 14a,* 16ab
(Horse) manure – *11,* 18
Horse shit – 7b
Litter – 7c
Short dung – 16a
Stable manure – 7c, 10
Nil – 2, 4ab, 5, 7a, 8, 12, 14b, 15, 17

Argyll

(Horse) dung – *1,* 5-*6, 10-12, 14-15,* 16, *17,* 18, *19,* 21, *22-24, 27, 39*
Horse manure – 2, 24, 37
Stable manure – 3, 7, 9, 19, 34
Tollies – 30
Nil – 4, 8, 13, 20, 25-26, 28-29, 31-33, 35-36, 38, 40

Bute

(Horse) dung – 1a*bd*, 2, *8a, 9*
(Horse) manure – 1a, *7*
Stable manure – 8b
Toalies – 9
Turds – 9
Nil – 1ce, 3-6

Ayr

Aidle – 48
(Horse) drappins – 24a, *41*
(Horse) droppin(g)s – *1a,* 27, *47, 57*
(Horse) dung – 2a*b, 4-6,* 8ab, *9*-10, 12*ab*, *13-14,* 15, *20bc,* 21, *24b, 28be,* 30ab, *31, 33-34, 35ab, 36,* 38-*39,* 41-46, 52, 53*ab*, *54,* 55, *56-57*
(Horse) manure – 1b, 26a, 29, 38, *57*
Horse skailing – 20f
Horse toalies – 8b, 28f
(Horse) tollies – 3, 11, *16b,* 20a*ce*, *32*
Horse turds – 57
Short dung – 33
Stable dung – 3, 26b, 42
Stable manure – 49
Nil – 7, 16a, 17, 18ab, 19, 20dgh, 22-23, 25, 26c, 28acd, 37, 40, 50-51

Renfrew

(Horse) dung – 1a*b*, 2*bd*, 4*acd*, 5, 11*acefl*, *12a, 13ac, 16b, 17,* 18a, 19, *20a*
(Horse) manure – 1b, 2a*di*, 11j, 16a
Horse oranges – 1b, 4d
Horse tollies – 20b, 21
Shairn – 11k
Stable manure – 15
Tolie – 11k
Turds – 2e, 11k, 14b, 16a
Nil – 2cfghj, 3, 4be, 6-10, 11bdghi, 12b, 13bd, 14a, 16cd, 18b

Lanark

Guiden – 46a
Het dung – 46c
(Horse) dovers – 32e, *39*
(Horse) drappins – 33cd
Horse droppings – 7a, 29cf, 46a, 48
(Horse) dung – *1-3,* 6, *8b, 9a, 12,* 15ac, 16ab, 17, 19, *22,*

Lanark cont'd

25c, 27b, 29cd, 31ad, *35abcd,* 36, 38ad, *39-40, 44-45, 46ab, 47-48,* 49ab, *51, 53, 58, 59b,* 60, *62,* 64b
Horse manors — 47
(Horse) manure — 3, 6, 7c, 14b*cd,* 18, *25b,* 26a, 28, 29ef, 30, 31a, 32abc*f,* 37, 38c
Horse shairn — 38d
Horse tollies — 5, 13, 20, 33bcd, 48
Manure orts — 17
Muck — 67a
Plunk — 42
Stable dung — 20
Stable manure — 15bc
Nil — 4, 7b, 8a, 9b, 10ab, 11, 14a, 21, 23-24, 25ad, 26b, 27a, 29abg, 31bc, 32d, 33a, 34, 38be, 41, 43, 50, 52ab, 54-56, 57abc, 59a, 61, 63, 64a, 65-66, 67b

West Lothian

Horse drite — 19b
(Horse) droppin(g)s — *8,* 11, *18*
(Horse) dung — 1abc, *2*-3, *5-8,* 9a, *10,* 11, *12,* 13, *15-16,* 20a, *21b,* 22
Manure — 3, 16, 17a, 19a
Minure — 1c
Muck — 21a
Stable dung — 1a
Stable manure — 16
Toalies — 1b
Tollies — 7
Nil — 1d, 4, 9b, 14, 17b, 20b

Midlothian

Droppings — 22, 23b, 26b
(Horse) dung — 2, 6ab, *7a, 8a, 9,* 10-11, 12ab, *13, 14a,* 15-16, *17-18,* 21, 23ab, 24, 25c, *27, 29, 32*
Horse's oranges — 3, 7a
Manure — 1, 6a, 11, 12b, 19-20, 22
Stable dung — 16
Tollies — 26a
Nil — 4-5, 7b, 8b, 14b, 25abd, 28, 30-31

East Lothian

Dirt — 14
Horse droppings — 16
(Horse('s)) dung — 1, 4b, 6a, *7,* 9, 13, *15, 17-18, 20-21*
Horse tollies — 16
Stable dung — 8, 19
Stable muck — 2, 9, 16
Toalies — 6b
Nil — 3, 4a, 5, 10-12

Berwick

Fose — 27
Horse dirt — 16a
Horse drippings — 8
(Horse) droppin(g)s — 4, 12, 16ce, *26, 30, 32*
(Horse) dung — *1, 7*, 7-8, *16b, 21, 26, 32*
Horse muck — 2-3, 6, 9-10, 13, 15, 19-20, 22-23, 26-27, 31
Nil — 5, 11, 14, 17-18, 24-25, 28-29

Peebles

Droppings — 10
(Horse) dung — *2-3,* 5, *6a,* 8
(Horse) manure — 1, *4b,* 5
Horse muck — 9
Horse shairn — 4a
Stable manure — 4b, 6b
Nil — 4c, 7

Selkirk

Horse dung — 1, 2ace
Horse muck — 3, 8
Purls — 2a
Nil — 2bd, 4-7

Roxburgh

Guding — 21c
(Horse) droppings — *3a,* 7-8, 15b, 21a, 24
(Horse) dung — 1-*2,* 3b, *4, 8, 10, 13, 17,* 19-*20,* 22-23
(Horse) manure — 15ab
(Horse) muck — 3b, 4, 8, *9ab, 15a,* 16, *17-18, 20,* 21bcdef, *25, 28*
Nil — 5-6, 11-12, 14, 26-27

Dumfries

Horse dirt — 17ab
(Horse) dung — *1a, 2, 4-5, 7, 8a, 12*-13, *16,* 19-*20, 21b, 22,* 28, 31*de,* 32-*33,* 45a, *46*-47
(Horse) manure — *11, 15,* 17b, *27,* 32
(Horse) muck — 6, 8b, *18, 26,* 31bc, *35, 37, 39*-40, 44, *46,* 49
Horse shairn — 29
Stable dung — 21b
Stable muck — 43
Nil — 1b, 3, 9-10, 14, 21a, 23-25, 30, 31af, 34, 36, 38, 41-42, 45b, 48

Kirkcudbright

Droppin — 17
(Horse) dung — *1-6,* 7, *10, 12b,* 18-*19,* 21b, *22*-23, *27*
(Horse) manure — *7,* 11
Horse muck — 15a, 21c
Shairn — 27
Stable — 9
Stable manure — 16
Stable muck — 18
Nil — 8, 12a, 13-14, 15b, 20, 21a, 24-26

Wigtown

Horse droppings — 5b
(Horse) dung — *2*-3, *5a,* 8, *11, 13*-14, *16*-17
Horse orts — 5a
Horse shite — 1
Purl — 5a
Nil — 4, 6-7, 9-10, 12, 15, 18

Northumberland

Doddles — 130e
Fegs — 127d
(Horse) dirt — *52,* 53b, *72d*
(Horse) dottles — 32, 69g, *72d,* 115, 122a
(Horse) droppin(g)s — *41c,* 44, *56,* 57, 59b, *72i,* 76, 79, 81, 95b, 111b, 126c
(Horse) dung — *1a,* 2b, *6, 14,* 19a, *28, 30, 35, 41c,* 59b
(Horse) manure — 20b, 24a, 40b, 45, 68, 69ah, 71*a*cd, 72*ab*d*i*, 85, 93, 113, 122b, 123, 126*b*ef, 127b*d*h, 130ce
(Horse) muck) — 1b, 2a, 5, 7-13, 15-18, 19a, 20b, *21,* 22, *24b, 26-28,* 29*ab*cde, 30, *31,* 33b, *34ab, 35,* 36-37, *38-39, 40ab,* 41a*b*cd, *42-46, 48-50* 51, *52,* 53ab, *54-58,* 59ac*df, 60,* 61, *62acegh, 63, 64ab, 65ab, 66-68, 69abcdefh, 70, 71abcd,* 72abdegkl, *74* 76-77, *78,* 79, *80-87, 88ab, 90-92,* 93, *94b, 95ab, 96, 98, 99bd, 100, 102,* 103ac, *104ab, 106, 108a, 109-110, 111ab, 112, 114, 116-117, 118ab, 119,* 120abc, 122ab, *123,* 124ab, *125,* 126*abd*f, 127abc*de* *129bc,* 130abcef, *131-133,* 134 *135-137,* 138, *139-142*
Horse shit — 82
(Horse) tods — 101b, *128,* 129b, 130*de, 143*
Manner — 37, 53b
Platter — 126e
Shite — 83
Slip — 126e
Stable manure — 59d, 68, 69b
Styeble muck — 69a
Nil — 1c, 3-4, 19b, 20a, 23, 25, 29f, 33a, 47, 59e, 62bdf, 71e, 72cfhj, 73, 75, 89, 94a, 97, 99ac, 101a, 103b, 105, 107, 108bc, 121, 127fg, 129a, 141

Cumberland

Dottles — 43
Dummock — 56
Horse cobs — 41
(Horse) droppings — 27, 41, *46*
(Horse) dung — *9, 57,* 60
Horse manure — 47, 50, 57
(Horse) muck — *2-3,* 4, *5a, 6-9, 11-12,* 13cd, *14, 15abc, 16-18,* 19, *20,* 21, *22-26, 28-29,* 31, 36, *37ab,* 38, *40, 42, 44-50,* 51, *52-53,* 54, *55, 57-62, 63b*
Horse shit — 9
Horse tiurd — 40
Stable muck — 33, 48
Tollies — 30
Nil — 1ab, 5b, 10, 13ab, 32, 34-35, 39, 63a

Down

Paughal — 27
Horse dung — 6, 15, 19, 22, 24, 29
(Horse) manure — *2a, 5-6,* 9, *17-18, 26*
Nil — 1, 2b, 3-4, 7-8, 10-14, 16, 20-21, 23, 25, 28, 30

Tyrone

Horse dung — 1, 7-8, 10
Horse manure — 8, 11
Nil — 2-6, 9, 12-16

Antrim

Dolders — 16b
Droppings — 4A
Horse balls — 33
Horse dung — 1, 15, 17, 19-20, 22, 25-26, 28
(Horse) manure — 13-*14,* 31
Nil — 2-4, 5ab, 6-7, 8ab, 9-12, 16ac, 18, 21, 23-24, 27, 29-30, 32, 34

Donegal

Horse dung — 5, 5A, 8, 10b, 12
Horse droppings — 5A, 6, 10a
Horse manure — 1, 10b
Nil — 1A, 2-4, 7, 7A, 9, 11, 13

Fermanagh

Horse dung — 2, 4
Horse manure — 2, 4, 8-9
Nil — 1, 3, 5-6, 7ab, 10

Armagh

Cadles — 3
Horse manure — 4, 6a
Nil — 1-2, 5, 6b

Londonderry

Dong — 3A
Horse dung — 2, 4
Nil — 1, 1AB, 3, 5-7

63 SHEEP'S DUNG (PQ1, 130)

See note (1) on 60 **cow dung.**

Shetland
Padles — 26
Sharn — 11
Sheep muck — 30
Sheep's dirt — 32
Sheep's dung — 1, 21a
(Sheep('s)) pirls — 2-10, 12-15, *16*-17, 18-20, *21ab, 22-23,* 24-28, 30-33
Nil — 29

Orkney
Sheep dirt — 2-3, 5-6, 9
Sheep droppings — 8
Sheep pertles — 7
Sheep('s) dung — 3-4, 8, 15, 17, 20
Sheep shit — 16
(Sheep('s)) pirls — *1,* 4, *7-8,* 11, 13ab, 14-*15, 17*-19
Nil — 10, 12, 21

Caithness
Currans — 11
Manure — 13
Purlies — 12a
Sheep's dirt — 2b, 5, 11
(Sheep's) droppings — 13, *16b*
(Sheep's) dung — 13-*14*
(Sheep's) pirlacks — *2a,* 12b
(Sheep's) purlags — 7-*8,* 11, 12b
Nil — 1, 3-4, 6, 9-10, 12c, 15, 16a, 17

Sutherland
Sharn — 15
(Sheep) droppings — *3,* 7, *11,* 15
(Sheep's) dung — 1, *4-5,* 8, 11, *12-13, 16*
Sheep's turds — 9ab
Nil — 2, 6, 10, 14, 17

Ross & Cromarty
Cackans — 14
Currants — 34
Dollars — 36
Dreeps — 18
Purl — 18
Purlies — 25b
Sheepie's pirlies — 25a
Sheep's dirt — 4, 33
(Sheep('s)) droppings — 8-9, 12-13, 17, *23, 27-29,* 31
(Sheep('s)) dung — *1, 5,* 16, *23, 27-29,* 31, 32ab, *39*
Turdies — 15
Turds — 25b
Nil — 2-3, 6-7, 10-11, 19-22, 24, 26, 30, 32c, 35, 37ab, 38

Inverness
Dolders — 35
(Sheep's) currants — 13a*c*
Sheep's dirt — 22
(Sheep('s)) droppings — 1, 6, 9-*10,* 12, 13*abc,* 16-17, 19 21ab, *26, 29, 31-32, 37,* 38-40
(Sheep's) dung — *1,* 2, *3, 5, 7, 13e, 23, 27,* 28, *29-30*
Turdies — 40
Turds — 13b
Nil — 4, 8, 11, 13d, 14-15, 18, 20, 24-25, 33-34, 36

Nairn
Droppings — 1c
Sheep's dung — 6
Nil — 1ab, 2-5

Moray
Drottle — 12
Manure — 14
Sheepie's tothins — 9a
Sheep('s) dirt — 8be
(Sheep's) droppin(g)s — *6b,* 7, 8c, 13, 15, *18,* 19-22
(Sheep's) dung — *4*-5, 14, *23*
Toldies — 3
Tollies — 8b
Trodlichs — 1
Trodlicks — 22
Trotlichs — 6a
Nil — 2ab, 8adf, 9b, 10-11, 16-17

Banff
Darlicks — 5
Drotlichs — 16
Drottles — 9
Sheepie's droppings — 9
(Sheep('s)) dirt — 4, *13, 17, 24, 27*
(Sheep('s)) droppin(g)s — *1,* 10, 15, *17,* 18d, 19, *23,* 32
Tallies — 12
Toddles — 5
Trodlicks — 29
Trotlags — 34
Trotlichs — 6a, 21
Trotlicks — 8, 14, 32-33
Turdie — 18d
Nil — 2abc, 3, 6b, 7, 11, 18abc, 20, 22, 25-26, 28, 30-31

Aberdeen
Beecham's pills — 27
Knapdarlochs — 71c
Pirlicks — 107
Pirlies — 60
Pushlets — 14
Pushlicks — 62
Pushlocks of hush — 28a
Puttles — 4
Puttlicks — 4
Sheep currans — 19
Sheep drottles — 34
Sheepies — 54
Sheepie's ballies — 11
Sheepie's dirt — 106
Sheepie's droppin(g)s — 63, 88
Sheepie's pirlies — 9
(Sheepie's) terdies — *47f,* 101
Sheep('s) dirt — 1, 8-11, 17, 21, 28a, 35-36, 47ae, 50-51, 56, 58, 65, 71a, 73, 81-82, 94, 105
(Sheep('s)) droppin(g)s — *3b,* 6, *9, 12,* 14, 16, 18, *21-22, 26,* 28a*c*, *29,* 31, 37, 40, *44,* 48, *59,* 69, *74,* 78, 84, *95,* 98, *104*
Sheep's drottles — 34
(Sheep('s)) dung — *5c,* 20, *34, 66, 70*
Sheep('s) muck — 2, 32, 70
Sheep's purlies — 104
(Sheep's) purls — *97,* 100
(Sheep) toldies — 10, *28a,* 101
Terrlies — 3a
Tirds — 76
Tollies — 108
Troddles — 98
Trollochs — 25, 46, 75
Trottlichs — 83
Trottlicks — 23, 53
V-gums — 14, 73
Yowies — 54
Nil — 5abd, 7, 13, 15, 24, 28b, 30, 33, 38-39, 41-43, 45, 47bcd, 49, 52, 55, 57, 61, 64, 67-68, 71b, 72, 77, 79-80, 85-87, 89-93, 96, 99, 102-103, 109

Kincardine
Currants — 24
Doldies — 24
Perlies — 14
Pirlies — 4
Sheepie's purlies — 17c
Sheep('s) dirt — 7, 11, 16, 17c, 21
(Sheep('s)) droppin(g)s — *3, 6, 8,* 13, *17b,* 20
Sheep('s) dung — 1, 5, 10, 17c, 26
(Sheep's) purlies — 12, 15, *18*-19, 22, 27-28
Nil — 2, 9, 17ad, 23, 25

Kinross
Sheep's droppins — 4
(Sheep's) purls — 1-2, *3,* 4-6, *7*

Angus
Boucht — 17a
Curlies — 17b
Pirls — 23
Sheep dirt — 35
Sheepie's perlies — 2
(Sheep's) droppings — *2,* 9, 14a, 17b
(Sheep('s)) dung — *10,* 17b, *18, 36*
(Sheep's) pirlies — *14b,* 24, 27
Sheep's porls — 14d
(Sheep's) purlies — 1, 5a*bc*, 6, 11, 13, 15, 19-20, *22,* 30
(Sheep's) purls — 5a, *7-8,* 14a, 20, *31,* 33b, *34-35,* 37
Sheep's toadles — 8
Sheep's tollies — 25
Sheep's turles — 28
Sheppie's tollies — 18
Tolies — 14acd, 27
Torrals — 13
Turtles — 17a
Nil — 3-4, 12, 16, 21, 26, 29ab, 32, 33a

Perth
Manure — 25
Perlies — 6
Perls — 41b
Pirlies — 37
(Sheep('s)) droppin(g)s — 2ab, *3,* 8, *24,* 34, *55, 57,* 66, *73*
(Sheep('s)) dung — *2a, 4, 9*-10, *24*-25, *52b, 60*
(Sheep('s)) pirls — *13,* 31, 39, *46,* 48, 64, 70
(Sheep('s)) purlies — *5,* 32, 38, *45,* 55, 69, 71
(Sheep's) purls — 1, 7, 12, *15-16,* 20, *23,* 25-28, *29ab,* 32-*33,* 40, 41a, 42-44, 49-*50,* 51a, 52acde *53,* 56, *57,* 58, *59,* 62-63, 65-*66,* 68, *71-72*
(Sheep's) tolies — 16-*17*
(Sheep) ted — *26*-27
Trintles — 67
Turlies — 73
Nil — 11, 14, 18-19, 21-22, 30, 35-36, 47, 51b, 54, 61, 74

Fife
Currants — 33
Messes — 16
Perls — 52
(Sheep's) droppin(g)s — 3, 9a, *14,* 23, 37, 54
Sheep's drops — 44e
Sheep's dung — 21
(Sheep's) pirls — *7,* 12-13, *44c, 51*
(Sheep's) purlies — *12,* 34, *37,* 44ab, 63, 64a
(Sheep's) purls — 1-2, 4-*5,* 6, *8,* 9b, *10-11, 14, 16,* 17-20, 22-23, *25-26, 27-28, 30,* 32, *33,* 34-35, 36ab, *38-39, 40ab,* 41abcd, 42, 43ab, 44*adef*, *45-46,* 47, *48,* 52-54, 55*bcdefg*, *56-57, 59,* 60-62, 64a
Taith — 64b
Ted — 17
Turds — 37
Nil — 15, 24, 29, 31, 49-50, 55a, 58

Clackmannan
Droppings — 3, 4c
Pirls — 4d
Purlies — 4b
(Sheep('s)) purls — *1-2, 4c,* 5, *6,* 7
Nil — 4a

Stirling
Dottles — 15
Manure — 23b
Nirls — 26e
Poodles — 37a
Purn — 26f
Sheep('s) dirt — 31, 41
(Sheep('s)) droppings — *4, 7f, 12,* 21a*b*, *35b,* 36
(Sheep('s)) dung — 23b*c*, *28, 31, 36*
Sheep's perls — 7a
(Sheep's) pirls — 7b*c*, 25a
(Sheep's) purlies — 2, 7b, 9, *21b*
(Sheep('s)) purls — 3, 7b*de*, 8, 10-11, 17, *18,* 19, *20,* 22ab, 25abcd, 26*acdef*, 31, 33-34, 35*ab*, 36, *37b,* 38, 39ab, 42ab
(Sheep's) tothins — 7bd, *26b*
(Sheep) troddles — 7bd, *26b*
Tradlucks — 9
Tradlucks — 9
Trintlucks — 13, 21a
Tritlucks — 30
Trunklets — 36
Nil — 1, 5-6, 14, 16, 23a, 24, 27b, 29, 40

Dunbarton
Pernurles — 10
Pirlies — 10
(Sheep('s)) droppin(g)s — 4a, *5-6, 10-11,* 14a*b*, 15, 16a
Sheep's dung — 11, 13bc, 16a
Sheep's trintlers — 13b
(Sheep) trincklets — 7abc, 9
(Sheep) turtles — 3, *7c*
Trinkles — 14a
Trintlocks — 1, 5, 13a
Nil — 2, 4b, 8, 12, 16b, 17-18

Argyll
Pirlies — 24
Sheep's dirt — 1
(Sheep('s)) droppings — 5, 7, *9-10,* 12, *15*-16, *19, 22, 27, 32, 35*
(Sheep('s)) dung — *6, 11, 14,* 17-18, *19, 22-23, 25,* 30, *33, 35, 39*
Sheep('s) manure — 2, 33
Sheep's perls — 16
Sheep's purls — 35
Turds — 30
Nil — 3-4, 8, 13, 20-21, 26, 28-29, 31, 34, 36-38, 40

Bute
Purlies — 9
Purls — 5, 9
(Sheep('s)) droppings — 1a*b*, *3-4, 7,* 8b, *9*
(Sheep('s)) dung — 2, *8a, 9*
Sheep's trintles — 1a
Tolies — 7
Trinklings — 6
Turds — 9
Nil — 1cde

Ayr
Crottles — 3
Purls — 7, 57
(Sheep) curran(t)s — 8b, *20b,* 29, *47*
Sheep dots — 21
(Sheep) dottles — 8a, 18b, 35b, *45*-46, 53a*b*, *56*
Sheep's curns — 20h
Sheep dripping — 10
(Sheep('s)) droppin(g)s — *1a,* 2a, 6, *8ab,* 14-*15, 18a,* 28af, 29

Ayr cont'd
31 38, 41, *49, 52, 53a, 57*
(Sheep('s) dung — *2b, 5, 26*b, *41 45, 53a,* 55
Sheep shit — 54
Sheep's marbles — 12b
Sheep's tardles — 48
(Sheep('s)) tartles — *9,* 20g, 30b, 32, *34,* 41
Sheep's tollies — 32
(Sheep's) trintles — 2a, 12a, 14, *17,* 18b, 20dh, *32,* 35b
Sheep's trintlets — 24b
Sheep's trotters — 29
Sheep's truntles — 24a
(Sheep('s)) turds — *12b,* 18b, *47*
(Sheep('s)) turtles — 3-4, 7, 8a, 11, *13, 15,* 20aceg, 23, *28b, 30a, 33, 35a, 36, 40,* 41-44, 46, *54*
(Sheep) tirtles — 22, *27*
Sheerans — 20b
Tollie trinkles — 37
Tritlocks — 12b
Trottles — 41
Turdles — 7, 12a
Nil — 1b, 16ab, 19, 20f, 25, 26ac, 28cde, 39, 50-51

Renfrew
Pebbles — 4d
Purlies — 5
Purls — 16a
(Sheep's) curran(t)s — *1b, 2bj,* 16a
(Sheep('s)) droppings — 2*aei*, 4d, 10, 11af, 12a*b*, 13c, 16*bc* *20a*
Sheep('s) dung — 1b, 2b, 4ac, 8, 11e, 19
Sheep's eggs — 11k
Sheep's trintlers — 11e, 14a, 15, 18a
(Sheep's) trintles — 11*c*i, 14b, 16ad, 17, 19
(Sheep's) trintlets — 11jk*l*, 21
Tartles — 4d
Tolies — 2f
Tollies — 11b
Tottles — 14b
Trentles — 10
Trinklocks — 20b
Trintlocks — 8, 13c
Turdies — 17
Nil — 1a, 2cdgh, 3, 4be, 6-7, 9, 11dgh, 13abd, 18b

Lanark
Churls — 27a
Curns — 7b
Driblets — 57c
Pirlies — 57b
Rowans — 29e
Sheep pen — 25b
(Sheep's) curran(t)s — *7a,* 29e
(Sheep's) dottles — 56, *67b*
(Sheep('s)) droppings — *1, 3,* 7a, 8b, *14d,* 15ab*c*, 23, *25c,* 26a, *29c,* 31d, 32adf, 33bc, 36-37, *38ac, 45, 46a, 49b,* 60, *67a*
(Sheep('s)) dung — *12,* 16b, *25c, 26a, 29c, 31a,* 44, *46a, 47,* 49a, *59b*
Sheep sheerin — 6
Sheep's manure — 14d
(Sheep('s)) pirls — *29f, 35c,* 40, *53,* 56
(Sheep's) purlies — 7b, 13, *19,* 27b, 29e, *35b*
(Sheep('s)) purls — *3,* 15c, *18,* 20, 32c, 35ad, 38bd, 39, 46a, 50
Sheep's tolies — 52b
(Sheep('s)) tollies — *9b,* 33d, 39, *47,* 56, *58, 62*
(Sheep's) trinklets — 5, 29d, *58*
(Sheep('s)) trintles — 7ac, *9a,* 15b, 30, 32*e*, *34,* 46bc, 61
(Sheep's) trintlets — *2,* 12
(Sheep's) trottles — *51,* 60
Sheep's trowlies — 65
Trindles — 42
Trintilicks — 30
Trintlicks — 17, 43
Trotlicks — 64ab
Truckles — 63
Turdies — 27b
Turdles — 13
Turds — 35d
Nil — 4, 8a, 10ab, 11, 14abc, 16a, 21-22, 24, 25ad, 26b, 28, 29abg, 31bc, 32b, 33a, 38e, 41, 48, 52a, 54-55, 57a, 59a, 66

West Lothian
Pirlies — 1d
Puddle — 20b
Purlies — 1c, 7, 21b
(Sheep's) droppings — *3,* 5, *13,* 15
Sheep's dung — 12
(Sheep's) pirls — 4, *9a,* 12
(Sheep('s)) purls — 1*ab*, 2-*3*, 5-6, *7,* 8, 9b, *10*-11, *13*-14, *16,* 17a, *18,* 19a*b*, 20b, 21ab, *22*
Nil — 17b, 20a

Midlothian
Manure — 11
Perlies — 8a
(Sheep) dung — 11, *23b*
(Sheep's) droppin(g)s — 7b, 8a, 15-16, 19, 31-*32*
Sheep's perls — 4
(Sheep's) pirlies — 3, *14a*
(Sheep's) pirls — 3, *14b, 24,* 27-28
Sheep's purlies — 7a, 14a
(Sheep's) purls — 1-*2,* 6b, 8b, *10,* 12a*b*, *13,* 16, *17-18,* 19-20, *21,* 23ab, 25*abcd*, 26*ab*, *29*-30, *32*
Nil — 5, 6a, 9, 22

East Lothian
Clits — 9
Dung — 15
(Sheep's) droppings — 2, 13, *16*
(Sheep's) pirls — *2*-3, 14
(Sheep('s)) purls — *1,* 4*ab*, 6ab, 7, *8,* 9, *11-13,* 15, *16-17,* 20-21
Trintles — 12
Nil — 5, 10, 18-19

Berwick
Carlins — 8
Pearlies — 8
Pirlins — 31
Purlies — 8, 12
(Sheep) droppings — *2,* 15, *16b, 17,* 26-27, *30*
(Sheep) pirls — *2,* 29
Sheep's currants — 10
Sheep('s) dung — 10, 26
Sheep shairn — 13, 32
Sheep sharn — 16a
Sheep sharrin — 20
Sheep's perls — 6
(Sheep('s)) purls — 1, 3-4, *7, 9, 11,* 14, 16c, 18, *20-21,* 22-23, *26,* 31-*32*
Skein — 27
Nil — 5, 19, 24-25, 28

Peebles
Dottles — 2, 7
Pirls — 3
Sharen — 3
(Sheep) droppings — 4b, 5, *6b,* 8, *10*
(Sheep) purls — *1,* 4b
Sheep shairn — 4a
Trotlicks — 10
Trottles — 9
Turls — 7
Nil — 4c, 6a

Selkirk
Clairt — 2d
Purls — 1, 2a, 3
Sharn — 5
(Sheep) droppin(g)s — 3, *8*
Sheep's trotters — 4
(Sheep('s)) trottle(s) — 2cde, *6*
Nil — 2b, 7

Roxburgh
Clarts — 22
Crop — 8
Dottles — 19
Sheep dung — 21f
(Sheep's) droppin(g)s — *3a,* 21ce
Sheep shairn — 2, 9a, 15b, 16
Sheep sharin — 5-6
(Sheep('s)) purls — 1-2, 4, 7-*8,* 9b, *10,* 13, *17-18,* 21d, 23-24
(Sheep('s)) trottles — 3b, *11*-12, *20,* 21*ace*, 25-26
Tricklets — 28
Trotlets — 15a
Nil — 14, 21b, 27

Dumfries
Currans — 15
Purls — 32
(Sheep) droppins — 6, *8a,* 19, *27,* 30, 31d, 45a, 46
(Sheep) muck — 40, *43*
(Sheep('s)) dottle(s) — 1a, 2, *3,* 4, 8b, 9, *10, 11-12,* 13-14, 21a*b*, *22, 31e,* 38, 41-42, 45a, 46-48
Sheep's drottles — 33
(Sheep('s)) dung — *1a, 12, 16, 19-20, 21b,* 31b
Sheep tes — 22
(Sheep) trottles — 5, 7, 15, 17ab, *18,* 23, 25-*26,* 28-*29,* 32, *35-36,* 37-38, 44, *45b,* 46, 49
Tritlicks — 39
Nil — 1b, 24, 31acf, 34

Kirkcudbright
Sheep dirt — 22
(Sheep) dottles — *1-2, 4,* 7-*10, 13,* 15ab, 16-17
Sheep pen — 18
(Sheep('s)) droppin(g)s — *5,* 12a*b*, *15b,* 17-*19,* 21ac, 24
Sheep's dung — 6
Sheep shairn — 27
Tottles — 7
Trottles — 3
Nil — 11, 14, 20, 21b, 23, 25-26

Wigtown
Dottle(s) — 5a, 10
Dung — 3
Perlies — 2
Pirl — 5a
Purl — 5a
(Sheep('s)) droppin(g)s — *5ab, 7*-11, *13,* 14-15, *16,* 17
Sheep shite — 1
Sheep's perls — 5a
Toll — 18
Nil — 4, 6, 12

Northumberland
Dirt — 82
Perlies — 10
Purls — 1a, 19a
(Sheep) cowans — *26,* 124b
Sheep dirit — 8
(Sheep) manure — 71d, *72i, 85,* 94b
Sheep perils — 9
(Sheep('s)) carlin(g)s — 6, 69g, 81, 96, 98, *109, 116,* 125, 128, 129b
(Sheep's) doddle(s) — *50,* 118b, 124b, 143
(Sheep('s)) dottles — 1ab, *2b,* 3, 6, 11, 14, 16-17, *18,* 20b, 22, 24, *26-27,* 28, 29bcdef, *33b,* 34b, 35, 37-38, 40b, *41ac,* 42, 44, *45, 48,* 49, 51, *52,* 53*a*b, 55, *56-58,* 59bcdef, 61, *62aegh, 63, 64b, 65b,* 66, 68, 69*abefgh*, *70, 71bc,* 72*ak*l, *73-74,* 75, *76,* 77, *78-79,* 81-82, *83,* 84, *85-86,* 88*ab*, *90, 92,* 95*ab*, 96-97, 102, *103bc, 104ab, 106,* 107, 108*ab*, *109-110,* 111*ab*, 114, *117,* 119, 120c, 122a, 124b, 125, 127*d*h, *130c, 132-133,* 136, *140,* 141, *142*
(Sheep('s)) droppin(g)s — 2ab, *10, 19a, 24b, 31, 41cd, 43,* 59b, 68, 69*cd*fh, *71c, 72bd, 80,* 82, *87,* 93, *99d, 103a,* 111a*b*, 112, 116, *123, 124a, 126c,* 127ac, 134
(Sheep's) dung — *28, 30, 35,* 59b, *64b, 69b, 72i*
Sheep sharn — 13
Sheep shearn — 13
(Sheep('s)) muck — 5, 12, *15, 21, 34a,* 36, *40a, 41d,* 44, 46, *48, 53a, 54,* 59c, *60,* 64a, *65a,* 71d, 72bg, *74, 83, 100, 111b, 113, 120a, 126bf, 127e, 129c, 133, 135, 137*-138, *140, 142*
Sheep stridlings — 135
Sheep's tritlicks — 57
Tridlicks — 53b
Nil — 1c, 4, 7, 19b, 20a, 23, 25, 29a, 32, 33a, 39, 41b, 47, 59a, 62bcdf, 67, 71ae, 72cefhj, 89, 91, 94a, 99abc, 101ab, 105, 108c, 115, 118a, 120b, 121, 122b, 126ade, 127bfg, 129a, 130abdef, 131, 139

Cumberland
Bratties — 25
Doddles — 55
Dottlings — 5a, 13bc
Frittlings — 13b
Parclins — 27
Partlicks — 19
Purtles — 38
(Sheep) droppings — 1b, *7,* 60
Sheep dung — 57
(Sheep) muck — *9, 11, 15a, 18,* 38, *46, 49, 53, 57-58,* 60
(Sheep) partles — *3*-4, *8,* 15abc, 16, *26*-28, *30*-31, *33,* 40, *41-42,* 43-44, *45-48, 54*-56, *59,* 61-62
Sheep partlings — 24
Sheep purdlicks — 22
Sheep purls — 9
(Sheep('s)) dottles — *1a,* 2-3, 5a, *8-9, 12,* 13*a*d, 14, *17,* 20-21, *23-24,* 25, 28-*29,* 36, *37ab, 38,* 40, *41-42,* 45, *50-54*
Sheep's purlicks — 38
(Sheep's) trun(d)lings — 56, *60,* 62, 63*ab*
Tittlings — 13c
Tottles — 32
Triddlings — 60
Nil — 5b, 6, 10, 34-35, 39

Down
Black balls — 26
Crackling — 13
Crutlins — 27
(Sheep's) droppings — *15,* 17, 23
Sheep's dung — 2a, 5, 15, 18-19, 24, 29
Sheep's pays — 22
Nil — 1, 2b, 3-4, 6-12, 14, 16, 20-21, 25, 28, 30

Tyrone
Crottles — 5
Cruttlings — 14
Drap — 1
(Sheep) droppings — 2, 8, *11*
Sheep's dung — 7
Sheep's pills — 12

Tyrone cont'd

Nil — 3-4, 6, 9-10, 13, 15-16

Antrim

Dirt — 25
Manure — 13, 31
(Sheep's) droppin(g)s — 1, 4A, 12, 22, *25*, *33*
(Sheep('s)) dung — *5a*, *15*, *17*, *19-20*, *25*-26
(Sheep's) tartles — 5ab, 9, *16b*
Nil — 2-4, 6-7, 8ab, 10-11, 14, 16ac, 18, 21, 23-24, 27-30, 32, 34

Donegal

Dottles — 2
Sheep manure — 5A
Sheep's droppings — 5A, 6, 10a, 13
Sheep's dung — 1, 5, 5A, 8, 12
Nil — 1A, 3-4, 7, 7A, 9, 10b, 11

Fermanagh

Crudlins — 2
Sheep's crotlins — 1, 5
Sheep's droppins — 4
Sheep's dung — 5
Nil — 3, 6, 7ab, 8-10

Armagh

Droppings — 6a
Sheep's dung — 4
Sheep's pills — 3
Nil — 1-2, 5, 6b

Londonderry

Droppings — 1A
Sheep's tartles — 2-3
Turtelins — 5
Nil — 1, 1B, 3A, 4, 6-7

64 PIGSTY (PQ1, 132)

Pigsty has not been mapped as it occurs nearly everywhere. Variants of SOW (**soo** very common), HOUSE and HOUSIE (**hoose, hoosie** nearly everywhere) have been subsumed.
Some of the second elements of the target items occur also in 66 **hen coop.**

Shetland

Bizzie — 21b
Grice sty — 1-10, 13-16, 18-20, 21a, 23-25, 31
Grish house — 17
(Pig)sty — *1*, 17, 22, 28, 30, 32-*33*
Nil — 11-12, 26-27, 29

Orkney

Paddy sty — 4, 8-9, 12, 15
Pig's ark — 13a
(Pig)sty — *1-5*, 7, *8-9*. 11, *13ab*, 15-*16*, 19, *20-21*
Swine's house — 17, 19
Swine sty — 2, 6
Swinsty — 13a
Nil — 10, 14, 18

Caithness

Ark — 7
Gaat's house — 12b
Mook's house — 3
Pen — 12a
Pig neuk — 7
Pig('s) house — 2b, 4-6, 8, 10-11, 14-15, 16b
Pig's housie — 15
(Pig)sty — *2ab*, 8-9, *10*, 13
Nil — 1, 12c, 16a, 17

Sutherland

Pig house — 3, 5, 9b
(Pig)sty — *1*, *3-8*, *10-13*, 16
Swine's house — 9a
Nil — 2, 14-15, 17

Ross & Cromarty

Bowan — 18-19
Pen — 33
Pig fold — 9-10
Pig fowld — 9
Piggerie — 27
Pig house — 25a, 29, 31, 34, 36
(Pig)sty — *1*, *3-6*, *8-9*, *13-14*, 16, *17*, 18-19, *20*, *22-24*, *25b*, *27-29*, *31*, *32ab*, 33, *36*, *39*
Sow's houseack — 37a
Nil — 2, 7, 11-12, 15, 21, 26, 30, 32c, 35, 37b, 38

Inverness

Piggerie — 26
Pig house — 9, 14, 20
(Pig)sty — *1-2*, 3, *4*, 5, *6-8*, *10-11*, *13abce*, 16-17, 21*ab*, *22-23*, *26-27*, 28, *29*, 30, *32-35*, 36, *37-40*
Nil — 12, 13d, 15, 18-19, 24-25, 31

Nairn

Pig house — 6
Pig ruv — 4
Pigsty — 2, 5
Nil — 1abc, 3

Moray

Cree — 9a
Criv — 21
Pigreeve — 5, 22
Pigriff — 3
(Pig) riv — 1, *4*, 6a, 8bf, 9ab, 18-19, 21
Pigrive — 8d, 16
(Pig) ruve — *3*, 14
Pig('s) house — 6b, 7, 8c, 15, 20, 23
(Pig)sty — *7*, 8*bde*
Ree — 9a
Swine's riv — 10
Nil — 2ab, 8a, 11-13, 17

Banff

Pig's house — 13, 15, 23-24
Pig's ree — 6b
(Pig's) riv — 6a, *7*-8, 12, *15-16*, 17, 18bcd, 20, *21*, 22, 25, 27-32
(Pig's) rive — *11*, 14
(Pig)sty — *1*, *2ab*, 3-*4*, *7-8*, *13*, *19*, *21*, 23, *34*
Rieve — 27
Sow's house — 33-34
Sow's riv — 34
Swine's cruive — 26
Swine('s) riv — 2c, 5, 10, 18c
Swine's ruive — 9
Nil — 18a

Aberdeen

Criv — 53
Crive — 24
Pen — 41
Piggerie — 28a, 70
Pigs('s) house — 8, 23, 47a, 54, 59, 70, 71bc, 85, 104, 107, 109
(Pig('s)) ree — 27, 51-*52*, *54*, 67, *69*, *72-73*, 77, *79*-80, 86, *97*, *99*, *100-101*, 104, *108*
(Pig's) rieve — 5b, *35*, 42, 46, 77
Pig's rin — 34
(Pig('s)) riv — 5d, 9, *11*, 14, 25, 28b, *31*, 39, 43, 47*ac*, 50-51, 53, 64, *69*, 80, 104
(Pig's) rive — *3a*, 6, 12, *15*, 24, 27, 29, 37, 40, 55, 67, 96
(Pig)sty— *2*, 6, *8*-9, *16*, *26*, *28c*, *44-45*, 47ef, *48-49*, *56*, *62*, *66-67*, *73-75*, 82-*83*, *95*, *98*, *105*-106
Riug — 10
Run — 27
(Sow's) house — *5a*, *17*, *19*, 92-93, *94*, *97*, *109*
Sow s ree — 78
Sow's reeve — 5c
Sow's riv — 17, 43, 45, 61
Sow's rive — 3b, 18, 21, 29, 36
Sty house — 107
Swine's house — 5b, 17, 71b, 75, 81
Swine's ree — 88
Swine's rieve — 5b, 22
Swine('s) riv — 9, 28a, 30, 32, 49, 65
Swine's rive — 58
Nil — 1, 4, 7, 13, 20, 33, 38, 47bd, 57, 60, 63, 68, 71a, 76, 84, 87, 89-91, 102-103

Kincardine

Cree — 22
Criv — 28
Croo — 22, 28
Cruve — 27
Cruvie — 24
Pig's crow — 26
(Pig('s) house — 1, 8-10, 19
(Pig's) ree — *5*, *7*, 17*abd*, 23
(Pig)sty — *3*, *10*, 12, *16*, *17c*, *21*
Sow's house — 6
Swine's croose — 15
Swine's house — 11, 14, 18
Swine('s) ree — 4-5, 13
Nil — 2, 20, 25

Kinross

Cravie — 2
Sow croo — 7
Sow cruive — 7
Sow('s) cray — 1-5
Nil — 6

Angus

Crave — 24
Cree — 9
Crev — 17a
Croe — 5a, 10
Crue — 1, 5b, 30, 35
Cruive — 18
(Pig's) cray — 3, *8-9*, 10-11, 13, 14ac, *15*, 20, 22-24, *26*-27, *29a*, 30, *32*, 34, *36*-37
Pigsty — 2, 4, 17a, 18, 34, 36
Sow croo — 14d
Sow('s) cray — 7, 31
Swine creve — 21
Swine('s) cray — 5c, 6, 12, 14abcd, 18-19, 25, 33a
Swine('s) crue — 28, 33b
Nil — 16, 17b, 29b

Perth

Crate — 67
Cruive — 24, 41a
Cruivie — 58, 62
Cry — 6
Pig crow — 16
Piggerie — 73
Pig house — 68, 70, 72-73
Pig's cavie — 68
(Pig's) cray — 11, 20-21, 23, 27-28, 29*ab*, 30, *33*, 37, 47-48, 51a, 52a, 54-*55*, *57*, 60, 69, *71*
(Pig('s)) cree — *1*, 3, 5, 10, 12, *18*, *26*, 37, 39
(Pig)sty — *2a*, *3-4*, *8-10*, *14-15*, *24-25*, *32*, *36*, *51b*, 52a, *57*, *71-72*, *74*
Riv — 67
Sow cravie — 66
Sow crue — 15
Sow('s) crae — 7, 13, 22, 25, 29a, 31-32, 44-46, 49-50, 52cde, 53, 56, 61-63, 65-66
(Sow('s)) cree — *17*, *26*, 39-*40*, *41ab*, *42-43*, *52b*
Sow stack — 13
Swine('s) cray — 32, 59
Swine's crue — 64
Nil — 2b, 19, 34-35, 38

Fife

Cra — 1
Cravie — 33
Craw — 18
Cray — 4, 44a, 64a
Creave — 23, 44b
Cruive — 23
Piggerie — 37, 41a
Pig house — 41a
(Pig's) crave — 1-2, 4-5, *6-7*, 8, *9a*, 11, 13, 17-18, 20, 22, *25*-26, *28*, 32, 35, 38, 41d, 42, 44d*e*, *45*, 47, 55b, 64ab
Pig's crue — 3
Pig's cruive — 27
(Pig)sty — *4*, 7, 11, *21*, *36b*, 41*ad*, *43a*, *44e*, 55e, *63*
Sowerie — 59
Sow's crafe — 44f
Sow('s) crave — 10, 14, 16, 19, 21, 29, 43a, 44af, 46, 48-49, 55f
Sow('s) cray — 36ab, 39, 40ab.

Fife cont'd

41c, 43b, 44c, 51-54, 55acdeg, 56-58, 60-62
Swine cruve — 9b
Swine('s) crave — 12, 25, 30, 33
Nil — 15, 24, 31, 41b, 50

Clackmannan

Piggerie — 4cd
Pigsty — 4c
Sookerie — 4c
Sow cray — 1-2, 4abc, 5-7
Nil — 3

Stirling

Crave — 25b
Cravie — 22a
Craw sty — 26b
Cray — 2-3, 7e, 18, 22a, 26ac, 35a
Creivie — 32
Crive — 7d
Grice sty — 26b
Pig crow — 7f
Piggerie — 7ae, 18, 26e
Pig house — 7c, 33
(Pig) pen — 22a, 25c, *26a*
Pig's crate — 9
(Pig)sty — *4, 7e, 8-9, 12-13,* 15-*16, 18,* 21a*b, 23bc,* 26bc*d, 27a, 28, 30-31, 34, 36,* 39a, *40-41,* 42a
Reed — 7b
Sookerie — 26f, 39b
Sow cray — 6, 7bd, 8, 10-11, 17-18, 20, 21b, 24, 26abdef, 35b, 36, 37ab, 42ab
Sow crive — 7b
Sow house — 22b, 25ad
Swine cray — 6
Nil — 1, 5, 14, 19, 23a, 27b, 29, 38

Dunbarton

Cruve — 14a
Cruvie — 14a
Pig cray — 5
Piggerie — 2, 6, 10, 18
Pig house — 3, 7c, 9, 16ab
Pig pen — 7c
(Pig)sty — *1,* 7bc, *10-11, 13abc,* 14a*b, 16ab*
Sow house — 6
Nil — 4ab, 7a, 8, 12, 15, 17

Argyll

Pig cray — 24
Piggerie — 11-12, 19, 30, 33-34, 37
Pig house — 7, 10, 19, 22-23, 31-33, 35, 37, 39
(Pig's) crow — 25, *29*
(Pig)sty — *1-3, 5-6,* 9-*10, 14-17, 22, 25, 27, 35*
Nil — 4, 8, 13, 18, 20-21, 26, 28, 36, 38, 40

Bute

Pig cray — 1a, 9
Piggerie — 1a
Pig house — 1c, 3, 4, 8b
Pigsty — 1acd, 2, 7, 8ab, 9
Nil — 1be, 5-6

Ayr

Pig craw — 20b
Piggerie — 4, 6, 20bc, 27, 28f, 38, 42, 57
Pig house — 1a, 2a, 3-5, 8b, 11, 14-15, 16a, 17, 18ab, 19, 20cdg, 21-22, 24b, 30ab, 33-34, 36, 40, 44-47, 51, 53a, 55
(Pig) pen — *5,* 38
(Pig) ree — *7, 20g,* 27, *28b,* 29, *42, 49, 56-57*
(Pig)sty — 2b, 3, *5, 8a, 9-10,* 12ab, *13, 15,* 16b, 21, *26bc, 28ce, 30a,* 31-32, 35ab, *36,* 41 *42-43, 45, 48, 52, 53a, 54, 56*
Runnel — 54
Sow cray — 7
Sow house — 28c
Nil — 1b, 20aefh, 23, 24a, 25, 26a, 28ad, 37, 39, 50, 53b

Renfrew

Crue — 21
Pen — 16a, 18b
Piggerie — 1a
Pig house — 11a
Pig's ree — 1b
(Pig)sty — *2abi, 4*a*cd, 5, 8,* 11cefjl, 12ab, *13c, 14a,* 16a*b, 17,* 18a, *19, 20a*
Swine ree — 21
Nil — 2cdefghj, 3, 4be, 6-7, 9-10, 11bdghik, 13abd, 14b, 15 16cd, 20b

Lanark

Crave — 30
Cravie — 46c, 59b
Cree — 30
Criv — 17
Crivvie — 33b
Cruive — 18
Midden — 6
Muck house — 32d
Piggerie — 29f, 32d, 33c, 46b
Pig house — 12, 15b, 18, 20, 23, 27b, 30, 33cd, 36, 38c, 40, 42, 46c, 47-48, 51, 57ab, 60, 62, 64ab, 65
Pig pen — 17
(Pig)sty — *1-3, 5-6, 7ac, 8*a*b, 9a, 12, 14bd,* 15abc, *16ab, 19, 22, 25bc, 26a,* 29bcf, *31ad,* 32af, *35bcd,* 36-37, *38ac, 39, 44-45, 46a,* 49a, 52b, *53,* 57b, *58, 60, 65*
Sow crave — 59a
Sow cray — 13, 29d, 50
Sow cree — 9b
Sow house — 15b, 45, 47-48, 49b, 56, 57c, 61, 63, 66, 67a
(Swine) cray — 30, 32bc, *38d*
Swine house — 29e
Nil — 4, 7b, 10ab, 11, 14ac, 21, 24, 25ad, 26b, 27a, 28, 29ag, 31bc, 32e, 33a, 34, 35a, 38be, 41, 43, 52a, 54-55, 67b

West Lothian

Crave — 1c, 14
Pen — 16
(Pig) cray — 1a, 6, 8, 9a, *12,* 19b
Piggerie — 13, 16, 17a, 21b
Pigsty — 1c, 3, 10-13, 15, 18, 20a, 22
Sow cray — 2-5, 7, 9b, 16, 19a, 20a
Sow crie — 18, 21a
Nil — 1bd, 17b, 20b

Midlothian

Cavie — 23b
Cray — 1, 3-4, 16
(Pig) cravie — 3, 8b, 12a, *21*
Pig criff — 31
Piggerie — 20
(Pig's) crave — 9, *17,* 23b, 25c, 26b
(Pig)sty — *6b,* 7a, *8a,* 10, *12a, 14a, 15-16,* 17, *18,* 19, *21-*22, 23a*b*
Ree — 7b
Sow crave — 24, 25ad, 27-30, 32
Sow cravie — 26a
(Sow) cray — *11, 12b, 13, 14ab,* 16, *31*
Sow's cruivie — 4
Nil — 2, 5, 6a, 25b

East Lothian

Cravie — 10
Cray — 15
Cree — 9
(Pig's) crave — *2*-3, 4ab, 5, 6b, *8,* 9-11, *13*-17, 20
(Pig)sty — 1, *19*
Sow crave — 6a, 7, 16, 21
Sow cry — 4a
Nil — 12, 18

Berwick

Cravie — 2-3, 6, 10, 17-18, 23, 25, 27, 31-32
Creave — 20
Cree — 20
Cruive — 17
Griand — 27
(Pig's) crave — *1, 7-8,* 17-18, 21, *26-27,* 29-*30*
(Pig)sty — 2, *12, 15, 26*
Sow crafe — 16c
Sow crave — 2-4, 7-8, 11-14, 16ab, 19, 23-24, 26-27, 30, 32
Sow criv — 31
Sow crive — 15
Sow cruive — 5, 9, 22
Nil — 28

Peebles

Cravie — 9
Pen — 6a
(Pig) crave — 1-*2*
Pig cruive — 2
Pig house — 5, 8
Pigsty — 4bc, 6ab, 8
Sow house — 10
Sow's crave — 3, 4b, 5, 6ab, 8
Nil — 4a, 7

Selkirk

Cravie — 1, 2ad, 6-7
Pig house — 4
(Pig)sty — *2ce,* 6
Sow crave — 1
Sow cravie — 3-4
Sow cray — 2b
Sow house — 8
Nil — 5

Roxburgh

Crave — 3b
Crivie — 7
Crue — 28
Cruivie — 3a, 15b, 21ad
(Pig) cravie — 1-2, *4*-5, 8, 11, 15a, 16, 19, 23-24, 26
Pig cruif — 25
Pig cruive — 15b, 17-18
Pig house — 20, 25, 28
Pigsty — 2, 13, 15b, 21af, 22, 25, 28
Puidge — 21c
Sow crave — 5-6, 9a, 12-13
Sow cravie — 8, 20, 26
Sow cri — 7
Sow criv — 9b
Sow crive — 10
Sow cruivie — 17
Sow house — 21c
Nil — 14, 21be, 27

Dumfries

Cray — 1a, 18, 32, 34
(Pig) crue — *36,* 45a, *46*
Pig house — 1a, 6-7, 8ab, 11-12, 15-16, 17ab, 19, 21b, 28, 31c, 32, 33, 39-40, 44
Pig pen — 31b
Pig ree — 13
Pigsty — 1a, 4, 9, 20, 22, 27, 31de, 32, 46
Sow cray — 4, 38
Sow house — 2-3, 10, 29
Swane house — 37
Swine cray — 5, 25, 35
Swine crew — 16, 43, 46
Swine house — 8a, 26, 34, 47
Swine ree — 31a, 33, 42
Nil — 1b, 14, 21a, 23-24, 30, 31f, 41, 45b, 48-49

Kirkcudbright

Crue — 17
Pig house — 1, 3-4, 6, 9, 11, 13, 18, 23
(Pig) ree — *5, 10, 12a, 15a,* 17, 21a*c, 22,* 24, *27*
(Pig)sty — *6-7,* 12b, 14, 16, *18-19*
Sow cray — 8
Sow house — 2, 4
Swine ree — 7
Nil — 15b, 20, 21b, 25-26

Wigtown

Piggerie — 15
Pig house — 2, 5a, 7, 11, 13-14, 16-17
(Pig) ree — *1, 5a,* 6, *9-10,* 12, 17
(Pig)sty — 1, *5a,* 10-12
Swine house — 18
Nil — 3-4, 5b, 8

Northumberland

Creer — 14
Crevie — 2ab, 10
Farrowing pen — 130d
Peg creevie — 8
(Pig) cree — 5, 14, 16-17, 20a, 22, 24ab, 25, *26-28,* 29*bc*def, *33b, 34b, 35,* 37, *38-39, 40a, 41abc, 45,* 47, *48-50,* 53ab, 56, 5*9bef,* 60-*61, 62adegh, 63, 64b, 65ab,* 68, 6*9abcegh, 71ab,* 72bdgjl, 73, 75, *76-78,* 79, *80-81, 83*-84, 86, *88ab,* 89, 91, 93, *94b, 95a, 96, 98, 99d,* 102, *103bc, 104ab, 105-107, 108ac, 110, 111ab, 112, 114, 116-117, 118b, 120c, 122ab, 124ab, 127e, 129bc, 130b, 132-133,* 134, *135-137, 140, 143*
Pig creef, 13, 15, 26, 28, 45
(Pig) creeve — 1a, *2b, 3-4, 6, 9-10,* 11, *15-18,* 19a, *20b,* 22, *34a, 122a, 124a*
Pig crey — 69d
Piggerie — 45, 59b, 69ab, 90, 126a, 130d, 131
Pig hole — 45
Pig pen — 71c, 130c
(Pig's) house — 12, 21, *83,* 104b, 111b, 138, 142
(Pig)sty — 1b, *2b, 4-5, 8, 13-14,* 28, *29d, 30-31, 35-36, 40a, 41ad, 42*-43, 46, 51-*52, 53a, 54, 56-57, 59bd, 62b, 64a, 66,* 68, *69c, 70, 71acd,* 72acdik, *82, 86-87, 88a, 89-90,* 91-92, *98, 100,* 101b, *103a, 104a, 106, 109-110, 112,* 118a, *119,* 120ab, 126*acf,* 127ad, *130e, 133, 140*
Sow crave — 29f, 71c
Swine cree — 135, 142
Swine creef — 124a
Swine house — 142
Swinerie — 59b
Nil — 1c, 7, 19b, 23, 29a, 32, 33a, 40b, 44, 55, 58, 59ac, 62cf, 67, 69f, 71e, 72efh, 74, 85, 94a, 95b, 97, 99abc, 101a, 108b, 113, 115, 121, 123, 125, 126bde, 127bcfgh, 128, 129a, 130af, 139, 141

Cumberland

Croo — 13b
Farrowing sty — 46
Pen — 56
Pig crea — 5b, 23
Piggerie — 37b
Pig hoal — 63b
Pig hol — 31
Pig house — 2

Cumberland cont'd

(Pig) hull — *1a, 2-3,* 4, *5a, 7-9, 11-12, 13d,* 14, *15abc, 16-22, 24-29, 31, 33-35,* 36, *37ab, 38-49, 51-52, 54,* 56-61, *62*
Pigsty — 1a, 3, 7, 9, 15c, 19, 24, 28, 42, 46, 50, 53, 56-58
Swine cra — 13c
Swine craw — 13a
Swine creuh — 5a
Swine hull — 30
Yard — 56
Nil — 1b, 6, 10, 32, 55, 63a

Down

(Pig) crew — *2b, 9-12,* 13-*14, 17-18,* 23, *24-27, 29*
Piggerie — 2a, 9, 15, 21
Pig house — 2a, 5, 21, 24
Pigsty — 2a, 5-6, 15, 19
Nil — 1, 3-4, 7-8, 16, 20, 22, 28, 30

Tyrone

(Pig) craw — 3, *4-5, 7, 9-10,* 11, 14, *16*
(Pig) crew — 9, *10-12,* 13-14
Pig crough — 6
Piggerie — 2, 11
Pig house — 1, 8
Pigsty — 1, 6, 11
Nil — 15

Antrim

(Pig) crew — 1-*2, 4, 5b,* 6-7, *10,* 11-12, *13, 16b, 18,* 21-*22, 25, 29*
Piggerie — 15, 20, 34
Pig house — 1, 5ab, 9, 12, 15, 17, 19-20, 26-28, 33-34
Pigsty — 1, 3, 8b, 9, 25, 28, 31
Nil — 4A, 8a, 14, 16ac, 23-24, 30, 32

Donegal

(Pig) craw — *1-2, 6, 8,* 10a*b, 12*
Piggerie — 5
Pig house — 4-5, 5A, 7A, 10a
Pig's crow — 13
Pigsty — 4-5, 12
Nil — 1A, 3, 7, 9, 11

Fermanagh

(Pig) craw — *1-2, 5,* 8, *10*
Pig crow — 6
Piggerie — 4
Pigsty — 4, 7a, 8-10
Nil — 3, 7b

Armagh

Pig craw — 6b
Pig house — 4-5, 6a
Pigsty — 3
Nil — 1-2

Londonderry

(Pig) craw — *3A, 4,* 5-*6*
(Pig) crew — 3, *7*
Piggerie — 5
Pig house — 1-2, 5
Toorie — 3
Nil — 1AB

65 THE YOUNGEST OF A BROOD (PQ1, 136)

Some of the items mapped are not very concentrated.

Shetland

Perrie een — 20
Pooster fitling — 22
Scoor da buggie — 6, 9, 15, 19, 30-31
Shakeens — 21b
Shakkins o' da pokki — 17
Shicken — 32
Water droger — 23
Nil — 1-5, 7-8, 10-14, 16, 18, 21a, 24-29, 33

Orkney

Dritie — 15
Hinmost hatched — 2
Oddity — 6
Peedie — 9
Shakin(g)s o' the poke — 15, 17
Tamas — 6
Youngest — 9, 19
Nil — 1, 3-5, 7-8, 10-12, 13ab, 14, 16, 18, 20-21

Caithness

Bairn — 12a
Chucken — 9
Coacher — 8, 11
Coojer — 15
Cosher — 3
Cottor — 14
Cotyer — 14
Couter — 7
Eeshan — 12b
Groshan — 13
Tail — 14
Tailag — 5, 7-8, 10-11, 12a, 14, 16b
Tailie — 14
Weakling — 13
Youngest chiel — 14
Nil — 1, 2ab, 4, 6, 12c, 16a, 17

Sutherland

Eeshan — 5, 14
Youngest — 13
Nil — 1-4, 6-8, 9ab, 10-12, 15-17

Ross & Cromarty

Baby — 1, 9, 26, 34
Bairn — 37b
Cheeper — 29
Coolan — 25b
Droichen — 11, 13, 31
Drone — 24
Dronie — 21, 23-24, 33
Eeshan — 3, 12, 14, 18, 32ab
Gillie frickan — 36
Goat — 7
Grechan — 12
Greeshan — 19, 28
Sharger — 7
Tor neat — 36
Youngest — 4-5, 9, 16, 18, 39
Nil — 2, 6, 8, 10, 15, 17, 20, 22, 25a, 27, 30, 32c, 35, 37a, 38

Inverness

Baby — 21a
Carneed — 15
Cheeper — 33
Chicken — 34, 39
Creenie — 31
Isean deireadh line — 26
Ishean — 9, 26
Tor neitch — 29
Youngest — 5, 22, 27, 37
Nil — 1-4, 6-8, 10-12, 13abcde, 14, 16-20, 21b, 23-25, 28, 30, 32, 35-36, 38, 40

Nairn

Carneed — 1ac, 3
Carneig — 1b
Eeshun — 1b
Nil — 2, 4-6

Moray

Brodmel — 8e
Cairnide — 8d
Carneed — 3
Chucken — 18
Crit — 22
Curneed — 6b, 12-15
Dirneed — 7
Doorneed — 8b, 9a, 10, 16, 19
Dorneed — 1, 3, 6a, 13, 17, 21
Dorneet — 22
Durneed — 7
Last of the cleckin — 20
Poot — 18
Runt — 6a
Torneach — 22
Torneecht — 23
Wrig — 22
Youngest — 4, 23
Nil — 2ab, 5, 8acf, 9b, 11

Banff

Doorneed — 15-17, 19, 21, 25, 29
Doorneedie — 2c, 17
Doorneet — 29, 33
Dorneed — 4-5, 7-9, 11, 14, 27, 30
Dorneedie — 6b, 10, 28
Dorneet — 32
Last o' the cleckin — 34
Little 'un — 13
Poot — 32
Youngest — 34
Nil — 1, 2ab, 3, 6a, 12, 18abcd, 20, 22-24, 26, 31

Aberdeen

Abblich — 31
Baby — 20, 56
Bairn — 108
Benjie — 88
Birdie — 94
Chicken — 94
Chucken — 29
Doorneed — 9, 27, 40
Dorneed — 5b, 10, 28a
Dorneedie — 23, 48, 80
Dorneight — 78
Dwiner — 107
Eppie's fleckin' — 3a
Hinmist ane — 81
Last o' the lauchter — 64
Littlest — 1
Littl'un — 5a, 46, 51, 53
Piner — 101, 104, 107
Runt — 47f
Shaggie — 31, 47e
Shakins o' the puock — 54
Shakkins o' the pyock — 69, 83
Sharger — 5c, 6, 10, 17, 19, 28a, 43, 47e, 48, 69, 73-74, 77, 99-101, 104-105, 109
Weaklin — 104
Youngest — 17, 82-83
Nil — 2, 3b, 4, 5d, 7-8, 11-16, 18, 21-22, 24-26, 28bc, 30, 32-39, 41-42, 44-45, 47abcd, 49-50, 52, 55, 57-63, 65-68, 70, 71abc, 72, 75-76, 79, 84-87, 89-93, 95-98, 102-103, 106

Kincardine

Chucken — 16
Erick — 4
Girbel — 3
Gorbel — 3
Latest hatched — 8
Litlin — 24
Sharger — 11-12, 15, 17cd, 22
Titlin — 26, 28
Young ane — 26
Nil — 1-2, 5-7, 9-10, 13-14, 17ab, 18-21, 23, 25, 27

Kinross

Cheeper — 1
End o' lachter — 6
Shakins o' the poke — 2
Weardie — 1
Nil — 3-5, 7

Angus

Bairn — 11, 18
Benjamin — 30
Cricket — 14d
Cricklet — 33b
Hatch — 17b
Kitlin — 17a
Kleckin — 17a
Piner — 33a
Rig — 9-10, 13, 14ad, 19, 21-23, 25, 31-32, 34-35
Riggie — 6, 8, 14cd, 21, 32, 34

Angus cont'd

Riglin — 37
Shakin o' the pock — 14a
Tiplin — 6
Titlin(g) — 1-2, 5abc, 7, 13, 15, 23, 27, 29a, 34, 37
Youngest — 14b
Youngest een — 18
Nil — 3-4, 12, 16, 20, 24, 26, 28, 29b, 36

Perth

Baby — 2a
Bairn — 29a
Cheeper — 40, 44
Chick — 41b
Dorneed — 67
Draidluck — 73
Dreddle — 70
Dredlock — 61, 70
Dreidlich — 66
Drich — 68
Dridlock — 71
Drochk — 37
Droich — 13, 39
Droichie — 13
Rig — 20, 23, 25, 30, 32-33, 42, 46, 48-50, 56, 58-60, 62, 65
Riggie — 26, 33, 41a, 57
Riglin — 20
Runt — 66
Scrunt — 13
Shake of the bag — 68
Shakin' o' the pockie — 33
Shott — 28
Stirk — 29a
Tail end — 51a
Titlin — 64
Voollie voorin — 17
Wee tot — 41a
Weirdie — 16
Wreckling — 26
Youngest — 4, 12, 52b
Youngest of cleckin — 52c
Nil — 1, 2b, 3, 5-11, 14-15, 18-19, 21-22, 24, 27, 29b, 31, 34-36, 38, 43, 45, 47, 51b, 52ade, 53-55, 63, 69, 72, 74

Fife

Antony — 55d
Bairn — 3
Benjamin — 3, 55d, 58
Benjie — 33
Broodie — 56
Chick — 37, 55g
Crit — 20, 23, 33-34, 55e, 61
Draidloch — 53
Last of the lachter — 16
Reg — 6
Rig — 1-2, 9a, 10-14, 21, 23, 25, 28, 34-35, 61
Riggie — 34
Runt — 23
Wairdie — 4, 37, 40a, 42, 44ef, 57, 61, 64a
Wardie — 39
Warrock — 12
Wee wairdie — 41d
Weirdie — 1, 9b, 14, 17-18, 36a, 39, 40b, 43ab, 44abc, 51, 54, 55bc, 59-60, 64a
Wuirdie — 44e
Youngest — 8
Young one — 21
Nil — 5, 7, 15, 19, 22, 24, 26-27, 29-32, 36b, 38, 41abc, 44d, 45-50, 52, 55af, 62-63, 64b

Clackmannan

Chicken — 7
Wairdie — 1-2, 4b
Weirdie — 4bcd, 5-6
Nil — 3, 4a

Stirling

Crit — 12, 31
Draidlie — 7b
Draidloch — 7a, 25b
Draidlock — 7bde, 9, 18, 21ab, 22ab, 23c, 25acd, 26acdef, 32, 37ab, 39b, 42ab
Draidlurk — 20
Draiglain — 6
Dredgelock — 35b
Dredlock — 7cf, 8, 33
Dreedlock — 7b, 17
Dridlock — 35ab
Droit — 2
Rickling — 2
Runt — 26a
Scud — 27a
Wairdie — 39b
Weakling — 35b
Weardie — 7bd
Nil — 1, 3-5, 10-11, 13-16, 19, 23ab, 24, 26b, 27b, 28-30, 34, 36, 38, 39a, 40-41

Dunbarton

Baby — 7b
Benjamin — 1
Crick — 3
Cricklet — 3
Crit — 7c, 9, 14a, 15
Draichle — 5
Dreight — 7c
Dridlock — 16b, 18
Drite — 13a
Gorbie — 7c, 9
Nil — 2, 4ab, 6, 7a, 8, 10-12, 13bc, 14b, 16a, 17

Argyll

Baby — 10, 15
Benjamin — 1
Crittling — 19
Deoran — 29
Droich — 35
Hinmost — 18
Jorran — 31, 33
Last — 15
Pock shakings — 40
Poke shakins — 31, 39
Rig — 23-24
Shot — 12, 23
Smallest — 33
Youngest — 11, 17, 22
Nil — 2-9, 13-14, 16, 20-21, 25-28, 30, 32, 34, 36-38

Bute

Chicken — 1a
Crit — 6
Dreggle — 2, 4
Poke shakings — 1d
Runt — 1a, 9
Weardie — 1a
Yunk — 1b
Nil — 1ce, 3, 5, 7, 8ab

Ayr

Baby — 43
Chick — 5-6, 27, 45
Chicken — 38
Cleckin — 10
Crecklet — 9
Crecklin — 9
Crick — 52
Cricklet — 2a, 3-4, 11, 20b
Crit — 18b
Crittle — 21
Crittlick — 41
Crowl — 20h, 53a
Cruilt — 30b
Crult — 12a, 17, 24b, 33, 35b
Himnest ane — 15
Last — 49
Last of the cleckin — 43, 47
Last of the litter — 56-57
Nestling — 28e
Pallie — 50
Piglet — 42
Poke shakins — 8b, 35b, 41, 48
Rig — 28af, 50-52, 53b, 54
Runt — 29, 48, 53b
Shakings — 56
Shakings o' the bag — 57
Shakins o' the pock — 8a
Shakins o' the poke — 20h, 36, 57
Weest yin — 34
Wee yin — 34
Nil — 1ab, 2b, 7, 12b, 13-14, 16ab, 18a, 19, 20acdefg, 22-23, 24a, 25, 26abc, 28bcd, 30a, 31-32, 35a, 37, 39-40, 44, 46, 55

Renfrew

Birdie — 20b
Chick — 2b, 5
Chicken — 2i
Cricklet — 17, 18b
Croul — 16a
Doreneed — 21
Draidlet — 11e
Droichen — 4d
Ewe lamb — 14b
Rant — 11j
Runt — 6, 11ij
Wallie draigle — 2h
Weakling — 10
Youngest — 2a, 8, 11ef
Nil — 1ab, 2cdefgj, 3, 4abce, 7, 9, 11abcdghkl, 12ab, 13abcd, 14a, 15, 16bcd, 18a, 19, 20a

Lanark

Chick — 18
Cricklet — 9b
Crike o' the cleekin — 9b
Crit — 15b, 17, 24, 27b, 29df, 32f, 34, 35a, 38acd, 39-40, 44-45, 47-48, 49b, 50-51, 52b, 53, 56, 57ab, 58, 59ab, 60-63, 64ab, 66, 67a
Crowl — 2, 27b
Last o' the poke — 20
Leavings — 32d
Rickling — 15c
Runt — 11
Shakins o' the poke — 42, 46c
Sharger — 11
Triplet — 27a
Wean — 16a, 30
Wee runt — 7c
Wee yin — 29e
Youngest — 16b, 25c, 29c, 35d
Younk — 25b
Nil — 1, 3-6, 7ab, 8ab, 9a, 10ab, 12-13, 14abcd, 15a, 19, 21-23, 25ad, 26ab, 28, 29abg, 31abcd, 32abce, 33abcd, 35bc, 36-37, 38be, 41, 43, 46ab, 49a, 52a, 54-55, 57c, 65, 67b

West Lothian

Cheaper — 1c
Crit — 1a, 7-8, 10, 12, 16, 19b, 20a
Draidlock — 1b, 2-3, 7, 11
Draiggle — 8
Draiglock — 3
Dridlet — 21b
Piner — 1a
Shakins o' the poke — 3
Squab — 17a
Timmins o' the poke — 3
Youngest — 6, 11
Nil — 1d, 4-5, 9ab, 13-15, 17b, 18, 19a, 20b, 21a, 22

Midlothian

Chicken — 1
Crit — 4, 9-11, 12ab, 14ab, 17-21, 23b, 24, 25ac, 26a, 27, 29, 31-32
Crite — 23b
Cruit — 23a, 30
Douterie — 23b
Gorb — 23b
Poke shakins — 7b
Runt — 7b, 10 12a, 25c
Youngest — 8a
Nil — 2-3, 5, 6ab, 7a, 8b, 13, 15-16, 22, 25bd, 26b, 28

East Lothian

Bairn — 1
Cheeper — 2
Crait — 16
Crit — 2, 5, 6ab, 7-11, 13-15, 17, 20-21
Runt — 9
Vraiglie — 4a
Young yin — 1
Youngest — 4b
Nil — 3, 12, 18-19

Berwick

Chick — 23
Crate — 12, 15, 23
Creet — 32
Cret — 32
Crit — 2-4, 6-8, 10, 13, 16ab, 18, 20, 23-24, 26, 29, 31
Cruit — 9, 11, 17, 21-22
Kid — 27
Lafie — 27
Nil — 1, 5, 14, 16c, 19, 25, 28, 30

Peebles

Baby — 8
Craitur — 2
Crit — 1-3, 4ab, 5, 6a, 7, 10
Nil — 4c, 6b, 9

Selkirk

Benjie — 2a
Crit — 2de, 4
Cruit — 1, 2b, 6-8
Nil — 2c, 3, 5

Roxburgh

Crait — 5, 10, 13
Crit — 1, 4, 7-8, 9a, 11, 19, 21c, 22-23, 25
Cruait — 13
Cruit — 2, 3a, 4, 8, 9b, 10, 16-17, 21abcd, 24, 26
Pock shakings — 28
Youngest — 21abc, 25
Nil — 3b, 6, 12, 14, 15ab, 18, 20, 21ef, 27

Dumfries

Babby — 46
Baby — 42, 46
Cleckin — 3
Cralt — 1a
Crit — 8a, 16, 28
Cruit — 26, 29
Crutlock — 32
Hin en — 17b
Last — 17b
Last hatched o' the cleckin — 12
Last yin o' the poke — 4
Midget — 13
Pallie — 43
Pawlie — 5
Piner — 46
Poke shakings — 11, 36
Ricklin — 19, 32
Rigglin(g) — 27, 34, 49
Runt — 27
Shakins o' the poke — 43
Wallie draigle — 2
Weakling — 42
Wean — 46
Wrecklin(g) — 35, 37-40, 45a, 46
Youngest — 4, 29, 32, 34-35, 37-38, 40, 45a, 49
Young yin — 17a
Nil — 1b, 6-7, 8b, 9-10, 14-15, 18, 20, 21ab, 22-25, 30, 31abcdef, 33, 41, 44, 45b, 47-48

Kirkcudbright

Chick — 18
Chicken — 21c
Clecken — 12b

Kirkcudbright cont'd

Crickilan — 24
Flo'er o' the flock — 1
Gorlin — 17
Pallie lamb — 4
Quiverfu' — 1
Ricklin(g) — 7, 12a, 15a, 21a, 22-23, 27
Riddling — 7
Rigglin — 18
Shilpit — 4
Shott — 27
Youngest — 7, 15a, 22-23
Nil — 2-3, 5-6, 8-11, 13-14, 15b, 16, 19-20, 21b, 25-26

Wigtown

Rig — 2, 5a, 6, 9-14, 17
Rig pig — 5b
Shot — 5a
Nil — 1, 3-4, 7-8, 15-16, 18

Northumberland

Babby — 77, 81, 83, 101b
Baby — 64b
Bairn — 46, 83, 103c
Cheeper — 58, 69ab
Chick — 59b, 72i, 111a
Chicken — 59b
Chickling — 59b
Chuck — 59b
Creet — 2b, 3, 7, 10-13, 15-16, 19a, 20ab, 39
Crit — 2a, 9-10, 16-18, 23, 24ab, 26, 28, 29cdef, 31, 33b, 35, 38-39, 40ab, 41abc, 46, 48, 59a, 59e, 61, 62ag, 63, 64b, 65a, 66, 69abd, 71b, 102, 130d
Crowl — 83
Crut — 1b, 14, 20a, 21, 25, 27, 30, 34ab, 36-37, 39, 42, 44-45, 49-52, 53ab, 55-57, 59cdf, 60, 63, 68, 71d, 73, 75-76, 79, 97, 122a, 124ab
Fledgling — 69ab
Kitlin(g) — 14, 17, 40b, 88b
Last oot e th' shell — 111b
Leveret — 112
Littlest — 101b, 130c
Nestling — 69ab
Poke shakin(g)s — 17, 29f, 79
Ricklin(g) — 73, 77, 115, 124a
Rigglin — 69a
Runster — 110
Runt — 1b, 57, 59d, 122b, 126e, 130d
Scrut — 56
Shakin of the poke — 122b
Shot — 77
Squeaker — 61
Weastrel — 102
Wreakling — 100
Wrecklin(g) — 47, 59d, 62c, 65b, 69f, 72dj, 74, 76, 79-81, 86-87, 88a, 89-90, 94b, 97-98, 99d, 100, 102, 103abc, 104a, 107, 108abc, 110, 114, 117, 118b, 120a, 122ab, 124b, 129bc, 130d, 132-135, 137-138, 142-143
Wrecknel — 124a
Wrig — 62f
Wrinklin(g) — 69a, 95a
Youngest — 30
Young un — 64a, 69b, 72i, 95b, 99d
Nil — 1ac, 4-6, 8, 19b, 22, 29ab, 32, 33a, 41d, 43, 54, 59a, 62bdeh, 64a, 67, 69cegh, 70, 71ace, 72abcefghkl, 78, 82, 84-85, 91-93, 94a, 96, 99abc, 101a, 104b, 105-106, 109, 113, 116, 118a, 119, 120bc, 121, 123, 125, 126abcdf, 127abcdefgh, 128, 129a, 130abef, 131, 136, 139-141

Cumberland

Chick — 50
Chicken — 16
Gorling — 39
Last un — 56
Little un — 4
Poke shakkins — 37a
Runt — 22
Suckling — 51
Weed — 2
Wrecklin(g) — 2, 4, 5a, 7-11, 13d, 14, 15b, 17, 19-20, 24-26, 28, 31, 33, 35, 37ab, 38-42, 45-46, 48-49, 51-52, 56-57, 59-61, 63b
Youngest — 57
Nil — 1ab, 3, 5b, 6, 12, 13abc, 15ac, 18, 21, 23, 27, 29-30, 32, 34, 36, 43-44, 47, 53-55, 58, 62, 63a

Down

Chick — 2a
Crowl — 5, 11-12
Dwarie — 22
Georie — 27
Gyurrie — 18
Kitlin — 25
Rig — 15, 24
Runt — 13, 24, 28
Squeller — 11
Youngest — 15
Nil — 1, 2b, 3-4, 6-10, 14, 16-17, 19-21, 23, 26, 29-30

Tyrone

Ba lamb — 13
Cappie — 12
Croil — 14
Dirrib — 5
Drawlye — 2, 7
Drolling — 1
Poke shakings — 5
Weaklin — 1
Nil — 3-4, 6, 8-11, 15-16

Antrim

Chick — 21
Crowl — 8b, 12-13, 15, 16b, 17, 19-20, 22, 28-30
Dorbie — 16b
Dortie — 5b
Hen — 31
Jorie — 1-2, 4, 5a, 6, 8a, 11
Poke shakin(g)s — 16b, 19
Wee yin — 25
Youngest of a brood — 25
Young yin — 15
Nil — 3, 4A, 7, 9-10, 14, 16ac, 18, 23-24, 26-27, 32-34

Donegal

Bag shake — 13
Drolie — 7A
Droylie — 4-5, 7-8, 13
Runt — 10a
Scaldie — 10a
Shakings o' the poke — 6
Skeeden — 10a
Nil — 1, 1A, 2-3, 5A, 9, 10b, 11-12

Fermanagh

Croil — 8
Droit — 1
Nil — 2-6, 7ab, 9-10

Armagh

Coppie — 4
Nil — 1-3, 5, 6ab

Londonderry

Doncie — 6
Dorbie — 6
Droic — 6
Droich — 3, 5
Drough — 1, 3
Droylie — 4
Duncie — 1A
Growlie — 5
Joree — 3
Nil — 1B, 2, 3A, 7

66 HEN COOP (not just the 'run') (PQ1, 140)

Hen coop has not been mapped as it occurs everywhere except in Shetland.

The variants of HOUSE, HOUSIE (**hoose, hoosie** in most cases: for distribution cf. forms with 'oo' in map 14 (cow), Appendix A) have been subsumed.

Some elements of target items also occur in 64 **pigsty.**

Shetland

Hennie house — 15-16
Hen run — 33
Hen's bauk — 12
Hen('s) house — 1-2, 4-8, 10-11 14 17, 20, 21a, 24-25, 27, 30-32
Ruist — 26
Nil — 3, 9, 13, 18-19, 21b, 22-23, 28-29

Orkney

Chicken house — 15
(Hen) coop — *7-8,* 15, 19, *21*
Hennie house — 6, 11-12, 13a, 16
Hen('s) house — 2, 4, 9, 20-21
Hen's peund — 5
Peerie hen housie — 7
Nil — 1, 3, 10, 13b, 14, 17-18

Caithness

Back — 12b
Chicken's house — 9
(Hen) coop — 8, *10,* 13-14, *16b*
Hen house — 2ab, 5, 12a, 16a
Nil — 1, 3-4, 6-7, 11, 12c, 15, 17

Sutherland

(Hen) coop — *6,* 8, *9b,* 11, *12-13*
Hen house — 1, 3, 5, 7, 10, 16
Hen's box — 9a
Nil — 2, 4, 14-15, 17

Ross & Cromarty

(Hen) coop — *1, 4,* 6, *8*-9, *13-14,* 17-18 *20* 22-23, *25b,* 27-29, *30-31,* 32ab, 34, *39*
Hen house — 3, 12, 14, 16, 19, 26, 33, 37b
Henus — 24
Nil — 2, 5, 7, 10-11, 15, 21, 25a, 32c, 35-36, 37a, 38

Inverness

Hen box — 32
(Hen) coop — 2, *4-8, 10-11,* 13*bce,* 16-17, 20, 21ab, 22-23, 26-28, *29-30,* 32-33, *34, 38-39*
(Hen) house — *3, 13a, 26, 32, 35-38,* 40
Nil — 1, 9, 12, 13d, 14-15, 18-19, 24-25, 31

Nairn

Coop and run — 2
Hen coop — 6
Hen house — 5
Nil — 1abc, 3-4

Moray

Cavie — 9a
Chicken coop — 7
Chicken house — 22
Coopie — 9a
Criv — 6a
Crivvie — 1
Hen box — 20
(Hen) coop — 5, 6b, *7,* 8d, 14, 18, 20, 22-*23*
Hen house — 4, 8bc, 10, 15, 21, 23
Hennin — 8d
Hen pen — 21
Hutch — 2a
Riv — 9a
Nil — 2b, 3, 8aef, 9b, 11-13, 16-17, 19

Banff

Chicken coop — 15
Chicken housie — 32
Chucken house — 10
Coopie — 4, 27
Crieve — 6b
Criv — 18b
(Hen) coop — *1,* 2b, 5, *8*-9, *17,* 18c, *19, 21,* 23, *25,* 27
Hen house — 2a, 6b, 16, 18c, 24, 28-30; 33-34
(Hen) riv — 5, *15*
Ree — 14
Nil — 2c, 3, 6a, 7, 11-13, 18ad, 20, 22, 26, 31

Aberdeen

Cavie — 25, 47b
Chicken coop — 14, 107
Choocken coop — 8
Chooken housie — 8
Chucken box — 47d
Chucken coop — 10, 17, 19, 80, 101
Chucken house — 81
Coopie — 23, 47b, 59, 61-62, 71c, 74, 77
Criv — 28b, 47a, 71b
(Hen) coop — 2, 3b, 4, *5c,* 6, 12, *15,* 20, *26, 28ac,* 31, *35,* 44, *46,* 50-51, 54, 59-60, 65, *66,* 67, 69-70, 71b, 73, *75,* 82, *83,* 84-85, 88, *94-95,* 98, 100, *104-105,* 106-108
Hennerie — 37
Hen ree — 93, 95, 105
Hen riv — 104
Hen('s) house — 1, 3a, 7, 15, 21-22, 26-27, 32, 45, 47aef, 48-49, 53, 56, 84, 99, 103, 106-107
Little hen house — 29
Quern — 24
Reive — 5b
Nil — 5ad, 9, 11, 13, 16, 18, 30, 33-34, 36, 38-43, 47c, 52, 55, 57-58, 63-64, 68, 71a, 72, 76, 78-79, 86-87, 89-92, 96-97, 102, 109

Kincardine

(Hen) coop — *1, 6,* 10-11, *14,* 15, *16,* 17b*cd,* 19, 21, 24, 26-28
Hen house — 3, 6, 8, 12, 17c
Henness — 7

Kincardine cont'd

Hen ree – 2
Nil – 4-5, 9, 13, 17a, 18, 20, 22-23, 25

Kinross

Cavie – 1
(Hen) coop – 1, *3-4*
(Hen) crib – *2*-3, *5,* 7
Nil – 6

Angus

Cavie – 17a
(Hen) coop – *1-3, 6*-7, *9*-10, *12,* 14b, 15, *17b,* 18, 22, 24, *26, 31-32,* 34, *35-36*
(Hen) crib – 7, 13, 14acd, 20-*21,* 23, *33b*
Hennis – 5c, 29a
Hen('s) house – 8, 12, 17b, 19, 25, 28, 33b
Pen – 4
Roostin portion – 33b
Nil – 5ab, 11, 16, 27, 29b, 30, 33a, 37

Perth

Brooder – 26
Chicken coop – 16
Crib – 20, 23, 29b, 31, 33, 49, 60, 65
(Hen) cavie – 25, 39, 52c, *66, 68,* 70-71
(Hen) coop – *2a, 4-5,* 7-10, 12, 15-16, *24-25,* 26-28, *32, 46,* 48, 50, 52*be*, *57, 62, 67-68,* 71, *72,* 73-74
Hen cray – 62
Hen house – 29a, 33, 36, 40, 41a, 51a, 59
(Hen) pen – 8, *25, 41b, 43*
Nil – 1, 2b, 3, 6, 11, 13-14, 17-19, 21-22, 30, 34-35, 37-38, 42, 44-45, 47, 51b, 52ad, 53-56, 58, 61, 63-64, 69

Fife

Ark – 24, 37
Cavie – 36a, 39, 51
Chicken coop – 43b
(Hen) coop – 7, *11, 14,* 16, *21,* 23-*24, 28, 36b, 41a,* 53, *55a, 62, 64a*
Hen house – 9a, 11, 13, 19-20, 25, 32, 38, 40b, 41bc, 42, 47, 55e, 57-58, 61, 63
Hen kip – 17
(Hen) pen – 36a, 37, *57*
(Hen('s)) crib – *1*-2, *4,* 8, 10, 12, 18, 20, 27, 30, 33, 35, 39, 40b, 41bd, 42, 43a, 44bef, *45,* 46-47, 51, *55cdefg, 56, 58-59,* 60, 64b
Nil – 3, 5-6, 9b, 15, 22, 26, 29, 31, 34, 44acd, 48-50, 52, 54, 55b

Clackmannan

Ark – 4c
(Hen) cavie – *4c,* 5
(Hen) coop – *6*-7
Hen house – 3, 4cd
Nil – 1-2, 4ab

Stirling

Bawk – 8
Brooder – 12
Cavie coop – 7bd
(Hen) cavie – 1, 3, 6, 7e, *8,* 10, *11,* 12, 17, *18,* 19, *20,* 21b, *22b, 23bc,* 25abd, 26acde, 27a, 28, 31, 34, 35b, 36, 37*ab,* 39b, 42a
(Hen) coop – *7c, 13,* 21a, 22a, *23b,* 25c, *26b, 31, 35a*
Hen cray – 27ab
Hen crib – 7f
Hen cry – 12
Hen house – 4, 7e, 12, 16, 21b, 22b, 25c, 33, 38, 39a, 41
(Hen) kivvie – *7a,* 32
Hen run – 17
Night ark – 12
Nil – 2, 5, 9, 14-15, 23a, 24, 26f, 29-30, 40, 42b

Dunbarton

Cavie – 9, 13a, 14a, 18
Clechin box – 5
(Hen) coop – 3, *6, 7bc,* 10-*11,* 13a, *14b*
(Hen) cray – 1, *7a, 9, 16b*
Hen house – 1, 10, 13bc, 16ab, 17-18
Hen run – 15
Nil – 2, 4ab, 8, 12

Argyll

Cavie – 26, 35
(Hen) coop – 1, 3, 5, *6,* 7, *9,* 10, *11-12, 14,* 15, *16,* 17, 19, *21,* 22, *23, 26*-27, 30, 32-*33,* 35, 38-*39*
Hen cot – 33
Hen house – 2, 16, 25, 30
Pen – 35
Rearing fold – 24
Nil – 4, 8, 13, 18, 20, 28-29, 31, 34, 36-37, 40

Bute

Cavie – 8ab
(Hen) coop – 1acd, 5
Hen house – 2, 7, 8ab
Nil – 1be, 3-4, 6, 9

Ayr

(Hen) cavie – 6, 8ab, 14, 19, 20c, 28f, 30b, 41, 43-44, *47,* 49-51, 54, 57
(Hen) coop – 2b, 3-4, *5,* 6, *10,* 12a, 13, 16b, *24b,* 28cf, 30ab, *31-32,* 33, *34, 35ab, 36, 45, 48-49, 52,* 53a, 54-56
(Hen) cray – *12b,* 18b, 20b*gh, 21, 24a,* 26b, *29,* 38, *43*
Hen house – 2a, 9, 15, 18a, 25, 26b, 36-38, 42, 56-57
(Hen) ree – 18b, 28d*e*
Hen run – 5
Nil – 1ab, 7, 11, 16a, 17, 20adef, 22-23, 26ac, 27, 28ab, 39-40, 46, 53b

Renfrew

Ark – 19
Brooder – 4d
Cavie – 16ad, 17, 20b, 21
Crive – 21
(Hen) coop – 2b*h, 4ac,* 5, *8,* 11ef*l,* 13c, 18b, *19, 20a*
(Hen) cray – *11i,* 13c, *16c, 17*
(Hen) house – 2a, *7-8, 11acj,* 15, 16*bd,* 18a, *20a*
Nil – 1ab, 2cdefgj, 3, 4be, 6, 9-10, 11bdghk, 12ab, 13abd, 14ab

Lanark

Ark – 27b
Chicken cavie – 6
Chicken coop – 58
Cray – 1
(Hen) cavie – *6,* 8b, 9b, 10a, *11,* 15bc, 17, 19-*20,* 24, 25c, 29deg, *30,* 31bd, 32d, 33bcd, 35d, 36, 38abcd, 39, 42, 46c, 47, 49b, *51,* 56, 59*a*b, 60, 62-63, 66
(Hen) coop – *1-3,* 5, *7a, 12,* 15b*c, 25c, 26a, 29cf,* 32af, 35a, *39-40, 44,* 46*a*b, *47,* 49a, *52b, 53,* 58, 65
Hen house – 1, 7ac, 8a, 9a, 13, 14abd, 15a, 16ab, 18, 22, 25b, 29cf, 30, 35bcd, 45, 46a, 64b
(Hen) run – *6,* 32f
Hopper – 37
Hutch – 13
Pen – 29b, 30, 32f, 45
Nil – 4, 7b, 10b, 14c, 21, 23, 25ad, 26b, 27a, 28, 29a, 31ac, 32bce, 33a, 34, 38e, 41, 43, 48, 50, 52a, 54-55, 57abc, 61, 64a, 67ab

West Lothian

Brooder – 14
Coopie – 19b
(Hen) cavie – 1acd, 6-8, 9a*b*, 14, 16, 17a, 21b
(Hen) coop – 1c, *2-3,* 5, 11-12, 15, *22*
Hen house – 3, 10, 13, 18, 21a
Hen roost – 18
Pen – 4
Nil – 1b, 17b, 19a, 20ab

Midlothian

(Hen) cavie – *1, 3,* 7b, 9, 11, 12ab, 13, *14b,* 15, 17-*18, 20,* 21-22, *23b,* 24, 25a, 26a, 27, 29-32
(Hen) coop – *6b, 8a,* 10, 12a, 14b, *15*-16, *18*-19, 21
Hen house – 7a, 18, 23ab, 25bc, 28
Hen kivie – 25a
Hen ree – 14a
Hutch – 25c
Nil – 2, 4-5, 6a, 8b, 25d, 26b

East Lothian

Ark – 13
(Hen) cavie – 2-3, 4b, 6a, 8-16, *17,* 19-20, *21*
(Hen) coop – 1, *7,* 15-*16*
Hen house – 5, 6b
Nil – 4a, 18

Berwick

Chicken coop – 25
Gwien – 27
(Hen) cavie – 1, 3-7, *8,* 9-15, 16abc, 17-18, 20-23, *24, 26*-27, 30-32
(Hen) coop – 2, 12, 15, *16b, 25, 31-32*
Hen house – 16c, 29
Nil – 19, 28

Peebles

Chicken cavie – 6a
(Hen) cavie – 1, 3, 4b, 5, 7, *9*-10
(Hen) coop – 2, 4b, 5, 6a*b, 8*
Hen house – 4b, 6a, 8
Nil – 4ac

Selkirk

Chicken coop – 8
(Hen) cavie – 1, 2abde, 3, *4,* 5, 7-*8*
Hen coop – 2c, 8
Nil – 6

Roxburgh

Bird coop – 22
(Hen) cavie – 1-2, 3ab, 4-8, 9ab, 10, *12*-13, 15ab, 16-*17,* 18-20, 21acdf, 23-26, 28
(Hen) coop – *8,* 20, *21a, 25*
Hen house – 28
Nil – 11, 14, 21be, 27

Dumfries

Chicken coop – 37
Coovie – 37, 46
(Hen) cavie – 3, 6-7, 9, 11-*12,* 14-15, 18, 25-29, 31d, *32,* 34-*35,* 38-39, 42, 45a
(Hen) coop – *1a 5,* 8ab, *12*-13, 16, 17ab, 19-*20,* 21b, *22, 24,* 32-*33, 40, 45a, 46*
Hen house – 2, 4, 47
Hutch – 42
Nil – 1b, 10, 21a, 23, 30, 31abcef, 36, 41, 43-44, 45b, 48-49

Kirkcudbright

Cavie – 15a, 17, 21c, 22, 26
Crue – 17
(Hen) coop – 2-3, *4,* 5, *6-7,* 10, 12b, 14, 16, 18-*19,* 21abc, *22*-23, 27
(Hen) house – *1,* 18
Nil – 8-9, 11, 12a, 13, 15b, 20, 24-25

Wigtown

(Hen) coop – 1, *5a, 11,* 13-14, 16-17
Hen house – 2, 7
Nil – 3-4, 5b, 6, 8-10, 12, 15, 18

Northumberland

Cavie – 22, 29f, 75
Cawel – 71c
Chicken coop – 21, 45
Creeve – 17
(Hen) coop – *1a,* 2a*b, 5-6,* 8-9, 11-12, *13-14,* 16, 18, 19a, *20b,* 26, 28, *30-31,* 34b *35-36, 38*-39, 42, 52, *53a,* 54, 59b, *61, 62b, 65a,* 68, 77-78, 82, *89, 106-107, 109, 112,* 120a*b*, *127c, 133, 137, 143*
Hen cote – 71c
Hen cray – 103a
(Hen) cree – 17, 24a*b*, 29*bcd*, 30, *35,* 39, *40ab, 41abd, 43*-44, 46, *48-50,* 51, *53ab,* 56, *57,* 58, 59ab*cdef, 60, 62acegh, 63,* 64ab, *65b,* 66-67, 69*abdef*gh, *70,* 71abd, 72*abcdefghijkl, 76*-77, 79, *80,* 81-86, 88ab, *89-93,* 94b, *95ab, 96-98, 99bd, 100,* 101a*b*, *103bc, 104b, 105, 108ac, 109-110, 111ab, 112,* 113, *114-117,* 118a*b*, *119, 120c, 122ab,* 123, *124ab, 125,* 126acdef, *127abcdefgh, 128, 129bc, 130abcdef, 131, 138-139,* 141, *142-143*
(Hen) creer – 102, *104a, 132*
(Hen) house – *1b,* 7, *12, 23, 29b, 40b, 45, 48, 57,* 59b, 69*abcfg, 71c, 72d, 82-83, 87, 103b, 104ab, 109, 111ab, 116, 126b, 132, 135, 142-143*
Hen loft – 114
Hennerie – 59b
Hen pen – 69ab, 71a, 87, 95a, 115, 122a
Hen rick – 41c
(Hen) roost – 69a, *114*
Hutch – 73
Whemmle – 134
Nil – 1c, 3-4, 10, 15, 19b, 20a, 25, 27, 29ae, 32, 33ab, 34a, 37, 47, 55, 62df, 71e, 74, 94a, 99ac, 108b, 121, 129a, 136, 140

Cumberland

Ark – 56
Chicken coop – 7, 57
Clocker box – 29
(Hen) coop – *2-4, 5a, 9, 12, 13c, 14, 15a,* 16, *24-25,* 31, *38, 40, 42, 49,* 56, *59, 62*
Hen cote – 57
Hen cree – 22
Hen house – 9, 23, 37b, 47, 58
(Hen) hull – 4, *7, 11, 15b, 19-20,*

Cumberland cont'd

24, 26, 30, *33, 37b, 41-43, 45-48,* 50, *52-54,* 55-56, *57-58, 60*
Hen pen — 15c, 53, 56
Nil — 1ab, 5b, 6, 8, 10, 13abd, 17-18, 21, 27-28, 32, 34-36, 37a, 39, 44, 51, 61, 63ab

Down

Cavie — 13
Hen coop — 2a, 5, 15, 17-18, 24
Hen house — 1, 19, 24, 26-27, 29
Hen hutch — 22
Nil — 2b, 3-4, 6-12, 14, 16, 20-21, 23, 25, 28, 30

Tyrone

Ark — 5
Hen coop — 1, 7, 10-11
Hen house — 1, 10, 12-13, 15-16
Nil — 2-4, 6, 8-9, 14

Antrim

(Bird) ark — 18, 20, 29, *33*-34
Hen coop — 13, 22, 31
Hen house — 1-2, 7, 9, 17, 25-26, 28-30
Henis — 5b
Roost — 16b, 25
Nil — 3-4, 4A, 5a, 6, 8ab, 10-12, 14-15, 16ac, 19, 21, 23-24, 27, 32

Donegal

Ark — 5
Hen coop — 1, 5A
Hen craw — 2, 10b, 12-13
Hen creel — 6, 10a
Hen house — 4, 5A, 7A, 13
Nil — 1A, 3, 7-9, 11

Fermanagh

Hen coop — 4, 9
Hen house — 2, 8
Nil — 1, 3, 5-6, 7ab, 10

Armagh

Pen (crate) — *1,* 4, 6a
Nil — 2-3, 5, 6b

Londonderry

Hen house — 3, 3A, 4, 7
Hen run — 2
Nil — 1, 1AB, 5-6

67 GIZZARD (of a fowl) (PQ1, 141)

Gizzard has not been mapped as it occurs fairly densely all over the area except in Shetland and parts of Aberdeenshire.

Shetland

Croopie — 14
Cropie — 10
Croppie — 24
Djuzerin — 15
Geuzereen — 1, 3, 19, 21a, 30
Gizereen — 5, 16
Gizzard — 20, 22, 25
Gizzen — 27
Gooshard — 21a
Guzereen — 2, 4, 6-9, 21b, 26, 30-33
Guzzarn — 17
Queerins — 11
Nil — 12-13, 18, 23, 28-29

Orkney

Geuzereen — 1, 16
Gizzard — 1, 5, 7-9, 11, 13ab, 15-17, 20-21
Gizzran — 15
Gizzring — 5
Goozerin — 4, 6
Grind — 17
Guzreen — 2
Quern — 18-19
Stench — 21
Whern — 17
Nil — 3, 10, 12, 14

Caithness

Cabie — 2a, 5
Croban — 16b
Crop — 12b, 15, 17
Gishren — 7
Gizzard — 2b, 8, 10-11, 13-14, 16b
Gizzerine — 8
Gizzrin — 9
Quern — 6
Scroban — 5, 11, 13
Wazzin — 12a
Nil — 1, 3-4, 12c, 16a

Sutherland

Cabban — 6
Cabie — 9a
Caiban — 2, 4
Crop — 14
Gizzard — 1, 3, 5-8, 9b, 11-13, 16
Scroban — 5, 8, 10, 15
Nil — 17

Ross & Cromarty

Crop — 6-7, 34
Geezerin — 12
Giblet — 15, 23, 26
Gizzard — 1, 3-4, 8-9, 13-14, 16-18, 22, 24, 25b, 26-30 32ab, 36, 39
Gurrie — 31
Keepan — 3
Kyeopie — 24
Mill — 26
Scroban — 32b
Thraple — 37a
Nil — 2, 5, 10-11, 19-21, 25a, 32c, 33, 35, 37b, 38

Inverness

Crop — 22, 25- 26, 35, 38
Giblet — 27, 30
Gizzard — 1-6, 8-11, 13ace, 16-17, 21ab, 23, 27-29, 32-34, 36-37, 39-40
Scroopan — 9
Nil — 7, 12, 13bd, 14-15, 18-20, 24, 31

Nairn

Crop — 2
Curan — 1a
Gizzard — 2, 5-6
Nil — 1bc, 3-4

Moray

Blue bag — 8c
Ciaban — 22
Crap — 3, 9b
Curin — 1, 6a, 20-21
Girzen — 3
Gizzard — 3, 5, 6b, 7, 8cd, 14, 23
Gizzen — 8b, 9a, 10, 19
Gizzivin — 15
Gizzrin — 4, 6b
Queerin — 20
Quern — 7, 8b, 22
Seed bag — 8c
Thrapple — 18
Nil — 2ab, 8aef, 11-13, 16-17

Banff

Cannel fir — 6b
Ceopan — 34
Coupan — 33
Crap — 18b, 28
Curin — 2c, 4, 6a, 9-10, 14, 16 18c, 19, 21-22, 30-31
Gizzard — 1, 8, 13, 15, 18c, 23, 25
Gizzen — 2a, 3, 5, 8
Queerin — 15, 27
Queern — 23, 26
Querin — 24, 32
Quern — 29
Quirin — 12
Throat — 20
Weezin — 6b
Wizzen — 2a, 6b
Nil — 2b, 7, 11, 18ad

Aberdeen

Crap — 16, 47f, 49
Crop — 36, 68
Cuern — 23, 51, 78
Curin — 9, 14, 22, 24-25, 48, 85
Gizzard — 26, 56, 60, 66, 104-105
Gizzen — 49
Keerin — 9
Miller — 53
Mizzen — 93
Mullart — 53
Purse — 108
Quairn — 12
Queerin — 2, 5d, 6, 8-9, 11, 14, 17, 19, 21, 27, 28c, 35, 39-40, 42, 44, 47ce, 50, 52, 54, 62, 64-65, 72, 82, 85-87, 94, 96, 98-100, 105
Queern — 3ab, 4, 5ab, 19-20, 28ab, 29-30, 32-34, 37, 43, 45, 51, 55, 61, 69, 71bc, 75, 79-81, 83-84, 88, 95, 97, 104, 107-109
Queernin — 47a
Querin — 15, 26, 47d, 59
Quern — 29, 31, 41, 46, 47b, 57-58, 60, 63, 67-68, 71a, 73-74, 76-78, 89, 101, 103-104
Quirin — 12
Quirn — 10, 70, 83, 106
Thrapple — 20, 47f
Nil — 1, 5c, 7, 13, 18, 38, 90-92, 102

Kincardine

Crap — 15, 22
Crop — 3
Gizzard — 6, 8, 17c, 19, 21, 24, 26-28
Queerin — 1-2, 7, 9-11, 13, 17abd, 18, 24
Queern — 3-5, 12, 23, 28
Quern — 6, 16, 17c
Thrapple — 14, 26
Nil — 20, 25

Kinross

Crop — 5
Gaibie — 3
Gebbie — 4
Gizzard — 1-2
Thrapple — 7
Nil — 6

Angus

Crap — 4, 5ac, 14abcd, 17b, 24, 34, 37
Crop — 9
Cuzzen — 17a
Gibbie — 6
Giblets — 13
Gizzard — 1-2, 8-10, 17b, 22, 25, 28,34-36
Goose horn — 7
Guts — 18
Innards — 18
Pudding — 18
Queern — 19, 31
Stomach — 33b
Thrapple — 26
Nil — 3, 5b, 11-12, 15-16, 20-21, 23, 27, 29ab, 30, 32, 33a

Perth

Chuckie bag — 65
Crap — 13, 37, 52d, 53, 65-66
Crop — 6-8, 12, 41b, 48-49, 64
Gabie — 20
Gebbie — 1, 55-56
Gibbie — 18, 20, 26, 32, 39, 42
Gibbot — 67
Gizzard — 2a, 4-5, 9-10, 15, 17, 25, 27-28, 32-33, 36, 41a, 50 52be, 57, 60, 65, 67-68, 71-72, 74
Gizzen — 52c
Grinder — 25
Mill — 16
Millie — 62
Queerin — 31
Queern — 39, 43
Scroban — 36
Stam(m)ach — 52c
Stomach — 73
Thrapple — 21, 29ab, 30, 46, 53, 58
Trapple — 40
Nil — 2b, 3, 11, 14, 19, 22-24, 34-35, 38, 44-45, 47, 51ab, 52a,

Perth cont'd

54, 59, 61, 63, 69-70

Fife

Chuckie bag — 44a
Crap — 7, 22, 24, 35, 36a, 44e, 46-47, 51, 55dg, 57
Crappen — 61
Crop — 2, 30, 35, 42, 44e, 53, 55b, 59
Gabie — 8, 10, 12, 31, 40b, 43a, 44a, 46
Gaw — 20
Gebbie — 41a, 51, 53-54
Geese horn — 16
Gillet — 49
Gizzard — 1, 4, 9a, 11, 13-14, 19, 21, 23, 25, 28, 36b, 37, 39, 44e, 47, 55e, 56-57, 62-63
Gizzen — 55e
Gizzie — 33
Mill — 1
Thrapple — 9a, 32-33, 39, 58
Thraps — 49
Wazzen — 12
Nil — 3, 5-6, 9b, 15, 17-18, 26-27, 29, 34, 38, 40a, 41bcd, 43b, 44bcdf, 45, 48, 50, 52, 55acf, 60, 64ab

Clackmannan

Crap bag — 4d
Crop — 4c
Gebbie — 4b
Gizzard — 7
Grebbie — 4d
Nil — 1-3, 4a, 5-6

Stirling

Chuckie bag — 27b
Crap — 7b, 8, 18, 25d, 30, 35a
Crappin — 27a
Crop — 7d, 9, 11, 14-15, 25bcd, 26c, 27a, 34, 35b, 37b
Gabie — 23c
Gebbie — 7cf, 15, 17, 21a, 23c, 39b
Geebie — 33
Gishorn — 25a, 26e
Gizzard — 4, 7e, 8, 17-18, 21ab, 26ad, 28, 31, 34, 36, 42a
Gizzen — 26f
Reistle — 23b
Thrapple — 7bd, 12, 17, 20, 26b, 31-32, 39a
Wise horn — 2
Nil — 1, 3, 5-6, 7a, 10, 13, 16, 19, 22ab, 23a, 24, 29, 37a, 38, 40-41, 42b

Dunbarton

Crap — 2, 5, 14a, 16a
Crappin — 14a
Crop — 4b, 6, 7a, 14b
Gebbie — 6, 9
Gizzard — 1, 3, 7bc, 10-11, 13bc
Gullet — 18
Peuchan — 4b
Thrapple — 16b
Nil — 4a, 8, 12, 13a, 15, 17

Argyll

Crap — 35
Crop — 2, 14, 35, 39
Geesron — 32
Giblets — 36
Gizzard — 1, 5-7, 10, 12, 15-17, 19, 22-25, 27, 30, 34-35, 37-39
Muscular stomach — 33
Sandbag — 2
Scroban — 9, 13, 30
Scrope — 11
Stomach — 33
Nil — 3-4, 8, 18, 20-21, 26, 28-29, 31, 40

Bute

Crop — 1ac, 5, 7, 8a
Gizzard — 1ad, 2-3, 7, 8b
Scrob — 9
Scroban — 9
Nil — 1be, 4, 6

Ayr

Crap — 2ab, 5, 7, 8b, 14, 17, 20ade, 30a, 36, 39, 41, 57
Crape — 27
Crapin — 28b, 33
Crappin(g) — 8a, 23, 36, 39, 41, 43, 51, 55-56
Craw — 57
Crop — 2ab, 8b, 30b, 57
Gebbie — 9, 19
Giblets — 1b, 20g, 28a
Gisset — 2a
Gizzard — 2a, 3-4, 6, 8a, 10, 12a, 13, 16b, 20b, 21, 26b, 28cf, 30a, 31-34, 35ab, 42, 44-45, 48-49, 52, 53a, 54, 57
Gizzen — 3, 12b, 20c, 37
Gizzer — 28d
Guzzorn — 19
Maw — 5, 7, 29, 54
Thrapple — 15, 18b, 20gh, 24ab, 25, 28a, 46, 53b
Wizzen — 11, 38
Nil — 1a, 16a, 18a, 20f, 22, 26ac, 28e, 40, 47, 50

Renfrew

Crap — 4d, 11b, 15, 17, 21
Craw — 21
Crop — 9, 11j
Gizzan — 11a
Gizzandie bag — 11e
Gizzard — 2bhi, 4ac, 5, 11efl, 12a, 13c, 16b, 18a, 20a
Gullet — 2j
Neck — 16a
Thrapple — 2ahi, 8, 10, 11k, 19, 20b
Throat — 2a, 16a
Win pipe — 16d
Nil — 1ab, 2cdefg, 3, 4be, 6-7, 11cdghi, 12b, 13abd, 14ab, 16c, 18b

Lanark

Bag — 33cd
Chuckie bag — 46c
Crap — 14a, 15c, 17, 23, 30, 49a, 62
Crapin — 47, 64a
Crappin — 9b, 51, 56, 57b, 58, 60-61, 67b
Craw — 35a
Croop — 15c
Crop — 1, 13, 14a, 15ac, 20, 29g, 30, 32adf, 38c, 45, 54, 59a, 64a
Food basket — 18
Fowl muscular stomach — 37
Gabbie — 15a
Gebbie — 20
Gibbie — 38d
Giblets — 27a
Gisset — 39
Gizzard — 2-3, 5-6, 7ac, 9a, 12, 14bd, 16b, 25c, 27b, 29cdef, 31a, 35abd, 40, 46a, 49b, 52b, 53, 64b
Gizzen — 10a, 42
Gizzern — 65
Gullet — 25bc, 31d, 44
Pluck — 52a
Thrapple — 8b, 15c, 16b, 22, 32df, 33bc, 38a, 39, 46b, 52b
Throat — 37
Nil — 4, 7b, 8a, 10b, 11, 14c, 15b, 16a, 19, 21, 24, 25ad, 26ab, 28, 29ab, 31bc, 32bce, 33a, 34, 35c, 36, 38be, 41, 43, 48, 50, 55, 57ac, 59b, 63, 66, 67a

West Lothian

Crap — 9b, 16, 20a
Crop — 1a, 5-6, 8, 12, 16
Croppin — 21a
Gebbie — 1b, 15
Giblet — 9a
Gisshorn — 7
Gizzard — 1a, 2-3, 5, 7-8, 10, 20a, 21b
Gritbag — 11
Gullet — 17a
Queern — 11
Thrapple — 4, 13, 17a, 19b
Nil — 1cd, 14, 17b, 18, 19a, 20b, 22

Midlothian

Chuckie bag — 14a
Crap — 7a, 14ab, 16, 20, 23b, 26a
Crappin — 30, 32
Crop — 11, 16, 18, 31
Gebbie — 13, 18
Gizzard — 1, 8a, 10, 12a, 15, 18, 21, 23ab, 24, 25c
Goinder — 12a
Gullet — 26b
Neck — 19
Thrapple — 6b, 9, 25d
Nil — 2-5, 6a, 7b, 8b, 12b, 17, 22, 25ab, 27-29

East Lothian

Crap — 2, 7-8, 12
Crop — 5, 6b, 8, 13
Gebbie — 2
Gizzard — 1, 7, 9, 15-17, 19-20
Gizzern — 9, 14
Thrapple — 4ab, 6a, 13, 21
Nil — 3, 10-11, 18

Berwick

Crap — 10, 12, 21
Crapin — 7, 26
Crappin — 8, 13, 27, 30
Crop — 23, 26, 29
Geezer — 9
Giblet — 16b
Gizzard — 1-2, 9, 12, 15, 29, 31-32
Wizer — 8
Nil — 3-6, 11, 14, 16ac, 17-20, 22, 24-25, 28

Peebles

Crap — 1
Crappin — 5
Crop — 5, 7-8
Gizzard — 2-3, 4b, 6ab
Muscular stomach — 6a
Queerin — 2
Thrapple — 4b
Nil — 4ac, 9-10

Selkirk

Crappin — 2a
Gizzard — 2d, 4, 8
Thropple — 2b
Nil — 1, 2ce, 3, 5-7

Roxburgh

Crap — 3b, 8, 13
Crappin — 16
Crop — 13, 15b
Cropine — 21d
Cropping — 21f, 28
Croup — 15b
Gizzard — 1-2, 4, 9a, 10, 17, 21af, 25, 28
Guizern — 17, 26
Guzner — 21c
Thrapple — 3a
Nil — 5-7, 9b, 11-12, 14, 15a, 18-20, 21be, 22-24, 27

Dumfries

Crap — 2, 31d
Crapin — 2, 8a
Crappin — 3, 5, 7, 8b, 13, 22, 24, 31b, 35-36, 42
Croop — 45a
Crop — 31c, 43, 46, 49
Croppin — 18, 35
Giblet — 33, 42
Gizzard — 1a, 4, 6, 12, 15-16, 17ab, 21b, 26-29, 31d, 33, 37, 40, 43, 47
Gizzern — 10-11, 22, 39, 46
Purse — 19
Scriffen — 4
Thrapple — 42, 44
Nil — 1b, 9, 14, 20, 21a, 23, 25, 30, 31aef, 32, 34, 38, 41, 45b, 48

Kirkcudbright

Crap — 1, 15a
Crapin — 2
Crappin — 1, 4, 8-9, 12b, 17, 19
Gizzard — 2-3, 6-7, 10, 18, 22-23
Gizzen — 5
Purse — 15a
Scrobban — 27
Watch — 8
Nil — 11, 12a, 13-14, 15b, 16, 20, 21abc, 24-26

Wigtown

Chuckie bag — 7
Crap — 6, 14
Crapin — 10
Crappin — 16-17
Gizzard — 5a, 11, 13
Gizzerin — 17
Gussar — 2
Maw — 12
Wizzern — 5b, 6
Nil — 1, 3-4, 8-9, 15, 18

Northumberland

Croop — 46
Crop — 2b, 8, 13-15, 19a, 22, 24a, 25, 29bd, 40a, 41b, 50, 53b, 57, 62g, 63, 65ab, 69abd, 71d, 74-76, 86, 90, 99d, 106, 108c, 111ab, 124b, 126b, 127de, 129c, 130d, 135, 137
Giblet — 49, 69d, 118b
Gissern — 25
Gizzard — 1a, 2a, 5-6, 13, 16-18, 20b, 21, 30-31, 34b, 35-38, 41cd, 42-43, 48, 52, 53a, 54, 56-57, 59b, 61, 62b, 64ab, 66, 69ac, 70, 71acd, 72cdg, 77-79, 83, 87, 88ab, 89, 94b, 95b, 98, 100, 101b, 103bc, 104a, 107, 109-110, 112, 117, 119, 120bc, 124b, 126cf, 127a, 130bde, 132-133, 135, 138, 140, 143
Gizzen — 131
Gizzern — 20a, 59b, 102, 107, 124a
Gizzren — 60, 73, 77, 140
Grit bag — 79
Gullet — 59b, 72b, 92, 125
Gyser — 71c
Jaade — 95a
Neck — 69c
Thropple — 29b, 62eh, 72i, 84, 103a, 127h, 130c, 134
Weezin — 56
Wisan — 29f
Wizand — 17
Nil — 1bc, 3-4, 7, 9-12, 19b, 23, 24b, 26-28, 29ace, 32, 33ab, 34a, 39, 40b, 41a, 44-45, 47, 51, 55, 58, 59acdef, 62acdf, 67-68, 69efgh, 71be, 72aefhjkl, 80-82, 85, 91, 93, 94a, 96-97, 99abc, 101a, 104b, 105, 108ab, 113-116, 118a,

Northumberland cont'd

120a, 121, 122ab, 123, 126ade, 127bcfg, 128, 129ab, 130af, 136, 139, 141-142

Cumberland

Crop — 15b, 22, 29, 37ab, 48
Fou — 61
Giblet — 47
Gizzard — 1a, 3-4, 9, 12, 13c, 14, 15ac, 23-26, 28, 30-31, 38, 40, 42, 46-50, 53-54, 56-60, 62
Gizzerin(g) — 28, 40, 53
Gizzern — 5ab, 7, 13a, 15a, 30, 46
Gizzin — 30
Keckle box — 56
Thropple — 41
Wesend — 56
Wezen — 56
Nil — 1b, 2, 6, 8, 10-11, 13bd, 16-21, 27, 32-36, 39, 43-45, 51-52, 55, 63ab

Down

Crappen — 15, 25
Gizzard — 2a, 3, 5-6, 9-10, 13-15, 17-19, 24, 26-29
Nil — 1, 2b, 4, 7-8, 11-12, 16, 20-23, 30

Tyrone

Crapen — 5
Craw — 16
Gizzard — 1, 4, 7-8, 10-11
Nil — 2-3, 6, 9, 12-15

Antrim

Crap — 25
Crapen — 7
Crappen — 22, 28, 31, 34
Fowl stomach — 33
Gizzard — 1, 9, 11, 13, 15, 16b, 17-21, 25-26, 29
Thrappen — 22
Nil — 2-4, 4A, 5ab, 6, 8ab, 10, 12, 14, 16ac, 23-24, 27, 30, 32

Donegal

Gizzard — 1, 5, 5A, 8, 12
San bag — 4
Scribben — 2
Slipper — 6
Wozan — 1
Nil — 1A, 3, 7, 7A, 9, 10ab, 11, 13

Fermanagh

Gizzard — 4-5, 7a, 8-9
Nil — 1-3, 6, 7b, 10

Armagh

Gizzard — 1-2, 4
Nil — 3, 5, 6ab

Londonderry

Crap — 3
Crappin — 3, 3A, 6
Craw — 3
Gizzard — 2, 3A
Grit bag — 1A
Nil — 1, 1B, 4-5, 7

68 FOWL DUNG (PQ1, 142)

Some of the items mapped are not very concentrated. See also note (1) on 60 **cow dung.**

Shetland

Hen pen — 11
Hens' dirt — 2, 17, 20, 21b, 22, 28, 30-33
Hens' droppins — 2
Hens' muck — 1, 3, 17, 22, 27, 30
(Hens') scottin(g)s — *6-7,* 8-9. *10, 15*
Hens' skeet — 18
Scoot(s) — 4-5, 14, 16, 19, 21a, 23-25
Nil — 12-13, 26, 29

Orkney

Fowl droppings — 8
Fowl dung — 1, 8
Hen dirt — 2-7, 9, 11, 14-16, 18-19
Hen dung — 3, 5, 13ab, 15, 17
Hen pen — 13a
Hen pin — 4
Nil — 10, 12, 20-21

Caithness

Hen's dirt — 2b, 5, 9, 11, 13, 17
(Hens') droppings — 7-*8,* 12a, 13, 16b
Hens' dung — 14
Nil — 1, 2a, 3-4, 6, 10, 12bc, 15, 16a

Sutherland

(Fowl) dung — 1, *5-6, 12*
Hen dung — 9b, 13, 16
Hens' dirt — 9a
(Hen(s')) droppings — *3,* 7-*8,* 10, *15*
Hens' sharn — 5
Poultry manure — 11
Nil — 2, 4, 14, 17

Ross & Cromarty

(Fowl) dung — *1, 8,* 16, *18,* 32b
Hen manure — 25b, 29
Hen pen — 25b
Hens' dirt — 4, 25a
(Hen(s')) droppings — 9-10, 13, 21-22, 27, 31, 32ab, 34, *36, 39*
Hen(s') dung — 3, 5, 19, 24, 29, 36
Hens' mess — 39
Poultry dung — 23
Poultry manure — 26
Nil — 2, 6-7, 11-12, 14-15, 17, 20, 28, 30, 32c, 33, 35, 37ab, 38

Inverness

(Fowl) droppings — *1,* 3, 6, 12, 13ab, 14, 17, 19, 21a, 28-29 32-33, 37, 39
Fowl dung — 2-3, 5-6, 27, 30
(Hen) manure — *22-23, 32,* 35-*36*
Hen pen — 22, 37
Hens' dirt — 9, 15
Hen(s') droppings — 8, 13c, 21b, 26, 38
Hens' dung — 7, 13e
Hens' mess — 16, 38
Poultry manure — 10
Nil — 4, 11, 13d, 18, 20, 24-25, 31, 34, 40

Nairn

Dropings — 2
Hen dung — 6
Nil — 1abc, 3-5

Moray

Dung — 5
Guana — 19
Hen dung — 6b, 21
Hen pen — 6a, 8bd, 16-17, 19-22
Hens' curneesh — 7
Hen(s') dirt — 2a, 15
(Hens') droppin(g)s — *4, 7,* 16, 18
Manure — 14
Skite — 9a
Skitters — 9a
Nil — 1, 2b, 3, 8acef, 9b, 10-13, 23

Banff

Carneesh — 30
Fowl dung — 1
(Hen) droppin(g)s — 1, 5, 9, 17, 18d, *19,* 21, 23
Hen(s') dirt — 4, 6b, 15, 17, 27, 32, 34
Hen(s') dung — 7, 16, 23
Hen(s') pen — 3, 8, 10, 14-15, 18c, 20, 24-25, 29, 31, 33-34
Keech — 28
Nil — 2bc, 6a, 11-12, 18ab, 22, 26

Aberdeen

Chucken dirt — 17
Dirt — 20
Heneretta — 87
Hen hoose muck — 71b
Hen pane — 89
Hen pen — 3ab, 5d, 10, 14-17, 20, 23-24, 27, 28c, 31, 36, 39, 41, 44, 46, 47bcef, 48-49, 51-53, 58-59, 62, 65, 70, 71c, 72, 75-77, 80, 83-84, 87-88, 96-97. 99-100, 104, 107
Hens' carneesh — 28a
Hen(s') dirt — 1, 4, 6, 8, 11, 19, 21, 23, 28a, 32, 34, 36, 51, 53, 62, 65-66, 69, 71ab, 73-74, 82-83, 85, 92, 97, 101, 103, 105, 108
(Hens') droppin(g)s — *15,* 21, 24, 26, 29, 32, 40, 47d, 59-*60, 67*
Hen(s') dung — 45, 56, 65, 67, 81-82, 95, 98, 106
Hens' litter — 104
(Hen(s')) muck — *2, 3a, 5c, 8, 10, 12, 18, 22,* 25, *29, 35, 37, 44-45, 47af,* 50, *54, 61, 70, 80-81, 86, 94,* 104
Nil — 5ab, 7, 13, 28b, 30, 33, 38, 42-43, 55, 57, 63-64, 68, 78-79, 90-91, 93, 102, 109

Kincardine

(Hen) droppin(g)s — *3, 8,* 20, 24
Hen manure — 15
Hen pen — 3-4, 6-7, 10-11, 13-15, 17b, 22-23, 26-27
Hen(s') dirt — 9-12, 16, 17c, 21, 26, 28
Hen(s') dung — 1, 5, 15, 17bc, 19, 28
Hen shit — 10
Muck — 23
Nil — 2, 17ad, 18, 25

Kinross

Hen dirt — 7
Hen pen — 1-7

Angus

Curlies — 17b
Hen manure — 17b
Hen muck — 10
Hen pen — 3-4, 5bc, 6-8, 11, 13, 14a, 17ab, 19-20, 22, 24, 31, 33b, 34, 37
Hen(s') dirt — 1, 5a, 14abcd, 25, 35-36
(Hens') droppins — 2, 12, *14cd,* 18, 27, 30, 32, 33a, 34, 36
Hen(s') dung — 1, 9-10, 17a, 22, 24, 28
Nil — 15-16, 21, 23, 26, 29ab

Perth

Fowl dung — 4, 52b
Hen dung — 5, 7, 28
Hen manure — 57
Hen pen — 2a, 12, 15, 18, 20-21, 23-25, 27-28, 29ab, 30-33, 37-40, 41a, 42, 44-46, 48-50, 51a, 52ce, 53, 55-57, 59-74
Hens' dirt — 1, 16
(Hen(s')) droppin(g)s — 2a, *3,* 8-10, 12, *24,* 41b, 47, 52ac, 58
Nil — 2b, 6, 11, 13-14, 17, 19, 22, 26, 34-36, 43, 51b, 52d, 54

Fife

Droppin(g)s — 37, 43b, 44b, 45
Hen pin — 3
Hen(s') pen — 1-2, 4-8, 9ab, 10-14, 16-35, 36ab, 37-39, 40ab, 41abcd, 42, 43a, 44acdef, 46-48, 51-54, 55bcdeg, 56-63, 64ab
Nil — 15, 49-50, 55af

Clackmannan

(Hen) pen — *1-3,* 4abcd, *5-7*

Stirling

Droppings — 37a
Fowl dung — 23b
Hen pen — 1-4, 6, 7abcdef, 8-20, 21ab, 22ab, 23c, 24, 25abcd,

Stirling cont'd
26abcdef, 27ab, 28-34, 35ab, 36, 37ab, 38, 39ab, 40-41, 42ab
Manure — 23b
Nil — 5, 23a

Dunbarton
Droppings — 4a
Hen pen — 1-3, 4ab, 5-6, 7abc, 9-11, 13abc, 14ab, 15, 16ab, 17-18
Poultry manure — 7c
Nil — 8, 12

Argyll
(Fowl) droppings — 1, 5, 30, *35*
(Fowl) dung — *6, 14,* 17, *33*
Fowl manure — 33
Hen manure — 2, 34
Hen pen — 7, 12-13, 15, 18-19, 21, 23, 25, 27, 31, 35, 40
Hen(s') droppings — 9, 16, 22
Hen(s') dung — 10, 22, 39
Midden — 24
Nil — 3-4, 8, 11, 20, 26, 28-29, 32, 36-38

Bute
Dung — 1a
Hen pen — 1abcde, 2-7, 8ab, 9

Ayr
Hen caw — 23
Hen droppins — 47
Hen dung — 55
Hen manure — 57
(Hen) pen — *1ab, 2ab, 3-7, 8ab, 9-11, 12ab, 13-15, 16ab, 17, 18ab, 19, 20abcdefgh, 21-23, 24ab, 25, 26abc, 27, 28abcf, 29, 30ab, 31-32,* 33, *34, 35ab, 36-37,* 38, *39-45,* 46, *47-52, 53ab, 54, 56-57*
Nil — 28de

Renfrew
Fowl dung — 2a, 11e
Hen dirt — 2j
(Hen) pen — *1ab, 2bfghi, 3, 4acd, 5, 7-10, 11abcfijkl,* 12a, *13ac, 14b, 15, 16abcd, 17, 18,* 19, *20ab, 21*
Nil — 2cde, 4be, 6, 11dgh, 12b, 13bd, 14a, 18b

Lanark
Droppings — 6, 15b, 32a, 35a
(Fowl) dung — 25bc, *49a*
Guana — 6
Hen dung — 59b
(Hen) pen — *1-3,* 5, *7abc, 8b, 9ab, 10a, 12-13, 14abd, 15abc, 16b, 17-24, 25a,* 26a, *27ab, 28, 29cdefg, 30, 31abcd, 32acdef, 33abcd, 34, 35abd, 36-37, 38abcde, 39-41,* 42, *44-45, 46abc, 47-48, 49b, 50-51, 52ab, 53-56, 57abc, 58, 59ab, 60-63, 64ab, 65-66, 67ab*
Moashie — 33a
Nil — 4, 8a, 10b, 11, 14c, 16a, 25d, 26b, 29ab, 32b, 35c, 43

West Lothian
Droppings — 11
Hen manure — 1c
Hen pen — 1abcd, 2-8, 9a, 10-16, 17a, 18, 19b, 20ab, 21ab, 22
Pigeon droppins — 15
Nil — 9b, 17b, 19a

Midlothian
Droppings — 6a, 10
Fowl dung — 8a
Hen pen — 1, 3-4, 6b, 7a, 8b, 9-11, 12ab, 13, 14ab, 15-21, 23ab, 24, 25abc, 26ab, 27-32
Hens' dirt — 7a
Nil — 2, 5, 7b, 22, 25d

East Lothian
Droppings — 2
Hen pen — 1-3, 4ab, 5, 6ab, 7-17, 19-21
Nil — 18

Berwick
Fowl manure — 26
Hen pen — 1-15, 16abc, 17-27, 29-32
Nil — 28

Peebles
Cock hen pen — 9
Droppings — 3
Hen pen — 1-3, 4bc, 5, 6ab, 7-10
Nil — 4a

Selkirk
Droppings — 2c, 3
Hen pen — 1, 2abde, 3-6, 8
Nil — 7

Roxburgh
Droppings — 21e
Hen pen — 1-2, 3ab, 4-5, 7-8, 9ab, 10-14, 15ab, 16-20, 21acdef, 23-26, 28
Nil — 6, 21b, 22, 27

Dumfries
Droppin(g)s — 42, 45a
Hen muck — 18, 43, 46
(Hen) pen — *1ab, 2-7, 8ab, 9-16, 17ab, 19-20, 21ab, 22, 24-30,* 31abcdef, *32-33, 35-44, 45a, 46-49*
Nil — 23, 34, 45b

Kirkcudbright
(Hen) droppins — 3, 5, *21c*
Hen pen — 1-4, 6-11, 12ab, 13-14, 15a, 16-19, 21ab, 22-27
Nil — 15b, 20

Wigtown
Hen dirt — 7, 16
(Hen) droppings — 5ab, *14*-15
Hen dung — 2
Hen manure — 13
Hen pen — 2, 6-8, 10-12, 17
Hen shite — 1
Nil — 3-4, 9, 18

Northumberland
Coke — 29c
Dort — 111b, 130e
Dottles — 9
Excreta — 69b
Fowl dirt — 52
(Fowl) droppin(g)s — 2b, 5, 14, 16, 20b, 22, 28, 29b, 39, 47, 49, 57, 59bc, 60-61, 62g, 69abd, 71d, 72b, 79, 82, *83,* 84, 87, 88ab, 93, 94b, 95ab, 99d, 101b, 104a, *106,* 107, 108a, *110,* 114, 125, 126*cf*, 127d, 128, 129b, 134, 143
Fowl dung — 30, 35, 52, 71c, 83
(Fowl) manure — 45, *52,* 71d
(Fowl) muck — 5, 12, 36, 41a, 46, *54,* 56, 71d, 102, 104a, 124b, 126a, 130*ef*, 138
Hen dirt — 41c, 64b
Hen dort — 71a
Hen manure — 68, 72bd, 117
Hen pennins — 28
Hen(s') dropping(s) — 58, 63, 72ad, 76, 103bc, 112
Hens' dung — 120c
(Hen(s')) muck — 10, 13, 15, 26, 40a, 41c, 42-44, 48, 50, 53ab, 55, 59c, 60, 62aeh, 64b, 65a, 68, 69acf, 70, 71ab, 72bg, 74, 77-78, 89-92, 98, 100 103b, 104b, 106, 109, 111ab, 118b, 120ab, 126b, 127a, 129bc, 132-133, 135-137, 139-140, 142
(Hen(s')) pen — *1abc, 2a, 3, 6-11, 13, 17-18, 19a, 21-23,* 24ab, *25-27, 29abef, 31, 33b, 34b, 36-39, 40a, 41cd, 45, 51, 58,* 59*bcdef, 60, 68, 71c, 75, 77, 82, 86, 106, 122a,* 124ab, *130c*
Lime — 130e
Pigeon dung — 59b
Pigeon muck — 111b
Poultry droppings — 40b
Nil — 4, 19b, 20a, 29d, 32, 33a, 34a, 37, 41b, 59a, 62bcdf, 64a, 65b, 66-67, 69egh, 71e, 72cefhijkl, 73, 80-81, 85, 94a, 96-97, 99abc, 101a, 103a, 105, 108bc, 113, 115-116, 118a, 119, 121, 122b, 123, 126de, 127bcefgh, 129a, 130abd, 131, 141

Cumberland
Bird droppings — 22
Doddles — 63b
(Fowl) droppin(g)s — 3-4, 13c, 14, 15b, 19, 24-25, 28, 40, 43, 46, 50, 52, 56, 58, *60,* 61-62
Fowl dung — 4, 9
Hen dirt — 42
Hen droppings — 6-7, 17, 57
(Hen) muck — *3, 8-9, 12, 15ac, 16, 18, 20-21, 23, 26, 29-31, 33,* 37ab, *38, 40, 42-46, 48-49, 52-53, 55,* 56, *57, 59,* 62, *63b*
Hen pen — 2, 8, 13ab
Manure — 51, 54
Shit — 56
Turd — 5a
Nil — 1ab, 5b, 10-11, 13d, 27, 32, 34-36, 39, 41, 47, 63a

Down
(Fowl) droppings — 3-*5,* 14-*15,* 17, 21, 23
Fowl dung — 2a, 15, 19, 24, 29
(Fowl) manure — 2a, *5*
Hen dung — 6
Hen manure — 18
Ka — 26
Turd — 13
Nil — 1, 2b, 7-12, 16, 20, 22, 25, 27-28, 30

Tyrone
Hen dirt — 11
Hen dung — 1, 7-8
Hen manure — 11
(Hen(s')) droppings — 1, 5-7, 10, *11-12,* 14
Scoot — 4
Nil — 2-3, 9, 13, 15-16

Antrim
Fowl dung — 5a, 22, 28
(Hen) droppin(g)s — 1, 5ab, 7, *9,* 10-12, 16b, 17-19, 31
Hen dung — 9, 20, 25-26, 33
Manure — 13, 31
Nil — 2-4, 4A, 6, 8ab, 14-15, 16ac, 21, 23-24, 27, 29-30, 32, 34

Donegal
Fowl dung — 1, 5, 12
Hen dirt — 12
Hen dung — 5A, 7A, 8
(Hens') droppings — 5-*6,* 10a
Hen shit — 4
Poultry droppings — 5A
Nil — 1A, 2-3, 7, 9, 10b, 11, 13

Fermanagh
Droppings — 1, 6, 7a
Hen dung — 4
Hen manure — 2, 4, 8-9
Nil — 3, 5, 7b, 10

Armagh
Fowl droppings — 2
Hen dung — 3-4
Nil — 1, 5, 6ab

Londonderry
Droppings — 1A, 3, 5
Hen dung — 1AB, 2, 3A
Pen — 3
Scoot — 6
Nil — 1, 4, 7

69 SNOW FLAKE (PQ1, 159)

Snow flake has not been mapped, as it occurs fairly densely all over the area.
For variants of SNOW see map 15, Appendix A.

Shetland
Flokra — 26
Flucker — 12, 17, 27-32
Fluckra — 3, 5-6, 10, 17-19, 21ab, 22, 24, 30
Koorie — 19
Moor cavie — 19
Murine — 13
Peask — 6
Scaelva — 7
Scalye — 5
Skalva — 3-4, 7-9, 13, 15, 17, 19, 21ab, 23, 26
Skalvi — 24
Snow flake — 1, 20, 21a, 33
Snow fleck — 2, 7, 15-16, 22, 25, 27
Nil — 11, 14

Orkney
Flakie — 3
Fleck — 14, 19
Fleuk — 11-12, 16
Fluck — 14
Fluken — 14
Hail puckle — 4
Snow — 8-9
Snowbunting — 15
(Snow) flake — *2, 4-5, 7-8, 13ab, 15, 17,* 20
Nil — 1, 6, 10, 18, 21

Caithness
Flag — 6
Flechter — 7
Snow — 8, 10
(Snow) flake — 2ab, *5-6, 9, 11, 13-14, 16b*
Nil — 1, 3-4, 12abc, 15, 16a, 17

Sutherland
Snow flake — 1, 3-8, 9ab, 10-13, 16
Soft snow — 3
Nil — 2, 14-15, 17

Ross & Cromarty
Feather — 34
Flagan — 25a
Fleichter — 21
Gentle Annie — 25b
Snow — 14
Snow blade — 37ab
(Snow) flake — 1, *3-6, 8-9, 13-14, 16-17,* 18, *22-24,* 25ab, *26-31,* 32ab, 36, *39*
Nil — 2, 7, 10-12, 15, 19-20, 32c, 33, 35, 38

Inverness
(Snow) flake — *1-3,* 4, *5-8,* 10-11, 13abce, 16-18, 20, *21ab, 22-23, 26-29,* 30, *32-40*
Nil — 9, 12, 13d, 14-15, 19, 24-25, 31

Nairn
Flechter — 1bc
Fleichter — 3
Snow flake — 2, 5
Nil — 1a, 4, 6

Moray
Flichter — 8b, 9a, 12
Fluchter — 3
Sleet — 21
Snow — 4
(Snow) flag — 1, 5, 16, *17,* 19, 22
(Snow) flake — *3,* 6b, 7, *8bd,* 10, *14,* 19, *23*
Nil — 2ab, 6a, 8acef, 9b, 11, 13, 15, 18, 20

Banff
Dingin on — 32
Drift — 20
Flacht — 18d
Snajve — 2b
Snjave — 2b
(Snow) flag — 2c, 3, 5, 6b, 8-9, 15, 17, 18c, 21, 23-27, *29,* 31-32, 34
Snow flaikie — 2b
(Snow) flake — *1, 2a,* 3, *8, 13,* 15-17, *19, 34*
Snow fleck — 4-5, 10, 14, 31
Nil — 6a, 7, 11-12, 18ab, 22, 28, 30, 33

Aberdeen
Blin drift — 47cf
Blinsmorg — 20
Buntin — 31
Ding — 47f
Drift — 10, 59
Flaisick — 33
Flay — 97
Fleck — 83
Fluggin — 47e
Snave — 15
Snow — 6, 54, 70
(Snow) flag — 3a, 5bcd, 6, 8-12, 14, 17-18, 21-*25,* 27, 28ab, 29-30, 32, *35,* 46, 47a, 48, 50-53, 61, 64, 71bc, 75, 77, 79-80, 84, 86-88, 91, 95, 101, 103-105
Snow flaiche — 92
(Snow) flake — *1, 3a,* 10, 20, *23,* 28c, *32, 35,* 37, *44-45, 47b, 49,* 56, *65, 67,* 68-69, *73-74, 81*-82, 85, *94-95, 98,* 104, *105,* 106, *107-108*
Nil — 2, 3b, 4, 5a, 7, 13, 16, 19, 26, 34, 36, 38-43, 47d, 55, 57-58, 60, 62-63, 68, 71a, 72, 76, 78, 89-90, 93, 96, 99-100, 102, 109

Kincardine
Flag — 4-6, 8-9, 12, 14, 17c
Snow — 7, 11, 15, 21
(Snow) drift — 7, *24*
(Snow) flake — 2, 5, *6,* 7, *8,* 10, *16, 17c, 19-20, 26*
(Snow) fleck — *1,* 13, 17b, 28
Snow leaf — 3
Nil — 17ad, 18, 22-23, 25, 27

Kinross
Flaffen — 5
Flichen — 2
Flicher — 3
(Snow) flake — 1, 3-*4*
Nil — 6-7

Angus
Flacher — 36
Flachin — 1, 5ab, 7-8, 12-13, 14d, 15, 21, 23, 30, 35, 37
Flacken — 10, 14d
Flaffin — 3, 19, 25, 27, 34
Fleckaw — 5c
Flichen — 31
Flocken — 2, 4, 5c
Snow — 15, 22, 25, 28
Snow buntin — 17a
Snow flaigh — 33b
(Snow) flake — *8-9,* 14bc, *18, 22, 34, 36*
Snow fleck — 6, 14a, 33b
Snow fluke — 17b
Nil — 11, 16, 20, 24, 26, 29ab, 32, 33a

Perth
Flachin — 7, 21, 23, 31, 37
Flaffan — 33
Flaghen — 72
Flechin — 22, 41a, 45, 52c, 55, 62
Fleckin — 66
Flichen — 20, 39-40, 52d, 65, 73
Flochon — 37
Flou — 20
Snow — 29a, 41a, 50
Snow bree — 41b
(Snow) flake — 1, *2a, 4-5,* 8-9, *10, 12-13, 15, 27-28, 32-33, 36, 43, 46, 48, 52be, 53, 57,* 60, *67*-68, *71,* 74
(Snow) fleck — *25, 59,* 70
Nil — 2b, 3, 6, 11, 14, 16-19, 24, 26, 29b, 30, 34-35, 38, 42, 44, 47, 49, 51ab, 52a, 54, 56, 58, 61, 63-64, 69

Fife
Drap — 8
Flaffer — 2, 38
Flaffin — 6, 9a, 12-14, 18, 21, 23, 25-27, 30, 51, 61
Flappin — 48
Flechan — 39, 64b
Fleck — 55d
Fleckin — 17
Flichan — 10, 55d, 59
Fluffin — 43a
Goose feather — 40b
Snow — 6-8, 19, 31
(Snow) flake — *1, 9a, 11, 14, 16, 21, 24, 28, 33, 36a, 37, 39, 40b, 41a, 42, 43a, 44bce, 46-48, 50,* 53, *55abe, 56-57, 62-63*
Nil — 3-5, 9b, 15, 20, 22, 29, 32, 34-35, 36b, 40a, 41bcd, 43b, 44adf, 45, 49, 52, 54, 55cfg, 58, 60, 64a

Clackmannan
Flachan — 2
Flichen — 4a
Purl — 4d
Snow — 3
Snow flake — 4bc, 5, 7
Nil — 1, 6

Stirling
Flachin — 10, 17
Flag — 26a
Flechin — 8, 26a
Flichen — 18
Flick — 7bd
Pile — 27a, 30
Purl — 27a
Snow — 25c
Snow drap — 25d
(Snow) flake — *4, 7ace, 8, 11, 17-18, 20, 21ab, 22b, 23bc, 26ad, 27a, 28, 30-31,* 34, *35a, 36, 37a, 41, 42a*
(Snow) fleck — *12,* 25b, *26b*
Nil — 1-3, 5-6, 7f, 9, 13-16, 19, 22a, 23a, 24, 25a, 26cef, 27b, 29, 32-33, 35b, 37b, 38, 39ab, 40, 42b

Dunbarton
Pile — 7c
Pirl — 13a
Snowfall — 14a
Snow flake — 1, 3, 6, 7bc, 8-11, 13ac, 16b
Snow fleck — 2, 7c
Nil — 4ab, 5, 7a, 12, 13b, 14b, 15, 16a, 17-18

Argyll
Claden — 6, 30
Flurry — 12
(Snow) flake — *1-3, 5-7, 9-10,* 11, *14-17, 19, 22,* 23, *24-25, 27, 30, 32-33, 35, 39*
Nil — 4, 8, 13, 18, 20-21, 26, 28-29, 31, 34, 36-38, 40

Bute
Snow flake — 1cd, 2, 7, 8ab
Nil — 1abe, 3-6, 9

Ayr
Flaffin — 19
Flichen — 45
Flurry — 41
Pick — 8a
Piffer — 57
Pile — 2a, 3, 8a, 12a, 20cg, 21, 24ab, 28f, 31-33, 42, 57
Snow — 10, 16a
Snowdrap — 15
(Snow) flake — 2a*b, 5-6, 8b,* 11, *12a, 18a, 20bg, 25, 26b, 28ce, 30a, 31,* 33-34, *35ab, 36, 38, 41-44,* 45, *47-48,* 49, *52, 53a,* 54, *56-57*
Nil — 1ab, 4, 7, 9, 12b, 13-14, 16b, 17, 18b, 20adefh, 22-23, 26ac, 27, 28abd, 29, 30b, 37, 39-40, 46, 50-51, 53b, 55

Renfrew
Fleck — 11a
Flurry — 2e
Goose feather — 15, 20b
Hogg reck — 20b
Pile — 4d, 11b
Purl — 14b
Sleet — 16a
Snow — 2j, 7
(Snow) flake — *1b, 2abchi, 4ace,* 5, *8, 11ael, 13c, 14a, 16bd, 17, 18a, 19, 20a*
Wee burd's fain — 2j
Nil — 1a, 2dfg, 3, 4b, 6, 9-10, 11cdfghijk, 12ab, 13abd, 16c, 18b, 21

Lanark
Auld wife's feather — 9b
Drap — 18
Flechan — 30
Fleck — 17, 31d
Flichin — 60
Goose feather — 32d
Pile — 15b, 16b, 30, 32c, 33c, 38a, 41-42, 46c, 49b, 56, 62, 64a
Piling — 15a, 33b, 39
Snow drap — 22
Snow fa' — 46c
Snow flaigh — 38d
(Snow) flake — *1-3, 5-6, 7ac, 8b, 9a, 10ab, 12-13, 14bd, 15ac,* 16a, *18, 20, 25bc, 26ab, 27b, 29cdf, 30, 31a, 32af, 33cd, 35abd, 38c, 39-40, 44-45, 46ab, 47-48,* 49a, *51, 53, 58, 59b, 64b*
Snow pile — 45
Nil — 4, 7b, 8a, 11, 14ac, 19, 21, 23-24, 25ad, 27a, 28, 29abeg, 31bc, 32be, 33a, 34, 35c, 36-37, 38be, 43, 50, 52ab, 54-55, 57abc, 59a, 61, 63, 65-66, 67ab

West Lothian
Drap — 1b
Flech — 11
Fleck — 16
Pile — 16, 19b
Piling — 4
Snow — 1c, 10, 22
(Snow) flake — *1a, 2-3, 5-6, 9a,* 11, *12-13, 15, 18,* 20a
Nil — 1d, 7-8, 9b, 14, 17ab, 19a, 20b, 21ab

Midlothian
Pile — 14b
Smirle — 1
Snow — 20-21, 25c
Snow drop — 17
Snow flake — 2, 6a, 8a, 10-11, 12a, 14a, 15, 18, 23b
Snow fluke — 32
Speck — 30
Nil 3-5, 6b, 7ab, 8b, 9, 12b, 13, 16, 19, 22, 23a, 24, 25abd, 26ab, 27-29, 31

East Lothian
Feather — 4a
Fleein' snow — 6a
Fleght — 17
Fliechen — 16
Perl — 14
(Snow) flake — 1, *4b, 6b, 7-9,* 15-*16, 18-21*
Nil — 2-3, 5, 10-13

Berwick
Feather — 8
Flachen — 23
Flaften — 18
Flechin — 21
Fleckin — 14
Flicht — 7
Flite — 9, 18
Leetie — 27
Minkle — 27
Pirl — 11, 24
Snow — 9
(Snow) flake — *1-2,* 4, *6, 8, 10, 12-13, 15, 16ab, 17, 22-23,* 25, *29-32*
Snow fleck — 19
White feather — 1
Nil — 3, 5, 16c, 20, 26, 28

Peebles
Fleckin — 10
Flichen — 2
Pile — 3
Pilin snow — 1
Purl — 3
Snow flake — 4b, 6b, 8-9
Snow fleck — 6a
Nil — 4ac, 5, 7

Selkirk
Pirl — 2a
Snow flake — 2ce, 4, 8
Nil — 1, 2bd, 3, 5-7

Roxburgh
Flaggin — 28
Flaucht — 28
Flicht — 4
Peal — 25
Pirl — 9b, 12
Purl — 25
Sneck — 11
Snow — 6
(Snow) flake — *1-2, 3a, 9a, 10, 15b, 16-17, 21adf*
Snow fleek — 28
Spitter — 8
Nil — 3b, 5, 7, 13-14, 15a, 18-20, 21bce, 22-24, 26-27

Dumfries
Flachen — 28
Flaffin — 39
Flechin — 32
Flichen — 4-5, 8a, 9-13, 21ab, 24, 31be, 33
Flicken — 19, 42
Flikker — 44
Fluchan — 7
Peelin — 4
Pile — 5
Pirl — 6, 26
Pyowlen — 5
Snow — 8b, 16, 45a
Snow flake — 12, 15, 17ab, 18, 20, 22, 27, 31bd, 37, 40, 43, 45b
Snow fleek — 29, 46
Nil — 1ab, 2-3, 14, 23, 25, 30, 31acf, 34-36, 38, 41, 47-49

Kirkcudbright
Flechin — 4, 14
Flecken — 18
Flichen — 2-3, 5-9, 12ab, 15ab, 21ab, 23
Flichter — 17, 19
Flickin — 16
Jenny's pluckin her feathers — 24
Pirl — 1
Snow — 22
Snow flake — 1, 6, 10
Snow flichen — 21c
Nil — 11, 13, 20, 25-27

Wigtown
Flaighter — 8
Pile — 6
Pirl — 7, 14
Sleet — 2
Snow — 2
(Snow) flake — *5a, 9, 11, 13,* 16-*17*
Snow fleck — 6
Nil — 1, 3-4, 5b, 10, 12, 15, 18

Northumberland
Feather — 76
Flighten — 68
Flighter — 73, 104b
Flitter — 75
Flockin — 122b
Snow — 3, 9, 13, 53b, 62e, 69b, 86, 88a, 94b, 111a, 113, 126c, 130c
Snow bunting — 124a
Snow drop — 72b
Snow flag — 17, 20b, 39, 138
(Snow) flake — *1a, 2b, 6, 8, 14,* 15, *16, 18, 19a, 20b, 21, 24b, 26, 28, 29bd, 30-31, 35-36, 38-39, 40a, 41cd,* 42, *45-46, 48, 52, 53ab, 54,* 56, *59bc, 60, 62bh, 64ab, 65a, 66, 69cdh, 70, 71abcd, 72acdgi, 77-78, 83, 87, 88b, 89-91, 95b, 99d, 100, 101a, 102, 103ac, 104a, 106*-107, *109-110, 111ab, 112, 119, 120abc, 124ab, 126cf, 127a, 130be, 132, 134-135, 142-143*
Snow fleak — 103b
(Snow) fleck — *47,* 67, *69ab, 98, 105, 117*
Snow flight — 34b
Snow flighter — 47, 104b
Nil — 1bc, 2a, 4-5, 7, 10-12, 19b, 20a, 22-23, 24a, 25, 27, 29acef, 32, 33ab, 34a, 37, 40b, 41ab, 43-44, 49-51, 55, 57-58, 59adef, 61, 62acdfg, 63, 65b, 69efg, 71e, 72efhjkl, 74, 79-82, 84-85, 92-93, 94a, 95a, 96-97, 99abc, 101b, 108abc, 114-116, 118ab, 121, 122a, 123, 125, 126abde, 127bcdefgh, 128, 129abc, 130adf, 131, 133, 136-137, 139-141

Cumberland
Drift — 44
Fleck — 40
Goose feather — 60
Mul — 60
Pickle o' snow — 56
Snow — 7, 62
Snow flake — 2-4, 5a, 9, 12, 13c, 14, 15ac, 16, 18, 20-26, 28, 42, 46-50, 53, 56-59
Snow fleak — 38, 41
Nil — 1ab, 5b, 6, 8, 10-11, 13abd, 15b, 17, 19, 27, 29-36, 37ab, 39, 41, 43, 45, 51-52, 54-55, 61, 63ab

Down
Snow skud — 13
(Snow) flake — *2a, 5, 7, 9, 15, 18-19,* 24, *26*
Nil — 1, 2b, 3-4, 6, 8, 10-12, 14, 16-17, 20-23, 25, 27-30

Tyrone
Blab — 9
Brade — 5
Snow — 8
Snow drop — 14
(Snow) flake — 1, *7, 10-11*
Nil — 2-4, 6, 12-13, 15-16

Antrim
Blab — 16b
(Goose) down — *16b,* 34
Goose feathers — 16b
Grain — 15
Pickle — 9, 15
Pile — 5b, 25
Snow — 21, 26
Snow flake — 1, 11, 13, 17, 19-20, 22, 25, 33
Nil — 2-4, 4A, 5a, 6-7, 8ab, 10, 12, 14, 16ac, 18, 23-24, 27-32

Donegal
Brattog — 2, 6, 12
Snow flake — 1, 5, 5A, 8
Nil — 1A, 3-4, 7, 7A, 9, 10ab, 11, 13

Fermanagh
Snow flake — 4, 8-9
Nil — 1-3, 5-6, 7ab, 10

Armagh
(Snow) flake — 3-*4*
Nil — 1-2, 5, 6ab

Londonderry
Snow feather — 5
(Snow) flake — *2*-3, 3A
Nil — 1, 1AB, 4, 6-7

70 CHAFFINCH (PQ1, 160)

Spinkie also appears in 75 **yellowhammer.**

Shetland
Chaffinch — 5, 15, 33
Lintie — 16
Stane chackler — 20
Nil — 1-4, 6-14, 17-19, 21ab, 22-32

Orkney
Chaffie — 20
Chaffinch — 2, 4, 7, 15, 19
Nil — 1, 3, 5-6, 8-12, 13ab, 14, 16-18, 21

Caithness
Bullfinch — 13
Chaffinch — 2b, 5, 9, 11, 16b
Nil — 1, 2a, 3-4, 6-8, 10, 12abc, 14-15, 16a, 17

Sutherland
Chaffie — 6, 9b, 14
Chaffinch — 4-8, 9a, 10-13, 16
Finch — 16
Finchie — 1
Nil — 2-3, 15, 17

Ross & Cromarty
Binkie — 28
Birkie — 10, 18
Brachtan — 37a
Breakie — 12, 20
Breckie — 8, 13
Burkie — 19
Chaffie — 9, 21, 23, 26, 31
Chaffinch — 1, 3-5, 8-9, 16-17, 22, 24, 25a, 26-27, 29-30, 32a, 34, 39
Finch — 36
Shilfie — 18
Spink — 29
Spinkie — 29
Nil — 2, 6-7, 11, 14-15, 25b, 32bc, 33, 35, 37b, 38

Inverness
Chaffie — 13a, 15-16, 21a, 27
Chaffinch — 2-8, 10-11, 13abce, 17, 20, 21b, 22-23, 26, 28-30, 34-37, 39-40
Chiff chaff — 26
Finch — 18, 32
Prink prink — 13a
Shelfie — 38
Nil — 1, 9, 12, 13d, 14, 19, 24-25, 31, 33

Nairn

Chaffie — 1bc, 2
Chaffinch — 2
Nil — 1a, 3-6

Moray

Chaffie — 2a, 4-5, 6a, 7, 8bc, 9a, 11, 13-14, 18, 21-23
Chaffinch — 8d
Chay — 20
Chy — 9b, 10, 19
Shilfa — 8a, 22
Shilfie — 1, 4
Shulfie — 9a
Spinkie — 8bd
Treeack — 8e, 12
Tree lintie — 3, 8f, 16
Nil — 2b, 6b, 15, 17

Banff

Chaffie — 5, 6b, 8-17, 18c, 19-21, 23-24, 26-27, 32-33
Chafftie — 9
Chay — 5, 6b, 18bd
Chiffie — 18d
Chy — 3-4, 7, 16, 18c
Finchie — 11
Jye — 10, 23
Robin dowl — 34
Spinkie — 25, 29
Yellow yite — 1
Nil — 2abc, 6a, 18a, 22, 28, 30-31

Aberdeen

Blue cap — 57
Chaffie — 2, 3ab, 4, 5ad, 10, 12, 14-15, 17-27, 28ab, 29-32, 34-37, 39, 41, 43-46, 47abe, 48-54, 56, 58, 62-67, 69, 71bc, 72-75, 79-84, 86-90, 92-94, 96-98, 100-101, 103-109
Chaffinch — 6, 9, 70, 95
Chavie — 80
Chy — 22, 29
Finch — 11, 16
Finchie — 1, 3b
Yaldie yite — 59
Yalla yerlin — 5c
Yallaywite — 5c
Nil — 5b, 7-8, 13, 28c, 33, 38, 40, 42, 47cdf, 55, 60-61, 68, 71a, 76-78, 85, 91, 99, 102

Kincardine

Boldie — 5, 14
Chaffie — 1-8, 10, 12-13, 15-16, 17bcd, 23-24
Chaisie — 3
Finch — 19
Shelfie — 4
Shellie — 21, 26-28
Shillie — 9, 17a, 22
Nil — 11, 18, 20, 25

Kinross

Sheelie — 2-3, 6-7
Shelfa — 5, 7
Shelfie — 1-2
Shiltie — 6
Nil — 4, 6

Angus

Chaffie — 9, 13, 17a, 18, 32
Chaffinch — 17b, 34
Finch — 14b, 17b, 25
Shelfie — 5c, 6-7, 11, 13, 19-21, 31, 33ab, 36
Shellie — 1-4, 5abc, 7-8, 12-13, 15, 22-24, 27, 30, 34, 37
Shilfa — 33b
Shilfie — 20, 37
Shillie — 28, 35
Shilpie — 14a
Shulfie — 23
Stane chackie — 33b
Wet chaff — 17a
Yite — 15
Nil — 10, 14cd, 16, 26, 29ab

Perth

Chaffie — 12, 21, 25-26, 30, 34, 36
Chaffinch — 2a, 4, 10, 25, 36, 52b
Fink — 70
Jink — 39
Shelfie — 1, 3, 5, 7-11, 13, 15-16, 20, 22-24, 26-28, 29ab, 31-33, 37, 39-40, 41ab, 43, 47, 49, 51b, 52acde, 53-56, 59-63, 66-69, 71, 73-74
Shellie — 64
Shilfa — 51a, 62
Shilfie — 44-46, 48, 50, 58, 65
Shulfie — 52a, 57, 62
Skelfie — 42
Spink — 24
Nil — 2b, 6, 14, 17-19, 35, 38, 72

Fife

Bullie — 54
Chaffie — 7-8, 11, 22, 28, 30, 36a, 37-38, 41c, 43b, 50, 55d, 61-62
Chaffinch — 4, 16, 19, 21, 24, 41a, 42, 55ab
Checkstane — 48
Cheelie — 44e
Cheffie — 34
Chilfa — 44a
Finch — 55e, 57, 63
Finchie — 33
Red lintie — 9a, 37
Sheekie — 50
Sheelie — 11, 36a, 39, 40b, 41cd, 43b, 53, 55bcd, 59-60
Shelfaw — 23, 29, 31
Shelfie — 7, 35, 55e, 56
Shellie — 10, 12, 17, 19, 22-23, 25, 48-49
Shellyfaw — 1, 4, 12-14, 18, 26, 28
Shelpet — 59
Sheltie — 56
Shilfa — 27, 44c, 46
Shilfie — 47, 49, 51, 64a
Shillie — 20, 40a, 44e
Shulfie — 61
Shullie — 44d
Snabbie — 21
Whinnie — 12
Nil — 2-3, 5-6, 9b, 15, 32, 36b, 41b, 43a, 44bf, 45, 52, 55fg, 58, 64b

Clackmannan

Chaffie — 2, 4b
Chaffinch — 5c
Chelfie — 4d
Finch — 4c
Shelfie — 1, 4d
Shilfie — 4a, 5-7
Shulfie — 2
Nil — 3

Stirling

Chaffie — 26abdf, 38, 39b
Chaffinch — 4, 7b, 8, 12, 21b, 31, 36, 39b
Chiffie — 26d
Chilfie — 23b
Finch — 34
Finchie — 38
Fink — 7e, 9-10
Finkie — 12
Lintie — 22a
Shelfa — 26a
Shelfie — 1-4, 6, 7ade, 9, 11, 13-18, 20, 21ab, 22b, 23c, 24, 25bcd, 27ab, 34, 35ab, 37b, 39b, 42ab
Shelvie — 7b, 22a, 40
Shilfa — 26ab
Shilfaw — 26b
Shilfie — 25a, 26b, 28, 30-32, 41
Shilpie — 33
Shoffie — 20, 26e
Shulfie — 21b, 23a, 36
Skelfie — 7b
Skittrie feltie — 8
Nil — 5, 7cf, 19, 26c, 29, 37a, 39a

Dunbarton

Chaffie — 1, 13abc, 17
Chaffinch — 11, 13bc
Finch — 7c
Shelfa — 14a
Shelfie — 2, 6, 7abc, 9-10, 13a, 16ab
Shilfa — 14b
Shilfie — 3, 4ab, 10, 16a
Shulfie — 18
Nil — 5, 8, 12, 15

Argyll

Chaffie — 1, 8, 16, 24
Chaffinch — 1-2, 5-7, 9-10, 15-17, 22, 27, 33, 35
Flinch — 11
Shelfie — 12-15, 18-19
Shell finch — 19
Sheltie — 37, 40
Shilfa — 23
Shilfie — 23, 29
Shiltie — 35, 39
Shultie — 31
Nil — 3-4, 20-21, 25-26, 28, 30, 32, 34, 36, 38

Bute

Chaffie — 1a
Chaffinch — 7, 8b
Chilfie — 1b
Shelfie — 1cde, 2, 5
Shilfie — 1b, 7, 8ab, 9
Shulfie — 4
Nil — 3, 6

Ayr

Chaffie — 7, 8b, 18b, 20g, 21, 55
Chaffinch — 28e, 45
Chilfa — 49
Chilfie — 28d, 49, 51, 56
Finchie — 28d
Shelfie — 3, 6, 12ab, 13, 17, 18ab, 19, 20abeg, 22, 24ab, 26c, 28b, 30a, 32-34, 35ab, 36-37, 43, 46, 54
Shilfa — 8a, 57
Shilfie — 1a, 2ab, 3-5, 7, 8b, 9-11, 14-15, 16ab, 20cdfh, 25, 26ab, 28acf, 29, 30b, 31, 38-42, 47-48, 50, 52, 53b, 57
Shilfinch — 28e
Shilpie — 53a
Shulfie — 5, 10, 20h, 44-45
Nil — 1b, 23, 27

Renfrew

Chaffie — 2de, 4d, 11i, 14a, 16b
Chaffinch — 1b, 2adhi, 4ac, 11ae, 13c, 20a
Chilfie — 5, 11e
Feltie — 12b
Finch — 11j
Finchie — 7
Shelfa — 14b
Shelfie — 9, 12b, 14a, 16ac, 20b
Shilfie — 1b, 2bg, 6, 8, 11bfkl, 12a, 13abd, 15, 16d, 19, 21
Shulfie — 17, 18a
Nil — 1a, 2cfj, 3, 4be, 10, 11cdgh, 18b

Lanark

Chaffie — 1-3
Chaffinch — 1, 7ac, 14d, 24, 25b, 26a, 29f, 31a, 35d, 44
Chilfie — 29a, 64a
Filchie — 27a
Finch — 1, 10a, 15ab, 21, 25c
Finchie — 12, 14b
Mavie — 51
Shelfie — 3, 5, 8b, 9a, 11, 15c, 29c, 31bd, 33cd, 42-45, 46bc, 47-48, 49b, 52b, 53, 56, 57ac, 59a, 60
Shelvie — 19
Shilfa — 9b, 29d, 37, 38bd
Shilfie — 5, 7bc, 9a, 12-13, 14d, 15b, 16b, 17-18, 23-24, 25b 27b, 29cefg, 30, 31c, 32adef, 33bd, 35bcd, 37, 38acde, 39-41, 46a, 48, 50, 55, 57b, 58, 59b, 61-62, 64b, 65-66, 67a
Shofie — 8a
Shulfie — 10a, 25c, 26b, 31b, 32bc, 33a, 34, 35a, 52a, 57a, 63
Skitterie feltie — 22
White wingie — 20, 46c
Yorlin — 38d
Nil — 4, 6, 10b, 14ac, 16a, 25ad, 28, 29b, 36, 49a, 54, 67b

West Lothian

Chaffie — 1c, 11
Chilfie — 20a
Finch — 11
Shelfie — 1c, 4-6, 8, 9b, 12-13, 15, 17a, 19b
Shilfa — 18
Shilfie — 1abd, 2-3, 7, 21a
Shulfie — 8, 16
Nil — 9a, 10, 14, 17b, 19a, 20b, 21b, 22

Midlothian

Chaffie — 3, 10, 18
Chaffinch — 6b, 8a, 15, 23b, 25c
Chelfie — 19
Chilfie — 21
Finch — 17, 19-20
Finchie — 23b
Sheilfie — 23a
Sheilie — 23a
Shelfie — 7b, 11, 12b, 14ab, 15-18, 24, 28-29, 32
Sheltie — 5
Shielfa — 26ab
Shilfie — 3-4, 8b, 12a, 14a, 22, 23b, 25a, 30-31
Shulfie — 13
Nil — 1-2, 6a, 7a, 9, 25bd, 27

East Lothian

Chaffie — 9, 13
Chaffinch — 4b, 17
Shelfa — 16
Shelfie — 2, 6a, 7, 10, 12-15, 18
Shielfie — 1, 8-9
Shilfa — 2
Shilfie — 3, 4b, 6b, 11, 15-16, 20-21
Shulfie — 19
Spink — 13
Nil — 4a, 5

Berwick

Bullfinch — 27
Chaffie — 27, 30
Chaffinch — 12
Cheddie — 27
Chilfie — 6, 16a
Shaffie — 8
Shelfie — 1-4, 9-10, 13, 15, 17-21, 23, 25-26, 29, 31
Shilfie — 7, 11-12, 16b, 22, 24, 27, 32
Shiltie — 31
Shulfie — 16c
Nil — 5, 14, 28

Peebles

Chaffie — 4a, 6a, 9
Chaffinch — 4c
Finch — 2
Sheelie — 4b
Shelfie — 1-3, 5
Shilfa — 6a
Shilfie — 4bc, 7-8, 10
Shulfie — 6b

Roxburgh

Chaffinch — 21a
Chilfie — 13, 21d, 24-25
Shelfie — 1, 7, 15a, 19, 22-23
Shilfa — 3a, 12, 15b, 17, 21a
Shilfie — 2, 3b, 4-6, 8, 9ab, 10, 16, 18, 20, 21cf, 26, 28
Nil — 11, 14, 21be, 27

Dumfries

Chaffie — 31d
Chaffinch — 4, 17b
Chilfie — 8a, 9, 12, 25, 33, 35, 42, 44
Cock o' the north — 15
Shelfie — 7, 20, 21b, 22, 28, 31c, 40, 49
Shilfa — 4, 31b
Shilfie — 1ab, 2-6, 8b, 10-11, 13-14, 16, 18-19, 24, 26-27, 29-30, 31a, 32, 37-39, 41, 43, 45ab, 46
Shilvie — 19
Shulfie — 21b, 27, 34
Snabbie — 31c
Nil — 17a, 21a, 23, 31ef, 36, 47-48

Kirkcudbright

Brichtie — 4, 12a, 14, 15ab, 17, 19-20, 21abc
Briskie — 18-19
Chaffie — 7, 11, 12b
Chaffinch — 6, 10
Chilfie — 24
Gooldie — 22
Green lintie — 12b
Shelfie — 8, 23
Shilfie — 1-2, 5, 8-9, 13, 15a, 16, 25
Shilpie — 17
Shulfie — 4
Nil — 3, 26-27

Wigtown

Brichtie — 10
Chaffie — 14
Guldie — 2
Mavis — 15
Shelfie — 4, 5b, 7, 9, 17-18
Sheltie — 1
Shilfa — 5a
Shilfie — 6, 8, 10-13, 16
Shiltie — 14
Nil — 3

Northumberland

Apple sheelaw — 22
Apple sheeler — 2b, 6, 14, 17-18, 19a, 20a, 23, 24ab, 30, 48
Apple sheelie — 2a, 15, 27, 33b, 35, 38, 41d, 47-48, 59f, 60, 62a, 65b, 68, 69de, 71cdj, 82, 94b, 108a
Apple shela — 32
Apple sheller — 41c
Applie — 2b, 3, 10-11, 18
Chaff — 62g
Chaffer — 101b
Chaffie — 1b, 5, 9, 12, 18, 21, 26, 28, 29bde, 31, 34b, 39, 41a, 42-43, 45-46, 52, 53a, 54, 59c, 63, 68, 69d, 70, 71c, 72l, 76, 78-79, 83, 97, 103abc, 105, 111ab, 118a, 124a, 125, 126ac, 127ab, 128, 130cf, 138
Chaffinch — 2b, 5, 13-14, 16, 23, 28, 29b, 35, 40a, 53b, 62b, 64a, 66, 69ch, 72dgik, 87, 88b, 99bd, 120ab, 124b, 127a, 132, 140, 143
Chappie — 88a
Chavie — 74
Chiff chaff — 79
Chiffie — 48
Chilfie — 68
Finch — 16, 40a, 59b, 69c, 122b, 127e, 130be
Finchie — 1a, 86, 99b
Gold spink — 69ab
Muck finch — 103bc
Paper sheelie — 65b, 114, 116
Peachie — 129b
Piebie — 20b
Pink — 69b
Scobbie — 102, 103bc
Shave apple — 133
Shaver — 56, 106, 108c, 136
Shavie — 56, 107, 108bc, 110, 112, 133-135, 137, 140
Sheeldie — 52, 90
Sheelie — 25, 29a, 34a, 36-37, 39, 41cd, 45-46, 49-50, 58, 59acde, 62f, 64b, 69fg, 71de, 72fj, 77, 79-82, 86, 95ab, 108a, 109, 111ab, 115-116, 118ab, 120c, 122a, 124a, 139, 141
Sheelie apple — 44
Shelfie — 8, 19a
Shevvie — 103a, 104ab
Shielapple — 36
Shilfa — 103b
Shilfie — 29f, 42, 51
Shilvie — 73
Spink — 35, 69ab, 98, 114
Spinkie — 69ab
Spink spink — 20b
Spuggie — 83
Tit — 122b
Nil — 1c, 4, 7, 19b, 29c, 33a, 40b, 41b, 55, 57, 61, 62cdeh, 66a, 67, 71ab, 72abceh, 75, 84-85, 89, 91-93, 94a, 96, 99ac, 100, 101a, 113, 117, 119, 121, 123, 126bdef, 127cdfgh, 129ac, 130ad, 131, 142

Cumberland

Bessie — 52
Chaffinch — 9, 15a, 23-24, 42, 56, 58
Chiff chaff — 26
Chittie — 1a
Finch — 50
Linkie — 60
Scobbie — 3, 5a, 6, 13cd, 14, 19, 21, 27, 31, 36, 37ab, 38-40, 43, 49, 60
Scop — 4, 15c, 27, 30, 41, 43-44, 46-47, 53-57, 61-62
Scoppie — 2, 5a, 7-12, 13ab, 15bc, 16-18, 20, 24-25, 28-29, 32-34, 40, 44-48, 56
Spink — 2, 12, 27, 41, 51, 53, 56-62, 63ab
Spinkie — 22, 54, 58, 60
Spinx — 40
Nil — 1b, 5b, 35

Down

Apple picker — 11
Chaffinch — 2a, 5, 7, 9, 13, 15, 18, 26
Chafflinch — 22
Finch — 17
Flinch — 23
Nil — 1, 2b, 3-4, 6, 8, 10, 12, 14, 16, 19-21, 24-25, 27-30

Tyrone

Chaffinch — 1-2, 7, 11
Nil — 3-6, 8-10, 12-16

Antrim

Chaffinch — 1, 11-13, 17, 19, 21, 25-26
Chafflinch — 4A, 14-15, 20, 22, 33
Finch — 9
Yellow yarnie — 34
Nil — 2-4, 5ab, 6-7, 8ab, 10, 16abc, 18, 23-24, 27-32

Donegal

Chaffinch — 1, 5A, 12
Chafflinch — 5
Hedge sparrow — 6
Righ rua — 12
White wing — 11
Nil — 1A, 2-4, 7, 7A, 8-9, 10ab, 13

Fermanagh

Chaffinch — 4, 8
Finch — 9
Nil — 1-3, 5-6, 7ab, 10

Armagh

Chaffinch — 4, 6a
Chafflinch — 6a
White wing — 1
Nil — 2-3, 5, 6b

Londonderry

Chaffinch — 2-3
Grey flinch — 5
Nil — 1, 1AB, 3A, 4, 6-7

71 SPARROW (PQ1, 161)

Variants of SPARROW have been subsumed (variations occur mainly in the unstressed vowel).

Shetland

Cheeky breeks — 26
Sparrow — 1-8, 10, 14-17, 19-20, 21ab, 22-25, 27-28, 30-33
Spyug — 11
Stirlin — 31
Nil — 9, 12-13, 18, 29

Orkney

Sparrick — 19
Sparrow — 1-9, 11, 13ab, 14-17, 20
Sprob — 15
Spuggie — 17
Spurkie — 4
Nil — 10, 12, 18, 21

Caithness

Sparrow — 2b, 3, 5, 10-11, 13
Spreug — 6
Spreugie — 9
Sprog — 3
Sproug — 2ab, 3-5, 8, 11, 12abc, 13-15, 16ab
Nil — 1, 7, 17

Sutherland

Sparrow — 1, 3-8, 9b, 10-13, 16
Speug — 8
Sproug — 9a
Nil — 2, 14-15, 17

Ross & Cromarty

Sparrach — 30
Sparrow — 1, 3-5, 8-9, 14, 16-20, 22, 24, 25b, 26-29, 32ab, 34, 36, 39
Speerack — 11
Speeugh — 23
Speug — 13, 18, 21-22, 25a
Sporrack — 6, 31
Spug — 19, 25b, 32b
Spurgie — 26
Nil — 2, 7, 10, 12, 15, 32c, 33, 35, 37ab, 38

Inverness

Sparrow — 1-11, 13abce, 16-17, 19-20, 21ab, 22-23, 26-30, 32-37, 39-40
Sperrick — 10
Speug — 15, 38
Spoarick — 14
Sporrick — 13ace
Sporrish — 9
Spug — 18
Spuig — 26
Nil — 12, 13d, 24-25, 31

Nairn

Sparrow — 2
Speug — 5
Spewach — 1b
Spurgie — 1b, 4
Nil — 1ac, 3, 6

Moray

Spardie — 6b, 8ef
Sparrow — 6b, 7, 8bde, 14, 23
Speug — 1, 6ab, 7, 8d, 9a, 20
Sprug — 18
Spruggie — 3
Spungie — 2a, 12-13
Spurdie — 4-5, 6a, 8bcd, 10, 14-15, 17-21
Spurgie — 9ab, 11, 16, 22
Nil — 2b, 8a

Banff

Sparrow — 2b, 30, 32, 34
Speug — 5, 15, 17, 18cd
Spog — 28
Spruggie — 1
Spug — 10, 30
Spuggie — 1, 23
Spurd — 18c
Spurdie — 1, 2abc, 3-5, 6ab, 7-17, 18b, 19-21, 23-29, 31-33
Spurgie — 6b, 13, 22
Nil — 18a

Aberdeen

Sparrow — 6, 8, 44, 70
Speug — 14
Sprottie — 71c
Spug — 75, 98
Spurdie — 8-9, 11-12, 15-16, 22-24, 26, 28abc, 29-30, 32, 53-55, 65, 91, 96, 104, 107
Spurg — 5cd, 43, 71c
Spurgie — 1-2, 3ab, 4, 5abd, 6-7, 10, 12-14, 16-21, 24-25, 27, 31, 33-46, 47abcdef, 48-52, 56-64, 66-67, 69-70, 71abc, 72-90, 92-106, 108-109
Nil — 68

Kincardine

Sparrow — 3, 5-6, 8, 12, 17c
Spug — 3, 6, 11, 15, 18, 20-21, 27
Spuggie — 18-19, 21-22, 24-26, 28
Spurg — 5
Spurgie — 1-5, 7-14, 16, 17abcd, 23

Kinross

Sparrow — 2
Speuch — 1, 3
Speug — 1-3, 5-7
Spug — 1, 4, 6

Angus

Sparrow — 17b, 18, 34
Speug — 10, 13, 19, 31-32, 37
Sprug — 33b
Spug — 1, 3-4, 5ac, 6-9, 12, 14abcd, 16, 17ab, 20-25, 27, 30, 33ab, 34-36
Spuggie — 2, 4, 5bc, 7, 9, 14bcd, 15, 18, 21-23, 26, 28, 29a, 32, 34
Nil — 11, 29b

Perth

Sparrow — 2a, 4, 8-10, 16, 24-25, 33, 36, 46, 50, 52c, 60
Speug — 1, 8, 13, 15-17, 21, 24-26, 35, 37-39, 41ab, 44-45, 48, 51b, 52abde, 53, 55, 59-61, 65-66, 68-73
Speugie — 33, 52ae, 59
Spig — 6
Sporrack — 14
Sprog — 1
Sprug — 41a, 46, 51a, 62
Spug — 2a, 3, 5, 7, 9-10, 12-13, 18, 20, 22-23, 25, 27-28, 29ab, 30-32, 33, 40, 42-43, 47-49, 51b, 52e, 54-56, 63-64, 67
Spuggie — 5, 20, 28, 29a, 31-32, 50, 52ace, 57-59
Spuig — 11, 62, 74
Spurdie — 62
Nil — 2b, 19, 34

Fife

Sparrow — 4, 8, 10-11, 16, 19, 21, 25, 33, 35, 37, 41b, 43a, 44b, 48-50, 55be, 56-58, 61, 63
Speug — 1-2, 7-8, 9a, 12-13, 16, 21, 23, 25-27, 29-30, 32, 34-35, 36ab, 37-39, 41d, 42, 43ab, 44bce, 45, 47, 49-54, 55abdef, 57, 59-60, 62-63, 64ab
Speuggie — 8
Speugh — 48
Speuk — 58
Spreech — 44e, 50
Spreug — 64a
Sproggie — 19
Sprogie — 64b
Sproogie — 33
Sproug — 44f
Sprug — 18, 20, 31, 33, 40a, 41c, 43b, 44d, 46, 55c, 59
Spruggie — 40b
Spug — 3-6, 9b, 11, 17, 24, 28, 34, 36b, 41a, 44a, 55g, 56
Spuggie — 34
Spurdie — 22, 42
Spurgie — 6, 14
Whinnie — 50
Whin sparrow — 50
Nil — 15

Clackmannan

Sparrow — 1, 4c
Speug — 1-3, 4abd, 5-7
Spug — 4cd
Spurdie — 4c

Stirling

Sparrow — 4, 7e, 8, 15, 21b, 23a, 26ad, 27a, 31-32, 35a, 36
Speug — 1, 3-4, 6, 7ace, 8-9, 11-20, 21b, 22b, 23ac, 25abcd, 26acde, 27a, 28-34, 35a, 36, 37a, 38, 39ab, 40-41, 42ab
Speugh — 7b
Sprug — 2
Spug — 7df, 10, 21a, 22a, 24, 25d, 26bf, 27b, 35b, 37b
Spuig — 23b
Spurdie — 9
Spurgie — 26f
Nil — 5

Dunbarton

Smool — 7ac
Smule — 6
Sparrow — 1, 3, 7bc, 13abc, 14b
Speug — 1-3, 4b, 5, 7abc, 8-10, 12, 13abc, 14ab, 15, 16ab, 18
Speugh — 11
Speuk — 10
Spug — 3, 4a, 6, 17

Argyll

Snapper — 3
Sparrow — 1-2, 5-7, 9-11, 14-17, 19, 22, 25, 27, 30, 33-35
Speuch — 33
Speug — 8-9, 12, 16, 21, 23-24, 28, 32, 34-39
Spiout — 39-40
Spowk — 13
Sprug — 35
Spug — 18-19, 35
Nil — 4, 20, 26, 29, 31

Bute

Sparrow — 1acd, 7, 8b
Speug — 1acde, 2, 4-7, 8a, 9
Spug — 3, 8b
Spurgie — 2
Nil — 1b

Ayr

Sparrow — 2b, 5, 9, 12a, 28ce, 30a, 34, 43, 45, 57
Speug — 1ab, 2ab, 3-7, 8ab, 9-11, 12ab, 14-15, 16a, 17, 18ab, 19, 20bcdgh, 22-23, 24ab, 25, 26b, 28abcef, 29, 30ab, 31-34, 35ab, 37-46, 48-52, 53a, 54-57
Speugh — 28d
Speuk — 53b
Spug — 7, 13, 16b, 20aef, 21, 26ac, 27, 36, 38, 47
Titlin — 19

Renfrew

Sparrow — 2adi, 4ace, 11abdel, 14a, 19, 20a
Speug — 1b, 2abcefghj, 3, 4de, 5-7, 9, 11abdefhijkl, 12ab, 13acd, 14ab, 16abcd, 17, 18ab, 19, 20a, 21
Speugh — 1a, 20b
Sphueg — 11c
Sphug — 18a
Spiout — 2j
Spout — 15
Spueg — 15
Spug — 2dg, 8, 10, 11be, 16b, 18a
Nil — 4b, 11g, 13b

Lanark

Sparrow — 1, 3, 6, 7c, 14ad, 15ac, 16b, 25bc, 26ab, 29acf, 35d, 44-45, 48, 58, 59b
Speug — 2, 4-6, 7ab, 8ab, 9ab, 10ab, 11-13, 14abc, 15ac, 16a, 17-19, 21-22, 24, 25abc, 26ab, 27ab, 28, 29cdfg, 30, 31abcd, 32abdef, 33abcd, 34, 35abcd, 36-37, 38ace, 41, 43-44, 46abc, 47-48, 49ab, 50-51, 52ab, 53, 55-56, 57bc, 58, 59ab, 60-63, 64b, 65-66, 67a
Speugh — 25d, 29g
Spiout — 46c
Spreug — 33c
Spueg — 16b, 23
Spug — 1, 3, 7c, 14d, 15b, 20, 29ae, 32c, 33b, 38bd, 39-40, 42, 45, 54, 57a, 64a
Nil — 29b, 67b

West Lothian

Sparrow — 1c, 2-3, 6-7, 11, 13, 15-16
Speug — 1ab, 2-3, 5-8, 9ab, 10, 12, 15-16, 17ab, 20ab, 21b, 22
Speuggie — 13
Sprug — 15
Spug — 1cd, 4, 11, 14, 18, 19ab, 21a
Spurgie — 11

Midlothian

Lum lintie — 23b
Sparrow — 2, 6a, 8ab, 10, 14a, 15, 18, 23b, 25c, 32
Speug — 2-3, 5, 6b, 7ab, 8b, 10, 12ab, 13, 14ab, 17-18, 21-22, 23a, 24, 25bc, 26ab, 27-28, 30
Spreig — 31
Spreug — 18, 31
Sprig — 26b
Sprug — 4-5, 7b, 8b, 14b, 15, 17, 19-20, 23a, 24, 25ad, 26a, 27, 29
Spug — 1, 4, 6a, 9, 11, 13, 16
Spugh — 23b
Spurdie — 32
Whinnie — 6b

East Lothian

Lum lintie — 4a
Sparrow — 4b, 8-9, 15-16, 18
Speug — 2, 4b, 5, 6ab, 10, 14, 19, 21
Speugh — 12
Spreug — 7
Sprig — 13
Sprug — 2, 6a, 9-11, 15, 17
Spruggie — 3, 14-16, 20
Spug — 1, 4a, 8, 10, 13
Spuggie — 1, 13

Berwick

Hempie — 5
Scallie — 27
Sparrow — 8, 12-13, 16bc, 27, 29, 31-32
Speug — 4, 6, 8, 13, 23, 27, 29
Sprig — 8, 14, 26
Sprug — 2, 11, 16a, 22-23, 31
Spug — 1-2, 8, 12, 15, 16b, 17, 21, 23, 25, 29, 32
Spuger — 5
Spuggie — 3, 7-10, 16b, 18-20, 23, 25, 27, 30-31
Spurdie — 11-12
Nil — 24, 28

Peebles

Sparrow — 4bc, 6ab
Speug — 1-2, 4c, 7, 9
Speugh — 5, 8
Sprug — 4b, 10
Spug — 3, 6a
Spuggie — 4a

Selkirk

Sparrow — 2acde, 4, 8
Speug — 2cd
Sprug — 2a
Spud — 2e
Spug — 1, 2d, 3, 6
Spuggie — 7
Spurdie — 2bc
Nil — 5

Roxburgh

Dykie — 21c
Fieldie — 21c
Sparrow — 1-2, 5-6, 9a, 13, 15b, 17, 20, 21a, 26, 28
Speug — 8, 14, 23
Speugie — 18
Sprug — 4, 15a
Spug — 1, 4-5, 9ab, 10, 13, 17, 20, 21acdf, 22, 25-26
Spuggie — 3b, 7-8, 16-17, 19-20, 24, 28
Spurdie — 3a
Nil — 11-12, 21be, 27

Dumfries

Spadger — 43
Sparrow — 4, 12, 46
Speug — 1b, 3-5, 8a, 10, 17a, 20, 21b, 22, 24-26, 31acdef, 32, 41
Speugh — 9
Sproog — 2
Spud — 33
Spug — 1a, 5-7, 8ab, 10, 12-16, 17b, 18-19, 21ab, 26-30, 31bcde, 32-44, 45ab, 46-47, 49
Spuggie — 29
Spuig — 11
Nil — 23, 48

Kirkcudbright

Sparrow — 6-7
Speug — 1, 3-8, 12b, 13-14, 15a, 19, 21ac, 22-24, 26-27
Speugh — 18
Spug — 2, 9-11, 15b, 16-17, 21b, 25
Spuig — 9, 12a
Nil — 20

Wigtown

Spag — 9
Sparrow — 2, 4, 7, 11-13, 16
Spatie — 17
Speug — 1, 5b, 6, 12-17
Speugh — 8
Sprug — 5a
Spug — 3, 7, 10
Nil — 18

Northumberland

Cuddie — 69b
Hoosie — 132
Jackie sparrow — 41c
Mountie — 95a
Smokie — 10
Smottie — 124a
Sooty wool — 37
Spadger — 33a, 62f, 63, 64a, 79, 127a, 129a, 135
Spadgie — 1c, 129b
Spaggie — 130a
Sparrow — 2b, 5, 7, 14, 16, 23, 28, 30, 35, 40a, 41cd, 42, 53b, 57, 59bd, 62b, 69c, 71d, 72c, 77, 87, 89, 99b, 103abc, 109, 111a, 112, 121, 127a, 130bce, 140, 142
Sping — 132
Spoggie — 100
Spogie — 89
Spoogie — 123
Sprug — 132
Spudger — 51
Spug — 1c, 28, 39, 59b
Spuggie — 1abc, 2ab, 3-10, 12-18, 19a, 20ab, 21-23, 24ab, 25-28, 29abcdef, 30-32, 33ab, 34ab, 35-39, 40ab, 41abcd, 42-52, 53ab, 54-58, 59abcdef, 60-61, 62abcdefgh, 63, 64ab, 65ab, 66-68, 69abcdefgh, 70, 71abcde,

Northumberland cont'd
72abcdefgijkl, 73-86, 88ab, 90-93, 94b, 95ab, 96-98, 99abcd, 101ab, 102, 103bc, 104ab, 105-107, 108abc, 109-110, 111ab, 112-117, 118ab, 119, 120abc, 121, 122ab, 123, 124ab, 125, 126abcdef, 127abcdefgh, 128, 129abc, 130bcdef, 131-143
Spur — 11
Nil — 19b, 72h, 94a

Cumberland
Blue dykie — 13d, 28, 38, 63a
Creepy dyke — 27
Dykie — 27
Scobbie — 40
Scoppie — 1a
Spadger — 7, 12, 13a, 15c, 16, 18, 20, 22, 25-27, 30, 41, 43-45, 56-57, 59-62, 63ab
Sparrow — 5a, 9, 15a, 21-24, 26, 39-40, 42, 45, 48-50, 57-58, 60
Spogie — 15c
Spudger — 52
Spug — 5a, 12, 29, 43
Spuggie — 1a, 2-4, 5a, 6, 8-9, 11, 13bcd, 14, 15ab, 16-19, 24, 28-29, 31, 33-34, 36, 37ab, 38-40, 42, 44-45, 47, 50, 53, 55, 57-58, 63a
Nil — 1b, 5b, 10, 32, 35, 46, 51, 54

Down
Blue bird — 24
Spadger — 2ab, 10
Sparrow — 2a, 3, 5, 7, 9, 13, 15, 17-19, 21, 24, 26-30
Nil — 1, 4, 6, 8, 11-12, 14, 16, 20, 22-23, 25

Tyrone
Sparrow — 1, 7-11, 13
Nil — 2-6, 12, 14-16

Antrim
Grey spadger — 34
Spadger — 23-24, 31, 33
Sparrow — 1, 3, 5ab, 9, 13, 15, 17, 19-22, 25-27, 29
Tweed spadger — 34
Nil — 2, 4, 4A, 6-7, 8ab, 10-12, 14, 16abc, 18, 28, 30, 32

Donegal
Gealabhain — 6
Sparrow — 4-6, 7A, 8, 10a, 12
Spyug — 2
Nil — 1, 1A, 3, 5A, 7, 9, 10b, 11, 13

Fermanagh
Sparrow — 4-5, 7a, 8-9
Nil — 1-3, 6, 7b, 10

Armagh
Sparrow — 4, 6a
Spug — 2-3
Nil — 1, 5, 6b

Londonderry
Sparrow — 2-3, 3A
Nil — 1, 1AB, 4-7

72 LAPWING (PQ1, 162)

Shetland
Cattifool — 10
Dockin fowl — 23
Green plover — 5
Lapwing — 1-3, 7-8, 15-17, 20, 21ab, 29-30, 33
Peewee — 24
Peeweep — 21a
Peewit — 2, 6, 11, 15, 18, 22
Tieves' nacket — 5, 21b, 26
Whaap — 25
Nil — 4, 9, 12-14, 19, 27-28, 31-32

Orkney
Lapwing — 8
Peewit — 5, 8, 15
Pheweep — 14
Teeack — 4, 8-12, 13ab, 14-17, 20-21
Teeo — 5-7, 13ab
Tee whip — 4
Tee whipo — 1, 4
Tee whoppo — 2
Tee whuppo — 3
Tee wup — 8
Thievnack — 17-19, 21

Caithness
Green plover — 13
Jochad — 13
Peewee — 12a
Peeweep — 6, 8, 10-11, 14-15, 16b
Peewit — 1, 2b, 16b
Scochad — 12a
Shochad — 2b, 3, 5-11, 12bc, 14-15, 16b, 17
Shochet — 6
Shouchad — 2a
Shuchad — 16a
Nil — 4

Sutherland
Green plover — 3
Lapwing — 3, 6-7, 12-13
Peesieweep — 15
Peesweep — 3, 13
Peeweep — 14-15
Peewit — 1-3, 5-8, 9b, 10-12, 15-17
Shochad — 3, 6, 9a
Shockat — 9b, 10
Sochad — 3
Teuchat — 8
Nil — 4

Ross & Cromarty
Lapwing — 1, 4-5, 16-17, 27, 32a
Peesweep — 19
Peevick — 24, 31
Peewee — 20
Peeweep — 8-9, 12-13, 18, 26, 28, 34-35
Peewick — 25b
Peewit — 2-3, 5-7, 9-11, 14, 16-17, 19-23, 25a, 27-31, 32bc, 33, 36, 39
Plover — 20,29
Nil — 15, 37ab, 38

Inverness
Derakin — 27
Lapwing — 2-3, 5, 21b, 23, 32, 36-37
Peeweep — 7-8, 13e, 17, 22, 25, 29, 40
Peewit — 1, 4, 6, 8-12, 13abcde, 15-16, 18-20, 21ab, 23-24, 26-35, 38-39
Plover — 6, 13e, 32
Wallapie — 29
Nil — 14

Nairn
Lapwing — 2
Peesie — 1c
Peewit — 1abc, 2-5
Nil — 6

Moray
Cheukat — 11
Lallack — 2a
Lapwing — 20, 23
Laverock — 21
Peesieweep — 9b
Peesweep — 6a, 8a
Peeweep — 1, 3-4, 7, 8e, 11-12, 22-23
Peewit — 5, 6b, 7, 8abcd, 9a, 11, 13-15, 19-20, 23
Teuchat — 3, 8bf, 9a, 12, 20, 22
Wallock — 7, 8f, 12-17
Wallockie — 5, 7, 13
Wallop — 18
Wallopie — 8b, 10-11, 22-23
Wallopie weep — 22
Wollackie — 18
Nil — 2b

Banff
Peesie — 1, 2c, 3-5, 6b, 7-12, 14-17, 18c, 21-25, 28, 31
Peesiewee — 2c
Peesieweep — 1, 2ac, 3, 7-8, 10, 17, 26
Peesieweet — 18b
Peesweep — 10, 18c, 21, 24, 29-30
Peeweep — 33-34
Peewit — 6a, 9, 18cd, 19-20, 27-28, 30, 32
Teuchit — 6b, 9, 11, 13-16, 22-24, 26-27, 29-32
Tuquheit — 29
Wallop — 18d
Wallopie — 14-16, 25, 31-33
Weep — 34
Nil — 2b, 18a

Aberdeen
Peesie — 2, 8, 11-13, 16, 19, 22-25, 27, 28abc, 29-30, 32-34, 45, 48-49, 51, 53-56, 58, 60, 62-65, 67-70, 71ab, 72, 74, 79, 81-85, 87-89, 93-96, 98-101, 103-108
Peesieweep — 4, 5b, 9, 16, 19-21, 29, 34, 44-45, 47ae, 51, 62, 66-67, 71abc, 73-74, 77, 80, 89, 97, 104, 107-108
Peesieweet — 3a, 6, 10, 38, 47a, 59, 90
Peeshieweep — 5a
Peesweep — 8-9, 28ab, 47a, 75-76, 85
Peesweet — 14, 76
Peeweep — 78, 92
Peewit — 7, 9-10, 12, 23-24, 26, 40, 47cd, 65, 70, 86, 102-103, 105-106
Teucat — 6, 67
Teuchat — 2, 3ab, 4, 5abcd, 6, 8-12, 15-21, 23-25, 27, 28abc, 30-46, 47abcdef, 48-53, 55-64, 69, 71abc, 72-77, 79-82, 85, 91-94, 96-98, 101, 103-106, 109
Teuchie — 14
Tuckat — 26, 86
Twechat — 5c
Wallop — 22, 53
Wallopie — 64
Wallopie weep — 33
Whaup — 16, 30
Nil — 1

Kincardine
Peesie — 1, 3-4, 7, 10-11, 13-14, 17abd, 18-19, 21, 23-24, 26-28
Peesieweep — 2-3, 5, 12, 17c
Peesieweet — 10, 14, 22-23
Peesweep — 17d
Peeweep — 11
Peewit — 8, 15, 17c, 18, 20, 22, 25, 27
Teuchat — 2, 4-13, 15-16, 17abcd, 18, 21, 23, 26, 28
Tuchet — 19
Whaup — 3

Kinross
Chuckit — 2-3
Peeser — 6
Peesweep — 2, 4, 7
Peeweep — 1, 3, 6
Peewit — 1, 5
Teuchat — 7

Angus
Chuchet — 2
Curlew — 14a
Lapwing — 17b
Peesie — 3, 5c, 6, 8-10, 12-13, 14bcd, 15, 19-20, 22-24, 26-27, 29a, 30-32, 33a, 34-35
Peesieweep — 5a
Peesieweet — 37
Peeweep — 18, 23, 28
Peewit — 1, 4, 5a, 7, 14acd, 16, 17b, 18, 21-22, 25, 27, 31, 33b, 34, 36
Plover — 14a, 17b
Teanchat — 22
Teuchat — 3, 5abc, 7, 13, 14ab, 15, 21, 23-27, 30, 32, 34, 36
Tuchet — 17a
Nil — 11, 29b

Perth
Chewit — 30
Chukit — 62
Herald davie — 49
Lapwing — 2a, 4, 24, 36
Peeser — 16, 61, 68
Peesie — 5-7, 11, 13, 16, 20, 22-23, 26-28, 29a, 31-33, 41a, 42-44, 50, 52a, 57-60, 62-63
Peesieweet — 20
Peesweep — 9-10, 33, 50, 51ab, 52b, 62, 66, 68-69, 72
Peesweet — 24, 53
Peewee — 24, 34
Peeweep — 5-6, 13, 15-16, 18, 25-26, 28, 29b, 39-40, 45-46, 52acde, 54, 56, 59, 61-62, 67-68, 71-72
Peewit — 1, 2b, 3, 8-12, 14, 17, 20-21, 25-26, 29ab, 34-35, 37-38, 41ab, 47-48, 51b, 53, 55, 57, 59, 63-64, 67, 70, 73-74
Pliver — 52c
Plover — 34, 55, 57
Teuchat — 13, 26, 29a, 32, 39, 45, 52cd
Nil — 19, 65

Fife
Lappie — 23, 48
Lapwing — 4
Peeser — 26
Peesie — 2, 7, 29, 63
Peesweep — 6, 21-22, 27, 30, 35, 36a, 44ad, 46
Peevie — 18
Peewee — 64a
Peeweep — 1, 3-5, 7-8, 9ab, 10, 12-14, 16, 23, 25-26, 31, 34, 36b, 38-39, 40a, 41abcd, 42, 43ab, 44ef, 48, 50, 54, 55bcef, 56-59, 61
Peewheep — 3
Peewit — 6, 11-12, 17-21, 24, 28-29, 32-35, 37, 40b, 43b, 44ce, 45, 47, 49, 51-54, 55abdg, 60, 62
Plover — 50, 55bd
Teuchat — 12, 23, 46
Whaup — 8, 12
Nil — 15, 44b, 64b

Clackmannan
Peesweep — 2, 4a
Peeweep — 1-3, 4cd, 5
Peewit — 4bd, 6-7
Plover — 4c

Stirling

Lark — 20
Peeser — 12
Peesie — 7abc
Peesieweep — 26b
Peesweep — 2, 15, 18, 21b, 25a, 26b
Peewee — 9, 24
Peeweep — 1, 3-4, 7abcde, 8-9, 12-14, 16-19, 21ab, 22ab, 23abc, 25cd, 26ade, 27a, 28, 30-34, 35a, 36, 37ab, 39b, 42a
Peewit — 4, 6, 7bef, 10-11, 15, 23a, 25ab, 26bcdf, 29, 35b, 36, 38, 39a, 40, 42b
Plover — 36, 39b
Teuchat — 6
Whaup — 18
Nil — 5, 27b, 41

Dunbarton

Peeser — 16b, 18
Peesweep — 2, 4a, 7c, 14b, 16a
Peesweet — 5
Peeweep — 1, 3, 4b, 6, 7abc, 9-12, 13a, 16b, 18
Peewit — 3, 5, 8, 13bc, 14a, 15, 17-18
Plover — 4a

Argyll

Green plover — 26-27, 33
Lapwing — 6, 17, 19, 26-27
Peesweep — 6, 14, 31-35, 39
Peeweep — 1, 7, 9-10, 12, 15-16, 18, 20, 24-26, 28-30, 36-38, 40
Peewit — 3, 5, 8, 16, 19, 21-24, 26, 34-35
Plover — 11, 15
Nil — 2, 4, 13

Bute

Green plover — 8b
Lapwing — 1a
Peesweep — 3, 6, 8b
Peeweep — 1e, 2, 4-5, 7, 8ab
Peewit — 1acd, 6, 9
Plover — 7
Nil — 1b

Ayr

Green plover — 57
Lapwing — 28ce, 43, 57
Peeser — 2a, 24ab
Peesie — 10, 18b, 22, 29, 37, 42-46, 48-49, 51, 53a
Peesweep — 1a, 2ab, 3-4, 6-7, 8ab, 11, 12a, 13, 17, 19, 20ae, 23, 26ac, 28abce, 30a, 32, 34, 37, 40, 43, 46-50, 52, 53ab, 54, 56-57
Peesweet — 16a, 20fh
Peewee — 18b, 20g, 27, 28a, 49
Peeweep — 1ab, 2a, 5-6, 8b, 9-11, 12b, 13, 15, 16b, 18a, 20abce, 21, 24ab, 25, 28def, 29, 30a, 33, 35ab, 36-37, 45, 51-52, 55
Peewist — 18b
Peewit — 1a, 3, 7, 14, 18b, 20d, 22, 26ab, 28ace, 29, 30b, 31, 38-39, 41, 49, 57
Plover — 28e, 35b

Renfrew

Lapwing — 2ai, 16b, 20a
Peeser — 7, 11l, 18a
Peesie — 14b
Peesweep — 2e, 3, 4c, 11bfil, 12b, 13b, 14b, 16bc
Peewee — 11k
Peeweep — 2bcdij, 5-10, 11adil, 12a, 14a, 16ad, 18a, 21
Peewit — 1b, 2fgh, 4ae, 11bejk, 12b, 13acd, 14a, 15, 16bc, 17, 18b, 19, 20ab, 21
Plover — 8
Nil — 1a, 4bd, 11cgh

Lanark

Curlew — 7a
Green plover — 29e
Lapwing — 7c, 14d, 26a, 35d
Peeser — 3, 16b, 21, 31b, 33a, 35ac, 41-43, 45, 46c, 47, 51, 52b, 56, 57ab, 58, 59a, 61-63
Peesie — 57c
Peesweep — 4, 9ab, 10a, 13, 15bc, 17, 20, 23-24, 29d, 30, 31ad, 32e, 33cd, 35d, 38bd, 39, 45, 46ac, 47-48, 49b, 52ab, 56, 57ab, 58, 59ab, 64ab, 65
Peesweet — 1
Peewee — 29g
Peeweep — 2-4, 6, 8b, 9a, 12, 14ab, 15a, 16b, 18-19, 22, 24, 25a, 26b, 27ab, 29cf, 30, 31d, 32abf, 33ab, 35abd, 36-37, 38ae, 39-40, 47, 50-51, 52b, 53-54, 57c, 59a, 60, 62-63, 66
Peewit — 1-3, 5-6, 7ac, 10a, 11-12, 14acd, 15bc, 21, 25abc, 27b, 29ae, 31b, 32cde, 33cd, 34, 35cd, 38cd, 43-44, 46b, 55
Plover — 7c, 14d, 29c, 32e
Teuchat — 38cd
Nil — 7b, 8a, 10b, 16a, 25d, 28, 29b, 31c, 49a, 67ab

West Lothian

Peeser — 17a, 20a
Peesie — 11
Peesweep — 2, 10, 18
Peewee — 9b
Peeweep — 1ad, 2-6, 8, 9a, 11-12, 15, 17ab, 20a, 21ab, 22
Peewit — 1bc, 7, 12-14, 16, 19b, 20a, 21b, 22
Plover — 16
Nil — 19a, 20b

Midlothian

Lapwing — 10, 23b
Peesweep — 4, 13, 14a, 26a, 30, 32
Peesweet — 7b
Peewee — 3, 22
Peeweep — 7b, 10, 12ab, 14a, 18, 23b, 24, 25c, 28-30
Peewit — 1, 3, 6ab, 7a, 8b, 10-11, 14b, 15-22, 25ac, 26b, 27, 31
Plover — 17
Socher — 11
Nil — 2, 5, 8a, 9, 23a, 25bd

East Lothian

Peesweep — 4b, 8-9, 14-15
Peesweet — 9
Peeweep — 3, 4ab, 6a, 7-9, 16-17, 19-21
Peewit — 1-2, 6b, 9-16, 18
Plover — 13
Nil — 5

Berwick

Peesweep — 3-5, 7, 10-11, 13-14, 16b, 18, 22, 26, 32
Peesweet — 31
Peeweep — 1-2, 8-10, 12, 16c, 18, 20, 25, 27
Peewit — 2, 6-8, 10, 15a, 16a, 17, 19, 21, 23-24, 29-30, 32
Plover — 8
Rikkitie — 27
Nil — 28

Peebles

Lapwing — 6b
Peeser — 5, 7
Peesweep — 3, 10
Peeweep — 1-2, 4bc, 5, 7, 10
Peewit — 6a, 8-9
Nil — 4a

Selkirk

Peesweep — 1, 3-4, 8
Peewee — 2d
Peeweep — 2be
Peewit — 2ac, 6-7
Nil — 5

Roxburgh

Lapwing — 21a, 28
Peesieweep — 10
Peesweep — 1-2, 3a, 4, 7-8, 9ab, 12-14, 15b, 16-18, 20, 21acdf, 23, 25-26, 28
Peesweet — 19
Peeweep — 5, 10, 13, 17, 20, 21d, 24
Peewit — 2, 3b, 4, 6, 15a, 22, 26
Pick maw — 21c
Nil — 11, 21be, 27

Dumfries

Peesie — 14, 21a, 25-28, 34-35
Peesweep — 1a, 4, 10-11, 13, 16, 17b, 18-19, 21b, 26-28, 31bc, 32, 34, 36-41, 45a, 46, 49
Peesweet — 9, 31b, 35
Peewee — 15
Peeweep — 2-3, 5, 10-11, 17a, 25, 29
Peewheet — 7
Peewit — 4, 8a, 11-12, 17b, 19, 21b, 22, 31abcef, 33, 42-44, 46
Plover — 4, 12, 46
Teeweet — 19, 22, 30, 31d, 32, 42, 46
Teewheet — 6, 8b, 20, 21b, 24, 41, 45b
Nil — 1b, 23, 47-48

Kirkcudbright

Lapwing — 7
Peesweep — 2, 6, 15a
Peesweet — 1, 18
Peeweep — 4
Peewheep — 19
Peewheet — 14, 19, 27
Peewit — 1, 3, 5, 7, 11, 12b, 15b, 23-24, 26
Tee weet — 20, 21c, 25
Teewheet — 6, 8-10, 12a, 13, 16-18, 21ab, 22, 27

Wigtown

Peesweep — 5a, 6, 10, 18
Peesweet — 7
Peeweep — 1-4, 5b, 6-9, 12-13, 15, 17-18
Peewit — 11, 14, 16
Plover — 5a

Northumberland

Curlew — 92
Curlui — 69c
Green plover — 6, 29e, 58, 69a
Lappin — 126c
Lapwing — 2b, 13, 28, 35, 64a, 70, 77, 86, 100, 120abc, 127a
Peeser — 53a, 60
Peesie — 7, 47
Peesweep — 1abc, 2ab, 3, 5, 11-16, 20a, 21, 23, 24b, 25-26, 34a, 39, 40b, 41c, 43-45, 48, 51, 59e, 62f, 68, 72j, 74, 77, 103bc, 104a, 107, 112, 133, 136-138
Peesweet — 45
Peewee — 92, 129a
Peeweep — 1a, 4, 6, 9, 27-28, 29b, 33b, 36, 38, 41bd, 45, 62bg, 63, 65ab, 69abdefg, 71b, 72gj, 76, 81-82, 84, 88a, 90, 101a, 103bc, 111ab, 117, 130f, 142
Peewheep — 32, 86, 118b
Peewheet — 58, 72d, 89, 98, 118b
Peewit — 1b, 2b, 8, 10, 14, 16-18, 19a, 20b, 22, 24a, 26, 28, 29abdef, 30-31, 34b, 35, 37, 39, 40ab, 41abd, 42-43, 46-50, 52, 53ab, 54-57 59abcdef, 60, 62abdef, 64b, 65b, 66, 68, 69abcgh, 71bcde, 72bfgijk, 73, 75-80, 82-83, 85, 87, 88b, 91, 94b, 95ab, 97, 99bcd, 101b, 102, 103a, 104ab, 105-106, 108abc, 109-110, 111ab, 114, 118a, 119, 121, 122ab, 124ab, 125, 126abef, 127acde, 128, 129b, 130cdef, 132-135, 138-139, 143
Plover — 2b, 5, 19a, 20b, 29a, 45-47, 53b, 58, 59b, 62a, 66, 69f, 71d, 72gi, 77, 79, 104a, 109-110, 122a, 127c
Teewit — 12
Tufit — 124a
Tyufit — 124a, 133
Waup — 46
Weep — 63
Whaup — 29d, 41c
Nil — 19b, 29c, 33a, 61, 62ch, 67 71a, 72acehl, 93, 94a, 96, 99a, 113, 115-116, 123, 126d, 127bfgh, 129c, 130ab, 131, 140-141

Cumberland

Chuffet — 14
Lapwing — 4, 12, 23, 42, 48
Peesweep — 2-3, 5a, 8, 13ac, 27, 30, 37b
Peeweep — 2
Peewhit — 15b, 29
Peewit — 1ab, 4, 6-9, 11-12, 13b, 14, 15ac, 16-28, 30, 32-34, 36, 37b, 38-47, 49-62, 63b
Plover — 4, 12, 25, 40, 42-43, 54, 56
Puett — 13a
Teuffet — 9, 13a, 15ac, 16, 27-28, 30-32, 38-40, 43-44, 46, 49, 57, 59-60
Tewet — 27, 37a, 56, 62, 63a
Twuffet — 21
Nil — 5b, 10, 13d, 35

Down

Green plover — 21, 24
Lapwing — 5, 7
Peesweep — 3, 8
Peeweep — 10-11, 13, 15, 21-23, 25, 28
Peeweet — 2b, 4, 8
Pliver — 2b
Plover — 2b, 6, 11, 14-15, 18, 26, 28
Nil — 1, 2a, 9, 12, 16-17, 19-20, 27, 29-30

Tyrone

Lapwing — 1, 11
Peeweep — 11
Peeweet — 14
Peewit — 2, 5, 11
Nil — 3-4, 6-10, 12-13, 15-16

Antrim

Lapwing — 1, 29
Peesweep — 15, 16b, 19-26
Peesweet — 19
Peewee — 18
Peeweep — 2, 7, 9, 11-13, 33
Peeweet — 7, 15, 19
Peewit — 4A, 8b, 9, 25-26, 28, 34
Ploomer — 17
Plover — 27
Whaup — 34
Nil — 3-4, 5ab, 6, 8a, 10, 14, 16ac, 30-32

Donegal
Corncrake — 10b
Lapwing — 12
Peeweet — 4, 6, 10a
Peewit — 5, 10a
Plover 12
Tappie — 5
Nil — 1, 1A, 2-3, 5A, 7, 7A, 8-9, 11, 13

Fermanagh
Lapwing — 9
Peeweep — 4-5
Peeweet — 8
Peewit — 4-5, 8, 10
Nil — 1-3, 6, 7ab

Armagh
Curlew — 4
Footan — 2
Peeweep — 5, 6a
Peeweet — 6a
Peewit — 1, 6b
Snipe — 3
Nil — 2

Londonderry
Curlew — 3, 5
Lapwing — 2
Peeweet — 1AB, 4, 6
Peewheet — 3
Nil — 1, 3A, 7

73 JACKDAW (PQ1, 164)

Jackdaw has not been mapped as it occurs densely nearly everywhere except in Shetland.
Variants of JACKDAW have been subsumed (**jakedaw** Stirlingshire, Dunbarton, Ayrshire, Renfrewshire, Lanarkshire and the Lothians; **jeckdaw** is more scattered).

Shetland
Cra — 22
Daw — 5
Jackdaw — 15
Nil — 1-4, 6-14, 16-20, 21ab, 23-33

Orkney
Jackdaw — 1-2, 13ab, 15, 17, 19
Rook — 5
Nil — 3-4, 6-12, 14, 16, 18, 20-21

Caithness
Craw — 8-9
Crow — 4, 9, 15
Daw — 2b, 6
Jackdaw — 5, 9, 11, 13, 16b
Little crow — 13
Nil — 1, 2a, 3, 7, 10, 12abc, 14, 16a, 17

Sutherland
Crow — 3
Jackdaw — 1, 7-8, 9ab, 10-13, 16
Jeckiedaw — 15
Nil — 2, 4-6, 14, 17

Ross & Cromarty
Jackdaw — 1, 3-6, 8-9, 16-20, 22, 24, 25ab, 27-29, 32ab, 34, 36, 39
Jackie — 13, 25b
Jeckie — 37a
Jeckiedaw — 31
Keeya — 33
Kyau — 36
Nil — 2, 7, 10-12, 14-15, 21, 23, 26, 30, 32c, 35, 37b, 38

Inverness
Crow — 20, 35
Daw — 6, 16
Jackdaw — 2-8, 10-11, 13abce, 17, 19, 21ab, 22-23, 26-29, 33-34, 36-39
Jackie — 7, 14-15, 26
Nil — 1, 9, 12, 13d, 18, 24-25, 30-32, 40

Nairn
Daw — 1b
Jackdaw — 2
Nil — 1ac, 3-6

Moray
Corbie — 21
Daw — 20
Hoodie craw — 21
Jackdaw — 8bd, 11, 23
Jackie — 5, 7, 8c, 9a, 14-15
Jackiedaw — 9b
Jakie — 11, 22
Kaise — 2a
Kay — 1, 3, 7, 8ab, 10, 18-19
Kya — 4
Kyaw — 3
Stirlin' — 6b
Nil — 2b, 6a, 8ef, 12-13, 16-17

Banff
Caw — 23
Daw — 5, 6b, 10, 17, 24
Jackdaw — 1, 2b, 15-16, 18c, 19, 21, 24
Jacker — 27
Jackie — 32
Jay — 9
Kay — 4, 7-8, 18c, 23, 26, 29, 31, 34
Nil — 2ac, 3, 6a, 11-14, 18abd, 20, 22, 25, 28, 30, 33

Aberdeen
Craw — 21, 32, 48, 50
Crow — 31
Daw — 17, 34, 41, 66
Jackdaw — 5a, 6, 12, 22-23, 28c, 44-46, 47f, 59, 69-70, 74, 79, 81-83, 94-95, 98, 100-101, 104, 107
Jackie — 17, 21, 49, 92
Jakie — 108
Jay — 35
Kay — 3a, 5cd, 9-10, 17, 28a, 75-76, 78, 82, 88
Nil — 1-2, 3b, 4, 5b, 7-8, 11, 13-16, 18-20, 24-27, 28b, 29-30, 33, 36-40, 42-43, 47abcde, 51-58, 60-65, 67-68, 71abc, 72-73, 77, 80, 84-87, 89-91, 93, 96-97, 99, 102-103, 105-106, 109

Kincardine
Craw — 5
Daw — 2, 24
Huddie craw — 26
Jackdaw — 5-8, 10, 16, 19
Jackie — 17c, 21
Jeck — 3
Kay — 14, 25, 27
Nil — 1, 4, 9, 11-13, 15, 17abd, 18, 20, 22-23, 28

Kinross
Jackdaw — 4, 6
Jeckie — 1-3, 7
Kay — 7
Nil -- 5

Angus
Craw — 28
Daw — 4, 5c, 14b, 25
Huddie — 15
Jackdaw — 10, 17b, 25, 31, 34, 36
Jackie — 5a, 8-9, 13, 15, 17a, 18, 20, 22, 24, 34-36
Jaikie — 7
Jay — 12, 17b
Jeckie — 19, 27, 31
Jockie — 17b
Kay — 3, 5c, 6-7, 13, 14acd, 24, 33b, 34, 37
Kay hattie — 33b
Nil — 1-2, 5b, 11, 16, 21, 23, 26, 29ab, 30, 32, 33a

Perth
Cavie — 41b
Daw — 51a, 71
Jackdaw — 2a, 4, 8-10, 21, 24-25, 32, 36, 40, 46, 52ab, 57, 61, 69-72, 74
Jackie — 1, 2ab, 8-9, 12-13, 17, 24-26, 28, 30, 50, 73
Jaikie — 5-6, 66-68
Jeckie — 7, 10-11, 13, 15, 18, 20, 25-26, 29a, 32, 42-43, 52cde, 55, 57, 59, 65, 73
Jeckiedaw — 16
Kay — 27, 29b, 32-33, 39, 41ab, 46, 48, 52cd, 56, 60, 62
Kyaw — 59, 69
Piet — 53
Nil — 3, 14, 19, 22-23, 31, 34-35, 37-38, 44-45, 47, 49, 51b, 54, 58, 63-64

Fife
Craw — 44a
Daw — 23, 36a, 39, 44c, 48, 50, 53, 55d, 57
Hoodie — 49
Jack — 37
Jackdaw — 4, 7-8, 16, 19-21, 24, 41a, 43a, 44cd, 46-47, 50, 55abef, 56-57, 62
Jackie -- 6, 21, 29, 33-35, 37, 53
Jaikie — 20, 30
Jeckie — 1-5, 7-8, 9a, 10-14, 17, 25-26, 28, 36ab, 39, 40b, 42, 43b, 44e, 45, 55b, 58-59, 61, 64ab
Kay — 18, 55f
Keeya — 32-34
Sma' craw — 6
Nil — 9b, 15, 22, 27, 31, 38, 40a, 41bcd, 44bf, 51-52, 54, 55cg, 60, 63

Clackmannan
Daw — 4bc
Jackdaw — 5-7
Jaikie — 1
K'yaw — 1
Nil — 2-3, 4ad

Stirling
Craw — 10,12
Daw — 25b, 26f, 35a, 40
Jack — 26b
Jackdaw — 4, 7ade, 8-9, 13, 15, 18, 20, 21ab, 22b, 23abc, 25ad, 26ae, 27a, 28, 30-34, 37a, 39b
Jackie — 7b
Jaikie — 17, 26c, 37b, 42a
Jaiko — 7b
Jeckie — 6, 7e, 11, 36
Kais — 26b
Kay — 2, 7d
Rookie daw — 25c
White headed crow — 7c
Nil — 1, 3, 5, 7f, 14-16, 19, 22a, 24, 26d, 27b, 29, 35b, 38, 39a, 41, 42b

Dunbarton
Corbie — 4b
Corbie crow — 6
Daw — 1, 6, 9, 14a
Jackdaw — 3, 6, 7abc, 9-11, 13bc, 14b, 16ab, 18
Jeck — 13a
Kay — 14a
Keyaw — 2
Stookie — 3
Nil — 4a, 5, 8, 12, 15, 17

Argyll
Corbie — 18
Craw — 18
Daw — 1, 35
Jackdaw — 2-3, 6-7, 9-11, 14-17, 19, 22-25, 27, 30, 33-37, 39
Jackie — 28
Sammie jay — 24
Nil — 4-5, 8, 12-13, 20-21, 26, 29, 31-32, 38, 40

Bute
Craw — 8a, 9
Jackdaw — 1abcd, 2-4, 7, 8b
Jaikie — 5
Nil — 1e, 6

Ayr
Chough — 57
Craw — 8b, 20e, 25
Daw — 2b, 12a, 17, 20c, 27, 28e, 30b, 41, 53b, 57
Hoodie craw — 19
Jackdaw — 2ab, 3-5, 7, 8a, 9-10, 13-15, 20bcdgh, 21, 24ab, 26c, 28cef, 30a, 31, 33-34, 35ab, 36, 43-45, 48-49, 55-57
Jackie — 26b, 28b, 53a, 56
Jaik — 12b, 41, 49
Jaikie — 6, 18a, 30a, 32, 37, 42, 48
Jeckie — 1a, 52
Kay — 18b, 47
Kyaw — 51, 54
Qua — 45
Quhaw — 18b
Nil — 1b, 11, 16ab, 20af, 22-23

Ayr cont'd
26a, 28ad, 29, 38-40, 46, 50

Renfrew
Daw — 11ab, 16a
Jackdaw — 2abi, 4ace, 8, 11aefjkl, 12a, 13c, 14a, 16b, 18a, 19, 20a
Jackie — 16d
Jackie daw — 7
Jacko — 21
Jaik — 15
Jaikie — 17
Jeckie — 1b
Kay — 20b
Nil — 1a, 2cdefghj, 3, 4bd, 5-6, 9-10, 11cdghi, 12b, 13abd, 14b, 16c, 18b

Lanark
Craw — 64a
Daw — 7c, 10a, 11, 14b, 15b, 20 26a, 30, 33b, 38b, 39, 42, 46ac, 47-48, 49a, 57b, 59a
Jack — 29f
Jackdaw — 1-2, 6, 7ac, 8b, 9a, 12-13, 14d, 15ac, 16b, 18-20, 25bc, 27b, 29cdf, 31ad, 32a, 33d, 35bd, 37, 40, 44-45, 46abc, 47, 51, 53, 57ab, 58, 59b, 64b, 65
Jackie — 13, 15b, 39, 56, 59a
Jaikie — 17, 29d, 38ac, 49b 50-51, 52a, 62-63
Kay — 38d
Kay wattie — 38d
Keya — 9b
Lipper jay — 38d
Rook — 29e
Nil — 3-5, 7b, 8a, 10b, 14ac, 16a, 21-24, 25ad, 26b, 27a, 28, 29abg, 31bc, 32bcdef, 33ac, 34, 35ac, 36, 38e, 41, 43, 52b, 54-55, 57c, 60-61, 66, 67ab

West Lothian
Daw — 2-3, 20a, 21a
Jackdaw — 1a, 3, 5-6, 9b, 10-13, 16, 17a, 18, 20a
Jackie — 1c, 7-8, 11, 14, 19ab
Jakie — 1bd, 2, 5-6, 15, 22
Jeckie — 4, 13
Joakie — 15
Nil — 9a, 17b, 20b, 21b

Midlothian
Daw — 6a
Grey neck — 17
Jackdaw — 6ab, 7a, 8a, 10-11, 12b, 14a, 15, 18, 21, 23ab, 32
Jackie — 4, 6b, 15-17, 26b
Jakie — 3, 7b, 8b, 9-10, 12ab, 13, 14b, 17-20, 23ab, 24, 25ac, 26a, 27-32
Jeckie — 11
Nil — 1-2, 5, 22, 25bd

East Lothian
Daw — 2, 4a
Jackdaw — 4b, 6a, 15-16, 21
Jackie — 10, 17, 19
Jaikie — 1-3, 4b, 6b, 7-10, 12, 14-16, 18, 20
Ja ka — 13
Jeckie — 11
Ka — 13
Nil — 5

Berwick
Blackie — 8
Gwain — 27
Jack — 5-6
Jackdaw — 10, 16b, 32
Jackie — 2, 8, 16a, 18-19, 24, 27
Jaik — 32
Jaikie — 1, 3-4, 11-13, 15, 16c, 17, 22-23, 25, 29-32
Jeck — 7, 9-10, 21, 26, 31-32,
Jeckie — 14, 20
Kay — 16a
Laver — 27
Nil — 28

Peebles
Daw — 6a
Ja ckdaw — 2, 6b
Jackie — 4b, 6ab
Jaikie — 1-3, 4c, 5, 7-10
Jeckie — 4b
Nil — 4a

Selkirk
Jackdaw — 2ac, 8
Jackie — 4
Jaikie — 1, 2bcde, 3, 6
Jeckie — 8
Nil — 5, 7

Roxburgh
Jack — 4
Jackdaw — 5, 15b, 21ad, 28
Jackie — 2, 3ab, 6, 9a, 12, 15a, 18, 25, 27
Jaikie — 1, 10, 19, 22, 26
Jauk — 28
Jeck — 7, 9b, 16-17
Jeckie — 5, 8, 17, 20, 23-24, 26
Jockie — 21c
Kay — 3a, 4, 13, 15a, 17, 21acf
Nil — 11, 14, 21be

Dumfries
Daw — 15, 17b, 32, 35, 42-43
Caw — 13
Chaw — 7
Corbie — 8a, 46
Craw — 31b, 45a, 46
Jackdaw — 4, 8a, 10, 12, 15-16, 17a, 18-20, 22, 24, 27, 31bd, 33, 40
Jackie — 12, 28, 43
Jaik — 10
Jeck — 29, 39
Kay — 12
Kya — 10, 21b
Kyaw — 8b, 11, 26
Quaw — 6
Raven — 5
Nil — 1ab, 2-3, 9, 14, 21a, 23, 25, 30, 31acef, 34, 36-38, 41, 44, 45b, 47-49

Kirkcudbright
Caw — 7, 21c
Cra — 21b
Craw — 12b
Daw — 16
Jackdaw — 1, 3-7, 10, 18, 22
Jackie — 18
Kaew — 2
Kiaaw — 23
Kwa — 17
Kwe — 17
Kya — 15a, 19, 21ab
Kyaw — 8
Paiet — 1
Pate — 1
Nil — 9, 11, 12a, 13-14, 15b, 20, 24-27

Wigtown
Daw — 10
Jackdaw — 2, 5a, 6, 8, 11, 14, 17
Kya — 11-13, 16, 18
Kyaw — 11
Quaa — 5b, 10
Nil — 1, 3-4, 7, 9, 15

Northumberland
Chough — 37
Corbie craw — 69b
Daw — 37, 90, 103b
Jack — 2b, 3-11, 13-16, 18, 19a, 20b, 22-23, 24ab, 26-28, 29f, 30-31, 33b, 34a, 35, 37-39, 40ab, 41abcd, 43-45, 47-50, 53a, 56-58, 59bd, 61, 62afgh, 63, 64b, 68, 69acde, 71d, 75, 79, 81, 84, 86, 88a, 98, 99d, 102, 103abc, 104a, 108a, 110, 111b, 114, 118a, 122b, 125, 126f, 130b, 132, 134-135
Jack craa — 69a, 124a
Jackdaw — 5, 21, 28, 29b, 34b, 35-36, 40a, 42-43, 52, 53b, 54, 56, 59bc, 62b, 64a, 65a, 66, 69bdfh, 70, 71acd, 72dgik, 76-77, 80, 82-83, 87, 89-90, 92-93, 99b, 100, 101b, 103bc, 104ab, 106-107, 109, 111ab, 112, 116, 120abc, 124b, 126c, 127a, 129c, 130e, 137, 140, 142-143
Jackie — 1b, 2a, 10, 12, 17, 29d, 42, 46, 51, 56, 60, 68, 72k, 74, 76, 78, 110, 111b, 128, 131, 136, 138, 141, 143
Jackiedaw — 1a
Jack jaa — 65b, 69a
Jaik — 95b
Jaw — 122b
Jay — 127e
Jock — 124a
Nil — 1c, 19b, 20a, 25, 29ace, 32, 33a, 55, 59aef, 62cde, 67, 69g, 71be, 72abcefhjl, 73, 85, 88b, 91, 94ab, 95a, 96-97, 99ac, 101a, 105, 108bc, 113, 115, 117, 118b, 119, 121, 122a, 123, 126abde, 127bcdfgh, 129ab, 130acdf, 133, 139

Cumberland
Daw — 56, 60
Dawp — 31
Grey pate — 5b, 43
Ja — 19
Jack — 2-4, 5a, 7-9, 11-12, 13c, 15abc, 16, 18-19, 21-22, 27-31, 33-34, 36, 38-40, 42, 44, 48, 54, 56-57
Ja ckdaw — 1a, 4, 7, 9, 13c, 14, 15a, 23-25, 38, 40, 42, 46-47, 50, 56-58
Jackie — 24, 37b, 43, 56, 59
Nil — 1b, 6, 10, 13abd, 17, 20, 26, 32, 35, 37a, 41, 45, 49, 51-53, 55, 61-62, 63ab

Down
Crow — 18, 26
Jackdaw — 2a, 4-5, 7, 9, 15, 17, 19, 24
Jaw — 13
Kae — 13
Nil — 1, 2b, 3, 6, 8, 10-12, 14, 16, 20-23, 25, 27-30

Tyrone
Crow — 8, 11
Jackdaw — 1, 5, 7, 10-11, 14
Rook — 8
Scald crow — 14
Nil — 2-4, 6, 9, 12-13, 15-16

Antrim
Crow — 20, 27
Grey head — 11
Jackda — 4A
Jackdaw — 1, 3, 5ab, 9, 13, 16b, 17, 19-20, 22, 25-26, 29
Nil — 2, 4, 6-7, 8ab, 10, 12, 14-15, 16ac, 18, 21, 23-24, 28, 30-34

Donegal
Crow — 10a
Jackdaw — 4-5, 5A, 6, 8, 10a, 12
Jakeda — 7A
Rook — 10a
Nil — 1, 1A, 2-3, 7, 9, 10b, 11, 13

Fermanagh
Crow — 8-9
Jackdaw — 4-5, 7a
Nil — 1-3, 6, 7b, 10

Armagh
Jackdaw — 4, 6a
Nil — 1-3, 5, 6b

Londonderry
Ca — 4
Jackda — 3A
Jackdaw — 2-3
Nil — 1, 1AB, 5-7

74 SEAGULL (PQ1, 165)

Seagull has not been mapped as it occurs fairly densely all over the area except in Caithness, Orkney and Shetland.
A raised + symbol was put after a locality in which the informant commented 'young gull'.

Shetland
Loch ma — 21b
Mar — 2-3, 7, 10-11, 13-20, 21ab, 22-26, 29, 33
Maw — 1, 4-6, 8-9, 12, 27-33
Peerie ma — 15, 21b
Scor(r)ie — 3^{+}-5^{+}, 7^{+}-10^{+}, 13, 15^{+}-16^{+}, 18^{+}-19^{+}, 21b^{+}, 22^{+}, 23, 24^{+}-25^{+}
Sea craw — 15
Swaabie — 10, 15, 21b
Swabbie ma — 17
White ma — 3, 21b
White maw — 5, 28

Orkney
Baakie — 4, 6
Black back — 15
Black hatto — 6
Cullya — 13a, 15
Kittack — 15
Ma — 21
Ritto — 13b
Scor(r)ie — 4^{+}, 6, 9^{+}, 13a^{+}, 15^{+}, 18^{+}, 21^{+}
(Sea)gull — *8,* 13a, 14-15, 21
Waiko — 1
White fall — 3
White fool — 2
White ma — 4-12, 13ab, 14-16, 18-21
White maw — 17

Caithness
Blue back — 8
Headie craw — 8
Ma — 5, 7, 11, 12ac, 15, 16a
Maw — 2ab, 3-4, 6, 8-10, 12b, 13-14, 16b, 17
Scor(r)ie — 2b, 5^{+}, 10-11^{+}, 12ab^{+}c^{+}, 13, 14^{+}, 15, 16b^{+}, 17
Nil — 1

Sutherland
Black back — 5
Scorrie — 10
Screchag — 15
(Sea)gull — *1, 3-4,* 5, *6-8,* 11-12, *13,* 15-16
Sea ma — 15
(Sea) maw — *2, 8,* 9ab, 10-*11,* 14
Spluie — 5
Nil — 17

Ross & Cromarty
Culla — 25ab
Cul waw — 31
Foolack — 6, 12, 14, 26
Mew — 37a
Screechack — 11
Screechan — 13-14
(Sea)gull — *1,* 3, *4,* 5, *8-9,* 12, *16-18,* 19-20, *22,* 23-24, 25b, *26-27, 29, 32a,* 39
(Sea)ma — *8,* 25a, *32b,* 33
(Sea) maw — *9, 11, 15,* 18, *19-21, 25b,* 28, *30-31, 34-36,* 37ab
Nil — 2, 7, 10, 32c, 38

Inverness
Gullack — 13a
Gullie — 13c
(Sea)gull — *1-8,* 9, *10-11,* 13abce, 16, *17,* 18-20, 21ab, 22-23, 26, *27-30,* 32, *33-39,* 40
Sea maw — 13e, 15, 20, 21a
Seamew — 11, 26
Stewartack — 28-29
Nil — 12, 13d, 14, 24-25, 31

Nairn
Gow — 1abc
Seagull — 2
Sea ma — 2
Sea miau — 1b
Nil — 3-6

Moray
Covesea gow — 7
Goo — 6a, 9a
Gowie — 7, 8b, 14
Gru Willie — 3^{+}
Gullie — 8c, 14, 22
Pickie tar — 8e, 18, 22
Pule — 6a
Pyowl — 8d
(Sea) gow — 1, 2*ab,* 3-5, 6*ab,* 7, 8abcde, 10, 11, *12,* 13,15-16 *17--18,* 19, *20-21*
Seagull — 23
Stewartack — 22
Nil — 8f, 9b

Banff
Black maggie — 13
Fisher's hennie — 21
Grey daw — 13^{+}
Grey Willie — 13^{+}
Mawve — 13
Pwuel — 6b
Scurrie — 13
(Sea) gow — 1, 2abc, 3-5, 6ab, 7, 9-10, 14, 16, 19, *25,* 29
(Sea)gull — 15, *16,* 17, 18c, 19, 31-32, 34
(Sea) maw — *10, 17,* 18c, *23-24, 31*
Sea myauve — 2c
(Sea) peul — 7-13, 18b, *20,* 22, 24, 27
Sea piet — 27
Nil — 18ad, 26, 28, 30, 33

Aberdeen
Gaw — 97
Gow — 53
Grey Willie maw — 9^{+}
Grey Wull — 4^{+}
Maeve — 3b
Meow — 55
Miauve — 3a, 5c
Miauvie — 7
Miav — 47e, 60
Peul — 1-2, 3a, 4, 8-15, 28a, 29, 32, 69, 88
Peulie — 4, 9, 48
Pottern hen — 101
Potterton hen — 51, 71b
Scerrie — 55
Scurdie — 5b
Scurrie — 2^{+}, 3b, 4, 5abd, 6, 16, 19, 21, 41, 44, 47abcdef, 61, 102
Sea gee — 79
Sea goo — 25, 27, 65, 84
Sea gue — 37
(Sea)gull — *8,* 12, 22-*23,* 28ac, *34, 43-45, 48, 50,* 51-52, 54, 59-60, *69-70,* 71b, *73*-74, *75,* 81-82, *83,* 84, 88, 92, *94-95,* 96, 98, 100, 103-*104,* 106, *107,* 108
(Sea) maa — *16, 19,* 28a, *64, 88*
(Sea) maw — *3a, 6, 8, 14, 17-18, 20, 27, 28ab, 31, 35, 39, 43, 45-46, 62, 71ac,* 73, *75, 77, 80, 87, 91, 105*
Sea mawa — 32
Sea mew — 28b
Skerrie miaver — 14
Tarie scurrie — 20
Nil — 24, 26, 30, 33, 36, 38, 40, 42, 49, 56-58, 63, 66-68, 72, 76, 78, 85-86, 89-90, 93, 99, 109

Kincardine
Gullie — 1
Plangie — 17d
Pleeng — 25
Plengie — 12
Pling — 14
Plingie — 17abc, 18, 21, 23-24, 27
Potterton hen — 5
(Sea)gull — *3, 5,* 6-7, *8,* 9-11, *12, 15-16,* 17c, 19, *20,* 21, 26, 28
Seagull pleen — 3
(Sea) maw — 4, 14
Nil — 2, 13, 22

Kinross
Gull — 1
Picktaurnie — 7
Sea maw — 1-5, 7
Nil — 6

Angus
Scaffie — 18
(Sea)gull — *1*-2, 4, 5ac, *6,* 8, *9-10,* 12-13, 14b, 15, *17ab,* 18, *22, 24-25,* 28, 32, *34, 36*
Sea ma — 3
Sea maw — 5ab, 7, 14a, 19, 21, 23, 33b, 35, 37
Sea mew — 37
Nil — 11, 14cd, 16, 20, 26-27, 29ab, 30-31, 33a

Perth
Gow — 30, 67
Pitarmie — 57
Pitarnie — 41a
(Sea)gull — 1, *2a, 4-5,* 8-9, *10,* 12, *16,* 18, *24-25,* 27-28, *29a, 36, 46, 52a, 57,* 59-*60,* 67-*68,* 71, *74*
Sea ma — 6, 33, 46
Sea maw — 7, 10-11, 15-17, 20-21, 23, 25-27, 29a, 31-32, 39-40, 41ab, 42-44, 48, 50, 51ab, 52bce, 53, 55-56, 58-59, 61-63, 65-66, 68-73
Sea mew — 24
Nil — 2b, 3, 13-14, 19, 22, 29b, 34-35, 37-38, 45, 47, 49, 52d, 54, 64

Fife
Coorie — 33-34
Cutsie — 3, 32
Cuttie —33-34
Gull maw — 50
Scurrie — 55d
(Sea)gull — 4, *8,* 10-*11,* 16, *19,* 20, *21, 24,* 36ab, *37,* 38, *39,* 40ab, 41ab, *42,* 43ab, 44ce, *50, 55ab,* 58, 62-63
(Sea) maw — *1-7, 9ab, 11-12, 14, 16-18,* 20-21, 23, *25-31,* 32, *33,* 34, *35, 36a, 39, 40a, 42, 44ac, 45-54, 55bdefg, 56-57, 59, 64ab*
Sea mawret — 50
Sea mew — 55d
Tornie — 44d
Nil — 13, 15, 22, 41cd, 44bf, 55c, 60-61

Clackmannan
Coorus doo — 2
(Sea)gull — 1, *4c*
Sea maw — 1-2, 4abcd, 6-7
Nil — 3, 5

Stirling
Puffin — 8
Sea gled — 26b
(Sea)gull — *4,* 7abcef, 8, *9,* 10, *12,* 15-16, 20, *21ab,* 23a*b,* 25abcd, 26a*d,* 27ab, *28, 30-32,* 34, 35a, *36,* 37b, 38, 40-41
Sea maw — 2-4, 6, 7bde, 11-12, 17-18, 21b, 22a, 23c, 24, 25acd, 26bcdef, 35b, 37a, 39ab, 42a
Sea mew — 26a
Nil — 1, 5, 13-14, 19, 22b, 29, 33, 42b

Dunbarton
(Sea)gull — *1, 3,* 5-*6,* 7bc, *8,* 9-11, 13abc, *14b,* 16ab
Sea maw — 4b, 6, 14a
(Sea) mew — *2,* 9
Nil — 4a, 7a, 12, 15, 17-18

Argyll
Grayluck — 16
Sclurach — 35
(Sea)gull — *1-2,* 3, *5-7, 9-10,* 11, *14,* 15-16, *17, 19, 22-23,* 24, *25, 27,* 30-31, 33, *34-35,* 36-37, 39
Nil — 4, 8, 12-13, 18, 20-21, 26, 28-29, 32, 38, 40

Bute
(Sea)gull — 1acd, *2*-3, 5, *7,* 8a*b,* 9
Nil — 1be, 4, 6

Ayr
Black backed pickmar — 45
Gow — 53a
Herngull — 47
Herring gull — 57
Kittie wick — 47
Patie — 53b
Pickie — 41, 56-57
Pickma — 49
Pickmar — 18b, 52
Pickmaw — 49, 54, 57
Sea bird — 28e
(Sea)gull — 1b, 2ab, *3,* 4, *5,* 6-7, 8ab, *9*-10, 12ab, *13,* 14-15, 16ab, 17, 18a, 20bch, 21, *24b,* 25, *26bc,* 28cdef, 29, 30a, *31,* 32-33, *34,* 35a*b,* 36, 38, 40, 42-43, *44,* 45, *48,* 52, 53ab, 54-*55,* 57
Sea maw — 1a, 19, 41, 57
Sea mew — 57
Nil — 11, 20adefg, 22-23, 24a, 26a, 27, 28ab, 30b, 37, 39, 46, 50-51

Renfrew
(Sea)gull — 1b, 2abcgh*i,* 4acd*e,* 5, 7-*8,* 11adef*il,* 12a, *13c, 14a,* 16a*b,* 17, *18a, 19, 20a*
Sea maw — 11l
Sma maw — 21
Nil — 1a, 2defj, 3, 4b, 6, 9-10, 11bcghjk, 12b, 13abd, 14b, 15, 16cd, 18b, 20b

Lanark
Paternick — 39
Pickent — 50
Pickmaw — 60
Picternie — 15c
Scorrie — 32f
Sea goo — 17
(Sea)gull — 1-2, *3,* 5-*6,* 7a*c,* *8b, 9a,* 10a, *12,* 14bd, 15abc 16ab, *17*-18, *19*-20, 23, *25bc,*

Lanark cont'd
26a, 27b, 29cdf, *31a,* 32ac, 33cd, *35bcd, 38ac,* 39, 42, *44*-45, 46abc, *47*-48, 49ab, 51, 53, 57a, *58,* 59a
(Sea) maw — *9ab, 13, 15a, 20, 29d, 30, 31d,* 38bd, *40, 47-48, 50, 52a,* 56, 59b, *61-62, 64b,* 65
(Sea) mew — 42, *54*
Whaup — 6, 38d
Nil — 4, 7b, 8a, 10b, 11, 14ac, 21-22, 24, 25ad, 26b, 27a, 28, 29abeg, 31bc, 32bde, 33ab, 34, 35a, 36-37, 38e, 41, 43, 52b, 55, 57bc, 63, 64a, 66, 67ab

West Lothian
Screamer — 11
(Sea)gull — 1c, 4, *5,* 6-7, *10,* 11, *12-13,* 14-16, 17a, *18, 20a,* 21a*b,* 22
Sea maw — 1abd, 2-5, 7-8, 16, 17a, 19ab
Sea mew — 22
Nil — 9a, 17b, 20b

Midlothian
Pickie maw — 31
Pitcairnie — 14a
(Sea)gull — 1-*2, 6ab, 7a, 8a, 10*-11, 12ab, 14*a*b, 16, 18-19, *21,* 23a*b, 24, 25c,* 28, *29,* 30
(Sea) maw — *3, 7b, 8b, 9, 12ab, 14a, 17, 20,* 25a, *26a, 27, 32*
Nil — 4-5, 13, 15, 22, 25bd, 26b

East Lothian
Gullie maw — 16
Pickie maw — 14
(Sea)gull — 1, *4b,* 6b, 8-*9,* 13, 16-17, *18-19*
Sea maw — 2, 4ab, 6a, 7-9, 11, 13-16, 20
Sea scavenger — 13
Nil — 3, 5, 10, 12, 21

Berwick
Furlie — 8
Gullie — 10
Peckie maw — 16c
Pickie ma — 16a
Pickie maw — 11-12, 17, 22-23, 31
Rooner — 27
(Sea)gull — *1,* 2-3, *6,* 7-10, *12, 15, 16bc,* 19-20, *21,* 29, *31*-32
(Sea) maw — *4,* 7, *13,* 17
Nil — 5, 14, 18, 24-26, 28, 30

Peebles
Pickie maw — 3, 9
Picternie — 7
(Sea)gull — 1-2, 4c, 5, *6b, 7*-8
Sea ma — 4b
Sea maw — 2-3, 4c, 5, 6a, 7, 10
Nil — 4a

Selkirk
Pickie — 2e
Pickie maw — 1, 2d, 4
Pickmaw — 2abce, 6
(Sea)gull — 2c, *4,* 8
Nil — 3, 5, 7

Roxburgh
Gormaw — 21c
Peckmaw — 22
Pickie maw — 4-6, 8, 10, 12-13, 18, 20
Pickmaw — 3b, 15a, 16-17, 21adf, 25-26, 28
Pixiemaw — 17
(Sea)gull — *1*-2, 6-7, 9a, *15b, 21a*
(Sea) maw — *3a,* 15a, 17
Nil — 9b, 11, 14, 19, 21be, 23-24, 27

Dumfries
Peagie — 26
Pickmar — 1a
Pickmaw — 2, 7
(Sea)gull — *4,* 5-6, 8*a*b, 10-11, *12,* 13, *15-16,* 17ab, *18-19,* 20, 21b, 22, *24,* 27, *28,* 29-30, 31*bd,* 33, *37,* 39-*40,* 42, *45a,* 46
Sea maw — 31b
Sea mawr — 35
Nil — 1b, 3, 9, 14, 21a, 23, 25, 31acef, 32, 34, 36, 38, 41, 43-44, 45b, 47-49

Kirkcudbright
Pickmar — 2
Pickmaw — 1
(Sea)gull — *1,* 3-5, *6-7,* 10, 12b, *15a,* 16, 18, *19,* 20, 21a*c,* 22-23, 27
Sea maw — 8, 17
Nil — 9, 11, 12a, 13-14, 15b, 21b, 24-26

Wigtown
Pirma — 5b, 12
Pirmaw — 10
(Sea)gull — *2,* 5a, 8-9, *11,* 12-14, 16-18
Nil — 1, 3-4, 6-7, 15

Northumberland
Annet — 124a, 134
Cuddie's chick — 134
Pick maw — 29f, 51
Plingie — 22
Sea bord — 69b
Sea cra — 69a, 109
Sea crow — 56, 103bc, 133
(Sea)gull — 1*ab,* 2*ab,* 3, *5-6,* 8-9, 11-13, *14,* 15, *16,* 17-18, 19a, 20b, *21,* 23, 26, *28,* 29bd, *30-31,* 34b, *35-36, 38, 40a, 41cd, 42*-43, *45,* 46-49, *52,* 53*a*b, *54, 56,* 59b, 60, *62b,* 63, 64*a*b, *65a, 66,* 68, 69bc*d*fh, *70, 71cd,* 72cd*g*i, 75-76, *77,* 78-79, 82-83, *86-87,* 88a, *89*-90, *92,* 94b, 95b, 98, 99*bd, 100, 101b,* 102, *103abc,* 104*a*b, *106-107, 109-110,* 111*a*b, *112,* 118a, *120abc, 121,* 124b, 126cf, 127*abd, 130be,* 131, *132-133,* 135, *137-138,* 143
Sea hare — 127e
Sea mew — 62f, 69a, 124a
White crow — 103bc, 132
Nil — 1c, 4, 7, 10, 19b, 20a, 24ab, 25, 27, 29ace, 32, 33ab, 34a, 37, 39, 40b, 41ab, 44, 50, 55, 57-58, 59acdef, 61, 62acdegh, 65b, 67, 69eg, 71abe, 72abefhjkl, 73-74, 80-81, 84-85, 88b, 91, 93, 94a, 95a, 96-97, 99ac, 101a, 105, 108abc, 113-117, 118b, 119, 122ab, 123, 125, 126abde, 127cfgh, 128, 129abc, 130acdf, 136, 139-142

Cumberland
Black heided gull — 56
Churr — 13a
Churr mo — 30
Dirt bird — 46
Drake catcher — 30
Grey gull — 56
Gurmaw — 13a
Pick maw — 13b
Sea a ma — 56, 63b
Sea crow — 37b
(Sea)gull — 1a, 2, *3,* 4, 7-*8,* 12, *13c, 14,* 15ac, 16, 18, *21-25,* 26, 28, *38,* 40, *42,* 46-48, 50, 54, *56-57,* 58, 60
(Sea) ma — 57, *63a*
Sea maw — 44-45
Sea mew — 11, 56
Sea mo — 7, 9, 13a, 27
Nil — 1b, 5ab, 6, 10, 13d, 15b, 17, 19-20, 29, 31-36, 37a, 39, 41, 43, 49, 51-53, 55, 59, 61-62

Down
(Sea)gull — 2a, 4, *5,* 6, *7, 9,* 15, 17, *18-19, 20, 24,* 26, *30*
Nil — 1, 2b, 3, 8, 10-14, 16, 21-23, 25, 27-29

Tyrone
(Sea)gull — *7-8, 10-11,* 12, 15
Seamers — 1
Nil — 2-6, 9, 13-14, 16

Antrim
(Sea)gull — *1, 3, 5b,* 7, 9, 11, *13,* 16b, 17, 19, *20-22, 25,* 26-27, 29, 33
Nil — 2, 4, 4A, 5a, 6, 8ab, 10, 12, 14-15, 16ac, 18, 23-24, 28, 30-32, 34

Donegal
(Sea)gull — *5, 5A,* 6, *8,* 10a, 12
Nil — 1, 1A, 2-4, 7, 7A, 9, 10b, 11, 13

Fermanagh
(Sea)gull — *2-5, 7a,* 8-*9*
Nil — 1, 6, 7b, 10

Armagh
(Sea)gull — *2,* 3-4, *6a*
Nil — 1, 5, 6b

Londonderry
(Sea)gull — *2*-3, 3A
Nil — 1, 1AB, 4-7

75 YELLOWHAMMER (PQ1, 166)

For variants of the element YELLOW see map 16, Appendix A (stressed vowel only).
Spinkie also occurs in 70 **chaffinch**

Shetland
Yellow hammer — 30, 33
Nil — 1-20, 21ab, 22-29, 31-32

Orkney
Yellow hammer — 2, 13b, 15, 19
Yellow yarling — 6-7, 11-12, 15
Nil — 1, 3-5, 8-10, 13a, 14, 16-18, 20-21

Caithness
Yellow hammer — 5, 11
Yellow yarlin(g) — 2b, 6, 8-9, 11, 12b, 13, 16ab
Yellow yeet — 12c, 15, 17
Yellow yewt — 15
Nil — 1, 2a, 3-4, 7, 10, 12a, 14

Sutherland
Yellow gite — 15
Yellow hammer — 1, 4-8, 11, 13, 16
Yellow yarling — 6, 9ab
(Yellow) yite — 14, *16*
Yournie — 15
Nil — 2-3, 10, 12, 17

Ross & Cromarty
Bouiack — 12, 20, 28
Bouian — 18
Whin linnet — 26
Yellow hammer — 1, 3-5, 8-9, 16-17, 25a, 26-27, 29, 32a, 36, 39
Yellow yarlack — 25b
Yellow yet — 37a
Yellow yite — 7-11, 13, 15, 17-19, 21-24, 25b, 29, 31, 32b, 33-35
Yellow yoit — 36
Nil — 2, 6, 14, 30, 32c, 37b, 38

Inverness
Little bit of bread and no cheese— 13a
Yellockie yite — 13e
Yellow hammer — 2-3, 5-6, 11, 13bce, 17, 19, 21a, 22-23, 27-28, 30, 32,34, 36-39
Yellow yite — 7-12, 13ace, 14-16, 18, 20, 21b, 24, 26, 29, 31-32, 35, 40
Yellow yurlack — 13a
Nil — 1, 4, 13d, 25, 33

Nairn
Yellockie yite — 1bc, 3
Yellow hammer — 2
Yellow yite — 1ab, 4-5
Nil — 6

Moray

Yaldie — 1, 3-5, 7, 8ef, 9ab, 10-11, 15-21
Yaldie yarlin — 8b
Yallacher — 6b, 8b
Yallachie — 8a, 9a, 14
Yallocker — 8f
Yallockie — 2a, 3
Yarlin — 3
Yellockie — 21
Yellockie yarlin — 12
Yellockie yite — 12-13
Yellow hammer — 8d
Yellow yarlin — 22
Yellow yite — 4, 6a, 8d, 9a, 13, 23
Yellow yitie — 8d, 22
Yellow yorlin — 8a
Yorlin — 8f, 9d
Nil — 2b, 8c

Banff

Yaldie — 1, 2ac, 3-5, 6b, 9, 14-15, 17, 18bcd, 25, 30-31
Yaldie yarlin — 16
Yaldie yite — 16-17
Yallockie — 32-33
Yallockie yite — 28
Yellow linkie — 32
Yellow lintie — 6b
Yellow yaldie — 29
(Yellow) yarlin(g) — *4, 9,* 18d, 32, *33-34*
Yellow yerlin — 11
(Yellow) yirlin — *2a,* 23
Yellow yite — 2c, 7-8, 11-12, 15, 18bc, 19-21, 26
Yellow yitie — 6b, 9-10, 13, 19, 22-24, 27
Nil — 2b, 6a, 18a

Aberdeen

Fun lintie — 64
Yaldie — 2, 5a, 14, 17, 19, 20-23, 28a, 35-36, 43, 53, 79, 85, 87
Yallockie yite — 13, 24
Yeldrin — 25
Yellachtie yite — 24
Yellow — 10
Yellow itie — 69, 73
Yellow lintie — 6
Yellow yarlin — 64, 78, 86, 92, 96, 108
Yellow yeat — 41
Yellow yerlin — 3b, 4, 14, 31, 71b, 82
Yellow yettie — 25, 27
Yellow yichtie —89, 101
Yellow yirlin — 17, 19, 28a, 65, 80
(Yellow) yite — *9, 11, 14 16 19, 28a, 33, 35, 38, 40 43-44, 47b, 50, 53, 56-58, 64-65, 71c, 76, 81,* 85, *93-95, 97, 103, 106-107*
(Yellow) yitie — *3a, 5bd, 6, 9, 12, 17,* 18, *19-21, 24, 26, 28bc, 29-30, 32, 37, 45-46, 47acdef, 48-49, 51, 54-55, 60-63, 66*-67, *70, 71bc, 72, 74-75, 77-80, 82-84, 87-88, 90, 96, 98-100, 104-106, 108*
Yellow yittie — 86
Yellow yoitie — 52
Yellow ypie — 20
Yerlin — 3a, 88
Yutie — 10
Nil — 1, 5c, 7-8, 34-42, 59, 68, 71a, 91, 102, 109

Kincardine

Yellitie yite — 26
Yellow yarlin — 6
Yellow yite — 1, 3-4, 6, 8-9, 14-16, 17bd, 18-23, 25, 27-28
Yellow yitie — 2, 5, 7, 10-13, 17ac, 21, 24
Yellow yittie — 3

Kinross

Scotch canary — 3, 6
Yellow yite — 1-7

Angus

Scotch canary — 5c,
Tit — 17b
Yellow bunting — 33b
Yellow hammer — 15, 17b, 34
Yellow yite — 1-4, 5abc, 6-10, 12-13, 14abcd, 17a, 19-28, 29a, 30-32, 33ab, 34-37
Yellow yitie — 14d, 15, 22
Nil — 11, 16, 18, 29b

Perth

Scotch canary — 33, 39, 59, 67-68, 71, 73
Yarlin — 39
Yellow hammer — 2a, 4, 9-10
Yellow yeet — 67
Yellow yeyt — 51b
Yellow yite — 1, 2a, 3, 6-13, 15-18, 20-22, 24-28, 29ab, 30-33, 38, 40, 41ab, 42-47, 50, 51a, 52abcde, 53-54, 56-59, 61-66, 68-74
Yellow yitie — 5, 23, 60
Yellow yoit — 48
Yoarlin — 62
Yorling — 24
Nil — 2b, 14, 19, 34-37, 49, 55

Fife

Hammer heed — 37
Scotch canary — 11, 41c, 42, 48-49, 52, 55d
Scotchie — 20, 38, 43b, 45
Yarlin — 20
Yellow hammer — 4, 16, 24, 37, 55b
Yellow head — 54
Yellow lintie — 9a
Yellow yeyt — 44d
(Yellow) yite — *1-2, 4-8, 10, 12-14, 17, 19-21, 23, 25-30, 33-35, 36ab, 37, 39, 40b, 41d, 42, 43ab, 44acef, 45, 47-51, 53, 55acdefg, 56-58,* 59-60, *61-62, 64ab*
Yellow yitie — 39, 40a
Yellow yorlin — 44a
Yellow yowt — 11-12, 18, 21, 27, 31-34, 46
Yertie — 12
Nil — 3, 9b, 15, 22, 41ab, 44b, 63

Clackmannan

Lintie — 4b
Scotch canary — 4d
Scots canary — 1, 3
Skitterie yite — 2
Yellow yite — 1-3, 4ad, 5-7
Yellow yoit — 4c

Stirling

Scotch canary — 7c, 10, 16, 21a, 25d, 28, 33-34
Scotchie — 40
Scots canary — 8, 15, 26a
Yellow gate — 4
Yellow hammer — 4, 21b, 31
Yellow lintie — 7e, 20
Yellow yike — 15
Yellow yite — 2-3, 6, 7abde, 8-9, 12, 14-15, 17-18, 21b, 22ab, 23c, 24, 25abcd, 26abcdef, 27ab, 30-31, 33, 35a, 36, 37ab, 38, 39ab, 40, 42a
Yellow yoit — 26b, 35b
Yirlin — 26b
Yorlin — 26e
Nil — 1, 5, 7f, 11, 13, 19, 23ab, 29, 32, 41, 42b

Dunbarton

Lintie — 7a
Scotch canary — 7a, 10, 13bc, 14a, 16b
Stane chapper — 16a
Yellow hammer — 3, 11, 13bc, 14b
Yellow yite — 1-2, 4ab, 5-6, 7ac, 9-10, 13abc, 14ab, 16ab, 17-18
Yoldrick — 14a
Yorling — 14a
Nil — 7b, 8, 12, 15

Argyll

Bunting — 11
Scotch canary — 25
Yellow hammer — 1-3, 5-7, 10-12, 14-17, 22, 25, 33
Yellow yeldrin — 28, 33, 35, 37, 39-40
Yellow yite — 1, 9-10, 16, 18-19, 23-24, 29, 31-32, 35, 37, 40
Nil — 4, 8, 13, 20-21, 26-27, 30, 34, 36, 38

Bute

Scotch canary — 1b, 3, 8a
Yellow hammer — 1a, 8b
Yellow yite — 1ae, 2, 4-7, 8ab, 9
Nil — 1cd

Ayr

Scotch canary — 18b, 20g, 24ab, 34, 35b, 46, 48
Scotchie — 24a
Skitterie feltie — 29
Yeldron — 19
Yellow bunting — 28e
Yellow hammer — 28ce
Yellow head — 9
Yellow yeldron — 24b
(Yellow) yite — *1a, 2ab, 3-7, 8ab, 9-11, 12ab, 13-15, 16ab, 17, 18ab, 19, 20abcdefgh, 21, 23, 24b, 25, 26abc, 28abcf, 29, 30ab, 31-34, 35ab, 36-44, 46-50,* 51, *52, 53a, 55, 57*
(Yellow) yoit — *45,* 49, *53b, 54, 56*
Yellow yorling — 57
Nil — 1b, 22, 27, 28d

Renfrew

Scotch canary — 2j, 17, 18a
Scots canary — 11j, 12a
Skitterie feltie — 11ej
Yellow bunting — 2d
Yellow hammer — 2ai, 8, 14a, 19, 20a
Yellow head — 12b
(Yellow) yite — *1b, 2bdehj, 4acd, 5-9, 11abefijkl, 13ac, 14ab, 15, 16abc,* 17, *18ab, 19, 20b, 21*
Yellow yoit — 16b
Nil — 1a, 2cfg, 3, 4be, 10, 11cdgh, 13bd, 16d

Lanark

Scotch canary — 1, 3, 13, 15a, 16b, 27b, 29c, 30, 32e, 33b, 34, 35ac, 39, 46ab, 60-61
Skitterie felter — 7b
Yellow hammer — 1, 7c, 14d, 35d, 39, 64b
Yellow yiet — 23
Yellow yike — 7c, 25b
(Yellow) yite — *1, 3-6, 7a, 8b, 9ab, 10a, 12-13, 14bd, 15abc, 16b, 17-24, 25c, 26b,* 27b, *29acdg, 30, 31abcd, 32abcdef,* 33abcd, *34, 35abd, 36-37, 38abce, 39-42, 44-45, 46ac, 47-48, 49b, 50-51, 52ab, 53-56, 57abc, 58, 59ab, 60, 62-63, 64a, 65-66*
Yellow yoit — 11, 38d, 46b
Yellow yorlin — 61
Yirlin — 38a
Yorlin — 46c, 57a
Nil — 2, 8a, 10b, 14ac, 16a, 25ad, 26a, 27a, 28, 29bef, 43, 49a, 67ab

West Lothian

Scotch canary — 1d, 3, 15
Scots canary — 1a
Yaurlick — 18
Yellow hammer — 5, 10
(Yellow) yite — 1ab*cd, 2-8, 9b, 11-13, 15*-16, 17a, *18,* 19b, *20a, 21a, 22*
Yorlin — 20a
Nil — 9a, 14, 17b, 19a, 20b, 21b

Midlothian

Lintie — 19
Scotch canary — 3, 12b, 14a, 18
Scots canary — 8b
(Yellow) hammer — *6a, 15,* 19
Yellow ite — 1
(Yellow) yite — *3-4, 6b, 7ab, 8ab, 10-11,* 12ab, *13, 14ab, 16-18, 20-22, 23b, 24, 25abc, 26a, 27-29, 31-32*
Yellow yittie — 9
Yellow yorling — 32
Yellow yuite — 25d
Yitie — 3, 23b, 30
Nil — 2, 5, 23a, 26b

East Lothian

Yellow hammer — 17
Yellow yite — 1-3, 4ab, 6ab, 7-21
(Yellow) yorlin(g) — *9*-10, *15-16*
Yitie — 10, 15-16
Nil — 5

Berwick

Fellock — 27
Scotch canary — 27
Skellie — 27
Uller — 27
Yellow hammer — 15
Yellow yite — 1-10, 12-13, 15, 16abc, 17-21, 23-25, 30-32
Yellow yorland — 23, 32
Yellow yorlin(g) — 2, 11-13, 22, 26-27, 29, 31
Yitie — 11
Nil — 14, 28

Peebles

Scotch canary — 8
Yellow hammer — 4c, 6b
Yellow yite — 1, 3, 4abc, 5, 6ab, 7-10
Yorlin(g) — 2, 8

Selkirk

Yellow hammer — 8
Yellow yite — 1, 2abcde, 3-4, 7
Yellow yorlin(g) — 2abe, 4, 7
Yellow yoit — 6
Nil — 5

Roxburgh

Yellow hammer — 21a
Yellow yite — 2, 3a, 4-5, 9ab, 11-13, 15a, 17, 20, 21ad, 23, 25-26
Yellow yodlin — 19
Yellow yoit — 9b
Yellow yorlene — 21d
Yellow yorline — 3b
Yellow yorlin(g) — 2, 3a, 5-8, 9a, 10, 13, 15ab, 16-18, 20, 21acf, 22-24, 26, 28
Yilie — 19
Yodlin — 1
Nil — 14, 21be, 27

Dumfries

Lintie – 31a
Scotch canary – 1b
Yellow buntin – 46
Yellow hammer – 4, 16
Yellow yite – 13, 17a, 20, 21ab, 30, 31d, 38
Yellow yoit – 1a, 3-7, 8ab, 9-11, 14-15, 17b, 18-19, 21b, 22, 24-29, 31bcde, 32-38, 40-43, 45a, 46
(Yellow) yorlin(g) – *10,* 29, *39*
Yellow yowt – 2, 12, 44
Yoitie – 26
Nil – 23, 31f, 45b, 47-49

Kirkcudbright

Gooldie – 27
Scots canary – 11
Yellow hammer – 7
Yellow tit – 18
Yellow yite – 11
Yellow yoicht – 23
Yellow yoit – 1-11, 12ab, 13-14, 15ab, 16-17, 19-20, 21abc, 22, 24-25
Yorling – 17
Nil – 26

Wigtown

Yellow yoit – 1-4, 5ab, 6-18

Northumberland

Bunting – 127e
Lintie – 118b
Scrape – 72k
Scribbler – 60
Scribblie – 71b
Scribblie jack – 63, 66, 69e, 72dk,125
Scribbling lark – 47
Scrubblie jack – 124b
Yallock – 14, 48
Yallockie – 41d, 48
Yellock – 29ad
Yellockie – 31, 40a, 41d, 66
Yellow buntin(g) – 26, 42, 103c
Yellow gowlin – 28
Yellow hammer – 2b, 5, 13-14, 16-17, 26, 28, 29b, 35 40a, 41c, 46, 48, 52, 53ab, 54, 56, 59b, 62b, 64a, 69c, 70, 71ad, 72i, 77-78, 87, 90-92, 100, 103ab, 106, 111a, 125, 127a, 130be, 132, 138, 140
Yellow howlie – 126c
Yellow itie – 2b, 3, 6, 9, 24b, 59d
Yellow owlie – 33a, 59d, 69abg, 78, 83, 94b, 101b, 104b, 118a, 120c, 122b, 129c
Yellow yarlin(g) – 20b, 32
Yellow yeollie – 59f
Yellow yite – 19a, 20a, 29f, 69c
Yellow yitie – 1b, 2a, 8, 10, 15, 41c
Yellow yittie – 1a
Yellow yorlie – 12
Yellow yorlin – 21, 43, 71c
Yellow yowler – 108c, 110
Yellow yowlie – 5, 14, 18, 22, 25, 27, 29b, 30, 34a, 35-39, 40b, 41ab, 44-45, 47, 49-51, 56-58, 59ce, 60, 62aef, 63, 64b, 65ab, 66, 68, 69defh, 71d, 72dfgijl, 73-74, 76-77, 79-82, 84-86, 88a, 90-91, 95ab, 96-98, 99bcd, 101a, 103bc, 104a, 106-107, 108ab, 109-110, 111ab, 112-117, 118b, 120ab, 122a, 124ab, 128, 130cf, 131, 133-137, 139-141, 143
(Yellow) yowlin(g) – *18, 24a,* 34b, *102*
Yellow yowrie – 129b
Yellow yowrling – 11
Yites – 79
Yorlin – 29f
Nil – 1c, 4, 7, 19b, 23, 29ce, 33b, 55, 59a, 61, 62cdgh, 67, 71e, 72abceh, 75, 88b, 89, 93, 94a, 99a, 105, 119, 121, 123, 126abdef, 127bcdfgh, 129a, 130ad, 142

Cumberland

A wish a wish 'twad rain – 56
Bessie – 3-4, 8-9, 11, 15bc, 17, 24, 27-29, 34, 36, 41-44, 50-52, 54-61
Bessie buntie – 28
Black gap – 61
Buntie – 7, 28
Little bit of bread and no cheese – 54
May the devil take you – 14
Spinkie – 15c, 16, 18, 32-33, 38-40, 46-47, 49
Sprinkie – 30-31
Yellow buntie – 7, 28, 58
Yellow bunting – 3, 57
Yellow hammer – 9, 13c, 14, 15a, 16, 22-23, 25, 37b, 40, 42, 46, 56-57, 62
Yellow yoit – 13a
Yellow yorling – 2-3, 5a, 13c
Yellow yowlie – 60
Nil – 1ab, 5b, 6, 10, 12, 13bd, 19-21, 26, 35, 37a, 45, 48, 53, 63ab

Down

Finch – 17
Gouldie – 3
Yellow hammer – 5, 9, 15
Yellow yarnie – 4
Yellow yoit – 7, 10
Yellow yorlie – 26
Yellow yorling – 24-25
Yellow yorn – 11, 18
Yellow yornie – 12-13, 24, 27-29
Yellow yornin – 14, 22
Yellow yout – 21
Yellow yurnie – 2b
Yeltie (yorn) – *23,* 27
Nil – 1, 2a, 6, 8, 16, 19-20, 30

Tyrone

Yellow hammer – 1, 11
Yellow yoit – 11
Yellow yolder – 4
Yellow yorldrin – 2
Yellow yorlin(g) – 6, 14, 16
Yellow yorn – 11
Yellow yornel – 9
Yellow yornie – 7, 12
Nil – 3, 5, 8, 10, 13, 15

Antrim

Yellow hammer – 1, 3, 25
Yellow yarling – 34
Yellow yeldering – 2
Yellow yeldern – 4A
Yellow yite – 12
Yellow yoit – 15, 16b, 25, 33
(Yellow) yorlin(g) – *1, 4,* 8b, *9-10, 12-13, 15, 16b, 17, 19-20, 22, 24, 26-27, 30*
Yellow yorn – 11
Yellow yornie – 29
Nil – 5ab, 6-7, 8a, 14, 16ac, 18, 21, 23, 28, 31-32

Donegal

Yedda yeldern – 4
Yellow anyrin – 2
Yellow hammer – 5A
Yellow yalder – 6
Yellow yaldern – 4
Yellow yaldherin – 10b
Yellow yander – 10a
Yellow yeldren – 5, 11
Yellow yenderen – 12
Yellow yorlin – 10a
Nil – 1, 1A, 3, 7, 7A, 8-9, 13

Fermanagh

Yellow hammer – 4
Yellow yorling – 2, 4-5
Nil – 1, 3, 6, 7ab, 8-10

Armagh

Yaltie – 3
Yellow yarn – 6a
Yellow yite – 4
Yellow yorlin(g) – 4-5
Yeltie – 1-2
Yeltie yarn – 6a
Yeltie yorn – 4
Nil – 6b

Londonderry

Yellow hammer – 2, 3A
Yellow yalderin – 1
Yellow yauldron – 5
Yellow yelded – 1A
Yellow yeldring – 1B
Yellow yeldron – 4-5
Yellow yorgle – 3
Yellow yorlin(g) – 6-7
Yildering – 5

76 ANT (PQ1, 167)

Ant has not been mapped as it occurs nearly everywhere. The variants of the unstressed vowel in **eemOck, em(m)Ock** have been subsumed

Shetland

Ant – 1, 7, 27, 32
Mooratoog – 3-6, 9-10, 12, 14-15, 17-20, 21b, 22, 24-26, 28-31
Mooriktoog – 23
Moortoog – 21a
Mouratoeg – 8, 16
Nil – 2, 11, 13, 33

Orkney

Aeman – 21
Ant – 2-5, 8-9, 13b, 15-17, 19, 21
Meero – 13b
Meeroo – 11-12
Miru – 7
Moorag – 17
Moorick – 15
Myroo – 10
Nil – 1, 6, 13a, 14, 18, 20

Caithness

Ant – 9, 11, 13, 16b
Shangin – 12a
Shannag – 2ab, 3, 5-6, 8, 11, 12bc, 14, 16b
Sneeag – 12b
Snian – 3, 12b
Nil – 1, 4, 7, 10, 15, 16a,17

Sutherland

Ant – 1, 3-8, 9b, 10-13, 16
Shannag – 9a
Nil – 2, 14-15, 17

Ross & Cromarty

Ant – 1, 3-6, 8-10, 14, 16-19, 22, 24, 25ab, 26-30, 32ab, 34, 36, 39
Shevan – 10, 12
Sneevan – 28
Snevan – 31
Snevyan – 18
Synèvan – 20
Nil – 2, 7, 11, 13, 15, 21, 23, 32c, 33, 35, 37ab, 38

Inverness

Ant – 1-6, 8, 10-11, 13abce, 16-19, 21ab, 22-23, 26-30, 32-40
Nil – 7, 9, 12, 13d, 14-15, 20, 24-25, 31

Nairn

Ant – 1ab, 2
Emmet – 4-5
Nil – 1c, 3, 6

Moray

Ant – 7, 8bd, 19, 21, 23
Eemert – 1, 2a, 3-5, 6b, 7, 8bf, 9ab, 12-17
Emert – 8e
Emerteen – 6a, 18
Emertine – 21
Emmert – 8d
Emmerteen – 20
Emmertine – 22
Emmet – 11
Hemerteen – 19
Hemmerteen – 10
Pismire – 8c
Nil – 2b, 8a

Banff

Aimerteen – 22
Ant – 1, 2ab, 5, 9, 13, 15, 17, 18c, 34
Emerteen – 2c, 15
Emertine – 6b, 8-11, 14, 24-26
Emmertain – 4
Emmerteen – 16, 18d, 25
Emmertine – 7, 12, 18c, 27, 29, 31
Emmock – 14
Hemertine – 19
Hemmerteen – 5
Pishack – 34
Piss hack – 33
Pushack – 32
Nil 3, 6a, 18ab, 20-21, 23, 28, 30

Aberdeen

Aimerteen – 93
Aimertin – 75
Amintin – 46
Ant – 3a, 6, 16-17, 20, 28ac, 29, 32, 45, 49, 53, 59, 70, 73, 82, 95, 98, 104-105

Aberdeen cont'd

Emantin — 21
Emert — 17, 107
Emertant — 6
Emerteen — 5b, 8, 25, 30, 34, 42, 49, 52, 56, 58, 66, 69, 71a, 79, 81, 85, 87, 99, 101, 105
Emertin — 17, 40, 45, 61-62, 77, 92
Emertine — 12, 22-24, 33, 43, 47e, 51, 100
Emmert — 109
Emmertain — 29, 32
Emmerteen — 9, 27, 28ab, 36, 50, 55, 74, 78, 80, 83-84, 88, 95, 97, 108
Emmertin — 3b, 14-15, 31, 44, 47b, 94, 104
Emmertine — 10, 37, 41, 47a, 48, 64, 72, 76, 86
Emmet — 19, 45, 47f
Enerteen — 71b
Ennenteen — 88
Ennerteen — 68, 70, 71c
Ennertine — 54, 106
Eppertine — 18
Etterkep — 3a
Foumart — 53, 96
Unt — 34-35, 44
Nil — 1-2, 4, 5acd, 7, 11, 13, 26, 38-39, 47cd, 57, 60, 63, 65, 67, 89-91, 102-103

Kincardine

Ant — 1, 5-8, 10, 12, 15-16, 17c, 19, 21, 24, 26, 28
Emert — 3, 6
Emertine — 9-10, 17a, 23
Emintin — 13
Emmert — 4
Emmerteen — 2
Emmertie — 5
Emmertine — 9, 17a, 23
Emmet — 7, 11, 13-15, 17abcd, 18, 22, 28
Ennetn — 12
Nil — 20, 25, 27

Kinross

Ant — 2-4
Emock — 2
Emickie — 1-3, 7
Emmet — 5
Nil — 6

Angus

Ant — 2, 8-10, 14ab, 17b, 18, 20, 25, 28, 32, 34, 36
Emmet — 1, 5ac, 13, 18
Emmoch — 34
Emmock — 3, 5a, 6-7, 12, 14ac, 15, 21-24, 29a, 31-32, 33b, 35-37
Emock — 13, 14d, 20, 27
Nil — 4, 5b, 11, 16, 17a, 19, 26, 29b, 30, 33a

Perth

Ant — 1, 2a, 4-5, 7-10, 12, 21, 24-25, 28, 29a, 32-33, 36, 40, 43, 51b, 52ae, 57, 71-72, 74
Aymock — 66, 70, 73
Emmet — 13, 15, 17, 24-25, 45, 52ab, 65, 69
Emmoch — 39
Emmock — 17, 20-21, 25-28, 29ab, 31-33, 37, 41a, 42, 45-48, 50, 52c, 53, 57, 60, 62, 67-68
Emock — 18
Nil — 2b, 3, 6, 11, 14, 16, 19, 22-23, 30, 34-35, 38, 41b, 44, 49, 51a, 52d, 54-56, 58-59, 61, 63-64

Fife

Ant — 4, 8, 9a, 11, 14, 16, 19, 21, 24, 28, 36ab, 37, 39, 41a, 42, 43a, 44c, 46, 50-51, 53, 55abe, 56-57, 59, 62-63

Emmet — 7, 12-13, 21, 23, 44a, 51, 53
Emmock — 1-3, 6, 8, 10, 14, 21, 27, 43b, 44a, 53
Emmockie — 59
Emock — 25, 55b, 61
Emockie — 58
Enimees — 29
Hornet — 20
Imick — 9b
Mite — 39
Nettercap — 56
Pismire — 21
Nil — 5, 15, 17-18, 22, 26, 30-35, 38, 40ab, 41bcd, 44bdef, 45, 47-49, 52, 54, 55cdfg, 60, 64ab

Clackmannan

Ant — 7
Emmet — 2
Emmock — 6
Emmockie — 5
Nil — 1, 3, 4abcd

Stirling

Ant — 4, 7acef, 8, 11, 13, 16-18, 21ab, 22a, 23bc, 25abcd, 26ac, 27a, 28-32, 34, 35a, 36, 37b, 41, 42a
Aymuck — 3
Black devils — 8
Crammock — 7b
Eemock — 21b
Emmet — 36
Emmock — 6, 7e, 18
Emoch — 7bd
Emock — 2, 7bd, 21a, 42a
Emockie — 39b
Ont — 20
Nil — 1, 5, 9-10, 12, 14-15, 19, 22b, 23a, 24, 26bdef, 27b, 33, 35b, 37a, 38, 39a, 40, 42b

Dunbarton

Ant — 1, 3, 6, 7b, 9-11, 13abc, 14b, 16ab
Eemock — 2, 4b, 7c
Emmet — 14a
Emock — 6
Pismire — 14a
Nil — 4a, 5, 7a, 8, 12, 15, 17-18

Argyll

Ant — 1-3, 5-7, 9-11, 14-17, 19, 22-25, 27, 33, 37, 39
Nil — 4, 8, 12-13, 18, 20-21, 26, 28-32, 34-36, 38, 40

Bute

Ant — 1acd, 2, 7, 8ab, 9
Nil — 1be, 3-6

Ayr

Ant — 1a, 2ab, 3, 5-6, 8ab, 10, 12a, 17, 18b, 20b, 21, 24b, 26b, 28cef, 30a, 31-32, 34, 35ab, 36, 41-45, 49, 52, 53a, 54-55
Dusty millers — 3
Emerteen — 18b
Emmet — 1a
Emmock — 1a
Ont — 10
Pish mither — 56
Pish mole — 19, 33, 41, 51, 54
Pish mool — 48, 57
Pish mule — 48
Pismal — 13, 52
Pismire — 8b, 39, 57
Pismole — 31
Pissmool — 50
Piss mule — 53a
Push money — 37
Nil — 1b, 4, 7, 9, 11, 12b, 14-15, 16ab, 18a, 20acdefgh, 22-23, 24a, 25, 26ac, 27, 28abd, 29, 30b, 38, 40, 46-47, 53b

Renfrew

Ant — 1b, 2abchi, 4ace, 5, 8, 11aefl, 12a, 13c, 14a, 16ab, 17, 19, 20a
Emmet — 16a
Shannag — 21
Nil — 1a, 2defgj, 3, 4bd, 6-7, 9-10, 11bcdghijk, 12b, 13abd, 14b, 15, 16cd, 18ab, 20b

Lanark

Ant — 1-3, 6, 7ac, 8b, 9a, 12, 14bd, 15ac, 16ab, 18-19, 25bc, 26a, 27b, 29cf, 30, 31a, 32a, 33cd, 35bcd, 38ac, 39-40, 44-45, 46abc, 48, 49ab, 51, 52b, 53, 58, 59b, 64b, 65
Beetle — 17
Cloak — 17
Eemock — 20, 38b, 47, 56, 60, 63
Emmet — 13, 17
Emmock — 9b, 13, 29d
Emock — 32c, 46a, 62
Pis minnie — 38d
Nil — 4-5, 7b, 8a, 10ab, 11, 14ac, 15b, 21-24, 25ad, 26b, 27a, 28, 29abeg, 31bcd, 32bdef, 33ab, 34, 35a, 36-37, 38e, 41-43, 50, 52a, 54-55, 57abc, 59a, 61, 64a, 66, 67ab

West Lothian

Ant — 1a, 2-3, 5-6, 8, 9b, 10-13, 15-16, 18, 20a
Eemock — 11
Emmet — 19a
Immick — 22
Nil — 1bcd, 4, 7, 9a, 14, 17ab, 19b, 20b, 21ab

Midlothian

Ant — 6a, 7a, 8a, 10-11, 12ab, 14ab, 15, 18-21, 23b, 24, 25c, 28-29, 32
Eemock — 3, 7a, 13
Eenuck — 30
Emmet — 26a
Immock — 12a
Nil — 1-2, 4-5, 6b, 7b, 8b, 9, 16-17, 22, 23a, 25abd, 26b, 27, 31

East Lothian

Ant — 1, 4b, 6ab, 7-8, 15-21
Eem(m)ock — 10-11, 16
Emmet — 16
Emmock — 2
Emock — 13
Nil — 3, 4a, 5, 9, 12, 14

Berwick

Ant — 1-2, 6-10, 12, 15, 16a, 17, 21, 31-32
Aughan — 27
Eemock — 16b, 21-22, 27
Eerick — 31
Elmick — 18
Emmet — 11, 17, 23
Emmie — 5
Emock — 4, 13, 16a, 20, 26
Midge — 8
Mounie — 27
Ont — 12, 29
Nil — 3, 14, 16c, 19, 24-25, 28, 30

Peebles

Ant — 1, 3, 4bc, 6ab, 8
Eemock — 10
Emmet — 2, 6a
Emock — 3
Nil — 4a, 5, 7, 9

Selkirk

Ant — 1, 2abc, 4, 8
Emmock — 2a
Nil — 2de, 3, 5-7

Roxburgh

Ant — 1-2, 4, 8, 9a, 13, 15b, 16-17, 21adf, 22, 25
Eemock — 21c
Emmet — 3a, 13, 17, 21c
Emmock — 8, 21c
Emock — 7
Pishmere — 8
Pishmother — 8, 26, 28
Pismire — 17
Pismuir — 15b
Scotch — 21c
Nil — 3b, 5-6, 9b, 10-12, 14, 15a, 18-20, 21be, 23-24, 27

Dumfries

Ant — 1a, 4, 8a, 12, 15-16, 18-20, 21b, 22, 24, 26-27, 29, 31de, 33, 40, 46
Emmet — 29
Pesh money — 11
Pish minnie — 4, 8b, 9, 13, 19, 22
Pish money — 5, 17ab, 21b, 24
Pish mother — 39
Pismenie — 26
Pismonger — 7
Piss mainer — 35
Piss minner — 28, 45a, 46, 49
Piss minnie — 7, 31a, 32, 41-42
Piss minnows — 31b
Piss mother — 29
Nil — 1b, 2-3, 6, 10, 14, 21a, 23, 25, 30, 31cf, 34, 36-38, 43-44, 45b, 47-48

Kirkcudbright

Ant — 1, 3, 6-7, 10, 21c
Bigglie — 14
Bug — 12a
Pees minnie — 18
Pish minnie — 1, 6, 9
Pish mithers — 19
Pish money — 24
Pismire — 17
Pissminnie — 4-5, 8, 12a, 16-17, 21ac, 22-23, 27
Piss minnow — 2, 15a
Nil — 11, 13, 15b, 20, 21b, 25-26

Wigtown

Ant — 2, 5a, 11, 14, 16-17
Pish maw — 1
Pish mither — 1, 13, 15, 18
Pis miller — 18
Pismire — 5b, 10
Pissminnie — 5a
Piss mither — 5a, 6, 12
Nil — 3-4, 7-9

Northumberland

Aant — 8
Amet — 69a
And — 72i
Ant — 1a, 2ab, 3, 5-6, 9, 13-18, 19a, 20b, 21-22, 26, 28, 29bd, 30-31, 35-38, 40a, 41cd, 42, 45-48, 52, 53ab, 54, 56, 59b, 60, 62b, 64ab, 66, 68, 69bcdh, 70, 71abcd, 72cdg, 77-78, 82-83, 86-87, 88b, 89-90, 94b, 98, 99d, 101ab, 102, 103abc, 104ab, 106-107, 109, 111ab, 112, 120abc, 124b, 126cf, 127a, 129b, 130ce, 132-133, 135, 137, 140, 142
Creeper — 30, 83
Emmet — 25, 69ab, 71c, 127e
Pessimore — 43
Pishmuther — 53a
Pismire — 34a, 69a, 124a, 134
Pissie meer — 142
Pissie moor — 34a, 44, 73-74, 77, 80, 103bc, 138, 140
Pissiemore — 37, 81, 110
Pissir moor — 136
Pizzie moor — 124a
Walker — 76

Northumberland cont'd

Nil — 1bc, 4, 7, 10-12, 19b, 20a, 23, 24ab, 27, 29acef, 32, 33ab, 34b, 39, 40b, 41ab, 49-51, 55, 57-58, 59acdef, 61, 62acdefgh, 63, 67, 69efg, 71e, 72abefhjkl, 75, 79, 84-85, 88a, 91-93, 94a, 95ab, 96-97, 99abc, 100, 105, 108abc, 113-117, 118ab, 119, 121, 122ab, 123, 125, 126abde, 127bcdfgh, 128, 129ac, 130abdf, 131, 139, 141, 143

Cumberland

Ant — 1a, 4, 9, 13c, 14, 15ac, 18, 21, 23-24, 40, 42, 46-48, 50, 53, 56-59
Emmet — 9
Ermit — 60
Pishie mother — 3
Pishie mudder — 8
Pishimer — 27
Pishmidder — 13a
Pismire — 9
Pissiemoor — 22, 49, 52, 57, 60, 62, 63b
Pissie mother — 2, 5a, 12, 15a, 16-17, 20, 29, 38
Pissie mudder — 9, 13a, 15c, 16 28, 33
Pissima — 31
Pissimer — 13a, 27-28, 30, 44-47, 56-57, 61, 63a
Pissiemire — 13a, 27, 41, 43
Nil — 1b, 5b, 6-7, 10-11, 13bd, 15b, 19, 25-26, 32, 34-36, 37ab, 39, 51, 54-55

Down

Ant — 2a, 5, 15, 19
Creeper — 19
Emmet — 2b
Gellick — 7
Pishmetter — 24
Pishmire — 2b, 4, 22, 26
Pishmowl — 18, 21, 29
Pissmedder — 27
Pissmeller — 11
Pissmellick — 13
Pissmire — 17, 23, 25, 27
Pissmither — 10
Nil — 1, 3, 6, 8-9, 12, 14, 16, 20, 28, 30

Tyrone

Ant — 1, 7, 11
Pishmire — 6, 8, 10, 12, 15
Pishmool — 4, 7
Pishmowl — 5
Pismugger — 13
Pissmether — 11
Pissmire — 4, 9, 11, 14, 16
Nil — 2-3

Antrim

Ant — 13, 20, 25, 27, 29
Granny needles — 34
Mollog — 34
Mullog — 34
Pish hule — 19
Pishmire — 6, 30, 33
Pishmowl(d) — 1-3, 4A, 5ab, 7, 9, 11, 16b, 17, 22-24, 26
Pis(h) mugger — 15, 21
Pissmire — 8b, 15, 18, 34
Pissmowl(d) — 15, 18
Pissmug — 15
Nil — 4, 8a, 10, 12, 14, 16ac, 28, 31-32

Donegal

Ant — 5, 5A
Insect — 5A
Mole — 1A
Pishe moolog — 7A
Pishimool — 4, 6, 8
Pish me logue — 10b
Pishmire — 2
shmowl — 5
Pissmire — 13
Shang gan — 12
Nil — 1, 3, 7, 9, 10a, 11

Fermanagh

Ant — 4-5, 9
Pishmire — 1-2, 7a, 8-9
Pissmire — 4-6, 10
Nil — 3, 7b

Armagh

Ant — 6a
Pishmire — 4
Pissmire — 1-2, 6b
Nil — 3, 5

Londonderry

Pishmool — 1
Pishmoul(d) — 2-3, 3A, 5-6
Pishmucker — 6
Pishmugger — 7
Nil — 1AB, 4

77 BEE (the wild variety) (PQ1, 168)

Bumble bee has not been mapped as it occurs nearly everywhere (in varying degrees of concentration). Variants of BUMBLE BEE (a number of **bummle bee, bummel bee**) have been subsumed.
Item PQ1, 169 BEE (the domesticated bee) did not yield any interesting mappable material. (**Bee, honey bee** occur nearly everywhere; a small area of **bumbee** in the middle of Central Scotland).

Shetland

Bee — 1-2, 15-16, 21a, 25, 27, 30, 33
Bumbee — 2
Drummer bee — 6, 8
Drummie bee — 3, 21ab, 23, 26
Honey bee — 4-5, 7
Stangie bee — 19-20, 30
Stingie bee — 7, 9, 17, 22, 24, 32
Stungie bee — 10
Nil — 11-14, 18, 28-29, 31

Orkney

Bumbee — 7
(Bumble) bee — 1-5, 7-9, *11*, 13ab, 19
Honey bee — 13a, 15-16
Ringo — 15
Stanger — 17
Sucko — 15
Nil — 6, 10, 12, 14, 18, 20-21

Caithness

Bumble bee — 2b, 8-9, 16b
Honey bee — 2a
(Wild) bee — 5, *11, 14*
Nil — 1, 3-7, 10, 12abc, 13, 15, 16a, 17

Sutherland

Bumbee — 11
Bumble bee — 1-6, 8, 9ab, 11, 13, 15
(Wild) bee — *3*, 5, 7-8, 10, 12, 16
Nil — 14, 17

Ross & Cromarty

Blairack — 24, 25b, 32c
Bombee — 9, 15, 18
Bumbee — 12-13, 22, 28, 32b
Bumber — 7, 20, 24, 25b, 32c, 33-36
Bumble bee — 3, 6, 8-9, 15, 17, 19, 21, 23, 25b, 26-27, 39
Foggie bee — 8, 12
(Wild) bee — 1, 4-5, 14, 16, 25a, 26, *29*, 30-31, 32a, 39
Nil — 2, 10-11, 37ab, 38

Inverness

Bodach ruadh — 19
Bumbee — 9, 27
Bumber — 7-12, 13e, 14-16, 19, 25, 31
Bumble (bee) — *1, 6, 8*, 13ac, *16, 21ab, 26*, 30, *32, 34-35, 39-40*
Bummer — 10, 13a
(Wild) bee — 1-5, 13bce, 17, 22-*23*, 28-29, 33, 36-38
Nil — 13d, 18, 20, 24

Nairn

Bee — 2
Bumber — 1ac, 2-4
Bumble (bee) — *1bc, 5*
Nil — 6

Moray

Bumbee — 1, 2a, 3-5, 6b, 7, 8bf, 9a, 10, 12, 14
Bumble bee — 4, 9a, 11, 13, 23
Bumbler — 12
Bumblie bee — 8ae
Bummer — 6a, 8f, 11, 16, 18, 22
Bummie — 3, 8b, 20
Foggie (bee) — *8b*, 16, 18-19, 22
Wasp — 7, 14
(Wild) bee — 8d, *23*
Nil — 2b, 8c, 9b, 15, 17

Banff

Bizzer — 6b
Bumbee — 2ac, 3, 5, 13-15, 18c, 21, 23-25
Bumble (bee) — *15-16, 23, 29*-30
Bumbler — 17
Bummel — 32
Bummer — 1, 6b, 9-11, 18c, 19-23, 26-27, 33
Bummie — 29, 31
Buzzer — 6b
Drondie — 7
Foggie bee — 4-5, 8-9, 16, 18bd, 26, 32
Foggie toddler — 6b
Humble bee — 19
Hummel — 18d
Wild bee — 2b, 34
Nil — 6a, 12, 18a, 28

Aberdeen

Big bummer — 37
Bumbee — 3b, 4, 6, 8, 10-12, 14, 17, 32, 35, 41-43, 45, 47ab, 56, 62, 65, 71bc, 76-78, 92-93, 95, 102
Bumble (bee) — *3a*, 4, *16, 20-21*, 47cf, *57, 59, 63, 70, 71a*, 72, 89
Bumble wasp — 31
Bummer — 2, 4, 5abcd, 8-11, 15-20, 22-27, 28ac, 30, 32-34, 36, 40, 43-46, 47acd, 48-54, 58, 60-61, 64-67, 69, 71ac, 72-75, 78-88, 90, 92, 94, 96, 98-101, 103-105, 107-109
Foggie bee — 27, 53, 55, 78, 97
Foggie bummer — 10, 51, 85, 104
Foggie toddler — 3a, 45, 71c, 73, 83, 98, 101, 104
Mossie toddler — 17
Red ersie — 98
Reid bummer — 104
Stanger — 7
Wasp — 22, 29, 40, 70, 75, 105
Wild bee — 8, 106
Nil — 1-2, 13, 28b, 38-39, 47e, 68, 91

Kincardine

Bee — 5, 16, 19
Black bumber — 13, 17bd
Brown nosie — 28
Bumbee — 7-8, 11-12, 17c, 24
Bumble (bee) — *6*, 15, *17d, 26, 28*
Bummer — 1-7, 9-10, 14-16, 17a, 21, 28
Foggie toddler — 5, 10-14, 17abcd, 21, 23-24, 26,28
Humle bee — 24
Red erse — 28
Snippie — 28
Wasp — 11, 20
White erse — 28
Nil — 18, 22, 25, 27

Kinross

Bumbee — 1-5
Earthie garie — 7
Foggie bee — 3, 7
Foggie toddler — 3, 7
Fuggie bee — 1-2
Nil — 6

Angus

Brakie — 7
Bumbee — 1, 18, 27, 30
Bumble bee — 2, 18, 33b
Bummer — 5bc, 17a, 19
Bummie — 1, 3, 5ac, 6-13, 14a, 15, 20, 22-24, 28, 32 33a, 34, 36-37
Dora hill — 14c
Foggie toddler — 2, 4, 5c, 6-7 9, 11, 14bcd, 21, 23, 31-32 33ab, 34, 37
Garie — 14d
Humble bee — 33b
Red ersie — 5c, 14a, 28
Reed doupie — 14d
Snippie — 5a, 35
Wasp — 14a, 25
(White) arsie — 23
White ersie — 5c, 14a, 31
(Wild) bee — *17b*, 34
Yellow endie — 23
Nil — 16, 19, 26, 29ab

Perth

Baker — 52a
Brakit bummie — 13
Bumbee — 10, 25, 29a, 32, 41b, 43-44, 51b, 52d, 53,

Perth cont'd

62 70
Bumble — 64, 66
(Bumble) bee — *1, 2ab,* 4, *8-10, 12, 16, 21, 23-25,* 26, *29a,* 32, *35-36, 49,* 52bde, *62, 67-68, 71-72,* 74
Bummer — 1, 15, 17, 25-26
Bummie — 5-7, 11, 20-21, 27-28, 29a, 32-33, 42, 45-46, 51a, 52ac, 55-57
Faggie toddler — 27
Foggie bee — 41b, 52c, 66-67
Foggie toddler — 1, 10, 13, 15-16, 18, 20-21, 31-33, 42, 44-45, 50, 52a, 54, 57
Fogie todler — 5-6
Fuggie (bee) — 28, 37, 39-40, 48, 68, *70*-71, 73
Fuggie toddler — 29b, 41a, 46, 52de, 53, 62, 65
Honey bee — 2a
Humble (bee) — *24,* 55
Hummie — 29a
Toddie foddler — 45
Toddler — 48
Wasp — 23, 60
Nil - 3, 14, 19, 22, 30, 34, 38, 47, 58-59, 61, 63, 69

Fife

Bumbee — 9ab, 12-13, 16, 21, 24, 26, 28-30, 32-34, 36a, 37, 41ab, 42, 43a, 44acde, 45-53, 55cdf, 56-58, 60, 63, 64a
(Bumble) bee — *4-5,* 7, 11, *20, 22, 35, 37, 40b, 43b,* 44b, 50, *53-54,* 55*abde, 58*-59, 62-63
Bummer — 23, 35, 44c, 55b
Bummie — 1-2, 5, 8, 11, 14, 17-18, 24, 27, 31, 33
Bummler — 23
Cannie annie — 27
Cannie nannie — 47, 55e
Foggie (bee) — 10, *42*
Foggie toddler — 21, 23, 27
Fogie (bee) — 7, 20, *44d,* 61
Fogie todler — 6
Fuggie — 8, 36b, 52
Fuggie toddler — 35
Fuggie todler — 25
Geordie bummer — 25
Red ersie — 44a
Wasp — 19, 25
Nil — 3, 5, 15, 38-39, 40a, 41cd, 44f, 55g, 64b

Clackmannan

Baker — 3
Bee — 4c
Bumbee — 3, 4d, 6-7
Bumble(bee) — 1, 4*ac*
Bummer — 5
Bummie — 4b
Cannie nannie — 3, 4d
Nil — 2

Stirling

Baker — 30
Bloober bee — 10
Bumbee — 1, 7abe, 9, 11, 15-20, 22b, 23abc, 24, 25abcd, 26acdef, 27ab, 28, 30, 32-34, 35b, 36, 37ab, 39a, 40-41, 42a
Bumble bee — 4, 7b, 10, 12, 15, 18, 21a, 22a, 25d, 31, 37b, 38, 39b
Bum geordie — 3
Bummer — 9, 11, 27a, 34
Bussock — 12
Cannie nannie — 26a
Connie nonnie — 38
Foggie (bee) — 7bd, *21b*
Foggie toddler — 7b
Fuggie — 2-3, 7b, 8-9, 13, 18, 26b, 35a
Fuggie todler — 7de
Mammie — 26a
Sodger — 26e
Soldier — 26a

(Wild) bee — 7*cf,* 21b, 23bc, 31
Nil — 5-6, 14, 29, 42b

Dunbarton

Baker — 7a, 16b
Bumbee — 2-3, 5, 10, 14a, 16ab, 17-18
(Bumble) bee — *6, 7b,* 8-9, 11, *13abc, 14ab*
Bummer — 13b
Bummie — 13b, 14a
Foggie bee — 13a
Fuggie (bee) — 7*ac,* 16a, 18
Hynee — 14b
Nipper — 16b
Nil — 1, 4ab, 12, 15

Argyll

Brown bee — 27
Bumbee — 10, 14, 19, 23, 28, 31, 35-40
Bumble bee — 2, 5, 11, 15, 24, 26, 29, 32, 34-35
Hornet wasp — 26
Sheilan — 12
Wasp — 33
(Wild) bee — 1-3, 5-*7, 9*-10, 16-17, *22,* 25, *33*
Nil — 4, 8, 13, 18, 20-21, 30

Bute

Baker bee — 8a, 9
Bumbee — 1acde, 3-5, 8a
(Bumble) bee — *1a,* 2, *7, 8b, 9*
Moss bummer — 9
Sand bee — 9
Wee hunch back — 8b
Nil — 1b, 6

Ayr

Baker — 8a, 10
Bumbee — 1a, 2a, 3-4, 6-7, 8ab, 9-11, 12ab, 13-15, 16ab, 18a, 19, 20bcdg, 23, 24ab, 25, 26bc, 28abd, 29, 30ab, 31-32, 36, 38-39, 41-43, 46-49, 52, 53a, 54, 56
Bumble bee — 2ab, 3, 10, 12ab, 15, 20f, 21, 24b, 27, 28f, 33, 35a, 50, 53b, 55, 57
Bummer — 36
Bummie — 28f
Foggie (bee) — 26b, 32, *34*
Fogie — 18b, 30a, 35b
Fuggie — 13
Humble bee — 57
Mammie bee — 2b
Meadie bee — 45
Moss bee — 57
Sodger — 6
Solitary — 57
Tiger wasp — 6
(Wild) bee — 2b, *5,* 12a, 20c, 28*ce,* 34, 44
Nil — 1b, 17, 20aeh, 22, 26a, 37, 40, 51

Renfrew

Baker — 12b, 17, 18a
Bakie — 11k
Broon bee — 17
Bumbee — 4de, 5, 7, 11adejkl, 13a, 14ab, 15, 16ad, 20ab, 21
Bumble bee — 2aei, 8, 16d, 18a, 19
Bummer — 16c
Bummie bee — 18a, 21
Fuggie — 21
Honey bee — 2j, 12b, 15
Hornie — 12a
Sojer — 11k
(Wild) bee — 2abc*i,* 4ace, 11f, 13c, *16b, 19*
Nil — 1ab, 2dfg, 3, 4b, 6, 9-10, 11bcghi, 13bd, 18b

Lanark

Baker — 17, 32c, 35d, 46c, 47, 61
Blackie — 15c, 17
Bumbee — 1-3, 6, 7abc, 8a, 9ab, 10a, 12-13, 15ab, 16b, 17, 20, 22-24, 25cd, 26a, 27ab, 29cdfg, 31ac, 32def, 33cd, 35abc, 38cd, 39-40, 42, 44-45, 46abc, 47, 53, 57bc, 58, 60-62, 64b, 65
Bumble bee — 10a, 14bc, 15bc, 16a 18, 21, 25a, 26a, 32b, 35d, 48, 51, 58, 66
Bummer — 35d
Bummie — 4, 24, 25b, 30, 31d, 32b, 33b, 38ce, 43-44, 46b, 57a, 58, 59a, 61
Foggie (bee) — 15b, *38d,* 48, *49b,* 51, 56, 59ab, 66
Foggie yirdie — 38b
Fogie — 47, 50, 52ab
Fuggie (bee) — 1, 15c, 20, *30,* 46a
Himie — 17, 25b, 30, 32ac, 33bi
Humble bee — 13
Mossie bee — 65
Sodger — 15c, 32c
Stinging bee — 5
Wasp — 11, 32f
(Wild) bee — 6, *8b,* 14d, 19, 26a, 35bcd, 38a, 46ab, 49a
Yirdie — 50
Nil — 10b, 14a, 26b, 28, 29abe, 31b, 33a, 34, 36-37, 41, 54-55, 63, 64a, 67ab

West Lothian

Bee — 1a, 10-11, 18, 20a
Bizzer — 11
Bumbee — 1abd, 3-8, 9ab, 11-15, 17a, 20a, 22
Bumble bee — 2-3, 8, 16, 19b, 21a
Bumbler — 11
Bummie — 1ac
Cannie nannie — 1a, 13
Fuggie (bee) — *3,* 19b, 21a
Puggie bee — 16
Red hot poker — 13
Sodjger — 1a
Nil -- 17b, 19a, 20b, 21b

Midlothian

Baker — 23a
Bumbee — 2-4, 6b, 7a, 8b, 10, 12b, 13, 14a, 17-18, 20, 23b, 25bc, 26a, 29, 32
Bumble bee — 3, 6a, 10, 12a, 16-18, 23ab
Bummer — 11, 15
Bummie — 8b, 12a, 18, 24, 25d, 27-28, 30-31
Cannie mammie — 12b
Cannie nannie — 23a, 24, 25c, 29
Foggie — 26a, 30
Foggie toddler — 23a
Fogie — 28
Fuggie — 13, 14b
Fuzzie -- 14b
Mammie bee — 14a
Puggie bee — 14a
Wappie — 23a
Wasp — 1
(Wild) bee — 8a, 14a, *15,* 19, *22*
Nil — 5, 7b, 9, 21, 25a, 26b

East Lothian

Big bee — 2
Bumbee — 2, 4ab, 6ab, 7-9
(Bumble) bee — *1, 3, 4a, 8, 11,* 18-19
Bummer — 1
Bummie (bee) — 1-*2,* 10, 12-17, 20-21
Cannie nannie — 2-3, 7, 14, 17, 21
Connie nonnie — 10
Foggie bee — 7, 9
Fuggie — 15
King bumie — 14

Nil — 5

Berwick

Bumbee — 8, 17, 22-23
Bumble (bee) — 6, *23,* 25, 31
Bummie — 3-5, 7-14, 16ab, 18-20, 23, 25-27, 29, 31
Bummle — 30
Bummler — 32
Cannie nannie — 11, 17-19, 32
Leph — 27
Wasp — 24
(Wild) bee — 1-2, 15, *21*
Nil — 16c, 28

Peebles

Bumbee — 1, 4ab, 6a, 8, 10
(Bumble) bee — *2,* 4c, *6b*
Bummer — 2
Bummie — 3, 4c, 9
Bummle — 7
Foggie — 4c, 6a, 8
Fogie — 3, 5
Yirdie — 5

Selkirk

Bumbee — 2a
Bummie (bee) — 1, 2abde, 3-*4,* 6, 8
Cannie nannie — 2d
Fogie (bee) — 2c
Nil — 5, 7

Roxburgh

Bumbee — 28
(Bumble) bee — 2, 3a, 9a, 21*ac*
Bummie (bee) — 1, 3ab, 4-8, 9b, 10, 13, 15ab, 17-20, 21acde, *22-24,* 25-26, 28
Cannie nannie — 17, 21c
Dusty miller — 21c
Foggie bee — 21c
Foggie toddler — 17
Red dowp — 17
Wasp — 21f
Nil — 11-12, 14, 16, 21b, 23, 27

Dumfries

Baigh — 37
Baker — 10
Bumbee — 1a, 13, 41, 46
Bumble (bee) — *4-5,* 6, *9-10, 11-12, 17b,* 20, *27,* 31*bcd, 33*
Bummel — 19, 21ab, 24, 30, 41-42
Bummie — 7, 14-16, 17ab, 18, 26, 28-29, 32, 34-39, 43-44, 45a, 46, 49
Fog bee — 1a
(Foggie) bee — *20,* 29
Foggie bummie — 18
Foggie toddler — 27
Wasp — 27-28
(Wild) bee — 8*ab,* 19-20, 22, 31e, 47
Yellow bee — 5
Nil — 1b, 2-3, 23, 25, 31af, 40, 45b, 48

Kirkcudbright

Bumbee — 1, 17, 27
Bumble (bee) — *3-4, 6-7, 11, 13, 15b, 18-19, 21bc,* 23
Bummle — 2, 5, 8-9, 14, 15a, 16, 21b, 22, 27
Wild bee — 10, 12b
Nil — 12a, 20, 21a, 24-26

Wigtown

Bumbee — 2, 4, 5a, 6-7, 10-12, 15, 17-18
Bumble bee — 5a, 13, 16
Bummie — 14
Bummle — 8
Yellow bee — 11
Nil — 1, 3, 5b, 9

Northumberland

Big bumbler — 15
Blue arstie — 72d
Bombus lapidarius — 69b
Bumble bee — 2b, 59b, 64b, 66, 68, 71a, 72d, 79, 103ac, 104b, 110, 126f, 127bc, 140, 143
Bumbler (bee) — 1c, 4, 7, 9-12, 17-18, 19a, 22-23, 26, 29ace, 31-32, 33b, 34a, 38, 48-51, *53ab,* 54-58, 59bcd, 60, 62ad, 64b, 65ab, 66, 69acg, 70, 71e, 72cdefhil, 73, 75, 77-78, 81, 84, 86-87, 88a, 89, 91, 94b, 96-98, 99a, *101b,* 103abc, 105, 107, 112, 116, 118ab, 122ab, 124b, 127dh, 128, 130c, 134-135, 138, 140-141, 143
Bummler — 1ab, 2ab, 3, 6, 8, 14, 20ab, 23, 24a, 25, 27, 29bdf, 30, 33a, 34b, 37, 39, 40ab, 41abd, 42-44, 47, 59ef, 61, 62cegh, 63, 64a, 67-68, 69deh, 71abcd, 72abgjk, 74, 76, 80, 82-83, 85, 90, 92, 95ab, 99bd, 103ab, 104a, 106, 108abc, 109, 111ab, 112-114, 116-117, 119, 120abc, 124a, 125, 126abcde, 127ceg, 129bc, 130abe, 131-133, 137, 139, 142
Cannie nannie — 25, 37, 60, 80, 122a
Dusty — 18
Dusty miller — 80
Gad flea — 69b
Hornet — 69b, 70
Hum — 69a
Humble bee — 59e, 103bc, 140
Queenie — 127h
Red arstie — 62a, 72d, 116
Sand bee — 5, 52
Sandie — 62a, 70, 76, 79
Sandie bummler — 62h
Small bee — 15
Wappie — 70, 78
Wasp — 69b, 78, 100, 123
Waspie — 70
White arstie — 62a, 72d
(Wild) bee — 5, 13, *16,* 28, 35-36, 40a, 42, 45-46, 52, 53b, 57, 59b, 62b, 69bc, 70, 71d, 72c, 82, 87, 88b, 127a, 130e, 137
Wild honey bee — 71c
Nil — 19b, 24b, 41c, 59a, 62f, 69f, 71f, 72h, 93, 94a, 99c, 101a, 102, 115, 121, 127f, 129a, 130df, 136

Cumberland

Bee — 1a, 5a, 14, 40, 42, 50, 53
Belted earl — 13a, 30-31
Boomlie — 63a
Bum bee — 13c
Bumble (bee) — 2, *12,* 13bcd, 18, 20, *23, 33, 42, 46, 57,* 61
Bumbler — 3, 13a, 29, 39
Bumblie (bee) — 4, 24, 41, 48, *51*-52, 54-55, 60
Bumlie (bee) — 13a, 15c, 16, 18, 25-28, 43-46, *56-57,* 58-59, 62,
Bummel — 7-9, 11, 13ad, 15abc, 17, 28, 30, 32, 34, 36, 37b, 38, 40, 49
Haytime bee — 56
Hornet — 47
Moss bumlie — 46
Red arsed bumlie — 46
Scotch bumble — 9
Sowljer bee — 46
Wamp — 47, 62
Wasp — 19, 47
Wild honey bee — 56
Yellow bumlie — 46
Nil — 1b, 5b, 6, 10, 21-22, 35, 37a, 63b

Down

Bumbee — 2b, 6-7, 11-13, 17-19, 21, 23-24, 26-27, 29
Bumble (bee) — *2b,* 5, 9, *15, 20,* 27
Humble bee — 2b
Nil — 1, 2a, 3-4, 8, 10, 14, 16, 22, 25, 28, 30

Tyrone

Bumbee — 1, 5-6, 10, 12
Bumble bee — 11
Wild bee — 7-8, 11
Nil — 2-4, 9, 13-16

Antrim

Bumbee — 3, 5b, 7, 9, 11-12, 14-15, 16b, 17, 19-21, 23-27, 30, 33
Bumble — 8b
(Bumble) bee — 1, *3, 13,* 19, *25,* 29
Foggie bee — 16b
Grun bee — 19
Wasp — 5b
Nil — 2, 4, 4A, 5a, 6, 8a, 10, 16ac, 18, 22, 28, 31-32, 34

Donegal

Bumbee — 1-2, 5-6, 7A, 8, 10a, 13
Bumble (bee) — *5A,* 6, *12*
Honey bee — 4
Meadow bee — 6
Red bee — 13
Nil — 1A, 3, 7, 9, 10b, 11

Fermanagh

Bumbee — 2, 8
Bumble bee — 1, 10
Wild bee — 4-5, 9
Nil — 3, 6, 7ab

Armagh

Bumbee — 2, 4-5, 6a
(Bumble) bee — 3, *6a*
Nil 1, 6b

Londonderry

Bumbee — 1B, 4-5, 7
Bumble (bee) — *2,* 3A
Nil — 1, 1A, 3, 6

78 BLACK BEETLE (large one) (PQ1, 170)

Italics (see Introduction p.13) have only been used in this item where the informant specified the size of the insect.
There is no essential difference in the distribution areas of PQ1, 171 BEETLE (small one) except that the items are often preceded by 'small, wee, peerie, etc.' There are also fewer instances of **cockroach** and **hundie clock.**
The unstressed vowel variants in **gollAch, gollAcher** have been subsumed (**-och, -uch, -ich,** etc.).
Some of the items occur also in 44 **crowbar** and 82 **earwig. Gowlack** also appears in 24 **forked stick.**

Shetland

Black clock — 10, 17, 19, 21a, 23-27, 29-30, 33
Blue clock — 21b
Fleein clock — 21b
Hointie clock — 3
Horn clock — 1-2
Hunchie clock — 9
Hundie clock — 4, 6-7, 13-15, 17, 23, 30
Hungie clock — 12
Muckle (black) clock — 10, *20,* 32
Peat clock — 5
Peat heundie clock — 16
Tur — 5
Witchie clock — 21b, 22, 31
Nil — 8, 11, 18, 28

Orkney

(Big black) beetle — 5, *8*-9, *13a,* 15, 17
(Big/black) clock — 7, 15, *18*-19, 21
Big gablack — 16
(Big *or* big black) gablo — 1, *2-3,* 7, 11-12
Cleg — 4
Cloak — 7
Clockie — 20
Clog — 4
Cockroach — 5, 14
Hard backed gablo — 6
Muckle gablo — 13a
Nil — 10, 13b

Caithness

Beetle — 2b, 10
(Big/black) clock — 1, 2a, 3, 5, *6,* 8-11, 12abc, 13-*14,* 16b
Black cloaker — 15
Clocker — 12c, 17
Nil — 4, 7, 16a

Sutherland

(Black) beetle — *5-8, 11,* 12-*13,* 16
Cloak — 4, 9b, 12
Cloaker — 10
Clock — 2, 9a, 14
Cockroach — 1
Nil — 3, 15, 17

Ross & Cromarty

(Big/black) beetle — 1, 3-6, 8-9, 14, 16-17, 20, 22, 24, 25a, *26,* 27-29, 32ab, 36, 39
Clock — 31, 37a
Clocker — 18, 25b
Clog — 33
Cockroach — 23, 34
Gullach — 36
Nil — 2, 7, 10-13, 15, 19, 21, 30, 32c, 35, 37b, 38

Inverness

(Big/black) beetle — 1-5, *8,* 10-11, 13abce, 17, 19, 21ab, 22-23, 27-29, 32, 34, 36-37, 39-40
Cloaker — 26
Cockroach — 6, 26, 35
Stag beetle — 38
Nil — 7, 9, 12, 13d, 14-16, 18, 20, 24-25, 30-31, 33

Nairn

Black beetle — 1a, 4
Cloak — 5
Cloaker — 1a
Clocker — 1b
Nil — 1c, 2-3, 6

Moray

Beetle — 2a, 8d
Clock — 3, 6b, 8f, 9a, 12-13
Clocker — 1, 9b
Clog — 3
Cockroach — 6a, 7, 19
Gol(l)ach — 5, 8def, 9a, 10, 12, 14, 18, 20-22
Gullach — 23
Muckle gollach — 8b
Nil — 2b, 4, 8ac, 11, 15-17

Banff

Beetle — 2b
Blue gollach — 34
Cloak — 2a, 13
Clock — 2c, 3
Cockroach — 2a, 10, 18c, 21
Gol(l)ach — 1, 2c, 4-5, 6b, 7-9, 11, 14-17, 18bcd, 19-20, 22-26, 28-31, 33
Golack — 32
Horn golach — 23
Horny golach — 23
Nil — 6a, 12, 18a, 27

Aberdeen

Beetle — 6, 105, 107
(Big/black) gol(l)ach — 1-2, 3b, 5cd, 8-9, 11-12, 14, 16-17, 19-22, 24, 26-27, 28abc, 30, 32-35, 37, *39,* 42-44, 46,

Aberdeen cont'd
47abe, 48-62, 64-69, 71abc, 72 73, 76, 78-87, 89, 92-93, *94,* 96 98, 100, 103-105, 108-109
Bum clock that flies 5c
Clock – 47f, 78
Cockroach – 14-15, 22, 48, 70, 74-75, 95
Colcroach – 6, 51
Cricket – 29
Fleein gollach – 31
Gramshie – 25
Horny gol(l)ach – 5bc, 10, 19, 34, 41, 45-46, 64, 77, 85, 88, 99, 101
Muckle gol(l)ach – 10, 23
Muckle horny golach – 3a
Nil – 4, 5a, 7, 13, 18, 36, 38, 40, 47cd, 63, 90-91, 97, 102, 106

Kincardine
Beetle – 6, 8, 19, 26
Cockroach – 15, 17c
Gol(l)ach – 2-5, 9-12, 14, 16, 18, 22-24, 28
Golack – 1
Horny gol(l)ach – 6-7, 10, 13, 17b
Nil – 17ad, 20-21, 25, 27

Kinross
Cloaker – 2-3, 6
Clocker – 7
Gowlack – 4-5
Sunny clocker – 1

Angus
(Black) beetle – 7, *9, 17b,* 18, 28, 29a, *32, 33b,* 34, 36
(Black) gol(l)ach – 3, 5a, 6, 12, 14abcd, 15, 17a, 19, 21-*22,* 23, 25, 27, 31-32, 34-36
Black goulach – 22
Bum cloak – 13
Canthard – 33b
Cloak – 5ab, 9, 18, 29a
Cloaker – 18
Clock (beetle) – *4,* 5c, 8, 10, 17a, 37
Clocker – 24
Cockroach – 18
Gollack – 23
Horny gollach – 11, 14b
May bug – 33b
Nil – 1-2, 16, 20, 26, 29b, 30, 33a

Perth
(Black) beetle – *1,* 2a, *4-5, 8*-9, 12, *24, 28,* 32-33, *36,* 48, 57, 74
(Black) clock – *18,* 20, 39-40, 41b, 49, 52b
Bum clock – 15, 29a, 31, 46, 52c
Burying beetle – 10
Clauk – 62
Cloak – 22, 32, 70, 73
Cloaker – 3, 25, 27, 29b, 32, 44, 51ab, 52de, 61-62, 64, 70-71
Clocker – 26, 37, 39, 41b, 46, 53, 56, 63, 66-69, 72
Cockroach – 21, 23, 25
Dor beetle – 41a
Fleein' cloaker – 41a
Gol(l)ach – 32, 43, 50, 52b, 58-60
Gollacher – 67
Goulack – 42, 65
Gullach – 7, 21, 31
Horn golach – 57
Horny golach – 33, 52a
Nil – 2b, 6, 11, 13-14, 16-17, 19, 30, 34-35, 38, 45, 47, 54-55

Fife
(Big) clocker – 9b, 12-13, 16, 22-23, 36b, 39, 41d, 44acf, *46,* 48, 54, 55d
(Black) beetle – *4, 37,* 44b, 50, 57, 63
Bum cloak – 8, 25
Bum cloaker – 10
(Bum) clock – 23, *44a,* 64a
Cloaker – 8, 9a, 12, 18-20, 24, 28, 36a, 38, 40ab, 41ad, 42, 43ab, 44ce, 45, 47, 49-52, 55abef, 56-59, 61-63, 64b
Cockroach – 35, 55d
Goulack – 28
Creeper – 41b
Crockroach – 41a
Fleein' clocker – 27
Forkie tailie – 3
Golack – 2, 4-5, 12, 14, 26, 29, 33, 47
Gol(l)ach – 8, 17, 33-34
Gollack – 32
Gowlack – 1, 6-8, 12, 19, 21, 31, 44a, 46, 55b, 64a
Gullach – 53
Hard back – 11
Horny golach – 37
Horny golack – 21
Nil – 15, 30, 41c, 44d, 55cg, 60

Clackmannan
(Big) cloaker – 1, 4abcd, 5-*6,* 7
Clock – 2
Clocker – 2
Gowlack – 1
Gowlet – 4d
Nil – 3

Stirling
(Big) cloaker – 3-4, 7acef, 8-10, 12, 16, *17,* 18-19, *20,* 21ab, *22b,* 23abc, 25*acd,* 26adef, 27b, 28, 31, *32,* 33-34, 35b, 36, 37a, 38, 39ab, 40, 42a
(Black) beetle – *4,* 7e, 21b, 26ad, 36
Bum clock – 7b
Cloak – 13, 18, 29, 33, 36
Clock – 2, 13-14
Clocker – 6, 7bd, 11, 15, 22a, 26b
Coatroach – 7f
Cockroach – 26c, 35a
Death beetle – 37b
Roach – 25b
Sunny cloak – 27a, 30
Sunny cloaker – 17
Nil – 1, 5, 24, 41, 42b

Dunbarton
Beetle – 7bc, 11, 13c
(Black) cloak – *5,* 10, 14a
Bum cloak – 14a
Cloaker – 10, 16ab, 17
Clock – 2, 4b, 7ac, 12, 13a
Cockie roach – 3
Cockroach – 1, 6, 14b
Flying clocker – 18
Sunny cloak – 9
Nil – 4a, 8, 13b, 15

Argyll
(Black) clock – 5, 18, 23-24, 28-31, *34,* 35-36, 38-40
Cloak – 19, 26-27, 38
Cloaker – 37
Clocker – 30
Clog – 3
Daoll – 6
(Large/black *or* big black) beetle – 1-2, 7, 9-11, 14-17, 19-*22,* 25-27, 30, *33*
Long legged beetle – 6
Nil – 4, 8, 12-13, 20-21, 32

Bute
Beetle – 2, 7
Cloak – 1cde, 7
Cloaker – 1a, 5
Clock – 2, 8ab, 9
Clocker – 8a
Nil – 1b, 3-4, 6

Ayr
(Big) cloak – 2ab, 4-7, 8b, 9-11, 12ab, 14-15, 16*a*b, 18b, 20abcdefgh, 21-23, 24ab, 25, 26b, 28acef, 30b, 31, 37, 40, *44,* 47-48, 52, 54
(Black) beetle – *5,* 13, 26b, *28c,* 35a, 42
Bum cloak – 18a
Bum clock – 41, 49, 57
Bumming beetle – 57
Cloaker – 6, 17, 18b, 26c, 28d
Cloakie – 18b
Clock – 1a, 3, 8a, 27, 28e, 29, 36, 53ab, 55
Coakie rochie – 32
Cocker roach – 51
Cockie roach – 34, 38
Cockie roachie – 30a, 34, 36, 45
Cockroach – 10, 19, 20f, 28e, 29, 33, 35b, 39, 43, 49, 56
Humming clock – 57
Sun cloak – 43
Sunny cloak – 18b
Sunny clock – 1b
Wachie – 18b
Nil – 26a, 28b, 46, 50

Renfrew
(Big) cloaker – *11a,* 16d, 17
(Big) clock – 1b, 2abcef*j,* 3, 4acd, 5-6, 13b, 16a
(Black) beetle – 2a, 8, 11al, 13c, *20a*
Cloak – 7, 9, 11abcefijkl, 12b, 13d, 14ab, 15, 16bcd, 17, 19
Cockroach – 2i, 4e, 8, 20ab
Flying cloak – 13c
Rainy beetle – 12b
Sunny cloak – 11a, 13a, 18a, 21
Nil – 1a, 2dgh, 4b, 10, 11dgh, 12a, 18b

Lanark
(Big) cloak – 1, 5-6, 7ac, 8a, 9a, 12, 14acd, *15b,* 16a, 17, 22, 25bcd, 27ab, 29acg, 30, 31ad, 32abd, 33bd, 34, 35b, 37, 38abde, 44-45, 46bc, 48, 50-51, 52a, 53, 55, 57b, 59ab, 62-63, 67a
(Big *or* big black) cloaker – 2, 7bc, *9a,* 12, 15c, 16b, 18-19, 26b, 27b, 30, 32d, 35bc, 38c, 39, *40,* 41, 49a, 52b, 61
(Black) beetle – 1, 3, 6, 7c, 10a, 12, 14bd, *25c,* 26a, *35d, 44*-45, 46b, 49b, 57b
Bum cloak – 56
Bum clock – 47
Bummer – 47
Clock – 1, 7a, 8b, 11, 25d, 29df, 31c, 33c, 42, 46a, 57c, 60, 65-66
Clocker – 3, 13, 32be
Cloker roach – 36
Cockie roach – 30
Cockroach – 4, 9b, 14c, 15a, 20, 25a, 29f, 35d, 37, 58
Lousy clock – 67b
Slater – 32df
Nil – 10b, 21, 23-24, 28, 29be, 31b, 32c, 33a, 35a, 43, 54, 57a, 64ab

West Lothian
Beetle – 6, 15, 17a, 18
(Big) cloaker – 1ad, 2-5, 7-8, 9a, 10, 12-14, *16,* 17a, 20ab, 21ab, 22
Clocker – 1b, 9b, 11, 18
Cockroach – 19b
Nil – 1c, 17b, 19a

Midlothian
(Big) cloaker – 2, 10, 12*ab, 14a,* 15-18, 23ab, 25ac, 26a, 27
(Black) beetle – 6a, 7a, *8a,* 10, 18, 21, 23b, 24, 26b, 29
Bum cloak – 3, 7a
Bum cloaker – 7b
Clocker – 4, 6b, 8b, 11, 19-20, 22, 25d, 26b, 32
Cockroach – 14b, 30
Nil – 1, 5, 9, 13, 25b, 28, 31

East Lothian
Beetle – 15, 17, 19
(Big) cloaker – 1-3, 4*a*b, 5, 6a, 7-8, 11, 13-14, 16, 18, 20-21
Bum clocker – 10
Clocker – 9
Coachman – 13
Coffin cutter – 6b
Scodger – 15
Scodgible – 15
Scodgie – 15
Nil – 12

Berwick
(Black) beetle – 7, *15,* 16b, 32
Black clock – 31
Bumclock – 27
Cloaker – 1, 5, 8, 10-13, 16b, 17-18, 21, 23, 29, 32
Clocker – 3-4, 6, 8, 27
Cockroach – 2, 9, 16a, 17, 20, 23, 31
Codgible – 13, 22
Sunny cloaker – 10
Nil – 14, 16c, 19, 24-26, 28, 30

Peebles
(Black) beetle – 4*bc, 6b*
Bum cloak – 5
Bum clock – 10
Cloak – 5, 7
Clock – 6a, 9
Clocker – 1-3, 6a
Scotchible – 8
Nil – 4a

Selkirk
(Black) beetle – 2c, *8*
Bum cloak – 2a
Cloaker – 2bd, 3-4, 6-7
Clocker – 1
Drone beetle – 2a
Nil – 2e, 5

Roxburgh
(Big) cloaker – *5,* 8, 9b, 10, 13, 17-20, 21cd, 26
(Black) beetle – 1-2, 21a*f, 22,* 25
(Black) clock – 13, *15b, 28*
Cloak – 23
Clocker – 2, 3ab, 4, 6, 8, 9a, 15a, 21ae, 24
Cochbill – 21c
Cockroach – 17, 28
Codgible – 4
Nil – 7, 11-12, 14, 16, 21b, 27

Dumfries
(Big) clock – 8b, *10, 12,* 13-14, 16, 19-20, 21b, 26-28, 31c, 32, 34, 38-39, 41, 45a, 47
Black beetle – 40
Bum clock – 4, 42
Cloak – 1a, 6-7, 18, 22, 24-25, 31ae, 37
Cloaker – 49
Clocker – 8a, 16
Cockie roachie – 17a
Cockroach – 4-5, 9-11, 15, 17b, 21a, 29, 33, 35-36, 44, 46
Cook roach – 3
Crow croach – 31d
Loozie cloak – 2
Sunny clock – 27

Dumfries cont'd

Nil — 1b, 23, 30, 31bf, 43, 45b, 48

Kirkcudbright

(Big) clock — 1, 4, 8, 14, 18-19, 21ab, *22*
Black beetle — 2, 7
Bum cloak — 27
Bum clock — 4, 6, 15a, 17, 24
Cloak — 9, 12b, 13, 15b
Cloaker — 12b
Clocker — 23
Coak roach — 10
Cockroach — 3, 5, 7-8, 16
Nil — 11, 12a, 20, 21c, 25-26

Wigtown

Bum clock — 12
Cloak — 6
Cloaker — 5b
Clock — 1, 4, 5a, 7-8, 10-11, 13, 15-16, 18
Cockroach — 7, 14, 17
Crockroch — 2
Nil — 3, 9

Northumberland

Beast — 8
(Black) beetle — *2b,* 3, 13, *16,* 21, *26, 28, 35-36, 40a, 41c, 42,* 46, *52, 54, 57, 59b, 62b 66, 69c, 71ad, 72c, 78, 82, 87, 89,* 103a, *104a, 130e,* 132-*133, 140*
Black cloak — 4
(Black) clock — *14, 17-18,* 25, *28, 29b,* 30, *33b, 37-39, 40ab, 41abd, 42-43, 45, 47-51, 53a, 55-57, 59cdef, 60-61, 62abcdegh, 63, 64b, 65ab, 66-68, 69abdefgh, 70, 71bcde, 72abcdgijkl, 74-78, 81, 84, 86*-87, *88ab, 89-93, 94ab, 95b, 96-98, 99abd, 100, 101b, 102, 103c, 104ab, 106-107, 108a 110, 111ab, 112, 114-117, 118ab, 119, 120abc, 122ab, 123, 124b, 125, 126abcdef, 127abcdefh, 129abc, 130abdef, 131, 133-134, 137-142*
(Black) clocker — 1c, 2a, 6, 9, 15, 18, 20a, 24a, 27-28, 29bd, 31, *34a,* 35-*36,* 38, 40b, 41bcd, *46,* 57, *103b, 135,* 137
Blyth clock — 83
Bum clock — 69a, 124a
Clacker — 29e
Cloaker — 1abc, 2b, 10, 102
Clock beetle — 107
Clock bell — 101a, 131
Clocke roach — 127b
Cloker beetle — 13
Cockroach — 14, 20b, 22, 29b, 32, 44, 60, 64ab, 69abc, 71d, 72di, 76, 79, 121, 123, 126f, 130cef
Cockrotch — 58
Coffin killer — 11
Fleein black clock — 109
Flying (black) clock — *95a,* 124a
Hard back — 47
Horse beetle — 103c
Muckle fleying cloaker — 7
Roach — 126f
Sunny clocker — 24b
Nil — 5, 12, 19ab, 23, 29acf, 33a, 34b, 53b, 59a, 62f, 72efh, 73, 80, 85, 99c, 105, 108bc, 113, 127g, 128, 136, 143

Cumberland

Bessie clocker — 17, 37a, 38
(Big black) clocker — 7-8, *9,* 12, 15c, 16, 18, 33, 40
(Black) beetle — *4,* 7, *13c* 15a, *21,* 22-23, 40, *42, 56, 58*
(Black) clock — 2-3, 5b, *6,* 13ab, 25, 27, 30, 47, *56*
Broon clock — 13a
Clock beetle — 12, 44
Cocker roach — 4, 60
Cockroach — 1ab, 5a, 12, 14, 15b, 16-17, 20, 24, 31, 36, 41-42, 44-45, 47-48, 50, 53-54, 57
Devil's coach horse — 44
Girt black beetle — 57
Great dor beetle — 27
Horse beetle — 28
Leather jacket — 52
Loozie bummle — 15c
Lousy beegle — 13a
Lousy beetle — 30, 43, 56
Thunner clock — 46
Tom beegle — 13a
Nil — 10-11, 13d, 19, 26, 29, 32, 34-35, 37b, 39, 49, 51, 55, 59, 61-62, 63ab

Down

Black beetle — 9, 15, 19
Bum clock — 2b, 11, 13
Clock — 2a, 4-8, 10, 18, 22-23, 26, 29-30
Cockroach — 3, 27
Horse clock — 24
Nil — 1, 12, 14, 16-17, 20-21, 25, 28

Tyrone

Black beetle — 8, 11
Bum clock — 1, 11
Clock — 1-2, 4-5, 7, 12
Cockroach — 11
Nil — 3, 6, 9-10, 13-16

Antrim

Black clock — 13
Bum clock — 15, 16b
Clock — 1-2, 4, 4A, 7, 9, 11-12, 15, 19-22, 24-26
Clockroach — 5b, 17
Cockroach — 27, 31
Coffin cutter — 27
Nil — 3, 5a, 6, 8ab, 10, 14, 16ac, 18, 23, 28-30, 32-34

Donegal

Beetle — 5A, 8
Clock — 1A, 5-6, 7A, 8-9, 10ab, 11-12
Clockroach — 1
Cockroach — 5, 8, 13
Nil — 2-4, 7

Fermanagh

Bum clock — 2
Clock — 2, 4, 7b, 8
Cockroach — 6, 10
Dung cock — 5
Nil — 1, 3, 7a, 9

Armagh

Bum clock — 2, 5
Clock — 1, 3-4, 6b
Cockroach — 6a
Coffin cutter — 6a

Londonderry

Black beetle — 2
Bum clock — 5
Clock — 1, 3
Cockroach — 3A, 4, 6
Nil — 1AB, 7

79 CATERPILLAR (PQ1, 172)

Caterpillar has not been mapped as it occurs nearly everywhere in the area.
Some of the items mapped are not very concentrated.
Granny also appears in 80 **centipede.**

Shetland

Caterpillar — 1, 6-7, 15-17, 20, 21a, 22, 25, 27, 32
Peter hacksie — 19
Stoorie — 14
Storie — 2, 14-16, 21b
Nil — 3-5, 8-13, 18, 23-24, 26, 28-31, 33

Orkney

Caterpillar — 3, 5, 11, 13ab, 15
Kailie worm — 7, 13a, 14, 17-18
Kail worm — 10, 19, 21
Keelie worm — 1-2, 4, 6, 8-9, 12, 13a, 16
Nil — 20

Caithness

Brittag — 12b
Brottag — 12b
Caterpillar — 11, 16b
Grub — 12a, 13
Hairy broddach — 16b
Hair brottag — 5-6, 11, 12c, 14, 16a
Kailie brockad — 15
Kailie worm — 2ab, 3, 5-6, 8-11, 12b, 14
Storie — 2a
Worm — 13
Nil — 1, 4, 7, 17

Sutherland

Caterpillar — 1, 3-8, 10-13, 16
Golloch — 14
Hairy granny — 8
Kailie worm — 9a
Kail worm — 9b
Nil — 2, 15, 17

Ross & Cromarty

Brown fellow — 20
Caterpillar — 1, 3-6, 8-9, 14, 16-18, 22, 24, 25ab, 26-31, 32ab, 34, 36, 39
Hairy granny — 23, 25b, 36
Jennie with the hundred legs — 20
Nil — 2, 7, 10-13, 15, 19, 21, 32c, 33, 35, 37ab, 38

Inverness

Caterpillar — 1-8, 10-11, 13abce, 16-17, 19, 21ab, 22-23, 26-30, 32, 34-40
Hairy granny — 13b
Hairy Jock — 31
Nil — 9, 12, 13d, 14-15, 18, 20, 24-25, 33

Nairn

Caterpillar — 1a, 2, 4
Hairy granny — 5
Nil — 1bc, 3, 6

Moray

Caterie — 22
Caterpillar — 6b, 7, 8bd, 14, 23
Cattie — 11
Green kail worm — 8b
Hairy golloch — 9a
Hairy grandfather — 4
Hairy granny — 2b, 8c, 21
Hairy oobit — 4
Hairy worm — 6a, 8f, 9ab, 19
Kail worm — 3, 22
Oubit — 8a
Torie worm — 10
Nil — 1, 2a, 5, 8e, 12-13, 15-18, 20

Banff

Broattach — 8
Caterpillar — 4-5, 8-9, 13, 15, 17, 19, 34
Green worm — 20
Hairy Geordie — 4
Hairy grub — 19
Hairy Jennie — 6b

Banff cont'd

Hairy loafie — 15
Hairy mannie — 1
Hairy Mary — 6b
Hairy worm — 2ac, 4, 11, 14, 16, 18bc, 24-25
Kail worm — 2b, 10
Torie worm — 18c
Nil — 3, 6a, 7, 12, 18ad, 21-23, 26-33

Aberdeen

Caterie — 46
Caterpillar — 3b, 4, 6, 8, 11-12, 14, 17, 20, 22-23, 28ac, 31, 34, 44-45, 49-51, 53, 59, 66, 70, 74-75, 82-83, 88, 94-95, 98, 100-101, 106-108
Green worm — 25
Grub — 48
Hairy golloch — 53
Hairy grand da — 90
Hairy grandfadder — 8
Hairy minister — 14
Hairy oobit — 4
Hairy oomit — 28a
Hairy worm — 3a, 5c, 12, 14, 16, 21, 27, 29-30, 32, 47bdf, 48, 52, 61, 64, 67, 69, 71b, 73, 78-81, 84, 86-87, 92, 97-99, 103-104
Hairy Wullie — 87
Hay worm — 6
Kail worm — 4, 5bd, 19, 40, 47e, 57, 61-62, 86
Worm — 21, 51, 79
Nil — 1-2, 5a, 7, 9-10, 13, 15, 18, 24, 26, 28b, 33, 35-39, 41-43, 47ac, 54-56, 58, 60, 63, 65, 68, 71ac, 72, 76-77, 85, 89, 91, 93, 96, 102, 105, 109

Kincardine

Caterpillar — 5-8, 10, 15-16, 17c, 19, 21, 24, 26, 28
Crawler — 20
Hairy grandfather — 17a, 21
Hairy worm — 2-4, 7, 10, 23, 28
Kail worm — 11-12, 14
Nil — 1, 9, 13, 17bd, 18, 22, 25, 27

Kinross

Caterpillar — 3-4
Hairy worm — 2
Kail worm — 5
Nil — 1, 6-7

Angus

Caterie — 34
Caterpillar — 6-7, 9-10, 17b, 18, 22, 31-32, 34-36
Green worm — 25, 28
Grozet maggot — 17a
Hair oobit — 24
Hairy worm — 2, 5c, 13, 14abcd, 19, 22, 24, 30, 37
Kail worm — 5a, 27, 33b
Worm — 12
Nil — 1, 3-4, 5b, 8, 11, 15-16, 20-21, 23, 26, 29ab, 33a

Perth

Caterie — 33
Caterpillar — 2a, 4-5, 7-10, 20-21, 24-25, 27-28, 29a, 32, 40, 43, 46, 50, 51b, 52abe, 57, 66-67, 71, 74
Granny — 16
Green worm — 60
Grub — 25, 52c
Hairy Jennie — 67
Hairy Jock — 68
Hairy oobit — 62
Hairy worm — 1, 12, 22, 25, 32, 39, 44, 48, 52ac, 53, 62
Jennie with the hunder legs — 41a
Maggot — 26
Woolly bear — 32
Nil — 2b, 3, 6, 11, 13-15, 17-19, 23, 29b, 30-31, 34-38, 41b, 42, 45, 47, 49, 51a, 52d, 54-56, 58-59, 61, 63-65, 69-70, 72-73

Fife

Caterpillar — 4, 7, 11, 14, 18-19, 24-25, 37-38, 41a, 42, 43a, 44b, 48, 50, 55abe, 56-57, 59, 62-63
Creepie crawlie — 37
Green kailie worm — 40b
Green kail worm — 20, 39, 40a, 41bc, 43a, 47, 60
Green worm — 48
Grub — 36a, 55b
Hairy Mary — 38
Hairy oobit — 27
Hairy worm — 8, 10, 12-13, 16, 21, 27, 38, 46, 51, 55df, 61
Kail worm — 4, 9a, 23, 31-32, 35, 36b, 41a, 46, 48
Oobit — 53
Woobit — 12
Nil — 1-3, 5-6, 9b, 15, 17, 22, 26, 28-30, 33-34, 41d, 43b, 44acdef, 45, 49, 52, 54, 55cg, 58, 64ab

Clackmannan

Caterpillar — 1, 4c, 6-7
Grandfather — 4d
Granny mutch — 4c
Green kail worm — 4d
Grub — 7
Hairy grandfaither — 4a
Nil — 2-3, 4b, 5

Stirling

Caterpillar — 4, 7cef, 8, 11, 13, 16-18, 20, 21ab, 23bc, 25bcd, 26ad, 27a, 28, 30-32, 35a, 36, 41
Crawlie — 35b
Creepie crawlie — 7bd, 26b
Grandfather — 7b
Greenie — 7a
Grub — 6, 42a
Hairy — 7a
Hairy daddie — 17
Hairy deddie — 25ad, 37a
Hairy deedie — 25a
Hairy grandfaither — 7e
Hairy granny — 34
Hairy Jock — 15
Jennie hunner legs — 22a
Kail worm — 26c
Mawk — 21b
Slug — 20
Nil — 1-3, 5, 9-10, 12, 14, 19, 22b, 23a, 24, 26ef, 27b, 29, 33, 37b, 38, 39ab, 40, 42b

Dunbarton

Caterpillar — 1, 3, 6, 7b, 10-11, 13abc, 14b, 16a
Cattie — 10
Furrie beast — 6
Grub — 2, 7c
Hairy jaiket — 9
Hairy oobie — 9
Nil — 4ab, 5, 7a, 8, 12, 14a, 15, 16b, 17-18

Argyll

Bourach — 6, 12
Caterpillar — 1-2, 5-7, 9-11, 14-17, 19, 22-23, 25, 27, 33, 35, 39
Hairy granny — 24, 29, 35
Hairy man — 16
Hairy oubit — 13
Slug — 32
Nil — 3-4, 8, 18, 20-21, 26, 28, 30-31, 34, 36-38, 40

Bute

Caterpillar — 1cd, 2, 7, 8ab
Hairy oobit — 2
Hairy worm — 1a
Heather Jock — 9
Nil — 1be, 3-6

Ayr

Cabbage worm — 28e
Caterpillar — 2ab, 5-6, 8a, 12a, 13, 20bc, 21, 24b, 26b, 28ce, 30a, 31, 33-34, 35ab, 36, 42-45, 48-49, 55-56
Farrie — 18b
Gramie — 18b
Grandfather — 8b
Granny — 10, 15, 18a, 20ae, 27, 28f, 29, 32, 41, 48, 53a, 54-55, 57
Granny mushie — 50, 53b
Grub — 28e, 38
Hairy oumit — 26b
Hairy Tam — 12a
Hairy Willie — 8b
Kail worm — 7, 16b, 35b, 46, 54, 57
Mawk — 3
Oobit — 28f
Nil — 1ab, 4, 9, 11, 12b, 14, 16a, 17, 19, 20dfgh, 22-23, 24a, 25, 26ac, 28abd, 30b, 37, 39-40, 47, 51-52

Renfrew

Caterpillar — 2abij, 4ace, 5, 8, 11aefl, 13c, 14a, 16b, 18a, 19, 20a
Crawlie — 20b
Granny — 1b
Grub — 11j, 16a, 17
Hairy uncle — 2j
Torie worm — 21
Nil 1a, 2cdefgh, 3, 4bd, 6-7, 9-10, 11bcdghik, 12ab, 13abd, 14b, 15, 16cd, 18b

Lanark

Big mawk — 27b
Butte fly (*sic*) — 23
Caterpillar — 1-3, 6, 7ac, 8b, 9a, 12, 14bd, 15ac, 16b, 18-19, 25bc, 26a, 29cf, 31a, 32ae, 35bcd, 38c, 40, 44-45, 46ab, 47, 49b, 53, 56, 58, 59b, 60, 64b
Comming (*sic*) butterfly — 37
Creepie crawlie — 35d
Green kail worm — 9b
Grub 6, 15a, 20, 48
Hairy granny — 64b
Hairy man — 33d, 38a
Hairy oobit — 65
Hairy oovite — 60
Hairy Willie — 33d, 46c, 47
Hairy worm — 14d
Hairy Wullie — 15b, 30, 33c, 48, 57b
Insect — 37
Kail worm — 17, 38bd, 46ac
Mawk — 31c, 39
Oobit — 29d
Slug — 58
Woolly bear — 13
Worm — 20
Nil — 4-5, 7b, 8a, 10ab, 11, 14ac, 16a, 21-22, 24, 25ad, 26b, 27a, 28, 29abeg, 31bd, 32bcdf, 33ab, 34, 35a, 36, 38e, 41-43, 49a, 50-51, 52ab, 54-55, 57ac, 59a, 61-63, 64a, 66, 67ab

West Lothian

Caterpillar — 1a, 3, 5-6, 8, 9a, 10-13, 15-16, 18, 22
Grandfaither — 7
Grub — 20a
Hairy Maggie — 1d
Hairy Willie — 4
Kail worm — 2, 16, 17a, 20a, 21a
Woolly back — 6
Woolly bear — 1a
Nil — 1bc, 9b, 14, 17b, 19ab, 20b, 21b

Midlothian

Caterpillar — 6a, 7a, 8a, 10-11, 12a, 14a, 15, 18, 21, 23b, 24, 25c, 29, 32
Crawler — 6a
Creepie — 5
Fuzzy wuzzy — 18
Grub — 16
Hairy Mary — 12b
Hairy oobit — 8b, 23a, 24, 30
Hairy oubit — 4, 17, 25a
Kail worm — 3, 7b, 14b, 17, 20, 23ab, 26a, 28, 30
Oobit — 3
Nil — 1-2, 6b, 9, 13, 19, 22, 25bd, 26b, 27, 31

East Lothian

Caterpillar — 1, 4b, 6b, 7, 9, 15-18
Crawler — 13
Grub — 19
Hairy oobit — 2, 6ab, 7, 11, 13-14, 20-21
Kail worm — 6ab, 9, 11, 16
Oobit — 13
Nil — 3, 4a, 5, 8, 10, 12

Berwick

Caterpillar — 2, 8, 10, 12, 15, 16b, 21, 31-32
Green worm — 31
Grub — 32
Hairy hoopit — 10
Hairy oobit — 2, 7, 12-13, 15, 19, 22-23, 29, 32
Hairy yoobit — 12
Kail worm — 3, 6, 8, 16a, 17-18, 20, 25-27
Oobit — 16b, 23
Slug — 9
Veen — 27
Nil — 1, 4-5, 11, 14, 16c, 24, 28, 30

Peebles

Caterpillar 4bc, 6b, 8
Hairy cat — 2
Hairy grossit — 10
Hairy oobit — 2-3, 4c, 9
Kail worm — 1
Nil — 4a, 5, 6a, 7

Selkirk

Caterpillar — 2bc, 8
Grub — 2d
Hairy oobit — 1, 2abe, 7
Oobit — 6
Woolly bear — 1
Nil — 3-5

Roxburgh

Caterpillar — 1-2, 3a, 9a, 10, 13, 15b, 17, 21ad, 22, 25
Hairy oobit — 3a, 5, 8, 9a, 10, 13, 15b, 17-18, 20, 21ace, 23-24, 26-28
Hairy oopie — 19
Hairy yoobit — 26
Kail worm — 5, 7, 16-17
Oobit — 3b, 4, 8, 13, 21ac, 28
Tammie noddie heid — 23
Nil — 6, 9b, 11-12, 14, 15a, 21bf

Dumfries

Caterpillar — 1a, 4-5, 7, 12-13,

Dumfries cont'd
15-16, 17ab, 18-19, 21b, 22, 24, 26, 31bd, 33, 40, 45a, 46
Granny – 5, 9-11, 20, 21ab, 25, 28, 31ac, 32-34, 38, 41
Grub – 6, 35, 46
Hairy Mary – 4
Hairy oobit – 20, 28-29, 46
Hairy wubbit – 38
Kail worm – 2
Oobit – 46
Slug – 46
Nil – 1b, 3, 8ab, 14, 23, 27, 30, 31ef, 36-37, 39, 42-44, 45b, 47-49

Kirkcudbright
Caterpillar – 5-7, 10, 12b, 15a, 18, 22
Granny – 4-5, 8, 19, 23, 27
Granny hairy 17
Granny mouldie – 14
Granny mush – 14, 16
Granny mushie – 15a
Grub – 2
Hairy – 11
Hairy witch – 24
Kail worm – 1
Moolie – 15a
Nil – 3, 9, 12a, 13, 15b, 20, 21abc, 25-26

Wigtown
Caterpillar – 11, 13-14, 16-17
Granny – 5ab, 6
Hairy hurchin – 10
Granny moolie – 4, 8, 14
Granny mush – 13
Kail worm – 5a
Poute – 2
Nil – 1, 3, 7, 9, 12, 15, 18

Northumberland
Cabbage worm – 20b
Caterpillar – 1a, 2b, 3, 5-6, 8-9, 13-18, 20b, 21-22, 26, 28, 30-31, 35-36, 38, 40a, 41cd, 42, 45-46, 48, 52, 53ab, 54, 56, 59b, 60, 62b, 64ab, 65ab, 66, 68, 69cdh, 70, 71abcd, 72abcdgi, 77-78, 82, 86-87, 88ab, 89-92, 94b, 99bd, 100, 101b, 102, 103ac, 106-107, 109, 111ab, 112, 120ab, 124b, 126f, 127ad, 130be, 132-133, 135, 137-138, 142
Cattie – 101b, 126c
Crawler – 137
Creeper – 77
Crowler – 12
Futbarler – 101b
Grub – 14, 69ab, 134
Hairy hoobit – 7, 26-27, 29b, 33b, 37-38, 40ab, 41ab, 44-45, 49, 62a, 69d, 71d, 124a
Hairy Hubert – 1a, 2a, 12, 29f, 34a, 39, 43, 46, 68
Hairy legs – 110
Hairy man – 59e
Hairy oobit – 2b, 25, 73, 124ab
Hairy ubbit – 19a
Hairy ubert – 20a
Hairy upid – 29d
Hairy worm – 45, 59c, 64a, 69ab, 72cg, 91, 95a, 98, 104a, 114, 116, 119, 120c, 127a, 130c
Hairy woubit – 71c
Larvae – 69b
Mawk – 117
Oobit – 124a
Pillar – 71c
Woolly bear – 99d
Worm – 28
Nil – 1bc, 4, 10-11, 19b, 23, 24ab, 29ace, 32, 33a, 34b, 47, 50-51, 55, 57-58, 59adf, 61, 62cdefgh, 63, 67, 69efg, 71e, 72efhjkl, 74-76, 79-81, 83-85, 93, 94a, 95b, 96-97, 99ac, 101a, 103b, 104b, 105, 108abc, 113, 115, 118ab, 121, 122ab, 123, 125, 126abde, 127bcefgh, 128, 129abc, 130adf, 131, 136, 139-141, 143

Cumberland
Caterpillar – 1a, 2-4, 7, 9, 12, 13c, 15ac, 16, 21-24, 28, 38, 40, 42, 46-50, 53, 56-58, 60
Fuzzy gannie – 38
Grub – 24, 52, 54
Hairy man – 56
Hair worm – 3, 5a, 14, 15c, 24-25, 28, 38, 41, 43-44, 46, 52, 57
Maggot – 37b
Moke – 37b
Nil – 1b, 5b, 6, 8, 10-11, 13abd, 15b, 17-20, 26-27, 29-36, 37a, 39, 45, 51, 55, 59, 61-62, 63ab

Down
Caterpillar – 2a, 7, 15, 19, 24, 26
Granny's needle – 11
Grub – 18
Hairy Mary – 23-24, 27
Powt – 18
Slug – 2a, 5
Nil – 1, 2b, 3-4, 6, 8-10, 12-14, 16-17, 20-22, 25, 28-30

Tyrone
Caterpillar – 7, 10-11
Grub – 8, 10, 14
Horse worm – 1, 4, 16
Slug – 9
Nil – 2-3, 5-6, 12-13, 15

Antrim
Caterpillar – 3, 9, 13, 15, 17, 22, 25-26, 29
Granny greybeard – 6, 8a, 15, 19-26, 30
Granny (mush) – 2, *31*
Green worm – 5a
Hairy Mary – 21
Kale worm – 11, 19
Leather jacket – 33
Slug – 5b, 33
Nil – 1, 4, 4A, 7, 8b, 10, 12, 14, 16abc, 18, 23-24, 27-28, 32, 34

Donegal
Cabbage worm – 8
Caterpillar – 1, 5A, 8
Green worm – 8
Grub – 6, 12
Horse worm – 6, 11
Maggot – 5
Nil – 1A, 2-4, 7, 7A, 9, 10ab, 13

Fermanagh
Caterpillar – 4-5, 7a, 9
Grub – 2, 8-9
Hairy Mary – 6
Nil – 1, 3, 7b, 10

Armagh
Caterpillar – 3, 6a
Granny grey baird – 6a
Hairy Mary – 4-5
Nil – 1-2, 6b

Londonderry
Caterpillar – 2
Horse worm – 6
Kale worm – 3
Nil – 1, 1AB, 3A, 4-5, 7

80 CENTIPEDE (PQ1, 173)

(1) Note the recurrence of some elements of target items in 81 **daddy long legs. Granny** also appears in 79 **caterpillar.**
(2) The variants of the following (elements of) items have been subsumed: AND, FOOT(ED) (**fit(ted)**), HUNDRED (**hunder, hunner**), JENNIE (**Jinnie, Jeanie**), MAG(GIE) (**Meg(gie)**), OF (**o**), THOUSAND (**t(h)oosan(d)**), WITH (**wi'**).

Shetland
Forty fitter – 1-7, 15-16, 27-31, 33
Forty footer – 25
Fower and forty fitter – 8
Hundred legs – 21ab
Hundred taes – 22
Spurrie tail – 14
Ten taed wirm – 10, 23
Thousand feet – 26
Thousand taes – 7, 12, 17, 19, 21a, 23-24
Nil – 9, 11, 13, 18, 20, 32

Orkney
Centipede – 13a, 15, 21
Check forty legs – 20
Forty feeter – 5, 17-20
Hundred feet – 13b
Hundred legs – 4, 11, 15
Jennie hundred feet – 1, 8
Jennie (with the) hundred legs – 2-3, 6, 9, 13a, 15
Maggie hundred feet – 7, 10
Maggie hundred legs – 16, 20
Maggie many feet – 7, 21
Maggie many taes – 15
Nil – 12, 14

Caithness
Cat o' nine tails – 5-6
Centipede – 16b
Creepie crawlie – 1
Forty feet – 16a
Hundred feet – 3, 14
Jeckie forty feets – 5
Jennie – 13
Jennie forty feet – 2b, 11
Jennie hundred feet – 9, 12b, 13
Slater – 8
Nil – 2a, 4, 7, 10, 12ac, 15, 17

Sutherland
Centipede – 1, 5-8, 13, 16
Hundred legger – 10
Jennie (with the) hundred feet – 2, 10-11, 15
Jennie with the hundred legs – 4, 6, 14
Nil – 3, 9ab, 12, 17

Ross & Cromarty
Centipede – 1, 3, 5, 8, 16-17, 19-20, 29, 32ab, 39
Creepie crawlie – 39
Hundred legger – 26
Jack the hundred leg – 4
Jennie (with the) hundred feet – 13, 18, 21-22, 24, 30-31, 33, 35-36, 37a
Jennie (with the) hundred legs – 9, 14, 17, 19, 23, 25ab, 27-29, 32a, 34
Nil – 2, 6-7, 10-12, 15, 32c, 37b, 38

Inverness
Centipede – 2-6, 8, 10, 13bce, 17, 19 21ab, 22, 26-29, 34, 37, 39-40
Jennie with the hundred feet – 15, 20
Jennie (with the) hundred legs – 13e, 14, 16, 23, 31, 38
Jennie with the many feet – 26
Johnnie with the hundred legs – 9, 13a
Nil – 1, 7, 11-12, 13d, 18, 24-25, 30, 32-33, 35-36

Nairn
Creepie crawlie – 1b
Forty footed Janet – 4
Jennie feeter – 1c
Jennie with the hundred legs – 1ab, 5
Nil – 2-3, 6

Moray
Centipede – 7, 8d
Forty feeted gollack – 3
Forty feeted Janet – 8f
Forty feeted Jennie – 2a, 7, 15, 22
Forty footed gollach – 9a, 12
Forty footed Janet – 7, 19
Forty footed januar – 9b, 10
Forty footed Jennie – 1, 7, 15
Forty legget granny – 14
Gollach – 8d
Hundred footed gollach – 6b
Jennie hundred feet – 11
Maggie forty feet – 23
Maggie many feet – 6a, 8bd, 9a, 18, 20
Slater – 21
Nil – 2b, 4-5, 8ace, 13, 16-17

Banff
Centipede – 5, 18c
Forty feeted Mary – 2a
Forty footed gollach – 2c, 3
Forty footed gollack – 3
Forty footed Jennie – 5, 15, 23
Forty footer – 2c
Forty legged Jennie – 19
Forty legged sandie – 24
Jennie many feet – 6b, 9, 11, 20-21, 28
Maggie many feet – 4, 7-10, 12-16, 18bd, 24-27, 29-34
Mag o' many feet – 17
Many feet – 18c
Slater – 27
Nil – 1, 2b, 6a, 18a, 22

Aberdeen
Centipede – 101
Forty feeted Jennie – 67, 71a, 108
Forty feeted Maggie – 37
Forty footed Janet – 53, 87-88, 95
Forty footed Jennie – 12, 15, 27, 28b, 29, 33-34, 50-51, 55-58, 62, 64, 66, 70, 71bc, 72, 75, 77, 82, 98, 101, 104
Forty footed Mag – 42, 46
Forty footed Maggie – 34, 45, 47a, 74
Forty legged janitor – 44, 87, 99
Forty legged Jennie – 16, 40, 54, 69, 74, 79, 86, 89
Forty legged Mag – 43
Hundred legged Jennie – 54
Hundred legged Jimmie – 4
Jennie many feet – 9-10
Jennie with the hundred legs – 74
Johnnie many feet – 11

Aberdeen cont'd

Maggie (with the) many feet – 3ab, 4, 5abcd, 6, 8, 13-14, 16-27, 28a, 30-32, 35-36, 39, 41, 44, 47aef, 48-52, 57, 60-62, 69, 71c, 75, 78-82, 84-85, 87-88, 92-94, 96-97, 99-100, 103-104, 107-108
Twenty pegged Jennie – 16
Nil – 1-2, 7, 28c, 38, 47bcd, 59, 63, 65, 73, 76, 83, 90-91, 102, 105 106, 109

Kincardine

Forty feeted Jennie – 1, 24
Forty footed Jennie – 9-10, 13
Forty footed Maggie – 12
Forty legged Janet – 4
Horner – 25
Hundred feeted Maggie – 16
Jennie with the hundred feet – 15
Maggie many feet – 4-8, 12-14, 17abc, 21, 26
Maggie with/and the many feet – 11, 15, 19, 23
Mag o' the many feet – 22, 28
Sixteen legged Jennie – 18
Slater – 3
Nil – 2, 17d, 20, 27

Kinross

Jennie hundred feet – 2-4, 7
Jennie hundred legs – 6
Johnnie hundred feet – 5
Nil – 1

Angus

Cat and nine tails – 28
Centipede – 9, 34-35
Daddy hundred feet – 3
Daddy long legs – 33a
Daddy (with the) hundred legs – 8, 32
Forty footed Jennie – 30
Hundred legged Johnnie – 34
Jackie forty feet – 17a
Jennie hundred – 30
Jennie with/and the/a hundred feet – 7, 9, 14acd, 21, 33b
Jennie with/and the/a hundred legs – 10, 13, 22-25, 27, 31-32, 36-37
Johnnie with/and a hundred legs – 6 19, 32 34
Johnnie and the/a hundred feet – 14bd
Maggie (with/and the) many feet – 2, 4, 5ac, 13, 15, 27, 37
Maggie with the hundred legs – 5b
Mag with the hundred legs – 1
Mag with the many feet – 14d
Nannie with the hundred legs – 5a
Slater – 10
Nil – 11, 12, 16, 17b, 18, 20, 26, 29ab

Perth

Centipede – 2a, 4, 8, 10, 20, 24-25, 32, 36, 52b, 67-68, 71, 74
Creepie crawlie – 32
Forkie – 66
Forty legged Jennie – 5
Fuzzy wuzzy caterpillar – 41a
Hairy Jennie – 56
Hairy worm – 29a, 61, 65
Hairy Wullie – 40
Hunder legs – 16, 44
Hundred legs – 9, 26, 56
Jennie – 33
Jennie long legs – 17
Jennie (with/and the/a) hundred legs – 1, 7, 10, 15, 21-22, 25, 28, 32, 37, 42, 57, 62, 70
Jennie (with/and the) hundred feet – 12, 20, 31, 39, 52e, 53
Johnnie and the hundred foot – 60
Johnnie with the/a hundred legs – 13, 33, 51b
Maggie many feet – 25, 45, 50
Maggie many legs – 52a
Maggie (with/and the /á) hundred feet – 18, 27, 45-46, 52cd, 53
Mag o' many feet – 25
Nathair ceud – 24
Nil – 2b, 3, 6, 11, 14, 19, 23, 29b, 30, 34-35, 38, 41b, 43, 47-49, 51a, 54-55, 58-59, 63-64, 69, 72-73

Fife

Centipede – 44b, 50, 62
Hairy Willie – 52e
Hairy worm – 43a
Hundred feet – 43b
Hundred legs – 4, 37-38, 49
Jennie hundred legs – 1-2, 5-8, 12-13, 21, 26, 36a, 40b, 42, 44ad, 45, 54, 55b, 58, 61-62, 64ab
Jennie long legs – 6, 33
Jennie (with the/a) hundred legs – 1-2, 5-8, 11-13, 17, 21, 26, 33, 36a, 40b, 42, 44ad, 45, 54, 55b, 58, 61-62, 64ab
Jennie (with the) hundred feet – 9a, 10, 12, 14, 16, 18-20, 23, 25, 27-28, 30-32, 39, 40a, 44ce, 46-48, 50-51, 53, 55acdfg, 56-57, 59-60
Nil – 3, 9b, 15, 22, 24, 29, 34-35, 36b, 41abcd, 44f, 52, 63

Clackmannan

Hairy Willie – 5
Hairy worm – 5
Hundred legs – 4b
Jennie hundred feet – 2, 4a, 7
Jennie hundred legs – 4d, 6
Nil – 1, 3, 4c

Stirling

Beast with the hundred legs – 27a
Centipede – 4, 7e, 22a, 23b, 31, 35a, 37b
Gallocher – 21b
Gallocker – 36
Grandfather – 26f
Hairy deddie – 20
Hairy Wullie – 31
Hundred legged beastie – 38
Hundred legger – 7c, 8, 23c
Hundred legs – 6, 7e, 25a, 26a, 30, 40
Jackie forty feet – 7bd
Jennie hundred feet – 2, 17-18, 23b, 25acd, 26de, 39b, 42a
Jennie (with the) hundred legs – 3, 7a, 8, 10, 21b, 25b, 26ac, 32, 34, 35b
Jock with the hundred legs – 27a
Kail worm – 7b
Mag forty feet – 7b
Maggie many feet – 26b
Mag many feet – 7b
Wire worm – 39a
Nil – 1, 5, 7f, 9, 12-16, 19, 21a, 22b, 23a, 24, 27b, 28-29, 33, 37a, 41, 42b

Dunbarton

Centipede – 7bc, 10-11, 13abc, 14b
Gallacher – 17
Hundred legs – 18
Jennie hundred feet – 6
Jennie hundred legs – 16a
Jennie spinner – 3
Maggie many feet – 14a
Man with the many feet – 6
Many feet – 2
Nil – 1, 4ab, 5, 7a, 8-9, 12, 15, 16b

Argyll

Centipede – 2, 7, 9-11, 14-17, 19, 22-23, 25, 29, 33
Hairy granny – 13, 38, 40
Jack with the hundred legs – 37
Jeck with the many feet – 39
Jennie (with a) hundred legs – 5, 30
Jennie with the many legs – 35
Maggie many feet – 35
Sclater – 31
Slater – 31
Nil – 1, 3-4, 6, 8, 12, 18, 20-21, 24, 26-28, 32, 34, 36

Bute

Centipede – 1a, 7, 8ab
Gallachero – 5
Hairy grandfather – 8b
Hairy granny – 8b
Hairy Jock – 8b
Hundred legged beastie – 8a
Hundred legs – 2, 8b
Jennie hundred leg – 1e
Jennie (with the) hundred/many feet – 1e, 9
Slater – 3
Nil – 1bcd, 4, 6

Ayr

Beast with hundred legs – 32
Centipede – 1a, 5, 26b, 28e, 43-44, 48, 53a, 56
Coffin cutter – 41, 49
Crawlie – 39
Creepie crawlie – 8b
Eel worm – 45
Gallacher – 18b
Granny – 20c, 29, 47, 51, 53b
Granny mushie – 50
Hundred legged beat(ie) – 5, 12a, 42, 55
Hundred legged worm – 9
Hundred legs – 2a, 15, 18ab, 20aeh, 25, 27, 28b, 31, 33-34, 35a, 36-38
Hundred feet – 28f
Jennie a' legs – 41
Jennie hundred legs – 18b, 24b, 49, 57
Jennie long legs – 40
Jennie many feet – 16a, 26b
Jennie (with a) hundred feet – 1a, 28a
Maggie many feet – 57
Mag Mag with a hundred feet – 31
Mag many feet – 3, 13, 19, 20g, 26c, 30b, 46, 54
Mag many legs – 8b, 16a, 35b
Mag o' many legs – 42
Mag with the many feet – 28e
Many feet – 9, 37, 41, 53a
Nil – 1b, 2b, 4, 6-7, 8a, 10-11, 12b, 14, 16b, 17, 20bdf, 21-23, 24a, 26a, 28cd, 30a, 52

Renfrew

Centipede – 2abi, 8, 11e, 13c, 14a, 16b, 20a
Cleg – 4e
Clipper – 18b
Creepie – 16a
Hundred legs 2i, 20b, 21
Hundred legger – 11d
Jennie (with the) hundred legs – 4ac, 11l, 14b, 17, 18a
Slater – 2h
Nil – 1ab, 2cdefgj, 3, 4bd, 5-7, 9-10, 11abcfghijk, 12ab, 13abd, 15, 16cd, 19

Lanark

Centipede – 1-2, 7c, 8b, 14bd, 15a, 18, 25c, 29cf, 31a, 40, 44, 46ab, 49a, 58
Creepie crawlie – 32e
Gollach – 17
Gullacher – 10a
Hairy grandfaither – 29a
Hairy legs – 16b
Hornie gornie – 60
Hundred feet – 9ab, 33cd, 48, 54, 65
Hundred legged – 7a, 65
Hundred legged Jennie – 25d
Hundred legger – 58
Hundred legs – 16b, 25b, 30, 32c, 38c, 53, 56
Jennie hundred legs – 11, 15c, 26a, 35d, 38a, 39, 44, 47, 51, 52ab, 57ab
Jennie (with the/a) hundred feet – 3, 6, 12, 14c, 20, 27b, 36
Jennie (with the) hundred legs – 1, 11, 13, 15c, 17, 21, 25c, 26a, 35ad, 38a, 39, 44, 47, 51, 52ab, 57ab
Jock 'n a hundred feet – 59b
Maggie many feet – 15b, 29d, 33d, 38d, 45, 46ac, 57a
Mag (o'/with) many feet – 13, 43, 61
Many feet – 33d
Nil – 4-5, 7b, 8a, 10b, 14a, 16a, 19, 22-24, 25a, 26b, 27a, 28, 29beg, 31bcd, 32abdf, 33a, 34, 35bc, 37, 38be, 41-42, 49b, 50, 55, 57c, 59a, 62-63, 64ab, 66, 67ab

West Lothian

Centipede – 5, 12, 15, 22
Forkie tail – 9b
Forty footed Janet – 11
Gollach – 15
Herrin Jennie – 18
Hundred legger – 21a
Hundred legs – 2-3
Jennie hundred feet – 1a, 5
Jennie hundred legs – 1a, 4, 6, 9a, 16, 17a, 19b, 22
Jennie (with the) hundred legs – 1a, 4, 6-8, 9a, 13, 16, 17a, 19b, 20a, 22
Nil – 1bcd, 10, 14, 17b, 19a, 20b, 21b

Midlothian

Centipede – 6a, 12a, 14a, 21
Hairy oobit – 32
Hundred legs – 14a
Jennie lang legs – 31
Jennie with a hundred feet – 11
Jennie (with the/a) hundred legs – 3 8ab, 10, 12b, 13, 14b, 17-19, 23ab, 24, 25c, 26a, 27
Maggie many feet – 30
Mag with many feet – 11
Slater – 25a
Twenty legger – 6a
Nil – 1-2, 4-5, 6b, 7ab, 9, 15-16, 20, 22, 25bd, 26b, 28

East Lothian

Centipede – 4b, 15, 19
Hundred legged Jennie – 17
Hundred legs – 13
Jennie many feet – 7
Jennie (with the) hundred feet – 4a, 6b, 16
Jennie (with the) hundred legs – 1-2, 6a, 8-9, 14-15, 18, 20-21
Maggie many feet – 10
Nil – 3, 5, 11-12

Berwick

Centipede – 10, 12
Hairy oubit – 17
Hundred legged beast – 6-7
Hundred legged Jennie – 18
Hundred legs – 3, 12, 19
Jennie hundred – 29
Jennie hundred feet – 13
Jennie lang legs – 31
Jennie (with the) hundred legs –

Berwick cont'd

1-2, 8, 14-15, 16b, 23
Lechan gorrie – 27
Maggie many feet – 7, 16a, 18, 20-22, 31-32
Maggie many legs – 4
Magna many feet – 26
Mag o' many feet – 11
Merrie many feet – 5
Nil – 9, 16c, 24-25, 28, 30

Peebles

Centipede – 4c, 6ab
Creepie crawlie – 2
Hundred legs – 7
Jennie with the hundred feet – 4b
Jennie (with the) hundred legs – 1, 3, 4c, 8-9
Maggie many feet – 3
Nil – 4a, 5, 10

Selkirk

Hundred leg – 3
Jennie hundred feet – 2ad
Jennie hundred legs – 2bc, 4, 6
Nil – 1, 2e, 5, 7-8

Roxburgh

Centipede – 21a, 22
Creepin Jennie – 18
Deil's darning needle – 28
Hundred legs – 15a, 18
Jennie (and the) hundred legs – 1, 5, 10 12-13, 16, 20, 21e, 25
Jennie hundred feet – 8, 21c
Jennie many legs – 20, 25
Leather jacket – 9a
Maggie many feet – 2, 3a, 4, 7-8, 9b, 15b, 17, 21a, 26, 28
Mag o' many feet – 21c
Nil – 3b, 6, 11, 14, 19, 21bdf, 23-24, 27

Dumfries

Centipede – 12, 18, 20, 21b, 40
Forty feeted kellock – 2
Granny – 1a, 7, 8a, 19, 22, 26-27, 37, 44
Hairy obit – 45a
Hundred footed gollick – 11
Hundred legged gellick – 21b
Hundred leg gellick – 12
Hundred legs – 13, 29
Jennie hundred legs – 28
Jock o' many feet – 32
Jock with a hundred feet – 7
Lizard – 33
Maggie many feet – 39
Maggie with the hundred feet – 17ab
Slater – 4, 8b, 41-42
Nil – 1b, 3, 5-6, 9-10, 14-16, 21a, 23-25, 30, 31abcdef, 34-36, 38, 43, 45b, 46-49

Kirkcudbright

Centipede – 2, 6-7, 16
Granny – 9-10, 18, 22
Granny hundred legs – 12a
Hundred footed worm – 21c
Hundred legged beast – 8
Hundred legged ether – 23
Jennie hundred legs – 1
Jennie (with the) hundred legs – 1, 15a
Maggie many feet – 15a
Mag many feet – 1, 17
Many feet – 4
Nil – 3, 5, 11, 12b, 13-14, 15b, 19-20, 21ab, 24-27

Wigtown

Centipede – 2, 13-14
Creepie crawlie – 7
Granny moolie – 17
Hairy oobit – 17
Hummer legs – 1
Mag many feet – 5a, 9, 11, 18
Mag o' many legs – 10
Nil – 3-4, 5b, 6, 8, 12, 15-16

Northumberland

Centipede – 2b, 6, 13-14, 30-31, 35, 41d, 42, 46, 48, 53ab, 54, 59b, 60, 64a, 65b, 66, 69cd, 70, 71cd, 72cd, 86-87, 88b, 94b, 101ab, 103a, 106-107, 109-110, 111a, 112, 120ac, 126c, 127a, 130e, 132, 137
Eel worm – 111b
Forkie tail – 83, 124b, 129c, 138
Forty feet – 59e
Forty legs – 69b
Hairy Hubert – 22
Hundred footer – 69a
Hundred legger – 1a
Hundred legs – 99d
Jennie hundred leg – 8, 11, 29f
Jennie many legs – 18
Knives and fork – 118b
Leather jacket – 100
Maggie many feet – 2ab, 3, 8-10, 15-18, 19a, 20a, 21, 25-27, 29be, 33b, 34ab, 35-39, 40b, 41c, 44-47, 51-52, 53a, 57, 60, 62a, 68, 71d, 79-81, 102, 104a, 122a, 124a, 136
Maggie many legs – 12, 20b, 28, 56, 76
Maggie millie feet – 86
Mag o' many feet – 29d, 55, 77, 114, 124a, 127d, 133-135, 142
Mag with/o' many legs – 73-74, 141
Minnie Maggie many feet – 6
Minnie many feet – 59c
Nannie many legs – 24ab
Peggie many feet – 58
Twitchbell – 103c
Tyler tarton – 6
Wire worm – 103a, 111b, 130c
Wirie worm – 88a
Nil – 1bc, 4-5, 7, 19b, 23, 29ac, 30, 32, 33a, 40a, 41ab, 43, 49-50, 59adf, 61, 62bcdefgh, 63, 64b, 65a, 67, 69efgh, 71abe, 72abefghijkl, 75, 78, 82, 84-85, 89-93, 94a, 95ab, 96-98, 99abc, 103b, 104b, 105, 108abc, 113, 115-117, 118a, 119, 120b, 121, 122b, 123, 125, 126abdef, 127bcefgh, 128, 129ab, 130abdf, 131, 139-140, 143

Cumberland

Cat o' nine tails – 16, 18
Centipede – 1a, 3-4, 7, 12, 13c, 14, 15a, 21-22, 24-25, 40, 42, 46-48, 53, 57-58
Earwig – 50
Hairy worm – 2
Hard back – 40
Hundred legs – 51
Mag many legs – 30-31
Mag o' many feet – 3
Many legs – 56
Teeas toes – 30
Wire worm – 52
Nil – 1b, 5ab, 6, 8-11, 13abd, 15bc, 17, 19-20, 23, 26-29, 32-36, 37ab, 38-39, 41, 43-45, 49, 54-55, 59-62, 63ab

Down

Centipede – 2a
Coffin cutter – 22
Coffin nailer – 6
Granny greybeard – 4
Granny's needle – 5
Hairy hundred legs – 28
Hairy Mary – 17, 24
Mag wae the many feet – 13, 29
Nil – 1, 2b, 3, 7-12, 14-16, 18-21, 23, 25-27, 30

Tyrone

Centipede – 1
Granny Greybaird – 15
Hairy hundred foot – 4
Harry hundred legs – 9, 13
Nil – 2-3, 5-8, 10-12, 14, 16

Antrim

Centipede – 25-26
Coffin cutter – 4A, 16b
Forty feet – 17
Granny greybeard – 7, 16b, 33
Hairy Mary – 10
Harry hundred feet – 13, 21
Hundred feet – 11
Maggie wae many feet – 5a, 9, 15, 16b, 19-20, 24, 30
Mag o' many legs – 25
Mary o' the many legs – 11
Slater – 34
Nil – 1-4, 5b, 6, 8ab, 12, 14, 16ac, 18, 22-23, 27-29, 31-32

Donegal

Forty feet – 6, 12
Grub – 2
Horse beetle – 5
Nil – 1, 1A, 3-4, 5A, 7, 7A, 8-9, 10ab, 11, 13

Fermanagh

Forty feet – 2, 4, 6
Hairy horse – 9-10
Harry hundred feet – 5
Nil – 1, 3, 7ab, 8

Armagh

Centipede – 4
Forty feet – 2
Nil – 1, 3, 5, 6ab

Londonderry

Daddy hundred feet – 6
Harry hundred feet – 5-6
Harry hundred legs – 7
Nil – 1, 1AB, 2-3, 3A, 4

81 DADDY LONG LEGS (crane fly) (PQ1, 174)

The variants of the following (elements of) items have been subsumed: DADDY LONG LEGS (negligible), JENNIE (a few **Jinnie** Northumberland), TAILOR (Northumberland a few **tail(l)yor, teelior**), KATIE (a few **Kittie**).
See also note (1) on 80 **centipede.**

Shetland

Daddy long legs – 33
Spin Willie – 4, 15-16
Willie bock – 9
Willie long legs – 1-10, 12-14, 17-20, 21ab, 22-30, 32
Nil – 11, 31

Orkney

Daddy long legs – 5, 9, 11, 13ab, 14, 16-17, 20
Long legged laru – 7
Long legs – 15
Spinnick – 16
Willie long legs – 1-4, 6, 8, 12, 17-21
Nil – 10

Caithness

Chinnie spinner – 2b, 12c
Daddy long legs – 3, 6, 8-11, 13-14, 16b
Grub – 13
Jennie spinner – 8
Storie – 12b
Nil – 1, 2a, 4-5, 7, 12a, 15, 16a, 17

Sutherland

Daddy long legs – 1, 3-8, 9ab, 10-13, 16
Nil – 2, 14-15, 17

Ross & Cromarty

Daddy long legs – 1, 3-6, 8 9, 14, 16-17, 20, 22-24, 25ab, 26 29, 31, 32ab, 36 39
Dandie – 34
Grass hopper – 18
Jennie long legs – 26
Spinning Jennie – 35
Nil – 2, 7, 10-13, 15, 19, 21, 30, 32c, 33, 37ab, 38

Inverness

Crane fly – 26
Daddy long legs – 1-6, 8, 10-11, 13abce, 16-17, 19, 21ab, 22-23, 26, 27-30, 32-40
Leerie leerie light the lamp – 26
Spin Maggie – 15
Nil – 7, 9, 12, 13d, 14, 18, 20, 24-25 31

Nairn

Daddy long legs — 1a, 2, 5
Nil — 1bc, 3-4

Moray

Daddy long legs — 3, 6b, 7, 8d, 14, 21, 23
Jennie langlegs — 9a
Jennie spinner — 1, 3, 7, 10, 18, 22
Maggie spinner — 19
Spinnin(g) Jennie — 2a, 8b, 9a, 13, 17
Spun Meg 12
Wallace braefiddler — 4
Nil — 2b, 5, 6a, 8acef, 9b, 11, 15-16, 20

Banff

Daddy — 27
Daddy long legs — 2a, 6b, 7, 9, 13, 15-17, 18c, 21, 23, 25-27, 34
Dandie long legs — 19
Jackie long legs — 1, 6b
Jennie long legs — 16
Jennie spinner — 5
Long Sandie — 20, 24
Maggie spinner — 4, 14, 31
Maggie spindle — 2b
Spinner — 6b
Spinnin(g) Jennie — 8, 18bc, 29
Nil — 2c, 3, 6a, 10-12, 18ad, 22, 28, 30, 32-33

Aberdeen

Daddy — 8
Daddy long legs — 3b, 5c, 6, 8, 11-12, 14, 17, 20-21, 23, 29, 32, 34, 39, 43-46, 47f, 49-51, 59, 66, 69-70, 74-75, 80-82, 84-86, 94-95, 98, 100, 103-108
Dandie long legs — 62
Dannie long legs — 19, 29, 47a, 67
Geordie long legs — 5d, 7
Jennie long legs — 71a
Jimmie long legs — 4, 10, 47a, 90, 93
Johnnie long legs — 3a, 102
Long legged Jimmie — 58, 101, 104
Long legged Sandie — 28b
Piper — 80, 95
Spinner — 14, 28a, 31
Spinnin Jennie — 22, 48
Spinnin Maggie — 98
Torie — 47e
Wyver — 47b
Nil — 1-2, 5ab, 9, 13, 15-16, 18, 24-27, 28c, 30, 33, 35-38, 40-42, 47cd, 52-57, 60-61, 63-65, 68, 71bc, 72-73, 76-79, 83, 87-89, 91-92, 96-97, 99, 109

Kincardine

Daddlie long legs — 19
Daddy long legs — 1, 3, 6, 8, 10-11, 15-16, 17bd, 21, 24, 26, 28
Jimmie long legs — 12, 17c
Leather jacket — 9
Long legged Jimmie — 5, 7, 12, 14, 17c
Nil — 2, 4, 13, 17a, 18, 20, 22-23, 25, 27

Kinross

Jennie long legs — 3
Spinnin(g) Jennie— 1, 3, 7
Spinnin Maggie — 2-4, 7
Nil — 5-6

Angus

Daddy long legs — 3-4, 5c, 14a, 15, 17b, 18-19, 22-25, 31-32, 34, 36
Daddy wi' the long legs — 35
Dandie long legs — 10
Dannie long legs — 9-10
Drummer — 7
Fiddler — 6, 10, 14cd
Jennie — 12
Jennie long legs — 13, 17b
Jennie (the) spinner — 5a, 30
Leather jeckit — 14a
Long legged tailor — 17a
Midgie long feet — 18
Piper — 7, 10, 12, 14d
Spether — 10
Spinner — 20-21, 27, 31, 33b
Spinnin Jennie — 37
Nil — 1-2, 5b, 8, 11, 14b, 16, 26, 28, 29ab, 33a

Perth

Daddy long legs — 1, 2a, 4-5, 8, 10, 12, 14-15, 21, 24-25, 29a, 32-33, 36, 46, 48, 52ae, 67, 71, 74
Fiddler — 7, 31, 60
Jennie — 34, 56
Jennie long legs — 1, 45, 49-50, 52a, 62, 68, 70-72
Jennie spinner — 73
Leather jacket — 55
Skinnie my linkie — 30
Spinnin(g) Jennie — 9, 12, 16, 18, 20, 25-28, 32-33, 40, 41ab, 45, 52d, 66-67
Spinnin(g) Maggie — 27-28, 29b, 39, 41a, 42, 47, 52bc, 53, 57, 62, 65
Nil — 2b, 3, 6, 11, 13, 17, 19, 22-23, 35, 37-38, 43-44, 51ab, 54, 58-59, 61, 63-64, 69

Fife

Daddy long legs — 4, 7-8, 9a, 11, 16, 18, 24, 36ab, 37, 44a, 46-47, 55be, 62
Herrin' Jennie — 39
Jennie hunder legs — 36b, 44f
Jennie long legs — 4, 12-13, 20-21, 25, 34, 37, 39, 41ab, 44bef, 45, 48, 50, 52, 54, 55abe, 58-60, 63
Jennie Meggie — 64a
Spindie Wullie — 32
Spinnin(g) Jennie — 2, 8, 10, 16, 19, 23, 27, 29, 35, 41c, 42, 43ab, 44de, 46, 51, 53, 55cd, 56-57
Spinnin(g) Maggie — 5, 8, 9b, 14, 19-21, 25-26, 28, 31, 38, 40ab, 44e, 48, 50, 55b, 61
Spinnin(g) Mary — 51, 55dg
Nil — 1, 3, 6, 15, 17, 22, 30, 33, 41d, 44c, 49, 55f, 64b

Clackmannan

Daddy long legs — 4b
Jennie hunder legs — 5
Jennie long legs — 1, 4c, 6-7
Jennie macspinner — 4b
Jennie spinner — 4c
Leegie — 4d
Spinnin(g) Jennie — 1-2, 4a
Nil — 3

Stirling

Bam piper — 25c
Daddy long legs — 4, 7ce, 16-17, 21b, 23b, 25c, 26acd, 28, 36, 37b, 39b, 42a
Jennie long legs — 3, 7abde, 8-9, 11-12, 15-16, 18-20, 21a, 22ab, 23abc, 25ad, 26ae, 27a, 28-34, 35ab, 36, 37a, 38, 39a, 40
Jennie nettle — 35a
Jennie spinner — 2
Johnnie hunder legs — 28
Leather jacket — 25b
Spinnin Jennie — 26b
Spinnin Maggie — 26b
Nil — 1, 5-6, 7f, 10, 13-14, 24, 26f, 27b, 41, 42b

Dunbarton

Daddy long legs — 3, 7b, 8, 11, 13a, 14ab, 16a, 17
Herring Jennie — 18
Jennie long legs — 1, 6, 7ac, 9-10, 12, 13abc, 14a, 16ab
Jennie nettle — 2
Nil — 4ab, 5, 15

Argyll

Crane fly — 2
Daddlie long legs — 22
Daddy long legs — 1-3, 5-7, 9-10, 14-17, 19, 23, 25-27, 29, 33, 35
Grasshopper — 30
Jennie long legs — 8, 11, 13, 15-16, 18, 24-25, 29, 40
Katie leelie — 36-37, 39
Katie lillie — 31, 33, 35
Long legged weaver — 26
Nil — 4, 12, 20-21, 28, 32, 34, 38

Bute

Daddy long legs — 1acd, 3, 8b
Jennie long legs — 2, 5, 7, 8ab, 9
Jennie nettle — 8a
Nil — 1be, 4, 6

Ayr

Daddy long legs — 1a, 2ab, 3, 6, 10, 21, 26b, 27, 28ef, 34, 35a, 45
Jennie — 18b
Jennie heron — 27, 28f, 31, 38
Jennie long legs — 1a, 2ab, 3-7, 8ab, 9-10, 12a, 14-15, 16ab, 18ab, 20abdegh, 21-22, 24b, 25, 26b, 28abde, 29, 30a, 32, 37, 39, 41, 47-49, 52, 53ab, 55-57
Jennie speeder — 34, 35ab, 36-37, 46
Jennie spindle — 32
Jennie spinner — 8b, 10, 13, 16ab, 17, 19, 20cd, 23, 29, 30ab, 33, 41-46, 50-51, 54, 57
Speeder Jennie — 15
Spinning Jennie — 1a
Spinning Maggie — 1a
Nil — 1b, 11, 12b, 20f, 24a, 26ac, 28c, 40

Renfrew

Daddy long legs — 2abhij, 4ac, 11defl, 13c, 14a, 16b, 19, 20a, 21
Devil's fly — 2i
Devil's needle — 2i
Jennie long legs — 1b, 2bj, 5, 7-9, 11acfkl, 12b, 13abc, 14b, 16ad, 17, 18a, 20b, 21
Jennie Maggie — 13c
Jennie spinner — 19
Jennie wi' the mony legs — 14b
Johnnie long legs — 4de
Leather jacket — 13c
Spinnin Meg — 21
Nil — 1a, 2cdefg, 3, 4b, 6, 10, 11bghij, 12a, 13d, 15, 16c, 18b

Lanark

Daddy long legs — 1-2, 8b, 14d, 15ac, 17, 25c, 29cf, 31a, 32e, 34, 35ad, 45, 46ab, 49a, 64b
Herrin Jennie — 33a
Jennie — 8a, 25d, 46a
Jennie long legs — 2-4, 6, 7c, 8a, 9a. 12-13, 14abd, 15bc, 16ab, 17 21, 24 25abc, 26ab, 27b, 28, 29ag, 30, 32adef, 33bd, 34, 35bcd, 37, 38c, 39, 42, 49b, 52a, 57a, 59b, 60, 65
Jennie Maggie — 9b, 10a, 15b, 34, 38abde, 39-40, 44, 47-48, 50-51, 52b, 53-54, 56, 57ab, 58, 59a, 62-63, 65
Jennie nickle — 46c
Jennie spinner — 7a, 32c, 46b, 60-61, 63, 64a, 65-66, 67ab
Spinnin(g) Jennie — 9b, 13, 15c, 21, 29d, 33cd
Spinning Maggie — 13
Nil — 5, 7b, 10b, 11, 14c, 22-23, 27a, 29be, 31bcd, 32b, 36, 41, 43, 55, 57c

West Lothian

Daddy long legs — 1a, 8, 11, 13, 15, 20ab
Dannie long legs — 1c
Granny long legs — 15
Herrin Jennie — 17a, 18
Jennie daing — 6
Jennie hunder legs — 1d
Jennie long legs — 1a, 2-8, 9b, 12, 15-16, 17a, 20ab, 22
Spinnin(g) Jennie — 1a, 10, 19b, 21a
Spinning Maggie — 20a
Nil — 1b, 9a, 14, 17b, 19a, 21b

Midlothian

Daddy long legs — 6ab, 10, 23b, 25c, 29
Jennie long legs — 3, 7ab, 11, 12ab, 13, 14ab, 16, 18, 21-22, 24, 25c, 30
Jennie spinner — 14a
Jennie wi' the hunder legs — 25a
Jennie wren — 12b
Spinnin(g) Jennie — 7b, 23ab, 26a, 28
Nil — 1-2, 4-5, 8ab, 9, 15, 17, 19-20, 25bd, 26b, 27, 31-32

East Lothian

Daddy long legs — 1, 15-16, 18-20
Herrin Jennie — 4b
Jennie long legs — 6a, 9, 13-14
Long legged flee — 6b
Spinnin(g) Jennie — 4a, 7, 16-17, 21
Spinnin Maggie — 2, 4b
Nil — 3, 5, 8, 10-12

Berwick

Daddy long legs — 1-2, 32
Dannie long legs — 12
Jennie good spinner — 21
Jennie long legs — 8-13, 16b, 17, 19, 24, 27, 29
Jennie spinner — 3
Long legged gitter — 27
Spinnin(g) Jennie — 3, 6-7, 12, 15, 16ab, 18, 20-23, 26-27, 31
Spinning Maggie — 4
Nil — 5, 14, 16c, 25, 28, 30

Peebles

Crane flee — 6a
Daddy long legs — 2, 4c, 6ab, 8
Heron Jennie — 4b
Jennie long legs — 1, 4a, 7
Jennie Meggie — 10
Jennie spinner — 2, 5, 9
Spinnin(g) Jennie — 3, 6a

Selkirk

Daddy long legs — 2bcd
Jennie long legs — 1, 2ae
Jennie spinner — 3-4, 8
Spinnin Meggie — 2a
Nil — 5-7

Roxburgh

Daddy long legs — 3a, 9a, 13, 20, 21a
Jennie long legs — 1, 7, 9b,

Roxburgh cont'd

11-12, 15a, 17, 19-20, 21abe, 22
Jennie speeder – 8
Jennie spinner – 13, 15ab, 17, 21f, 23, 26, 28
Long legged tailor – 21c
Spinner – 19
Spinner langlegs – 8
Spinnin(g) Jennie – 2, 4-5, 9b, 10, 16, 21acd, 25
Tammie noddie heid – 21c
Nil – 3b, 6, 14, 18, 24, 27

Dumfries

Daddy long legs – 4, 8b, 12, 19, 22, 31d
Jennie – 14
Jennie dang – 2
Jenny long legs – 1a, 5, 25, 31c, 32-34, 41
Jennie spinner – 3, 5-7, 8a, 9-13, 15-16, 17ab, 18-20, 21ab, 22, 24, 26-29, 31be, 32, 35-41, 43-44, 45ab, 46
Mirdie moider – 7
Spinning Jennie – 42
Nil – 1b, 23, 30, 31af, 47-49

Kirkcudbright

Daddy long legs – 1, 7
Jennie long legs – 16, 21a, 23
Jennie spinner – 1-10, 12ab, 13-14, 15ab, 17-20, 21bc, 22, 24-26
Nil – 11, 27

Wigtown

Jennie long legs – 2, 8-9, 11-12, 14-18
Jennie spinner – 4, 5a, 6-7, 10-13
Nil 1, 3, 5b

Northumberland

Crane fly – 22
Daddy long legs – 2ab, 4-5, 8-9, 13-18, 20b, 26, 28, 29b, 30-31, 34b, 35-37, 40a, 41c, 42-43, 46, 48, 53ab, 54, 56, 59be, 66, 69c, 71ac, 72adi, 77, 82, 85, 87, 89, 100, 103ac, 104ab, 106, 111ab, 112, 117, 119, 120a, 126a, 127ad, 130bce, 133, 137, 140, 143
Gnat – 71a
Harry long legs – 124a
Harvestman – 69b
Jennie long legs – 1a, 3, 45, 129a
Jennie spinner – 19a, 21, 25, 29bc, 39, 41c, 42-43, 45, 47, 52, 55, 59cef, 60-61, 62a, 63, 65a, 68, 69g, 72ik, 73, 78, 84, 89, 91, 95a, 96, 98, 99a, 102, 103b, 110, 116, 124a, 126f, 129c, 132-133
Jennie the spinner – 130d
Jimmie spinner – 130c
Johnnie long legs – 45, 70, 71d, 90, 99d, 129b
Johnnie spinner – 17, 29b, 34a, 37-39, 40b, 41ab, 44, 47, 49-50, 57, 60, 62abcegh, 63, 64ab, 66-67, 69abdefh, 70, 71bde, 72bcefgkl, 83-84, 86, 88ab, 90-93, 94ab, 96-97, 99b, 107, 114-115, 118a, 122ab, 124b, 129c
Knife and fork – 118a
Leather jacket – 14, 52, 134
Logger – 121
Long legged allor – 24b
Long legged Jennie/Joannie spinner – 7, 59d
Long legged Johnnie spinner – 40a, 41d, 59bd, 65b, 72hj, 95b, 99b
Long legged tailor – 29b, 36, 48, 51, 53b, 78-79, 101b, 103bc, 107, 108a, 109, 111b, 116, 120bc, 124a, 127adh, 134-136, 138, 140
Long legged terrier – 64a
Long leg tailor – 24a, 126d, 142
Spinning Jennie – 77
Tailor tartan – 11, 15, 41c
Nil – 1bc, 6, 10, 12, 19b, 20a, 23, 27, 29adef, 32, 33ab, 58, 59a, 62df, 74-76, 80-81, 99c, 101a, 105, 108bc, 113, 118b, 123, 125, 126be, 127bcefg, 128, 130af, 131, 139, 141

Cumberland

Daddy long legs – 1a, 23, 37b, 40, 47-48, 50, 53, 57-58
Jennie long legs – 50-52, 54-55, 57
Jennie spinner 2-4 5a, 6-12, 13abcd, 14, 15abc, 16-20, 22, 24-26, 28-34, 36, 37ab, 38-42, 44, 46-47, 49, 52-53, 57, 59-62, 63ab
Jerrie long legs – 56
Jimmie crane – 43, 56
Jimmie long legs – 43, 56
Nil – 1b, 5b, 21, 27, 35, 45

Down

Click beetle – 4
Daddy long legs – 2a, 5-7, 9, 12, 15, 19, 24
Dannie long legs – 6
Granny long legs – 26
Granny(s) needle – 13, 18, 22, 24, 26-27, 29
Leather jacket – 17
Nil – 1, 2b, 3, 8, 10-11, 14, 16, 20-21, 23, 25, 28, 30

Tyrone

Daddy long legs – 1, 7-11
Deil's needle – 5
Devil's needle – 5
Harry long legs – 16
Nil – 2-4, 6, 12-15

Antrim

Daddy long legs – 1, 3, 5a, 9, 11, 13, 15, 17, 19-20, 25-26
Deil's needle – 16b, 19, 24, 30, 33
Devil's needle – 5b, 7, 15, 21
Granny's needle – 23-25, 30
Jennie spinner – 23
Paddy – 20
Tammie lang legs – 16b
Nil – 2, 4, 4A, 6, 8ab, 10, 12, 14, 16ac, 18, 22, 27-29, 31-32, 34

Donegal

Daddy long legs – 1, 5, 8, 12
Deil's needle – 4, 8
Devil's darning needle – 1A
Devil's needle – 6, 12-13
Nil – 2-3, 5A, 7, 7A, 9, 10ab, 11

Fermanagh

Daddy long legs – 4-5, 9
Devil's (big) needle – 6, 8
Harry long legs – 1, 9-10
Nil – 2-3, 7ab

Armagh

Daddy long legs – 1, 3-4
Tommy long legs – 1-2, 6a
Nil – 5, 6b

Londonderry

Daddy long legs – 2-3, 3A, 4
Deil's needle – 3A
Devil's needle – 5
Granny's needle – 5
Nil – 1, 1AB, 6-7

82 EARWIG (the fork tailed insect with six legs) (PQ1, 176)

Variants of the unstressed vowel followed by 'ch' in items like **gollAch, gollAcher, gullAch** have been subsumed. Where the unstressed vowel was followed by 'ck' as in **gowlack, gowlick,** the majority spelling has been adopted (but -**ack** appears where there was no predominant form). In items like gol(l)ach, gel(l)ick, etc. where one 'l' appears in brackets, the forms with 'll' are in the majority.
See the recurrence of some items in 44 **crowbar** and 78 **black beetle. Gowlack** also appears in 24 **forked stick.**

Shetland

Forkietail – 1-10, 12, 14, 17, 19, 21ab, 22-33
Scurdie – 10
Spurrietail – 15-16
Nil – 11, 13, 18, 20

Orkney

Earwig – 8
Forkie – 4-7, 13b, 20
Forkietail – 2-4, 6-12, 13a, 14-21
Muaro – 1

Caithness

Clipshear – 1
Cloaker – 13
Eariewig – 16a
Forkietail – 2ab, 3-11, 12abc, 13-15, 16ab
Gavelag – 6, 12c
Gevlag – 5
Gollach – 15
Nil – 17

Sutherland

Earwig – 1, 3, 6-8
Forkie – 9a
Forkietail – 1-8, 9b, 10-16
Golach – 15
Gollachan – 5, 8, 10, 14, 16
Hornie gollach – 16
Nil – 17

Ross & Cromarty

Earwig – 1, 4-5, 8-9, 16-17, 27, 29, 32a, 39
Forkie – 19
Forkietail – 6, 8-11, 16, 18, 20-22, 25b, 26, 28-29, 32b, 35- 36
Ghoulachan – 24
Gloileachan – 7
Goalachan – 28, 32a
Gobhlachan – 29
Golieachan – 31
Gol(l)ach – 13, 17, 22-23
Gol(l)achan – 3, 21, 23, 26-27, 30, 32bc, 35
Gollackan – 20
Goolachan – 34
Gull – 37b
Gullach – 25b, 37a
Gullachan 8, 12, 14, 18-19, 25ab, 33
Gullachie 6
Gullackan 15
Gullieach – 37b
Gullieachan – 37b
Hornie gollach – 26
Nil 2, 38

Inverness

Eariewig – 38, 40
Earwig – 1-6, 10-11, 13ce, 17, 21a, 22-23, 27, 30, 32, 34, 36-37, 39
Forkietail – 8-10, 13abd, 17, 21b, 23, 29, 33, 35
Forkietailie – 28
Gobhlachan – 7
Goilachan – 11
Goilleach – 15
Golach – 29
Goliachan – 9
Gol(l)achan – 8, 12, 13cd, 18-19, 33
Goolach – 26
Goolachan – 13abe, 14, 16, 26
Gooliachen – 21a
Goulachan – 24
Gurachan – 31
Nil – 20, 25

Nairn

Earwig – 2
Forkie – 1ab
Forkietail – 1ac, 4-5
Gol(l)ach – 1c, 2, 5
Gollacher – 1abc
Nil – 3, 6

Moray

Eariewig – 7
Earwig – 23
Forkie – 5, 8bcf, 10, 14
Forkie gol(l)ach – 8def, 9a, 13
Forkietail – 1, 2ab, 3-4, 6ab, 7, 8bdf, 9ab, 11, 15-23
Forkit gollach – 8f
Forkit tail – 8f
Gol(l)ach – 1, 2a, 3-5, 6b, 7 8bc, 13, 15-17
Gullach – 4
Hornie gol(l)ach – 8ab, 12, 22

Banff

Forkie – 5, 16, 23
Forkie gol(l)ach – 2c, 4, 9
Forkietail – 1, 2ac, 3-5, 6b, 7-17, 18bcd, 20-34
Forkietailie – 19
Gol(l)ach – 2ab, 3, 6a, 13
Hornie gol(l)ach – 6b, 17, 31-32
Nil – 18a

Aberdeen

Forkie – 3a, 4, 6, 8-9, 16, 19, 28a, 30, 34, 43, 51, 67, 74, 77-78, 85, 89-90, 94
Forkie golach – 28a
Forkietail – 2, 3ab, 5abcd, 6-15, 17-24, 26-27, 28abc, 29-37, 39-46, 47abcdef, 48-62, 64-70, 71abc, 72-89, 91-93, 95-101, 103-109
Gol(l)ach – 4, 7, 63, 102
Hornie gol(l)ach – 4, 16, 44, 47abcdef, 62, 107-108
Midget – 25
Midgie – 25
Nil – 1, 38

Kincardine

Earwig – 6
Forkie – 1, 3, 9-10, 14, 18, 21, 25
Forkietail – 2-8, 10-13, 15-16, 17abcd, 18-19, 21-24, 26
Forkietailie – 28

Kincardine cont'd

Hornie gol(l)ach — 12, 15, 17ac, 18, 21, 24, 26-28
Hornie gollack — 17d, 22
Nil — 20

Kinross

Clippie — 2
Clipshear — 1-6
Eariewig — 1
Forkietail — 5-6
Forkietailie — 7
Gowlack — 3, 7
Hornie gollach — 1
Hornie gollack — 5

Angus

Clippie — 32
Clipshear — 34
Eariewig — 32
Earwig — 17b
Forkie — 9, 14ab, 18, 23-24, 29a, 34
Forkietail — 2-4, 5ac, 7, 10, 15, 17a, 19-20, 22, 24, 30-32, 34-35
Forkietailie — 1, 6, 8-9, 11-13, 14abcd, 18, 21-23, 25-28, 33ab, 36-37
Forkit tailie — 14d
Golack — 5c
Horn gollach — 1, 17b, 27-28, 29a, 33b
Hornie gol(l)ach — 4, 5b, 9, 13, 14acd, 24-25, 30, 32, 33a, 34-35, 37
Hornie gollack — 5c, 23
Jennie — 17a
Nil —16, 29b

Perth

Clippie — 45
Clipshear — 52a, 56, 65
Eariewig — 29a, 34, 72
Earwig — 2a, 4, 9-10, 24, 36, 57, 67, 74
Forker — 69
Forkie — 8, 11, 22, 26-27, 32-33, 40, 43, 49, 52d, 54-55, 58, 60, 71
Forkietail — 1, 2ab, 3, 5-7, 9-10, 12-18, 20-21, 24-28, 29a, 31-33, 35, 37, 39, 41ab, 42, 44, 47, 50, 51ab, 52abde, 53, 56, 61-62, 64-65, 67-68, 70-71, 73
Forkietailie — 23, 45, 57, 59
Gallacher — 49, 68, 72-74
Gellack — 73
Gollach — 30
Gol(l)acher — 24, 46
Golliewog — 29a
Gowlach — 37, 41b, 45, 52c, 61
Gowlack — 25, 27, 29b, 39, 41a, 42-43, 46, 48, 53, 62-63
Horn golacher — 52d
Horn gol(l)ach — 15, 37
Hornie gol(l)ach — 13, 20, 29a, 32, 52b, 66
Hornie gollack — 53
Hornie gowlach — 16
Kittle forkie — 38
Nil — 19

Fife

Cleppie — 6
Clepshear — 6, 44d, 64b
Clippie — 2, 5, 31, 45-46
Clipshear — 5, 7, 9ab, 10, 12-13, 16-27, 29-30, 32-35, 36a, 37-39, 40ab, 41abcd, 42, 43ab, 44abcef, 45-54, 55abcdefg, 56-61, 63, 64a
Clocker — 37
Cluppie — 8
Clupshear — 4, 8, 14, 28, 36b
Eariewig — 38, 55b
Earwig — 50, 57
Ermit — 56
Forkie — 3, 33, 37, 41d, 47, 52, 62
Forkietail — 1, 4-5, 7-8, 11-13, 19, 21-23, 27, 34, 36ab, 39, 43a, 44ce, 55cdf, 62-63, 64a
Forkietailie — 12, 37, 46, 53, 55e, 62
Gowlack — 51, 55c, 56-58
Gowlig — 61
Hoarn golach — 12
Hoarnie gollach — 43a
Hornie gol(l)ach — 12, 55f
Nil — 15

Clackmannan

Clipshear — 1, 4abcd, 7
Eariewig — 1
Earwig — 4c
Forkietail — 1, 4abcd, 5-6
Galacher — 4d
Gowlach — 5
Gowlack — 1-3, 4ac, 6-7
Gowlect — 4d
Gullach — 6

Stirling

Clipshear — 2, 7abdf, 9, 25ab
Cliptail — 9
Cloacker — 26a
Eariewig — 7bc, 8-9, 12-13, 15-16, 21a, 22a, 23ab, 25c, 28-30, 32, 34, 35b, 38, 41, 42a
Earwig — 4, 7ce, 15, 21b, 26a, 27a, 30-31, 36
Forker — 26b
Forkie — 7ae, 9, 26a, 38
Forkietail — 4, 6, 7f, 8, 12, 17, 21b, 22a, 24, 25ac, 31, 33-34, 35b, 39a
Forkit tail — 26b
Forktailie — 7bd
Gal(l)acher — 3, 6, 7ab, 11, 13, 22ab, 23b, 25b, 26def, 27a, 29-30, 35a, 37ab, 42a
Gallicar — 26a
Gollach — 18
Gollacher — 3, 10, 14, 18
Gowlacher — 7bde, 10
Gowlack — 7b, 26d
Gowlaker — 8, 10
Gullach — 7e, 17
Gullacher — 7e, 17, 23c, 25acd, 26ce, 33, 39b
Hornie golach — 23b
Hornie gollacher — 2
Switchtible — 12
Switch poll — 31
Nil 1 5,19-20,27b,40 42b

Dunbarton

Eariewig — 3, 4b, 5-6, 7a,9-12, 13bc, 16ab, 17-18
Earwig — 1, 4b, 6, 10bc, 14b, 16a
Forkie — 2, 13a, 16b
Forkietail — 1, 7c, 14a
Gallach — 13b, 14a
Gal(l)acher — 7abc, 10, 12, 13a, 14a, 16a
Gallie cloaker — 16b
Nil — 4a, 8, 15

Argyll

Callangleen — 31
Calliegleean — 32
Clipshear — 5, 8
Colanglean — 33, 35
Collieglean — 34, 38-40
Colliguleen — 36
Culagleane — 30
Cullieglean — 37
Eariewig — 11
Earwig — 1-3, 5-6, 9-10, 14-17, 19, 22-23, 25-27, 30, 32-33, 35-36
Forkietail — 7, 16, 24-25, 35
Forkie weevil — 26
Hairy oobit — 24
Horn gollach — 35
Nil — 4, 12-13, 18, 20-21, 28-29

Bute

Eariewig — 1b, 3, 7, 8b
Earwig — 1cd, 8ab
Forkietail — 8b, 9
Forkietailie — 1a
Gallacher — 5
Golach — 1e
Goulach — 2
Gullucher — 9
Nil — 4, 6

Ayr

Clipshear — 7
Eariewig — 1a, 2ab, 3-5, 8ab, 16b, 18a, 20g, 34, 44, 53a, 55, 57
Earwig — 28ce
Forkie — 20f, 41
Forkie gullack — 28d
Forkietail — 1a, 16b, 18a, 28f
Forkit gellack — 42
Gaellack — 46
Gallach — 3, 18b
Gallacher — 8a, 18b
Gavelach — 53a
Gavelack — 41, 47, 49, 53b, 54, 56
Gellack — 1a, 35ab, 36-39, 45, 52, 57
Gillach — 15, 32
Gillack — 22, 26a, 30b, 34, 41, 47-51
Gol(l)ach — 1a, 19, 30a, 41, 52
Gowlack — 56-57
Gullach — 2a, 3, 5-6, 9-10, 12ab, 15, 16a, 18b, 20abefg, 24ab, 25, 28b, 29, 30a
Gul(l)acher — 7, 8b, 20h, 26c
Gullack — 8a, 13-14, 16b, 17, 18ab, 20cdh, 21-23, 26b, 27, 28abcdf, 29, 31, 33, 40, 43
Hornie gollach — 1a, 18b
Hornie gullach — 2a
Hornie gullack — 53b
Nil — 1b, 11

Renfrew

Clipshear — 21
Eariewig — 1b, 2acghj, 3, 4acd, 7, 11acdeijkl, 12b, 13c, 14ab, 16abd, 17, 18a
Earwig — 2ij, 4e, 5, 19, 20a
Forkie — 2b
Forkietail — 2e, 4d, 5, 11b, 15, 16c
Gal(l)acher — 8, 11bfl, 13c, 16c, 17
Gellack — 20b
Gillach — 19
Gillack — 14b
Golack — 14b
Gul(l)acher — 11cijkl
Hornie gallacher — 21
Hornie gollach — 14b
Rainie beast — 2a
Nil — 1a, 2df, 4b, 6, 9-10, 11gh, 12a, 13abd, 18b

Lanark

Clipshear — 13, 32a, 39, 48, 59a
Clip the shears — 38c
Cloak — 15a
Clocker — 3
Cochbell — 38d, 46a
Doctor draw bluid — 46c
Eariewig — 2-3, 5-6, 8a, 9a, 12, 14abd, 15c, 16ab, 18, 22, 24, 25abcd, 26ab, 27b, 28, 29cef, 30, 31ad, 32e, 33a, 35cd, 37, 42, 44-45, 46b, 49a, 57a, 58, 60
Earwig — 1, 6, 7ac, 14d, 15a, 20, 25c, 29c, 31a, 35bd, 39, 44, 46a, 52b
Forker — 8b
Forkie — 57a
Forkietail — 4, 7a, 15c, 17, 21, 23, 32a, 34, 36, 38d, 56
Forkietailie — 15b, 20
Gal(l)acher — 13, 17, 29cd, 35d
Gallack — 9b
Gellack — 38d, 63
Gol(l)ach — 17, 32c, 35d
Gollacher — 22
Gowlack — 15b
Hornie gallacher — 9b
Hornie goalie — 50
Hornie godouch — 39
Hornie gogle — 39
Hornie goler — 39-40, 59b, 61
Hornie gollach — 15b, 32cd
Hornie goller — 15b, 39, 49b, 51, 52a, 56, 62, 65
Hornie gollie — 53
Hornie goral — 54
Hornie gullach — 27a
Hornie solar — 48
Sclater — 11
Scodgible — 56
Scotchible — 65
Switchabell — 44
Switchpeeler — 38c
Switchple — 33d, 38a
Switch pol — 19, 33b, 38bc
Switchpole — 30, 31b
Switchpool — 15b, 31b, 32f, 33cd, 38d, 41, 43, 56, 57ac, 58
Switchtible — 33a
Switchtiple - 57b
Swutchipol — 47
Swutchple — 48
Swutchpool — 48
Witchpool — 30, 45
Nil — 7b, 10ab, 14c, 29abg, 31c, 32b, 35a, 38e, 55, 64ab, 66, 67ab

West Lothian

Clippie — 12
Clippieshear — 9a
Clipshear — 1ad, 2-3, 5-8, 9b, 10, 12-16, 19a, 20a
Codgible — 20a
Eariewig — 1ac, 2, 5-7, 9a, 10-13, 17a, 20a, 21a
Earwig — 18, 22
Forkie — 8, 11
Forkietail — 1d, 3-4 13, 22
Gallacher — 3
Gullack — 17a
Hedgible — 10
Scotchbull — 2
Scotchible — 1ac, 9a, 21a
Nil — 1b, 17b, 19b, 20b, 21b

Midlothian

Clippie — 5, 6b, 17
Clipshear — 1-4, 6ab, 7ab, 8ab, 10-11, 12ab, 14ab, 15-21, 23ab, 24, 25acd, 26ab, 27-29
Coachable — 13
Eariewig — 12a, 14ab, 22
Earwig — 10, 23b
Forker — 23ab, 25a, 26a, 28, 30
Forkie — 17, 23a, 32
Forkietail — 7b, 8ab, 10-11, 12b, 14a, 15, 24, 27, 30
Gellick — 18
Gollach — 26a
Gollacher — 26a
Gowlack — 4
Hornie golach — 24
Scodgie — 27
Nil — 9, 25b, 31

East Lothian

Clippie — 20
Clipshear — 2-3, 4ab, 5, 6a, 7-18, 20-21
Coachbill — 11
Earwig — 4b, 15, 18
Forker — 1, 4a, 6b, 7, 10, 14-15, 19-21
Forkie — 9, 13-14

East Lothian cont'd

Forkietail — 4b, 6a, 8-9, 13
Forkietailie — 15
Hornie gollach — 2
Scodgbill — 13
Scotchbill — 16-17
Scotchiebill — 16

Berwick

Clipshear — 7, 12, 27, 29
Earie — 27
Earwig — 2, 9, 12, 19
Forker — 2, 11-13, 15, 19, 22-24, 26, 29, 31
Forkie — 4, 17, 29, 31
Forkie hornie — 21
Forkietail — 16b, 17-18, 23, 30, 32
Scodgibell — 16c
Scodgible — 1-3, 7, 9, 15, 16a, 19, 31-32
Scodgibull — 16b
Scodgie — 4, 16a, 25
Scogabell — 17
Scotchbell — 6, 8
Scotchible — 18, 20-21
Scotchie — 20
Scotchiebell — 5, 8, 10, 27
'Wig — 12
Nil — 14, 28

Peebles

Clipshear — 3, 4abc, 5, 6a
Eariewig — 5, 7
Earwig — 3, 4bc, 5, 6ab
Forker — 4bc, 8
Forkie — 2, 10
Forkietail — 1, 6a
Forktailie — 2
Gallacher — 8
Gellack — 2
Hornie gollach — 7
Hornie goller — 3, 6a
Scoachible — 9
Scotchible — 4c, 7
Scrochible — 10

Selkirk

Clipshear — 2a
Forker — 1, 2abcde, 3, 6-8
Scodgibald — 4
Scodgible — 3, 7
Nil — 5

Roxburgh

Clipshear — 4, 13, 21c
Coadgible — 26
Codgible — 9b
Cotchibol — 3a
Earwig — 21a
Forker — 1-2, 3b, 4-5, 7, 9ab, 10-13, 15ab, 16-17, 20, 21abcdef, 22-27
Forkie — 21c, 26
Forkietail — 3a, 8, 19-20, 21c
Scoadgie — 26
Scodgebell — 21c
Scodgible — 9a, 10, 16-18
Scodgie — 19, 21a
Scotchbald — 21c
Scotchbol — 21c
Scotchbolt — 21c
Scotchible — 5-6, 8, 10
Scotchie — 21c
Switchbell — 4, 21c, 25, 28
Touchspale — 21c
Twichiebell — 27
Nil — 14

Dumfries

Blood sooker — 29
Clipshear — 7
Cloch — 8b
Earwig — 4, 12, 16, 17b
Ettercup — 35
Foorkie leg — 46
Forkie — 3, 17ab, 29
Forkietail — 16, 31c, 34
Gailick — 18, 31d
Geleock — 3
Gelick — 6, 19, 21a, 32, 37, 45a
Gellick — 1a, 4-5, 7, 8a, 9-11, 13-16, 17ab, 20, 21b, 22-28, 30, 31abcdef, 34-36, 38, 40-44, 46-47, 49
Glellick — 33
Gowlick — 19
Switchbell — 18, 34, 39
Swutchbell — 29
Nil — 1b, 2, 45b, 48

Kirkcudbright

Earwig — 1, 6
Forkietail — 1
Gellick — 1, 3-11, 12ab, 13-14, 15b, 16-19, 21abc, 22-27
Gowlick — 15a, 17
Nil — 2, 20

Wigtown

Eariewig — 6, 18
Earwig — 16
Gowlach — 5a, 10
Gowlack — 1-4, 5ab, 6-9, 11-18

Northumberland

Cat with two tails — 71c
Cochiebell — 41c
Codgiebell — 134
Critchiebell — 29cf
Crochiebell — 18, 59b
Crutchie — 66
Crutchie beetle — 33b
Crutchiebell — 20a, 23, 24ab, 40a, 41ab, 45, 48, 66, 68, 69d
Crutchie bug — 17
Cutchiebell — 22
Eariewig — 71c
Earwig — 2b, 14, 20b, 26, 28, 29b, 31, 35, 40a, 41c, 42-43, 46, 52, 53b, 54, 56, 59de, 62b, 69c, 71ad, 78, 82, 87, 104a, 106, 111a, 112, 120b, 121, 127a, 130e, 132-133, 140
Earworm — 69a
Forker — 22, 71c
Forkietail — 1b, 8, 10, 16, 21-22, 24a, 25, 28, 29abde, 30, 33a, 39, 40ab, 41bc, 45, 47, 49-50, 57, 59ae, 60-61, 62abcdefgh, 63, 64ab, 65ab, 66-68, 69abcdefgh, 70, 71abde, 72abcdegijkl, 76, 80, 82-87, 88ab, 90-93, 94b, 95ab, 96-98 99abcd, 100, 101ab, 104b, 107, 111a, 115, 122b, 123, 124a, 125, 126bcdef, 127dh, 129ac, 130abcdef, 134
Scodgibell — 4, 59b
Scodgible — 16
Scodible — 2b
Scotchabell — 11, 19a
Scotchie beetle — 1b
Scotchiebell — 1abc, 2ab, 5-6, 10, 12-15, 20b, 59d, 134
Scotchieble — 8-9
Scratchiebelle — 18
Scrutchiebell — 26
Twitch — 77
Twitchie — 66, 111b, 112, 127a, 130d
Twitchbell — 25, 34b, 43, 61, 69g, 73-75, 91, 96, 101a, 103abc, 104ab, 107, 108ab, 109-110, 111ab, 112, 120a, 126f, 127ac, 133-134, 137-138, 140-141, 143
Twitchie back — 86, 125
Twitchiebell — 7, 17-18, 21, 26-27, 29abcdef, 30, 32, 33a, 34a, 35-39, 40ab, 41bd, 44-46, 48-51, 53ab, 57, 59bcd, 60, 62bc, 68, 69b, 71b, 72f, 74, 76-77, 79-82, 97, 99cd, 102, 105, 114, 116-117, 118ab, 119, 120c, 121, 122a, 124b, 125, 126ade, 127dh, 129b, 130cd, 131, 135, 139
Nil — 3, 19b, 55, 58, 59f, 72h, 89, 94a, 108c, 113, 127befg, 128, 136, 142

Cumberland

Cat nine tail — 8
Cat o nine tails — 7, 13a, 28, 33, 43
Cattie nine tails — 9
Cat with two tails — 27
Eariewig — 14, 16, 18, 26, 42, 53, 56-57, 62
Earwig — 1a, 4, 9, 13c, 15ac, 24-25, 40, 46-50, 52-53, 57-59
Erriewig — 46
Forkietail — 9, 25, 57
Twitchbell — 2-3, 5ab, 10, 12, 13abc, 17, 19-22, 27-28, 30-31, 37b, 38-39, 49
Nil — 1b, 6, 11, 13d, 15b, 23, 29, 32, 34-36, 37a, 41, 44-45, 51, 54-55, 60-61, 63ab

Down

Eariewig — 1, 3, 6, 8-9, 11-12, 14, 19-20, 23-24, 28
Earwig — 2a, 7, 22
Gaelic — 13, 21
Gallick — 5, 18, 26
Gallig — 25
Geelick — 12
Gelick — 3
Gellick — 2b, 10, 29
Gel(l)ig — 11, 27
Gillick — 24
Midge — 15
Nil — 4, 16-17, 30

Tyrone

Dyeelog — 5
Eariewig — 1, 6, 9, 11-13, 15
Earwig — 7, 10
Gaelig — 8
Galack — 3
Gwyliegleen — 2
Nil — 4, 14, 16

Antrim

Coligaleen — 5b, 7
Creeper — 34
Eariewig — 3, 4A, 10-11, 13-15, 16b, 18, 21, 24-26, 28-29, 31, 34
Gaelick — 8b, 28
Galag — 5b
Gallick — 16a, 29
Gallyub — 1
Geelick — 3
Geelig — 1, 5a
Gelach — 2
Gelig — 1, 12, 18, 22
Gellick — 4, 4A, 9, 15, 16b, 17, 20-21, 23-24, 27, 30-31, 33
Gellie galeen — 16b
Gillick — 19
Gillig — 19
Sissie wig — 34
Nil — 6, 8a, 16c, 32

Donegal

Eariewig — 10b
Earwig — 5, 5A, 12
Gale — 6
Geelick — 9
Geelog — 7, 7A, 10b, 11
Gollie gleen — 1
Gullie gleen — 4-5
Slater — 13
Nil — 1A, 2-3, 8, 10a

Fermanagh

Dheel — 6
Dheelog — 6
Eariewig — 2, 5
Earwig — 4, 7a, 8-9
Geelug — 1, 7b, 10
Nil — 3

Armagh

Eriewig — 1-5, 6ab

Londonderry

Eariewig — 3A, 4-7
Gaellick — 1B
Gallagh — 5
Gallick — 1
Gillig — 3, 5
Gillick — 2
Nil — 1A,

83 MAGGOT (PQ1, 177)

Maggot has not been mapped as it occurs fairly densely everywhere except the south-west of Scotland including Ayrshire.

Shetland
Maeo – 9
Maetho – 19
Maggot – 1, 3, 7, 15-16, 29, 32
Maid – 12, 17, 20, 21b, 23-25, 27-29
Maith – 30-31, 33
Mead – 4, 15
Med – 26
Mite – 2, 14
Moch – 21a
Warbeck – 22
White wirm – 15, 30
Wirm – 1, 5-6, 22, 30
Nil – 8, 10-11, 13, 18

Orkney
Fish worm – 5, 13a
Leather jacket – 6
Maggot – 2-3, 5, 7-9, 11, 13ab, 14-17, 19, 21
Maith – 15, 17-18, 20-21
Sma white worm – 4
Storie – 6
Warble – 12
Warbo – 12
Worm – 4
Nil – 1, 10

Caithness
Grub – 13
Maggot – 2b, 4-5, 7-11, 12b, 13-14, 16b
Maith – 2a, 5, 12b
Mank – 15
Moch – 16a
Nil – 1, 3, 6, 12ac, 17

Sutherland
Creeag – 5
Maag – 16
Mack – 14-15
Maggot – 1, 3-8, 9b, 11-13, 16
Mawk – 6, 8, 9ab, 10, 15
Nil – 2, 17

Ross & Cromarty
Crayack – 3, 29
Grub – 32b
Maak – 19, 27, 32bc, 33-34, 37a
Maggot – 1, 3-6, 8-9, 16-18, 20, 26-27, 29-30, 32a, 39
Mawk – 9-11, 13-15, 17, 20-24, 25ab, 28-29, 31, 35-36
Tick – 17
Nil – 2, 7, 12, 37b, 38

Inverness
Creeach – 31
Fly – 13c
Grub – 6
Meach – 12
Maak – 13e, 21a
Maggot – 2-6, 8, 10-11, 13abce, 17, 21ab, 23, 26-28, 30, 32-40
Mauch – 26
Mawk – 8-9, 13cd, 14-16, 18-20, 22, 24-25, 29
Worm – 1
Nil – 7

Nairn
Mack – 1ab, 2
Maggot – 2
Mawk – 1c, 3-5
Nil – 6

Moray
Mach – 2a, 8b, 15, 18, 20-21
Mack – 4, 6b, 7, 11, 14, 17, 22
Magg – 22
Maggot – 7, 23
Mauch – 2b, 3, 6a, 7, 9b, 10, 12, 19
Maw – 3
Mawk – 1, 8abd, 9a, 13, 16, 23
Nil – 5, 8cef

Banff
Kabe – 20
Mach – 9, 16-17, 25, 31
Maggot – 4, 8, 15, 18c, 19, 27, 30, 34
Maith – 2abc, 3, 6b, 10-11, 13, 21-24, 28, 32, 34
Mauch – 4-5, 6b, 14, 29, 33
Mauck – 6b, 8, 34
Mech – 1
Mite – 10
Warble – 18d
Nil – 6a, 7, 12, 18ab, 26

Aberdeen
Beastie – 53, 71b
Fite – 104
Golach – 53
Grub – 48, 82, 104
Mach – 40
Mack – 77
Maggot – 6, 8, 11, 23, 32, 34, 43-44, 49-51, 54, 56, 63, 66-67, 71b, 74, 79, 81, 85-86, 94-95, 98, 101, 103, 105-108
Maith – 3ab, 4, 5acd, 6-10, 12, 14, 17, 19-21, 23, 28abc, 29-32, 35, 37, 39, 41-46, 47abef, 48, 51-52, 59, 61-62, 71c, 75-76, 78, 80, 83-86, 88-89, 92, 97, 102
Maithse – 49
Maize – 69
Mauch – 19, 22, 24-25
Mave – 16, 60
Mawk – 105
Mite – 9, 28b, 87, 100
Mythe – 27
Tick – 104
Warble – 66
Warble fly – 70
Weevil – 73
Worm – 20, 104
Nil – 1-2, 5b, 13, 15, 18, 26, 33, 36, 38, 47cd, 55, 57-58, 64-65, 68, 71a, 72, 90-91, 93, 96, 99, 109

Kincardine
Grub – 11
Maggot – 1, 3, 5-8, 10, 15-16, 17bc, 18-19, 24, 26, 28
Maid – 25, 27-28
Maith – 4, 9, 12, 14-15, 17c, 21-22
Mawk – 17b
Mays – 10
Mite – 7
Weevel – 2
Nil – 13, 17ad, 20, 23

Kinross
Mauch – 1-5, 7
Nil – 6

Angus
Grub – 22
Maak – 10
Mach – 9, 11, 13, 15, 19, 22-23, 27, 34
Macht – 13
Mae – 13
Maggot – 2, 6, 8, 12, 17b, 20, 24-25, 32, 34-36
Maid – 14abc, 17b, 33b, 34
Maidie – 18
Maig – 28
Math – 13
Mauch – 1, 3-4, 5ab, 7-8, 13, 21, 31
Maw – 13
Meath – 33b
Mite – 14cd, 37
Nil – 5c, 16, 17a, 26, 29ab, 30, 33a

Perth
Crawler – 21
Grub – 25
Maak – 12
Mach – 5, 15, 23, 30-31, 51a
Mag – 64
Maggot – 2a, 4, 8-10, 15-16, 21, 24, 27-28, 29a, 32-33, 36, 46, 50, 52bc, 60
Mauch – 7, 9-10, 13, 18, 20, 22, 26, 29ab, 32-33, 38-40, 41ab, 42-43, 46-47, 50, 51b, 52d, 53, 56-57, 59, 61-62, 65
Mawk – 1, 16, 26, 48, 66-68, 70-74
Mawkit – 41b
Mite – 25
Moock – 67
Worm – 25
Nil – 2b, 3, 6, 11, 14, 17, 19, 34-35, 37, 44-45, 49, 52ae, 54-55, 58, 63, 69

Fife
Cob – 37, 43b
Mach – 9b
Made – 32-34
Maggie moth – 55d
Maggot – 4, 21-22, 24, 36b, 37, 41a, 44b, 46-48, 50, 55ab, 56, 62-63
Mauch – 2, 5-8, 9a, 10-14, 16-17, 19-21, 23, 25-28, 30, 35, 36ab, 38-39, 40ab, 41ad, 42, 43a, 44acdef, 46, 48-52, 55bcdefg, 57-59, 57-59, 61, 64ab
Mawk – 12, 29, 41b, 53
Moak – 52
Nil – 1, 3, 15, 18, 31, 41c, 45, 54, 60

Clackmannan
Mack – 4c
Maggot – 1, 4c, 6
Mauch – 1-2, 4b, 5-7
Mawk – 4ad, 5
Nil – 3

Stirling
Grub – 6, 7c, 21b, 23a, 38
Maggot – 4, 7ae, 12, 21b, 25c, 26ad, 27a, 28, 31, 34, 36, 37b
Mauch – 7bdf, 10, 12, 18, 20, 25c, 26f, 34
Mawk – 2-3, 7abe, 8-17, 21ab, 22ab, 23abc, 24, 25abd, 26abcdef, 27ab, 29-33, 35ab, 36, 37ab, 38, 39ab 40, 42a
Milluck – 33
Moke – 23a
Nil – 1, 5, 19, 41, 42b

Dunbarton
Grub – 10, 16b, 17
Maggot – 1, 6, 7b, 11, 13abc, 14b
Mauck – 2-3, 4ab, 6, 7ac, 9-10, 12, 13abc, 14ab, 15, 16ab
Mouk – 17
Nil – 5, 8, 18

Argyll
Grub – 2
Maach – 32
Mack – 5, 28, 33, 37, 39-40
Mag – 36
Maggot – 1-3, 5-7, 9-11, 14-17, 19, 22-27, 30, 33, 35
Maug – 26
Mawk – 7, 9, 18-19, 21, 31, 34-35, 38-39
Nil – 4, 8, 12-13, 20, 29

Bute
Maggot – 1a, 2, 7, 8a
Mawk – 1ace, 2-7, 8ab, 9
Moke – 1d
Nil – 1b

Ayr
Gentle – 57
Grub – 6, 43
Mack – 18b, 21, 27, 47, 53b
Maggot – 2b, 28ce, 45
Mauch – 19
Mawk – 1ab, 2ab, 3-7, 8ab, 9-11, 12ab, 13-15, 16ab, 17, 18ab, 19, 20abcdefgh, 22-23, 24ab, 25, 26bc, 27, 28abcdf, 29, 30ab, 31-34, 35ab, 36-52, 53a, 54-57
Mite – 3, 28e
Moke – 18b
Tick – 8b
Weevil – 28e
Nil – 26a

Renfrew
Grub – 3, 16ad
Maggot – 2abhi, 4e, 11ae, 14a, 16b, 19, 20a
Mawk – 1b, 2bfgij, 4acd, 5, 7-9, 11aefijkl, 12ab, 13abc, 14ab, 15, 16ac, 17, 18ab, 19, 20b, 21
Moch – 21
Mocket – 2e
Tick – 11b
Worm – 16a
Nil – 1a, 2cd, 4b, 6, 10, 11cdgh, 13d

Lanark
Blue bottle – 37
Fluke – 31d
Grub – 6, 15c, 16b, 29f, 32a, 59a
Insect – 29f, 37
Mack – 67b
Maggot – 1, 3, 6, 7c, 14bd, 15ac, 18, 25c, 26a, 29cf, 32e, 35ad, 45, 49a, 58
Mauch – 31c
Mawk – 1-3, 5, 7abc, 8b, 9ab, 10a, 11-13, 15abc, 16a, 17, 19-20, 22, 24, 25abcd, 26a, 27ab, 28, 29deg, 30, 31abd, 32bcdf, 33abcd, 34, 35abcd, 36, 38abcde, 39-42, 44, 46abc, 47-48, 49b, 50-51, 52ab, 53-56, 57abc, 58, 59ab, 60-63, 64ab, 65-66
Weevil – 30
Worm – 20
Nil – 4, 8a, 10b, 14ac, 21, 23, 26b, 29ab, 43, 67a

West Lothian
Grub – 15
Mack – 1c, 14
Mag – 15
Maggot – 11, 13, 16, 18, 20a, 22
Mauch – 3
Mawk – 1abd, 2, 4-8, 9ab, 10, 12-13, 15-16, 17a, 18, 19b, 21a
Nil – 17b, 19a, 20b, 21b

Midlothian
Grub – 6a
Mack – 7a, 8a, 20, 23a, 25a, 26ab, 31-32
Maggot – 6ab, 7a, 10, 14a, 23b
Maque – 4
Mauch – 26a
Mauk – 3, 6b, 7b, 8b, 10-11, 12ab, 13, 14ab, 16-18, 21, 23b, 24, 25cd, 27-30
Nil – 1-2, 5, 9, 15, 19, 22, 25b

East Lothian
Grub – 6b
Mach – 8
Mack – 2, 4b, 6a, 7, 9, 13, 15-18, 20-21
Maggie – 1
Maggot – 4b, 16-17, 19
Mauch – 4ab
Mawk – 3, 10-12, 14, 20
Nil – 5

Berwick
Mack – 1-4, 8, 11, 15, 16ab,

Berwick cont'd

17-18, 20-21, 23-24, 26, 30-32
Maggot — 12, 16b, 29
Mawk — 5-7, 9-10, 12-14, 16c, 19, 22, 27
Stoat box — 27
Nil — 25, 28

Peebles

Mack — 2-3, 4c, 6b, 9
Maggie — 4b
Maggot — 4bc, 6b
Mawk — 1-2, 5, 6a, 7-10
Mawkie flee — 6a
Nil — 4a

Selkirk

Mack — 1, 2bcde, 4, 6-7
Mawk — 2a, 3, 8
Nil — 5

Roxburgh

Mack — 1-2, 3ab, 5, 7-8, 9ab, 11-13, 15ab, 16, 18-20, 21bdf, 22, 24-25, 27-28
Maggot — 21a
Mawk — 4, 6, 10, 17, 21ace, 23, 26
Nil 14

Dumfries

Mack — 4, 6-7, 8ab, 9-10, 12-15, 18-19, 21a, 24-30, 31abcdef, 36-37, 39-43, 45ab, 46-47, 49
Macket — 23
Mackworm — 32
Maggot — 4, 20, 33
Mawk — 1a, 2-3, 5, 11, 16, 17ab, 21b, 22, 25, 34-35, 38, 41
Nil — 1b, 44, 48

Kirkcudbright

Grub — 16
Mack — 2-3, 5-11, 12ab, 13-14, 15b, 17-19, 21abc, 22-23, 25-27
Maggot — 6-7
Mawk — 1, 4, 15a, 24
Nil — 20

Wigtown

Mack — 2-4, 8-16, 18
Mawk — 1, 5ab, 6-7, 17

Northumberland

Blow fly — 22
Fly strike — 77
Gentle — 56, 129b
Grub — 14, 41c, 69abc, 72i, 79, 118a, 125, 126f, 129b, 142
Jumper — 26
Little worm — 101b
Mack — 1ac, 2b, 3, 5, 8-11, 15-18, 19a, 20b, 21-23, 24ab, 25, 27-28, 29abcd, 30, 33b, 34ab, 35-36, 38-39, 40ab, 41abd, 42-43, 45-46, 48-50, 53ab, 54-55, 57-58, 59bcde, 61, 62abcdeg, 63, 64ab, 65ab, 66, 68, 69abde, 70, 71abe, 72cgij, 74, 76-77, 79-86, 88ab, 90-93, 94ab, 95b, 97-98, 100, 106, 116, 118b, 122ab, 124ab, 126f, 127h, 134
Mackie — 13, 99b
Mag — 32, 89
Maggot — 2b, 5-7, 14, 28, 29b, 30-31, 35, 40a, 41c, 42, 52, 53b, 56, 59b, 62b, 64b, 65a, 66, 69c, 71cd, 72cdi, 77-78, 82, 86-87, 99bd, 101a, 103ac, 104b, 106, 109, 111ab, 112, 119, 120ab, 121, 126c, 127ad, 130bce
Maggotie — 110
Mairk — 91
Malk — 59c, 130c
Maork — 139
Mawk — 1a, 2a, 16, 22, 25-26, 29af, 37, 44, 47, 51, 59c, 60, 62f, 69h, 70, 71d, 75, 77, 83, 91, 95a, 98, 107, 108a, 114, 117, 120c, 124a, 126d, 131
Mawkie — 41a
Merk — 112
Mite — 130c
Moke — 34a, 53a, 73-74, 78, 102, 103bc, 104a, 108bc, 110, 112, 132-139, 142
Molk — 137
Warble — 71c
Nil — 1b, 4, 12, 19b, 20a, 29e, 33a, 59af, 62h, 67, 69fg, 72abefhkl, 96, 99ac, 105, 113, 115, 123, 126abe, 127bcefg, 128, 129ac, 130adf, 140-141, 143

Cumberland

Crowler — 56
Fleeblow — 56
Kyadd — 15c
Maak — 63b
Maggot — 1a, 9, 12, 15c, 23-24, 40, 46, 50, 53, 56-58
Mawk — 1a, 3, 5b, 12, 13bc, 20-22, 25, 27, 33, 36, 39-41, 46-47, 49, 52, 54, 57, 62
Moke — 1a, 3-4, 5a, 6-9, 11-12, 13d, 14, 15a, 16-19, 21, 23-24, 28-31, 34, 37ab, 38, 42-43, 45, 51, 54, 59-61
Whick — 2, 33, 38, 44, 56
Wick — 4, 15ab, 18, 32, 41, 46, 48, 54, 57, 61-62, 63a
Nil — 1b, 10, 13a, 26, 35, 55

Down

Blue bottle — 17
Grub — 4
Maggot — 2a, 5-7, 13, 15, 18-19, 24, 26
Mough — 21
Nil — 1, 2b, 3, 8-12, 14, 16, 20, 22-23, 25, 27-30

Tyrone

Creeper — 6
Grub — 5, 8, 11-12, 16
Maggot — 1, 7-8, 10-11
Worm — 1
Nil — 2-4, 9, 13-15

Antrim

Grub — 9, 16b, 25
Maggot — 1-3, 5ab, 9, 12-13, 15, 16b, 17, 19-20, 25-26, 33
Mite — 16b
Worm — 21-22
Nil — 4, 4A, 6-7, 8ab, 10-11, 14, 16ac, 18, 23-24, 27-32, 34

Donegal

Crawler — 10a
Maggot — 1, 4-5, 5A, 6, 7A, 8, 10a, 12
Mite — 5
Weevil — 6
Nil — 1A, 2-3, 7, 9, 10b, 11, 13

Fermanagh

Grub — 1-2
Maggot — 2, 4-5, 7a, 8-9
Nil — 3, 6, 7b, 10

Armagh

Grub — 2, 4
Maggot — 3-4, 6a
Nil — 1, 5, 6b

Londonderry

Grub — 5
Maggot — 2-3, 3A, 7

84 SPIDER (PQ1, 178)

For variants of SPIDER see map 17, Appendix A.

Shetland

Creepie craalie — 24
Ettercap — 2, 30
Maamie spider — 17
Paamie — 23
Spider — 1-10, 13-16, 18-20, 21ab, 22, 24-25, 27-33
Nil — 11-12, 26

Orkney

Aiter kep — 15
Ettercap — 11-12, 13b
Kipie kringlie — 13a
Spider — 1-9, 11, 13ab, 15-21
Nil — 10, 14

Caithness

Sheepard — 2a
Spider — 2ab, 5, 8-9, 11, 13-14, 16b
Weaver — 12b
Web spinner — 8
Nil — 1, 3-4, 6-7, 10, 12ac, 15, 16a, 17

Sutherland

Spider — 1, 3-8, 9ab, 10-13, 16
Nil — 2, 14-15, 17

Ross & Cromarty

Pochcan salyin — 31
Sautie pock — 22
Spider — 3-6, 8-9, 13-14, 16-18, 20, 22-24, 25ab, 26-27, 29-31, 32ab, 34, 36, 39
Spinner — 26
Nil -- 1-2, 7, 10-12, 15, 19, 21, 28, 32c, 33, 35, 37ab, 38

Inverness

Pocan salann — 9, 26
Spider — 1-6, 8-11, 13abce, 16-19, 21ab, 22-23, 26-30, 32-40
Nil — 7, 12, 13d, 14-15, 20, 24-25, 31

Nairn

Spider — 1ab, 2, 5
Nil — 1c, 3-4

Moray

Ettercap — 6a, 8d
Jennie spinner — 6a, 21
Spider — 4, 6b, 7, 8abdf, 11, 14, 18-19, 23
Spinning Jennie — 19
Weaver — 6b, 21
Weyver — 7, 8bf
Wyver — 1, 3-4, 6a, 8de, 9a, 10, 12, 16-17, 20, 22
Nil — 2ab, 5, 8c, 9b, 13, 15

Banff

Cobweb — 24
Ettercap — 27
Spider — 1, 2a, 5, 13, 15-16, 18c, 19, 21, 23, 30, 34
Spinner — 31
Weaver — 2bc, 9, 15-17, 18c, 29-30, 34
Weyver — 11, 34
Wyver — 3-4, 6b, 7-8, 10, 12, 14, 17, 18d, 25-26, 29-30, 33-34
Nil — 6a, 18ab, 20, 22, 28, 32

Aberdeen

Cappie — 58
Ettercap — 17, 19, 21, 28b, 31, 35, 37, 41, 43-44, 47ac, 62, 71a, 97
Ettercapper — 21
Jennie spinner — 69
Moos — 16
Naetrie — 25
Nettercap — 46
Spider — 3ab, 6, 8, 11-12, 14, 17, 20-21, 26, 28ac, 32, 43-45, 47bef, 49-50, 56, 59, 63, 66-67, 70, 73-75, 85, 98, 100, 105-106, 108
Weaver — 5b, 11, 30, 39, 57, 77, 91, 96, 105
Wiver — 4, 5d, 8-11, 15, 22-23, 25-27, 28a, 29, 34, 40, 47a, 48-49, 51, 53, 57-58, 60, 64-65, 67, 69, 71bc, 72, 75, 78-88, 92-95, 97-101, 103-104, 107-109
Nil — 1-2, 5ac, 7, 13, 18, 24, 33, 36, 38, 42, 47d, 52, 54-55, 61, 68, 76, 89-90, 102

Kincardine

Cappertie — 25, 27
Nettercap — 21-22, 28
Netterie — 22, 28
Spider — 3, 5-6, 8, 10, 15-16, 17bc, 19, 24, 26
Spinnin' Jennie — 10
Weiver — 13
Weyver — 3
Wiver — 4-9, 11-12, 14, 23
Nil — 1-2, 17ad, 18, 20

Kinross

Ettercap — 5, 7
Nettercap — 2
Spider — 2-4, 7
Nil — 1, 6

Angus

Cob — 19
Ettercap — 27
Ettrie — 35
Naiterte — 13
Nettercap — 3-4, 7, 25, 37
Netterie — 2-3, 5ac, 6-8, 10, 12, 14abcd, 15, 20-25, 27, 32, 33ab, 34, 36-37
Spider — 6, 8-10, 15, 17b, 18, 20, 28, 32, 34, 36
Wabster — 17a
Wyver — 23
Nil — 1, 5b, 11, 16, 26, 29ab, 30-31

Perth

Aetin — 66
Ettercap — 39, 62
Ettercaup — 45
Ettrie — 60
Gollach — 25
Nettercap — 33, 46, 53, 57, 59, 62, 65
Netterie — 20-21, 31-32, 50, 52a, 58
Netterkep — 20
Spider — 1, 2a, 5, 7-10, 12, 14-15, 21, 24-25, 27-28, 29a, 32-33, 36, 40, 41ab, 43, 46, 48, 51b, 52abce, 56-57, 62, 67-74
Spidie — 4
Spinner — 25-26
Wabster — 20, 47
Nil — 2b, 3, 6, 11, 13, 16-19,

Perth cont'd

22-23, 29b, 30, 34-35, 37-38, 42, 44, 49, 51a, 52d, 54-55, 61, 63-64

Fife

Cob — 53
Ettercap — 13
Etterie — 7
Jennie spinner — 33
Nether crap — 45
Nettercap — 4, 8, 9ab, 10, 12, 21, 23, 27, 29, 39, 56
Netter cawp — 46
Netter crab — 32
Nettercrap — 6, 12, 20, 26, 35, 44f
Netterie — 1, 4, 6
Spider — 4, 6, 8, 11, 13-14, 16, 19, 21, 23-25, 28, 36ab, 37, 39, 40b, 41a, 42, 43a, 44abcd, 46-47, 50-51, 53, 55adef, 56-57, 59, 61-63
Spinner — 51, 55f
Spinnin' Jennie — 33
Nil — 2-3, 5, 15, 17-18, 22, 30-31, 34, 38, 40a, 41bcd, 43b, 44e, 48-49, 52, 54, 55bcg, 58, 60, 64ab

Clackmannan

Spider — 1-2, 4c, 5-7
Wabster — 5
Nil — 3, 4abd

Stirling

Ethercap — 7b
Ettercap — 7b, 23c, 26d
Nettercap — 7bd, 26d
Speedart — 26b
Spider — 3-4, 6, 7abcdef, 8, 11, 13, 15-18, 20, 21ab, 22ab, 23b, 25abcd, 26ad, 27a, 28, 30-32, 34, 35a, 36, 37ab, 39ab, 41, 42a
Spidert — 26b
Weaver — 26c
Nil — 1-2, 5, 9-10, 12, 14, 19, 23a, 24, 26ef, 27b, 29, 33, 35b, 38, 40, 42b

Dunbarton

Speedert — 7a, 13b
Spider — 1-3, 5-6, 7bc, 8-11, 13abc, 14b, 15, 16ab
Nil — 4ab, 12, 14a, 17-18

Argyll

Jennie spinner — 35
Robert Bruce — 24
Spider — 1-3, 5-7, 9-11, 14-17, 19, 22-27, 30, 33, 35, 39
Weaver — 26
Nil — 4, 8, 12-13, 18, 20-21, 28-29, 31-32, 34, 36-38, 40

Bute

Spider — 1acd, 2, 7, 8ab, 9
Nil — 1be, 3-6

Ayr

Ettercap — 12a, 18b, 19
Spider — 1a, 2ab, 3-7, 8ab, 9-11, 12ab, 13-15, 16ab, 17, 18ab, 20bcdfgh, 21-23, 24ab, 25, 26bc, 27, 28adef, 30ab, 31-34, 35ab, 36-38, 40-46, 48-52, 53a, 54-57
Wabster — 13, 41
Nil — 1b, 20ae, 26a, 28bc, 29, 39, 47, 53b

Renfrew

Speedert — 11afkl, 13a, 18b, 21
Spider — 1b, 2abghij, 4acde, 5, 7-8, 11abcejl, 12a, 13bc, 14ab, 16abd, 17, 18a, 19, 20ab
Wabster — 14a
Nil — 1a, 2cdef, 3, 4b, 6, 9-10, 11dghi, 12b, 13d, 15, 16c

Lanark

Daddy long legs — 29e
Jennie long legs — 29f
Netterie — 4
Speedert — 9b, 38bd, 47, 57a, 63, 67a
Speeker — 41
Spider — 2-3, 5-6, 7ac, 8b, 9a, 10a, 11-13, 14bd, 15abc, 16ab, 17-20, 25bc, 26a, 27b, 29cd, 30, 31ad, 32aef, 33b, 35bcd, 37, 38ac, 39-40, 42, 44-45, 46abc, 47-48, 49ab, 50-51, 52ab, 53, 56, 57b, 58, 59b, 60, 62, 64ab, 65
Wabster — 33cd
Weaver — 65
Wyver — 15a, 30, 38d, 46c
Nil — 1, 7b, 8a, 10b, 14ac, 21-24, 25ad, 26b, 27a, 28, 29abg, 31bc, 32bcd, 33a, 34, 35a, 36, 38e, 43, 54-55, 57c, 59a, 61, 66, 67b

West Lothian

Spider — 1a, 2-8, 9a, 10-13, 15-16, 17a, 18, 19b, 20a, 21a, 22
Nil — 1bcd, 9b, 14, 17b, 19a, 20b, 21b

Midlothian

Spider — 1-3, 6ab, 7ab, 8ab, 10-11, 12ab, 13, 14ab, 16-18, 20-22, 23ab, 24, 25ac, 26ab, 27-32
Nil — 4-5, 9, 15, 19, 25bd

East Lothian

Spider — 1-2, 4b, 6ab, 7-21
Nil — 3, 4a, 5

Berwick

Ettercap — 5
Spider — 1-4, 6, 13, 15, 16abc, 17-23, 26-27, 29-32
Nil — 14, 24-25, 28

Peebles

Spider — 1-3, 4bc, 5, 6ab, 7-9
Nil — 4a, 10

Selkirk

Spider — 1, 2abcde, 3-4, 6-8
Nil — 5

Roxburgh

Spider — 1-2, 3ab, 4-8, 9ab, 10-13, 15ab, 16-17, 19-20, 21acdef, 22-28
Nil — 14, 18, 21b

Dumfries

Meggie — 29, 39, 45a
Speedert — 4, 23
Spider — 1a, 2,4-7, 8ab, 9-13, 15-16, 17ab, 18-20, 21b, 22, 24-29, 31bcde, 32-35, 37, 40-42, 44, 45b, 46
Nil — 1b, 3, 14, 21a, 30, 31af, 36, 38, 43, 47-49

Kirkcudbright

Ethercap — 17
Ettercap — 11
Speedert — 4, 8, 15a, 21b
Spider — 1-3, 5-10, 12ab, 14, 15b, 16-19, 21abc, 22-23
Nil — 13, 20, 24=27

Wigtown

Spider — 2, 4, 5a, 6-8, 11-14, 16-17
Weaver — 5a, 10, 18
Nil — 1, 3, 5b, 9, 15

Northumberland

Creepie — 46
Ettercap — 62f
Jennie spinner — 37, 134
Spider — 1a, 2ab, 3, 5-9, 13-18, 19a, 20b, 21, 26, 28, 29ab, 30-31, 34b, 35-36, 38, 40a, 41cd, 42, 45-46, 48, 52, 53ab, 54, 56, 59b, 60, 62bg, 64ab, 65ab, 66, 68, 69abcd, 70, 71abcd, 72bcdgi, 77-78, 82-83, 86-87, 88ab, 89-91, 94b, 98, 99bd, 100, 101ab, 102, 103ac, 104ab, 106-107, 109-110, 111ab, 112, 117, 119, 120abc, 122b, 124b, 126cf, 127ad, 130bce, 132-133, 135, 137-138, 142
Spidert — 69a
Spindly legs — 69b
Spinner — 71c, 127e
Spyther — 69a, 71c, 124a
Nil — 1bc, 4, 10-12, 19b, 20a, 22-23, 24ab, 25, 27, 29cdef, 32, 33ab, 34a, 39, 40b, 41ab, 43-44, 47, 49-51, 55, 57-58, 59acdef, 61, 62acdeh, 63, 67, 69efgh, 71e, 72aefhjkl, 73-76, 79-81, 84-85, 92-93, 94a, 95ab, 96-97, 99ac, 103b, 105, 108abc, 113-116, 118ab, 121, 122a, 123, 125, 126abde, 127bcfgh, 128, 129abc, 130adf, 131, 136, 139-141, 143

Cumberland

Atter — 13a, 30-31, 60, 63b
Attercop — 27
Attercope — 56
Crowley — 43
Money spider — 37b
Spid — 56
Spider — 1a, 3-4, 5a, 7-9, 12, 13c, 14, 15ac, 16, 18, 20-26, 28, 38, 40, 42, 46-50, 52-53, 56-58, 62
Webber — 57
Nil — 1b, 2, 5b, 6, 10-11, 13bd, 15b, 17, 19, 29, 32-36, 37a, 39, 41, 44-45, 51, 54-55, 59, 61, 63a

Down

Spider — 2a, 5-7, 9, 12, 15, 19, 24
Waver — 22
Weaver — 10
Willie waver — 24, 29
Willie weaver — 12, 18, 25-26
Wullie weaver — 13
Nil — 1, 2b, 3-4, 8, 11, 14, 16-17, 20-21, 23, 27-28, 30

Tyrone

Daddy long legs — 12
Spider — 1, 7-8, 10-11
Willie weaver — 4, 11
Wullie weaver — 5
Nil — 2-3, 6, 9, 13-16

Antrim

Atter cap — 24
Spelder — 16b
Spider — 1, 3, 9, 11, 13, 16b, 17, 19-20, 25-29
Waver — 28
Weaver — 4A, 5a, 8b, 10, 15, 16b, 20, 23, 25, 30, 33
Willie waver — 7
Willie weaver — 18, 34
Nil — 2, 4, 5b, 6, 8a, 12, 14, 16ac, 21-22, 31-32

Donegal

Weaver — 6, 7A, 12-13
Willie weaver — 4
Spider — 1, 5, 5A, 8, 10a, 12
Nil — 1A, 2-3, 7, 9, 10b, 11

Fermanagh

Spider — 4-5, 7a, 8-9
Nil — 1-3, 6, 7b, 10

Armagh

Spider — 3-4, 6a
Nil — 1-2, 5, 6b

Londonderry

Spider — 2
Waver — 3, 6
Willie waver — 3A
Willie weaver — 5
Nil — 1, 1AB, 4, 7

85 TADPOLE (PQ1, 179)

Tadpole has not been mapped as it occurs densely nearly everywhere.
The variants of HEAD have been subsumed (**heid** very frequent). Variants of the unstressed vowel in **puddOck** have been subsumed (**-ick, -uck**).
For **puddock** see also 36 **leapfrog.**

Shetland

Tadpole – 16, 21b, 22, 25
Nil – 1-15, 17-20, 21a, 23-24, 26-33

Orkney

Paddo – 1, 12
Paddock – 14
Peerie huppo – 7
Tadpole – 3, 11, 13b, 15-17, 19-20
Young frog – 5
Nil – 2, 4, 6, 8-10, 13a, 18, 21

Caithness

Pellao – 2a, 6
Puddle aid lag – 16a
Tadpole – 2b, 5, 8-9, 11, 13-14, 16b
Young frog – 13
Young puddag – 7, 12b
Nil – 1, 3-4, 10, 12ac, 15, 17

Sutherland

Pellad – 9a
Puddock – 9b
Tadpole – 1, 3-8, 9a, 10-13, 16
Nil – 2, 14-15, 17

Ross & Cromarty

Frog's egg – 25b
Minnow – 24
Paddock – 37a
Tadder – 19
Taddie – 36
Taddock – 6
Tadpole – 1, 3-6, 8-9, 14, 16-18, 20, 25ab, 26-31, 32ab, 34, 39
Nil – 2, 7, 10-13, 15, 21-23, 32c, 33, 35, 37b, 38

Inverness

Tadder – 40
Tadlock – 15
Tadpole – 2-8, 10-11, 13abce, 16-19, 21ab, 22-23, 26-29, 32-39
Nil – 1, 9, 12, 13d, 14, 20, 24-25, 30-31

Nairn

Baanie – 1a
Taddie – 1bc
Tadpole – 1a, 2, 4-5
Nil – 3, 6

Moray

Bandie – 19
Ladle – 3, 8f
Ladlock – 8bf
Paddie – 6a
Paddie ladles – 9a
Taddie – 3, 7, 8c, 9a, 11, 13, 21-22
Tadpole – 4, 6b, 7, 8bd, 14, 23
Tiddlie – 21
Young paddock – 2a
Young puddock – 18
Nil – 1, 2b, 5, 8ae, 9b, 10, 12, 15-17, 20

Banff

Crood – 16
Poddock – 32
Powat – 29
Puddock – 16, 19, 25
Tadder – 23
Taddie – 1, 5, 6b, 17, 18c, 21, 30
Tadpole – 2ab, 4, 8-9, 13, 15, 18c, 21, 23, 34
Willie poorie – 14
Young puddock – 10
Nil – 2c, 3, 6a, 7, 11-12, 18abd, 20, 22, 24, 26-28, 31, 33

Aberdeen

Pow head – 4, 78, 92
Puddock – 15, 40
Spergie – 25
Tad – 47a, 105
Tadder – 5d, 10, 28a, 55, 71c, 72, 85
Taddie – 4, 8-9, 19, 28a, 29, 31, 34, 41, 44, 46, 47a, 48-49, 54, 57, 61, 67, 69, 73-74, 79, 90, 96, 104, 106
Tadpole – 3ab, 6, 8, 11-12, 14, 17, 20-23, 26, 28c, 32, 35, 44-45, 47ef, 49-51, 56, 59-60, 66-67, 70, 74-75, 81-83, 86, 88, 95, 98, 100-101, 103-104, 107-108
Tiddler – 23, 26
Young poddock – 5c
Young puddock – 5a, 10, 28a, 32, 37, 63, 94, 97
Nil – 1-2, 5b, 7, 13, 16, 18, 24, 27, 28b, 30, 33, 36, 38-39, 42-43, 47bcd, 52-53, 58, 62, 64-65, 68, 71ab, 76-77, 80, 84, 87, 89, 91, 93, 99, 102, 109

Kincardine

Bandie – 2, 20
Pow head – 6
Tadder – 1
Taddie – 7, 9, 26
Tadpole – 3, 5-8, 10, 15-16, 17bcd, 19, 21, 24, 28
Tiddler – 15
Puddock – 11-12
Young puddock – 23
Nil – 4, 13-14, 17a, 18, 22, 25, 27

Kinross

Puddock gener – 5
Tadpole – 2-3
Young puddock – 4
Nil – 1, 6-7

Angus

Bandie – 17b
Paddock's egg – 14a
Poutie – 10
Preen headie – 4
Puddock – 18
Taddie – 7, 10, 12-13, 15, 17a, 19, 24, 26-27, 30, 34, 37
Tadpole – 3, 6, 8-9, 14b, 17b, 18, 20, 22, 25, 28, 32, 34-36
Teddie – 14a
Tiddler – 32
Toddie – 18
Young paddock – 31
Nil – 1-2, 5abc, 11, 14cd, 16, 21, 23, 29ab, 33ab

Perth

Baggie – 25
Froggie – 29b
Mute – 55
Paddock splewin – 7
Peenie – 18
Powdie – 20
Pow head – 20
Pownie – 39
Puddock – 39-40, 41b, 51a
Puddock eggs – 25
Puddock span – 67
Taddie – 5, 12-13, 21, 23, 29b, 33, 42-43, 50, 51b, 52c, 56-57, 59, 62, 65-66
Tadpole – 1, 2a, 4, 8-10, 15, 21, 24-25, 27-28, 29a, 32-33, 36, 41a, 46, 48, 52ab, 57,60, 67-68, 71, 74
Tailie puddock – 31
Tiddler – 24, 73
Young puddock – 30
Nil – 2b, 3, 6, 11, 14, 16-17, 19, 22, 26, 34-35, 37-38, 44-45, 47, 49, 52de, 53-54, 58, 61, 63-64, 69-70, 72

Fife

Froggie – 56
Kail ladle – 12, 27
Minnow – 41a
Pin head – 10
Poodlie – 12, 43a, 55d
Polliewig – 55f
Poolie – 40b
Puddock – 56
Taddie – 1, 4, 8, 13, 17, 21-23, 33-34, 36b, 37-39, 41bc, 43ab, 44a, 48, 50, 52, 55g
Tadpole – 4, 9a, 11, 14, 16, 19, 21, 25, 36ab, 37, 41a, 42, 43a, 44b, 46-47, 50, 53, 55abe, 57, 59, 62-63
Tiddie – 33
Tiddlie – 7, 33
Toad – 51
Wullie powrit – 21
Young piddock – 32
Young puddock – 35, 46
Young toad – 56
Nil – 2-3, 5-6, 9b, 15, 18, 20, 24, 26, 28-31, 40a, 41d, 44cdef, 45, 49, 54, 55c, 58, 60-61, 64ab

Clackmannan

Taddie – 4bc, 5-7
Tadpole – 1, 4c
Nil – 2-3, 4ad

Stirling

Baggie – 19
Baggie minnin – 31
Bull head – 26b
Bullie head – 7bd
Pow head – 17, 25abd, 26e, 31, 35ab, 36, 37a, 39b
Puddie doo – 7bd
Puddock – 13
Taddie – 7ae, 8, 10, 22a, 23b, 25ad, 26b, 32-33, 38, 39a, 41, 42a
Tadpole – 4, 7ace, 11, 16, 18, 20, 21ab, 23c, 25c, 26ac, 27a, 28, 30-31, 34, 35a, 36, 37b
Tiddler – 7f, 39b
Tiddlie – 21b
Nil – 1-3, 5-6, 9, 12, 14-15, 22b, 23a, 24, 26df, 27b, 29, 40, 42b

Dunbarton

Beetle head – 6, 10, 16a
Pow head – 9, 14a,
Taddie – 10, 13a, 16b
Tadpole – 1, 3, 6, 7bc, 8, 11, 13bc, 14b, 16ab
Young puddock – 2
Nil – 4ab, 5, 7a, 12, 15, 17-18

Argyll

Beetle head – 29, 31, 39
Tadpole – 1-3, 5-7, 9-11, 14-17, 19, 22-25, 27, 33, 35-36
Young frog – 33
Young puddock – 32
Nil – 4, 8, 12-13, 18, 20-21, 26, 28, 30, 34, 37-38, 40

Bute

Taddie – 8b
Tadpole – 1acd, 2, 7, 8ab, 9
Nil – 1be, 3-6

Ayr

Beetle head – 3
Frog spawn – 47
Pollie wog – 53a
Pow head – 2a, 8b, 11, 12a, 13, 17, 18b, 19, 20cg, 28d, 29, 30a, 32, 35b, 40-41, 49, 57
Puddock – 15, 18b
Taddie – 7, 8b, 9-10, 12a, 14, 18ab, 20g, 28af, 33, 41, 43, 53b
Tadpole – 2ab, 3, 5-6, 8ab, 9-10, 12a, 20bc, 21, 24b, 26b, 28ce, 30ab, 31, 34, 35a, 41-42, 44-45, 48, 52, 53a, 54-57
Teedlie – 36
Tiddlie – 36
Young frog – 15
Young puddock – 47
Nil – 1ab, 4, 12b, 16ab, 20adefh, 22-23, 24a, 25, 26ac, 27, 28b, 37-39, 46, 50-51

Renfrew

Baggie minnin – 2b
Baggie minnow – 16d
Beetle head – 13b, 15
Pow head – 21
Puddock – 2i
Taddie – 5, 11abdi, 16ad, 17, 18ab
Tadpole – 1b, 2ahi, 4acd, 8, 11adefl, 13c, 14a, 16b, 19, 20a
Tiddler – 2b
Nil – 1a, 2cdefgj, 3, 4be, 6-7, 9-10, 11cghjk, 12ab, 13ad, 14b, 16c, 20b

Lanark

Bairdie – 32f
Beardie – 32f
Big head – 38c
Black head – 7c
Laidlock – 17
Newt – 14c
Paddock reed – 11
Paw head – 39
Peen head – 48
Pow head – 9ab, 11, 13, 15b, 20, 27b, 29d, 30, 31d, 32c, 33acd, 36, 38abc, 40, 42, 46a, 47-48, 49b, 53, 56, 59a, 60-61, 65
Puddock – 23, 29f, 32e
Puddock's trawlick – 67a
Taddie – 3, 7a, 16ab, 19, 22, 26a, 27b, 37, 38c, 39, 63
Tadler – 9b
Tadpole – 1-3, 6, 7c, 8ab, 9a, 12, 14b, 15ac, 16ab, 17-19, 25bc, 26a, 29c, 30, 31a, 32a, 33a, 35abcd, 44-45, 46bc, 48, 49ab, 51, 52b, 58, 59b, 60, 62, 64b
Taedred – 38d
Tiddler – 10a
Wee puddock – 45
Young puddock – 17
Nil – 4-5, 7b, 10b, 14ad, 21, 24, 25ad, 26b, 27a, 28 29abeg, 31bc, 32bd, 33b, 34, 38e, 41, 43, 50, 52a, 54-55, 57abc, 64a, 66, 67b

West Lothian

Bandie – 11

West Lothian cont'd

Pow head – 7-8, 17a, 18, 20a, 21a
Puddock – 5
Taddie – 6, 13, 15, 19b
Tadpole – 1a, 3, 6, 9a, 10-13, 15-16, 20a, 22
Nil – 1bcd, 2, 4, 9b, 14, 17b, 19a, 20b, 21b

Midlothian

Minnow – 1
Pow head – 4, 10, 14b
Tad – 5
Taddie – 3, 12ab, 16-18, 25a, 26b
Tadpole – 6ab, 7a, 8a, 10-11, 14a, 18, 21, 23ab, 24, 25c, 28-30
Tiddler – 32
Toad – 20
Towt – 26a
Nil – 2, 7b, 8b, 9, 13, 15, 19, 22, 25bd, 27, 31

East Lothian

Paddie ladle – 6a, 21
Paddie taddle – 2
Paudie – 10
Paw head – 11
Peen head – 4b
Pow head – 9
Puddock – 6b
Taddie – 1, 13
Tadpole – 1, 7, 15-20
Taedie – 13
Nil – 3, 4a, 5, 8, 12, 14

Berwick

Paddie – 4, 14
Paddie ladle – 5, 8, 11, 16b, 22, 26
Pin head – 17
Taddie – 3, 12, 18, 23-24, 27, 31
Tadpole – 1-2, 9-10, 12-13, 15, 16b, 21, 29, 32
Podlie – 13
Wee paddie – 6
Nil – 7, 16ac, 19-20, 25, 28, 30

Peebles

Paddie – 5
Paddie ladle – 4b
Paddie's egg – 4e
Tadder – 2
Tadpole – 1, 3, 4bc, 6ab
Young paddie – 8
Nil – 4a, 7, 9-10

Selkirk

Paddie ladle – 2a
Taddie – 2d
Tadpole – 2bc, 4, 8
Nil – 1, 2e, 3, 5-7

Roxburgh

Paddie – 1, 7-8, 21c
Paddie ladle – 3a, 13, 21ac
Paddie red – 24
Powart – 21c
Pow head – 4, 15b, 21ac, 23, 28
Taddie – 19-20, 22, 26-27
Tadpole – 2, 4, 9a, 13, 16-17, 21adf, 25
Taed – 19
Tammie noddie head – 21c
Nil – 3b, 5-6, 9b, 10-12, 14, 15a, 18, 21be

Dumfries

Frog spawn – 17a
Padda – 29
Paddock – 6, 8b
Paddock rowk – 9, 13
Pow head – 2, 7, 11, 27-28, 42
Taddie – 10, 15, 29, 31d, 35, 45b, 46
Tadpole – 1a, 4-5, 7, 9, 12, 16, 18, 20, 21b, 22, 26, 33, 40
Tiddler – 8a, 24, 46
Young padda – 17b
Young paddock – 17b
Nil – 1b, 3, 14, 19, 21a, 23, 25, 30, 31abcef, 32, 34, 36-39, 41, 43-44, 45a, 47-49

Kirkcudbright

Paddock reed – 4
Paddock rid – 27
Paddock rud – 2
Pow head – 1, 4-5, 15a, 17
Taddie – 1, 12a, 23
Tadpole – 6-7, 10, 12b, 16, 19, 21c, 22
Tiddler – 21c
Young paddock – 17
Nil – 3, 8-9, 11, 13-14, 15b, 18, 20, 21ab, 24-26

Wigtown

Minner – 6
Paddoch red – 8
Paddock – 2
Pow head – 5a, 10, 17
Taddie – 8
Tadpole – 11, 13-14, 16-17
Tiddler – 9
Nil – 1, 3-4, 5b, 7, 12, 15, 18

Northumberland

Baggie – 127b
Bo head – 131
Bull head – 64a, 95a
Bullie head – 79
Frog – 69ab
Little paddock – 98
Logger head – 69b
Mennon – 1a
Newt – 20b
Paddered – 53b
Paddock – 8, 27, 62f, 69ab, 111a, 130c
Pie head – 62a
Po head – 47, 69e, 86, 103bc, 106, 109, 111ab, 124a, 133-134, 138
Pole head – 76
Pow head – 30, 107, 124a
Spawn – 130c
Tad – 94b
Tadder – 84, 118a
Taddie – 12, 26, 28, 45, 49, 52, 53a, 59c, 60, 64b, 68, 69c, 71a, 72b, 76, 83, 92, 99d, 101b, 114, 127c, 143
Taddie pole – 46
Tadger – 71d, 125
Tadpole – 2b, 3, 5-6, 8-9, 13-16, 18, 19a, 21, 26, 28, 29b, 30-31, 34b, 35-36, 38, 40a, 41cd, 42, 45, 53a, 54, 56, 59b, 62ab, 64b, 65ab, 66, 69cdh, 70, 71bcd, 72cdgi, 77-78, 82, 86-87, 88a, 89-90, 95a, 100, 101b, 102, 103abc, 104ab, 106, 111a, 112, 117, 119, 120abc, 124b, 126cf, 127ad, 130ce, 132-133, 135, 137
Tartar – 124b
Tiddler – 5, 18, 22, 64b, 69b, 71c, 78, 88b, 110, 126b, 135, 143
Toad – 69ab, 127e
Tommie noddie – 39
Young paddock – 44
Nil – 1bc, 2a, 4, 7, 10-11, 17, 19b, 20a, 23, 24ab, 25, 29acdef, 32, 33ab, 34a, 37, 40b, 41ab, 43, 48, 50-51, 55, 57-58, 59adef, 61, 62cdegh, 63, 67, 69fg, 71e, 72aefhjkl, 73-75, 80-81, 85, 91, 93, 94a, 95b, 96-97, 99abc, 101a, 105, 108abc, 113, 115-116, 118b, 121, 122ab, 123, 126ade, 127fgh, 128, 129abc, 130abdf, 136, 139-142

Cumberland

Bull head – 13ad, 18, 21, 24, 30-31, 37a, 38, 45-47, 52, 54, 56, 60
Bullie – 38
Frog spawn – 46
Pow head – 3, 5a, 13c
Taddie – 2, 9, 13a, 15ac, 18, 24-25, 28, 33, 37b, 40-43, 56-58, 61
Tadpole – 1a, 4, 7, 9, 12, 13c, 14, 15a, 16, 22-24, 26-27, 40, 48, 50, 53, 56-58, 60
Tiddler – 24
Tommie tiddler – 15b
Nil – 1b, 5b, 6, 8, 10-11, 13b, 17, 19-20, 29, 32, 34-36, 39, 44, 49, 51, 55, 59, 62, 63ab

Down

Beetle head – 5, 11, 13, 17, 19, 22, 26
Frog – 15
Tadpole – 2a, 7, 9, 18, 24
Nil – 1, 2b, 3-4, 6, 8, 10, 12, 14, 16, 20-21, 23-25, 27-30

Tyrone

Beetle – 16
Beetle head – 14
Frog spawn – 8
Spricklie – 15
Tadpole – 1, 7, 10-11
Young frog – 11
Nil – 2-6, 9, 12-13

Antrim

Beetle head – 4A, 12, 15, 16b, 20, 23, 25, 27, 34
Beetlie head – 9, 15
Frog spawn – 18
Puddock – 30
Spawn – 33
Tadpole – 1, 3, 9, 13, 16b, 17, 22, 25-26
Nil – 2, 4, 5ab, 6-7, 8ab, 10-11, 14, 16ac, 19, 21, 24, 28-29, 31-32

Donegal

Frog spawn – 6, 10a
Sprickle back – 5
Spricklie – 5
Tadpole – 1, 5A, 12
Young frog – 8
Nil – 1A, 2-4, 7, 7A, 9, 10b, 11, 13

Fermanagh

Beetle head – 2
Tadpole – 4, 7a, 8
Young frog – 9
Nil – 1, 3, 5-6, 7b, 10

Armagh

Beetle head – 1, 3
Spricklie – 2
Tadpole – 4, 6a
Nil – 5, 6b

Londonderry

Beetle head – 3, 6
Nil – 1, 1AB, 2, 3A, 4-5, 7

86 THE FRY OF THE MINNOW (PQ1, 180)

Some of the items mapped do not show high concentrations. The variants of unstressed vowel in items like **minnIn, mennIn, minnIm**, etc., have been subsumed.

Shetland

Bandie — 21b, 25
Banstickle — 15, 22
Benstickle — 16
Benstinkle — 6
Bonstickle — 9
Fry — 21a, 27
Prigatroot — 2
Stickle back — 16
Nil — 1, 3-5, 7-8, 10-14, 17-20, 23-24, 26, 28-33

Orkney

Brandie — 6, 9, 13a, 20
Brandstickle — 6, 9
Branstickle — 4, 7
Nil — 1-3, 5, 8, 10-12, 13b, 14-19, 21

Caithness

Bitlings — 16b
Brandles — 8
Bran lag — 9
Brannle — 7
Minnow — 16b
Young minnow — 11
Nil — 1, 2ab, 3-6, 10, 12abc, 13-15, 16a, 17

Sutherland

Fry — 6, 8
Minnow fry — 13
Nil — 1-5, 7, 9ab, 10-12, 14-17

Ross & Cromarty

Bairdie — 20
Bantle — 36
Fry — 1, 32a, 34, 39
Geet — 31
Minnow — 16, 20, 27, 32bc
Paddock's spewing — 24
Pars — 27
Rawn — 18
Roe — 18
Smug — 37b
Tiddler — 29, 32b, 35
Nil — 2-15, 17, 19, 21-23, 25ab, 26, 28, 30, 33, 37a, 38

Inverness

Baggie minnow — 8, 40
Bandie — 26
Beelan — 13a
Fry — 1-2, 13b, 18, 29-30
Minnow — 4, 37
Rawn — 27
Tiddler — 14, 19
Nil — 3, 5-7, 9-12, 13cde, 15-17, 20, 21ab, 22-25, 28, 31-36, 38-39

Nairn

Bandie — 1c
Bandlie — 4
Bannie — 1bc
Bawnie — 1c
Nil — 1a, 2-3, 5-6

Moray

Bandie — 2a, 7, 8bcdf, 9a, 11-12, 15-17, 22
Banler — 13, 22
Beardie — 9a
Brodie — 9a
Tiddler — 21-22
Nil — 1, 2b, 3-5, 6ab, 8ae, 9b, 10, 14, 18-20, 23

Banff

Bandie — 2c, 3, 5, 7, 13, 15, 17, 24, 31-32
Bannie — 19, 22
Bawnie — 9
Minnin — 8c, 20, 30, 34
Minnin's crood — 14
Poddlie — 2c
Ran — 6b
Tiddler — 18c, 32
Nil — 1, 2ab, 4, 6a, 8, 10-12, 16, 18abd, 21, 23, 25-29, 33

Aberdeen

Bairnie — 51
Bandie — 3a, 5b, 16-17, 19-20, 27, 28ab, 29, 31, 34-35, 39-40, 45, 47ae, 48, 51, 54-57, 63, 67, 69, 73-75, 77, 87-90, 96-99, 103-108
Bawdie — 46
Fry — 12, 66
Geek — 2
Minnin — 11, 44, 47f
Minnow — 51, 69, 81
Perrie — 3a, 6
Rawn — 14, 23, 25,104
Span — 50
Spawn — 70
Tiddler — 3b, 5b
Tiddler eel — 5b
Trootie — 15
Nil — 1, 4, 5acd, 7-10, 13, 18, 21-22, 24, 26, 28c, 30, 32-33, 36-38, 41-43, 47bcd, 49, 52-53, 58-62, 64-65, 68, 71abc, 72, 76, 78-80, 82-86, 91-95, 100-102, 109

Kincardine

Bandie — 1, 3-4, 7-8, 10, 12, 15-16, 17bd, 19, 21, 26
Pin head — 17c
Ran — 28
Tiddler — 24
Nil — 2, 5-6, 9, 11, 13-14, 17a, 18, 20, 22-23, 25, 27

Kinross

Baggie — 2-3
Baggie minnin — 3
Tiddler — 3
Nil — 1, 4-7

Angus

Baggie — 37
Baggie minnin — 9
Bandie — 5c, 25, 27, 29a
Minnin — 9, 12, 14cd, 22, 34, 36
Parr — 31
Pin head — 13, 20-21, 24
Preen head — 7, 23
Preen headie — 4, 5c
Stickle back — 33b
Tiddler — 6, 14a, 25
Nil — 1-3, 5ab, 8, 10-11, 14b, 15-16, 17ab, 18-19, 26, 28, 29b, 30, 32, 33a, 35

Perth

Attock — 14
Baggie — 28, 29a, 37, 40, 52ac, 62-63, 70
Baggie minnin — 1, 7, 16, 41b, 51b, 56, 62-63
Baggie minnow — 8, 21, 67
Beldie — 39
Brannie — 59
Fry — 4, 52b, 57
Minnin — 46, 69
Minnow — 8, 21
Needleck — 39
Needlie — 67
Parr — 57
Pin head — 5, 11-12, 15, 24, 27, 29b, 31-32, 41a, 44, 48, 52cd, 66, 71
Pinnie head — 52d
Prannie — 60
Preen head — 13, 20, 32
Spawn — 8, 25
Tiddler — 26-27, 41a, 45, 50, 52a, 53, 64
Nil — 2ab, 3, 6, 9-10, 17-19, 22-23, 30, 33-36, 38, 42-43, 47, 49, 51a, 52e, 54-55, 58, 61, 65, 68, 72-74

Fife

Baggie — 18, 46
Baggie minnin — 21
Bairdie — 25, 36b
Brannie — 7
Mennin — 51
Minnie — 30, 33
Minnin — 8, 13, 16, 37, 40b, 44c, 46, 55b
Pin head — 11, 20, 37, 39, 40b, 53-54, 55dfg, 62
Podlie — 12, 44ac
Spawn — 10, 57, 61, 63
Tiddler — 28, 42, 44b, 49, 55deg
Tiddlie — 55e
Nil — 1-6, 9ab, 14-15, 17, 19, 22-24, 26-27, 29, 31-32, 34-35, 36a, 38, 40a, 41abcd, 43ab, 44def, 45, 47-48, 50, 52,55ac, 56, 58-60, 64ab

Clackmannan

Baggie — 4c, 6
Baggie mennin — 4b
Mennin — 1, 4c
Pin head — 4b
Tiddler — 5
Nil — 2-3, 4ad, 7

Stirling

Baggie — 7be, 9, 21ab, 25c, 27a
Baggie mennin — 21b, 23c, 26df, 37a, 39b
Baggie minnin — 23b, 27a
Baggie minnow — 6, 7be, 8
Fry — 36
Guttie — 9
Guttie minnow — 8
Mennin — 25c
Mennin's egg — 37b
Minnow — 30
Pin head — 7ac, 8-10, 17-18, 25bd, 26abe, 33, 35a, 38, 40, 42a
Pinkhead — 4
Pinnie — 20, 26b
Spang — 28, 32
Spawn — 36
Sprawn — 35b
Tiddler — 7bde, 12
Nil — 1-3, 5, 7f, 11, 13-16, 19, 22ab, 23a, 24, 25a, 26c, 27b, 29, 31, 34, 39a, 41, 42b

Dunbarton

Baggie — 1, 3, 6, 7bc, 9, 11
Baggie minnin — 7c, 15
Baggie minnow — 8
Baggie ride — 14a
Minnow — 13c
Minnow ride — 14a
Pin head — 2, 7a, 10, 13bc, 14b, 16ab
Spawn — 16a
Tiddler — 12
Nil — 4ab, 5, 13a, 17-18

Argyll

Baggie — 36
Baggie minnow — 2, 8, 19, 24
Cuddie — 18
Fry — 7, 9, 11, 17, 27, 33
Minnow fry — 22
Pin head — 15
Pinnie head — 37
Shachle — 36-38
Shachles doctors — 35
Start — 33
Nil — 1, 3-4, 10, 12-14, 16, 20-21, 23, 25-26, 28-32, 34, 39-40

Bute

Baggie mennin — 5
Baggie minnow — 1cd, 7
Elf — 2
Nil — 1abe, 3-4, 6, 8ab, 9

Ayr

Baggie — 20c, 41, 53ab, 54, 57
Baggie minnin — 54
Baggie minnow — 18b
Bainie — 56
Beardie — 16a
Minnin — 1a, 2b, 16a
Minnit — 17
Minnow — 2b, 43
Mintie — 10, 18b, 43, 48
Needles — 49
Needles and pins — 24b
Needles and preens — 15
Paddock ride — 19
Pin head — 7,8b, 10, 12ab, 13-15, 16b, 18b, 20abdeg, 21, 28f, 34, 35b, 37-38, 42, 46, 55
Pinnie — 20bg, 33
Pins and needles — 5, 24a
Powan — 57
Preen head — 30a, 36
Spawn — 51
Tiddler — 6, 18ab, 31-32
Nil — 1b, 2a, 3-4, 8a, 9, 11, 20fh, 22-23, 25, 26abc, 27, 28abcde, 29, 30b, 35a, 39-40, 44-45, 47, 50, 52

Renfrew

Baggie — 2e, 11a, 16cd
Baggie mennin — 21
Baggie minnin — 11ace, 16a
Baggie minnow — 11bf, 14a
Bogie — 11j
Bogie minnin — 11c
Fry — 8, 16b
Minnin — 2ahi, 5
Minnow — 2i
Pin head — 2bhi, 8, 11kl, 14a, 16b, 17, 20b
Podlie — 6
Preen head — 14b
Spawn — 4d, 16a
Tiddler — 11d
Nil — 1ab, 2cdfgj, 3, 4abce, 7, 9-10, 11ghi, 12ab, 13abcd, 15, 18ab, 19, 20a

Lanark

Baggie — 4-5, 7ac, 10a, 18, 22, 25bd, 27b, 28, 29c, 30, 31c, 32a, 33b, 64b
Baggie mennin — 20, 32d, 35a, 60, 64a
Baggie minnie — 25c
Baggie minnin — 27b, 29f, 61
Baggie minnow — 7c
Bairdie — 60
Fry — 49a
Mennin — 33b, 35c, 52a, 59b
Minnow — 29f
Needle — 45, 47, 57c, 65
Pin head — 1-3, 7b, 9a, 15b, 16b, 25c, 29c, 30, 31bd, 33bcd, 34, 35d, 38ce, 39, 41, 44-45, 46bc, 49b, 51, 52ab, 58, 59a, 63, 66
Pins and needles — 57b
Pow head — 23, 38d
Preen head — 9a, 13

Lanark cont'd

Roe – 62
Spawn – 17
Swarm – 44
Tiddler – 14b, 15a, 32d, 38a
Young mennin – 15c, 47
Young minnow – 26a
Nil – 6, 8ab, 9b, 10b, 11-12, 14acd, 16a, 19, 21, 24, 25a, 26b, 27a, 29abdeg, 31a, 32bcef, 33a, 35b, 36-37, 38b, 40, 42-43, 46a, 48, 50, 53-56, 57a, 67ab

West Lothian

Baggie – 20a
Bainie – 19b
Bandie – 11
Mennin – 1b, 4, 9a, 12, 15, 20a, 21a
Minnin – 7
Minnow – 22
Pin head – 1a, 9b, 11, 13, 16, 18
Young minnin – 8
Nil – 1cd, 2-3, 5-6, 10, 14, 17ab, 19a, 20b, 21b

Midlothian

Baggie – 24
Bessie bairdie – 32
Mennant – 30
Mennin – 4, 11, 17, 20, 24
Minnin – 7a, 19
Pin head – 3, 6a, 10, 12a, 14b, 16, 18-19, 23b, 29
Tiddler – 6a
Nil – 1-2, 5, 6b, 7b, 8ab, 9, 12b, 13, 14a, 15, 21-22, 23a, 25abcd, 26ab, 27-28, 31

East Lothian

Baggie minnin – 7
Fry – 6a, 17
Mennin – 6a, 14
Pin head – 8-9, 13
Red – 2
Spawn – 4ab, 6b
Nil – 1, 3, 5, 10-12, 15-16, 18-21

Berwick

Bairdie – 9
Mennant – 4
Mennet – 11
Mennin – 10, 18
Mentie – 3, 27
Mintie – 8
Needle – 8
Needle preen – 17
Padarine – 27
Pin head – 15, 16b, 21-23, 27, 29, 31-32
Stickle back – 27
Tiddler – 17, 32
Tiddlie – 17
Nil – 1-2, 5-7, 12-14, 16ac, 19-20, 24-26, 28, 30

Peebles

Baggie – 5
Baggie minnin – 9
Fry – 8
Mennin – 1, 3
Minnow fry – 6a
Needle – 4b
Pin head – 2, 4bc, 5, 6a, 7
Preen head – 2
Red breast – 5
Tiddler – 10
Nil – 4a, 6b

Selkirk

Baggie – 2e
Baggie mennin – 2a
Mennant – 2cd
Needle – 2d
Pin head – 2cd, 3
Preen head – 1
Nil – 2b, 4-8

Roxburgh

Baggie – 19-20, 21cf, 22
Bag mentie – 22
Bessie bairdie – 10
Mennant – 6, 9a
Mennet – 7
Mennet red – 13
Menning – 18
Needle – 3a, 15b, 21c
Pin head – 9b, 13, 21d
Preen head – 5, 8, 12, 15b, 16-17, 21a, 23
Roe – 25
Nil – 1-2, 3b, 4, 11, 14, 15a, 21be, 24, 26-28

Dumfries

Alevin – 35
Baggie – 3-4, 6, 11-12, 16, 22, 28, 31d, 39, 41, 45a
Baggie minnie 44
Baggie minnin – 15, 20, 32
Baggie minnow – 46
Beardie – 4
Minnin – 19, 24
Parr – 31b
Pin head – 2, 8a, 9, 21b, 26, 31c, 32
Preen head – 17a
Rowan – 13
Rowk – 8b
Tiddler – 1a
Watch pointer – 29
Wee baggie – 5, 32
Wee minnin – 10
Nil – 1b, 7, 14, 17b, 18, 21a, 23, 25, 27, 30, 31aef, 33-34, 36-38, 40, 42-43, 45b, 47-49

Kirkcudbright

Baggie – 5, 9, 15a, 16-17, 21b
Baggie minnin – 9, 14
Bairdie – 12b
Beel goit – 15a
Fry – 7
Minnin – 2
Minnow – 6
Pin head – 1, 4, 11
Span – 10
Tiddler – 3, 16
Wee baggie – 18
Nil – 8, 12a, 13, 15b, 19-20, 21ac, 22-27

Wigtown

Baggie – 1, 10
Baggie minnow – 1, 7-8
Minnie fry – 14
Minnow spawn – 11
Pickie – 2
Pin head – 7
Tiddler – 12
Wee herrin – 18
Nil – 3-4, 5ab, 6, 9, 13, 15-17

Northumberland

Baggie – 42, 51, 59f
Baggie minnim – 68
Baggie minnow – 46
Fry – 2b, 22, 31, 59b, 88b, 112
Fry of the mennim – 45
Harnie – 76, 118ab
Kelk – 124a
Lie – 77
Meddum – 17, 40a, 41b, 47, 50, 59d, 62bdegh, 64a, 65b, 71a, 72d, 82
Melt – 20b, 30, 110
Mennant – 29f
Mennim – 13, 29bd, 49, 63, 106
Mennin – 51
Mentie – 8
Midgie – 118a
Minnim – 17, 53b, 62g, 71d, 98, 122b
Minnow – 26, 82, 103c, 118b, 138
Minnow's egg – 126c
Mintie – 9, 59c, 124b
Pin head – 26, 43, 56, 59e, 79, 101b, 104a, 118a
Roe – 64b, 69c, 81, 124a
Shoal – 16
Shoal of baggus – 118b
Small fry – 69ab
Small minnim – 111ab
Spawn – 21, 41c, 81, 87, 124a, 130ce
Spawn lockie – 59c
Stickler – 11, 72d
Tiddler – 2a, 18, 25, 29b, 33b, 39, 46-48, 50, 53b, 59bc, 61, 62egh, 68, 69a, 71ad, 72i, 73, 75 79-80, 83-84, 88a, 100, 104a, 105-106, 111ab, 118ab, 122a, 124b, 126f, 127bcdhi, 129ab, 130af, 141-142
Tommie – 72d
Tommie lie lodger – 77
Tommie lie loucher – 78
Young meddum – 62a
Young mennim – 62a
Young minnow – 40a
Nil – 1abc, 3-7, 10, 12, 14-15, 19ab, 20a, 23, 24ab, 27-28, 29ace, 32, 33a, 34ab, 35-38, 40a, 41ad, 44, 52, 53a, 54-55, 57-58, 59a, 60, 62cf, 65a, 66-67, 69defgh, 70, 71bce, 72abcefghjkl, 74, 85-86, 89-93, 94ab, 95ab, 96-97, 99abcd, 101a, 102, 103ab, 104b, 107, 108abc, 109, 113-117, 119, 120abc, 121, 123, 125, 126abde, 127aefg, 128, 129c, 130bd, 131-137, 139-140, 143

Cumberland

Fry – 4
Liggie – 13d
Little mennim – 24
Mennim – 46
Minnim – 54, 60
Minnow fry – 47-48
Pin head – 9, 12, 16, 43, 47
Tiddler – 2, 8, 15b, 17, 21, 28, 40, 42, 46, 50, 56-57, 61, 63b
Tommie – 15b
Tommie mennim – 30-31
Tommie minnim – 51, 57
Tommie minnin – 62
Tommie minnow – 28, 53
Young menner – 56
Young mennim – 56
Nil – 1ab, 3, 5ab, 6-7, 10-11, 13abc, 14, 15ac, 18-20, 22-23, 25-27, 29, 32-36, 37ab, 38-39, 41, 44-45, 49, 52, 55, 58-59, 63a

Down

Spreckle back – 13
Sprick – 7, 12, 20, 26
Sprickle bone – 15
Spricklie back – 23-24
Stickleback – 5
Sticky back – 23
Tiddler – 27
Nil – 1, 2ab, 3-4, 6, 8-11, 14, 16-19, 21-22, 25, 28-30

Tyrone

Jinkin – 5
Minnie – 6
Sprick – 11
Spricklie – 2, 13, 15
Nil – 1, 3-4, 7-10, 12, 14, 16

Antrim

Gillygowan – 31
Minnow – 9
Pin heed – 15
Sprick – 17, 31
Spricklie back – 31
Spricklie bag – 17
Stickle back – 4A
Sticky bag – 17
Stricklie – 16b
Stricklie back – 11
Stricklie bag – 13, 16b, 19
Tadpole – 33
Nil – 1-4, 5ab, 6-7, 8ab, 10, 12, 14, 16ac, 18, 20-30, 32, 34

Donegal

Gilleog – 12
Pinkeen – 13
Spawn – 6, 10a
Sprat – 13
Sprick – 5
Sprickle bag – 7A
Nil – 1, 1A, 2-4, 5A, 7-9, 10b, 11

Fermanagh

Minnow – 5
Striddlie – 1, 4-6
Tiddler – 6
Nil – 2-3, 7ab, 8-10

Armagh

Sprick – 4
Spricklie beg – 4
Nil – 1-3, 5, 6ab

Londonderry

Spricklie back – 3
Spricklie bag – 1B, 4, 6
Nil – 1, 1A, 2, 3A, 5, 7

87 COUCH GRASS (PQ1, 181)

Variants of the element GRASS have been subsumed (**girs** Orkney, Aberdeenshire, Kincardineshire; a few scattered **gress**).

Shetland

Aukrabong – 6
Burra – 10
Couch grass – 22
Floss – 2
Kwigga – 21b, 30
Soorike – 7
Trow's cairds – 26
Whigga – 5, 9, 17, 19, 30
Nil – 1, 3-4, 8, 11-16, 18, 20, 21a, 23-25, 27-29, 31-33

Orkney

Bent – 4
Harle grass – 20
Hen pen – 17
Mettus – 7
Moors – 1-2
Runnin grass – 7
Sinnie grass – 11-12, 13ab
Swinie beeds – 16
Wire grass – 13a, 15-16, 18-19
Nil – 3, 5-6, 8-10, 14, 21

Caithness

Couch grass – 11, 16b
Knot grass – 8, 14
Knottie grass – 15
Lelan grass – 5
Stolon – 12b
Taa – 12b
Nil – 1, 2ab, 3-4, 6-7, 9-10, 12ac, 13, 16a, 17

Sutherland

Bindweed – 4
Couch grass – 7-8, 10, 16
Grass – 11
Knottie grass – 8
Weed grass – 1
Nil – 2-3, 5-6, 9ab, 12-15, 17

Ross & Cromarty

Bindweed – 18, 32b
Couch grass – 1, 3, 8-9, 16-17, 20, 28-29, 31, 32a, 34, 39
Cur knot – 18
Knot weed – 35
Onion couch – 9
Quickens – 11
Scuttch grass – 27
Sook sooracks – 24
Stringers – 6
Stringie weeds – 33
String weed – 37a
Twich grass – 27
Vases – 25b
Nil – 2, 4-5, 7, 10, 12-15, 19, 21-23, 25a, 26, 30, 32c, 36, 37b, 38

Inverness

Bent – 1
Couch grass – 2, 6, 10-11, 13abe, 21b, 22-23, 26-29, 34, 37
Feur a' phuint – 26
Knot grass – 6
Quickens – 13e, 15
Weed – 38
Nil – 3-5, 7-9, 12, 13cd, 14, 16-20, 21a, 24-25, 30-33, 35-36, 39-40

Nairn

Fluff grass – 1b
Knot grass – 5
Quicken(s) – 1bc, 3
Nil – 1a, 2, 4, 6

Moray

Couch grass – 2a, 7, 8d, 20
Cra' fit grass – 19
Grass – 8b
Knap grass – 1, 6b, 7, 17-18, 21
Knot grass – 7
Lonachies – 9a
Quicken(s) – 11, 16, 22
Rack – 22
Runner weed – 3
Sprotts – 9a
Weeds – 14
Weyds – 7
Nil – 2b, 4-5, 6a, 8acef, 9b, 10, 12-13, 15, 23

Banff

Bent – 2b, 20
Couch grass – 8, 27
Deer grass – 6b
Grass – 2a
Knap grass – 16, 18cd, 25, 32, 34
Knot grass – 1, 10, 15-16, 19, 23, 26
Pluff grass – 31
Quicken – 9
Stringie weed – 4, 22
Stringle – 8
String weed – 32
Trailie weed – 24
Twitch grass – 5
Weed – 17
Nil – 2c, 3, 6a, 7, 11-14, 18ab, 21, 28-30, 33

Aberdeen

Bent(s) (grass) – 3a, 9, 23, *47f*, 95
Cock's fit – 105
Cooth grass – 101
Couch grass – 5d, 6, 12, 22, 32, 44, 51, 67, 104-105, 108
Gosk – 21
Grass – 66
Growth – 3a, 47ab
Knaps – 105
Knobs – 105
Knot grass – 2, 3b, 10-11, 28b, 29, 34, 39-40, 46, 48, 50, 56, 58, 64, 69. 71bc, 72. 74, 104, 106
Nater grass – 97
Pluff grass – 24-25
Quicken – 28a
Reemick(s) – 79-80, 82, 93
Remmicks – 86
Rimmicks – 96
Rinnin grass – 14, 51
Runner grass – 60
Runnin grass – 47e
Rymmachs – 81
Saut grass – 9
Sea bent – 9
Siller grass – 19
Stickie Willie – 52
Stickie Wullie – 91
String grass – 5b, 17, 20, 35, 37, 41, 44-45, 47bc, 75, 88
Stringie weed – 28a
String weed(s) – 6, 86, 98
Timothy grass – 70
Trailie grass – 100
Trailie growth – 31
Trailie wides – 27
Wild running grass – 15
Wrack – 107
Nil – 1, 4, 5ac, 7-8, 13, 16, 18, 26, 28c, 30, 33, 36, 38, 42-43, 47d, 49, 53-55, 57, 59, 61-63, 65, 68, 71a, 73, 76-78, 83-85, 87, 89-90, 92, 94, 99, 102-103, 109

Kincardine

Couch grass – 6, 8, 10, 14, 17b, 19
Grass – 23, 25
Knot grass – 26
Lonach – 7, 24, 28
Natur' grass – 5
Pluff grass – 21
Reemach – 7
Reemicks – 4, 6
Reemish – 3
Stringie grass – 1
Stringie weeds – 5
Twitch – 6
Wrack – 17b
Nil – 2, 9, 11-13, 15-16, 17acd, 18, 20, 22, 27

Kinross

Knot grass – 4
Quicken(s) – 2, 5
Wrack – 2-3
Nil – 1, 6-7

Angus

Couch grass – 18
Knot grass – 2, 14a
Lonach – 4, 5bc, 13, 17a, 18, 27
Lornach – 18
Quick – 25
Quicken – 3, 9, 13, 14ab, 15, 21-23, 25, 31, 33b, 34, 36
Rough grass – 35
Stickie Willie – 10
Tnot grass – 14a
Wrack – 9, 11, 20, 22, 24, 26, 28, 30, 32, 33b, 34, 37
Nil – 1, 5a, 6-8, 12, 14cd, 16, 17b, 19, 29ab, 33a

Perth

Bent – 25
Couch grass – 4, 8, 24, 29a, 52b, 67
Couck grass – 28
Craw tae – 41b
Dog grass – 66
Fail grass – 25
Grass – 74
Knot grass – 9, 13, 24-25, 33, 62
Moss crop – 7
Purl grass – 73
Purlie grass – 68
Quicken(s) – 13, 15-16, 18, 20, 29a, 31, 33, 39, 44-45, 50, 51a, 52d, 62
Quitch grass – 24
Skelloch – 51b
Wrack – 1, 10, 15, 20, 27, 29ab, 31, 40, 41a, 46, 52a, 60, 64-65, 71
Nil – 2ab, 3, 5-6, 11-12, 14, 17, 19, 21-23, 26, 30, 32, 34-38, 42-43, 47-49, 52ce, 53-59, 61, 63, 69-70, 72

Fife

Bear grass – 55f
Bent – 52, 55d
Chain grass – 40b
Couch (grass) – 44*ac*, *50*
Grass – 43a
Knot grass – 35, 36a, 42, 44a, 59
Onion grass – 35
Quecken – 6
Quick – 40b
Quicken(s) – 2, 4, 7, 12-14, 21, 59
Threshes – 54
Twitch grass – 53
Wrack (grass) – 2, 4, 6, 8, 10-13, 16-17, *20*-21, 23, 28-30, 36a, 39, 41d, 43a, 44d, 45, 47-*48*, 50-51, 55bce, 57, 61-63
Nil – 1, 3, 5, 9ab, 15, 18-19, 22, 24-27, 31-34, 36b, 37-38, 40a, 41abc, 43b, 44bef, 46, 49, 55ag, 56, 58, 60, 64ab

Clackmannan

Coorse grass – 4d
Rough grass – 4d
Wrack – 2, 5-7
Nil – 1, 3, 4abc

Stirling

Bent – 7b
Coorse grass – 22b
Couch grass – 4, 12, 17, 23c, 25c, 36
Felt – 31
Fog – 27b
Green grass – 20
Knot grass – 6, 7e, 10, 18, 35b, 42a
Knotted grass – 34
Puck – 8
Purl grass – 15, 30
Quicken(s) – 7d, 35b
Quitch grass – 25d
Rough grass – 12
Scoutch – 7a
Scutch grass – 28
Stickie Willie – 31
String grass – 33
Twitch – 33, 36
Wrack – 7b, 9, 21ab, 22a, 24, 25b, 26ac, 27a, 37a, 39a
Yorkshire fug – 2
Nil – 1, 3, 5, 7cf, 11, 13-14, 16, 19, 23ab, 25a, 26bdef, 29, 32, 35a, 37b, 38, 39b, 40-41, 42b

Dunbarton

Couch grass – 4b, 7b, 13c, 14b, 16a
Felt – 3, 13a
Gorse – 1
Gowt grass – 7c
Grass – 11
Knaps – 14a
Quick – 14b
Quickens – 14a
Scotch grass – 7a
Scutch grass – 5, 9
Sword grass – 2
Twitch – 4a
Wrack – 4a, 13a
Nil – 6, 8, 10, 12, 13b, 15, 16b, 17-18

Argyll

Bents – 35
Couch grass – 2-3, 6, 9, 11, 18, 22-23, 33
Gonnyer – 39
Grass – 15, 17, 25
Hill grass – 1
Knot grass – 7, 10, 32
Knotted grass – 33
Knottie grass – 29, 39
Pearl grass – 29
Pirl grass – 39
Quickens – 19
Twitch (grass) – 19, *24*, 33
Nil – 4-5, 8, 12-14, 16, 20-21, 26-28, 30-31, 34, 36-38, 40

Bute

Bent – 8a
Couch grass – 1a, 2, 8b, 9
Goinyer – 9
Gonyer – 7
Keeb – 8a
Twitch – 4, 7
Weld grass – 3
Nil – 1bcde, 5-6

Ayr

Bent(s) – 36, 53b
Cock's fit – 24b
Couch grass – 1a, 2b, 6, 8a, 24b, 36, 45
Cowrce grass – 21
Cowt's grass – 9

Ayr cont'd

Dog grass — 8a
Factor — 10
Flig — 3
Knot(ted) grass — 1a
Quicken(s) — 6-7, 8a, 9-11, 12a, 13-14, 16ab, 18ab, 20adegh, 26b, 28bef, 29, 30a, 31-34, 35b, 41-42, 44-48, 51, 53a, 54, 56-57
Quick (grass) — 8b, *20g*
Reegrass — 4
Runches — 56
Scruibie grass — 19
Sprowt grass — 35b
Tenant grass — 1a
Tenant weed — 8a
Tiger grass — 1b
Twitch grass — 8a, 20c, 57
Wrack — 5
Nil — 2a, 12b, 15, 17, 20bf, 22-23, 24a, 25, 26ac, 27, 28acd, 30b, 35a, 37-40, 43, 49-50, 52, 55

Renfrew

Bent — 16d
Couch grass — 2abi, 4ac, 8, 11bf, 16b, 17, 19, 20a
Creepers — 16a
Deil's grass — 14b
Felt — 9, 13c
Grass — 13c
Ket — 21
Quick — 13c
Quickens — 19
Rank grass — 11a
Scutch grass — 5
Stringie wicker — 20b
Wire grass — 2a
Wrack — 21
Nil — 1ab, 2cdefghj, 3, 4bde, 6-7, 10, 11cdeghijkl, 12ab, 13abd, 14a, 15, 16c, 18ab

Lanark

Bent — 32d, 60, 64b
Bishop's weed — 33d
Coarse grass — 7a, 15c
Couch grass — 1-2, 7c, 8b, 9a, 15ac, 25c, 26a, 29d, 35d, 39, 43-44, 46a, 47, 49a
Felt (grass) — 9ab, 16b, 17, 22, *35a*
Furze — 29f
Grass — 27b, 29c
Hiucck grass — 3
Ingin grass — 20
Knot grass — 32c
Lonnachs — 17
Pearl weed — 52a
Purl (grass) — *15a, 16b, 30,* 31d, *45,* 46c, *58*
Quick(s) — 12, 32f, 34, 37, 38abd, 48, 57b
Quitch (grass) — 13, *15c*
Shekels — 27a
Silver shekle — 18
Spear grass — 47
Twitch — 13, 31c, 55
Whin — 29f
Winnle strae(s) — 42, 66
Wrack (grass) — 13, 15b, 24, 31d, 32c, 33bcd, 35d, 38c, 39, 48, 49b, 50-51, 52b, 53, 55-56, 57abc, 58, 59ab, *62*-63
Nil — 4-6, 7b, 8a, 10ab, 11, 14abcd, 16a, 19, 21, 23, 25abd, 26b, 28, 29abeg, 31ab, 32abe, 33a, 35bc, 36, 38e, 40-41, 46b, 54, 61, 64a, 65, 67ab

West Lothian

Coarse grass — 2
Couch fit — 15
Couch grass — 6
Horse grass — 17a
Knotted grass — 3
Rank grass — 16
Rats' tails — 11
Wrack — 1a, 5, 7-8, 9a, 12-13, 17a, 19b
Nil — 1bcd, 4, 9b, 10, 14, 17b, 18, 19a, 20ab, 21ab, 22

Midlothian

Cocktail grass — 4
Couch grass — 6a, 18, 21
Knot grass — 14b, 26a
Quicks — 10
Twitch — 30
Wrack — 3, 6b, 7a, 8b, 10-11, 12ab, 13, 14a, 16, 18, 23b, 25c, 26a, 27, 29-30, 32
Wrawk — 23a
Nil — 1-2, 5, 7b, 8a, 9, 15, 17, 19-20, 22, 24, 25abd, 26b, 28, 31

East Lothian

Bent(s) — 4a, 6b, 9, 11
Cocks fit — 10
Couch grass — 4b
Twitch (grass) — 8, *13*
Wrack — 2-3, 4a, 6ab, 7-8, 14-20
Nil — 1, 5, 12, 21

Berwick

Bent — 23
Couch grass — 32
Quickens — 31
Sketch rot — 27
Twitch — 23
Whicken — 8
Wrack — 3, 5, 8, 10, 12, 14, 16ab, 17-19, 21-22, 25, 27, 31-32
Nil — 1-2, 4, 6-7, 9, 11, 13, 15, 16c, 20, 24, 26, 28-30

Peebles

Couch grass — 4b, 6b
Quitch — 2
Wrack — 5, 6a, 7-9
Nil — 1, 3, 4ac, 10

Selkirk

Bull grass — 2d
Lady's garter — 2b
Wrack — 2a, 6
Nil — 1, 2ce, 3-5, 7-8

Roxburgh

Bull snoots — 15b
Couch grass — 21f
Cricken grass — 13
Crickens — 17, 21c
Quickens — 7, 10, 17, 21c
Spret — 23
Twutch — 28
Whickens — 21c
Wrack — 2, 3a, 4-6, 8, 9b, 12-13, 17-18, 20, 21a, 24-25, 28
Wrawck — 26
Nil — 1, 3b, 9a, 11, 14, 15a, 16, 19, 21bde, 22, 27

Dumfries

Bent — 27
Bull snoots — 5
Couch grass — 4, 12, 17a
Johnnie weet the feet — 21a
Knot grass — 46
Quicken(s) — 1a, 9-10, 13, 19, 21b, 22, 24, 26, 28, 31cde, 42
Shivering grass — 29, 39
Twitch (grass) — 8a, 15-*16,* 18, 25, 34-37, 40, 43, 45a, 46
Twutch — 46
Winnle strae — 8b
Winnle straws — 20
Wullie wat the feet — 37
Wundle strae — 19
Wunnle straw — 12, 19
Nil — 1b, 2-3, 6-7, 11, 14, 17b, 23, 30, 31abf, 32-33, 38, 41, 44, 45ab, 47-49

Kirkcudbright

Bent — 27
Blaw grass — 4
Couch grass — 6
Knot grass — 24
Quicken(s) — 1-3, 7-9, 12ab, 13, 15a, 17, 19, 21c
Rashes — 23
Twitch (grass) — *7,* 9
Whinnle straw — 16
Wild cocks fit — 10
Wunnle strae — 4, 18
Nil — 5, 11, 14, 15b, 20, 21ab, 22, 25-26

Wigtown

Coolts grass — 6
Doggins — 14
Quicken grass — 5a, 11
Quicken(s) — 1-3, 5b, 6, 10, 12, 15-18
Nil — 4, 7-9, 13

Northumberland

Bent (grass) — *20b,* 24a, 72b, 124a
Blue grass — 64b
Bull's face — 102
Bull's lug — 29d
Couch grass — 13, 29b, 31, 35, 41c, 42, 46, 54, 64a, 71c, 72d, 88a, 103a, 112, 127a
Ditherie dock — 76, 99c
Dog grass — 69b
Fannie grass — 69a, 134
Grass — 87
Lady grass — 134
Quick — 77, 114
Quicken(s) — 2a, 10-11, 20a, 25, 27, 29a, 69a, 104a, 134
Quitch — 71c, 124a
Rack — 1b, 2a, 8, 16, 25, 29a, 59b, 69a, 134
Soldier's buttons — 59b
Tannie grass — 25
Twitch (grass) — 1b, 29f, 33a, 34a, 44, 47, 51, *71c,* 73-74, 78, *81,* 103bc, 105-106, *110,* 114, *129b,* 132
Weed — 127e
Whick — 77
Whicken grass — 6, 18, 59d, 74, 133
Whicken roots — 34a
Whicken(s) — 3-4, 9-10, 12, 14-16, 19a, 20b, 21, 26, 30, 33b, 37-38, 41a, 44, 51, 53a, 60, 62f, 65b, 66, 68, 72a, 75, 77, 104a, 107, 110, 122a, 126f, 142
White couch — 71c
White rut — 120b
Wick — 50
Wicken grass — 35, 40a, 80, 86, 88b, 98, 99d, 111ab, 117, 119, 122b, 124b, 126c, 127f, 128, 130bc
Wicken(s) — 1bc, 2a, 7, 17, 22, 24b, 27-28, 29cf, 33a, 39, 43, 45, 47-48, 50, 52, 53b, 54, 57, 59ace, 62f, 63, 64b, 65a, 66, 68, 69deg, 71d, 72ef, 78, 81, 83, 90, 99b, 101a, 103bc, 106, 108c, 109, 114, 116, 118b, 120c, 126ae, 127bdgh, 129b, 130a, 131-132, 134-138, 141
Nil — 1a, 2b, 5, 19b, 23, 29e, 32, 34b, 36, 40b, 41bd, 49, 55-56, 58, 59f, 61, 62abcdegh, 67, 69cfh, 70, 71abe, 72cghijkl, 79, 82, 84-85, 89, 91-93, 94ab, 95ab, 96-97, 99a, 100, 101b, 104b, 108ab, 113, 115, 118a, 120a, 121, 123, 125, 126bd, 127c, 129ac, 130def, 139-140, 143

Cumberland

Bent — 61
Black twitch — 13a
Button grass — 13a
Button twitch — 13a
Couch grass — 4, 13c, 46
Doddering grass — 25
Grass — 50
Havver grass — 13a
Rattle grass — 16
Rib grass — 13c
Scrag — 56
Scutch — 55
Stitch — 60
Trash — 56
Twitch — 1a, 2-3, 5a, 7-9, 12, 13b, 14, 15abc, 16-18, 20-22, 24, 26-29, 31-33, 36, 37ab, 38-42, 44-46, 48-49, 51-52, 54, 56-60, 62, 63a
Whing — 60
Whitlow grass — 46
Wick — 57, 63ab
Winnel — 15c
Nil — 1b, 5b, 6, 10-11, 13d, 19, 23, 30, 34-35, 43, 47, 53

Down

Quckney — 11
Quicken (grass) — *5, 8,* 10-11, 17-18, 24-25, 27-28
Quickens — 29
Scutch (grass) — 4, *10,* 13-*14,* 15, 18, *22-24,* 26
Twitch — 18
White grass — 23
Nil — 1, 2ab, 3, 6-7, 9, 12, 16, 19-21, 30

Tyrone

Couch grass — 1, 11
Keeb — 5
Scutch (grass) — 2, *7,* 10-*11, 14-15*
Switch grass — 11
Nil — 3-4, 6, 8-9, 12-13, 16

Antrim

Couch grass — 16b
Robin run the hedge — 33
Scutch (grass) — *2* 8b, 9, *12,* 25
Switch (grass) — *4A, 6-7,* 13, 18, 22, *25*
Swutch — 16b, 19
Nil — 1, 3-4, 5ab, 8a, 10-11, 14-15, 16ac, 17, 20-21, 23-24 26-32, 34

Donegal

Bent — 5-6
Fawreen — 12
Kanawan — 6
Pirle — 1, 11
Ripple grass — 2
Scorch grass — 10a
Scutch grass — 1, 5, 10b
Switch grass — 5A, 8
Nil — 1A, 3-4, 7, 7A, 9, 13

Fermanagh

Scutch grass — 1-2, 5, 7b
Nil — 3-4, 6, 7a, 8-10

Armagh

Quicken grass — 4
Scutch grass — 2
Star grass — 6a
Nil — 1, 3, 5, 6b

Londonderry

Scutch (grass) — 1, 1B, *5*
Nil — 1A, 2-3, 3A, 4, 6-7

88 FOXGLOVE (PQ1, 182)

Foxglove has not been mapped as it occurs everywhere except in parts of Northern Ireland.
The variants of the following elements of items have been subsumed: DEAD (many **deid**), BLOODY, (**bluidy, bliddy**).

Shetland

Digatail — 9
Ferrie's umbrella — 6
Foxglove — 2, 5, 16, 21ab, 22, 25, 30
Nil — 1, 3-4, 7-8, 10-15, 17-20, 23-24, 26-29, 31-33

Orkney

Deadman's thimble — 18
Devil's thimble — 15
Fairy's thimble — 20
Foxglove — 4-5, 7-9, 11, 13ab, 15-17, 19
Trowie glove — 7, 10, 12, 13a, 15
Nil — 1-3, 6, 14, 21

Caithness

Deadman's bell — 15
Digatilis — 15
Foxglove — 2b, 8-9, 11, 16b
Lady's thumble — 13
Nil — 1, 2a, 3-7, 10, 12abc, 14, 16a, 17

Sutherland

Dead man's finger — 5
Devil's finger — 16
Devil's thimble — 9ab
Digitalis — 3
Foxglove — 1, 3-8, 10, 13, 16
Lady's thimble — 6
Nil — 2, 14-15, 17

Ross & Cromarty

Badman's bonnie flower — 10, 36
Dead man's bell — 13, 24
Dead man's finger — 3, 20, 29
Dead woman's finger — 2
Devil's finger — 28, 36
Fairy glove — 26
Fairy pixie — 26
Foxglove — 1, 3-6, 8-10, 14, 16-20, 25ab, 29, 31, 32ab, 34, 39
Wishing finger — 26
Witch's finger — 19
Nil — 7, 11-12, 15, 21-23, 27, 30, 32c, 33, 35, 37ab, 38

Inverness

Dead man's finger — 7, 11, 16, 26
Devil's thimble — 9
Fairy thimble — 40
Foxglove — 2-6, 8-11, 13abce, 17-19, 21ab, 22-23, 26-30, 32, 34-39
Lus nam ban sith — 26
Nil — 1, 12, 13d, 14-15, 20, 24-25, 31, 33

Nairn

Bad man's bonnie thing — 5
Foxglove — 1a, 2
Nil — 1bc, 3-4, 6

Moray

Bad man's finger — 21
Bloody bell — 22
Bluebell — 14
Caffie moo — 8c
Dead man's bell — 1, 4, 6ab, 8b, 9ab, 10, 12, 16, 19, 22-23
Dumb bell — 2a
Dumb man's bell — 18
Foxglove — 7, 8d, 23
Witch's thimble — 9a, 22
Nil — 2b, 3, 5, 8aef, 11, 13, 15, 17, 20

Banff

Blin' man's bell — 11
Dead man's bell — 2c, 3-5, 6b, 7-10, 14-15, 17, 18bcd, 29-32, 34
Dead man's glove — 31
Dumbbell — 11
Foxglove — 1, 2b, 15, 19
Nil — 2a, 6a, 12-13, 16, 18a, 20-28, 33

Aberdeen

Bell — 77
Blind man's bell — 24
Blin' man's bell — 25, 52, 82, 108
Bummer's bell — 81
Dead man's bell — 3a, 5b, 8, 10, 12, 18, 27, 28b, 29, 32, 35, 53, 57-58, 64, 71c, 72, 75-76, 78, 80, 84, 86, 88, 92, 94, 97-98, 100-101, 103
Dead man's glove — 26
Dumb bell — 22
Fairy's hat — 60
Foxglove — 3b, 6, 11, 17, 23, 26, 28c, 31, 34, 44-45, 50-51, 56, 59, 66-67, 69-70, 74, 81-82, 100, 104, 106-107
Gowk's thummle — 64
Granny's mutch — 47e
Thummle — 21
Thummlie — 46
Nil — 1-2, 4, 5acd, 7, 9, 13-16, 19-20, 28a, 30, 33, 36-43, 47abcdf, 49, 54-55, 61-63, 65, 68, 71ab, 73, 79, 83, 85, 87, 89-91, 93, 95-96, 99, 102, 105, 109

Kincardine

Blin' man's bell — 4
Dead man's bell — 5-7, 10-15, 17abcd, 24
Foxglove — 1, 3, 5-6, 8, 12, 15-16, 17c, 19, 26, 28
Red bell — 9
Nil — 2, 18, 20-23, 25, 27

Kinross

Dead man's bell — 1-2, 5, 7
Foxglove — 2-5
Nil — 6

Angus

Dead man's bell — 14ad
Deevil's thummle — 14d
Deil's thimmle — 35
Devil's thimmle — 14c
Foxglove — 3-4, 7, 9-10, 12-13, 22-24, 32, 33b, 34, 36
Foxter leaf — 17a
Mappies moo — 25
Witch's thimmle — 32
Nil — 1-2, 5abc, 6, 8, 11, 14b, 15-16, 17b, 18-21, 26-28, 29ab, 30-31, 33a, 37

Perth

Bloody finger — 25, 40
Dead man's bell — 20, 27, 37-39, 41ab, 44-48, 61-62, 65-71
Dead man's finger — 41a
Dead man's thimble — 24
Dumb bell — 40
Fairy's thimble — 41a
Foxglove — 1, 2a, 4-5, 7-10, 12, 15, 20, 24-25, 28, 29a, 32-33, 36, 50, 52b, 57, 60, 67, 73-74
Nil — 2b, 3, 6, 11, 13-14, 16-19, 21-23, 26, 29b, 30-31, 34-35, 42-43, 49, 51ab, 52acde, 53-56, 58-59, 63-64, 72

Fife

Dead man's bell — 7-8, 10, 12-13, 18, 23, 43b, 51, 55d, 61
Dug's lug — 55a
Foxglove — 4, 9a, 11, 13, 16, 19, 21, 25, 36ab, 37, 40b, 41a, 42, 43a, 44a, 50-51, 53, 55de, 56-57, 62-63
Foxter — 56
Granny mutch — 55c
Granny's coul — 18
Lady's finger — 23, 48, 53
Leddy's finger — 57
Mappie's moo — 37
Mappie's mouth — 35
Nightshade — 61
Thummel — 20
Witch's thimble — 55d
Nil — 1-3, 5-6, 9b, 14-15, 17, 22, 24, 26-34, 38-39, 40a, 41bcd, 44bcdef, 45-47, 49, 52, 54, 55bfg, 58-60, 64ab

Clackmannan

Bloody finger — 4c
Dead man's bell — 1-2, 4ad, 5
Foxglove — 1, 4bc, 7
Nil — 3-6

Stirling

Auld wife's finger — 30
Bella dona — 25b
Clover — 20
(Deadly) nightshade — 10, *25b*
Dead man's bell — 2-3, 6, 7abcde, 9-13, 16-18, 21ab, 22a, 23ac, 26be, 27ab, 28, 31-33
Dead man's bluebell — 8
Dead man's finger — 31
Dead man's glove — 38
Dug's lugs — 26e
Foxglove — 4, 7cef, 11, 17, 21b, 23b, 26a, 30-31, 35a, 36, 42a
Granny's purse — 12
Lady's finger — 27a
Lady's thimble — 35b
Nil — 1, 5, 14-15, 19, 22b, 24, 25a, 26cdf, 29, 34, 37ab, 39ab, 40-41, 42b

Dunbarton

Dead man's bell — 2, 4b, 5-6, 9, 13a, 14ab, 18
Foxglove — 1, 3, 6, 7bc, 11, 13ac, 14b, 16a
Granny's thimble — 9-10
Witch's thimble — 14b
Nil — 4a, 7a, 8, 12, 13b, 15, 16b, 17

Argyll

Bad man's thimble — 13, 23
Dead man's thimble — 9
Devil's thimble — 11, 16
Fairy thimble — 25
Foxglove — 1-3, 5-7, 9-10, 14-17, 19, 22, 24-25, 27, 30, 33, 35, 39
Granny's mutch — 29
Witch's pap — 30, 34-35, 37, 39-40
Witch's paup — 31
Nil — 4, 8, 12, 18, 20-21, 26, 28, 32, 36, 38

Bute

Bad man's finger — 3
Foxglove — 1acd, 2, 7, 8ab
Nil — 1be, 4-6, 9

Ayr

Bad man's thimble — 8b
Blin' man's finger — 56
Bloody bell — 45
Bloody finger — 8a
Bloody man's finger — 56
(Deadly) nightshade — 9, *35a*
Dead man's bell — 32, 46
Dead man's finger — 3
Elve's hat — 8b
Fairy bell — 8b
Fairy glove — 26b
Finger still — 41
Foxglove — 2b, 3, 5-6, 8ab, 9-10, 12a, 20bc, 21, 24b, 28ef, 30a, 31, 34, 35b, 36, 42-43, 48, 55, 57
Frog's mouth — 28f
Gien — 3
Gudsie — 18b
Lady's thimble — 41, 49
Lady's thumble — 54
Old man's bell — 33
Thimble — 41
Witch's pap — 8a
Witch's thimble — 18b, 54
Nil — 1ab, 2a, 4, 7, 11, 12b, 13-15, 16ab, 17, 18a, 19, 20adefgh, 22-23, 24a, 25, 26ac, 27, 28abcd, 29, 30b, 37-40, 44, 47, 50-52, 53ab

Renfrew

Bad man's poison — 1b
Coo's pop — 21
Dog's lug — 20b
Fairy thimble — 2j, 12b
Foxglove — 2ahij, 4ace, 5, 11acefl, 13c, 16ab, 17, 19, 20a
Granny's thimble — 2f, 4bcde
Gun — 14b
Lady's thimble — 8
Man's thumble — 18b
Thumble — 21
Nil — 1a, 2bcdeg, 3, 6-7, 9-10, 11bdghijk, 12a, 13abd, 14a, 15, 16cd, 18a

Lanark

Bloody finger — 9a, 61
Coo paup — 46c
Coo's pop — 31d
Dead man's bell — 1, 8b, 9be, 12-13, 14a, 15b, 25c, 38acde, 63
Dead man's finger — 17
Digitalis — 26a, 30, 44
Dog's lug — 38d
Foxglove — 1-3, 6, 7ac, 12, 14d, 15ac, 16b, 18-19, 25bc, 26a, 27b, 29cd, 31a, 32a, 35d, 40, 44-45, 46ab, 47, 49a, 53, 56, 58, 59b, 60, 64b, 65
Granny mutchie — 36
Lady's finger — 33cd
Lady's slipper — 29f
Lady's smock — 14d
Lady's thimble — 60
Mappy's mou — 38d
Rose bay willow herb — 32f
Thumble — 20, 57b
Witch's thimble — 9b
Witch's thumble — 17
Nil — 4-5, 7b, 8a, 10ab, 11, 14bc, 16a, 21-24, 25ad, 26b, 27a, 28, 29abeg, 31bc, 32bcde, 33ab, 34, 35ac, 37, 38b, 39, 41-43, 48, 49b, 50-51, 52ab, 54-55, 57ac, 59a, 62, 64a, 66, 67ab

West Lothian

Dead man's bell — 9b, 11
Digitalis — 16
Foxglove — 1a, 3, 5-6, 8, 10-12, 15-16, 20a, 22
Nil — 1bcd, 2, 4, 7, 9a, 13-14,

West Lothian cont'd

17ab, 18, 19ab, 20b, 21ab

Midlothian

Dead man's bell — 11
Dell — 19
Foxglove — 3, 6ab, 10-11, 12a, 14a, 18, 20-21, 23b, 25c, 29
Foxterleaf — 7b
Granny mutch — 12b
Witch's thimble — 27, 30
Nil — 1-2, 4-5, 7a, 8ab, 9, 13, 14b, 15-17, 22, 23a, 24, 25abd, 26ab, 28, 31-32

East Lothian

Antireenum — 6b
Dead man's bell — 7
Devil's thimble — 14
Dog's lug — 13
Fairy thumble — 11
Foxglove — 4b, 15-19, 21
Frog's mooth — 6ab
Witch's thimble — 2, 21
Nil — 1, 3, 4a, 5, 8-10, 12, 20

Berwick

Campine — 27
Dog's heid — 31
Dog's lug — 17
Foxglove — 1-2, 6, 8-10, 12, 15, 16b, 21, 29, 31-32
Mipmip — 8
Thimble — 18
Witch's thimble — 2, 11, 13, 23
Witch's thumble — 12
Nil — 3-5, 7, 14, 16ac, 19-20, 22, 24-26, 28, 30

Peebles

Dead man s bell — 2
Fairy thimble — 2
Foxglove — 1, 4bc, 6ab, 8
Granny's thimble — 4c
Tintock bell — 6a
Nil — 3, 4a, 5, 7, 9-10

Selkirk

Foxglove — 2c, 4, 8
Witch's thimble — 2bd, 6-7
Wutch's thimble — 2ae
Nil — 1, 3, 5

Roxburgh

Dead man's bell — 8, 21c
Foxglove — 1-2, 4, 8, 13, 15b, 16, 20, 21acdf, 22, 25
Foxterleaf — 8, 21c
King — 21c
Thimble — 8, 21ac
Tod mit — 3a, 13
Tod tail — 4, 21c, 28
Witch's thimble — 3b, 7, 18, 20
Wutch's thimble — 17
Nil — 5-6, 9ab, 10-12, 14, 15a, 19, 21be, 23-24, 26-27

Dumfries

Bee's glove — 15
Bloody bell — 1a
Bloody finger — 5-6, 8a, 9-13, 19-20, 21ab, 22, 24, 28, 31abef, 32, 41-42
Coo's pop — 5
Cracker — 7
Finger still — 8b
Foxglove — 1a, 4, 12, 15-16, 17ab, 21b, 22, 24, 26-28, 31d, 33, 40, 45a
Thimble — 26, 37
Toad stool — 29
Tod tail — 18, 39
Nil — 1b, 2-3, 14, 23, 25, 30, 31c, 34-36, 38, 43-44, 45b, 46-49

Kirkcudbright

Bloody finger—2-9, 12ab, 14, 15ab, 18-20, 21abc, 22-24, 26-27
Bloody man's finger — 1, 17
Foxglove — 1, 6-7, 10, 16
Thimble — 1
Nil — 11, 13, 25

Wigtown

Blin' man's finger — 6, 13
Bloody finger — 5a, 16-17
Bloody man's finger — 7-8, 10-13
Deil's finger still — 18
Finger stule — 2
Foxglove — 4, 5a, 14
Nil — 1, 3, 5b, 9, 15

Northumberland

Bloody finger — 69b
Dead man's bell — 69b, 124a, 127b, 134
Digitail — 103b
Dog's mouth — 22
Fairy finger — 29b, 59c, 79
Fairy's glove — 69b
Fox finger — 76
Foxglove — 2a, 6-7, 12-14, 16, 18, 20b, 21, 26, 28, 29b, 30-31, 34b, 35-36, 40a, 41cd, 42, 45-48, 52, 53ab, 54, 56, 59b, 60, 62b, 64a, 65ab, 68, 69cdh, 70, 71acd, 72bcdi, 78, 82, 87, 88b, 89-90, 94b, 98, 99d, 100, 102, 103abc, 104a, 106-107, 109-110, 111ab, 112, 120ab, 124ab, 126c, 127a, 130e, 132-135, 137-138
Granny's night cap — 29d
Lady's finger — 69a, 73, 103a, 120c
Lady's glove — 59c
Lady's thimble — 71c
Rabbit's lug — 130c
Rabbit's mouth — 87
Shepherd's purse — 1a
Snap dragon — 22, 69h, 83
Sugar dumpling — 9
Witch's finger — 59c
Witch's thimble — 124a
Nil — 1bc, 2b, 3-5, 8, 10-11, 15, 17, 19ab, 20a, 23, 24ab, 25, 27, 29acef, 32, 33ab, 34a, 37-39, 40b, 41ab, 43-44, 49-51, 55, 57-58, 59adef, 61, 62acdefgh, 63, 64b, 66-67, 69efg, 71be, 72aefghjkl, 74-75, 77, 80-81, 84-86, 88a, 91-93, 94a, 95ab, 96-97, 99abc, 101ab, 104b, 105, 108abc, 113-117, 118ab, 119, 121, 122ab, 123, 125, 126abdef, 127cdefgh, 128, 129abc, 130abdf, 131, 136, 139-143

Cumberland

Dead man s thimble — 27
Digitalie — 57
Fairy finger — 13a, 30, 42
Fairy thimble — 30-31
Fox glev — 49
Foxglove — 1a, 3-4, 5a, 7, 12, 13c, 15ac, 16, 21-25, 28, 37b, 38, 40, 42, 46-48, 50, 56-58
Lady's finger — 56
Lady's thimble — 24, 27
Thimble — 13a
Tod tail — 13bc
Nil — 1b, 2, 5b, 6, 8-11, 13d, 14, 15b, 17-20, 26, 29, 32-36, 37a, 39, 41, 43-45, 51-55, 59-62, 63ab

Down

Fairy finger — 21, 30
Fairy thimble — 13, 15, 28
Finger lady — 10
Foxglove — 19, 24
Lady finger — 4-5, 9-11, 14, 17-24, 26-27
Nil — 1, 2ab, 3, 6-8, 12, 16, 25, 29

Tyrone

Fairy finger — 3, 5-7, 9-10, 12, 14, 16
Fairy thimble — 1
Foxglove — 7, 11
Wee folk's thimble — 2
Nil — 4, 8, 13, 15

Antrim

Cuckoo thimmel — 4A
Divil's thimble — 15
Fairy finger — 6
Fairy thimble — 7, 10-11, 13, 16b, 19-22, 34
Foxglove — 1, 3, 9, 25-26
Lady's finger — 25, 34
Lady's thimble — 8b, 20
Wee folk's thimble — 5b, 10
Nil — 2, 4, 5a, 8a, 12, 14, 16ac, 17-18, 23-24, 27-33

Donegal

Cracker — 6
Fairy finger — 13
Fairy thimble — 1-2, 6-9, 10ab, 12
Foxglove — 5, 5A
Lady finger — 10b
Wee folk's thimmel — 5A, 11
Nil — 1A, 3-4, 7A

Fermanagh

Fairy finger — 2, 5-6, 8
Fairy thimble — 1
Foxglove — 4, 7a, 9
Nil — 3, 7b, 10

Armagh

Fairy finger — 1-2
Foxglove — 6a
Lady finger — 4-5, 6a
Nil — 3, 6b

Londonderry

Fairy finger — 7
Fairy thimble — 3-5
Foxglove — 2, 6
Sheegie — 5
Wee folk's thimble — 1B, 3A, 5-6
Nil — 1, 1A

89 GOOSEBERRY (PQ1, 183)

Variants of GOOSEBERRY have been subsumed (**geuseberry** Cumberland), but they remain for the element **goose** in other compounds.

Shetland

Gooseberry — 1-2, 4-7, 10, 16, 20, 21ab, 22, 25, 30, 32-33
Nil — 3, 8-9, 11-15, 17-19, 23-24, 26-29, 31

Orkney

Gooseberry — 2, 4-5, 7-9, 11, 13ab, 15-17, 19-20
Grocer — 15
Grosset — 19
Grozer — 8
Nil — 1, 3, 6, 10, 12, 14, 18, 21

Caithness

Gooseberry — 2ab, 5, 8-9, 11, 13, 16b
Groset — 15, 16a
Grossag — 5
Grosset — 1
Grozet — 12b
Nil — 3-4, 6-7, 10, 12ac, 14, 17

Sutherland

Gooseberry — 1, 3-8, 9a, 10-13, 16
Goose gog — 16
Groserd — 4
Grossag — 9b
Grossert — 2
Grosset — 6
Nil — 14-15, 17

Ross & Cromarty

Gooseberry — 1, 3-5, 8-9, 14, 16-18, 20, 23, 26, 28-30, 32ab, 36, 39
Goosegog — 14-15, 19, 25ab, 34
Gooser — 6
Groosie — 15
Grosert — 18
Groset — 24, 32b
Grosie — 25b, 37ab
Grossack — 31
Grosset — 11
Grossie — 31
Grozer — 22
Grozie — 25a
Hairy berry — 26
Nil — 2, 7, 10, 12-13, 21, 27, 32c, 33, 35, 38

Inverness
Gooseberry — 1-11, 13abce, 16-19, 21ab, 22-23, 26, 29-30, 32, 34-37, 39
Goose gog — 8, 21a, 38, 40
Goosie — 14
Groset — 9, 13a, 26
Grossack — 27
Grosset — 14, 22, 28, 31, 35
Grozet — 29
Nil — 12, 13d, 15, 20, 24-25, 33

Nairn
Berry — 2
Gooseberry — 1a, 2
Groser — 1a, 5
Grosert — 1b
Grosset — 1bc
Nil — 3-4, 6

Moray
Gooseberry — 3, 6b, 7, 8bd, 23
Goosegog — 2b
Gooser — 3, 6b
Goosie — 8c, 11, 13-16, 21
Gossert — 21
Grauser — 7
Groser — 1
Grosert — 6a
Groset — 8be, 9a, 14, 23
Grossert — 8a, 19
Grosset — 4, 17, 22
Grozack — 12
Grozer — 18
Grozert — 10, 12
Grozet — 5, 16
Grozzet — 20
Nil — 2a, 8f, 9b

Banff
Gooseberry — 4, 9, 30, 34
Gooser — 20-24
Goosie — 5, 6b, 8, 10, 15-16, 19
Grosert — 2bc, 5, 7-9, 11, 16, 18c, 24, 29
Groset — 12, 18d, 32, 34
Grosser — 1
Grossert — 13, 15, 18b, 26, 30-31
Grosset — 1, 10, 23, 27
Grozer — 4, 6ab
Grozert — 2a, 14-15, 17, 25
Grozet — 33
Grozzert — 3
Gruser — 20
Hairy berry — 2b
Nil — 18a, 28

Aberdeen
Gooseberry — 6, 8, 14, 28ac, 35, 44, 59, 70, 82, 86
Goosegog — 14, 34, 60, 90
Gooser — 2, 3b, 4, 5b, 11, 16, 19-21, 27, 28c, 29-30, 34, 39, 44-45, 47acdf, 49-51, 54-57, 60-61, 63, 65-67, 72-74, 79, 86, 89, 94, 96, 98-99, 103-106, 108
Goosie — 19
Gosser — 5c, 37, 101
Green berry — 28a
Groser — 24, 79, 81, 92, 96, 98
Grosert — 5bd, 14, 22, 25, 27, 30, 34, 39, 47f, 48, 51-53, 58, 64, 71b, 80, 82, 84, 87, 99
Groset — 5d, 11, 23, 42, 71a, 73
Grosser — 31, 46, 94-95
Grossert — 9, 12, 15-16, 32, 40, 57, 76, 83, 88, 97
Grosset — 3a, 10, 16, 18, 33, 35, 38, 41, 60, 69, 71a, 77, 93
Growser — 17
Grozer — 19, 62, 65, 75, 78, 98, 100, 104, 108
Grozert — 28ab, 47be, 71c, 85, 107
Grozet — 49
Hairy grosset — 102
Nil — 1, 5a, 7, 13, 26, 36, 43, 68, 91, 109

Kincardine
Gooseberry — 5-6, 8, 16, 17bcd
Gooser — 1-3, 5, 9-12, 14, 17c, 18, 21
Goosie — 19, 26
Groser — 7, 17bd, 26, 28
Grosert — 12
Groset — 27
Grossert — 13-14, 17ad, 23
Grosset — 3-4, 24
Grozer — 15, 17c, 20, 22
Grozert — 6, 10
Grozet — 5, 21, 25
Grozzer — 21

Kinross
Berry — 2
Goosegog — 3
Groser — 4-5
Grosser — 3
Grosset — 1
Grozer — 1, 7
Nil — 6

Angus
Gooseberry — 17b, 18, 20, 34
Goosegog — 30, 32
Gooser — 17a
Groser — 5bc, 10-13, 14a, 16, 21, 23, 30-31, 33b, 34-35
Grosser — 3, 28
Grozer — 1-2, 4, 5a, 6-9, 14bc, 15, 17b, 18-20, 22, 24-27, 29a, 32, 33a, 35-37
Grozet — 17ab, 18
Grozzer — 14d
Nil — 29b

Perth
Gooseberry — 2a, 4, 8-10, 24-25, 36, 74
Goosegog — 12, 26, 57, 65, 68, 72, 74
Grooser — 50
Grooset — 67
Groser — 1, 2a, 3, 5, 11-12, 15, 17, 19, 21-22, 29ab, 30, 51a, 52abce, 55, 58, 60, 63, 65
Groset — 10, 12, 24, 29a, 51a, 52e, 56, 67, 72
Grosser — 42
Grossert — 18, 45
Grosset — 8, 37, 39-40, 41ab, 43, 45, 49, 53-54, 61, 64, 66, 68, 71, 73
Grozer — 6-7, 9, 13, 15, 18, 20, 23, 25, 27-28, 31-32, 41a, 44, 46-48, 51b, 52d, 53, 57, 59
Grozert — 62
Grozet — 15-16, 20, 41b, 46, 62, 69-70
Grozzer — 26, 33
Nil — 2b, 14, 34-35, 38

Fife
Berry — 36b
Gasegog — 25
Gooseberry — 4, 25, 37, 43a, 46
Goosegob — 7
Goosegog — 16, 23, 36ab, 37-39, 41bc, 43a, 44c, 45, 50, 52, 55bd, 63
Greister — 6
Groser — 1, 3, 5, 9a, 10, 12, 14, 18-19, 21, 24, 30, 39, 40b, 44adf, 48, 52-53, 55e, 56, 58, 61, 64a
Grosert — 33, 41b, 51
Groset — 20, 27, 36b, 39, 44af, 51-52, 64a
Grosser — 9b, 17, 23, 32, 36a, 55d
Grossert — 21, 56
Grosset — 29, 38, 41a, 42, 43b, 55d
Growk — 52
Grozer — 2, 4, 6-8, 11-13, 20, 22, 25-26, 33-35, 40a, 41d, 42, 43a, 44ce, 45-47, 49-50, 54, 55abcfg, 57, 59, 62, 64b
Grozet — 8, 26, 46, 55c
Grozert — 55f
Grozzer — 27-28, 60
Grozzet — 28
Rozer — 44e
Nil — 15, 31, 44b

Clackmannan
Gooseberry — 4c
Goosegog — 1-2, 4bc, 7
Grosert — 4a, 5
Groset — 4d, 5
Grosset — 1, 7
Grozer — 4c, 6
Grozet — 2, 4b
Grunk — 4c
Nil — 3

Stirling
Berry — 7e, 25c, 37a
Gooseberry — 4, 7ce, 21b, 25c, 26ad, 31-32, 36
Goosegog — 7abcef, 8, 16-18, 20, 21ab, 22a, 23bc, 24, 25a, 26abe, 28, 30, 34, 35b, 37b, 41, 42a
Goosiegog — 38, 39b, 40
Grizzle — 26b
Grosack — 42a
Groser — 12
Grosert — 10, 25d, 26e, 34, 35b
Groset — 10, 14, 22b, 23a, 27a, 33
Grossack — 19
Grosser — 26b
Grossert — 7bdf, 25b, 26abc
Grosset — 2, 4, 6, 7abe, 8, 12-13, 16-17, 21a, 26bf, 31, 35a, 37b
Growset — 26a
Grozert — 18, 22a, 25ad, 26d
Grozet — 1, 3, 9, 11, 15, 23c, 25a, 27b, 29-30, 32, 37a, 39a, 42b
Grozzet — 6, 21b, 36
Grudgock — 30
Grunk — 22b
Gudgie — 28
Gudgock — 3
Hairy groset — 38
Nil — 5

Dunbarton
Gooseberry — 1, 7c, 13bc, 14b, 16b
Goosegog — 2, 4b, 10-12, 13a, 16b
Gouget — 2
Grooset — 17
Groset — 1, 3, 4a, 5, 7a, 12, 13b
Grossert — 2
Grosset — 4b, 13a, 14b
Grossock — 16a
Growzet — 6, 9
Grozet — 7bc, 10, 13c, 14a, 16a, 18
Grozer — 15
Grozert — 14a
Grozock — 16b
Grunter — 7a
Gudget — 9
Gudgie — 16ab
Gudgock — 5, 7ab, 18
Nil — 8

Argyll
Gooseberry — 1-2, 5-7, 9-11, 14-17, 19, 22, 25-27, 30, 33, 35, 39
Goosegog — 8, 24, 36
Grawset — 1
Groisid — 3
Groset — 12, 16, 21, 26-27, 30, 32-33, 36-38
Groozet — 20
Groshet — 29
Grosset — 5, 9, 11, 13, 15, 19, 23-24, 28, 34
Grozet — 18, 31, 35, 39-40
Nil — 4

Bute
Gooseberry — 7, 8ab
Goosegog — 1a, 8b
Groset — 1ae, 4-5, 8a
Grosette — 3
Grosset — 6-7, 9
Growset — 8b
Grozet — 1bcd, 2
Hairy grosette — 3

Ayr
Berry — 45
Gooseberry — 5, 9, 28ce
Goose gob — 8b
Goosegog — 1a, 2b, 6-7, 15, 18b, 23, 37, 53b, 55
Grooset — 43
Groset — 1a, 2b, 7, 8a, 13, 18b, 26ab, 28ef, 42-44, 49
Grossert — 35a
Grosset — 21, 27, 28d, 35a, 38, 50-51, 56-57
Growset — 28f
Grozert — 16a
Grozet — 1b, 2a, 3-6, 8b, 9-11, 12ab, 14-15, 16ab, 17, 18a, 19, 20abcdefgh, 22-23, 24ab, 25, 26c, 28abc, 29, 30ab, 31-34, 35b, 36-37, 39, 41, 45-49, 52, 53ab, 54-55
Grozzet — 40
Grudget — 5, 43
Grugguck — 23
Gubuck — 38
Gudget — 2a, 15, 24b
Gudgie — 12b
Gudock — 12b, 14, 18b, 20bdg, 22, 25, 32, 35b, 36-38, 46, 51, 54
Gudyock — 49
Oudguck — 16a

Renfrew
Gooseberry — 2adi, 4de, 8, 11ade, 19, 20a
Goosegob — 12b
Goosegog — 2b, 9, 11k, 14b, 18ab, 20a
Grooset — 13d
Groset — 2dj, 3, 4d, 6-9, 11ac, 13a, 14ab, 16abc, 17, 18b
Grosock — 2i
Grossert — 15
Grosset — 2abfg, 11f, 13c, 16d, 19, 20ab
Grossock — 10
Grozet — 1b, 2ch, 4ace, 5, 11bdijkl, 12a, 13b, 18a, 21
Grozock — 18a
Grozzet — 11l
Grudget — 11bl, 14a, 16a
Gudget — 15
Gudgock — 16c, 17
Hairy grosset — 2ae
Nil — 1a, 4b, 11gh

Lanark
Berry — 64a
Gob — 47
Gooseberry — 1, 3, 6, 7ac, 12, 14d, 15ac, 25bc, 26a, 29cf, 32d, 35abcd, 40, 44, 60
Goosegog — 2-4, 7ab, 14b, 15b, 16ab, 17-19, 21-23, 25abcd, 26b, 28, 29bg, 30, 31b, 32ab, 33ad, 35acd, 36-37, 38e, 39, 41, 46ab, 49a, 51, 52ab, 54, 56, 58, 59a, 60, 64b
Goosie — 27b, 51
Goosiegog — 26a, 27b, 32e, 38c

Lanark cont'd

Groiset – 14d
Groser – 4
Groset – 1, 6, 8a, 9b, 12, 15c, 23, 29cd, 31ad, 32b, 33d, 37, 40, 44-45, 46ac, 59ab, 64a, 65
Grosock – 3
Grossert – 15b, 31c, 63
Grosset – 7abc, 8b, 11, 14abc, 18, 20, 22, 25ac, 26a, 27a, 29afg, 32cdef, 33b, 34, 35ab, 38abd, 42-43, 49b, 51, 52ab, 53, 55-56, 58, 62, 67b
Grozet – 5, 9a, 10ab, 13, 14c, 15c, 16b, 17, 24, 29e, 30, 33bc, 35cd, 39, 46b, 47-48, 50, 57ab, 61, 67a
Grozock – 9a, 13
Grozzet – 15a, 66
Gudgeup – 44
Gudgit – 57c
Gudgock – 30, 33a, 34, 58
Guggie – 7a
Hairy grozzet – 15a
Sooreck – 29f

West Lothian

Gooseberry – 2-3, 7, 16, 22
Goosegog – 1acd, 4-7, 9a, 11-16, 17ab, 18, 19b, 20ab, 21a
Gooser – 11
Goosie – 19a
Goosiegog – 21b
Grosert – 3
Groset – 2, 21b
Grosset – 1b, 4, 7, 9ab, 11, 13, 19b, 21a
Grozet – 8, 16, 17a, 20ab, 22
Grozzet – 1a, 18
Nil – 10

Midlothian

Gooseberry – 6a, 8a, 10, 14a, 21, 23b
Goosegag – 25d
Goosegog – 1, 3, 5, 6a, 7a, 8b, 10-11, 12ab, 14ab, 16-19, 21, 23ab, 25abc, 26b, 27, 29-32
Goosegug – 20
Groset – 14b, 28
Grossert – 17, 23a, 26a, 27, 29
Grosset – 4, 6b, 7b, 8b, 9-11, 13, 22, 29-30
Grozert – 3
Grozet – 7a, 23b, 24
Gudshop – 11
Nil – 2, 15

East Lothian

Gooseberry – 15-17
Goosegag – 9
Goosegog – 1-3, 4ab, 5, 8-13, 18-20
Groser – 13, 15
Grosert – 15
Groset – 2, 6b, 14
Grosser – 15
Grossert – 6a, 15
Grosset – 6a, 8, 10-11, 16, 21
Grossin – 2
Grozet – 7
Grozzie – 9

Berwick

Berry – 10
Gooseberry – 1-2, 6, 8, 16b, 21, 32
Goosegog – 2-3, 8, 10-12, 15, 16bc, 17-20, 23-24, 27, 29, 31
Goosie – 12, 27
Groser – 32
Groset – 7, 16c
Grossert – 21
Grosset – 4-5, 9, 13, 16a, 22-23, 26
Grozet – 12, 16c, 32
Nil – 14, 25, 28, 30

Peebles

Gooseberry – 4bc, 6b, 7
Goosegog – 1-3, 4bc, 5, 6ab, 9
Grosset – 1-3, 4abc, 5, 6a, 7-8, 10
Gudget – 4b

Selkirk

Berry – 1
Gooseberry – 2c, 4, 8
Goosegog – 2cd
Goosegrog – 2b
Grosert – 4
Grosset – 2a, 3, 6-7
Nil – 2e, 5

Roxburgh

Berry – 3b, 13, 21d, 27
Gooseberry – 1, 5, 9a, 15b, 16, 20, 21af, 22-23, 26, 28,
Goosegog – 2, 8, 9b, 11, 15ab, 18-20, 21c, 24-25
Gooser – 17
Groosel – 15a, 21c
Grossel – 21c
Grosser – 7
Grossert – 3a, 4, 13, 15a, 21c
Grosset – 2, 3b, 8, 21ab, 23, 28
Grozel – 21c
Grozert – 28
Grozet – 4, 9a, 20
Guissgog – 17, 26
Nil – 6, 10, 12, 14, 21e

Dumfries

Berry – 8b, 21b, 24, 26, 31e, 32, 42, 46
Goose – 15
Gooseberry – 4, 7, 12, 16, 17b, 18, 20, 22, 27, 31d, 33, 37, 39-40
Goosegob – 22, 45a, 47
Goosegog – 8b, 15, 19, 21ab, 28-29, 31cd, 32, 34-35, 44, 45b, 46
Green berry – 17a
Groset – 1a, 2-3, 6, 13, 15, 22-23, 31a, 34, 38
Grosset – 1b, 7, 8a, 9-11, 19, 21a, 25-26, 29, 32, 35-36, 41-43, 47, 49
Grozet – 4, 22, 31b, 39
Grozzet – 5
Hairy berry – 44
Hairy grosset – 14
Nil – 30, 31f, 48

Kirkcudbright

Berry – 4, 7-8, 12a, 21ac, 22, 27
Gooseberry – 6-7, 10, 12b, 15a, 18-19
Goosegog – 1, 3, 11, 12a, 16, 18, 21b, 23-25
Grosert – 14, 18
Groset – 1, 3, 6
Grosset – 2, 4-5, 7, 9, 11, 12b, 15a, 16-17, 21b, 24
Grozet – 10, 21c
Huskie – 26
Nil – 13, 15b, 20

Wigtown

Berry – 8, 13
Blob – 5a
Gooseberry – 11, 16-18
Goosegog – 5a, 7, 14-15, 17
Groset – 2, 7-8
Grosset – 1, 5ab
Grozet – 6
Sidberry – 5a
Nil – 3-4, 9-10, 12

Northumberland

Cockle berry – 103a
Googer – 118b
Gooseberry – 5, 8, 13-16, 23, 30, 35-36, 40a, 41c, 42, 46, 48, 53b, 54, 56-57, 59b, 62ab, 64b, 66, 69bc, 71c, 72c, 77, 87, 89, 99b, 104a, 111b, 121, 127ag, 132, 140-141
Goosegob – 20a, 68, 71c, 84, 92, 122a, 127b, 129a, 132
Goosegog – 1abc, 2a, 7, 12, 17-18, 22, 26, 28, 29f, 32, 37, 39, 45-46, 48, 52, 53a, 54-56, 58, 59abce, 60, 62bd, 64a, 67, 69ce, 71e, 72deil 73, 76, 79, 81-82, 99d, 102, 104a, 105, 108b, 114, 116, 118ab, 121, 122b, 124b, 125, 126abdef, 127acdfgh, 129bc, 130abdef, 131, 143
Gooser – 3-5, 9, 16-17, 19a, 22, 24ab, 28, 29cd, 33b, 40a, 41b, 42-45, 48, 50, 59abcd, 60, 62begh, 63, 65b, 68, 69a, 71d, 72adei, 78, 82, 84, 86, 90-91, 93, 94b, 95b, 97-98, 100, 101b, 102, 113-114, 120a, 125, 126bef, 127ab, 130c, 139
Goosher – 20b
Goozer – 1b, 12, 21, 23, 29f, 39, 40a, 41d, 47, 62ac, 66, 69defh, 70, 71b, 72k, 76-77, 104a, 116, 118a, 120c, 126d, 127g, 130cd, 131, 135
Goslin – 10
Grawser – 126f
Grocer – 72h, 110
Grooser – 18, 52, 103b, 123
Groozer – 6, 18, 34b
Groser – 25, 27, 32, 36-37, 41bc, 44-45, 51, 53a, 55, 59de, 60, 62f, 65a, 67, 69g, 74, 78-79, 82-83, 89-90, 95a, 98, 99c, 101ab, 103b, 104b, 112, 119, 120b, 122b, 127f, 130c, 132, 134, 136, 141
Grosert – 11, 20a
Groset – 29f
Grosser – 34a, 71d, 127h
Grossert – 17
Grosset – 34a
Growser – 59f, 68, 85, 106, 120a, 142
Grozer – 14, 22, 24b, 29ab, 30-31, 33a, 34a, 35, 38-39, 40b, 41ad, 43, 46-47, 49, 56-58, 59bc, 61, 62egh, 64b, 69abe, 71ac, 72bcfgjl, 73, 75, 77, 80-81, 85-86, 88ab, 91, 93, 96, 99abd, 103c, 104a, 107, 108ac, 109-110, 111ab, 114, 116-117, 120c, 121, 122a, 124ab, 126acde, 127deg, 128, 130de, 133, 135, 137-138, 140, 143
Grozet – 124a
Nil – 2b, 19b, 29e, 94a, 115

Cumberland

Berry – 13a, 38, 42
Geesgob – 40
Geesgog – 48
Geusecob – 24
Geusegob – 8-9, 12, 13b, 16-18, 26, 28, 33, 37b, 39, 43, 46, 56, 58
Gooseberry – 1a, 4, 8-9, 13cd, 15ac, 18, 22-24, 28, 30, 38, 40, 46-47, 49-50, 56-58
Goosebob – 27
Goosegob – 3-4, 5a, 7, 10, 13d, 14, 16, 19, 25, 29, 31-32, 36, 37a, 42-43, 45, 47, 52, 61
Goosegog – 2, 21, 27, 44, 51, 54, 57, 60, 62, 63ab
Gooser – 6
Grosert – 22
Grosser – 13a
Grostle berry – 13c
Guesgob – 15a
Guusgob – 15b
Hairy back – 30
Hairy berry – 30
(Yella) hamber – 57
Nil – 1b, 5b, 11, 20, 34-35, 41, 53, 55, 59

Down

Gooseberry – 2a, 3, 9, 12, 15, 19, 24
Goosegab – 1, 2a, 4-7, 11, 17-21, 23-24, 26, 30
Goosegob – 12, 22-23, 29
Goosen – 13
Groset – 13
Nil – 2b, 8, 10, 14, 16, 25, 27-28

Tyrone

Gooseberry – 1, 7-8, 10-11
Goosegab – 1-2, 5, 11-12
Goosegog – 9
Nil – 3-4, 6, 13-16

Antrim

Berry – 28
Gissgab – 33
Gooseberry – 1, 3, 9-10, 13, 15, 17, 19-20, 22, 25, 28
Goosegab – 1, 4A, 6, 8a, 11-12, 14-15, 16ab, 17, 21, 23-26, 28, 30-31, 34
Goosegog – 2, 9, 24
Grozet – 8b
Hairy grosset – 7
Nil – 4, 5ab, 16c, 18, 27, 29, 32

Donegal

Gooseberry – 1, 5, 5A, 8, 12
Goosegab – 4
Nil – 1A, 2-3, 6-7, 7A, 9, 10ab, 11, 13

Fermanagh

Gooseberry – 4-5, 8-9
Goosegab – 5
Goosegob – 7b
Goosegog – 7a
Nil – 1-3, 6, 10

Armagh

Gooseberry – 6a
Goosegab – 1-4
Nil – 5, 6b

Londonderry

Gooseberry – 2, 3A
Goosegab – 1B, 3, 4
Goosegob – 5
Goosegog – 4
Nil – 1, 1A, 6-7

90 PEA POD (PQ1, 184)

Pea pod has not been mapped as it occurs everywhere. The variants of the following items have been subsumed: PEA (**pey** Banffshire, Aberdeenshire, Angus, Kincardineshire; **pay** Moray; **pye** Aberdeenshire), PEASE (**piz(z)** Aberdeenshire).

Shetland

(Pea) pod — *1-2, 6, 15-16, 20,* 21ab, *25,* 30, *32-33*
Nil — 3-5, 7-14, 17-19, 22-24, 26-29, 31

Orkney

Pea case — 4
Pea cod — 1, 12, 15
(Pea) pod — *3, 7-9, 11, 13a, 15-17, 19*-20
Peas — 2
Peas cod — 16
Nil — 5-6, 10, 13b, 14, 18, 21

Caithness

Pea — 2b
Pea cod — 8
(Pea) pod — *2a,* 9, *11,* 16b
Nil — 1, 3-7, 10, 12abc, 13-15, 16a, 17

Sutherland

Pea — 9ab, 16
Pea pod — 1, 3-8, 10-13
Peas pod — 16
Nil — 2, 14-15, 17

Ross & Cromarty

Cod — 25b, 31, 37b
(Pea) pod — *1, 3-6, 8-9, 14, 16-20, 22-23,* 24, 25ab, *26, 28-30, 32ab, 34, 36,* 39
Peas — 32c
Shuck — 36
Nil — 1-2, 7, 10-13, 15, 21, 27, 33, 35, 37a, 38

Inverness

Fitchack — 19
(Pea) pod — 1, *2-6, 8, 10*-11, *13abce,* 16-17, 21ab, *22-23, 26-29, 32, 34-40*
Peas cod — 26
Pessair — 22
Pod of tares — 19
Rusg — 26
Nil — 7, 9, 12, 13d, 14-15, 18, 20, 24-25, 30-31, 33

Nairn

Pea pod — 1a, 2
Shap — 1b
Nil — 1c, 3-6

Moray

Green peas — 2a
Hool — 9a
Pea — 10
Pea cod — 4, 8f, 22
(Pea) pod — *3, 6b, 7, 8bd, 14,* 19, *21, 23*
Pea shell — 11, 19
Pea slough — 8b
Shaap — 9a
Shill — 7
Sluck — 6a
Nil — 1, 2b, 5, 8ace, 9b, 12-13, 15-18, 20

Banff

Pea — 16, 26
(Pea) cod — *10-11,* 18cd, *23*
Pea pod — 1, 2b, 4-5, 6b, 8-9, 15, 19, 25, 30, 34
Pease cod — 27
Pea shell — 2a, 13
(Pea) sloch — 7-*8, 14,* 17, *22*
Shalloch — 17
Slouch — 6b
Slough of a pea — 21
Sluch — 20, 24
Nil — 2c, 3, 6a, 12, 18ab, 28-29, 31-33

Aberdeen

Hool — 25
Hull — 48
Pea — 4, 22, 62, 69
Pea bean — 5d
Pea cod — 60, 103, 105
(Pea) pod — *3b, 17, 28c, 44, 47f, 48-49,* 50, *56, 59,* 70, *71b, 82, 86, 94, 100, 105-106,* 107, *108*
Pease — 74, 78, 83, 92, 95, 104
Pease pod — 34-35, 66, 84, 97
Pease sha — 49
Pease shall — 39, 67, 75, 80-81, 85, 98
Pease shaw — 27
Pease shell — 67
(Pea) shall — *8, 29,* 54, *65, 67,* 73, 96, *104*
(Pea) shaw — *23,* 64, *101*
Pea slouch — 10
Pea slough — 5b, 11
(Pea) sluch — 5d, 11-12, *28a,* 31, *75*
Pea(s) wham — 47a
Peas whap — 75
Peas whaup — 77
(Pea) whap — 3a, 16, 18, 41, *44, 46,* 47ae, *75*
(Pea) whaup — *5c, 6,* 14, 19, 21, 32, *35-36,* 37, 42, *45,* 47b, *58, 61, 72,* 76, *88*
Shaup — 87-88
Shell — 70
Shuch — 52
Sloch — 9, 51, 53
Nil — 1-2, 5a, 7, 13, 15, 20, 24, 26, 28b, 30, 33, 38, 40, 43, 47cd, 55, 57, 63, 68, 71ac, 79, 89-91, 93, 99, 102, 109

Kincardine

Pea cod — 14
(Pea) pod — *3, 5-6, 8, 11, 16,* 17bcd, *24, 26*
Peas — 1
Pease — 10
Pea shall — 24
(Pea) shell — *7,* 17bd
(Pea) sloch — 15, *21-23, 25,* 28
Slough — 19
Sluch — 18
Nil — 2, 4, 9, 12-13, 17a, 20, 27

Kinross

Pea cod — 3
Pea hale — 4
Pea huil — 2
Pea pang — 6
Pea pod — 2-3
Pea scod — 5
Pea shaup — 2
Shale — 1
Nil — 7

Angus

Pea cod — 5c, 6, 10, 14abcd, 17ab, 20-22, 25, 27-28, 29a, 33b, 34
Pea pod — 12, 17b, 18, 20, 32, 34, 36
Peas — 8
Peas cod — 4, 13, 18, 23
(Pea) sloch — 3, 5a, *7, 9,* 11-*12,* 24, 30-31, 35, 37
(Pea) slouch — 2, *22,* 26
Shelloch — 5b
Slock — 23
Slough — 34
Nil — 1, 15-16, 19, 29b, 33a

Perth

Huil — 65
(Pea) coad — 27, 62
Pea cod — 25, 29b, 52e, 62
(Pea) pod — *1, 2a, 4-5, 8-10, 12, 21, 24-25, 28, 29a, 32-33, 36, 43, 46,* 48, *52b, 53, 57, 67,* 71, 74
Peas cod — 41a, 57
Pease pod — 67
Pea shap — 68, 71
(Pea) shell — *9, 13,* 18, *25, 29b,* 49, *51a, 73*
Peas hope — 55
Pea shot — 8
Pea shuck — 61
(Pea) sloch — 15, 18, *32-33,* 39-40, *45*-46, *50,* 52c, 60
Shap — 66, 69-70
Slagh — 47
Slauch — 62
Sloach — 27
Slouch — 29a
Slough — 20
Nil — 2b, 3, 6-7, 11, 14, 16-17, 19, 22-23, 26, 30-31, 34-35, 37-38, 41b, 42, 44, 51b, 52ad, 54, 56, 58-59, 63-64, 72

Fife

Cob — 56
Green peas — 63
Hull — 55d
Pea cod — 7, 40a, 41d, 43a, 46-47, 51, 55c, 64a
Pea hale — 1, 14, 32, 35
Pea hill — 51, 55g
(Pea) pod — *4,* 7-8, *9a, 11, 13, 19, 21, 23, 25, 28, 36ab, 37, 39, 40b, 41a, 42, 43a,* 44abc, *46,* 50, 55ae, *57, 62*
Peas cod — 10, 12-13, 16, 20-22, 33, 53, 55f
Pease — 6
(Pea) shaup — *29, 53,* 55e
Pea shell — 1, 30, 37, 44c
Pea stock — 3
Sheeprit — 26
Shop — 18
Nil — 2, 5, 9b, 15, 17, 24, 27, 31, 34, 38, 41bc, 43b, 44def, 45, 48-49, 52, 54, 55b, 58-61, 64b

Clackmannan

Hull — 4ac
Pea pod — 4c, 7
(Pea) shap — *4a,* 6
Shaup — 5
Shuch — 4b
Nil — 1-3, 4d

Stirling

Pea chop — 35a
Pea cod — 7a, 32
Pea hull — 26d
Pea pod — 4, 17, 20, 21ab, 23abc, 25c, 26a, 28, 31, 34, 36
Pease cod — 42a
(Pea) shap — *6,* 7abc*d*ef, *10,* 11-12, *18,* 25d, 26ace, *39a*
(Pea) shaup — *2-3,* 7be, *8-10, 14,* 21b, 22a, 25*bd*, *31,* 37a, *42a*
(Pea) shell — *6,* 12, 25c, 39b
(Pea) shop — *13,* 16, 21b, *22b, 25a, 27a,* 30, *33, 35b,* 36
Pea shup — 17
Shod — 39b
Nil — 1, 5, 15, 19, 24, 26bf, 27b, 29, 37b, 38, 40-41, 42b

Dunbarton

Pea pod — 3, 6, 11, 13abc, 14b, 16ab
Peas cod — 16b
(Pea) shap — *14a,* 17
Pea shaup — 2
Pea shop — 1, 3, 4b, 5-6, 7abc, 9-10
Pea shot — 1, 12, 13bc, 14b
Nil — 4a, 8, 15, 18

Argyll

(Pea) pod — 1, *2-3,* 5, *6-7, 9-10, 14-17, 19, 22-24, 27,* 30, *33, 35*
(Pea) shap — *28, 36*-37, 39-40
Pea shaup — 35
(Pea) shell — *11, 19,* 30
Pea shill — 32
Nil — 4, 8, 12-13, 18, 20-21, 25-26, 29, 31, 34, 38

Bute

Pea pod — 1a, 2, 7, 8ab, 9
Peas cod — 1b
(Pea) shaup — *3,* 9
Pea shell — 8b
Pea shoch — 1a
Pea shop — 1cd
Pea shot — 1a
Nil — 1e, 4-6

Ayr

Chaup — 32
Hull — 45
Husk — 45
Pea — 2b
Pea holm — 26b
(Pea) pod — *5*-6, *10, 20b, 28ce,* 45, *55*
(Pea) shap — *18ab, 28b, 29, 35b, 37-38, 41, 43-44, 46-48,* 49-50, *51-52, 53b,* 54, *56-57*
(Pea) shaup — *2a, 7,* 8b, *11,* 12a, *13-14,* 16ab, 17, *18b, 19,* 20cgh, 22, *24b, 26c,* 28*bc*f, 30ab, 31, *34, 36-37, 40,* 42
(Pea) shaw — 18b, *27*
Pea shell — 3, 56
Pea shod — 18b
(Pea) shop — *1a, 4*-5, 8a, *10-11, 15,* 19, *20ade, 21,* 23, *24a, 25,* 28d, *29, 53a, 57*
Nil — 1b, 9, 12b, 20f, 26a, 28a, 35a, 39

Renfrew

Pea cod — 11f, 13b
Pea code — 11k
Pea pod — 2i, 4e, 5, 8, 11acel, 13c, 14a, 16b, 19, 20a
Peas cod — 14a, 16a
Pea shap — 17
(Pea) shaup — 12a, *13a, 14b,* 21
Pea shoot — 2aei
Pea shop — 2b, 6, 11bk, 15, 16a, 18a, 20ab, 21
Pea shot — 2fij, 4acd, 7
Nil — 1ab, 2cdgh, 3, 4b, 9-10, 11dghij, 12b, 13d, 16cd, 18bc

Lanark

Chaup — 32c
Fitch — 18
Holm — 66
Pea chop — 14ad, 27b, 32b, 36
Pea cod — 46c
Pea hool — 38d
Pea hull — 38d
Pea pod — 2-3, 6, 7c, 8ab, 9a, 14bd, 15a, 16a, 26a, 29a, 35d, 45, 46b, 49a, 60
Peas cod — 7b, 8a, 32e

Lanark cont'd
(Pea) shap — *1, 15c, 50, 52b,* 56, *67ab*
(Pea) shaup — 9b, *15b, 17, 20,* 24, 29d, 31d, *32f,* 33bcd, *34, 35b,* 38ad, *39-40, 45, 46a, 47*-48, 49b, *51,* 52a, 53, *55,* 59a, *61-62, 65*
Pea shaw — 17
Pea shell — 6, 38c
(Pea) shop — *1, 6, 7a, 10a, 11-13, 15c, 16b, 18-19, 22-23, 25bc, 26ab, 27ab, 28,* 29acfg, *30, 31ab, 32ad, 35acd, 37,* 38e, *40,* 42, *46bc,* 57abc, *58, 59b,* 63, *64a*
Pea shot — 25d
Pea shup — 31c, 38b
Nil — 4-5, 10b, 14c, 21, 25a, 29be, 33a, 41, 43-44, 54, 64b

West Lothian
(Pea) cod — 1b, *9a, 13*
Pea code — 2
(Pea) pod — *1a, 2-3, 6, 12,* 15, *20a, 22*
Peas — 11
Pea shap — 5-6, 8, 19b
Pea shaup — 18
Pea shop — 4, 16, 17a, 20a, 21ab
Pizzer — 11
Nil — 1cd, 7, 9b, 10, 14, 17b, 19a, 20b

Midlothian
Pea cod — 2, 4, 8b, 29
(Pea) hill — 24, *25a, 27*
(Pea) huil — 23a, *30,* 32
(Pea) pod — *3, 6ab, 7a, 8a, 10, 14a, 18,* 19, *20-21, 23b,* 25c, *28*
Peas cod — 21
Pea shap — 12a, 13
(Pea) shaup — 11, *12b,* 23b
Pea shop — 14ab, 25b
Sheil — 26a
Nil — 1, 5, 7b, 9, 15-17, 22, 25d, 26b, 31

East Lothian
Hail — 17
Pea cod — 4b, 5, 9
(Pea) hill — *7,* 10, *21*
Pea huil — 8, 16
(Pea) hull — *2,* 6b, *14*-15
Pea pod — 9, 15, 18-20
(Pea) shell — *1-2, 6a,* 13, 15-*16*
Shap — 4a
Nil — 3, 11-12

Berwick
Pad — 27
(Pea) hail — 1, 4, *6, 12*
Pea heel — 32
(Pea) hill — *16a,* 18
(Pea) huil — *9,* 21
Pea hule — 13
(Pea) hull — 1, *3, 17,* 20, 23, *31*
(Pea) pod — *2, 8, 10,* 12, *15, 16b, 29, 31-32*
Shell — 27
Slough — 23
Swap — 5
Yhale — 4
Nil — 7, 11, 14, 16c, 19, 22, 24-26, 28, 30

Peebles
Pea hule — 1
Pea hull — 8
Pea pod — 3, 4c, 5, 6ab
(Pea) shap — 1, *4bc,* 5
Pea shaup — 3, 7
Pea shop — 2
Shalp — 9
Nil — 4a, 10

Selkirk
Huil — 3-4, 7
Pea hule — 2a
(Pea) pod — *2bcd, 4, 8*
Nil — 1, 2e, 5-6

Roxburgh
Green peas — 13
Pea hail — 3a, 5-6, 13
Pea hill — 8, 15a, 23
Pea huil — 2, 4, 9ab, 15b, 16, 20, 21ad, 24, 26
Pea hule — 4, 12
(Pea) hull — 7-*8*
(Pea) pod — 1, *9a, 17,* 20, *21af, 22, 25, 27*
Pea swap — 4, 21c, 28
Shill — 3b
Whop — 21c
Nil — 10-11, 14, 18-19, 21be

Dumfries
Hool — 29
Pea — 6
(Pea) hull — 8b, 9-10, 13, 31a, 32, *35*
Pea husk — 35
Pea pang — 8a, 21b, 24, 31bcdef, 34, 41-42
Pea pod — 1a, 4-5, 7, 8a, 12, 16, 17b, 19-20, 22, 24, 26, 29, 33, 40, 43, 45a, 46
Pea shap — 2, 32
Pea shaup — 1a
(Pea) shell — 17*ab*
Pea shull — 11
Pea sleugh — 16
(Pea) slugh — 25, 37-*38,* 46
Shill — 14, 37
Sleuch — 28, 35
Sloosh — 29
Slouch — 6
Slough — 34, 39
Sluch — 15, 27
Sluf — 18
Nil — 1b, 3, 21a, 23, 30, 36, 44, 45b, 47-49

Kirkcudbright
Pea hulk — 7
(Pea) hull — 2, *4*-5, *7*-8, 12ab, 15a, 17, 20, 22-23, *26*
Pea pod — 6-7, 10, 16, 18
Pea shap — 7
Pea shaum — 1
Pea shaw — 1
Pea shol — 19
(Pea) shull — *1,* 17, 21a*c*, 22
Shell — 9, 11
Shuck — 22, 25
Nil — 3, 13-14, 15b, 21b, 24, 27

Wigtown
Pea — 16
Pea pod — 2, 13-14
Pea hull — 5a, 11, 16
Pea shap — 17
Pea shop — 18
(Pea) shull — 10, *17*
Shell — 5a, 6
Nil — 1, 3-4, 5b, 7-9, 12, 15

Northumberland
Horm — 37
Husk — 29b, 59b, 86
Hyull — 37
(Pea) hull — 1a, 2ab, 5-6, 9, *10,* 11, *15-16,* 17-18, 19a, 20b, 24a, 29c, 39, 40b, 45, 59b, 68
(Pea) pod — 2b, *5-6, 8, 12-14, 16, 21, 30-31, 34b, 35-36,* 37, 40a, *41cd, 42, 45-46, 48, 53ab, 54, 57, 59b, 60, 62b, 64b, 65b, 66, 69c, 70, 71bcd, 72cg,* 82, 86-*87, 88b, 89, 91, 94b, 95b, 99d, 101a,* 106, *110, 112, 120a, 127a, 140*
Pea scod — 73, 108a, 130d
(Pea) shaa — 71a, *72f, 90,* 129c
Pea shaw — 69ab, 98, 100
(Pea) shell — *7, 18,* 26-*27,* 29b, 39, 40a, 41b*d,* 53a, 59b, 68, 69*bd,* 71a, 72*bi,* 93, 114
Pea shuck — 64a, 99d, 127b
(Pea) skin — 71a, 93, *95b, 111b*
Peaskit — 124a
(Pea) squab — 25, 64a, *71c, 101b, 118a, 126b, 127d, 129a, 130acdf*
Peasquad — 74
(Pea) swab — 51, *59d, 62a, 71c, 72cd, 87, 92, 96, 103a, 118ab, 120b, 123, 126bcdf,* 127abcfh, *128, 130be, 131*
(Pea) swad — 22, 29a*bf, 32,* 33b, *35, 38, 44, 47-49,* 50-51, *52, 53a, 54-55,* 56-57, 59cf, 60, *62cf,* 64b, *65a,* 67-68, 69*aegh,* 72egij, 75-81, *83*-84, 86, 88a, 89-*90, 95a,* 102, *103bc, 104ab, 105-106,* 107, 108*abc, 109, 111ab,* 114, *116-117, 119, 120c, 122ab,* 124ab, *126a,* 127eg, *129b, 132-133,* 134, *135,* 136-137, *138, 140-142*
Swag — 46
Nil — 1bc, 3-4, 19b, 20a, 23, 24b, 28, 29de, 33a, 41a, 43, 58, 59ae, 61, 62degh, 63, 69f, 71e, 72ahkl, 85, 94a, 97, 99abc, 113, 115, 121, 125, 126e, 139, 143

Cumberland
Hull — 56
Pea — 56
Pea pod — 1a, 13c, 23-24, 42, 49, 56-60
Pea scod — 41
Pea skell — 37b
Peas pod — 50
Pea swab — 20
(Pea) swad — *1a, 2-3,* 4, *5ab, 6-9,* 11-12, *13abcd, 14, 15abc, 16-19,* 21-*22, 24-34, 36, 37a, 38-47,* 48, *49, 51-58, 60-62,* 63*ab*
Pea wad — 12
Scob — 40
Nil — 1b, 10, 35

Down
Ear — 29
(Pea) hull — 11, 14, *22,* 27
Pea husk — 22
Pea pod — 2a, 6-7, 9, 15, 18-19, 24-26
(Pea) shap — 3, 8, *13*
(Pea) shell — *2a,* 5-*6, 15*
Shaup — 10
Shill — 2b, 5
Shull — 23
Nil — 1, 4, 12, 16-17, 20-21, 25, 28, 30

Tyrone
Hull — 5, 8, 14, 16
(Pea) pod — 1, *7*-8, *10-11*
Pea shell — 11
Nil — 2-4, 6, 9, 12-13, 15

Antrim
Hull — 5b, 15, 16b, 29, 34
Hulm — 16a
(Pea) pod — *1, 3, 9, 13,* 17, *19, 22, 29*
Shap — 5b, 11, 26, 33
Nil — 2, 4, 4A, 5a, 6-7, 8ab, 10, 12, 14, 16c, 18, 20-21, 23-25, 27-28, 30-32

Donegal
Finger — 10a
(Pea) pod — 1, 5, 5A, *8, 12*
(Pea) shell — 5-*6*
Skin — 6
Nil — 1A, 2-4, 7, 7A, 9, 10b, 11, 13

Fermanagh
(Pea) hull — 2, *10*
Pea pod — 4, 8-9
Nil — 1, 3, 5-6, 7ab

Armagh
Hull — 6ab
Pea pod — 4
Nil — 1-3, 5

Londonderry
Hull — 2
(Pea) pod — *3,* 3A
Shell — 4
Nil — 1, 1AB, 5-7

APPENDIX A . PHONETIC ORTHOGRAPHICAL MAPS

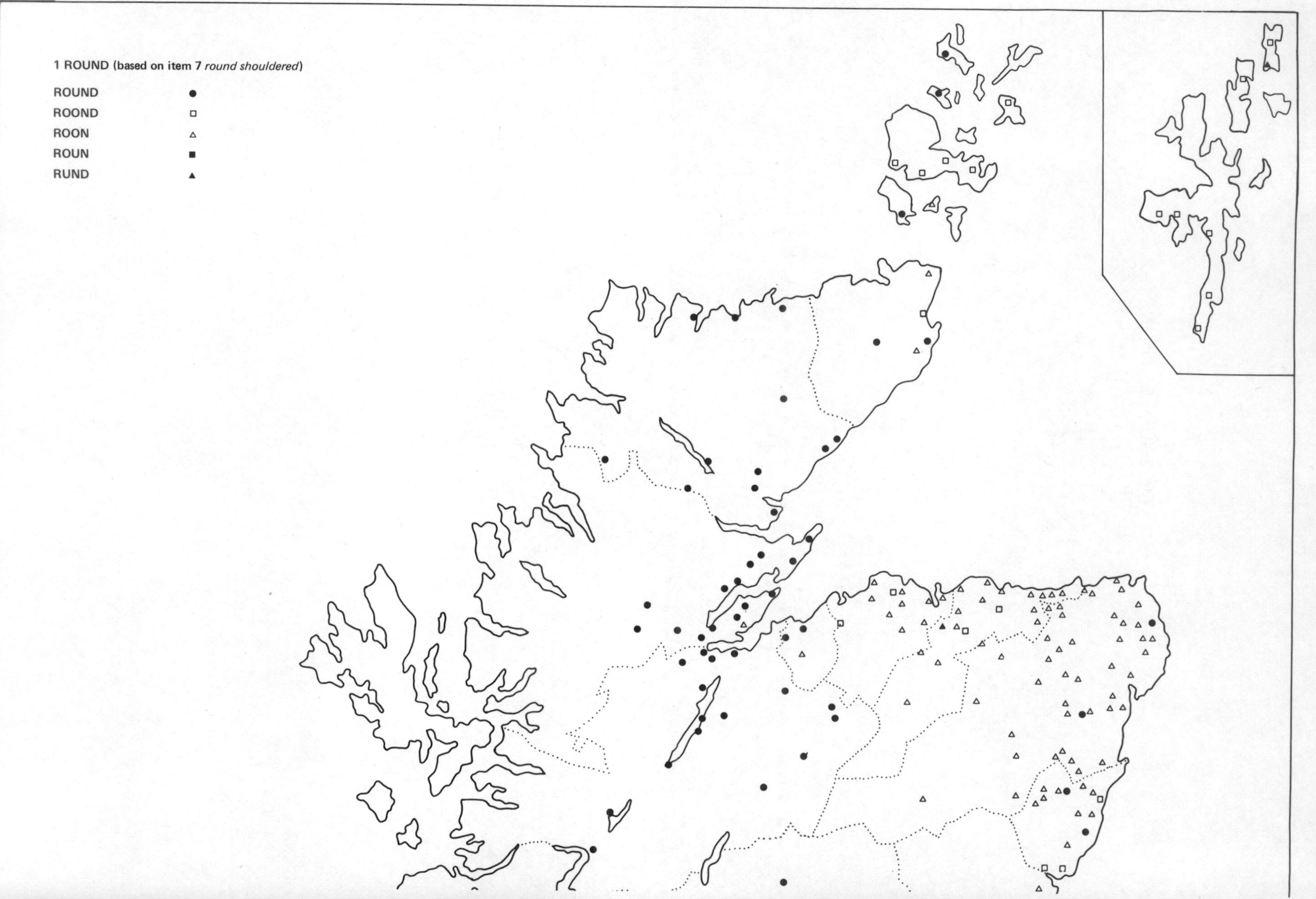
1 ROUND (based on item 7 *round shouldered*)
ROUND ●
ROOND □
ROON △
ROUN ■
RUND ▲

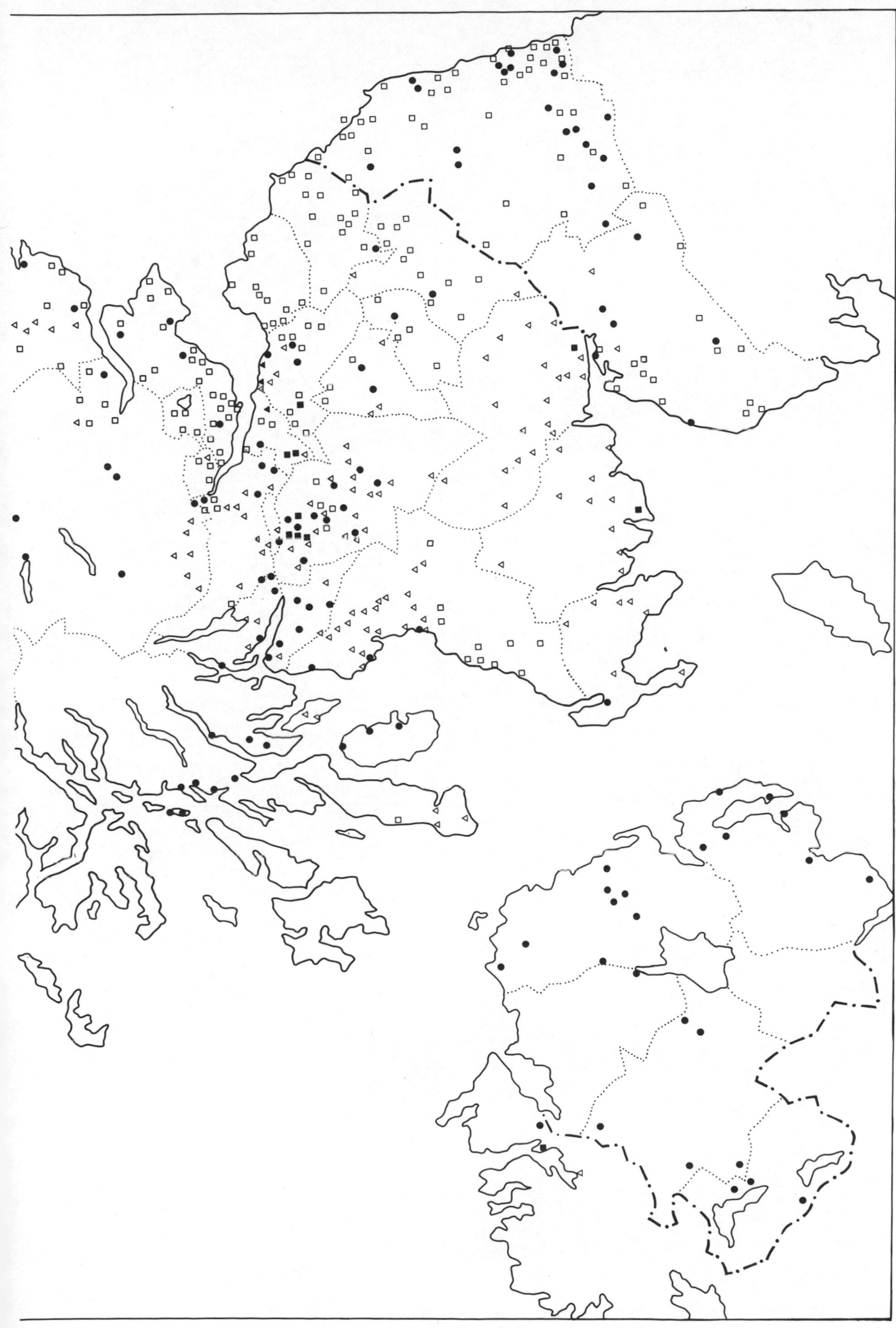

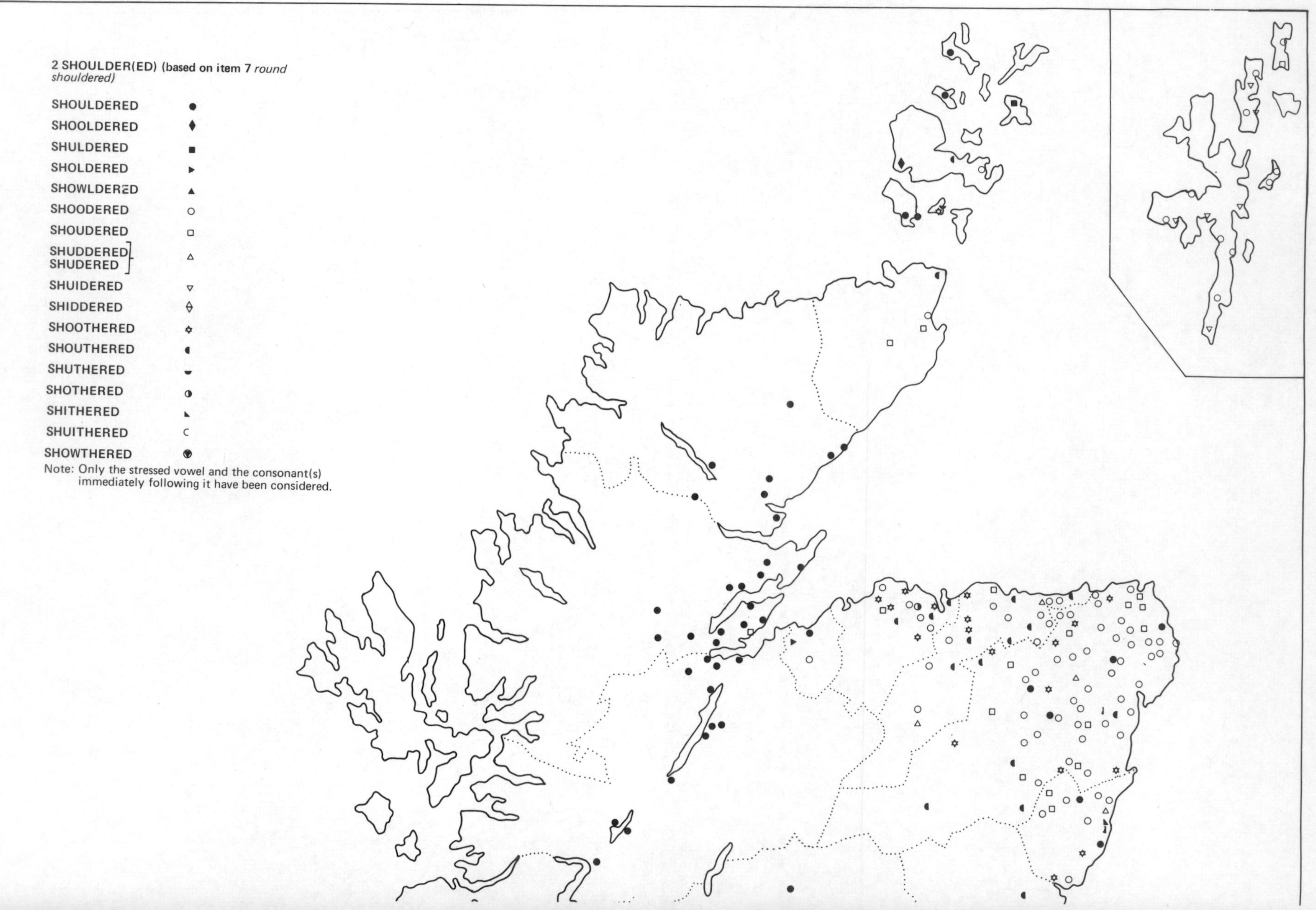
2 SHOULDER(ED) (based on item 7 *round shouldered*)
SHOULDERED ●
SHOOLDERED ◆
SHULDERED ■
SHOLDERED ▶
SHOWLDERED ▲
SHOODERED ○
SHOUDERED □
SHUDDERED, SHUDERED △
SHUIDERED ▽
SHIDDERED
SHOOTHERED
SHOUTHERED
SHUTHERED
SHOTHERED
SHITHERED
SHUITHERED
SHOWTHERED
Note: Only the stressed vowel and the consonant(s) immediately following it have been considered.

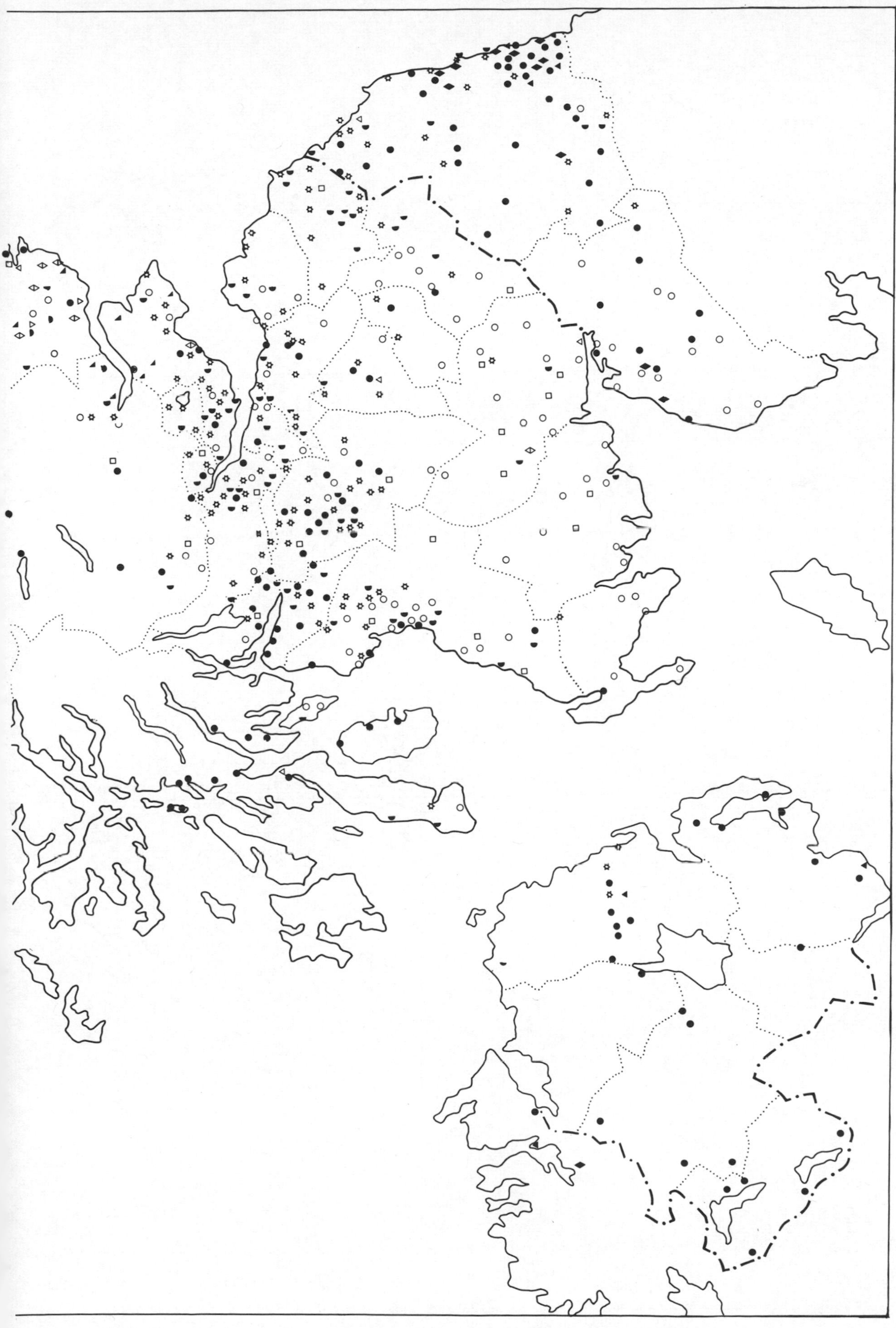

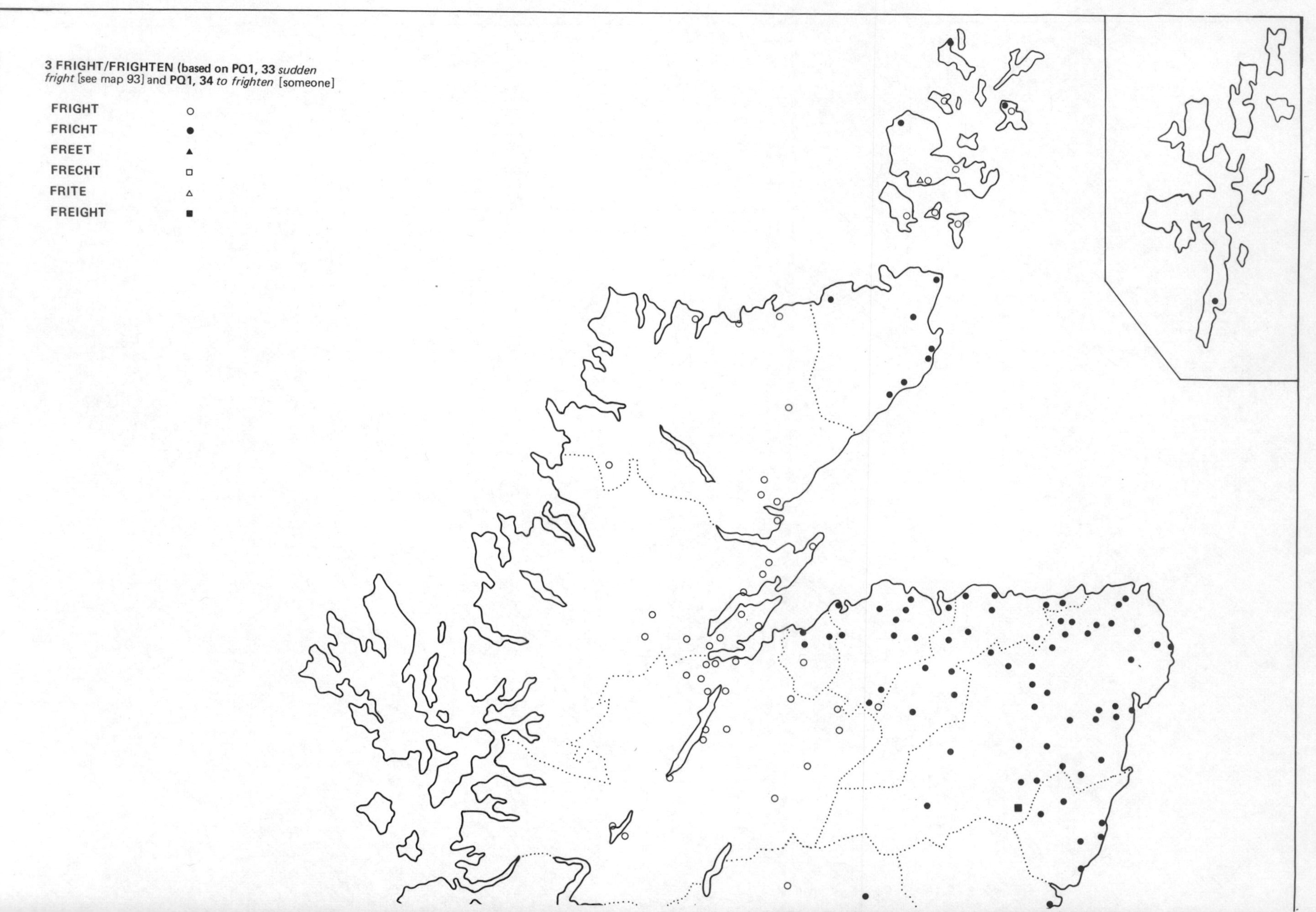
3 FRIGHT/FRIGHTEN (based on PQ1, 33 *sudden fright* [see map 93] and PQ1, 34 *to frighten* [someone]
FRIGHT ○
FRICHT ●
FREET ▲
FRECHT □
FRITE △
FREIGHT ■

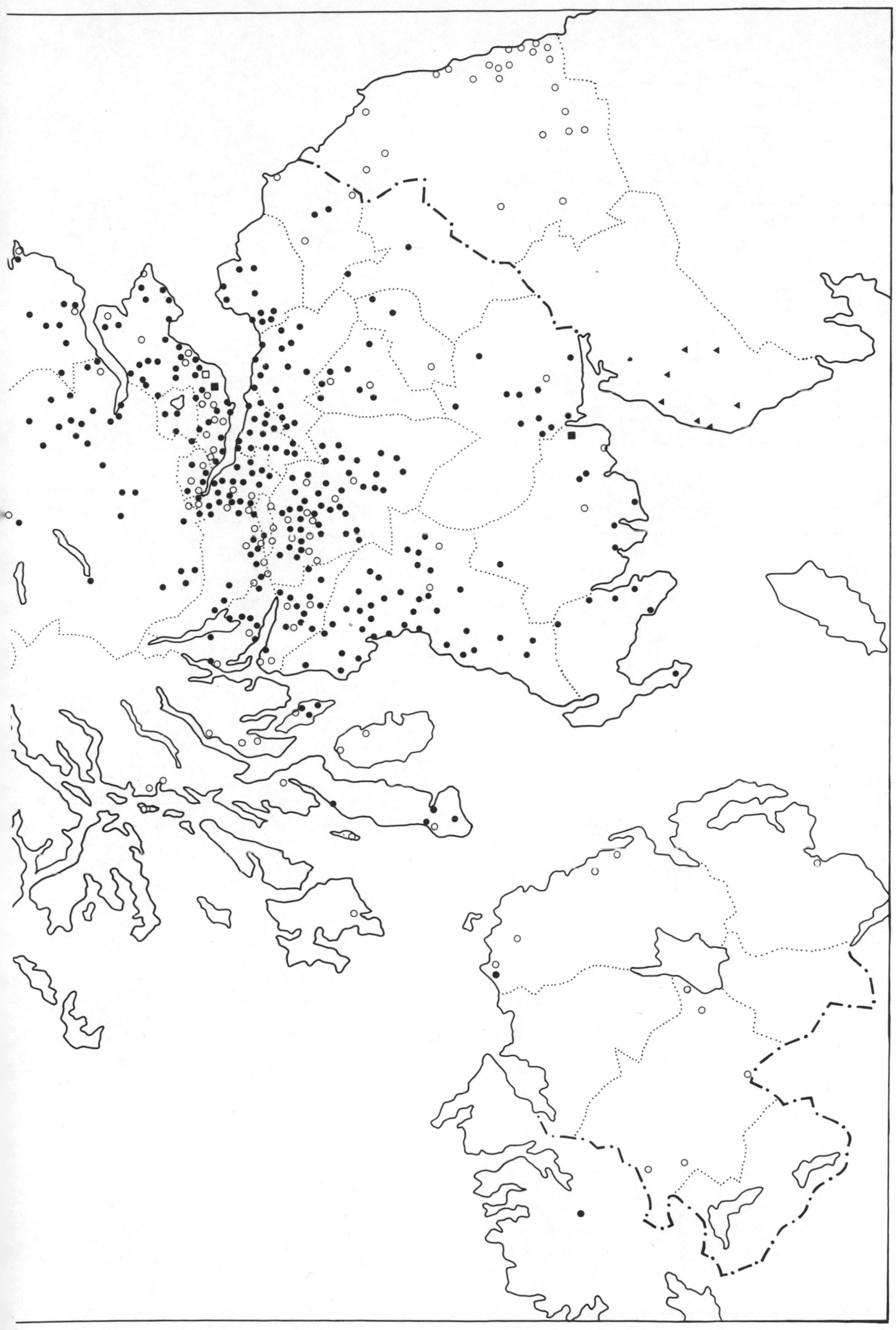

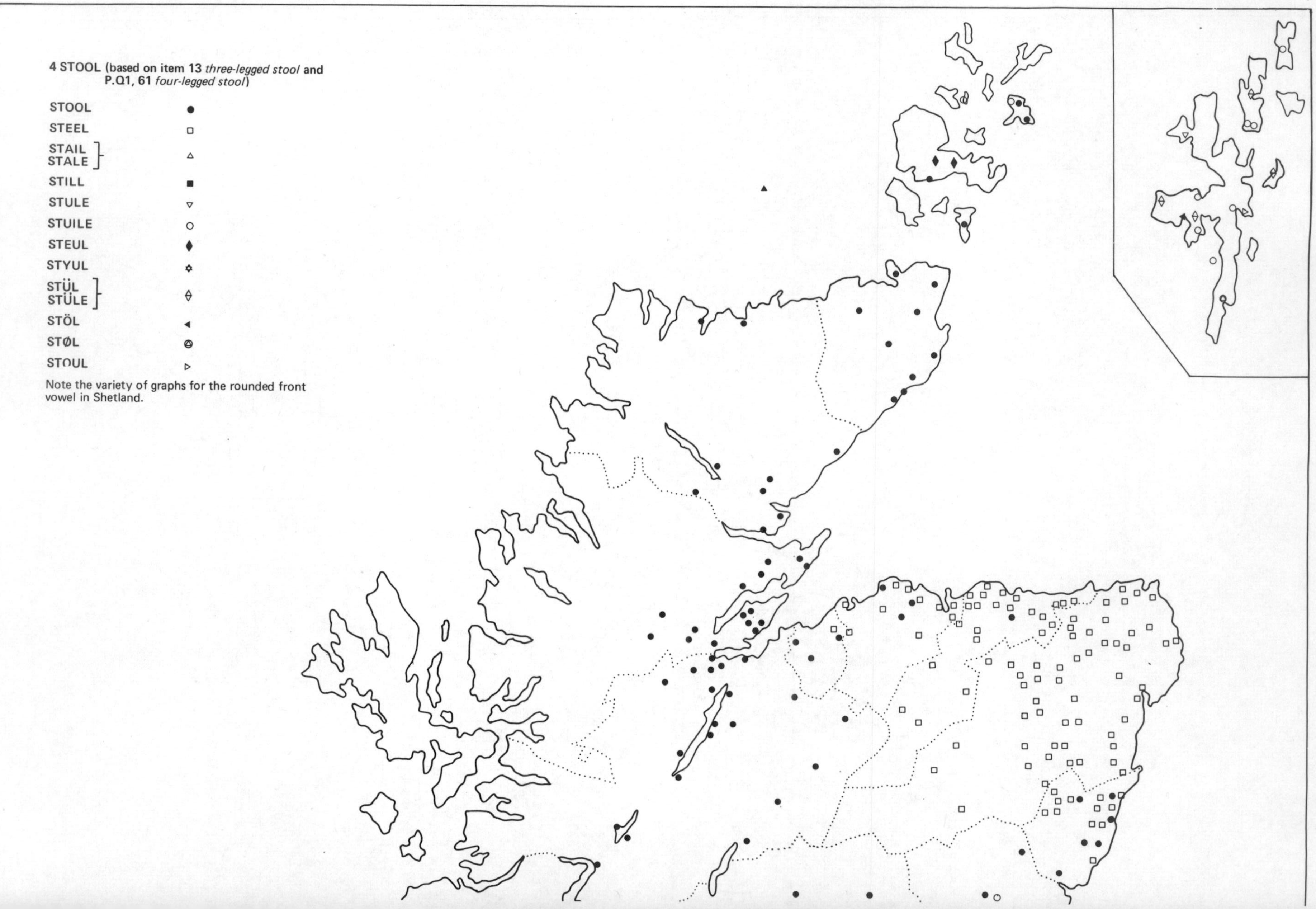
4 STOOL (based on item 13 *three-legged stool* and P.Q1, 61 *four-legged stool*)
STOOL
STEEL
STAIL
STALE
STILL
STULE
STUILE
STEUL
STYUL
STÜL
STÜLE
STÖL
STØL
STOUL
Note the variety of graphs for the rounded front vowel in Shetland.

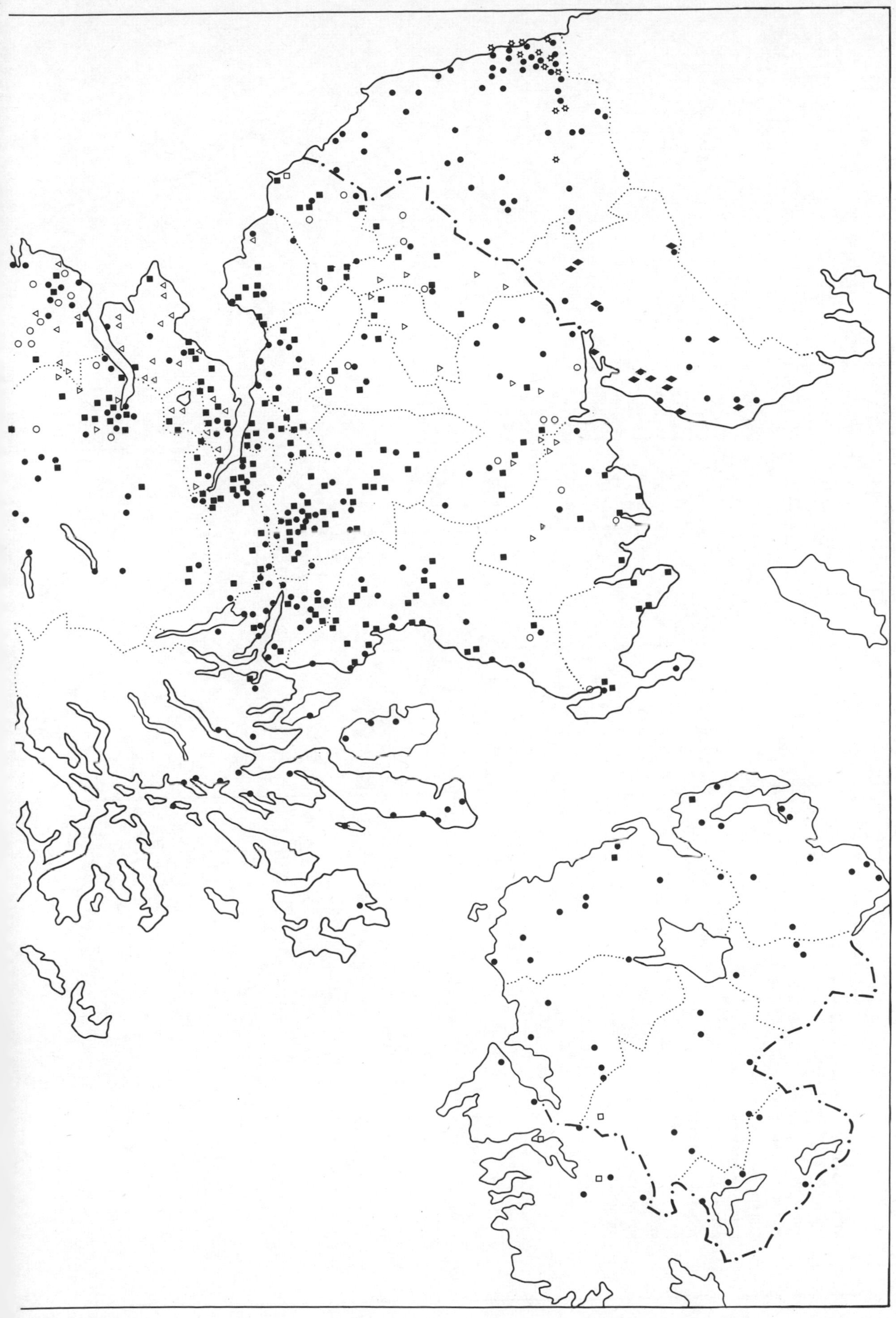

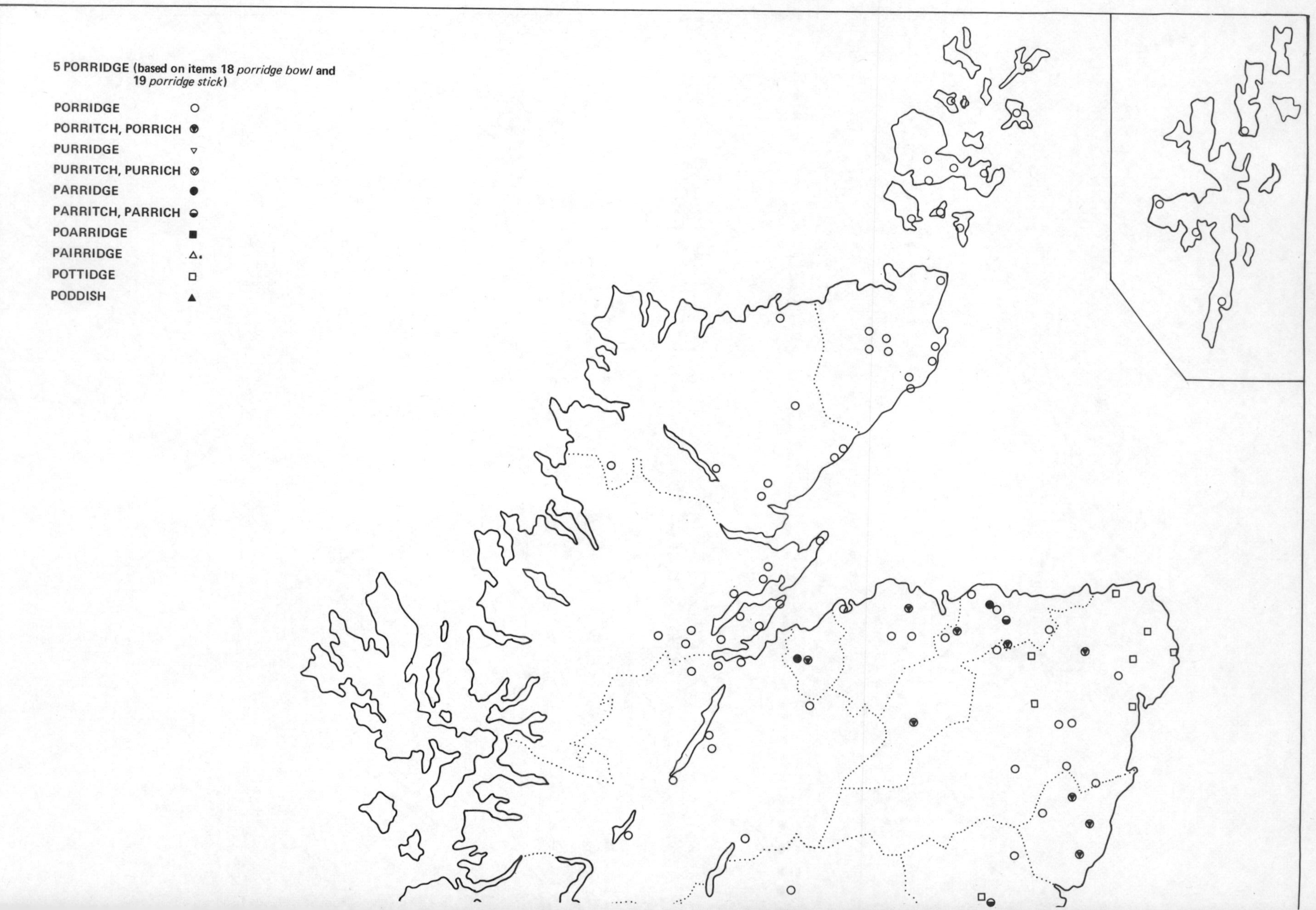
5 PORRIDGE (based on items 18 porridge bowl and 19 porridge stick)
PORRIDGE
PORRITCH, PORRICH
PURRIDGE
PURRITCH, PURRICH
PARRIDGE
PARRITCH, PARRICH
POARRIDGE
PAIRRIDGE
POTTIDGE
PODDISH

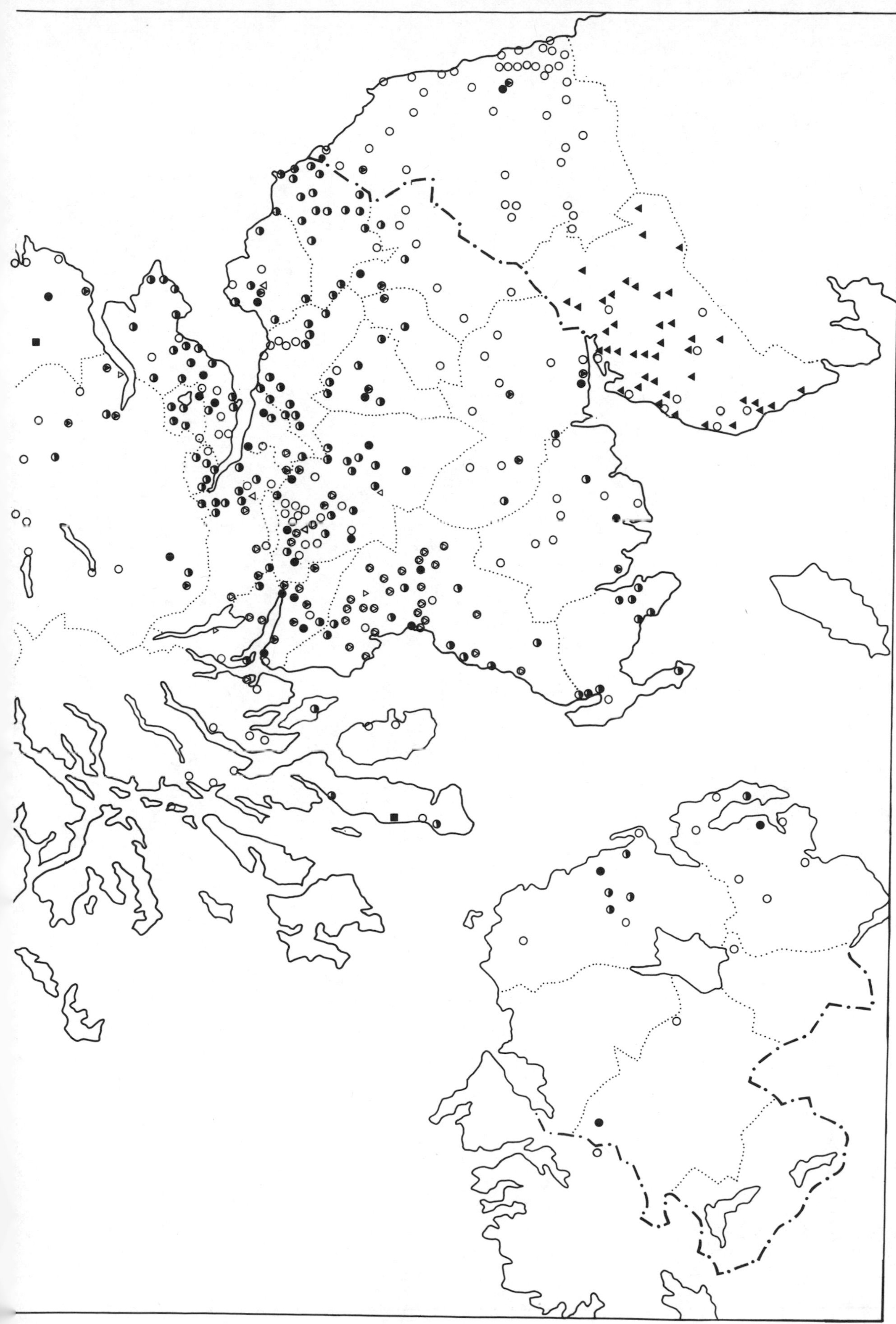

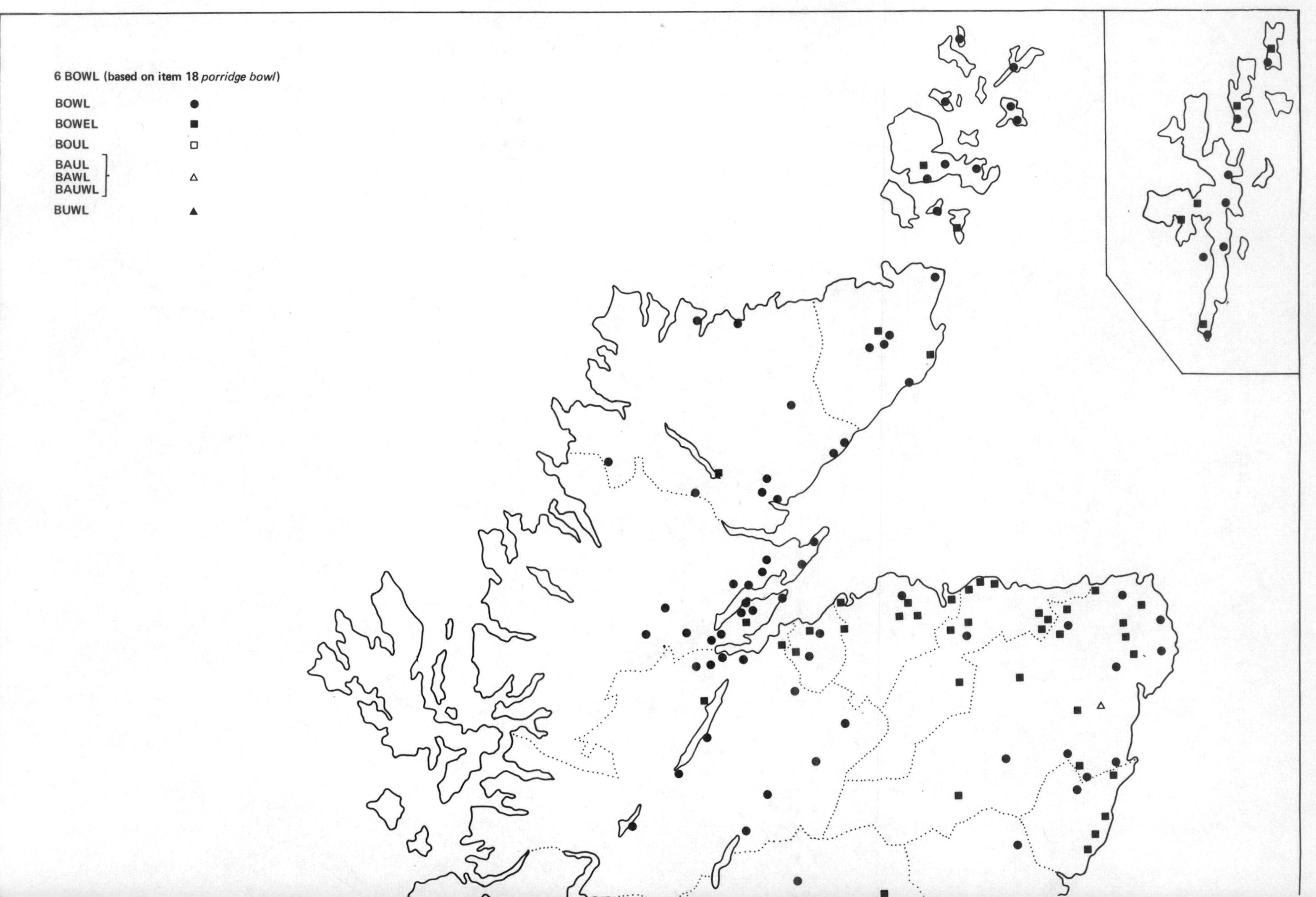
6 BOWL (based on item 18 *porridge bowl*)
BOWL
BOWEL
BOUL
BAUL
BAWL
BAUWL
BUWL

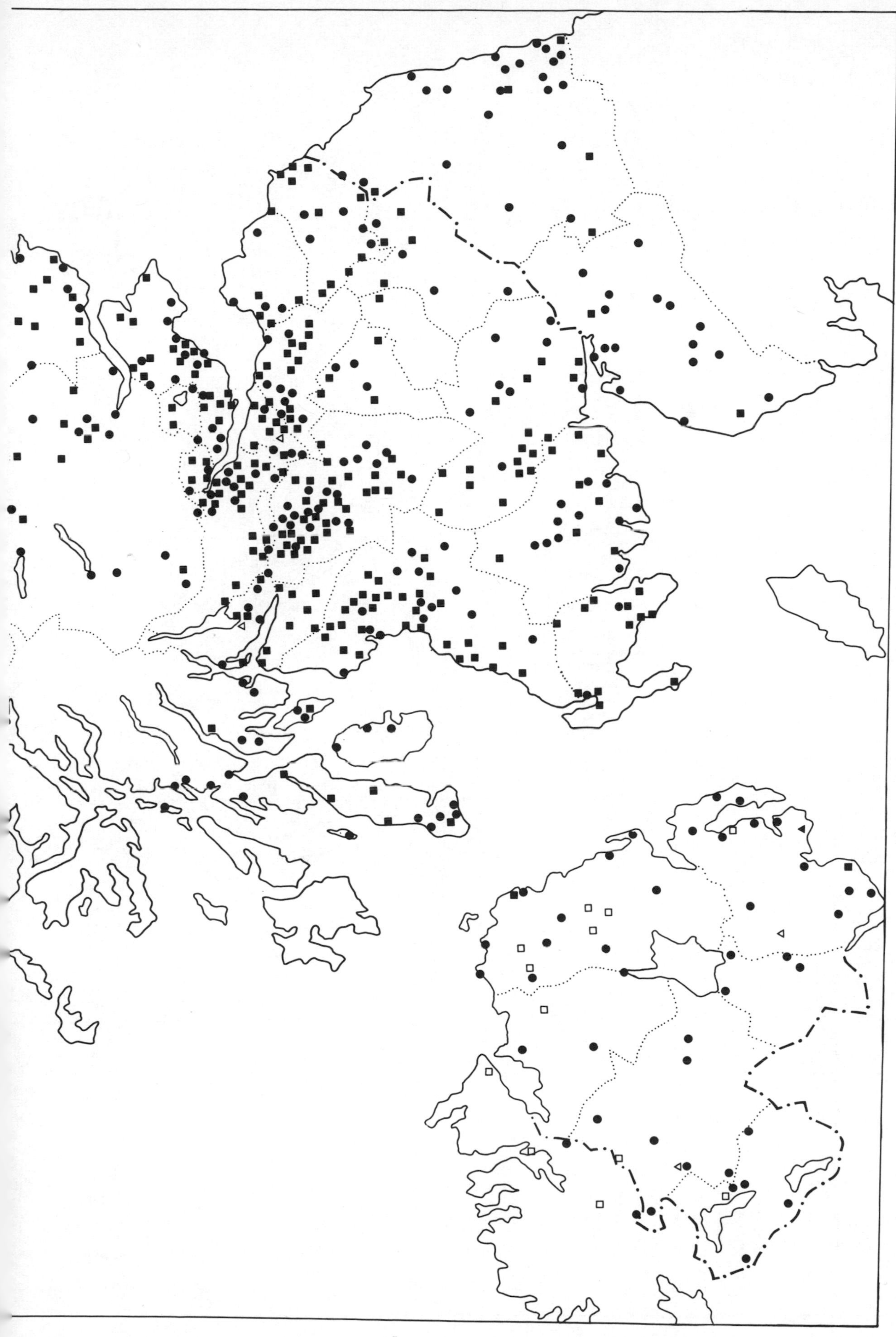

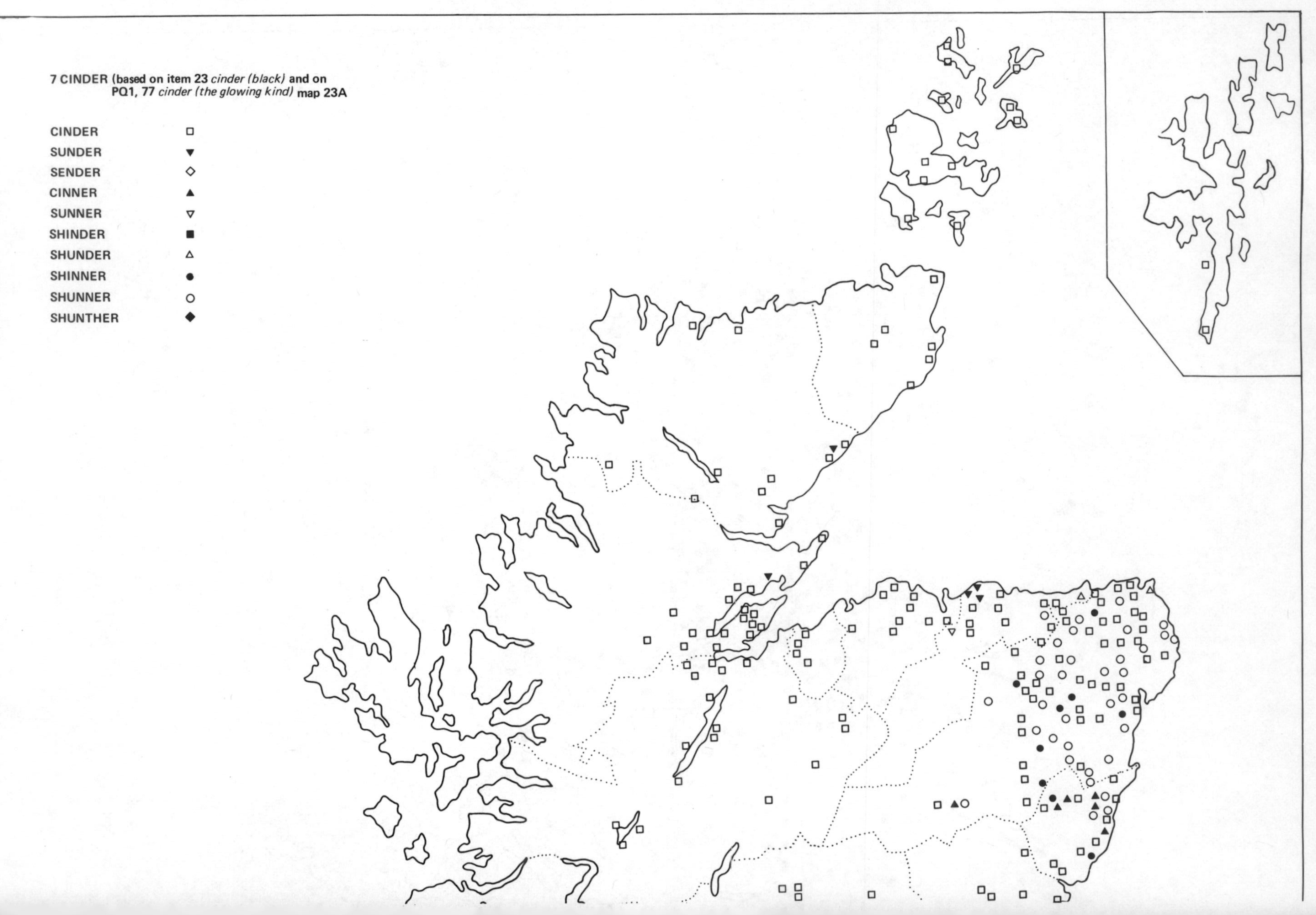
7 CINDER (based on item 23 *cinder (black)* and on
PQ1, 77 *cinder (the glowing kind)* map 23A
CINDER
SUNDER
SENDER
CINNER
SUNNER
SHINDER
SHUNDER
SHINNER
SHUNNER
SHUNTHER

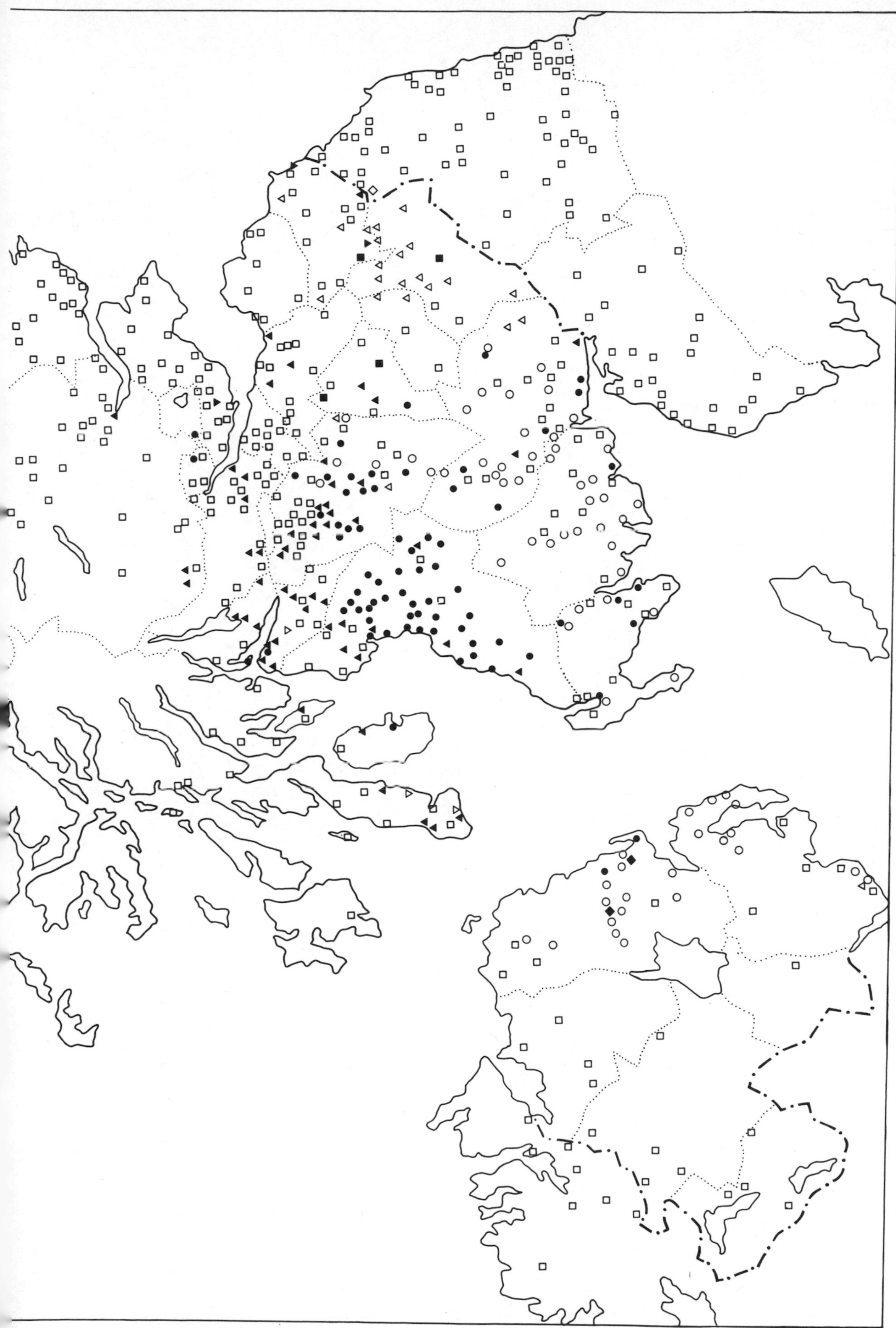

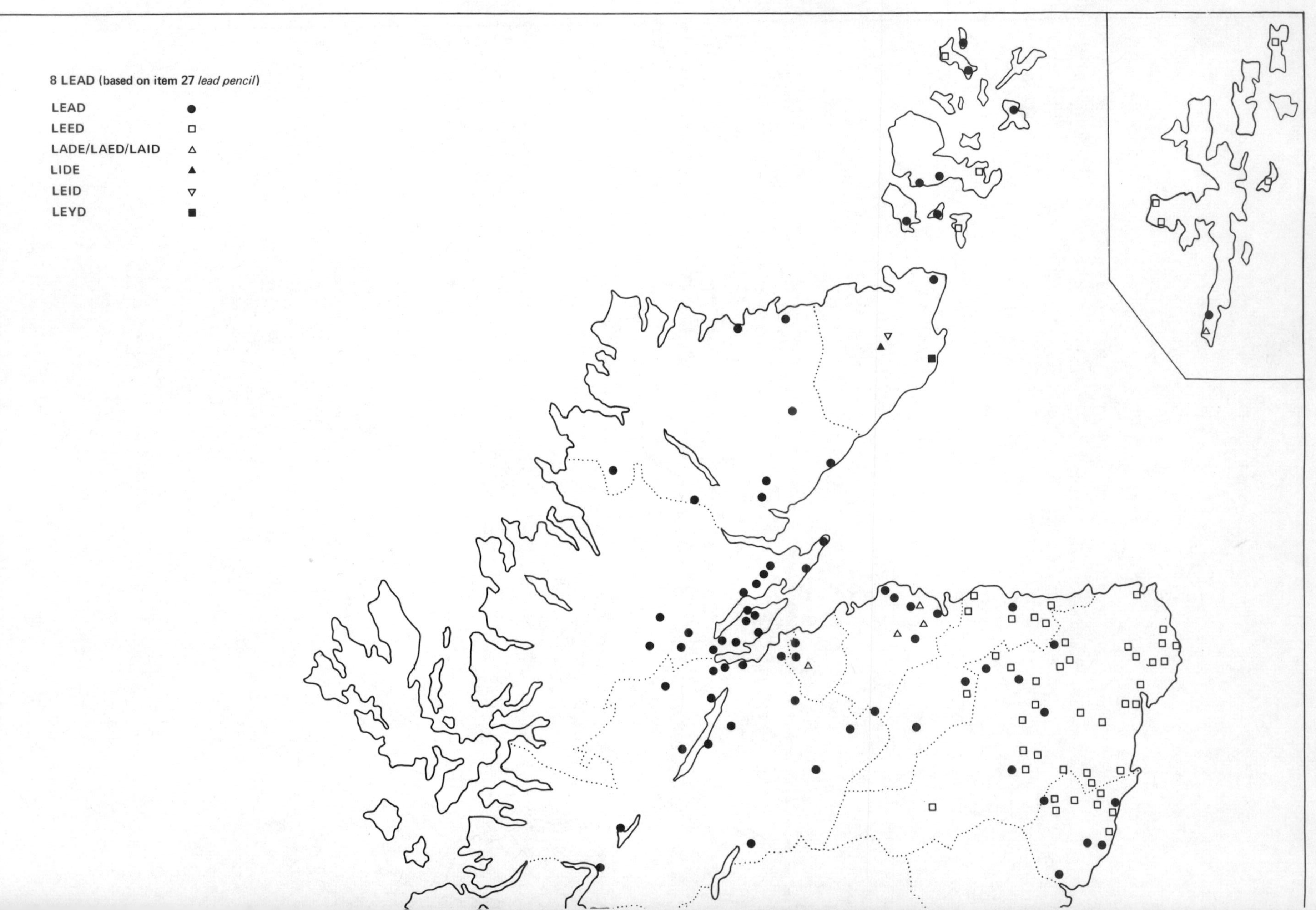
8 LEAD (based on item 27 *lead pencil*)
LEAD ●
LEED □
LADE/LAED/LAID △
LIDE ▲
LEID ▽
LEYD ■

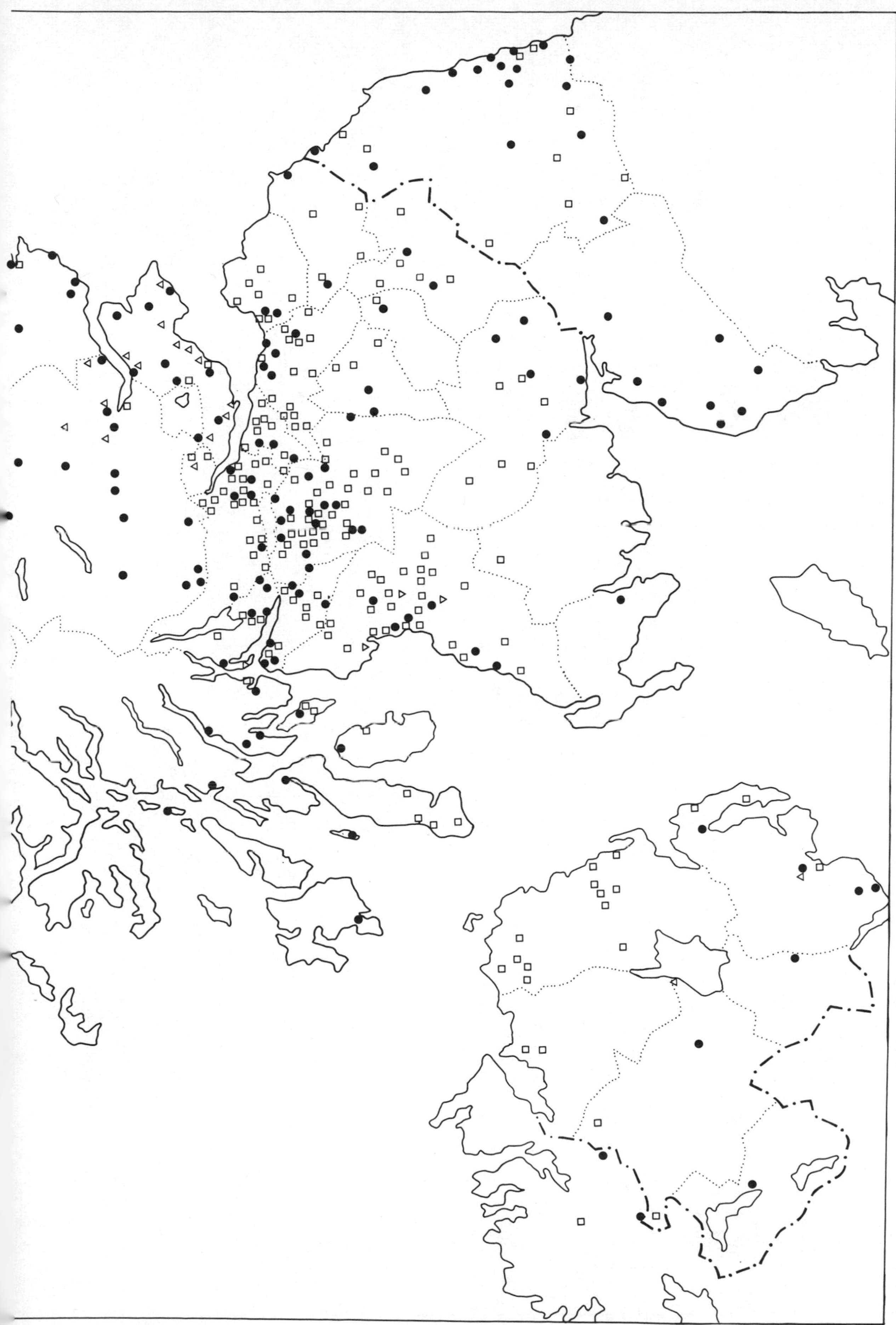

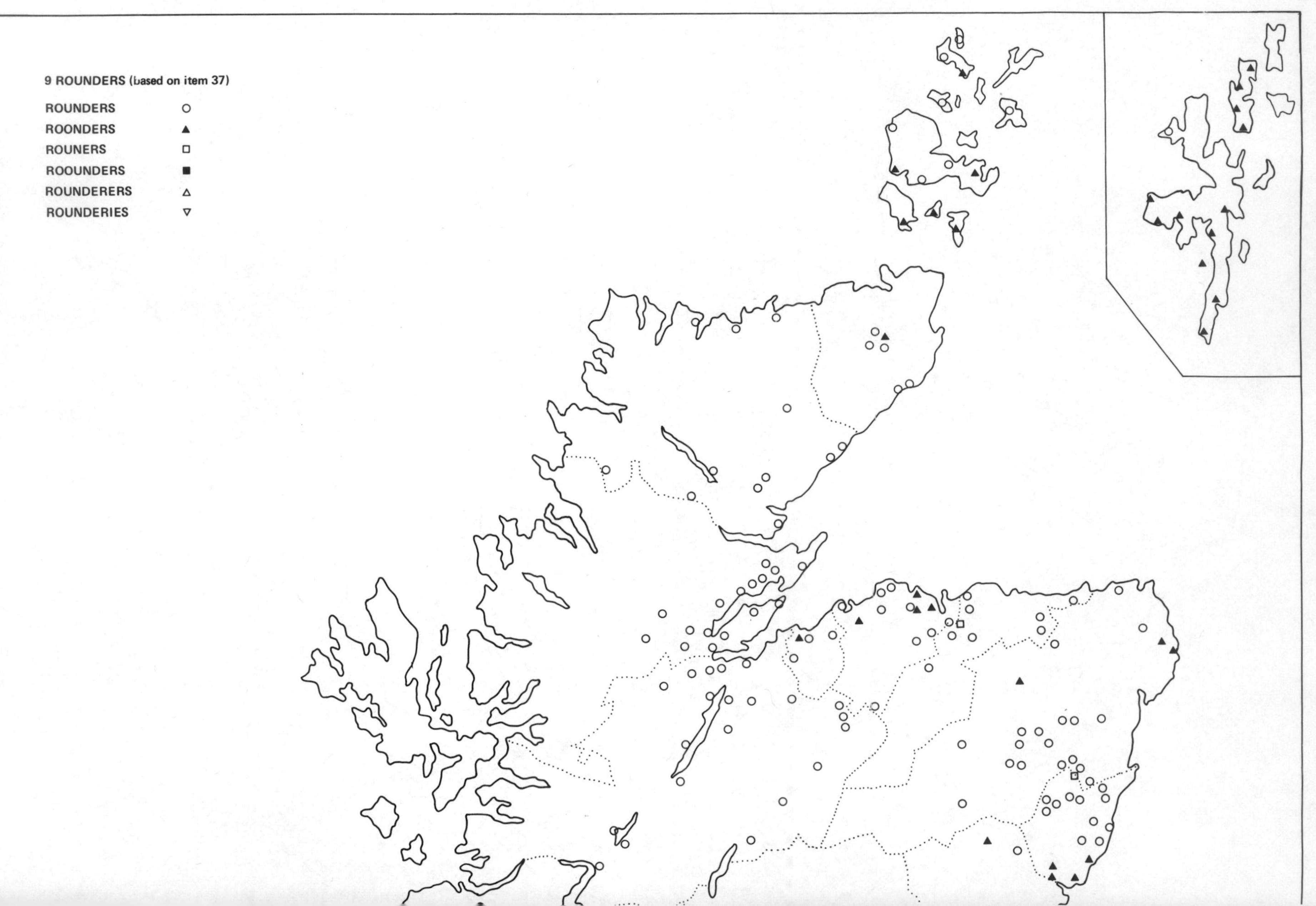
9 ROUNDERS (based on item 37)
ROUNDERS ○
ROONDERS ▲
ROUNERS □
ROOUNDERS ■
ROUNDERERS △
ROUNDERIES ▽

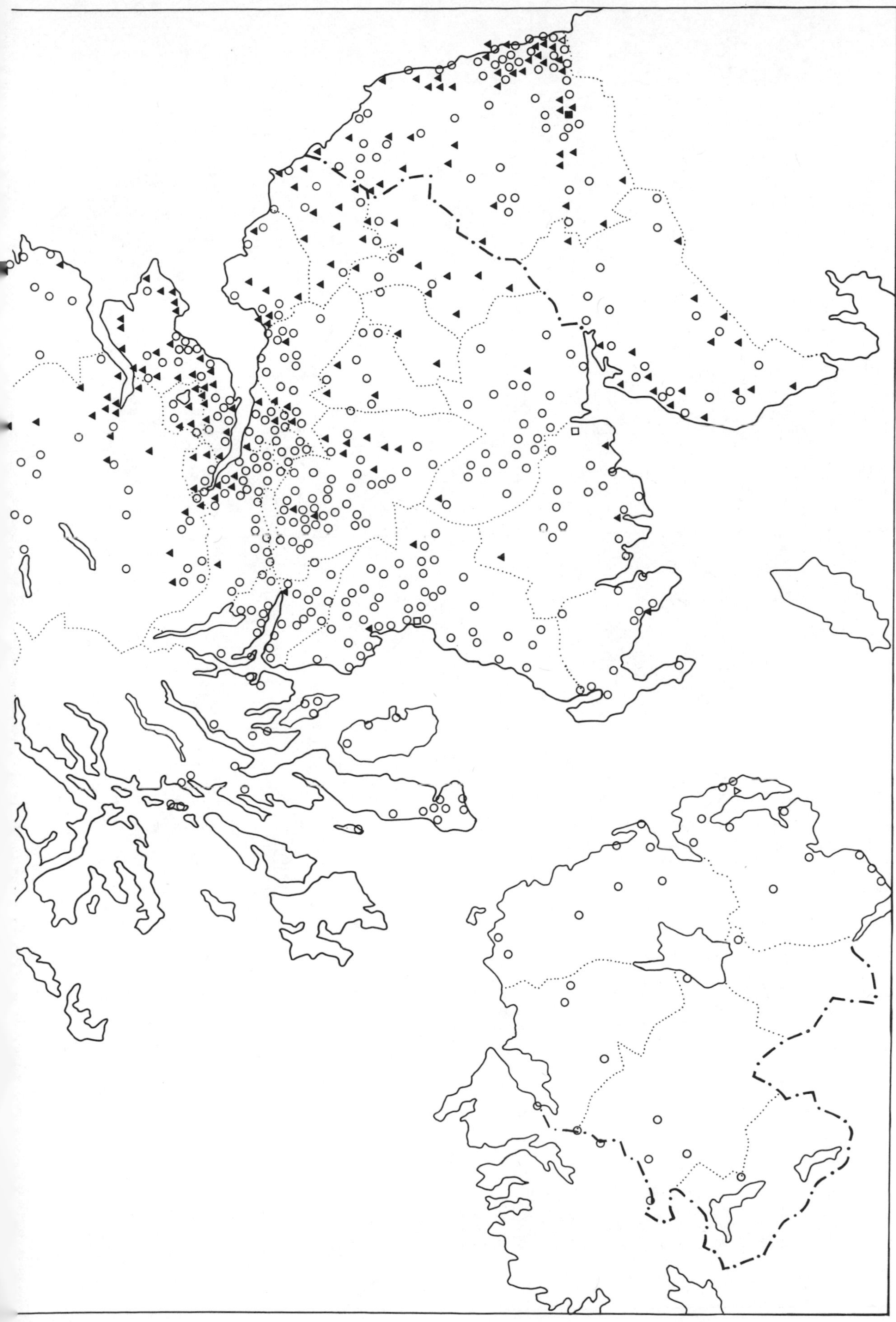

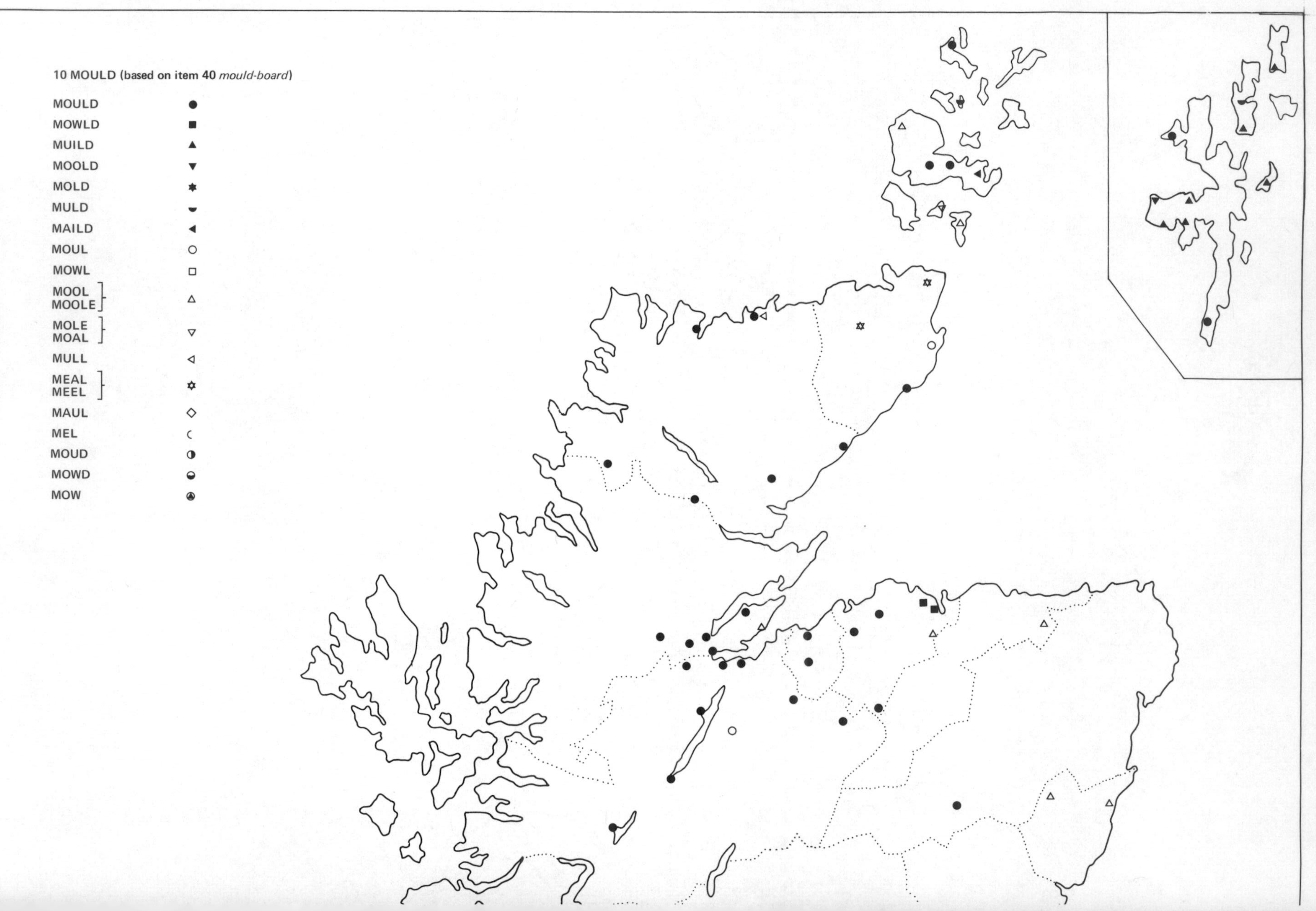
10 MOULD (based on item 40 *mould-board*)
MOULD
MOWLD
MUILD
MOOLD
MOLD
MULD
MAILD
MOUL
MOWL
MOOL
MOOLE
MOLE
MOAL
MULL
MEAL
MEEL
MAUL
MEL
MOUD
MOWD
MOW

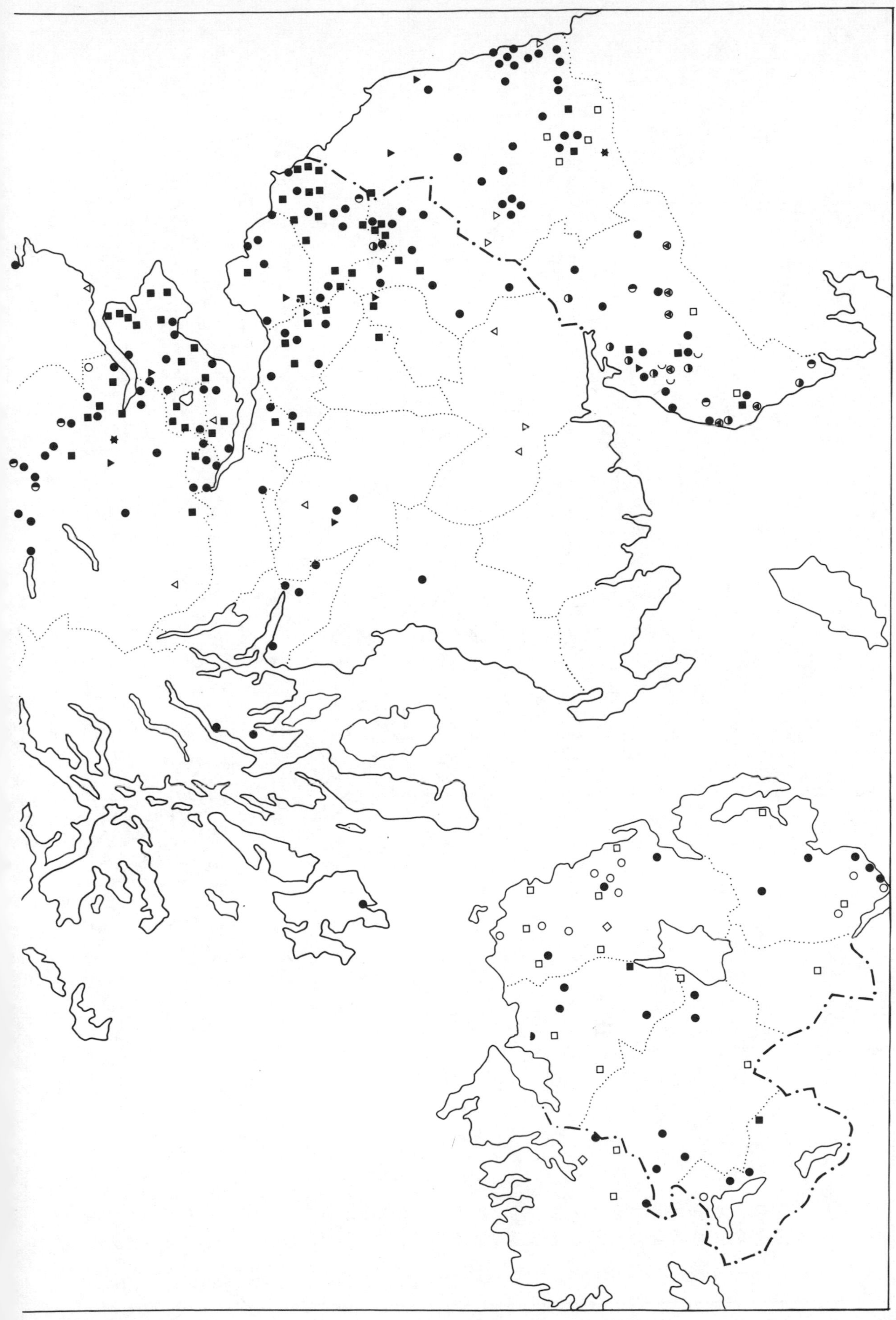

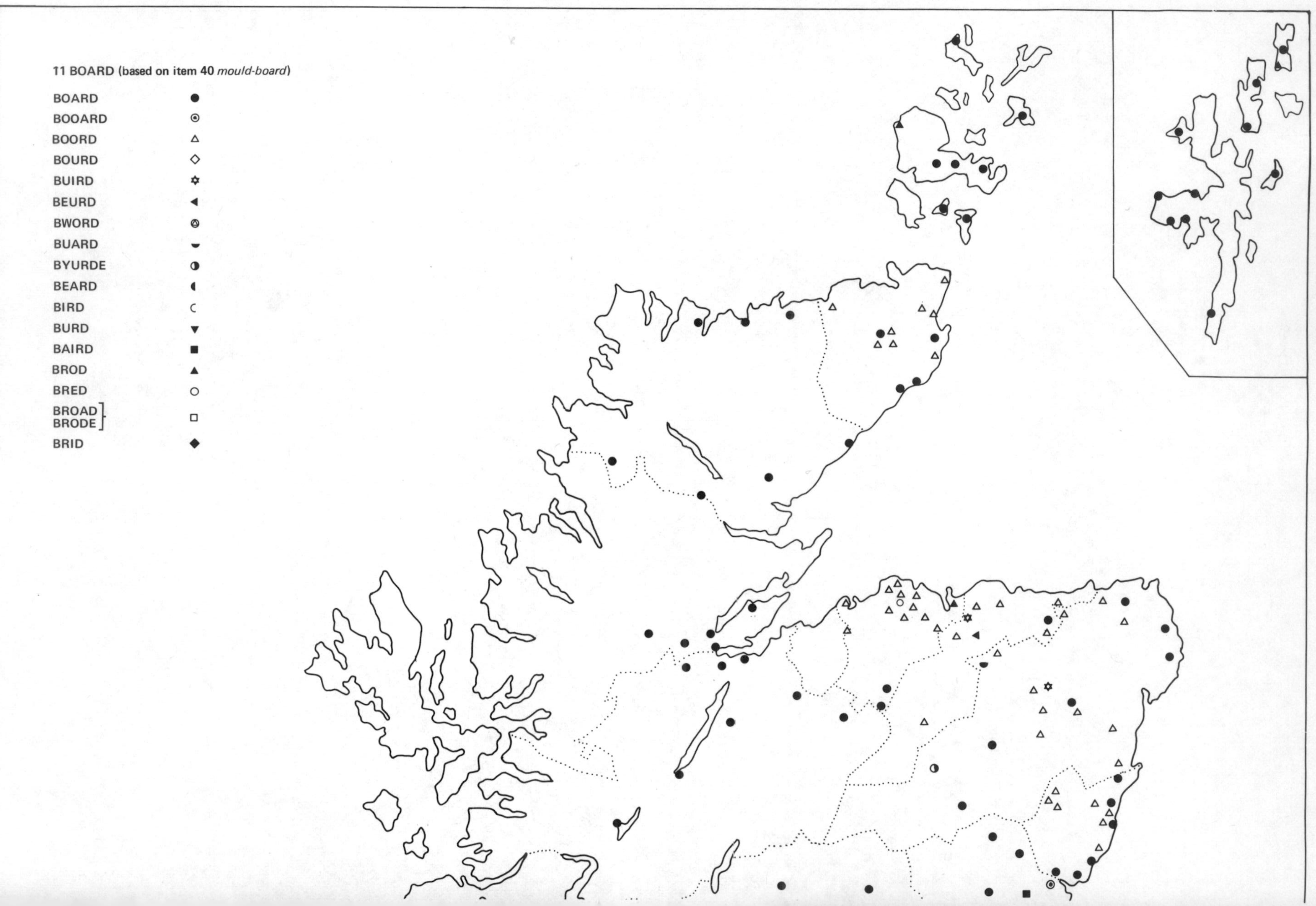
11 BOARD (based on item 40 *mould-board*)
BOARD
BOOARD
BOORD
BOURD
BUIRD
BEURD
BWORD
BUARD
BYURDE
BEARD
BIRD
BURD
BAIRD
BROD
BRED
BROAD
BRODE
BRID

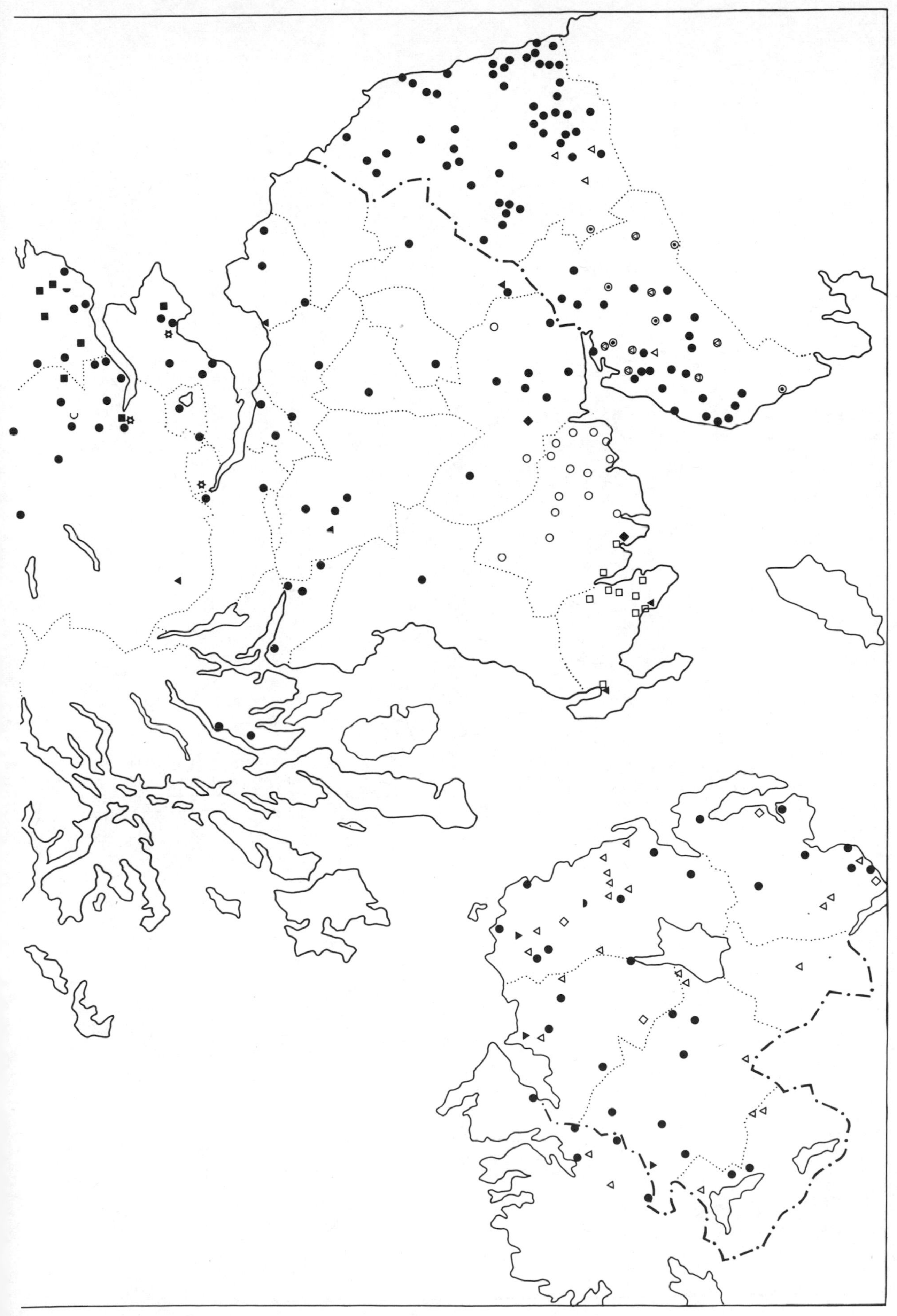

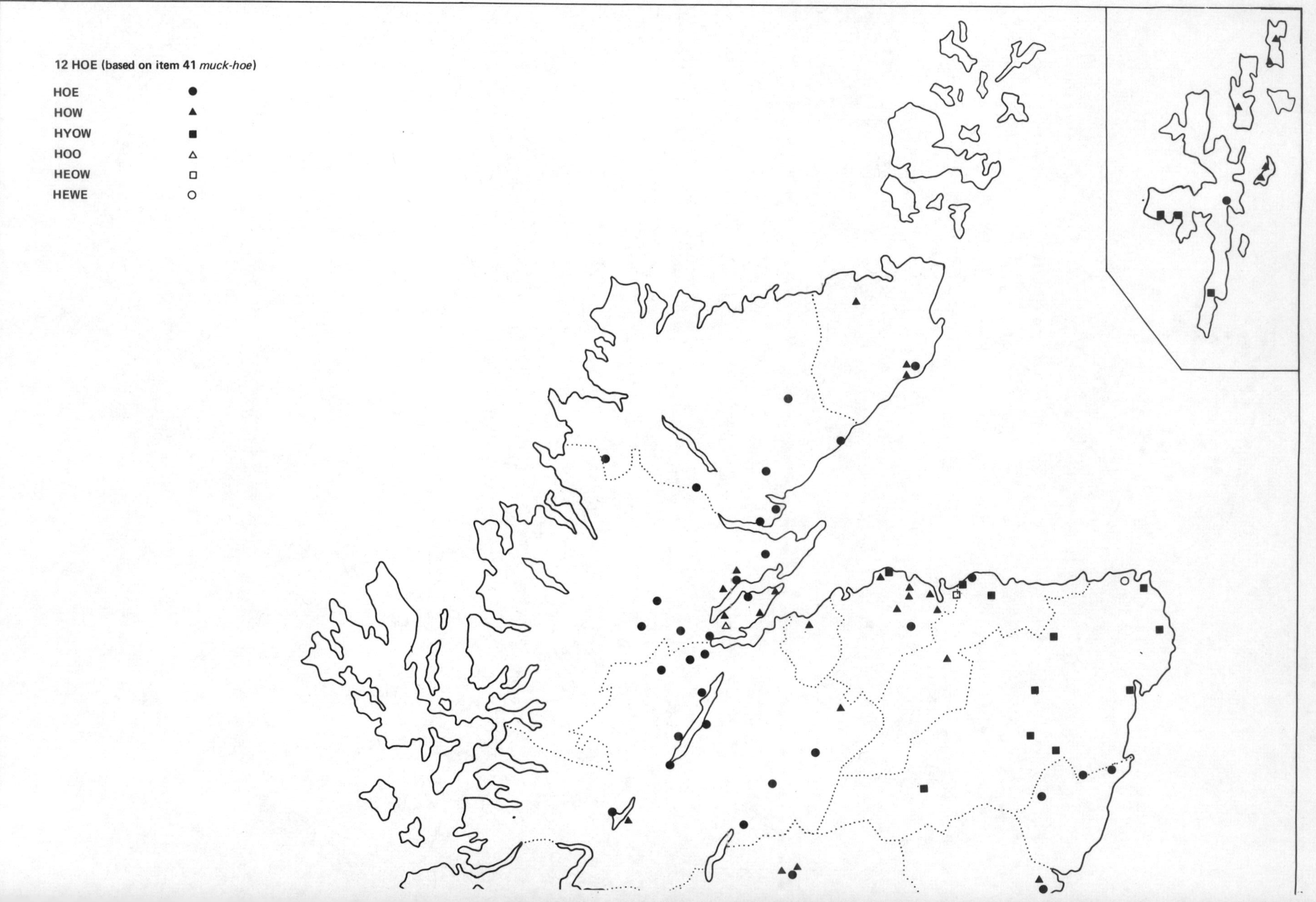
12 HOE (based on item 41 *muck-hoe*)
HOE
HOW
HYOW
HOO
HEOW
HEWE

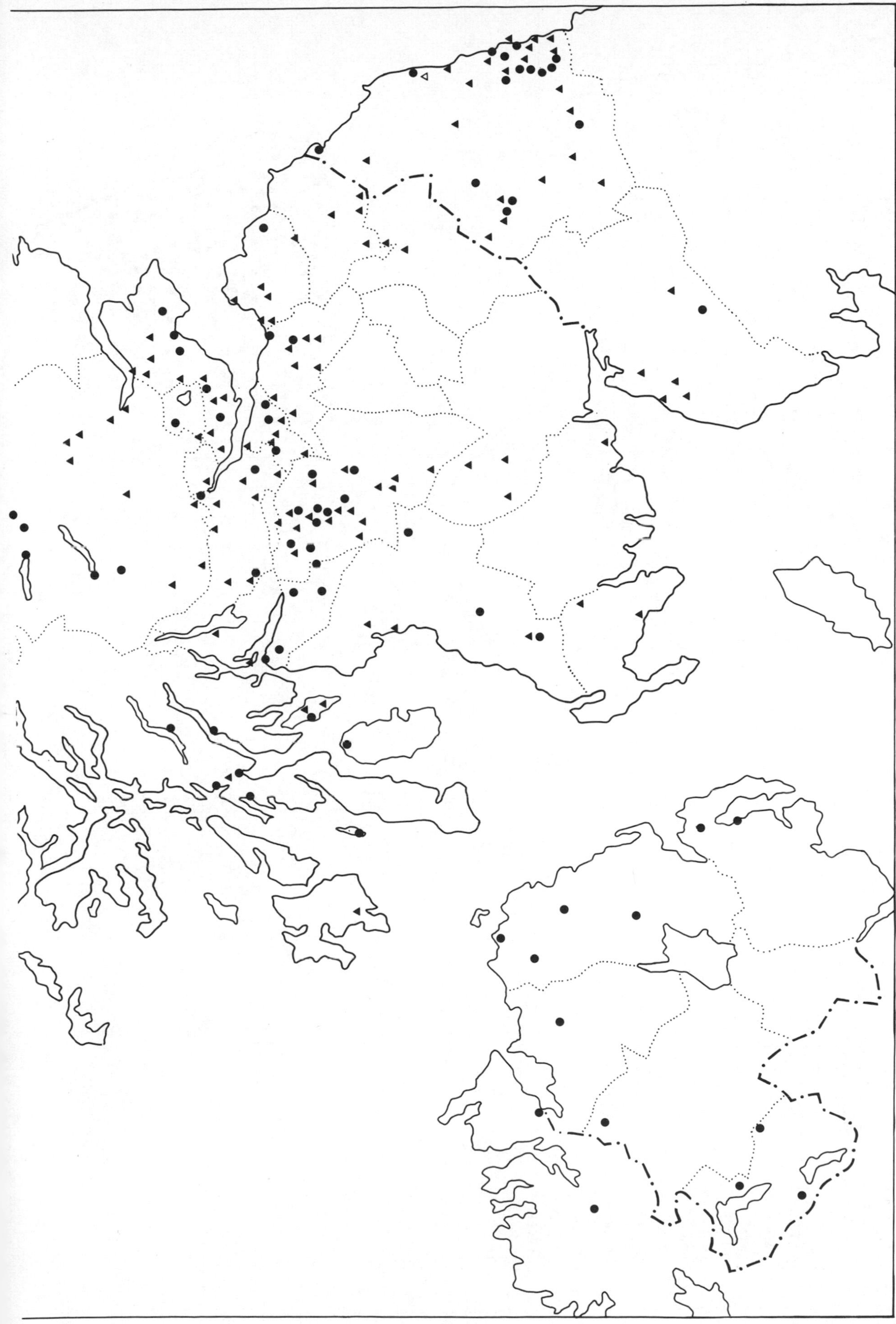

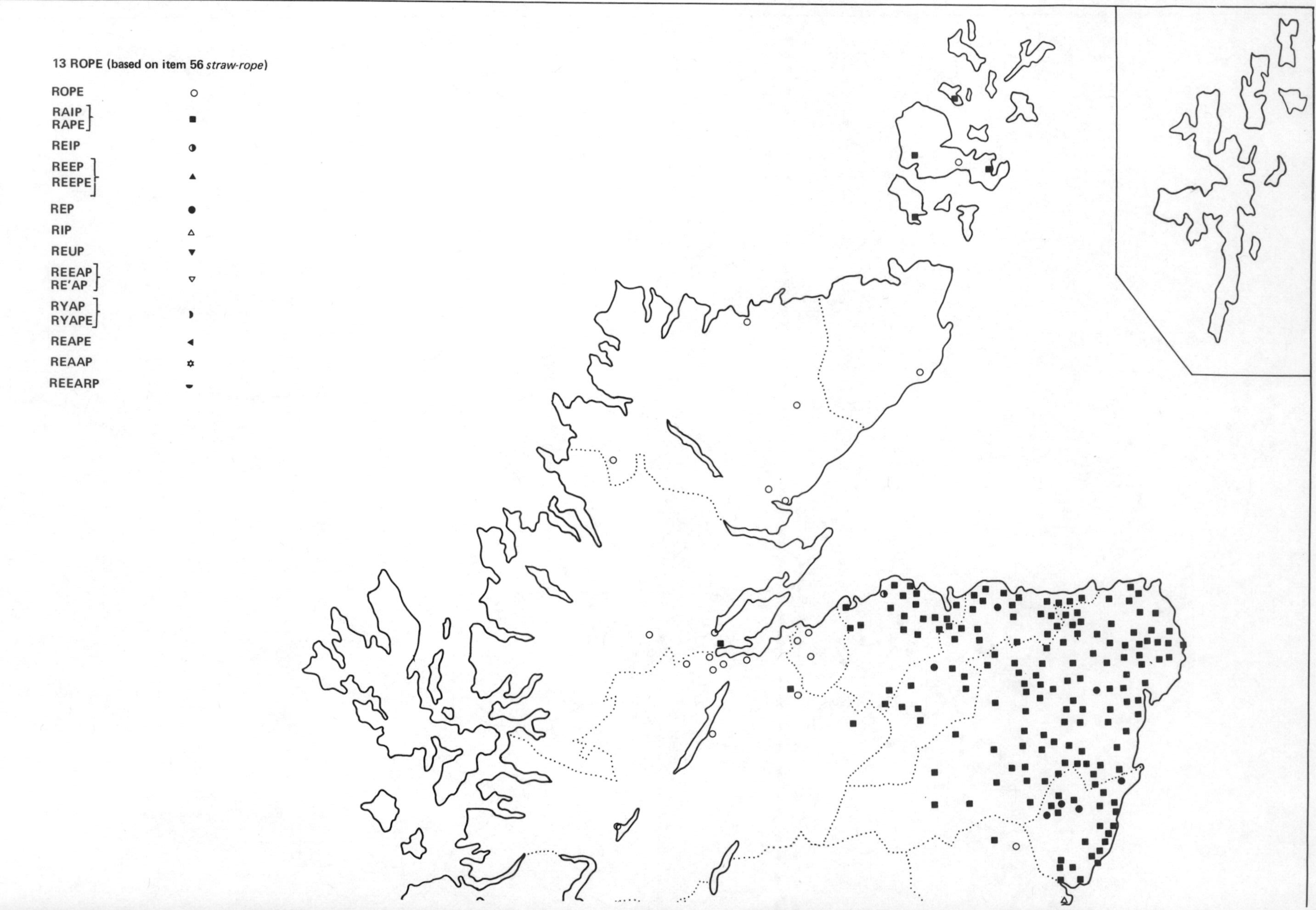

13 ROPE (based on item 56 *straw-rope*)
ROPE
RAIP
RAPE
REIP
REEP
REEPE
REP
RIP
REUP
REEAP
RE'AP
RYAP
RYAPE
REAPE
REAAP
REEARP

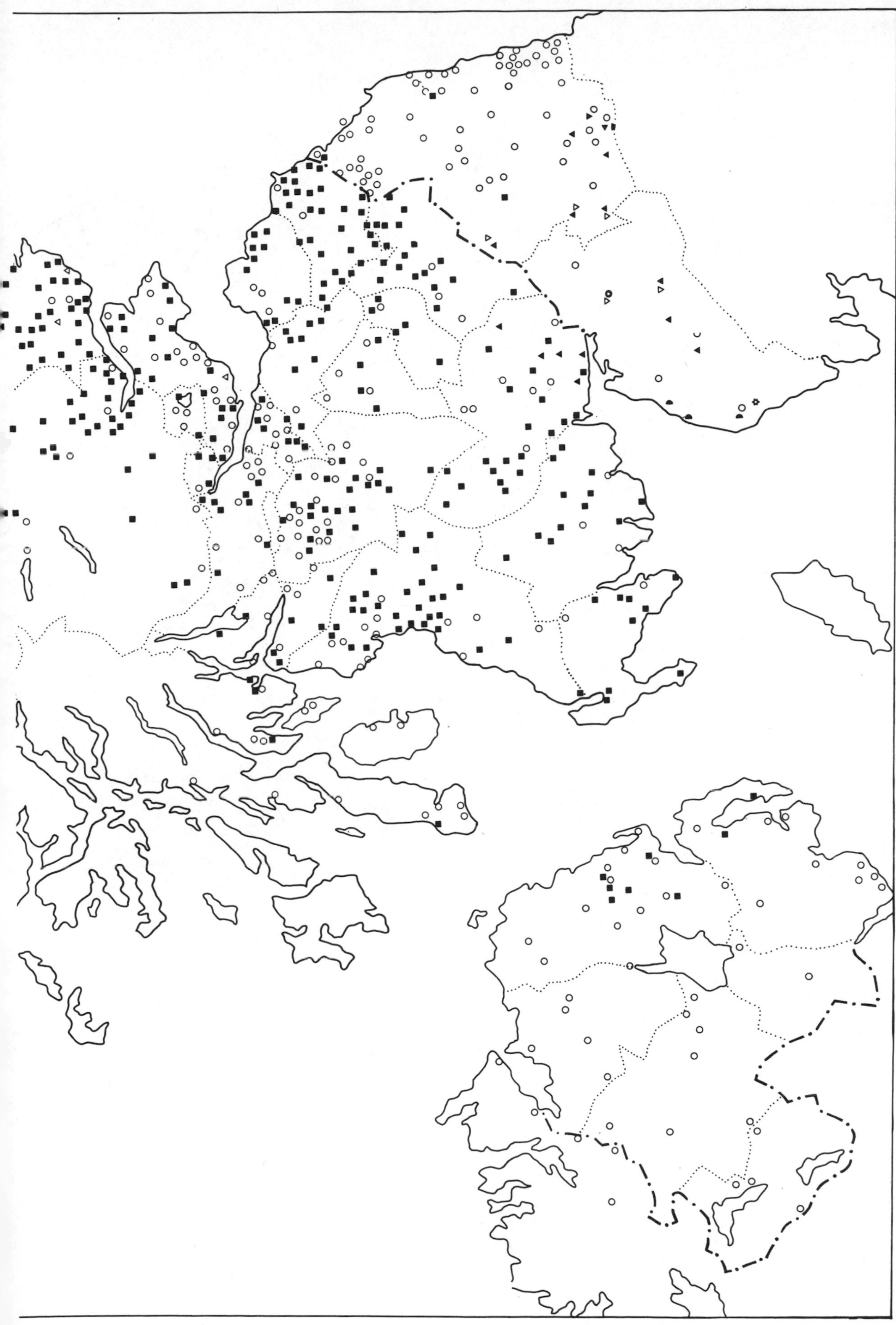

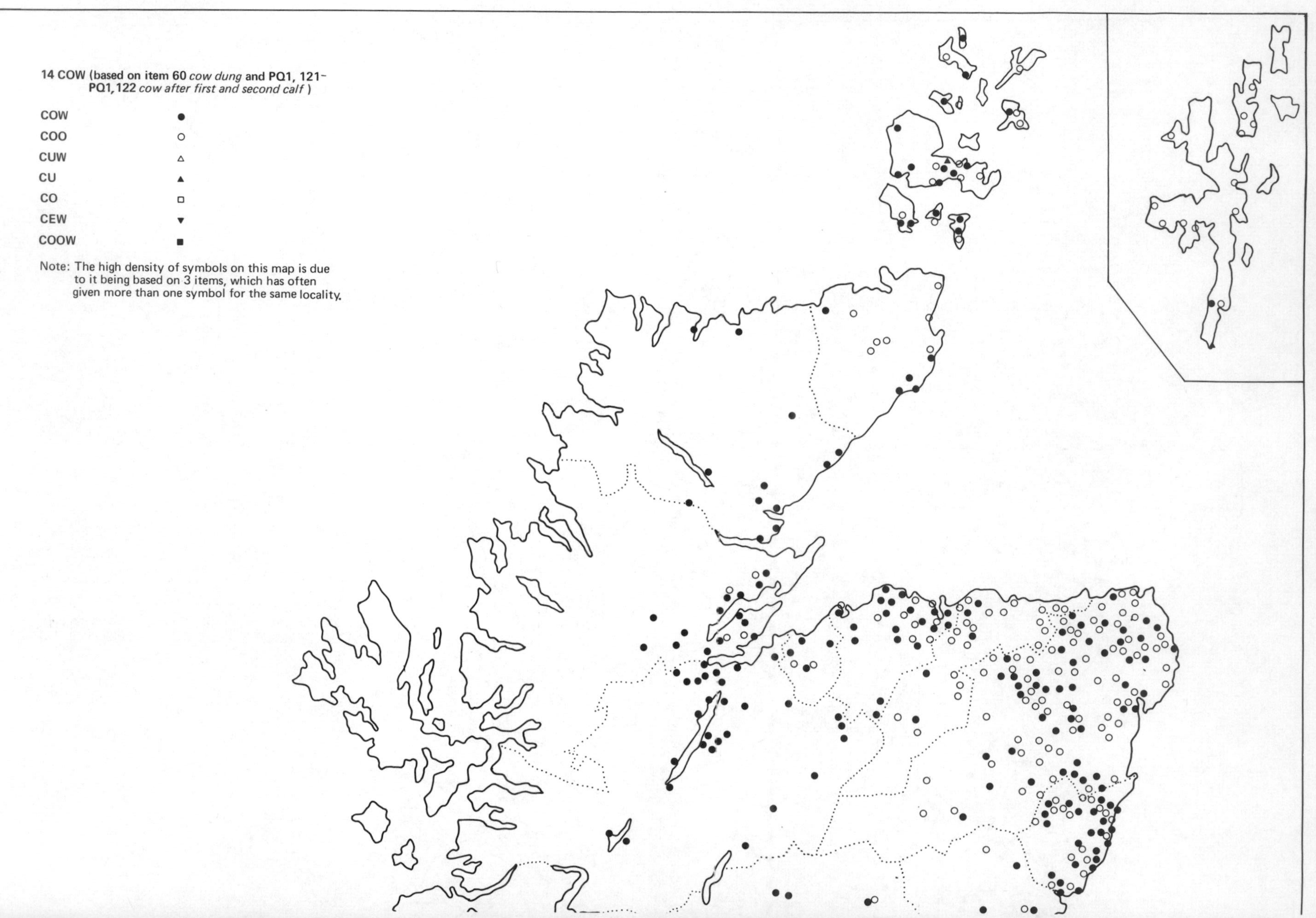
14 COW (based on item 60 *cow dung* and PQ1, 121–
PQ1, 122 *cow after first and second calf*)
COW ●
COO ○
CUW △
CU ▲
CO □
CEW ▼
COOW ■
Note: The high density of symbols on this map is due
to it being based on 3 items, which has often
given more than one symbol for the same locality.

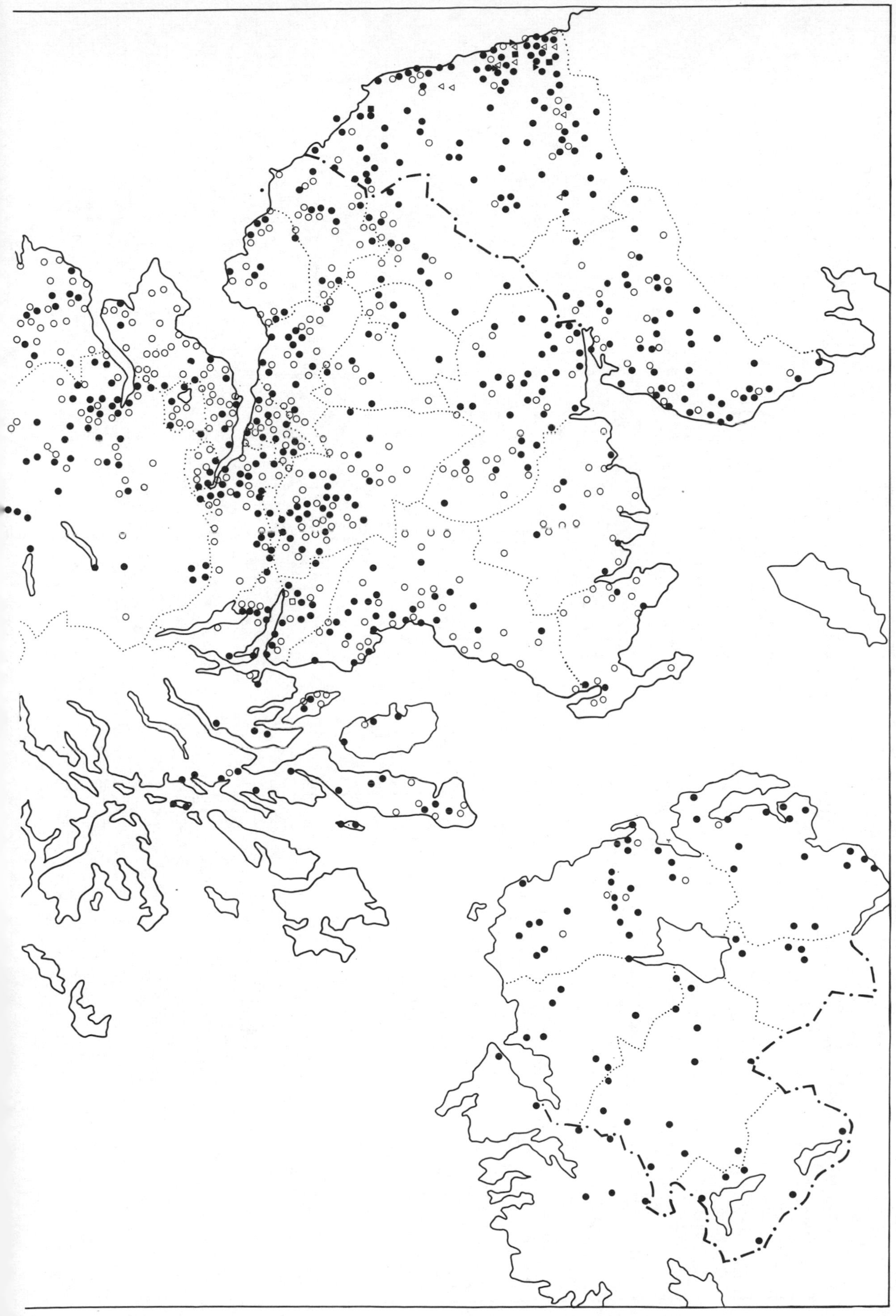

15 SNOW (based on item 69 *snowflake*)
SNOW ●
SNAW ○
SNA ▲
SNAA △
SNAE ■
SNAAW □

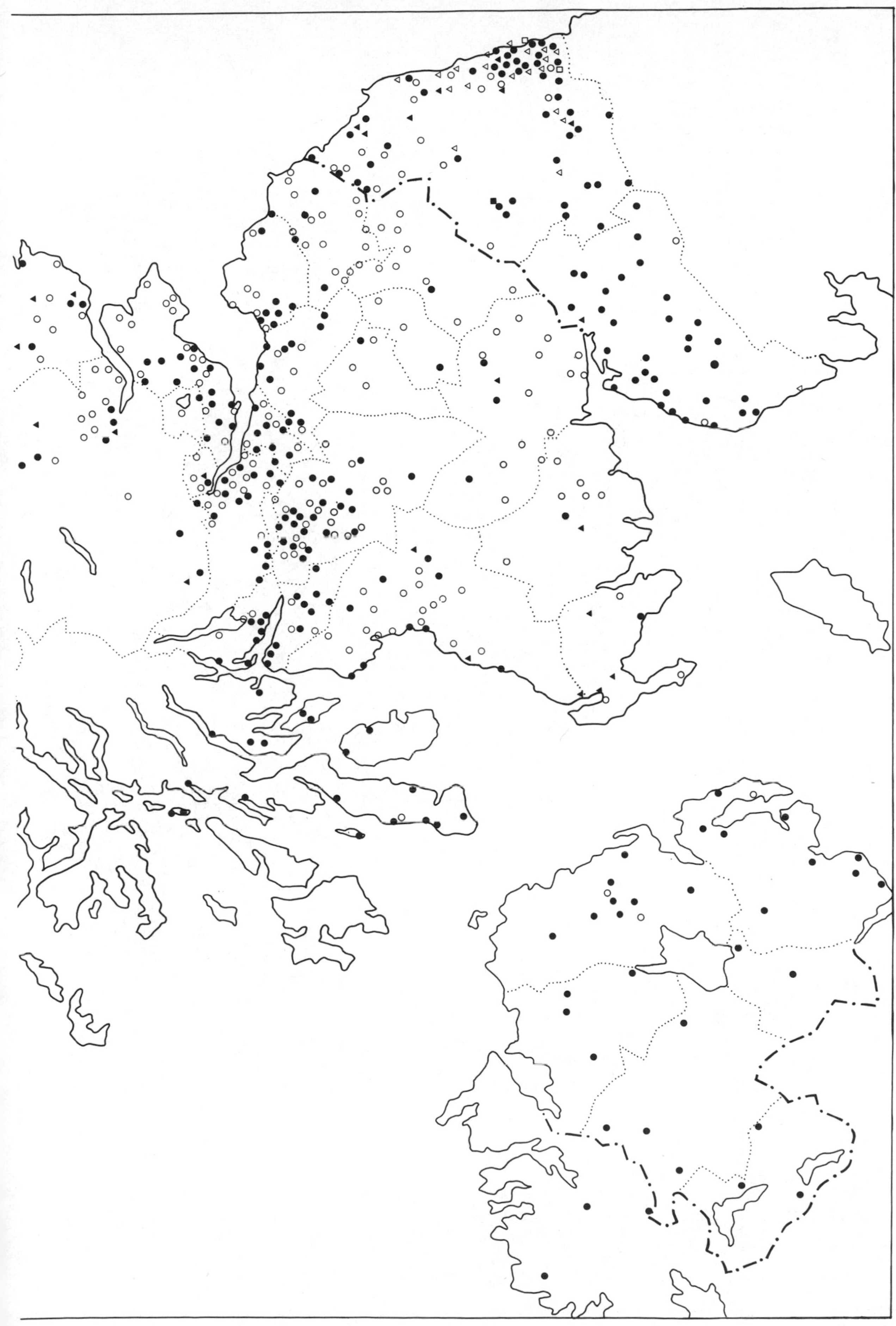

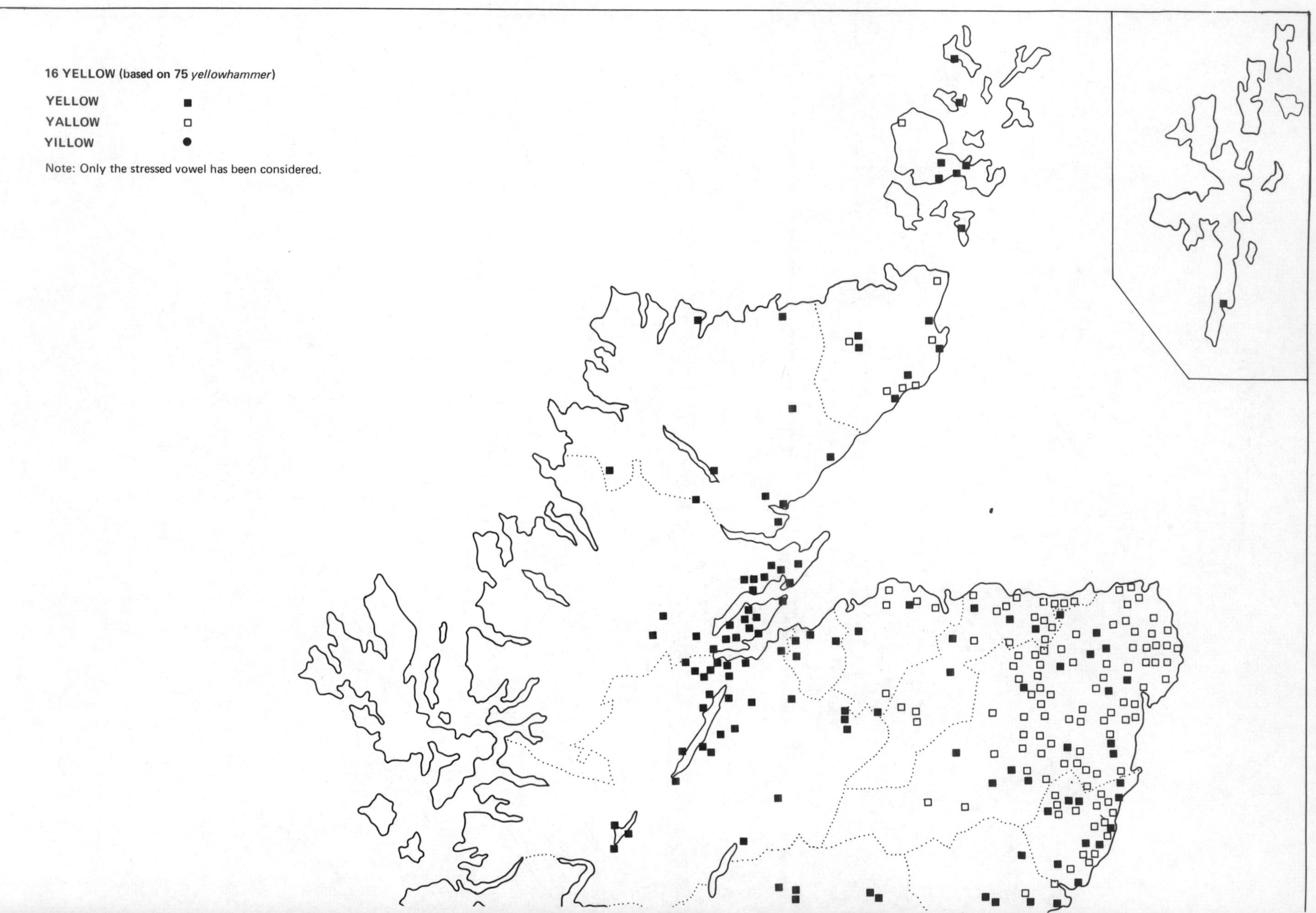
16 YELLOW (based on 75 *yellowhammer*)
YELLOW ■
YALLOW □
YILLOW ●
Note: Only the stressed vowel has been considered.

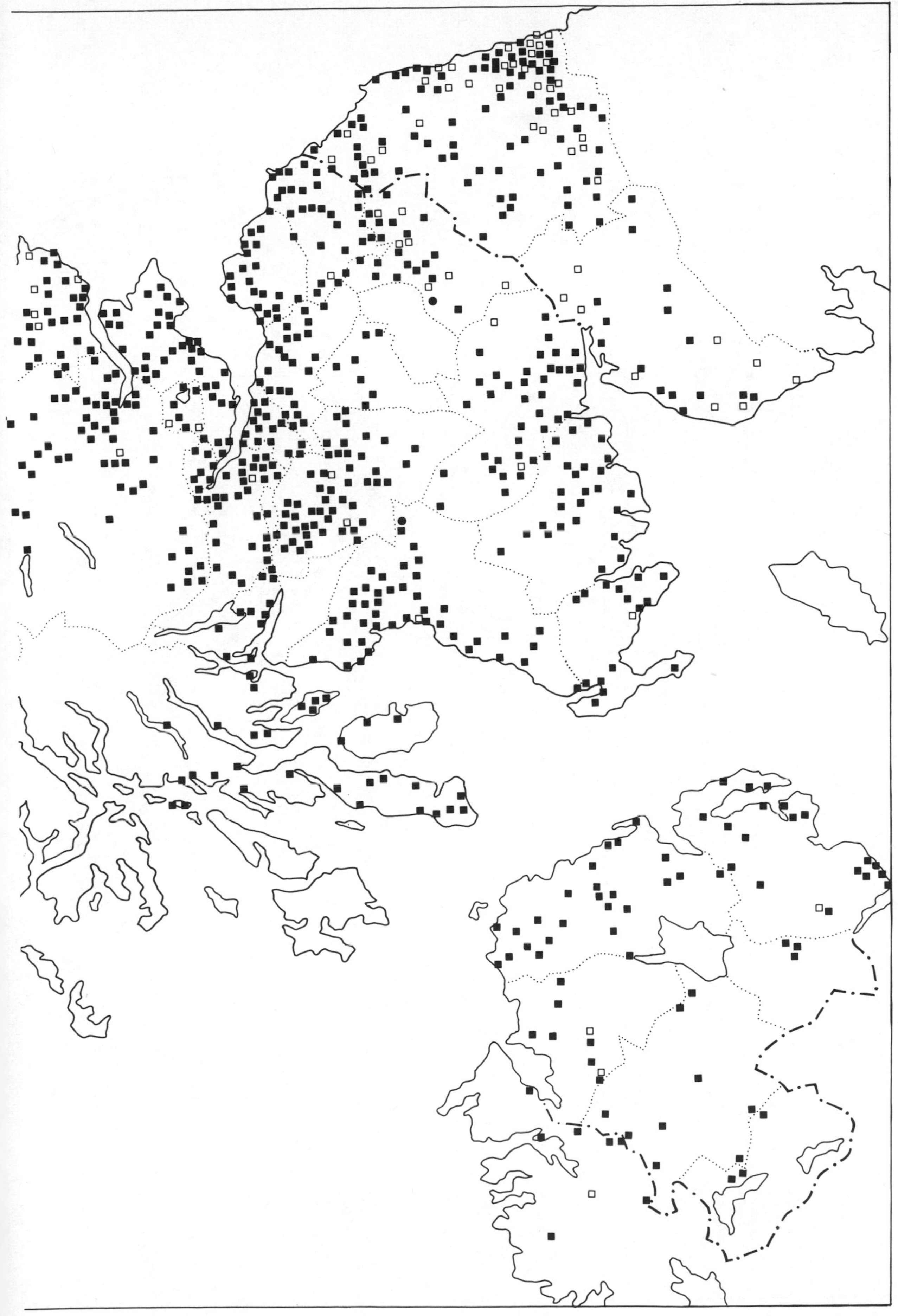

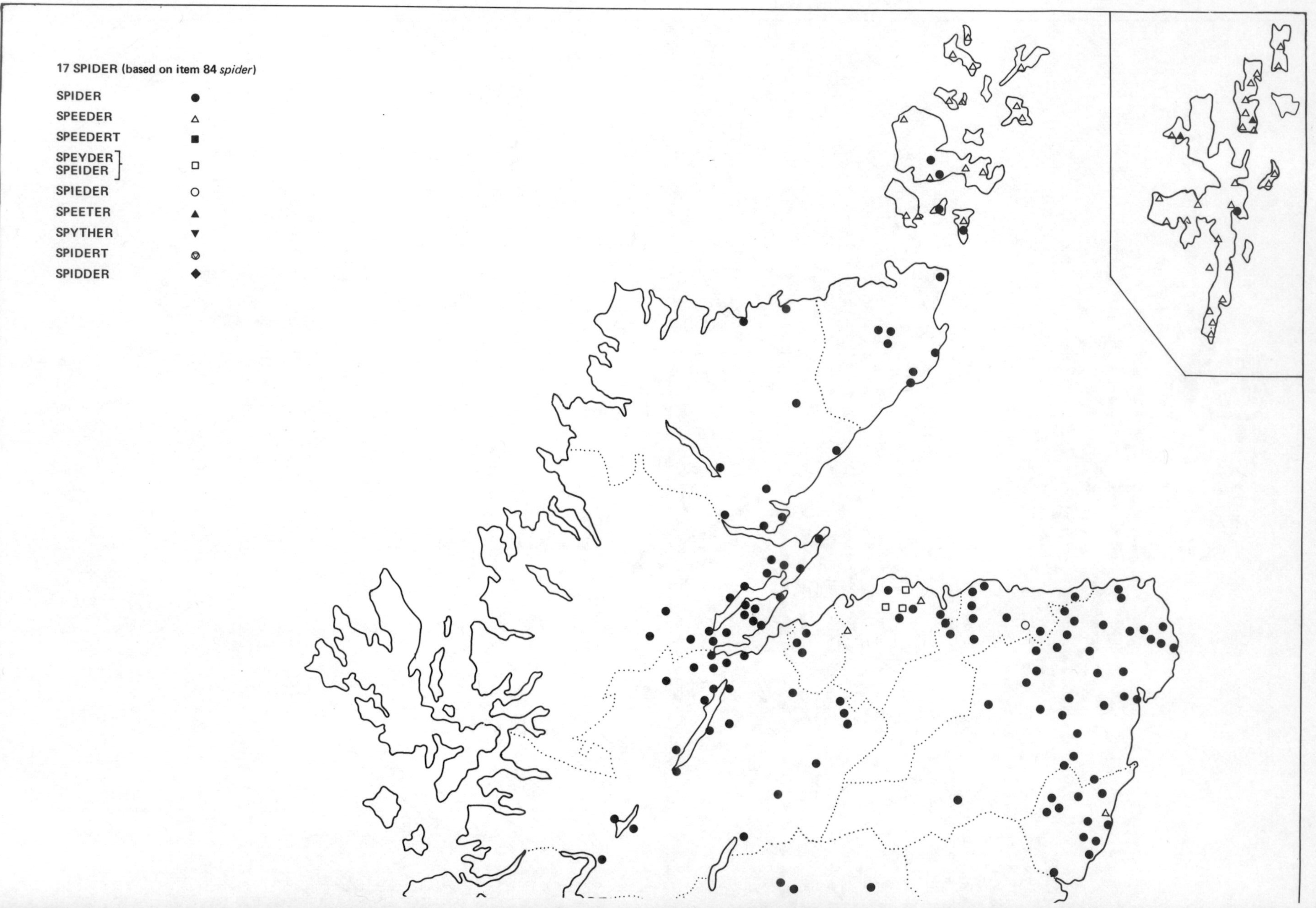
17 SPIDER (based on item 84 *spider*)
SPIDER ●
SPEEDER △
SPEEDERT ■
SPEYDER
SPEIDER □
SPIEDER ○
SPEETER ▲
SPYTHER ▼
SPIDERT ⊗
SPIDDER ◆

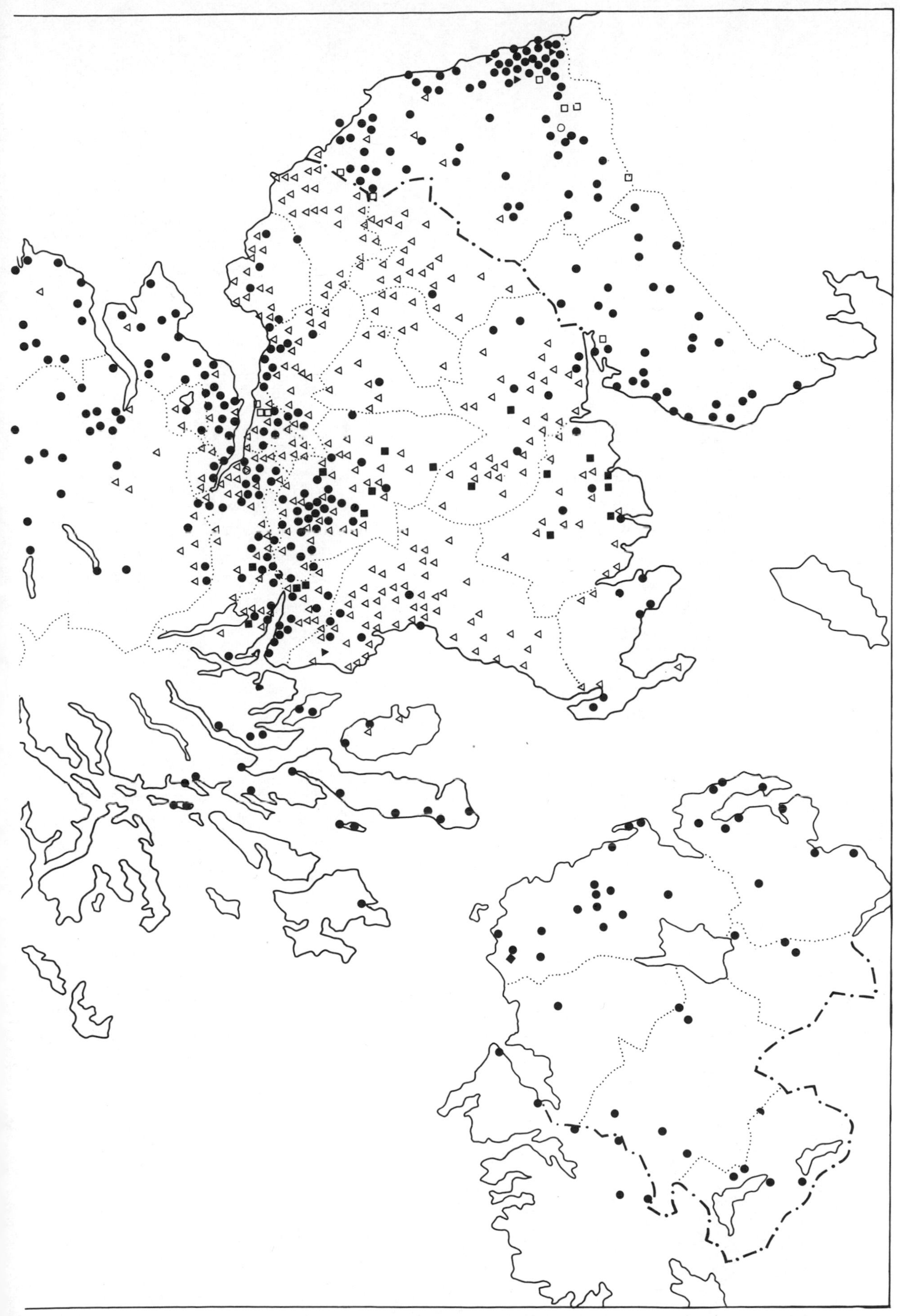

APPENDIX B . ADDITIONAL PHONETIC ORTHOGRAPHICAL MAPS

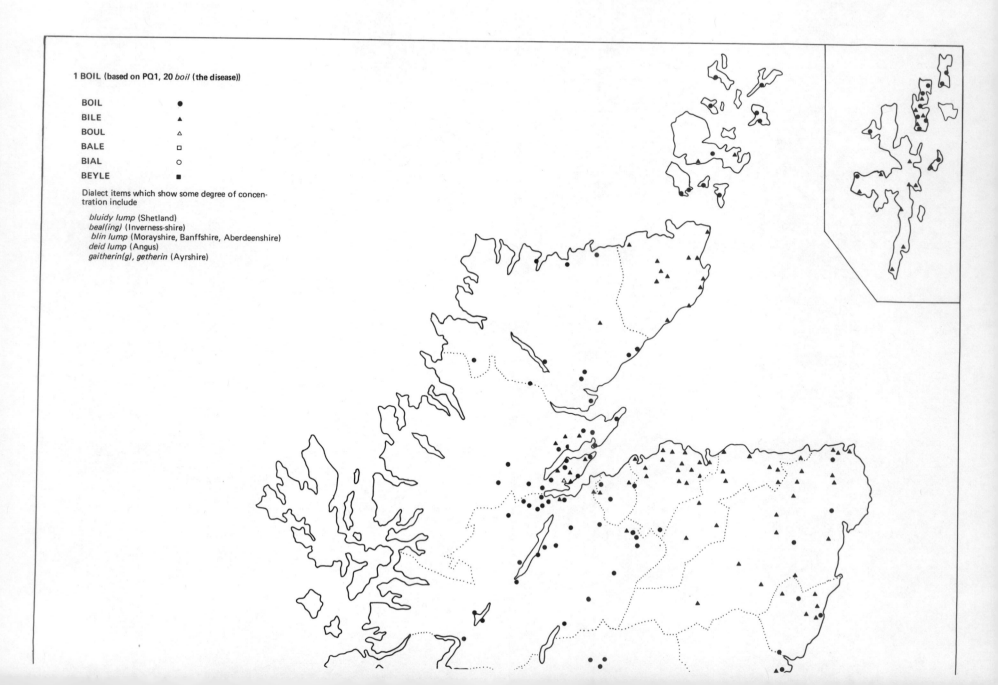

1 BOIL (based on PQ1, 20 *boil* (the disease))

BOIL	●
BILE	▲
BOUL	△
BALE	□
BIAL	○
BEYLE	■

Dialect items which show some degree of concentration include

bluidy lump (Shetland)
beal(ing) (Inverness-shire)
blin lump (Morayshire, Banffshire, Aberdeenshire)
deid lump (Angus)
gaitherin(g), getherin (Ayrshire)

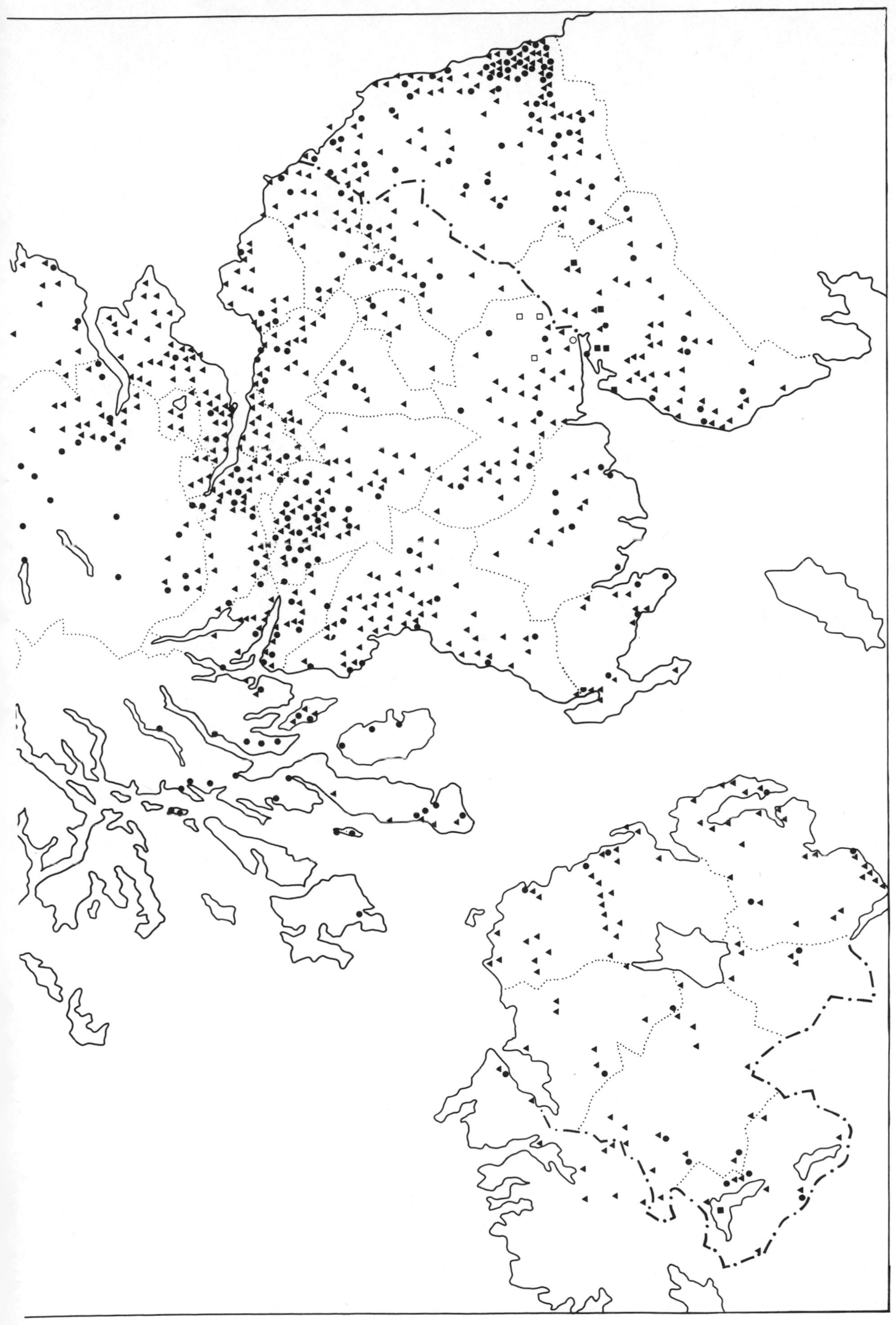

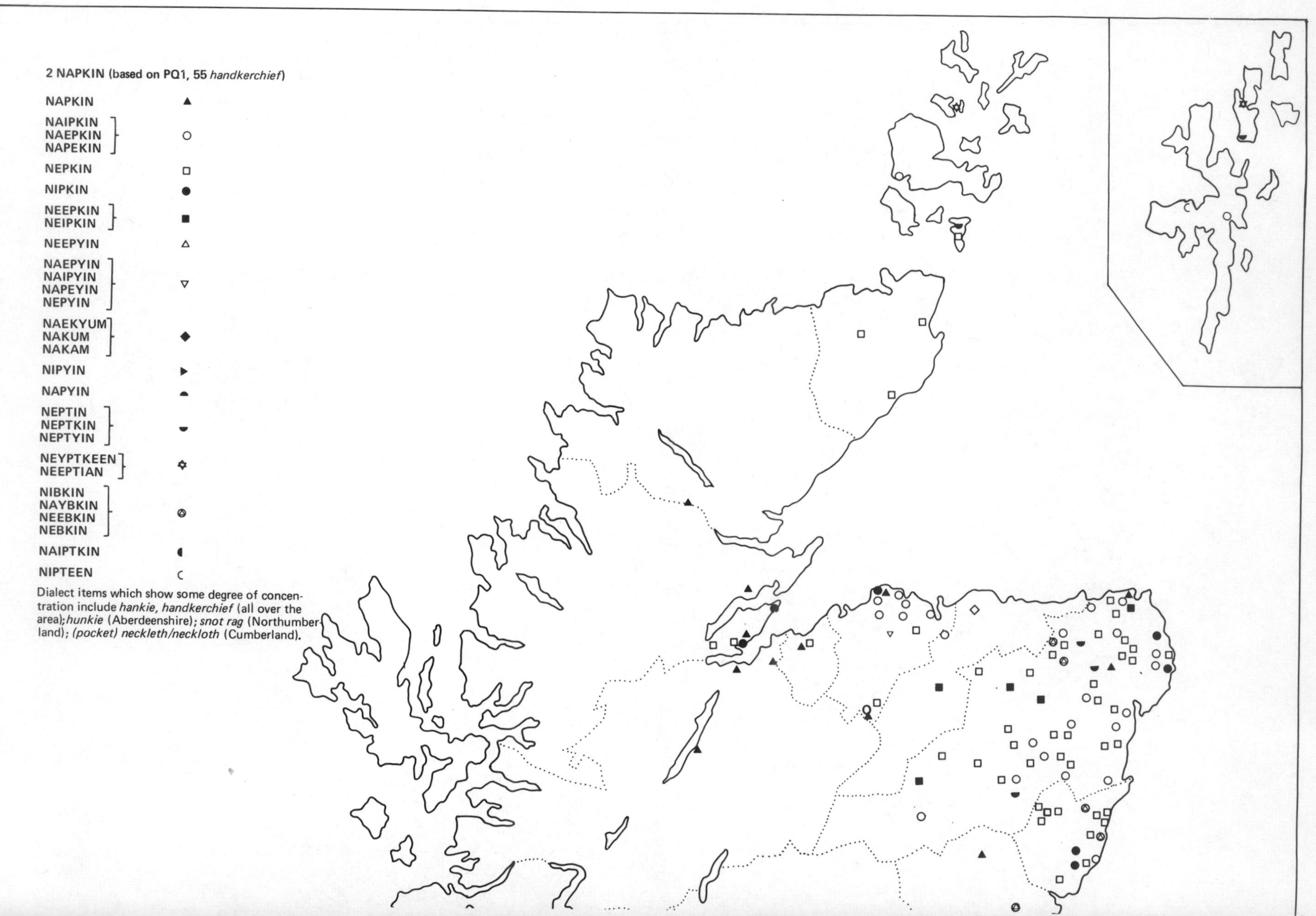
2 NAPKIN (based on PQ1, 55 *handkerchief*)
NAPKIN
NAIPKIN
NAEPKIN
NAPEKIN
NEPKIN
NIPKIN
NEEPKIN
NEIPKIN
NEEPYIN
NAEPYIN
NAIPYIN
NAPEYIN
NEPYIN
NAEKYUM
NAKUM
NAKAM
NIPYIN
NAPYIN
NEPTIN
NEPTKIN
NEPTYIN
NEYPTKEEN
NEEPTIAN
NIBKIN
NAYBKIN
NEEBKIN
NEBKIN
NAIPTKIN
NIPTEEN
Dialect items which show some degree of concentration include *hankie, handkerchief* (all over the area); *hunkie* (Aberdeenshire); *snot rag* (Northumberland); *(pocket) neckleth/neckloth* (Cumberland).

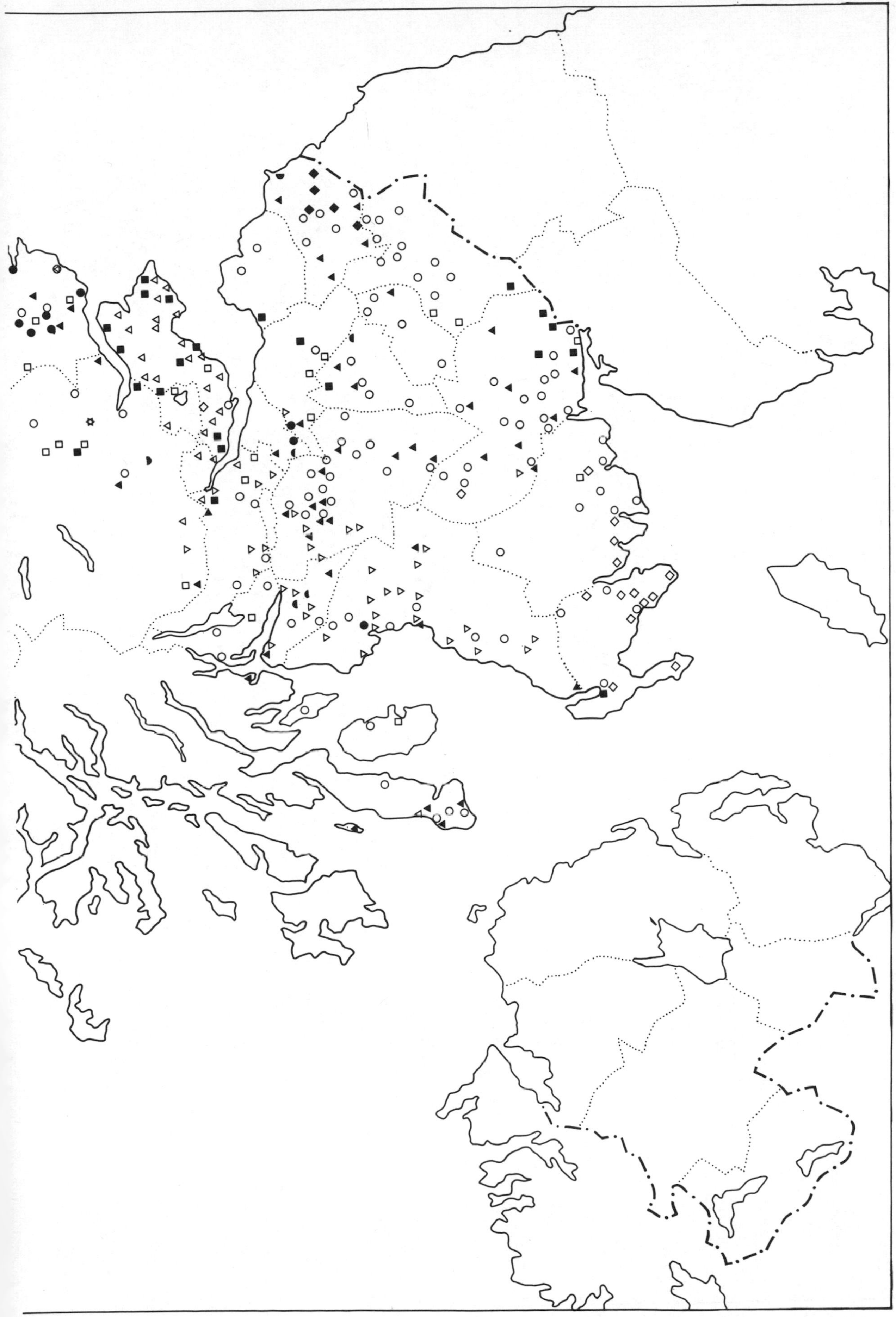

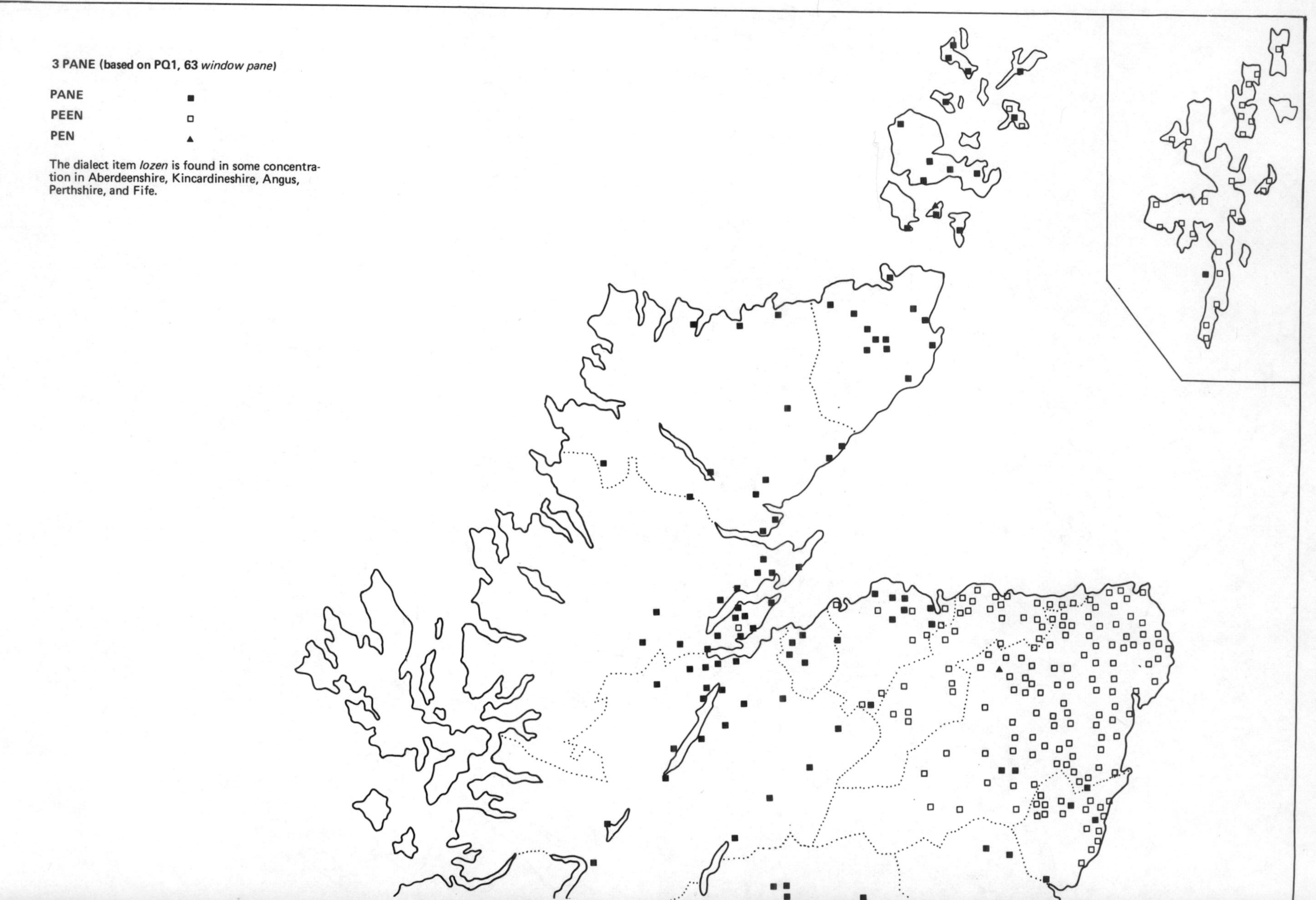
3 PANE (based on PQ1, 63 *window pane*)
PANE ■
PEEN □
PEN ▲
The dialect item *lozen* is found in some concentration in Aberdeenshire, Kincardineshire, Angus, Perthshire, and Fife.

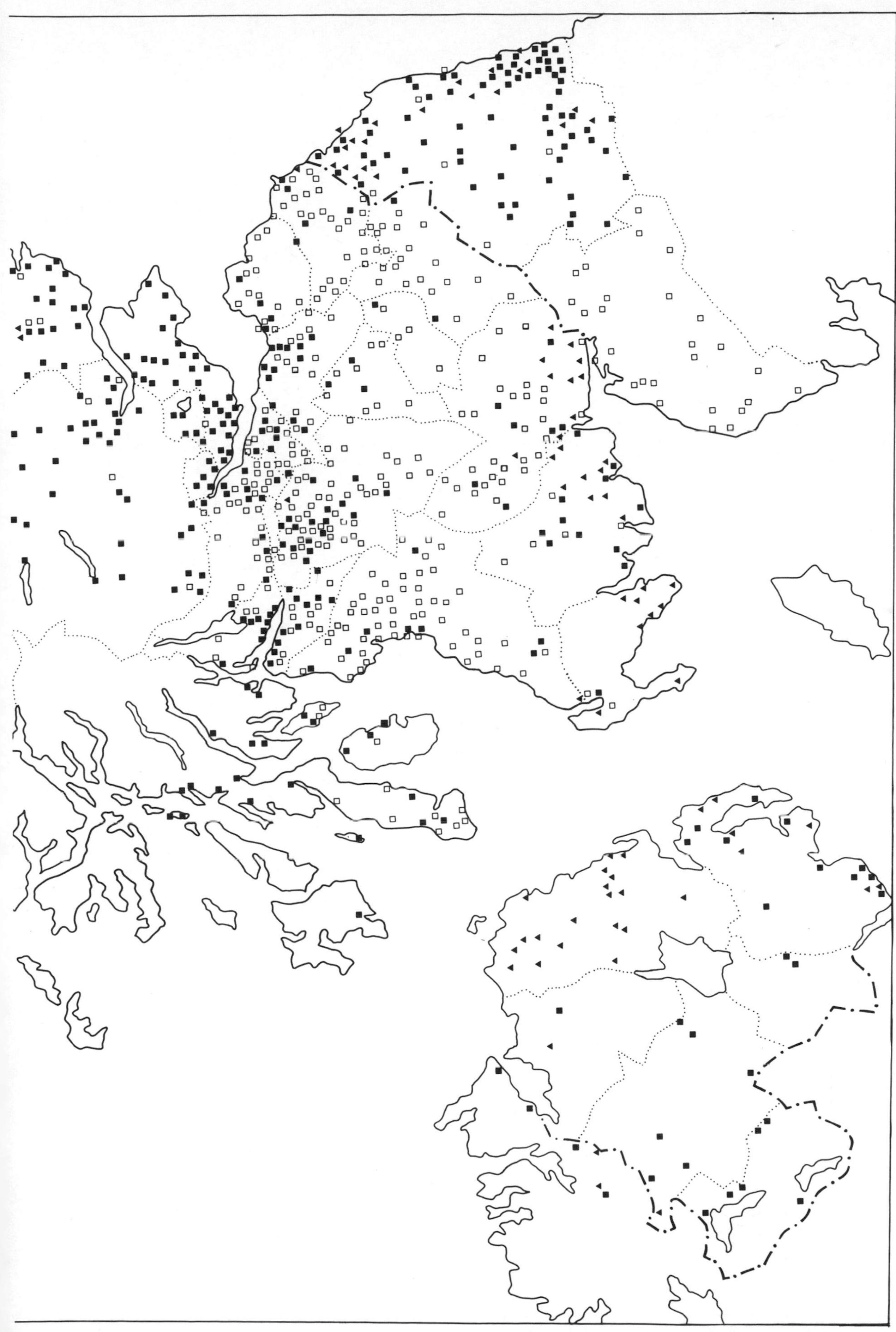

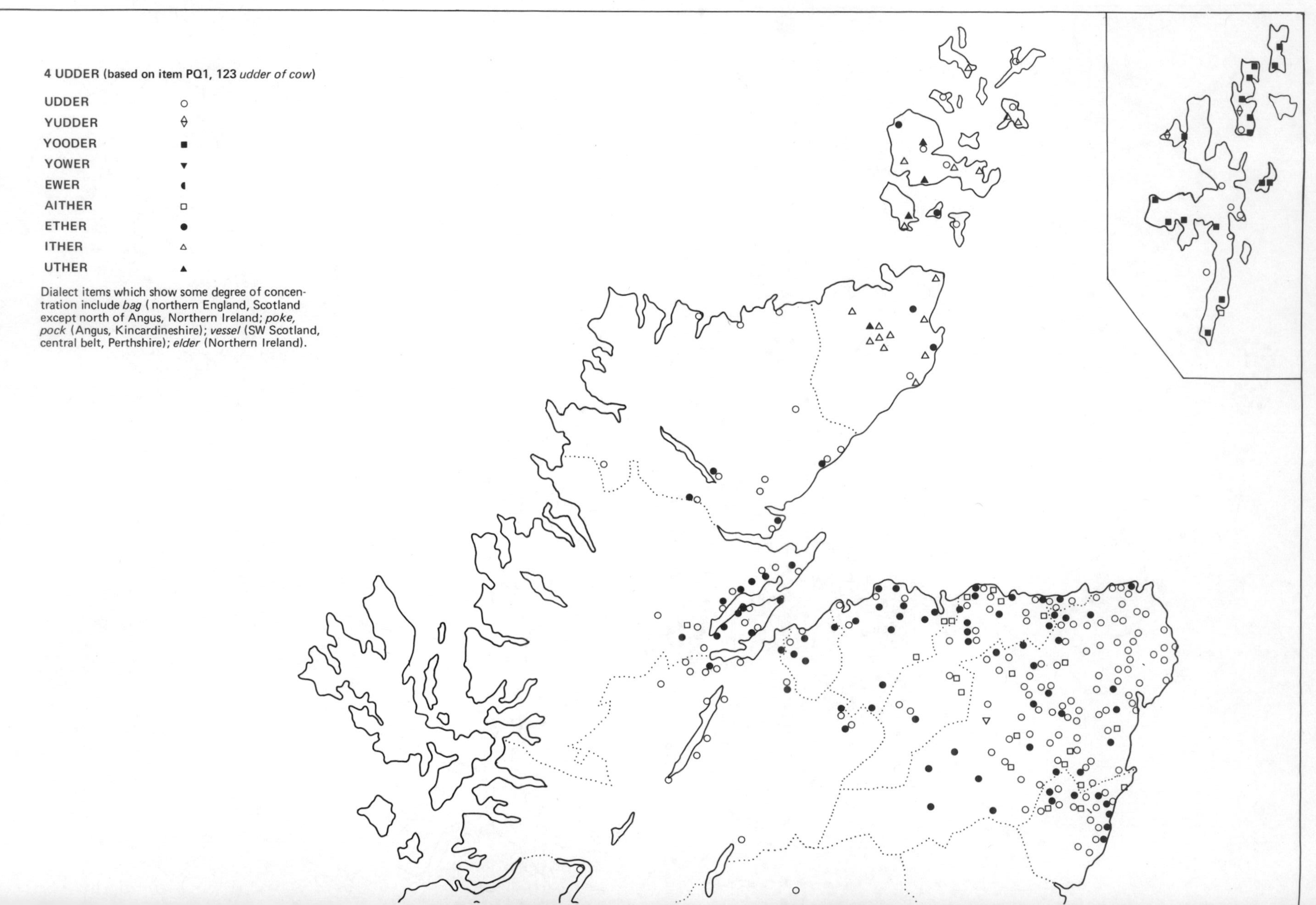
4 UDDER (based on item PQ1, 123 *udder of cow*)
UDDER ○
YUDDER
YOODER ■
YOWER ▼
EWER
AITHER □
ETHER ●
ITHER △
UTHER ▲
Dialect items which show some degree of concentration include *bag* (northern England, Scotland except north of Angus, Northern Ireland; *poke, pock* (Angus, Kincardineshire); *vessel* (SW Scotland, central belt, Perthshire); *elder* (Northern Ireland).

APPENDIX C. INFORMANTS

APPENDIX C: INFORMANTS

We publish here information from the name-slips provided by the individual informants *or* by intermediaries who worked with informants, but gave their own personal particulars.[1] The latter cases account for the seemingly disturbing examples where 'informants' (of middle or old age) have only resided for a few years in the district for which they offer information.[2] The Detailed Instructions (cf. p. 10) do not *explicitly* request that only the name of the actual local informants and not of the local teacher or other distributors or helpers should be given, although this is strongly implied. Where the Detailed Instructions have been disregarded to the extent that a person filled in the questionnaire for another area than requested or where the information was spurious, the completed books were rejected and the material does not, therefore, appear in this work. The present editors had, however, no part in this process of selection which took place before 1955.

The first eight columns in the following list contain information on the informant or intermediary who is referred to be his initials (col. 4). All informants' *places of residence* (col. 2) have been located on the Ordnance Survey one-inch maps of Great Britain and given their National Grid[3] reference (col. 3) and their atlas locality number (col. 1). Additional information concerning a questionnaire locality has, in general, been left out, if the place is identifiable on the one-inch map by its grid reference.[4] Birthplaces in the UK occurring in the last three colums (cols. 8-10) have been checked, as far as they can be traced, against the *Gazetteer of Great Britain* published by the Ordnance Survey,[5] and failing this with W. and A. K. Johnston's *Gazetteer of Scotland* (Edinburgh and London) 1937). Place-name spellings have been changed to conform to these sources.

The name of the county in which a place is situated has been added, if it is outside the county under which it appears in the list. For the benefit of readers who are not familiar with the geography of the area this has been done even in obvious or even obsolete cases e.g., Edinburgh, Midlothian, but where the name of a county town and a county coincide, as e.g., Aberdeen, Aberdeenshire, Antrim, Co. Antrim, the county name has been omitted. English county names have been given in their customary abbreviations e.g., Bucks. = Buckinghamshire etc. Where the informant has not specified the county for a place-name which occurs more than once in the UK, we have not attempted to identify it, although in many cases it will be the locality closes to the present place of residence of the informant.

The questionnaire was sent out in 1952 (cf. 10) and books continued to come in throughout the next decade but the bulk had arrived by 1954. As there exists no record of the actual date of completion of a questionnaire the *age* (col. 6) of Informants has been calculated for 1954. It was not possible to follow the same procedure for the *length of residence* (col. 7) where the informants usually supplied the number of years of residence rather than a date. If, therefore, there is only a slight discrepancy, say of one to three years, between columns 6 and 7, it can in many cases be reasonably assumed that the informant has resided at the locality all his life.

Sch = School m = male f = female Co. = County

NOTES

1 Gaelic questionnaires are not included,
2 The addition of ((Sch.) = school) after the locality often points to such cases.
3 The method by which the grid reference is obtained is described on the Ordnance Survey one-inch maps. (N.B. Northern Ireland has a separate grid.)
4 Readers who have no access to the Ordnance Survey one-inch series are advised to refer to our key map where they will find the relative position of localities within each county. For Shetland and Orkney we have left more additional details than elsewhere.
5. Chessington, Surrey, 1953, 'giving the position of all features named on the Ordnance Survey Quarter-inch Maps in terms of the National Grid'. Unfortunately there is no Ordnance Survey Gazetteer for the one-inch series.

SHETLAND

	Place of Residence	Grid	Name	Sex	Age	Length of residence (yrs)	BIRTHPLACE OF Informant	Mother	Father
1	Ordale, Unst	412/6108	J.T.J.	m	61	22	Uyeasound, Unst	same	same
2	Uyeasound, Unst	412/5901	A.T.C.	m	64	46	Uyeasound, Unst	same	same
3	Cullivoe, Yell	412/5402	A.W.	m	79	70	Gloup, Cullivoe, Yell	Yell	Gloup, Cullivoe, Yell
4	Colvister, Yell	411/5197	A.W.	m	29	26	Colvister, Yell	Houlland, Yell	Colvister, Yell
5	Mid Yell	411/5190	C.J.I.	m	80	67	Setter, Burra Isle	Herra	Vatsie, Yell
6	Westsandwick, Yell	411/4488	M.M.	m	87	80	Westsandwick, Yell	same	same
7	Ulsta, Yell	411/4680	J.I.	m	32	21	Delting	South of England	Delting
8	Midgarth, Yell	411/5285	A.J.	m	23	23	Otterswick, Yell	Aywick, Yell	Otterswick, Yell
9	Burravoe	411/5280	E.J.W.	f	75	75	Kettlester, Burravoe	Burravoe	Lunnasting
10	Eshaness	411/2178	J.H.J.	m	53	53	Eshaness	same	same
11	Hillswick	411/2877	A.A.	f	58	12	Hillswick	Old Deer, Aberdeenshire	Hillswick

SHETLAND Cont'd

	Place of Residence	Grid	Name	Sex	Age	Length of residence (yrs)	Informant	BIRTHPLACE OF Mother	Father
12	Firth, Mossbank	411/4473	C.M.L.	f	64	60	—	—	Yell
13	East Isle, Skerries	411/6771	J.L.J.	m	65	62	West Isle, Skerries	Whalsay	West Isle, Skerries
14	Laxo, Vidlin	411/4463	A.L.	m	55	51	Lunnasting	same	same
15	Whalsay	411/5565	J.S.	m	51	24	Whalsay	same	same
16	Huxter, Whalsay	411/5662	J.P.	m	68	65	Huxter, Whalsay	Railsbrough, Nesting	Huxter, Whalsey
17	Sandness	411/1957	J.C.P.	m	73	71	Sandness	Papa Stour	Papa Stour
18	East Burrafirth, Aith	411/3658	J.M.A.	f	46	11	Lerwick	Yell	Fetlar
19	Skellister, Nesting	411/4654	I.A.	f	46	12	Lerwick	Delting	Lunnasting
20	Ling Ness, Nesting	411/4954	G.G.	m	37	34	Ling Ness, Nesting	Ling Ness, Nesting	Eswick, Nesting
21a	Walls	411/2449	A.P.	m	41	5	Lunnasting	same	same
21b	Walls	411/2449	T.A.R.	m	45	14	Sandsting	same	same
22	Gruting (Sch.) Walls	411/2749	E.G.L.C.	f	59	18	Delting	Nesting	Delting
23	Sandsound, Tresta	411/3548	–.L.	f	–	80	Sandsound, Tresta	—	—
24	Veensgarth	411/4244	L.G.	m	30	25	Stromfirth, Weisdale	Houll, Weisdale	Stromfirth, Weisdale
25	Lerwick	411/4741	T.M.	m	38	38	Lerwick	Lerwick	Sandness
26	Foula	311/9638	V.C.	f	–	5	—	—	—
27	Hamnavoe, Burra Isle	411/3735	J.P.	m	57	31	Setter, Burra Isle	Sandsting	Burra Isle
28	Quarff	411/4235	J.D.T.	f	45	21	Lerwick	Yell	Gulberwick
29	Brecks of Bigton	411/3721	R.L.	m	66	63	Mewhouse, Bigton	Brecks of Bigton	Mewhouse, Bigton
30	Sandwick (Sch.)	411/4323	R.W.T.	m	63	39	Sandwick	same	same
31	Boddam (Sch.), Dunrossness	411/3916	L.H.G.	f	47	33	Dunrossness	Noss, Dunrossness	Symblisetter, Dunrossness
32	Breck of Quendale	411/3713	M.E.L.	f	27	24	Quendale	Hillwell, Quendale	Breck of Quendale
33	Fair Isle	410/2071	J.E.	m	42	14	Fair Isle	same	same

ORKNEY

	Place of Residence	Grid	Name	Sex	Age	Length of residence (yrs)	Informant	Mother	Father
1	Habreck, Westray	310/4552	G.M.R.	m	76	–	Habreck, Westray	Pierowall, Westray	Habreck, Westray
2	Mount Pleasant, Westray	310/4444	J.B.	m	62	59	Mount Pleasant, Westray	same	same
3	Ness, Rapness, Westray	310/4939	D.L.B.	m	44	44	Ness Farm, Rapness, Westray	Newbigging, Rapness	Sotteroshan, Rapnes
4	Central (Sch.), Sanday	310/6841	J.D.M.	m	45	4	Papa Westray	same	same
5	Bigland, Rousay	310/4332	H.I.G.	m	54	51	Rousay	Rendall Parish	Rousay
6	Egilsay (Sch.)	310/4630	I.M.H.	f	40	3	Kirkwall	—	Kirkwall
7	Birsay	310/2427	M.S.	f	70	70	Birsay	same	same
8	School Brae, Stronsay	310/6426	J.P.S.	m	72	65	Stronsay	same	same
9	Stronsay	310/6622	J.R.F.	m	51	48	Stronsay	Sanday	Stronsay
10	Appiehouse, Stenness	310/2815	P.L.	m	68	68	Stenness	same	same
11	Finstown	310/3513	J.R.W.	m	73	70	Finstown	Sanday	Rendall
12	Tankerness	310/5108	W.T.	m	70	1	Sanday	Sanday	North Ronaldsay
13a	Kirkwall	310/4410	C.M.C.	f	–	since birth	Kirkwall	Walls, Hoy	Rousay
13b	Kirkwall	310/4410	H.M.	m	73	73	Rousay	same	same
14	Stromness	310/2509	P.L.E.	m	74	72	Stromness	same	same
15	Burnside, Kirbister	310/3508	E.A.W.	f	72	50	Orkney	South Ronaldsay	Orphir
16	Hawill, Tankerness	310/5006	R.W.G.	m	54	22	Crofty, Tankerness	Hawill	Sandsquoy
17	Windbreck, Flotta	39/3593	A.S.S.	m	51	48	Windbreck, Flotta	Saraquoy	Flotta
18	St Margaret's Hope	39/4493	J.L.	m	71	68	South Ronaldsay	same	same
19	Quoybanks, South Ronaldsay	39/4290	E.H.	f	45	14	Kirkwall	same	same
20	Melsetter, Hoy	39/2789	J.H.	m	74	50	Melsetter, Hoy	Melsetter, Hoy	Edinburgh, Midlothi
21	South Walls (Sch.), Hoy	39/3189	T.M.W.	m	–	–	—	—	—
			(Completed by several local people, all over middle age)						

CAITHNESS

	Place of Residence	Grid	Name	Sex	Age	Length of residence (yrs)	Informant	Mother	Father
1	Dunnet	39/2271	J.C.	f	92	75	Dunnet	same	same
2a	John O'Groats	39/3873	J.S.B.	m	63	60	John O'Groats	same	same
2b	John O'Groats (Sch.)	39/3872	J.M.L.	f	38	3	Lyth	John O'Groats	Bower
3	Dounreay	29/9966	N.B.	m	–	since birth	—	—	—
4	Janetstown	39/0965	A.C.	f	40	25	North Berwick, East Lothian	Janetstown	Ross-shire
5	Lyth (Sch.)	39/2963	G.S.	m	55	25	John O'Groats	same	same
6	Keiss (Sch.)	39/3461	A.M.	m	–	–	—	—	—
			Completed by four natives of district						
7	Gerston	39/1259	J.I.T.	f	62	62	Halkirk	same	same
8	Achalone	39/1556	A.D.B.	f	52	38	Sibster	Bower Parish	Olrig, Wick
9	Dunn	39/1956	B.G.A.	f	46	43	Dunn	Dunn	Castletown

CAITHNESS Cont'd

	Place of Residence	Grid	Name	Sex	Age	Length of residence (yrs)	Birthplace of Informant	Birthplace of Mother	Birthplace of Father
10	Harpsdale (Sch.)	39/1354	A.S.	f	49	2	Thurso	Ross-shire	Dunbeath
11	Spittal (Sch.)	39/1653	M.C.M.	f	47	22	Grangemouth, Stirlingshire	Berriedale	Lybster
12a	Wick	39/3650	D.B.	m	74	71	Wick	same	same
12b	Wick	39/3650	R.J.G.M.	m	88	88	Latheron	Caithness	Caithness
12c	Wick	39/3650	J.R.	m	–	–	—	—	—
13	Camster	39/2545	T.M.	m	77	47	Rhinivie, Bethy Hill, Sutherland	Sutherland	Kildonan, Stirlingshire
14	Old Stirkoke	39/3249	D.B.M.	m	40	40	Stirkoke	Latheron	Halkirk
15	Latheron	39/1933	J.M.	m	73	23	Halkirk	Latheron	Strathmore, Halkirk
16a	Mid-Clyth	39/2837	C.C.	f	69	29	Mid-Clyth	Camster	Roster
16b	Mid-Clyth	39/2837	J.A.M.	m	63	60	East Clyth	Clyth Mains	Boultach
17	Achow	39/2236	J.M.	m	43	30	Achow, Lybster	Clyth	Achow

SUTHERLAND

	Place of Residence	Grid	Name	Sex	Age	Length of residence (yrs)	Birthplace of Informant	Birthplace of Mother	Birthplace of Father
1	Talmine	29/5862	H.M.	f	27	25	Talmine	Erribol, Durness	Talmine
2	Armadale	29/7864	D.M.F.	m	60	18	Halladale	same	same
3	Naver Bridge	29/7060	G.W.M.	m	71	71	Naver	Bettyhill	Bettyhill
			A.M.	m	69	69	Achina	Bettyhill	Bettyhill
4	Strathy West	29/8404	C.M.	f	77	42	Bettyhill	same	same
5	Scourie	29/1544	A.M.	f	49	9	Glasgow	Parish of Assynt	Stoer, by Lairg
6	Kinbrace	29/8631	E.M.	m	59	50	Eriboll, Durness	Parish of Assynt	Ness, Lewis, Ross and Cromarty
7	Elphin	29/2111	H.M.	m	74	–	Elphin	Ullapool, Ross and Cromarty	Elphin
8	Colaboll	29/5610	M.G.	f	62	47	Colaboll, Lairg	Lairg Muir	Colmaily, Lairg
9a	Culgower	29/9711	D.C.	m	64	16	Caithness	same	same
9b	Kilmote	29/9711	A.B.M.	m	60	28	Loth	Braemore, Caithness	Backies, Golspie
10	Helmsdale	39/0215	R.G.	f	–	–	Portgower, Helmsdale	Navidale	Gartymore
11	Altassmore	29/5000	A.M.	m	68	–	Altassmore	Tongue	Rosehall
12	Rhilochan	29/7407	A.M.	m	70	70	Rhilochan	Morness, Rogart	Morness
13	Rogart	29/7303	W.A.S.M.	m	55	52	Reidchalmie	Watten, Caithness	Reidchalmie
14	Bonar Bridge	28/6191	W.B.U.	m	51	14	Ousdale, Caithness	Aberdeenshire	Ross-shire
15	Golspie	28/8399	B.B.P.	f	34	31	Golspie	Strath, Halladale	Dornoch
16	Embo	28/8192	W.A.C.	m	52	14	Bonar Bridge	same	same
17	Clashmore	28/7389	M.J.G.	f	43	43	Dornoch	Wick, Caithness	Fearn, Ross-shire

ROSS AND CROMARTY

	Place of Residence	Grid	Name	Sex	Age	Length of residence (yrs)	Birthplace of Informant	Birthplace of Mother	Birthplace of Father
1	Kershader (Sch.)	19/3420	D.M.	m	48	1	Shader Point, Lewis	same	same
2	Laide (Sch.)	18/9091	A.M.	f	53	28	Badluarach, Ross-shire	same	same
3	Ullapool	28/1294	J.R.M.	m	62	–	Ullapool	Stornoway	Ullapool
4	Melvaig (Sch.)	18/7486	C.M.	f	47	29	Melvaig, Gairloch	same	same
5	Midtown	18/8185	A.J.M.	m	50	44	Inverness-shire	Inverasdale	Inverasdale
6	Portmahomack	28/9184	M.C.B.S.	f	29	26	Portmahomack.	Isle of Lewis	Tain
7	Ardross (Sch.)	28/6473	J.H.R.	m	53	22	Urray	Urquhart	Fearn
8	Newfield	28/7877	A.M.D.	m	73	70	Calrossie, Nigg Station	Fearn	Nairn
9	Tullich	28/7373	J.R.	f	45	42	Delny	same	same
10	Reiskmore	28/7072	D.J.R.	m	67	64	Reiskmore	Fearn	Reiskmore
11	Rhynie	28/8479	A.C.R.	f	–	since birth	Fearn	Inverness	Fearn
12	Fearn	28/8377	A.R.	m	51	51	Fearn	Munlochy	Fearn
13	Nigg Station	28/8076	A.M.	m	66	40	Logie-Easter	Black Isle	Logie-Easter
14	Hilton of Cadboll	28/8776	J.R.	f	49	49	Hilton	same	same
15	Pitcalnie	28/8072	D.M.	m	59	28	Burnside, Avoch	Strathconon	Strathconon
16	Diabaig	18/8060	W.M.	m	53	50	Diabaig	same	same
17	Garve	28/3961	A.M.	f	56	15	Brahan, Cononbridge	Muchernich, Tore	Brahan
18	Alness	28/6569	L.M.	m	73	50	Alness	Richailin, Rosskeen	Alness
19	Rosskeen	28/6869	D.M.	m	26	9	Brechin, Angus	Cowdenbeath, Fife	Motherwell, Lanarkshire
20	Evanton	28/6066	M.M.	m	50	15	Carrbridge, Inverness-shire	Inverness-shire	Inverness-shire
21	Auchmartin	28/6966	M.J.F.	f	39	36	Auchmartin	Parish of Cromarty	Parish of Resolis
22	Resolis	28/6665	E.C.	f	67	67	Resolis	Morayshire	Resolis
23	Newhall (Sch.)	28/6965	G.M.C.	m	44	12	Stornoway	Garve Ross-shire	Stornoway
24	Cullicudden	28/6564	C.M.	f	68	65	Toberchurn, Cullicudden	Broomton, Culbokie	Toberchurn
25a	Cromarty	28/7967	L.B. (Cromarty Youth Club)	f	–	30	Wales	Cornwall	Cromarty
25b	Cromarty	28/7867	J.M.	f	60	58	—	Beauly, Inverness-shire	Ardgay, Ross-shire
26	Torridon (Sch.)	18/8956	M.A.F.	f	64	11	Dingwall	Lochcarron	Black Isle

ROSS AND CROMARTY Cont'd

	Place of Residence	Grid	Name	Sex	Age	Length of residence (Yrs)	BIRTHPLACE OF Informant	Mother	Father
27	Bridge End	28/3255	D.K.S.	m	76	4	Dochfour, Inverness-shire	Tarvie, Contin	Tarvie
28	Strathpeffer	28/4858	M.R.	f	62	62	Strathpeffer	Dingwall	Strathpeffer
29	Fairburn	28/4653	J.A.M.	f	40	40	Urray, Fairburn	Inverness	Contin
30	Lochussie	28/5157	A.S.	f	44	3	Ferintosh	same	same
31	Balreillan	28/5856	D.G.	m	73	71	Cononbridge	Avoch	Cononbridge
32a	Muir of Ord	28/5250	M.C.	f	49	44	Inverness	Allanfearn, Inverness-shire	Muir of Ord
32b	Muir of Ord	28/5250	A.F.	m	73	40	Urquhart	same	same
32c	Muir of Ord	28/5250	A.L.	m	62	62	Muir of Ord	same	same
33	Culbokie	28/6059	J.F.	m	69	65	Culbokie	Shoreton	Culbokie
34	Killen	28/6758	A.S.H.	m	53	18	Dunbar, East Lothian	Newcastle, Northumberland	Manchester, Lancs.
35	Balnakyle	28/6454	D.M.	m	52	52	Balnakyle	Knockbairn, Munlochy	Balnakyle
36	Fortrose	28/7256	M.J.M.	f	—	38	Auldearn, Narinshire	Speybay, Banffshire	Knockbain, Ross-shire
37a	Avoch	28/7055	D.S.	m	73	73	Avoch	same	same
37b	Avoch	28/7055	J.S.	f	55	52	Avoch	same	same
38	Balmacara	18/8028	F.M.	f	48	45	Balmacara	Glenelg, Inverness-shire	Gairloch
39	Invershiel	18/9319	I.M.	f	25	22	Totaig, Glenshiel	Lochinver, Sutherland	Totaig

INVERNESS

	Place of Residence	Grid	Name	Sex	Age	Length of residence (Yrs)	Informant	Mother	Father
1	Scarp (Sch.)	09/9813	D.C.	m	41	3	Argyllshire	same	same
2	Cliasamol (Sch.)	19/0806	M.M.	f	40	1	Scarp	same	same
3	Uig	18/3864	D.M.	m	67	64	Uig	same	same
4	Kyles Floddy (Sch.) Benbecula	08/8255	K.M.M.	f	28	2	Carinish	Leirinish	Carinish
5	Colbost (Sch.)	18/2049	M.A.M.	f	24	21	Colbost	Colbost	Shiader, by Dunvegan
6	Portree	18/4843	R.M.C.	m	78	71	Portree	Glenelg	Tote, Skye
7	Farley	28/4645	W.F.	m	72	72	Farley	Cromarty	Kiltarlity
8	Kiltarlity	28/4943	J.F.	m	75	75	Dores	Kiltarlity	Kiltarlity
9	Kirkhill	28/5545	M.P.	f	48	43	Inverness	Kirkhill	Haddington, East Lothian
10	Lentran	28/5844	J.F.	m	83	70	Inverness	Lentran	Alves, Morayshire
11	Milifiach	28/5443	J.M.	f	—	—	—	—	—
12	Auchvaich	28/5340	C.F.	f	48	48	Auchvaich	Stratherrick	Clunes, Kirkhill
13a	Inverness	28/6645	J.A.C.	m	46	43	Inverness	Kilmarack, Beauly	Crieff, Perthshire
13b	Inverness	28/6645	H.H.	m	46	43	Inverness	Invershin, Sutherland	Wick, Caithness
13c	Inverness	28/6645	J.H.	m	60	50	Skye	Aberdeen	Fife
13d	Inverness	28/6645	D.J.M.	m	54	27	Lochcarron, Ross-shire	Gairloch, Ross-shire	Lochcarron
13e	Inverness	28/6645	E.J.T.	m	83	80	Inverness	Dingwall, Ross-shire	Inverness
14	Battlefield	27/6040	J.R.	m	81	78	Battlefield	Inverness	Battlefield
15	Croy	28/7949	—, R.	f	70	35	Little Dalcross, Croy	Hardhill, Dalcross	Little Dalcross
16	Struy (Sch.)	28/3939	E.M.	f	—	—	—	—	—
17	Abriachan (Sch.)	28/5535	E.F.	f	43	32	Abriachan	same	same
18	Drumnadrochit	28/5130	A.C.M.	m	54	40	Inverness	Glenurquhart	Dundee, Angus
19	Aldourie (Sch.)	28/6036	D.C.	m	55	26	Inverness	Strathconon, Ross-shire	Conon, Ross-shire
20	Farr (Sch.)	28/6833	J.C.M.	f	46	1	Nigg, Ross-shire	Nigg, Ross-shire	Kildary, Ross-shire
21a	Ruthven	28/8133	A.M.	m	73	70	Ruthven	Farr	Ruthven
21b	Ruthven	28/8133	L.R.	m	70	67	Ruthven	Invereen, Tomatin	Dores
22	Kyleakin	18/7526	F.N.R.	f	39	36	Kyleakin	Portree, Skye	Lossiemouth, Morayshire
23	Foyers	28/4920	J.G.	m	60	23	Aultnagoire	Dores	Dores
24	Gorthlick	28/5521	T.F.	m	73	68	Gorthlick	same	same
25	Glenlia	28/5020	D.A.M.	m	69	61	Inverness	Boat of Garten	Parish of Boleskine
26	Dunmaglass	28/6023	E.K.	f	73	3	Inverness	Kirkhill	Invern, nr. Dunkeld, Perthshire
27	Auchnahannet	28/9727	G.G.G.	m	53	49	Dulnain Bridge	Dulnain Bridge	Kingussie
28	Dulnain Bridge	28/9925	J.M.	m	71	68	Dulnain Bridge	Banffshire	Dulnain Bridge
29	Nethybridge	38/0020	M.M.G.	f	66	63	Nethybridge	Duthill	Nairn
30	Invermoriston	28/4216	A.G.	m	86	—	Invermoriston	—	—
31	Lochgarthside	28/5219	A.C.	m	77	67	Gorthlick	—	—
32	Fort Augustus	28/3709	M.B.	f	29	9	Kirkwall, Orkney	Beauly	Beauly
33	Alvie	28/8709	C.M.M.	f	52	6	Lairg, Sutherland	Dornoch, Sutherland	Ardgay, Ross-shire
34	Morar	17/6793	D.M.	m	62	60	Morar	Mallaig	Morar
35	Newtonmore	27/7199	N.F.	f	—	26	Kinlochlaggan	Newtonmore	Rannoch, Perthshire
36	Lochailort	17/7682	C.M.	f	54	3	Arisaig	Arisaig	Beauly
37	Achnacarry (Sch.)	27/1887	J.L.K.	f	51	42	Glasgow, Lanarkshire	Glasgow, Lanarkshire	Achnacarry
38	Spean Bridge	27/2282	A.G.	m	59	55	Parish of Kilmally, Argyllshire	Uachan, Lochielside	Morar district
39	Dalwhinnie	27/6384	—. M.	f	57	—	Corrievackie	Rannoch, Perthshire	Ross-shire

INVERNESS Cont'd

	Place of Residence	Grid	Name	Sex	Age	Length of residence (Yrs)	Informant	BIRTHPLACE OF Mother	Father
40	Tomacharich (Sch.)	27/1477	J.A.N.	f	82	–	Fort William	Glen Nevis, Fort William	Glenelg
			Words supplied by M.C.						

N A I R N

	Place of Residence	Grid	Name	Sex	Age	Length of residence (Yrs)	Informant	Mother	Father
1a	Tradespark	28/8856	A.C.	f	45	22	Tradespark	Aberdeenshire	Delnies
1b	Nairn	28/8856	I.R.	f	52	12	London	Nairn	Aberdeen
1c	Nairn	28/8856	A.R.R.	m	50	4	Glasgow, Lanarkshire	Kilbirnie, Ayrshire	Glasgow, Lanarkshire
2	Knockanbuie	28/8352	J.C.	m	51	20	Woodlands	Inverness-shire	Knockanbuie
3	Raitloan	28/8853	J.C.	m	58	58	Raitloan	Nairnshire	Nairnshire
4	Moyness	28/9553	S.L.M.	f	67	20	Cawdor	Banffshire	Morayshire
5	Barevan	28/8347	I.R.P.	f	65	16	Milton of Cawdor	Inverness	Forres, Morayshire
6	Clunas	28/8846	T.M.	m	76	–	Knockandhu, Cawdor	Cabrach, Beauly, Inverness-shire	Ballachrochan, Cawdor

M O R A Y

	Place of Residence	Grid	Name	Sex	Age	Length of residence (Yrs)	Informant	Mother	Father
1	Stotfield	38/2270	E.G.	f	65	56	Lossiemouth	Stotfield, Lossiemouth	Barmuckity, nr. Elgin
2a	Findhorn	38/0364	D.F.	m	61	20	Kellas, Dallas	Kellas	Duffus
2b	Findhorn	38/0364	I.M.	f	65	40	Findhorn	Burghead	Findhorn
3	Hopeman	38/1469	V.W.H.P.	m	49	4	Orkney	same	same
4	Burghead	38/1168	H.M.M.	m	50	4	Inverness	Bernera, Lewis, Ross and Cromarty	Gairloch, Ross-shire
5	Duffus	38/1768	E.F.	f	22	19	Duffus	Morayshire	Morayshire
6a	Crook of Alves	38/1362	F.M.	m	66	34	Oban, Argyllshire	Benderloch, Argyllshire	Perthshire
6b	Crook of Alves	38/1362	J.S.	m	89	86	Alves	Black Isle, Ross and Cromarty	Alves
7	Kinneddar	38/2269	W.D.M.S.	m	35	30	Elgin	Morayshire	Aberdeenshire
8a	Elgin	38/2162	E.S.H.	m	–	50	—	—	—
8b	Elgin	38/2162	M.H.	f	64	50	Dufftown, Banffshire	Elgin	Dufftown, Banffshire
8c	Elgin	38/2162	K.M.K.	f	44	24	Ireland	same	same
8d	Elgin	38/2162	E.I.R.	f	49	40	Elgin	Gamrie, Banffshire	Boharm, Banffshire
8e	Elgin	38/2162	H.S.	m	74	74	Morayshire	same	same
8f	Elgin	38/2162	J.S.S.	m	77	17	Elgin	Kildrummy, Aberdeenshire	Mosstodloch, nr. Fochabers
9a	Garmouth	38/3364	E.T.D.	f	55	43	Garmouth	Garmouth	Rothes
9b	Garmouth	38/3364	E.M.M.	f	62	59	Garmouth	Banffshire	Banffshire
10	Nether Dallachy	38/3663	M.R.	f	50	46	Byres, Spey Bay	Tugnet, Spey Bay	Slackbuie, Mulben Banffshire
11	Conicavel	28/9953	A.W.	m	55	22	Archiestown	Knockando, Banffshire	Aberchirder, Banffshire
12	Forres	38/0358	A.G.S.	m	–	22	—	—	—
13	Pilmuir	38/0257	J.F.	m	75	72	Forres	London	Forres
14	Easter Manbeen	38/1959	G.C.	m	41	30	Pluscarden	Pluscarden	Brodie
15	Kellas	38/1754	J.M.	m	71	68	Kellas	same	same
16	Strypes	38/2758	L.R.G.	f	54	50	Lhanbryd	Aberdeen	Drainie
17	Cranloch (Sch.)	38/2858	J.D.N.	Information obtained from various local residents					
18	Mosstodloch	38/3259	J.R.	m	75	75	Dipple, Fochabers	Dallas, Nr. Elgin	Orton, Fochabers
19	Fochabers	38/3458	S.D.M.	f	73	50	Banff	Fochabers	Fochabers
20	Mains of Orton	38/3154	G.L.W.	m	59	50	Fraserburgh, Aberdeenshire	Rathen, Fraserburgh, Aberdeenshire	Fraserburgh, Aberdeenshire
21	Archiestown	38/2344	M.S.	f	60	26	Banffshire	same	same
22	Advie	38/1234	J.T.S.	m	69	1	Echt, Aberdeenshire	London	Banff
23	Cromdale	38/0728	E.S.	f	–	–	Cromdale	same	same

B A N F F

	Place of Residence	Grid	Name	Sex	Age	Length of residence (Yrs)	Informant	Mother	Father
1	Findochty	38/4667	J.W.O.	m	59	23	Castletown, Caithness	Castletown, Caithness	Thurso, Caithness
2a	Buckie	38/4265	N.L.B.	f	62	50	Buckie	Buckie	Rosehearty, Aberdeenshire
2b	Buckie	38/4265	W.C.	m	77	74	Aberdeen	Buckie	Buckie
2c	Buckie	38/4265	J.P.	f	39	30	Buckie	same	same
3	Rathven (Sch.)	38/4465	J.S.M.	m	62	23	Buckie	Buckie	Portsoy
4	Drybridge	38/4362	–.W.	f	74	50	Raemore, Marnoch	Keith district	Keith district
5	Clochan	38/4060	W.F.J.	m	45	6	Buckie	Buckie	Bishophill, Elgin, Morayshire
6a	Cullen	38/5167	J.H.G.	f	56	53	Deskford	—	—
6b	Cullen	38/5167	P.H.	m	51	12	Aberdeenshire	Aberdeenshire	Kincardineshire

	Place of Residence	Grid	Name	Sex	Age	Length residence (Yrs)	Informant	BIRTHPLACE OF Mother	Father
7	Portsoy	38/5866	M.A.M.	f	54	40	Portsoy	Banffshire	Banffshire
8	Fordyce	38/5563	J.W.C.	f	71	43	Keith	Angus	Kinross
9	Kirktown of Deskford	38/5061	M.E.B.	f	52	49	Deskford	Deskford	Deskford
10	Banff	38/6864	A.S.M.	m	56	15	Carron, Morayshire	Grange	Cornhill
11	Macduff	38/7064	R.H.	m	48	5	Gamrie	King Edward, Aberdeenshire	Macduff
12	Bonnyton	38/7463	W.M.R.	m	47	45	Mill of Cullen, Gamrie	Turriff, Aberdeenshire	Banff
13	Gamrie	38/7962	J.S.	m	58	25	Lossiemouth	same	same
14	Upper Forgie	38/4052	H.M.	f	65	62	Keith	same	same
15	Mulben	38/3550	H.M.G.	m	–	–	Farr, Sutherland	—	—
16	Glen of Newmill	38/4354	J.M.S.	f	39	36	Glen of Newmill	Grange	Glen of Newmill
17	Newmill	38/4352	R.M.	m	58	47	Auchinblae	—	—
18a	Keith	38/4350	M.A.	f	53	22	Eire	same	same
18b	Keith	38/4350	H.M.C.	f	25	22	Keith	Fife Keith	Fife Keith
18c	Keith	38/4350	H.D.	m	79	38	Keith	same	same
18d	Keith	38/4350	R.Y.B.	m	75	20	Keith	Cairnie, Aberdeenshire	Cairnie
19	Bogmuchals	38/5559	–.G.	f	–	12	Grange	same	same
20	Rawgowan	38/6258	A.M.	f	79	–	—	—	—
21	Hungryhill	38/6858	J.G.	f	27	4	Glenlivet	same	same
22	Peatknowe	38/6256	R.T.	m	52	20	Alvah	same	same
23	Forglen House	38/6951	A.C.W.S.	m	44	14	Inverness	Macduff	Inverness
24	Muirden	38/7053	G.S.	m	52	–	Muirden	Turriff, Aberdeenshire	Ellon, Aberdeenshire
25	Aberlour	38/2642	J.W.	m	56	53	Aberlour	same	same
26	Milltown	38/5448	C.P.	m	70	70	Rothiemay	—	—
27	Bogower	38/6345	G.H.	m	31	28	Forgue, Aberdeenshire	Forgue, Aberdeenshire	Inverkeithney
28	Inveravon (Sch.)	38/1837	W.J.B.	m	–	8	—	—	—
29	Dufftown	38/3240	I.I.	f	70	60	Dufftown	Tulloch, Dufftown	Georgetown, Demerara, British Guinea
30	Auchindoun	38/3639	B.H.G.	f	65	21	Dufftown	Lower Cabrach, Aberdeenshire	Dufftown
31	Mains of Lesmurdie	38/3932	D.K.C.	f	46	46	Lesmurdie	Fordyce	Lesmurdie
32	Glenlivet (Sch.)	38/1929	With assistance from various local residents.						
33	Tomnavoulin	38/2126	A.J.I.	m	79	79	Tomnavoulin	UpperDrumin, Glenlivet	Braes of Glenlivet
34	Achnarrow	38/2123	R.L.	m	51	48	Braes of Glenlivet	same	same

ABERDEEN

	Place of Residence	Grid	Name	Sex	Age	Length residence (Yrs)	Informant	Mother	Father
1	Pennan	38/8465	A.S.	m	61	40	New Pitsligo	same	same
2	New Aberdour	38/8863	D.B.G.	m	59	29	Sanday, Orkney	same	same
3a	Rosehearty	38/9367	A.H.	f	57	54	Montrose, Angus	Rothes	Muchalls, Kincardineshire
3b	Peathill	38/9366	J.R.	f	69	69	Peathill, Rosehearty	Ironhill, New Aberdour	Peathill
4	Sandhaven	38/9667	C.G.J.	m	42	8	Inverurie	Rosehearty	Inverurie
5a	Fraserburgh	38/9966	A.M.	f	–	–	Fraserburgh	Ross-shire	Fraserburgh
5b	Fraserburgh	38/9967	G.R.	m	59	4	Deer	Longside	Deer
5c	Fraserburgh	38/9967	C.S.	m	63	–	Rathen	—	—
5d	Fraserburgh	38/9966	A.B.W.	f	50	5	Alvah, Banffshire	Banffshire	Banffshire
6	Hatton	38/9558	J.E.	m	56	22	Fraserburgh	Rathen	Pitsligo
7	Inverallochy	48/0465	G.T.R.	m	23	15	Slains	Halkirk, Caithness	Wick, Caithness
8	Milton of Fishrie	38/7558	G.K.	m	56	50	Fishrie	same	same
9	King Edward	38/7157	–.S.	f	70	30	Blairmaud	Boyndie, Banffshire	Boyndie, Banffshire
10	Fishrie (Sch.)	38/7557	A.I.G.	f	54	8	Peterculter	Banchory, Kincardineshire	Kildrummy
11	Walker Hill	38/7756	S.D.M.	m	46	43	Crudie	Crudie	Forglen, Turriff
12	Fintry (Sch.)	38/7554	H.M.B.	f	61	25	Monymusk	Keig, nr. Alford	Tarves
13	Den of Glasslaw (Sch.)	38/8558	J.J.R.G.	f	43	3	King Edward	Auchterless	Monymusk
14	New Pitsligo	38/8855	W.F.	f	76	8	New Aberdour	same	same
15	Newbyth	38/8254	–.C.	f	80	50	Auchterless	Daviot	Rayne
16	Strichen	38/9455	R.F.B.	m	46	10	Inverurie	Cults	Alford
17	Fetterangus (Sch.)	38/9850	C.A.C.	f	–	16	Banffshire	—	—
			Information gathered from several old residents of Fetterangus						
18	Nether Cortes	48/0058	A.F.	m	63	60	Nether Cortes	N.E.Aberdeenshire	N.E. Aberdeenshire
19	Lonmay	48/0158	–.K.	f	65	65	Crimond	New Pitsligo	Lonmay
20	St Fergus	48/0952	D.D.	m	65	27	Dunfermline, Fife	same	same
21	Hythie	48/0051	M.H.	f	65	62	Kininmonth	Fetterangus, Old Deer	Sandhole, Fraserburg
22	Cairnie	38/4844	J.H.	m	60	57	Cairnie	Huntly	Cairnie

ABERDEEN Cont'd

	Place of Residence	Grid	Name	Sex	Age	Length of residence (Yrs)	BIRTHPLACE OF Informant	Mother	Father
23	Ruthven	38/5047	J.M.	f	69	69	Cairnie	same	same
24	Kinnoir (Sch.)	38/5543	A.M.A.	f	47	10	Banff	Cornhill, Banffshire	Cornhill, Banffshire
25	Huntly	38/5340	—	—	—	—	—	—	—
26	Yonders Bognie	38/6046	J.T.	f	43	43	Forgue	Forgue	Fintry
27	Newtown of Auchaber	38/6240	B.R.S.S.	m	—	13	Culsalmond	Clatt	Drumblade
28a	Turriff	38/7249	W.C.	m	76	44	Fordyce, Banffshire	Gamrie, Banffshire	Banff
28b	Turriff	38/7249	J.H.F.	f	—	60	—	—	—
28c	Turriff	38/7249	R.W.S.N.	m	—	—	—	—	—
29	Steinmanhill (Sch.)	38/7642	W.E.D.D.	f	66	11	Newmill, Keith, Banffshire	Newmill, Banffshire	Grange, Banffshire
30	Kirktown of Auchterless	38/7141	G.W.R.	m	46	29	Rothienorman	Rothienorman	Cuminestown
31	Mains of Culsh	38/8848	J.W.	m	74	28	Hillhead, Strichen	Old Pitsligo	Rathen
32	Greenfield	38/8246	A.P.	m	73	31	Old Deer	Bonnykelly, New Deer	Overside, St Fergus
33	Cairnorrie	38/8641	W.F.D.	m	63	23	Edinburgh, Midlothian	Edinburgh, Midlothian	East Lothian
34	Maud	38/9248	D.M.	m	57	14	Grange, Banffshire	Grange, Banffshire	Keith, Banffshire
35	Milladen	38/9846	P.E.	m	57	57	Fetterangus	Fetterangus	St Fergus
36	Stuartfield	38/9745	G.H.D.	m	60	50	Mintlaw	Parish of King Edward	Paris of Longside
37	Smithy Croft	38/9844	A.M.	m	61	59	Ardallie Parish	New Aberdour	St Fergus
38	Shannas (Sch.)	38/9943	L.W.	f	—	20	Manse of Savoch, Auchnagatt	Charlottetown, Prince Edward Isle, Canada	Beith, Ayrshire
39	Brownhill of Annochie	38/9343	A.W.	m	56	56	Brownhill of Annochie	Brownhill Croft	Brownhill of Annochie
40	Auchnavaird	38/9440	A.W.	m	72	69	Auchnavaird, Auchnagatt	Gibseat, Auchnagatt	Slains
41	Lunderton	48/1049	G.C.	m	82	60	Inverugie	Kininmonth	Kininmonth
42	Mintlaw	48/0048	J.T.G.	m	58	24	Peterhead	—	St Fergus
43	Longside	48/0347	J.F.	m	49	5	New Deer	same	same
44	Torterston	48/0847	R.G.B.	m	44	5	Stoneywood	Aberdeen	Bucksburn
45	Kinmundy	48/0444	J.T.	m	78	45	Peterhead	Auchnagatt	Auchnagatt
46	Blackhills	48/0843	J.M.	f	78	75	Blackhills, Peterhead	Cruden	Blackhills
47a	Peterhead Academy	48/1346	I.S.	f	per I.S., Principal Teacher of Geography and Woman Adviser				
47b	Peterhead	48/1346	C.D.F.	f	52	52	Peterhead	same	same
47c	Peterhead	48/1346	B.E.G.	f	—	16	Fraserburgh	Pitsligo	Fraserburgh
47d	Peterhead	48/1346	E.F.M.	f	52	30	Peterhead	Peterhead	Aberdeen
47e	Peterhead	48/1346	H.M.S.	f	34	32	Peterhead	same	same
47f	Peterhead	48/1346	M.T.	f	63	63	Peterhead	same	same
48	Drumblade Parish	38/5739	M.S.	f	78	41	Rothiemay, Banffshire	Huntly	Cairnie
49	Wells of Ythan	38/6338	W.G.S.	m	43	4	Newhills	same	same
50	Glens of Foudland	38/6034	T.M.D.	m	37	2	Carmyle, Lanarkshire	Stair, Ayrshire	Drongan, Ayrshire
51	Kirkton of Culsalmond	38/6532	J.G.D.	m	48	15	Fraserburgh	Portsoy	Whitehills, Banffshire
52	Largie	38/6131	W.W.	m	64	50	Cairnie	Cairnie	Drummuir, Banffshire
53	Rayne (Sch.)	38/6931	A.W.	m	52	8	Cairnie	same	same
54	Rothienorman	38/7235	E.M.J.K.	f	47	16	Alford	Ballater	Alford
55	St Katherine	38/7834	C.G.	f	29	2	Ayrshire	Ayrshire	Dingwall, Ross and Cromarty
56	Methlick	38/8537	H.B.	f	61	38	Tarves	Tarves	Methlick
57	Tulloch (Sch.)	38/7932	L.A.H.	f	63	30	Aberdeenshire (East)	Central Aberdeenshire	North Aberdeenshire
58	Tarves	38/8631	C.R.M.	m	50	8	Kemnay	Cairney	Monquhitter
59	Mains of Inkhorn	38/9239	J.S.	f	64	36	Stockbridge, Peterhead	Boghead, Kininmonth	Mintlaw, Kininmonth
60	Mill of Dumbreck	38/9030	H.M.	f	43	25	Strathdon	same	same
61	Aulton	48/0735	E.D.	f	45	2	Cruden Bay	Cruden Bay	Wellbank, Peterhead
62	Tassathill	48/0033	Anonymous						
63	Rhynie	38/4927	J.F.	m	59	19	Knock, Sleat, Skye, Inverness-shire	Dingwall, Rosshire	Beauly, Inverness-shire
64	Premnay (Sch.)	38/5924	M.M.S.	f	46	46	Glass	Inverurie	Glass
65	Insch	38/6328	J.A.	m	75	40	Turriff	Turriff	Garioch
66	Hatton of Ardoyne	38/6526	—.R.	f	49	30	Culsalmond	Culsalmond	Kennethmont
67	Daviot (Sch.)	38/7528	E.M.	m	66	20	Westray, Orkney	Orkney	Orkney
68	Durno	38/7128	A.M.F.	m	61	58	Durno	Methlick	—
69	Bourtie (Sch.)	38/7824	B.M.M.	f	46	21	Cluny	Banchory	Midmar
70	Balquhain	38/7322	J.W.W.	f	66	31	Keith-Hall, Inverurie	Keith-Hall	same
71a	Inverurie	38/7721	G.S.B.	m	70	32	New Deer	same	same
71b	Inverurie	38/7721	D.B.	f	49	13½	Keith-Hall	same	same
71c	Inverurie	38/7721	N.D.	m	Information obtained from two old residents.				
72	Denend	38/8825	J.A.	m	76	73	Udny	Oldmeldrum	Tarves
73	Whiterashes	38/8523	L.M.	f	34	12	Cluny	Garlogie, Echt	Cluny
74	Littlemill of Esslemont	38/9228	G.M.	m	58	56	Littlemill of Esslemont	Ellon	Littlemill of Esslemont
75	Craigieford	38/9727	E.P.C.	f	76	53	Deepheather, Ellon	—	—
76	Newburgh	38/9925	A.M.	m	86	86	Newburgh	Longside	New Deer
77	Cultercullen	38/9124	A.M.	f	61	35	—	Morayshire	—
78	Forbestown	38/3612	L.F.	f	67	59	Wilton, Roxburghshire	Strathdon	Coull, Deeside
79	Newseat	38/4911	A.C.	m	73	36	Tarland	Cushnie	Lumphanan
80	Montgarrie	38/5717	I.D.K.	f	54	24	Grange, Banffshire	Cairnie	Cairnie
81	Haughton	38/5816	A.S.	m	58	56	Old Strathlunach	Monymusk	Keig
82	Keig (Sch.)	38/6118	W.B.	m	44	16	Rhynie	Ellon	Strichen

ABERDEEN Cont'd

	Place of Residence	Grid	Name	Sex	Age	Length of residence (Yrs)	BIRTHPLACE OF Informant	Mother	Father
83	Monymusk	38/6815	E.D.M.M.	f	61	26	Aboyne	Skene	Methlick
84	Tough	38/6113	A.K.S.	f	74	74	Tough	Tough	Garioch
85	Kintore	38/7816	W.H.A.	m	—	3	—	—	—
86	Kemnay	38/7315	D.W.S.	m	52	24	Lumphanan	Cushnie	Torphins
87	Lyne of Skene	38/7610	E.A.S.	f	63	31	Aberlour, Banffshire	Morange, Banffshire	Aberlour, Banffshire
88	Monykebbuck	38/8718	–.W.	f	59	56	Ord, Newmachar	Kinghorn, Newmachar	Newmachar
89	Overton (Sch.)	38/8614	M.H.R.	f	64	13	Orkney	same	same
90	Bankhead (Sch.)	38/8910	A.S.R.	m	Completed with the help of schoolchildren				
91	Craigie (Sch.)	38/9119	—	m	—	—	—	—	—
92	Corgarff	38/2708	J.R.	m	67	60	Tarland	Corgarff	Corgarff
93	Tarland	38/4804	H.G.	m	53	2	Caithness	same	same
94	Milton Corse	38/5507	J.R.	m	67	65	Milton Corse, Coull, Lumphanan	Kincardine O'Neil	Milton Corse, Coull, Lumphanan
95	Waulkmill	38/5507	I.T.	f	—	25	—	—	—
96	Lumphanan	38/5804	J.F.D.	m	53	19½	Portsoy Banffshire	Cullen, Banffshire	Rathven, Banffshire
97	Milton of Campfield	38/6400	J.C.F.	m	73	70	Glassel	Raemoir, Kincardine-shire	Glassel
98	West Kinnernie	38/7109	J.C.	m	58	10	Cluny	Kemnay	Inverness
99	Dunecht	38/7509	J.B.	f	49	18	Newhills	Kininmonth	Midmar
100	Midmar	38/7005	C.I.D.	f	56	40	Midmar	Huntly	Ruthven
101	Garlogie (Sch.)	38/7805	C.D.W.	f	55	20	Fintary	Fintary	Newmachar
102	Bucksburn	38/8909	–.W.	m	—	—	—	—	—
103	Westhill	38/8306	M.J.F.C.	f	63	25	Aberdeen	Tough	Skene
104	Eddieston (Sch.)	38/8003	E.H.C.	f	58	9	Tulloch, Old Meldrum	Leslie, Insch	Old Meldrum
105	Peterculter	38/8300	A.I.M.	m	48	45	Peterculter	Forgue	Lonmay
106	Craighill	38/9301	J.M.	m	72	70	Nigg	Banchory	Broomhill Farm, Aberdeenshire
107	Crathie	37/2695	A.A.T.	m	50	50	Crathie	Braemar	Crathie
108	Ballater	37/3695	I.L.U.	f	59	18	Port Elphinstone	Parish of King Edward	Savoch, Nr. Auchnag
109	Finzean	37/5993	A.M.	m	62	22	Glasgow, Lanarkshire	Ayr	Old Kilpatrick

KINCARDINE

	Place of Residence	Grid	Name	Sex	Age	Length of residence (Yrs)	Informant	Mother	Father
1	Cove	38/9500	C.E.M.	m	—	12	—	—	—
		and	A.S.	m	—	—	—	—	—
2	Raemoir	37/7099	A.H.H.	f	38	2½	Glasgow, Lanarkshire	Old Meldrum, Aberdeenshire	Skene, Aberdeenshire
3	Upper Lochton	37/6997	M.R.G.	f	57	54	Upper Lochton, Banchory	Strachan, by Banchory	Upper Lochton, Banchory
4	Inchmarlo	37/6796	J.C.	f	65	31½	Lonmay, Aberdeenshire	Fraserburgh, Aberdeenshire	St Fergus Aberdeenshire
5	Banchory	37/6995	W.R.	m	72	4	Drumoak, Aberdeenshire	Birse, Aberdeenshire	Drumoak, Aberdeenshire
6	Strachan	37/6692	A.A.	f	56	38	Lumphanan, Aberdeenshire	same	same
7	Crathes	37/7596	J.M.H.	f	50	6½	Newtonhill, Nr. Stonehaven	Newtonhill	Auchnagatt, Aberdeenshire
8	Little Tulloch	37/7795	J.A.B.	m	54	12	Tarland, Aberdeenshire	Cabrach, Banffshire	Glenkindie, Aberdeenshire
9	Cairnfauld	37/7593	A.R.	m	47	44	Durris	Old Rayne, Aberdeenshire	Durris
10	Maryculter	37/8497	J.M.	m	59	37	Portlethan	Aberdeen	Rothienorman, Aberdeenshire
11	Netherly	37/8493	–.N.	f	64	36	East Blackburn, Urie	Echt, Aberdeenshire	Banchory-Devenick
12	Cookney	37/8793	E.G.	-	50	50	Aberdeen	Savoch Aberdeenshire	Methlick, Aberdeens
13	Bridge of Muchalls (Sch.)	37/8991	E.L.G.	f	48	—	—	—	—
14	Newtonhill	37/9093	J.M.	m	56	50	Newtonhill	same	same
15	Drumlithie	37/7880	I.H.M.	f	68	65	Glenbervie	Angus	Ayrshire
16	Rickarton (Sch.)	37/8189	E.T.	f	52	5	Ellon, Aberdeenshire	St Fergus, Aberdeenshire	Maud, Aberdeenshire
17a	Stonehaven	37/8786	A.G.	m	Completed with the assistance of several local residents				
17b	Stonehaven	37/8785	G.J.	m	78	9	Netherley	Netherley	Cookney
17c	Stonehaven	37/8785	J.M.	f	53	50	Stonehaven	Stonehaven	Stranathro
17d	Stonehaven	37/8786	H.R.W.	f	65	39	Stonehaven	same	same
18	Stonehaven	37/8582	M.H.	f	65	61	Brucklaywaird, Stonehaven	Rickarton, Stonehaven	Dunnottar, Stonehav
19	Upper Westown	37/8280	D.F.	m	48	48	Upper Westown	—	Upper Westown
20	Pitnamoon	37/6874	D.F.	m	68	39	Fordoun	Fordoun	Stonehaven
21	Mill of Mondynes	37/7779	J.S.	m	55	50	Drumlithie	Fordoun	By Fordoun
22	Laurencekirk	37/7171	A.T.	m	48	35	Laurencekirk	Stonehaven	Laurencekirk
23	Barras	37/8178	–.B.	f	66	28	Barras	Stonehaven	Laurencekirk

KINCARDINE Cont'd

	Place of Residence	Grid	Name	Sex	Age	Length of residence (Yrs)	Informant	BIRTHPLACE OF Mother	BIRTHPLACE OF Father
24	Kirkton	37/8074	A.F.	m	58	20	Drumlithie	Rathen, Aberdeenshire	Parkseat, Aberdeenshire
25	Gourdon	37/8270	J.S.	m	49	44	Gourdon	Arbroath, Angus	Gourdon
26	Dubton	37/6867	F.A.	m	35	33	Marykirk	Angus	Marykirk
27	Marykirk	37/6865	C.K.C.	m	—	52	Marykirk	Anstruther, Fife	Marykirk
28	East Braidieston	37/7468	A.P.	m	79	70	St Cyrus	Dumfries	Kinneff

KINROSS

	Place of Residence	Grid	Name	Sex	Age	Length of residence (Yrs)	Informant	BIRTHPLACE OF Mother	BIRTHPLACE OF Father
1	Carnbo	37/0503	M.S.A.	f	72	68	Mawcarse	Stonehouse, Lanarkshire	Strathven, Lanarkshire
2	Fossoway	37/0202	M.W.	f	61	57	Orwell Parish	Blairingone	Kinghorn, Fife — Kinross-shire since age 16
3	Milnathort	37/1204	A.F.G.	f	44	41	Milnathort	Milnathort	Arbroath, Angus
4	Balleave	37/1102	A.B.	m	78	42	Coldrain, Kinross	Kinnesswood	Forgandenny, Perthshire
5	Portmoak	37/1700	W.A.	m	73	25	Stonehaven	same	same
6	Blairingone	26/9897	B.C.N.M.	f	50	22	Milnathort	Kilkerran, Ayrshire	Fossoway
7	Rumblingbridge	36/0199	W.S.	m	—	—	Fossoway	—	Fossoway

ANGUS

	Place of Residence	Grid	Name	Sex	Age	Length of residence (Yrs)	Informant	BIRTHPLACE OF Mother	BIRTHPLACE OF Father
1	Tarfside	37/4880	A.C.	m	73	70	Lochlee	same	same
2	Hillock	37/5578	D.M.	m	52	49	Glenesk	same	—
3	Glenogil	37/4462	A.R.	m	62	26	Menmuir, By Brechin	Fern, by Brechin	Carseburn, by Forfar
4	Fern Den	37/4861	H.T.	f	76	49	Perth	Lindores, Fife	Ceres, Fife
5a	Brechin	37/5960	O.H.A.H.	f	37	35	Lunan, by Arbroath	Roseley, Arbroath	Chapelton, Arbroath
5b	Brechin	37/5960	J.R.	m	66	35	Inverbervie, Kincardineshire	St Cyrus, Montrose	Dun, Montrose
5c	Brechin	37/5960	E.S.	m	54	51	Brechin	same	same
6	West Kinwhirrie	37/3758	W.L.	m	75	40	Airlie	Tannadice	Airlie
7	Little Kenny	37/3054	J.L.	m	75	34	Glenisla, Perthshire	same	same
8	Kirriemuir	37/3853	A.P.F.	m	—	—	—	—	—
9	Craigton of Airlie	37/3250	A.H.	m	54	51	Craigton of Airlie	—	Craigton of Airlie
10	Memus	37/4258	C.H.	m	79	9	Glamis	Westmuir	Glamis
11	Meadows	37/4454	H.E.	m	43	10	Carse of Gowrie	Angus	Carse of Gowrie
12	Padanaram (Sch.)	37/4151	E.W.	f	56	8	Kirriemuir	Kirriemuir	Meigle, East Perthshire
13	Forfar	37/4150	G.F.M.	m	58	16	Drymen, Stirlingshire	Thurso, Caithness	Girloch, Ross-shire
14a	Forfar	37/4550	G.R.C.	f	64	57	Forfar	Midmar, Aberdeenshire	Forfar
14b	Forfar	37/4550	A.C.D.	m	84	80	Forfar	same	same
			F.D.R.M.	m	54	50	Forfar	same	same
14c	Forfar	37/4550	J.N.	f	—	50	Forfar	same	same
14d	Forfar	37/4550	J.C.R.	f	49	43	Forfar	same	same
15	Guthrie (Sch.)	37/5650	M.M.	f	65	11	Dundee	Angus	Angus
16	Westerton (Sch.)	37/6654	—.K.	f	—	13	Montrose	Elgin, Morayshire	Montrose
17a	Montrose	37/7157	G.D.	m	68	21	Aberdeen	Buchan, N.E. Aberdeen	Aberdeen
17b	Montrose	37/7157	W.D.	m	77	26	Dundee	Longside, Aberdeenshire	Dundee
18	Ferryden	37/7156	J.P.	f	63	59	Ferryden	same	same
19	Newtyle	37/2941	W.W.C.	m	54	7	Peterhead, Aberdeenshire	same	same
20	Kirkinch	37/3144	M.T.	f	23	20	Kirkinch	Dufftown, Banffshire	—
21	Kingsmuir (Sch.)	37/4749	H.M.S.	f	66	13	Dundee (brought up in Forfar)	Coupar Angus, Perthshire	Barry
22	Kinnettles	37/4346	J.F.E.	m	45	4	Inverbervie, Kincardineshire	same	same
23	S. Tarbrax	37/4241	P.G.	m	79	76	Inverarity	same	same
24	Friockheim	37/5949	S.A.M.	m	34	30	Earlston, Berwickshire	Earlston, Berwickshire	Glasgow, Lanarkshire
25	Letham	37/5248	M.W.S.	f	76	64	Letham	Letham	Guthrie, by Forfar
26	Arbirlot	37/5940	W.R.	m	42	4	Motherwell, Lanarkshire	Montrose	Montrose
27	Chapelton	37/6247	A.B.	f	75	45	Kinblethmont Muir	Chapelton	Kingennie
28	Auchmithie	37/6744	A.S.	m	78	75	Auchmithie	Crail, Fifeshire	Chapelton
29a	Arbroath	37/6441	R.J.C.	m	48	45	Arbroath	same	same
29b	Arbroath	37/6441	E.J.J.	m	63	16	Montrose	Angus	Aberdeenshire
30	Old Balkello	37/3638	A.F.	m	78	25	Westmarch, Mains	Carnoustie	Mattocks, Wellbank
31	Fowlis Easter	37/3233	W.W.	m	81	39	Cargill, Perthshire	Kinclaven, Perthshire	Rattray, Perthshire
32	Kellas	37/4535	K.M.O.	f	28	26	Dundee	Inverness	Largo, East Fife
33a	Monifieth	37/4932	A.C.B.	f	56	50	Belfast	Dundee	Dundee
33b	Monifieth	37/4932	D.J.	m	86	30	Forfar	same	same

ANGUS Cont'd

	Place of Residence	Grid	Name	Sex	Age	Length of residence (Yrs)	BIRTHPLACE OF Informant	Mother	Father
34	Monikie	37/5038	D.G.D.	m	53	14	Kinneff, Kincardineshire	Dundee	Arbroath
35	Muirdrum	37/5637	A.S.J.	f	83	80	Muirdrum	Kilconquhar, Fife	Muirdrum
36	Downieken	37/5035	R.W.	m	58	55	Downieken	Kirkden	Auchterlonie
37	Carnoustie	37/5634	I.R.	f	73	44	Arbroath	same	same

PERTH

	Place of Residence	Grid	Name	Sex	Age	Length of residence (Yrs)	Informant	Mother	Father
1	Dail-na-mein	27/7569	C.D.G	m	67	64	Calvine	Strathtay	Calvine
2a	Calvine	27/8065	M.D.	f	73	4 months	Blair Atholl	Blair Atholl	Rannoch
2b	Calvine	27/8065	A.R.	f	47	40	Edinburgh, Midlothian	Edinburgh, Midlothian	Blair Atholl
3	Kindrochit	27/8064	W.M.	m	81	81	Ardgie, Pitlochry	Grantown-on-Spey, Morayshire	Ardgie
4	Strathtummel	27/8160	M.U.	f	69	–	Strathtummel	Strathtummel	Fortingall
5	Bridgend	37/0464	F.M.M.	f	51	51	Straloch	Blair Atoll	Blair Atoll
6	Enochdhu	37/0662	E.L.	f	49	49	Enochdhu	Perthshire	Perthshire
7	Kirkmichael	37/0760	C.M.	f	47	23	Blairgowrie	Alyth	Kintyre, Argyllshire
8	Kinloch Rannoch	27/6658	A.M.	m	66	27	Glasgow, Lanarkshire	Kilwinning, Ayrshire	Glasgow, Lanarkshire
9	Foss	27/7958	D.A.W.	m	46	43	Tummel Bridge, Foss	Aberdeen	Fife
10	Pitlochry	27/9458	J.A.M.	m	43	40	Bohally	Cumnock, Ayrshire	Strathtummel
11	Pitnacree	27/9253	J.C.	m	58	55	Strathtay	Inchture	Grandtully
12	Logierait	27/9751	E.D.	f	40	40	Logierait	Logierait	Dalguise
13	Alltreoch, Ballintuim	37/0956	R.S.R.	m	65	65	Dalnabreck, Ballintuim	Balnabeggan, Ballintuim	Balnabroich, Ballintuim
14	Acharn	27/7543	J.M.	m	80	77	Acharn	same	same
15	Dalguise	27/9947	A.G.	m	68	40	Moulin	Moulin	Tullymet
16	Trochrie	27/9740	J.S.	m	64	21	Amulree	Aberfeldy	Strathtummel
17	Dowally, Ballinluig	37/0048	M.E.C.	f	–	–	—	—	—
			B.C.	f	–	–	—	—	—
			D.F.	m	–	–	—	—	—
18	Dunkeld	37/0242	A.H.	f	78	70	Blair Atoll	Tullymet	Dunkeld
19	Birnam	37/0341	J.S.	m	82	80	Birnam	Dowally	Murthly
20	Culthill	37/0941	S.B.	m	53	53	Caputh	Caputh	Wexford, Ireland
21	Rattray	37/1845	M.W.T.L.	f	39	36	Rattray	same	same
22	Marlee	37/1543	J.A.M.	m	41	41	Marlee	Clunie	Marlee
23	Meigle	37/2844	E.D.N.T.	f	32	32	Meigle	same	same
24	Killin	27/5732	M.A.M.	f	80	50	Ardchattan, Argyllshire	Kirkhill, Inverness	Ardchattan, Argyll-shire
25	Bankfoot	37/0635	M.G.S.	f	82	54	Bankfoot	Aberdeenshire	Morayshire
26	Kinglands (Sch.)	37/0233	C.J.C.	f	48	10	Dunkeld	Thirsk, Yorks.	Ballinluig
27	Luncarty	37/0930	J.G.	m	76	73	Luncarty	same	same
28	Drummond Hall	37/1036	A.A.	m	–	10	Tibbermore	Braco	Comrie
29a	Newbigging Farm	37/1236	D.G.B.	m	66	44	Benchill, Redgorton	Carey, Abernethy	Newbigging, Kinclaven
29b	Stanley	37/1033	J.R.	m	84	55	Dunfermline, Fife	same	same
30	Wolf Hill	37/1533	A.R.	m	75	72	Wolfhill	Cargill	Cargill
31	Loanhead	37/1432	–.M.	f	66	22	Fintry	Bendochty	Kettins
32	Woodside	37/2037	J.W.M.	f	42	33	Burrelton	Ardler	Dundee, Angus
33	Longforgan	37/3130	D.R.	m	57	48	Dundee, Angus	Abernyte	Broughty, Ferry Angus
34	Crianlarich	27/3825	A.R.	f	Completed with the help of various local residents				
35	Lochearnhead	27/5823	D.M.	m	25	22	Lochearnhead	Lochearnhead	Brig O'Turk
36	Balquhidder	27/5320	F.M.	f	65	10	Gairloch, Ross-shire	same	same
37	St Fillans (Sch.)	27/6924	A.B.R.	f	–	–	—	—	—
38	Coishavachan	27/7427	W.M.	m	–	50	—	—	—
39	Comrie	27/7722	J.G.	m	77	54	Comrie	Comrie	Fowlis Wester, by Crieff
40	Gilmerton	27/8823	A.M.	f	60	60	Gilmerton	Crieff	Crieff
41a	Crieff	27/8621	M.M.M.	f	70	57	Auchterarder	Dunkeld	Kiltarlity, Inverness-shire
41b	Crieff	27/8621	N.M.	f	60	25	Glasgow, Lanarkshire	same	same
42	Culnacloich	27/9429	P.A.	m	69	66	Culnacloich	Castlehill, Logiealmond	Kipney, Logiealmond
43	Buchanty	27/9238	H.G.E.	f	62	28	Huntly	Aberdeen	Aberdeenshire
44	Newbigging	27/9424	J.Y.	m	67	64	Methven	Crieff	Methven
45	Fowlis Wester	27/9223	M.M.	f	70	70	Fowlis Wester	—	—
46	Pitcairngreen	37/0627	J.A.	m	72	72	Pitcairngreen	Moneydie	Cromwellpark
47	Methven	37/0225							
48	Ruthvenfield	37/0825	D.L.	m	70	67	Ruthvenfield	same	same
49	Tibbermore	37/0523	W.J.	m	73	70	Tibbermore	Baldernock, nr. Glasgow, Lanark-shire	Mollinsburn, nr. Glasgow, Lanark-shire
50	Balbeggie	37/1629	M.G.	f	61	29	Guildtown	Redstone (Cargil)	Guildtown
51a	New Scone	37/1325	A.H.	m	–	–	—	—	—

PERTH Cont'd

	Place of Residence	Grid	Name	Sex	Age	Length of residence (Yrs)	Informant	BIRTHPLACE OF Mother	Father
51b	New Scone	37/1325	J.Y	m	70	25	Perth	same	same
52a	Perth	37/1123	W.T.C.	m	43	19	Kirkcudbright	Lockerbie, Dumfries-shire	Dumfries
52b	Perth	37/1123	S.G.	m	72	45	Tullymet	Kinclaven	Tullymet
52c	Perth	37/1022	J.H.	m	84	20	Aberdalgie	Aber-Ruthven	Crieff
52d	Perth	37/1023	A.M.	m	66	50	Perth	same	same
52e	Perth	37/1123	C.C.R.	m	65	62	Perth	St Andrews,Fife	Fowlis Wester
53	Kinnoull	37/1223	R.G.T.	m	–	–	—	—	—
54	Glencarse	37/1921	–.G.	f	–	–	—	—	—
55	Craigend (Sch.)	37/1220	S.W.	m	–	–	—	—	—
56	Rhynd	37/1520	D.C.	m	81	78	Rhynd	Kinfauns	Rhynd
57	Baledgarno	37/2828	E.W.M.	f	62	59	Baledgarno	Abernyte	Newtyle, Angus
58	Rait	37/2226	W.B.	f	71	68	Rait	Kilspindie	Pitlessie, Fife
59	Errol	37/2522	R.S.	m	62	26	Bellshill, Lanarkshire	Airdrie, Lanarkshire	Bellshill, Lanarkshire
60	Pilmore	37/3229	C.P.	m	69	50	Dundee, Angus	—	—
61	Muthill	27/8617	C.D.	f	84	84	Muthill	—	—
62	Auchterarder	27/9412	J.L.T.	m	50	8	Blackford	Ayr	Auchterarder
63	Newton of Pitcairns	37/0214	D.H.	m	72	68	Dunning	same	same
64	Bridge of Earn	37/1318	J.A.F.	m	66	29	Montrose, Angus	Montrose, Angus	Laurencekirk, Kincardineshire
65	Abernethy	37/1916	M.B.	f	89	87	Abernethy	Not certain	Abernethy
66	Glenbruach	27/5106	J.S.	m	68	65	Cambusmore	Scone	Perth
67	Aberfoyle	27/5200	M.M.	f	72	49	Dufftown, Banffshire	—	—
68	Malling West	27/5600	D.G.	m	81	–	Port of Mentieth	Islay, Argyllshire	nr. Stirling
69	Callander	27/6207	A.M.	m	65	62	Callander	same	same
70	Thornhill	27/6600	D.A.	m	–	–	Thornhill	same	same
71	Deanston	27/7101	C.S.	m	Completed by various aged local residents.				
72	Doune	27/7201	P.M.	m	38	36	Doune	—	—
73	Gartmore	26/5297	J.F.	m	76	–	Gartmore	Balfron, Stirlingshire	Gartmore
74	Dykehead	27/5997	C.S.N.	f	–	–	—	—	—

FIFE

	Place of Residence	Grid	Name	Sex	Age	Length of residence (Yrs)	Informant	Mother	Father
1	Pittachope	37/3120	H.F.	m	52	52	Brunton	—	—
2	Tayport	37/4528	A.M.S.	f	55	29	Forgan	Blair Atholl, Perthshire	Kilmany
3	Newport	37/4127	A.B.M.S.	f	65	54	Dundee, Angus	Newport	Tealing, Angus
4	Leuchars	37/4521	J.E.	m	55	48	Lochgelly	Cardenden	Lochgelly
5	Logie	37/4020	–.M.	f	71	35	nr. Dundee, Angus	Strathmore	Crail
6	Balmullo	37/4220	J.G.M.	f	59	18	Leuchars	Forgan	Mains of Strath martine, Angus
7	Newburgh	37/2318	D.A.T.	m	55	7½	Dunfermline	same	same
8	Abdie (Sch.)	37/2516	C.S.C.	f	44	44	Auchtermuchty	Newburgh	Gifford town, nr. Ladybank
9a	Auchtermuchty	37/2311	B.L.D.	f	60	48	Auchtermuchty	Auchtermuchty	Ladybank
9b	Auchtermuchty	37/2311	A.S.	m	80	40	Dunshelt	Auchtermuchty	Portobello, Midlothian
10	Strathmiglo	37/2110	J.P.S.	f	63	60	Strathmiglo	Strathmiglo	Strathmiglo
11	Letham	37/3014	M.I.S.	f	73	70	Letham	Dundee, Angus	nr. St Andrews
12	Cupar	37/3714	J.E.D.	m	50	5½	Blantyre, Lanarkshire	Glasgow, Lanarkshire	Lanarkshire
13	Ladybank	37/3010	J.G.C.	f	48	44	Ladybank	same	same
14	Wester Dron	37/4116	H.G.	m	65	40	Leuchars	Not known	Kingskettle
15	Strathkinnes	37/4516	–.L.	f	88	36	Kinaldy, St Andrews	Cupar	Falkland
16	Kingsbarns	37/5911	W.S.W.	m	63	24	Kirkcaldy	same	same
17	Woodend	37/5312	R.B.	m	60	40	St Andrews	Newport	St Andrews
18	Gateside	37/1809	J.S.H.	m	75	–	Glasgow, Lanarkshire	Gateside	Leith, Midlothian
19	Leslie	37/2401	T.C.S.	m	69	66	Leslie	Cleish, Kinross-shire	Anstruther
20	Markinch	37/2901	W.W.	m	84	44	Leslie	Auchtertool	Kinross-shire
21	Kingskettle	37/3008	J.D.N.	f	63	27	Markinch	London	Arngask, Perthshire
22	Kennoway	37/3502	S.P.C.C.	f	63	63	Kennoway	Stonehaven, Kincardineshire	Lairg, Sutherland-shire
23	Leven	37/3801	J.M.	m	81	68	Kinross	Kinross	Guay, Perthshire
		Assisted by	G.B.	m	76	30	Buckhaven	Abdie	Kirkcaldy
24	Milton of Balgonie	37/3200	D.C.	m	74	70	Methil	—	—
25	New Gilston	37/4208	W.M.	m	65	36	Appleton, New Gilston	same	Woodside, nr. New Gilston
26	Largoward	37/4607	E.N.D.	f	43	40	Largoward	same	same
27	Upper Largo	37/4203	A.B.I.	f	73	24	Muthill, Perthshire	Fife	Perthshire
28	Drumeldrie	37/4403	R.P.	m	34	31	Drumeldrie, Lower Largo	Anstruther	By Leven
29	Elie	37/4900	W.B.T.	m	Completed with assistance of various old residents.				
30	Carnbee	37/3306	J.A.I.	m	64	22	Hawick, Roxburghshire	same	same
31	Arncroach	37/5105	E.G.C.	f	53	52	Arncroach	Gasstown, Dumfries-shire	Peatinn, Fife

FIFE Cont'd

	Place of Residence	Grid	Name	Sex	Age	Length of residence (Yrs)	BIRTHPLACE OF Informant	Mother	Father
32	Cellardyke	37/5703	P.S.	m	80	77	Cellardyke	same	same
33	Pittenweem	37/5402	M.N.H.	f	78	20	Pittenweem	Pittenweem	Crail
34	St Monance	37/5201	D.D.	m	45	5	Crail	Arbroath, Angus	Crail
35	Crail	37/6107	A.M.H.	f	53	31	Crail	same	same
36a	Saline	36/0292	J.H.B.	f	66	50	Saline	Dunfermline	Dunfermline
36b	Saline	36/0292	J.N.	m	51	48	Saline	Saline	Edinburgh, Midlothian
37	Lochore and Ballingry	36/1797	I.M.C.	m	38	2	St Andrews	Brechin, Angus	Boarhills
38	Crosshill	36/1896	Mr – A.	m	91	40	Capledrae	Roscobie	Milnathort
			Mrs – A.	f	78	–	Lochgelly	Capledrae	Lochgelly
39	Kelty	36/1494	I.T.	m	39	36	Kelty	Kelty	Bo'ness, West Lothian
40a	Lochgelly	36/1893	B.G.F.	f	61	58	Lochgelly	Lochgelly	Lassodie
40b	Lochgelly	36/1893	E.C.H.	f	63	60	Lochgelly	Cowdenbeath	Lochgelly
41a	Cowdenbeath	36/1691	G.S.H.	m	43	35	Cowdenbeath	Kirkcaldy	Chirnside, Berwick-shire
41b	Cowdenbeath	36/1691	J.C.M.	m	49	40	Cowdenbeath	Falkirk	Dunning, Perthshire
41c	Cowdenbeath	36/1691	R.N.	m	60	15	Broxburn, West Lothian	Ireland	Ireland
41d	Cowdenbeath	37/1691	J.K.O.	m	48	20	Kirkcaldy	same	same
42	Thornton	36/2897	M.L.C.	f	54	47	Markinch	Leslie	Leslie
43a	Cardenden	36/2195	J.C.	f	57	50	Kirkcaldy	West Wemyss	West Wemyss
43b	Cardenden	36/2195	C.A.M.	m	78	49	Dunfermline	Lochgelly	Midlothian
44a	Kirkcaldy	36/2791	J.B.T.C.	f	61	48	Kirkcaldy	Dysart	Auchtertool
44b	Kirkcaldy	36/2791	A.M.	m	Information supplied by man of 80 years.				
44c	Kirkcaldy	36/2791	M.D.N.	f	52	49	Kirkcaldy	Stirling	Kirkcaldy
44d	Kirkcaldy	36/2791	A.G.N.	f	58	50	Kirkcaldy	same	same
44e	Kirkcaldy	36/2791	D.L.K.T.	m	62	36	Kirkcaldy	Leven	Ceres
44f	Kirkcaldy	36/2791	——	m	Completed with the assistance of various local people.				
45	Methilhill	36/3699	J.F.	m	39	36	Windygates	Birmingham, Warwick-shire	Warwickshire
46	Methil	36/3799	J.S.	m	68	65	Methil	Methil	Methilhill
47	Denbeath (Sch.)	36/3598	J.A.	m	62	1	Kirkcaldy	Dysart	Dysart
48	Buckhaven	36/3698	J.C.G.	m	85	62	Buckhaven	Buckhaven	St Andrews
49	East Wemyss	36/3496	M.G.	f	–	27	Dunshalt	Kirkcaldy	Dusart
50	West Wemyss	36/3294	A.J.G.	m	–	–	——	——	——
51	Kincardine-on-Forth	26/9387	J.T.	m	73	70	Kincardine-on-Forth	Kincardine-on-Forth	Buckhaven
52	Blairhall (Sch.)	26/9987	Words have been supplied by school children.						
53	Culross	26/9885	A.F.	f	56	30	Dunfermline	Cumbernauld, Dunbartonshire	Dunfermline
54	Oakley	36/0289	M.S.R.	f	66	9	Oakley	Coatbridge, Lanark-shire	Carnock, nr. Oakley
55a	Dunfermline	36/0987	M.C.D.	f	51	48	Dunfermline	Dunfermline	Cults
55b	Dunfermline	36/0987	W.R.J.	f	28	25	Dunfermline	Kinross	Dunfermline
55c	Dunfermline	36/0987	A.M.	f	65	56	Thornton	Dunfermline	Dunfermline
55d	Dunfermline	36/0987	J.M.M.	f	67	64	Dunfermline	same	same
55e	Dunfermline	36/0987	A.W.S.	f	68	65	Dunfermline	Dunfermline	Culros
55f	Dunfermline	36/0987	J.S.	m	51	48	Dunfermline	same	same
55g	Dunfermline	36/0987	–.V.	f	65	62	Dunfermline	same	same
56	Torryburn	36/0286	J.W.	m	69	66	Torryburn	same	same
57	Charlestown	36/0683	C.R.	f	69	69	Limekilns	Low Valley Field	Edinburgh, Midlothian
58	Limekilns	36/0783	J.T.	m	Answers provided by a local resident.				
59	Halbeath	36/1288	R.W.	m	43	4½	Portnockie, Banffshire	Cullen, Banffshire	Portnockie, Banffshire
60	Crossgates	36/1488	T.M.B.	m	63	60	Crossgates	same	same
61	Aberdour	36/1985	M.R.M.R.	f	Information obtained from various local residents.				
62	Inverkeithing	36/1383	C.M.	m	45	42	Inverkeithing	Inverkeithing	St Davids
63	North Queensferry	36/1380	E.M.	m	45	30	Malta	Kettlehill	Portsmouth, Hants.
64a	Burntisland	36/2386	A.M.	m	–	10	Information obtained from various local people		
64b	Burntisland	36/2386	J.L.M.	m	57	12	Kirkcaldy	same	same

CLACKMANNAN

	Place of Residence	Grid	Name	Sex	Age	Length of residence (Yrs)	Informant	Mother	Father
1	Menstrie	26/8597	R.M.	m	58	10	Alva	same	same
2	Alva	26/8897	J.N.J.	m	68	25	Alva	Cambusbarn	Alva
3	Sauchie	26/8995	P.H.H.	m	47	5	Ayrshire	Ayrshire	Lanarkshire
4a	Alloa	26/8892	M.R.T.	f	64	64	Alloa	Pleanmill, Stirlingshire	Bannockburn, Stirlingshire
4b	Alloa	26/8892	T.S.	m	62	50	Sauchie	Sauchie	Menstrie
4c	Alloa	26/8892	A.H.G.	f	64	61	Sauchie	same	same
4d	Alloa	26/8892	–.P.	f	60	60	Alloa	Comrie, Perthshire	Alloa
			–.M.	f	92	92	Alloa		Alloa
			–.M.	f	59	30	Alloa	Stirling	Airdrie
5	Dollar	26/9698	M.W.	f	64	60	Tillicoultry	Newmilns, Ayrshire	Strathaven, Lanarkshire
6	Forest Mill	26/2593	C.S.L.	f	59	27	Carron, Stirlingshire	Parish of Kilmuir, Skye, Inverness-shire	Laurieston, Stirlingshire

CLACKMANNAN Cont'd

	Place of Residence	Grid	Name	Sex	Age	Length of residence (Yrs)	BIRTHPLACE OF Informant	Mother	Father
7	Clackmannan	26/9191	L.S.	m	70	66	Clackmannan	same	same

STIRLING

	Place of Residence	Grid	Name	Sex	Age	Length of residence (Yrs)	Informant	Mother	Father
1	Buchanan (Sch.)	26/4490	C.G.E.	f	Completed with the assistance of local residents				
2	Buchlyvie	26/5793	M.C.S.	f	71	–	Buchlyvie	same	same
3	Kippen	26/6594	W.D.	m	72	72	Kippen	St Ninians	Kippen
4	Bridge of Allan	26/7997	J.J.M.	m	78	78	Dunblane, Perthshire	Ceres, Fife	Ruthvenfield, nr. Perth
5	Kildean	26/7895	–	–	–	–	——	——	——
6	Gargunnock	26/7094	D.M.	m	67	55	Gargunnock	Argyllshire	Argyllshire
7a	Stirling	26/7993	A.A.	m	62	14	Kilsyth	same	same
7b	Stirling	26/7993	J.L.F.	m	57	15	Glasgow, Lanarkshire	Antrim, Northern Ireland	Devon
7c	Stirling	26/7993	M.C.H.	f	50	47	Stirling	Paisley, Renfrewshire	Alva, Clackmannan-shire
7d	Stirling	26/7993	J.K.	m	83	70	Alva, Clackmannanshire	Alloa, Clackmannan-shire	Alloa, Clackmannan-shire
7e	Stirling	26/7993	J.M.T.	f	55	55	Stirling	St Ninians	Newhouse
7f	Stirling	26/7993	H.C.W.	f	69	27	Alloa, Clackmannanshire	Alloa, Clackmannan-shire	Paisley, Renfrew-shire
8	Cambusbarron	26/7792	E.J.	f	43	21	Stirling	Minnigaff, Kirkcud-brightshire	Cambusbarron, Stirling
9	St Ninians	26/7991	J.R.	f	64	35½	Cumbernauld, Dunbartonshire	same	same
10	Causewayhead	26/8095	J.S.	m	60	57	Causewayhead	Culross, Fife	Cupar, Fife
11	Kersie Mains	26/8791	A.G.	m	80	77	Kippen	Near Stirling	
12	Bannockburn	16/8090	D.M.	m	63	5	Eskdalemuir, Dumfriess-shire	Croy, Nairnshire	Drumnadrochit, Inverness-shire
13	Drymen	26/4788	M.G.G.	f	67	67	Drymen	same	same
14	Balfron	26/5589	–.S.	f	68	64	Balfron	Coatbridge, Lanarkshire	Longtown, Cumberland
15	Killearn	26/5286	P.M.J.	m	41	33	Glasgow, Lanarkshire	Leith, Midlothian	Loch Lomond side, Dunbartonshire
16	Banknock	26/7980	R.P.	f	52	38	Grangemouth	Tullibody, Clackmannanshire	Banknock
17	Cowie	26/8389	A.W.	m	63	7	Carronshore	Kinnaird	Carronshore
18	Dunmore	26/8989	H.C.G.	f	67	22	Dunmore	Bridge-end	Edinburgh, Midlothian
19	Plean	26/8386	H.T.	m	58	–	Plean	Drongan, Ayrshire	Little Mill, Ayrshire
20	Carronshore	26/8983	C.W.	m	73	73	Bothkennar	Larbert	Bothkennar
21a	Denny	26/8182	M.M.	f	71	5	Dunipace	Dennyloanhead	Dunipace
21b	Denny	26/8182	A.C.	f	67	64	Denny	Denny	Ireland
22a	Larbert	26/8582	T.H.	m	69	67	Larbert	East Linton, East Lothian	Haddington, East Lothian
22b	Larbert	26/8582	P.R.	m	78	75	Stenhousemuir, Larbert	Torwood, Larbert	Stenhousemuir, Larbert
23a	Bonnybridge	26/8280	P.D.	m	55	1	Kilsyth	Airdrie, Lanarkshire	Kilsyth
23b	High Bonnybridge	26/8280	E.F.F.	f	22	19	High Bonnybridge	Coatbridge, Lanark-shire	High Bonnybridge
23c	Bonnybridge	26/8280	I.G.R.	f	61	58	Bonnybridge	Carron	Stirling
24	Camelon	26/8680	J.C.	m	76	49	Falkirk	same	same
25a	Falkirk	26/8880	D.C.	m	71	46	Dunoon, Argyllshire	Achahoish, Argyll-shire	Ardrishaig, Argyll-shire
25b	Falkirk	26/8880	A.H.	m	73	66	Glasgow, Lanarkshire	Falkirk	Falkirk
25c	Falkirk	26/8880	M.C.M.	f	49	16	Bothkennar, Falkirk	Carronshore, Falkirk	Carronshore
25d	Falkirk	26/8880	A.R.W.	m	73	65	Harthill, Lanarkshire	Barrhead, Renfrew-shire	Shieldhall, by Falkirk
26a	Grangemouth	26/9281	A.B.	m	52	43	Falkirk	Glasgow, Lanarkshire	Glasgow
26b	Grangemouth	26/9281	F.C.D.	f	61	50	Grangemouth	Dalry, Ayrshire	West Wemyss, Fife
26c	Grangemouth	26/9281	J.J.H.	m	Completed with the help of various local residents.				
26d	Grangemouth	26/9281	J.M.R.	f	68	54	Kincardine-on-Forth	Kincardine-on-Forth	Perth
26e	Grangemouth	26/9281	R.T.	m	47	33	Girvan	Camelon	Camelon
26f	Grangemouth	26/9281	J.W.	f	66	66	Grangemouth	Grangemouth	Banffshire
27a	Lennoxtown	26/6277	M.C.K.	f	62	59	Lennoxtown	Lesmahagow, Lanarkshire	Lennoxtown
27b	Lennoxtown	26/6277	E.S.	m	68	65	Lennoxtown	Lennoxtown	Eire
28	Queenzieburn	26/6977	R.H.	m	37	32	Kilsyth	Carronshore, Falkirk	Coleraine, Northern Ireland
29	Milton	26/6576	D.C.	m	64	56	Milton	Old Kilpatrick, Dunbartonshire	Kirkintilloch Dunbartonshire
30	Torrance	26/6174	C.O.J.C.	m	62	59	Torrance	Torrance	Norway
31	Balmore	26/6073	J.B.	m	–	–	Balmore	——	Balmore
32	Kilsyth	26/7178	P.S.	m	61	61	Kilsyth	Banton, nr. Kilsyth	same

STIRLING Cont'd

	Place of Residence	Grid	Name	Sex	Age	Length of residence (Yrs)	BIRTHPLACE OF Informant	Mother	Father
33	Castlecary (Sch.)	26/7978	I.H.S.	f	Completed by various local residents.				
34	Greenhill	26/8279	A.F.	m	59	56	Greenhill	Durris, Aberdeenshire	Duns, Berwickshire
35a	Slamannan	26/8573	J.F.	m	59	50	Limerigg	Greengairs, Lanarkshire	Low Limerigg
35b	Slamannan	26/8573	E.G.	f	72	40	Slamannan	Fife	Slamannan
36	Laurieston	26/9079	J.H.M.	m	85	49	Coatbridge, Lanarkshire	Dundonald, Ayrshire	Airdrie, Lanarkshire
37a	Polmont	26/9378	E.R.	f	54	–	Polmont	Fife	Grangemouth
37b	Polmont	26/9378	J.S.	m	57	54	Falkirk	Greenock, Renfrewshire	Hawick, Roxburghshire
38	Redding Muirhead	26/9177	A.J.W.W.	f	23	20	Redding Muirhead	Newhouse, Lanarkshire	Camelon, Falkirk
39a	Brightons	26/9277	W.T.A.	m	37	16	Falkirk	same	same
39b	Brightons	26/9277	I.D.G.R.	f	26	23	Brightons	Polmont	Brightons
40	Maddiston	26/9476	M.K.T.	f	25	22	Edinburgh, Midlothian	Plains, Airdrie, Lanarkshire	Maddiston
41	Blackbraes	26/9075	D.P.J.	m	43	8	Auchinstarry, Dunbartonshire	Penicuik, Midlothian	Auchinstarry, Dunbartonshire
42a	Avonbridge	26/9172	J.A.E.	f	60	48	Bathgate, West Lothian	Bellshill, Lanarkshire	Airdrie, Lanarkshire
42b	Avonbridge	26/9172	J.J.	f	46	43	Avonbridge	Old Monkland, Lanarkshire	Torphichen, West Lothian

DUNBARTON

	Place of Residence	Grid	Name	Sex	Age	Length of residence (Yrs)	Informant	Mother	Father
1	Garelochhead	26/2391	M.H.	f	69	66	Garelochhead	Easthouse, Lanarkshire	Auchterarder, Perthshire
2	Luss	26/3592	J.F.	m	77	74	Luss	Buchanan, Stirlingshire	Muthill, Perthshire
3	Roseneath	26/2583	M.H.C.	m	44	–	Roseneath	Roseneath	Kilmarnock, Ayrshire
4a	Helensburgh	26/2982	J.B.	m	Assisted by others.				
4b	Helensburgh	26/2982	I.S.	f	–	–	——	——	——
5	Balloch	26/3982	A.S.	f	–	–	——	——	——
6	Jamestown	26/3981	E.G.	f	64	60	Balloch	Balloch	Lochgelly, Fife
7a	Alexandria	26/3980	J.A.	m	55	50	London	England	Bonhill
7b	Alexandria	26/3980	A.B.	m	67	64	Alexandria	Renton	Alexandria
7c	Alexandria	26/3980	M.B.J.	f	72	69	Alexandria	Drymen, Stirlingshire	Alexandria
8	Cardross	26/3477	J.S.M.	m	50	4½	Alexandria	Bonhill	Forres, Morayshire
9	Kirktonhill	26/3875	M.N.H.	f	71	68	Glasgow, Lanarkshire	Glasgow, Lanarkshire	Dunbarton
10	Dunbarton	26/3975	R.W.M.	m	63	12	Birkenhead	Brechin, Angus	Ettrick, Selkirkshire
11	Milton	26/4274	M.F.S.	f	–	13	Glasgow, Lanarkshire	Fife	Banff
12	Old Kilpatrick	26/4672	W.I.	m	62	25	Newton, Lanarkshire	Lochgoilhead, Argyllshire	Bishopbriggs, Lanarkshire
13a	Milngavie	26/5574	J.F.	f	65	45	Newton Don, Roxburghshire	Balfron, Stirlingshire	Buchlyvie, Stirlingshire
13b	Milngavie	26/5574	C.H.	m	63	32	Edinburgh, Midlothian	Banff	Wishaw, Lanarkshire
13c	Milngavie	26/5574	W.N.	m	61	30	Sandbank, Argyllshire	Paisley, Renfrewshire	Paisley, Renfrewshire
14a	Bearsden	26/5372	D.F.M.	m	83	36	Old Cumnock, Ayrshire	Old Cumnock, Ayrshire	Huntly, Aberdeenshire
14b	Bearsden	26/5372	J.K.R.	f	71	29	Glasgow, Lanarkshire	Glasgow, Lanarkshire	East Lothian
15	Kessington	26/5571	G.H.	m	Information obtained from the local farm workers.				
16a	Kirkintilloch	26/6574	J.P.	m	With the assistance of various people.				
16b	Kirkintilloch	26/6574	G.M.T.	m	43	40	Kirkintilloch	Kilsyth, Stirlingshire	Twechar
17	Lenzie	26/6571	A.D.C.	m	70	60	Kirkintilloch	Carluke, Lanarkshire	Carstairs, Lanarkshire
18	Croy	26/7275	J.W.	m	45	40	Smithston, Croy	Smithston, Croy	Denny, Stirlingshire

ARGYLL

	Place of Residence	Grid	Name	Sex	Age	Length of residence (Yrs)	Informant	Mother	Father
1	Ardgour	27/0974	D.C.M.	f	65	37	Tobermory, Mull	Kinloch, Mull	Greenock, Renfrewshire
2	Kinlochleven	27/1861	J.S.L.	m	56	11	Kirkcaldy, Fife	Dysart, Fife	Kennoway, Fife
3	Tobermory	17/5055	D.M.M.	m	45	42	Tobermory	Isle of Mull	Isle of Mull
4	Port Appin	17/9045	I.J.M.	f	63	60	Port Appin	Kilbrandon	Easdale
5	Auchnacraig	17/7330	W.R.F.	m	48	38	Auchnacraig	Island of Erraid	Auchnacraig
6	Leob	17/4023	D.C.	m	83	14	Uisken, Mull	Aharacle, Ardnamurchan	Aharacle
7	Cullipool	17/7413	H.M.	m	60	57	Cullipool	Easdale	Black Mill Bay
8	Ardchoonel (Sch.)	17/9711	F.C.	f	33	6	Oban	Sutherlandshire	Oban
9	Toberonochy	17/7408	P.M.	m	85	40	Glasgow, Lanarkshire	Luing	Seil
10	Ford	17/8603	A.C.	m	41	38	Ford	South Uist	Appin
11	Ardfern	17/8004	J.M.	m	64	30	Ardrishaig	Knapdale	Colonsay

ARGYLL Cont'd

	Place of Residence	Grid	Name	Sex	Age	Length of residence (Yrs)	BIRTHPLACE OF Informant	Mother	Father
12	Ballymeanoch	16/8296	J.C.	m	75	10	North Knapdale	Island of Jura	North Knapdale
13	Kilmichael, Glassary	16/8593	E.G.	f	–	–	Kilmichael	same	same
14	Strathlachlan	26/0296	J.M.	m	78	74	Greenock, Renfrewshire	Strathlachlan	Greenock, Renfrewshire
15	Ashfield (Sch.)	16/7685	P.A.M.	f	28	13	Ardrishaig	Barnashalaig, Tayvallich	Castle Sween, Achnamara
16	Lochgilphead	16/8687	J.S.	m	51	15	Ardrishaig	Ardrishaig	Loanhead, Midlothian
17	Clachan of Glendaruel	16/9984	A.M.	m	–	5	Islay	——	——
18	Blairmore	26/1982	T.M.	m	69	69	Strone	Kent, England	Glencoe
19	Kilmun	26/1781	R.S.	m	67	64	Kilmun	Kilwinning, Ayrshire	Dalry, Ayrshire
20	Achahoish	16/7777	H.M.	f	46	5	Dunmore	Isle of Gigha	Creag
21	Tighnabruaich	16/9873	W.M.	m	79	79	Tighnabruaich	Tighnabruaich	Skipness, Kintyre
22	Fearn'ach Farm	26/0176	D.B.	m	58	58	Fearn'ach Farm	Tarbert	Fearn'ach Farm
23	Tarbert	16/8668	G.G.	m	72	72	Tarbert	Skipness	Kilberry
24	Clachan	16/7656	J.H.R.	f	44	5	Edinburgh, Midlothian	Edinburgh, Midlothian	Galashield, Selkirkshire
25	Port Ellen, Isle of Islay	16/3645	M.E.	f	48	43	Greenock, Renfrewshire	Isle of Mull	Isle of Islay
26	Ardminish, Isle of Gigha	16/6448	D.M.	m	63	60	Parish of Gigha and Cara	same	same
27	Ferry House, Isle of Gigha	16/6548	A.M.	m	78	75	Isle of Gigha	Isle of Gigha	Kintyre
28	Rhunahaorine	16/7048	M.L.	f	45	30	Campbeltown	Campbeltown	Mull
29	Kilmichael, Glassary	16/7840	D.M.	m	67	15	Sunadale, Grogport	Craigmore, Carradale Glen	Sunadale, Grogport
30	Glenbarr	16/6636	M.B.	f	65	55	Glenbarr	same	same
31	Ugadale	16/7828	A.S.	m	75	25	Darlochan, Campbeltown	Campbeltown	Darlochan
32	Ballochgair	16/7727	J.S.	m	58	24	Carradale	Carradale	Strathaven, Lanarkshire
33	Darlochan Farm, Campbeltown	16/6823	W.M.S.	m	73	73	Darlochan Farm Campbeltown	Campbeltown	Darlochan Farm, Campbeltown
34	Craigs	16/6923	T.Y.	m	64	47	Drum Kilkenzie	Peninver, Kintyre	Dalry, Ayrshire
35	Machrihanish	16/6320	J.McN.	m	79	76	Machrihanish	Arbroath, Angus	Machrihanish
36	Campbeltown	16/7220	A.M.	m	32	20	Campbeltown	Southend, Kintyre	Campbeltown
37	Woodbank	16/6816	—.M.	f	80	16	Tangy	Gigha	Islay
38	Culinlongart	16/6511	A.R.	m	49	49	Southend	same	same
39	Southend	16/6908	A.M.	m	64	55½	Southend	same	same
40	Aucharua	16/7008	D.B.	m	68	68	Aucharua	Dalrioch, Campbeltown	West Kilbridge, Ayrshire

BUTE

	Place of Residence	Grid	Name	Sex	Age	Length of residence (Yrs)	Informant	Mother	Father
1a	Rothesay	26/0864	D.M.	f	62	–	North Bute	same	same
1b	Rothesay	26/0864	E.M.	f	38	38	Port Bannatyne	Rothesay	Argyll
1c	Rothesay	26/0864	W.M.	m	48	45	Rothesay	Kingarth	Mountstuart
1d	Rothesay	26/0864	E.M.	f	53	50	Rothesay	Rothesay	Clachan, Argyllshire
1e	Rothesay	26/0864	A.M.O.	m	59	23	West Calder	Bishop Auckland, Co. Durham	Airdrie, Lanarkshire
2	Straad	26/0462	A.M.	f	47	44	Straad	Wishaw, Lanarkshire	Bute
3	Kerrycroy	26/1061	E.C.	f	82	79	Kerrycroy	Bute	Cambushbarron, Stirlingshire
4	Gallachan	26/0757	J.M.	m	57	54	Bute	Maybole, Ayrshire	Bute
5	Kingarth	26/0956	M.M.	f	68	25	Scoulag Moor Butts, Kingarth	Islay, Argyllshire	Scoulag Moor Butts, Kingarth
6	Kilchattan Bay	26/0955	J.B.	f	64	64	Kingarth	Bute	Aryshire
7	Lochranza	16/9250	E.I.B.	f	41	35	Machrie, Isle of Arran	Paisley, Renfrewshire	Machrie, Isle of Arran
8a	Corrie	26/0243	R.L.	m	64	64	Corrie, Arran	Shiskine, Arran	Corrie, Arran
8b	Corrie	26/0243	J.M.K.	f	59	40	Lamlash, Arran	Ardross, Ross-shire	Cardross, Dunbartonshire
9	Lamlash	26/0231	J.S.	m	67	67	Brodick, Arran	Northern Ireland	Brodick, Arran

AYR

	Place of Residence	Grid	Name	Sex	Age	Length of residence (Yrs)	Informant	Mother	Father
1a	Largs	26/2059	H.S.M.	m	64	16	Newburgh, Fife	Markinch, Fife	Newburgh, Fife
1b	Largs	26/2059	J.Q.	m	37	–	Glasgow, Lanarkshire	Donegal, Eire	Antrim, Northern Ireland
2a	Beith	26/3454	C.K.B.	f	45	42	Beith	Muirkirk	Beith
2b	Beith	26/3454	R.R.F.	m	57	14	West Calder, Midlothian	same	same

AYR Cont'd

	Place of Residence	Grid	Name	Sex	Age	Length of residence (Yrs)	Informant	BIRTHPLACE OF Mother	Father
3	Gateside	26/3653	A.W.D.	f	72	60	Parish of Dalry	Parish of Dalry	Galston
4	Burnhouse	26/3850	M.G.B.	m	66	66	Kilbirnie	Greenhills, Beith	South Barr, Beith
5	Dalry	26/2949	W.B.S.	m	43	40	Dalry	Inver-Fearn, Ross-shire	Dalry
6	West Kilbride	26/2048	J.H.G.	m	85	82	West Kilbride	same	same
7	Ardrossan	26/2342	J.M.N.	m	63	30	Carnoustie, Angus	Brechin, Angus	Edzell, Angus
8a	Saltcoats	26/2441	W.D.K.	m	75	49	Dumfries	Lochfoot, Kirkcud-bright	Dumfries
8b	Saltcoats	26/2441	M.M.K.	f	57	57	Saltcoats	Beith	Lugton
9	Kilwinning	26/3043	R.H.	m	84	54	Glasgow, Lanarkshire	Dunfermline, Fife	St Ninians, Stirlingshire
10	Cunninghamhead	26/3641	J.M.B.	m	44	1	Saltcoats	Saltcoats	Maybole
11	Dunlop	26/4049	M.C.G.	f	58	–	Dunlop	Dunlop	Hurlford
12a	Stewarton	26/4246	J.A.	m	41	38	Stewarton	Kirkconnel, Dumfr.	Riccarton
12b	Stewarton	26/4246	C.K.R.	m	34	30½	Kilmarnock	Kilmarnock	Dover, Kent
13	Fenwick	26/4643	R.W.	m	78	75	Fenwick	Fenwick	Beith
14	Kilmaurs	26/4141	G.W.	m	78	–	Kilmaurs	Ayr	Ayr
			J.S.	m	63	–	Galston	Hurlford	Galston
15	Moscow	26/4840	J.A.M.	m	44	1½	Bellshill, Lanarkshire	same	same
16a	Irvine	26/3239	J.S.B.	m	73	66	Irvine	Irvine	Paisley, Renfrew-shire
16b	Irvine	26/3239	W.D.J.	m	49	3½	Glasgow, Lanarkshire	Dumfries	Dumfries
17	Crosshouse	26/3938	E.W.B.	f	47	35	Bathgate, West Lothian	Lochgoilhead, Argyllshire	Glasgow, Lanark-shire
18a	Troon	26/3231	J.K.	m	56	49	Monkton, Fife	Muirkirk	Coylton
18b	Troon	26/3231	A.M.	m	45	4	Edinburgh, Midlothian	Perth	Edinburgh, Midlothian
19	Symington	26/3831	D.F.	m	58	30	Kilmarnock	Darvel	Cumnock
20a	Kilmarnock	26/4238	J.H.	f	58	25	Dreghorn	Mauchline	Dreghorn
20b	Kilmarnock	26/4238	E.S.S.	f	63	–	Kilmarnock	Stewarton	Ayr
20c	Kilmarnock	26/4238	J.S.	f	66	43	Craigie Parish	Sorn	Craigie Parish
20d	Kilmarnock	26/4238	S.H.S.	m	50	30	Kilmarnock	Troon	Irvine
20e	Kilmarnock	26/4238	A.C.M.	f	73	73	Kilmarnock	Riccarton	Auchinew, Isle of Arran, Bute
20f	Kilmarnock	26/4238	J.Q.	m	76	70	Kilmarnock	same	same
20g	Kilmarnock	26/4238	J.M.W.	m	48	30	Kilmarnock	Kilmarnock	Kirkmichael
20h	Kilmarnock	26/4238	T.M.Y.	m	65	20	Galston	Galston	Tarbolton
21	Crookedholm	26/4537	W.A.B.	m	68	37	Largs	Largs	Maybole
22	Craigie	26/4232	J.S.	f	56	53	Craigie	Tarbolton	Craigie
23	Sidehead	26/4532	G.D.	m	42	40	Sidehead Crossroads, Hurlford	——	——
24a	Newmilns	26/5337	R.M.P.	m	65	62	Newmilns	same	same
24b	Newmilns	26/5337	R.W.P.	m	42	10	Darvel	Glasgow, Lanark-shire	Kilmarnock
25	Galston	26/5036	C.D.	f	60	57	Galston	Galston	Strahaven, Lanarkshire
26a	Prestwick	26/3525	M.F.F.	m	68	–	——	Glasgow, Lanark-shire	Mauchline
26b	Prestwick	26/3525	H.G.	m	39	36	Prestwick	Stevenston	Kilmarnock
26c	Prestwick	26/3525	S.W.	m	53	50	Ayr	Straiton	Ayr
27	Annbank Station	26/4024	J.G.	m	62	51	Whitletts	Ayr	Gatehead
28a	Ayr	26/3422	W.B.D.	m	73	73	——	——	——
28b	Ayr	26/3422	J.H.B.L.	m	73	73	Ayr	Bo'ness, West Lothian	Glasgow, Lanarkshire
28c	Ayr	26/3422	J.M.	m	77	57	Ayr	Whitletts	Ochiltree
28d	Ayr	26/3422	M.M.	f	69	4	Patna	same	same
28e	Ayr	26/3422	A.K.J.M.	f	65	57½	Glasgow, Lanarkshire	Ayr	Dalrymple
28f	Ayr	26/3422	J.M.	m	69	66	Highfield	West Kilbride	Whitletts
29	Ayr	26/3521	A.H.H.K.	f	Answers supplied by various people.				
30a	Mauchline	26/4927	J.C.	m	70	68	Mauchline	same	same
30b	Mauchline	26/4927	J.& E.H.	f	94 & 93	80	Mauchline	Tarbolton	Mauchline
			M.B.	f	90	20	Sorn	Auchinleck	Sorn
31	Annbank	26/4023	M.R.	f	42	39	Annbank	same	same
32	Stair	26/4323	R.T.W.S.	m	61	22	Mauchline	Perth	Ayr
33	Sorn	26/5526	R.J.	m	61	25	Galston	Galston	Glenbuck
34	Ochiltree	26/5021	A.S.	m	74	67	Auchinleck	Auchinleck	Ochiltree
35a	Auchinleck	26/5521	W.D.K.	m	51	48	Auchinleck	Dailly	Girvan
35b	Auchinleck	26/5521	E.M.	f	65	62	Auchonleck	Lugar	Cumnock
36	Cumnock	26/5720	M.R.D.	f	70	30	Cumnock	Montrose, Angus	Montrose, Angus
37	Muirkirk	26/6927	A.W.T.	m	43	30	Muirkirk	Coylton	Blackwood, Lanarkshire
38	Cronberry	26/6022	J.M.	m	67	–	Auchinleck	——	——
39	Alloway	26/3318	F.P.W.	m	48	5	Ayr	Glasgow, Lanarkshire	Old Cumnock

AYR Cont'd

	Place of Residence	Grid	Name	Sex	Age	Length of residence (Yrs)	Informant	BIRTHPLACE OF Mother	Father
40	Laurieston	26/4014	R.R.	f	59	35	Sorn	Sorn	Douglas Water
41	Maybole	26/3010	E.M.	f	68	59	Girvan	Girvan	Maybole
42	Coylton	26/4219	M.T.	f	44	40	Coylton	Coylton	Greenock, Renfrewshire
43	Rankinston	26/4513	T.P.S.	m	55	47	Holytown, Lanarkshire	Motherwell, Lanarkshire	Mossend, Lanarkshire
44	Garrallan	26/5418	R.W.	m	52	25	Kilmarnock	Ellan, Kincardineshire	Drybridge
45	Dalblair	26/6419	M.G.I.	f	58	50	Sanquhar	Cumnock	Sanquhar, Dunfriesshire
46	New Cumnock	26/6113	J.T.	m	76	73	New Cumnock	same	same
47	Maidens	26/2108	M.L.H.	f	45	42	Maidens	Maidens	Kirkoswald
48	Kilgrammie (Sch.)	26/2502	M.M.	f	59	8	Dalry	same	same
49	Dailly	26/2602	S.S.	m	77	73	Dailly	Killinchy, Northern Ireland	Kilgrammie
50	Rowanston	26/3105	R.A.	m	71	71	Rowanston	Newmilns district	Rowanston
51	Straiton	26/3804	J.E.	m	74	74	Straiton	Dalmellington	Straiton
52	Dalmellington	26/4806	C.T.	f	68	68	Dalmellington	Isle of Arran, Bute	Dalmeny, West Lothian
53a	Girvan	25/1898	G.W.F.	m	69	27	Glasgow, Lanarkshire	Glasgow, Lanarkshire	St Ninians, Stirlingshire
53b	Girvan	25/1898	J.W.H.	f	63	60	Girvan	same	same
54	Barr	25/2794	J.M.	m	76	73	Kirkcudbright	Colmonell	Barr
55	Pinwherry (Sch.)	25/1986	J.F.P.	f	62	13	Newmilns	Ballantrae	Newmilns
56	Barrhill	25/2382	B.B.	f	57	54	Barrhill	Stranraer	Barrhill
57	Corwar (Sch.)	25/2880	W.M.	m	75	6	Ballantrae	Sanquhar, Dumfriesshire	Ballantrae

RENFREW

	Place of Residence	Grid	Name	Sex	Age	Length of residence (Yrs)	Informant	BIRTHPLACE OF Mother	Father
1a	Gourock	26/2477	H.R.C.	f	66	60	Greenock	Port Glasgow	Port Glasgow
1b	Gourock	26/2477	C.L.	f	70	24	Greenock	Loch Sween, Mid-Argyllshire	Isle of Jura, Argyllshire
2a	Greenock	26/2875	J.M.B.	m	59	55	Greenock	Greenock	Donegal, Ireland
2b	Greenock	26/2875	J.W.C.	m	—	—	——	——	——
2c	Greenock	26/2875	N.M.C.	m	67	4	Greenock	Southend, Kintyre, Argyllshire	Bridgend, Islay, Argyllshire
2d	Greenock	26/2875	A.K.	m	77	77	Greenock	Mull, Argyllshire	Greenock
2e	Greenock	26/2875	E.M.	f	88	65	Kilmeny, Islay, Argyllshire	Islay, Argyllshire	Islay, Argyllshire
2f	Greenock	26/2875	A.M.	m	67	65	Greenock	Greenock	Kilmarnock, Ayrshire
2g	Greenock	26/2875	W.M.	m	48	45	Greenock	Liverpool, Lancs.	Greenock
2h	Greenock	26/2875	J.N.M.	m	46	30	Greenock	same	same
2i	Greenock	26/2875	J.B.S.	m	77	77	Greenock	Ballyconly, Co. Antrim	Ahoghill, Co. Antrim
2j	Greenock	26/2875	D.W.S.	m	80	80	Greenock	Glendaruel, Argyllshire	Greenock
3	Inverkip	26/2072	J.A.	m	78	70	Greenock	Isle of Mull, Argyllshire	Balfron, Stirlingshire
4a	Port Glasgow	26/3274	J.H.	m	80	77	Port Glasgow	Greenock	Greenock
4b	Port Glasgow	26/3274	M.J.	f	21	18	Port Glasgow	same	same
4c	Port Glasgow	26/3274	J.K.	m	74	65	Greenock	Beith, Ayrshire	Beith, Ayrshire
4d	Port Glasgow	26/3274	E.D.L.	f	54	51	Port Glasgow	same	same
4e	Port Glasgow	26/3274	I.M.	f	52	49	Port Glasgow	Port Glasgow	Yoker nr Glasgow, Lanarkshire
5	Bogside Farm	26/3672	J.D.	m	51	15	Kilmacolm	Jura, Argyllshire	Greenock
6	Kilmacolm	26/3569		f	64	5	Kilmacolm	Glasgow, Lanarkshire	Kilmacolm
7	Bridge of Weir	26/3766	–.L.	m/f	Information supplied by family.				
8	Bridge of Weir	26/3865	R.M.	m	66	30	Paisley	same	same
9	Fulwood Mains	26/4367	W.N.Y.	m	73	70	North Mains, Houston	Arran, Bute	Wester Fulwood, Houston
10	Linwood	26/4464	J.W.	m	75	75	Linwood		
11a	Paisley	26/4864	A.H.C.	f	52	49	Paisley	London	Paisley
11b	Paisley	26/4864	J.S.C.	f	—	—	——	——	——
11c	Paisley	26/4864	G.D.	m	64	60	Paisley	same	same
11d	Paisley	26/4864	M.G.	f	45	22	Maybole, Ayrshire	Kilmarnock, Ayrshire	Ayr
11e	Paisley	26/4864	J.H.	m	45	42	Paisley	Paisley	Renfrew
11f	Paisley	26/4864	T.H.	m	76	76	Paisley	same	same
11g	Paisley	26/4864	E.M.H.L.	f	38	35	Paisley	Paisley	Renfrew

RENFREW Cont'd

	Place of Residence	Grid	Name	Sex	Age	Length of residence (Yrs)	BIRTHPLACE OF Informant	Mother	Father
11h	Paisley	26/4864	J.M.	m	36	16	Paisley	same	same
11i	Paisley	26/4864	T.D.M.	m	47	39	Cathcart, Lanarkshire	Turnberry, Ayrshire	Irvine, Ayrshire
11j	Paisley	26/4864	J.M.	m	60	57	Hawkhead, Paisley	Clachan, Kintyre, Argyllshire	Paisley
11k	Paisley	26/4864	J.W.M.	m	66	63	Paisley	Paisley	Vale of Leven, Dunbartonshire
11l	Paisley	26/4864	—.S.	f	67	12	Paisley	Aberdeenshire	Fife
12a	Kilbarchan	26/4063	C.B.A.	m	71	12	Paisley	same	same
12b	Kilbarchan	26/4063	A.W.	m	43	4	Clydebank, Dunbartonshire	Sorn, Ayrshire	Cleland, Lanarkshire
13a	Johnstone	26/4263	F.E.B.A.	f	56	53	Johnstone	Johnstone	Kilbirnie, Ayrshire
13b	Johnstone	26/4263	J.D.	m	73	73	Johnstone	Johnstone	Co. Cavan, Eire
13c	Johnstone	26/4263	R.W.F.	m	68	12	Paisley	Paisley	Hamilton, Lanarkshire
13d	Johnstone	26/4263	C.A.S.	m	62	58	Johnstone	same	same
14a	Elderslie	26/4463	F.D.	m	44	1	Paisley	Dublin, Eire	New Cumnock, Ayrshire
14b	Elderslie	26/4463	T.C.M.	m	55	25	Maybole	Edinburgh, Midlothian	Maybole
15	Thornliebank	26/5459	T.P.S.	m	74	71	Thornliebank	Barrhead	Thornliebank
16a	Renfrew	26/5067	J.N.	m	75	41	Greenock	same	same
16b	Renfrew	26/5067	J.S.	m	63	61	Renfrew	Barr, Ayrshire	——
16c	Renfrew	26/5067	J.Y.	f	52	50	Renfrew	Paisley	Renfrew
16d	Renfrew	26/5067	J.B.	f	40	24	Inchinnan	Drem, East Lothian	Renfrew
17	Lochwinnoch	26/3558	J.N.	m	66	10	Cleland	same	same
	Lochwinnoch		J.D.M.	m	75	72	Lochwinnoch	Paisley	Paisley
18a	Neilston	26/4757	A.L.	m	44	40	Neilston	Glasgow, Lanarkshire	Leeds, Yorks.
18b	Paisley	26/4757	A.R.T.R.	m	57	38	Paisley	Paisley	Glasgow, Lanarkshire
19	Uplawmoor	26/4255	E.B.M.	m	—	41	Edinburgh, Midlothian	Hawick, Roxburghshire	Dumfries
20a	Clarkston	26/5757	J.B.H.	m	70	16	Glasgow, Lanarkshire	Kilmarnock, Ayrshire	New Cumnock, Ayrshire
20b	Clarkston	26/5757	C.M.	f	66	63	Busby, Lanarkshire	Clarkston	Ballymoney, Northern Ireland
21	Newton Mearns	26/5355	S.T.	m	—	60	Newton Mearns	Rutherglen, Lanarkshire	Newton Mearns

LANARK

	Place of Residence	Grid	Name	Sex	Age	Length of residence (Yrs)	Informant	Mother	Father
1	Chryston	26/6870	J.M.	m	64	46	Chryston	Glasgow	Catrine, Ayrshire
2	Annathill	26/7370	A.F.	m	67	51	Glasgow	Coatbridge	Glasgow
3	Longriggend	26/8270	J.B.	m	69	69	Longriggend	Co. Antrim, Northern Ireland	Co. Antrim, Northern Ireland
4	Glasgow	26/5965	L.L.H.J.	f	51	48	Glasgow	Singapore	Glasgow
5	Auchinairn	26/6169	J.B.B.	m	64	9	Saltcoats, Ayrshire	Glasgow, Lanarkshire	Irvine, Ayrshire
6	Stepps	26/6568	T.M.	m	73	12	Millerston	Stepps	Baillieston
7a	Rutherglen	26/6161	J.R.B.	f	43	21	Blantyre	Wishaw	Rathen, Aberdeenshire
7b	Rutherglen	26/6161	W.A.M.	m	48	40	Glasgow	Liverpool, Lancs.	Old Meldrum, Aberdeenshire
7c	Rutherglen	26/6161	J.N.	f	57	17	Coatbridge	Glasgow	Denny, Stirlingshire
8a	Burnside	26/6260	A.M.L.	f	50	34	Cambuslang	Paisley	Cambuslang
8b	Burnside	26/6260	T.A.M.	m	71	66	Longridge, Midlothian	Kirkintilloch, Dunbartonshire	Thornhill, Perthshire
9a	Cambuslang	26/6460	J.C.F.	m	71	68	Cambuslang	Glasgow	Cambuslang
9b	Cambuslang	26/6460	G.M.	m	79	46	Dalmellington, Ayrshire	St Quivox, Ayrshire	Old Cumnock, Ayrshire
10a	Uddingston	26/6960	C.M.B.	f	69	69	Blantyre	Troon, Ayrshire	Carluke
10b	Uddingston	26/6960	M.R.D.	f	53	24	Glasgow	Shilford, Renfrewshire	Coatbridge
11	Gartcosh	26/7067	J.M.D.	m	65	46	Ruthwell, Dumfriesshire	Woodside, Aberdeenshire	New Machar, Aberdeenshire
12	Glenmavis	26/7567	J.M.I.	m	62	62	Glenmavis	Glenmavis	Slamannan, Stirlingshire
13	Plains	26/7966	J.R.	m	75	62	Kiltarlity Parish Inverness-shire	Methlick Parish Aberdeenshire	Parish of Birse
14a	Coatbridge	26/7265	I.I.P.	f	46	19	Coatbridge	Coatbridge	Muirkirk, Ayrshire
14b	Coatbridge	26/7265	T.P.	m	59	25	Edinburgh, Midlothian	same	same
14c	Coatbridge	26/7265	E.C.R.	f	72	—	Coatbridge	Coatbridge	Hurlford, Ayrshire
14d	Coatbridge	26/7265	J.S.	f	53	53	Coatbridge	Waterside, Dunbartonshire	Waterside, Dunbartonshire
15a	Airdrie	26/7665	J.M.M.	m	62	59	Airdrie	Oban, Argyllshire	Coatbridge

LANARK Cont'd

	Place of Residence	Grid	Name	Sex	Age	Length of residence (Yrs)	Informant	BIRTHPLACE OF Mother	Father
15b	Airdrie	26/7665	J.P.	m	67	11	Holytown	Holytown	Newhouse
15c	Airdrie	26/7665	R.S.S.	m	69	23	Fauldhouse, West Lothian	same	same
16a	Bargeddie	26/7064	C.M.C.	f	44	41	Bargeddie	Bargeddie	Cleland
16b	Bargeddie	26/7064	R.F.	m	53	27	Balla, Co. Mayo, Eire	Kilsyth, Stirling-shire	Garnkirk, Lanarkshire
17	Calderbank	26/7662	M.S.	f	80	78	Calderbank	——	Lanarkshire
18	Bellshill	26/7360	J.N.	m	84	50	Airdrie	same	same
19	Salsburgh (Sch.)	26/8262	W.L.W.	m	51	–	Harthill	Whitburn, West Lothian	Whitburn, West Lothian
20	Harthill	26/9064	A.L.	m	71	68	Harthill	Harthill	Strathaven
21	Hayhill	26/5953	E.L.	f	37	35	Thornton Hall	East Kilbride	East Kilbride
22	Low Blantyre	26/6958	W.G.	m	65	15	Glasgow	Glasgow	Barrhead, Renfrew-shire
23	Auchentibber	26/6755	C.G.	f	77	77	Auchentibber	East Kilbride	Auchentibber
24	Blantyre	26/6856	J.A.D.	m	58	5	Douglas	Nemphlar	Kirkfieldbank
25a	Bothwell	26/7058	S.A.	m	54	4	Glasgow	same	same
25b	Bothwell	26/7058	G.H.	m	55	6½	Hamilton	Hamilton	Muirkirk, Ayrshire
			Completed with the assistance of various local residents.						
25c	Bothwell	26/7058	M.M.	f	67	50	Glasgow	Taynuilt, Argyllshire	Arrochar, Dunbarton-shire
25d	Bothwell	26/7058	–.M.	f	Words collected by local senior girls.				
26a	Carfin	26/7758	J.A.	m	47	35	Newarthill	Cleland	Holytown
26b	Carfin	26/7758	M.H.	f	53	49	Wilsontown	Carnwath	Fauldhouse, West Lothian
27a	Cleland	26/7958	M.L.A.	f	59	59	Cleland	Annan, Dumfries-shire	Cleland
27b	Cleland	26/7958	J.C.C.	m	69	66	Cleland	Newmains	Cleland
28	Bothwellhaugh	26/7257	G.L.	f	42	40	Bothwellhaugh	Blantyre	Liverpool, Lancs.
29a	Motherwell	26/7557	W.B.	m	82	67	Motherwell	Cleland	Monkland
29b	Motherwell	26/7557	T.G.	m	42	11	Motherwell	Wishaw	Longford, Eire
29c	Motherwell	26/7557	J.H.	m	62	45	Mossend	Glasgow	Dudley, Worcs.
29d	Motherwell	26/7557	J.S.M.	m	83	68	West Lothian	West Lothian	Berwickshire
29e	Motherwell	26/7557	–.O.	f	75	75	Motherwell	Motherwell	nr. New Stevenston
29f	Motherwell	26/7557	A.Q.	f	71	60	Workington, Cumber-land	Darlington, Co. Durham	Harrington, Cumberland
29g	Motherwell	26/7557	——	—	—	—	——	——	——
	Wishaw	26/7955							
30	Burnbank	26/7056	M.M.	f	61	27	Burnbank	Shotts	Shotts
31a	Hamilton	26/7255	A.J.C.	m	66	63	Blantyre	Renfrewshire	Blantyre
31b	Hamilton	26/7255	T.L.	m	52	50	Hamilton	same	same
31c	Hamilton	26/7255	J.M.	m	81	54	Edinburgh, Midlothian	Near Cupar, Fife	Edinburgh, Midlothian
31d	Hamilton	26/7255	J.A.T.	m	69	69	Hamilton	Glassford	Glassford
32a	Wishaw	26/7955	A.M.B.	f	–	10	——	——	——
32b	Wishaw	26/7955	E.C.	f	58	40	Falkirk, Stirlingshire	Ceres, Fife	Cupar, Fife
32c	Wishaw	26/7955	A.H.	m	75	75	Wishaw	same	same
32d	Wishaw	26/7955	A.A.M.	f	56	40	Kirk of Shotts	Harthill	Shotts
32e	Wishaw	26/7955	J.V.	m	33	3½	Cleland	Haywood	Greenhill
32f	Wishaw	26/7955	A.P.W.	m	66	34	Catrine, Ayrshire	New Cumnock, Ayrshire	Irvine, Ayrshire
33a	Larkhall	26/7651	J.E.	m	43	17	Larkhall	same	same
33b	Larkhall	26/7651	J.F.	m	80	80	Larhall	——	Larkhall
33c	Larkhall	26/7651	W.M.	m	73	41	Roughrigg	——	——
33d	Larkhall	26/7651	A.S.	m	69	67	Larkhall	Glenbuck, Ayrshire	Glasgow
34	Dalserf (Sch.)	26/7949	J.C.	m	56	14	Coatbridge	Glasgow	Coatbridge
35a	Shotts	26/8759	W.K.	m	41	37	Paisley, Renfrewshire	Paisley, Renfrewshire	Co. Derry, Northern Ireland
35b	Shotts	26/8759	A.M.K.	f	69	66	Shotts	Cambusnethan	Hamilton Parish
35c	Shotts	26/8759	J.L.	m	44	40	Shotts	Shotts	Peebles
35d	Shotts	26/8759	G.R.B.S.	m	68	54	Shotts	same	same
36	Newmains	26/8255	B.M.	f	72	60	Newmains	Co. Down, Northern Ireland	Co. Down, Northern Ireland
37	Overton	26/8052	——	–	50-86	Information supplied by three local people.			
38a	Carluke	26/8450	J.C.A.	f	55	55	Carluke	same	same
38b	Carluke	26/8450	J.B.	m	81	78	Carluke	Shotts	Ayrshire
38c	Carluke	26/8450	F.R.C.	f	60	60	Carluke	Huntly, Aberdeen-shire	Carluke
38d	Carluke	26/8450	J.G.	m	77	48½	Ecclefechan, Dumfriesshire	Gatehouse-of-Fleet, Kirkcudbrightshire	Kirkpatrick-Fleming, Dumfriesshire
38e	Carluke	26/8450	–	m	–	–	——	——	——
39	Forth	26/9453	W.B.S.	m	61	7	Ayrshire	Glasgow	Glasgow

LANARK Cont'd

	Place of Residence	Grid	Name	Sex	Age	Length of residence (Yrs)	Informant	BIRTHPLACE OF Mother	Father
40	Auchengray	26/9953	A.L.	m	64	61	Auchengray	Elsrickle	Longridge, West Lothian
41	Chapelton	26/6848	R.H.	m	72	69	Chapelton	Strahaven	Chapelton
42	Hookhead	26/6541	–.S.	m	–	60	Auldhouse	Drumclog	Drumclog
43	Glassford	26/7247	J.P.T.	m	59	56	Glassford	same	same
44	Netherburn	26/7947	J.C.H.	m	62	59	Netherburn	Rosebank, Carluke	Rosebank, Carluke
45	Stonehouse	26/7546	S.H.	m	85	83	Stonehouse	same	same
46a	Strathaven	26/7044	J.B.	m	73	42	Fauldhouse, West Lothian	Breich, Midlothian	Fauldhouse, West Lothian
46b	Strathaven	26/7044	J.C.	m	46	46	Strathaven	Glasgow	Auchenheath
46c	Strathaven	26/7044	E.L.H.	f	82	79	Strathaven	Glencoe, Argyllshire	Strathaven
47	Kirkmuirhill	26/7043	J.C.	m	77	60	Kirkmuirhill	same	same
48	Crossford	26/8246	D.S.F.	m	73	70	Crossford	Auchenheath	Carluke
49a	Lanark	26/8843	T.H.	m	–	30	Kirkfieldbank	Kirkfieldbank	Lanark
49b	Lanark	26/8843	T.P.J.	m	53	20	Covington	Carmichael	Glenbuck, Ayrshire
50	Scabgill	26/9449	T.W.	m	69	67	Scabgill Farm, Braehead	Auchengray	Scabgill Farm, Braehead
51	Carstairs Junction	26/9546	W.C.	m	55	46	Lanark	Lamington	Beattock, Dumfriesshire
52a	Carnwath	26/9846	R.B.	f	28	22	Carnwath	Carstairs Junction	Carnwath
52b	Carnwath	26/9846	J.W.	m	–	–	——	——	——
53	Prett's Mill	26/9040	A.C.	m	60	58	Prett's Mill	Lesmahagow	Prett's Mill
54	Dunsyre	36/0748	J.G.	m	65	59	Thankerton	Lanark	Lanark
55	Walston	36/0545	J.W.	m	52	30	Pettinain	Carluke	Carluke
56	Logiebank	36/0946	C.R.D.	f	59	59	Dunsyre	Meikle Earnock	Strathaven
57a	Lesmahagow	26/8139	J.L.T.A.	f	54	54	Lesmahagow	same	same
57b	Lesmahagow	26/8139	H.E.R.	f	49	40	Kirkmuirhill	Strathaven	Auchenheath
57c	Lesmahagow	26/8139	J.L.S.	f	56	2½	——	——	——
58	Auchlochan	36/8037	T.D.	m	44	32	Lesmahagow	Hamilton	Kirkmuirhill
59a	Rigside (Sch.)	26/8734	J.H.	m	60	50	Coalburn	Carluke	Rigside
59b	Douglas Water	26/8736	A.S.	m	26	17½	Douglas Water	Lanark	Lanark
60	Douglas West	26/8231	W.S.	m	68	17	Yarrow, Selkirkshire	Biggar	Yarrow, Selkirkshire
61	Douglas	26/8330	J.S.	m	76	28	Dumfries	——	——
62	Quothquan	26/9939	C.M.	f	46	46	Biggar	Carnwath	Walston
63	Lamington	26/9831	I.M.	f	48	40	Crawfordjohn	Durrisdeer, Dumfriesshire	Lesmahagow
64a	Stonehill Farm	26/8321	M.L.	f	54	22	Crawfordjohn	same	same
64b	Crawfordjohn	26/8723	W.S.M.	m	78	71	Douglas	Douglas	Biggar
65	Abington	26/9428	C.C.	f	62	30	Carmichael	Lesmahagow	Carmichael
66	Crawford	26/9520	J.F.	m	76	70	Crawford	Crawford	Lamington
67a	Leadhills	26/8815	A.M.G.	f	Information supplied by various people.				
67b	Leadhills	26/8815	W.W.	m	80	65	Leadhills	Carsphairn, Kirkcudbrightshire	Carsphairn, Kirkcudbrightshire

WEST LOTHIAN

	Place of Residence	Grid	Name	Sex	Age	Length of residence (Yrs)	Informant	Mother	Father
1a	Bo'ness	26/9981	M.B.	f	50	38	Linlithgow	Thornhill, Perthshire	Selkirk
1b	Bo'ness	26/9981	J.C.B.	m	72	65	Bo'ness	Greengairs, Lanarkshire	Airdrie
1c	Bo'ness	26/9981	R.R.	m	Completed by a local farmer.				
1d	Bo'ness	26/9981	–.R.	f	87	87	Bo'ness	same	same
			–.R.	f	55	55	Bo. ness	Bo'ness	Lanark
2	Carriden	36/0281	W.J.M.	m	67	35	Bo'ness	Coatdyke, Lanarkshire	Co. Antrim, Northern Ireland
3	Linlithgow	26/9977	J.M.	m	74	39	Grangemouth, Stirlingshire	Skinflats, nr. Grangemouth, Stirlingshire	Glasgow, Lanarkshire
4	Westfield (sch.)	26/9371	A.R.	m	47	13	Bo'ness	Edinburgh, Midlothian	Bo'ness
5	Torchichen	26/9672	L.S.M.	m	43	4	Kinbrace, Sutherlandshire	Caithness	Sutherlandshire
6	Bridgend (Sch.)	36/0475	J.A.W.H.	m	Information supplied by various people.				
7	East Philipstoun	36/0577	A.C.F.	f	53	44	Linlithgow	Dunblane, Perthshire	Linlithgow
8	Winchburgh	36/0874	J.F.	m	66	45	West Calder, Midlothian	Walls, Shetland	West Calder, Midlothian
9a	Broxburn	36/0872	M.F.	f	62	49	Bathgate	West Calder, Midlothian	Bathgate
9b	Broxburn	36/0872	A.W.	f	51	5	Linlithgow	Linlithgow	Lanarkshire
10	Kilpunt, Broxburn	36/0971	J.P.	m	75	45	Pumpherston, Midlothian	Broxburn area	Broxburn area
11	Dechmont	36/0370	R.A.G.C.	m	39	35	Dechmont	Ballantrae, Ayrshire	By Insch, Aberdeenshire
12	Uphall Station	36/0670	J.A.	f	44	41	Uphall Station	Edinburgh, Midlothian	Pumpherston, Midlothian

WEST LOTHIAN Cont'd

	Place of Residence	Grid	Name	Sex	Age	Length of residence (Yrs)	BIRTHPLACE OF Informant	Mother	Father
13	South Queensferry	36/1278	W.C.T.	m	29	3	Burntisland, Fife	Hawick, Roxburgh-shire	Wiltshire
14	Wester Dalmeny	36/1477	W.T.	m	75	43	Stobhill, East Lothian	——	——
15	Kirkliston	36/1274	R.S.	m	65	15¾	West Calder, Midlothian	West Calder, Mid-lothian	West Calder, Mid-lothian
16	Blackridge	26/8967	J.P.	m	72	28½	Glasgow, Lanarkshire	same	same
17a	Armadale	26/9368	H.Y.	f	51	48	——	Blackburn	Armadale
17b	Armadale	26/9368	C.R.	f	–	20	——	——	——
18	Whitburn	26/9465	H.C.	m	–	44	Newarthill, Lanarkshire	Baillieston, Lanark-shire	Newarthill, Lanark-shire
19a	Blackburn	26/9865	P.C.	m	73	–	——	——	——
19b	Blackburn	26/9865	D.N.T.	m	–	–	——	——	——
20a	Stoneyburn	26/9862	M.M.	f	55	24	Addiewell, Midlothian	West Calder, Mid-lothian	Stobo, Peeblesshire
20b	Stoneyburn	26/9862	–	–	–	–	——	——	——
21a	Fauldhouse	26/9360	G.C.	f	65	–	Fauldhouse	Whitburn	Whitburn
21b	Fauldhouse	26/9360	D.E.C.	m	48	2½	Kirknewton, Midlothian	Blairgowrie, Perth-shire	Kirriemuir, Angus
22	Livingston Station	36/0268	J.D.	m	42	2½	Blantyre, Lanarkshire	Airdrie	Airdrie

MIDLOTHIAN

	Place of Residence	Grid	Name	Sex	Age	Length of residence (Yrs)	Informant	Mother	Father
1	Newbridge	36/1272	C.M.	f	74	71	Newbridge	Ratho	——
2	Leith	36/2776	J.M.	m	66	62	Leith	same	same
3	Davidson's Mains	36/2075	J.K.A.	m	46	16	Edinburgh	Lesmahagow, Lanarkshire	Edinburgh
4	Blackhall	36/2174	G.N.	m	75	40	Torphichen, West Lothian	Loudoun, Ayrshire	Slamannan, Stirlingshire
5	Edinburgh, 3	36/2574	N.A.M.	m	49	30	Dundee, Angus	same	same
6a	Edinburgh, 11	36/2171	M.M.	f	24	14	Edinburgh	London	Isle of Skye, Inverness-shire
6b	Edinburgh, 11	36/2171	A.S.	m	77	14	Midlothian	Lanarkshire	Lanarkshire
7a	Edinburgh, 9	36/2570	A.D.M.	m	50	5	Edinburgh	Edinburgh	Keith, Banffshire
7b	Edinburgh, 9	36/2570	–.Y.	f	65	30	Crichton Parish	Edinburgh	Edinburgh
8a	Musselburgh	36/3473	J.H.	m	–	–	——	——	——
8b	Musselburgh	36/3473	T.T.	m	70	44	Lasswade	Aberdeenshire	Cockpen
9	Musselburgh	36/3471	E.P.	f	78	72	Musselburgh	——	——
10	Pumpherston	36/0669	W.M.	m	54	22	Oak Bank	Newton Grange	Newton Stewart
11	Mid-Calder	36/0767	J.D.C.	m	60	26	Helmsdale, Sutherland	Dornoch, Sutherland	Kinloch Rannoch, Perthshire
12a	East Calder	36/0867	A.B.	m	73	71	East Calder	East Calder	Ratho
12b	East Calder	36/0867	M.F.W.	f	67	67	East Calder	Mid-Calder	Colinton district
13	Bellsquarry	36/0465	I.W.	f	78	54	Parkhall, West Calder	Whitburn, West Lothian	Whitburn, West Lothian
14a	West Calder	36/0163	H.H.	m	48	45	Addiewell, West Calder	Glasgow, Lanarkshire	Ecclefechan, Dumfriess-shire
14b	West Calder	36/0163	J.W.	m	–	–	West Calder area	same	same
15	Currie	36/1867	J.B.	m	46	46	Currie	Slateford	Currie
16	Balerno	36/1666	J.L.C.	m	47	18	West Calder	Dalkeith	West Calder
17	Roslin	36/2763	G.L.	m	81	79	Balerno	Cousland	Bonnyrigg
18	Milton Bridge	36/2562	R.S.	m	57	54	Milton Bridge	Edinburgh	Roslin
19	Rosewell	36/2862	R.M.	m	57	17	Dornoch, Sutherland	same	same
20	Danderhall	36/3069	W.Y.	m	66	11	Adams Row	Tarves, Aberdeen-shire	Belhaven, Dunbar, East Lothian
21	Dalkeith	36/3367	M.A.Y.	f	64	64	Dalkeith	same	same
22	Muirpark, Eskbank	36/3166	C.M.S.	f	54	30	Lasswade	Glasgow, Lanark-shire	Lasswade
23a	Newton Grange	36/3364	A.G.	m	49	36	Newton Grange	Edinburgh	Forfarshire
23b	Newton Grange	36/3364	G.H.	m	77	45	Kilmarnock, Ayrshire	same	same
24	Ford	36/3864	M.S.	f	–	–	——	——	——
25a	Gorebridge	36/3461	I.C.	f	54	54	Gorebridge	Haddington, East Lothian	Gorebridge
25b	Gorebridge	36/3461	R.Y.D.	m	45	42	Gorebridge	Holytown, Lanark-shire	Carluke, Lanarkshire
25c	Gorebridge	36/3461	A.M.K.J.	m	37	6	Newlandrig	Shettleston, Lanark-shire	Hawick, Roxburgh-shire
25d	Gorebridge	36/3461	J.T.	f	71	68	Gorebridge	Millerhill	Millerhill
26a	Penicuik	36/2359	G.A.	f	78?	78	Penicuik	same	same
26b	Penicuik	36/2359	C.M.	m	69	66	Penicuik	same	same
27	Howgate (Sch.)	36/2458	–.C.	f	50	10	Edinburgh	Leith	Leith
28	Borthwick (Sch.)	36/3659	W.F.H.	m	39	10	Orkney	same	same
29	Tynehead	36/3959	J.S.	m	49	20	Cranshaws, Duns,	Dunbar, East Lothian	Yarrow, Selkirkshire
			A.B.	m	49	40	Pathhead	Pathhead	——

MIDLOTHIAN Cont'd

	Place of Residence	Grid	Name	Sex	Age	Length of residence (Yrs)	BIRTHPLACE OF Informant	Mother	Father
			A.B.	m	49	40	Pathhead	Pathhead	
30	Heriot	36/3952	J.S.	m	72	41	Headshaw, Roxburghshire	Kirkcaldy, Fife Berwickshire	Oxton, Berwickshire
31	Fountainhall	36/4249	J.P.S.	m	59	26	Cousland	Orkney	Blackshields, East Lothian
32	Stow	36/4644	J.L.F.	m	64	60	Stow	same	same

EAST LOTHIAN

	Place of Residence	Grid	Name	Sex	Age	Length of residence (Yrs)	Informant	Mother	Father
1	Gullane	36/4882	W.B.	m	40	2	East Lothian	same	same
2	North Berwick	36/5585	I.W.	f	59	56	North Berwick	Auchinleck, Ayrshire	North Berwick
3	Dirleton	36/5183	W.J.S.	m	64	59	Ratho, Midlothian	West Kilbride, Ayrshire	West Kilbride, Ayrshire
4a	Cockenzie	36/3975	J.H.	m	78	74	North Shields, Northumberland	Cockenzie	Cockenzie
4b	Cockenzie	36/3975	E.M.M.	f	50	44	Kirkcaldy, Fife	Dumfermline, Fife	Armadale, Sutherland
5	Prestonpans	36/3874	J.S.	m	75	50	East Linton	North Berwick	North Berwick
6a	Tranent	36/4072	M.S.H.	f	71	68	Tranent	East Lothian	East Lothian
6b	Tranent	36/4072	P.M.	m	76	74	Tranent	same	same
7	Macmerry	36/4372	P.O.	m	68	65	Macmerry	Penston	Penston
8	Athelstaneford	36/5377	G.T.B.	m	67	64	Needless, Athelstaneford	West Fortune	Leith, Midlothian
9	Haddington	36/5173	F.F.R.	m	43	40	Haddington	Dunbar	Colchester, Essex
10	Bolton (Sch.)	36/5070	J.F.F.	f	Information given by man over seventy — native who has lived all his life in district.				
11	Tynninghame (Sch.)	36/6079	E.C.G.	f	Information given by several local residents.				
12	West Barns	36/6578	J.D.	m	47	14	Kilbirnie, Ayrshire	Kilbirnie, Ayrshire	Dalry, Ayrshire
13	Dunbar	36/6778	C.G.L.D.	f	42	39	Dunbar	Ayton, Berwickshire	Dunbar
14	Spott	36/6775	W.S.	m	54	54	Spott	Spott	——
15	Whittingehame	36/6073	C.B.A.	m	66	4	Bolton, Haddington	Muthill, Perthshire	Yetholm, Kelso, Roxburghshire
16	Innerwick	36/7273	T.D.H.	m	82	79	Innerwick	Spott parish	Norham, Northumberland
17	Oldhamstocks	36/7370	G.D.	m	79	41	Coldstream, Berwickshire		
18	Ormiston	36/4169	A.S.	m	67	11	Haddington	Whitekirk	Haddington
19	Pencaitland	36/4468	W.Y.	m	46	43	Pencaitland	same	same
20	East Saltoun	36/4767	P.F.P.	m	59	12½	Wishaw, Lanarkshire	Lanarkshire	Wishaw, Lanarkshire
21	Humbie	36/4662	A.C.	f	63	12	Ormiston, Midlothian	Norham, Northumberland	Crichton, Midlothian

BERWICK

	Place of Residence	Grid	Name	Sex	Age	Length of residence (Yrs)	Informant	Mother	Father
1	Cockburnspath	36/7771	E.H.	m	42	23	Cockburnspath	Gavinton	Chirnside
2	Cranshaws (Sch.)	36/6961	E.A.	f	47	16	Duns	Galashiels, Selkirkshire	Duns
3	Abbey St Bathans	36/7662	A.I.O.	f	62	4	Strichen, Aberdeenshire	Gartly, Aberdeenshire	Strichen, Aberdeenshire
4	Greenwood	36/8304	M.I.D.W.	f	52	52	Cockburnspath	Berwickshire	Berwickshire
5	Greenhead	36/7561	N.S.	m	67	64	Greenhead	——	——
6	Auchencrow	36/8560	D.W.	m	74	70	Auchencrow	——	——
7	St Abbs	36/9167	A.N.	m	59	40	St Abbs	Co. Durham	St Abbs
8	Eyemouth	36/9464	M.H.G.	f	77	77	Eyemouth	Dunfermline, Fife	Arbroath, Angus
9	Ayton	36/9261	A.W.G.	f	60	56	Ayton	Coldingham	Morebattle, Roxburghshire
10	Burnmouth	36/9561	Q.B.	m	47	1	Bathgate, West Lothian	West Calder, Midlothian	Perth
11	Oxton	36/4953	A.M.C.	f	67	–	Oxton	Midlothian	Oxton
12	Lylestone	36/5251	–.C.	f	70	46	Duns	Duns	Ireland
13	Longformacus	36/6957	J.S.L.	m	61	58½	Longfarmacus	Humbie, East Lothian	Hume
14	Westruther	36/6350	J.R.	m	70	67	Westruther	Westruther	Selkirk
15	Cumledge	36/7856	M.F.M.	f	37	35	Elgin, Morayshire	same	same
16a	Duns	36/7853	A.M.C.	m	78	–	West Blanerne	Chirnside	Fernieside, Ayton
16b	Duns	36/7853	G.M.	m	84	17	Abbey St Bathans	Ladykirk	Cockburnspath
16c	Duns	36/7853	A.M.	m	64	40	Glasgow, Lanarkshire	Glasgow, Lanarkshire	Crieff, Perthshire
17	Crunklaw	36/7850	J.E.	f	61	40	Ladykirk	Milne Graden	Twizel, Northumberland
18	Chirnside	36/8656	P.M.	m	61	15½	Edinburgh, Midlothian	same	same
19	Whitsome	36/8650	R.E.	m	42	6	Coatbridge, Lanarkshire	Stirling	Lanarkshire
20	Foulden	36/9255	J.A.C.	m	60	24	Mordington	Ancroft, Northumberland	Foulden
21	Hutton	36/9053	J.A.	m	60	–	Hutton	Coldstream	Hutton
22	Blythe	36/5849	A.R.M.	m	75	72	Blythe	Flass, Westruther	Gordon
23	Lauder	36/5247	D.W.H.	m	44	32	Lauder	Aberdeen	Lauder

BERWICK Cont'd

	Place of Residence	Grid	Name	Sex	Age	Length of residence (Yrs)	BIRTHPLACE OF Informant	Mother	Father
24	Gordon	36/6443	D.L.R.	m	54	4½	Galashiels, Selkirkshire	Heiton, Roxburgh-shire	Edinburgh, Mid-lothian
25	Fogo	36/7749	J.C.T.H.	m	54	25	Edinburgh, Midlothian	Kirriemuir, Angus	Mid-Calder, Mid-lothian
26	Greenlaw	36/7146	W.M.T.	m	71	–	Greenlaw	Gordon	Hume
27	Leitholm	36/7844	W.M.T.	m	47	1	Motherwell, Lanarkshire	Dalserf, Lanarkshire	Wanlockhead, Dumfriesshire
28	Eccles	36/7641	D.P.	m	77	77	Eccles	West Lothian	Eccles
29	Earlston	36/5738	N.S.B.	f	25	22	Earlston	Gorebridge, Mid-lothian	Earlston
30	Mellerstain	36/6439	T.H.	m	67	31	Ancrum, Roxburghshire	Roxburghshire	Roxburghshire
31	Birgham	36/7939	J.S.	m	63	60	Birgham	same	same
32	Coldstream	36/8439	R.O.	m	57	54	Coldstream	Coldstream	Roxburghshire

PEEBLES

	Place of Residence	Grid	Name	Sex	Age	Length of residence (Yrs)	Informant	Mother	Father
1	West Linton	36/1451	J.H.	m	47	45	Deanfoot, West Linton	Gorebridge, Mid-lothian	Bonnyrigg, Mid-lothian
2	Lamancha (Sch.)	36/2051	M.M.G.	f	59	6	Glasgow, Lanarkshire	Cruden, Aberdeen-shire	Ballantrae, Ayrshire
3	Eddleston	36/2447	M.B.	f	47	20	Walkerburn,	West Linton	Caddonfoot
4a	Peebles	36/2540	E.A.H.	f	89	–	Peebles	Dechmont, West Lothian	Mull of Kintyre Argyllshire
4b	Peebles	36/2540	J.A.J.	m	76	73	Peebles	Carnoustie, Angus	Peebles
4c	Peebles	36/2540	M.P.M.	f	46	43	Peebles	Peebles	Selkirk
5	Skirling	36/0738	M.B.M.	f	42	3	Glasgow, Lanarkshire	same	same
6a	Bellspool	36/1635	W.M.T.	m	77	20	nr. Peebles	Edinburgh, Mid-lothian	nr. Peebles
6b	Stobo	36/1837	G.A.	m	75	59	Stobo	Kirknewton, Mid-lothian	Cockburnspath, Berwickshire
7	Broughton	36/1136	W.R.	m	67	64	Broughton	same	same
8	Innerleithen	36/3337	J.F.	m	68	60	Thankerton, Lanarkshire		Traquair
9	Traquair (Sch.)	36/3334	B.W.	f	–	2	Information supplied by natives about fifty years of age.		
10	Oliver	36/0924	L.T.	f	68	14	Eskdalemuir, Dum-friesshire	Skirling	St Andrews, Fife

SELKIRK

	Place of Residence	Grid	Name	Sex	Age	Length of residence (Yrs)	Informant	Mother	Father
1	Blackhaugh	36/4338	J.E.	m	64	64	Meigle, Clovenfords	Laidlawstiel	Blackhaugh
2a	Galashiels	36/4936	I.M.B.	f	–	83	Selkirk	Edinburgh, Mid-lothian	——
			M.T.B.	f	–	82	——	——	——
			M.M.B.	f	–	77	——	——	——
2b	Galashiels	36/4936	G.F.	f	53	32	Hawick, Roxburghshire	Hawick, Roxburgh shire	Langholm, Selkirk-shire
2c	Galashiels	36/4936	R.M.M.	m	54	51	Galashiels	same	same
2d	Galashiels	36/4936	D.H.M.	m	50	50	Galashiels	Melrose, Roxburgh-shire	Dumfries
2e	Galashiels	36/4936	T.G.M.	m	49	46	Galashiels	same	same
3	Catslackburn	36/3326	W.D.	m	54	54	Catslackburn	Yarrow	Liddlesdale, Roxburghshire
4	Ettrickbridge End	36/3824	J.D.B.	f	49	41	Haltwhistle, North-umberland	Ewes, Dumfriesshire	Yarrow
5	Foulshiels	36/4229	W.C.	m	52	30	Ettrick	——	——
6	Ashkirk	36/4722	J.A.T.	m	66	18	Langholm, Dumfriesshire	——	——
7	Nether Whitlaw	36/5129	J.S.M.	f	68	65	Nether Whitlaw	Colmslie, Roxburgh-shire	Lilliesleaf, Roxburghshire
8	Brockhoperig	36/2312	J.S.	m	56	26	Yarrow	Dumfriesshire	Ettrick

ROXBURGH

	Place of Residence	Grid	Name	Sex	Age	Length of residence (Yrs)	Informant	Mother	Father
1	Blainslie	36/5544	G.S.R.	m	69	66	Blainslie	Midlothian	Blainslie
2	Melrose	36/5433	W.R.	m	57	12	Hawick	Bridge of Cally, Perthshire	Hawick
3a	St Boswells	36/5930	L.D.L.	m	83	50	St Boswells	Blairgowrie, Perthshire	St Boswells
3b	St Boswells	36/5930	J.S.	f	63	60	St Boswells	Roxburghshire	Roxburghshire
4	Smailholm	36/6436	R.C.K.	m	68	14	Lowick, Northumber-land	Wark-on-Tweed, Northumberland	Kelso
5	Rutherford Station	36/6530	J.R.M.	m	57	26	Lochside, Yetholm	Gladsmuir, East Lothian	Jedburgh

	Place of Residence	Grid	Name	Sex	Age	Length of residence (Yrs)	BIRTHPLACE OF Informant	Mother	Father
6	Stitchill	36/7138	W.B.	m	49	–	Stitchill	Berwickshire	Stitchill
7	Ednam	36/7337	–.P.	f	–	10	Kelso	Carlisle, Cumb.	Penrith, Cumb.
8	Kelso	36/7233	M.R.	f	61	50	Edinburgh, Midlothian	Ross-shire	Ross-shire
9a	Heiton	36/7130	A.P.	m	76	44	Ferney Hill, Kelso	Sprouston	Sprouston
9b	Heiton Mill	36/7130	J.S.S.	f	69	69	Heiton Mill, Kelso	Heiton, Kelso	Howden, Ancrum
10	Sandystones	36/5926	M.J.R.	f	59	14	Kirkden, Angus	Airlie, Angus	Forfar, Angus
11	Lilliesleaf	36/5325	J.I.H.	m	78	78	Lilliesleaf	——	Lilliesleaf
12	Minto	36/5620	W.S.	m	53	37	Jedburgh	Jedburgh	Oxnam
13	Ancrum	36/6224	M.K.	f	57	55	Ancrum	same	same
14	Crailing (Sch.)	36/6724	J.J.	f	64	18	Garmouth, Morayshire	Buckie, Morayshire	Aberdeen
15a	Jedburgh	36/6420	J.R.	m	67	67	Jedburgh	same	same
			I.H.H.	m	67	67	Jedburgh	Yetholm	Yetholm
15b	Jedburgh	36/6420	A.R.	m	74	73	Edgerston	Jedburgh	Hobkirk
16	Eckford Moss	36/7025	C.J.	m	64	64	Eckford Moss	Jedburgh	Eckford Moss
17	Morebattle	36/7724	M.O.F.	m	75	75	Morebattle	Cavers	Morebattle
18	Yetholm	36/8228	A.G.	m	56	50	Yetholm	Borders	Yetholm
19	Roberton (Sch.)	36/4214	C.A.R.D.	f	61	26	Dundee, Angus	Dundee, Angus	Perth
20	Denholm	36/5618	J.E.D.B.	f	54	30	Stobs	Appletreehall	Wiltonburn
21a	Hawick	36/5014	R.B.	m	65	55	Hawick	same	same
21b	Hawick	36/5014	B.P.E.	m	54	51	Hawick	Nottingham	Hawick
21c	Hawick	36/5014	I.C.H.	f	75	72	Hawick	Jedburgh	Roberton
21d	Hawick	36/5014	J.L.	m	43	2½	Denny, Stirlingshire	Denny, Stirlingshire	Coatbridge, Lanarkshire
21e	Hawick	36/5014	I.D.T.	f	42	–	Hawick	Carluke, Lanarkshire	Hawick
21f	Hawick	36/5014	J.T.	m	57	38	Edgerston	Jedburgh	Jedburgh
22	Gatehousecote	36/5812	A.M.H.	f	38	23	Gatehousecote	Crowton, Cheshire	Hindhope, Jedburgh
23	Mackside	36/6010	T.G.T.	m	66	44	Edgerston Rigg	Edgerston	Bedrule
24	Swineside Hall	36/7216	J.D.	m	64	62	Swineside Hall, Oxnam	Swineside Hall, Oxnam	Swineside, Townfoo[t]
25	Teviothead	36/4005	M.H.M.	f	65	20	Fraserburgh, Aberdeen-shire	Fraserburgh, Aber-deenshire	St Fergus, Aberdeen-shire
26	Cogsmill (Sch.)	36/5108	–.W.	f	63	3	Hobkirk	Oxnam	Teviotdale
27	Riccarton Junction	35/5393	J.H.	f	88	20	Canonbie, Dumfriesshire	same	same
28	Newcastleton	36/4887	J.B.	m	75	75	Newcastleton	Castleton	——

DUMFRIES

	Place of Residence	Grid	Name	Sex	Age	Length of residence (Yrs)	Informant	Mother	Father
1a	Kirkconnel	26/7312	W.B.	m	–	67	Nethercairn, Kirkconnel	Kirkconnel	Kirkconnel
1b	Kirkconnel	26/7312	T.D.	m	–	90	Kirkconnel	same	same
2	Wanlockhead	26/8712	R.D.	m	74	71	Wanlockhead	same	same
3	Mennock	26/8107	J.R.	m	73	42	Lochrutton, Kirkcud-brightshire	New Abbey Kirkcud-brightshire	New Abbey, Kirkcud-brightshire
4	Mid-Nithsdale	26/8603	T.E.M.L.	m	46	1	Thornhill	Thornhill	Crocketford, Kirkcudbrightshi[re]
5	Durisdeer	26/8903	W.H.	m	55	48	Galston, Ayrshire	same	same
6	Moffat	36/0805	E.A.	f	74	74	Moffat	Moffat	Ettrick, Selkirkshire
7	Beattock	36/0702	W.W.	m	68	68	Palace Knowe	Kirkmichael	Kirkpatrick-Juxta
8a	Moniaive	25/7790	–.C.	f	54	52	Moniaive	Moniaive	Kirkmichael
8b	Moniaive	25/7790	W.H.	m	66	63	Stewarton	same	same
9	Carronbridge	25/8697	A.J.H.	f	54	50	Carronbridge	Carronbridge	Durisdeer
10	Thornhill	25/8795	W.M.M.	m	45	17	Coshogle, Durisdeer	Croydon, Mddx.	Ingleston, Durisdeer
11	Penpont	25/8494	M.M.	f	72	63	Tynron	Glencairn parish	Patna Parish, Ayrshir[e]
12	Closeburn	25/8992	T.S.	m	71	71	Closeburn	Closeburn	Stoup
13	Gatelawbridge	25/9096	F.F.	m	75	69	New Cumnock, Ayrshire	Christchurch, Hants.	Closeburn
14	Wamphray	35/1296	W.E.	m	60	18	Crawford, Lanarkshire	——	——
15	Johnstonebridge	35/1092	M.F.	f	65	40	Hoddam	Kirkpatrick Fleming	Ecclefechan
16	Boreland	35/1690	J.H.	m	79	75	Boreland	Ayrshire	Johnstone
17a	Eskdalemuir	35/2597	–.M.	f	–	60	——	——	——
17b	Eskdalemuir	35/2597	C.M.	f	80	60	Fife	Perthshire	Perthshire
18	Bentpath	35/3190	R.J.	m	71	25	Kirktonhill	Ecclefechan	Billholmshiel, Westerkirk
19	Dunscore	25/8682	T.E.	m	65	63	Dunscore	Dunbar, East Lothian	Irongray
20	Newtonairds	25/8980	R.S.	m	75	52	Midlothian	Aberdeenshire	Peeblesshire
21a	Auldgirth	25/9086	G.B.	f	54	18	Glasgow, Lanarkshire	England	Ireland
21b	Auldgirth	25/9086	W.A.R.	m	47	35	Dunscore	Sorn, Ayrshire	Mauchline, Ayrshire
22	Duncow	25/9683	M.J.S.	f	82	82	Duncow	Duncow	Dumfries
23	Parkgate	35/0288	–.L.	f	–	–	——	——	
24	Amisfield Town	35/0082	J.L.	m	85	82	Tinwald	same	same
25	Lochmaben	35/0882	P.A.C.	m	64	60	Tynninghame, East Lothian	Carron	Stenton, East Lothian
26	Newbigging	35/1489	R.J.	m	58	5½	Lockerbie	Beattock	Lockerbie
27	Dryfesdalegate	35/1182	G.B.	m	63	57	Applegarth	Ruthwell	Canonbie
28	Corriemains	35/1982	A.A.	m	–	–	——	——	——
29	Langholm	35/3684	J.B.W.	f	60	60	Langholm	Canonbie	Langholm

DUMFRIES Cont'd

	Place of Residence	Grid	Name	Sex	Age	Length of residence (Yrs)	Informant	BIRTHPLACE OF Mother	Father
30	Newbridge	25/9479	J.F.	m	54	45	Glasgow, Lanarkshire	——	——
	Holywood		J.C.	m	33	30	Glasgow, Lanarkshire	——	——
31a	Dumfries	25/9776	J.D.	m	66	31	Kirkgunzeon, Kirkcudbrightshire	Dumfries	Kirkgunzeon, Kirkcudbrightshire
31b	Dumfries	25/9776	J.C.J.	m	50	41	Dumfries	same	same
31c	Dumfries	25/9776	W.J.	m	46	46	Dumfries	——	——
31d	Dumfries	25/9776	T.M.	m	50	45	Moffat	Lockerbie	Stranraer, Wigtownshire
31e	Dumfries	25/9776	J.M.	f	64	61	Dumfries	Dumfriesshire	Dumfriesshire
31f	Dumfries	25/9776	St Andrew's Girls' High School.						
32	Torthorwald	35/0378	G.J.M.	f	64	12¼	Lockerbie	Lockerbie	Glasgow, Lanarkshire
33	Hightae	35/0978	M.L.	f	74	70	Hightae	Wigtownshire	Hightae
34	Lockerbie	35/1477	D.D.B.	m	47	17	Ireland	Perth	Pitlochry, Perthshire
35	Ecclefechan	35/1974	J.R.	m	87	77	Lockerbie	Dryfesdale	Lockerbie
36	Brydekirk	35/1870	D.J.T.	m	54	51	Brydekirk	Near Annan	Manchester, Lancs.
37	Middlebie	35/2176	M.I.	f	61	50	Middlebie	Canonbie	Canonbie
38	Eaglesfield	35/2374	A.B.C.	m	56	21	Glasgow, Lanarkshire	Stirlingshire	Islay, Argyllshire
39	Canonbie	35/3976	N.T.	f	50	50	Glasgow, Lanarkshire	Larkhall, Lanarkshire	Canonbie
40	Becktonhall	35/3072	T.I.	m	49	46	Chapelknowe	Cumberland	Cumberland
41	Glencaple	25/9968	I.T.	f	59	59	Dumfries	New Cumnock, Ayrshire	Glasgow, Lanarkshire
42	Glenhowan Farm, Caerlaverock	35/0166	J.E.	m	60	57	Glenhowan Farm, Caerlaverock	Dumfries	Glenhowan Farm, Caerlaverock
43	Blacketlees	35/1868	G.A.	m	–	–	——	——	——
44	Cummertrees	35/1366	A.F.	m	82	–	Dumfries	Dumfries	Cummertrees
45a	Annan	35/1966	–.C.	f	76	40	Middlebie	Ecclefechan	Ecclefechan
45b	Annan	35/1966	J.W.	m	73	71	Annan	Breconbeds, nr Annan	Annan
46	Eastriggs	35/2466	J.S.	m	54	14	Dornock	same	same
47	Rigg of Gretna	35/2966	T.F.	m	64	64	Mount Pleasant	Canonbie	Stonehaven, Kincardineshire
48	Springfield	35/3208	M.H.J.	f	39	36	Springfield	Springfield	Rigg
49	Gretna	35/3167	R.J.L.	m	Information obtained from local residents.				

KIRKCUDBRIGHT

	Place of Residence	Grid	Name	Sex	Age	Length of residence (Yrs)	Informant	BIRTHPLACE OF Mother	Father
1	Carsphairn	25/5693	I.H.B.	f	69	21	Carsphairn	Edinburgh, Midlothian	Carsphairn
2	Dalry	25/6281	W.W.	m	74	46½	Glencairn, Dumfriesshire	Carsphairn	Glencairn, Dumfriesshire
3	Balmaclellan	25/6579	J.M.	f	57	54	Balmaclellan	same	same
4	New Galloway	25/6377	A.B.	m	–	–	Thornhill	same	same
5	Mossdale	25/6570	C.W.	f	79	72	Glasgow, Lanarkshire	Bridge-of-Dee	Kirkpatrick-Durham
6	Diamonds Laggan	25/7171	J.R.	m	55	33	Kells	Tongland	Creetown
7	Kirkpatrick-Durham	25/7870	M.J.M.	f	77	40	Kirkpatrick-Durham	Kirkcudbright	Twynholm
8	Bomerick	25/9076	W.A.W.	m	69	55	Glenkiln	Buittle	Glenkiln
9	Drumsleet (Sch.)	25/9474	J.J.M.	f	65	15	Crocketford	Kirkcudbrightshire	Dumfriesshire
10	Laurieston	25/6865	A.L.	m	Information obtained from various local residents.				
11	Kirkmichael	25/7562	W.S.	m	75	40	Crossmichael	——	——
12a	Castle Douglas	25/7662	J.S.P.	f	61	50	Beith, Ayrshire	same	same
12b	Castle Douglas	25/7662	P.T.	m	71	60	Castle Douglas	Castle Douglas	Ireland
13	Killymingan	25/8567	J.C.	m	–	–	Kirkgunzeon	——	Kirkgunzeon
14	Hardgate (Sch.)	25/8166	T.F.	m	44	5	Inverurie, Aberdeenshire	Aberdeenshire	Aberdeenshire
15a	Dalbeattie	25/8361	M.A.G.	f	64	61	Dalbeattie	Glenluce, Wigtownshire	Corsock
15b	Dalbeattie	25/8361	M.M.L.	f	26	20	Dalbeattie	Kirkpatrick-Durham	Dalbeattie
16	New Abbey	25/9666	W.A.M.	m	59	50	Lincluden, Dumfriesshire	Maxwelltown, Dumfriesshire	Crocketford, Dumfriesshire
17	Creetown	25/4758	A.B.	m	87	84	Anwoth	Anwoth	Gretna, Dumfriesshire
18	Skyreburn (Sch.)	25/5754	M.U.	f	–	3 mths	Chester, Cheshire	same	same
19	Kirkdale (Sch.)	25/5153	J.P.W.	m	46	1	Leadhills, Lanarkshire	Hutton, Dumfriesshire	Leadhills, Lanarkshire
20	Ringford	25/6857	W.M.	m	–	–	——	——	——
21a	Kirkcudbright	25/6851	J.G.	m	61	58	Kirkcudbright	Dundrennan	Kirkcudbright
21b	Kirkcudbright	25/6851	G.C.H.	m	50	47	Kirkcudbright	Kirkcudbright	Castle Douglas
21c	Kirkcudbright	25/6851	N.M.	m	66	30	Inverness-shire	Inverness-shire	Argyllshire
22	Breoch Cottage, Gelston	25/7759	J.G.	m	57	54	Breoch Cottage, Gelston	Kirkpatrick-Durham	Breoch Farm, Gelston
23	Palnackie	25/8156	J.C.	f	–	50	Palnackie	——	——
			M.H.	f	–	40	Creetown	——	——
24	Lochside, Colvend	25/8654	C.S.M.	m	82	23	Southwick	Irvine, Ayrshire	Cumnock, Ayrshire
25	Kirkbean	25/9859	J.C.	m	57	54	Southerness, Kirkbean	Hardgate	Loaningfoot, Kirkbean
26	Southwick	25/9258	R.J.	m	Information obtained from local inhabitants.				

KIRKCUDBRIGHT Cont'd

	Place of Residence	Grid	Name	Sex	Age	Length of residence (Yrs)	BIRTHPLACE OF Informant	Mother	Father
27	Dundrennan	25/7447	–.C.	f	61	58	Dundrennan	Dundrennan	Balmachie

WIGTOWN

	Place of Residence	Grid	Name	Sex	Age	Length of residence (Yrs)	Informant	Mother	Father
1	Creebank	25/3476	A.M.M.	m	48	42	Kingston-upon-Thames Greater London	Newton-Stewart	Newton-Stewart
2	Cairnryan	25/0668	E.M.	f	64	30	Kirkcolm	same	same
3	Beoch, Stranraer	25/0865	J.H.M.	m	50	21	Glenluce	Barrhill, Ayrshire	Stoneykirk
4	Leswalt	25/0163	–.L.	f	–	–	———	———	———
5a	Stranraer	25/0660	A.H.	m	80	50	Kirkcolm	Wigtownshire	Kirkcolm
5b	Stranraer	25/0660	J.M.	m	58	27	Glenluce	same	same
6	Dhuloch (Sch.)	25/0960	J.H.R.	m	54	7	Kirkmuirhill, Lanark-shire	Strathaven, Lanark-shire	Auchenheath, Lanarkshire
7	Challoch	25/3867	M.F.M.C.	f	Completed with help of various local residents.				
8	Newton-Stewart	25/4165	J.M.	f	62	55	Kirkcowan	Inch	Kirkmabreck, Kirkcudbrightsh
9	Dunragit	25/1557	J.D.B.	f	48	45	Newton-Stewart	Wigtown	Newton-Stewart
10	Wigtown	25/4355	T.G.	m	67	–	Newton-Stewart	Newton-Stewart	Creetown
11	Barglass	25/4151	W.C.	m	70	70	Barglass	Kirkinner	Barglass
12	Kirk of Mochrum	25/3446	W.M.	m	58	40	Balmaclellan, Kirkcud-brightshire	New Galloway, Kirk-cudbrightshire	Balmaghie, Kirkcud brightshire
13	Port William	25/3343	A.M.	m	87	40	Auchengallie, Mochrum	Chilcarroch	Milton
14	Monreith	25/3641	J.A.M.	f	51	21	Moffat, Dumfriesshire	Upper Lanarkshire	Upper Lanarkshire
15	Whauphill	25/4049	P.W.W.	m	53	50	Monreith	Govan, Glasgow, Lanarkshire	Govan, Glasgow, Lanarkshire
16	Whitehills	25/4546	J.K.W.	m	47	33	Glasserton	Sorbie	Port William
17	Drummore	25/1336	J.A.	f	–	–	———	———	———
18	Isle of Whithorn	25/4736	T.R.	m	–	–	———	———	———

NORTHUMBERLAND

	Place of Residence	Grid	Name	Sex	Age	Length of residence (Yrs)	Informant	Mother	Father
1a	Berwick-on-Tweed	36/9953	–.B.	f	52	40	Scremerston	Berwick-on-Tweed	Glasgow, Lanarkshi
1b	Berwick-on-Tweed	36/9953	L.F.G.	m	52	38	Gateshead	Flintshire, Wales	Perth
1c	Berwick-on-Tweed	36/9953	W.M.	m	61	50	Berwick-on-Tweed	Nesbit	Howtel
2a	Norham-on-Tweed	36/8947	J.W.G.E.	m	60	32	nr. Cornhill-on-Tweed	Chirnside, Berwickshire	Cornhill-on-Tweed
2b	Norham-on-Tweed	36/8947	M.A.J.	f	60	29	nr. Berwick-on-Tweed	Ancroft	Harelaw, Berwickshi
3	Duddo	36/9342	J.O.K.	f	–	–	———	———	———
4	Cheswick	46/0346	C.D.	f	80	50	Lowick	Horncliff	Lowick
5	Beal	46/0642	–	–	–	–	———	———	———
6	Fenwick, Beal	46/0640	J.D.G.	–	–	–	———	———	———
7	Holy Island	46/1342	G.R.	m	50	3	West Sleekburn	Dinnington	Pegswood, nr. Morp
8	Wark-on-Tweed	36/8238	F.C.	m	39	1	Bedlington	Bedlington	Newcastle-upon-Tyne
9	Mindrum	36/8533	C.B.C.	m	–	–	———	———	———
10	Crookham	36/9138	–.R.	f	61	58	Crookham	Spittal	Berwick-on-Tweed
11	Branxton	36/9037	W.R.	m	64	62	Branxton	Tillmouth	Branxton
12	Ford	36/9437	I.H.M.	f	–	–	———	———	———
13	North Doddington	36/9935	W.W.	m	47	29	Kilham	Blythe, Berwickshire	Venchen, Roxburgh shire
14	Milfield	36/9333	W.H.W.	m	58	23	Rothbury	Ingram	Rothbury
15	Kirknewton	36/9130	A.S.	m	65	48	Goswick	Allerdean, nr. Berwick	Bowmonthill, Mindrum
16	South Hazelrigg	46/0532	R.B.	m	45	9	East Horton, Chatton	Norham	Doddington
17	Bamburgh	46/1835	M.J.R.	f	61	58	Bamburgh	Bare Lees, Ford	North Sunderland
18	Belford	46/1033	J.H.	m	45	6	Beanley	Chatton	Alnwick
19a	Cornhill-on-Tweed	36/8639	W.J.	m	59	24	Donaldson's Lodge	Prior House	Donaldson's Lodge
19b	Cornhill-on-Tweed	36/8639	T.J.	m	70	70	Cornhill-on-Tweed	Newcastle-on-Tyne	Cornhill-on-Tweed
20a	Wooler	36/9928	W.B.	m	76	72	Belford	Glendale	Berwickshire
20b	Wooler	36/9928	W.D.	m	74	72	Wooler	same	same
21	Goldscleugh	36/9123	R.J.	m	46	24	Goldscleugh	Harbottle	Newcastleton, Roxburghshire
22	Chatton	46/0528	Information obtained from various people.						
23	Beadnell	46/2329	E.M.E.	m	–	–	———	———	———
24a	Embleton	46/2322	J.E.B.	m	45	6	Newton-by-the-Sea	Shilbottle	Newton-by-the-Sea
24b	Embleton	46/2322	J.S.B.	m	72	70	Embleton	Swinhoe	Lucker
25	Alnham	36/9910	C.B.	f	–	23	Belsay	Norham	Norham
26	Ingram	46/0116	E.P.	f	48	28	Alnwick	Alnwick	Forres, Inverness-shire
27	Glanton	46/0714	C.D.	f	75	70	Glanton	same	same
28	Eglingham	46/1019	T.B.B.	m	83	81	Eglingham	Embleton	Eglingham

NORTHUMBERLAND Cont'd

	Place of Residence	Grid	Name	Sex	Age	Length of residence (Yrs)	Informant	Birthplace of Mother	Birthplace of Father
29a	Alnwick	46/1813	G.A.	m	84	48	Longhorsley	Morpeth	Felton
29b	Alnwick	46/1813	E.S.	m	78	75	South Charlton	Yorkshire	South Charlton
29c	Alnwick	46/1813	G.H.T.	m	35	33	Alnwick	Embleton	Warenford
29d	Alnwick	46/1813	T.W.	m	37	–	Alnwick	same	same
29e	Alnwick	46/1813	J.Y.	m	34	32	Alnwick	same	same
29f	Alnwick	46/1813	Alnwick Young Farmers' Club						
30	Dunstan	46/2419	J.B.	m	59	26	Choppington	same	same
31	Rennington	46/2118	F.T.M.	m	71	60	London	Suffolk	Rennington
32	Howick	46/2517	E.L.T.	f	Assisted by other inhabitants of Howick.				
33a	Alnmouth	46/2410	C.E.	f	76	76	Alnmouth	Coldingham, Berwickshire	Alnmouth
33b	Boulmer (Sch.)	46/2614	J.E.S.	f	61	22	Alnwick	Alnwick	Denwick
34a	Harbottle	36/9304	M.M.	f	49	6	Cartington	Hepscott	North Heugh
34b	Harbottle	36/9304	D.T.	m	48	12	Southdean, Roxburghshire	——	——
35	Campville	36/9402	E.M.	m	67	–	Warkworth	same	same
36	Flotterton	36/9902	W.M.	m	54	14	Netherton, Thropton	Sharperton, Thropton	Netherton, Thropton
37	Rothbury	46/0501	M.F.M.	f	62	59	Rothbury	Rothbury	Cockermouth, Cumb.
38	Shilbottle	46/1908	W.M.D.	m	64	26	Warkworth	Berwick	——
39	Newton-on-the-Moor	46/1705	A.E.	m	Compiled with help of various local residents.				
40a	Warkworth	46/2406	N.G.	m	44	3	Amble	Alnmouth	Leeds, Yorks.
40b	Warkworth	46/2406	H.I.M.	f	63	4	Amble	same	same
41a	Amble	46/2604	A.R.C.	f	67	67	Amble	Alnwick	Newcastle-on-Tyne
41b	Amble	46/2604	W.B.D.	m	54	54	Amble	——	——
41c	Amble	46/2604	R.L.	m	78	60	Wooler	nr. Wooler	Redden, nr. Kelso Roxburghshire
41d	Amble	46/2604	R.L.	m	65	65	Amble	same	same
42	Kielder	35/6293	R.W.H.	m	27	24	Kielder	same	same
43	Rochester	35/8398	J.A.	m	76	74	Rochester	same	same
44	Otterburn	35/8893	G.W.	m	64	61	Otterburn	Cumberland	Otterburn
45	East Thirston	45/1999	E.M.T.	f	56	53	East Thirston, Felton	West Thirston, Felton	nr. Seahouses
46	Netherwitton	45/1090	E.P.H.	f	54	9	Rothbury	Not known	Rothbury
47	Widdrington	45/2494	D.E.	f	54	54	Pegswood	Morpeth	Netherton
48	Tritlington	45/2092	J.E.A.	m	62	13	Craster	same	same
49	Ellington Village	45/2791	A.T.B.	f	74	47	Blake Law	Stannington	Blake Law
50	Lynemouth	45/2991	R.H.	m	68	22	Widdrington	Doddington	Gateshead-on-Tyne
51	Falstone	35/7287	J.R.C.	m	65	12	Hazelentonrigg	Cairn Glassenhope	Langburnshiels
52	The Eals, Tarset	35/7686	S.D.	m	50		Humshaugh	Hexham	Fenham, nr. Newcastle
53a	Hott Farm, Tarset	35/7785	L.D.	m	24	18	Australia	Capheaton	Hexham
53b	Greystead, Tarset	35/7785	P.R.	f	75	72	Tarset	Kielder	Greenhaugh, Tarset
54	Tarset	35/7885	A.G.T.	m	62	62	Tarset	Southdean Rigg, Roxburghshire	Hownan, Roxburghshire
55	West Woodburn	35/8986	J.M.R.	m	63	60	Dyke Nook	Haydon Bridge	Haydon Bridge
56	Bellingham	35/8383	R.J.B.	m	64	64	Bellingham	same	same
57	Kirkwhelpington	35/9984	J.R.S.	m	49	1	Belsay	Kirkley	Belsay
58	Mitford Hall	45/1685	W.J.R.	m	70	70	Mitford	——	——
59a	Morpeth	45/1985	W.A.D.	m	63	33	Jarrow-on-Tyne, Co. Durham	Hylton-on-Wear, Co. Durham	Darlington, Co. Durham
59b	Morpeth	45/1985	D.E.	m	75	29	Horncliffe	Roxburgh	Horncliffe
59c	Morpeth	45/1985	I.H.	f	55	52	Cambo	Belsay	Warworth
59d	Morpeth	45/1985	J.E.P.	f	60	18	Berwick-on-Tweed	Newcastle-on-Tyne	Newcastle-on-Tyne
59e	Morpeth	45/1985	F.S.	m	61	58	Morpeth	Morpeth	Hepscott
59f	Morpeth	45/1985	–	–	–	–	——	——	——
60	Longhirst	45/2289	E.R.	f	–	8	——	——	——
61	Pegswood	45/2287	M.D.	f	–	–	——	——	——
62a	Ashington	45/2687	J.H.B.	m	80	60	Banna Moor	Edlingham	Banna Moor
62b	Ashington	45/2687	E.C.	f	49	46	Ashington	Netherton	Hartley
62c	Ashington	45/2687	E.H.G.	f	61	59	Ashington	Bellingham	Bellingham
62d	Ashington	45/2687	R.G.	m	74	72	Ashington	Belford	Belford
62e	Ashington	45/2687	R.A.R.	m	51	36	Blaydon-on-Tyne, Co. Durham	Allendale	Allendale
62f	Ashington	45/2687	–.R.	m	–	–	——	——	——
62g	Ashington	45/2687	M.M.W.	f	59	56	Ashington	Northumberland	Scremerston
62h	Ashington	45/2687	R.H.W.	m	47	18	Shankhouse	Sunnyside, Co. Durham	Shankhouse
63	North Seaton (Sch.)	45/2986	T.W.H.	m	55	8	Co. Durham	same	same
64a	Sheepwash	45/2585	A.R.F.	m	63	60	Barrow-in-Furness, Lancs.	Sunderland, Co. Durham	Newcastle-on-Tyne
64b	Guide Post	45/2585	J.C.S.	m	67	65	Choppington	Bothal	Earsdon
65a	Stakeford	45/2685	G.E.C.	m	66	19	Ravensworth, Co. Durham	Gateshead, Co. Durham	Greenside, Co. Durham

NORTHUMBERLAND Cont'd

	Place of Residence	Grid	Name	Sex	Age	Length of residence (Yrs)	BIRTHPLACE OF Informant	Mother	Father
65b	Stakeford	45/2685	P.S.	m	80	70	North Seaton	Northumberland	Leics.
			C.M.	f	75	70	North Seaton	Northumberland	Leics.
66	West Sleekburn	45/2784	C.R.H.	m	54	—	Newbiggin	Blyth	Newbiggin
67	Choppington	45/2583	G.S.	m	57	55	Choppington	Bedlington	Hepscott
68	Netherton	45/2382	E.F.	f	48	10	Whittingham	Lowick	Portobello Midlothian
			Helped by various local residents.						
69a	Bedlington	45/2581	W.D.E.	m	—	50	Bedlington	same	same
69b	Bedlington	45/2581	W.H.G.	m	69	39	Bedlington	Holywell, Flintshire, Wales	Bedlington
69c	Bedlington	45/2581	A.H.O.	f	—	—	——	——	——
69d	Bedlington	45/2581	R.O.	m	54	50	Bedlington	same	same
69e	Bedlington	45/2581	R.S.	m	88	45	Earsdon	Cramlington	Earsdon
69f	Bedlington	45/2581	A.D.S.	m	46	43	Bedlington	Narberth, Wales	Bedlington
69g	Bedlington	45/2581	W.T.	m	67	22	Lowick	Gateshead-on-Tyne, Co. Durham	Shildon, Co. Durham
69h	Bedlington	45/2581	I.P.W.	f	48	45	Bedlington	same	same
70	Cowpen	45/2981	J.D.	m	36	22	Haltwhistle	Brampton, Cumber-land	Newbiggin, Cumberland
71a	Newbiggin-by-Sea	45/3087	C.S.	f	72	40	Bedlington	same	same
71b	Newbiggin-by-Sea	45/3087	G.W.R.	m	44	42	Ashington	Haltwhistle	Ashington
71c	Newbiggin-by-Sea	45/3087	W.S.	m	72	27	South Shields	Glasgow	Knarsdale, Cumberland
71d	Newbiggin-by-Sea	45/3087	W.W.	m	59	42	North Shields	Sheepwash	Tynemouth
71e	Newbiggin-by-Sea	45/3087	School staff.						
72a	Blyth	45/3181	J.C.	m	64	25½	Gateshead	Hexham	Hexham
72b	Blyth	45/3181	T.F.	m	75	75	Blyth	Lanarkshire	Norther Ireland
72c	Blyth	45/3181	F.H.	f	64	64	Blyth	Ashington	Blyth
72d	Blyth	45/3181	A.H.	m	75	73	Blyth	same	same
			L.H.	f	75	73	Blyth	same	same
			M.A.C.	f	49	47	Blyth	same	same
			J.W.C.	m	55	38	Gateshead, Co. Durham	Cumberland	Westmorland
72e	Blyth	45/3181	T.B.P.	m	54	42	Newsham	Fakenham, Norfolk	South Shields, Co. Durham
72f	Blyth	45/3181	–.P.	m	65	40	——	——	——
72g	Blyth	45/3181	G.S.	m	60	47	Seghill	Co. Durham	South Yorkshire
72h	Blyth	45/3181	G.S.	m	67	30	Northumberland	same	same
72i	Blyth	45/3181	A.W.	f	43	32	Blyth	same	same
72j	Blyth	45/3181	R.W.	m	65	62	Blyth	same	same
72k	Blyth	45/3181	H.B.W.	f	47	45	Blyth	Norfolk	Blyth
73	Stooprigg	35/8472	E.N.	f	59	42	Shepherd Shields	Kirkharle	Gofton
74	Hallington Home Farm	35/9977	C.M.	m	83	46	North Heugh	Hallington New	North Heugh
75	Colwell	35/9575	R.C.	m	85	76	Northumberland	Northumberland	Roxburgh
76	Ingoe	45/0374	D.R.	f	With the help of children of Ingoe School.				
77	Stamfordham	45/0772	J.E.D.	m	67	43	Milbourne High House	Ponteland	Elsden Mill
78	Great Whittington	45/0070	E.H.	f	–	16	——	——	——
79	Milbourne	45/1275	G.P.	m	70	20½	Sunderland, Co. Durham	same	same
80	Dalton	45/1072	E.E.P.	f	39	7	Westerhope	Heddon	Dereham, Cumberland
81	Ponteland	45/1672	G.H.	m	76	76	Ponteland	——	——
82	Stannington	45/2179	N.G.	m	52	23	Heddon-on-Wall	Ashington	Morpeth
83	Hartford Colliery	45/2679	W.C.	m	87	42	Shankhouse	Cornwall	Cornwall
84	Shankhouse	45/2778	–.B.	f	–	–	——	——	——
85	Cramlington	45/2677	E.N.S.	m	65	40	Killingworth	Cramlington	Cramlington
86	East Cramlington	45/2876	E.H.	m	34	31	Cramlington	Horton Grange	Cramlington
87	Annitsford	45/2674	E.Q.	m	42	42	Felling-on-Tyne, Co. Durham	same	same
88a	Seghill	45/2874	D.K.M.	f	50	26	Seaton Delaval	Holywell	Seghill
88b	Seghill	45/2874	A.E.S.	m	62	30	Whalton	Seaton Delaval	Morpeth
89	Dinnington	45/2073	A.B.	f	87	87	Dinnington	——	——
90	Dudley	45/2573	L.C.	f	35	6	Dudley	Seaton Burn	Dudley
91	Backworth	45/2972	W.F.	m	43	40	Shiremoor	Shiremoor	Cambois
92	Westmoor	45/2670	M.C.	f	Information collected from local residents.				
93	Newsham	45/3079	F.H.	m	72	69	Newsham	Durham	Gloucester
94a	New Hartley	45/3076	M.J.D.	f	65	30	New Delaval	same	same
94b	New Hartley	45/3076	J.G.F.	m	50	47	NewHartley	New Hartley	Seaton Delaval
95a	Seaton Sluice	45/3376	T.W.G.	m	80	53	Seaton Delaval	Backworth	Long Benton
95b	Seaton Sluice	45/3376	F.N.S.	m	51	48	Seaton Sluice	Seaton Sluice	Birmingham
96	Seaton Delaval	45/3075	M.F.	f	64	64	Blyth	New Hartley	Caldbeck, Cumb.
97	Holywell	45/3174	T.J.B.	m	82	52	Seaton Delaval	——	Berwick-on-Tweed

NORTHUMBERLAND Cont'd

	Place of Residence	Grid	Name	Sex	Age	Length of residence (Yrs)	BIRTHPLACE OF Informant	Mother	Father
98	Earsdon	45/3272	J.A.S.	m	59	59	Earsdon	Shiremoor	Earsdon
99a	Whitley Bay	45/3572	E.G.	m	–	–	———	———	———
99b	Whitley Bay	45/3572	J.G.R.	m	69	20	Annitsford	Burradon	Burradon
99c	Whitley Bay	45/3572	W.H.T.	m	77	74	Tynemouth	North Shields	Howdon-on-Tyne
99d	Whitley Bay	45/3572	M.T.	f	58	43	Newcastle-on-Tyne	Tynemouth	Newcastle-on-Tyne
100	Shiremoor	45/3171	A.W.	f	53	50	Shiremoor	same	same
101a	Cullercoats	45/3671	G.D.	m	77	76	Cullercoats	same	same
101b	Cullercoats	45/3671	M.B.S.	f	44	18	Wallsend	same	same
102	Greenhead	35/6665	C.R.	f	43	43	Greenhead	same	same
103a	Hatlwhistle	35/7164	W.C.F.	m	73	73	Haltwhistle	Durham	Haltwhistle
103b	Haltwhistle	35/7164	M.P.	m	62	40	Haydon Bridge	Fourstones	Allendale
103c	Haltwhistle	35/7164	J.S.T.	m	54	11	Haydon Bridge	Stamfordham	Wall, Hexham
104a	Bardon Mill	35/7764	E.M.D.	f	44	42	Bardon Mill	Acomb	Hexham
104b	Bardon Mill	35/7764	R.S.J.	m	53	50	Bardon Mill	Tow House	Henshaw
105	Newburgh	35/8867	G.R.W.	m	54	10	East Northumberland	Newcastle	East Northumberland
106	Wall	35/9169	J.T.R.	m	54	12	High Warden, Hexham	Wall, Hexham	Linnolds, Hexham
107	Fern Hill	35/9567	G.W.S.	m	60	28	Hexham	Pitlochry, Perthshire	Gt Bavington
108a	Hexham	35/9364	J.C.	m	65	33	Newcastle	———	———
108b	Hexham	35/9364	R.G.	m	60	–	Fourstones	Haltwhistle	Hexham area
108c	Hexham	35/9364	C.W.W.	m	69	66½	Hexham	Halesworth, Suffolk	Thorp Arch, Yorks.
109	Horsley	45/0965	J.T.	m	67	64	Horsley	Wearhead, Co. Durham	Ryal, nr. Barrasford
110	Farnley	45/0062	T.H.	m	67	61	Langley	Acomb	Whitfield
111a	Prudhoe	45/0962	H.A.	m	44	42	Prudhoe	Leadgate, Durham	Sanquhar, Dumfriesshire
111b	Prudhoe	45/0962	H.P.	m	73	58	Upper Weardale, Co.	Allendale	Upper Weardale, Co. Durham
112	Ridingmill	45/0161	G.W.F.C.	m	74	45	Durham	Wylam-on-Tyne	Shiremoor
113	Stockfield	45/0650	M.H.Y	m	65	20	Newcastle-on-Tyne	Glanton	Gateshead, Co. Durham
114	Throckley	45/1567	T.E.D.	m	61	58	Throckley	———	Rothbury
115	Westerhope	45/1967	W.D.R.	m	67	30	Bedlington	Alnwick	North Shields
116	Heddon-on-the-Wall	45/1366	S.E.	f	62	–	Heddon-on-the-Wall	same	same
117	Wallbottle	45/1666	B.A.C.	f	76	73	Newcastle-on-Tyne	Felling-on-Tyne, Co. Durham	Newburn-on-Tyne
118a	Newburn-on-Tyne	45/1665	D.H.	m	61	10	Earsdon	Newcastle-on-Tyne	Blaydon-on-Tyne, Co. Durham
118b	Newburn-on-Tyne	45/1665	G.W.	m	42	40	Newburn-on-Tyne	same	same
119	Ryton	45/1564	J.J.	f	62	4½	Lemington	Chester-le-Street, Co. Durham	Corbridge
120a	Lemington	45/1864	H.C.	m	69	32	Wallbottle	same	Not known
120b	West Denton	45/1864	J.W.J.	m	48	44	Lemington	Felling-on-Tyne, Co. Durham	Newburn-on-Tyne
120c	Lemington	45/1864	G.B.S.	m	65	65	Denton Burn	Haltwhistle	Ireland
121	Fawdon	45/2269	G.W.C.	m	63	50	Hovingham, Yorks.	Farndale, Yorks.	Kirkbymoorside, Yorks.
122a	Forest Hall	45/2769	G.H.	m	57	50	Burradon	Seghill	Burradon
122b	Forest Hall	45/2769	W.G.W.	m	67	63	Corpusty, Norfolk	same	same
123	Coxlodge	45/2268	J.D.	m	69	54	Durham	Edinburgh, Midlothian	Bonnyrigg, Midlothian
124a	Gosforth	45/2368	R.H.	m	81	79	Gosforth	same	same
124b	Gosforth	45/2368	J.S.S.	m	56	–	Durham	Durham	Hutton-Rudby, Yorks.
125	Jesmond	45/2566	T.H.S.	m	48	40	Stakeford	same	same
126a	Wallsend-on-Tyne	45/2966	J.J.	m	47	45	Wallsend	Coatbridge, Lanarkshire	Coatbridge, Lanarkshire
	Words supplied by		J.S.	m	–	76	Tyneside	same	same
126b	Wallsend	45/2966	M.N.T.	f	53	53	Wallsend	Jarrow, Co. Durham	Weardale, Co. Durham
126c	Wallsend	45/2966	J.H.W.	m	72	72	Wallsend	Felling-on-Tyne, Co. Durham	North Sunderland
126d	Wallsend	45/2966	Staff of Girls' School						
126e	Wallsend	45/2966	Grammar School						
126f	Wallsend	45/2966	Staff of Infants' School.						
127a	Newcastle-on-Tyne	45/2464	G.B.B.	m	59	57	Newcastle-on-Tyne	same	same
127b	Newcastle-on-Tyne	45/2464	M.I.	f	Information supplied by various local residents.				
127c	Newcastle-on-Tyne	45/2464	M.L.	f	–	–	———	———	———
127d	Newcastle-on-Tyne	45/2464	W.M.	f	36	25	Heworth, Co. Durham	Ouston, Co. Durham	Heworth, Co. Durham
127e	Newcastle-on-Tyne	45/2464	R.T.M.	m	–	57	Co. Durham	Gateshead, Co. Durham	Co. Durham
127f	Newcastle-on-Tyne	45/2464	J.A.P.	m	66	63	Newcastle-on-Tyne	same	same
127g	Newcastle-on-Tyne	45/2464	I.R.	f	83	80	Newcastle-on-Tyne	Maryport, Cumb.	Newcastle-on-Tyne
127h	Newcastle-on-Tyne	45/2464	Staff of Infants' School.						

NORTHUMBERLAND Cont'd

	Place of Residence	Grid	Name	Sex	Age	Length of residence (Yrs)	BIRTHPLACE OF Informant	Mother	Father
128	Tynemouth	45/3669	J.T.R.	m	74	72	Wallsend-on-Tyne	Birtley, Co. Durham	Wallsend-on-Tyne
129a	North Shields	45/3648	P.G.	m	59	57	North Shields	same	same
129b	North Shields	45/3648	M.R.	f	—	—	———	———	———
129c	North Shields	45/3648	E.M.T.	f	49	8	Killingworth	Jesmond	Seghill
130a	Willington Quay	45/3266	D.M.	m	47	40	Willington Quay	Ireland	Ireland
130b	Willington Quay	45/3266	C.D.	m	51	49	Willington Quay	Suffolk	Yarmouth, Norfolk
130c	Willington Quay	45/3266	H.G.	f	—	—	Willington	Berwick-on-Tweed	Willington
130d	Willington Quay	45/3266	R.O.	f	41	20	Corbridge	———	Alnwick
130e	Willington Quay	45/3266	J.S.	m	73	71	Howdon-on-Tyne	Thursby, Carlisle, Cumb.	South Shields, Co. Durham
130f	Willington Quay	45/3266	Information supplied by the Head Teacher, Willington Quay R.C. School.						
131	South Shields	45/3666	J.E.C.	m	70	67	South Shields	same	same
132	Slaggyford	35/6752	E.W.B.	f	48	32	Penrith	Kirkhaugh	Slaggyford
133	Keenleyside	35/7955	E.H.S.	f	61	61	Keenleyside	Birtley, Co. Durham	Greysouthen, Cumb
134	Catton	35/8257	F.W.N.	m	73	12	Blackhill, Durham	Castleside, Co. Durham	Blackhill, Durham
135	Allendale	35/8355	H.S.	m	68	65	Allendale	same	same
136	Steel	35/9358	F.A.	m	64	54	Ryton	Tyneside	Tyneside
137	Slaley	35/9758	G.H.	m	79	50	———	———	———
138	Steel, Hexham	35/9152	T.N.	m	79	5	Hexham	Allenheads	Allendale
139	Stocksfield	45/0749	P.S.	m	31	28	Newcastle	Newcastle	Hedley-on-the-Hill
140	Healey	45/0158	T.F.	m	80	57½	Slaley	———	———
141	Newlands	45/0955	M.P.	f	63	46	Newcastle-on-Tyne	Stocksfield	Wall
142	Allenheads	35/8665	A.J.	m	59	59	Allenheads	same	same
143	Castleside	45/0748	K.M.	f	67	25	Castleside	Healeyfield	Aydon

CUMBERLAND

	Place of Residence	Grid	Name	Sex	Age	Length of residence (Yrs)	Informant	Mother	Father
1a	Bowness-on-Solway	35/2262	I.M.H.	f	54	42	Penrith	nr. Aspatria	nr. Alston
1b	Bowness-on-Solway	35/2262	M.A.S.	f	63	60	Bowness-on-Solway	Carlisle	Bowness-on-Solway
2	Blackford	35/3962	G.P.	m	69	50	Scaleby	Kirklinton	Kirklinton
3	Kirklinton	35/4367	R.T.D.	m	77	74	Kirklinton	Easton	Newby West
4	Walton	35/5264	M.J.	f	—	20	Lorton	Salter Hall	Ennerdale
5a	Brampton	35/5261	N.D.	f	67	46	Houghton	Knaresdale, Alston	Scaleby
5b	Brampton	35/5261	H.R.	m	60	18	Allensteads	Tercrossit	Shap
6	Gilsland	35/6266	J.B.	m	36	36	Haltwhistle, Northld.	same	same
7	Silloth	35/1153	J.A.	m	73	50	Mawbray	Mawbray	Beckfoot
8	Fingland	35/2557	A.M.	f	52	36	Fingland	Saltcoats, Ayrshire	nr. Fingland
9	Gamelsby	35/2552	–.G.	f	—	—	———	———	———
10	Dockrayrigg	35/2550	O.H.W.	f	66	—	Bothel	Kinniside	Arlecdon
11	Great Orton	35/3254	J.H.	m	60	23	Blind Bothel	St John's-in-the-Vale	Santon Bridge
12	Cumwhinton Station	35/4552	A.G.	m	—	30	———	———	———
13a	Carlisle	35/4056	F.A.	m	62	16	Carlisle	same	same
13b	Carlisle	35/4056	W.F.	m	41	9	Bewcastle	same	same
13c	Carlisle	35/4056	I.M.	f	35	35	Roweltown	Carlisle	Longtown
13d	Carlisle	35/4056	A.T.T.	f	66	2	Stockdalewath	Penrith	Penrith
14	Thursby (Sch.)	35/3250	H.A.	m	59	21	Carlisle	Carlisle	Maryport
15a	Aspatria, Carlisle	35/1441	J.B.	m	49	—	Aspatria	same	same
15b	Aspatria	35/1441	W.C.	m	39	—	Oughterside	Aspatria	Broughton Moor
15c	Aspatria	35/1441	W.S.	m	67	67	Aspatria	Lorton	Parsonby
16	Blennerhasset	35/1741	A.B.	m	—	70	Information supplied by Blennerhasset Discussion Group.		
17	Bolton Low Houses	35/2344	S.G.	f	62	50	Roslyn Castle	Buck Farm	Bewcastle
18	Mealsgate	35/2142	M.J.I.	f	49	1	Aspatria	Carlisle	Aspatria
19	Southwaite	35/4744	J.B.	m	44	5	Maryport	same	same
20	Armathwaite	35/5046	W.T.	m	67	54	Dufton, Westmoreland	———	Brampton
21	Kirkoswald	35/5541	D.H.E.W.	f	55	40	Essex	Kirkoswald	Kirkoswald
22	Hazelrigg	35/6140	J.T.	m	83	80	Gamblesby	same	same
23	Garrigill	35/7441	H.R.	f	—	—	———	———	———
			R.H.	m	—	—	———	———	———
24	Maryport	35/0336	J.I.C.	f	66	66	Maryport	Maryport	Workington
25	Dovenby	35/0933	C.I.B.	f	49	14	Workington	Blackford	Mealsgate
26	Seaton	35/0130	G.S.	m	63	—	Seaton	same	same
27	Brigham	35/0830	B.P.W.	m	—	—	———	———	———
			A.M.	m	—	—	———	———	———
28	Arkleby	35/1439	R.H.	m	68	20	Frizington	Keswick	Keswick
29	Bothel	35/1838	E.G.	m	64	26	Whitrigglees	Bolton, Wigton	Bolton, Wigton
30	Cockermouth	35/1230	E.R.D.	m	72	—	Cockermouth	Kirkoswald	Cockermouth
31	Embleton	35/1630	D.A.G.	m	—	—	———	———	———
32	Longlands	35/2736	J.F.	m	76	41	Sebergham	Ivegill	Matterdale
33	Upton	35/3239	F.A.	f	62	60	Caldbeck	Caldbeck	Uldale
34	Hesket Newmarket	35/3438	A.M.	m	45	18	Wigton	Carlisle	Allonby
35	Mungrisdale	35/3630	B.B.	f	62	32	Hayton	Cumberland	London

CUMBERLAND Cont'd

	Place of Residence	Grid	Name	Sex	Age	Length of residence (Yrs)	BIRTHPLACE OF Informant	Mother	Father
36	Skelton	35/4335	N.G. Assisted by local residents.	f	49	6	Bolton, nr. Wigton	Bolton	Bewcastle
37a	Greystoke	35/4430	W.D.A.	m	66	27	Newcastle-on-Tyne, Northumberland	Chirnside, Berwickshire	Berwick-on-Tweed, Northumberland
37b	Greystoke	35/4430	M.E.M.	f	53	20	Calthwaite	Kirklinton	Cumrew
38	Great Salkeld	35/5536	J.L.P.	m	76	74	Lazonby	Kirkoswald	Lazonby
39	Little Salkeld	35/5636	J.H.T.	m	84	64	Northumberland	Alston	Kirkoswald
40	Penrith	35/5130	J.J.	m	67	40	Whitefield, Manchester, Lancs.	same	same
41	Lowca	25/9821	J.B.J.	m	66	30	Keswick	Cleator Moor	Longtown
42	Workington	35/0028	E.M.S.	f	62	60	Workington	Aspatria	Harrington
43	Little Clifton	35/0528	J.C.F.	m	—	18	Beckermet	Udford	Dalston
44	Pardshaw	35/0924	T.E.W.	m	80	68	Pardshaw	Whitehaven	Allonby
45	Lorton	35/1625	M.C.	m	60	22	Broughton Moor, Maryport	same	same
46	Braithwaite	35/2323	C.B.	m	57	54	Braithwaite	Gilcrux	Braithwaite
47	High Hill	35/2623	T.W.	m	67	65	Keswick	same	same
48	Beckthorns	35/3220	E.S.C.	m	67	65	Keswick	Lincolnshire	Suffolk
49	Culgaith	35/6029	A.F.H.	f	59	34	Culgaith	Milburn, Westmorland	Culgaith
50	Branstey	25/9819	T.B.	m	57	25	Whitehaven	same	same
51	Whitehaven	25/9718	E.J.	f	63	55	Whitehaven	Mylor Bridge, Cornwall	Mylor Bridge Cornwall
52	St Bees	25/9711	—.B.	f	55	52	St Bees	Brigham	Distington
53	Arlecdon	35/0419	J.C.	m	44	20	Frizington	Harrington	Frizington
54	Keekle (Sch.)	35/0115	L.C.	f	—	5	———	———	———
55	Egremont	35/0111	W.G.C.	m	49	46	Egremont	Egremont	Beckermet
56	Borrowdale	35/2514	W.N.	m	73	32	Littlelangdale, Westmorland	Skelwith, Westmorland	Hill o'Millom
57	Calder Bridge	35/0406	J.W.T.	m	45	26	Kinniside	Flimby	Cleator Moor
58	Gosforth	35/0603	W.W.	m	56	20	Maryport	Maryport	Aspatria
59	Black How Farm	35/0401	T.C.	m	79	40	Frizington	Bigriff	Haile
60	Boot	35/1701	M.G.A.	f	64	40	Keswick	Workington	Borrowdale
61	Drigg	34/0698	D.M.	m	62	20	Sellafield	Beckermet	Beckermet
62	Bootle	34/1088	M.H.	f	58	38	Keswick	Lorton	Borrowdale
63a	Millom	34/1780	D.C.	m	—	—	———		———
63b	Millom	34/1780	F.W.	m	50	50	Millom	Ormskirk, Lancs.	Haverigg

DOWN

	Place of Residence	Grid	Name	Sex	Age	Length of residence (Yrs)	Informant	Mother	Father
1	Holywood	J3978	J.H.W.	m	21	16	Belfast, Co. Antrim	Newtown Hamilton, Co. Armagh	Belfast, Co. Antrim
2a	Newtownards	J4874	A.M.T.	f	21	11	Downpatrick	Ardglass	Downpatrick
2b	Ards Peninsula	J4874	S.S.	m	—	7	———	———	———
3	Millisle	J5976	A.B.	f	40	39	Belfast, Co. Antrim	Millisle	Ballyblack
4	Lisnoe	J2661	D.W.	f	38	17	Taghnabrick	Lisburn	Taghnabrick
5	Drumhirk	J4565	D.K.	m	—	—	Drumhirk, Comber	same	same
6	Ardmillan	J5063	S.J.J.	m	—	21	Belfast, Co. Antrim	same	same
7	Ballywalter	J6268	J.B.	m	23	22	Ballywalter	same	same
8	Ballyhalbert	J6464	D.M.	m	72	72	Ballyhalbert	same	same
9	Dromara	J2849	V.S.	f	21	19	Dromara	same	same
10	Saintfield	J4058	J.G.	m	—	—	Ballygowan	Carryduff	Ballygowan
11	Killyleagh	J5353	E.B.	m	51	—	Ballygawley	Terminane	Ballygawley
12	Portaferry	J5953	I.S.	f	29	29	Portaferry	Dublin, Eire	Portaferry
13	Ardkeen	J6056	—.M.	f	52	12	Ballygelagh	Cloughey	Ballygelagh
14	Saul	J5146	W.S.	m	84	60	Downpatrick	Loughinisland	Saul
15	Raholp	J5347	J.F.	m	70	68	Raholp	same	same
16	Bishops Court	J5543	G.S.M.	m	59	59	Bishops Court	same	same
17	Loughbrickland	J1337	E.J.E.K.	f	38	7	Jerrettspass	Drumbanagher, Co. Armagh	Dromantine
18	Leitrim	J3016	A.C.	f	50	15	Leitrim	same	same
19	Annsborough	J3537	H.G.O'N.	m	22	19	Ballylough	———	———
20	Newcastle	J3730	W.G.S.	m	22	20	Newcastle	Downpatrick	Portadown
21	Ardglass	J5537	M.W.	f	—	—	Ardglass	———	———
22	Mayobridge	J1527	T.C.	f	40	21	Mayobridge	same	same
23	Newry	J0926	N.C.	f	55	16	Newry	same	same
24	Annalong	J3719	S.T.P.	m	33	30	Annalong	Annalong	Co. Down
25	Greencastle	J2512	W.M.	m	52	50	Greencastle	Co. Down	Co. Down
26	Kilkeel	J3014	J.G.	m	78	78	Kilkeel	———	———
27	Aughnaloopy	J3116	E.V.B.	f	25	25	Aughnaloopy	same	same

DOWN Cont'd

	Place of Residence	Grid	Name	Sex	Age	Length of residence (Yrs)	Informant	BIRTHPLACE OF Mother	Father
28	Ballymartin	J3416	J.C.	m	22	20	Ballymartin	Glenravel, Co. Antrim	Glenravel, Co. Antrim
29	Moneydorragh	J3518	S.M.	m	75	73	Annalong	same	same
30	Annalong	J3719	J.H.	m	—	—	Annalong	same	same

TYRONE

	Place of Residence	Grid	Name	Sex	Age	Length of residence (Yrs)	Informant	Mother	Father
1	Dunnamanagh	H4402	G.D.	f	19	19	Dunnamanagh	same	same
2	Strabane	H3497	T.B.	m	71	71	East Donegal	———	Strabane
3	Strabane	H3497	M.Y.	f	66	30	Omagh	same	same
4	Stranagalwilly	H5400	—.D.	f	—	—	———	———	———
5	Tullycar	H1282	A.M.M.	f	39	39	Castlederg	Killygordon, Co. Donegal, Eire	Castlederg
6	Castlederg	H2685	M.C.	f	22	20	Castlederg	Glasgow, Lanarkshire	Castlederg
7	Newtownstewart.	H4085	M.T.	f	48	48	Newtownstewart	same	same
8	Drumquin	H3274	N.M.A.T.	f	24	21	Drumquin	same	same
9	Carrickmore	H6472	—.M.	f	86	84	Carrickmore	Cregnadvesky	Carrickmore
10	Rock, Dungannon	H7572	E.M.D.	f	58	35	Donaghmore	same	same
11	Cookstown	H8177	J.B.K.	m	54	30	Downpatrick, Co. Down	Co. Down	Downpatrick, Co. Down
12	Stewartstown	H8772	M.D.	f	22	7	Drumhubbert	Drumhubbert	Stewartstown
13	Coagh	H8978	A.W.	f	22	20	Ballymoyle, Co. Wicklow	same	same
14	Kilskeery	H3054	C.M.	m	67	65	Kilskeery	same	same
15	Aughnacloy	H6652	W.M.B.	f	36	14	Garvagh, Co. Londonderry	Kilrea, Co. Londonderry	Garvagh, Co. Londonderry
16	Fivemiletown	H4447	R.E.C.	f	38	4	Co. Donegal, Eire	same	same

ANTRIM

	Place of Residence	Grid	Name	Sex	Age	Length of residence (Yrs)	Informant	Mother	Father
1	Portballintrae to Ballintoy	C0445	J.M.	f	36	12	Belfast	Belfast	Ballymoney
2	Portballintrae	C9342	J.C.F.	f	44	—	Port Ballintrae	Ballyclough, Co. Cork	Ballyhackett, Co. Londonderry
3	Bushmills	C9440	H.S.	m	23	23	Bushmills	Belfast	Bushmills
4	Dervock	C9731	H.H.	f	—	—	———	———	———
4A	Moss Side	D0135	A.C.	m	—	—	———	———	———
5a	Armoy	D0632	M.M.	f	22	19	Armoy	same	same
5b	Armoy	D0632	A.M.	f	55	34	Ballycastle	same	same
6	Glendun	D2332	—.S.	f	and family.		———	———	———
7	Cushendun	D2432	P.P.D.	m	45	12	Glenravel	Co. Mayo, Eire	Glenravel
8a	Ballymoney	C9426	M.T.H.	f	37	4	South Antrim	———	———
			Collected from elderly residents of Ballymoney						
8b	Ballymoney	C9426	—.H.	f	—	—	Scotland	Scotland	North Antrim
9	Ballymoney	C9426	J.B.	m	51	16	Ballymoney	Ballymoney	Coleraine, Co. Londonderry
10	Loughguile	D0726	T.M.	m	57	30	Belfast	same	same
11	Crushybracken (Sch.) Rasharkin	D9913	M.C.F.	f	37	9	Carclinty	Craigs	Carclinty
12	Clogh Mills	D0617	J.M.	m	64	12	Clogh Mills	Clough	Clogh Mills
13	Crooknahaya	D1615	A.O.	m	22	20	Crooknahaya	Glenravel	Martinstown
14	Portglenone	C9703	A.K.W.	m	51	38	Belfast	Co. Antrim	Co. Down
15	Tullaghgarley	D0800	R.B.N.	m	55	32	Tullaghgarley	Glarryford	Tullaghgarley
16a	Ballymena	D1003	T.P.M.	m	—	—	Ballymena	Co. Down	Ballymena
16b	Broughshane (Sch.)	D1506	A.L.H.	f	60	22	Rasharkin	same	same
16c	Omerbane	D1219	J.W.C.	m	22	20	Ballymena	Clogh Mills	Ballymena
17	Glenwhirry	D2200	J.C.	f	29	24	Ballymena	Glarryford	Ballymoney
18	Broughshane	D1506	G.G.	f	58	50	Ballymena	Galgorm	nr. Randalstown
19	Buckna	D2006	C.B.	m	21	21	Buckna, Broughshane	Co. Tyrone	Buckna, Broughshane
20	Carnalbanagh	D2607	I.W.	f	31	13	Ballygarvey	Glasgow, Lanarkshire	Galashiels, Selkirkshire
21	Aughagash (Sch.)	D2808	M.A.C.	f	—	35	Moneymore, Co. Londonderry	Moneymore, Co. Londonderry	Draperstown, Co. Londonderry
22	Deerpark East	D3109	M.D.	m	40	14	Portglenone	Larne	Portglenone
23	Kilwaughter	D3500	J.C.	m	54	35	Enniskillen, Co. Fermanagh	Larne	Carrickfergus
24	Larne	D4003	H.T.B.	m	—	—	———	———	———
25	Larne	D4003	M.M.G.	f	61	56	Larne	Magheramorne	Braid district
26	Kells	J1497	P.L.E.H.	f	23	18	Kells	Dublin, Eire	Kells

ANTRIM Cont'd

	Place of Residence	Grid	Name	Sex	Age	Length of residence (Yrs)	BIRTHPLACE OF Informant	Mother	Father
27	Ballykeel, Islandmagee	J4796	–.H.	f	59	59	Ballykeel, Islandmagee	Belfast	Islandmagee
28	Islandmagee	J4895	W.A.	f	–	13	Belfast	Portrush, Co. Londonderry	Larne
29	Ballymather, Muckamore	J2281	J.R.F.	f	22	5	Belfast	same	same
30	Carnmoney	J3283	J.E.D.	f	88	–	———	Carnmoney	Carnmoney
31	Woodburn (Sch.) Carrickfergus	J3888	S.F.	m	43	10	Co. Antrim	same	same
32	Nutt's Corner	J1977	W.E.R.	m	17	16	Ballysculty	Kilgreel	Ballyrobin
33	Browndod Doagh	J2391	–.C.	m	–	–	———	———	———
34	Lisburn	J2665	L.N.B.	m	–	–	———	———	———
35	Toome	H9990	T.H.E.	m	36	25	Creagh	Uddingston, nr. Glasgow, Lanarkshire	Creagh

LONDONDERRY

	Place of Residence	Grid	Name	Sex	Age	Length of residence (Yrs)	Informant	Mother	Father
1	Ballyleighery	C6832	W.H.A.B.	m	36	24	Belfast, Co. Antrim	Rasharkin, Co. Antrim	Bellarena
1A	Bellarena	C6630	S.M.	f	–	50	———	———	———
1B	Limavady	C6723	L.D.	m	–	55	———	———	———
2	Ringsend	C8021	M.F.K.	f	25	22	Ringsend	Ringsend	Co. Donegal, Eire
3	Aghadowey	C8721	M.E.	f	39	39	Aghadowey	nr. Maghera	Co. Clare, Eire
3A	Park	C5902	M.C.M.	f	–	23	Park	same	same
4	Feeny	C6205	M.S.N.	f	15	14	Feeny	Claudy	Feeny
5	Dungiven	C6809	A.V.B.	m	49	22	Liverpool, Lancs.	Cumberland	Norfolk
6	Benady Glen	C7207	S.M.	m	22	18	Dungiven	same	same
7	Corick	H7790	B.B.	f	23	20	Corick	same	same

FERMANAGH

	Place of Residence	Grid	Name	Sex	Age	Length of residence (Yrs)	Informant	Mother	Father
1	Kesh	H1465	J.S.	f	74	68	Clonelly	Kesh	Omagh, Co. Tyrone
2	Cooneen	H4547	R.M.	m	49	3	nr. Fivemiletown	Clogher Valley, Co. Tyrone	nr. Enniskillen
3	Garrison	G9452	J.J.G.	m	23	20	Garrison	same	same
4	Irvinestown	H2358	J.J.M.	m	41	14	Kinine, Co. Tyrone	Co. Tyrone	Co. Tyrone
5	Ballinamallard	H2652	W.C.	m	61	23	Ballinamallard	Kilbrea, Co. Londonderry	Newtownstewart, Co. Tyrone
6	Cashel	G9650	M.B.	f	43	20	Kiltyclogher, Co. Leitrim, Eire	same	same
7a	Enniskillen	H2344	T.L.	f	22	19½	Enniskillen	same	same
7b	Enniskillen	H2344	V.G.C.	m	20	18	Enniskillen	Enniskillen	Pettigo
8	Cooneen	H4547	J.M.	m	62	38	Monaghan, Eire	Co. Meath, Eire	Monaghan, Eire
9	Mackan	H2134	K.G.	f	21	19	Enniskillen	Enniskillen	Liverpool, Lancs
10	Wattle Bridge	H4220	S.H.	m	–	70	———	———	———

ARMAGH

	Place of Residence	Grid	Name	Sex	Age	Length of residence (Yrs)	Informant	Mother	Father
1	The Birches	H9360	–.K.	f	–	–	———	———	———
2	Portadown	J0255	D.J.H.	m	69	2	Drumcree, West Meath, Eire	Annaghmore	Drumcree, West Meath, Eire
3	Lurgan	J0758	P.M.	m	23	20	Lurgan	same	same
4	Mount Norris	H9934	E.R.F.	f	44	22	Moy, Co. Tyrone	Clentyclay, Co. Tyrone	Moy, Co. Tyrone
5	Poyntzpass	J0639	M. and S.S.	f	–	–	———	———	———
6a	Jerrettspass	J0636	R.B.W.	m	43	1	Jerrettspass	Ballymena, Co. Antrim	Jerrettspass
6b	Newtownhamilton	H9227	R.B.W.	m	70	35	Dublin, Eire	———	Dublin, Eire

DONEGAL

	Place of Residence	Grid	Name	Sex	Age	Length of residence (Yrs)	Informant	Mother	Father
1	Greencastle	C6642	F.W.	f	19	16	Greencastle	same	same
1A	Carrickart	C1236	–.M.	m	–	50	———	———	———
2	Bunbeg	B7724	J.W.	m	42	7	Donaghadee, Co. Down	Belfast	Clintnagoolan, Co. Down
3	Gweedore	B8222	C.G.	m	57	25	Gweedore	same	same
4	Inch Isle	C3223	E.M.	f	21	18	Londonderry	Inch	Inch
5	Muff	C4826	J.T.	m	48	21	Ture	Muff	Ture

DONEGAL Cont'd

	Place of Residence	Grid	Name	Sex	Age	Length of residence (Yrs)	Informant	BIRTHPLACE OF Mother	Father
5A	Carrigans	C3612	T.B.	m	39	38	Cloon, Carrigans	same	same
6	Newmills	C1209	J.C.O.	m	60	31	Termon	same	same
7	Galdonagh	C2309	J.R.	f	18	16	Galdonagh	Raphoe	St Johnston
7A	Drumoghill	C2610	L.H.	m	–	32	Drumoghill	same	same
8	Ballybofey	H1495	B.M.	f	–	14	Ballyconley	Killybegs	Letterkenny district
9	Stranorlar	H1696	L.M.	f	–	17	——	——	——
10a	Lifford	H3297	L.P.K.	m	70	70	Co. Donegal	same	same
10b	Lifford	H3297	I.S.	f	–	29	Co. Tyrone	Cootehill, Co. Cavan, Eire	Portadown, Co. Armagh
11	Ballindrait	H3000	A.L.	m	82	80	Ballindrait	nr. Raphoe	Scotland
12	Carrick	H1387	J.C.	m	68	68	Carrick	same	same

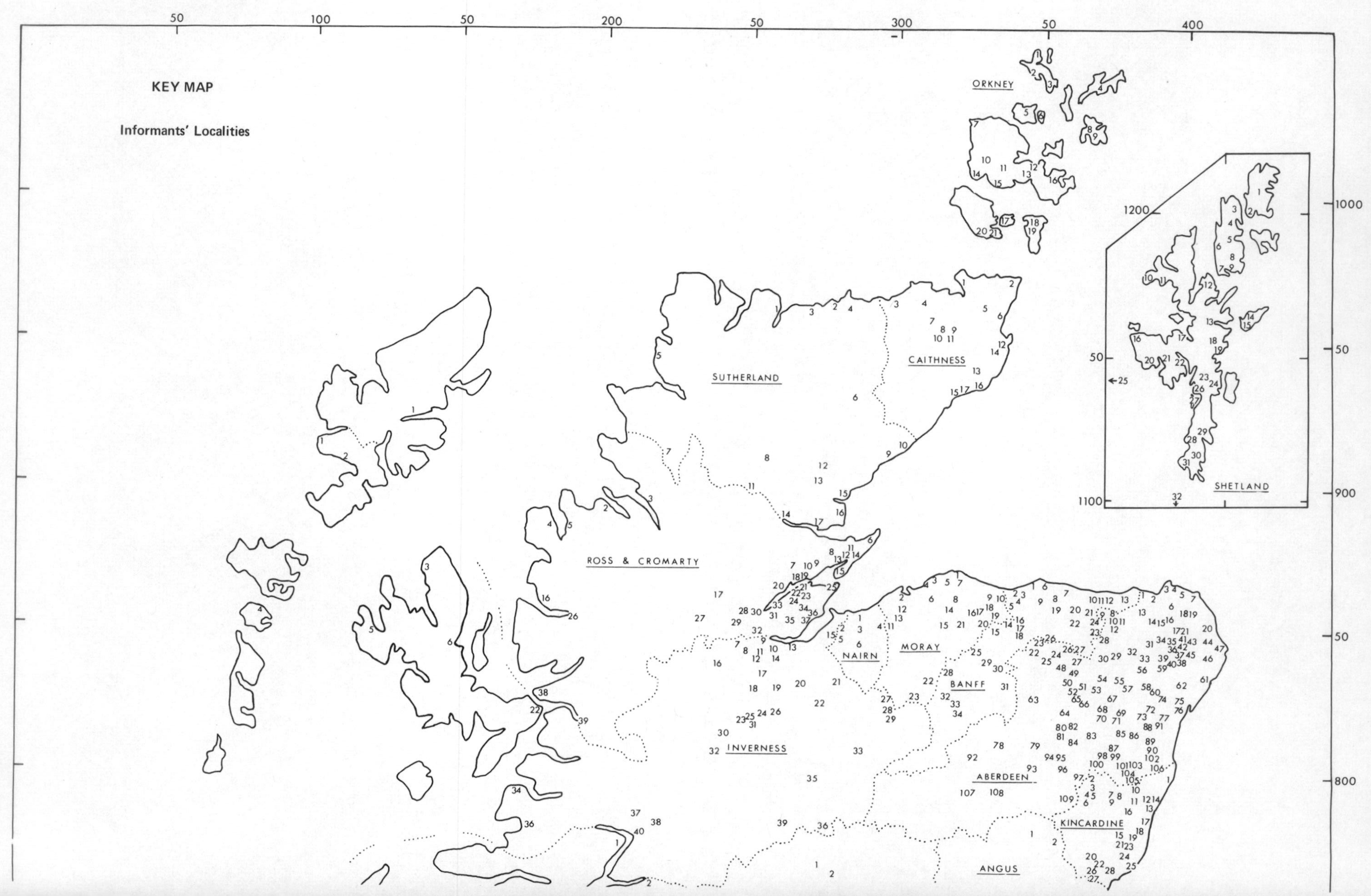
KEY MAP
Informants' Localities
ORKNEY
SHETLAND
CAITHNESS
SUTHERLAND
ROSS & CROMARTY
NAIRN
MORAY
BANFF
INVERNESS
ABERDEEN
KINCARDINE
ANGUS

ARGYLL
PERTH
FIFE
CLACK.
KINROSS
STIRLING
DUNBARTON
RENFREW
BUTE
MIDLOTHIAN
E. LOTHIAN
BERWICK
LANARK
PEEBLES
AYR
SELKIRK
ROXBURGH
NORTHUMBERLAND
KIRKCUDBRIGHT
DUMFRIES
WIGTON
CUMBERLAND
DONEGAL
LONDONDERRY
ANTRIM
TYRONE
FERMANAGH
ARMAGH
DOWN

APPENDIX D . OTHER MAPS

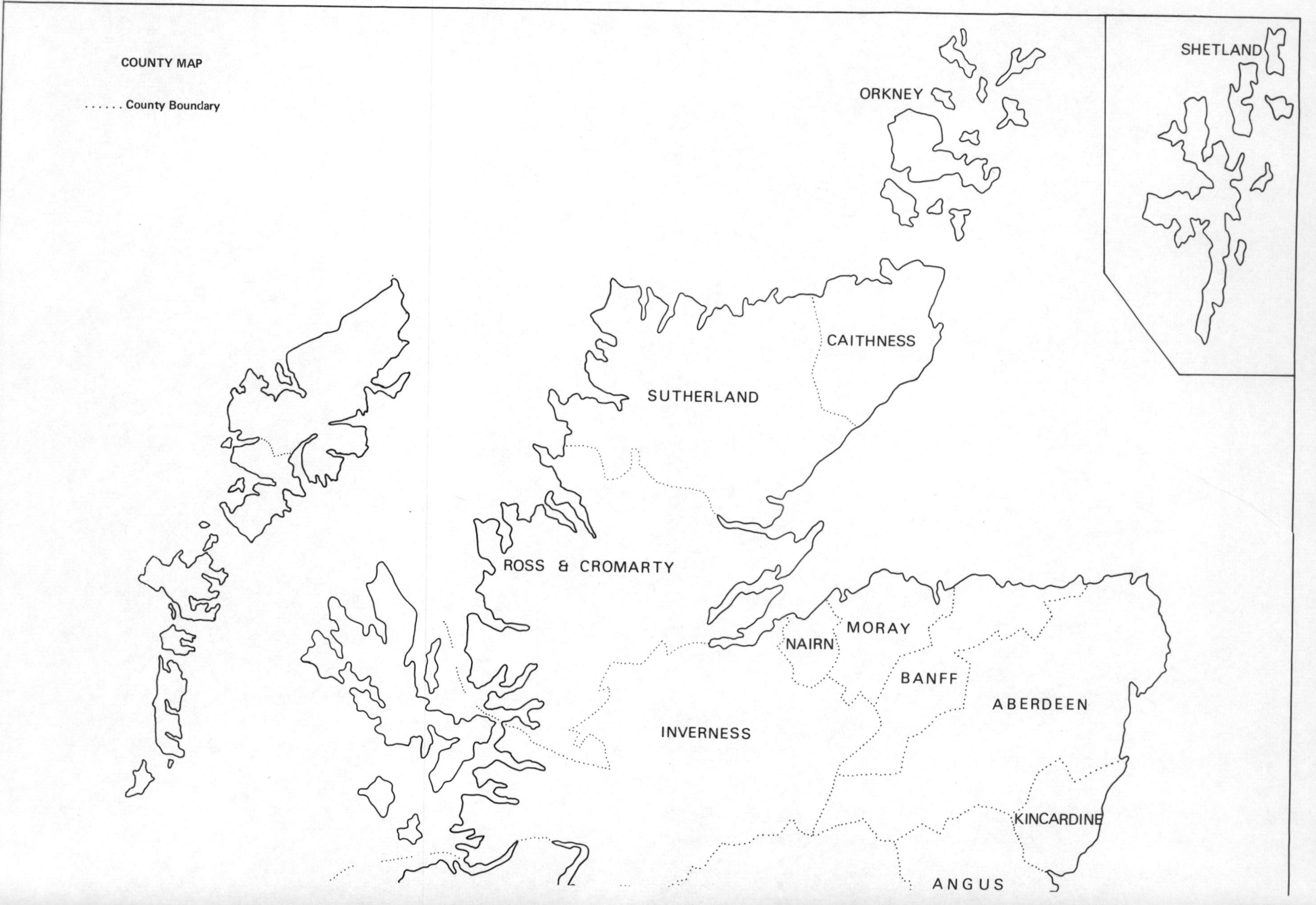

COUNTY MAP
. . . . . . County Boundary
ORKNEY
SHETLAND
CAITHNESS
SUTHERLAND
ROSS & CROMARTY
NAIRN
MORAY
BANFF
ABERDEEN
INVERNESS
KINCARDINE
ANGUS

PERTH
ARGYLL
FIFE
CLACK.
KINROSS
DUNBARTON
STIRLING
DUNBARTON
W.LOTHIAN
E. LOTHIAN
MIDLOTHIAN
RENFREW
BERWICK
BUTE
LANARK
PEEBLES
SELKIRK
AYR
ROXBURGH
NORTHUMBERLAND
DUMFRIES
KIRKCUDBRIGHT
WIGTON
CUMBERLAND
LONDONDERRY
DONEGAL
ANTRIM
TYRONE
FERMANAGH
ARMAGH
DOWN

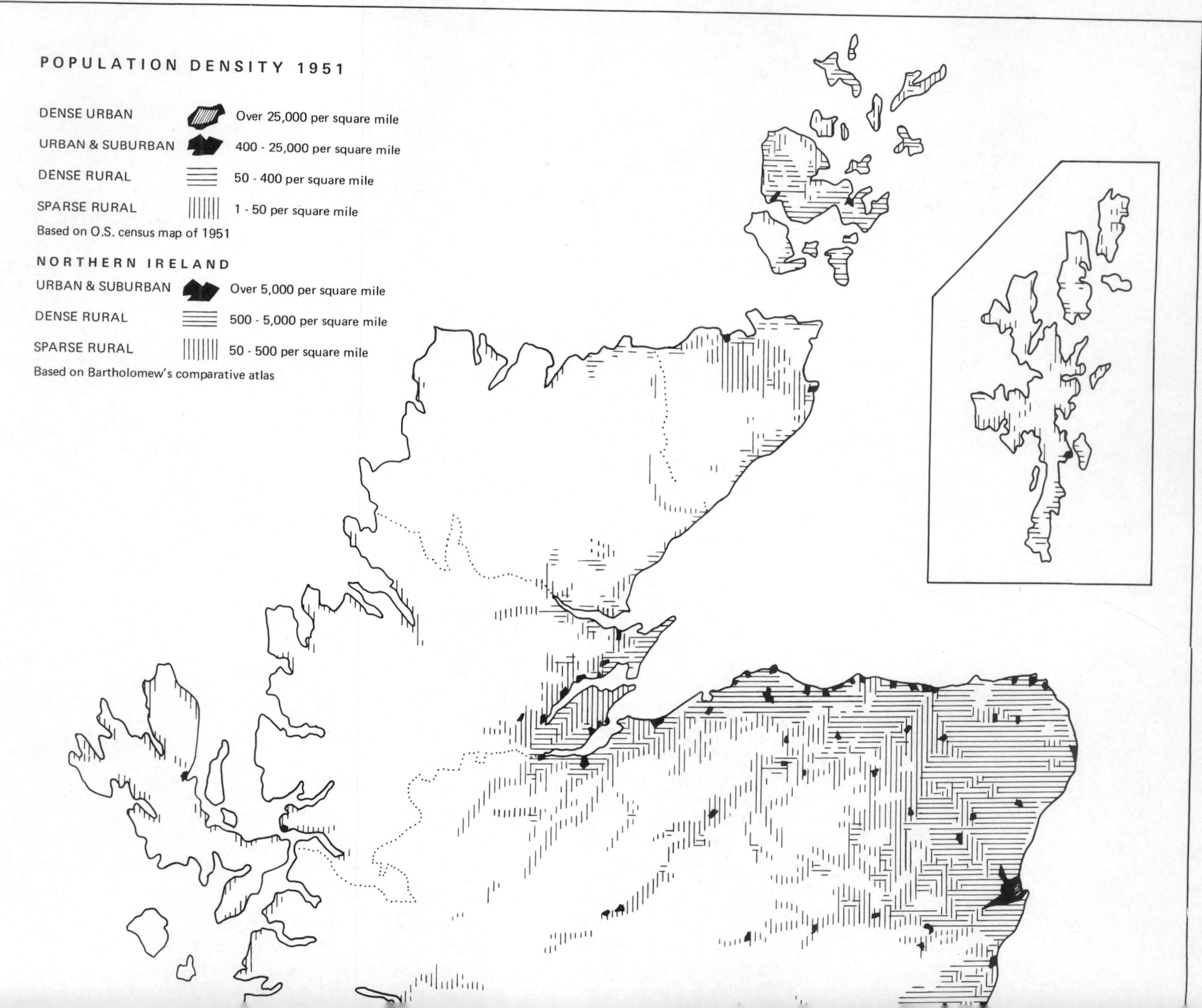
POPULATION DENSITY 1951
DENSE URBAN
Over 25,000 per square mile
URBAN & SUBURBAN
400 - 25,000 per square mile
DENSE RURAL
50 - 400 per square mile
SPARSE RURAL
1 - 50 per square mile
Based on O.S. census map of 1951
NORTHERN IRELAND
URBAN & SUBURBAN
Over 5,000 per square mile
DENSE RURAL
500 - 5,000 per square mile
SPARSE RURAL
50 - 500 per square mile
Based on Bartholomew's comparative atlas

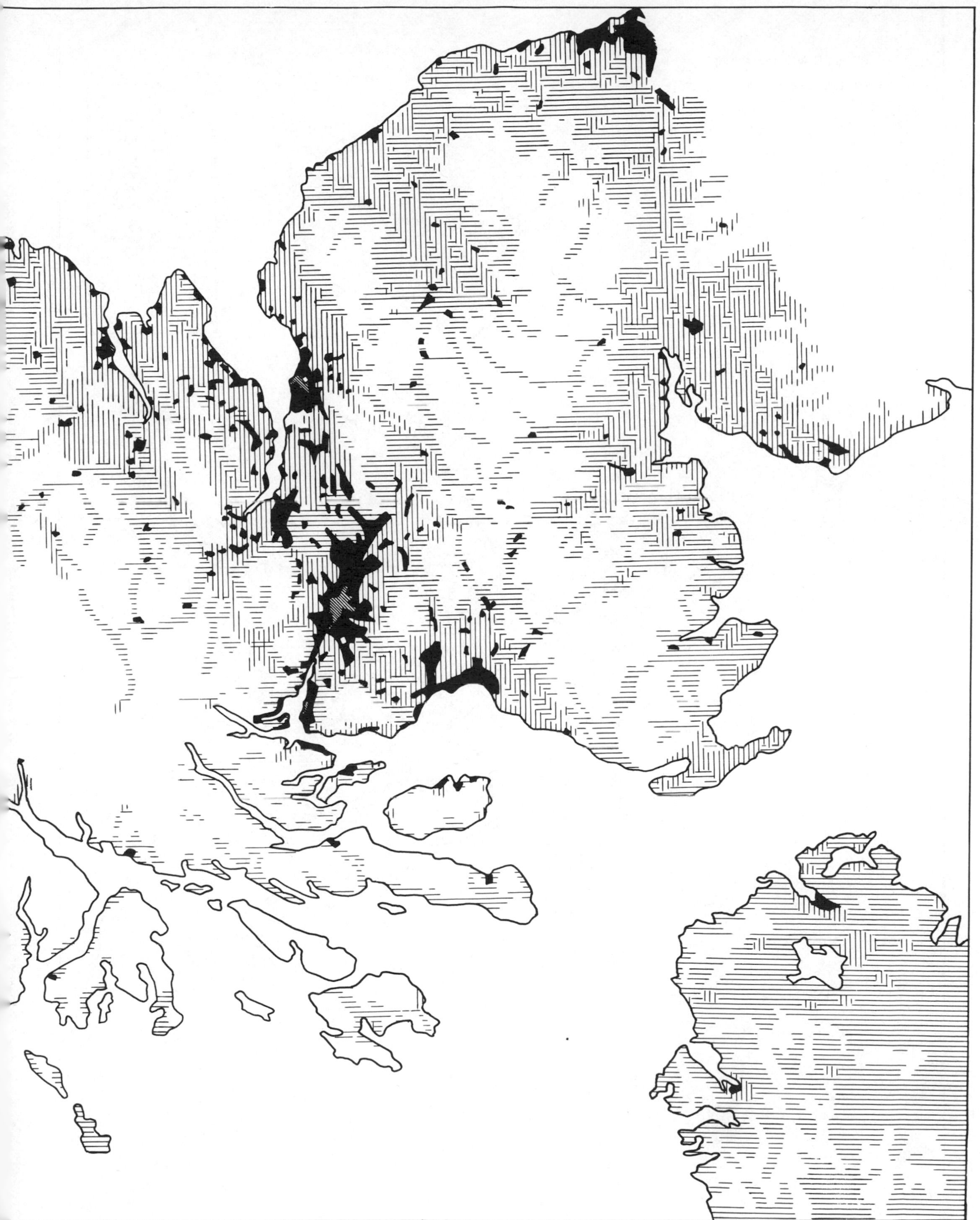

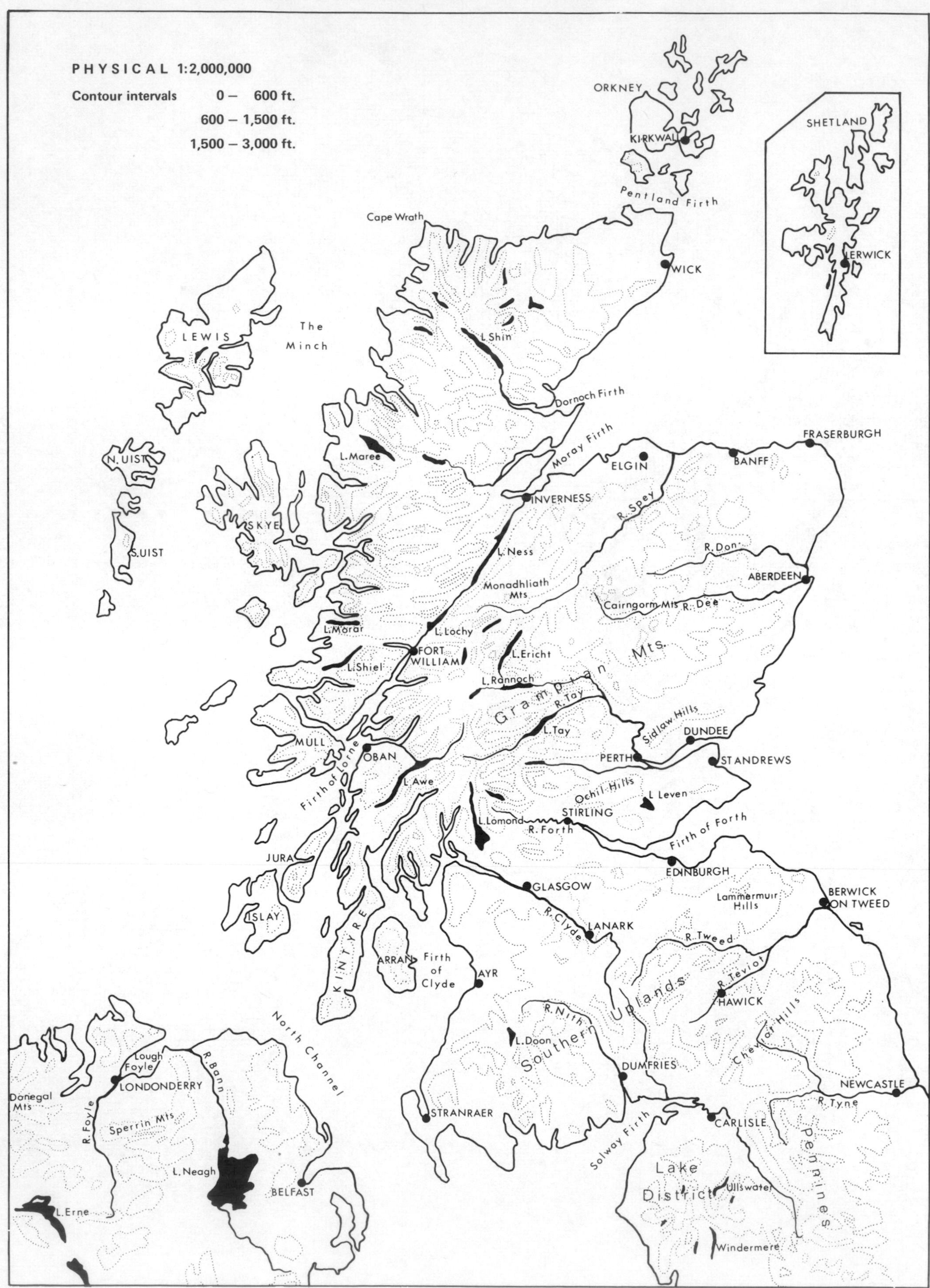
PHYSICAL 1:2,000,000
Contour intervals 0 – 600 ft.
600 – 1,500 ft.
1,500 – 3,000 ft.
ORKNEY
KIRKWALL
SHETLAND
LERWICK
Pentland Firth
Cape Wrath
WICK
LEWIS
The Minch
L.Shin
Dornoch Firth
Moray Firth
FRASERBURGH
BANFF
ELGIN
L.Maree
N.UIST
INVERNESS
R.Spey
SKYE
S.UIST
L.Ness
R.Don
ABERDEEN
Monadhliath Mts
Cairngorm Mts
R.Dee
L.Morar
L.Lochy
FORT WILLIAM
L.Ericht
Grampian Mts.
L.Shiel
L.Rannoch
R.Tay
L.Tay
Sidlaw Hills
DUNDEE
MULL
OBAN
PERTH
ST ANDREWS
Firth of Lorne
L.Awe
Ochil Hills
L.Leven
L.Lomond
STIRLING
R.Forth
Firth of Forth
JURA
EDINBURGH
GLASGOW
Lammermuir Hills
BERWICK ON TWEED
ISLAY
R.Clyde
LANARK
R.Tweed
KINTYRE
ARRAN
Firth of Clyde
AYR
R.Teviot
HAWICK
Southern Uplands
R.Nith
L.Doon
Cheviot Hills
North Channel
Lough Foyle
R.Bann
LONDONDERRY
Donegal Mts
DUMFRIES
NEWCASTLE
R.Tyne
STRANRAER
CARLISLE
R.Foyle
Sperrin Mts
Solway Firth
Pennines
L.Neagh
BELFAST
Lake District
Ullswater
L.Erne
Windermere

APPENDIX E. CONTENTS OF QUESTIONNAIRES

APPENDIX E: CONTENTS OF QUESTIONNAIRE

Items which also appear in Orr's questionnaires (see p.10) are marked + ((+) where the identification is doubtful or difficult). A marks items which appear *only* in the Appendices.

Atlas No.	PQ1 No.	
	+1.	CHILD
	+2.	BOY (aged about 12) (Have you different words for a boy according to his age?)
	+3.	GIRL (aged about 12) (Have you different words for a girl according to her age?)
	4.	YOUNG MAN (around 20)
	5.	YOUNG WOMAN (around 20)
	6.	COBBLER
	7.	FOOLISH PERSON
	+8.	CROWD (of people)
	9.	Say here whether the word BOURACH (or something very similar) is used in your locality and if so what meaning(s) it has.
	10.	BOGLE (hobgoblin)
	11.	A SMALL AMOUNT (as applied to separate things like stones, grains, etc.)
	12.	A SMALL AMOUNT (as applied to inseparable things like hay or snow)
	13.	A SMALL AMOUNT (as applied to liquids)
	+14.	A GOOD DEAL (as applied to separate things like stones, grains, etc.)
	15.	A GOOD DEAL (as applied to inseparable things like snow or hay)
	16.	A GOOD DEAL (as applied to liquids)
1	+17.	ANKLE
2	18.	LITTLE FINGER
3	+19.	BLISTER (on skin)
A	20.	BOIL (the disease)
	21.	COUGH
	22.	MUMPS
	23.	Say here whether the word BRANKS is used in your locality and if so what meaning(s) it has.
	+24.	PIMPLE
4	+25.	SPLINTER (tiny fragment of wood driven into finger, etc.)
	26.	Say here whether the word STOB (or something very similar) is used in your locality and if so what meaning(s) it has.
91	+27.	TO SPRAIN (a muscle, the ankle, etc.)
92	28.	TO STAMMER or STUTTER
5	29.	TO PRICK (one's finger)
6	30.	LEFT HANDED
7	31.	ROUND SHOULDERED
8	32.	STARK NAKED
93	33.	SUDDEN FRIGHT
	34.	TO FRIGHTEN (someone)
	35.	A THUMP (heavy blow)
96	36.	EVENING
	37.	AUTUMN
	38.	BAD (in the sense of "lame," "gammy" as in "bad leg," "bad finger")
	39.	DRENCHED, SOAKED (with rain)
	40.	NIGGARDLY, STINGY
	41.	TO CRY (referring to a child)
	42.	TO SHIVER (with cold)
	43.	TO SMACK (a child)
	44.	TO QUARREL
94	45.	TO THROW (ball, stone, etc.)
	46.	TO TURN (something) UPSIDE DOWN
	47.	TO INTEND
	48.	TO DWELL, RESIDE (in or at a certain place)
	49.	How do you say "WHO OWNS IT"?
	50.	How do you say "SHE'S IN THE SULKS"?
9	51.	The kind of GLOVES with one compartment for the thumb and another for all the fingers together.
10	52.	SOCKS WITHOUT FEET
11	53.	UNDERVEST (man's)
12	54.	UNVERVEST (woman's)
A	55.	HANDKERCHIEF
	56.	TO DRY (clothes) IN THE OPEN AIR
	57.	CLOTHES-STRETCHER
	58.	PIN-CUSHION
	59.	LAMP (the oil and wick kind for indoors)
13	60.	THREE-LEGGED STOOL
	61.	FOUR-LEGGED STOOL
	62.	DOOR-CATCH
A	+63.	PANE (of glass)
14	64.	SOAP SUDS
15	+65.	DOWN DRAUGHT (in chimney)
16	66.	PAIL
17	67.	TWO PAILFULS OF WATER CARRIED TOGETHER
	68.	HIGH TEA
	(+)69.	PIECE OF OATCAKE (Orr: small piece of bread (scone, farl, row, etc.))
95	70.	OATMEAL MIXED WITH WATER
18	+71.	PORRIDGE BOWL
19	+72.	PORRIDGE STICK
	+73.	GRIDIRON
20	(+)74.	MEAL BIN (Orr: flour bin)
21	+75.	CRUMBS
22	76.	QUARTER OF A PECK
	77.	CINDER (the glowing kind)
23	78.	CINDER (black)
24	79.	FORKED STICK (e.g. for making a catapult)
25	80.	PASSAGE BETWEEN HOUSES
	81.	DUST (e.g. in street, on furniture)
	82.	Say here whether the word STOOR (or something very similar) is used in your locality and if so what meaning(s) it has.
26	83.	BRADAWL
27	84.	LEAD PENCIL
28	85.	SLATE PENCIL
29	+86.	TO PLAY TRUANT (from school)
	87.	TAWSE
30	88.	A STROKE with the tawse
31	89.	BROKEN PIECES OF CHINA (used as playthings)
	90.	HIDE AND SEEK
32	+91.	HOLE (used in playing marbles)

Atlas No.	PQ1 No.	
33	92.	The word used of the action of SHOOTING A MARBLE by flicking the thumb over the forefinger.
34	93.	HOME (in the sense of the "base" used in playing certain games)
35	94.	HOP SCOTCH
36	95.	LEAP FROG
37	96.	ROUNDERS
38	97.	(A child's) SWING
39	98.	The name for the STRIP OF ICE children slide on.
	+99.	LANTERN (as used on a farm)
40	100.	MOULD BOARD (of a plough)
41	101.	MUCK HOE
42	102.	FENCE POSTS
43	103.	POST RAMMER (for firming earth round fence posts, etc.)
44	104.	CROWBAR (Say whether you have separate word for kind with a forked end)
45	105.	DITCH (e.g. alongside a country road)
46	106.	GUTTER (the kind running along the side of a paved street)
47	107.	The GRATING over a drain opening in such a gutter.
48	108.	The DRAIN OPENING itself.
49	109.	GUTTER (the kind running along the edge of a roof)
50	110.	GUTTER (the kind running through a byre)
51	111.	PIPE down the side of a house draining water from the roof.
52	+112.	HAY-RACK (in byre, etc.) (Are there different words according to the animal it is for? Is there a different word if it is in the fields?)
53	113.	HAYSTACK (If there is more than one word, say how they differ in meaning)
54	114	HEAP OF HAY (the first small heap, usually about three feet high, made by haymakers)
55	115.	HEAP OF HAY (the big one, usually about six feet high, made afterwards, which stands about in the fields before stacking)
56	116.	STRAW ROPE (especially the kind used in thatching ricks)
57	117.	SCARECROW
58	118.	BULLOCK
59	119.	HEIFER (young cow that has not had a calf)
	120.	HEIFER (in sense beast in first calf)
	121.	COW after her first calf
	122.	COW after her second calf
A	123.	UDDER (of a cow)
60	124.	COW DUNG
	(+)125.	FOAL } (Orr: young horse (male), young horse (female))
61	(+)126.	COLT }
62	127.	HORSE DUNG
	128.	Give here the different names of sheep according to sex, age, etc.
	129.	FLOCK (of sheep)
63	130.	SHEEP'S DUNG
	131.	PIG (If you live by the sea, say if this word is avoided by fishermen, and if so what they say instead)
64	+132.	PIGSTY
	+133.	HARE (If you live by the sea, say if this word is avoided by fishermen, and if so what they say instead)
	134.	RABBIT (If you live by the sea, say if this word is avoided by fishermen, and if so what they say instead)
	135.	Mention here any other words you know which are traditionally avoided for some superstitious reason, and say by whom.
65	136.	THE YOUNGEST OF A BROOD
	137.	PULLET
	138.	BROODY HEN
	139.	COCK
66	+140.	HEN COOP (not just the "run")
67	141.	GIZZARD (of a fowl)
68	142.	FOWL DUNG
97	+143.	The call used when calling CALVES (In 143 to 158, if you cannot write down the call exactly, try to describe it)
	+144.	The call used when calling COWS
	+145.	The call used when calling HORSES
98	+146.	The call used when calling PIGS
	+147.	The call used when calling DOGS
	+148.	The call used when calling CATS
	+149.	The call used when calling HENS
	+150.	The call used when calling DUCKS
	151.	Any other calls to animals (excluding orders to horses, for which see 152-158)
	+152.	What do you say to a horse when you want it to start?
	+153.	What do you say to a horse when you want it to stop?
	154.	What do you say to a horse when you want it to go faster?
	+155.	What do you say to a horse when you want it to back?
99	+156.	What do you say to a horse when you want it to turn left?
100	+157.	What do you say to a horse when you want it to turn right?
	158.	Any other words telling a horse what to do (with meanings)
69	159.	SNOWFLAKE
70	160.	CHAFFINCH
71	161.	SPARROW
72	(+)162.	LAPWING (Orr: plover)
	+163.	MAGPIE
73	164.	JACKDAW
74	165.	SEAGULL
75	166.	YELLOWHAMMER
76	167.	ANT
77	168.	BEE (the wild variety) (List any words for wild bees of different kinds or colours)
	169.	BEE (the domesticated bee) (List any words for domesticated bees of different kinds of colours)

Atlas No.	PQ1 No.	
78	(+)170.	BLACK BEETLE (large one) (Orr: beetle (other than cockroach))
	(+)171.	BLACK BEETLE (small one) (Orr: beetle (other than cockroach))
79	172.	CATERPILLAR
80	173.	CENTIPEDE
81	174.	DADDY LONG LEGS (crane fly)
	175.	EARWIG (the fork-tailed insect with six legs)
82	+176.	MAGGOT
83	+177.	SPIDER
84	+178.	TADPOLE
85	179.	THE FRY OF THE MINNOW
86	180.	COUCH GRASS
87	181.	FOXGLOVE
88	182.	GOOSEBERRY
89	183.	PEA POD
90	184.	PEA POD

185. How do you say "I'm not ready yet"? How do you say "I don't know"?
How do you say "He wants to go to the auction"?

186. What word(s) do you use for THAN in sentences like "John is taller THAN Alec"?
What word(s) do you use for VERY in sentences like "It's VERY stormy to-night"?
What word(s) do you use for EXCEPT in sentences like "They all jumped over the fence EXCEPT two"?

187. For "these men" which would you say, THESE men, THAE men, THIR men, THIS men?
For "those men" which would say, THOSE men, THAE men, THON men, YON men, THAT men? (If none of these say what)

188. Do you speak of porridge as "they" e.g. "THESE ARE good porridge"? Are there any other word(s) (e.g. for broth), where you do this?

189. Say whether you use the expression "half three"
If so, which does it mean, 2.30 or 3.30?
How do you say, "the day after to-morrow"?

190. Do you pronounce the word SINGING in *exactly* the same way in these two sentences?
1. He likes singing. 2. He is aye singing.
What do you say for WITHOUT in sentences like "He did it WITHOUT my knowledge"?

191. Do you say "These horses PULLS well" or "These horses PULL well"?
Do you say "They PULL well" or "They PULLS well"?

192. In some parts of Scotland, the words EAST and WEST are used where *along* or *across* or *over* would be used in English. E.g. "Who's that coming WEST there?" or "I'm just going EAST to the henhouse." In your locality are either or both words used in this way? If so, state whether they are used generally, or only by old people.

193. Do you ever use the words THOU and THEE instead of YE and YOU in talking to a person?
If so, to what kinds of person?
Do children use them in talking to their parents?

194. Opposite the following sentences write what you would say for the English words in capitals.
She is going to BAKE the pie.
She BAKED the pie.
The pie is BAKED.
She wants to EAT the cakes.
She ATE the cakes.
The cakes ARE all EATEN.

195. Opposite the following sentences write what you would say for the English words in capitals.
He SHOULD FETCH some water.
He FETCHED it.
He has FETCHED it.
These soldiers DO NOT FIGHT well.
They FOUGHT well.
The soldiers HAVE FOUGHT well.

196. Opposite the following sentences write what you would say for the English words in capitals.
They MUST SOW the oats.
They SOWED the oats.
The oats WERE SOWN yesterday.
He COULDN'T SPLIT the log.
He SPLIT the log.
The log WAS SPLIT with a wedge.

In rectangles 197 to 205 please put a tick opposite the suggested spelling which seems to you to show as nearly as possible the pronunciation of the words as said in your locality. If you feel that none of the spellings gets near enough to your pronunciation, please make a spelling of your own at the bottom in the space opposite "Pronounced in this way." If two or more different pronunciations are used in the district, give them.

197. TWO

1. As in English "two"
2. Rhyming with English "law"
3. 3. Rhyming with English "spa" or "calm"
4. Rhyming with English "day" — TWAE
5. Rhyming with English "see" — TWEE
6. Rhyming with English "idea" — TWEEA
7. Pronounced in this way:

198. THREE

1. As in English "three" — THREE
2. With *th* pronounced t — TREE
3. With *th* pronounced as *ch* in "loch" — CHREE
4. With *th* pronounced almost like *sh* — SHREE
5. Rhyming with "gey" — THREY
6. Rhyming with "gey" — SHREY
7. Pronounced in this way:

Atlas No.	PQ1 No.		
	199.	EIGHT	
		1. As in English "eight"	AET
		2. Same as 1, but with extra *ch*	AECHT
		3. With *e* as in "bed"	ECHT
		4. With *aw* as in "law"	AWCHT
		5. With *a* as in "lass"	ACHT
		6. With *e* as in "bed" followed by a short *ee* as in "feet"	E-EECHT
		7. The same as 6. but without *ch*	E-EET
		8. Pronounced in this way:	
	200.	ENOUGH	
		1. As in English	ENUFF
		2. With *o* as in "hot"	ENOCH
		3. With *u* as in "but"	ENUCH
		4. With *yu* as in "young"	ENYUCH
		5. With *yo* as in "yon"	ENYOCH
		6. With *oo* as in "hoose"	ENOOCH
		7. With *oo* as in "do"	ENOO
		8. With *yoo* as in "you"	ENYOOCH
		9. With *o* as in "hot"	ENOFF
		10. With *ee* as in "feet"	ENEECH
		11. With *ee* followed by short *oo*	ENEEOCH
		12. Pronounced in this way:	
	201.	WHO	
		1. hoo	2. faa
		3. aa	4. faw
		5. hwaa	6. hweea
		7. hwaw	8. hwoe
		9. hwee	10. waw
		11. hwae	12. wee
		13. woe	14. wae
		15. hwoo	16. waa
		17. Pronounced in this way:	
	202.	1. stone	
		2. stae-een	
		3. steen	
		4. steean	
		5. stane (*a* as in English "day")	
		6. styan (*ya* as in English "yap")	
		7. styaen (*yae* as in English "yea")	
		8. Pronounced in this way:	
	203.	GOOD	
		1. As in English "good"	GOOD
		2. Exactly rhyming with your local pronounciation of "deed"	GEED
		3. Exactly rhyming with your local pronounciation of "deed"	GWEED
		4. Exactly rhyming with your local pronounciation of "did"	GID
		5. Not exactly rhyming with either	GUID
		6. Pronounced in this way:	
	204.	HOOK	
		1. With *yu* as in English "young"	HYUK
		2. With *yoo* as in English "you"	HYOOK
		3. With long *oo* as in English "do"	HOOK
		4. With *ui* as in Scots "guid"	HUIK
		5. Pronounced in this way:	
	205.	KNEE	
		1. With *e* as in "bed" followed by short *ee* as in English "feet"	NE-EE
		2. Similarly, but starting with *k*	K-NE-EE
		3. Starting with *t*	T-NE-EE
		4. As in English "knee"	NEE
		5. Starting with *k*	K-NEE
		6. Starting with *t*	T-NEE
		7. Starting with *kr*	KREE
		8. Starting with *ch* as in "loch"	CH-NEE
		9. Pronounced in this way:	

Atlas No.	PQ1 No.	

206 Answer these questions with "yes," "no" or "sometimes"
Is the *d* pronounced locally in
THUNDER? LAND? COLD?
Is *cht* pronounced as *th* in
MICHT? DOCHTER?
Is *f* pronounced as *th* in
FRAE?

207. Is the *g* ever pronounced locally in GNAW?
Is the *w* ever pronounced in WRANG?
If so, is it pronounced as a *w* or as a *v*?
Is *ch* pronounced as *sh* in CHEW?

208. GENERAL
The word you use to express a certain thing will in some cases not be in use all over Scotland; in some other place a different word may be employed instead. If you have first-hand knowledge of any such words (or phrases) not found in this booklet please give details below. One specimen is given by way of example. There is no need for you to do anything with 208, 209, and 210 unless you wish to.

209. GENERAL
The word you use to express a certain thing will in some cases have a different meaning in some other place. If you know of any cases of this kind which have not cropped up in this booklet please give details below.

210. GENERAL
This page and the next one are reserved for any strange or out-of-the-way words in your dialect that you may wish to write down.

211. GAELIC
A. Is any Gaelic spoken in your parish?
B. If so, (a) only by the old (over 60)?
(b) by the middle-aged (30-60) and old but not by the young?
(c) by all ages?
C. What is the mother-tongue of the children below school age?
D. Is Gaelic taught in the local school?
E. Are there any people over school age who cannot speak English?
F. Are church-services held in Gaelic? If so are they regularly in Gaelic or only sometimes?
G. Can you estimate roughly what proportion of the local population speaks Gaelic? If possible do this by age-groups: e.g. 90% of the old, 50% of the middle-aged, 10% of the young.
H. Has there been any clear decrease of Gaelic speaking within memory, and if so to what extent?
I. Has there been any noticeable immigration of Gaelic speakers within memory?
J. Do local Gaelic speakers feel that their dialect is markedly like or unlike that of neighbouring areas? If so, which areas are felt to be very similar in dialect and which different?